DICTIONARY OF
American History

Third Edition

EDITORIAL BOARD

DICTIONARY OF
American History

Third Edition

Stanley I. Kutler, *Editor in Chief*

Volume 6
Native to Pyramid

New York • Detroit • San Diego • San Francisco • Cleveland • New Haven, Conn. • Waterville, Maine • London • Munich

Dictionary of American History, Third Edition

Stanley I. Kutler, *Editor*

Charles Scribner's Sons is an imprint of The Gale Group, Inc., a division of Thomson Learning, Inc.

For more information, contact
Charles Scribner's Sons
An imprint of the Gale Group
300 Park Avenue South
New York, NY 10010

LIBRARY OF CONGRESS CATALOGING-IN-PUBLICATION DATA

Dictionary of American history / Stanley I. Kutler.—3rd ed.
p. cm.
Includes bibliographical references and index.
ISBN 0-684-80533-2 (set : alk. paper)
1. United States—History—Dictionaries. I. Kutler, Stanley I.
E174 .D52 2003
973'.03—dc21

Printed in United States of America
10 9 8 7 6 5 4 3 2 1

CONTENTS

DICTIONARY OF American History

Third Edition

N

(Continued)

NATIVE AMERICAN CHURCH. The Native American Church, a development that evolved out of the Peyote Cult, is a religion combining some Christian elements with others of Indian derivation. It features as a sacrament the ingestion of the peyote cactus, which may induce multicolored hallucinations. Christian elements include the cross, the Trinity, baptism, and some Christian theology and eschatology. The peyote rite is an all-night ceremonial, usually held in a Plains-type tipi. Prominent rituals include singing, prayers, testimonials, and the taking of peyote. First incorporated in Oklahoma in 1918, the Native American Church has become the principal religion of a majority of the Indians living between the Mississippi River and the Rocky Mountains, and it is also important among the NAVAJO in the Great Basin, in east-central California, and in southern Canada.

Peyote Cult. Quanah Parker, shown here with one of his seven wives, was a Comanche Indian leader who founded the Native American Church, which combined traditional Christian elements with the ingestion of the peyote cactus, a strong hallucinogenic drug. Polygamy was also one of the church's central tenets. SMITHSONIAN INSTITUTION

Peyotism's legal standing met a serious challenge in 1990, when the U.S. SUPREME COURT decreed, in *Employment Division v. Smith* (1990), that the free exercise clause of the FIRST AMENDMENT did not exempt Indians from criminal prosecution for the use of peyote in states where its use was outlawed as a controlled substance. The decision placed minority religions in jeopardy. In response Oregon passed a 1991 law permitting the sacramental use of peyote by American Indians in the state, and Congress passed the Religious Freedom Restoration Act in 1993, which required the government to demonstrate a compelling state interest to justify any measure restricting religious practices.

BIBLIOGRAPHY

LaBarre, Weston. *The Peyote Cult.* Norman: University of Oklahoma Press, 1989.

Slotkin, James Sydney. *The Peyote Religion: A Study in Indian-White Relations.* New York: Octagon Books, 1975.

Stewart, Omer C. *Peyote Religion.* Norman: University of Oklahoma Press, 1987.

Vecsey, Christopher, ed. *Handbook of American Indian Religious Freedom.* New York: Crossroad, 1991.

Christopher Vecsey
Kenneth M. Stewart/J. H.

See also **Bill of Rights; Indian Policy, U.S.: 1900–2000; Indian Religious Life; Religious Liberty.**

NATIVE AMERICAN GRAVES PROTECTION AND REPATRIATION ACT. In 1989, the U.S. Congress passed the National Museum of the American Indian (NMAI) Act (Public Law 101-185), which preceded the Native American Graves Protection and Repatriation Act (NAGPRA) by one year. The NMAI Act created a new museum within the Smithsonian Institution devoted to American Indians that incorporated the collections of the Heye Foundation in New York City. One part of the NMAI Act provided for the repatriation to lineal descendants or culturally affiliated tribes of Native American human remains and funerary objects held at the Smithsonian. This repatriation was to be monitored by a five-person review committee, at least three of whom were recommended by Native American tribes.

The following year, 1990, Congress passed NAGPRA (Public Law 101-601); it was signed by President George Bush on 16 November 1990. The act gives Native Americans, including Native Hawaiians, ownership or control of Native American cultural objects and human remains found on federal and tribal lands. The act also mandates the repatriation to lineal descendants or culturally affiliated tribes of human remains, funerary objects, objects of cultural patrimony, and sacred objects that are held by any federal agency and any museum or institution that receives federal funds. Agencies, museums, and institutions receiving federal funds were given five years to inventory human remains and funerary objects associated with human remains in their collections—with the possibility of extending time deadlines—and notify relevant Native American groups. They were given three years to provide summary inventories to Native American groups of unassociated funerary objects, objects of cultural patrimony, and sacred objects.

NAGPRA mandates the creation of a seven-person review committee to monitor and administer the provisions of the act. The secretary of the interior appoints the committee from a roster of nominated individuals, three of whom must be nominees of Native American tribes; two must be "traditional Indian religious leaders."

NAGPRA provides for fines and prison terms of up to one year for a first offense by individuals who obtain or traffic in Native American human remains or objects. Civil penalties set by the secretary of the interior apply to agencies, museums, and institutions that violate NAGPRA. The Smithsonian Institution is specifically exempted from the act, as it operates under the guidelines of the NMAI Act, as amended in 1996, which defines objects of cultural patrimony and sacred objects as subject to repatriation.

As the two major repatriation laws were being developed, Native American groups and museums and other institutions had very different views as to the impact of the laws. Native Americans assumed repatriation of human remains and objects would be simple and straightforward, while many museum employees were fearful that their institutions would lose their Native American human remains and artifacts. As the laws were passed and implemented, however, both groups were incorrect. Repatriation has often proved to be a difficult, time-consuming, and frequently expensive undertaking for Native Americans, and museums have not been emptied.

Part of the problem with implementing repatriation legislation has been refining the definitions of the law. "Cultural affiliation" is difficult to define. "Affiliation" may be established by a variety of means, but experts and Native American groups do not always agree. For example, the controversy over the remains of Kennewick Man pitted traditionalists, who claimed the ancient skeleton was an ancestor of modern tribesmen, against archaeologists, who believed the person was part of an unrelated prehistoric community. Native American groups have sometimes competed for remains or objects, all claiming affiliation. (Multiple ancestry is possible because a historic Native American group could be culturally affiliated with a number of contemporary tribes.)

Federal law has jurisdiction only over federally recognized tribes, thus excluding many American Indian groups, such as state-recognized tribes, terminated tribes (no longer federally recognized), and groups actively seeking federal recognition. In addition, it will surely be impossible to establish reasonable cultural affiliation for many human remains; this leaves the question of what to do with "culturally unaffiliated remains" unanswered. The definitions of human remains, funerary objects (associated or unassociated), objects of cultural patrimony, and sacred objects contained in the law are not as unambiguous as one might think. For example, do human hairs and fingernail clippings constitute "human remains"? Likewise, Native American groups and those charged with implementing the law define a funerary object, sacred object, or an object of cultural patrimony in varying ways.

Significant repatriations representing thousands of human remains and cultural objects have occurred, many from the Smithsonian Institution. The Smithsonian's National Museum of Natural History has itself returned several thousand human remains, primarily to Alaska, with particularly large numbers going to Alaskan native communities on Kodiak Island and St. Lawrence Island. The Smithsonian has also returned human remains associated with major nineteenth-century massacres of Native Americans, such as the Sand Creek Massacre of Southern Cheyenne and other Indians and the Fort Robinson Massacre of Northern Cheyenne. Included in the human remains the Smithsonian has repatriated is the brain of Ishi, the well-known California Indian. Sitting Bull's braid, cut from him during his autopsy, is still at the Smithsonian, but has been offered for repatriation. Numerous cultural objects have also been repatriated by the Smithsonian, including Ghost Dance shirts and other objects obtained from those Lakota massacred at Wounded Knee Creek. Likewise, the Smithsonian's National Museum of the American Indian has returned numerous sacred objects and objects of cultural patrimony to their rightful owners.

Under the mandate of NAGPRA, as of 2002, large numbers of human remains had not been returned, and significant Native American objects of cultural patrimony and sacred objects remained in museums and other institutions. Successes have occurred, however: for example, the Zuni Pueblo has had many of its Ahayu:da (war gods) repatriated, and the Pawnee tribe of Oklahoma has had the remains of ancestors returned from the State of Nebraska as well as from the Smithsonian.

BIBLIOGRAPHY

Mending the Circle: A Native American Repatriation Guide. New York: American Indian Ritual Object Repatriation Foundation, 1996.

Mihesuah, Devon A., ed. *Repatriation Reader: Who Owns American Indian Remains?* Lincoln: University of Nebraska Press, 2000.

Price, H. Marcus. *Disputing the Dead: U.S. Law on Aboriginal Remains and Grave Goods.* Columbia: University of Missouri Press, 1991.

Thornton, Russell. "Who Owns Our Past? The Repatriation of Native American Human Remains and Cultural Objects." In *Studying Native America: Problems and Prospects.* Edited by Russell Thornton. Madison: University of Wisconsin Press, 1997.

Trope, Jack F., and Walter R. Echo-Hawk. "The Native American Graves Protection and Repatriation Act: Background and Legislative History." *Arizona State Law Journal* 24 (1992): 35–77.

Russell Thornton

See also **Indian Policy, U.S.: 1900–2000; National Museum of the American Indian; Smithsonian Institution.**

NATIVE AMERICAN RIGHTS FUND (NARF) was established in 1970 by the staff of California Indian Legal Services, a poverty law program, with principal support from the Ford Foundation. The next year NARF became a separate entity, established its headquarters at Boulder, Colorado, and launched its information project, the National Indian Law Library. Offices in Washington, D.C., and Anchorage, Alaska, were added later. The NARF board of directors is comprised of prominent Native American leaders from across the United States. John E. Echohawk, a leading national figure in Indian law, was NARF executive director in 2002, a position he had held for more than a quarter century.

NARF provides legal advice and representation to Native American tribes, communities, and individuals in matters of major significance. Its declared priorities are preservation of tribal existence, protection of tribal resources, promotion of human rights, accountability of governments to Indian people, and development of and education about Indian law. NARF has played a central role in defending Native American tribal sovereignty, preserving Indian land and other natural resources, and protecting Indian treaty fishing rights and Indian religious rights. It has gained federal recognition for tribes around the country, particularly in the eastern United States; addressed the unique needs of Alaskan Native communities; and enforced the federal government's trust responsibility to tribes and individuals. Since its founding, the NARF

John E. Echohawk. The attorney and longtime executive director of the Native American Rights Fund stands outside its headquarters in Boulder, Colo., 1984. AP/WIDE WORLD PHOTOS

has participated in nearly every Indian law case before the U.S. Supreme Court.

BIBLIOGRAPHY

McCoy, Melody. *Tribalizing Indian Education: Federal Indian Law and Policy Affecting American Indian and Alaska Native Education.* Boulder, Colo.: Native American Rights Fund, 2000.

Sanders, Susan, and Debbie Thomas. "Native American Rights Fund: Our First Twenty Years." *Clearinghouse Review* 26 (1992): 49–56.

Wind, Wabun. *The People's Lawyers.* New York: Holt, Rinehart and Winston, 1973.

Richard B. Collins

See also **Indian Rights Association; Indian Self-Determination and Education Assistance Act.**

NATIVE AMERICAN STUDIES involves the study of American Indians and their history, culture, literatures, laws, and related subjects. It is cross-disciplinary and appeals both to Indians and non-Indians.

Attempts to establish Native American studies programs date back to 1914, when Senator Robert Owen of Oklahoma introduced a resolution calling for an Indian studies program at the University of Oklahoma; a similar attempt was made in 1937. But it was not until 1968 that the first Native American studies program was established at San Francisco State University.

That same year American Indian studies programs emerged at the University of Minnesota; the University of California, Berkeley; and later at the University of California, Los Angeles. In 1969, Trent University in Ontario started the first Native studies program in Canada. By the end of 2000, one survey reported that there were 112 American Indian studies programs, 84 in the United States and 28 in Canada. Many were part of an ethnic studies program or a unit of an anthropology department. The majority offered courses on Native Americans with about a third offering minors or majors in Native American Studies. Less than a dozen offered graduate degrees in Native American Studies.

BIBLIOGRAPHY

Morrison, Dane, ed. *American Indian Studies: An Interdisciplinary Approach to Contemporary Issues.* New York: Peter Lang, 1997.

Price, John A. *Native Studies: American and Canadian Indians.* Toronto and New York: McGraw-Hill Ryerson, 1978.

Thornton, Russell. *Studying Native America: Problems and Prospects.* Madison: University of Wisconsin Press, 1998.

Donald L. Fixico

See also **Education, Indian.**

NATIVE AMERICANS. "Native American" is the official term used by the U.S. government to refer to the original inhabitants of the lower 48 states. It was adopted by the Bureau of Indian Affairs in the 1960s after considerable "consciousness raising" on the part of Native activists to abandon the official use of the misnomer "Indian."

Although accepted by many tribal groups and people, many Native people reject the term because it is the "official" government designation and therefore immediately suspect. Also, the term still refers to "America," considered by many to be an inappropriate Eurocentric term. Finally, the term is confusing because it is also used to refer to people born in the United States—"native Americans."

BIBLIOGRAPHY

Bellfy, Phil. *Indians and Other Misnomers: A Cross-Referenced Dictionary of the People, Persons, and Places of Native North America.* Golden, Colo.: Fulcrum Press, 2001.

Phil Bellfy

NATIVISM, the fear and loathing of and hostility toward immigrants or other perceived "aliens," has run through American history ever since the European settlement of this continent. Though technically it refers to a person's place of birth, nativism is not simply xenophobia; it may be (and has been) directed toward native-born Americans whom nativists view as "un-American." The targets and the rhetoric of nativism shift over time, making difficult a single detailed description of it. However, all the disparate forms of nativism include a hostility toward those perceived as "outsiders," whether ethnic, religious, or political, and an emphasis on the purported moral, economic, and/or political dangers those people pose to America.

One prevalent strain of nativism has taken the form of antagonism toward the Roman Catholic Church and its members. Until well into the twentieth century, many Americans believed that this church endangered both the traditional Protestantism and the democratic institutions of the United States. Brought to America by the first Protestant English colonists, anti-Catholic sentiment was fostered in the new country by New England Puritans who taught their children that Catholics were corrupt and by the eighteenth-century wars with Catholic France and Spain. Colonial laws and colonial writing both reflected this intolerance.

After a brief post-Revolution respite, anti-Catholicism reappeared in the late 1820s as a response to Catholic immigration. The movement was nourished by English propaganda that Catholics could not be loyal American citizens because they were controlled by the Pope. By 1834 intolerance was such that the mob destruction of an Ursuline convent at Charlestown, Massachusetts, was condoned rather than condemned by most Americans. This sign of popular favor encouraged nativists to launch two new anti-Catholic papers, release a flood of anti-Catholic books and pamphlets, and form the Protestant Reformation Society in 1836. In the 1840s, when Catholics protested against reading the King James version of the Scriptures in the New York public schools, propagandists misrepresented their protests as opposition to all reading of the Bible. The resulting Protestant panic gave nativists sufficient strength to organize the American Republican Party with an anti-Catholic, antiforeign platform. In 1845, however, a series of bloody riots over Catholicism in Philadelphia turned popular sentiment against the party's anti-Catholic crusade. Reforming into the American Protestant Society, nativists influenced hundreds of clergymen to deliver anti-Catholic sermons. In 1849 it merged with two lesser anti-Catholic organizations to form the American and Foreign Christian Union, which pledged to win both the United States and Europe to Protestantism. These organized efforts, combined with heavy immigration from famine-stricken Ireland and Germany, paved the way for the Know-Nothing, or American, Party, which enjoyed remarkable success in 1854 and 1855, carrying a number of states and threatening to sweep the nation in the presidential election of 1856 before splitting over the slavery issue. Before the party's demise, former President Millard Fillmore ran for president again in 1856 on the Know-Nothing ticket.

The 1890s brought another wave of nativism, this one against the millions of Jews, Italian Catholics, Russians, and other southern and eastern European people who had immigrated to the United States after the Civil War. Nativist organizations flourished; the largest of them, the American Protection Association, had 500,000 members. After World War I the United States developed an intense nationalism that bred antagonism toward immigrants, Jews, communists, and Catholics—toward all groups that were not conservative Protestant Americans. In 1924 Congress passed sweeping immigration restrictions particularly targeting southern and eastern Europeans, and outright banning Asians. During the early 1920s, the Ku Klux Klan enjoyed a resurgence before its excesses and political corruption brought it down. In the presidential campaign of 1928, Alfred E. Smith, the Democratic candidate, encountered bitter anti-Catholic propaganda that contributed to his defeat. German immigrants and German-Americans also suffered harassment during this period. Before World War I German-language publications flourished, and numerous public schools offered instruction in German. However, anti-German sentiment led the government to ban the language from schools.

Immigrants from many areas of Asia, and their descendants have suffered grievously under nativist laws and attitudes since they first began coming to America. During the nineteenth century Chinese, Japanese, and Filipino immigrants, brought to the West Coast to drive down labor costs, encountered harsh discrimination; Anglo-Americans labeled them the "yellow peril," and labor unions excluded them. In 1870 U.S. law made Asian immigrants ineligible for citizenship, and Congress banned Chinese immigration outright from 1882 to 1943. In 1906, the San Francisco school board segregated Asian children, and Japanese Americans' land ownership was restricted in California. Then, in World War II, in one of the most notorious expressions of nativism and racism in U.S. history, the United States forced more than 110,000 Japanese Americans into camps solely on the basis of their nationality background, keeping some there from 1942 until 1946.

In the late 1930s through the 1940s, nativist sentiment turned to political targets in a frenzy of anticommunism. Though purportedly carried out as a protection from the Soviet threat, in practice anticommunists targeted leftist, feminist, and racial justice movements, harnessing the nativist term "anti-American" to discredit homegrown political dissent. The name of the congressional committee investigating supposed disloyalty, the "House Committee on un-American Activities" (HUAC), aptly expressed the conflation of "American" identity with adherence to rigid political orthodoxy. Founded in 1938, the committee was active into the late 1940s. Well into the 1980s U.S. critics of social injustice found themselves dismissed with jibes of "Go back to Russia!"

Though Catholics celebrated the election of a Roman Catholic, John F. Kennedy, to the presidency in 1960, nativism burst out in numerous other forms throughout the rest of the twentieth century, and into the twenty-first. In the 1990s, "English-only" campaigns thrived, directed particularly toward the increasing numbers of Spanish-speakers in the United States. In 1994, California voters passed Proposition 187, which required doctors and teachers to deny assistance to undocumented immigrants and report them to the government; other states followed suit. A 1996 federal law made it easier to deport immigrants and allowed for their immediate deportation, without a hearing or judicial review.

After Islamic terrorists flew planes into the World Trade Center and the Pentagon on 11 September 2001, killing thousands, many terrified Americans found refuge in nativist expressions, advertising "American-owned" businesses and aiming prejudice and violence at fellow Americans who did not fit their idea of what an "American" was—especially with respect to religious, ethnic, and racial identity. The federal government arrested huge numbers of Islamic and Middle-Eastern immigrants and in some cases held them for months without evidence or charges. In the months after 11 September, many Americans found themselves treated as "strangers in a strange land."

BIBLIOGRAPHY

Bennett, David Harry. *The Party of Fear: From Nativist Movements to the New Right in American History.* 2d ed. New York: Vintage Books, 1995.

Higham, John. *Strangers in the Land.* New Brunswick, N.J.: Rutgers University Press, 2002.

Hing, Bill Ong. *To Be an American: Cultural Pluralism and the Rhetoric of Assimilation.* New York: New York University Press, 1997.

Irving, Katrina. *Immigrant Mothers: Narratives of Race and Maternity, 1890–1925.* Urbana: University of Illinois Press, 2000.

Knobel, Dale T. *America for the Americans: The Nativist Movement in the United States.* New York: Twayne Publishers, 1996.

Pozzetta, George E., ed. *Nativism, Discrimination, and Images of Immigrants.* New York: Garland, 1991.

Ross, William G. *Forging New Freedoms: Nativism, Education, and the Constitution, 1917–1927.* Lincoln: University of Nebraska Press, 1994.

Ray Allen Billington / D. B.

See also **Alien and Sedition Laws; Alien Landholding; Aliens, Rights of; America First Committee; American Protective Association; Anti-Catholicism; Anti-Semitism; Espionage Act; Eugenics; Frank, Leo, Lynching of; German Americans; Immigration Restriction; Internment, Wartime; Know-Nothing Party; McCarthyism; Palmer Raids; Pledge of Allegiance; Relocation, Italian-American; Sacco-Vanzetti Case; Ursuline Convent, Burning of.**

NATIVIST MOVEMENTS (AMERICAN INDIAN REVIVAL MOVEMENTS). Sent to study the Ghost Dance among the "hostile" Sioux in the 1890s, James Mooney, an Irish nationalist and an employee of the Bureau of American Ethnology, quickly realized parallels with anticolonial expressions in his own homeland against occupation by the British. He combed available literature, and his 1896 report provided a historical overview of prior attempts, successful or not, to revitalize overstressed and disillusioned communities. Later works by Leslie Spier, Cora Du Bois, June Helm, Jean-Guy Goulet, and Robin Ridington traced such prophet or

Handsome Lake. The Seneca religious prophet preaches his Longhouse Religion—a blend of Indian traditions and elements of Christianity, with an emphasis on nonviolence, temperance, community, and land—to the Iroquois, c. 1800. New York State Library

messianic movements across western North America in great detail. Scholars working in modern New Guinea called similar phenomena "cargo cults" for their emphasis on material possessions, while Vittorio Lanternari summarized this worldwide variety as expressing "religions of the oppressed."

Careful further study, however, has shown that such efforts rarely occur at the moment of greatest stress and despair. Indeed, such rallying only comes after the crisis has passed, as though mere survival took every ounce of time and effort. Reflection afterward leads to well-formulated revelation about how best to avert such disasters in the future, allowing an effective strategy to be proposed, implemented, and integrated into existing patterns by enthusiastic community participation. Every situation requires its own solution, however, so the varieties of nativistic response are endless and ongoing.

Nativistic movements, initially called prophet cults, then messianic reforms, are inherent in the worldview of Native Americans, though their pace and number quickened considerably after and because of the arrival of Europeans. The high value placed on the individual and his or her willingness to sacrifice for the well-being of the community is underlain by a core belief in revelation, the basis of such prophecy.

For most of the Americas, this insight is provided by the fasting and successful quest for an immortal partner, a supernatural ally to help self and others gain success in life. Often called the guardian spirit complex, based in personal revelation, some individuals, such as the famous Lakota holy man Black Elk, received a message that had bearing on the well-being of the whole community. Black Elk never implemented his call, but others have done so.

An important corollary belief is that humans occupy a pivotal (but never superior) position in the world, where they bear direct and oblique moral responsibility for its stability. Storms, earthquakes, floods, and other natural disasters were likely triggers for prehistoric reforms, urged and proclaimed by prophets who came forward under divine sanction to institute better behavior. Recalled in mythic epics, such reformers included Payatamo for the Pueblos, Erect Horns for the Cheyennes, Dekanawidah for the Iroquois Confederacy, and a variety of Changers among the Coast Salishans.

From the moment of European impact, either via earlier pathogens or later face to face (blow for blow) contact, prophets arose to rally and redirect native survivors along healthful reforms. At the 1540 start of his brutal march through the Southeast, Hernando de Soto encountered a local leader in Florida whose dire threats and heaped curses have all the hallmarks of a call for nativistic resistance. Later explorers set off other reactions, and eventual settlements led to full-blown rebellions, such as those of the Powhatans in 1610, 1622, and 1644. Indeed, the advance of the frontier summoned a backfire of messianic efforts, highlighted by that of Popé, who led a rebellion in the Southwest in 1680, and the Delaware prophet Neolin ("Fourfold"), who inspired Pontiac in 1763.

Around 1800, the Seneca league prophet Handsome Lake successfully reformed Iroquois society to accord with European notions of the family and farming, at the same time safeguarding ancestral rituals and religion. The Shawnee Tenskwatawa, however, failed in his attempted anti-European stance, advocated by his brother Tekumtha (Tecumsah).

Throughout the Southeast, tribal communities reforged themselves after massive slaving raids and epidemics. Often they heeded the call of one of their native priests, sponsors of farming rituals throughout the year who felt compelled to turn to prophecy to provide direction and cohesion to these often fragile communities.

Across the Plains the depopulation from microbes and wholesale displacement as some tribes got guns before others was offset by the wondrous arrival of the horse, enhancing much needed mobility. Prophets arose to stabilize new tribal cohesions, often based in rituals such as the variety of expressions gathered under the term "sun dance." The Civil War caused a variety of reactions in Native communities. Among many similar unifying expressions in the Midwest was the 1864 effort of Baptiste Peoria to consolidate Kansas survivors of the Illinois and Miami Confederacies into what became the Peoria tribe of Oklahoma.

As Mormons and others entered the Great Basin, these highly practical and streamlined native societies became the cradle for important historic movements. The simplicity of their round dances and their inherent respect for nature carried compelling messages. In 1870, Wodziwob (Fish Lake Joe) moved to Walker River and tried to introduce his community's mourning rite, setting off the first GHOST DANCE movement throughout the West. In 1890, Wovoka of Walker River, facilitated by transcontinental railroads, sparked the second and more famous Ghost Dance, whose bearers included the famous Lakota Sioux holy man Sitting Bull.

The spread of the horse into the Plateau led to huge mobile groups hunting bison in the northern Plains under the command of recently emerged heads of intertribal confederacies such as Weowich of the Yakamas and Split Sun (Eclipse) of the Interior Salishans. Prophets reacting to these sweeping changes, espousing a strict localization of tribal sentiments, included Smohalla along the mid–Columbia River and Skolaskin along the Sanpoil.

In 1881, near the capitol of Washington Territory, John Slocum, a man of chiefly family, died but soon was revived to found the Indian Shaker Church under the inspiration of his wife, Mary Thompson Slocum, who received the divine gift of "the shake," a Native religious manifestation akin to that of the original Quakers and other ecstatic cults. Brilliantly combining outward forms of Catholicism, Protestant hymns, notions of personal salvation, and core Native beliefs, several thousand international Shakers from northern California to southern British Columbia survived into the twenty-first century.

Wovoka. Known as the Paiute messiah for his visions that sparked the rapidly spreading Ghost Dance revival of 1889–1890, he renounced the movement after white attempts to suppress it led to the murder of Sitting Bull and the massacre at Wounded Knee, S.D., in 1890. NEVADA STATE HISTORICAL SOCIETY

Along the Canada-Alaska border, many prophets emerged in reaction to the fur trade, disease, disruption, and disillusionment. The most famous of these was Bini (Mind), a Carrier Athapascan, whose name became hereditary in his matriline and so passed to at least one woman who continued his message.

While women have been rare among prophets (as was Joan of Arc), they have had impact proportional to the intensity of their revelations. Before 1878, the Sioux Tailfeather Woman lost four of her sons in one battle with U.S. soldiers. Out of the depths of her grief came the Dream Dance Drum, an international peace based on the ceremonial transfer of large drums from one tribe to another that continued in the twenty-first century.

Indian Shakers. John Slocum (*left*) founded the Indian Shaker Church, a mixture of Native beliefs and varied elements of Christianity, which spread across the Pacific Northwest after 1882. With him is an early convert and church leader, Louis Yowaluck, who later founded an offshoot of the church. SMITHSONIAN INSTITUTION

Among the most successful of such reforms for over a century is the Native American Church, based on the sacramental use of a spineless cactus button, peyote, that grows in northern Mexico and was featured in pre-Columbian rituals. Adapted to use on the Plains by the Caddo-Delaware John "Moonhead" Wilson (Nishkantu) and Kiowa-Comanche leaders like Quannah Parker, this religion spread across North America. Several court challenges to such "drug use" were upheld until issues of religious freedom successfully were raised. Peyotists oppose the recreational use of alcohol and drugs, countering that the public, communal, ritual use of peyote is above misguided if not racist laws.

In the decades before 2000, prophets appeared in western Canada, target for extractive exploitation. Using special flags and dance pavilions, the people among the Dogribs, Dene Thas, and Dunne-zas have small but loyal followings.

Not to be overlooked is the role of Natives in the spread of world religions, in particular Baha'i, in both the United States and Canada. Indeed, Black Elk himself turned from his own vision to serve as a catechist for the Roman Catholic Church for the rest of his long life.

Overall, based in notions of personal revelations from powerful immortal beings (spirits), nativistic reforms emerge from prophetic messages intended for a larger audience within or across communities. Ever expanding, these audiences are the familial, the community, and the international, each directed toward the welfare of the larger community of all interacting beings in time and space. What makes these movements stand out moreover is that they represent a moment when channels of communication are unclogged and renewed in the hope that better understanding will follow into the future.

BIBLIOGRAPHY

Goulet, Jean-Guy A. *Ways of Knowing: Experience, Knowledge, and Power among the Dene Tha.* Lincoln: University of Nebraska Press, 1998.

Lanternari, Vittorio. *The Religions of the Oppressed: A Study of Modern Messianic Cults.* Translated from the Italian by Lisa Sergio. New York: Knopf, 1963.

Mooney, James. *The Ghost-Dance Religion and the Sioux Outbreak of 1890.* Chicago: University of Chicago Press, 1965. A reprint of the 1896 original.

Spier, Leslie. *The Prophet Dance of the Northwest and Its Derivations: The Source of the Ghost Dance.* New York: AMS Press, 1979.

Wallace, Anthony F. C. "Revitalization Movements." *American Anthropologist* 58 (1956): 264–281.

Wallis, Wilson. *Messiahs: Their Role in Civilization.* Washington, D.C.: American Council of Public Affairs, 1943.

Jay Miller

See also **Indian Missions; Indian Religious Life; Indian Social Life;** *and vol. 9:* **Letter from Wovoka.**

NATO. *See* **North Atlantic Treaty Organization.**

NATURAL GAS INDUSTRY. Before being used for energy purposes, the natural gas seeping from the earth produced "burning springs" that were of ritual and religious significance to early Greek, Persian, and Indian cultures. The British first commercialized natural gas around 1785. In the United States, natural gas was primarily a curiosity until the middle of the nineteenth century, but thereafter its importance as an energy resource increased significantly. As early as 1626, French missionaries recorded incidents of Indians igniting natural gas springs off Lake Erie and its surrounding streams. Early explorers noticed natural gas being emitted from the ground on both the east and west coasts of the United States. Gas springs were found near Charleston, West Virginia, as early as 1775. In 1796, M. Ambroise and Company, Italian fireworkers in Philadelphia, made the first recorded demonstration of burning natural gas in the United States. It aroused so much interest that in 1816 Rembrandt Peale put natural gas on display at his famous museum in Baltimore. But perhaps the best-known natural gas well during these years was in Fredonia, New-York, discovered in 1824 by William A. Hart, a local gunsmith. This spring was used to fuel thirty streetlights in the village and led to the founding in 1858 of the Fredonia Gaslight and Waterworks Company, which undertook commercial exploitation of this new source of energy. During the next fifty years scores of promoters developed similar natural gas wells in Ohio and Indiana, supplying factories as well as homes. By 1900 natural gas had been discovered in seventeen states, and the value of the gas produced in the United States amounted to $24 million annually.

Natural Gas. Beyond marshland near Port Sulphur, La., a natural gas installation burns off unwanted emissions in December 1972. NATIONAL ARCHIVES AND RECORDS ADMINISTRATION

During the first four decades of the twentieth century the natural gas industry grew, but its expansion was held up by a lack of suitable transportation. Increasing production of petroleum after 1900 boosted available natural gas enormously, since it appeared as a by-product. In 1920 the total annual value of natural gas produced had reached $196 million. Producers still faced serious problems in transporting the gas to the large urban centers that constituted their most lucrative markets. Ten years later engineers developed seamless electrically welded pipes that were capable of transmitting natural gas cheaply and efficiently over long distances, but in the midst of the Great Depression, investors were loath to develop such new pipelines to any appreciable extent.

WORLD WAR II inaugurated a tremendous boom in natural gas consumption and production, as this energy resource became the foundation for a major new industry. In the ensuing thirty years, prosperity and population growth stimulated investors to build thousands of miles of new pipelines from the vast natural gas fields in the Southwest to the great metropolitan areas of the East, the South, the Middle West, and the Far West. Natural gas quickly displaced coal and fuel oil in millions of homes and factories. It was far more versatile, and also cheaper, than its competitors. Gas could be used as readily for heating as for air conditioning and refrigeration. Moreover, it was cleaner and more convenient to use than coal or fuel oil and much easier to transport. Many industries came to utilize natural gas as a source of energy, including cement and synthetics manufacturers. In 1950 the natural gas industry served 8 million users with an income of about $1.5 billion. In 1960 it had 31 million customers and revenues totaling about $6 billion. By 1970 natural gas producers supplied more than 42 million individuals and corporations, who paid $11 billion for the product. Between 1950 and 1970 the number of natural gas wells in the United States more than doubled, totaling about 120,000 in 1970. At that point, the natural gas industry had emerged as one of the ten most important in the nation. In 1999 the industry had almost 62 million customers and earned over $46 billion for providing natural gas to them. By 2002 the number of natural gas wells in the United States had increased steadily to over 306,000. Roughly 85 percent of the natural gas consumed in the United States is extracted within the country, with the remainder mostly imported from Canada and Mexico.

This period of intensive growth was accompanied by increasing federal regulation of the industry. In the years between 1914 and 1938, state governments had been the prime regulators of gas production, seeking to reduce the excessive waste that was then so common. But their regulations varied greatly and frequently were not enforced. Thus, representatives of the industry as well as conservationists prevailed upon Congress in the New Deal era to extend federal control over the interstate transmission of natural gas. Their efforts resulted in the Natural Gas Act of 1938, which placed responsibility for national regulation in the hands of the Federal Power Commission. Since locally produced gas often mingled with gas crossing state boundaries, the commissioners found it difficult to determine clear boundaries of federal jurisdiction. Between 1942 and 1970, both the Federal Power Commission and the federal courts aggressively extended federal control over virtually all natural gas produced in the United States. In particular, the SUPREME COURT decision in *Phillips Petroleum Company v. Wisconsin* (347 U.S. 672 [1954]) greatly expanded the Federal Power Commission's authority over the industry. Despite protests from natural gas producers that federal regulation was hampering their expansion, the natural gas industry became one of the most closely government-regulated industries in the nation. The Clean Air Act Amendments of 1990 require municipal fleets with ten or more vehicles to replace all retired autos with "clean fuel vehicles." Taxi cabs, school buses, transit buses, street sweepers, and delivery trucks have been increasingly replaced with or converted to natural gas vehicles. The number of natural gas fueling stations is increasing rapidly, providing fuel that is, on average, one-third the cost of gasoline. Today there are over 110,000 natural gas vehicles on U.S. roads.

BIBLIOGRAPHY

De Vany, Arthur S., and David Walls. *The Emerging New Order in Natural Gas: Markets Versus Regulation.* Westport, Conn: Quorum Books, 1995.

Herbert, John H. *Clean Cheap Heat: The Development of Residential Markets for Natural Gas in the United States.* New York: Praeger, 1992.

Ingersoll, John G. *Natural Gas Vehicles.* Lilburn, Ga.: Fairmont Press, 1996.

MacAvoy, Paul, and Robert S. Pindyck. *The Economics of Natural Gas Shortage, 1960–1980.* New York: American Elsevier, 1975.

———. *The Natural Gas Market: Sixty Years of Regulation and Deregulation.* New Haven, Conn: Yale University Press, 2000.

Nash, Gerald D. *United States Oil Policy, 1890–1964: Business and Government in Twentieth-Century America.* Pittsburgh, Pa.: University of Pittsburgh Press, 1968.

Gerald D. Nash / H. S.; A. E.

See also **Air Pollution; Automobile Industry; Coal; Conservation; Energy Industry; Energy, Renewable; Heating; Petrochemical Industry.**

NATURAL RIGHTS. Natural rights, according to American tradition, are those rights granted to humankind by their Creator, or as Jefferson put it in the DECLARATION OF INDEPENDENCE—essentially borrowing from John Locke's *Second Treatise on Government* (1690)—the rights accorded by "Nature and Nature's God." In the Declaration, these are described as "unalienable" rights, and include the recognition that "all men are created equal" and that all have rights to "Life, Liberty, and the Pursuit of Happiness."

Locke himself formulated man's basic natural right as "to preserve his property, that is, his life, liberty and estate," and both Jefferson's and Locke's ideas found echoes in some of the early American state constitutions. The Pennsylvania Constitution of 1776 was typical. It declared "That all men are born equally free and independent, and have certain natural, inherent and unalienable rights, amongst which are the enjoying and defending life and liberty, acquiring, possessing and protecting property, and pursuing and obtaining happiness and safety." The Pennsylvania document added to this enumeration of its citizens' rights, among others, the "natural and unalienable right to worship Almighty God according to the dictates of their own consciences and understanding," and it made clear that "the community hath an indubitable, unalienable and indefeasible right to reform, alter or abolish government, in such manner as shall be by that community judged most conducive to the public weal." Natural rights, then, protect particular individual freedoms, but also give the community the right to self-government, so long as that government continues to protect and preserve the basic natural rights of individuals. When government fails to protect those rights, revolution—as Locke and the Declaration affirmed—is justified.

While natural rights are, in theory at least, the gift of a benevolent creator, American documents of fundamental law, following the English example, have tended to enumerate these basic protections against the government in documents called "bills of rights." The most important consists of the first ten amendments to the U.S. Constitution, passed in 1791. These include, among others, rights of freedom of religion, freedom of speech, freedom of the press, freedom from unreasonable searches and seizures, rights to trial by jury, and the guarantee that no one will be deprived of life, liberty, or property without due process of law.

Over the course of American history there has been a great deal of debate over whether the broad generalizations regarding natural rights in the Declaration of Independence ought to be regarded as incorporated within the more specific guarantees of the U.S. Constitution, or even regarded as "supra-Constitutional principles" that are nevertheless binding on all American governments. The suggestion that there are such principles can be found in some early American federal and state cases. For example, in *CALDER V. BULL* (1798) U.S. Supreme Court Justice Samuel Chase declares that whether or not there are express prohibitions against it in a Constitution, no "republican" government can make a person judge and party in his own case, pass a law that makes criminal an act legal when committed, or take one person's property without compensation and grant it to another. Similarly, in *Currie's Administrators v. The Mutual Assurance Society* (1809), Virginia supreme court judge Spencer Roane observed that "all free governments" were instituted for the protection of "our rights of person and property," and that the powers of legislatures are bounded by "the principles and provisions of the constitution and bill of rights, and by those great rights and principles, for the preservation of which all just governments are founded."

The sentiments in the Declaration that all men are created equal led the abolitionists, in the antebellum years, to resist the American law of slavery and to argue, based on natural rights, that the provisions in the Constitution that supported slavery were null and void. This view was rejected by Chief Justice Roger Taney in the DRED SCOTT CASE of 1857, in which he essentially ruled that the property rights of the slaveholders trumped any words of the Declaration. Taney's view was repudiated by many speeches of Abraham Lincoln, most notably in his GETTYSBURG ADDRESS (1863), where he reaffirmed the idea that the United States had been "conceived in liberty, and dedicated to the proposition that all men are created equal" and that, further, the Civil War was being fought to reaffirm those principles and to preserve "government of the people, for the people, by the people." The Thirteenth Amendment's abolition of slavery and the Fourteenth Amendment's guarantee that state governments may not deprive anyone of the "equal protection of the laws" have come to be viewed as vital protections of the natural rights of Americans.

Thus, in the 1950s and 1960s the Supreme Court under Earl Warren, chiefly employing the Fourteenth Amendment, rendered a series of decisions, based on simple principles of equality and individual rights, that were viewed by their champions as essential implementations of justice or natural rights. These included prohibitions on racial segregation in schools and public services, prohibitions on mandatory school prayer and Bible reading, guarantees that state legislatures had to be organized around the principle of "one man, one vote," and restrictions on police practices that encroached on the rights of the accused. None of these decisions was dictated by the text of the Constitution, or by the historical understanding of its provisions, but all had in common an expansive and egalitarian notion of individual rights quite consistent with Lincoln's address, if not Jefferson's Declaration.

In the late twentieth and early twenty-first century, jurisprudential approaches based on natural rights were falling out of favor at the federal level because they gave judges too much discretion. Thus, Clarence Thomas's nomination to the Supreme Court foundered briefly because he had given speeches indicating a commitment to the implementation of the kind of "natural law" thinking in the Declaration. While the Supreme Court seemed to be shying away from the expansive implementation of individual natural rights, however, it was becoming increasingly common for state court judges to reject civil justice reform efforts of state legislatures on the grounds that they interfered with state constitutional guarantees of natural rights such as the right to trial by jury or to enjoy the benefits of the separation of governmental powers. Finally, the revolutionary American ideas of natural rights were being metamorphosed or superseded in international law by conceptions of human rights. These were often invoked by insurgents who sought to throw off oppressive governments and by countries, including the United States, that sought, often in concert, to intervene in other sovereign nations' affairs where human rights had been infringed.

BIBLIOGRAPHY

Gerber, Scott Douglas. *To Secure These Rights: The Declaration of Independence and Constitutional Interpretation.* New York: New York University Press, 1995.

Jaffa, Harry V. *A New Birth of Freedom: Abraham Lincoln and the Coming of the Civil War.* Lanham, Md.: Rowman and Littlefield, 2000.

Perry, Michael J. *The Constitution, the Courts, and Human Rights: An Inquiry into the Legitimacy of Constitutional Policymaking by the Judiciary.* New Haven, Conn.: Yale University Press, 1982.

Presser, Stephen B. "Liberty under Law under Siege" *ORBIS: A Journal of World Affairs* 45 (2001): 357–369.

———, and Jamil S. Zainaldin. *Law and Jurisprudence in American History.* 4th ed. St. Paul, Minn.: West Group, 2000

Stephen B. Presser

See also **Constitution of the United States.**

NATURALISM, a literary mode developed in the late nineteenth and early twentieth centuries, characterized by detailed description, scientific and sociological themes, an objective, documentary quality, and a deterministic philosophy. The term "naturalism" is especially, but not exclusively, applied to novels. French writers such as the Goncourt brothers and Émile Zola pioneered naturalism in the late 1860s and 1870s. In the following three decades, naturalism appeared in Germany (the plays of Gerhart Hauptmann) and England (the novels of George Gissing and Arnold Bennett).

When transplanted to American soil near the turn of the twentieth century, naturalism flourished in the hands of such novelists as Harold Frederic, Frank Norris, Theodore Dreiser, Jack London, Stephen Crane, Hamlin Garland, David Graham Phillips, and Upton Sinclair. Many later works also have naturalistic qualities—including John Dos Passos's *U.S.A.* trilogy (1930, 1932, 1936), John Steinbeck's *Grapes of Wrath* (1939), James Farrell's *Studs Lonigan* trilogy (1932, 1934, 1935), Richard Wright's *Native Son* (1940), Norman Mailer's *Executioner's Song* (1979), Tom Wolfe's *Bonfire of the Vanities* (1987), and Bret Easton Ellis's *American Psycho* (1991). Naturalism's endurance suggests that it has become a fixture in the American literary landscape.

Influences

Naturalism's most important theorist, Émile Zola, was perhaps its leading practitioner. His preface to the second edition of *Thérèse Raquin* (1868) defines naturalism, while his "The Experimental Novel" (1880) elaborates on its method. Zola urges novelists to work like scientists, placing characters in controlled environments and studying temperaments rather than individualized characters. This strategy results in a narrative posture of detached objectivity and clinical observation. Zola exemplified these qualities in his twenty-volume *Rougon-Macquart* series, illustrating the effects of heredity and environment on several generations.

Naturalism absorbed scientific and social scientific ideas, in particular Charles Darwin's theory of evolution and Karl Marx's theory of class struggle. These influences suggest why naturalists deliberately depict limited characters—not autonomous agents but creatures acted upon by biological or social forces. That Dreiser's Carrie Meeber "drifts" through *Sister Carrie* (1900), or that Sinclair's Jurgis Rudkis is pummeled by circumstances throughout THE JUNGLE (1906) is precisely the point. Coercion or chance will more likely determine events than will choice, deliberation, or morality.

Naturalist works respond as much to material changes as to intellectual currents. Industrialization and urbanization occurred rapidly in America following the Civil War, and naturalists responded by addressing new literary subjects such as factory work (*The Jungle*), immigrant populations (Abraham Cahan's *The Rise of David Levinsky*, 1917), slums (Crane's *Maggie: A Girl of the Streets*, 1893), the closing of the western frontier (Norris's *The Octopus*, 1901), and the growth of consumer culture (*Sister Carrie*). Despite a characteristic interest in dislocations brought on by the modern economy—or perhaps because of it—some naturalist authors trace a retreat from civilization, such as to the high seas (London's *The Sea Wolf*, 1904), or examine the provincial countryside that was increasingly being eclipsed by urban centers (Garland's *Main-Travelled Roads*, 1891).

Characteristics

Naturalists often depict biological, social, and economic determinants as interdependent, though dominant preoccupations can be isolated. Racial or genetic conditions may prevail (as in *McTeague* or *The Octopus*), or environmental ones (as in Wright's *Native Son*, 1940, or *Maggie*); economic class may be decisive (Dreiser's *An American Tragedy*, 1925), as may gender (as in Edith Wharton's *The House of Mirth*, 1905). Often naturalistic narrators, or their mouthpieces, engage in lengthy disquisitions explaining abstract concepts incomprehensible to their hapless characters (as in book three of *Native Son*, where the defense lawyer provides a Marxist analysis of why Bigger Thomas committed murder). Such lectures may seem digressive, while also placing the characters at a distance from the author and the reader. Such narrative interpolations also suggest the overlap of naturalism with social science. Indeed, naturalist novels share topics and rhetorical strategies with such nonfiction treatises as Charlotte Perkins Gilman's *Women and Economics* (1898), Thorstein Veblen's *The Theory of the Leisure Class* (1899), Jacob Riis's *How the Other Half Lives* (1890), the criminology of Cesare Lombroso, and the time-motion studies of Frederick Winslow Taylor.

Degeneration or "devolution" is a dominant naturalistic motif, manifesting itself in studies of crime and violence (such as *Native Son* and *American Psycho*) and in the liberal use of animal imagery to describe human conduct, as in the famous lobster and squid episode at the beginning of Dreiser's *The Financier* (1912). The animal fixation extends to one of Norris's characters thinking he becomes a wolf (*Vandover and the Brute*, 1914), and to London making a dog the protagonist of *The Call of the Wild* (1903).

Although some American naturalists attempt the objectivity lauded by Zola, most write more like journalists than like scientists. Many worked for newspapers and magazines before adapting journalism's characteristic descriptiveness into fiction. Sinclair's on-site research for *The Jungle* helped make his exposé of the meatpacking industry so shocking. Norris's research for *McTeague* ranged from dentistry to actual murder cases. In describing the trolley strike in *Sister Carrie*, Dreiser drew liberally from an account he had written for the *Toledo Blade*. Furthermore, journalism itself becomes a literary motif: in *An American Tragedy*, Clyde Griffiths reads a news account that inspires him to murder his pregnant girlfriend; in *Native Son*, Wright uses newspapers to expose the racist bias of the press; in the *U.S.A.* trilogy, Dos Passos combines actual news clippings to produce the "Newsreel" sections. American naturalism's documentary strategies have made it a reliable source for historians.

Another hallmark is a fixation on sexuality and gender. Naturalism has been described as hypermasculine, with its rugged male characters such as Norris's plainspoken Buck Annixter in *The Octopus*, the virile tycoon Frank Cowperwood of Dreiser's *Financier* trilogy (1912, 1914, 1947), or London's brutal sea captain Wolf Larsen of *The Sea-Wolf.* Naturalists often depict women in similarly exaggerated terms: Dreiser's Carrie is more aroused by shopping than by her lovers; the large-armed Hilma Tree of *The Octopus* seems more nature goddess than human; and the miserly Trina McTeague parodies the frugal housewife. Women have not written as many naturalist novels, though Ann Petry's *The Street* (1946), Edith Wharton's *The House of Mirth* (1905), and Kate Chopin's *The Awakening* (1899), all profound studies of environmental pressures on women, certainly qualify.

Despite naturalist authors' overarching interest in ideologically charged subjects, it is impossible to generalize about their political positions. London and Sinclair were proud to be socialist reformers, and the development of proletarian literature in the 1930s owes much to naturalism. Norris, by contrast, looks down on his working-class characters, especially in *McTeague.* Authors frequently change positions over time: Dreiser, for instance, is critical of capitalism in *Sister Carrie* (the beginning of which shows factories exploiting workers, especially women) and in *An American Tragedy* (where Griffiths's unquestioning acceptance of the dominant ideology of success and ambition causes his downfall), but he glorifies capitalist unscrupulousness in the *Financier* trilogy.

Naturalism and Literary History

American naturalism has never been a self-conscious school, nor have its practitioners issued systematic theories. Naturalism is often situated alongside the more polite realism of such writers as William Dean Howells or Henry James. The comparison is both necessary and inconclusive, for some authorities maintain naturalism is an outgrowth of realism, and others, that naturalism repudiates the genteel premises of realism. An additional complication is that some authors said to exemplify naturalism, such as Dreiser, are also hailed as landmark realists. Further confusion results from archetypal naturalist Norris defining his writing (and also Zola's) as romanticism in *The Responsibilities of the Novelist* (1903). That text, along with Garland's *Crumbling Idols* (1894) and Dreiser's "True Art Speaks Plainly" (1903), are important manifestos of American naturalism with widely different emphases.

One way of resolving this confusion is to consider realism and naturalism as existing on a continuum. Both employ descriptive detail and social themes, but realism tends to adopt more conventionally moral positions, while seeming less extreme, less pessimistic, and simply less bizarre than naturalism. Thus, Howells's *Rise of Silas Lapham* (1885) shows its allegiance to realism by locating a businessman's "rise" in his decision to place morality above money making, while Dreiser's *The Titan* (1914) exemplifies naturalism in depicting a businessman's being rewarded for his amorality through financial success and multiple sexual partners.

The case of American naturalism demonstrates that literary modes are not absolute categories but flexible ap-

Sherwood Anderson. A photograph by Alfred Stieglitz of the early-twentieth-century writer, whose best-known book, *Winesburg, Ohio* (1919), contains elements of naturalism as well as modernism. LIBRARY OF CONGRESS

proaches that authors can shape, combine, and rework. The treatment of the oppressive urban environment in Henry Roth's *Call It Sleep* (1934), for example, is naturalistic while its stream-of-consciousness narration is a modernist technique. Much of the nightmarish imagery of *The Street* is expressionistic, notwithstanding its naturalistic treatment of the effects of the ghetto on character. The compulsive characters in *Winesburg, Ohio* (1919) suggest naturalism, while Sherwood Anderson's Freudian emphasis on dreams and sexuality aligns his book with modernism.

This fluidity is especially significant because neither naturalism nor realism has ever enjoyed the éclat of the literary modes that flourished before it (the romanticism of Nathaniel Hawthorne and Herman Melville) or after it (the modernism of Gertrude Stein and William Faulkner). Naturalism's detractors have claimed its penchant for plots of decline, deterministic vision, and limited characters demonstrate its impoverished vision. Such unpleasant features caused many early twentieth-century readers to complain of barbarous and even immoral writing. Dreiser's response is exemplary: "True art speaks plainly. . . . The sum and substance of literary as well as social morality may be expressed in three words—tell the truth" (reprinted in Becker, p. 155). Even if unwilling to grant naturalists the ground of superior truthfulness that they prized, we can still appreciate their widening of the literary canvas, their engagement with important social issues, and their often unembarrassed political engagement. The mode that struck earlier readers as "immoral" is indeed strong medicine, but has opened up countless literary possibilities that have yet to be exhausted.

BIBLIOGRAPHY

Becker, George J., ed. *Documents of Modern Literary Realism.* Princeton, N.J.: Princeton University Press, 1963.

Howard, June. *Form and History in American Literary Naturalism.* Chapel Hill: University of North Carolina Press, 1985.

Kazin, Alfred. *On Native Grounds: An Interpretation of Modern American Prose Literature.* Fortieth Anniversary Edition. New York: Harcourt Brace Jovanovich, 1982.

Michaels, Walter Benn. *The Gold Standard and the Logic of Naturalism: American Literature at the Turn of the Century.* Berkeley: University of California Press, 1987.

Pizer, Donald. *Realism and Naturalism in Nineteenth-Century American Literature.* Rev. ed. Carbondale: Southern Illinois University Press, 1984.

Pizer, Donald, ed. *The Cambridge Companion to American Realism and Naturalism: Howells to London.* Cambridge, U.K.: Cambridge University Press, 1995.

Wilson, Christopher P. *The Labor of Words: Literary Professionalism in the Progressive Era.* Athens: University of Georgia Press, 1985.

Clare Virginia Eby

See also **Literature.**

NATURALIZATION. U.S. citizenship—a legal status making one a member of the political community—is acquired at birth or through naturalization. With few exceptions, those born on U.S. territory or abroad to American parents automatically acquire U.S. citizenship. Other foreign-born persons, called aliens in legal terminology, must "naturalize" to acquire the status and rights of native-born citizens.

Historically naturalization was considered critical in building America. In colonial America, only the British parliament could naturalize aliens and make them British subjects. Colonies established local naturalization procedures, but London banned these practices in 1773. The conflict over naturalization is evident in the Declaration of Independence, which charges that King George III "has endeavoured to prevent the Population of these States; for that purpose obstructing the Laws for Naturalization of Foreigners." The Articles of Confederation (article 4) left naturalization to the states, but the U.S. Constitution (article 1, section 8, clause 4) gave this power to the federal legislative branch. The first Congress quickly exercised its authority, passing the first U.S. naturalization law on 26 March 1790.

Naturalization can be collective, an individual judicial process, or derivative. Collective naturalization grants citizenship to a group of people, usually after territorial acquisition. Residents of Louisiana, Florida, the Mexican territories, and Alaska received citizenship through treaties of incorporation, and Texans acquired citizenship through a joint resolution of Congress in 1845. American Indians received citizenship through statute (in 1924), as did people in Hawaii (1900), Puerto Rico (1917), the U.S. Virgin Islands (1927), and Guam (1950).

Individual judicial naturalization is perhaps most familiar, used by adult immigrants to become American citizens. From 1790 to 1802 a series of naturalization laws set the core regulations for the next century. Many provisions continue today, including a five-year residence requirement, the need to demonstrate "good moral character," and the obligation to swear an oath of allegiance. Congress gave the courts authority to administer and grant naturalization.

In 1905 a presidential commission investigated lack of standardization and abuses to the naturalization system. At the time, courts charged varying fees, had their own forms, and sometimes turned a blind eye to fraud. The Naturalization Act of 29 June 1906 established a new federal agency, the Bureau of Immigration and Naturalization, to help administer citizenship and establish nationwide standards. The act also made oral English ability a requirement of citizenship.

Today, the Immigration and Nationality Act of 27 June 1952 (the McCarran-Walter Act) and subsequent amendments governs naturalization. Under this act, applicants must demonstrate basic ability in written English. The Immigration Act of 29 November 1990 extended exceptions to the English requirement and assigned exclusive jurisdiction over naturalization to the attorney general.

Unlike many countries, the United States has had no religious requirements for naturalization since 1790. However, throughout the nineteenth and early-twentieth centuries significant racial, gender, and marital status restrictions existed. The 1790 act limited naturalization to "free white persons." Following the Civil War and the Fourteenth Amendment, the Naturalization Act of 14 July 1870 expanded this to "persons of African nativity and African descent." Chinese were barred from naturalization under the Chinese Exclusion Act of 6 May 1882. Subsequent court decisions denied most individuals from Asia access to U.S. citizenship. Racial restrictions only began to disappear during World War II, first for Chinese (1943), then East Indians and Filipinos (1946), and finally for any group in 1952.

Finally, citizenship can also be derived from a close relation. Historically, married women derived citizenship from their husband and in some periods had no control over their status. Under the Act of 10 February 1855, a woman automatically became an American upon marrying a U.S. citizen or following the naturalization of her foreign husband. The 1907 Expatriation Act (2 March) extended this logic by taking away the citizenship of a U.S.-born or naturalized American woman if she married an alien. The 1922 Married Women's Act (or the Cable Act) finally severed the link between naturalization and marital status for most women. However, women who married foreign-born Asian men ineligible for naturalization did not retain independent citizenship until 1931.

Since 1790, children can derive citizenship from a parent when the parent naturalizes. The Child Citizenship Act of 2000 added a new provision making citizenship automatic for children adopted from foreign countries, provided at least one parent is American at the time of adoption.

BIBLIOGRAPHY

Smith, Rogers M. *Civic Ideals: Conflicting Visions of Citizenship in U.S. History.* New Haven, Conn.: Yale University Press, 1997.

Ueda, Reed. "Naturalization and Citizenship." In *Immigration.* Edited by Richard A. Easterlin et al. Cambridge, Mass.: Belknap Press, 1982.

United States Immigration and Naturalization Service. Home page at http://www.ins.usdoj.gov.

Irene Bloemraad

See also **Immigration Restriction.**

NAUTILUS. The *Nautilus,* a "diving boat" armed with a torpedo, designed and built at Rouen, France, by Robert Fulton, was launched on 24 July 1800. After several successful submersions of it, Fulton submitted his plans for submarine operations against England's navy to Napoleon Bonaparte, who advanced ten thousand francs for repairs and improvements to the *Nautilus.* Although Fulton blew up a French sloop with the *Nautilus,* at Brest, 11 August 1801, he dismantled it when Napoleon offered no further encouragement. The U.S. Navy resurrected the name for the first nuclear powered submarine, the U.S.S. *Nautilus,* completed in 1954.

BIBLIOGRAPHY

Hoyt, Edwin P. *From the Turtle to the Nautilus: The Story of Submarines.* Boston: Little, Brown, 1963.

Hutcheon, Wallace. *Robert Fulton, Pioneer of Undersea Warfare.* Annapolis, Md.: Naval Institute Press, 1981.

Louis H. Bolander / A. R.

See also **Arms Race and Disarmament; Submarines; Torpedo Warfare.**

NAUVOO, MORMONS AT. Nauvoo, Illinois, was the central gathering place for the Church of Jesus Christ of Latter-day Saints from 1839 to 1846. Joseph Smith, the founder of the church, purchased the site of the town of Commerce, located on a spit of land extending into the Mississippi River near Quincy. Soon after he changed the name to Nauvoo, a word signifying, he said, "a beautiful location, a place of rest." Mormons collected at Nauvoo from all over the United States and from Great Britain, where a vigorous missionary effort was conducted. Eventually, the population of Mormons in Nauvoo and the immediate vicinity reached about fifteen thousand. The state charter obtained from the legislature in 1840 permitted the city to form a militia and to organize municipal courts, which Smith hoped would protect the Mormons from the persecution they had experienced elsewhere.

Smith attempted to develop Nauvoo as a capital city for the church. The Mormons began a temple on a bluff overlooking the city, organized a company to construct a large hotel, and laid plans for a university. Smith served as mayor and was chosen lieutenant general of the militia. Smith revealed some of his most distinctive and controversial doctrines at Nauvoo. The Mormons began the practice of baptism for the dead, which enabled the deceased to receive the benefits of the Christian ordinance vicariously. He instituted rituals that were available only to selected church members in the privacy of the temple and taught the doctrine of eternal and plural marriage. Plural marriage, in which men married multiple wives, turned some highly placed Mormons against Smith. They organized a reformist movement and published a newspaper exposing the prophet. When Smith as mayor closed down the paper and destroyed its press, non-Mormon citizens in the surrounding towns demanded his arrest. Opposition had already been building against the Mormons because of their growing influence in county politics. On 27 June 1844, while Smith was awaiting trial, a lynching party invaded the jail where he was held and shot and killed him.

Brigham Young, who succeeded Smith as president of the church, remained in Nauvoo until opposition rose again. On 6 February 1846, the first party of Mormons left Nauvoo for the West, and the remainder of the saints followed within a year. The temple was burned, and Nauvoo lapsed into quiescence. The church restored the town as a tourist site and completed reconstruction of the temple in 2002.

BIBLIOGRAPHY

Ehat, Andrew F., and Lyndon W. Cook. *The Words of Joseph Smith: The Contemporary Accounts of the Nauvoo Discourses of the Prophet Joseph.* Orem, Utah: Grandin Book Company, 1991.

Flanders, Robert Bruce. *Nauvoo: Kingdom on the Mississippi.* Urbana: University of Illinois Press, 1965.

Hampshire, Annette P. *Mormonism in Conflict: The Nauvoo Years.* New York: Edwin Mellen Press, 1985.

Leonard, Glen M. *Nauvoo: A Place of Peace, A People of Promise.* Salt Lake City: Deseret Books, 2002.

Miller, David E., and Della S. Miller. *Nauvoo: The City of Joseph.* Salt Lake City: Peregrine Smith, 1974.

Oaks, Dallin H., and Marvin S. Hill. *Carthage Conspiracy: The Trial of the Accused Assassins of Joseph Smith.* Urbana: University of Illinois Press, 1975.

Richard Lyman Bushman

See also **Latter-day Saints, Church of Jesus Christ of.**

NAVAJO. The Navajos, or Dine (the People), as they call themselves in their own language, are the most populous Indian community in the United States. A majority of the community's more than 225,000 members reside within the boundaries of the Navajo Nation, a sprawling enclave of 25,000 square miles, approximately the size of West Virginia, that is situated in northeastern Arizona, northwestern New Mexico, and southeastern Utah.

Until the late twentieth century most archaeologists thought that the Navajos, and their linguistic relatives the Apaches, had arrived perhaps two centuries before the Spanish incursion in the region in the sixteenth century. They generally portrayed the Dine as dependent upon the Puebloan peoples for survival in a harsh, new land. Further research, however suggests that the Navajos came to the Southwest a century or two earlier than had been assumed. It also suggests that the Navajos absorbed other peoples, including some of the Anasazi, forming a dynamic, expansionist culture that by the time of Coronado had become a significant force in New Mexico. The Navajo clan system reflects the incorporation not only of Puebloan peoples but also of Utes, Apaches, Paiutes, and Spanish or Mexican individuals and groups.

The Spanish presence created many difficulties for the Navajos, including the evolution of a vast slave trade that forced many Dine women and children into involuntary servitude. However, the Spaniards also brought livestock, the addition of which transformed the Navajo world. It would be hard for later observers to imagine the Dine without sheep, horses, goats, and cattle. Livestock, especially sheep, quickly became central to the workings of Navajo society. The Navajos became extraordinary weavers. Sheep also fed people and helped pay for ceremonial services. To be sure, the Dine gave no credit to Spain for introducing these animals. Rather, the elders told the children that the Holy People had brought these wonderful beings to the Navajos, charging the Dine with the responsibility of caring for them properly.

The Navajos often raided Spanish communities in order to obtain additional livestock and to seek revenge for their relatives who had been incarcerated. From their administrative headquarters in the northern Rio Grande valley, the Spanish dispatched punitive expeditions against the Dine. But the Navajos remained elusive; any treaty or agreement signed with one group of the Dine was not considered binding on another group some distance away. After gaining independence from Spain in 1821, the Mexicans experienced comparable problems. When the United States claimed the region during and following the war

Navajo Weaver. A woman spins wool in front of her loom in Torreon, N.M.; weaving and sheep are central to Navajo society. NATIONAL ARCHIVES AND RECORDS ADMINISTRATION

with Mexico in the late 1840s, it was determined to assert its authority over these uncooperative residents.

American aggression brought about what the Navajos would call "the fearing time." Within a generation, most of the Dine had been forced to surrender and, in the early to mid-1860s, departed on forced marches into captivity hundreds of miles from their home country. "The Long Walk," as it became known, took them to Fort Sumner, a newly constructed post in east-central New Mexico. There the head military officer for New Mexico Territory, James Carleton, expressed the hope that away from "the haunts and hills and hiding places" of their own country, the Navajos would become a contented and peaceful people.

Fort Sumner, or Hweeldi, as the Navajo termed it, never came close to fulfilling Carleton's dreams.Instead, it brought enormous hardship and anguish to the captive Dine. Disease and despair swept through the people, who desperately wanted to return to their homeland. In 1868 two members of the U.S. Peace Commission, William Tecumseh Sherman and Lewis Tappan, arrived at Fort Sumner to negotiate what turned out to be one of the final treaties signed by the United States with an American Indian nation. Sherman had suggested the possibility of the Navajos moving to Indian Territory, but this notion was immediately protested by Barboncito, the head Dine spokesperson, who argued that the Holy People had intended that the Navajos should live only within the boundaries of the four sacred mountains of their home country.

The Treaty of 1868 represented in many ways a triumph for the Navajos. Not only did they return to a portion of their homeland, but they succeeded in adding substantial amounts of acreage through a series of executive orders. Land became more difficult to obtain after New Mexico and Arizona became states in 1912, but by that time the essential Navajo land base had been established. In the early 1900s the photographer Edward Curtis used a group of Navajos on horseback to exemplify the notion of Indians as a vanishing race, but the twentieth century would prove him to be incorrect.

In the 1930s Commissioner of Indian Affairs John Collier imposed a drastic program of livestock reduction upon the Navajos. Although launched in the name of soil conservation and the well-being of the Dine, the program brought trauma and enormous suffering to thousands of Navajos. It also began to prompt a movement by many of the Dine into the wage economy, a movement that accelerated with the Navajo participation in World War II. Finally, the program initiated the transformation of the Navajo Tribal Council from an entity initially imposed upon the Navajos in the 1920s as a means to approve oil leases to a unit that represented the people.

The Navajo Code Talkers—a special unit in the U.S. Marines that employed the Navajo language as the basis

Navajo Nation. A desolate stretch of Dine Bikeyah (the Navajo country), the Navajos' large reservation, which is mostly in northeastern Arizona. AP/WIDE WORLD PHOTOS

for an effective code—played a vital role in the Pacific Campaign during World War II. Several hundred Dine became Code Talkers, and thousands worked in war-related industries. After the war the Dine leadership launched a program of sweeping modernization, including a new emphasis on formal education, industrialization, and road construction. Aided by funds from the Navajo-Hopi Long Range Rehabilitation Act of the 1950s, the Navajo tribal government began a nationalistic movement to gain greater control over Dine lives and lands.

The last decades of the twentieth century brought sweeping, and at times overwhelming, social and cultural change to Dine Bikeyah (the Navajo country). Only a minority of the people, most of them elderly, herded sheep, and most Navajo children grew up speaking English as a first language. Yet many of the traditional values within Navajo society are still observed and honored. The Dine bring new elements into their culture and, over time, make them Navajo. Members of the Navajo Nation struggled to control their own educational systems, to develop their economies in an appropriate way, and to live within the sacred mountains. Their very presence, the continuation of their language and their arts, and their successful incorporation of old and new means of competing and achieving (ranging from chess, basketball, and rodeos to tourism, education, and the arts) deny the old image of the vanishing Indian. As the twenty-first century began, the Navajos were clearly here to stay.

BIBLIOGRAPHY

Iverson, Peter. *Dine: A History of the Navajos.* Albuquerque: University of New Mexico Press, 2002. Photographs by Monty Roessel (Navajo).

Iverson, Peter, ed. *"For Our Navajo People": Navajo Letters, Speeches, and Petitions, 1900–1960.* Albuquerque: University of New Mexico Press, 2002. Photographs by Monty Roessel (Navajo).

Peter Iverson

See also **Tribes: Southwestern.**

NAVAJO CODE TALKERS were Native Americans who encoded, transmitted, and decoded messages for the U.S. Marine Corps during World War II. Philip Johnston, the son of a missionary to the Navajos, broached the idea of using Navajo tribesmen to send secure communications for the marines in 1942. Johnston was aware that Native Americans, notably Choctaws, had been used by the U.S. Army in World War I to encode messages. Following successful demonstrations of the Navajos' ability to encode, transmit, and decode messages, the Marine Corps began recruiting Navajos in May 1942. The first group of twenty-nine Navajos created the Navajo code, devising a dictionary and numerous words for military terms. As they were trained, the Navajo code talkers were assigned to marine units deploying in the Pacific theater. The code talkers transmitted information on tactics,

Navajo Code Talkers. A two-man team in the Pacific relays orders in the Navajos' native language.

troop movements, orders, and other battlefield communications over tactical telephones and radios in their native language, a code the Japanese never broke. They served in all six marine divisions, marine raider battalions, and marine parachute units in the Pacific, taking part in every assault the marines conducted. As of 1945, about 540 Navajos had enlisted in the Marine Corps; from 375 to 420 of those were trained as code talkers. About twenty Navajos along with Native Americans from other tribes served with the army in the same capacity in Europe.

BIBLIOGRAPHY

Paul, Doris A. *The Navajo Code Talkers.* Philadelphia: Dorance, 1973.

Vincent H. Demma

NAVAJO LANGUAGE. The Navajo language is the most heavily used language of Native North America. The NAVAJO tribe itself has about 220,000 members, the second largest Native American tribe in the United States. During the 1990s it was estimated that about 145,000 spoke the language, by far the largest number of speakers of any Native North American language—about 45 percent of all speakers of such languages—as well as the highest ratio of speakers among tribal members.

Navajo, with other languages such as Jicarilla, Mescalero-Chiricahua, and Western Apache, form a language complex called Apachean. At the time of the European contact Apachean was spoken over a large area of the southwestern United States, centered in New Mexico and Arizona, and that is still the case. Apachean is part of the large Athapaskan family of languages that is centered in northwestern Canada, the area generally believed to be the Athapaskan homeland. In addition to Apachean, there is another small cluster of extinct or nearly extinct Athapaskan outliers, such as Hupa, on the Pacific Coast of northern California. This linguistic configuration supports the generally accepted view that the Apacheans are relatively recent immigrants into their present homeland, probably about one thousand years ago. However, details such as the route of migration, whether the migration was unitary or came in waves, and its relationship to cultures in the Southwest known from the archeological record are matters of controversy.

During World War II, the U.S. Marines created a unit of so-called NAVAJO CODE TALKERS as a way to encrypt messages at the tactical level in the Pacific theater. The so-called code was a jargon that the Navajos in the unit developed amongst themselves orally to describe necessary battlefield information. Its effectiveness was demonstrated by the fact that a Navajo soldier who had been captured by the Japanese before the development of the code was unable to decipher the messages despite being tortured by his captors.

In the late twentieth century, the use of Navajo has been displaced by English, especially in and around urban areas and among younger Navajos. In response to this threat to the survival of the language, tribal agencies have instituted a vigorous program of language maintenance and renewal through bilingual schools and through Diné College, which provides instruction in Navajo language and literacy and training of Native Navajo-speaking teachers for certification in Navajo bilingual education.

BIBLIOGRAPHY

Field, Margaret. "Navajo." In *Facts About the World's Major Languages, Past and Present.* Edited by Jane Garry and Carl Galvez Rubino. New York: H. W. Wilson, 2001.

Gary Bevington

See also **Indian Languages; Indians in the Military.**

NAVAJO WAR. Following the American conquest of the Southwest after the Mexican War (1846–1848), U.S. military and political leaders attempted to reduce the autonomy and power of the region's largest Indian nation, the Navajos, or Diné as they call themselves. After several failed treaties, the U.S. government, under the military leadership of Brigadier General James Carleton and Colonel Christopher ("Kit") Carson, instituted a scorched earth policy against Navajos in northwestern New Mexico, Arizona, and southern Utah. Destroying Navajo herds, orchards, and resources, the U.S. Army brought nearly eight thousand Navajos into army forts, where beginning in 1863 they were forced to march more than three hundred miles to Fort Sumner on a tiny reservation in eastern New Mexico known as Bosque Redondo. For four years the Navajos lived in extreme poverty and bitterly resisted the army's attempt to destroy their culture. By 1868 new government policies recognized the disastrous effects of Navajo imprisonment, and the Navajos secured their rights to return to their homelands on a newly established reservation. The forced march to Fort Sumner is remembered as the Long Walk among Navajo peoples. An estimated two thousand Navajos lost their lives during the Long Walk and imprisonment at Bosque Redondo due to disease, malnutrition, and murder.

BIBLIOGRAPHY

Iverson, Peter. *The Navajos: A Critical Bibliography.* Newberry Library Center for the History of the American Indian Bibliographic Series. Bloomington: Indiana University Press, 1976.

McNitt, Frank. *Navajo Wars: Military Campaigns, Slave Raids, and Reprisals.* Albuquerque: University of New Mexico Press, 1972.

Ned Blackhawk

See also **Indian Reservations; New Mexico; Wars with Indian Nations: Later Nineteenth Century (1840–1900).**

NAVAL ACADEMY. The United States Naval Academy was established in 1845 by Secretary of the Navy George Bancroft as the Naval School in Annapolis, Maryland, and was renamed the U.S. Naval Academy in 1851. Known from the start for its high standards of discipline and efficiency, after the Civil War the academy added new buildings, modernized its curriculum, and began emphasizing athletics. Throughout its history it has conservatively reflected the soundest trends in U.S. engineering institutions, while keeping uppermost the fundamental mission of educating professional officers rather than technicians. Women have been admitted to the academy since 1975. The brigade of midshipmen is kept at a strength of approximately four thousand by a dozen methods of entry, of which congressional appointment supplies the greatest number.

BIBLIOGRAPHY

Sweetman, Jack. *The U.S. Naval Academy.* Annapolis: Naval Institute Press, 1995.

R. W. Daly/c. w.

See also **Engineering Education; Navy, Department of the; Navy, United States.**

NAVAL OIL RESERVES. In September 1909 Secretary of the Interior R. A. Ballinger suggested to President William Howard Taft that the United States should maintain naval oil reserves. After the necessary legislation had been passed, Presidents Taft and Wilson permanently withdrew from entry three Naval petroleum reserves—at Elk Hills, California; Buena Vista, California; and Teapot Dome, Wyoming—altogether involving about fifty thousand acres of public land. Between 1915 and the mid-1920s, the United States also set aside three Naval oil shale reserves, two in Colorado and one in Utah. Legislation permitting the Navy Department to take possession of the reserves, drill wells, erect refineries, and produce its own supply of fuel oil was not given until 1920. An act of Congress authorized the Navy Department to take possession of that part of the reserves against which no claims were pending, to develop them, and to use, store, and exchange their products.

Early in 1921, Albert Fall, the secretary of the interior, with the consent of the secretary of the navy, Edwin Denby, convinced President Warren G. Harding to transfer custody of the naval petroleum reserves to the Interior Department. This was done in comparative secrecy, imposed by the Navy Department on the ground that the action taken was part of its war plans, but in 1923 the measure came to the attention of the Senate, which began an investigation. This investigation discredited the Republican administration when the Senate discovered that

Fall had received more than $400,000 from the companies that had leased Elk Hills and Teapot Dome. Through the ensuing scandal, Denby and Fall were forced to resign; Fall was convicted of bribery; and in 1927 the SUPREME COURT invalidated the leases Fall had granted.

By the mid-twentieth century, the strategic needs of the navy had changed such that petroleum reserves were no longer a priority. Because domestic demands for oil had increased, the DEPARTMENT OF ENERGY took control of the reserves and, in the 1970s, opened them for commercial production. In 1996 the Department of Energy sold the government's share of the Elk Hills field to Occidental Petroleum Corporation for $3.65 billion, the largest PRIVATIZATION of federal property in U.S. history. Shortly thereafter, the government transferred the two Naval Oil Shale Reserves in Colorado to the DEPARTMENT OF THE INTERIOR, and in 1998 the Department of Energy returned the land designated as Naval Oil Shale Reserve number three in Utah to the Uintah and Ouray Reservation, home to the Northern UTE Indian Tribe. In 2000, the Department of Energy retained control of the Teapot Dome and Buena Vista reserves, leasing 90 percent of the Buena Vista reserves to private oil companies.

BIBLIOGRAPHY

Werner, Morris, and John Starr. *Teapot Dome.* Viking Press, 1959.

Stratton, David H. *Tempest over Teapot Dome: The Story of Albert B. Fall.* Norman: University of Oklahoma Press, 1998.

La Botz, Dan. *Edward L. Doheny: Petroleum, Power, and Politics in the United States and Mexico.* New York: Praeger, 1991.

T. T. Read / F. B.

See also **Teapot Dome Oil Scandal; Navy, Department of the.**

NAVAL OPERATIONS, CHIEF OF. The post of chief of naval operations (CNO) was established on 3 February 1915 to give the navy a military chief "charged with the operations of the Fleet and with the preparations of plans for use in war." Legally, the CNO was only an adviser to the secretary of the navy, but the structure was adequate during WORLD WAR I. The CINCUS (an unhappy acronym for commander in chief, changed after Pearl Harbor to COMINCH) was, in practice, the commander of the Atlantic, the Pacific, or the Asiatic Fleet. In March 1942 the titles of CNO and COMINCH merged in the person of Ernest J. King. His administration resulted in a general order abolishing COMINCH to vest CNO with clear supremacy.

BIBLIOGRAPHY

Hone, Thomas. *Power and Change: The Administrative History of the Office of the Chief of Naval Operations, 1946–1986.* Washington, D.C.: Naval Historical Center, 1989.

R. W. Daly
D. W. Knox / A. E.

See also **Navy, Department of the; Navy, United States; World War II.**

NAVAL STORES, a phrase applied to the resinous products of longleaf and other pines, such as tar, resin, pitch, and, to a lesser degree, turpentine, that were historically used in the shipping industry. Mariners used tar to preserve ropes from decay and applied the pitch of resin to seams in the planking to make them watertight, and shipbuilders used turpentine in connection with paint. Naval stores were important in England's colonial commercial policy, for England had normally purchased these goods from Sweden, which meant an unfavorable balance of trade to the mercantilists and the danger that an enemy might cut off the supply. The vast pine forests in the British colonies of New England and the Carolinas proved a bountiful new resource for naval stores. The British Board of Trade saw obtaining these stores from the colonies as an important move toward a self-sufficient empire and arranged for a bounty to be paid to colonial producers by the Royal Navy. This encouraged production, though members of the Royal Navy felt the American tar was not of as high a quality as European-produced tar. Although a group of German Palatines operated in upstate New York, the major center of naval store production shifted to the southeastern colonies through the eighteenth century.

The British continued to import naval stores from the colonies until the American Revolution, at which point they traded with the Dutch for Swedish products. The tar and pitch were obtained by burning chunks of pinewood in kilns. Turpentine was procured by a team of workers, called "chippers," who tapped a metal strip into a pine, allowed the tree to heal over it, then collected the rosin to be distilled into turpentine. Americans continued to produce naval stores, although eastern forests were being rapidly depleted as the growing population cleared lands and moved west. In the early nineteenth century the southern states, especially the Carolina "tarheels," began to dominate the industry. Naval store production continued in Georgia, Alabama, Mississippi, Louisiana, Texas, and Florida. By 1900 the pine forests of Georgia and northern Florida produced the major stores of rosin and turpentine.

The original naval aspect of these products ended with the coming of steamships and the introduction of iron- and steel-hulled ships. Although one can still smell the tarred rope in shops serving yachtsmen, naval stores have otherwise lost their nautical aspect and have been absorbed among the numerous products of industrial chemistry. Today wood turpentine is used in exterior paints and varnishes. Tar is used in paints, stains, disinfectants, soaps, and shampoos. Pine tar is used in the cordage industry. Other naval stores are now used in the production of linoleum, shoe polish, lubricants, and roofing materials. There is still a substantial trade based in Georgia, about half of the product being exported.

BIBLIOGRAPHY

Gamble, Thomas. *Naval Stores: History, Production, Distribution, and Consumption.* Savannah, Ga.: Review Publishing and Printing, 1921.

Knittle, Walter A. *Early Eighteenth-Century Palatine Emigration.* Philadelphia: Dorrance, 1936.

Malone, Joseph. *Pine Trees and Politics: The Naval Stores and Forest Policy in Colonial New England.* Seattle: University of Washington Press, 1964.

Robert G. Albion / H. S.

See also **Industries, Colonial; Colonial Ships; Tar.**

NAVIGATION ACT OF 1817. The Navigation Act of 1817 was one of many American steps toward national self-sufficiency that followed the WAR OF 1812. An effort to regain the lucrative West Indian trade, which the British had closed after the war, this act stated that all cargo between American ports must only be carried in ships entirely owned by American citizens or belonging to West Indian merchants. Tonnage duties on vessels licensed for coastwise trade were set at six cents a ton on vessels manned by Americans and fifty cents for others.

BIBLIOGRAPHY

Dangerfield, George. *The Awakening of American Nationalism, 1815–1828.* New York: Harper and Row, 1965.

White, Patrick Cecil Telfer, ed. *The Critical Years: American Foreign Policy, 1793–1823.* New York: Wiley, 1970.

John Haskell Kemble / H. S.

See also **Coasting Trade; Triangular Trade.**

NAVIGATION ACTS had their origin in Britain's regulation of its coastal trade, which was extended to the British colonies as they developed. Parliament enacted the first Navigation Act in 1660, although this legislation had its roots in earlier policy. By the close of the seventeenth century, Parliament had put other Navigation Acts in place and had installed colonial officials to enforce them through a system of admiralty courts, which had jurisdiction in cases involving trade law. The purpose of the Navigation Acts was twofold: to protect British shipping against competition from the Dutch and other foreign powers, and to grant British merchants a monopoly on colonial commodities such as TOBACCO and SUGAR. The Navigation Acts came about in the context of MERCANTILISM, the dominant economic system of the time among the European powers. According to mercantilist thought, a nation could measure its wealth in bullion, or its accumulated supply of gold. According to conventional wisdom, because there existed a finite supply of gold in the world, there also existed a finite supply of wealth. An imperial power acquired colonies for the purpose of expanding its wealth—preferably through the discovery of gold, but also through the production of natural resources, which colonists would ship to the mother country, where manufacturers would process these raw materials into wealth-producing finished products. According to the mercantilist economic model, therefore, a system of open trade could only result in the loss of wealth. To retain material wealth in the imperial realm, a trading power had to utilize its colonies' resources within a closed-trade system, such as the one that the Navigation Acts implemented.

Under these acts, British colonies in Asia, Africa, and America could import and export goods only in English vessels, and three-fourths of each crew was to be English. Other clauses stipulated that England could import products from its colonies in Asia, Africa, or America on English vessels and that goods from foreign countries could arrive in England only on English vessels or on the vessels of the country from which the goods originated. In effect, the Navigation Acts gave English subjects (defined as anyone living within the British realm) and English ships a legal monopoly of all trade between various colonial ports and between these ports and England. Even the trade between colonial ports and foreign countries was limited to English vessels. Thus, foreign vessels were excluded entirely from colonial ports and could trade only at ports in the British Isles.

Another field of legislation related to commodities. The Navigation Acts "enumerated" certain colonial products, which could be exported from the place of production only to another British colony or to England. At first the list included tobacco, sugar, INDIGO, COTTON, WOOL, ginger, and fustic and other dyewoods. Later, Parliament extended the list to include NAVAL STORES, HEMP, RICE, MOLASSES, BEAVER skins, FURS, COPPER ore, IRON, and LUMBER. In addition, the colonies could import Asian goods and European manufactures only from England—although an exception was made in the case of SALT or wine from the Azores or the Madeira Islands and food products from Ireland or Scotland. Parliament implemented a system of bonds to enforce the trade of enumerated commodities under the Navigation Acts. These bonds required the master of the vessel to comply with the provisions of the acts. Such arrangements operated so as to give American shipowners a practical monopoly of the trade between the continental and West Indian colonies. Residents of Great Britain in turn had a general monopoly of the carrying of the heavy enumerated goods from the colonies to the British Isles.

Colonists were largely limited to buying British manufactures. This was not necessarily a disadvantage, because an elaborate system of export bounties was provided so that British goods were actually cheaper in the colonies than similar foreign goods. These bounties averaged more than £38,000 per year for the ten years preceding the Revolution. From 1757 to 1770 the bounties on British linens exported to the colonies totaled £346,232 according to British treasury reports. In addition to bounties, there was a series of rebates, or drawbacks, of duties on European goods exported to the colonies. These, too, ran into formidable sums. Those to the West Indies alone amounted to £34,000 in 1774. The average payments from the British treasury in bounties and drawbacks on exports to the colonies in 1764 amounted to about £250,000 sterling per year.

Closely related to the Navigation Acts was another series of measures called the Trade Acts, which are usually confused with the Navigation Acts proper. Most of these were enacted after 1700, and they gradually developed into a complicated system of trade control and encouragement. The general plan was to make the entire British Empire prosperous and the trade of one section complementary to that of other sections. The Trade Acts employed a variety of measures to encourage the colonial production of goods desired in Britain. These laws gave colonial tobacco a complete monopoly of the home market by prohibiting its growth in England and imposing heavy import duties on the competing Spanish tobacco. The Trade Acts encouraged production of other colonial goods through tariff duties, which discriminated sharply in favor of the colonial product and against the competing foreign product. The legislation also granted rebates for some colonial commodities for which production exceeded British demand. Rebates facilitated the flow of these items through British markets to their foreign destinations. In other cases, regulations permitted exports of surplus colonial products, such as rice, directly to foreign colonies and to southern Europe without passing through England. In still other cases, Parliament allowed direct cash bounties on such colonial products as hemp, indigo, lumber, and SILK upon their arrival in England. These alone totaled more than £82,000 from 1771 to 1775. Naval stores also received liberal bounties, totaling £1,438,762 from 1706 to 1774, and at the time of the Revolution were averaging £25,000 annually.

Overall, the navigation system was mutually profitable to colonies and mother country. Resistance to the acts emerged periodically, however. In the late seventeenth century, for example, colonists complained that James II used the Navigation Acts to hamper colonial economic autonomy. Colonists also resisted British attempts to use trade law as taxation measures. Occasionally, parliamentary prohibitions discouraged colonial industries if they threatened serious competition with an important home industry. Notable examples include prohibitions of the intercolonial export of hats made in the colonies (1732; see HAT MANUFACTURE, COLONIAL RESTRICTION ON) and wool grown or manufactured in the colonies (1699). In this case, the powerful Company of Felt-Makers in London became alarmed at the increasing number of hats that colonial manufacturers were distributing throughout the British colonies and in southern Europe. In response to these complaints, Parliament passed legislation that regulated apprenticeships for hatmakers and slowed the growth of this industry. In another instance, Parliament—responding to English manufacturers who feared colonial competition—forbade the establishment of new mills to produce wrought iron and steel (1750). The same legislation encouraged the production and export of pig iron and bar iron, which benefitted both the colonies and the mother country. Laws such as these produced some local complaint, although they evidently affected few people, because many ignored the more restrictive aspects of the regulations.

More common than resistance to the law was simple negligence—either by ignoring specific restrictions, as hat and iron manufacturers often did, or by SMUGGLING. Evidence indicates that smuggling flourished in the colonies throughout the seventeenth and eighteenth centuries. Parliament's delays in empowering customs agents, the distance between Britain and its colonies, and the length and complex geography of the North American coastline all made thorough enforcement of the Navigation and Trade Acts nearly impossible. As a result, foreign goods proliferated throught the colonies, and many colonial materials left North America on foreign vessels. Other evidence of smuggling included the frequent abuse of customs agents and the preponderance of bribery, forgery, and other fraud among customs agents and colonial merchants alike. Smuggling was so prevalent that, in the mid-eighteenth century, measures such as the Revenue Act (also known as the SUGAR ACT, 1764) and the Tea Act (1773), which reduced duties in the legitimate trade while cracking down on smugglers, sparked some of the fiercest patriot resistance.

As long as the trade and navigation laws were limited to the regulation of trade and the promotion of the total commerce of the empire, they generally found support in eighteenth-century America. The enumerated products came largely from the colonies that remained loyal. The bounties went largely to the colonies that revolted. The New England shipping industry depended greatly on the protection that the Navigation Acts ensured. Consequently, the First CONTINENTAL CONGRESS approved the navigation system in its resolutions, and Benjamin Franklin offered to have the acts reenacted by every colonial legislature in America and to guarantee them for a hundred years if Britain abandoned efforts to tax the American colonies.

BIBLIOGRAPHY

Andrews, K. R., et al. *The Westward Enterprise: English Activities in Ireland, the Atlantic, and America, 1480–1650.* Detroit, Mich.: Wayne State University Press, 1979.

Carr, Lois Green, et al., eds. *Colonial Chesapeake Society.* Chapel Hill: University of North Carolina Press, 1988.

Church, R. A., ed. *The Coal and Iron Industries.* Oxford: Blackwell, 1994.

Kammen, Michael G. *Empire and Interest: The American Colonies and the Politics of Mercantilism.* Philadelphia: Lippincott, 1970.

McCusker, John J., and Kenneth Morgan, eds. *The Early Modern Atlantic Economy.* New York: Cambridge University Press, 2000.

McCusker, John J., and Russell R. Menard. *The Economy of British America, 1607–1789.* Chapel Hill: University of North Carolina Press, 1985.

Shelby Balik
O. M. Dickerson

See also **Board of Trade and Plantations; Bounties, Commercial; Culpeper's Rebellion; Dominion of New England; Enumerated Commodities; Mercantilism; Townshend Acts; Triangular Trade.**

NAVY, CONFEDERATE, was established by act of the Confederate Congress on 21 February 1861. On the same day, President Jefferson Davis appointed S. R. Mallory secretary of the Confederate navy. By an act of 21 April 1862 the navy was to consist of four admirals, ten captains, thirty-one commanders, and a specified number of subaltern officers. The naval service consisted of three main classes, including ships that served inland waters and commissioned cruisers to harass Union commerce and privateers. Before the outbreak of hostilities, Raphael Semmes was sent North to purchase ships and materials. No ships were secured but some materials were. Two U.S. shipyards fell to the Confederacy—one when the Gosport Navy Yard at Norfolk, Virginia, was abandoned and the other when the yard at Pensacola, Florida, was seized. All shipping in the Norfolk yard had been destroyed, but the Confederates raised the hull of the *Merrimac* and converted it into an ironclad ram. The Pensacola yard was of little value. On 9 May 1861 Mallory commissioned James D. Bulloch to go to England to secure ships for the Confederacy. Bulloch had some success, contriving to secure several ships that did much damage, as Confederate cruisers, to U.S. commerce.

The Confederacy had ample naval personnel, as 321 officers had resigned from the U.S. Navy by 1 June 1861 and tendered their services. Lack of all necessary facilities, however, and the increasing effectiveness of the Union blockade presented grave obstacles to the building of a Confederate navy. The Confederacy is credited with introducing the ironclad vessel, which revolutionized naval warfare. Confederates also contributed to perfecting the torpedo.

BIBLIOGRAPHY

Fowler, William M. *Under Two Flags: The American Navy in the Civil War.* New York: Norton, 1990.

Luraghi, Raimondo. *A History of the Confederate Navy.* Annapolis, Md.: Naval Institute Press, 1996.

Silverstone, Paul H. *Civil War Navies, 1855–1883.* Annapolis, Md.: Naval Institute Press, 2001.

Haywood J. Pearce Jr.
Honor Sachs

See also **Ironclad Warships; *Merrimac,* Sinking of; Torpedo Warfare.**

NAVY, DEPARTMENT OF THE. The unsatisfactory administration of naval affairs by the War Department led Congress to create the Department of the Navy in April 1798, following the recommendation of President John Adams. Benjamin Stoddert of Georgetown, in the District of Columbia, was appointed the first secretary and directed operations during the undeclared naval war with France (1798–1800). The War of 1812 demonstrated the need for adequate and responsible professional assistants for the secretary, and in 1815 the Board of Navy Commissioners, consisting of three senior officers, was created to meet that need. The first appointees were commodores John Rodgers, Isaac Hull, and David Porter—but by the rulings of the secretary, the functions of the board were restricted to naval technology, naval operations being excluded from its purview. In 1842 an organization of technical bureaus was instituted, and it continued to be a main feature of the organization.

The first bureaus to be created were those of Navy Yards and Docks; Construction, Equipment, and Repairs; Provisions and Clothing; Ordnance and Hydrography; and Medicine and Surgery. The duties of the bureaus were performed under the authority of the secretary of the Department of the Navy, and their orders had full force and effect as emanating from him. In 1862 the five bureaus were supplanted by eight: two new bureaus were created, those of Navigation and of Steam Engineering, and the responsibilities of the Bureau of Construction, Equipment, and Repairs were divided between two bureaus, those of Construction and Repairs, and of Equipment and Recruiting. The Bureau of Equipment was abolished in 1910, and in 1921 the Bureau of Aeronautics was established. The Office of the Judge Advocate General, independent of any bureau, was created in 1865.

The defect of inadequate professional direction of strategy and the general operations of the fleet was manifest in all the nation's early wars. In the Civil War it was minimized by the advice of Gustavus V. Fox, a former naval officer who was appointed temporary assistant secretary. The office was created permanently in 1890 but is usually occupied by civilian appointees with jurisdiction over industrial functions. During the war with Spain in 1898, a temporary board of officers advised the secretary on strategy but had no responsibility or authority respecting fleet operations. In 1900 the secretary appointed a general board of high-ranking officers, which remained in existence as an advisory body without executive functions. But by 1909 the scope and extent of the Navy Department had grown too much to permit coordination of the bureaus by the office of the secretary, and in that year Secretary George von Lengerke Meyer appointed four naval officer-aides to assist him—one each for the functions of operations, personnel, matériel, and inspections. This functional organization seemed sound and worked well and was continued in principle.

Secretary Josephus Daniels abolished the position of aide for personnel in 1913, but the duties were continued by the Bureau of Navigation. Similarly, the function of inspection was delegated to the Board of Inspection. Matters related to matériel passed largely to the jurisdiction of the assistant secretary. The creation by law in 1915 of a chief of naval operations served to rectify many previous administrative defects and to lead to further coordination within the department, the chief having authority commensurate with his great responsibilities as the principal adviser of the secretary and the person under the secretary having charge of the operations of the fleet. The Office of Operations absorbed many of the lesser boards and offices outside the normal province of the bureaus. During World War I the new organization worked extremely well.

World War II necessitated minor changes in organization that carried into 1947, when the National Security Act was passed. This act created the Department of Defense, within which the secretary of the navy lost cabinet status in 1949. The year 1949 also proved contentious for relations between the navy and the Truman administration, particularly when some high-ranking naval officers resisted Truman's changes in naval force structure—an event sometimes called the "revolt of the admirals."

The Kennedy administration also battled with navy leadership over perceived inefficiency, and by the mid-1970s navy officials were struggling with the consequences of reduced military spending and reduced administrative attention to naval forces. Organizational changes also marked the 1970s. By 1974 refinements in organization had resulted in a structure consisting of the secretary of the navy, an undersecretary, and four assistant secretaries for manpower and reserve affairs, installations and logistics, financial management, and research and development. The military arm included the chief of naval operations, a vice-chief, and six deputy chiefs for surface, submarine, and air warfare, logistics, plans and policy, manpower, and reserve, supported by a complex system of bureaus and commands.

During the mid-1980s, the Navy underwent a resurgence under the leadership of Secretary of the Navy John Lehman. Lehman pushed successfully for an expansion of the Navy's fleet and a greater defense buildup.

By 2000 the Department of the Navy consisted of two uniformed services, the U.S. Navy and the U.S. Marine Corps. Within the department there were 383,000 service men and women on active duty and 90,000 reserve sailors; 172,000 active duty and 40,000 reserve marines; and 184,000 civilians. The deparment encompassed 315 warships, 4,100 aircraft, and an annual budget of over $100 billion.

BIBLIOGRAPHY

Hewlett, Richard G., and Francis Duncan. *Nuclear Navy, 1946–1962.* Chicago: University of Chicago Press, 1974.

Howarth, Stephen. *To Shining Sea: A History of the United States Navy, 1775–1998.* Noman: University of Oklahoma Press, 1999.

Morison, Samuel E. *History of United States Naval Operations in World War II.* Urbana: University of Illinois Press, 2002.

Smelser, Marshall. *The Congress Founds the Navy, 1787–1798.* Notre Dame, Ind.: University of Notre Dame Press, 1959.

R. W. Daly
Dudley W. Knox / F. B.

See also **Coast Guard, U.S.; Defense, Department of; Defense, National; Marine Corps, United States; Naval Academy, United States; Naval Operations, Chief of; Navy, Confederate.**

NAVY, UNITED STATES, dates its existence from 13 October 1775, when the Continental Congress voted to purchase a small number of warships in defense of American liberties, then being abused by the British colonial power. In the course of the War of Independence, the Continental Navy operated more than fifty warships, including thirteen frigates Congress ordered built. Their mission was to protect trade and to prey on British commerce. John Paul Jones, captain of warship *Bonhomme Richard*, brought the war to the enemy's shores when he led daring raids on the English coast. When asked to surrender his ship during a fierce battle with Royal Navy warship *Serapis* in 1779, Jones answered, "I have not yet begun to fight," and led his sailors to victory. In October 1781, combined American and French land and sea forces finally compelled the surrender of British Lord Cornwallis and his army at Yorktown, Virginia. American independence followed this decisive victory.

A New Nation's Navy

During the next twenty years, corsairs controlled by the Barbary powers of North Africa repeatedly sortied from Algiers, Tunis, and Tripoli to seize the merchant ships and cargoes of the new and energetic, but virtually defenseless, American nation. In the last years of the eighteenth century, Congress established a Department of the Navy, which soon included a U.S. Marine Corps, and authorized construction of six fast, powerfully armed frigates and other vessels to deal with overseas threats. USS *Constitution* and the other warships of the United States eventually convinced the rulers of the Barbary states that preying on American overseas commerce could be disastrous to their fortunes.

The navies of France and Great Britain also interfered with American trading vessels. U.S. and French warships fought pitched sea battles during the so-called Quasi-War of 1798–1800 over maritime trade and other issues (see France, Quasi-War with). The British often angered Americans by stopping their ships and seizing or "impressing" into the Royal Navy American merchant sailors and even U.S. Navy bluejackets. In 1812, impressment and other contentious issues finally led to war. The

U.S. Navy was heavily outgunned by the Royal Navy, but the speed and firepower of the American frigates and the professional skill of their sailors routinely brought victory to the American side. Commodore Thomas Macdonough won an impressive victory on inland waters in the Battle of Lake Champlain. Peace in Europe removed the principal irritants that had led to war between the United States and Great Britain, prompting an end to the last war between these two nations. American success in battle ensured a peace treaty in 1814 that protected U.S. interests.

During the next forty-five years, U.S. naval vessels sailed in all the world's oceans while charting new lands and seas, promoting U.S. diplomatic interests, and protecting American merchantmen. The navy fought Caribbean pirates, established a patrol off the coast of Africa to stop the transportation of slaves to the Americas, and played a prominent role in the MEXICAN-AMERICAN WAR of 1846–1848.

Civil War and Postwar Decline

The focus of the U.S. Navy turned toward home during the 1860s, as the issues of slavery and states' rights brought on internal conflict. Soon after eleven Southern states seceded from the Union to form the Confederate States of America, President Abraham Lincoln directed the navy to blockade Norfolk, New Orleans, and other key ports.

To counter the blockade, the Confederate navy launched steam-powered ironclad warships, including CSS *Virginia.* In March 1862, the vessel boldly attacked the Union squadron off Norfolk and in a matter of hours destroyed two wood-hull sailing ships. With disaster looming, the North's own revolutionary ironclad, USS *Monitor*, arrived on the scene and fought a pitched battle that prevented the *Virginia* from destroying more Union ships. The Battle of Hampton Roads heralded a new era of naval warfare.

In addition to blockading Southern ports, the U.S. Navy mounted combined operations with the U.S. Army on the Mississippi and other major rivers to control those waterways and divide the Confederate states. David Farragut led naval forces that won the battles of New Orleans and Mobile Bay while David Dixon Porter helped General Ulysses S. Grant seize Vicksburg on the Mississippi. In short, the U.S. Navy was vital to Union victory in the long, bloody Civil War that ended in April 1865.

The absence of a threat from overseas and the small size of the post–Civil War merchant marine convinced Congress that funding for a large, modern fleet was not warranted. By the 1880s, the huge, powerful wartime fleet had declined to a small force of obsolete, rotting sailing ships and rusting monitors.

Emergence of a Sea Power

The navy's prospects began to change in the 1880s, when Congress authorized construction of the fleet's first steel-hull cruisers—USS *Atlanta*, USS *Boston*, and USS *Chicago.*

The "Mother Ship." The U.S.S. Holland—photographed here with ten S-type and one V-5 submarines lined up alongside it and five smaller boats waiting at the end of the ship—exemplifies U.S. naval might at its zenith. In World War II, the navy proved crucial in defeating Germany and Japan, especially the latter's island outposts scattered throughout the Pacific Ocean. LIBRARY OF CONGRESS

Naval strategists Theodore Roosevelt and Captain Alfred Thayer Mahan argued that the new industrial power and maritime commercial interests of the United States demanded a modern fleet capable of winning a major sea battle against any European naval power.

Their sea power theories passed the test in the SPANISH-AMERICAN WAR (partly ignited by the destruction of USS *Maine* on 15 February 1898 in the harbor of Havana, Cuba). U.S. naval forces under George Dewey and William T. Sampson destroyed enemy squadrons in the battles of Manila Bay and Santiago de Cuba.

American expansionists and navalists stressed anew that the United States needed a first-rank navy to protect its newly won overseas empire. As president, Theodore Roosevelt championed construction of a battle fleet of heavily armed and armored battleships, propelled by coal-fired boilers and capable of seizing and maintaining control of the sea. During this period, the U.S. Navy and its foreign counterparts also developed two weapon systems that would revolutionize twentieth-century naval warfare—the submarine and the airplane.

Naval leaders recognized that to operate the machinery of the new steel warships they needed more technically skilled bluejackets, professionally prepared officers, and a more rational naval organization. This era witnessed the creation of technical schools for enlisted personnel and establishment of the Naval War College in Newport, Rhode Island. In 1915, in response to the efforts of reformist naval officers, Congress established the Office of the Chief of Naval Operations to improve direction of the battle fleet.

The U.S. Navy's most important accomplishments during World War I were twofold. First was the provision of warship escorts to Allied convoys bringing supplies and American troops to the European theater. Second was the laying of a massive minefield in the North Sea where German submarines operated.

With international agreements restricting the construction of battleships during the period between the world wars, the navy focused on developing improved weapon systems and battle tactics. The future of naval aviation got a boost when aircraft carriers USS *Langley*, USS *Saratoga*, and USS *Lexington* entered the fleet. Almost yearly during the 1930s, the navy refined its battle tactics in "fleet problems," or exercises. The Marine Corps, tasked in war plans with establishing advanced bases in the vast Pacific Ocean, developed a doctrine for amphibious warfare.

The surprise Japanese attack on Pearl Harbor, Hawaii, on 7 December 1941 heralded a war in which sea power would figure prominently. As the naval, air, and ground forces of Japan seized U.S. and Allied possessions throughout the western Pacific in early 1942, the Kriegsmarine of Adolf Hitler's Nazi Germany unleashed U-boats against merchant ships all along America's East Coast. The U.S. Navy defeated both threats with decisive victories against the Japanese at the Battle of Midway in June 1942 and against the Germans in a long antisubmarine campaign in the Atlantic Ocean. Allied codebreaking and other intelligence units played key roles in both victories. The start of operations on and around Guadalcanal Island by U.S. Navy and Marine Corps units in August 1942 marked the opening of a major Allied counteroffensive in the South Pacific.

Meanwhile, U.S. and British naval forces had deployed Allied armies ashore in North Africa that went on to help destroy German and Italian forces in the combat theater. Following on this success, U.S. Navy and Royal Navy amphibious assault forces put American and British troops on Italian soil with landings in Sicily and on the mainland at Salerno.

To strengthen the Allied advance on Japan, in November 1943 Admiral Chester W. Nimitz launched his Pacific Fleet on a major thrust across the central Pacific. The bloody but successful marine landing on Tarawa in the Gilbert Islands was followed by the seizure of the Japanese-held Marshall Islands. The Japanese fleet tried to prevent Allied capture of the Marianas in June 1944 but lost hundreds of first-line aircraft in the attempt during the Battle of the Philippine Sea.

On 6 June 1944—D-Day—the U.S. and British navies executed one of the most masterful amphibious operations in history when they deployed ashore on the Normandy coast of France five combat divisions. The Allied armies that followed them ashore in succeeding months joined Soviet forces in bringing about the defeat of Nazi Germany and the end of the war in Europe in May 1945.

Admiral Nimitz's fleet helped pave the way for the defeat of the Pacific enemy with its decisive victory over the Imperial Japanese Navy in the October 1944 Battle of Leyte Gulf. The elimination of enemy forces in the Philippines and on the islands of Iwo Jima and Okinawa during the first half of 1945, combined with the destruction of the Japanese merchant marine by the U.S. submarine force, foretold the demise of the Japanese empire. That end, hastened when American planes dropped atomic bombs on the cities of Hiroshima and Nagasaki, came with the Japanese surrender onboard battleship USS *Missouri* on 2 September 1945.

A Global Navy

The navy suffered severe cutbacks in ships and sailors during the post–World War II years but still mustered enough strength to oppose the invasion of South Korea by North Korean communist forces on 25 June 1950. In this first conflict of the Cold War, navy and marine units executed one of the most decisive amphibious operations in history with the landing at Inchon behind enemy lines. Aircraft carriers, battleships, destroyers, minesweepers, hospital ships, and supply vessels proved indispensable to success in this war, which ended on 27 July 1953.

Throughout the Cold War, powerful U.S. naval forces remained permanently deployed on the periphery of the Soviet Union, the People's Republic of China, and other communist countries. Throughout the era, carrier task forces responded to threats and crises in the Mediterranean and the western Pacific. During the Cuban Missile Crisis of October 1962, the navy was instrumental in isolating communist Cuba from outside support and monitoring the removal of Soviet nuclear-armed missiles from the island nation.

A vital national mission of the navy throughout the Cold War was to deter a direct attack on the United States by the Soviet Union. To that end, the navy developed nuclear-powered Polaris, Poseidon, and Trident submarines, carrying nuclear-armed, long-range ballistic missiles, and deployed those vessels deep under the surface of the world's oceans. Fast, quiet, and lethal attack submarines prepared to destroy Soviet naval vessels if it came to war.

During the long struggle for Southeast Asia in the 1960s and early 1970s, navy carrier aircraft struck enemy bridges, railways, and supply depots. Battleships and destroyers bombarded troops concentrations; patrol ships and "Swift" boats prevented coastal infiltration; and riverine warfare units teamed up with army troops to fight Viet Cong and North Vietnamese Army units on the waterways of Indochina.

A new concern developed in the late 1970s and early 1980s when the Soviet Union increasingly put to sea heavily armed and capable warships and built a powerful military establishment in Russia. To counter the threat, the navy developed a new operational approach—a Maritime Strategy—that emphasized offensive action. If the

Soviet Union started a war, the navy planned to launch attacks by powerful carrier and amphibious groups against enemy forces in northern Russia and in the Soviet Far East.

Even after the demise of the Soviet Union in the late 1980s, the need for international peace and order demanded that the navy remain on station in distant waters. The unprovoked invasion of Kuwait by Saddam Hussein's Iraqi armed forces on 2 August 1990 signaled that naked aggression would continue to plague the world. As part of an international coalition, the navy deployed ships, planes, and troops to the Persian Gulf region to defend America's allies and to liberate Kuwait from the Iraqis. In Operation Desert Storm, which began on 17 January 1991, Tomahawk ship-launched cruise missiles and carrier aircraft struck targets throughout Iraq and Kuwait. A massive ground assault by U.S. Marine, U.S. Army, and coalition units, assisted by a naval feint operation, ended the short war on 28 February.

The end of the twentieth century and the beginning of the twenty-first brought the navy no respite. Ethnic conflict in the Balkans required navy carriers and cruise missile–launching surface ships and submarines to take part in strike operations against Serbian forces in Bosnia and Kosovo. The bloody terrorist attack on the United States on 11 September 2001 and the subsequent U.S.-led war on terrorism involved aircraft carriers, missile-launching ships, SEAL special warfare units, and other naval forces in military operations from Afghanistan to the Philippines. In short, throughout its more than 225 years of existence, the U.S. Navy has defended the United States and its interests at sea, on land, and in the air all across the globe.

BIBLIOGRAPHY

Baer, George W. *One Hundred Years of Sea Power: The U.S. Navy, 1890–1990.* Stanford, Calif.: Stanford University Press, 1994.

Bradford, James C., ed. *Quarterdeck & Bridge: Two Centuries of American Naval Leaders.* Annapolis, Md.: Naval Institute Press, 1997.

Godson, Susan H. *Serving Proudly: A History of Women in the U.S. Navy.* Annapolis, Md.: Naval Institute Press, 2001.

Holland, W. J., Jr., ed. *The Navy.* Washington: Naval Historical Foundation, 2000.

Howarth, Stephen. *To Shining Sea: A History of the United States Navy, 1775–1991.* New York: Random House, 1991.

Marolda, Edward J. *By Sea, Air, and Land: An Illustrated History of the U.S. Navy and the War in Southeast Asia.* Washington, D.C.: Naval Historical Center, 1994.

Marolda, Edward J., and Robert J. Schneller, Jr. *Shield and Sword: The U.S. Navy and the Persian Gulf War.* Annapolis: Naval Institute Press, 2001.

Millett, Allan R. *Semper Fidelis: The History of the United States Marine Corps.* Rev. ed. New York: The Free Press, 1991.

Morison, Samuel E. *The Two Ocean War: A Short History of the United States Navy in the Second World War.* Boston: Little Brown, 1963.

Spector, Ronald H. *Eagle Against the Sun: The American War with Japan.* New York: Free Press, 1984.

Edward J. Marolda

See also **Battle Fleet Cruise Around the World; Naval Academy; Naval Operations, Chief of; Navy, Confederate; Navy, Department of the; World War II, Navy in.**

NAZARENE, CHURCH OF THE. The Church of the Nazarene was formed by the merger of three Pentecostal and Holiness churches in 1907–1908: the Association of Pentecostal Churches in America, the Church of the Nazarene, and the Holiness Church of Christ. The church has dissociated itself from the more extreme Pentecostal groups and generally adheres to the teachings of late-nineteenh-century Methodism. The Nazarenes believe that regeneration and sanctification are different experiences, and they practice faith healing and abstain from the use of tobacco and alcohol. The ecclesiastical structure of the church is similar to that of Methodism. At the turn of the twenty-first century, 1.2 million Nazarenes worshipped in 11,800 churches worldwide.

BIBLIOGRAPHY

Jones, Charles Edwin. *Perfectionist Persuasion: The Holiness Movement and American Methodism, 1867–1936.* Metuchen, N.J.: Scarecrow Press, 1974.

Smith, Timothy Lawrence. *Called unto Holiness: The Story of the Nazarenes: The Formative Years.* Kansas City, Mo.: Nazarene Publishing House, 1983.

Glenn T. Miller / A. R.

See also **Fundamentalism; Religion and Religious Affiliation.**

NEAR V. MINNESOTA, 283 U.S. 697 (1931), invalidated an act of the state of Minnesota that provided for the suppression of, as a public nuisance, a "malicious, scandalous, and defamatory newspaper, magazine, or other periodical." The *Saturday Press* of Minneapolis had been so suppressed, and the editor was perpetually enjoined from further engaging in the business. The Supreme Court declared the statute unconstitutional on the grounds that it violated freedom of the press and therefore the due process clause of the Fourteenth Amendment. The measure also went far beyond existing libel laws.

BIBLIOGRAPHY

Rosenberg, Norman L. *Protecting the Best Men: An Interpretive History of the Law of Libel.* Chapel Hill: University of North Carolina Press, 1986.

Harvey Pinney / A. R.

See also **Censorship, Press and Artistic; Due Process of Law; Libel.**

NEBBIA V. NEW YORK, 291 U.S. 502 (1934), a U.S. Supreme Court case that favored New Deal economic reforms by widening the definition of a business "affected with a public interest." New York State in 1933 impaneled a milk control board to fix maximum and minimum retail prices. A dealer, convicted of underselling, claimed that price fixing violated the Fourteenth Amendment's due process clause, save as applied to businesses affected with a public interest, such as public utilities or monopolies. The Supreme Court, upholding the law five to four, declared that such a class includes any industry that, "for adequate reason, is subject to control for the public good."

BIBLIOGRAPHY

Leuchtenburg, William E. *The Supreme Court Reborn: The Constitutional Revolution in the Age of Roosevelt.* New York: Oxford University Press, 1995.

Maidment, Richard A. *The Judicial Response to the New Deal.* New York: St. Martin's Press, 1991.

Ransom E. Noble Jr. / A. R.

See also **Due Process of Law; Government Regulation of Business; New Deal.**

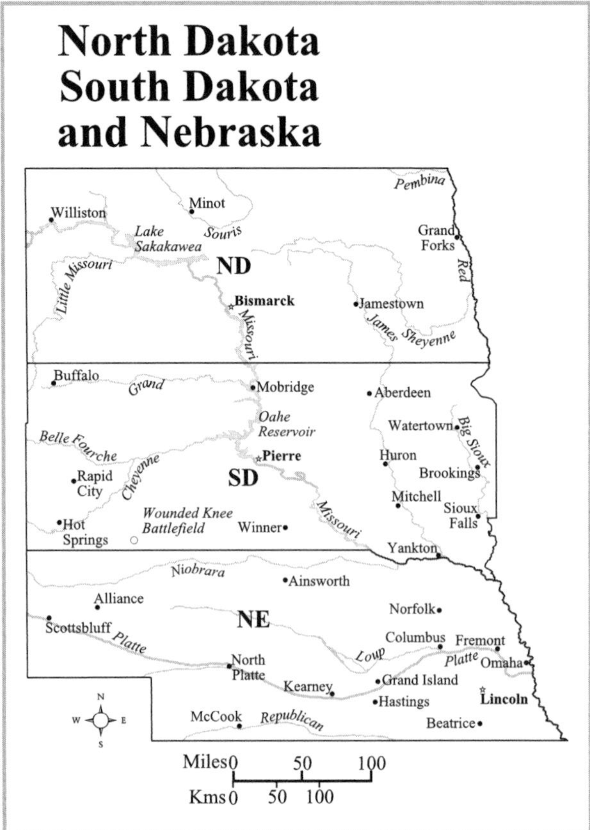

NEBRASKA looks like a diesel locomotive facing eastward. When it became a territory of the United States in 1854, its northern border extended all the way to Canada and its western border extended deep into the Rocky Mountains, but between 1854 and statehood in 1867, it was whittled down by Congress to please its various constituencies. It is now bounded to the north by South Dakota. The Missouri River flows southeastward out of South Dakota, forming part of Nebraska's border with South Dakota and its eastern border with Iowa and then northwest Missouri. Nebraska's southern border forms Kansas's northern border, meets Colorado, makes a sharp corner northward to southeast of Ogallala, Nebraska, and then turns sharply westward along Colorado's border until meeting Wyoming. The border then goes north until meeting South Dakota, where it turns sharply eastward.

The climate and land of Nebraska can be divided into four parts. The eastern part of Nebraska, along the Missouri, is part of the Central Lowlands of the Missouri River region. It is usually moist, prone to flooding, and rich for agriculture. West of the Lowlands, in south central Nebraska, are the Loess Hills. Loess is fine-grained silt deposited on the land by winds. The Loess Hills region has many rivers that have carved the land into hills and valleys; it is prone to drought, and even the rivers may go dry. The Sand Hills are in the western part of the state. In the early era of Nebraska's settlement, they were often mistakenly thought to be just part of the High Plains farther to the west because of their vast expanses of sand dunes, the third largest expanse of sand dunes in the world, behind only the Sahara Desert and the Arabian Desert. Yet the Sand Hills harbor lakes and streams that enabled those who knew about them to farm and survive even during droughts. The High Plains fill the far western part of Nebraska and are highlands that begin the continent's westward rise into the Rocky Mountains. The High Plains have Nebraska's highest spot, Panorama Point, at 5,424 feet above sea level. This is part of a steady westward rise from 480 feet above sea level at the Missouri River, meaning that Nebraska is tilted. The High Plains tend to be dry and windy, but irrigation and pumping water from underground aquifers have made it good land for raising cattle.

Prehistory

There have been several significant migrations from northeast Asia into North America, the first probably occurring over 100,000 years ago. There is evidence that people were on the land that is now Nebraska 25,000 years ago, probably migratory people who did not settle in one place. When the last glacial era was ending around 11,000 B.C., nomads known as Paleo-Indians, likely a mix of several cultures, judging by the distinct varieties of their spearheads, lived in or migrated through the Nebraska area. These people hunted the big game that was abundant in the Great Plains of the time.

The region of Nebraska gradually warmed, and a great forest grew. About 7000 B.C., new cultures were evolving; archaeologists call the people of those cultures Archaic Indians. These people moved into and off of the land over several thousand years. Most of the really big game had disappeared. Thus the Archaic Indians hunted small game as well as what big game they could find, such as deer, and they foraged for fruits and vegetables. They made advancements in technology that made their survival easier.

About 2000 B.C., a revolution in how people lived in Nebraska began with the migration into the area of people who had lived east of the Missouri River, sometimes called the "Plains Woodland" culture. Perhaps originally attracted by Nebraska's woodlands, they adjusted to a climate change that diminished the forest and generated open grasslands. One of their important contributions to life in the region was the development of pottery, especially vessels in which food or water could be stored. Some large vessels were used for cooking. They probably moved encampments with the seasons, but they were a fairly settled people who built dwellings and even villages that they would return to as the seasons dictated. Some evidence indicates that near the end of their era, the Plains Woodlanders were experimenting with agriculture. Burial mounds from this era indicate a society that was becoming larger and more complex.

In about A.D. 1000, the climate seems to have become drier. The Native Americans in Nebraska of that era often were farmers. Maize had been imported from the southwest, probably along an ancient trading route that extended all the way into Mexico, and it was cultivated along with varieties of squash and beans. Hunting and foraging for wild food plants was still very important for survival. Probably most of the native Nebraskans of the time lived in villages, in rectangular lodges with wooden frames, wattle-and-daub walls, and roofs plastered with mud and covered by grass and tree branches. The pottery became varied and was often simply decorated by carved incisions made before firing.

By the time Europeans were taking an interest in the area of Nebraska, the Native Americans there were in flux, rapidly moving in and out of the area in response to wars and invasions. The Pawnees were in the middle of what became Nebraska; they were settled farmers who probably had been there longer than any of their neighbors. The Poncas occupied the northeast part of modern Nebraska; the Cheyennes were moving in from the west; the Otos had recently settled into the southeast corner; and the Arapahos were hanging onto lands to the southwest. Wars far to the north were sending refugees southward, and the Brule and Oglala Dakota (aka Lakota) Sioux tribes had been forced into northern Nebraska from the other side of the Missouri River by the Chippewas. The Dakotas were violent nomads who raided the villages of the settled peoples of Nebraska; they were very suspicious of outsiders. In addition, the Apaches were following the herds of bison and were pressing the Arapahos and some Pawnees out of their homes.

Frontier

In 1682, René Robert Cavalier, Sieur de La Salle, led a French expedition down the Mississippi River to the Gulf of Mexico, claiming for France all the land that drained water into the Mississippi, which included the territory that became Nebraska. The region was named "Louisiana" for Louis XIV. At the time, Spain had already laid claim to most of the same land, including Nebraska. Many French trappers and traders visited the Nebraska region without arousing much interest until 1714, when Étienne Veniard de Bourgmont, something of a reprobate adventurer, traveled to the Platte River, which flowed through the middle of what is now Nebraska. Alarmed by this, Spain sent a military expedition north to drive out the French, but there were no French to be found. A couple of years later, in 1720, another Spanish expedition was sent, led by Pedro de Villasur, with forty or so Spanish soldiers and about sixty Native American warriors. They found no French, but they managed to thoroughly antagonize the local population, including the Pawnees, who were on a war footing because of their conflicts with the Dakotas; the Pawnees attacked the Spanish and only thirteen members of the Spanish expedition survived to return south.

In 1739, the French explorers Paul and Pierre Mallet named the Platte River and traveled its length westward and beyond, past the western border of modern Nebraska. French traders continued to visit Nebraska's tribes. In 1800, France forced Spain to surrender its claims to Louisiana, and in 1803 the United States purchased Louisiana from France. In 1804, the Lewis and Clark Expedition stopped briefly in Nebraska while traveling up the Missouri River, gathered some local tribesmen, and offered American friendship; the tribesmen listened patiently, but they had no authority—the leaders who could have made a pact with the explorers were away on other business. In 1812, trader Manuel Lisa established a trading post near the same spot. Robert Stuart led an expedition that trekked eastward from Oregon, reaching the Platte River in 1813 and following the river to the Missouri; his route became the Oregon Trail on which hundreds of thousands of people traveled through Nebraska to the Far West. Major Stephen Long led an expedition into the Great Plains in 1820, and what he saw seemed "barren and uncongenial" to him. He therefore called it a "Great Desert."

Even so, in 1823, Americans established the town of Bellevue across the Missouri River from Council Bluffs in Iowa. It was the first permanent American settlement in the future Nebraska. In 1834, the United States Congress passed the Indian Intercourse Act, forbidding Americans from settling in Nebraska's lands and providing that the United States Army would remove people who violated the law. The Native Americans of the area also reached an agreement whereby they would be compensated annually for Americans using roads and establishing forts in their territory. Beginning with Moses and Eliza Merrill in

1833, missionaries came to live with the Native Americans. In the 1830s, two trails in addition to the Oregon Trail became important in the mass migration of Americans to the West: the Mormon Trail that followed the north bank of the Platte River, and the Denver Trail, which followed the Blue River and the Platte River and then went to Denver.

The Oto name for the Platte River was Nebrathka, which meant "flat water," because even though very long, the Platte River was shallow and easy to cross on foot in many places. Explorer Lieutenant John C. Frémont referred to the river as the Nebraska in a report in 1842, and in 1844 Secretary of War William Wilkins said that given the river's importance, either Nebraska or Platte should be the official name of the region. An effort in Congress on 17 December 1844 to recognize Nebraska as a territory failed, but on 30 May 1854 Nebraska was recognized as an American territory in the Kansas-Nebraska Act. In the Missouri Compromise of 6 March 1820, all lands from Kansas northward were supposed to become free states—no slavery allowed; the Kansas-Nebraska Act repealed the Missouri Compromise and left it up to the citizens of the Kansas and Nebraska to decide whether to be free or slave states.

The Kansas-Nebraska Act gave Nebraska a vast territory, from Kansas to Canada, from the Missouri River into the Rocky Mountains. A census in 1854 found 2,732 Americans living in Nebraska. The citizens of Bellevue and much of southern Nebraska were upset when Omaha was chosen to be the territorial capital instead of Bellevue. In 1863, Congress divided the territory into smaller ones, leaving Nebraska close to its modern form. The Civil War (1861–1865) was going on at the time, but Nebraska felt the effect primarily in the 3,000 troops it contributed to the Union. From 1865 to 1867, the Union Pacific Railroad built a line out from Omaha, westward past the Nebraska border.

In 1866, Nebraska submitted a proposal for a state constitution to Congress. It included a clause that said only white males could vote, which outraged a Congress controlled by the Radical Republicans, who opposed racial discrimination. The offending clause had to be eliminated in order for the constitution to be acceptable; the change was made, allowing Nebraska to become the thirty-seventh state in the Union on 1 March 1867. The new state government resolved to build a new city for its capital, naming it "Lincoln" because it was unlikely that anyone would complain about the name of the martyred President. In 1875, a new state constitution was approved to replace the first one, because the first one had been put together in haste and had not provided a clear framework for laws.

Early Statehood

Although Arbor Day was begun by Nebraska on 10 April 1872, the 1870s were difficult times, with droughts and plagues of locusts between 1874 and 1877. The 1880s, however, saw a boom in the economy. During that decade, the population increased from 453,402 to 1,062,656, an amazing jump in ten years. By 1885, the bison of Nebraska had been exterminated. The 1890s saw a severe reversal of fortune because the United States was hit by a depression that lasted most of the decade. Land prices plummeted, crop prices dropped, and water was scarce. The population only increased to 1,066,300 during the decade. During the 1890s and 1900s, dry land farming techniques and irrigation opened the High Plains to farming, but growing crops there proved to be too difficult for farmers, and thus much of the land became pasture for cattle. Congress's Reclamation Act of 1902 proved especially helpful to Nebraska by providing funds for the development of state water projects.

During the 1890s, one of Nebraska's most famous public figures rose in prominence: William Jennings Bryan, "the Boy Orator of the Platte," from Lincoln. He served Nebraska in the House of Representatives from 1890 to 1894. In 1896, 1900, and 1908, he won the Democrats' presidential nomination. His public speaking was galvanizing, thrilling his listeners. He advocated farmers' rights, and in his best-known speech, he declared that farmers should not be crucified "on a cross of gold."

In the 1920s, Nebraska had another boom. Like that of the 1880s, it was cut down by a depression, the Great Depression that lasted until America entered World War II (1939–1945). In the 1930s, a drought dried the land in most of Nebraska. The soil was composed of fine grains from decades of tilling, and high winds out of the southwest would pick it up and blow tons of it into the sky, blotting out the sun and penetrating everything from clothing to stored food. This was the era of the DUST BOWL. During Nebraska's worst year, 1935, Congress passed the Tri-County Pact, a federal irrigation project designed to help Nebraskans. By 1954, 1,300,000 acres were irrigated.

In 1937, Nebraska revised its constitution to create a unicameral legislature. Until 1937, Nebraska had a bicameral legislature, meaning it had two houses, a senate and a house of representatives, but the new unicameral legislature had only one house, the Senate. The constitution was further amended to make the Senate nonpartisan. The idea was to streamline the process of making laws and to minimize partisan bickering. The amendment became law partly because Nebraska's very popular United States Senator George W. Norris supported it. He went so far as to leave the Republican Party and run as an independent for reelection to the United States Senate, winning a fifth term.

Modern Era

In 1944, near the end of World War II, the Pick-Sloan Missouri Basin Project was passed by Congress, authorizing hydroelectric plants and reservoirs in states along the Missouri River. This contributed to the expansion of irrigation in Nebraska and to a boom in the 1950s that managed to defy another drought. This boom attracted investors, and corporations began buying farms, with farm sizes nearly doubling from 1950 to 2000, while the number of farms dropped by about 40 percent. People who had worked on farms moved to cities to work in manufacturing plants. In 1960, 54.3 percent of the population of 1,411,921 lived in cities, the first time a census recorded more Nebraskans living in urban areas than in rural areas. African Americans in Nebraskan cities began civil rights protests in 1963. The nationally recognized civil rights leader Malcolm X was born in Omaha.

In 1966, the state property tax seemed too much of a burden for small farmers, and Nebraska was trying to discourage out-of-staters from owning farms in the state and to encourage family ownership of farms. Thus, it revamped its tax structure, eliminating the state property tax while beginning an income tax and a sales tax to finance the state government.

During the 1970s, times were generally good, but in the 1980s, Nebraska went into a recession. Many people lost their farms. The Family Farm Preservation Act of 1982 passed by Nebraska's legislature was intended to help the small farmers with low-interest loans and tax breaks. In 1987, the legislature passed tax incentives to encourage more manufacturing in the state, hoping to create jobs. In 1986, Nebraska's race for governor featured for the first time two female nominees for the Republican and Democratic Parties, with Republican Kay Orr winning over Helen Boosalis.

In the 1990s, Nebraska slowly pulled out of its recession. Advances in farm equipment made it easier for a few people to manage a large farm or ranch, and investments in expensive new equipment were being paid off in an average of three years. This brought with it a significant increase in population, from 1,578,417 in 1990 to 1,713,235 in 2002.

BIBLIOGRAPHY

Andreas, A. T. *History of Nebraska.* Lincoln: Nebraska State Historical Society, 1976 (circa 1882).

Creigh, Dorothy Weyer. *Nebraska: A Bicentennial History.* New York: Norton, 1977.

Johnson, J. R. *Representative Nebraskans.* Lincoln, Nebr.: Johnsen Publishing, 1954.

Mattes, Merrill J. *The Great Platte River Road: The Covered Wagon Mainline Via Fort Kearney to Fort Laramie.* Lincoln: Nebraska State Historical Society, 1969. About the Overland Trail.

McNair, Sylvia. *Nebraska.* New York: Children's Press, 1999.

Nebraska State Historical Society. Home page at http://www.nebraskahistory.org.

Olson, James C. *History of Nebraska.* Lincoln: University of Nebraska Press, 1955.

Wills, Charles A. *A Historical Album of Nebraska.* Brookfield, Conn.: Millbrook Press, 1994.

Kirk H. Beetz

NEGATIVE INCOME TAX. The economist Milton Friedman coined the term "negative income tax" (NIT) in *Capitalism and Freedom* (1962). Under an NIT, transfers are based on how far income falls below a "break-even" level. Those with no income receive the maximum payment, but payments fall as income rises up to the break-even point. An NIT makes it possible to subsidize the working poor, without requiring that welfare recipients earn nothing or reducing payments by one dollar for every dollar earned. The NIT was the subject of several federally funded local experiments in the late 1960s and early 1970s, and some welfare programs, including food stamps and supplemental security income, have operated as negative income taxes. However, the earned income tax credit, rather than the NIT, has become the principal subsidy giving the poor an incentive to work.

BIBLIOGRAPHY

Killingsworth, Mark R. *Labor Supply.* New York: Cambridge University Press, 1983.

Robert Whaples

See also **Taxation.**

NEOCONSERVATISM was primarily an intellectual movement of Cold War liberal Democrats and democratic socialists who moved rightward during the 1970s and 1980s. The term was apparently coined in 1976 by an opponent, the socialist Michael Harrington. By and large, neoconservatives either repudiated the label or accepted it grudgingly. Nonetheless, the term usefully describes an ideological tendency represented by a close-knit group of influential political intellectuals. In the early 1980s, the short-hand designation "neocon" was a standard part of the American political vocabulary.

Most of the leading neoconservatives were in their forties or early fifties when they began their ideological transition. Many were Jewish and several prided themselves on being "New York intellectuals" no matter where they lived at the moment. All of the leading neocons engaged in cultural politics by writing books or articles, but they came from varied professional backgrounds. Foremost among them were the sociologists Daniel Bell, Nathan Glazer, Peter Berger, and Seymour Martin Lipset; the *Commentary* magazine editor Norman Podhoretz and his wife, the writer Midge Decter; the political activists Ben Wattenberg, Penn Kemble, and Carl Gershman; the foreign policy specialists Walter Laqueur, Edward Luttwak, and Robert Tucker; the traditionalist Catholic academics Michael Novak and William Bennett; and the art critic Hilton Kramer. Daniel Patrick Moynihan and Jeane Kirkpatrick straddled the realms of scholarship and politics. No one was more important to the movement's rise to prominence than the intellectual entrepreneur Irving Kristol, who sometimes joked that he was the only self-confessed neoconservative.

Many of the older neoconservatives had briefly been radical socialists in their youth. By the 1950s, they affirmed centrist liberalism in philosophy and practice. The sociologists Bell, Glazer, and Lipset formulated an influential interpretation of American politics in which a pragmatic, pluralist center was besieged by parallel threats from "extremist" ideologues: Communists and "anti-Communists" on the left and a "radical right" represented most visibly by Senators Joseph McCarthy and Barry Goldwater. This position did not preclude nudging the center slightly leftward. In the early 1960s, for example, Podhoretz at *Commentary* published articles holding the United States partly responsible for the start of the Cold War.

The future neocons began to reevaluate liberalism, which was itself in flux, in response to the domestic turmoil and international crises of the late 1960s and early 1970s. Great Society antipoverty programs seemed utopian in conception or flawed in implementation. "Affirmative action" especially violated their belief, often reinforced by their own experiences, that success should come through merit. New Left demonstrators not only disdained the civility they cherished, but also disrupted their classrooms. Feminist and gay activists challenged the bourgeois values they considered essential underpinnings of a democratic order. Although few future neoconservatives supported the Vietnam War, many believed that the United States lost more than it gained from detente with the Soviet Union. Jewish neoconservatives were especially upset by the growing anti-Semitism within the black community and the increasing criticism of Israel by the left. All of these trends, they contended, were at least tolerated by the "new politics" wing of the Democratic Party that won the presidential nomination for Senator George McGovern in 1972.

These disaffected liberals moved rightward with varying speed. As early as 1965, Kristol and Bell founded *Public Interest* magazine to critically examine the flaws in Great Society programs. Appointed ambassador to the United Nations by Republican President Gerald Ford in 1975, Moynihan defended both American foreign policy and Israel's legitimacy. Bell and Glazer endorsed McGovern in 1972. The next year, however, both joined Lipset, Podhoretz, Decter, Kirkpatrick, Novak, and Wattenberg in creating the Coalition for a Democratic Majority in order to save their party from the "new politics." The future neoconservatives overwhelmingly favored Senator Henry Jackson, a staunch cold warrior, friend of Israel, and supporter of the welfare state, for the Democratic presidential nomination in 1976.

Jimmy Carter, who won the nomination and the election, soon disappointed the neoconservatives. Despite their concerted efforts, none received a high-level appointment in his administration. Moreover, Carter enthusiastically practiced affirmative action, remained committed to detente, and sympathized with Third World nationalism. Jewish neoconservatives complained that he pressed Israel harder than Egypt while negotiating peace between the two countries in 1978 through 1979. Such behavior was only part of a foreign policy that looked like weakness or a "new isolationism" at best, "appeasement" at worst. Writing in *Commentary* in 1979, Kirkpatrick claimed that Carter not only overlooked human rights abuses by the Soviet Union, but also drove from power "friendly authoritarians" like the Shah of Iran, who were then succeeded by full-fledged "totalitarian" regimes.

By 1980, the increasingly visible neoconservative network had formulated a comprehensive critique of American politics, culture, and foreign policy. Essentially they updated the pluralist theory of the 1950s to account for recent social changes and to justify their own turn rightward. According to this interpretation, the Democratic Party—and much of American culture—had been captured by "ideologues" whose ranks now included social radicals, black nationalists, self-indulgent feminists, and proponents of gay rights. These extremists scorned the values cherished by most Americans, that is, faith in capitalism, hard work, sexual propriety, masculine toughness, the nuclear family, and democracy. Indeed, disdain for democracy explained both their snobbish rejection of middle-class life at home and their sympathy for communist or Third World tyranny abroad. Such views had wide currency not because they appealed to ordinary Americans, but because they were disseminated by a powerful "new class" of academics, journalists, and others in the cultural elite.

Although a caricature in many respects, this interpretation of American life and recent politics attracted the attention of Republicans seeking to build a majority coalition. Ronald Reagan courted the neoconservatives during the 1980 presidential campaign and subsequently recruited many of them into his administration. Kirkpatrick was appointed ambassador to the United Nations, Novak served as lower level diplomat there, and Gershman headed the newly created National Endowment for Democracy. Second-generation neocons from the political rather than the intellectual world held important midlevel positions. Richard Perle, a former aide to Henry Jackson, became assistant secretary of defense. Assistant Secretary of State Elliott Abrams, Podhoretz's son-in-law, helped to formulate policy toward Central America and played a major role in the Iran-Contra scandal. Other neocons served on government advisory boards dealing with education and foreign policy. Outside of the Reagan administration, neoconservatism thrived in the more conservative climate of the 1980s. In 1981, Decter organized the Committee for the Free World, an international collection of writers, artists, and labor leaders dedicated to mounting a cultural defense against the "rising tide of totalitarianism." The next year, Kramer founded *New Criterion* magazine to defend high culture and aesthetic modernism against leftist detractors. Kristol began publishing *National Interest* in 1985 to analyze foreign policy from a "realist" perspective. The centrist *New Republic* and many mainstream newspapers welcomed articles by neoconservatives.

Success brought division and controversy. Moynihan, elected senator from New York in 1976, drifted back into the ranks of liberal Democrats. Kristol thought the Reagan administration was too harsh on the welfare state. Leading the most avid cold warriors, Podhoretz denied that the Soviet Union was becoming more democratic in the late 1980s and chided Reagan for pursuing detente in fact if not in name. The most bitter debates arrayed neoconservatives against traditionalist conservatives (who sometimes called themselves paleocons). These two intellectual factions within the Reagan coalition were separated by background, worldview, and questions of patronage. The neoconservatives were disproportionately Jewish, accepted much of the welfare state, and enthusiastically endorsed efforts to defeat international communism. The paleocons were devoutly Christians, opposed activist government in principle, and expressed reservations about both internationalist foreign policy and the cultural impact of capitalism. Tensions became apparent in 1981 when Reagan chose neocon William Bennett instead of a traditionalist to chair the National Endowment for the Humanities.

By 1986, traditionalists were accusing neoconservatives of excessive devotion to Israel. Neocons countered with some warrant that paleoconservatives harbored anti-Semites in their ranks. These factional disputes obscured the fact that neoconservatives fitted better into a coalition led by Ronald Reagan, a former liberal Democrat, who still celebrated the New Deal and wanted above all to win the Cold War.

By the early 1990s at the latest, a coherent neoconservative movement no longer existed, even though many erstwhile neocons remained active. As the Cold War ended and memories of the volatile 1960s faded, the serious scholars among them returned to scholarship. Bell, Glazer, and Lipset in particular wrote thoughtful analyses of American society. Moynihan served in the Senate until 2001. The most polemical neocons, notably Podhoretz and Kramer, persisted in attacking feminism, gay activism, and the alleged triumph of "political correctness" in higher education. Yet, after years of ideological cross-fertilization, such polemics were virtually indistinguishable from those of traditionalists. Second-generation neocons increasingly emphasized foreign policy, rarely defended the welfare state, and thus fit easily into the Republican coalitions that elected Presidents George H. W. Bush and George W. Bush. Irving Kristol's son William, who served as chief-of-staff to Vice President Dan Quayle and then edited the conservative magazine *Weekly Standard,* joked that any neoconservative who drifted back to the Democrats was a "pseudo-neocon." Although neoconservatism as a distinctive intellectual enterprise congealed and dispersed in less than two decades, the neocons provided a serious intellectual rationale for the Reagan administration's policies and helped to reorient the broader conservative movement that remained influential into the twenty-first century.

BIBLIOGRAPHY

Bloom, Alexander. *Prodigal Sons: The New York Intellectuals and Their World.* New York: Oxford University Press, 1986.

Dorrien, Gary J. *The Neoconservative Mind: Politics, Culture, and the War of Ideology.* Philadelphia: Temple University Press, 1993.

Ehrman, John, *The Rise of Neoconservatism: Intellectuals and Foreign Affairs 1945–1994.* New Haven, Conn.: Yale University Press, 1995.

Gottfried, Paul, and Thomas Fleming. *The Conservative Movement.* Boston: Twayne, 1988.

Kristol, Irving. *Neoconservatism: The Autobiography of an Idea.* New York: Free Press, 1995.

Lora, Ron, and William Henry Longton, eds. *The Conservative Press in Twentieth-Century America.* Westport, Conn.: Greenwood Press, 1999.

Peele, Gillian. *Revival and Reaction: The Right in Contemporary America.* Oxford: Oxford University Press, 1984.

Steinfels, Peter. *The Neoconservatives: The Men Who Are Changing America's Politics.* New York: Simon and Schuster, 1979.

Leo R. Ribuffo

See also **Conservatism; Liberalism; New York Intellectuals;** *and vol. 9:* **The New Right: We're Ready to Lead.**

"NESTERS." *See* **Homesteaders and the Cattle Industry.**

NEUTRAL RIGHTS, both the capability of a state to remain neutral toward other states at war with one another and the freedom of a neutral state from hindrance by the belligerents, including undisturbed commerce with non-belligerents, and even including commerce with belligerents, if that commerce does not aid in war. Neutrals do not, however, have rights to trade in munitions with belligerents, to allow their territory to be used by a belligerent, or to allow recruitment or other support from their nationals. With occasional reservations and violations, the United States has led the international community of states in the recognition and protection of these rights, practically since its founding, although the significance of these rights may have diminished as a result of changes in the legal nature of state responsibility and the legitimation of war.

The idea that a state could remain outside of war between other states has classical origins, but was first comprehensively stated by Hugo Grotius in the seventeenth century. It did not, however, initially find acceptance among the state powers of Europe.

In 1793 the United States, under the presidency of George Washington, asserted a right to neutrality in the wars between Great Britain and France—a right, among other claims, for which it fought an undeclared war with France in the 1790s and a declared war with Great Britain between 1812 and 1815. Neither conflict, however, led to a resolution of the American claims or to international recognition of a national right to neutrality.

In 1856, with the Declaration of Paris, the United States sought but failed to achieve international recognition of the rights of neutrals to protection from belligerents' seizure of non-contraband property. Contrary to this attempt, and despite a series of proclamations of neutrality in domestic law, the United States sought a narrowed understanding of neutrality during the Civil War, in order to enforce its blockade against Confederate ports. Even so, assertions of neutrality under American law survived the Civil War and were the basis of much of nineteenth-century U.S. foreign policy. Great Britain acknowledged the duty of a neutral state to refrain from permitting its territory to serve as a base for belligerent operations in the *Alabama* Claims Arbitration of 1871. In the case of *The Paquete Habana* in 1900, the U.S. Supreme Court declared the neutrality of fishing vessels to be a custom of international law binding upon states, including the United States, even in the absence of treaties.

In 1907 the Second Hague Peace Conference set forth standards of neutrality and the treatment of neutrals, based largely on rules drafted by law professor Francis Lieber and adopted by the U.S. Army as General Order 100 (1863) to guide the behavior of Union troops during the American Civil War. These rules were often violated, sometimes by the United States, but still served as the basis for American neutrality in the early years of World Wars I and II, as well as the neutrality of Switzerland, Spain, and other states during those conflicts.

With the adoption of the United Nations (UN) Charter in 1945, principles of a just war established by Grotius have been enacted into international law. Under these principles, only states that act in self-defense are legally justified in war; further, expanded definitions of individual and state responsibility for acts of aggression against a state have diminished the scope of possible neutrality. As a result, the nineteenth-century concept of neutral rights has been limited to a state's right, as provided by Article 51 of the UN Charter, to engage in either collective security enforcement actions or in collective defense.

BIBLIOGRAPHY

Jessup, Philip, et al. *Neutrality: Its History, Economics, and Law.* New York: Columbia University Press, 1935–1936.

Jessup, Philip, and Francis Deák, eds. *Treaty Provisions: Defining Neutral Rights and Duties, 1778–1936.* Washington, D.C.: U.S. Government Printing Office, 1937.

Tucker, Robert W. "The Law of War and Neutrality at Sea." *Naval War College Review* 50 (May 1955): 25–49.

Steve Sheppard

NEUTRALITY is the principle of classical international law and politics that allows a nation-state to remain friendly with both sides in a war. Neutrality and the international law of war from which it derives have been significant at times in U.S. history, but at the close of the twentieth century neutrality was less central than doctrines of the United Nations Charter, customary notions of state responsibility, and new concepts of individual criminal liability.

State neutrality is an invention of early modern Europe. Ancient states frequently forced other states to abet their wars or to suffer the consequences, although the ancient Greeks did recognize the neutrality of temples, the Olympic Games, and, sometimes, states. Still, the notion of a claim protected and enforceable by law that could be asserted by a state demanding that other states respect its neutrality awaited the development of the modern law among nations.

The Dutch jurist and ambassador Hugo Grotius published *On the Law of War and Peace* in 1625. The third book of this influential work set forth two rules of state neutrality: Neutral states should do nothing to strengthen a belligerent whose cause is unjust or to impede the cause of a belligerent whose cause is just. When there is no clear view as to the justice or injustice of a war between two states, a third state should treat each alike, offering both or neither the passage of troops over its territory, supplies or provisions, or assistance to the besieged. Despite considerable discussion of this approach, seventeenth-century states tended toward customs of neutrality with no regard for just or unjust wars. Instead states applied a Machiavellian notion that war is a supreme right of the state, and that there is no customary right of neutrality.

In the eighteenth century the foreign policy of the newly formed United States encouraged a custom of neutrality based on impartiality. Its weak military, coupled with economic ambition, led the new state to seek to "avoid foreign entanglements" and yet to profit from both sides. In 1793, as France once again declared war on England, George Washington's administration declared the United States to be neutral and forbade the French recruitment of soldiers on American soil. The American declaration of neutrality was based on the sovereign rights of states to control such matters as the raising of armies, and Congress passed laws forbidding U.S. citizens to participate in foreign wars without government orders.

This position of neutrality was not easily maintained, and the United States found itself in a quasi-war with France over neutral rights between 1798 and 1800. Thomas Jefferson sought in 1807 to protect American neutral rights through embargoes against belligerents who consistently violated those rights. The embargoes, attempted for two years, seem not to have been successful, in part owing to violations by American smugglers and in part to the availability of alternative markets. They did, however, establish a principle of economic embargo as a tool of enforcement of national rights without armed attack. One tool by which U.S. merchants attempted to circumvent both embargo and the possibility of seizure by the belligerents was by transshipping goods through neutral ports to ports controlled by a belligerent. American merchants complained when the British naval blockade seized ships as prizes for carrying cargo from the French West Indies to France via U.S. ports. Over U.S. objections British courts applied a doctrine of "continuous voyage," and ruled that such cargoes were intended for a belligerent power, notwithstanding the period in the neutral port or lands, and the voyages were not neutral.

Further, the unavailing protests against the British practice of impressing American seaman into the British navy was a leading cause of the War of 1812. The war itself, something of a sideshow to the Napoleonic Wars (1799–1815) between France, and Britain and its allies, was inconclusive.

Two events in the mid-nineteenth century led to a strengthened international resolve in favor of neutrality and to a weakened recognition of it by the United States. First, the diplomatic convention leading to the Declaration of Paris in 1856 was a turning point in the law of neutrality. The United States sought, but failed to achieve, recognition of the rights of private neutral property aboard neutral ships subject to search for war contraband bound for a belligerent, and therefore did not sign the declaration. Despite this failing, the agreement did abolish privateering, the commissioning of private ships so as to give them belligerent status to raid enemy shipping.

The position of the United States regarding neutrals changed abruptly with the declaration of a blockade and embargo on all Southern ports during the Southern rebellion of the 1860s. The newly muscular U.S. Navy adopted many of the practices the United States had complained of only a decade earlier, particularly the seizure of British ships with commercial cargoes. The United States adopted the doctrine of continuous voyage and seized supplies bound for the Confederacy that were being transshipped through British and French possessions and Mexico.

Even after the war American policy regarding neutrality was contradictory and self-serving. On the one hand America complained of British violations of its neutrality. In the Alabama Claims Arbitration of 1871, the United States sought compensation from Great Britain for losses to U.S. shipping caused by Confederate raiders outfitted and based in British territory. The result was a precedent of continuing importance, because Great Britain agreed that neutral territory may not be used as a base for belligerent operations, thus establishing the principle of state responsibility for the use of its territory as a base for civil war, terrorism, subversion, or other kinds of indirect aggression. On the other hand the general position of the United States in demanding its claims of neutrality be honored by other states contradicted some of its specific foreign policies, such as the Monroe Doctrine (1823), the Open Door policy in China, and the military opening of Japan to U.S. trade. These difficulties, as well as the U.S. positions during the 1860s, would be used against American arguments for neutrality in World War I.

One important step toward recognition of neutrality in U.S. interpretations of international law arose when the United States took some fishing packets as prize vessels during the Spanish-American War (1898). In *The Paquet Habana* (1900) the U.S. Supreme Court held that international law arising from custom, not just treaty, applied in the United States, and that by custom nonbelligerent coastal fishing vessels were neutral, and so could not be taken as prizes of war.

Despite such steps in one nation or another, World War I commenced with little international agreement on the nature of war and neutrality. The Hague conferences of 1899 and 1907 were unsuccessful in defining neutrality at sea, although there were agreements as to the treatment of neutrals on land at the conference of 1907.

For the first years of World War I, the United States vainly attempted to maintain a policy of neutrality and to protect its neutral rights. To the Central Powers it appeared that the Allies' heavy dependence on U.S. trade and financial support made the United States biased, and its policies injurious, particularly to Germany. Of course, U.S. corporations were turning a vast profit from the war, predominantly from supplying the Allies, which, along with effective Allied propaganda and ham-fisted German diplomacy, led to even greater American support for the Allies. As German submarines increasingly violated U.S. claims to neutral rights, the United States declared war on Germany and its allies, citing these violations as the dominant cause.

After the war isolationist sentiment and policy grew increasingly powerful in the United States. Congressional investigations of the munitions industries in the 1930s fueled suspicion of industrial instigation of U.S. entry into the war. U.S. diplomats attempted through bilateral treaties and conventions, such as the unenforceable Kellogg-Briand Pact for the Renunciation of War (1928) outlawing war as a matter of policy, and the abortive Geneva Conference of 1932, to establish not only neutrality but also peace, or at least disarmament—or, failing that, mutual defense with a broad array of states. In addition to these international efforts, a domestically framed policy of isolationism was written into neutrality acts, reflecting Congress's worries over war in South America and the increasing threat of war in Europe, in 1935, 1936, 1937, and 1939 that were unevenly enforced by President Franklin D. Roosevelt. The most ambitious American neutrality law of this period was a treaty enacting U.S. policy, the Declaration of Panama (October 1939), which, quite ineffectually, banned belligerent action within a security zone covering much of the Western Hemisphere.

The 1930s also saw an increased attempt to use trade sanctions as a mechanism for state policy short of war. The United States and other nations enacted sanctions against Japan after its takeover of Manchuria in 1931–1932 and against Italy during its conquest of Ethiopia in 1935–1937. Neither effort was successful.

America proclaimed its neutrality during the first years of World War II, in accord with statute and widespread sentiment. But from September 1939 until the Japanese attack on Pearl Harbor, Hawaii, in December 1941, President Franklin Roosevelt provided increasing aid to the Allies, both by authorizing and funding private arms sales and by direct supply of ships and materiel. The most famous of these neutral but supportive acts was the Lend-Lease Act, proposed by Roosevelt in 1940 and enacted in March 1941, authorizing the president to aid any nation whose defense he believed vital to the United States and to accept repayment "in kind or property, or any other direct or indirect benefit which the President deems satisfactory." Lend-lease sales to Great Britain, and then to China, to the Soviet Union, and ultimately to thirty-eight nations, eventually amounted to nearly $50 billion in aid.

World War II left few states untouched, yet it is important to note the willingness of both the Allies and the Axis to respect the neutrality of Switzerland and of Spain. In part these nations were left alone for lack of strategic necessity—and, indeed, the strategic benefit of some neutral spaces during war. In part their claims to neutrality were respected owing to the costs of invasion. Still, fundamentally their claims to neutrality and their relative impartiality were successes of the international framework established at the Hague Conference of 1907.

On the other hand World War II was a total war in which combatants attempted to destroy their opponents' means of production, and so brought war to civilian populations and agriculture. Total war was particularly manifested in the German attacks on London, in British and U.S. destruction of cities by bombing and firestorm, and U.S. use of nuclear weapons to destroy the Japanese cities of Hiroshima and Nagasaki, ending World War II. The power and number of such weapons increased, making possible a global holocaust. In this age of thermonuclear war, neutral countries are as liable to destruction as combatant states.

The concept of state use of war, and therefore the idea of neutrality in war, fundamentally altered with the adoption of the United Nations Charter in 1945. The charter enshrines the idea of the Kellogg-Briand Pact that aggressive war is a crime against all nations, although it allows for a state's self-defense and for its defense of another state. Thus it establishes much of the principle of just war envisioned by Grotius as a matter of international law. This idea was underscored in indictments by the international military tribunals in Nuremberg and Tokyo, which convicted individuals for causing states to wage wars of aggression.

In an international legal climate that distinguishes states waging a war of aggression from those engaged in self-defense, the presumption of state neutrality is also changed, although it is not obsolete. The Cold War, from the 1950s through the 1980s, established standing alliances in the North Atlantic Treaty Organization and the Warsaw Pact states. Many states, particularly European states such as Switzerland and Austria, and Third World states with more to gain as clients than as players, proclaimed themselves nonaligned with either alliance, despite pressure against such neutrality from the United States.

In one of the most protracted hot wars during the Cold War, the U.S. intervention in the Vietnam War (1955–1975), U.S. policy toward neutrals generally recognized both neutrality and the limits of neutrality for states supporting a belligerent. According to the Final Declaration of the Geneva Accords of 1954, Cambodia claimed neutrality in the struggle between North and South Vietnam. Both of those states accepted the claim and agreed to refrain from establishing military bases on Cambodian territory. In 1957 Cambodia's National Assembly enacted its neutrality into domestic law. Although the United States never signed the 1954 Geneva Accords, it agreed to abide by its terms and did so even though, throughout the 1960s, North Vietnam used Cambodian territory to move troops and supplies on the Ho Chi Minh Trail, established military bases there, and staged offensive operations from it. In the spring of 1970 U.S. forces bombed and invaded Cambodia, sparking increased domestic opposition to the U.S. intervention, which ended in 1975, two years after America ended its war with Vietnam by signing the Paris Peace Accords (1973).

A major U.S. initiative of the late twentieth century was the assurance of the neutrality of Antarctica, outer space, and the Moon. Ratified in 1961 after a U.S. initiative to draft and adopt it, the Antarctic Treaty specifies that Antarctica shall be used only for peaceful purposes, and prohibits "any measures of a military nature, such as the establishment of military bases and fortifications, the carrying out of military maneuvers, as well as the testing of any types of weapons." The Treaty on Principles Governing the Activities of States in the Exploration and Use of Outer Space, Including the Moon and Other Celestial Bodies, another American initiative, entered into force in 1967; it bars claims of states to sovereignty over the Moon or other celestial bodies, decrees that the Moon shall be used for peaceful purposes, bars the same military acts barred in Antarctica, and decrees that no satellite shall carry weapons of mass destruction. In the year 2000 there were 2,671 artificial satellites in Earth's orbit, of which 741 were registered to the United States, 1,335 to Russia, and the remainder belonging primarily to smaller countries and international organizations but often under the control of corporations. It is believed by most intelligence observers that many of these are armed, and that some are capable of intersatellite warfare, but that none are capable of destroying terrestrial targets.

In 2001 terrorists apparently sheltered in Afghanistan hijacked commercial airplanes and crashed them into the

World Trade Center in New York City and the Pentagon in Washington, D.C., killing thousands of people. The U.S. response included the bombardment of Afghanistan, the de facto government of which proclaimed itself uninvolved in the dispute between the terrorists and the United States, but refused to surrender the terrorists. The legal disputes arising from these actions will continue for decades, and the significance both for claims of neutrality and for the conception of states will likely be profound.

BIBLIOGRAPHY

Bauslaugh, Robert. *The Concept of Neutrality in Classical Greece.* Berkeley: University of California Press, 1991.

Bemis, George. *American Neutrality: Its Honorable Past, Its Expedient Future. A Protest Against the Proposed Repeal of Neutrality Laws, and a Plea for Their Improvement and Consolidation.* Boston: Little, Brown, 1866.

Borchard, Edwin, and William Potter Lage. *Neutrality for the United States.* New Haven, Conn.: Yale University Press, 1937, 1940.

Crabb, Cecil V., Jr. *The Elephants and the Grass: A Study in Nonalignment.* New York: Praeger, 1965.

Morris, Gouverneur. *An Answer to "War in Disguise," Or, Remarks upon the New Doctrine of England, Concerning Neutral Trade.* New York: Hopkins and Seymour, 1806.

Ogley, Roderick, comp. *The Theory and Practice of Neutrality in the Twentieth Century.* New York: Barnes and Noble, 1970.

Tucker, Robert W. *The Law of War and Neutrality at Sea.* Washington, D.C.: U.S. Government Printing Office, 1957.

Steve Sheppard

See also **"Alabama" Claims; Geneva Conferences; Hague Peace Conferences; Impressment of Seamen; Lend-Lease;** *and vol. 9:* **The Monroe Doctrine and the Roosevelt Corollary; Washington's Farewell Address.**

NEVADA was the fastest growing state in the United States during the last half of the twentieth century. Its population increased from a mere 160,000 in 1950 to just over 2,000,000 in 2001. It was the thirty-sixth state to be admitted to the Union, its official statehood proclaimed on 31 October 1864, with Carson City designated as its capital.

Early History and Exploration

The area that became Nevada was first inhabited between 10,000 and 12,000 years ago, and small stone dart points, called Clovis points, have been found among rock shelters and caves, indicating that early peoples gathered and hunted their food. Around 300 B.C., the culture of the Anasazis appeared; the Anasazis dominated the area for more than a thousand years, living in caves and houses made with adobe and rock and eventually developing a more agriculturally based culture. Migrating tribes replaced the Anasazis, and by the time Europeans first entered the area it was dominated by three Native American tribes—the Paiutes, the Shoshones, and the Washoes. Spanish explorers ventured into areas of Nevada in the late eighteenth century but never established settlements in the mostly arid environment. In 1821, Mexico laid claim to the territory after a successful revolt against Spain, and in 1848 the Treaty of Guadalupe Hildago ceded the land to the United States.

Much of the Nevada territory had by that time been explored, primarily by Peter Skene Ogden of Canada and the Hudson's Bay Company and Jedediah Smith of the Rocky Mountain Fur Company. Smith, on his way overland to California, entered Nevada in the late summer of 1826 (near present-day Bunkerville). In 1827, he traveled east and north from California, across the Sierras and into the central part of Nevada, the first white man to cross the territory. Ogden made three important expeditions, in 1828, 1829, and 1830, discovering the Humboldt River (he called it the Unknown River) and tracing its path from its source to its sink, where the river empties into marshy flats and evaporates.

In 1843 and 1844, John C. Frémont explored the area from the northwestern corner of the state south to Pyramid Lake and then southwest across the Sierras to California, calling it the Great Basin. His publicized expeditions and mappings of the territory helped establish settlements and routes for westward-bound settlers and miners, especially after the discovery of gold in California in 1849.

Statehood and Economic Boom

In 1850, the federal government created the Utah Territory, which included almost all of what is now Nevada. Much of it was Mormon-dominated territory after 1851, but the discovery of gold in the late 1850s drew non-Mormons into western Nevada, including a flood of miners from California who came upon hearing the news of the Comstock Lode silver strike, the richest deposit of silver in American history. After the Comstock, small towns sprang up and Virginia City became an important crossroads, trading post, and mining camp.

The importance of the Comstock silver helped gain approval from the federal government for the creation of the Territory of Nevada in 1861. In 1863, a constitutional convention was held in Carson City and a state constitution was drafted. A bitter battle between those who favored small mining interests and the political power of the large San Francisco mining companies ensued, and ratification of the newly drawn state constitution was hotly contested. Although the majority of residents favored statehood, in early 1864 voters rejected the constitution, effectively ending their chances for admission into the Union. However, the U.S. Congress and President Abraham Lincoln, waging the Civil War (1861–1865) and in need of additional support for the Thirteenth Amendment, strongly desired Nevada's admission into the Union. A second constitution was ratified in March of 1864 and, in spite of not meeting the population requirements for statehood, by October, Nevada was a new state. Its entry into the Union during the Civil War earned it the nickname "The Battle Born State."

The early years of statehood were dominated by economic issues of the mining industry, specifically the silver industry. In 1873, the federal government discontinued the minting of silver coins and the Comstock declined. The 1880s and 1890s were marked by economic depression and a consequent population decrease, but a revival of the mining industry, spurred by silver and copper ore discoveries in southwestern and eastern Nevada, brought in new investment capital, and the completion of the transcontinental railroad caused another boom.

The Twentieth Century

Nevada politics in the twentieth century were dominated by land-use issues. In the early part of the century, federal irrigation projects helped stimulate agriculture, expand farmland, and encourage cattle and sheep ranching. Hoover Dam and the creation of Lake Mead in the 1930s was welcomed for the economic stimulus provided, but other federal projects have been greeted with less enthusiasm. In the 1950s, the Atomic Energy Commission conducted aboveground nuclear tests at Frenchman Flat and Yucca Flat—events that met with little protest at the time but that nonetheless chafe many Nevadans in retrospect. During the 1970s, Nevadans led other western states in an attempt to regain control of the land from the federal Bureau of Land Management. In 1979, the state legislature passed a law requiring the return of 49 million acres of federally owned land to the State of Nevada. The movement, dubbed the "Sagebrush Rebellion," caused a brief controversy and ultimately lost in the federal courts, and the issue remains a sore point for many Nevadans. In 1987, the Department of Energy named Yucca Mountain as its primary high-level nuclear waste depository, a decision the State of Nevada continued to fight at the beginning of the twenty-first century.

Economic changes also took place throughout the twentieth century. The 1930s saw a transformation in the Nevada economy. In 1931 gambling was legalized throughout the state, with the exception of Boulder City, where housing had been built for government employees working on Hoover Dam. Earlier in the state's history, as with much of the United States, gambling had been legal. In the early 1900s, however, gambling prohibition swept the country, and in 1910 gambling was outlawed in Nevada. In spite of severe restrictions, illegal gambling still thrived in many parts of the state, especially in Las Vegas. During the Great Depression the need for state revenues and economic stimulus led Nevadans to approve the return of legalized gambling, and Nevada passed some of the most liberal gambling laws in the country.

World War II (1939–1945) brought military air bases to Las Vegas and Reno, and federal agencies such as the Bureau of Land Management and the U.S. Forest Service, which managed more than 85 percent of Nevada's land, brought public employees and some measure of prosperity to the more urban regions of the state. But it was the tourism industry that was shaping Nevada's economic future. During the 1940s, as other states cracked down on legalized gambling, Nevada's embrace of the gaming industry drew developers and tourists and boosted the state's economy, but it also drew organized crime. Criminal elements from the east coast and from nearby Los Angeles were instrumental in the development of some of the more famous casinos, including The Flamingo, opened in 1946 by New York mobster Benjamin "Bugsy" Siegel.

After World War II, the gaming and entertainment industries were expanded, especially in Reno, Las Vegas, and on the California border at Lake Tahoe. The tourism industry benefited from low tax rates, and legal gambling and top entertainers brought in visitors as well as new residents. Although organized crime played a significant role in the early development of Nevada's urban centers, especially in Las Vegas, the federal government pressured the state to strengthen license regulations and by the 1960s the stigma of gangster-owned casinos was on the wane.

During the late 1950s and early 1960s, Las Vegas and the surrounding area in Clark County grew tremendously and soon became the home of a quarter of the state's residents. Several large hotels and casinos opened and became internationally famous, including The Dunes (1955), The Tropicana (1957), and The Stardust (1958). The 1960s saw the boom continue with the openings of The Aladdin (1963), Caesar's Palace (1966), and Circus Circus (1968). The glamour and legal legitimacy of casinos and hotel resorts began to draw corporate development from beyond the gambling industry, and by 1970 Las Vegas was more associated with billionaire Howard Hughes than with gangsters such as Bugsy Siegel.

Although Nevada's population continued to increase during the 1980s, a sluggish economy meant a decline in casino and resort development. In 1988, voters overwhelmingly approved a constitutional amendment prohibiting state income tax. The 1990s saw a burst of development in the Reno-Sparks area and, more dramatically, in Las Vegas and Clark County. Las Vegas reshaped itself as a destination for families, not just gamblers, and many of the old casinos from the 1950s and 1960s were closed and demolished. They were replaced by bigger, more upscale hotels and theme casinos such as The Mirage (opened in 1989), The Luxor (1993), The Monte Carlo (1996), New York-New York (1997), and Paris, Las Vegas (1999). In 1996 The Stratosphere casino was opened in Las Vegas, inside the tallest building west of the Mississippi.

Although much of Nevada is open land, the population is predominantly urban. The state's total area is about 110,000 miles, but because much of the eastern side is federal land designated for military use or grazing and mining territory, the population centers are on the western side, near the California border to the south and west and the Arizona border to the south and east. The city of Las Vegas at the time of the 2000 census had a population of nearly 500,000, but the metropolitan area, including part of northern Arizona, had a total population of over 1.5 million. The Reno-Sparks metropolitan area had a population of 339,486 in 2000.

More than 75 percent of the state's population were born outside Nevada. The 2000 census reported that more than 75 percent of the population identified themselves as white, 6.8 percent as African American, and 4.5 percent as Asian. Those who identified themselves as being of Hispanic ancestry increased from just over 10 percent to more than 19 percent.

Although the service industry, through casinos and resorts, employs most Nevada residents, there is some manufacturing (gaming machines, aerospace equipment, and products related to irrigation and seismic monitoring) and a significant number of employees of the federal government, especially the military. U.S. military installations in Nevada include Nellis Air Force Base in Las Vegas, the Naval Air Station in Fallon, and the Army and Air National Guard Base in Carson City. Perhaps Nevada's most famous military base is the so-called secret or underground base known as "Area 51," located north of Las Vegas near Groom Lake. Self-proclaimed "ufologists" have perpetuated a rumor for decades that Area 51 is the location of nefarious U.S. government schemes that include secret spy planes and an alleged craft from outer space, said to have crashed near Roswell, New Mexico, in 1947.

The state flag, modified in 1991 from the original design approved in 1929, features a cobalt blue background behind a five-pointed silver star that sits forming a wreath between two sprays of sagebrush. Across the top of the wreath it reads "Battle Born" in black letters, with the state name in gold letters below the stars and above the sagebrush. Besides the Battle Born moniker, Nevada is also called "The Silver State" and "The Sagebrush State" (sagebrush is the state flower), and the state motto, of undetermined origin, is "All for Our Country."

Although it consists mostly of mountainous and desert terrain with altitudes between 1,000 and more than 13,000 feet (the state's highest point, Boundary Peak, is 13,145 feet), Nevada also has rivers and lakes. These include the Humboldt, Colorado, and Truckee Rivers and Pyramid Lake (the state's largest natural lake) and Lake Mead (the state's largest artificial lake, backed up by Hoover Dam on the Colorado River), and 5 million acres of designated national forestland.

BIBLIOGRAPHY

Elliott, Russell R. *History of Nevada.* Lincoln: University of Nebraska Press, 1973.

Farquhar, Francis Peloubet. *History of the Sierra Nevada.* Berkeley: University of California Press, 1965.

Laxalt, Robert. *Nevada.* New York: Coward-McCann, 1970.

Smith, Grant H. *The History of the Comstock Lode, 1850–1997.* Reno: Nevada Bureau of Mines and Geology, 1998.

The Official State of Nevada Web Site. Home page at http://silver.state.nv.us/.

Paul Hehn

See also **Hoover Dam; Las Vegas.**

NEW AGE MOVEMENT. The New Age movement was an international cultural current that arose in the late 1960s, when Eastern religions became popular in the United States. It combined earlier metaphysical beliefs such as Swedenborgianism, mesmerism, transcendentalism, theosophy, and often primitivist beliefs about the spiritual traditions of nonwhite peoples. As expressed by Baba Ram Dass (born Richard Alpert), its first recognized national exponent, the New Age movement propounded the totality of the human body, mind, and spirit in a search for experiences of transformation through rebirthing, meditation, possessing a crystal, or receiving a healing.

Stressing personal transformation, New Agers envision a universal religion placing emphasis on mystical self-knowledge and belief in a pantheistic god as the ultimate unifying principle. The New Age movement is perhaps best known for its emphasis on holistic health, which emphasizes the need to treat patients as persons and offers alternative methods of curing, including organic diet, naturopathy, vegetarianism, and a belief in the healing process of crystals and their vibrations. New Age techniques include reflexology, which involves foot massage; acupuncture; herbalism; shiatsu, a form of massage; and Rolfing, a technique named after Ida P. Rolf, the originator of structural integration, in which deep massage aims to create a structurally well-balanced human being. Music is also used as therapy and as a form of meditation. While the term "New Age music" in the mid-1990s was a marketing slogan that included almost any type of music, true New Age music carries no message and has no specific form because its major use is as background for meditation.

BIBLIOGRAPHY

Melton, J. Gordon, et al. *New Age Encyclopedia.* Detroit: Gale Research, 1990.

York, Michael. *The Emerging Network: A Sociology of the New Age and Neo-Pagan Movements.* Lanham, Md.: Rowman and Littlefield, 1995.

John J. Byrne/F. H.

See also **Asian Religions and Sects; Cults; Medicine, Alternative; Spiritualism; Utopian Communities.**

NEW ALBION COLONY. The New Albion colony was a project that never materialized. Had well-intentioned plans come to fruition, the colony would have encompassed Long Island and all of New Jersey by virtue of a charter issued on 21 June 1634 to Sir Edmund Plowden. The precise terms of the charter have been var-

Earliest View of New Amsterdam. This engraving of the Dutch fort and houses at the southern tip of Manhattan was originally printed in reverse, in *Beschrijvinghe Van Virginia, Nieuw Nederlandt, Nieuw Engelandt, En d'Eylanden Bermudes, Berbados, en S. Christoffel*, published by Joost Hartgers in Amsterdam, 1651. LIBRARY OF CONGRESS

iously interpreted by historians. Additionally, what became known as the island of Manhattan, lying between New Jersey and Long Island, was then New Amsterdam, a Dutch colony. Despite Plowden's long-standing intentions to settle the area, four attempts failed because of either financial, legal, or family problems. After his death in 1659, the New Albion charter was apparently misplaced. In 1664 Charles II granted the lands to the Duke of York, who in turn granted the area between the Hudson and Delaware Rivers (New Jersey) to John Lord Berkeley and Sir George Carteret.

BIBLIOGRAPHY

Craven, Wesley Frank. *New Jersey and the English Colonization of North America.* Princeton, N.J.: Van Nostrand, 1964.

Pulsipher, Jenny Hale. "The Overture of This New-Albion World: King Phillip's War and the Transformation of New England." Ph.D. diss., Brandeis University, 1999.

Christine E. Hoffman

See also **Colonial Charters; New Jersey.**

NEW AMSTERDAM. In 1625, officials of the Dutch West India Company, a commercial confederation, founded New Amsterdam, which became New York City, in New Netherland, later New York Colony. In 1626, the director Peter Minuit bought the island of Manhattan for sixty guilders, or $24, from the Canarsee Indians, although the Weckquaesgeeks of the Wappinger Confederation actually had claim to the island. Dutch pioneers and black slaves owned by the Dutch West India Company settled and cleared the island into bouweries, or farms. The buildings, windmills for grinding grain, and livestock were all owned by the company and were leased to tenants. The company also gave out land grants, sixteen miles wide and extending inward indefinitely, along the waterways to any member of the West India Company who settled fifty persons over the age of fifteen. These owners, or patroons, held manorial rights on these estates and were free from taxes for eight years.

Dutch middle-class values and distinct cosmopolitan traits spread from the beginning. By 1639, eighteen different languages were spoken within the small community. While seventeen taverns served the city, it had only one Reformed Protestant Dutch Church, established in 1628. The Dutch West India Company finally allowed self-rule in 1653 with the "burgher government" led by Peter Stuyvesant. Two burgomasters (mayors), and five *schepens* (magistrates) met weekly at the Stadt Huys and exercised judicial, administrative, and, after 1654, taxing powers. This weekly court decided matters related to trade, worship, defense, and schooling. After 1657 the municipal corporation retained business and officeholding privileges. England and Holland vied for economic supremacy during forty years of Dutch rule. With the power of four frigates, the English gained control of the city in 1664, although the Dutch government was not completely ousted until 10 November 1674.

BIBLIOGRAPHY

Condon, Thomas J. *New York Beginnings: The Commercial Origins of New Netherland.* New York: New York University Press, 1968.

Innes, J. H. *New Amsterdam and Its People: Studies, Social and Topographical, of the Town under Dutch and Early English Rule.* New York: Scribners, 1902.

Rink, Oliver A. *Holland on the Hudson: An Economic and Social History of Dutch New York.* Ithaca, N.Y.: Cornell University Press, 1986.

Singleton, Esther. *Dutch New York.* New York: B. Blom, 1968.

Michelle M. Mormul

See also **Manhattan; New Netherland; New York City; New York Colony.**

NEW CASTLE, a colonial settlement in DELAWARE founded by the Dutch in 1651 as Fort Casimir, was established to compete with the Swedish-controlled trade with the Indians along the Delaware River. Three years later, in May of 1654, it was surrendered to the Swedish governor and renamed Fort Trinity, only to be recaptured in 1655 by Peter Stuyvesant to operate under the Dutch West India Company. It was renamed again in 1656, this time New Amstel, by the burgomasters of the city of Amsterdam, and finally renamed New Castle in 1664 after surrender to Sir Robert Carr. It was governed by the Duke of York until 1682, when ownership was transferred to William Penn.

William Penn's colony, a haven for Quakers and other persecuted sects attracted by his policy of religious toleration, had been formed with a proprietary charter received in 1681 from the Crown designating him governor. In 1682, Penn was granted the three lower Delaware counties of Newcastle, Kent, and Sussex, all of which eventually separated from Pennsylvania to become the colony of Delaware in 1773. Under Penn's governorship, New Castle was the seat of the assembly of the Lower Counties, the seat of New Castle County at the outbreak of the Revolutionary War in 1776, and the capital of Delaware until the British invaded in 1777 and moved the capital to Dover.

New Castle was part of the Middle Colonies (New York, New Jersey, Pennsylvania, and Delaware), the only part of British North America initially settled by non-English Europeans. Society in the Middle Colonies was a mix of Dutch Calvinists, Scandinavian Lutherans, German Baptists, Swiss Pietists, Welsh Quakers, French Huguenots, Scots Presbyterians, and a sizable African slave population. The English were a clear minority. New settlers tended to stay with their own kind, creating a region characterized by a cultural localism that expressed itself in politics, thus creating a burgeoning conflict with the English settlers committed to British imperial objectives and English culture, including the Anglican Church. Local government included an elected assembly representing the people, and assemblymen were expected to advocate for their constituents' cultural, religious, and economic concerns. These concerns frequently were at odds with the governors' imperial objectives. English policy was intent on subordinating the interests of the colonies to those of the mother country and frequently was the cause of disputes between various colonial leaders. In one such incident, in 1696, Francis Nicholson, the governor of Maryland, took offense at Pennsylvania governor William Markham's reluctance to carry out imperial reform and dispatched troops to New Castle to arrest the pirate John Day, whom Markham had hired to defend the Delaware Capes against French privateers. Political success in such an atmosphere involved complex compromises that, although beneficial in the short term, ultimately proved divisive, diluting local power and undermining local leaders largely incapable of sustained stability. The growth of the Atlantic economy after the decline of the fur trade, the increasing importance of the major port cities of Philadelphia and New York, and the spread of Anglican congregations beyond their origin communities forecast the future social configurations and political culture of what would eventually become the United States.

BIBLIOGRAPHY

Cooper, Constance J., ed. *350 Years of New Castle, Del.: Chapters in a Town's History.* Wilmington, Del.: Cedar Tree, 2001.

Munroe, John A. *Colonial Delaware: A History.* Millwood, N.Y.: KTO Press, 1978.

Weslager, C. A. *The Swedes and Dutch at New Castle.* New York: Bart, 1987.

Christine E. Hoffman

NEW DEAL. The New Deal was a defining moment in American history comparable in impact to the Civil War. Never before had so much change in legislation and policy emanated from the federal government, which, in the process, became the center of American political authority. The progressive surge was also unique because it came at a time of economic collapse. Previously, in such crises government curtailed reform and reduced spending to balance the budget and so provide the stability thought necessary to help economic progress resume. The activist New Deal reversed that pattern in its effort to lift the country out of hard times and so altered American social and economic policy forever.

Origin and Design

Three factors stand out as the impetus for revolutionary change. First, the nation in the 1930s had sunk into the deepest economic depression in its history, an unprecedented catastrophe that called for measures that would necessarily break down old constraints on the use of federal powers. Second, an arsenal of progressive reform ideas that had been frustrated during the conservative years following World War I was available to resolve depression issues. Third, large numbers of racial and ethnic minorities had gained a strong enough position in American life to be ready to redress their long-standing grievances and disadvantages. By adding disaffected Republican victims of the Great Depression, reformers, and minorities, mostly in northern cities, to the traditional working-class and southern Democratic constituency, the New Deal forged an irresistible voting bloc.

The unwieldy coalition of sometimes rival interests and beliefs found the leadership it needed in Franklin Roosevelt, the most adept and inspiring president since Abraham Lincoln. Roosevelt rooted his approach in a simple set of moral precepts that he summed up in answering a question about his beliefs: "I am a Christian and a democrat, that's all." By Christian Roosevelt meant the social gospel message of shared service to those in need that he had absorbed in his youth, and by democrat, fealty to a similar progressive reform ethic. That outlook spanned both political parties. Raised a privileged only child on a large Hudson River estate at Hyde Park, New York, Franklin followed his father's lead in everything, including membership in the Democratic Party. But he was also the admiring cousin of Theodore Roosevelt, Republican president and leader of the Progressive movement in the early twentieth century. In 1910 Franklin made his successful entry into politics as a state senator devoted to reform of urban political corruption. Two years later, in support of Woodrow Wilson's campaign for the presidency, he began devising the formula that would envelop both Democratic and Republican progressive traditions.

Roosevelt's youth in the countryside and his admiration for Thomas Jefferson tied him to the decentralized ideal proclaimed in Wilson's New Freedom platform of a nation rooted in small towns and family farms. But he also accepted Theodore Roosevelt's New Nationalism argument that large concentrations of economic power were a feature of modern life that the government through expert guidance should harness to serve the general welfare. From these competing visions Franklin Roosevelt sought cooperative means to realize the ideal balance between individual liberty and democratic institutions that had eluded the nation from its beginning. In the popular term of the day, Roosevelt was an advocate of a cooperative commonwealth, and in approaching economic and political life he thought far more in terms of interdependence than of competition.

Roosevelt's political education was rounded out by his wife, Eleanor. It was she, serious, bookish, compassionate, who showed Franklin the terrible conditions she had discovered as a settlement house worker in lower Manhattan and introduced him to the remarkable women volunteers who were leading the fight to improve the lives of the poor and outcast. In drawing Franklin deeper into the lower-class world, Eleanor was able to convince him that he should learn to work with big-city machines, like Tammany Hall, as the only effective fighters for the interests of ethnic and immigrant groups. Throughout Roosevelt's presidency Eleanor would continue to stretch the inclusiveness of the New Deal by forcefully pressing for action that would serve the rights and needs of minorities, women, children, and others who usually had little influence on practical politics.

During his victorious campaign for the presidency in 1932, Roosevelt gathered a group of advisers around him who became known as the Brains Trust because they were mostly drawn from universities. Rexford Tugwell and Adolf Berle led the way in pressing for a planned approach to economic recovery and reform. Their ideas reflected a broad progressive band of thought, some of it drawn from European cooperative ventures and national systems of social insurance. Behind Tugwell's plans for a "concert of interests" lay the tutelage of Simon Patten at the University of Pennsylvania, whose advocacy of an economy of abundance early in the century opened the way for challenging orthodox conceptions of chronic scarcity and a competitive free marketplace. Berle used the devotion to facts and practical experience pressed upon him by institutional economists like John Commons and Charles Van Hise to carry out the monumental study *The Modern Corporation and Private Property* (1932) with his Harvard colleague Gardiner Means, which showed that control of America's large corporations had fallen into the hands of a small group of managers. Either that concentration should be broken up, concluded those who read the highly acclaimed book, or, as Berle thought, the bigness driving modern economic life should be made to benefit the public through careful control by the democratic government that alone was responsible for the general welfare. At the center of interest in planning was the memory of how the nation's productive capacity had been mobilized in World War I. The popular economist Stuart Chase captured the mood by calling for a Peace Industries Board to defeat the depression as the War Industries Board had defeated the Germans.

In his inaugural address Roosevelt promised "a New Deal for the American people" and rightly concluded that "this nation asks for action, and action now." With 13 million people, or one-quarter of the workforce, unemployed, and the local and private means relied upon to help the victims nearing collapse, the general public was ready for the torrent of legislation that flowed immediately from the White House and its congressional allies.

The New Deal in Action

Guiding the torrent during what came to be known as the Hundred Days was a remarkable group of bright, mostly young, people who wanted to be part of the promised action. It was they, as well as Roosevelt, who gave the New Deal its air of optimistic excitement. As one observer noted, "they have transformed [Washington] from a placid leisurely Southern town . . . into a breezy, sophisticated and metropolitan center." Within the new buzz of activity, the New Deal had first to revive and change the banking system that had almost completely stopped functioning. On 6 March a "bank holiday" was declared, and three days later Congress passed the Emergency Banking Act, empowering the secretary of the Treasury to decide which banks were stable enough to reopen and authorizing federal funds to restart banking operations. To make the revived system safe, the Federal Deposit Insurance Corporation (FDIC) was created to insure bank deposits. The stage was then set to help the millions of unemployed. On 31 March Congress enacted Roosevelt's favorite program, the CIVILIAN CONSERVATION CORPS (CCC), to enroll idle youth in conserving natural resources, and followed up on May 12 with the Federal Emergency Relief Administration (FERA), which distributed cash payments to those unable to work.

Having addressed the immediate emergency, the New Deal could proceed with its comprehensive designs for planned reform. The Agricultural Administration Act (AAA), passed on 12 May, permanently altered American agriculture through its provision to pay farmers to keep land out of production and so raise prices by making commodities scarcer. Roosevelt's intent to stress conservation as a national priority received its greatest boost on 18 May from the passage of the TENNESSEE VALLEY AUTHORITY Act (TVA), which authorized dams on the Tennessee River that would provide the hydroelectric power needed to transform vast portions of Tennessee and adjoining states from abject poverty into the prosperity of model towns and reclaimed farmland. Most central to the integrative design, though, because industry and commerce had long been the focal point for planners, including those in the Brains Trust, was the National Industrial Recovery Act (NIRA), enacted on 16 June, which sought to create a system of fair practice for the nation's business firms. With parades and other promotional fanfare to drum up support, the NATIONAL RECOVERY ADMINISTRATION (NRA) spread the New Deal activist spirit nationwide and persuaded most of the nation's businesses to devise codes to govern working conditions and prices.

On the Alphabetical Front. This 1934 political cartoon by Daniel Robert Fitzpatrick, the editorial cartoonist for the *St. Louis Post-Dispatch* for forty-five years, shows a few of the many acronyms representing the New Deal programs that the Democrats introduced—while the Republicans here offer only a cry for help. LIBRARY OF CONGRESS

Resistance and Realignment

Despite enthusiasm for New Deal initiatives, registered in sweeping Democratic victories in Congress in 1934, the New Deal suffered setbacks. Many businesses slanted their NRA codes to provide higher profits rather than the better wages for labor and lower prices for consumers that the cooperative design called for. In agriculture large farms garnered most of the benefits of payments for reducing crops. And within the Supreme Court a majority of justices regarded some New Deal measures as unconstitutional invasions of state authority and free enterprise. Taking the opposite view, radicals of left and right criticized the New Deal for not changing the capitalistic system more drastically.

New Dealers were willing to concede that the rise in gross national product from $56 billion in 1933 to $72 billion in 1935 was a slow pace, and they were particularly disturbed that over 10 million people were still without jobs. To spur the economy toward full employment and a decent standard of living for the "common man," the administration in 1935 made three successful proposals to Congress. First, a $4.8 billion fund to create the WORKS PROGRESS ADMINISTRATION (WPA) was rushed through Congress. Then to care for those unable to work, the SOCIAL SECURITY Administration was formed on the model of an insurance company, using payroll deductions from workers for a trust fund that would provide unemployment insurance, aid for dependent mothers, children, and the blind, and a monthly income to those over sixty-five who had contributed to the system. Finally, after reluctantly giving up hope for agreement between labor and management within the NRA, Roosevelt supported the passage on 5 July 1935 of the NATIONAL LABOR RELATIONS ACT (NLRA), or Wagner Act after its sponsor, Senator Robert F. Wagner of New York, guaranteeing the right of labor to bargain collectively and have disputes with management decided by the National Labor Relations Board (NLRB).

The Wagner Act, labor's "Magna Carta," indicated how pressures were forcing the administration to change its approach to what some historians have described as the Second New Deal. Even as the Wagner Act conferred on labor means to contend against management rather than futilely attempting to cooperate with it, the New Deal faced a need to cope with forces determined to thwart its planning designs. In 1936 the Supreme Court invalidated the AAA and the NRA as unconstitutional delegations of power to the federal government. Business leaders echoed conservative judges with attacks on the New Deal as a threat to individual liberty, while critics on the radical left and right contradicted those charges by rejecting the New Deal as too closely tied to the prevailing capitalist system to enact necessary reforms. In response Roosevelt set aside his preference for cooperative inclusiveness. During his reelection campaign in 1936, he ignored the left as a minor threat and excoriated the "economic royalists" on the right, bent on blocking plans to share America's wealth and opportunity with those who had been left out. The shift of the New Deal focus from a fully cooperative system of all elements in society to advancement of the fortunes of members of the New Deal coalition against those in opposition caused some historians to conclude that the New Deal had become a "broker state," trading favors with special interests rather than acting in the full national interest. However, Roosevelt never lost his intent to find some way to achieve his cooperative commonwealth ideal.

Enthused by his overwhelming reelection, Roosevelt moved quickly to drag the Supreme Court out of the "horse and buggy" era by sending Congress a plan to enlarge the Court with a new justice for every old justice over seventy. The rebuff that followed indicated that Roosevelt had failed to realize the public's reverence for the Court. Congress shelved the "court packing" plan, and only the chance to replace retiring justices with more liberal judges saved the New Deal from further court disasters. The administration then compounded its problems. An ill-advised attempt by Roosevelt, urged on him by his fiscally conservative secretary of the Treasury Henry Morgenthau, to cut spending and balance the budget threw the country into a recession in 1937 that almost wiped out the economic gains made since 1933.

Roosevelt sought to reverse the downslide by establishing the Temporary National Economic Committee (TNEC) in 1938 to investigate industry practices that might be retarding recovery. In support of that move he appointed Thurman Arnold, an influential critic of what he called the symbols of government and folklore of capitalism, to carry out the most extensive campaign to break up monopolies ever undertaken. Roosevelt also attempted to strengthen his political coalition by supporting candidates running against Democratic congressmen who had opposed New Deal initiatives. But the New Deal had lost much of its focus and leverage. The TNEC could not agree on what ailed the economy, Arnold's campaign alienated business, and the attempt to purge anti–New Deal congressmen bagged only Representative John Taber of New York. Congressional conservatism also showed its rising force in the defeat of an antilynching bill and the reduction of progressive taxes on high income and capital gains, which the New Deal Revenue Act of 1938 proposed to fund recovery and distribute income more equitably.

Congress did agree to several important measures. In 1937 the Resettlement Administration (established in 1935) was transformed into the Farm Security Administration (FSA) with broadened powers to move poor farmers to better land; a new AAA was drafted that passed muster with a liberalized Supreme Court; a weak National Housing Act was passed in 1937 to provide low-income housing; and the Fair Labor Standards Act of 1938 established a minimum wage and a forty-hour week for many workers and at last prohibited child labor.

The Final Phase

Especially significant for the way it signaled an important shift in New Deal economic thinking was the $3 billion Emergency Relief Appropriation Act of 1938, designed to combat the recession with increased relief work for the unemployed. Preceding the passage of the act was a contentious discussion of how to regain momentum toward full recovery. Against Morgenthau's orthodox argument that a balanced budget and increased credit for business investment would place the economy on a firm footing, a growing number of advisers pressed for spending on public projects, even if it meant deficits, and using antitrust action to break up big businesses that refused to contribute to the general recovery. There was some awareness within their midst of the publication in 1936 of the most important economic work of the century, John Maynard Keynes's *A General Theory of Employment, Interest, and Money*, but the strongest impetus came from Keynes's American counterparts, who decried the resistance of business leaders to planning. In their manifesto, *An Economic Program for American Democracy* (1938), a team of Harvard and Tufts economists proclaimed that "Here in America we can save our free democratic institutions only by using them to expand our national income." Government action was essential, for "private enterprise, left to its own devices, is no longer capable of achieving anything." Especially to be checked were businessmen who seemed "obsessed with a devil theory of government" that might tempt them to try replacing democracy with a plutocratic dictatorship. Roosevelt had long looked at businessmen that way but was only finally persuaded to the Keynesian case when the chairman of the New York Federal Reserve, Beardsley Ruml, reminded him that governmental stimulation of business was an old story, stretching back to nineteenth-century grants to railroads, the distribution of public lands, and the setting of tariffs.

In another important departure from past practice in the direction of greater executive authority, Congress acceded to Roosevelt's urging in 1939 to pass the Administration Reorganization Act, which, in the name of streamlined efficiency, placed many government agencies under the president's control. By also transferring the Bureau of the Budget to the executive office and creating a National Resources Planning Board, Roosevelt further expanded the scope of the executive branch to a degree that has prompted some historians to call that development the Third New Deal, bent on using expanded executive power to revive the original New Deal ardor for cooperative planning.

Significant reform initiatives did not follow, however, partly because of conservative resistance, partly because the approach of World War II diverted attention to foreign dangers. Industrial recovery continued to lag and unemployment remained high. Only the entry of America into the war ended the impasse. Mobilization of resources and manpower eliminated the most central and persistent curse of the Great Depression by absorbing the jobless so thoroughly that the WPA could be phased out in 1943. Wartime pressures did not, however, lay the groundwork for completion of New Deal plans to end hardship and injustice by assuring full employment at good wages, extend the SOCIAL SECURITY system to include those originally denied coverage, enact a national health system, and revise the law to grant civil rights and fair opportunity to women and minorities.

Despite these shortfalls, the New Deal changed America from a nation whose political focus was in regional localities and offered little in the way of welfare or national planning. In the wake of New Deal activism, Americans came to assume that the government would take significant responsibility for their material and spiritual needs. That expectation has remained intact even though the New Deal coalition has weakened as the prosperity it promoted moved many of its members from inner-city New Deal strongholds to the conservative suburbs, where reformist zeal and ethnic and labor union solidarity ebbed. Civil rights reform had a similarly ironic outcome. As the desegregation movement advanced in the 1960s, bearing the New Deal social justice spirit with it, many southerners rejected their traditional loyalty to the Democratic Party and joined in the Republican Party's continuing efforts to check New Deal reform in the name of states' rights and free enterprise.

An overall assessment of the New Deal's effectiveness indicates that most of its problems stemmed from not carrying its policies far enough to achieve a planned economy of abundance for all Americans, partly because of traditional individualism and to a lesser extent because the New Dealers themselves wished to revitalize the system, not displace it. Thus New Deal initiatives tended to stall. The NRA did not get enough money in the hands of consumers for them to support a fully productive economy. Commitment to deficit spending toward the end of the 1930s was not sufficient to end unemployment. New taxes on the wealthy did not go far enough to redistribute income to the desperate have-nots. Relief spending never reached more than 40 percent of those in need. And Social Security excluded several categories of needy people. In some cases, New Deal policies had unwanted results. The agricultural price support system did not eliminate the surplus and funneled payments mainly to large-scale farms. Nor were hopes for urban revitalization realized. Housing policies did not achieve the New Deal goal of eliminating city slums but instead encouraged flight to the suburbs, away from the meager low-cost housing that underfunded New Deal programs were able to build.

Yet the New Deal had lasting success in establishing the principle Lincoln enunciated that the federal government should do for people what they cannot do for themselves. Thus the NRA enacted a minimum wage standard and the right of workers to join unions of their own choosing. Regulation stabilized banking and finance. Civil rights became a significant part of the Democratic and then national agenda. And to extend recovery to mind and spirit, the WPA devised an arts program that inspired the later creation of the National Endowments for the Arts and Humanities. From the socially conscious art, regional guides, and documentary film and photography sponsored by the program has come a significant share of what Americans have learned about their history and culture.

Roosevelt stated at the outset that his New Deal would be a war on depression miseries comparable to previous military wars. But in the end it was the actuality of World War II, which the nation avoided as long as it could, that ended the depression by generating the economic stimulus the New Deal had not gone far enough to provide. In the years since the depression ended, admiration for the New Deal has remained high; but debate has also persisted as to whether the New Deal devotion to planned cooperation is a necessary part of maintaining a stable and prosperous American democracy.

BIBLIOGRAPHY

Allswang, John M. *The New Deal and American Politics: A Study in Political Change.* New York: Wiley, 1978. A convincing explanation of the formation of the New Deal coalition, buttressed by detailed case studies.

Badger, Anthony J. *The New Deal. The Depression Years, 1933–40.* New York: Hill and Wang, 1989. Provides a thorough account of the history and historiography of the New Deal.

Bernstein, Irving. *A Caring Society: The New Deal, the Worker, and the Great Depression.* Boston: Houghton Mifflin, 1985.

Brinkley, Alan. *The End of Reform: New Deal Liberalism in Recession and War.* New York: Knopf, 1995.

Brock, William R. *Welfare, Democracy, and the New Deal.* Cambridge, U.K.: Cambridge University Press, 1988.

Fite, Gilbert C. *American Farmers: The New Majority.* Bloomington: Indiana University Press, 1981. The most incisive overview of New Deal agricultural policy and its effects.

Harris, Jonathan. *Federal Art and National Culture: The Politics of Identity in New Deal America.* Cambridge, U.K.: Cambridge University Press, 1995. The most tightly drawn account of the links between the social populism of the New Deal and the Federal Arts Projects.

Hawley, Ellis W. *The New Deal and the Problem of Monopoly.* Princeton, N.J.: Princeton University Press, 1966. The cornerstone for understanding the New Deal's relations with business.

Leuchtenburg, William E. *Franklin D. Roosevelt and the New Deal, 1932–1940.* New York: Harper and Row, 1963. Still the best one-volume account. Detailed but highly readable.

Patterson, James T. *The Welfare State in America, 1930–1980.* Durham, U.K.: British Association for American Studies, 1981.The best, brief discussion of the creation and evolution of Social Security.

Reagan, Patrick D. *Designing a New America: The Origins of New Deal Planning, 1890–1943.* Amherst: University of Massachusetts Press, 1999. Engaging portraits of the architects of national planning in modern America.

Rodgers, Daniel T. "New Deal." In *Atlantic Crossings: Social Politics in a Progressive Age.* Cambridge, Mass.: Harvard University Press, 1998. An erudite and sweeping discussion of the European influences on American progressive reform thought.

Rosenof, Theodore. *Economics in the Long Run: New Deal Theorists and Their Legacies, 1933–1993.* Chapel Hill: University of North Carolina Press, 1997. A uniquely valuable account of how New Deal economic policy drew upon the changing economic thought of the time.

Schlesinger, Arthur S., Jr. *The Age of Roosevelt.* 3 vols. Boston: Houghton Mifflin, 1956–1960. An epic account of the New Deal era by a master of panoramic synthesis.

Sitkoff, Harvard. *A New Deal for Blacks: The Emergence of Civil Rights as a National Issue.* New York: Oxford University Press, 1978.

Tugwell, R. G. *The Brains Trust.* New York: Viking, 1968. A shrewd appraisal that has special value because it is by an insider.

Ware, Susan. *Beyond Suffrage: Women in the New Deal.* Cambridge, Mass.: Harvard University Press, 1981.

Alan Lawson

See also **Great Depression.**

NEW ENGLAND. Embracing the six states of Maine, New Hampshire, Vermont, Massachusetts, Rhode Island, and Connecticut, New England formed a distinct section with a character of its own from the beginning of European settlement in North America. It is significant that New England was the first to develop the idea of complete independence from Great Britain, that it opposed the unrestrained westward expansion of the new nation, and that it was the first to propose secession from the Union (see Hartford Convention). Its sectional identity and local character were deeply rooted in its history.

Geographically, New England is separated from the rest of the United States by the northern spurs of the Appalachian Mountains, and its lack of river systems, such as the Mohawk-Hudson, denies it easy access to the hinterland. Although Puritanism was widespread in all the colonies during the period of early English settlement, New England was settled by the most orthodox Puritans. In Massachusetts the first government was a conservative theocracy, which, owing to the transfer of the charter to Boston, was practically independent of England (1630–1686). Connecticut and Rhode Island colonies never had royal governors. Owing to altered conditions in England, immigration declined sharply for the two centuries after 1640, thus limiting New England's exposure to outside influences. The early establishment of Harvard College in 1636 further increased parochialism, for potential leaders who might have been broadened by an education in England remained in the provincial atmosphere of the colony. The poor soil and rough terrain precluded development of large estates or staple crops, as well as of slavery. The region became a land of small farmers, hardy fishermen, and versatile traders, all ingenious in finding ways of making money.

There were local differences, such as the religious intolerance of Massachusetts and the freedom of Rhode Island, but the "Yankee" character dominated all of New England by 1830. The limited number of immigrants, the lack of outside contacts, and stubborn control by the clerical oligarchy were all major factors in shaping the region. Moreover, when New Englanders migrated, they often did so in groups of families or entire congregations whose group solidarity maintained customs and character.

The typical New England institutions developed in isolation—public schools, Congregational churches, town government, and the "New England conscience"—as did the New England preoccupation with religion and morality. The 1825 opening of the Erie Canal, linking Lake Erie to New York City, further isolated New England, and even the first local railroad lines did not link it to the expanding nation. However, self-reliance, ingenuity, and industrious habits made New Englanders the most skilled workmen in America, and New England merchants developed manufactures to an extent that no other region did. The growth of mills and factories demanded an increase in cheap labor, and by 1840 foreign immigration reshaped the New England population and character. Even Puritan Massachusetts became an overwhelmingly Roman Catholic state.

Despite the arrival of immigrants from Canada and Europe, the New England character, established through two centuries of struggle and separation, persisted, and contributed much to other regions through migration and by example. Among the earliest migrations were those to Long Island, New Jersey, and South Carolina, and later to the Mohawk Valley, Pennsylvania, Ohio, Illinois, Michigan, and Oregon. Towns and districts all across the northern United States seem transplanted from New England, possessing as they do New England ideas of education, Congregational churches, town meetings, and Yankee character and attitudes, all introduced by New England migrants. Americans educated in New England colleges and universities also transmitted New England traditions to other states. Sectional as New England's history has been, the region's influence on the rest of the United States is out of all proportion to its size and population.

BIBLIOGRAPHY

Brown, Richard D., and Jack Tager. *Massachusetts: A Concise History*. Amherst: University of Massachusetts Press, 2000.

Peirce, Neal R. *The New England States: People, Politics, and Power in the Six New England States*. New York: Norton, 1976.

Peter C. Holloran

NEW ENGLAND ANTISLAVERY SOCIETY (NEAS). This group was the first antislavery association among white activists to demand immediate, unconditional abolition of slavery and equal rights for black Americans, without compensation to the slaveowners and without colonization (forced expatriation) of the freed slaves. William Lloyd Garrison helped to found the NEAS in 1831. By the next year it had several thousand members, white and black, male and female, and a dozen local affiliates, and had served as inspiration for nearly fifty local groups distributed across the North from Maine to Ohio. In 1835 the NEAS bowed to its own success by agreeing to become a state auxiliary of the American Antislavery Society and renaming itself the Massachusetts Antislavery Society.

Garrison was inspired to establish the NEAS because of his attraction in the 1820s to the morality and discipline of the temperance benevolent movement. Garrison committed himself to abolitionism in 1828 after meeting Benjamin Lundy, a zealous Quaker newspaper editor. Garrison founded the NEAS because he believed that abolitionism needed an organization on the model of other benevolent organizations. Garrison recruited to help him Isaac Knapp and Oliver Johnson, journalists he knew through his abolitionist newspaper, *The Liberator*; Samuel J. May, who, as a Unitarian minister, illustrated how abolitionism did not originate only in evangelical sects; Ellis Gray Loring, an attorney, who in 1851 would be involved in the celebrated rescue of a black man; Frederick Jenkins, who a slaveowner claimed was his escaped slave Shadrach; Lydia Maria Child, a novelist and historian of the condition of women; and Arnold Buffum, a Quaker businessman who became the first president of the NEAS.

From its outset the Society maintained petition campaigns against the slave trade and formed committees to inquire into the problem of segregated schooling, to protect free Negroes against the danger of kidnappers, and to develop opportunities for young black youths as apprentices in the skilled trades. However, its most important achievement was its attack on the American Colonization Society (ACS). Before the 1830s the ACS was the main abolitionist organization among whites in the United States. Its philosophy was that abolition had to be accompanied by the physical and political separation of the races. Its supporters by and large saw the establishment of a colony in Africa as an act of benevolence for freed slaves and poor free people of color, as well as a safety valve for troublesome elements. NEAS lecturers used Garrison's book, *Thoughts on African Colonization* (1832), to attack the ACS as a racist organization that actually pandered to the slaveowners' interests. When the ACS publicly attacked the NEAS as a low-class organization, the strategy backfired. Thousands of Northern working-class laborers became alienated from the ACS, and began to consider NEAS's commitment to immediate abolition. Colonization lost its support among abolitionists as a result of the attacks on the NEAS. Around 1835 Garrison began urging his followers to nonviolent civil disobedience of laws that required private citizens to assist in the return of fugitive slaves. At the same time the abolitionists also began circulation of antislavery tracts to ministers, legislators, and editors in the South. These strategies would be the most controversial component of abolitionism until the late 1850s.

BIBLIOGRAPHY

Mayer, Henry. *All On Fire: William Lloyd Garrison and the Abolition of Slavery*. New York: St. Martin's Press, 1998. The best biography of Garrison and his leadership of the NEAS.

Stewart, James B. *Holy Warriors: The Abolitionists and American Slavery*. New York: Hill and Wang, 1976.

Timothy M. Roberts

NEW ENGLAND COLONIES. Settled by Europeans, primarily the English, in the seventeenth century, New England included the PLYMOUTH COLONY (1620, absorbed by Massachusetts Bay in 1691), the MASSACHUSETTS BAY COLONY (1630), Connecticut (1636), New Haven (1640), Rhode Island (1636), and New Hampshire (separated from Massachusetts Bay in 1741). The New England Colonies are best known as the destination for Puritan religious reformers and their followers. Diverse European fishermen, however, had been tapping into the vast resources off Cape Cod since the late 1500s. Religious and economic motivations merged in each New England Colony.

Prompted by just those two motivations, in 1630 approximately one thousand people set sail from England under the auspices of the Puritan-controlled Massachusetts Bay Company. Led by John Winthrop, the Puritan founders of the Massachusetts Bay Colony sought to establish a religious utopia made up of Christians who operated in a strict covenant with God.

Tensions in Massachusetts Bay—the product of disagreements over what would constitute a theocratic community and government, relationships with Native Americans, and the role of wealth, status, and land in the colony—resulted early on in a threat of deportation for Roger Williams, a Puritan minister from Salem who openly challenged both church and government policy. In 1635 Williams fled south with a small band of followers to establish Providence, the first settlement in Rhode Is-

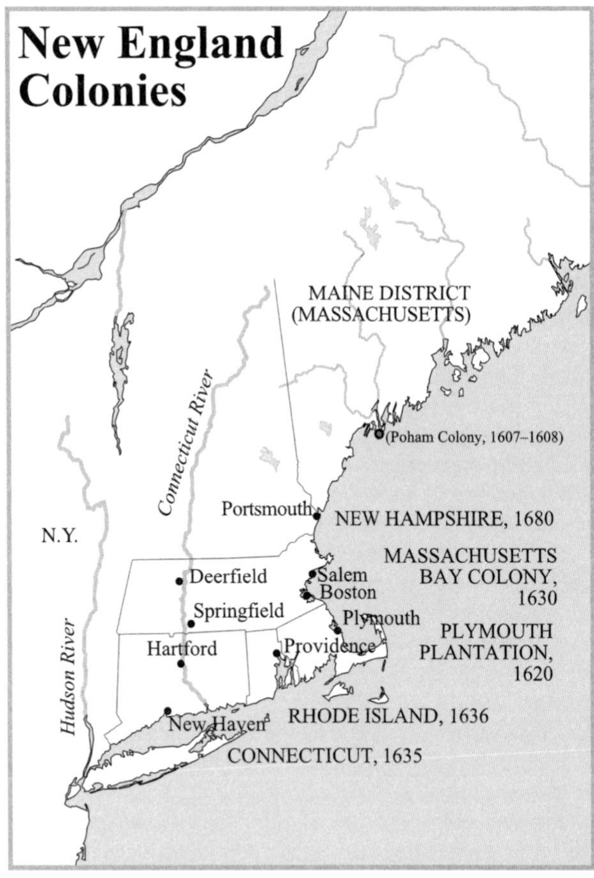

land. In like manner, Puritans from Massachusetts Bay also migrated to Connecticut, settling in Hartford (under the leadership of Thomas Hooker), New Haven (under John Davenport), and in towns along the Connecticut River Valley.

BIBLIOGRAPHY

Bremer, Francis J. *The Puritan Experiment: New England Society from Bradford to Edwards.* Rev. ed. Hanover, N.H.: University Press of New England, 1995. The original edition was published in 1976.

Leslie J. Lindenauer

See also **New Haven Colony; Pilgrims; Providence Plantations, Rhode Island and; Puritans and Puritanism; Separatists, Puritan.**

NEW ENGLAND COMPANY. Known officially as the Society for the Propagation of the Gospel in New England, the New England Company was initially an unincorporated joint stock venture, founded in 1649 for the purpose of converting New England Indians. The members were Puritans and principally prosperous London merchants; together they collected and invested funds, the interest from which paid missionaries' salaries. In 1660 the Society sought a royal charter to protect its assets and ensure its continued existence. According to the Charter's preamble, the corporation would draw New England's Indians away from "the power of darknesse and the kingdome of Sathan, to the Knowledge of the true and only God."

BIBLIOGRAPHY

Kellaway, William. *The New England Company, 1649–1776: Missionary Society to the American Indians.* New York: Barnes and Noble, 1962.

Leslie J. Lindenauer

NEW ENGLAND CONFEDERATION, the United Colonies of New England, consisting of Connecticut, New Haven, Massachusetts, and Plymouth colonies, founded on 19 May 1643. Only "heretical" Rhode Island was excluded from this, the first attempt at major intercolonial cooperation.

The confederation's main purpose was mutual defense. The English civil war and its aftermath had thrown England into chaos, leaving the colonies to fend for themselves. They were vulnerable to attack from the Dutch and French, but, most importantly, the New England colonies were growing ever more concerned about deteriorating Indian relations. Rapid expansion caused friction with neighboring Indian tribes, especially in the Connecticut Valley. In forming an alliance for mutual defense, the Puritan colonies were defending their continuing expansion as much as their existing settlements.

The first Articles of Confederation set up a "firm and perpetual league of friendship and amity for offense and defense." Each colony maintained full jurisdiction within its borders and selected two commissioners, who collectively formed the confederation's council. The commissioners were empowered by their respective general courts to determine matters of war and peace, handle diplomatic affairs, and treat other intercolonial matters at regular annual meetings. Six commissioners had to approve policy, or the matter could be referred to the colonial legislatures. In the event of war, the colonies would divide the costs, but no colony was allowed to initiate a war without six commissioners' approval. Yet the commissioners had no coercive power over the colonies. Sovereign power remained with the legislatures.

From 1643 to 1655, the confederation successfully exercised broad intercolonial powers in areas including education, Indian missions, and extradition of criminals, but it mainly focused on diplomacy. The commissioners practiced aggressive Indian diplomacy and maintained a favorable balance of power by shifting alliances and pitting one tribe against another. The United Colonies were also successful in keeping peace with the French and Dutch, even negotiating a treaty with the Dutch in 1650 that confirmed the English-Dutch border.

Problems arose as colonies asserted their independence. Massachusetts's refusal to support a war against the

Dutch and the confederation's inability to prevent Connecticut's encroachments on New Haven (beginning in 1662 and concluding with Connecticut's annexation of New Haven in 1664) exposed the confederation's lack of coercive power. A royal commission recommended reconstituting the confederation in 1664, and from that time the commissioners were limited to only triennial regular meetings. From 1655 to 1675 the confederation focused on Indian missions, administering funds raised in England for the "Society [later Corporation] for the Propagation of the Gospel." New Articles of Confederation were signed in 1672, but the commissioners remained essentially powerless to affect policy, and continued to focus on Indian missions, neglecting diplomacy and defense.

Failure to manipulate alliances with Indian tribes, aggressive and unregulated expansion, and Plymouth's harsh treatment of Metacom and the Wampanoag Indians led to the outbreak of Metacom's War (King Philip's War) in June 1675. For the first six months, the confederation successfully organized an intercolonial war effort, but initiative fell to the individual colonies as attacks became more dispersed and the war devolved into one of attrition. The confederation's last major piece of business was settling the colonies' war debts at its 1678 meeting. The official record ends in 1684 with the revocation of Massachusetts's charter, but commissioners met again in 1689, hoping to frame new articles. None were adopted, and the final blow to any hope of reviving the confederation came when Massachusetts absorbed Plymouth and became a royal colony in 1691.

BIBLIOGRAPHY

Bradford, William. *History of Plymouth Plantation, 1620–1647.* Edited by Samuel Eliot Morison. New York: Russell and Russell, 1968.

Drake, James D. *King Philip's War: Civil War in New England, 1675–1676.* Amherst: University of Massachusetts Press, 1999.

Leach, Douglas E. *Flintlock and Tomahawk: New England in King Philip's War.* New York: Norton, 1958.

Shurtleff, Nathaniel, and David Pulsifer, eds. *Acts of the Commissioners of the United Colonies of New England, 1643–1679.* Volumes 9–10 of *Records of the Colony of New Plymouth in New England.* 1855. Reprint, New York: AMS Press, 1968.

Vaughan, Alden T. *New England Frontier: Puritans and Indians, 1620–1675.* 3d ed. Norman: University of Oklahoma Press, 1965.

Ward, Harry M. *The United Colonies of New England, 1643–1690.* New York: Vantage Press, 1961.

Aaron J. Palmer

See also **King Philip's War.**

NEW ENGLAND EMIGRANT AID COMPANY.

Founded by Eli Thayer, of Worcester, Massachusetts, and seeking to assist Northern emigrants to settle in the West, mainly in the Kansas territory, the New England Emigrant Aid Company was incorporated as the Massachusetts Emigrant Aid Company on 26 April 1854; it changed its name in February 1855. Thayer and his supporters were alarmed that the Kansas-Nebraska Act of 1854, which overturned a territorial ban on slavery imposed by the Missouri Compromise of 1820, would close off economic opportunities to non-slaveholding laborers and immigrants. The Company was both a philanthropic undertaking and a money-making operation. It solicited investors and negotiated discounted transportation, provided conductors, and financed construction of hotels, schools, churches, and mills. Its expenditures totaled approximately $192,000. Company-backed settlers who went to Kansas, some three thousand in all, founded Lawrence, named for Amos A. Lawrence, the Massachusetts antislavery captain of industry and largest financial backer of the Company; Topeka; Manhattan; and Osawatomie, a town made famous when the zealot John Brown fought proslavery forces in its vicinity. The Company involved itself in the Kansas free-state movement by dispatching antislavery political advice and covertly supplying settlers with hundreds of the deadly Sharps breechloading rifle as well as cannons and a howitzer. When these operations were discovered they outraged proslavery forces, as well as the Democratic administration of Franklin Pierce. In the fight to determine whether Kansas would enter the Union slave or free, proslavery Missourians pointed to the Company's covert operations to justify their fraudulent voting. On the other hand, the rising Republican Party used the controversy surrounding the Company to build momentum. By 1857 settlement in Kansas by free labor migrants had grown to the thousands and the Company's efforts subsided. In 1861 the Company's assets, valued at $100,000, were liquidated to pay debts. During and after the Civil War the Company funded token efforts to establish colonies in Oregon and Florida.

BIBLIOGRAPHY

Johnson, Samuel A. *Battle Cry of Freedom: The New England Emigrant Aid Company in the Kansas Crusade. 1954.* Reprint, Westport, Conn: Greenwood Press, 1977.

Timothy M. Roberts

NEW ENGLAND INDIANS. *See* **Tribes: Northeastern.**

NEW ENGLAND PRIMER.

The New England Primer, first published about 1690, combined lessons in spelling with a short catechism and versified injunctions to piety and faith in Calvinistic fundamentals. Crude couplets and woodcut pictures illustrated the alphabet, and the child's prayer that begins "Now I lay me down to sleep" first appeared in this book. The primer fulfilled the purposes of EDUCATION in New England, where Puritan colonists stressed literacy as conducive to scriptural study. For about fifty years, this eighty-page booklet, four and

Now the Child being entred in his Letters and Spelling, let him learn these and such like Sentences by Heart, whereby he will be both instructed in his Duty, and encouraged in his Learning.

The Dutiful Child's Promises,

I Will fear GOD, and honour the KING.
I will honour my Father & Mother.
I will Obey my Superiours.
I will Submit to my Elders.
I will Love my Friends.
I will hate no Man.
I will forgive my Enemies, and pray to God for them.
I will as much as in me lies keep all God's Holy Commandments.

Early Textbook. The New England Primer was the standard teaching tool in early seventeenth-century classrooms throughout the colonies for more than 100 years. Shown here is a page from the earliest known extant version of the primer, printed in 1727.

a half by three inches in size, was the only elementary textbook in America, and for a century more it held a central place in primary education.

BIBLIOGRAPHY

Crain, Patricia. *The Story of A: The Alphebetization of America from the* New England Primer *to* The Scarlet Letter. Stanford, Calif.: Stanford University Press, 2000.

McClellan, B. Edward. *Moral Educaiton in America: Schools and the Shaping of Character from Colonial Times to the Present.* New York: Teachers College Press, 1999.

Harry R. Warfel / s. b.

See also **Literature: Children's Literature; New England Colonies; Printing Industry; Puritans and Puritanism.**

NEW ENGLAND WAY refers to the ecclesiastical polity, relation to the civil powers, and general practices of the Massachusetts Bay Colony churches and, sometimes, to those of Connecticut or Rhode Island. English reformers inquired into the system (1637), and after the Long Parliament began ecclesiastical "reform" (1641), interest in Massachusetts polity led John Cotton to expound its principles in *The Way of the Churches of Christ in New England . . .* (1645), later retitled *The New England Way.*

Originally a platform of opposition to English prelacy, based upon teachings of Henry Jacob, William Ames, and others, the "New England Way" evolved into New England Congregationalism. The church, originating neither in princes nor parliaments but in God's Word, was a body of professed regenerates (the "elect") who subscribed to a "covenant" (or creed), selected officers, chose and ordained its minister, and was subject to no interchurch organizations save "consociations" for counsel and advice. Being "visible saints," they admitted only persons who approved the covenant and whose piety and deportment recommended them to the congregation. They denied separation from the Anglican church; they separated only from its "corruptions," considered themselves true "primitive churches of Christ," and were supremely intolerant of others. Magistrates, "nursing fathers of the churches," were limited in civil authority by the Word (in practice, as interpreted by ministers) and compelled both to conform and to purge churches and state of heterodoxy (opposition to normal beliefs). Citizenship depended on church membership. Church and state were indestructibly united. The "New England Way" did not appeal to English separatists, whose multiple sects required embracing toleration, and New England Congregationalists parted company with their English brethren.

BIBLIOGRAPHY

Foster, Stephen. *The Long Argument: English Puritanism and the Shaping of New England Culture, 1570–1700.* Chapel Hill: University of North Carolina Press, 1991.

Simpson, Alan. *Puritanism in Old and New England.* Chicago: University of Chicago Press, 1955.

Raymond P. Stearns / a. r.

See also **Church and State, Separation of; Church of England in the Colonies; Covenant, Church; Meetinghouse; Puritans and Puritanism; Religious Thought and Writings.**

NEW ERA. A widely used label for the period of American history preceding the Great Depression and the New Deal, New Era usually refers to1921–1929 but sometimes is used to indicate 1919–1933. It was initially used during the period, particularly by those viewing the innovations in industrial technology, managerial practice, and associational formation as components of a new capitalism capable of keeping itself in balance and realizing the nation's democratic ideals. Among those to use it in this fashion were the investment banker Elisha Friedman in *America and the New Era* (1920), the Harvard economist Thomas Nixon Carver in *The Present Economic Revolution in the United States* (1925), Secretary of Commerce Herbert Hoover in numerous public statements, and the economists responsible for *Recent Economic Changes in the United States* (1929). Subsequently, as the Great Depression produced negative interpretations of the period, the term took on connotations of foolishness and illusion and was replaced by such labels as the Republican Era, the Age of Normalcy, and the Roaring Twenties. But as scholars in the 1950s and 1960s rediscovered the period's innovations and were impressed with the extent to which they did represent a new and distinctive stage in social modernization, governmental development, and the coming of a managerial capitalism, the term came back into academic use.

BIBLIOGRAPHY

Alchon, Guy. *The Invisible Hand of Planning: Capitalism, Social Science, and the State in the 1920s.* Princeton, N.J.: Princeton University Press, 1985.

Barber, William J. *From New Era to New Deal: Herbert Hoover, the Economists, and American Economic Policy, 1921–1933.* Cambridge, U.K.; New York: Cambridge University Press, 1985.

Hawley, Ellis W., ed. *Herbert Hoover as Secretary of Commerce: Studies in New Era Thought and Practice.* Iowa City: University of Iowa Press, 1981.

Ellis Hawley

NEW FRANCE. For nearly two and a half centuries up to 1763, the term "New France" designated those regions of the Americas claimed in the name of French kings or occupied by their subjects. Early in the eighteenth century, New France reached its greatest extent. On official maps, it then stretched from Plaisance (present-day Placentia) in Newfoundland, through Acadia, Canada, the Great Lakes region (with a northern, recently conquered outlier on Hudson Bay), and the Mississippi Valley to the Gulf of Mexico. French settlers were concentrated in only a few parts of this vast arc of territory. The authorities laid claim to the rest by dint of a network of posts and forts, a minimal French presence made possible by an alliance with the Native nations whose land this was. While French power in this area tended to grow, it remained limited until the British conquest of 1759–1760 (confirmed, for the territory east of the Mississippi, in 1763 by the Treaty of Paris).

Early Settlement of New France

The idea of a new France situated an ocean away from the old gained currency after explorer Giovanni da Verrazano's 1524 voyage along the east coast of North America. If the notion contained an element of projection up to the very end, in the beginning, it was only that—a name on a 1529 map proclaiming eastern North America to be Nova Gallia. Other early New Frances were associated with exploration and, beginning in the early 1540s, short-lived settlements: in the St. Lawrence Valley, Brazil, and Florida. Only later would such efforts prove successful, as the trade with Native people, initially a by-product of the fishery, grew more intense after 1580. This both encouraged and permitted French merchant interests, official charter in hand, to establish permanent bases in the Northeast. The nuclei of the colonies of Acadia and Canada were created in 1605 and 1608, respectively, at Port-Royal (Annapolis Royal, N.S.) and Quebec. Neither of these mainly commercial establishments attracted many settlers in the early years. Be it with the Mi'kmaqs and the Abenakis in Acadia or the Innus, the Algonquins, and soon the Hurons in Canada, trade implied some form of military cooperation. Missionaries, who initiated exchanges of another, more unilateral sort, were a logical part of the bargain from the French point of view.

Such were the foundations of a long collaboration between the French and a growing number of Amerindian nations. Bringing together peoples of contrasting cultures and of opposing long-term interests, the arrangement was by no means preordained. Even after it became a tradition, much hard work on the part of intermediaries on either side of the cultural divide (and a few of mixed origin who were in the middle) was required to maintain it, and their blunders could threaten it. But for the moment, the two groups' interests often converged, for reasons that ultimately had much to do with demography. While the French colonial population would grow rapidly by natural increase, by British American standards a paltry number of immigrants set the process in motion. For the moment, the French posed a correspondingly limited threat to Native lands. Moreover, as conflicts among aboriginal nations and colonial and European rivalries gradually merged, both the French and a growing number of Native peoples, facing population decline, found an alliance to their advantage.

New France's Colonial Population

Meanwhile, a colonial population took root. Most of New France's colonists would live in the St. Lawrence Valley. With over 65,000 inhabitants in the late 1750s, Canada was France's flagship colony on the continent, its settlers accounting for some three-fourths of the total colonial population under French rule. Colonial development accelerated noticeably in the 1660s, thanks to a series of royal measures. These included substituting for company rule a royal administration headed by a governor-general and an intendant; sending troops to encourage the Iroquois to make peace; organizing the recruitment of emigrants, including some 800 marriageable women, in France; and permitting Jean Talon, the first intendant, to spend freely on various development projects, most of them premature. The emergence late in the decade of a new group, the coureurs de bois, illegal traders who soon all but replaced their Native counterparts in the trade linking Canada and the Great Lakes region, signaled growing specialization in the colonial economy. By the1720s, licensed traders, who recruited canoemen mostly in rural areas and dealt with a handful of Montreal merchants, had largely replaced the coureurs. By then, the vast majority of "Canadiens" gained their livelihood on family farms or in ar-

tisan shops, most of the latter concentrated in the colony's main towns of Quebec and Montreal. The colonial elite comprised the top government and church officials sent from France, as well as a local noblesse whose men usually served as officers in the colonial regular troops. They and the religious orders, active in education and hospitals, held most of the colony's seigneuries. Merchants, those in Quebec oriented more toward Atlantic markets and the Montrealers toward the interior, maintained a discreet but influential presence in this ancien régime society. Several groups of Native allies residing on a half-dozen reserves in the valley provided military aid; some helped carry out the Montreal-Albany contraband trade. With a few companions in misfortune of African origin, other, enslaved Natives generally performed domestic service for the well off.

Acadia in peninsular Nova Scotia, with smaller settlements in present-day New Brunswick and Prince Edward Island, contained the Atlantic region's largest French population—some 13,000 by 1755. The Nova Scotia Acadians, most of whom grew wheat and raised livestock behind dikes in the Fundy marshlands, experienced both the advantages and the disadvantages of life in a borderland: trade with all comers (including Bostonians), a weak official or even noble presence, and extended periods of rule by the rival colonial power. The last of these began in 1710 with the British conquest of the peninsula. It would

New France. This engraving by Thomas Johnston is called *Quebec, Capital of New France*, and shows all of France's holdings in area of present-day Quebec, Ontario, Canada, and along the St. Lawrence River in 1758, five years before most of New France was turned over to the British in the Treaty of Paris (1763). © THE GRANGER COLLECTION LTD.

be marked by the deportation and dispersal from 1755 to 1762 of the Acadians, whom the new rulers came to regard, no doubt erroneously in the vast majority's case, as a security risk. The Fundy marshlands having been reserved for New Englanders, Acadian fugitives, and returning exiles settled mainly in New Brunswick, now British territory, after the return of peace to the region.

Plaisance in Newfoundland, which had emerged in the 1680s as a year-round base for the French fishery, was by then but a distant memory; the French had ceded it to the British in 1713. Many of its inhabitants moved to Île Royale (Cape Breton Island). Here, fishing villages sprang up and construction soon began on the fortress of Louisbourg. In the town (its population of about 4,000 in 1752 counting for some three-fourths of the colony's), merchants set the tone. This port, strategically located for the intercolonial trade and the banks fishery, became one of eastern North America's busiest. As the eastern buttress of New France, Louisbourg was twice captured, in 1745 and again, for good, in 1758. The British demolished the fortress in the early 1760s.

At New France's other extremity, Louisiana, founded at Biloxi in 1699, would for some twenty years amount to little more than a shaky French foothold on the Gulf of Mexico. Mobile, established in 1702, was the main French base in this early period, marked by an expanding trade with the nations of the interior. From 1718 to 1721, at great human cost, a chaotic period of speculation and ineptly administered settlement laid the basis for a plantation society with newly founded New Orleans at its center. Indigo, tobacco, and rice headed the list of crops. By 1730, African slaves were in the majority among the colony's non-Native inhabitants, whose total number would reach about 9,000 by the end of the French regime. Distant from France, Louisiana maintained commercial relations with neighboring colonies, be they French, British, or Spanish, as well as with the metropole. New Orleans and the lands west of the Mississippi were ceded to Spain in 1762, and the rest of Louisiana to Britain the following year. Native people were not consulted.

The evolving modus vivendi with Native people both attracted French people toward the heart of the continent and increased the chances that even the settlers among them would be tolerated there. By the 1750s, some forty posts and forts in the Great Lakes region and beyond were supplied from Montreal and a few more from New Orleans or Mobile. Some were garrisoned, and many were entrusted to commandants interested in the fur trade and charged with conducting diplomacy with the Natives. While some French traders and their employees ended up remaining in the interior, often marrying Native women, only in a few places did substantial French settlements eventually emerge. All but one had non-Native populations of a few hundred people at the end of the French regime. At Detroit, a major center of the Canadian fur trade, migrants from Canada began arriving soon after the construction of the French fort there in 1701. Louisiana's major interior dependencies were situated at Natchitoches and in the Natchez country. Finally, the Illinois country, an offshoot of Canada but increasingly tied to Louisiana, offered fertile bottomlands, a mild climate, and a ready market downriver for agricultural produce. Here, the first settlers took root discreetly around 1700, nearly two decades before an administration arrived from lower Louisiana. They practiced a productive open-field agriculture increasingly reliant on slave labor. By the early 1750s, the population of the area's six colonial villages reached about 1,400, more than a third of them slaves.

Founded at different times in a wide range of environments and with varying degrees of official participation, the principal settled areas of New France were a study in contrasts. They formed an expanding, shifting archipelago of lands where colonists and sometimes their slaves outnumbered free Native people. Beyond, among tens of thousands of Native people, the French presence was much more tenuous. That contrast takes a different form in the early twenty-first century: old French family and place names are spread across the continent, while French-speakers are concentrated in a few regions, Quebec first among them.

BIBLIOGRAPHY

Ekberg, Carl J. *French Roots in the Illinois Country. The Mississippi Frontier in Colonial Times.* Urbana: University of Illinois Press, 1998.

Greer, Allan. *The People of New France.* Toronto: University of Toronto Press, 1997.

Griffiths, Naomi E. S. *The Contexts of Acadian History, 1686–1784.* Montreal: McGill-Queen's University Press, 1992.

Harris, R. Cole, ed. *Historical Atlas of Canada.* Vol. 1: *From the Beginning to 1800.* Toronto: University of Toronto Press, 1987.

Ingersoll, Thomas N. *Mammon and Manon in Early New Orleans: The First Slave Society in the Deep South, 1718–1819.* Knoxville: University of Tennessee Press, 1999.

Krause, Eric, Carol Corbin, and William O'Shea, eds. *Aspects of Louisbourg: Essays on the History of an Eighteenth-Century French Community in North America.* Sydney, N.S.: University College of Cape Breton Press, Louisbourg Institute, 1995.

Miquelon, Dale. *New France, 1701–1744: "A Supplement to Europe."* Toronto: McClelland and Stewart, 1987.

Moogk, Peter N. *La Nouvelle France: The Making of French Canada: A Cultural History.* East Lansing: Michigan State University Press, 2000.

Trudel, Marcel. *Histoire de la Nouvelle-France.* Montréal: Fides, 1963.

Usner, Daniel H., Jr. *Indians, Settlers, and Slaves in a Frontier Exchange Economy: The Lower Mississippi Valley before 1783.* Chapel Hill: University of North Carolina Press, 1992.

———. *American Indians in the Lower Mississippi Valley: Social and Economic Histories.* Lincoln: University of Nebraska Press, 1998.

White, Richard. *The Middle Ground: Indians, Empires, and Republics in the Great Lakes Region, 1650–1815.* Cambridge, U.K., and New York: Cambridge University Press, 1991.

Thomas Wien

See also **Explorations and Expeditions: French.**

NEW FREEDOM. The reform philosophy of Woodrow Wilson, enunciated during the 1912 presidential race and embodied in the legislation of his first term. During the campaign, Wilson contrasted the New Freedom to Theodore Roosevelt's New Nationalism. Whereas Roosevelt argued that industrial concentration was inevitable and that government should regulate business for the common good, Wilson countered that economic concentration in any form threatened individualism and personal liberties. Wilson and his political adviser Louis Brandeis, chief architect of the New Freedom, believed government's responsibility lay in preserving competition by preventing the establishment of trusts. Their thinking reflected the doctrines of nineteenth-century political liberalism as well as the Jeffersonian belief in equality of rights and suspicion of all forms of concentrated power.

The implementation of this philosophy in subsequent legislation, however, contributed significantly to the growth of government regulation, in apparent contradiction to Wilson and Brandeis' stated aims. The New Freedom's legislative accomplishments included the Underwood Tariff Act of 1913 (which included a progressive income tax), the Federal Reserve Act of 1913, the Clayton Antitrust Act of 1914, and the Federal Trade Commission Act of 1914, all passed during the first session of the Sixty-third Congress, and most of which increased the regulatory power of government. Although Wilson's Jeffersonian pedigree made him opposed to measures benefiting special interests (including labor) or social welfare, or designed to reconcile government and business, political circumstances following the midterm elections in 1914 and his own political evolution pushed the New Freedom's agenda further leftwards in 1916. Beginning with the appointment of Brandeis to the Supreme Court in January, Wilson and the Democratic Congress enacted legislation furthering the reform agenda. This included the Federal Farm Loan Act of 1916, workers' compensation for federal employees, a law prohibiting the products of child labor from interstate commerce, and the Adamson Act of 1916, which mandated an eight-hour workday on interstate railways.

Growing involvement in World War I shifted the country's attention to military matters, and after 1916 the reform impulse withered. The New Freedom remains significant, however, in that it confirmed the modern Democratic Party's commitment to positive government as a means of preserving competition and the rights of economic smallholders, and established the foundations of the modern regulatory state.

BIBLIOGRAPHY

Gould, Lewis L. *Reform and Regulation: American Politics, 1900–1916.* New York: Wiley, 1978.

Link, Arthur S. *Wilson: The New Freedom.* Princeton, N.J.: Princeton University Press, 1956.

Sarasohn, David. *The Party of Reform: Democrats in the Progressive Era.* Jackson and London: University Press of Mississippi, 1989.

C. Wyatt Evans

See also **Antitrust Laws; Brandeis Confirmation Hearings; Clayton Act, Labor Provisions; New Nationalism.**

NEW FRONTIER. The term "New Frontier" refers to the economic and social programs of the presidency of John F. Kennedy. The concept of a "New Frontier" epitomized Kennedy's commitment to renewal and change. He pitched his 1960 presidential campaign as a crusade to bring in a "new generation of leadership—new men to cope with new problems and new opportunities." Standing in the Los Angeles Memorial Coliseum before 80,000 people, accepting the Democratic presidential nomination, Kennedy used "the New Frontier" to root himself in the past and evoke a new and rosy future. In a characteristic intellectual and political pastiche, Kennedy and his speechwriters built on President Theodore Roosevelt's "Square Deal," President Franklin D. Roosevelt's "New Deal," President Harry S. Truman's "Fair Deal," and Professor Frederick Jackson Turner's lament about "the closing of the frontier." Nearly seven decades after Turner's famous 1893 essay, Kennedy noted that "today some would say" that the pioneering struggles Turner praised "are all over, that all the horizons have been explored, that all the battles have been won, that there is no longer an American frontier. But . . . the problems are not all solved and the battles are not all won, and we stand today on the edge of a New Frontier—the frontier of the 1960s, a frontier of unknown opportunities and paths, a frontier of unfulfilled hopes and threats."

Kennedy claimed that his frontier was "a set of challenges. It sums up not what I intend to offer the American people, but what I intend to ask of them"—foreshadowing his more famous "ask not what your country can do for you" formulation in his inaugural address. And those challenges were essential in generating the great liberal excitement of Kennedy's magical "thousand days." But the New Frontier was also very much a "set of promises," and a legislative agenda "to get the country moving again." Detailed in the Democratic platform, the New Frontier called for advancing "the civil and economic rights essential to the human dignity of all men," raising the minimum wage, guaranteeing equal pay for women, rebuilding the inner cities, increasing federal aid for education, initiating a Peace Corps, and developing a Medicare program to assist the elderly.

Kennedy was more successful in setting a tone than in enacting his program. True, in Kennedy's first two years as president, Congress passed 304 bills that the White House proposed. But that represented less than half of the 653 bills actually championed and, many historians agree, "domestically, it was not the important half." Congress raised the minimum wage from $1.00 to $1.25 and broadened eligibility requirements. Congress did provide $4.9 billion in federal grants for urban development. But Congress defeated Kennedy's proposals for Medicare, for a Department of Urban Affairs, and for mass transit aid. The big, dramatic, Kennedyesque legislative program known as the Great Society was only enacted during President Lyndon B. Johnson's tenure—partially as a tribute to the martyred president after Kennedy's assassination, and partially as a result of Johnson's tenacity and talent. John F. Kennedy's New Frontier, thus, was more evocative than effective, more style than substance, more a mark of Kennedy's great potential and inspiring oratory than the high-point of liberal reform he hoped it would be.

BIBLIOGRAPHY

Bernstein, Irving. *Promises Kept: John F. Kennedy's New Frontier.* New York: Oxford University Press, 1991.

Reeves, Richard. *President Kennedy: Profile of Power.* New York: Simon and Schuster, 1993.

Schlesinger, Arthur M., Jr. *A Thousand Days: John F. Kennedy in the White House.* Boston: Houghton Mifflin, 1965.

Gil Troy

See also **Fair Deal; Great Society; New Deal; Square Deal.**

NEW HAMPSHIRE is roughly the shape of a fist, with its index finger pointed north. The tip of the finger forms a rough border with Quebec, Canada. Its eastern border is along the western border of Maine. What would be the bottom knuckle of the finger is New Hampshire's seacoast, only eighteen miles long, where the city of Portsmouth is found. The southern border of the state is along the northern border of Massachusetts. New Hampshire's western border is along the eastern border of Vermont. The state is 180 miles north-to-south and 93 miles at its widest, east-to-west, with an area of 9,283 square miles.

The Coastal Lowlands of the southeast were the first part of New Hampshire to be settled, partly because the fishing off the coast was extraordinarily good, attracting fishermen to settle there, and partly because there was good farmland to be found along the rivers that flowed into the sea. Even though farmers were the first to settle the rest of the state, most of New Hampshire's land is rocky and difficult to farm, The Eastern New England Upland is to the west of the Coastal Lowlands, with the north-to-south dividing line between the areas being the Merrimack River Valley, where the capital city Concord is found. Beginning in the middle of New Hampshire and extending northward are mountains, beginning with the White Mountains. The rough terrain of the north is

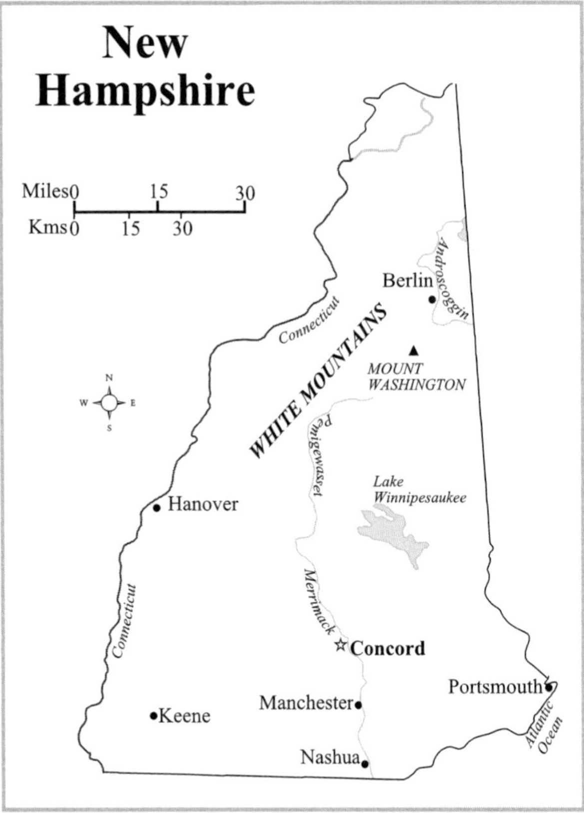

sparsely populated, mostly by farmers, who work in valleys and along the Androscoggin River.

There are over 40,000 miles of rivers and 1,300 lakes in New Hampshire, making it one of the wettest states in the Union, and earning the state the sobriquet "Mother of Rivers." Its border with Vermont is traced by the Connecticut River; both sides of the river belong to New Hampshire, which therefore bears most of the responsibility for building bridges over it. Much of the early colonial history of the state focuses on the Piscataqua River, which flows into the Atlantic Ocean and offered a trading route into the dense woods of ancient New Hampshire. The Merrimack River begins in the White Mountains and flows south through New Hampshire and into Massachusetts. In the southeastern foothills of the White Mountains is the Lakes Region, which includes New Hampshire's largest lake, Lake Winnipesaukee, which covers seventy-two square miles and contains 274 islands.

An imposing sight in the White Mountains is Mount Washington, which at 6,288 feet is the tallest point in New Hampshire. New Hampshire's average temperature in July is 68 degrees Fahrenheit. The winters in New Hampshire can be bitter, with the average temperature in January being 19 degrees.

Prehistory

At about 9000 B.C., a people known as Paleo-Indians occupied New Hampshire. They are hard to study in New Hampshire because they apparently lived by the sea, and the ocean level in their time was 150 feet lower than it is now, meaning many of their villages, if they had any, are now likely underwater. Around 7000 B.C. people known as Archaic Indians began to replace the Paleo-Indians. By then, New Hampshire had become very heavily forested with hundreds of different species of trees. The Archaic Indians consisted of many different cultural groups. In New Hampshire, they were nomadic, probably migrating from place to place according to the seasons, avoiding New Hampshire's very cold winters.

Around 2000 B.C., Native Americans began settling New Hampshire with small villages. From 2000 B.C. to A.D. 1000, they adopted the bow and arrow for hunting, developed sophisticated fishing techniques, and introduced agriculture. Near the end of the period, maize was introduced from the west. It is possible but unlikely that Vikings visited New Hampshire around A.D. 1004, even though there are tourist attractions in the state that claim otherwise. Before the coming of Europeans in the 1600s, the Native Americans of the New Hampshire area were divided into two cultural groups: to the north were the Abenakis, and to the south were the Pennacooks. These subdivided into seven important subgroups: the Ossipees in the north, near the Androscoggin River; the Coosucs in the west near the Connecticut River; the Winnipesaukees in the White Mountains south of the Coosucs; the Nashuas in the south, living also in what is now northern Massachusetts; the Pennacooks, who lived in the southeast and along the Merrimack River; and the Piscataquas, who lived in the southeast in the region where the city of Dover was established.

Colonial Era

Martin Pring, twenty-three years old from Bristol, England, was the first recorded European to lead an expedition to present-day New Hampshire. In 1603, his ship anchored in a bay, and he traced inland some of the Piscataqua River. In 1614, John Smith passed by along the coast during a mapping expedition and recorded the area as very heavily wooded with great mountains to the west, and he reported very favorably on what he saw. At the time, there were about 5,000 Native Americans in New Hampshire. From then on, their population declined.

In 1622, the king granted Captain John Mason of England ownership of much of the land in present-day New Hampshire. It was he, in honor of his homeland Hampshire, who gave the name "New Hampshire" to his large tracts of land. In 1622, he and Sir Ferdinando Gorges founded the Company of Laconia, which was intended to support colonization and development of Mason's holdings.

Mason and Gorges planned missions to the new lands carefully, using good ships, well provisioned with what people would need to survive in New Hampshire's climate. This planning helped make the New Hampshire colonies among the most successful in the 1600s. On 16 April 1623, David Thomson led one such mission, settling two sites near the sea. These early sites attracted fishermen because of the bountiful fishing waters in the nearby ocean, and they became very prosperous by selling salted cod to Europeans. They got along well with the local Native Americans, mostly Piscataquas and Pennacooks, who liked trading with the new settlers and who hoped the settlers would be good allies against what seemed like imminent invasions from warlike tribes to the west and south. The Native Americans were soon struck down by the measles and other imported diseases.

In the 1630s, John Wheelwright and his followers fled the Massachusetts colony because of religious persecution by the Congregationalist Church. He founded Exeter, which in 1641 had about 1,000 people living in or near the town. His hopes for freedom of religion were not immediately realized. In 1641, the towns of New Hampshire asked for protection from Massachusetts. Among the results was the introduction of slavery in 1645. Another result was religious persecution: In the 1660s, men were hanged and women stripped bareback and whipped for being Quakers. Religious laws were burdensome and sometimes downright irrational, such as the laws that forbade rest but forbade working on Sunday.

From 1684 to 1688, Kings Charles II and James II tried to force all the New England colonies into one large province, something the colonists resented. In 1679, monarchs William and Mary declared New Hampshire a royal province. By then, Portsmouth was becoming an important site for building ships, and the tall pines of New Hampshire were being shipped to England for use on English warships.

New Hampshire was fortunate in its royal governors. In December 1717, the king appointed John Wentworth the elder to be "lieutenant governor" in charge of New Hampshire, but serving under the governor of Massachusetts. The previous lieutenant governor, George Vaughn, had been ignoring orders from Massachusetts governor Samuel Shute. Wentworth proved to be a good diplomat, easing tensions while slowly separating the administration of New Hampshire from that of Massachusetts. In 1717, a large group of Scots Irish from northern Ireland came to New Hampshire. A careful, intelligent planner, Wentworth had hoped to establish a series of settlements in the interior of his colony, and the Scots Irish proved a welcome beginning of new settlers; in 1722, they dubbed their community Londonderry.

In 1740, the king of England settled disputes over New Hampshire's borders, awarding it twenty-eight townships claimed by Massachusetts and establishing the colony's western border to the west of the Connecticut River. John Wentworth had died in 1730, but in 1741, his son Benning Wentworth was made governor. He was one of the most contradictory and fascinating people in New Hampshire's history. He was self-indulgent, always cut himself in on any moneymaking proposal, lived lavishly in a house that perpetually expanded, and threw many parties for playing games and eating feasts. At the same time, he was a brilliant planner. He created a policy for not only establishing new townships but also for making sure they were all equal politically and in size. He oversaw the creation of sixty-seven new towns. In 1767, he was driven out of office because as a royal governor, he had supported the much loathed stamp tax.

His nephew, John Wentworth, known as "Long John," then became the governor. He loved New Hampshire. All his life, he referred to it as home. Among the wise choices he made was the establishment of three well-trained and supplied regiments of New Hampshire militia, a prudent precaution against the possibility of Native American raids from out of state. When in 1774 the colony's assembly met to consider independence, Wentworth tried to disband it—a right he had as royal governor. The assembly moved to a tavern and held its meeting anyway. Wentworth soon had to flee to Boston. On 17 June 1775, at the Battle of Bunker Hill (actually Breed's Hill), the regiments Wentworth had made sure were ready for war put themselves to use, for they formed the majority of Americans who defended the hill against British regulars, helping prove that Americans could stand up to England's best. Of the 911 New Hampshire volunteers, 107 were killed or wounded.

Live Free or Die

In 1776, the population of New Hampshire was 82,000 and increasing. Its growing industrialization was already causing problems: Its numerous sawmills had so polluted its rivers that the native salmon had gone extinct. The number of slaves was peaking at 626, soon to decline. On 5 January 1776, New Hampshire recorded two American firsts when the Fifth Provincial Congress of New Hampshire met. It was the first state to declare independence from England; it was also the first state to write its own constitution.

Portsmouth became a major naval manufacturer with the building of three warships, including the *Ranger*, which John Paul Jones commanded. The seaport also outfitted hundreds of privateers, privately owned merchant ships remade into warships with permission to raid, capture, or sink British ships. The privateers were successful enough to make many investors rich. Although New Hampshire was not the site of a single major battle, it was the site of bloody fighting. Native Americans from Canada were encouraged to raid New Hampshire settlements; they would kill anyone, although they sometimes took captives to be sold into slavery. Many of the soldiers of New Hampshire were skilled woodsmen and wise in the ways of guerrilla warfare, and they often drove off the invaders. In 1777, the British planned to drive through Vermont to the sea to divide the northern colonies in two. On 16 August 1777, American forces commanded by General John Stark fought the British force at the border of New York and Vermont, near Bennington, where the Americans won, taking hundreds of British soldiers prisoner. Thirty-two years later, veterans of the battle met, but John Stark was too sick to attend; instead, he sent them a message: "Live Free or Die."

The 1775 constitution was awkward and sometimes unclear. It took until 1 July 1784, after the end of the Revolutionary War, for a more permanent constitution to be adopted. As of 2002, it was still in effect. It was prefaced by thirty-eight articles that formed New Hampshire's bill of rights. When the Articles of Confederation proved to be inadequate for America's needs, in 1787, an American constitutional convention was held, with New Hampshire sending Nicholas Gilman and John Langdon as its representatives. In Concord, in June 1888, a convention on the proposed Constitution of the United States was held. The people of New Hampshire were not about to be rushed into anything and had taken their time considering the proposal. On 21 June 1788, voting fifty-seven to forty-seven, the delegates made New Hampshire the ninth state to ratify the Constitution; the agreement had been that if nine states ratified the Constitution, then it would officially be America's governing document.

Age of the Spindle

In 1800, the population of New Hampshire was 183,858. There were eight slaves in the state then. In 1819, New Hampshire outlawed slavery and abolished debtors' prison. In 1830, the legislature declared that any adult male could vote. There were 800 to 900 African Americans in the state at the time. The Democrats gained almost absolute control over New Hampshire politics in the first couple of decades of the nineteenth century, a grip they would maintain until tripping over the issue of slavery.

In the early 1800s, canals had been built around the Amoskeag waterfalls on the Merrimack River, allowing barges to travel between Concord, and Boston. Beside those falls, four local farmers built a mill. It had eighty-five spindles for the spinning of cloth. In 1822, financier Samuel Slater was brought in to help with expansion. By 1835, there were nineteen investors, and the mill was called the Amoskeag Manufacturing Company. The investors who had made textile mills in Lowell, Massachusetts, the models of enlightened industrial development also invested in the Amoskeag Manufacturing Company, buying land and laying out a model city, Manchester. From 1838 to 1846, the city grew from 500 to 10,000 in population. Amoskeag Manufacturing Company would become one of the world's industrial giants, making miles of cloth each day.

Meanwhile, prominent New Hampshire politician John Parker Hale had undergone a significant transformation. He was a stalwart Democrat; in 1835, when meeting with an abolitionist minister, he had taken the party line that slaves were merely beasts shaped like humans. While representing New Hampshire in the United States House of Representatives, he had held to his party's position. Yet, through contemplation, he changed his mind. In January 1845, he proposed legislation limiting slavery in the proposed new state of Texas. For this, the Democrats ousted him from their party. He managed to be elected to the Senate as an independent, and in 1853, he joined with dissident Democrats and some Whigs to help form the Republican Party, which called for the ending of slavery. This marked a great shift in New Hampshire politics, as over the next decade New Hampshirites joined the Republican Party, giving it a hold on local politics that it still had not lost by the 2000s.

Although New Hampshire contributed troops to the Civil War (1861–1865), major battles were not fought there. The state contributed much of the cloth used for Union uniforms and some of the munitions. The federal shipyard in Portsmouth contributed warships. In 1853, New Hampshire had passed laws restricting child labor, and throughout the nineteenth century the state passed laws further restricting child labor, and limiting hours and days industrial laborers could be required to work. In 1849, Amoskeag Manufacturing Company began manufacturing locomotives, and in 1869, the first railroad that could climb steep grades was built on Washington Mountain. It was a "cog railroad," meaning one that had a center rail that was gripped by a cogwheel attached under the center of a locomotive. In 1859, Amoskeag Manufacturing Company began producing fire engines. In 1870, farming was declining in the state, and in response the legislature created a Board of Agriculture to help farmers.

By 1895, the Boston and Maine Railroad, called the "Great Corporation," dominated the economic life of the state and was well known to use gifts to purchase votes in its favor from the legislature. In 1911, Robert Bass became governor and, helped by reform-minded members, he managed to push through the legislature laws extensively restricting child labor, a workers' compensation law, a "pure food" law, and a factory safety and inspection law. He and the legislature also created a commission to regulate public utilities and the railroads, eliminating such favors as free passes for the railroad, ending the Great Corporation's control over state politics.

In the 1920s, New Hampshire began a long shift in its economy. On 13 February 1922, the United Textile Workers struck against the Amoskeag Manufacturing Company over wages and working hours. Amoskeag already paid some of the highest wages in the textile industry and wanted to lower pay to its workers so that its products could compete with those manufactured in southern states where wages were much lower than those paid in New Hampshire. After a very unhappy nine months, the United Textile Workers accepted the terms of the Amoskeag Manufacturing Company, but the end of Amoskeag was in sight. By World War II (1939–1945), only a few manufacturers of specialty fabrics remained in the state.

During the middle of the twentieth century, New Hampshire's population declined. Once over 1,000,000 people, the population was 606,921 in 1960. The loss of manufacturing companies accounted for much of the exodus, but farms were failing, too. By the mid-1930s, many farms were abandoned, left to decay and yield to grasses, bushes, and trees. The land was not worth enough to sell, and there were too few buyers, anyway. World War II improved the economy; the shipyards at Portsmouth were very busy building submarines. During the 1920s and 1930s, one aspect of the economy picked up markedly: tourism.

Beautiful Land

New Hampshire is a beautiful state. In the 1920s, people from out of state would rent or purchase bungalows near beaches to spend a weekend or a whole summer relaxing. Some farmers rented rooms in their homes to vacationers, a practice that was still continuing at the turn of the twenty-first century. Writers and artists came to the state to enjoy quiet in small towns while pursuing their callings. One such writer, the American author Winston Churchill, even ran for governor in 1912.

After World War II, tourism became ever more important to the state, although it did not entirely stop the diminishing of New Hampshire's population. One effort to keep New Hampshire on people's minds was the beginning of the first-in-the-nation presidential primary in 1952. The primary brought politicians and money to the state. During the 1960s, skiers discovered the slopes of the White Mountains, some of which can support skiing into July. Traditional New Hampshire manufacturing businesses continued to decline in the 1960s, but a new group of employers discovered the state. The state's lack of income tax, its beautiful countryside, and its low crime rate were attractive to professionals. Finance and life insurance companies set up shop in the Granite State (a reference to its rocky terrain). High-technology companies also settled in New Hampshire in the hope that the skilled workers the industry needed would be attracted to a state with wonderful natural beauty. The high-technology companies established themselves in what became known as the "Golden Triangle" formed by Nashua, Manchester, and Portsmouth. By 1970, the state's population had grown to 737,681.

In 1976, the Seabrook nuclear power plant was built in New Hampshire amid protests from people who thought the plant would be dangerous. The plant went into operation in 1990. From 1989 to 1992, New Hampshire experienced a very tough recession, with 50,000 jobs leaving the state, and in 1990, Pease Air Force Base closed. The state's recovery was slow and focused on tourism, fishing, shipbuilding, and high-technology industries. In 1990, the state population was 1,113,915, and grew to almost 1,200,000 by 2000, so the state seemed to be recovering. In 1996, New Hampshire elected its first woman governor, Jeanne Shaheen. By 2000, only 7.7 percent of the people in New Hampshire lived below the federal poverty level, and the state had the third lowest crime rate among America's states.

BIBLIOGRAPHY

Belknap, Jeremy. *The History of New Hampshire*. Boston: Belknap and Young, 1792.

Fradin, Dennis B. *The New Hampshire Colony*. Chicago: Children's Press (Regensteiner), 1988.

Morison, Elizabeth Forbes, and Elting E. Morison. *New Hampshire: A Bicentennial History*. New York: W. W. Norton, 1976.

Robinson, J. Dennis. "Seacoast NH History." http://www.SeacoastNH.com.

Squires, J. Duane. *The Granite State of the United States: A History of New Hampshire from 1623 to the Present*. New York: American Historical Company, 1956.

Stein, R. Conrad. *New Hampshire*. New York: Children's Press, 2000.

Kirk H. Beetz

See also **New England.**

NEW HAVEN COLONY. Between 1638 and 1662, the New Haven Colony was an independent entity, separate and legally apart from the Connecticut Colony. Following a common pattern, New Haven was simply taken from the Quinnipiac Indians for token value by John Davenport and Theophilus Eaton and their followers. "New Haven" was both a name connoting an English port and, more importantly, a literal signifier of what the Puritan

New Haven Colony. A photograph, c. 1900, of the New Haven Colony Historical Society building. LIBRARY OF CONGRESS

founders hoped the American port colony would be: a purer Bible commonwealth than even the Massachusetts Bay Colony, from which the New Haven settlers had migrated.

In its one generation of independent existence, the colony at first lived up to its commitment to religious zealotry. The Puritans adopted a "plantation covenant" so pure that it bound every inhabitant to governance by literal Mosaic law. Reality intruded in short order, of course, and within a few years a civil government was reluctantly established, subject still to church dictates. Both the strength of the colony and its significance resides in the fact of its immaculate religious commitment, perhaps the most extreme of all the independent Puritan entities in the seventeenth-century New World colonies.

Its 1639 constitution mentions neither the king nor English common law; it forbade, for example, trial by jury. "Seven pillars" of religious strength (men) were elected to head both the church and the state in the colony. The term "theocracy" probably applied nowhere more aptly in the New World than in New Haven. Only church members could vote, and the community remained true to the vision of the Reverend John Davenport, its primary founder. (Old Testament blue laws in New Haven remain justly famous, with most on local books until well into the twentieth century.) Outsiders were turned away at the colony's borders, Quakers violently. These borders originally included what is now the city of New Haven and its hinterland, the towns of North Haven, Wallingford, and Hamden; over time the colony added the towns of Guilford, Milford, and even briefly Southold, Long Island. With hostile Dutch nearby in New Amsterdam, and assorted Baptists and omnipresent Quakers seeking entry, the colony was always a tense place, driven by its sense of religious mission to both hold its ground and expand where possible.

When the monarchy was restored in England in 1660, the influential John Winthrop left Connecticut for London to secure a charter. He did that in 1662, bringing home a charter that included title to New Haven. Sporadic rebellion ensued for a year or so, but with so many enemies waiting nearby (labeled "royalists, Romans, and Stuarts" by the locals), enemies even more odious than the backsliding Connecticut Congregationalists, the New Haven Colony submitted to the inevitable. On 13 December 1664 the colony reluctantly merged its fate with (by comparison) the more liberal and less theological Connecticut Colony. John Davenport, as zealous as ever, announced that the New Haven Colony had been "miserably lost." Even though independent no more, New Haven remained an obstreperous orphan within the larger Connecticut for at least a generation.

Its heritage is largely as a symbol of the heights of devotion to which these most committed of Puritans could aspire. New Haven in its brief existence was a living, breathing Bible commonwealth that endured for a single glorious generation.

BIBLIOGRAPHY

Calder, Isabel. *The New Haven Colony*. New Haven, Conn.: Yale University Press, 1934. Reprint, Hamden, Conn.: Archon, 1970.

Taylor, Robert J. *Colonial Connecticut*. Millwood, N.Y.: KTO Press, 1979.

Works Progress Administration. *Connecticut: Guide to Its Roads, Lore, and People*. Boston: 1938.

Carl E. Prince

See also **Colonial Settlements; Puritans and Puritanism.**

NEW JERSEY. While ranked forty-sixth among the states in size, in 2002 New Jersey ranked ninth in terms of population, with nearly 8.5 million people. New Jersey is by far the nation's most urbanized and most densely populated state, with 1,144 persons per square mile. In contrast, the national population density in 2000 was just 80 persons per square mile.

Between 1991 and 2001, New Jersey saw its population rise steadily, by 0.85 percent per annum. In 2000, 8,414,350 people lived in New Jersey. By July 2001, the state had 8,484,431 residents; New Jersey's population grew faster than any other state in the northeast region during 2000–2001. During those years, the state lost 39,200 inhabitants through domestic migration, but this was offset by the influx of 60,400 international immigrants. As a result, New Jersey ranked sixth among the states in foreign immigration between 2000 and 2001. While the state's population grew, the average household size actually shrank during the 1990s.

New Jersey's radical transformation from rural to industrial society, from vast regions of farmland to suburban sprawl, did not happen quickly but rather very gradually beginning in the seventeenth century.

Colonial Era

New Jersey began as a British colony in 1664, when James, duke of York, granted all his lands between the Hudson and Delaware Rivers to John, Lord Berkeley, and Sir George Carteret. On 10 February 1665 the two new proprietors issued concessions and agreements setting forth their governmental and land policies. Berkeley then sold his interest in the colony in March 1674 to John Fenwick, a Quaker who represented Edward Byllynge, for £1,000. The trustees for Byllynge, including William Penn, tried to establish a Quaker colony in West Jersey, but Fenwick seceded from the Byllynge group and settled at Salem in November 1675, thereby becoming lord proprietor of his tenth of the proprietary lands. In July 1676, the Quintpartite Deed legally separated the lands of New Jersey into east and west; Carteret remained proprietor of East Jersey while Byllynge, William Penn, and two other Quakers became the proprietors of West Jersey. In February 1682, after the death of Carteret, twelve men purchased his lands for £3,400. Following this transaction the Board of Proprietors of East Jersey was formed in 1684; four years later nine men established the Council of Proprietors of West Jersey.

The Crown refused to grant the proprietors of East and West Jersey governmental authority until 1702. Under the new terms of agreement, the British government allowed both groups to retain the rights to the soil and to the collection of quitrents (rents paid on agricultural lands). The boards of proprietors are still in existence and hold meetings at Perth Amboy (for East Jersey) and Burlington (for West Jersey).

Disputes over land titles in the colony resulted in land riots between 1745 to 1755. The English immigrants that settled in East Jersey during the 1660s argued that they did not need to pay proprietary quitrents, since they had purchased the land from indigenous Native Americans. In response to the dispute, James Alexander, an influential councillor of East Jersey, filed a bill in chancery court on 17 April 1745. On 19 September 1745, Samuel Baldwin, one of the claimants to land in East Jersey, was arrested on his land and taken to jail in Newark. One hundred fifty men rescued him from prison. This incident incited sporadic rioting and disruption of the courts and jails in most East Jersey counties. The land rioters did not stop rebelling until 1754, in response to fears of English retaliation, the coming of the French and Indian War, as well as unfavorable court decisions.

From the beginning colonial New Jersey was characterized by ethnic and religious diversity. In East Jersey, New England Quakers, Baptists, and Congregationalists settled alongside Scotch-Irish Presbyterians and Dutch migrants from New York. While the majority of residents lived in towns with individual landholdings of 100 acres, a few rich proprietors owned vast estates. West Jersey had fewer people than East Jersey, and both English Quakers and Anglicans owned large landholdings. Both Jerseys remained agrarian and rural throughout the colonial era, and commercial farming only developed sporadically. Some townships, though, like Burlington and Perth Amboy, emerged as important ports for shipping to New York and Philadelphia. The colony's fertile lands and tolerant religious policy drew more settlers, and New Jersey boasted a population of 120,000 by 1775.

New Jersey's "madness" for "municipal multiplication," notes one recent scholar, could clearly be observed in the colonial partisan politics of many founding townships, and is especially evident in the historical balkanization of dozens of large townships that developed along the lower bank of the Raritan. South Amboy, for example, would split into nine separate communities—and, by the end of the nineteenth century, there was very little left of the once-huge township. Similar patterns were duplicated throughout the state, such as in the huge township of Shrewsbury in East Jersey. Eventually that single township would be fragmented into seventy-five separate towns spreading over two counties.

Transportation and growth spurred rivalries between townships. During the seventeenth, eighteenth, and early nineteenth centuries, before the advent of the railroad, South Amboy's growing port served as the link in ferry transportation from Manhattan and Philadelphia. Equally important, a major roadway also took passengers through the township of Piscataway, which then included most of what would become Middlesex and Mercer Counties. After the coming of the railroad, rivalry between South Amboy and New Brunswick eventually altered the role of each township and the relations of power between the two competitive communities.

Hundreds of tales of factional disputes illustrate the pettiness and quarrelsomeness of the issues that came to divide New Jersey's municipalities: struggles involving railroad lands, school district control, moral regulation, and greedy individualism all led to the fracture of townships, towns, and cities. Many factors thwarted the consolidation of large and medium-sized cities, including antiurban prejudices that prevented the early creation of an urban way of life. New Jersey's geography and topography clearly helped shape the state's long tradition of divisiveness and fragmentation. The state's rivers, woodlands, and salt marshes divided towns, boroughs, and villages. Economic considerations and political pressures contributed to the crazy zigzag development of New Jersey's 566 municipalities, as did personal whims and interests. All of these factors combined to draw each boundary line of those hundreds of municipalities as the state's geopolitical map was drawn—every line has a story to tell. Hardly ever practical, functional, or straight, the boundary line designs eventually became to resemble, in the words of Alan Karcher, "cantilevered and circumlinear" shapes that formed "rhomboids and parallelograms—geometric rectangles and chaotic fractals." As New Jersey evolved, these "often bizarre configurations" became less and less defensible while their boundaries remained "immutable and very expensive memorials" to the designers who concocted them.

From the reunification of East Jersey and West Jersey in 1702 until 1776, the colony was ruled by a royal governor, an appointive council, and an assembly. While the governor of New York served as the governor of New Jersey until 1738, his power was checked and reduced by the assembly's right to initiate money bills, including controlling governors' salaries. From 1763 on, both political factionalism and sectional conflict hindered the role New Jersey played in the imperial crisis that would eventually erupt into the American Revolution. One important prerevolutionary incident, however, was the robbery of the treasury of the East Jersey proprietors on 21 July 1768, resulting in increased tensions between Governor William Franklin and the assembly. Although most New Jerseyites only reluctantly engaged in brief boycotts and other forms of protest over the Stamp Act and Townshend duties, the colonists of New Jersey found themselves being swept along by their more militant and powerful neighbors in New York and Pennsylvania. Once the Crown had shut down the port of Boston, however, New Jersey quickly joined rank and formed a provincial congress to assume control of the colony. After participating in both sessions of the Continental Congress and the signing of the Declaration of Independence, the colony's representatives ratified a state constitution on 2 July 1776.

During the days of the American Revolution, few states suffered as much or as long as New Jersey. In the first few years of war, both British and American armies swept across the state, while Loyalists returned in armed forays and foraging expeditions. Triumphant battles at Trenton on 26 December 1776, Monmouth on 28 June 1778, and Springfield, 23 June 1780, helped ensure American independence. Because of the weak government under the Articles of Confederation, though, New Jersey suffered immensely from the aftershocks of war's devastation and a heavy state debt. At the Constitutional Convention of 1787, New Jersey's representative William Paterson addressed the problem of indebtedness by speaking for the interests of smaller states, and advocating the passage of the New Jersey Plan.

Growth of Industry

After the instability of the 1780s, in the Federalist era the young state turned to novel kinds of industrial activities and began to erect a better transportation system to bolster its nascent economy. In November 1791, Alexander Hamilton helped create the Society for the Establishment of Useful Manufactures, which began operating a cotton mill in the new city of Paterson. As a promoter of national economic growth, Hamilton spearheaded other industrial ventures. After they had purchased land, Hamilton and other New York and New Jersey Federalists incorporated themselves as the Associates of New Jersey Company on 10 November 1804. Hamilton was shot while dueling with Aaron Burr in New Jersey, and died of his wounds; after his death, neither of his ventures proved successful until the 1820s.

During the first three decades of the nineteenth century, the nation experienced a transportation revolution, stimulated by capital investment and new manufacturing ventures. Improved roads—especially the Morris Turnpike of 1801—invigorated the state's economy, and steamboats linked New Jersey to the ports of New York and Philadelphia. Furthermore, the construction of the Morris Canal (1824–1838) and the Delaware and Raritan Canal (1826–1838) brought coal and iron to eastern industry, and the Camden and Amboy Railroad was completed in 1834. All these transportation advances increased internal trade and stimulated the infant manufacturing sector and rapid urbanization.

Disputes over school district boroughs, religion, prostitution, gambling, prohibition, exclusivity, zoning and prezoning, and the construction of canals, railroads, roads, and pathways all contributed to New Jerseyites' antiurban bias, myopic sense of community, and preoccupation with the control of property. Every key decision made at the state capital in Trenton regarding taxes, schools, transportation, preservation of natural resources, and a myriad of other issues, observed one political insider, faces the obstacle "that it must accommodate 566 local governments."

Because of these disputes, the number of New Jersey's boroughs rose from 5 to 193 between 1850 and 1917, when more than one hundred of the municipalities still consisted of less than 2,000 inhabitants. After 1930, this fragmentation slowed, with only ten new municipalities created and just three eliminated. New Jersey's communities became more isolated, particularly after the 1947 regulations on zoning took effect.

As the state's political landscape shifted and fragmented over the centuries, in the mid-nineteenth century New Jersey's economic and industrial landscape also underwent massive changes, transforming from a rural farming region into an urban, industrial state. Cities like Camden and Hoboken grew as a result of increased shipping and railroad facilities, while Newark and Jersey City mushroomed with the concentration of specialized industries like leather, shoemaking, and iron. The demand for both skilled and unskilled labor fostered a surge in the urban population of the state's major cities, while the need for cheap, unskilled workers in building and rail construction and factory production was met in part by new waves of immigrants. Starting in the 1840s, Germans, Irish, Poles, and other European immigrants—Protestant, Jewish, and Roman Catholic—added to New Jersey's ethnic and religious diversity. At the turn of the twentieth century, African Americans from the South pushed into the state's already overcrowded urban slums.

The Twentieth Century

New Jersey's political development reflected the changing social and economic climates, and changing demographic patterns. Because New Jersey's state constitution of 1776 envisioned a weak executive with no veto powers, it was not until modern times (like the years under Governor Woodrow Wilson) that the governor wielded more power than the state legislature.

The New Jersey state government has always been sensitive to the demands of business. During the political awakening of the Jacksonian era, the Whig Party forged the first ties between business and state government. Following the Civil War, liberal incorporation laws—and the unremitting pressure industrial giants like Standard Oil and the Pennsylvania Railroad Company placed on legislators—helped establish the corporate control of state politics. Then during the height of the Progressive age at the end of his 1911–1913 governorship, Woodrow Wilson used his newly expanded executive power to begin his assault on these corporations with his "Seven Sisters" monopoly legislation. These political reforms, though, did not prevent the political parties of the early twentieth century from being controlled by urban bosses, such as Frank Hague of Jersey City.

Even with Wilson's gains, it was not until the passage of the new state constitution of 1947 that the governor of New Jersey become a more independent figure with broader discretionary powers. By then, postwar New Jersey had become an even more urbanized and industrialized state, boasting a high standard of living but struggling with a concomitant array of social problems, including environmental pollution, urban decay, racial tension, and rising unemployment among growing minority populations.

With the proliferation of the automobile culture in the 1920s, New Jersey's population quickly decentralized into suburbs along the state's main highways. The rapid suburbanization and population growth (the state had surpassed the seven million mark by 1970), made New Jersey the nation's most urbanized state.

Through the twentieth century, the state developed a varied economic landscape. Its principal industries included recreation facilities, particularly along the Jersey shore; scientific research; chemical and mineral refining; and insurance. By the 1970s, New Jersey led the nation in the production of chemicals and pharmaceuticals. The state had also developed into four distinct topographical areas: the Hudson-to-Trenton great manufacturing hub, with its heavy concentration of chemical and major pharmaceutical, apparel, petroleum, and glass industries; the Atlantic coastal region (from New York Harbor to Atlantic City and Cape May), the state's vacation land; the Pinelands; and the southern, western, and northern regions, composed primarily of farms, forests, and wealthy suburbs.

The removal, relocation, and decentralization of the state's old manufacturing plants away from older areas in or near the major cities caused dramatic shifts in New Jersey's industrial economy, prompting the Trenton legislature to adopt new public policies toward the wholesale, retail, service, transportation, utilities, and finance industries.

Although urban centers declined in the postwar era—Camden by 13.4 percent, Jersey City by 6.7 percent, and Newark by 7.4 percent—commercial activities in the state's tertiary sector provided jobs for an even larger share of the labor force than industry had. Hudson County suffered the heaviest loss of jobs in the state (with just 2.1 percent growth in the 1980s and grim projections into the 1990s). Only two of New Jersey's major cities—Paterson and Elizabeth—experienced significant growth during these years. Another hard-felt drop in urban population would occur in the 1990s among the largest cities: Camden, Newark, Hoboken, Jersey City, Bayonne, Trenton, Passaic, and Paterson. These changes—combined with decreasing fertility rates, reduced movement of jobs from New York and Philadelphia to New Jersey, a marked decline in jobs in the Middle Atlantic states, and the state's transient status—led to New Jersey's population increasing by only 5 percent during the 1980s (from 7,365,011 to 7,730,188).

While many cities' populations plummeted after the 1970s, New Jersey retained the distinction of being America's most suburbanized state. By 1990, with practically 90 percent of its population classified as living in urban areas, New Jersey ranked ninth in the nation for population size. The state had an unemployment rate of just 5 percent in 1990, and boasted a per capita income rate second only to Connecticut.

In 1990, the state's largest ethnic group was Italian Americans, while African Americans constituted about 13 percent and Hispanics another 7 percent of the population. Asians were the fastest-growing racial group in the state in the 1990s, with a 77.3 percent growth rate. Dispersal patterns suggest that more than one in every two New Jersey Asians clustered in just three counties (Middlesex, Bergen, and Hudson), making them the largest minority group in Middlesex and Bergen Counties. Among New Jersey's Asian residents, the Indian Asian population ranked first in size and grew the fastest, followed by the Vietnamese, Koreans, Filipinos, Chinese, and Japanese. The Japanese population was the only Asian group to decline in the 1990s.

People of Hispanic descent accounted for more than half of New Jersey's demographic growth in the 1990s. Puerto Ricans constituted the largest Hispanic group, accounting for nearly a third of the state's Hispanic population, with large concentrations in Essex, Hudson, Passaic, and Camden counties. Mexicans comprised the fastest growing group among the state's Hispanic population. Cubans were the only Hispanic group to experience a population decline in the 1990s.

During the 1990s, the proportion of non-Hispanic whites in the state dropped from 74 percent to 66 percent, echoing the nationwide pattern of decline.

The decade of the 1990s proved to be another painful one for New Jersey's cities, with the total value of property dropping slightly even as values in suburban and rural towns continued to escalate. New Jersey attempted to improve its battered image by opening of the Garden State Arts Center and the Meadowlands sports complex. By the end of the 1990s, with a booming national economy and the state's concentration of skilled and specialized labor (especially in biotech and pharmaceuticals), most New Jersey cities began to experience a slight rebound.

New Jersey's Future

The State Plan for the early 2000s sought to channel growth by restricting state infrastructure spending in many rural and suburban areas and focusing instead on urban redevelopment. The recession that gripped the nation in 2001 also affected development schemes, and New Jersey's cities faced a difficult future.

One experiment in redevelopment would be watched closely, to see if former industrial sites could be successfully transformed into residential properties. After decades of decline, the Middlesex County city of Perth Amboy (population 47,000) welcomed $600 million in housing and retail development to be built on former industrial sites. One problem facing many of New Jersey's cities was the brownfields, contaminated vacant or underutilized industrial properties. The state attempted to reward developers interested in cities by reducing the red tape associated with brownfields. Before most other industrial cities in New Jersey, Perth Amboy secured an early federal grant and worked out an arrangement with the state environmental officials.

According to the state Planning Commission chairperson, Joseph Maraziti, the city's redevelopment plan had widespread implications for the entire state. "I have seen an evolution in Perth Amboy, and not just a visual change but a spiritual one. . . . That is exactly the message of the State Plan. We are trying to revitalize New Jersey's cities and towns. If that does not happen, nothing else in the state will work well." Other older industrial cities like New Brunswick, Jersey City, and Newark were also looking at Perth Amboy's example. They were all hoping that a fifty-year history of urban flight was about to be reversed.

When Governor Christine Todd Whitman gave her state-of-the-state address in early January 2001, New Jersey had the sixteenth largest economy in the world and the second highest per capita income in America. Perhaps her biggest accomplishment as governor was the creation of over 435,000 jobs in the state, but budget deficits accrued and a $2.8 billion budget gap developed under Whitman's Republican administration. With the Garden State Preservation Trust, though, Governor Whitman preserved nearly as much land as the combined administrations of governors Jim Florio, Brendan T. Byrne, William T. Cahill, and Richard J. Hughes. Before stepping down as governor in 2001, Whitman boasted that her administration had already created ten new business incubators and thirty "cyberdistricts" in New Jersey, with a focus on promoting high technology.

At the beginning of 2002, the state under Governor James E. McGreevey faced a $2.9 billion to $5 billion shortfall. To address this shortfall, the governor demanded 5 percent cutbacks in all agencies, and laid off 600 non-union public employees. McGreevey suggested that a Newark sports arena would be a catalyst for development, and proposed a stimulus package that would include public investment in the state's other urban centers, such as Camden, and job training programs to improve the quality of the state's work force.

Despite the governor's optimism, in 2002 New Jersey faced revenue shortfalls, pollution that ranked the worst in the nation, problems with the black business economy in northern New Jersey, issues surrounding the state's redevelopment areas, and problems facing New Jersey's "urban 30" cities.

BIBLIOGRAPHY

Cunningham, Barbara, ed. *The New Jersey Ethnic Experience.* Union City, N.J.: Wise, 1977.

Frank, Douglas. "Hittin' the Streets with Clem." *Rutgers Focus* (19 October 2001): 4–5.

Glovin, Bill. "The Price of Progress." *Rutgers Magazine* 81, no. 2 (Spring 2001): 20–27, 42–43.

Jackson, Kenneth T. *Crabgrass Frontier: The Suburbanization of the United States.* New York: Oxford University Press, 1985.

Karcher, Alan J. *New Jersey's Multiple Municipal Madness.* New Brunswick, N.J.: Rutgers University Press, 1998.

Kauffman, Matthew. "New Jersey Looks at Itself." *New Jersey Reporter* 14 (March 1985): 13–17.

Mappen, Marc. *Jerseyana: The Underside of New Jersey History.* New Brunswick, N.J.: Rutgers University Press, 1992.

McCormick, Richard P. *New Jersey from Colony to State, 1609–1789.* Newark: New Jersey Historical Society, 1981.

New Jersey Department of Labor Division of Labor Market and Demographic Research. *Southern Region: Regional Labor Market Review.* July 1998.

New Jersey Department of Labor Division of Labor Market and Demographic Research. *Atlantic Region: Regional Labor Market Review.* January 1998.

Projections 2008: New Jersey Employment and Population in the Twenty-First Century, Volume 1, Part B. Trenton: New Jersey Department of Labor Division of Labor Market and Demographic Research, May 2001.

"Remarks of Governor Christine Todd Whitman State of the State, Tuesday, January 9, 2001." In *New Jersey Documents.* 9 March 2001.

Roberts, Russell, and Richard Youmans. *Down the Jersey Shore.* New Brunswick, N.J.: Rutgers University Press, 1993.

Salmore, Barbara G., and Stephen A. Salmore. *New Jersey Politics and Government: Suburban Politics Comes of Age.* Lincoln: University of Nebraska Press, 1993.

Schwartz, Joel, and Daniel Prosser, eds. *Cities of the Garden State: Essays in the Urban and Suburban History of New Jersey.* Dubuque, Iowa: Kendall-Hunt, 1977.

Sullivan, Robert. *The Meadowlands: Wilderness Adventures at the Edge of a City.* New York: Scribners, 1998.

Wu, Sen-Yuan. *New Jersey Economic Indicators.* Trenton: New Jersey Department of Labor, Division of Labor Market and Demographic Research, January 2002.

Timothy C. Coogan

See also **Atlantic City; East Jersey; Newark; Suburbanization; Urbanization.**

NEW LIGHTS. George Whitefield, an English evangelist who appeared in New England in 1740, gave impetus to a religious movement, led by Jonathan Edwards, that propounded the doctrine of sanctification by faith alone. The New Lights, as they came to be known, split the Congregational establishment in New England, swelled the numbers of Baptists in the South, and drained parishioners away from the Anglican and Presbyterian Churches everywhere. Charismatic preachers such as Whitefield and Gilbert Tennent staged massive revivals across New England. Though denounced by Old Lights like Charles Chauncey as madmen and apostates, New Lights gained ground until the 1770s. They founded several of the Ivy League universities, and their continuing influence set the stage for the evangelical revivals, led by the Baptists and Methodists, of the next century.

New Lights. After evangelist George Whitefield used his theatrical preaching style to spread a revival frenzy known as the Great Awakening, Jonathan Edwards, shown here, became the leader of a religious movement known as the New Lights. The New Lights, who divided the Congregationalist movement, believed in sanctification by faith alone. LIBRARY OF CONGRESS

BIBLIOGRAPHY

Gaustad, Edwin S. *The Great Awakening in New England.* New York: Harper, 1957.

Lambert, Frank. "'Pedlar in Divinity': George Whitefield and the Great Awakening, 1737–1745," *The Journal of American History* 77 (1990): 812–837.

Alvin F. Harlow / A. R.

See also **Congregationalism; Evangelicalism and Revivalism; Princeton University; Protestantism; Religious Thought and Writings.**

NEW MEXICO. Having encountered unfathomable wealth and high civilization among the Aztecs in the Valley of Mexico, Spaniards quickly turned their attention northward, hoping to find another Mexico. New Mexico acquired its name and its early European visitors and residents from this misplaced belief in its potential mineral wealth. The Europeans found a dry, mountainous land of few trees and even less water populated by indigenous descendants of Anasazi Indians, whom the Spaniards named "Pueblos" for their towns that occupied the best lands along the banks of the Rio Grande. Seminomadic Athapascan and Shoshonean peoples, the Apaches and the Navajos, also called the high desert plateau home. The descendants of all of these groups inhabit the "Land of Enchantment" in the twenty-first century. New Mexico's history revolves around the relationships, sometimes tense, sometimes violent, sometimes friendly, among these groups and the land.

Another Mexico

The miraculous return in 1536 of Alvar Núñez Cabeza de Vaca, the Moorish slave Esteban, and two others from the disastrous 1528 Florida expedition of Pánfilo de Narváez piqued the curiosity of Spaniards. Cabeza de Vaca and his compatriots did not return with glowing reports of northern wealth, just rumors of a populous country to the north with large houses and trade in turquoise and other valuable items. These rumors sparked wild speculation as to the existence of another Mexico. When Cabeza de Vaca refused Viceroy Antonio de Mendoza's offer to return to the north, Mendoza selected the Franciscan

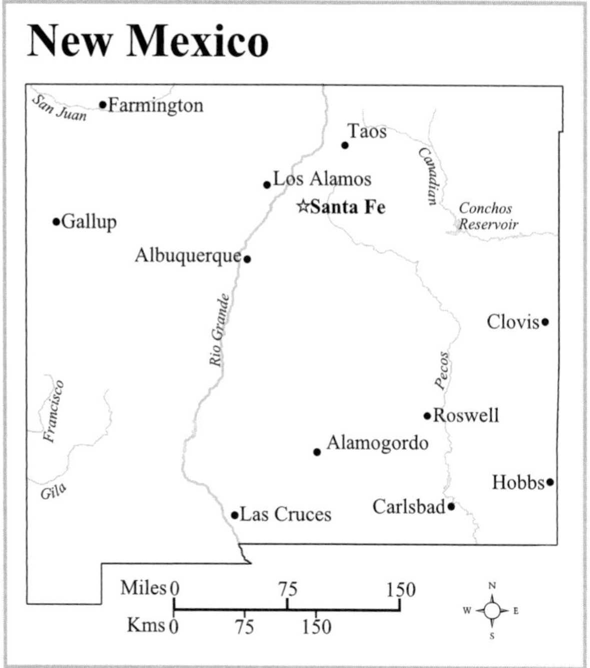

Fray Marcos de Niza to lead the expedition to verify the presence of wealthy northern cities. He was accompanied by the experienced Esteban.

After departing from Culiacán in 1539, Esteban and his Native retinue ranged ahead of Fray Marcos. In accordance with their plans, Esteban sent to Fray Marcos crosses of varying sizes, depending on his findings. When Esteban heard of Cíbola, he sent a large cross to Fray Marcos. The friar instructed Esteban to wait but to no avail. Esteban forged ahead, arriving at one of the Zuni pueblos, Háwikuh, where the Zunis seized and killed Esteban. Horrified at his companion's fate and eager to return to Mexico City, the Franciscan friar caught a glimpse of the Zuni village from afar, declared it Cíbola, and returned to Mexico City.

Fray Marcos's report of the golden glories of the north prompted Viceroy Mendoza to appoint his protégé Francisco Vásquez de Coronado to lead an expedition northward. The expedition seemed a mobile colony, including 350 Spaniards outfitted in armor and weaponry, 1,000 Native Mexican auxiliaries, six Franciscans, and hundreds of support staff. In July 1540 the expedition's vanguard arrived at the Zuni villages Fray Marcos had identified as the legendary Seven Cities of Cíbola, a rival to the wealth and size of Mexico City. Coronado and his forces discovered an adobe pueblo of some one hundred families. Disgusted with the friar's apparent lies, Coronado sent him back to Mexico City. The expedition settled down at Zuni for five months, where Coronado entertained delegations from other pueblos. The delegation from Pecos Pueblo told him all about the Great Plains, prompting Coronado to send Captain Hernando de Alvarado to return to Pecos with the delegation. At Pecos, a citadel of some two thousand people on the western edge of the Plains, Alvarado learned from an Indian slave called "the Turk" of a rich kingdom known as Quivira out on the Plains.

Alvarado brought the Turk to Coronado, who had relocated to Tiguex Pueblo. The expedition settled into a pueblo vacated for them north of present-day Albuquerque, where they spent the severe winter of 1540–1541. When spring finally arrived, almost the entire expedition headed for the Plains in search of Quivira, which proved elusive. Coronado, at the behest of the Turk, took thirty Spaniards and support persons deep into the Plains of central Kansas. Although other Indians claimed the Turk was lying, Coronado pushed onward. At last he located Quivira, not a rich kingdom but a village of grass lodges. In league with Pecos Pueblo, the Turk had hoped the Spaniards would be enveloped by the Plains and never return to New Mexico. For his treachery the Turk was garroted. Now convinced that no kingdom or city filled with riches lay hidden in the north, Coronado returned to Mexico in the spring of 1542. Although Coronado took no gold or riches back with him, his expedition mapped out much of the American Southwest, transforming the region from a mystery into an area ripe for permanent European settlement.

European Settlement

The scion of a silver-rich Zacatecas family, don Juan de Oñate received royal permission to colonize New Mexico in 1595. He spent three years organizing the privately funded expedition and recruiting colonists. After six months of travel, Oñate and his colonists arrived at San Juan Pueblo on the banks of the Rio Grande in northern New Mexico. The San Juans graciously shared their food and homes with their new neighbors, who soon founded their first capital at San Gabriel. Oñate and his colonists hoped New Mexico would prove rich in mineral wealth, and to that end the governor made several early forays into the New Mexican wilderness. While Oñate was out on one such journey in the late fall of 1598, his nephew Juan de Zaldivar, who was second-in-command, was killed in a battle with the Acomans at the summit of their sky city fortress. In retaliation Oñate launched a successful war party against Acoma. Determined to send a message to would-be rebels among the Pueblos, Oñate passed harsh punishments onto the Acomans, the severity of which set the stage for rebellion against the Spaniards.

Finding no mineral wealth, Oñate's colony failed, leading the Spanish government to take it over in 1608. No longer proprietary, New Mexico became a royal colony maintained to secure the thousands of indigenous souls Franciscan friars had baptized during Oñate's tenure. Spain also found it prudent to maintain New Mexico as a buffer zone against foreign encroachment on the profitable mining areas of northern New Spain. The royal governor Pedro de Peralta replaced Oñate in 1608 as a symbol of Spain's takeover of the colony. In 1610 Peralta removed the San Gabriel settlement to a site further from Pueblo settlements and renamed it SANTA FE.

Franciscans established missions along the Rio Grande in or near existing Pueblo Indian communities. In addition the Franciscans launched a harsh campaign of eradication against the Pueblo religion, particularly against Native priests, which angered the Pueblos. Peralta almost immediately clashed with religious authorities in New Mexico, inaugurating a competition for authority that endured until the 1680 Pueblo revolt. Civil and religious leaders argued over which group held control of and authority over Pueblos and their tributes. In essence the contest between the two groups was over control of New Mexico itself. Such squabbles revealed to Pueblo Indians the weaknesses of the sparsely populated northern colony of less than two thousand Europeans.

Pueblo Revolt

In one of their first acts of unity, most of the Rio Grande and western Pueblos (Tanos, Tewas, and Keres), with the exception of Socorro, which did not get the word of revolt in time, and Isleta, which was hampered by the presence of too many Spaniards, organized to drive the Spaniards out of New Mexico. Plans were to revolt on 11 August 1680. The New Mexico governor Antonio de Otermín found out about the plan, however, so the revolt was moved up one day to 10 August. On that day Pueblos rose up against everyone and everything Spanish, killing twenty-two Franciscan missionaries and some four hundred Spanish settlers and destroying mission churches as the most hated symbols of Spanish domination. The Pueblo Indian Popé directed the rebellion, allegedly hiding from the Spanish in a Taos Pueblo kiva. The revolt was largely successful. The Spanish survivors, many of them female heads of households, accompanied by some Isleta and Socorro Pueblos, spent twelve years in exile in the El Paso area.

Santa Fe. The one-story adobe Palace of the Governors, now a state museum, was built in the current state capital in 1610, soon after the city was founded as the capital of a Spanish royal colony—the oldest capital in what is now the United States. AP/WIDE WORLD PHOTOS

In 1692 don Diego de Vargas arrived in El Paso as New Mexico's new governor and led a "bloodless" and largely symbolic reconquest of New Mexico. The Pueblos had lost their unity, and some sought to ally themselves with the Spanish. Vargas's bloodless reconquest had to be followed by force, including a room-by-room siege of Pueblo-held Santa Fe. The Spanish victory in Santa Fe provided Vargas with a stronghold, from which he conducted a difficult military campaign against the Pueblos throughout 1694. The Pueblos answered his campaign with another revolt in 1696, during which they killed five Franciscan priests and twenty-one other Spaniards and burned churches and convents. Determined to subdue the Pueblos, Vargas launched a war of attrition that lasted six months, targeting food supplies as well as rebellious Natives. By the war's end all but the three western pueblos (Acoma, Zuni, and Hopi) were subdued. The resumption of trade in European goods beckoned the rest of the Pueblos, and they fell in line.

Accommodation

New Mexico after Vargas was largely a different place from what it had been in the seventeenth century. The eighteenth century ushered in more accommodation between Spanish settlers and Pueblos, ending the "mainly missions" atmosphere of the seventeenth century and the religious intolerance of the Franciscans. The two groups intermingled on a daily basis, sometimes intimately. Most New Mexicans eked out a meager existence, combining agriculture with raising small livestock. Merchants, soldiers, and government officials fared better, often employing a retinue of servants to tend their fields and care for their families. Roman Catholicism provided a central focus for many New Mexicans, including the Pueblo Indians, who practiced a form of Catholicism that left much of their Native religion intact.

In the eighteenth century raids by Comanche and Apache Indians and foreign encroachment from the French, British, and later the upstart Americans posed the largest threats to New Mexico. In 1786 Governor Juan Bautista de Anza engineered a "Comanche peace" by defeating the Comanche leader Cuerno Verde. Spaniards learned from the French that "peace by purchase" was far cheaper in the long run than continual raids and protracted battles. Anza convinced the Comanches to join with the Spanish against their common enemy the Apaches. The joint forces were successful in ending the Apache raids that had impoverished New Mexico's Spanish and Pueblo communities. The independence-oriented turmoil in Mexico in the 1810s and 1820s brought an end to "peace by purchase" payments to the two tribes and therefore an end to the peace.

Although Spanish officials frowned upon foreign trade, a few tenacious foreign souls attempted to reach Santa Fe and its markets prior to Mexican independence in 1821. In the late 1730s the French traders Pierre Mallet and Paul Mallet embarked on a mission to establish a trade route from New France (the modern-day upper Midwest) to Santa Fe. En route to New Mexico in 1739 they lost their six tons of trade goods in the Saline River in Kansas. Spanish authorities in Mexico denied the Mallet brothers' request for a trade license, but the brothers made a private agreement to trade with Santa Feans despite the government's decision.

Over the next few decades dozens of French traders from the Illinois country carried implements, cloth, and manufactured goods to Santa Fe in exchange for furs, gold, and silver. The international trade made Santa Fe a thriving town, and by the advent of the Missouri–Santa Fe highway, Santa Fe boasted nearly two thousand inhabitants. A few intrepid Americans, such as Zebulon Pike, rediscovered the trail to Santa Fe in the early 1800s. The trade remained the same as with the French, furs and silver in exchange for textiles, cutlery, and utensils.

The American purchase of the Louisiana Territory in 1803 put New Mexico on the defensive. Spanish officials justifiably feared invasion, as American explorers and traders kept appearing along the border and even in Santa Fe. But Spain, weak and on the verge of collapse, was in no position to guard New Mexico from the Americans. Mexican independence from Spain in 1821 brought looser trade policies to New Mexico, but Mexico had as much difficulty protecting its northern frontier from foreign intrusion as had Spain.

Santa Fe Trail

Thanks to the fortune of good timing, William Becknell, an Indian trader from Missouri, first broke open the Santa Fe trade. In so doing Becknell paved the way for American traders to tap into the pent-up consumer desires of New Mexicans. In the autumn of 1821 Becknell followed the Arkansas River west from Franklin, Missouri, with twenty men and a pack train of horses loaded with trade goods. As Becknell's group crossed Raton Pass north of Santa Fe to trade with Indians, they by chance encountered Mexican soldiers, who told them of Mexican independence and predicted that Santa Feans would gladly welcome the Missouri traders. To Becknell's delight the Mexican soldiers were correct. From trading with the New Mexicans, Becknell earned a healthy profit in silver. New Mexicans were pleased as well, for Becknell sold them higher-quality goods than what they received from the Chihuahua, Mexico, merchants, who had been their only legitimate source of trade goods prior to Becknell's visit to Santa Fe.

Becknell returned to Santa Fe in June 1822 with even more goods and men, including three wagons loaded with trade items worth $5,000. Seeking a shorter and easier route for wagon travel than the long and arduous trip across Raton Pass, Becknell forged the alternate Cimarron route, crossing the Cimarron River west of modern Dodge City, Kansas. This route, despite its heat and lack of water, became the SANTA FE TRAIL. By 1824 a well-established highway marked the route between Independence, Missouri, and Santa Fe.

Under Mexican Rule

American fur trappers also made their way into New Mexico in the 1820s, and Taos became the focus of the western American fur trade. By 1826 more than one hundred MOUNTAIN MEN trapped beaver along the Rio Grande and the Gila. While Mexican authorities saw these mountain men as a threat, presciently recognizing them as the advance wave of American movement into the Southwest, they were not willing to interrupt the lucrative trade the trappers ushered into New Mexico. For the most part Mexican authorities left New Mexico to its own devices. Accustomed to benign neglect, New Mexicans reacted strongly to Mexican dictator Antonio López de Santa Anna's attempts to centralize Mexico. Heavy-handed attempts at imposing order on the province by Governor Albino Pérez, the only nonlocal governor of New Mexico during the Mexican period, ended in chaos in 1837 as rebellion swept through the province. The fleeing Pérez lost his life to a rabble and was replaced by the native New Mexican Manuel Armijo, who restored order. In 1844 Governor Armijo successfully warded off attempts by land-hungry Texans to claim all the land east of the Rio Grande to its source, an episode that engendered a long-held antipathy toward Texans.

The U.S.–Mexican War

Texas's bid to join the United States launched a war between Mexico and the United States in 1846. U.S. general Stephen Kearney took New Mexico without a fight. Rather than organizing a defense, Governor Armijo departed for Chihuahua after meeting with the trader James Magoffin, who somehow negotiated a peaceful conquest, although no one knows for certain what happened. All did not remain peaceful, however. Discontented New Mexicans planned an uprising for 24 December 1846, but rumors reached officials, who managed to squelch the opposition's plans. On 19 January 1847 a rebel mob scalped the appointed U.S. governor Charles Bent and twelve others sympathetic to the American cause. Rebellion spread throughout northern New Mexico. In February 1847 Colonel Sterling Price marched on Taos Pueblo, where the rebels had gathered. After a bloody battle the ringleaders were hanged, bringing an end to the armed resistance to the American occupation of New Mexico.

In the Treaty of Guadalupe Hidalgo, which officially ended the war in 1848, New Mexico became part of the United States, and its people became American citizens. New Mexico had the necessary population for statehood, sixty-one thousand Hispanics and thirty thousand Indians in the 1850 census, and the support of Presidents James K. Polk and Zachary Taylor, but circumstances changed as gold was discovered in California. The Compromise of 1850 declared New Mexico a territory without restrictions on the issue of slavery and adjusted the long-contested boundary between New Mexico and Texas. New Mexico lost its bid for statehood to the politics of slavery and remained a territory for sixty-two years, until 1912.

The Civil War

During the 1850s the U.S. military built an elaborate defense system in New Mexico consisting of six military posts designed to keep hostile Indian tribes under control. The military thereby became the mainstay of the territory's economy and allowed the population to spread out from the Rio Grande valley. In 1861, however, Federal troops returned home to fight the Civil War, abandoning the defense system protecting those settlers and disrupting the orderly development of New Mexico. The territory sided with the Union, mostly out of hatred for the Confederate Texans. The few Civil War battles, including Valverde and Glorieta Pass (1862), that took place in New Mexico were more a reassertion of Texas imperialism than an integral part of Confederate strategy. Indeed most of the fighting in New Mexico during the Civil War years was against Indians. Colonel James H. Carleton ordered Colonel Christopher "Kit" Carson, a former mountain man, to campaign against the Mescalero Apaches (1863) and then the Navajos (1864). Carson prevailed against both tribes. Survivors were marched to Bosque Redondo, the first experiment in Indian reservations, which failed utterly. An 1868 treaty allowed the Navajos to return to their much-reduced homeland. The U.S. military confronted the Comanches and the Apaches in the 1870s and 1880s and confined both groups to reservations by the end of the 1880s.

The Civil War was a watershed in New Mexico history, bending the territory toward the United States and away from Mexico. After the war New Mexico shared much of the history of the rest of the American West, range wars, mining booms, railroad construction, Indian wars, nationalized forests, and military bases. As Anglo-Americans moved into the territory, Hispanic New Mexicans found it more difficult to hold onto their ancestral lands. The 1878–1879 Lincoln County War reflected the tensions among New Mexico's various populations, especially Hispanic sheepherders and Anglo cattle ranchers.

Statehood

New Mexico finally achieved statehood in 1912, beginning a new era. Statehood meant that a satisfactory level of Americanization had been reached, and participation in the twentieth century's major military efforts continued the process. Some 50,000 New Mexicans served their country in World War II, including Navajo Code Talkers. The state had the highest volunteer rate of any state. Many of these volunteers died in the Bataan death march. Northern New Mexico's mountains hid the secret Los Alamos labs and the Manhattan Project during World War II, and the first atomic bomb was detonated at the Trinity Test Site at White Sands on 16 July 1945, establishing the state as a major location for federal defense projects. Investments reached $100 billion by the end of the Cold War. Military defense continued to boost New Mexico's economy in the early twenty-first century along with tourism and some manufacturing. The legendary Route 66 bisected the state, passing through Albuquerque and bringing tourists who sampled the state's blend of cultures and drank in the romanticized Spanish and Indian past provided by boosters.

Albuquerque. A view of Second Street, in the city's business district, c. 1915—not long after New Mexico became the forty-seventh state. Library of Congress

Indians maintained a significant presence in New Mexico. Unlike most Native Americans, the Pueblos, Navajos, and Apaches remained on a portion of their ancestral homelands, while many other Native Americans settled in Albuquerque. India agent John Collier and the General Federation of Women's Clubs helped New Mexican Pueblos successfully overturn the 1922 Bursum bill, which would have given squatters land ownership and water rights in traditional Pueblo lands. The Pueblo Lands Act of 1924 protected Pueblo lands from squatters and recognized the land rights Pueblos had enjoyed under Spanish and Mexican rule. In recent years, Indian gaming brought an influx of cash to some of New Mexico's tribes and added punch to their political presence.

After 1848 Hispanics sought redress for the loss of their ancestral lands, mostly through the U.S. court system. In the last half of the twentieth century the issue of land grants generated some isolated violence, namely the July 1967 takeover of the county courthouse at Tierra Amarilla by the activist Reies Lopes Tijerina and his followers. New Mexican Indians also fought the loss of their lands, particularly sacred sites such as Taos Pueblo's Blue Lake, which had been swallowed by the Carson National Forest. President Richard M. Nixon returned Blue Lake to them in the 1970s. The twentieth century also put New Mexico on the map as a center for the arts. Early in the century Taos became an arts colony, attracting artists, writers, and other intellectuals. In 1914, artists Ernest L. Blumenschein and Bert Philips founded the Taos Society of Artists, prompting the development of a distinctive New Mexican style. Santa Fe, the state capital, also draws artists and the tourists who support them. The mix of three cultures, Indian, Hispanic, and Anglo, makes the forty-seventh state a vibrant laboratory for race relations.

BIBLIOGRAPHY

Boyle, Susan Calafate. *Los Capitalistas: Hispano Merchants and the Santa Fe Trade.* Albuquerque: University of New Mexico Press, 1997.

DeBuys, William. *Enchantment and Exploitation: The Life and Hard Times of a New Mexico Mountain Range.* Albuquerque: University of New Mexico Press, 1985.

DeMark, Judith Boyce, ed. *Essays in Twentieth-Century New Mexico History.* Albuquerque: University of New Mexico Press, 1994.

Deutsch, Sarah. *No Separate Refuge: Culture, Class, and Gender on an Anglo-Hispanic Frontier in the American Southwest, 1880–1940.* New York: Oxford University Press, 1987.

Gutiérrez, Ramón A. *When Jesus Came, the Corn Mothers Went Away: Marriage, Sexuality, and Power in New Mexico, 1500–1846.* Stanford, Calif.: Stanford University Press, 1991.

Jensen, Joan M., and Darlis A. Miller, eds. *New Mexico Women: Intercultural Perspectives.* Albuquerque: University of New Mexico Press, 1986.

Kessell, John L. *Kiva, Cross, and Crown: The Pecos Indians and New Mexico, 1540–1840.* Washington, D.C.: National Park Service, U.S. Department of the Interior, 1979.

Simmons, Marc. *New Mexico: An Interpretive History.* Albuquerque: University of New Mexico Press, 1988.

Szasz, Ferenc Morton. *The Day the Sun Rose Twice: The Story of the Trinity Site Nuclear Explosion, July 16, 1945.* Albuquerque: University of New Mexico Press, 1984.

Vargas, Diego de. *Remote beyond Compare: Letters of Don Diego de Vargas to His Family from New Spain and New Mexico, 1675–1706.* Edited by John L. Kessell. Albuquerque: University of New Mexico Press, 1989.

Weber, David J. *The Mexican Frontier, 1821–1846: The American Southwest under Mexico.* Albuquerque: University of New Mexico Press, 1982.

———. *The Spanish Frontier in North America.* New Haven, Conn.: Yale University Press, 1992.

Dedra S. McDonald

See also **Exploration and Expeditions: Spanish; Mexican War; Mexico, Relations with;** *and vol. 9:* **Glimpse of New Mexico.**

NEW NATIONALISM is the term used to describe Theodore Roosevelt's political philosophy that the nation is the best instrument for advancing progressive democracy. In 1910, former President Theodore Roosevelt returned from safari to plunge into the 1910 congressional elections. The Republican Party was deciding, Roosevelt believed, whether to be "the party of the plain people" or "the party of privilege." On 31 August in Osawatomie, Kansas, Roosevelt called for a "New Nationalism" to "deal with new problems. The New Nationalism puts the national need before sectional or personal advantage."

Roosevelt's New Nationalism sought a transcendent idealism and a renewed faith through the power of democratic nationalism and activist government. The phrase came from Herbert Croly's 1909 work, *The Promise of American Life*, which was itself inspired by Roosevelt's presidency. Roosevelt collected his 1910 campaign speeches under the title "The New Nationalism."

"The New Nationalism" became Roosevelt's campaign platform in fighting his handpicked successor William Howard Taft for the Republican presidential nomination in 1912. Roosevelt advocated a strong, Hamiltonian government to balance big business. He advocated more corporate regulation, the physical evaluation of railroads, a graduated income tax, a reformed banking system, labor legislation, a direct primary, and a corrupt practices act.

During an unprecedented popular primary campaign in a dozen states, Roosevelt ripped into Taft and the Republican old guard, as the defenders of "privilege and injustice." Responding, Taft became the first president to stump for his own renomination. Eventually, Roosevelt won Republican hearts but Taft won the nomination, thanks to the party "steamroller" of bosses and officeholders.

The Democratic candidate, New Jersey Governor Woodrow Wilson, positioned himself between Taft, the hostage of big business, and Roosevelt, the apostle of big government. Wilson advocated a "New Freedom." Influenced by the progressive reformer Louis D. Brandeis, Wilson viewed decentralized government and constrained corporations as the recipe for a just democracy. Roosevelt's run for the presidency under the Progressive Party banner kept the central issues—and these two outsized personalities—in the forefront of Wilson's winning 1912 campaign.

Yet, the Roosevelt-Wilson contrast was not as dramatic as it appeared, then or now. Even as Roosevelt championed the rights of labor over property, he asked Americans "whenever they go in for reform," to "exact justice from one side as much as from the other." While the difference in emphasis was significant—and pointed to two major trends in American progressivism—both the New Nationalism and the New Freedom highlighted the reform consensus. Roosevelt reflected more of the fire-breathing moralism of the politician Robert La Follette; Wilson displayed more the crisp, rational, monastic efficiency of the social crusader Jane Addams. Yet both men and both doctrines reflected a growing commitment in the early twentieth century to face the challenges of bigness, of modern corporate power, of the dislocations wrought by industrial capitalism. And both ideas helped shape the great reform movements of the twentieth century, including the New Deal and the Great Society.

BIBLIOGRAPHY

Blum, John Morton. *The Republican Roosevelt.* Cambridge, Mass.: Harvard University Press, 1954.

Cooper, John Milton, Jr. *The Warrior and the Priest: Woodrow Wilson and Theodore Roosevelt.* Cambridge, Mass.: Harvard University Press, 1983.

Gil Troy

See also **New Freedom; Taft-Roosevelt Split.**

NEW NETHERLAND. Founded by maritime entrepreneurs, New Netherland's beginnings lay with sea captains, traders, and investors principally from the Dutch provinces of Holland, North Holland, and Zeeland. In 1609 Henry Hudson explored the entrance to the North River (Hudson River) and navigated as far north as present-day Albany. Following his exploits, the United Provinces issued contracts for short-term voyages of discovery in the area north of Virginia and south of "nova Francia," lands claimed by France. In 1614 the New Netherland Company won a charter permitting it to send out four voyages and trade with native peoples, especially those living near the entrances to three rivers: the South River (Delaware River), the North River or River Mauritius (Hudson River), and the Fresh River (Connecticut River).

In 1621 the United Provinces awarded a charter to the West India Company (WIC). It received a monopoly to trade between thirty-nine and forty-one degrees north latitude. This was not a land patent. Indigenous peoples were presumed to hold rightful title to lands in New Netherland. Any properties acquired would be by purchase or contractual agreement.

In 1624 the WIC began its search for a proper base of operations in New Netherland. Jan Cornelisse May led several ships to locations already described and occupied by the earlier navigators and traders. May was particularly looking for an offshore island to serve as a *middelpunt,* a central location for the company's enterprises. Prince's Island in the Delaware River seemed a possibility, as did each of the two islands set at the entrance to the North River and separated by a narrow channel, the "island of the Manahates" (Manhattan Island) and Nut Island (Governor's Island.)

Willem Verhulst succeeded May, arriving on the southern shores of New Netherland in 1625. He came as "Provisional Director" with "Instructions" to decide on a permanent central site for the company's employees and possibly forty-three colonists. Once settled, he and the engineer Crijn Fredericksz were to oversee the building of a fort, one of the shore forts found at home and in the East Indies. Settlement on the island of the Manahates looked promising. But it was not until 1626 and after Verhulst's dismissal and replacement by Peter Minuit as first director-general that the island was purchased and occupancy legitimated.

Manhattan Island was not intended to be an agricultural colony. The company pursued its commercial monopoly by making bilateral agreements with coastal and inland peoples. But it had no intention of acquiring extensive native lands. And its directors were, like those of the East India Company, divided over the value of encouraging colonists. Overseas they meant to be the opposite of the Spanish: *kooplieden* not *conquistadors,* merchants not conquerors.

In 1629 Kiliaen van Rensselaer and other influential merchants forced the company to accept the Charter of Freedoms and Exemptions. This required it to assist those who would put themselves forward as patroons, men prepared to plant colonies. Van Rensselaer established his patroonship, Rensselaerswijck, on land 180 miles up the Hudson from Manhattan Island. There the company had earlier built Fort Orange and after 1652 promoted a successful fur-trading town, Beverwijck (later Albany). No other patroonship eventuated.

Population on Manhattan Island grew slowly. During the late 1630s, however, some Dutch colonists were moving farther away from the center of the settlement, Fort Amsterdam. They were creating persistent disputes with Algonquian-speaking natives who were farming nearby and fishing for shells that were highly valued by inland people and soon served as currency (wampum) in New Netherland.

At the same time the Dutch and natives were experiencing a shortage of maize (corn). The policy of Willem Kieft, the director general who had replaced Wouter van

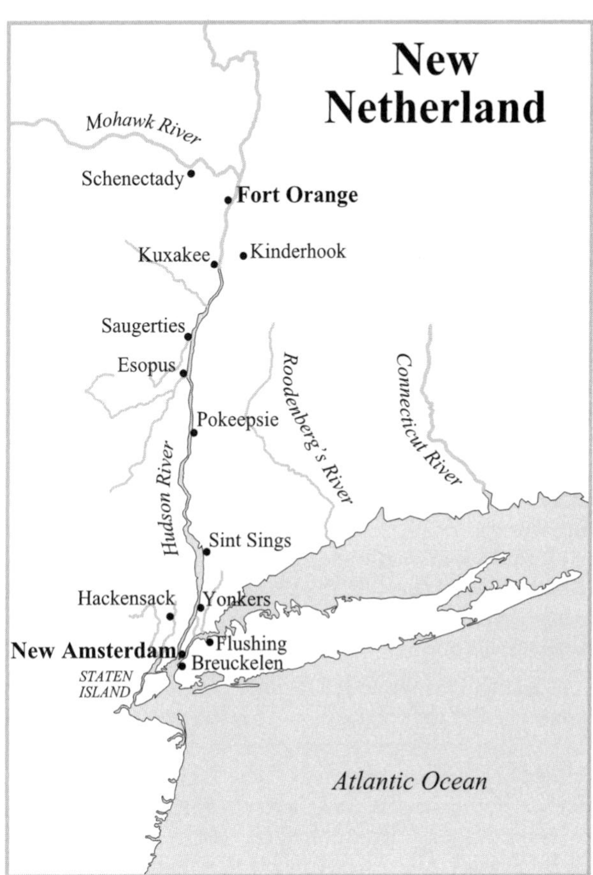

Petrus Stuyvesant. The director general of New Netherland from 1647 until 1664, when the arrival of an English fleet at New Amsterdam forced him to surrender the Dutch colony in America. LIBRARY OF CONGRESS

Twiller (1631–1637), was to extort the maize (and wampum and furs) from native villages. Clans such as the Raritans learned that unless they paid "fire money"—the same *brandschatting* that armies or brigands extracted from isolated farming villages in the Low Countries—the Dutch could not protect them from enemies or their own depredations. Kieft's War, as it has been called, resulted in the deaths of possibly a thousand natives.

Kieft denied responsibility. However, leading burghers, constituting themselves as the Twelve Men in 1641 and then the Eight Men in 1643, charged him with bringing the company's enterprise into peril and bearing the guilt for massacring innocent natives in September 1643. They made certain that the States General and the company directors knew of these affairs. The natives remembered them into the1650s.

Kieft's War was not a turning point in Dutch-native relations. But the fragile peace that had existed from 1624 to the late 1630s never returned. Petrus Stuyvesant assumed the administration of New Netherland in 1647. He was authoritarian but also competent, intelligent, and, in many respects, far-sighted. He saw to the foundation of Beverwijck. He agreed (reluctantly) that NEW AMSTERDAM (New York City) deserved the status of a chartered city in1653. He concluded the Treaty of Hartford in 1650, which established boundaries between New Netherland and Connecticut.

During Stuyvesant's administration and especially after the mid-1650s, immigration to New Netherland grew steadily. Transatlantic commerce was regularized, as were partnerships with Amsterdam's merchant houses. Ordinary burghers of New Amsterdam and Beverwijck (women among them) traveled to the *patria* seeing to business affairs. Well-developed legal and notarial systems gave protection to ordinary townspeople caught up in daily matters as well as to merchants engaged in international trade. In 1660 one of Stuyvesant's councillors profiled New Netherland for the company directors, listing two cities, thirteen villages, two forts, and three colonies. In 1664 New Amsterdam's burgomasters praised the city for its fine houses, surpassing nearly every other place in North America. The province's population was 10,000 people. Among them were small numbers of Africans. After their first arrival in 1626, some of these men and women remained as slaves on Manhattan Island. Others lived as free persons or were given considerable freedom and manumitted. Beyond the colony, the New Netherlanders played a major role in the African slave trade, with the first cargo of slaves probably arriving in New Amsterdam in 1655 for transshipment to the southern colonies and the West Indies.

But Stuyvesant inherited Kieft's legacy. In 1655 hostilities ignited, largely around Manhattan Island. In 1660 settlers in Esopus (Kingston) began a year of hostilities with the Esopus people. Stuyvesant and his council debated whether they could retaliate on the grounds of a "just war." They decided they could not. They urged the natives to relocate and sued for Mohawk mediation and peace. But it failed to hold. In 1664 Esopus was attacked and fighting resumed.

In August 1664 and in the absence of a declared war, an English fleet forced Stuyvesant's surrender of New Netherland. The province became the property of James, duke of York.

BIBLIOGRAPHY

Klooster, Wim. *The Dutch in the Americas, 1600–1800.* Providence, R.I.: The John Carter Brown Library, 1997.

Merwick, Donna. *Death of a Notary: Conquest and Change in Colonial New York.* Ithaca, N.Y.: Cornell University Press, 1999.

Rink, Oliver A. *Holland on the Hudson: An Economic and Social History of Dutch New York.* Ithaca, N.Y.: Cornell University Press, 1986.

Stokes, I. N. P., ed. *The Iconography of Manhattan Island: 1498–1909.* 6 vols. New York: Robert H. Dodd, 1915–1928.

Donna Merwick

See also **Dutch West India Company; Explorations and Expeditions: Dutch; New York Colony.**

NEW ORLEANS is located along a crescent-shaped portion of the Mississippi River, 120 miles from where it flows into the Gulf of Mexico. Bounded on the north by Lake Pontchartrain, much of the city lies below sea level and is protected from flooding by natural and human-made levees. Between 1699 and 1762 the French who colonized Louisiana struggled with many problems and received only limited support from their government. However, they left an enduring imprint, reinforced by later French-speaking immigrants from Acadia and Saint Domingue. That legacy has remained evident in New Orleans. In 1718 Jean-Baptiste Le Moyne, Sieur de Bienville, founded La Nouvelle Orléans. His assistant laid out streets in a gridiron pattern for the initial site, later known as the Vieux Carré. New Orleans became the capital of French Louisiana in 1722. French architecture, language, customs, and identity as well as the dominance of Roman Catholicism persisted across time. African slaves formed a large part of the colonial population and also shaped the city's culture.

By treaties in 1762 and 1763, the French government transferred most of Louisiana to Spain. Spanish governors generally proved to be effective administrators and operated in association with members of the city's government, the Cabildo. Spanish policies fostered an increase in the city's population of free people of color. During the latter part of the American Revolution, Governor Bernardo de Gálvez used New Orleans as a base for successful

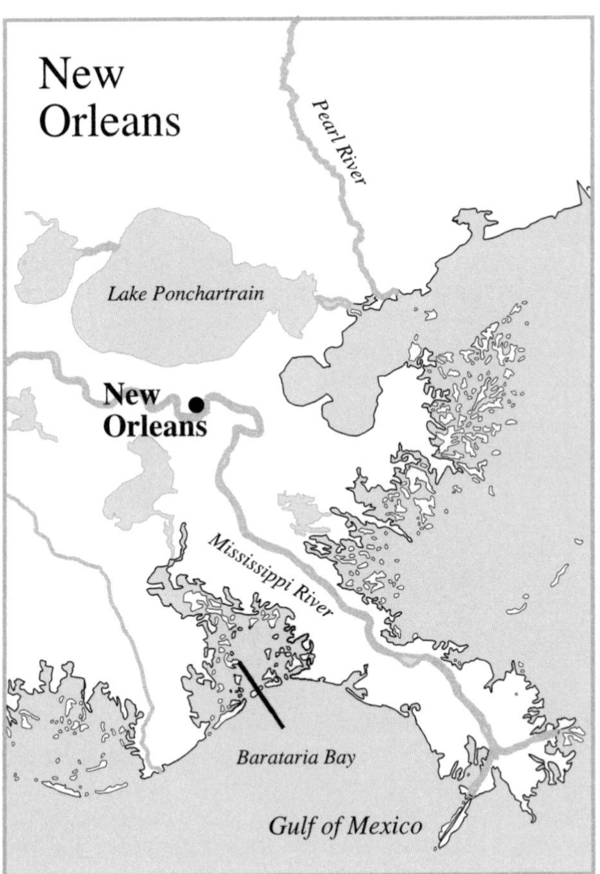

New Orleans. In Arnold Genthe's photograph from the early 1920s, ironwork around a balcony frames the back of St. Louis Cathedral and rooftops in the Vieux Carré (French quarter). Library of Congress

military campaigns against British forts along the Gulf Coast. As farmers living in the western United States began shipping their produce down the Mississippi River, the port of New Orleans became vital to the new nation's economy. Alarmed by reports that Spain had ceded Louisiana back to France, U.S. president Thomas Jefferson sent ministers to Europe to engage in negotiations that led to the Louisiana Purchase in 1803. At the Battle of New Orleans on 8 January 1815, General Andrew Jackson decisively defeated the British in the final military contest of the War of 1812, gaining national fame for himself and the city.

During the antebellum period, New Orleans thrived economically. Steamboat navigation and cotton production from Deep South plantations helped to make the city an entrepôt that briefly ranked as the nation's greatest export center. The New Orleans slave market became the country's largest. Slaves and free people of color sustained their own culture, particularly evident in gatherings at Congo Square. In addition to an influx of Anglo-Americans, Irish and German immigrants swelled the population. Repeated epidemics of yellow fever and cholera, however, killed thousands of residents. With traditions dating to the colonial period, Mardi Gras became an increasingly elaborate celebration. Friction between citizens of French ancestry and Anglo-Americans gave way to the combative nativism manifested by the Know-Nothing Party of the 1850s.

Despite a large Unionist vote in the presidential election of 1860, New Orleans succumbed to secessionist hysteria following the victory of Abraham Lincoln. After an inept military defense of the Confederacy's largest port, the city was occupied by Union admiral David Farragut on 29 April 1862. Thereafter, General Benjamin Butler

Mardi Gras. The parade of the Krewe of Rex, the King of Carnival (since 1872), c. 1907. Library of Congress

earned local enmity for his forceful but effective management of the city. During Reconstruction, racial and political conflict erupted in a deadly race riot on 30 July 1866 and in the Battle of Liberty Place fought between the White League and city police on 14 September 1874.

In the late nineteenth century, New Orleans permitted its port facilities to deteriorate and its economy stagnated. The corrupt political leaders of the New Orleans Ring neglected basic public services. The completion of jetties at the mouth of the Mississippi River in 1879, however, enabled larger oceangoing vessels to dock at the city. Large numbers of Italian immigrants arrived, between 1890 and 1920, and the early twentieth century brought a resurgence of trade, particularly with South America. A community with a rich and complex musical heritage, New Orleans promoted and nurtured early jazz. The city also housed the nation's most famous legalized vice district, Storyville. In the 1920s the Vieux Carré became a magnet for artists and writers, and a significant historic preservation movement began to emerge in the 1930s. As mayor from 1904 to 1920 and as boss of a powerful political machine, Martin Behrman brought many improvements in municipal services. His successors became ensnarled in political wars with governors Huey P. Long and Earl K. Long, periodically costing the city its powers of self-government.

World War II brought a surge in population and a booming economy, thanks to war-related industries, particularly shipbuilding. After the war, Mayor deLesseps Morrison initiated an ambitious building program, attracted new industries, and successfully promoted the city as an international port. Statewide support for segregation and weak local leadership produced the New Orleans school desegregation crisis of 1960, which branded the city as a stronghold of racism. In subsequent years whites in particular relocated to the suburbs, and by 2000 the city's population had shrunk to 484,674. In 1977 voters elected the city's first African American mayor, Ernest F. Morial. The completion of the Superdome in 1975, the hosting of a world's fair in 1984, and the opening of the Riverwalk shopping mall in 1986 and the Aquarium of the Americas in 1990 reflected a renewed vitality as well as an emphasis on tourism. Celebrated restaurants, medical facilities, and educational institutions also constitute important attractions of the Crescent City.

BIBLIOGRAPHY

Din, Gilbert C., and John E. Harkins. *The New Orleans Cabildo: Colonial Louisiana's First City Government, 1769–1803.* Baton Rouge: Louisiana State University Press, 1996.

Haas, Edward F. *DeLesseps S. Morrison and the Image of Reform: New Orleans Politics, 1946–1961.* Baton Rouge: Louisiana State University Press, 1974.

Hirsch, Arnold R., and Joseph Logsdon, eds. *Creole New Orleans: Race and and Americanization.* Baton Rouge: Louisiana State University Press, 1992.

Ingersoll, Thomas N. *Mammon and Manon in Early New Orleans: The First Slave Society in the Deep South, 1718–1819.* Knoxville: University of Tennessee Press, 1999.

Jackson, Joy J. *New Orleans in the Gilded Age: Politics and Urban Progress, 1880–1896.* Baton Rouge: Louisiana State University Press, 1969.

Tyler, Pamela. *Silk Stockings and Ballot Boxes: Women and Politics in New Orleans, 1920–1963.* Athens: University of Georgia Press, 1996.

Samuel C. Shepherd Jr.

See also **Jazz; Louisiana; Louisiana Purchase; New France; New Orleans Riots; New Orleans, Battle of; New Orleans, Capture of.**

NEW ORLEANS, the first steamboat on western waters, was built at Pittsburgh by Nicholas J. Roosevelt under patents held by Robert Fulton and Robert R. Livingston, during 1810–1811. A sidewheeler of between three hundred and four hundred tons, the *New Orleans* left Pittsburgh on 20 October 1811, braved the Falls of the Ohio and the New Madrid earthquake, and reached New Orleans 10 January 1812. It never returned to Pittsburgh, plying in the New Orleans–Natchez trade until snagged on 14 July 1814.

BIBLIOGRAPHY

Petersen, William J. *Steamboating on the Upper Mississippi.* New York: Dover Publications, 1995.

William J. Petersen / A. R.

See also **Mississippi River; Steamboats; Waterways, Inland.**

NEW ORLEANS, BATTLE OF (8 January 1815). The United States declared war on Great Britain in June 1812, but the contest did not threaten Louisiana until 1814, when Napoleon Bonaparte's abdication freed England to concentrate on the American war. In the autumn of 1814 a British fleet of more than fifty vessels, carrying 7,500 soldiers under Sir Edward Packenham, appeared in the Gulf of Mexico and prepared to attack New Orleans, the key to the entire Mississippi Valley. Gen. Andrew Jackson, who commanded the American army in the Southwest, reached New Orleans on 1 December 1814 to begin preparing the city's defenses.

Battle of New Orleans. Warships fire on one another near New Orleans in the prelude to the climactic—if unfortunately timed—battle of the War of 1812. © Bettmann/corbis

The superior British navy defeated the small American fleet on Lake Borgne, southwest of the Mississippi River's mouth; landed troops on its border; and marched them across the swamps to the river's banks, a few miles below New Orleans. Jackson had assembled more than 6,000 troops, mainly Kentucky, Tennessee, and Louisiana militia, with a few regulars. After a few preliminary skirmishes, the British attempted to overrun the American position with a full-scale offensive on the morning of 8 January 1815. The American defense held firm. The British were completely repulsed, losing more than 2,000 men, of whom 289 were killed, including Packenham and most of the other higher officers. The Americans lost only seventy-one men, of whom thirteen were killed.

The British soon retired to their ships and departed. New Orleans and the Mississippi Valley were saved from invasion. Coming two weeks after the peace treaty was signed that ended the war, the battle had no effect upon the peace terms; but it did bolster the political fortunes of Andrew Jackson, the "hero of New Orleans."

BIBLIOGRAPHY

Brooks, Charles B. *The Siege of New Orleans.* Seattle: University of Washington Press, 1961.

Brown, Wilburt S. *The Amphibious Campaign for West Florida and Louisiana, 1814–1815.* Tuscaloosa: University of Alabama Press, 1969.

Remini, Robert V. *Life of Andrew Jackson.* New York: Perennial Classics, [1988] 2001.

Tregle, Joseph George. *Louisiana in the Age of Jackson.* Baton Rouge: Louisiana State University Press, 1999.

Walter Prichard / A. R.

See also **Ghent, Treaty of; Mexico, Gulf of; Mississippi River; New Orleans; War of 1812.**

NEW ORLEANS, CAPTURE OF. At the outbreak of the Civil War, the Union authorities recognized the strategic importance of seizing New Orleans, the commercial emporium of the entire Mississippi Valley and the second port of the United States. In the spring of 1862 a naval squadron under Union Adm. David G. Farragut, carrying an army commanded by Gen. Benjamin F. Butler, entered the lower Mississippi and succeeded in passing two Confederate forts in the night. Farragut's fleet followed shortly thereafter. Realizing that resistance was useless, the city's small Confederate garrison withdrew northward, leaving New Orleans to fall into the hands of Union forces on 1 May 1862.

BIBLIOGRAPHY

Capers, Gerald M. *Occupied City: New Orleans under the Federals, 1862–1865.* Lexington: University of Kentucky Press, 1965.

Hearn, Chester G. *When the Devil Came down to Dixie: Ben Butler in New Orleans.* Baton Rouge: Louisiana State University Press, 1997.

Walter Prichard/A. G.

See also **"Damn the Torpedoes"; Gunboats; Mortars, Civil War Naval; Rams, Confederate; River Navigation; Warships.**

NEW ORLEANS RIOTS (1873–1874), clash of political factions led by Louisiana gubernatorial rivals Republican W. P. Kellogg and Democrat John McEnery. The disorder began 5 March 1873, when McEnery's partisans attacked two police stations. On 6 March the members of McEnery's legislature were arrested and jailed. In response to the violence, federal troops were ordered into Louisiana to protect Republican officials, which angered the McEneryites. In response, McEnery's supporters formed the WHITE LEAGUE in the spring of 1874. On 14 September 1874, the league launched a successful attack on Kellogg's forces; twenty-seven people were killed in the melee. McEnery took over the state government the following day, but U.S. troops hurried into the city and restored Kellogg on 17 September. The uprising paved the way for the overthrow of the Republican regime in Louisiana three years later.

BIBLIOGRAPHY

Lestage, Henry O. *The White League in Louisiana and Its Participation in Reconstruction Riots.* New Orleans, La.: 1935.

Taylor, Joe Gray. *Louisiana Reconstructed, 1863–1877.* Baton Rouge: Louisiana State University, 1974.

John S. Kendall/A. R.

See also **Louisiana; Reconstruction; Riots.**

NEW REPUBLIC, THE. *The New Republic* has been one of the most important journalistic outlets for a new form of LIBERALISM that appeared in the United States, particularly in its eastern and midwestern cities, during the decades around 1900. This new liberalism, which arose as a response to the industrialization of the nation's economy, stressed the recognition of mutual obligation and the development of an integrated public interest rather than the pursuit of private, individual interests.

The magazine was founded in New York City by Willard and Dorothy Straight, a wealthy couple active in humanitarian social causes, and journalist Herbert Croly. Croly recruited Walter Lippmann and Walter Weyl as fellow editors. All three men had recently published important statements of the new liberal faith and they hoped to use the journal, which debuted on 7 November 1914, to steer American political culture along a middle course between laissez-faire individualism and Marxist socialism.

Each week's issue opened with short editorial paragraphs, continuing with longer editorials, signed articles by contributors and editors, correspondence, and literary and artistic material. New York City icons such as the philosopher John Dewey and the historian Charles A. Beard quickly took advantage of the new publishing outlet. Articles on reforms such as feminism, civil rights, and workers' right to organize were accompanied by important statements of the new cultural modernism from artists such as Robert Frost and critics Randolph Bourne, Van Wyck Brooks, and Floyd Dell.

Circulation leapt to around forty thousand during American involvement in World War I during 1917 and 1918, as the journal was widely seen as an unofficial voice of President Woodrow Wilson's administration. Editors and contributors strongly supported American intervention, alienating many of their political allies. They hoped that the war would lead to national unity and a worldwide democratic revolution, and were shocked by the punitive terms of the Versailles Treaty.

During the politically conservative 1920s, circulation plummeted. Weyl died in 1919 and Lippmann abandoned the journal along with his hopes for a rational public. Croly continued as editor, increasingly identifying liberalism as a moral phenomenon. Critics Edmund Wilson, Robert Morss Lovett, Waldo Frank, and Lewis Mumford offered expanded cultural coverage. The journal pushed for an alternative to the major parties, and was guardedly hopeful that the Communist reforms in the Soviet Union after 1917 would produce a mature, democratic state.

A new editorial staff of the long-time journalist Bruce Bliven, the economist George Soule, and the literary critic Malcolm Cowley turned the magazine away from Croly's philosophical approach after his death in 1930. They remained aloof, however, from President Franklin D. Roosevelt's New Deal, which seemed insufficiently radical even though it consolidated the farmer-labor-professional coalition for which Croly had long hoped. Only in 1937 did they shift course, vigorously defending Roosevelt against his increasingly vocal detractors.

Increasingly distrustful of the capitalist economy, liberals heatedly debated the Soviet experiment during the 1930s. Bliven's and Cowley's faith that Communism would evolve into democracy was countered by contributors Beard and Dewey, whose critical views of Joseph Stalin's regime finally won over the editors after the Nazi-Soviet pact of 1939. The editors were, like many liberals, reluctant to involve themselves in another European conflict, calling for war on Germany only in August 1941. They continued throughout World War II to promote domestic issues, including the protection of civil liberties and full employment.

Former vice president and outspoken internationalist Henry A. Wallace, who became editor in 1946, opposed the anticommunist foreign policy of President Harry S. Truman, but his controversial third-party presidential candidacy led to a split with the magazine in January 1948. Soviet intervention in Czechoslovakia two months later solidified the journal's support for the containment of communism abroad, although it opposed the domestic anticommunism of Wisconsin Senator Joseph McCarthy.

The editors moved their office from New York City to Washington in 1950 to gain greater access to the nation's political machinery, but during the conservative decade that followed they once again emphasized cultural criticism over politics. They found a new political focus with the election of President John F. Kennedy in 1960, concentrating particularly on civil rights. Inspired by the spending programs of Kennedy's successor, Lyndon B. Johnson, the journal also reaffirmed its support for an activist federal government while strongly opposing the war in Vietnam. The antiauthority stance of the counterculture and the violent rhetoric of the black power movement disturbed the editors, although they agreed that fundamental social reforms were necessary.

New owner and editor-in-chief Martin Peretz steered the journal toward a stronger anti-Soviet line in the mid-1970s, leading to an intense debate among the editors over support for the Nicaraguan contra rebels in 1986. Writers also began to question the ability of the state to promote social equality, and criticized the interest-group politics of the Democratic Party while reluctantly supporting its presidential candidates. As the century closed, *The New Republic* remained a preeminent forum for liberal debate.

BIBLIOGRAPHY

Diggins, John Patrick. "The New Republic and Its Times. *New Republic* 191, no. 24 (10 December 1984): 23–34.

Levy, David W. *Herbert Croly of the New Republic: The Life and Thought of an American Progressive.* Princeton, N.J.: Princeton University Press, 1985.

Seideman, David. *The New Republic: A Voice of Modern Liberalism.* New York: Praeger, 1986.

Wickenden, Dorothy. "Introduction: Little Insurrections." In *The New Republic Reader: Eighty Years of Opinion and Debate.* Edited by Dorothy Wickenden. New York: BasicBooks, 1994.

Andrew Jewett

See also **Magazines.**

NEW SMYRNA COLONY. During 1767 and 1768, Andrew Turnbull, a Scottish physician who had traveled widely in the Mediterranean, brought some 1,400 persons from Greece, Italy, and Minorca to Florida to cultivate sugarcane, rice, indigo, cotton, and other crops. Colonists were supposed to work for seven to eight years, and then, at the end of the period, receive tracts of fifty or more acres of land. The settlement, named New Smyrna, lasted until 1776, when the colonists marched as one to Saint Augustine to ask for relief from their indentures, claiming cruel treatment. Only 600 of the original immigrants by that time remained, and they settled in Saint Augustine after they were released by the governor.

BIBLIOGRAPHY

Corse, Carita Doggett. *Dr. Andrew Turnbull and the New Smyrna Colony of Florida.* St. Petersburg, Fla.: Great Outdoors Publication Company, 1967.

W. T. Cash / A. R.

See also **Florida; Immigration; Indentured Servants.**

NEW SOUTH. *See* **South, the.**

NEW SWEDEN COLONY. "New Sweden" (a term applied only long after the fact) was an amorphous product of a series of scattered settlements in the parts of Delaware, New Jersey, and Pennsylvania that make up the Delaware River Valley. Sweden reached its apogee as a player in the European search for North American colonies in the first half of the seventeenth century, in keeping with a national need to pursue a mercantilist agenda. Dutch mercantilists William Usselinx and Peter Minuit furthered their own and Holland's economic and political interests by encouraging the Swedish Crown to establish a colony, mainly as a means of thwarting England.

But few Swedes would be lured to the Americas, so the economic and political potential for a New Sweden was undermined from the outset. In political terms, New Sweden had only a brief twelve-year existence (1643–1655) under the Swedish Crown and the inept and despotic rule of governor Johan Printz; his misrule contributed mightily to Sweden's demise as a possessor of Crown settlement in North America.

The cultural significance of the Swedish colonies persisted long after the end of their political existence, however. Fort Christina, settled at present-day Wilmington, Delaware, by a small Swedish contingent in 1638, was short-lived, but left a lasting legacy nonetheless by contributing a Swedish cultural component to the rich ethnic and religious mix of the middle colonies. The most promising Swedish settlement, it never fulfilled the mercantilist promise its founders envisioned. The same fate awaited Fort Nya Elfsborg, founded on Salem Creek in West Jersey in 1643. In this case the failure was attributed largely to the famed Jersey mosquito, a claim New Jersey residents of any era will find easy to believe. Sweden's nationalist effort succumbed completely to overwhelming Dutch force in 1655.

Short-lived New Sweden never counted more than four hundred people, and many of those were Finns, not Swedes. Yet the cultural and ethnic impact endured, as can be inferred from place names like Swedesboro, Finn's Point, Elinsboro, and Mullica Hill, all in New Jersey, and Swede's Ford in Pennsylvania. More importantly, this handful of settlers left behind a strong presence in West Jersey in the form of several Swedish Lutheran churches, the last of which closed its doors in 1786, nearly a century and a half after its founding. In ethnic terms, Swedes remain a permanent surviving element of the diversity that has always characterized New Jersey.

While cause and effect are hard to pin down, Sweden was one of the European nations committed to American independence. It lent money to the American cause in 1782, and entered into a treaty with the new United States in 1783, not only helping to secure Sweden's loans and future trading rights, but placing the nation among the first to recognize American independence. In sum, Swedish linkage to the middle colonies and to New Jersey in particular may have started badly with the abortive creation of "New Sweden" in 1638, but the connection persisted in religious, ethnic, and diplomatic terms through and beyond the American Revolution. In broad cultural terms, it still survives at the start of the twenty-first century.

BIBLIOGRAPHY

Johnson, Amandus. *The Swedes in America, 1638–1938.* Philadelphia: 1953.

McCormick, Richard P. *New Jersey from Colony to State, 1609–1789.* Rev. ed. Newark: New Jersey Historical Society, 1981. The original edition was published in 1964.

Prince, Carl E., ed. *The Papers of William Livingston.* New Brunswick, N.J.: New Jersey Historical Commission, 1979–1988.

Carl E. Prince

NEW YORK CITY. While it shares characteristics with a thousand other cities, New York City is also unique. At the southern tip of New York State, the city covers 320.38 miles and is divided into five boroughs, Manhattan, Brooklyn, Queens, Staten Island, and the Bronx. By the twenty-first century New York City was well established as the preeminent financial and cultural center of American society and an increasingly globalized world economy. Its stature is anchored in part on one of the great, natural deep-water ports in the world; on its resultant concentration of financial services, commercial ven-

A City of Businesses. New York has always been filled with small stores, like Caruso's Fruit Exchange, as well as upscale shops and corporate offices. NATIONAL ARCHIVES AND RECORDS ADMINISTRATION tures, and media outlets; and on its long and colorful history as the "front door" to the United States for millions of immigrants.

Prior to European settlement in 1624, Native Americans, including the Rockaways, the Matinecooks, the Canarsies, and the Lenapes, populated the region. While northern European and Spanish explorers had contact with these groups before 1600, the establishment of a Dutch fort on Governor's Island began New York's modern history. The Dutch West India Company christened the settlement New Amsterdam, and it became the central entrepôt to the Dutch colony of New Netherland. Dutch officials had trouble attracting settlers from a prosperous Holland and eventually allowed in non-Dutch settlers from nearby English colonies and northern and western Europe. As a result, by the 1660s the Dutch were close to being a minority in New Amsterdam. Led by Colonel Richard Nicolls, the British seized New Amsterdam on 8 September 1664. Nicolls renamed the city "New York City" to honor the brother of King Charles II, the duke of York (later King James II).

For its first hundred years the city grew steadily in diversity, population, and importance as a critical economic bridge between Britain's southern, agricultural colonies and its northern mercantile possessions. The first Africans arrived in 1626, and by the eighteenth century African slaves comprised approximately one-fifth of the city's population. At times the city's ethnic and racial diversity led to social unrest. In 1712 and 1741 city authorities brutally crushed slave insurrections. By 1743 New York was the third largest American city, and by 1760 it surpassed Boston to become second only to Philadelphia.

New York City saw substantial anti-British sentiment during the early years of the American Revolutionary period as radical Whig leaders organized militant Sons of Liberty and their allies in anti-British violence. As the Revolution progressed, however, the city became a bastion of Loyalist sympathy, particularly following the defeat of George Washington's forces at Brooklyn Heights and Harlem Heights in 1776. The British occupied the city for the remainder of the war.

After the British departed in 1783, New York City grew in economic importance, particularly with the establishment of the stock exchange in 1792. As European powers battled in the Napoleonic Wars, New York City supplied all sides with meat, flour, leather, and cloth among other goods and by 1810 emerged as the nation's premier port and the single most lucrative market for British exports.

The Nineteenth Century

To a significant extent New York City's subsequent rise in the nineteenth century stemmed from the opening of the Erie Canal in 1825. Originally advocated in 1810 by Mayor (and later governor) DeWitt Clinton, the canal allowed New York to overshadow New Orleans and St. Louis as an entry point to the western territories and pro-

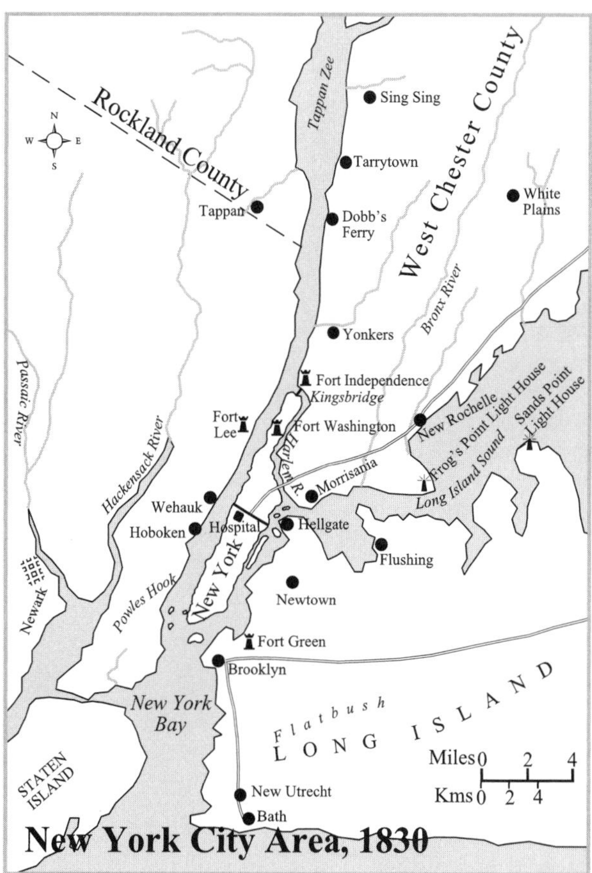

vided cheap access to the "inland empire" of the Great Lakes region. As a result the city's population surged from 123,706 in 1820 to 202,589 by 1830, surpassing Philadelphia as the largest city in the hemisphere. While it prospered, New York City also became more ethnically diverse as German, French, and Irish arrivals joined older Dutch and English groups. By mid-century, a large influx of German and Irish Catholics into a city still strongly dominated by Protestant groups led to significant social conflict over jobs, temperance, municipal government, and what it meant to be an "American."

As the population and diversity increased, New York's political environment became more fractious. Ignited by desire for political patronage and inclusion and fueled by class and ethnic resentments toward the city's traditional elite, the Democratic Party developed the notorious political machine Tammany Hall. Originally formed in 1788 to challenge the city's exclusive political clubs, Tammany garnered political influence by helping immigrants find work, gain citizenship, and meet other needs. Tammany also developed a well-deserved reputation for graft, scandal, and infighting. Under the leadership of Fernando Wood in the 1850s, William Marcy "Boss" Tweed after the Civil War, and Richard Crocker and Charles Murphy, Tammany became entrenched in the city's political operations and was not routed out until the 1930s.

A City of Homes. A New Deal–era view of East Sixty-third Street in Manhattan; about 1.5 million people from all socioeconomic classes live even in the heart of New York, after the commuters and visitors have departed. LIBRARY OF CONGRESS

The American Civil War dramatically stimulated New York's industrial development and made the city the unquestioned center of American finance and capitalism. Buoyed by federal war contracts and protected by federal tariffs, New York manufactures of all types expanded rapidly. As a result many of New York's commercial elite made unprecedented fortunes. In 1860 the city had only a few dozen millionaires; by the end of the war the city had several hundred, forming the basis for a culture of conspicuous consumption that continued into the twenty-first century.

Between 1880 and 1919, 17 million immigrants passed through New York City, among them growing numbers of Jewish, Hungarian, Italian, Chinese, and Russian arrivals. This surge in immigration placed significant pressure on the city's resources and led to the creation of a distinctive housing type, the tenement. As the tenant population grew, landlords subdivided single-family houses and constructed flimsy "rear lot" buildings, railroad flats, and from 1879 to 1901 the infamous "dumbbell" tenement, all noted for overcrowding, filth, and danger.

As a consequence New York City became a testing ground for regulatory reform, most notably in the areas of housing, public health, and occupational safety. Jacob Riis's landmark 1890 photo essay *How the Other Half Lives* detailed the overcrowding and unsanitary living conditions in the tenements and marked a major turning point in urban reform. Such efforts increased after the Triangle Shirt Waist Factory fire of 1911, which inspired a generation of local and national reformers, including Francis Perkins, Harry Hopkins, Robert F. Wagner, and Al Smith.

The Twentieth Century

Until the late nineteenth century "New York City" meant Manhattan. Two developments at that time, however, greatly expanded the city's boundaries. Led by Andrew Haswell Green, the consolidation of the city in 1898 unified the four outer boroughs with Manhattan, combining the country's largest city, New York, with the third biggest, Brooklyn, and raising the city's population from 2 million to 3.4 million overnight. In addition the subway system, which first began operation in 1904, eventually grew to over seven hundred miles of track in the city, the most extensive urban rail system in the world.

The city grew up as well. The construction of the Equitable Building in 1870 began the transformation of New York City's skyline. With the development of safety elevators, inexpensive steel, and skeleton-frame construction, office buildings leapt from six stories (or less) to twenty, forty, or sixty floors (or more). The construction of the Manhattan Life Building (1895), the Flatiron Building (1903), and the Woolworth Building (1913) among many others represented important architectural and engineering improvements. New York's love affair with the skyscraper culminated in 1930 with the race between H. Craig Severence's Bank of Manhattan on Wall Street and Walter Chrysler's eponymous Chrysler Building on Forty-second Street to claim the prize for the tallest building in the world. Both structures were quickly overshadowed in 1931 by the 102-story Empire State Building on Fifth Avenue and eventually by the twin towers of the 110-story World Trade Center in 1974. At the beginning of the

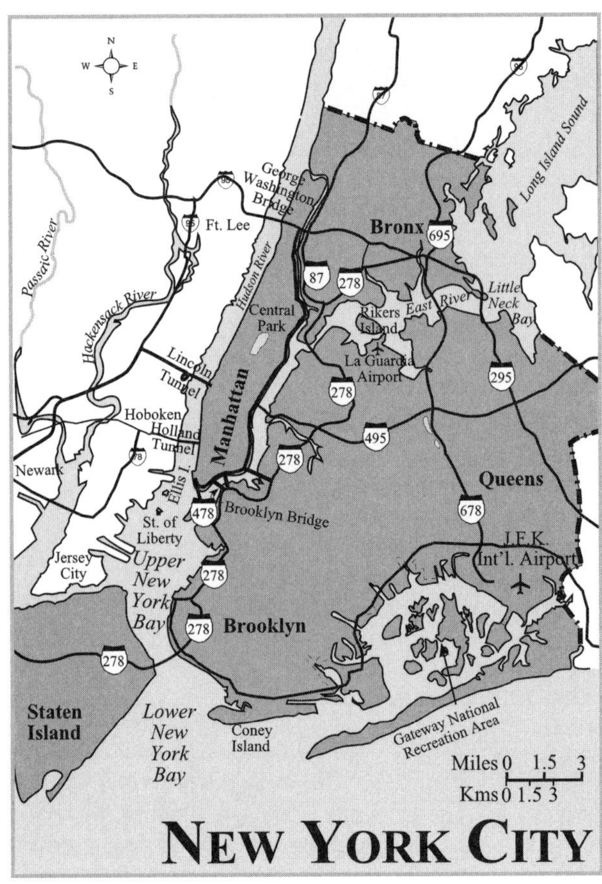

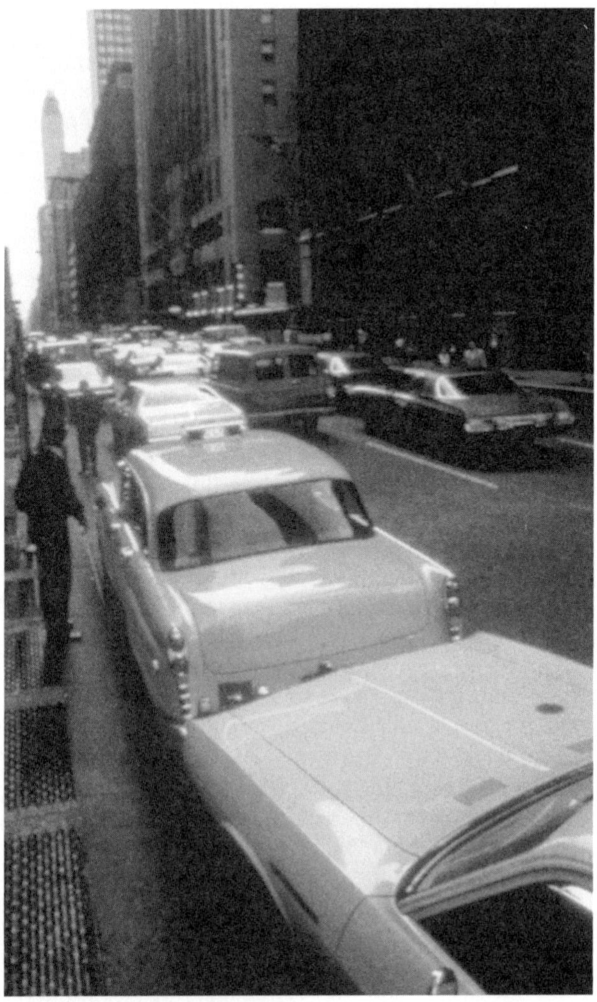

A City of Traffic Jams. Congested streets and excruciatingly slow-moving traffic have long been common in New York City. NATIONAL ARCHIVES AND RECORDS ADMINISTRATION

twenty-first century New York had more skyscrapers than any other place on Earth, and as business and residential structures, hotels and public housing, they have come to articulate American economic vitality. Sadly this symbolism made these structures attractive targets for attack. The Trade Center was bombed in 1993 by a group of Muslim fundamentalists. On 11 September 2001 two commercial airliners were hijacked and flown into the towers, destroying the entire complex and killing almost three thousand people, making it the most lethal terrorist attack to that date.

From the 1930s to the 1960s the city's landscape was further transformed as Mayor Fiorello La Guardia, Parks Commissioner Robert Moses, and other planners channeled state and federal money into massive highway and park projects, shifting the city from its nineteenth-century reliance on horses, trains, and streetcars to accommodation of the automobile. Public works projects such as the Triborough Bridge (1936), the Lincoln Tunnel (1937), the Brooklyn-Battery Tunnel (1950), and the Cross-Bronx Expressway (1963) made it possible for white, middle-class New Yorkers to move to the suburbs, leaving many older, inner-city communities neglected and consequently vulnerable to economic decline.

Beginning in the early nineteenth century New York City became the cultural capital of the United States, serving as the focal point for American literature, publishing, music, theater, and in the twentieth century movies, television, advertising, fashion, and one of America's unique musical contributions, jazz. The interactive artistic, literary, intellectual, and commercial life of New York has evolved into one of the city's most distinctive features.

Immigration continued to flavor the city. After World War II and the passage of the Hart-Cellar Act of 1965, which ended discrimination based on national origin, New York City became even more ethnically diverse. Large numbers of Middle Eastern, Latino, Caribbean, Asian, African, and eastern European immigrants settled in neighborhoods such as the Lower East Side, Flushing, Bay Ridge, Fordham, and Jackson Heights in Queens. In 1980 immigrants made up about 24 percent of the city's population; of them 80 percent were from Asia, the Caribbean, and Latin America. With the city's still vigorous communities of Italians, Irish, African Americans, and Chinese, the city's diversity has proven a source of both ethnic and racial tensions on the one hand and cultural enrichment and the promise of a more tolerant social order on the other.

BIBLIOGRAPHY

Burrows, Edwin G., and Mike Wallace. *Gotham: A History of New York City to 1898.* New York: Oxford University Press, 1999.

Caro, Robert A. *The Power Broker: Robert Moses and the Fall of New York.* New York: Vintage Books, 1975.

Kammen, Michael. *Colonial New York: A History.* New York: Oxford University Press, 1996.

Plunz, Richard. *A History of Housing in New York City.* New York: Columbia University Press, 1990.

Reimers, David M. *Still the Golden Door: The Third World Comes to America.* New York: Columbia University Press, 1992.

Stokes, I. N. Phelps. *The Iconography of Manhattan Island, 1498–1909.* 6 vols. Reprint, Union, New Jersey: The Lawbook Exchange, 1998.

Jared N. Day

See also **Brooklyn; Manhattan; New Amsterdam.**

NEW YORK CITY BALLET, one of the premier American dance companies, founded in 1948 by ballet artisans George Balanchine and Lincoln Kirstein, and originally known as the Ballet Society. The company's ballets were mostly Balanchine's creations, and he often used company classes at New York's City Center to rehearse a

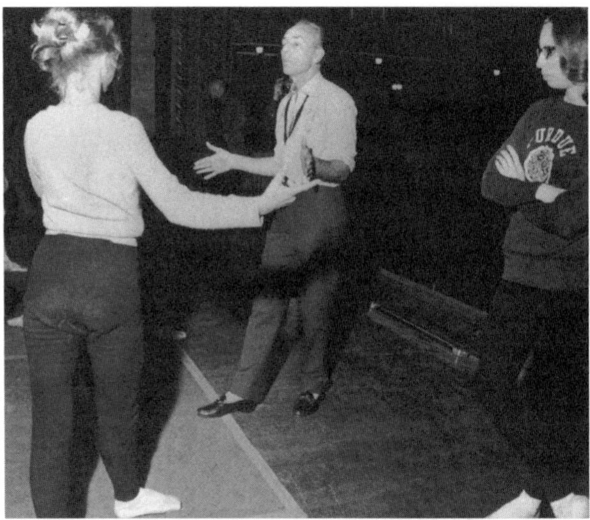

George Balanchine. The cofounder, artistic director, and prolific principal choreographer of the New York City Ballet—and one of the most significant creative figures in the history of dance. GETTY IMAGES

choreographic technique. The signature costume of the company became black leotards, pink tights, and pink pointe shoes, primarily because of limited finances for costuming. Known for their beautiful and intricate footwork, Balanchine's dancers developed a distinctly American style of dancing, combining Russian, Italian, and French traditions with a unique flair for musicality and extreme emotional control.

BIBLIOGRAPHY

Garafola, Lynn, and Eric Foner, eds. *Dance for a City.* New York: Columbia University Press, 1999.

Jennifer Harrison

See also **American Ballet Theatre; Ballet; Dance.**

NEW YORK CITY, CAPTURE OF. Nine years after losing the city to the English, the Dutch sent a squadron of twenty-three ships, under the joint command of Cornelius Evertsen Jr. and Jacob Binckes, to recapture New York. On 28 July 1673 the fleet appeared off Sandy Hook. The fleet approached the fort on 30 July, giving Manning and his hastily assembled corps of volunteers a half an hour to yield the fort. When the time expired, the Dutch fleet opened fire. The fort held out for four hours and then surrendered. Briefly rechristened New Orange, the city of New York was returned to England in 1674 pursuant to the Treaty of Westminster.

BIBLIOGRAPHY

Archdeacon, Thomas J. *New York City, 1664–1710: Conquest and Change.* Ithaca, N.Y.: Cornell University Press, 1976.

A. C. Flick / A. R.

See also **Long Island; New Amsterdam; New York City.**

NEW YORK CITY, PLOT TO BURN. After the Confederate raid on Saint Albans, Vermont, in October 1864, Confederates attempted to burn NEW YORK CITY on 25 November. Participants fired Barnum's Museum, the Astor House, and a number of other hotels and theaters with phosphorus and turpentine, but the damage was trifling.

BIBLIOGRAPHY

Burrows, Edwin G. *Gotham: A History of New York City to 1898.* New York: Oxford University Press, 1999.

Thomas Robson Hay / S. B.

See also **Civil War; Insurrections, Domestic.**

NEW YORK COLONY began as the Dutch trading outpost of New Netherland in 1614. On 4 May 1626, officials of the Dutch West India Company in New Netherland founded New Amsterdam, which subsequently became New York City. The English captured the colony in 1664, though a complete ousting of Dutch rule did not occur until 10 November 1674. Dutch residents received generous terms of surrender. Religious toleration and the verification of property rights assured that most stayed when the colony became the province of New York. Charles II gave the colony as a proprietorship to his brother James, duke of York, upon the English claim on 12 March 1664. Only when its proprietor became King James II on 6 February 1685 did New York become a royal colony. Settlement during the colonial era was confined to the Hudson Valley, Long Island, and the eastern one hundred miles of the Mohawk River.

Ethnic and Religious Heterogeneity

The diverse colony was almost 50 percent Dutch but also included English, various European nationalities, African slaves, and freedmen. By the mid-eighteenth century, New York held the highest slave population of all the northern colonies, at 7 to 10 percent of the population. With the religious toleration after the changeover to English rule, the predominant Dutch Reformed Church split into New York City's sophisticated and wealthy orthodox and rural Pietistic wings. By 1750, the Reformed churches were still in the majority, but Presbyterian, Lutheran, Anglican, Congregational, and Baptist denominations also existed. The city also had one Roman Catholic church and one Jewish synagogue.

La Nouvelle Yorck. A hand-colored eighteenth-century etching by André Basset of the New York City waterfront. © CORBIS

Economics

The central economic commerce was the Dutch and Indian fur trade through Fort Orange, now Albany. After the English takeover in 1664, the Dutch traders in Albany continued to dominate the inland northern fur trade, expanding to a provincial trading post at Fort Oswego on Lake Ontario in 1727. Foodstuffs, especially grain, became the major exports for the remainder of the colonial period. A landlord-tenant existence developed, taking the lead from the Dutch patroons' land grants. Continuing the grants of land under the English, farms dominated the lower Hudson River valley, where powerful families controlled great land tracts of manorial estates. In the 1760s, New Englanders encroached into the area, and land riots against the owners of Hudson Valley manors were suppressed by British troops.

Indian Relations

The Five Nations of the Iroquois Confederation (Cayuga, Mohawk, Oneida, Onondaga, and Seneca) who lived in the lower Hudson Valley controlled all the western area and much of the Mohawk Valley during the colonial era. Settlement of the interior remained moderate due to the Indian resistance. In 1701, the Iroquois conveyed to the king of England the title to their conquered western lands in the Iroquois Beaver Land Deed. Throughout much of the eighteenth century, despite claims of neutrality, Iroquois Confederacy diplomats manipulated Britain and France against each other.

Rise of the Assembly

In 1683, James II guaranteed New York a representative legislature and personal freedoms through the governor's authority. The governors sought advice and assistance from local powerful citizens, became entangled in local party politics, and made political concessions in return for increased revenues as their authority declined. Because New York was the most vulnerable of England's colonies, it was the most oppressed with expenditures for defense, and it hosted a body of English regulars throughout most of its existence. The governor's corruption and antagonism with the assembly culminated when John Peter Zenger's *New York Weekly Journal* printed an accusation of maladministration on the part of Governor William Cosby. Cosby ordered Zenger's arrest, and the outcome of the case that ensued set the precedent in 1735 that criticism was not libel, the first triumph for freedom of the press in the colonies. During King George's War, 1744–1748, a feud broke out between Governor George Clinton and New York chief justice James De Lancey over the conduct of the war and the assembly's appropriation of funds, shifting the focus away from the war and toward recurrent internal factional struggles. The elite leadership of the two major factions, the cosmopolitan Court Party and the provincial Country Party, tried to control the general population through ethnic, social, economic, constitutional, religious, geographic, and familial differences throughout the rest of the eighteenth century.

Dominion of New England and the Glorious Revolution

The Dominion of New England annexed New York in 1688, and Governor Edmund Andros's representative in New York, Captain Francis Hutchinson, fled when Captain Jacob Leisler seized control and created an arbitrary government of his own in 1689. When King William's

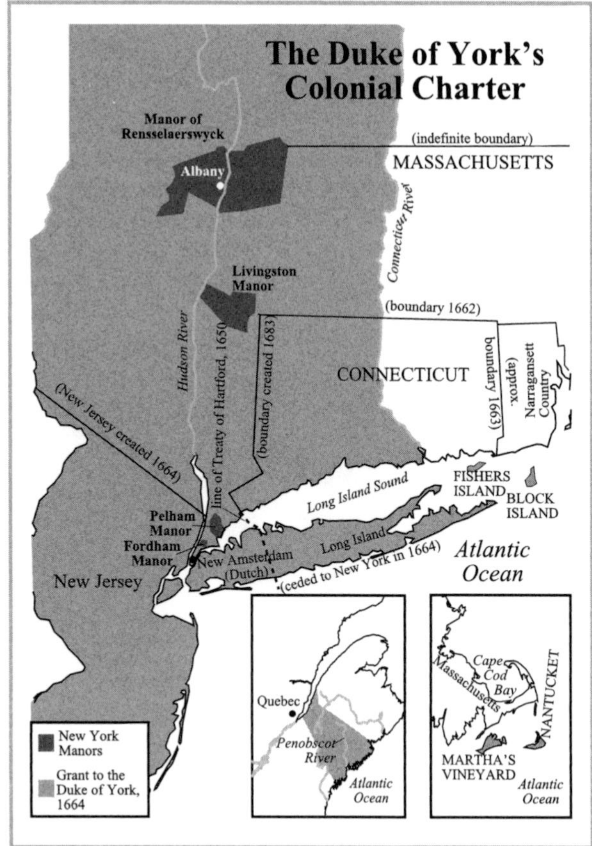

commissioned governor, Colonel Henry Sloughter, arrived, Leisler and his lieutenant, Jacob Milbourne, were executed. Leislerian and anti-Leislerian factions worked against each other for many subsequent years. Following the accession of William and Mary to England's throne in 1691, New York again became a royal colony.

Revolutionary Era

The unsuccessful Albany Congress in 1754 set a quasi precedent for an American union. The Proclamation of 1763 placed a limit on expansion and also infuriated merchants in New York by moving the fur trade to Montreal. Delegates from nine colonies met in New York in October 1765 to protest the Stamp Act, and the following spring the act was repealed. When the Townshend duties put a tax on glass, paint, paper, and tea, New York merchants signed a nonimportation agreement against British goods. In 1768, in noncompliance with the Quartering Act, the assembly refused to vote supplies for the British troops, but it reversed the decision in 1769. In 1770, the Sons of Liberty renewed their protest activities, culminating in the Battle of Golden Hill. A committee of correspondence met in January 1774 to communicate with like-minded colonies. New Yorkers had their own tea party in April 1774, when patriots dressed as Indians threw eighteen cases of tea into the harbor. After local and state authorities took over the government, the Fourth Provincial Congress of New York approved the Declaration of Independence on 9 July 1776. New York was declared a free state the next day, and a state constitution was created and approved in 1777.

BIBLIOGRAPHY

Becker, Carl Lotus. *The History of Political Parties in the Province of New York, 1760–1776.* Madison: University of Wisconsin Press, 1960.

Goodfriend, Joyce D. *Before the Melting Pot: Society and Culture in Colonial New York City, 1664–1730.* Princeton, N.J.: Princeton University Press, 1992.

Kammen, Michael. *Colonial New York: A History.* New York: Scribners, 1975.

Kim, Sung Bok. *Landlord and Tenant in Colonial New York: Manorial Society, 1664–1775.* Chapel Hill: University of North Carolina Press, 1978.

Rink, Oliver A. *Holland on the Hudson: An Economic and Social History of Dutch New York.* Ithaca, N.Y.: Cornell University Press, 1986.

Ritchie, Robert C. *The Duke's Province: A Study of New York Politics and Society, 1664–1691.* Chapel Hill: University of North Carolina Press, 1977.

Trelease, Allen W. *Indian Affairs in Colonial New York: The Seventeenth Century.* Ithaca, N.Y.: Cornell University Press, 1960.

Michelle M. Mormul

See also **Assemblies, Colonial; Colonial Policy, British; Dominion of New England; Dutch West India Company; Leisler Rebellion; New Amsterdam; New Netherland.**

NEW YORK INTELLECTUALS. The "New York Intellectuals"—an interacting cluster of scholars, editors, and essayists—formed an influential force in American intellectual life from the 1930s to at least the 1970s. Nevertheless, they promoted no cohesive body of ideas or singular purpose. They did not name themselves but were labeled by others, sometimes with a mixture of admiration and resentment. And no event or common project defined either a beginning or an end to their collective experience. Yet as an evolving circle, the New York Intellectuals brought to American discourse a seriousness about the import of ideas, a readiness for polemic, an engagement with (though not necessarily an adoption of) radical and modernist thought, an interest in theory and in European perspectives, and an attentiveness to one another that was distinctive.

Attracted at first to communism in the 1930s, members of the circle often came together around their anti-Stalinism, particularly through the rebirth of *Partisan Review* in 1937 and the defense of Leon Trotsky from charges made during the Moscow Trials. The politics of the Left, whether they stood in sympathy or opposition, remained a preoccupying concern. The majority of the New York Intellectuals were Jewish and the children of immigrants. Comfortable neither with ethnic particularism nor assimilation, they joined with non-Jews to develop a more cosmopolitan intellectual culture and found a creative edge in the tensions between individual and national identity. In addition to the literary commitments that carried particular force in the 1930s, the New York Intellectuals staked their claims in philosophy, analysis of the visual arts, and, especially after World War II, the social sciences.

The New York Intellectuals favored the essay, sprinkled with wide-ranging references, lifting individual reactions toward broader significance, and seeking definite leverage on questions of cultural and political import. Magazines and journals provided primary outlets for published work: *Partisan Review*, while edited by Philip Rahv and William Phillips; *politics*, Dwight Macdonald's 1940s antiwar magazine; *Commentary*, replacing the *Contemporary Jewish Record; Dissent*, founded by Irving Howe; and even the *New York Review of Books*, whose first issue (1963) was dominated by members of the New York Intellectual circle. Influential books, including Lionel Trilling's *The Liberal Imagination* (1950) and Daniel Bell's *The End of Ideology* (1961), were often collections of essays.

The circle divided over McCarthyism and the Cold War, proved skeptical of student radicalism in the 1960s, and lost its identity in the 1970s through the death of older members and the identification of some younger members with neoconservatism.

BIBLIOGRAPHY

Bloom, Alexander. *Prodigal Sons: The New York Intellectuals and Their World.* New York: Oxford University Press, 1986.

Cooney, Terry A. *The Rise of the New York Intellectuals: Partisan Review and Its Circle.* Madison: University of Wisconsin Press, 1986.

Jumonville, Neil. *Critical Crossings: The New York Intellectuals in Postwar America.* Berkeley: University of California Press, 1991.

Terry A. Cooney

NEW YORK SLAVE CONSPIRACY OF 1741.

Beginning in early 1741, enslaved Africans in New York City planned to overthrow Anglo American authority, burn the city, and turn it over to the Spanish, possibly setting up a black governor. Emboldened by the War of Jenkins' Ear, recent slave revolts in South Carolina and the West Indies, and personal attacks on local slave owners and Atlantic slave ships, groups of conspirators in and around New York City planned a massive uprising. At meetings in taverns, on wharves and street corners, and at homes of free Negroes, dozens of enslaved Africans swore their allegiance to the plot. Participants included enslaved people owned by masters from every ethnicity and rank in local society, South American free blacks captured by privateers and sold into slavery, and criminal gangs of escaped slaves. Among white people implicated were John Hughson, a tavern keeper; Peggy Kerry, common-law wife of Caesar, alias Jon Gwin, a black conspirator; and John Ury, a dancing instructor. The plot was discovered after an arson investigation of the fire that destroyed Fort George on the tip of New York. Municipal authorities tried dozens of conspirators whose confessions were later published by Daniel Horsmanden, the city recorder. Reaction by local officials was merciless. After quick trials, thirteen conspirators were burned at the stake, seventeen blacks and four whites were hanged, and seventy enslaved people were transported to the West Indies.

New York Slave Conspiracy of 1741. This engraving shows two slaves in the witness box during one of the trials resulting from the burning of Fort George in the city. Library of Congress

Horsmanden's record of the trials has become a classic piece of evidence for legal, African American, and Atlantic culture scholars. Within the slaves' confessions are fascinating glimpses of black culture. At Hughson's tavern, for example, black conspirators met on weekends and holidays, ate large meals and drank numerous toasts to their plans, gambled, danced to fiddle music, and swore loyalty oaths inside a chalk circle.

Historical memory of the event remains controversial. Throughout the eighteenth century, the conspiracy was seen as fact. During the antebellum period, a combination of historical amnesia about the cruelty of slavery in New York and abolitionist views of blacks as loyal citizens cast doubt on the veracity of Horsmanden's journal and the reality of a plot. During most of twentieth century, scholars believed that no extended conspiracy existed and that the affair revealed murderous white hysteria toward rumors of revolt. The prevailing view now accepts that enslaved people did conspire to overthrow the slave society. A short-term effect of the conspiracy was an increased emphasis on slave imports directly from Africa, avoiding seasoned slaves from the West Indies, who had proven to be troublemakers. Long-term effects were worsening racism and the preparation of enslaved Africans around New York for military roles during the American Revolution.

BIBLIOGRAPHY

Hodges, Graham Russell. *Root and Branch: African Americans in New York and East Jersey, 1613–1863.* Chapel Hill: University of North Carolina Press, 1999.

Horsmanden, Daniel. *The New York Conspiracy.* Edited by Thomas J. Davis. Boston: Beacon Press, 1971.

Linebaugh, Peter, and Marcus Rediker. *The Many-Headed Hydra: Sailors, Slaves, Commoners, and the Hidden History of the Revolutionary Atlantic.* Boston: Beacon Press, 2000.

Graham Russell Hodges

See also **Jenkins' Ear, War of; Slave Insurrections; Slavery.**

NEW YORK STATE

Location, Geography, and Climate

New York State is located in the northeast region of the United States. New York City and Long Island border on the Atlantic Ocean, and the state stretches westward to the Great Lakes of Ontario and Erie. These lakes, along with the St. Lawrence River, form the northern border of the state with Canada. To the east, New York borders Vermont, Massachusetts, and Connecticut; to the south, New Jersey and Pennsylvania; to the west, a short stretch of the state borders Ohio. The topography of the state is made up primarily of mountains, hills, woodlands, valleys, and fertile meadows. Ancient glacier formations and movements created rivers, gorges, and waterfalls that are among the most spectacular in the world. Niagara Falls, for example, which straddles the border with Canada in the northwest section of the state, is one of the most notable of the state's outstanding geographical features and is considered one of the natural wonders of the world.

Mountain ranges include the Adirondack and the Catskill Mountains, running north to south in the eastern portion of the state, and the foothills of the Allegheny Mountains in the southwestern area of the state. In addition to the Great Lakes, which border Canada to the north, notable lakes include the Finger Lakes in the center of the state, which is also the location of many gorges, and Lake Champlain, which forms part of the border with Vermont to the east. Noteworthy rivers in New York State include the Hudson River, which travels along the southeastern border to New York City, the St. Lawrence River, which separates the state from Canada on the eastern portion of the northern border, and the Mohawk River, which cuts through the center of the state on the eastern side.

New York has four distinct seasons every year. Winter lasts from approximately November through February and can see temperatures ranging from several degrees below zero Fahrenheit to averages in the forties and with several inches of snowfall. Spring can arrive in March or as late as May, with temperatures ranging from forty to sixty-five degrees. June, July, and August are the summer months, with temperatures ranging from an average of sixty to ninety degrees. Autumn is particularly spectacular in New York, with colorful foliage that begins turning in late September through mid-October, and sunny days and moderate temperatures in the sixties and seventies.

Peoples, Pre-1664

The area of North America that would come to be known as New York State was first populated by a Paleolithic culture from as far back as 5000 B.C., followed by Archaic cultures lasting until around 1000 B.C. Woodland native peoples arrived about the time of the fall of the Roman empire and lasted until about the time of the First Crusades, or about A.D. 1100. The Algonquin and Iroquoian cultures that flourished in the region when the first European settlers arrived had been there since about the twelfth century.

The Algonquin peoples, including the Raritans and the Delawares, lived near the coastal plains and shallow river valleys of the eastern regions. Algonquins usually lived near water, either the coastlines or rivers and streams, and ate fish and mollusks, with some plants in their diet. They collected shells, which they made into beads and sewed into ceremonial and historical keepsakes such as belts, known as wampum. Later, Europeans confused wampum with currency because it was valuable to the natives.

The Iroquoians lived along hills, in woodlands, along lakes, and in meadows in the interior of the state. They grew crops such as beans, squash, and corn, and hunted and fished in the forests and lakes. The Iroquois had an organized system of government made up of six member nations: Senecas, Onondagas, Cayugas, Mohawks, Oneidas, and later Tuscaroras. Each nation took its name from some physical aspect of its homeland or its place within the Iroquois League. The Senecas, for example, were "Keepers of the Western Door" because of their homeland at the western end of Iroquois territory, which would become western New York State years later. The Cayugas were called the "People of the Mucky Land" because of the marshy land around Cayuga Lake, one of the Finger Lakes. The Onondagas were the "People of the Hills" and the "Keepers of the Council Fire" because they ran council meetings and were located near the center of Iroquois lands. The Oneidas were the "People of the Standing Stone" and the Mohawks were the "People of the Flint." Within each nation, a system of self-government involved clans of families, which were headed up by the elder women of each clan and appointed leaders, or chiefs, called sachems. Clans, such as the Bear Clan, the Beaver Clan, etc., derived their names from the natural creatures or habitat where the nation of clans lived. When war broke out among nations threatening the way of life of all in the fourteenth century, a peace agreement was drawn up among them, forming what would come to be called the Iroquois League. This league would later become a model for the establishment of the U.S. Constitution.

Native legends described the formation of the league when a mythic figure and prophet, Deganawidah, sent Hiawatha to walk among the Five Nations and spread a message of peace, proposing an alliance. Fifty representatives from the nations were sent to a meeting called the grand council. Matters of interest and concern to all nations were discussed at the council meetings, and votes were taken to make decisions that would be binding on all parties. Sachems could only be removed from their responsibilities if they were proved to be incompetent by the elder clan women.

The Iroquois League is still in existence among the Native peoples who occupy reservations in New York State and Canada. Until the American Revolution, the League was a formidable force of military, political, and social resistance against European incursion.

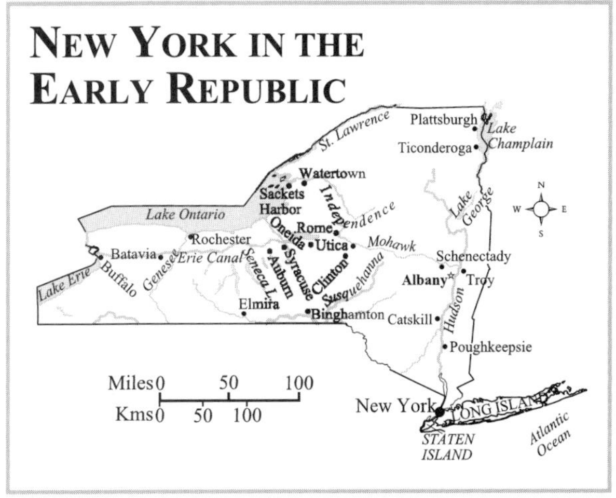

First Europeans and Africans

In 1524, the Italian explorer Giovanni da Verrazano, under commission of the king of France, sailed his ship the *Dauphine* near the coastline of what is now New York. He was the first European to see its shores. Although he dropped anchor off what is now Staten Island, he did not stay or claim the land for any colonizing power. A year later, the Portuguese explorer Esteban Gomes also sailed near, but did not make any claims. By 1540, fur traders were making their way up the Hudson to trade with the Native peoples in beaver fur; however, it was not until 1609, when the explorer Henry Hudson came to the area, sailed up the Narrows, and continued up the river to what is now Albany, that it was claimed for the Dutch. Later, the area was named New Netherland.

In 1624, the *Nieu Nederlandt* anchored in the East River, bringing the first European colonial settlers to New York State. Settlement, trade, and war with the Indians continued for some time. The Dutch brought new animals and diseases to the New York environment and fought many violent battles, particularly against the Algonquins and the Mohawks, for control of land. By 1650, under the leadership of Peter Stuyvesant, New Netherland had established itself as a growing and prosperous colony, which attracted more European settlers to New York's shores. Settlers from Portugal and many other countries left Europe for New Amsterdam, later called New York City, creating an early society of mixed cultures and backgrounds. By the middle of the seventeenth century, the Dutch had also brought African Americans to the area as slaves.

Events, 1664 to 1825

King Charles II of England authorized his brother, James, duke of York, to sponsor an expedition to seize New Netherland as a prize for England against the Dutch as well as for the promise of the colony's potential prosperity through trade. This was accomplished fairly easily, given the military superiority of the British, but for long into the eighteenth century, New York remained the least British in composition of all of the British American colonies. New Amsterdam became New York City and very quickly grew in prosperity as a port, even as early as the mid-1700s. At the arrival of the British, expansion moved westward, venturing into more of the Iroquoian territory. By 1775, clashes with the Mohawks were tempered by occasional treaties that aligned the British and the Mohawks against the revolutionaries.

New York experienced the Revolutionary War with perhaps the most violent and active engagements on many fronts and for a longer period of time than any other colony. The war in New York began 10 May 1775, when Ethan Allen, Benedict Arnold, and the Green Mountain Boys took Fort Ticonderoga; the war was also marked by important battles at Saratoga and General John Sullivan's invasion of Iroquois territory from the south. New York State ratified the United States Constitution on 26 July 1788 at the Dutchess County courthouse. The war brought to the attention of the British, New Englanders, and other Europeans the fertile wilderness of western New York, which changed quickly in character and settlement in the decades following the Revolutionary War. In 1825, Governor George Clinton's idea for a canal that would join the Great Lakes to the Hudson River and the sea and would move westward expansion even beyond the lands of New York State was realized when the Erie Canal was opened for trade.

Nineteenth Century: Abolition, Women's Movement, Civil War, and Immigration

While trade boomed with the opening of the Erie Canal, and New York City continued to increase in population, wealth, and power as a metropolitan and cultural center, New York State was also a focal point for social change including abolitionism, the women's movement, and the effects of the first massive influx of immigrants.

As the final stop for many runaway slaves before reaching Canada, Underground Railroad routes flourished throughout the state, particularly in the central and western regions, such as the Finger Lakes area. After escaping slavery, Frederick Douglass founded his newspaper *The North Star* in Rochester, and that city and other New York cities and smaller towns became hubs of discourse and activism against slavery. Harriet Tubman also settled in Rochester.

Not too far south of Rochester, in Seneca Falls, in July 1848, Elizabeth Cady Stanton and Lucretia Mott organized the first convention dedicated to women's rights. Adopting the Declaration of Sentiments they had written, modeled after the Declaration of Independence, the men and women who gathered at Seneca Falls advocated equal legal rights, property ownership, educational and employment opportunities, and voting rights for women. Meetings and speeches continued throughout the state, involving and elevating many women to national prominence in relation to the issue. Included among these were Susan B. Anthony and Amelia Bloomer, the editor of *The Lily*, a monthly temperance paper that also dealt with issues of importance to women. Bloomer also popularized a style of more healthy and convenient women's clothing comprising baggy pantaloons and overblouse, hence the later term "bloomers."

New Yorkers fought for the Union in the Civil War, most notably at the Battle of Gettysburg, some 200 miles south of the state line in Pennsylvania. Although most New Yorkers favored keeping the Union intact and supported President Lincoln, New York City became a hotbed of protests and speeches both supporting and opposing the war. Perhaps one of the most notable contributions New York made to the Civil War was the formation of the only entirely black Union regiment.

The great potato famine of the 1840s in Ireland resulted in a massive increase in Irish emigrants coming to the United States through the port of New York City. The influx grew and continued through the beginning of the next century, when millions of immigrants from Ireland, Italy, Germany, and the countries of Eastern Europe poured into the United States through Ellis Island. From the late 1800s through the early twentieth century, Ellis Island processed millions of immigrants into the country. Ellis Island was allowed to decline after limits were placed on immigration, but in the late twentieth century it was restored and opened to the public.

Twentieth Century

The rise of the stock market caused unprecedented wealth and power to emanate from New York City, resulting in what has been called the Gilded Age in the early twentieth century. Millionaires such as the Vanderbilts and the Roosevelts built mansions along the Hudson River the size and likes of which have rarely been seen since. As the upper class was gaining in wealth and political power, the lower classes were falling further into poverty, and the gap between the classes widened.

Industry thrived in New York State in the early twentieth century. New York City had major markets in finance, clothing, publishing, entertainment, and commerce. Institutions such as Madison Avenue's advertising center, Times Square, and Broadway's theater district took firm hold during this time. Ironically, skyscrapers and landmarks in New York City such as the Empire State Building and the Brooklyn Bridge were built in large part by descendants of the Mohawk nation that had been adversely affected by European incursion. The Mohawks had become skilled steelworkers, building bridges across the St. Lawrence River and other locations in the 1800s. Upstate, exploiting the railroad system as an active connection to the "Big Apple," as New York City was called, factories of glass and machinery grew and thrived. The state continued a significant agricultural business upstate as well, primarily in apples, beef, dairy products, and winemaking. The Great Depression hit New York State hard, as weaknesses in New York City's economy spread across the state. After World War II, the railways decreased in use, and this severed tie between upstate and New York City caused many smaller upstate towns to decline financially in the 1950s and 1960s. Politically, the divide widened even more as New York City became more liberal in its thinking and Democratic in its voting, while upstate dug in as a conservative, Republican stronghold.

By the end of the twentieth century, New York State was losing some of its political clout nationally. The 2000 national census resulted in the demotion of the state from second in electoral votes behind California to third, behind Texas as well. High state taxes drove many companies out of New York and kept many new ones from locating there. Family farms suffered from high costs and lack of federal support and many were forced to close. The suburban sprawl of chain stores and shopping malls drove commerce away from locally owned Main Street shops in upstate small towns. Tourism across the state remained strong, from Niagara Falls to Manhattan. The financial district in Manhattan also remained strong at the end of the century, enjoying an economic boom due to record-breaking stock market highs driven by hopes and prospects of the computer age.

In the final senatorial election of the twentieth century, New York State once again made women's history by electing Hillary Rodham Clinton, the former first lady of the United States, to Congress as its junior senator. This was the first time in the nation's history that a former first lady had been elected to public office.

Early Twenty-First Century

Nostalgia for the golden days of New York City and what the city has meant to the history and development of the United States on a national scale increased after the terrorist attacks on the World Trade Center on 11 September 2001. Two commercial jet airliners full of passengers on their way from Boston, Massachusetts, to Los Angeles, California, were hijacked and piloted by members of the Al Qaeda terrorist network into the sides of both Trade Center towers. (The Pentagon was also attacked, and a plane bound for the White House was downed by passengers in a field in Pennsylvania.) With nearly 3,000 dead in New York City alone, the attacks caused the most casualties of American civilians due to foreign action on American soil in the history of the United States. The terrorists clearly felt that the World Trade Center was a visible symbol of American financial strength and power throughout the world.

Visitors poured into the city to help first with the recovery and the rebuilding of the World Trade Center area in particular, then the economy of the city in general. The state economy continued to suffer as resources had to be diverted to rebuild the affected areas and support the affected families. Thus the cuts for education, libraries, and other social services throughout the state that had started in the 1990s continued into the start of the new century.

BIBLIOGRAPHY

Klein, Milton M., ed. *The Empire State: A History of New York.* Ithaca, N.Y.: Cornell University Press, 2001.

Snow, Dean R. *The Iroquois.* Cambridge: Blackwell, 1994.

Connie Ann Kirk

See also **Albany; Catskill Mountains; Empire State Building; Erie Canal; Hudson River; Lake Erie, Battle of; Leisler Rebellion; Long Island; Manhattan; New Amsterdam; New Netherland; New York City; New York Colony; Niagara Falls; 9/11 Attack; Patroons; Saint Lawrence Seaway; Saratoga Springs; World Trade Center.**

NEW YORK TIMES, newspaper and benchmark for distinguished journalism in the twentieth century, founded by Henry J. Raymond in 1851. In a crowded field, Raymond's daily found a niche among merchants and opponents of New York Democrats. It had ample capital, membership in the new Associated Press wire service, and a handsome building in lower Manhattan. The title read *New-York Daily Times.* ("The" was added and "Daily" was dropped in 1857; the hyphen lasted until 1896; a period survived until 1967.) The *Times* championed the Union and the unpopular draft during the Civil War. Raymond manned a Gatling gun from an office window at the height of antiwar feeling in the city.

The publisher, George Jones, continued to take risks after Raymond's death in 1869. The *Times*'s publication of extensive "secret accounts" in 1871 led to the fall of the city "Boss" William M. Tweed. In its first quarter century, the *New York Times* did not have the intellectual reach of Horace Greeley's *New York Tribune*; it was not as lively as Charles Dana's *New York Sun* or James Gordon Bennett's *New York Herald.* But the paper was known as a reliable and energetic paper of the ascending Republican Party. However, when Joseph Pulitzer (*New York World*) and William Randolph Hearst (*New York Journal*) reinvented the New York daily, Jones was unable to compete, and after his death in 1891 it was just a matter of time before the *Times*'s presses stopped unless new leadership was found.

The *Times*'s savior was the thirty-eight-year-old Adolph S. Ochs from the *Chattanooga Times.* In 1896 he purchased the failing New York daily for $75,000, using the money of wealthy Democrats who saw in Ochs a man who would sincerely defend "sound money" against the Populists. (The paper had first crossed party lines in 1884.) Ochs told New Yorkers that he would "give the news impartially, without fear or favor" and he branded the front page with "All the News That's Fit to Print."

Ochs's business plan was simple: spend money on quality and profits will follow. In the first twenty-five years of his management, the paper put 97 percent of what it earned back into the enterprise. His son-in-law and successor, Arthur Hays Sulzberger, placed news above extra revenue during World War II by limiting ads in the paper. A second Ochs principle was at work here: in contrast to modern corporate theory, family ties mattered. The line of succession in publishers was to Sulzberger's son-in-law Orvil E. Dryfoos, then to Arthur Ochs "Punch" Sulzberger, then to Arthur Ochs Sulzberger Jr.

"All the News That's Fit to Print."

The New York Times.

TITANIC SINKS FOUR HOURS AFTER HITTING ICEBERG; 866 RESCUED BY CARPATHIA, PROBABLY 1250 PERISH; ISMAY SAFE, MRS. ASTOR MAYBE, NOTED NAMES MISSING

Col. Astor and Bride, Isidor Straus and Wife, and Maj. Butt Aboard.

"RULE OF SEA" FOLLOWED

Biggest Liner Plunges to the Bottom at 2:20 A.M.

RESCUERS THERE TOO LATE

The Lost Titanic Being Towed Out of Belfast Harbor.

PARTIAL LIST OF THE SAVED.

CAPT. E. J. SMITH.

The *New York Times*. The newspaper's front page on the sinking of the *Titanic* in April 1912. © CORBIS

The family's paper expanded coverage as the United States became a world power, with uneven performance. The *Times* and its sister periodical, *Current History*, reported the concealed genocide of Armenians during the break-up of the Ottoman Empire after 1915. On the other hand, as the *New Republic* pointed out in damning detail in 1920, the paper's account of the civil wars following the Russian Revolution was "nothing short of a disaster." The depth of reporting during World War II set the *Times* apart from all rivals. The Truman administration trusted the paper and the reporter William L. Laurence with advance knowledge of the atomic bomb to be dropped on Japan. To critics of the Cold War, the *Times*'s relationship to the government was too close. The paper yielded to the Kennedy administration's request to report less than it knew about the pending Bay of Pigs invasion of Cuba in 1961; two years later, the publisher, Punch Sulzberger, stood up to the young president when he asked for softer coverage of American intervention in Vietnam. The paper became the leading "establishment" critic of that war, memorialized by its decision to print the PENTAGON PAPERS in 1971. This secret history of the war, assembled by the government, put the future of the paper at risk until the decision to publish was vindicated by a Supreme Court ruling on 30 June 1971.

In domestic coverage, the *Times* (especially its Washington bureau under James Reston) set an agenda for the nation's press. (A notable lapse was the Watergate conspiracy of 1972, where the *Times* played catch-up to the *Washington Post*.) After supporting the Republican president Dwight D. Eisenhower for his two terms, the paper settled into a pattern of Democratic presidential endorsements. General news coverage grew more interpretive, with a broader interest in social movements and mores. The paper was at the center of coverage of the civil rights struggle, for example, and *New York Times v. Sullivan* (1964) extended First Amendment protection. *Times* reviews had great impact on Broadway, where producers and actors believed the paper was the key to a long run. New voices came from the op-ed page, begun in 1970. Sections were added to hold upscale readers: "Science Times," "Weekend," "SportsMonday," "Living," "Home," "Circuits." Here the paper was learning from magazine pioneers such as Clay Felker's *New York*. The "old gray lady" was not literally that after 1993, when investments in printing allowed the paper to use color.

Religion and gender have frequently been cited in critiques of the paper. The Jewish identity of the Ochses and Sulzbergers explains little about news judgments. In coverage of the Holocaust and the formation of the state of Israel, for example, the paper did not step ahead of American public opinion. But patriarchy has been a powerful influence. Women from the families were not taken seriously as people who could lead the paper. Iphigene Sulzberger (Adolph Ochs's only child) made a key decision about succession, but no woman within the family was given the opportunity of Katharine Graham of the Meyer family, owners of the *Washington Post*. In 1974 women from both the editorial and business side sued the paper for discrimination. The *Times* agreed to an affirmative-action plan four years later in a settlement that was similar to agreements made by other large media companies. "Ms." as a term of address entered the *Times* style book in 1986.

No news enterprise has inspired more writing about internal dramas. Two books about the paper, *The Kingdom and the Power* by Gay Talese and *The Trust* by Susan E. Tifft and Alex S. Jones, are particularly well informed. Joined by *Times* writers such as William Safire, far-reaching debates about clear writing and thinking swirl around what the paper prints. With the success of its national edition (launched in 1980) and www.nytimes.com, a counterpoint to *Times* coverage and opinions occurs round-the-clock. The essayist Dwight Macdonald saw what lay ahead when he recalled that in the 1930s, "the N.Y. *Times* was to us what Aristotle was to the medieval scholastics—a revered authority, even though Pagan, and a mine of useful information about the actual world."

BIBLIOGRAPHY

Robertson, Nan. *The Girls in the Balcony: Women, Men, and the New York Times*. New York: Random House, 1992.

Rudenstine, David. *The Day the Presses Stopped: A History of the Pentagon Papers Case.* Berkeley: University of California Press, 1996.

Talese, Gay. *The Kingdom and the Power.* New York: World, 1969.

Tifft, Susan E., and Alex S. Jones. *The Trust.* Boston: Little, Brown, 1999.

Thomas C. Leonard

See also **New York City; Newspapers.**

NEW YORK TIMES V. SULLIVAN, 376 U.S. 254 (1964). Prior to *New York Times Company v. Sullivan*, libelous speech—speech that defames or slanders—was regarded as a form of personal assault unprotected by the First Amendment to the U.S. Constitution. Courts assumed that libelous speech injured, and merely "more speech" was an inadequate remedy, since the truth rarely catches the lie. Thus, in *Chaplinsky v. New Hampshire*, 315 U.S. 568 (1942), the Supreme Court ruled that libel was outside the scope of First Amendment protection because it was "no essential part in the exposition of ideas," and in *Beauharnais v. Illinois*, 343 U.S. 250 (1952), the Court concluded that libelous statements regarding a group were also unprotected.

In *Times v. Sullivan*, a watershed case in the history of the law of libel and a free press, a unanimous Supreme Court concluded that "libel can claim no talismanic immunity from constitutional limitations. It must be measured by standards that satisfy the First Amendment." Thus, for the first time since the adoption of the Constitution, the Supreme Court granted the press constitutional protection when sued for damages by public officials because of criticism relating to their official conduct. In *Times v. Sullivan*, L. B. Sullivan, a police commissioner of Montgomery, Alabama, sued the *New York Times* and four African American clergymen because of statements contained in a full-page fund-raising advertisement printed in the *Times*. The advertisement, which did not mention Sullivan by name, contained charges, some inaccurate, of police brutality and harassment aimed at civil rights protesters on the Alabama State College campus in 1960. Similar to many states, Alabama made a publisher strictly liable for defamatory falsehoods, and the state recognized no privilege for good-faith mistakes of fact. The jury granted Sullivan a $500,000 damage award which the Alabama Supreme Court affirmed. Although the outcome was in accord with Alabama law, many interpreted it to mean that the South was prepared to use the state law of libel to punish and stifle the civil rights movement.

In reversing the judgment, the Supreme Court stated that there existed a "profound national commitment to the principle that debate on public issues should be uninhibited, robust, and wide-open," and that such debate may well include "sharp attacks on government and public officials." The Court observed that erroneous statements are inevitable in a free debate and that they must be protected if a free press is to have the "breathing space" it requires to survive. The Court noted that although the constitutionality of the Sedition Act of 1798, which imposed criminal penalties upon those who criticized the government or public officials, was never tested in court, "the attack upon its validity has carried the day in the court of history." Because civil damage awards may be as inhibiting of free expression as the criminal sanction, the "central meaning" of the First Amendment requires that the amendment limit the potential devastating reach of a civil libel judgment. Accordingly, the Court ruled that a public official seeking a damage judgment because of a libelous statement critical of his official conduct could only prevail by proving, through clear and convincing evidence, "that the statement was made with 'actual malice'—that is, with knowledge that it was false or with reckless disregard of whether it was false or not."

The Supreme Court's decision in *Times v. Sullivan* has sparked many debates that still continue over its meaning and application. The Court's "actual malice" standard defies sound summary except for emphasizing that the term "actual malice" as used by the Court should not be confused with the concept of common-law malice that requires evidence of ill will or bias. Subsequent judicial decisions have parsed the meaning of who is a public official, what constitutes official as opposed to private conduct, who is a public figure, and to what extent the underlying meaning of *Times v. Sullivan* undermines a person's right to keep personal information private.

It is difficult to gauge, and perhaps difficult to exaggerate, the impact of *Times v. Sullivan* on protecting the mass media from damages arising out of defamation claims. Many criticize this development and point to mass-media abuses that allegedly needlessly injure individuals, erode civil discourse, and deter individuals from entering public life out of fear of having their reputations tarnished. Others applaud the development as essential to a vigorous and robust public discourse that strengthens the democratic process by providing the governed with critical information about the governors and their policies.

BIBLIOGRAPHY

Epstein, Richard. "Was *New York Times v. Sullivan* Wrong?" 53 *University of Chicago Law Review* 782 (1986).

Lewis, Anthony. *Make No Law: The Sullivan Case and the First Amendment.* New York: Random House, 1991.

David Rudenstine

See also **Libel; Mass Media; *New York Times*.**

NEW YORKER, THE. Harold Ross (1892–1951) founded The *New Yorker* as a weekly magazine in New York City in 1925. Ross had quit high school to become a reporter, and during World War I he edited the *Stars and Stripes*, a military newspaper. The *New Yorker* was his attempt to create a "reflection in word and picture of met-

Harold Ross. The founder of the *New Yorker,* and the guiding light of the witty, sophisticated magazine for its first quarter century. GETTY IMAGES

ropolitan life . . . with gaiety, wit, and satire." It was highly successful, weathering the Great Depression when many of its older competitors did not. Initially a humor magazine for urban sophisticates or those who wanted to become such, it dealt with social life and cultural events in Manhattan. The magazine quickly broadened its scope to include serious political and cultural topics, a shift in emphasis that became evident in the 1946 issue on Hiroshima, featuring an article by the novelist John Hersey. Under William Shawn, who took over as editor in chief in 1952, the *New Yorker* became known for its lengthy, probing journalistic essays while maintaining its stylistic flair and humor pieces. In 1987 Robert Gottlieb, a former book editor at Alfred A. Knopf and Company, succeeded Shawn. Tina Brown was brought on as editor in chief in 1992. Formerly the editor of *Vanity Fair,* which was seen as a more advertising-driven, less intellectual magazine, she was a controversial choice. The *New Yorker* had been facing some financial difficulties, and Brown increased coverage of popular culture, turned to slightly shorter articles, and revamped its look, changing the layout and including more color and photography. In 1998 David Remnick, a staff writer for the *New Yorker* since 1992, became its fifth editor in chief.

A typical issue of the *New Yorker* comprises "The Talk of the Town," short pieces written anonymously for many years by E. B. White; reviews of books, movies, art, music, and theater; a short story, poetry, and cartoons; and often a "Letter" from a foreign correspondent or a "Profile" of a person, place, or thing. Several times a year a themed issue appears, focusing, for example, on fashion or fiction. The *New Yorker* has attracted numerous writers, including James Agee, Hannah Arendt, Rachel Carson, John Cheever, Janet Flanner, Wolcott Gibbs, Brendan Gill, Clement Greenberg, John Hersey, Pauline Kael, Alfred Kazin, A. J. Liebling, Andy Logan, Dwight Macdonald, Mary McCarthy, St. Clair McKelway, Lewis Mumford, Dorothy Parker, Lillian Ross, J. D. Salinger, Irwin Shaw, John Updike, and Edmund Wilson. Poets such as John Ashbery and Ogden Nash and fiction writers like John O'Hara, S. J. Perelman, and Eudora Welty have contributed as well. The *New Yorker* cartoonists have included Charles Addams, Alajalov, Peter Arno, Rea Irvin, who created the first cover featuring the monocled dandy Eustace Tilley, which is repeated on every anniversary, Art Spiegelman, William Steig, Saul Steinberg, and James Thurber.

The *New Yorker* was aimed at an audience primarily made up of white, liberal, well-educated, upper-middle-class professionals. Unlike the *Nation, Harper's,* and the *Atlantic Monthly,* older magazines with a similar audience, the *New Yorker* was subsidized primarily by advertising, not subscriptions. The magazine has been known for its liberal, if privileged, politics. During the McCarthy era the *New Yorker* was one of the few magazines bold enough to stand up to the anticommunists in print, mocking the language of the House Un-American Activities Committee, lamenting the decline of privacy, and even suggesting its own "un-American" tendencies according to the restrictive definitions. White wrote about the silliness of the word "un-American."

Numerous anthologies have been made of the different departments in the *New Yorker.* Insiders, such as Thurber, Gill, Ross, Emily Hahn, and Renata Adler, have written books about the experience of writing for the magazine. Two late-twentieth-century academic studies attempt to examine its readership and influence. The *New Yorker* has become one of the most prestigious venues for short fiction in the United States and an influential voice in American culture.

BIBLIOGRAPHY

Corey, Mary F. *The World through a Monocle: "The New Yorker" at Midcentury.* Cambridge, Mass.: Harvard University Press, 1999.

Gill, Brendan. *Here at "The New Yorker."* New York: Da Capo Press, 1997.

Yagoda, Ben. *About Town: "The New Yorker" and the World It Made.* New York: Scribners, 2000.

Ruth Kaplan

See also **Literature: Popular Literature.**

NEWARK, New Jersey, is America's third-oldest major city (founded 1666) but among the country's smallest in

Newark. An aerial view of New Jersey's most populous city, which has seen numerous efforts at the start of the twenty-first century to bring the city back from a long period of severe decline and negative publicity. © CHARLES E. ROTKIN/CORBIS

land area: today it occupies only twenty-four square miles, of which nearly 75 percent are exempt from taxation. New Jersey's largest city, with a population of only 267,000 (in 2000), is the center of activity for an area of 2 million people spread over four counties. Since its founding it has had several forms of government including the original township, a charter from Queen Anne in 1713, a commission, and now a mayor-council government under which the city is divided into five political wards.

Four distinct periods characterize Newark's history. The first period belonged to the Puritans. Its merchants produced leather goods and quarried brownstone; its farmers worked their landholdings in what is today the Ironbound section and to the west along First and Second Mountains. The rise of industry and commerce in the nineteenth century marked a second era. From home or cottage industries, Newark produced fine silver and fancy chairs and cabinets, and within a half century it had become a major manufacturing complex. The rise of banks, insurance companies, and newspapers in the second half of the period marked Newark's commercial growth. In 1872, the city sponsored the nation's first Industrial Exposition to show the nation that it made everything from "asbestos to zippers."

Newark's third epoch belonged to the first half of the twentieth century and resembled a roller-coaster ride. The two world wars saw Newark's shipyards, plants, and factories feverishly busy, but Prohibition resulted in the shutdown of its breweries and the rise of organized crime, and with the Great Depression came the death of 600 factories. The race riots of 1967 severely damaged both the physical and emotional fabric of the city, and it was more than a quarter century before change for the better was noticeable.

No longer the city of the 1940s or 1960s, Newark has focused on developing a sophisticated transportation network, with its airport, monorail, extensive highway system, and construction of a light rapid transit system. Newark is also a university city, with five institutions of higher learning.

Newark's Cultureplex includes the Newark Public Library, Newark Museum, New Jersey Historical Society, New Jersey Symphony Orchestra, Newark Boys Chorus, Garden State Ballet, WBGO Jazz Radio, and several smaller art galleries. In addition, the city boasts two important concert halls—Symphony Hall and the New Jersey Performing Arts Center—heavily used by Newarkers and New Jerseyans alike.

BIBLIOGRAPHY

Cummings, Charles F., and John F. O'Connor. *Newark: An American City.* Newark, N.J.: Newark Bicentennial Commission, 1976.

Cummings, Charles F., and John T. Cunningham. *Remembering Essex.* Virginia Beach, Va.: Donning, 1995.

Cunningham, John T. *Newark.* 3d ed. Newark: New Jersey Historical Society, 2002.

Charles Cummings

See also **New Jersey; Riots, Urban, of 1967.**

NEWBERRY LIBRARY, in Chicago, Illinois, was founded in 1887 with a bequest of $2.15 million left by Walter Loomis Newberry, a Chicago businessman, to establish a public library. Since the Chicago Public Library had a circulating collection, the Newberry from its beginnings was a reference and research library with noncirculating materials. Early in the twentieth century, the scope of the Newberry became focused on the humanities, while the Crerar and Chicago Public Libraries concentrated respectively on science and social science. From the outset, collection development came from private funds and endowments. Grants from federal agencies and other sources support research projects and fellowships. Educational activities include an undergraduate research seminar program, faculty fellowships, and a variety of adult education courses. Research centers in the history of cartography, American Indian history, family and community history, and Renaissance studies, founded in the 1970s, continue to be active.

The holdings of the library in manuscripts, maps, microforms, and some 1.4 million books cover a broad range of western European and American culture and history. Strong collections include materials on the Americas, music, cartographic history, midwestern culture, the history of printing, and a range of other topics in the humanities. The extensive use of the collections in published research has made an invaluable contribution to scholarship and knowledge.

BIBLIOGRAPHY

Towner, Lawrence W. *An Uncommon Collection of Uncommon Collections: The Newberry Library.* 3d ed. Chicago: Newberry Library, 1985.

Wyly, Mary. "Chicago's Newberry Library—Independent Research Library and National Resource." *Alexandria* 7 (1995): 181–193.

Adele Hast

See also **Libraries.**

NEWBURGH ADDRESSES were two unsigned letters circulated among officers at the Continental Army's winter quarters in Newburgh, New York, after the British surrender at Yorktown in 1781. Both expressed the suspicion of many officers that the Congress would not settle their financial claims before demobilization. The first letter even urged direct action—an appeal from "the justice to the fears of government." Gen. George Washington, who was present in camp, denounced the call for direct action and urged patience and confidence in the good faith of Congress. Resolutions approving his counsel and reprobating the addresses were adopted. Maj. John Armstrong Jr., a young soldier on Gen. Horatio Gates's staff, later admitted to authorship of the letters.

BIBLIOGRAPHY

Carp, E. Wayne. *To Starve the Army at Pleasure.* Chapel Hill: University of North Carolina Press, 1984.

Royster, Charles. *A Revolutionary People at War.* Chapel Hill: University of North Carolina Press, 1979.

Charles Winslow Elliott / T. D.

See also **Pennsylvania Troops, Mutinies of; Revolution, American: Military History; Yorktown Campaign.**

NEWPORT, FRENCH ARMY AT. On 10 July 1780, a French fleet arrived off Newport, Rhode Island, in support of the American Revolution. Carrying 6,000 French soldiers under the command of Jean Baptiste Donatien de Vimeur, Comte de Rochambeau, the troops began to disembark the next day. Some 600–800 cavalrymen departed for Connecticut for the winter, and a part of the infantry traveled to Providence, Rhode Island. On 10 June 1781, the remainder of the French army left Newport by boat for Providence and then marched to Yorktown, where it participated in the siege that resulted in the surrender of Gen. Charles Cornwallis and the end of the war.

BIBLIOGRAPHY

Schaeper, Thomas J. *France and America in the Revolutionary Era.* Providence, R.I.: Berghahn Books, 1995.

Howard M. Chapin / C. W.

See also **French in the American Revolution; Revolution, American: Military History; Yorktown Campaign.**

NEWSPAPERS. The story of America's newspapers has been one of change. Newspapers have changed with and have been changed by their target readers, whether members of a particular ethnic, racial, or religious group; a political party; or society's most elite or poorest members. From the first American newspaper printed in 1690 through the beginning of the twenty-first century, when the United States boasted 1,480 daily and 7,689 total newspapers, the industry has sought always to appeal to Americans experiencing immigration, adjustment to a new land, acculturation, and stability. For the American newspaper the equation has been simple, change or die. Many have died.

Americans have started newspapers for many reasons, including to support religious or political beliefs, to express outrage over social issues, and simply to make a buck. For those newspapers to last, however, the one imperative was to attract readers. At its heart the U.S. newspaper industry was a commercial enterprise, and readers led to profits. For even those newspapers supported by special interest groups, like unions, religious or ethnic organizations, or political parties, the need to appeal to readers has been a constant.

Newspapers have evolved throughout the years so much that some scholars liken its progress to the natural sciences, a matter of evolution from one form into another. The earliest newspapers were simple affairs, often composed of only four small pages distributed to only a few elites in colonial New England's small cities. By the twenty-first century American newspapers offered more words than a novel, hundreds of pages, thousands of advertisements, and a circulation spanning the globe. Thousands of people throughout the world read online versions. Others, reminiscent of earlier newspapers, are simple sheets targeting small, often marginalized groups.

The American newspaper story has been filled with flamboyant figures, cultural changes, technological revolutions, and a brashness mirroring that of the United States itself. Newspapers swept west along with the settlers and helped turn small towns into cities. They thundered at injustice and battled the elite. They preached to the converted and to those disdaining their messages. They attacked minorities and were minorities' voices. They gave communities not only a place to read about themselves but also a place that turned the eyes of community members outward upon the world. The story of American newspapers is one of a window on life in America.

Getting a Foothold

The earliest-known newspaper, *Publick Occurrences Both Forreign and Domestick*, lasted only one edition. Benjamin Harris, who published it in Boston, on 25 September

1690, had neglected to get official permission, and perhaps worse, he printed news from the colonies, which disturbed colonial officials. It was banned. Fourteen years later the Boston postmaster John Campbell, who had been sending handwritten newsletters to a select few in New England, bought a wooden press, and the first successful newspaper, the *Boston News-Letter*, was born. His was more acceptable. He got permission from authorities beforehand and focused on foreign news. Published by authority of the government and reporting foreign news, it copied the British press, which was licensed and forbidden to criticize the government. But just as America was beginning to chafe under restrictive British rules in the eighteenth century, the young American newspaper industry became unruly as well. Papers were generally published part-time by printers, and publishers objected to the licensing requirements and prior restraints on publication imposed by the British rules.

The early years were marked by repeated disputes between publishers and authorities. Benjamin Franklin first became noticed because of such a dispute. His brother James Franklin had started the *New England Courant* in Boston in 1821, and Benjamin Franklin was apprenticed to him as a printer at age twelve. James Franklin, a fiery sort, was imprisoned for criticizing the governor, and at age seventeen Benjamin Franklin took over the paper while his brother was imprisoned. Benjamin Franklin later moved to Philadelphia and started a number of newspapers, including one in German.

Colonial newspapers were generally politically neutral, and some publishers did not want to offend anyone. Their news was that of interest mainly to the upper and middle classes, especially news from Britain and news of shipping. Publishers were frequently related to each other, and some had patrons, wealthy individuals who found it useful to sponsor a newspaper. Boston was the center of the early colonial newspaper world, but Philadelphia became a second center by the middle of the eighteenth century. American newspapers were urban institutions, and they spread with the growth of towns and cities. Thus they followed the urbanization of America. The first newspapers were centered in New England, then they moved into the South, then slowly they moved into the West. Publishers were mostly men, although Elizabeth Timothy took over the *South Carolina Gazette* in 1738, when her husband, Lewis Timothy, died.

In colonial America religion and religious leaders were influential, and they played significant roles in the early newspapers. Many newspapers were founded for religious purposes, printing sermons, supporting an immigrant group's religion, and performing missionary functions as with those printed to convert Native Americans to Christianity. New England's well-educated clergy promoted the press, although Puritan leaders often engaged in spirited debates with newspaper leaders. In truth these vigorous debates helped the fledgling newspaper industry become profitable in New England, and their absence is considered one significant reason that the newspaper industry grew more slowly in the South.

The colonial era was a time of immigration, and many immigrants spoke foreign tongues. Immigrants often settled in enclaves, distinct groups of one ethnic origin within larger settlements of different backgrounds. Immigrant enclaves found newspapers in their languages welcome aids in creating a sense of community, teaching newcomers how to adjust to this new culture, and bringing news of their compatriots both in America and in the Old World. Benjamin Franklin's *Die Philadelphische Zeitung* of 1732 was typical of the foreign-language press as it was located in a city with a sizable German-speaking population. Literate Germans dominated the foreign-language newspapers for a century and a half, although virtually every other immigrant group published newspapers in its native tongue. Among the first were French and Scandinavian language newspapers.

However, a German writing in English epitomized the growing dissatisfaction of American newspapers with colonial rulers. John Peter Zenger immigrated to America from Germany with his family in 1710 and was apprenticed a year later to the printer William Bradford in New York. After seven years Zenger started his own paper, bankrolled by a group opposed to the newly appointed governor William Cosby. One of Zenger's sponsors, James Alexander, wrote a number of articles recasting British libertarian thought, especially the need for freedom of expression, for the New World. The articles were published anonymously in Zenger's paper, and the editor was arrested in 1734 for "printing and publishing several seditious libels." He spent nine months in jail. At the trial Zenger's attorney argued basically that the articles were true. The prosecution correctly cited the law, which said truth did not matter. But a jury sided with Zenger, and truth as a defense persisted into the twenty-first century.

Newspaper disputes with colonial authorities were only one source of dissent during the middle of the eighteenth century. American newspapers began reporting perceived British injustices. When in 1765 the British Parliament passed the STAMP ACT, levying taxes on admittance to the bar, legal documents, business papers, and newspapers, many publishers abandoned political neutrality. Patriot newspapers, such as the *Boston Gazette* of 1755–1775, opposed Boston taxes and urged boycotts. It covered the BOSTON MASSACRE in 1770, when several Bostonians were killed in struggles with British soldiers. Not all newspapers sided with the colonies, but those remaining loyal to England suffered. For example, in 1773 the New York Loyalist James Rivington founded *Rivington's New York Gazetter*, which supported the British. He was embattled almost from the start and was jailed for a short time in 1775. After his printing house was destroyed by a mob on 10 May 1775, he fled to England, then returned with British troops. His Revolutionary War Loyalist newspaper, the *New-York Royal Gazette*, became synonymous with Toryism.

Following the Revolution the United States was a good place for newspapers. Advertising increased dramatically, and the excitement of a new nation led to increased readership. The new country's first successful daily newspaper, the *Pennsylvania Packet and Daily Advertiser*, started in 1784. More efficient presses lowered production costs, which led to a rapid increase in newspapers, especially dailies. Distribution was mostly by mail, and low postal rates helped. The increased importance of advertising was evident even in the names of newspapers. Twenty of the nation's twenty-four dailies in 1800 carried the word "advertiser" as part of their names. Even the government seemed to be on the side of newspapers. In 1788 the First Amendment to the Constitution aimed to protect the press. As the nation opened the West, newspapers went along and became local boosters of the frontier towns in Pennsylvania and Kentucky.

While the official name of the new nation was the United States, its citizens were anything but united in viewpoints, and the country became embroiled in a dispute over federalism. Political parties formed behind those wanting a strong federal government and those urging state sovereignty. Early debates over postal laws indicated that legislators recognized the effects of communication on modernity, and newspapers soon became leading weapons in the struggle. Both sides started or supported their own newspapers. The era was highlighted by partisan newspapers, like the *Federalist Gazette of the United States*, to which Alexander Hamilton was a frequent contributor, and the *Jeffersonian National Gazette*. One result of the struggle between the two factions was the Alien and Sedition Acts of 1798, aimed at silencing Thomas Jefferson's followers. One of the four laws, the Sedition Act, outlawed newspaper criticism of government officials and effectively nullified the First Amendment. Nearly 10 percent of existing American newspapers were charged under the act. However, it did provide for truth as a defense, thereby putting the Zenger verdict into law. The Sedition Act was allowed to expire in 1801, after national elections put Jefferson's party into power.

The first third of the nineteenth century was a time of expansion for the United States. The *National Intelligencer* was founded in 1800 as a paper of record, and it was the first to cover Congress directly. Newspapers changed their emphasis from advertising vehicles, although advertising was still a major part of their incomes. Most of their financing came from either political parties or circulation. Papers remained expensive, costing about six cents a paper. Only the mercantile and political elites could afford to buy newspapers. Ever catering to readers, editors focused on politics, business, and the comings and goings of ships in the port. Nevertheless many newspapers were feisty, fighting political or social battles. Not at all atypical of the time were lengthy attacks on immigrants, abolitionists, or black Americans, such as those in the *New York Examiner* in 1827 that led the Reverend Samuel Cornish and John Russwurm to found the nation's first black newspaper, *Freedom's Journal*. It lasted only a short time but was quickly followed by about thirty black newspapers in the next decade and even more as the abolition question heated up in the years preceding the Civil War. This lively press set the stage for the most dramatic evolution in American newspapers, the penny press.

The Era of the Reporter

The penny press derived its name from its cost, a penny apiece. It challenged the existing elite and the newspapers that served them by developing a new attitude toward advertising, cutting prices to become accessible to the masses, and by paying reporters to cover the news. Earlier newspapers had depended upon friends of the editor or publisher to provide news. The penny press revolutionized the way news was produced, distributed, and consumed. Due to faster presses and cheaper newsprint, penny papers cost less to produce. Advertising underwent a dramatic shift during this period. Previously those who advertised were those who read the paper, and advertising was seen as a mechanism for spreading information among an elite class. But the penny papers catered to the needs of all, and business advertised to inform readers about available products. These new newspapers were sold by street vendors one paper at a time. Thus the paper was available to all and needed to appeal to all for those sales. This led to a change in the kind of news covered. Readers wanted something other than strong opinions. With the rise in reporting, news became more local.

The first penny paper was Benjamin Day's *New York Sun* in 1833, quickly followed in 1834 by the *Evening Transcript* and in 1835 by James Gordon Bennett's *New York Herald*. The successful format spread quickly from New York to other East Coast newspapers and a bit slower to the West. But all followed Day's formula for success, that is, expanded advertising; low price to customers; street sales; new technology in gathering news, printing, and distribution; and paid reporters. Penny papers ushered in a lively time for the United States and for its newspapers, which experienced dramatic changes in technology, distribution, and format. Technological changes during this period included a steam-powered cylindrical press, much cheaper papermaking processes, the growth of railroads, and in the 1840s the advent of the telegraph, which directly led to the establishment in 1848 of the Associated Press, an association of New York newspapers.

Alongside the penny press arose an advanced specialized press appealing to special interests, such as those advocating the abolition of slavery, labor unions, and women's issues. Amelia Bloomer started the first woman's newspaper, the *Lily*, in 1849 initially as a temperance then as a suffrage paper. Others quickly followed. This era also experienced a growth in racial and ethnic newspapers. Virtually all these newspapers were published weekly, and their influence on their specialized audiences was great. Before the Civil War more than twenty black newspapers emerged, some edited by towering figures such as Frederick Douglass, who started the *North Star* in 1847. This paper lasted sixteen years, a long time for an abolitionist paper, during which the name was changed to *Frederick Douglass' Weekly*. The abolitionist papers published by both black and white advocates were among the most controversial. The abolitionist publisher Elijah Lovejoy of the *Observer* in Alton, Illinois, was killed by a mob in 1837. No counterpart for abolitionist newspapers existed in the South. Southern legislators had virtually banned comment on the slavery situation. The story was different in the West as the U.S. frontier expanded. Newspapers frequently were boosters of their new cities and often engaged in ideological battles, especially in "Bloody Kansas," split by the slavery issue.

All this was a prelude to the Civil War, which not only permanently changed the United States but also permanently changed American newspapers. The media had never covered a war before, and the emotional fervor of the war coupled with the increasing competitiveness of the nation's newspapers prompted a host of changes. The Civil War was the first modern war, and newspapers became modern as well. Major newspapers sent correspondents, a first, and the reliance on the telegraph led to two major developments in the way stories were written. The telegraph was expensive, so the writing style became less florid, using fewer words. The telegraph also was unreliable, which popularized the inverted pyramid style of writing in which the most important news is first in the story, followed in succession by less important facts. Photography, especially that of Mathew Brady, brought further developments, although it was a decade before photos could be engraved. Newspapers used Brady's photos as models for staff artists. Sometimes the heated competition led to bribery and fakery. At other times news correspondents faced heavy censorship. For instance, General William T. Sherman ordered the arrest and trial of a reporter, who faced the death penalty. General A. E. Burnside ordered the *Chicago Tribune* closed and prohibited the *New York World* from circulating in the Midwest, but President Abraham Lincoln rescinded the orders.

After the Civil War newspapers faced new challenges and opportunities. The pace of urbanization sped up, creating large cities and another spurt of immigration. Mass production replaced artisan craftsmanship, giving further impetus to advertising. Along with the nation, the news became bigger, more costly to report, and reliant on commercial advertising. Newspapers reflected city life, and publishers identified strongly with local business. Frequently publishers realized that extreme partisanship drove away valuable readers, and their political tones moderated.

Despite their growing numbers, immigrants and African Americans in the North felt left out of the competitive mainstream newspapers, which focusing on attracting the largest number of readers, appealed to native-born Americans. Consequently, these groups created their own newspapers. In 1870 the United States had 315 foreign-language newspapers, a number that grew to 1,159 in 1900, two-thirds of which were German. More than one and a half million German-language newspapers were sold in 1900, followed by 986,866 Polish newspapers, 827,754 Yiddish papers, and 691,353 Italian papers. More than one thousand black newspapers were founded between 1865 and 1900, but most quickly failed. Black newspapers took the lead in challenging the scaling back of Reconstruction in the South. The editor and writer Ida B. Wells, a former slave, documented lynching throughout the South.

In 1868 the Fourteenth Amendment to the Constitution enfranchised all men, including African Americans, but not women. This sparked a second wave of feminism, much of which was centered around newspapers edited and published by women. They were split into two factions, those concentrating on obtaining the vote for women and those seeking broad political and social reform. The latter group included the *Revolution*, started in 1868 by Susan B. Anthony with Elizabeth Cady Stanton as editor. As shown by its motto, "Men, their rights and nothing more; women, their rights and nothing less," the paper was radical. It lasted only two and a half years. On the other hand, Lucy Stone's more moderate *Women's Journal*, which was started in 1870, lasted until 1917 despite never having more than six thousand subscribers. These papers maintained pressure for woman suffrage until its eventual passage in 1920.

A short-lived agrarian press had more subscribers. But from its start in the 1880s it primarily served the Populist Party, and it died along with the party after the beginning of the twentieth century. A vociferously anti-urban press, it stood up for farmers' issues. The most notable paper was the *National Economist* with more than 100,000 readers at its peak. However, more than one thousand Populist newspapers spread throughout the nation's midsection.

By 1920 half of the people in the country lived in cities, where newspapers thrived. This was especially true at the end of the nineteenth century, when two of the most controversial figures in American newspapers took control of New York papers. They led a revolution in coverage and display that earned their style of journalism the sneering label of "yellow journalism" after a comic strip character, the "Yellow Kid." Joseph Pulitzer and William Randolph Hearst arrived on the New York City scene at a time when its mainstream newspapers were segmenting the audience by focusing on news of interest mostly to one type of reader. For example, the *New York Times* and *Chicago Tribune* appealed to the business classes. Hearst and Pulitzer's sensationalized newspapers were aimed directly at the working classes, adding to audience segmentation.

From its beginnings under Henry Raymond in 1851 the *New York Times* had grown in substance to become the newspaper most appealing to those wanting information. Pulitzer's *New York World* and Hearst's *New York*

Journal most appealed to those wanting entertainment. Pulitzer, who had started with a German-language newspaper and had merged the *St. Louis Dispatch* with the *Post* before moving to New York in 1883, added display flair. His newspaper emphasized sports and women's news, and he attracted good reporters, including Elizabeth Cochrane. Known as "Nellie Bly," Cochrane became famous for her stunts, such as rounding the world in seventy-two days, beating the time needed in the Jules Verne classic *Around the World in 80 Days.* Pulitzer's chief rival, Hearst, had turned around his family's failing *Examiner* in San Francisco and purchased the struggling *Journal.* Aiming at sensationalism of the highest order, Hearst raided Pulitzer's staff, including Richard Outcalt, creator of the "Yellow Kid" comic strip, and introduced color printing. The war for subscribers between Hearst and Pulitzer became sensationalized, and many blamed Hearst for the U.S. involvement in a war with Cuba. The rest of the nation's press splintered into two groups, those growing more sensational and those emphasizing solid reporting of the news. However, all were affected, and following this period multicolumn headlines and photographs became the norm for American newspapers.

By the beginning of the twentieth century many editors had college degrees and came from the ranks of reporters, not from the owner class. This led to an increase in professionalism, as did the general philosophy of the newspaper business that news was a separate division, funded by but not directly affected by advertising. Reporters, often paid on a space-rate system, earned salaries comparable to skilled craftspeople, such as plumbers.

World War I was an unsettling time for the industry. Foreign-language newspapers reached their peak in 1917, but wartime restrictions and prejudices hit them hard, especially those papers printed in German. They began a steep decline. The number of all newspapers peaked in 1909, when a total of 2,600 newspapers were published in the United States. Circulation continued to rise as the country became more urban. Newspapers had another war to cover, an all-out war that brought a rise in American nationalism. As has happened frequently when the nation was engaged in war, the federal government sought to control newspapers. The Espionage and Sedition Act provided a legal basis for shutting down newspapers. The former newspaperman George Creel directed the new Committee on Public Information and worked hard to determine what newspapers printed and omitted, relying generally on cooperation but lapsing into coercion when he felt he needed it. Socialist and black newspapers were particularly hard hit by government actions. Notably Victor Berger, editor of the socialist newspaper the *Milwaukee Leader,* was jailed. Because it refused to support U.S. involvement in the war, the *Leader* lost its mailing privileges, which crippled its ability to circulate and to gather news. Lack of support for the war effort, especially attacks on racial discrimination in the armed forces, created problems for black newspaper publishers as well. Creel believed those stories hurt the war effort, and in 1919 the Justice Department claimed the papers' racial stance was caused by Russian sympathizers.

Reflecting the great migration of African Americans from the rural South to the urban North, black newspapers achieved their greatest success in the first half of the twentieth century. The number of black newspapers rose from about two hundred in 1900 to a peak of five hundred by the 1920s, then the number began a slow decline to slightly higher than two hundred at the start of the twenty-first century. While most of these were small-town southern papers, in the 1920s four large black newspapers in the North developed circulations of more than 200,000, Marcus Garvey's *Negro World,* which lasted only from 1918 to 1933, Robert L. Vann's *Pittsburgh Courier,* Carl Murphy's *Baltimore Afro-American,* and Robert Abbott's *Chicago Defender.* The *Defender* was probably the best known of them, particularly in the 1920s. Abbott, who founded the paper in 1905, was one of the leaders in urging African Americans to move north. Some historians consider his newspaper, which was circulated throughout the South, one of the most effective institutions in stimulating the migration.

Newspapers in a Modern World

The year 1920 marks the line designating when a majority of Americans lived in urban areas. The United States was changing, and news adapted to the modern urban, technological, consumer society. The years since the era of yellow journalism's sensationalism had seen an end to the massive growth in the number of newspapers, although circulation continued to grow. The industry had stabilized, advertising had become national in scope, reporters were becoming higher educated and more professional, and the ownership of newspapers by chains and groups became more common, a trend that continued into the twenty-first century. Newspapers gained new competitors in broadcast media. Newsreels in theaters provided an alternative in presenting news, with moving pictures of events. The growth of the advertising industry pushed the United States toward a consumer society and greater use of brand names, and a professional public relations industry developed.

Newspaper content continued to evolve, especially in the 1930s. Competition pushed newspapers beyond presenting only the facts. Journalists sought to put facts into context. Newspaper content and style became interrelated, and the industry moved toward interpretation, photos, political columns, weekly review of news, and faster, more efficient technology in gathering, printing, and distributing news. Full-time columnists and editorial writers became more common. It was a time of journalism of synthesis, as newspapers attempted to add to the news via such techniques as daily and weekly interpretive news summaries, like the *New York Times* "Week in Review" section. Consolidation of mainstream papers continued, and President Franklin D. Roosevelt attacked what he called the "monopoly press." Roosevelt's antagonism toward the press had long-term ramifications as he started regular radio chats to bypass reporters. With the Great Depression afflicting most people, the alternative and socialist press thrived, especially social action newspapers like Dorothy Day's *Catholic Worker*, an influential alternative voice that actively opposed U.S. involvement in World War II, costing it much of its circulation.

The war emphasized some of the weaknesses and strengths of American newspapers. Their lack of coverage overseas left Americans unprepared for the strength of the Axis forces, and they have taken some justified criticism over the years for the lack of reporting on German restrictions on Jews during this period. But the war also emphasized newspapers' strength in their ability to change as needed. During the war the number of correspondents blossomed, and they reported in a vast variety of styles, ranging from the solid hard news of the wire services; through personal journalism like that of Ernie Pyle, one of an estimated forty-nine correspondents killed in action; to cartoonists like Bill Mauldin, whose "Willie" and "Joe" debated the war; to photographers like Joe Rosenthal, whose photo of the flag raising on the Pacific island of Iwo Jima symbolized American success.

Federal authorities censored and attempted to control newspapers, especially the black press, which had more than doubled its circulation between 1933 and 1940 to 1.3 million people. J. Edgar Hoover's Federal Bureau of Investigation (FBI) had monitored the black press since World War I and was concerned because it was becoming increasingly militant on racial matters. The growth of the big three black newspapers, the *Courier*, the *Afro-American*, and the *Defender*, changed the black press from small, low-circulation southern newspapers to mass-circulation, highly influential northern ones. During World War II the black press was investigated by seven government agencies, and an eighth, the War Production Board, was accused of cutting newsprint supplies to black newspapers. Wildly popular among African Americans was the *Courier*'s Double V platform, standing for "victory abroad [on the battlefield] and victory at home" over racial restrictions.

Much of the press faced a chill from government regulation and the public in the Cold War period following World War II. The SMITH ACT (1940), the nation's first peacetime sedition act since 1801, prohibited advocacy of the violent overthrow of the government. It was rarely used before 1949, when public opinion turned violently anticommunist. Twelve journalists were indicted. Many newspapers, now facing severe competition from television for advertising dollars, turned right along with the nation. Although a lonely few remained on the left, newspapers still attracted congressional anticommunist investigations. Though some questioned Wisconsin Senator Joseph McCarthy from the start of his anticommunist crusade, he easily manipulated most American newspapers and wire services. McCarthy followed a pattern of launching vague charges shortly before deadlines so they could not be questioned.

The growing disenchantment with newspapers by the public during the Cold War intensified during the tumultuous 1960s and 1970s as a generational divide among Americans was duplicated in newsrooms. Young reporters pushed editors to challenge authority on such controversial topics as civil rights, the counterculture, and antiwar activities. New forms of journalism included personalized and activist reporting, which led to even more public dissatisfaction with newspapers. The "new journalism" and criticism by government figures caused a steep decline in public respect for the media accompanied by circulation declines. In 1968 the pollster George Gallup reported that the media had never been as poorly regarded by the public.

Then came Watergate. The press reported events in the investigation of a break-in by Republican operatives at the Democratic Party national headquarters in Washington's Watergate Hotel that culminated in the resignation of President Richard Nixon in 1974, and public dissatisfaction with the press grew. Nixon's popularity had reached a peak of 68 percent after a Vietnam peace treaty was signed in 1973, and many Americans felt the media was out of touch.

The growing use of computers dramatically changed how newspapers were produced, with significant savings in labor and improvement in quality. Computers added depth to coverage and increased the use of color and graphics, especially after the 1980s. Serious reporting during Watergate was notable, as was the courage of the *New York Times*, the *Washington Post*, and the *St. Louis Post-Dispatch* in publishing the Pentagon Papers, a secret report detailing governmental decisions during the Vietnam War.

Continued newspaper consolidation coupled with more media companies going public resulted, in the view of many, in a thirst for high profit margins and caused continued concern in the industry, especially as the number of independent metropolitan dailies declined to fewer than the fingers on one hand by the beginning of the twenty-first century. Circulation actually was rising, but at a rate far less than that of the population. In an attempt to reverse the circulation weakness, the industry turned to consultants. A study in 1979 for the American Society of Newspaper Editors changed the kinds of news covered. It spotlighted as hot areas economic news, business news, financial news, health news, personal safety, technology, and international news. Many newspapers changed to include more of those areas, cutting coverage of more traditional areas, such as government. Other studies added to the changes in news focus, and the influence of market research reached its peak with the founding in 1982 of *USA Today*, a five-day-a-week national newspaper published by Gannett Corporation behind the guiding light of its chairman Allen Neuharth. Gannett's research indicated that readers wanted short stories that would not "jump" (would not continue on another page). Readers liked sports, charts, and graphs and wanted information presented in ways that could be absorbed quickly. The paper's success led many other newspapers, especially those with continued readership weakness, to copy the *USA Today* formula. After Neuharth's retirement, *USA Today* changed some of its emphasis and by the twenty-first century was garnering the journalists' praise that had eluded it earlier.

The new century found the newspaper industry in the same position as at the founding of the nation, facing uncertainty and change. New challenges to its prime product, news, came from the Internet and all-news cable television channels. Most newspapers established online publications, but as with the Internet in general, few had figured out how to make a consistent profit. Change started the newspaper story, and change ends it.

BIBLIOGRAPHY

Cahan, Abraham. *The Education of Abraham Cahan.* Translated by Leon Stein, Abraham P. Conan, and Lynn Davison. Philadelphia: Jewish Publication Society of America, 1969.

Emery, Michael, Edwin Emery, and Nancy L. Roberts. *The Press and America.* Boston: Allyn and Bacon, 2000.

Errico, Marcus. "Evolution of the Summary News Lead." Media History Monographs 1, no. 1. Available from http://www.scripps.ohiou.edu/mediahistory/mhmjour1-1.htm.

Fishman, Joshua A., et al. *Language Loyalty in the United States: The Maintenance and Perpetuation of Non-English Mother Tongues by American Ethnic and Religious Groups.* Hague: Mouton, 1966.

Folkerts, Jean, and Dwight L. Teeter Jr. *Voices of a Nation.* Boston: Allyn and Bacon, 2002.

Hindman, Douglas Blanks, Robert Littlefield, Ann Preston, and Dennis Neumann. "Structural Pluralism, Ethnic Pluralism, and Community Newspapers." *Journalism and Mass Communication Quarterly* 76, no. 2 (Summer 1999): 250–263.

Janowitz, Morris. *The Community Press in an Urban Setting.* 2d ed. Chicago: University of Chicago Press, 1967.

Kent, Robert B., and E. Maura. "Spanish-Language Newspapers in the United States." *Geographic Review* 86 (July 1996): 446–456.

Lippmann, Walter. *Public Opinion.* New York: Macmillan, 1922.

Miller, Sally M., ed. *The Ethnic Press in the United States: A Historical Analysis and Handbook.* New York: Greenwood Press, 1987.

Park, Robert E. *The Immigrant Press and Its Control.* New York: Harper and Brothers, 1922.

Reed, Barbara Straus. *The Antebellum Jewish Press: Origins, Problems, Functions.* Journalism Monographs, vol. 84. Columbia, S.C.: Association for Education in Journalism and Mass Communication, 1993.

Rhodes, Jane. *Mary Ann Shadd Cary: The Black Press and Protest in the Nineteenth Century.* Bloomington: Indiana University Press, 1998.

Schudson, Michael. *Discovering the News.* New York: Basic Books, 1978.

Simmons, Charles A. *The African American Press: A History of News Coverage during National Crises, with Special References to Four Black Newspapers, 1827–1965.* Jefferson, N.C.: McFarland, 1998.

Stamm, Keith R., and Lisa Fortini-Campbell. *The Relationship of Community Ties to Newspaper Use.* Columbia, S.C.: Association for Education in Journalism and Mass Communication, 1983.

Suggs, Henry Lewis, ed. *The Black Press in the South, 1865–1979.* Westport, Conn.: Greenwood Press, 1983.

———. *The Black Press in the Middle West, 1865–1985.* Westport, Conn.: Greenwood Press, 1996.

Wilson, Clint C., II, and Félix Gutiérrez. *Minorities and Media.* Beverly Hills, Calif.: Sage Publications, 1985.

Stephen R. Byers

See also ***New York Times*****; Press Associations; Publishing Industry.**

NEZ PERCE. The Nez Perces speak of themselves as Nimiipuu, "the real people," and are one of several Sahaptian branches of the Penutian language group found in the Pacific Northwest. They were called the Nez Percé or "Pierced Nose" Indians by early French and Anglo explorers because some of the tribe pierced the septum of their noses with dentalium, a custom more common along the Northwest Coast. Numbering between 6,000 to 8,000 when first contacted by Lewis and Clark in 1805, the Nez Perces located themselves at a crossroad between Plains and interior Plateau tribes, and thus had already been introduced to many material items of white origin by 1800.

The Nez Perces were friendly to white trappers. Some Nez Perce women married white or mixed-blood fur traders following the construction of Fort Nez Perce (later Walla Walla) in 1818 by the North West Company. After missionaries Eliza and Henry Spalding arrived in 1836 to live among the Nez Perces, nearly all continued to practice traditional religion and foodways, which integrated salmon fishing and camas gathering into a seasonal ceremonial calendar. These resources were supplemented with hunting of local game, especially deer and elk, and with procuring buffalo hide on biannual trips to the plains of Montana.

At the time of their first treaty with the United States in 1855, the Nez Perces were considered among the more cooperative people in the entire region. That atmosphere changed in the 1860s after whites trespassed on Nez Perce Reservation lands, establishing illegal gold mining camps and the supply center of Lewiston, Idaho, in violation of treaty provisions. This led to the Treaty of 1863, or the "Steal Treaty," signed in 1863 by one faction of the tribe, thereafter known as the "Treaty Band," under the United States' designated leader, Hallalhotsoot, "The Lawyer," who gave further concessions in 1868, reducing a land base of 7.5 million acres under the 1855 treaty to 750,000 acres.

Non-treaty Nez Perces remained scattered in the former reservation area under various headmen, among

Chief Joseph. A photograph of the leader of the non-treaty Nez Perce at the end of the group's extraordinary—but ultimately unsuccessful—walk toward safety in Canada, with U.S. troops in pursuit; he is perhaps best known today for his eloquent surrender speech. © CORBIS

them Tuekakas (Old Joseph) in the Wallowa Mountains of eastern Oregon. Following Tuekakas's death in 1871, Non-Treaty Nez Perces were pressured to move on to the diminished Nez Perce Reservation in Idaho. Violence escalated and when the murder of several Nez Perces went unpunished, young warriors determined to avenge the loss of their kinsmen, killing several whites in the Salmon River country. This led to an unofficial "war" in 1877 that escalated and eventually involved over 2,000 federal and territorial troops in pursuit of bands of Nez Perces not on the reservation. Led by warrior chief Looking Glass and guided by Lean Elk (also called Poker Joe), the non-treaty survivors were stopped after a heroic 1,500-mile trek through Idaho, Wyoming, and Montana. Only a few miles short of their goal of the Canadian border, the survivors stopped to rest and were confronted with superior numbers of U.S. troops. Upon Looking Glass's death in the final battle of the Nez Perce War at Bear's Paw, leadership was assumed by Hinmahtooyahlatkekht (Young Joseph), who surrendered, along with 86 men, 184 women, and 147 children, expecting to be returned to the Nez Perce Reservation. Instead, they faced incarceration on the Ponca Reservation in Indian Territory (later Oklahoma), remembered to this day as "the hot place" where all suffered and many died. A few, who had refused to surrender with Joseph, escaped into Canada with Chief White Bird, where they joined Sitting Bull's band of Sioux in political exile following victory at Little Bighorn the previous year.

In 1885, survivors of 1877 who agreed to convert to Christianity were allowed to return to Idaho; those who refused went to the Colville Reservation in Washington State. Struggling to the end for restoration of a reservation in the Wallowas, Joseph died on the Colville Reservation in 1904. By then, the official Nez Perce Reservation in Idaho had been allotted under the Dawes Severalty Act, which opened up "surplus lands" to non-Indian farmers in 1895.

During the twentieth century, Nez Perce men and women served in the U.S. Armed Services; many followed the lead of tribal member Dr. Archie Phinney and became professionals. Those in Idaho rejected the INDIAN REORGANIZATION ACT OF 1934, approving their own constitutional system in 1948 with an elected General Council that meets semi-annually. A nine-member elected body known as the Nez Perce Tribal Executive Committee (NEPTEC) makes day-to-day decisions and serves as the liaison with all federal agencies.

Enrolled Nez Perces numbered around 3,200 in the 2000 census. In Idaho, their political economy has benefited recently from the return of college graduates, tribal purchase of former lands lost during the Allotment Era, casino revenues, and an aggressive program in language revitalization.

BIBLIOGRAPHY

Gulick, Bill. *Chief Joseph Country: Land of the Nez Percé.* Caldwell, Idaho: Caxton, 1981.

Josephy, Alvin M., Jr. *The Nez Perce Indians and the Opening of the Northwest.* New Haven, Conn.: Yale University Press, 1965.

Slickpoo, Allen P., Sr., and Deward E. Walker Jr. *Noon Nee Me-Poo* (We, The Nez Percés): *Culture and History of the Nez Perces.* Lapwai, Idaho: Nez Perce Tribe of Idaho, 1973.

Stern, Theodore. *Chiefs and Chief Traders: Indian Relations at Fort Nez Percés, 1818–1855.* Corvallis: Oregon State University Press, 1996.

William R. Swagerty

See also **Indian Land Cessions; Nez Perce War.**

NEZ PERCE WAR, or Chief Joseph's War, was the result of efforts by the federal government to deprive the Nez Perces of their lands in northeastern Oregon's Wallowa Valley.

Title to Wallowa Valley lands was recognized in a treaty negotiated between territorial governor Isaac I. Stevens and the Nez Perces in 1855. The treaty was signed by fifty-eight Nez Perces, including tribal leaders Old Joseph and Lawyer, who were Christian converts. In return for a cession of land and the establishment of a reservation of about five thousand square miles, the Nez Perces were promised a monetary payment and goods and services from the government. They were also guaranteed the right to travel, fish, and hunt off the reservation.

The Nez Perces grew dissatisfied with the 1855 agreement. At a meeting in September 1856, Old Joseph and several other Nez Perce leaders complained to the whites that their acceptance of the treaty did not mean they had agreed to surrender their lands. Added to the tribe's dissatisfaction was the fact that the government had failed to render the promised services and payments.

Following the discovery of gold on the reservation in 1860, federal commissioners convened at Fort Lapwai in Idaho in 1863 to negotiate a new treaty that would protect the Nez Perces from an escalating level of white intrusion that threatened their grazing lands, while keeping the gold country open. The resulting treaty of 1863 reduced the boundaries of the reservation to about a tenth of its 1855 size, and the new reservation included primarily those lands belonging to the Christian Nez Perces, perhaps about three-fourths of the tribe. Moreover, the reduction of the reservation would exclude the tribe from the Wallowa Valley. The non-Christian bands refused to recognize the 1863 treaty, although they were given a year to settle within the boundaries of the restructured reservation. Old Joseph renounced his conversion, and anti-white feelings intensified, especially among those bands—called nontreaty bands—which rejected the agreement. They continued to use the Wallowa lands, despite growing white settlement there.

Pressure to give up more land continued over the next several years, while relations were strained further by the murder of over twenty Nez Perces by whites. Finally, in 1877, General Oliver O. Howard met with nontreaty Nez Perce leaders at Fort Lapwai in order to induce them to leave the Wallowa lands and return to the reservation. As the nontreaty leaders prepared to comply, some warriors attacked and killed a group of whites, and Howard responded by pursuing the so-called hostiles. The nontreaty Nez Perces resisted.

Led by Chief Joseph (the son of Old Joseph), the Nez Perces defeated Howard's troops at White Bird Canyon on 17 June, and conducted an inconclusive engagement at Clearwater on 11 July. Realizing he could not hold off the army indefinitely, Joseph, 200 warriors, and 350 women, children, and elderly opted to flee, beginning a remarkable 1,300-mile, three-month-long journey. Prevented from entering Montana by the Flatheads, and unable to persuade their old allies, the Crows, to join them, the Nez Perces decided their only alternative was to join Sioux Chief Sitting Bull, who had recently entered Canada. After an inconclusive engagement with troops led by General John Gibbon at the Big Hole River on 9 August and Seventh Cavalry forces at Canyon Creek on 30 September, Chief Joseph and his people were intercepted at Bear Paw Mountain, about forty miles from the Canadian border, by Colonel Nelson Miles. Surrounded, Joseph surrendered to Miles and General Howard on 5 October 1877 in order to save his remaining followers, some 400 in all. Most of Joseph's followers were sent to Oklahoma after their defeat at Bear Paw, but many would later return to the Colville reservation in Washington.

BIBLIOGRAPHY

Beal, Merrill D. *"I will fight no more forever": Chief Joseph and the Nez Perce War.* Seattle: University of Washington Press, 1963.

Greene, Jerome A. *Nez Perce Summer 1877: The U.S. Army and the Nee-Me-Poo Crisis.* Helena: Montana Historical Society Press, 2000.

Stadius, Martin. *Dreamers: On the Trail of the Nez Perce.* Caldwell, Idaho: Caxton Press, 1999.

Walker, Deward E., Jr. *Conflict and Schism in Nez Perce Acculturation: A Study of Religion and Politics.* Pullman: Washington State University Press, 1968.

Gregory Moore

See also **Indian Land Cessions; Tribes: Northwest.**

NIAGARA, CARRYING PLACE OF. Passage by water between Lakes Ontario and Erie being obstructed by Niagara Falls, a portage road between the lakes was constructed and maintained by the French in Canada. In 1720, Louis Thomas de Joncaire constructed and occupied the Magazin Royal, a trading house at the lower landing of the portage. In 1751, Daniel de Joncaire, succeeding his father, erected Fort Little Niagara to protect the portage road. On 7 July 1759, Fort Little Niagara was destroyed by its commandant when the British attacked to keep it out of their hands. After becoming masters of the portage, the British fully realized its importance. In 1764, they received from the Senecas the full right to its possession, and in 1796 they relinquished its control in accordance with JAY'S TREATY.

BIBLIOGRAPHY

Eccles, W. J. *The French in North America, 1500–1783.* East Lansing: Michigan State University Press, 1998.

Trigger, Bruce G. *Natives and Newcomers: Canada's "Heroic Age" Reconsidered.* Kingston, Ontario: McGill-Queen's University Press, 1985.

Robert W. Bingham / A. E.

See also **Fur Trade and Trapping; Niagara Falls; Portages and Water Routes.**

NIAGARA CAMPAIGNS. The American army's ill-fated invasion of Canada during the WAR OF 1812 touched off a series of clashes with British forces across the Niagara frontier. In October 1812, the Americans crossed the Niagara River and attacked the British at Queenston, opposite Fort Niagara, but retreated for lack of reinforcements. After Col. Winfield Scott captured neighboring Fort George in May 1813, the British were forced to abandon Fort Niagara, only to retake it in December. Now on the offensive, the British pushed south into American territory, defeating the Americans at Black Rock and burning that settlement and the village of Buffalo. After prevailing at Fort Erie, Chippawa, and the Battle of Lundy's Lane (which the British also claimed as a victory) in July 1814, the Americans withdrew to Fort Erie. In the last important engagement of the campaign, the British army's siege was raised 17 September by the sortie of Gen. Peter B. Porter's volunteers.

BIBLIOGRAPHY

Babcock, Louis L. *The War of 1812 on the Niagara Frontier.* Buffalo, N.Y.: Buffalo Historical Society, 1927.

Berton, Pierre. *The Invasion of Canada.* Boston: Little, Brown, 1980.

Graves, Donald D. *The Battle of Lundy's Lane.* Baltimore: Nautical and Aviation Publication Company of America, 1993.

Whitfield, Carol M. *The Battle of Queenston Heights.* Ottawa, Ontario, Canada: National Historic Sites Service, 1974.

Robert W. Bingham/A. R.

See also **Stoney Creek, Battle of.**

NIAGARA FALLS is a stunning 167-foot drop between Lakes Erie and Ontario, on the United States-Canada border. A major tourist attraction, it also generates huge amounts of hydroelectric energy. Composed of the American Falls and the Canadian, or Horseshoe, Falls, Niagara Falls obstructed early European navigation, and because Fort Niagara was extremely strategically significant, its portage road was precious to both Britain and France.

During the 1880s, a group of U.S. investment bankers formed the Niagara Falls Power Company and enlisted many eminent scientists and engineers for a hydroelectric project. By 1902 Niagara Falls power stations were producting about one-fifth of the total U.S. electrical energy. In the 1920s technological advances enabled the company to transmit power economically for hundreds of miles, in a large distribution network that established the pattern for twentieth-century electric power. Its abundant, inexpensive power also stimulated massive growth in such energy-intensive industries as the aluminum and carborundum industries. In 1961, after a U.S.-Canadian treaty increased the amount of water allowed for power generation, the Niagara Falls Power Company built a new, 1.95-million kilowatt plant. It was the largest single hydroelectric project in the Western Hemisphere up to that time.

BIBLIOGRAPHY

Berton, Pierre. *Niagara: A History of the Falls.* New York: Kodansha International, 1997.

———. *A Picture Book of Niagara Falls.* Toronto: McClelland & Stewart, 1993.

Irwin, William. *The New Niagara: Tourism, Technology, and the Landscape of Niagara Falls, 1776–1917.* University Park: Pennsylvania State University Press, 1996.

McKinsey, Elizabeth R. *Niagara Falls: Icon of the American Sublime.* New York: Cambridge University Press, 1985.

Robert W. Bingham
James E. Brittain/D. B.

See also **Canadian-American Waterways; Electric Power and Light Industry; Energy Industry; Explorations and Expeditions: British; Explorations and Expeditions: French; Hydroelectric Power; Tourism.**

NIAGARA MOVEMENT, a short-lived but influential civil rights group primarily organized by W. E. B. DuBois. The founding of the Niagara movement in 1905 marked DuBois's definitive split with Booker T. Washington, principal of the black Tuskegee Institute and considered by many the leader of black America. While Washington advocated gradual economic advancement at the expense of political rights for African Americans, DuBois agitated for total racial equality. After they quarreled repeatedly in 1904, DuBois called like-minded activists to a meeting in Buffalo, New York, to create a new organization dedicated to "Negro freedom and growth" and open dialogue, both withering attacks on Washington.

Thirty black intellectuals and professionals attended the first meeting, which was moved to Fort Erie, Ontario, Canada, because the Buffalo hotel refused to accommodate blacks. A "Declaration of Principles," composed at the first meeting, affirmed that "the voice of protest of ten million Americans must never cease to assail the ears of their fellows, so long as America is unjust." The Niagara movement was officially incorporated in January 1906. It would survive until 1910, publishing thousands of pamphlets that, along with the tightening Jim Crow regime in the South, undermined Washington's primacy and established DuBois's approach as the dominant civil rights philosophy for decades to come.

The second meeting of Niagarites took place at Harper's Ferry, West Virginia. Conceived as a celebration of abolitionist and insurrectionary leader John Brown, the event cemented the movement's reputation for radicalism. The 1907 meeting in Boston's FANEUIL HALL marked the height of the Niagara movement. Women sat in on sessions for the first time (though some men, led by the outspoken newspaper editor William Monroe Trotter, resisted), and 800 Niagarites representing thirty-four state chapters were in attendance.

Internal strife, however, had started to take its toll on the organization. Trotter and Clement Morgan, both friends of DuBois from Harvard University, fought bitterly in 1907 over the Massachusetts gubernatorial election, and Trotter eventually left the Niagara movement to form his own Negro-American Political League, and later, the National Equal Rights League. The Niagara movement conferences in 1908 and 1909 were poorly attended.

The National Association for the Advancement of Colored People (NAACP), formed over the course of 1909 and 1910, never formally absorbed the Niagara movement, but it informally adopted most of its points of view. At first, the NAACP's white founders clashed over how interracial and radical the organization should be, but when DuBois was hired for a salaried position, it was clear that the conservatives had lost. DuBois sent a circular to members of the sagging Niagara movement in 1911, announcing that the annual meeting was cancelled and asking them to join the new organization. Most of them did. In his career as editor of the NAACP's magazine, *The Crisis*, DuBois built on the propaganda work begun by the Niagara movement.

BIBLIOGRAPHY

DuBois, W. E. B. *The Autobiography of W. E. B. DuBois: A Soliloquy on Viewing My Life From the Last Decade of its First Century.* New York: International Publishers, 1968.

Fox, Stephen R. *The Guardian of Boston: William Monroe Trotter.* New York: Atheneum, 1970.

Lewis, David L. *W. E. B. DuBois: Biography of a Race.* New York: Holt, 1993.

Jeremy Derfner

See also **Civil Rights Movement; Discrimination: Race; Jim Crow Laws; *Souls of Black Folk*.**

NIBLO'S GARDEN was a famous nineteenth-century coffeehouse and theater on lower Broadway Avenue in New York City. Operas, concerts, and plays were presented there for several decades beginning in 1824. The 1866 opening of Charles M. Barras's *The Black Crook* at Niblo's Garden is considered by some to have been the first performance of an American musical. The structure was destroyed by fire in 1846, but it was rebuilt, and the new theater opened in 1849. It burned again in 1872, was rebuilt, and was transformed into a concert hall. The building was finally demolished in 1895.

BIBLIOGRAPHY

Stokes, Isaac N. P. *The Iconography of Manhattan Island, 1498–1909.* New York: Arno Press, 1967.

Alvin F. Harlow / D. B.

See also **Music: Classical, Early American, Theater and Film; Opera; Theater.**

NICARAGUA, RELATIONS WITH. Nicaragua's 1838 declaration of independence from the United Provinces of Central America was originally of little interest to U.S. officials. Yet by the late 1840s, growing interest in building a transoceanic canal across Central America caused American diplomats to devote closer scrutiny to Nicaragua. American officials quickly identified rising British influence in Nicaragua as a major obstacle to U.S. control of an isthmian canal. Yet since both Washington and London concluded that achieving supremacy in Central America was not worth an armed conflict, both nations agreed to joint control of a future canal by signing the Clayton-Bulwer Treaty in 1850.

As the debate over slavery expansion in the United States became more contentious during the 1850s, individual American adventurers, called filibusters, attempted to conquer parts of Central America and turn them into new slaveholding states. In Nicaragua, the site of sporadic warfare since independence, one political faction recruited the filibuster William Walker to Nicaragua in 1855, only to see Walker push it aside, declare himself president, and legalize slavery. Walker, who enjoyed the unofficial support of the American President Franklin Pierce, quickly alienated neighboring Central American leaders, the powerful financier Cornelius Vanderbilt, and most Nicaraguans, who together forced Walker to flee Nicaragua in 1857.

The birth of the Nicaraguan coffee industry in the 1860s fueled an economic boom that financed many improvements in transportation, communication, and education. Although the rise of the coffee economy also exacerbated poverty and widened the gap between rich and poor, Nicaraguan elites viewed the future with optimism, expecting that an American-financed isthmian canal would further accelerate Nicaragua's economic progress. Unsurprisingly, U.S.-Nicaraguan relations soured after Washington selected Panama as the site for an isthmian canal in 1903. When the Nicaraguan president José Santos Zelaya decided to attract non-American capital to finance a Nicaraguan canal, U.S. officials supported an anti-Zelaya coup in 1909. But the new government, lacking both political clout and popularity, soon turned to its American patron for support. At the request of the Nicaraguan government, the United States invaded Nicaragua in 1912, crushed the antigovernment insurgency, assumed control of Nicaraguan customs, and began a military occupation that would last intermittently until 1933.

In response to renewed violence in Nicaragua in 1927, the American diplomat Henry Stimson negotiated a peace settlement acceptable to all, save for the highly nationalistic Augusto Sandino, who recruited a peasant army and spent the next five years fighting a guerilla insurgency against the American marines. In 1933, the marines withdrew in favor of the National Guard, a native police force trained by American officials to provide internal security and political stability to Nicaragua. U.S. officials hoped that the guard would function apolitically, but Anastasio

Somoza García, the commander of the guard, instead used his position to assassinate Sandino, his main rival, in 1934. Somoza proceeded to use the National Guard to create a political dictatorship and amass considerable personal wealth.

Although many American officials frowned upon Somoza's corrupt and authoritarian regime, they nevertheless supported him because he created a stable environment for U.S. investments and opposed communism. After Somoza was assassinated in 1956, the United States continued to support his sons Luis and Anastasio, who continued both the family dynasty and the low living standards and political repression that characterized it. Opponents of the regime founded the National Sandinista Liberation Front (FSLN or Sandinistas) in 1961, but the Sandinistas remained isolated and ineffective until the 1970s, when rampant government corruption and the increasingly violent suppression of opposition leaders turned many urban, middle-class Nicaraguans against the government.

President Jimmy Carter spent the late 1970s searching desperately for an alternative to Somoza, yet determined to prevent a Sandinista victory. After the FSLN took power on 17 July 1979, the Carter administration shifted tactics and attempted to steer the new revolutionary junta toward moderate policies. But the defection of prominent moderates from the revolutionary junta, the postponement of national elections, and the FSLN's support of leftist rebels in El Salvador ensured the hostility of Ronald Reagan, the winner of the 1980 presidential election. Shortly after assuming office, Reagan approved plans to sponsor an opposition army, known as the Contras, to overthrow the Sandinista government. The U.S. Congress, fearing that these policies would invite a replay of the Vietnam War, responded in June 1984 by prohibiting all lethal aid to the Contras. The debate over Contra aid, a hotly contested and controversial issue during the mid-1980s, culminated in a major political scandal after revelations in late 1986 that Lieutenant Colonel Oliver North and a small cadre of officials had secretly and illegally diverted funds from Iranian arms sales to the Contras.

Although the Sandinistas still controlled Nicaragua when Reagan left office in 1989, the Contra war left Nicaragua war-weary and economically devastated. Sandinista leaders subsequently agreed to free elections in 1990 as part of a broader peace initiative proposed by the Costa Rican President Oscar Arias. To the surprise of many, the opposition leader Violeta Chamorro defeated the Sandinistas on a platform of restoring a free market economy and liberal democracy. Although U.S. officials widely approved of these developments, American entrepreneurs have yet to match Washington's political endorsement with their own, as ongoing conflicts regarding the ownership of property confiscated by the Sandinistas during the 1980s have led U.S. investors to avoid the country.

BIBLIOGRAPHY

LaFeber, Walter. *Inevitable Revolutions: The United States in Central America.* 2d ed. New York: Norton, 1993.

Langley, Lester D., and Thomas Schoonover. *The Banana Men: American Mercenaries and Entrepreneurs in Central America, 1880–1930.* Lexington: University Press of Kentucky, 1995.

Pastor, Robert A. *Condemned to Repetition: The United States and Nicaragua.* Princeton, N.J.: Princeton University Press, 1987.

Schoonover, Thomas. *The United States in Central America, 1860–1911: Episodes of Social Imperialism in the World System.* Durham, N.C.: Duke University Press, 1991.

H. Matthew Loayza

See also **Iran-Contra Affair; Nicaraguan Canal Project.**

NICARAGUAN CANAL PROJECT. A U.S. Army regiment sent in 1887 to survey Nicaragua as a possible site for a canal across Central America reported that it was possible to build a sea-level canal using the San Juan River and Lake Nicaragua for much of the canal's length. In 1889, Congress authorized J. P. Morgan's Maritime Canal Company to build the canal, and construction began. In 1893, the stock market crashed and an economic depression began, causing the Maritime Canal Company to lose its financial support.

The Isthmian Canal Commission, appointed in 1899, again reported that Nicaragua was the best place for the canal, and President William McKinley apparently planned to sign the authorization but was assassinated 6 September 1901. His successor, Theodore Roosevelt was persuaded that Panama was a more suitable site.

BIBLIOGRAPHY

Cameron, Ian. *The Impossible Dream: The Building of the Panama Canal.* London: Hodder and Stoughton, 1971.

Folkman, David I. *The Nicaragua Route.* Salt Lake City: University of Utah Press, 1972.

Kamman, William. *A Search for Stability: United States Diplomacy toward Nicaragua, 1925–1933.* Notre Dame, Ind.: University of Notre Dame Press, 1968.

Kirk H. Beetz

See also **Panama Canal.**

NICKELODEON, an early type of motion picture theater, so named for its five-cent admission price. ("Odeon" is derived from a Greek term for theater.) Nickelodeons were preceded by penny arcades, where patrons peered through viewers at short moving pictures. The arrival of narrative-style films, like Edwin Porter's famous 12-minute *The Great Train Robbery* (1903), created the need for a new form of presentation. The name "nickelodeon" is usually credited to entrepreneurs John Harris and Harry Davis, who in 1905 opened a simple theater in Pittsburgh where projected films were accompanied by piano. By 1910, thousands of nickelodeons had appeared nationwide, many of them little more than converted storefronts with wooden benches for seating. Nickelodeons often repeated the same films all day and evening, and were popular with working-class patrons who could not afford live theater, the leading entertainment of the day. The success of nickelodeons increased demand for more and better movies, leading in turn to the creation of new motion picture studios and helping establish film as a mass entertainment medium. Ironically, that rising popularity led to the end of nickelodeons, as they were replaced by larger, custom-built movie theaters. "Nickelodeon" later also became a term for a coin-operated musical jukebox.

BIBLIOGRAPHY

Bowers, Q. David. *Nickelodeon Theaters and Their Music.* Vestal, N.Y.: Vestal Press,1986.

Mast, Gerald, and Bruce F. Kawin. *A Short History of the Movies.* 7th ed. Boston: Allyn and Bacon, 1999. For scholars and serious buffs.

Naylor, David. *Great American Movie Theaters.* Washington, D.C.: Preservation Press, 1987.

Ryan F. Holznagel

See also **Film.**

NICOLET, EXPLORATIONS OF. Jean Nicolet de Belleborne became an interpreter, clerk, and trader in New France, as well as an explorer. The son of a royal postal messenger, he was born about 1598 near Cherbourg, Normandy. His colonial career seems to have begun in earnest in 1619/20, when he was sent to Canada by the Rouen and Saint-Malo Company, possibly after a brief initial visit in 1618. According to the Jesuits, with whom he had close ties—and who would eulogize him in glowing terms in their *Relations*—his good character and excellent memory impressed those with influence in the colony. Samuel de Champlain, the de facto governor, soon dispatched Nicolet to winter among the Kichesipirini Algonquins, who occupied Allumette Island (near Pembroke, Ontario) and levied tolls on the Ottawa River trade route. Here the future interpreter began to familiarize himself with the Algonquins.

After a stay of two years, Nicolet moved closer to Lake Huron to live among the Nipissings, a neighbouring Algonquian people, engaging in trade and participating in Nipissing councils. This last honor would have reflected his status as Champlain's representative as well as his own growing diplomatic experience. In 1634, Nicolet was sent on a combined peace mission and exploratory voyage to the upper Great Lakes. Like the rest of Nicolet's career, this expedition is poorly documented, and scholars disagree over his precise destination and the parties to the negotiations.

Nicolet visited the Winnebagos, most likely in the Green Bay region of Wisconsin, and negotiated an end to hostilities between them and a neighboring Native American nation. While it lasted, the peace favored an expansion of the fur trade. Officials seem to have pinned high hopes on Nicolet the explorer, providing him with an embroidered Chinese robe to impress his hosts, who had been described to the French as "people of the sea" (the sea being, it was hoped, the Pacific). Nicolet stayed only briefly in the region, but he brought back information that, while scarcely clarifying official French geography of the Upper Lakes, confirmed that the Pacific and China lay farther west than some had thought. His visit must also have increased the Winnebagos' knowledge of the French, once they had gotten over their astonishment at their elaborately-dressed, pistol-packing visitor.

After being recalled from his duties among the Nipissings—possibly because the Jesuits judged the presence of interpreters in the region disruptive of their Huron mission—Nicolet was named clerk and Algonquian interpreter for the Company of New France at Trois-Rivières. Apparently already the father of a Nipissing woman's child, in 1637, Nicolet married Marguerite Couillard, the daughter of a well-connected colonial family.

In October 1642, the interpreter drowned in the St. Lawrence, just upstream from Quebec, when the boat taking him on a diplomatic errand to Trois-Rivières capsized. A skillful negotiator with Native people and with influential members of colonial society, Nicolet is representative of a handful of able intermediaries who helped shape Franco-Native relations in New France's early years. In the process, he explored both Native territory and Native culture.

BIBLIOGRAPHY

Hamelin, Jean. "Nicollet de Belleborne, Jean." *Dictionary of Canadian Biography: 1000–1700.* Toronto: University of Toronto Press, 1981.

Heidenreich, Conrad. "Early French Exploration in the North American Interior." In *North American Exploration: A Continent Defined.* Edited by John Logan Allen. Lincoln: University of Nebraska Press, 1997.

Trigger, Bruce. *The Children of Aataentsic. A History of the Huron People to 1660.* Montreal: McGill-Queen's University Press, 1976.

Thwaites, Reuben Gold, ed. *The Jesuit Relations and Allied Documents: 1642–1643.* Vol. 23. Cleveland, Ohio: Burrows Brothers, 1896/1901.

Trudel, Marcel. *Histoire de la Nouvelle-France: Le comptoir.* Montreal: Fides, 1966.

———. *Histoire de la Nouvelle-France: La seigneurie des Cent-Associés: La société.* Montreal: Fides, 1983.

Thomas Wien

See also **Huron/Wyandot; New France; Winnebago/Ho-Chunk.**

NICOLLS' COMMISSION. In 1664 King Charles II of England determined to seize NEW NETHERLAND in order to eliminate the Dutch as an economic and political competitor in the region. He also intended to turn over the Dutch colony, once conquered, to his younger brother James Stuart, the duke of York, as a proprietary colony. To accomplish this he sent a military expedition comprised of four warships carrying three hundred soldiers. At the head of this expedition was Colonel Richard Nicolls. In anticipation of success the king also named Nicolls head of a commission of four to visit New England. This commission was to investigate boundary disputes, the state of defenses, laws passed during the Puritan revolution, attitude toward the recently enacted Navigation Acts, and was to report back on the general state of New England. As they moved from place to place, the commissioners were to hear complaints and appeals and to make such decisions as they deemed necessary. Their private instructions were to clear the way for a peaceful transition to English rule and to make it clear that freedom of conscience would be respected. The king also enjoined the commissioners to persuade those colonies to consent to the king's nominating or approving their governors. Although New England received the commissioners respectfully, the local authorities, particularly in Massachusetts, opposed them at every turn. In their final report they listed numerous irregularities occurring in Massachusetts and described a defiant and arrogant attitude that promised little hope of an amicable settlement of a unified and consistent colonial policy in New England.

BIBLIOGRAPHY

Rink, Oliver. *Holland on the Hudson: An Economic and Social History of Dutch New York*. Ithaca, N.Y.: Cornell University Press, 1986.

Taylor, Alan. *American Colonies*. New York: Viking, 2001.

Faren Siminoff

NIGHTCLUBS. In the United States and in much of the world, the term "nightclub" denotes an urban entertainment venue, generally featuring music, sometimes a dance floor, and food and drink. With nineteenth-century roots in the European cabaret, the nightclub evolved in the United States in the early twentieth century along with the popular music forms of RAGTIME and JAZZ, as well as modern social dance, and an urban nightlife centered on heterosexual dating. Nightclubs eventually incorporated features of turn-of-the-century restaurants (particularly the "lobster palace"), cafes, dance halls, cabarets, and vaudeville theaters. The term "club" became attached to American cafés during PROHIBITION in the 1920s and the development of so-called private "clubs," which supposedly deflected scrutiny by liquor law enforcers.

The growth of American nightclubs came in the mid-1920s and through the early Depression years. The popular clubs combined illicit liquor and lively music often available all night. Pre–World War II nightclubs promoted new music, musicians, and dance styles; became a staging ground for interracial contests and observation; and helped foster integration. The dominance of ragtime between 1890 and 1910, the emergence of southern African American blues forms after the turn of the century, and the northward migration of New Orleans jazz marked an immense historical shift in the sources and acknowledged masters of American popular music. Creative white musicians could no longer avoid reckoning with African American musicians.

White-owned cabarets, theatres, and clubs remained segregated into the 1950s. In the 1920s, "slumming" became a popular, somewhat daring pastime among urban whites, who would travel uptown to Harlem after hours for the music, food, and excitement. Many visited large, fancy clubs like Connie's Inn and the Cotton Club, both white, gangster-controlled clubs that featured black musicians playing to white-only audiences. Other whites sought out the smaller African American clubs like Pods and Jerry's Log Cabin, where Billie Holiday began singing. Harlem's club heyday lasted into the 1930s, and then succumbed to violent organized crime and expanding opportunities for black musicians and workers in neighborhoods beyond Harlem. As musical tastes have changed, so have American nightclubs' entertainment rosters. Big bands and swing combos dominated nightclub entertainment in the 1930s and 1940s. In the 1950s, clubs' tendency to specialize was exacerbated with the emergence of bebop, rhythm and blues, and then ROCK AND ROLL. Las Vegas casinos offered lavish clubs with headliners that might find a loyal following over decades. The male entertainers of the "Rat Pack" (Frank Sinatra, Dean Martin, Sammy Davis, Jr., and Peter Lawford) offer just one example of this kind of act. The folk "revival" found a home in certain clubs of San Francisco, Greenwich Village, and Cambridge, Massachusetts, in the early 1960s. Rock became the dominant, but not the only, popular form of musical entertainment in the later 1960s. Disco music emerged simultaneously with the rapid growth of openly gay nightclubs in the post-Stonewall era of the 1970s, though disco's constituency cut across sexual, racial, and class lines. Hosting disk jockeys and reducing the stage to expand the dance floor attracted club owners looking to maximize their profits. The 1980s and 1990s saw a renewed focus on live entertainment with new as well as older forms of popular music.

BIBLIOGRAPHY

Erenberg, Lewis A. *Steppin' Out: New York Nightlife and the Transformation of American Culture, 1890–1930*. Westport, Conn.: Greenwood Press, 1981.

Kenney, William Howland. *Chicago Jazz. A Cultural History 1904–1930*. New York: Oxford University Press, 1993.

Ward, Geoffrey C. *Jazz: A History of America's Music*. New York: Knopf, 2000.

Mina Julia Carson

See also **Harlem Renaissance; Jazz Age.**

9/11 ATTACK. On Tuesday, 11 September 2001, nineteen members of the Islamic terrorist group Al Qaeda perpetrated a devastating, deadly assault on the United States, crashing airplanes into the Pentagon and the World Trade Center, killing thousands. The attacks shattered Americans' sense of security, threw the nation into a state of emergency, and triggered a months-long war in Afghanistan and an extended worldwide "war on terrorism."

On the morning of 11 September, four teams of terrorists hijacked jetliners departing from Boston; Newark, New Jersey; and Washington, D.C. Once airborne, the terrorists, some of whom had gone to flight school in the United States, murdered the planes' pilots and took control of the aircrafts. At 8:46 A.M., the first plane flew directly into the north tower of the World Trade Center in southern Manhattan, tearing a gaping hole in the building and setting it ablaze. Seventeen minutes later, a second plane flew into the center's south tower, causing similar damage. At 9:43 A.M., a third plane plunged into the Pentagon in Virginia, smashing one wing of the government's military headquarters. The fourth plane appeared headed for Washington, D.C., but at 10:10 A.M. it crashed in western Pennsylvania, apparently after passengers, who had learned of the other attacks through conversations on their cellular phones, rushed the terrorists. Compounding the horror, the south and north towers of the Trade Center, their structures weakened by the heat of the blazes, collapsed entirely, at 10:05 and 10:28 A.M., respectively. The attack was seen as an act of war, likened to Japan's 1941 attack on Pearl Harbor that brought the United States into World War II.

The scope of the carnage and devastation, especially in Manhattan, overwhelmed Americans. Besides the towers, several smaller buildings in the World Trade Center complex also collapsed. People trapped on upper floors of the towers jumped or fell to their deaths. Hundreds of firefighters and rescue crews who had hurried to the buildings were crushed when the towers collapsed. All told, 2,819 people died (because of confusion and difficulty in tracking down individuals, early estimates put the toll at more than 6,000). Thousands more suffered severe physical injury or psychological trauma. Others were displaced from their homes and offices for weeks or months. Some businesses lost large portions of their workforces or sustained financial setbacks. Neighborhood restaurants and shops, which depended on the World Trade Center population for business, struggled to stay solvent.

Americans responded to the atrocities with shock and panic. Early in the day, television news reported (but retracted) false rumors of other attacks, including a bombing at the State Department, heightening the uncertainty of what might still happen. States of emergency were declared in Washington and New York. The Federal Aviation Agency grounded all flights in the United States and diverted all incoming foreign air traffic to Canada. Federal officials evacuated the White House and Congress and then closed all federal buildings. The military was put on worldwide alert.

President George W. Bush, attending a political event in Florida, gave a brief statement at 9:30 A.M. noting an "apparent terrorist attack." He then flew around the country, to Air Force bases in Louisiana and Nebraska, as Vice President Dick Cheney supervised operations from a White House bunker. Bush drew criticism for his decision and for promulgating a story, which the White House later admitted was false, that his plane was a target of the terrorists. Shortly before 7 P.M., with the threat of further attacks diminished, Bush returned to the White House. At 8:30 P.M., he spoke from the Oval Office, vowing retaliation against not just the terrorists responsible for the assaults, but also those governments that supported or sheltered them. As Bush's comments suggested, American intelligence agencies already believed the Al Qaeda terrorist ring, run by the Saudi Osama bin Laden, was responsible, and that it was operating in Afghanistan under the protection of the dictatorial Islamic regime known as the Taliban.

As Washington, D.C., coped with a national crisis, New York City faced an unprecedented urban emergency. Businesses closed for the day (and in some cases much longer), as did the subways. Manhattan became a sea of human beings fleeing the lower end of the island by foot. Bridges and tunnels leading into the borough were closed. The municipal primary elections scheduled for that day, including the mayoral contest, were postponed for two weeks. The stock market, located near the Trade Center, closed for the rest of the week. Rudolph Giuliani, the city's controversial mayor, won widespread praise for his confident, candid, and humane public posture during the crisis. In December, *Time* magazine named him "Man of the Year."

American officials had little trouble identifying the terrorists or how they achieved their feat. Mostly Egyptians, Saudis, and Yemenis, the perpetrators included both recent immigrants and those who had lived in the United States for several years. Some had already been under suspicion but had managed to conceal their whereabouts. Authorities also alleged that Zacarias Moussaoui, a French Muslim of Moroccan descent who had been arrested in August after suspicious behavior at a flight school, was intended to be the twentieth hijacker in the plot.

Officials also determined quickly that the hijackers belonged to bin Laden's Al Qaeda group. For several years, bin Laden had been organizing and bankrolling terrorist activities around the world, directed against the United States, other Western nations and individuals, and pro-Western Arab governments. He worked with a coalition of fanatical Islamic groups, mostly in the Arab world, but also in Southeast and Central Asia, including Egyptians who had assassinated their leader, Anwar Sadat, in 1981. These extremists opposed secular, modern, and Western values, called for the withdrawal of American troops from Saudi Arabia, and adopted unremitting violence against civilians as their instrument.

Bin Laden and his associates had struck before. They engineered the 1993 World Trade Center bombing, the 1996 assault on an American military barracks in Saudi Arabia, the 1998 bombings of the American embassies in Kenya and Tanzania, and the 2000 bombing of the USS *Cole*, a destroyer anchored in Yemen. The Bill Clinton administration had responded to these attacks by prosecuting those perpetrators whom it could apprehend, by (unsuccessfully) seeking legal changes to ease the tracking of terrorists, and by launching military strikes in 1998 against Sudan and Afghanistan, which supported Al Qaeda. The administration had also successfully thwarted earlier conspiracies, including a planned series of bombings on New Year's Eve 2000.

Few doubted, however, that more severe reprisals were needed after 11 September. On 14 September, Congress passed a resolution authorizing the use of military force to fight terrorism. The United States also secured a resolution on 12 September from the United Nations Security Council endorsing antiterrorism efforts, which, while not explicitly approving military action, was generally interpreted as doing so. After a mere four weeks—longer than some war hawks wanted—American and British forces began bombing Afghanistan. Despite a massive call-up of military reserves, the U.S. government remained wary of using American ground forces. Instead, Western forces bombed key targets while providing aid and coordination to the Northern Alliance, a coalition of Afghan rebels who did most of the actual fighting. On 13 November, Kabul, Afghanistan's capital, fell to the allies. On 22 December, a new, interim government friendly to the United States took power.

The domestic response to the 11 September attacks was almost as dramatic as the military action abroad. A surge of patriotism gripped the nation. Citizens flew flags, sang "God Bless America," and donated money to the victims' families, the Red Cross, and firefighters' and police officers' associations. The efficient performance of many federal and state agencies—law enforcement, emergency relief, environmental protection, and others—boosted public confidence in government to levels not seen in decades. President Bush appointed Pennsylvania Governor Tom Ridge to his cabinet as the director of "homeland" security, while other officials ordered the closer monitoring of sites ranging from nuclear reactors to reservoirs.

Congress granted new powers to law enforcement officials. The so-called USA Patriot Act, passed in October, gave authorities greater latitude in placing wiretaps and reading E-mail, prompting a national debate about whether civil liberties were being needlessly curtailed. Also controversial was a massive Justice Department dragnet that caught up hundreds of immigrants, mostly Middle Easterners, many of whom were jailed for months for technical violations of immigration laws.

In the immediate aftermath of the attacks, fear was pervasive. For several days, bomb scares proliferated. More troubling, starting in late September, several politicians and prominent news organizations received in the mail packages containing deadly high-grade anthrax spores. Five people died from the disease, although many more who were exposed recovered by taking antibiotics. Federal officials suspected that the anthrax was circulated not by Al Qaeda terrorists, but by Americans; nonetheless, the weeks-long scare, marked by news of sudden deaths and hospitalizations, fueled Americans' sense of insecurity.

Fear also centered on air travel, which decreased in the short term as many Americans realized how lax airport security was. Airports immediately tightened their security procedures after 11 September, creating long lines and frequent delays, but their policies remained erratic and far from foolproof. Months later, airplanes were still transporting bags that had not been screened, and private firms, not public employees, remained in control. Although air travel rebounded to normal levels, the airlines benefited from a perception after 11 September that they faced bankruptcy, and Congress passed a bailout bill giving them $15 billion in federal subsidies. Republican legislators blocked a plan to extend federal support to laid-off airline employees as well.

Within a few months after the attacks, daily life across America had essentially returned to normal. Fighting in Afghanistan sporadically erupted to top the news, and developments in the "war on terrorism"—whether the apprehension of alleged Al Qaeda members or the administration's plan to create a new cabinet department devoted to domestic security—attracted much comment. But other events, notably a wave of corruption scandals at several leading corporations, also vied for public attention. The war effort, which had successfully ousted the Taliban, still enjoyed wide support, as did President Bush. The administration began planning for an attack on Iraq; although the regime had no demonstrable links to Al Qaeda, its program to develop nuclear and chemical weapons now appeared, in the wake of 11 September, to be an intolerable danger. A year after the 9/11 attack, no end of the "war on terrorism" seemed imminent, as bin Laden and most of his top aides remained at large, and polls showed that a majority of Americans considered it likely that there would be another terrorist attack on their own soil.

David Greenberg

See also **Terrorism; World Trade Center;** *and vol. 9:* **George W. Bush, Address to a Joint Session of Congress and the American People.**

9 TO 5, NATIONAL ASSOCIATION OF WORKING WOMEN, a grassroots organization aimed at assisting working women, also functions as a national research and advocacy group. With members in all fifty states and twenty chapters, it is the biggest nonprofit membership association of working women in the country. A group of clerical workers founded the organization in Boston in 1973. Since its early days as a small newsletter, the organization has been an important force in the fight for pay equity, for family and medical leave, for protection for nonstandard work, and against sexual harassment.

BIBLIOGRAPHY

Kwolek-Folland, Angel. *Incorporating Women: A History of Women and Business in the United States.* New York: Twayne, 1998.

Zophy, Angela Howard, ed. *Handbook of American Women's History.* New York: Garland, 1990.

Eli Moses Diner

See also **Discrimination: Sex.**

NISEI. *See* **Japanese Americans.**

NITRATES. Nitrate (NO_3) is a compound of the elements nitrogen and oxygen. Nitrates are important to all living systems. Plants, especially, require it to develop and produce seeds. Nitrogen, the main component of Earth's atmosphere, is a relatively inert substance. To be useful, it must be converted into active forms. Lightning and radiation create nitrates in the atmosphere, where rainstorms carry them to the ground. Bacteria on roots of crops such as alfalfa and clover fix nitrogen in the soil. Microorganisms form nitrates as they break down animal matter. Since the early twentieth century, nitrates have been produced industrially.

Nitrates are present naturally in sewage and in some mineral deposits. Chile's Atacama Desert is the world's leading supplier of the mineralized form. Approximately 86 percent of the nitrate produced in the United States is used for fertilizer, though the chemicals have other uses. Potassium nitrate (KNO_3), also known as saltpeter, is the key ingredient in gunpowder. Saltpeter is formed naturally in warm climates by bacteria decomposing accumulations of excreta and animal refuse. Contact among putrefying material, alkaline soil, plant ashes, air, and moisture causes nitrates to form and penetrate the ground. After evaporation of rainwater, saltpeter appears as white powder on the surface.

Since the temperate climates of Europe and North America did not favor the formation of saltpeter, its supply was a vital concern for American colonists. European countries obtained saltpeter from India. When the American Revolution cut off the colonies from this source, some colonial governments offered bounties and established "artificial nitrate works," without much success. France saved the Continental Army from running out of gunpowder after having taken great pains to develop its own domestic supply. In the early nineteenth century, saltpeter was discovered in large quantities in caves in Kentucky and Tennessee. This resource helped fuel the Confederate armies during the American Civil War, though 90 percent of their powder likely came from foreign sources that managed to get through the Union blockade. After this period, the United States and Europe imported nitrate from Chile.

As the nineteenth century progressed into the twentieth, demand for nitrate fertilizers increased dramatically. Many countries experimented with methods of converting atmospheric nitrogen. All processes seemed expensive and complex. The outbreak of World War I drove the United States to attempt its own synthetic production by 1917. In preparation, a hydroelectric dam was built at Muscle Shoals, Alabama. Soon after, the process introduced in Germany by Fritz Haber in 1912 proved its superiority and the power plant was abandoned. In the 1930s, it became the foundation of the Tennessee Valley Authority.

Nitrates have become an environmental concern. Elevated levels of nitrogen flowing down the Mississippi River enter the Gulf of Mexico and nourish algal blooms. When algae die and decompose, they consume oxygen, depleting that vital element from the water. Fish and other creatures suffocate in affected areas that can cover thousands of square miles, causing problems for commercial fishing and other coastal industries. Sources of the nitrogen include sewage treatment water, industrial wastes, and atmospheric pollutants; large loads also come from livestock operations and nitrate fertilizer runoff from farmland. Nitrates infiltrate ground water as well as surface waters. According to the Environmental Protection Agency, when nitrates are present in quantities in excess of ten milligrams per liter, the water supply can pose a potentially fatal threat to infants under six months and to young and pregnant animals.

BIBLIOGRAPHY

Hill, Michael J., ed. *Nitrates and Nitrites in Food and Water.* New York: Ellis Horwood, 1991.

Keleti, Cornelius. *Nitric Acid and Fertilizer Nitrates.* New York: Dekker, 1985.

Wilson, W. S., A. S. Ball, and R. H. Hinton. *Managing Risks of Nitrates to Humans and the Environment.* Cambridge: Royal Society of Chemists, 1999.

Robert P. Multhauf
Christine M. Roane

See also **Fertilizers.**

NIXON, RESIGNATION OF. On 9 August 1974, Richard M. Nixon resigned the presidency of the United States as a result of his involvement in the Watergate scandal. He remains the only president ever to resign the office.

Nixon's Farewell. President Richard M. Nixon speaks emotionally to his staff and Cabinet on 9 August 1974, as his daughter Tricia and son-in-law Edward Cox Jr. look on. LIBRARY OF CONGRESS

On 17 June 1972, burglars working for Nixon's reelection campaign were arrested breaking into Democratic party headquarters at the Watergate building in Washington, D.C. For the next two years, Nixon and his top aides concealed information from prosecutors and the public about the break-in and related illegal activities. Eventually Senate hearings, the burglars' trials, and investigative reporting unearthed evidence that suggested Nixon had joined in the cover-up and abused the power of his office. On 30 October 1973, the House Judiciary Committee began hearings on whether to impeach him. On 27–30 July 1974, it passed three articles of impeachment. The House of Representatives appeared likely to approve the articles (it did so as a pro forma matter on 20 August)—a decision that would put Nixon on trial before the Senate.

To remove Nixon from office, two-thirds of the Senate (67 senators) would have to support conviction. By early August Nixon's support was clearly eroding. On 24 July, the Supreme Court had unanimously ordered the president to surrender the transcripts of 64 conversations that Nixon had secretly taped. On 5 August Nixon finally made public the transcripts of three of those discussions. In those discussions, which took place on 23 June 1972, Nixon had instructed H. R. Haldeman, his chief of staff at the time, to have the CIA, under false pretenses, order the FBI to curtail the Watergate probe. The tape-recorded evidence starkly contradicted Nixon's longstanding claims of his own innocence.

With the disclosure of the contents of this so-called "smoking gun" tape, many of Nixon's own aides and lawyers concluded he should resign. On 6 August, Nixon's congressional liaison, Bill Timmons, told the president that only seven senators supported his continuation in office. Later that day Nixon told family members and top aides that he would resign imminently. On 7 August Senators Hugh Scott of Pennsylvania and Barry Goldwater of Arizona and Representative John Rhodes of Arizona, all leaders of the Republican party, visited Nixon to tell him directly how meager his Congressional support was. Nixon was alternately emotional and stoic. The next day he told aides that he did not fear going to prison, since Lenin, Gandhi, and others had written great works from jail.

On 8 August, at 9:00 P.M., Nixon delivered a 15-minute televised address. Admitting to bad "judgments" but not to serious wrongdoing, he announced that he would resign the next day. The next morning he delivered an emotional speech to his staff and supporters in the White House East Room. Speaking about his parents, his boyhood, and the premature death of two of his brothers, he concluded by stating, "Always remember: others may hate you, but those who hate you don't win unless you hate them, and then you destroy yourself."

Nixon and his wife, Pat, then boarded a helicopter and flew to the nearby Andrews Air Force Base; they then flew to California, where he would live for the next six years. At 11:35 A.M. on 9 August his letter of resignation was given to Secretary of State Henry Kissinger, and at 12:03 P.M. Vice President Gerald R. Ford was sworn in as president. In his inaugural statement, Ford declared, "Our long national nightmare is over."

BIBLIOGRAPHY

Kutler, Stanley I. *The Wars of Watergate: The Last Crisis of Richard Nixon.* New York: Knopf, 1990.

New York Times, Staff of. *The End of a Presidency*. New York: Holt, 1974.

Nixon, Richard M. *RN: The Memoirs of Richard Nixon*. New York: Grosset and Dunlap, 1978.

White, Theodore H. *Breach of Faith: The Fall of Richard Nixon*. New York: Atheneum, 1975.

David Greenberg

See also **Impeachment; Watergate;** *and vol. 9:* **Constitutional Faith; Proclamation 4311: Nixon Pardoned; Nixon's Watergate Investigation Address.**

NIXON IMPEACHMENT. *See* **Impeachment; Nixon, Resignation of.**

NIXON TAPES. Although several presidents tape recorded White House conversations, none did so as extensively, or with such consequences, as Richard Nixon. In February 1971, Nixon installed tape machines in the Oval Office and elsewhere to record his conversations. In July 1973, one of his aides, Alexander Butterfield, told the Senate committee investigating the burgeoning WATERGATE scandal about the recordings. Butterfield's bombshell led the Senate committee and the Watergate special prosecutor to subpoena tapes pertaining to Nixon's role in covering up the June 1972 Watergate burglary. For nine months, Nixon refused, harming his cause, which suffered further when the White House revealed in November 1973 that someone had erased eighteen and one-half minutes of one key tape. In April 1974, Nixon finally made public edited transcripts of selected tapes, which failed to satisfy the special prosecutor. In July 1974, the Supreme Court ordered Nixon to turn over more tapes, including the "smoking gun" tape of 23 June 1972 on which Nixon explicitly plotted the cover-up. Days later, he resigned. In 1974, Congress mandated the release of all tapes relating to Watergate. It gave Nixon control of tapes deemed personal. The National Archives planned to make available the remainder of the tapes, which ran to almost 4,000 hours, but Nixon fought the release in court. After a lawsuit, the National Archives agreed to make those tapes public starting in late 1996.

BIBLIOGRAPHY

Kutler, Stanley I. *Abuse of Power: The New Nixon Tapes*. New York: Simon and Schuster, 1998.

David Greenberg

See also **Nixon, Resignation of.**

NOBEL PRIZES. *See* **Prizes and Awards.**

NOISE POLLUTION generally refers to unwanted sound produced by human activities—unwanted in that it interferes with communication, work, rest, recreation, or sleep. Unlike other forms of pollution, such as air, water, and hazardous materials, noise does not remain long in the environment. However, while its effects are immediate in terms of annoyance, they are cumulative in terms of temporary or permanent hearing loss. Society has attempted to regulate noise since the early days of the Romans, who by decree prohibited the movement of chariots in the streets at night. In the United States, communities since colonial days have enacted ordinances against excessive noise, primarily in response to complaints from residents. It was not until the late 1960s, however, that the federal government officially recognized noise as a pollutant and began to support noise research and regulation. Federal laws against noise pollution included the National Environmental Policy Act of 1969, especially sections concerning environmental impact statements; the Noise Pollution and Abatement Act of 1970; and the Noise Control Act of 1972, which appointed the Environmental Protection Agency (EPA) to coordinate federal research and activities in noise control.

Charged with developing federal noise-emission standards, identifying major sources of noise, and determining appropriate noise levels that would not infringe on public health and welfare, the EPA produced its so-called Levels Document, now the standard reference in the field of environmental noise assessment. In the document, the EPA established an equivalent sound level (Leq) and a day–night equivalent level (Ldn) as measures and descriptors for noise exposure. Soon thereafter, most federal agencies adopted either the Leq, Ldn, or both, including levels compatible with different land uses. The Federal Aviation Administration (FAA) uses Ldn as the noise descriptor in assessing land-use compatibility with various levels of aircraft noise. In 1978 the research findings of Theodore J. Schultz provided support for Ldn as the descriptor for environmental noise. Analyzing social surveys, Schultz found a correlation between Ldn and people who were highly annoyed by noise in their neighborhoods. The Schultz curve, expressing this correlation, became a basis for noise standards.

As part of its effort to identify major noise sources in the United States, the EPA set about determining the degree to which noise standards could contribute to noise reduction. During the 1970s, EPA-sponsored research on major noise sources led to regulation of the products that most affected the public, including medium and heavy trucks, portable air compressors, garbage trucks, buses, and motorcycles. Missing from the list was aircraft, which was considered the responsibility of the FAA. During the administration of President Ronald Reagan in the 1980s, the power of the EPA and its Office of Noise Abatement and Control was curtailed and most of its noise regulations rescinded. Even so, efforts continued to curb noise pollution. The Department of Transportation maintains standards for highways, mass transit, and railroads, as well as aircraft. The environmental review process, mandated by the National Environmental Policy Act of 1969, remains the single most effective deterrent to noise pollution.

BIBLIOGRAPHY

Kryter, Karl D. *The Handbook of Hearing and the Effects of Noise: Physiology, Psychology, and Public Health*. San Diego, Calif.: Academic Press, 1994.

Saenz, A. Lara, and R. W. B. Stephens, eds. *Noise Pollution: Effects and Control*. New York: Wiley, 1986.

Schultz, Theodore J. "Synthesis of Social Surveys on Noise Annoyance," *Journal of the Acoustical Society of America* 64 (August 1978): 377–405.

Carl E. Hanson / W. P.

See also **Environmental Movement; Environmental Protection Agency; Epidemics and Public Health.**

NOMINATING SYSTEM. The method of choosing candidates for the presidency of the United States has undergone dramatic changes since the adoption of the Constitution. The caucus, a loose collection of members of a political group that had been used in local elections during the colonial period, was first adopted as a means of choosing candidates for local elections and for nominating governor and other state officials. The first "congressional caucus," composed of members of Congress belonging to the same political party, was an informal meeting called by Alexander Hamilton in 1790 for the Federalist Party to choose candidates for the presidency and the vice presidency. It took the opposition ten years to officially form a similar group, a "congressional nominating caucus," which supported Thomas Jefferson in his bid for the presidency in 1800. Henry Clay, a member of the Democratic-Republican Party and Speaker of the House of Representatives, institutionalized the caucus as a means to foster congressional voting along the party line in 1811.

In the absence of a unified national party structure, the congressional caucuses soon became the most important groups for coordinating the nomination of candidates for the presidency for both parties. As long as the first two-party system worked, and as long as each party was relatively homogeneous and could easily reach a compromise on its candidates, this system was effective. After the demise of the Federalist Party the nomination of the Democratic-Republican John Quincy Adams was challenged in the campaign of 1824 by a number of strong competitors from within his own party, and the system began to break down. The caucus, favoring William H. Crawford, was boycotted by a vocal minority so that in the end only about one-fourth of its members participated. The other three candidates from the Democratic-Republican Party, Adams, Henry Clay, and Andrew Jackson, were nominated by state assemblies or regional caucuses and staged regional trial votes to gain public endorsement. No one candidate received a majority in the electoral college, and the election was decided in the House of Representatives.

After the split of the Democratic-Republican Party, no new caucuses were established and the new parties continued to use the supposedly more democratic decentralized nominating process. Regional party conventions had been staged, and in 1831 the newly established Anti-Masonic Party, having no elected representatives to form a congressional caucus, came up with the idea of inviting delegates from regional party chapters to a national convention to nominate the presidential candidate. Within months, the National Republicans copied the concept. Soon, committees were created to devise delegate credentials, rules, and a party platform. Delegates were selected either by caucuses, party members who served in state legislatures, or regional party leaders. The Democratic Party decided that the number of delegates from the individual states should be equal to the number of that states' members in the electoral college, and in 1832, the Democrats devised a "two-thirds rule" for selecting candidates. Established to prevent the nomination of John C. Calhoun, it was not challenged for a century and gave strong minorities a veto power.

Franklin D. Roosevelt, who had barely succeeded in 1932 in reaching a two-thirds majority for his nomination, was instrumental in changing the required margin for victory to a simple majority for the convention in 1940. The Democrats from the southern states, who had held a ruling minority under the old system, were compensated by the introduction of a bonus system that increased the number of delegates from those states that had been won for the Democrat's candidate in previous presidential elections. The Republican Party had already introduced a negative bonus system that reduced the number of delegates from states lost to the Democrats in 1916 and added a positive bonus in 1924. A unit rule had been introduced in 1844, forcing delegates from each state to vote as a block. The Democratic Party kept this rule until 1968, while the Whigs and later the Republican Party abided by it only at some conventions and only until 1880.

The convention system for choosing candidates was criticized almost from the start. Originating in 1903 in Wisconsin, a new system of using primaries was introduced by the Progressive Party. In 1904, Florida became the first state to adopt primaries to select delegates for national party conventions, and by 1916, the Democratic and Republican Parties in twenty states used this system. It failed, however, to attract a large number of voters, and many candidates over the next several decades avoided primaries or ran in only a select few to demonstrate that they could attract popular votes. Primaries thus were hardly consequential and in 1912 Theodore Roosevelt's name was not even proposed for the nomination at the Republican convention despite his winning nine of thirteen primaries that year. In 1952, the Democrats nominated Adlai Stevenson as presidential candidate even though Estes Kefauver had won twelve of fifteen primaries. In the wake of the unrest at the 1968 Democratic convention in Chicago, the McGovern-Fraser Commission was established; it proposed a series of sweeping changes for most aspects of delegate selection. The Democratic Party's National Committee adopted nearly all recommendations, which were subsequently taken over by the state parties and converted by many state legislatures into statutes for both parties. Measures for translating public support for candidates into delegates, eliminating automatic ex-officio slots, and ensuring equitable representation of women and minorities led to invigoration of the primaries. While in 1968, about one-third of all delegates to Democratic and Republican conventions had been selected in primaries, this share increased to 85 percent for the Democratic Party and 90 percent for the Republican Party in 2000.

Because of the increasing coverage of primaries and their results through the media, they have become highly contested. Primaries are conducted mostly from February to June, and early primaries in Iowa and in New Hampshire have become particularly important for lesser-known candidates who seek crucial media coverage and rely on establishing financial support for their campaign. On "Super Tuesday" (which in the year 2000 fell on March 7), a large number of delegates are selected in about one-third of the states (particularly in states, such as California, New York, and Ohio, that send a high number of delegates to the conventions), possibly pointing toward the establishment of a national primary day.

BIBLIOGRAPHY

Coleman, Kevin J., Thomas H. Neale, and Joseph E. Cantor. *Presidential Elections in the United States: A Primer.* Huntington, N.Y.: Novinka, 2001.

Keeter, Scott, and Cliff Zukin. *Uninformed Choice: The Failure of the New Presidential Nominating System.* New York: Praeger, 1983.

Michael Wala

See also **Caucus; Conventions, Party Nominating; Elections, Presidential; Two-Party System; Voting.**

NONFERROUS METALS. Other than tin and nickel, the United States produces in commercial quantities all the major nonferrous metals, which include aluminum, copper, lead, and zinc. Since 1993, no tin mines have operated in the United States, and China and Indonesia together produce over half of the world's supply. The American nickel industry has little or no impact on the world market, which Russia, Canada, and, increasingly, Australia dominate. By 1999 primary production of nickel in the United States at least temporarily ceased because it became cheaper to import the metal than to mine and refine it domestically. By contrast, American production of copper, lead, zinc, and aluminum remains influential in the world market and of great significance to the domestic economy. Moreover, the demand for metals with special qualities, such as light weight, high electrical conductivity, and noncorrosive finish, is increasing, and nonferrous metals represent the major source of supply to meet these demands. For example, the importance of titanium, increasingly used as a pigment in aeronautics and in medical implants, has grown, although the United States imports rather than exports this metal.

During the latter part of the nineteenth century, following the already established pattern in other basic industries, the entire nonferrous metals industry underwent a period of rapid expansion and development, after which came concentration and consolidation. During the last decade of that century the Aluminum Company of America (Alcoa) emerged to monopolize that industry, and the same period also witnessed the incorporation of the Anaconda Copper Company, American Smelting and Refining, United States Mining Company, Phelps-Dodge Corporation, American Metals Company, and most of the other leading producers of zinc, lead, and copper. The large corporate units that characterize the nonferrous metals industry resulted mostly from the advantages enjoyed by well-financed, large-scale operations in finding, extracting, processing, and marketing minerals.The "delivered price" or "basing point" price system characteristic of the metals industries prevails throughout the nonferrous metals market. While in itself the system does not ensure price uniformity, in actuality industries so in harmony on one aspect of pricing seldom have serious difficulty agreeing on others.

The first nonferrous metal to be mined and smelted in the United States was lead. English colonists exploited the small deposits along the eastern seaboard, and by 1720 the French had begun to work the Missouri lead mines. The Missouri mines have been in continuous production since the first underground mining began in 1798. Missouri and Alaska are the two largest domestic producers of lead.

The opening of the Missouri lead region to American settlers and the discovery of lead in the Wisconsin-Illinois Fever River district occasioned one of the first mineral rushes into the American West by eager miners. The rapid influx of miners, coupled with strong pressure from aspiring entrepreneurs, prevented the federal government from enforcing its policy of retaining ownership of some mineral deposits and led it to grant leases to miners and smelters to exploit the deposits. Even in the Fever River district, where the federal leasing policy existed in some form until the 1840s, the government agents experienced chronic difficulty in collecting rents and regulating smelters. By the end of the 1840s, the federal government had abandoned the leasing policy and opened mineral lands to unrestricted exploitation.

Development of the extensive western mines after the Civil War greatly augmented domestic lead production, and by 1881 the United States was the leading lead producer in the world. During the years immediately prior to World War I, the United States annually accounted for more than one-third of the total lead output. After World War II, domestic production averaged slightly over 1 million tons annually, about 20 percent short of domestic consumption. At the end of the twentieth century, only Australia ranked ahead of the United States in lead production. Although traditional uses for lead in water pipes, paint, and pigments declined, the increased demand for automobile batteries, gasoline additives, and chemicals more than offset the loss of the former markets. In 1999 lead-acid batteries stood as the single most significant use of lead in the United States.

Nonetheless, awareness of the extreme toxicity of lead, especially to small children, increased in the mid-twentieth century. By 1970 federal legislation banned lead in household paint, while 1990 marked the last year that leaded gasoline was available for purchase. Old lead water pipes continue to present a potential public health hazard, as they can leach metal into drinking water.

Unlike lead, zinc was not put into commercial production until toward the end of the nineteenth century. Only small quantities were smelted before the first commercially successful smelter in the United States began production in 1860. The then-known zinc deposits were not easily beneficiated, and the smelting process was difficult and costly, which rendered zinc too expensive for widespread use The only substantial demand for zinc was as a component in brass. The opening of the Joplin, Missouri, zinc ore district in 1871–1872 provided an easily mined, easily concentrated, and comparatively easily smelted ore. More importantly, the concurrent huge growth in the galvanizing and munitions industries created an effective demand for zinc metal. By 1907 the United States led the world in zinc production, and ten years later, it annually supplied more than 60 percent of the world output. Until World War II, the United States continued to be a net exporter of zinc, and only since then has domestic production been insufficient to supply national demand. As long as the United States remained a net exporter, the domestic price, often protected by tariffs, operated without dependence on the world market. In 2000 the United States ranked fifth in the world in zinc production, after China, Australia, Canada, and Peru, but it was still the largest consumer of the metal.

Most zinc is now used for galvanizing and die-casting. The next most prevalent use has been in brass products and zinc pigments. The rapid growth of the zinc industry in the early twentieth century relates in part to the development of the froth flotation process for mineral concentration. This process provided smelters with so many additional ore supplies that it practically revolutionized the entire nonferrous metals industry prior to World War I. The later development of differential media separation, which provided an inexpensive means of separating different components of complex ores, allowed the economic exploitation of lower-grade and more complex ores than before, which again greatly expanded domestic production.

Long before Europeans made contact with the Western Hemisphere, American Indians were working copper, perhaps the world's oldest metal, for fishhooks and ornaments. Nevertheless, the commercial copper industry in the United States started only in the 1840s with the discovery of old Indian mines in Michigan, and for the next forty years the Lake Superior region produced most of the copper in the United States. With the discovery of the great western mines, especially at Butte, Montana, in the 1880s, the United States became the principal producer of copper in the world. Today, the United States remains a leading producer of this nonferrous metal, second only to Chile, although American production has leveled off while Chile's continues to rise. Whereas the Lake Superior copper occurs as native metal and requires no complicated metallurgical process, some of the more complex western ores require leaching with an acidified solution and the separation of the copper from the resulting copper sulfate solution by an electrolytic process.

The most dramatic development in copper mining and manufacturing occurred at the beginning of the twentieth century when massive deposits of porphyritic ores, often containing no more than 1 percent copper, were first successfully exploited by D. C. Jackling, a prominent American mining engineer. Jackling demonstrated that the huge porphyry deposits at Bingham, Utah, could be profitably developed by utilizing open-pit mining and large-scale operations that permitted significant economies of scale. A large portion of the world copper supply subsequently came to be produced from porphyritic ore bodies.

The rapid growth of the copper industry paralleled the expansion of the major copper-consuming industries—electrical, automobile, construction, and mechanical refrigeration. In addition, large quantities of copper are used as alloys, especially by the American brass industry. Under favorable price ratios, aluminum and magnesium are close substitutes for copper in transmission lines and in certain die castings, but for the most part the demand for copper has increased within normal price ranges.

Although aluminum is the most abundant of all metallic elements found in the earth's crust, it was the last of the common nonferrous metals to be commercially exploited. Until the introduction of the electrolytic process in 1886, developed simultaneously but independently by Charles Martin Hall and Paul Louis Toussaint Héroult, the price of aluminum had been much too high for industrial uses. Within five years after its development, the Hall-Héroult process reduced the price from more than eight dollars to less than one dollar a pound. In 1888 Hall convinced a group of Pittsburgh entrepreneurs to form the Pittsburgh Reduction Company, later the Aluminum Company of America, to exploit his process, and until 1941 Alcoa was the sole producer of primary aluminum in the United States. In 1937 the Justice Department filed an antitrust suit against Alcoa but lost the appeal in 1945 when Judge Learned Hand ruled that, whereas Alcoa did have a monopoly when the suit was first filed, the existence and pending disposal of government-built wartime facilities threatened that monopoly. Judge Hand ruled that, pending "judicious" disposal of the government facilities, remedial action should be held in abeyance. The lease and ultimate sale of those facilities to the Reynolds Metals Company and Kaiser Aluminum and Chemical Company ended the Alcoa monopoly, and since 1946, a number of metal firms have entered the aluminum reduction industry. However, as of 2002, Alcoa still exerted strong leadership in the industry.

The demand for aluminum accelerated rapidly after World War II as both domestic and world production increased and the price of aluminum dropped, which made it competitive with other nonferrous metals for a great variety of uses. In the 1970s the United States accounted for nearly 40 percent of the world output and consumed approximately the same proportion. By the beginning of the twenty-first century, the American aluminum industry was producing 22 billion pounds of metal a year, a level of output that has allowed the United States to remain the leading producer of aluminum. Leading domestic consumers included the building and construction, transportation, electrical, and containers and packaging industries.

Although the automotive industry is the single biggest domestic market for aluminum, most American consumers most likely associate aluminum with soft-drink cans. Because of this metal's sustained recyclability, manufacturers may repeatedly use and reuse aluminum without a decline in quality. Thus, during the last two decades, aluminum recycling has become a widespread and cost-effective practice. Most recycled aluminum comes from beverage cans, and most beverage cans now undergo recycling.

BIBLIOGRAPHY

Fahey, John. *Hecla: A Century of Western Mining.* Seattle: University of Washington Press, 1990.

Francaviglia, Richard V. *Hard Places: Reading the Landscape of America's Historic Mining Districts.* Iowa City: University of Iowa Press, 1991.

Graham, Margaret B. W., and Bettye H. Pruitt. *R&D for Industry: A Century of Technical Innovation at Alcoa.* Cambridge, U.K.: Cambridge University Press, 1990.

Lankton, Larry D. *Cradle to Grave: Life, Work, and Death at the Lake Superior Copper Mines.* New York: Oxford University Press, 1991.

———. *Beyond the Boundaries: Life and Landscape at the Lake Superior Copper Mines, 1840–1875.* New York: Oxford University Press, 1997.

Smith, Duane A. *Mining America: The Industry and the Environment, 1800–1980.* Lawrence: University Press of Kansas, 1987.

Smith, George David. *From Monopoly to Competition: The Transformations of Alcoa, 1888–1986.* Cambridge, U.K.: Cambridge University Press, 1988.

Angela Ellis
James D. Norris

See also **Aluminum; Anaconda Copper; Copper Industry; Lead Industry; Mineralogy; Recycling; Smelters; Trusts; Zinc Industry.**

NONIMPORTATION AGREEMENTS were a series of commercial restrictions adopted by American colonists to protest British revenue policies prior to the American Revolution. Britain's STAMP ACT of 1765 triggered the first nonimportation agreements. To protest taxation without representation, New York merchants agreed collectively to embargo British imports until Parliament repealed the stamp tax, and they persuaded the merchants of Boston and Philadelphia to do likewise. Under pressure from British exporters who lost business, Parliament repealed the Stamp Act within a year.

After Parliament imposed the Townshend duties on imports in June–July 1767, colonists implemented a second, uneven round of nonimportation agreements. Boston promptly resumed its embargo of British imports, and New York followed in 1768. But Philadelphia signed on to the idea only in 1769, after stockpiling imports. Southern merchants refused to cooperate, and smuggling reportedly occurred everywhere. By 1770, the embargo began to squeeze British exporters as international tensions mounted in Europe. Parliament repealed the Townshend duties on all commodities except tea.

A third wave of economic embargo formed in 1774. To protest various parliamentary restrictions, the Continental Congress created the Continental Association, which imposed nonimportation, nonconsumption, and limited nonexportation terms on the colonies. In disregard of colonial wishes, however, British merchants opened new export markets, and the government in London resolved to crush colonial rebelliousness. War soon followed.

The nonimportation agreements of the late colonial era were important precursors to the American Revolution. The agreements stoked tensions that led to violence. Negotiation of the agreements thrust Boston patriots into prominence and demonstrated to colonists the potential of united action. On a deeper level, the agreements helped awaken colonists to their emerging national identity as Americans by helping them promote their cultural value of thrift on a national stage.

BIBLIOGRAPHY

Crowley, John E. *The Privileges of Independence: Neomercantilism and the American Revolution.* Baltimore: Johns Hopkins University Press, 1993.

Schlesinger, Arthur M. *The Colonial Merchants and the American Revolution, 1763–1776.* New York: Frederick Ungar, 1966.

Thomas, Peter D. G. *The Townshend Duties Crisis: The Second Phase of the American Revolution, 1767–1773.* Oxford: Clarendon, 1987.

Peter L. Hahn

See also **Townshend Acts;** *and vol. 9:* **The Continental Association.**

NONINTERCOURSE ACT. In 1807, in response to violations by France and England to American sovereignty, Congress closed its ports and prohibited international trade. The Embargo Act, however, failed to change the French and English policy toward the United States. As a result, Congress lifted the comprehensive embargo on American commercial activity and passed a new act designed to punish only those nations who violated American neutrality.

On 1 March 1809, the Nonintercourse Act replaced the Embargo Act, allowing transatlantic trade to resume. The act, which went into effect on 20 May, suspended trade with only France and England until one of them would "revoke or modify her edicts, as that they shall cease to violate the neutral commerce of the United States." The act prohibited their ships from entering American ports and decreed it illegal for citizens of the United States to have "any intercourse with, or to afford any aid or supplies" to any French or English ships. The act also authorized naval officers and customs officials to seize merchandise from ships in violation of the law.

Unfortunately, the Nonintercourse Act, like the Embargo Act, failed to change French and English policy. It was repealed on 1 May 1810 in favor of what became known as Macon's Bill No. 2, which conceded defeat and reopened trade with both nations.

BIBLIOGRAPHY

Smelser, Marshall. *The Democratic Republic: 1801–1815.* New York: Harper, 1968.

Keith Pacholl

See also **Embargo Act; Macon's Bill No. 2.**

NONINTERVENTION POLICY honors the principle of noninterference and nonintervention in the internal affairs of sovereign states. President George Washington's guideline for early U.S. foreign relations implied this principle when he warned his peers in his "Farewell Address" to have commercial relations with other nations but as "little political connection as possible." The first statement directly expressing nonintervention as the backbone of U.S. foreign policy came in 1823 in the Monroe Doctrine. President James Monroe said in his state of the nation address on 2 December 1823 that American policy in regard to Europe had been and would continue to be "not to interfere in the internal concerns of any of its powers." In that speech he declared a nonintervention policy for European nations on the American continents. This policy was reaffirmed in the Polk Doctrine, announced on 2 December 1845.

American policy prohibiting other nations from intervening in the Western Hemisphere was reinforced at the beginning of the twentieth century, as European governments used force to pressure several Latin American countries to repay their debts. In his annual message to Congress on 6 December 1904, President Theodore Roosevelt stated what became known as the Roosevelt Corollary to the Monroe Doctrine. He said chronic wrongdoing or unrest might require intervention by some civilized nation; in the Western Hemisphere this was a prerogative of the United States. American policy after World War I was based on the principle of self-determination of the people, but the United States did not hesitate to break up and reshape states. On the American continents the Roosevelt Corollary was finally abandoned in 1936, when the United States, at the Special Inter-American Conference for the Maintenance of Peace, for the first time bound itself to nonintervention in an international agreement. The nonintervention policy was applied in the Spanish civil war in 1937.

As a guiding principle, nonintervention was reaffirmed in the United Nations (UN) charter of 1945. Article 2.7 of the charter prohibits intervention "in matters which are essentially within the domestic jurisdiction of any State." However, in the wake of the UN Convention on the Prevention and Punishment of the Crime of Genocide of 1948 and the development of international understanding on human rights issues, the United States has had increasing difficulty justifying a rigorous nonintervention policy. Since human rights violations and genocide are often committed with the collusion or even the direct participation of the authorities, a strict nonintervention policy began to seem infeasible. In interventions by the United States in the late twentieth century, in Grenada, Panama, Libya, Somalia, Haiti, Bosnia, and Kosovo, human rights and the American national interest were the guiding forces.

BIBLIOGRAPHY

Graber, Doris A. *Crisis Diplomacy: A History of U.S. Intervention Policies and Practices.* Washington, D.C.: Public Affairs Press, 1959.

Haas, Richard N. *Intervention: The Use of American Military Force in the Post–Cold War World.* Washington, D.C.: Brookings Institution Press, 1999. Also available at http://brookings.nap.edu/books/.

Mayal, James. "Non-intervention, Self-determination, and the 'New World Order.'" *International Affairs* 67, no. 3 (July 1991): 421–429.

Michael Wala

See also **Human Rights; Intervention; Monroe Doctrine; Polk Doctrine; Roosevelt Corollary.**

NONPARTISAN LEAGUE, NATIONAL. First organized in 1915 in North Dakota by Arthur C. Townley and the leaders of the Socialist and Equity Parties, the Nonpartisan League (also known as the Farmers' Nonpartisan League and, later, the National Nonpartisan League) was the outcome of a grassroots farmers' revolt against monopolistic control of the wheat trade by financial speculators and government officials at the expense of wheat farmers. The original demands of this alliance of wheat farmers included the establishment of state-owned elevators, grain mills, and packing plants; state-provided hail insurance and rural tax credits; as well as the reform of state tax laws. Townley, along with colleagues William Lemke and William Langer, successfully and rapidly created a united politicized group of farmers and sympathizers, which he then used to endorse political candidates of either party (thus, the word "nonpartisan" in the league's name) who pledged to improve the working and living conditions of the farmers by supporting their agenda.

The North Dakota gubernatorial election of 1916 brought the league's first victory with the election of Republican Lynn J. Frazier, a dirt farmer who captured nearly 80 percent of the vote. Within four years, because of the league's aggressive organizing, the state legislature had effectively adopted the league's entire slate of reform measures within a far-reaching and legally mandated socioeconomic program. This program provided, among other things, production incentives by taxing unused farmland and exempting capital improvements on farmland, increased funding for rural education, established a shorter (nine-hour) work day for women, and created the Bank of North Dakota, a state-owned bank that made capital improvement loans to farmers. Although the league was not an established political party like the Republican or Democratic Parties, it nevertheless enjoyed widespread influence and power in local elections and legislative matters.

Membership fees created significant financial resources that enabled the league to expand throughout North and South Dakota, Minnesota, Montana, Wisconsin, Iowa, Nebraska, Kansas, Colorado, Oklahoma, Idaho, Washington, and Oregon. League funds were used to finance various legal challenges, brought for the purpose of strengthening the economic and political standing of member farmers. Strong farmer-labor coalitions emerged, highlighting issues unique to each market and culminating in favorable election results across the region.

Various political, economic, and social aftereffects of World War I, including the economic depression and a national unease with socialist concepts, lead to diminished coffers among the league's membership and eventually crippled its political effectiveness. By 1920 political conservatism was on the rise, further eroding the league's left-leaning political base. For the next thirty years, increasing political impotence, mismanagement, and financial scandal haunted the league, until it became affiliated with the Democratic Party in 1956, obscuring its original characteristics.

BIBLIOGRAPHY

Jenson, Carol E. *Agrarian Pioneer in Civil Liberties: The Nonpartisan League in Minnesota during World War I.* New York: Garland, 1986.

Christine E. Hoffman

See also **Agrarianism.**

NONRECOGNITION POLICY. *See* **Recognition Policy.**

NORMALCY. In a Boston address on the eve of the 1920 presidential campaign, Senator Warren G. Harding said, in part, "America's present need is not heroics but healing, not nostrums but normalcy. . . ." The word "normalcy" came quickly to symbolize to many Americans a respite from the activist policies of President Woodrow Wilson. Specifically, it signified a return to a high protective tariff, a drastic reduction in income and inheritance taxes, a government crackdown on organized labor, a restoration of subsidies and bounties to favored corporate groups, an absence of government interference in private enterprise, and a nationalistic foreign policy. Harding's "back to normal" slogan propelled him to victory in the 1920 presidential election.

BIBLIOGRAPHY

Ferrell, Robert H. *The Strange Deaths of President Harding.* Columbia: University of Missouri Press, 1996.

Russell, Francis. *The Shadow of Blooming Grove: Warren G. Harding in His Times.* New York: McGraw-Hill, 1968.

Thomas S. Barclay / A. G.

See also **Dark Horse; Depression of 1920; Fourteen Points; Laissez-Faire; Lost Generation.**

NORMANDY INVASION, Allied landings in France on 6 June 1944 (D Day), the prelude to the defeat of Nazi Germany in World War II. Known as Operation Overlord, the invasion was scheduled for 5 June but was postponed because of stormy weather. It involved 5,000 ships, the largest armada ever assembled. Although more men went ashore on the first day in the earlier Allied invasion of Sicily, it was overall the greatest amphibious operation in history.

Under command of General Dwight D. Eisenhower, with General Bernard L. Montgomery as ground commander, approximately 130,000 American, British, and Canadian troops landed on beaches extending from the mouth of the Orne River near Caen to the base of the Cotentin Peninsula, a distance of some fifty-five miles. Another 23,000 landed by parachute and glider. Allied aircraft during the day flew 11,000 sorties. Airborne troops began landing soon after midnight; American seaborne troops at 6:30 A.M.; and, because of local tidal conditions, British and Canadian troops at intervals over the next hour. The Allies chose Normandy because of its relatively short distance from British ports and airfields, the existence of particularly strong German defenses of the Atlantic Wall at the closest point to Britain in the Pas de Calais, and the need for early access to a major port (Cherbourg).

On beaches near Caen christened Gold, Juno, and Sword, one Canadian and two British divisions under the British Second Army made it ashore with relative ease, quickly establishing contact with a British airborne division that had captured bridges over the Orne and knocked out a coastal battery that might have enfiladed (heavily fired upon) the beaches. By nightfall the troops were short of the assigned objectives of Bayeux and Caen but held beachheads from two to four miles deep.

The U.S. First Army under Lieutenant General Omar N. Bradley sent the Fourth Infantry Division of the VII Corps ashore farthest west on Utah Beach, north of Carentan, at one of the weakest points of the Atlantic Wall. The 82d and 101st Airborne divisions landing behind the beach helped insure success. Although the air drops were badly scattered and one division landed amid a reserve German division, most essential objectives were in hand by the end of the day.

Under the V Corps, two regiments of the First Infantry Division and one of the Twenty-ninth landed on Omaha Beach, between Bayeux and Carentan. Sharp bluffs, strong defenses, lack of airborne assistance, and the presence of a powerful German division produced near-catastrophic difficulties. Throughout much of the day the fate of this part of the invasion hung in the balance, but inch by inch American troops forced their way inland, so that when night came the beachhead was approximately a mile deep. At a nearby cliff called Pointe du Hoe, the First Ranger Battalion eliminated a German artillery battery.

The invasion sector was defended by the German Seventh Army, a contingent of Army Group B, under overall command of Field Marshal Gerd von Rundstedt. Deluded by Allied deception measures, based in large part on intelligence known as ULTRA, obtained as a result of the British having broken the German wireless enciphering code, the Germans believed, even after the landings had begun, that a second and larger invasion would hit the Pas de Calais and for several weeks held strong forces

D Day. American troops move ashore in Normandy, finally taking and holding the western beaches code-named Omaha and Utah.

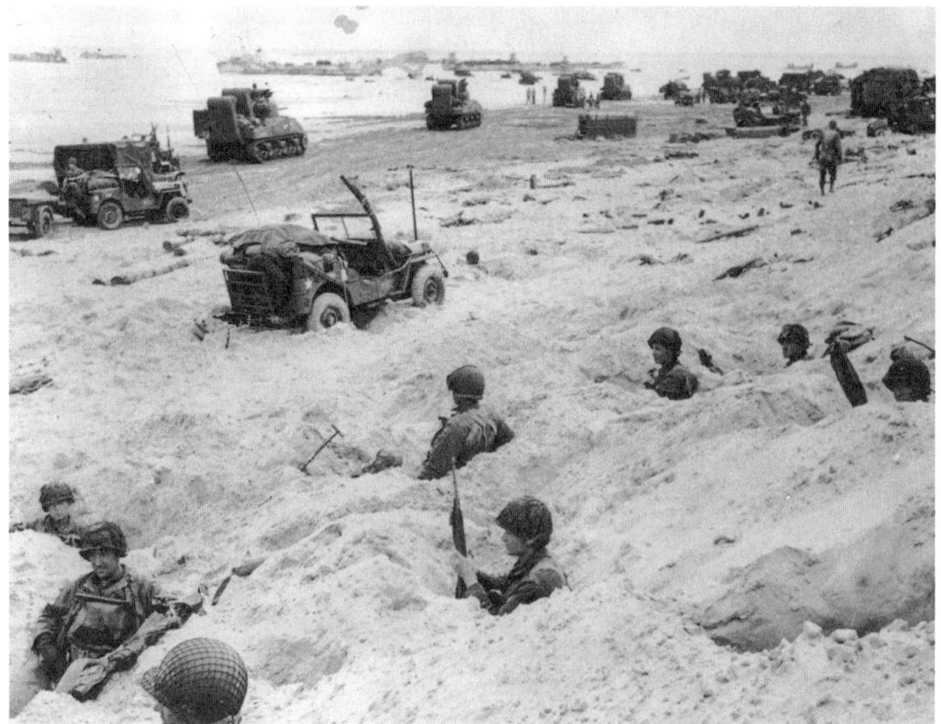

Manning Foxholes. Soldiers maintain the Allies' tenuous first foothold in France as vehicles are brought onto the beach. GAMMA LIAISON NETWORK

there that might have been decisive in Normandy. German defense was further deterred by difficulty in shifting reserves, because of preinvasion bombing of French railroads, disruption of traffic by Allied fighter bombers that earlier had driven German planes from the skies, and French partisans. The bad weather of 5 June and continuing heavy seas on 6 June lulled German troops into a false sense of security. Reluctance of staff officers back in Germany to awaken the German dictator, Adolf Hitler, for approval to commit reserves and tanks delayed a major counterattack against the invasion. The only counterattack on the first day, by a panzer division against the British, was defeated by fire from naval guns.

At the end of D Day, only the Canadians on Juno and the British on Gold had linked their beachheads. More than five miles separated the two American beachheads; the Rangers at Pointe du Hoe were isolated and under siege; and the Fourth Division at Utah Beach had yet to contact the American airborne divisions. Nevertheless, reinforcements and supplies were streaming ashore, even at embattled Omaha Beach, and unjustified concern about landings elsewhere continued to hamper German countermeasures. By the end of the first week, all Allied beachheads were linked and sixteen divisions had landed; only thirteen German divisions opposed them. By the end of June a million Allied troops were ashore.

Several innovations aided the invasion and subsequent buildup. Amphibious tanks equipped with canvas skirts that enabled them to float provided some early fire support on the beaches, although many of the customized tanks sank in the stormy seas. Lengths of big rubber hose (called PLUTO, for Pipe Line Under The Ocean) were laid on the floor of the English Channel for transporting fuel. Given the code name Mulberry, two artificial prefabricated harbors were towed into position at Omaha Beach and Arromanches. These consisted of an inner breakwater constructed of hollow concrete caissons six stories high, which were sunk and anchored in position, and a floating pier that rose and fell with the tide while fixed on concrete posts resting on the sea bottom. Old cargo ships sunk offshore formed an outer breakwater. Although a severe storm on 19 June wrecked the American Mulberry, the British port at Arromanches survived. A sophisticated family of landing craft delivered other supplies directly over the beaches.

Allied casualties on D Day were heaviest at Omaha Beach (2,500) and lightest at Utah (200). American airborne divisions incurred 2,499 casualties. Canadian losses were 1,074; British, 3,000. Of a total of more than 9,000 casualties, approximately one-third were killed.

BIBLIOGRAPHY

Ambrose, Stephen E. *D-Day, June 6, 1944: The Climactic Battle of World War II.* New York: Simon and Schuster, 1994.

Harrison, Gordon A. *Cross-Channel Attack.* Washington, D.C.: Office of the Chief of Military History, Department of the Army, 1951.

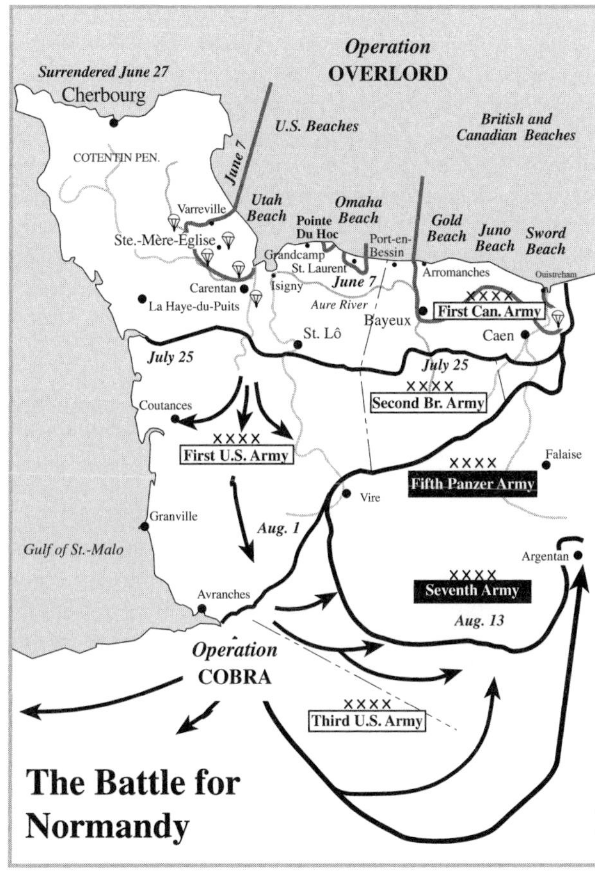

Keegan, John. *Six Armies in Normandy: From D-Day to the Liberation of Paris.* New York: Penguin, 1994.

Ryan, Cornelius. *The Longest Day.* New York: Simon and Schuster, 1994.

Charles B. MacDonald/A. R.

See also **D Day; Navy, United States; World War II, Air War against Germany; World War II, Navy in.**

NORRIS-LAGUARDIA ACT. In 1932, Congress passed the Norris-LaGuardia Anti-Injunction Act in response to what many saw as the abuse of federal court injunctions in labor disputes. An injunction is a judicial order that either commands an individual to perform an act or forbids performing a particular act. As the United States became a more industrialized nation in the late nineteenth and early twentieth centuries, it experienced increasing industrial strife, leading many employers to request federal courts to issue orders prohibiting the activities of strikers. For example, between 1880 and 1930, federal and state courts issued roughly 4,300 antistrike decrees.

The first antistrike decrees appeared during the 1877 railroad STRIKES. When local and state officials expressed reluctance to arrest the strikers, employers turned to the federal courts. Court orders restraining the strikers could often be obtained without any union input into the decision. Although often issued only temporarily, the injunction often succeeded in breaking the strikers' momentum and effectively ended the strike. Federal courts based their authority to issue injunctions chiefly on the Interstate Commerce Act (1887) and the Sherman Antitrust Act (1890). The Supreme Court unanimously upheld the use of such injunctions against striking labor unions in IN RE DEBS (158 U.S. 564, 1895).

Early in the twentieth century, federal court injunctions against labor activities began to fall into increasing disfavor. Labor unions began to lobby Congress for legislation that would abolish the courts' use of labor injunctions. In 1914 labor officials appeared to have achieved their goal when Congress passed the Clayton Act, whose labor provisions seemed to bar federal courts from enjoining peaceful picketing and certain other activities connected with strikes or boycotts. Nevertheless, lower federal courts construed the ambiguous language of the act's anti-injunction provisions in a limited fashion. In 1921 the Supreme Court announced in *Duplex Printing Press Company v. Deering* (254 U.S. 453) that the Clayton Act merely codified the existing common law of the injunction.

The Norris-LaGuardia Act, unlike the ambiguously drafted Clayton Act, ensured that procedural barriers and safeguards limited the use of labor injunctions. The act declared it to be the public policy of the United States that employees be allowed to organize and bargain collectively free of employer coercion. The act treated unions as entities with rights and interests of their own. It granted unions greater authority to engage in strikes and in most cases barred altogether the issuance of injunctions in labor disputes. The Senate report on the bill stated: "A man must work in order to live. If he can express no control over his conditions of employment, he is subject to involuntary servitude" (S.R. 163, 72d Cong., 1st Sess., p. 9).

Beginning in the late 1930s, the federal courts affirmed and extended the Norris-LaGuardia Act's protection of strike and boycott activities to include immunity for labor leaders not only from injunctions but also from civil actions for damages. Nevertheless, the Norris-LaGuardia Act was not as effective as it could have been because it contained no means of enforcing its provisions for labor representation, except through the courts, which sometimes proved hostile to labor's interests.

BIBLIOGRAPHY

Gorman, Robert A. *Basic Text on Labor Law: Unionization and Collective Bargaining.* St. Paul, Minn.: West, 1976.

Leslie, Douglas L. *Labor Law in a Nutshell.* St. Paul, Minn.: West, 2000.

Katherine M. Jones

See also **Clayton Act, Labor Provisions; Injunctions, Labor; Labor Legislation and Administration.**

NORSEMEN IN AMERICA. Generations of American schoolchildren have been taught that America was "discovered" by the Italian explorer Christopher Columbus in 1492 and that the first European colonies were established in the following years. This view of the history of European activities on the North American continent both reflects a relatively narrow view of history centered upon the colonial powers of western Europe during the period beginning in the fifteenth century and ignores a tradition in Scandinavian history about earlier North American expeditions mounted by the Norse.

The Norsemen, under economic and political pressure, were great explorers and launched expeditions to Britain, Iceland, and Greenland from the end of the eighth century through the beginning of the eleventh century. They were able to do this because of their long tradition of seafaring and the technological developments in maritime design that marked this period in Norse history. They established a permanent colony in what is now Iceland sometime around the year 870. This colony survived and became the basis for the modern Icelandic nation. The Norse also established what was intended to be a permanent colony in Greenland about a century later. Greenland, however, was climatically far less hospitable than Iceland, and because of this and possibly because of inter-family feuds, the Greenland colony failed within a century.

There is both literary and archaeological evidence to suggest that at about the same time that the Norse established their Greenland colony they also ventured across the North Atlantic and made their way to the North American coast. Most likely the Norse made landings somewhere along the Canadian coast and may well have established small colonies there. Literary sources refer to these as Vinland, Helluland, and Markland, Vinland being the best known of the three. Adam of Bremen, in a history dated about 1075, refers to Vinland. More importantly, there are several Scandinavian sources that give more details.

Both *Groenlendinga saga* ("Saga of the Greenlanders") and *Eiríks saga rauda* ("Saga of Erik the Red") make explicit references to Norse explorations in Vinland. The information contained in these sagas is rather detailed, although its historicity must be questioned since both sagas are the results of long oral traditions and were not reduced to writing until two centuries after the events related. Nevertheless, the picture that emerges from the sagas is quite fascinating. It would appear that the Norse settlers in Greenland decided to mount several expeditions across the Atlantic. The most notable member of these expeditions was Leif Eriksson, whose father, Erik the Red, had established one of the most important Greenland farms, Brattahlid.

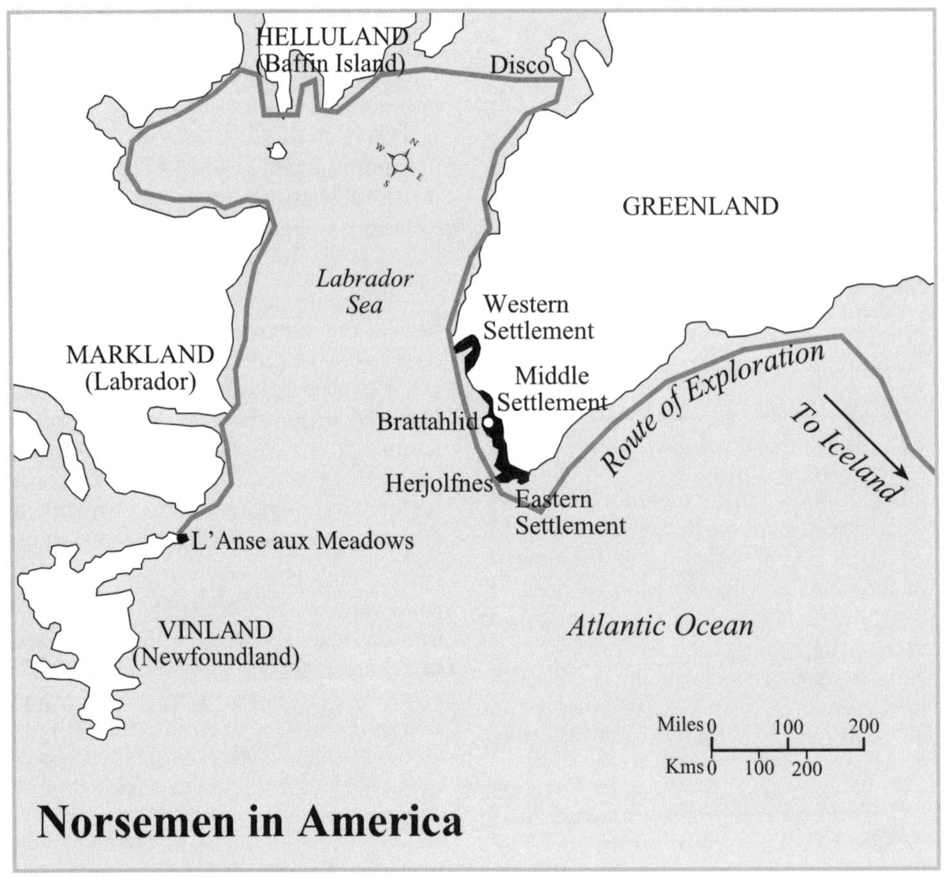

Norsemen in America

North African Campaign. General, then Field Marshal, Erwin Rommel (*pointing*) was the highly regarded German commander called the Desert Fox, but ultimately even he could not hold back the Allied advance in early 1943. ARCHIVE PHOTOS, INC.

Although we have strong literary evidence for Norse incursions into North America, there is no way to discover the exact sites of Vinland, Markland, or Helluland from these literary sources. However, the archaeological evidence can be of great help in this matter. Helge and Anne Stine Ingstad excavated what was quite clearly a Norse settlement on the northern tip of Newfoundland at what is now known as L'Anse aux Meadows. These excavations during the 1960s and 1970s provided confirmation, at least in the generalities, of the Scandinavian sources' claims of Norse settlements in North America. Unfortunately the archaeological evidence does not disclose whether the L'Anse aux Meadows site was intended to be a permanent settlement, a temporary stopover point, or a way station for other expeditions. We do know that whatever the use, it did not last long.

Norse artifacts have been found around the L'Anse aux Meadows site and at other locations, but these have been few, for example, a pin with strong Viking and Celtic influence found in Newfoundland and a Norse coin from the reign of King Olaf Kyrre (1066–1093) in Maine at the remains of a Native American village.

The question of Norse exploration in North America took on a more public aspect with the controversy surrounding the 1965 publication of the so-called Vinland Map. This map, which is alleged to date from the fifteenth century and to document pre-Columbian Norse voyages to North America, has engendered two quite heated debates. The first relates to the authenticity of the map itself, with some scholars strongly supporting the map and its authenticity and others, notably scientists and those using various dating techniques, claiming that the map is a later forgery. The second debate, despite the evidence at L'Anse aux Meadows, goes to the very question of whether the Norse did indeed reach the North American coast before Columbus. Nevertheless, most scholars agree that the archaeological and historical evidence strongly supports an at least temporary Norse presence somewhere in North America prior to 1492.

BIBLIOGRAPHY

Fitzhugh, William W., and Elisabeth I. Ward, eds. *Vikings: The North Atlantic Saga.* Washington, D.C., Smithsonian Institution/National Museum of Natural History, 2000.

Roesdahl, Else. *The Vikings.* Translated by Susan M. Margeson and Kirsten Williams. London and New York: Penguin, 1992; 2d ed., 1998.

Wooding, Jonathan. *The Vikings.* New York: Rizzoli, 1998.

Karenbeth Farmer
M. H. Hoeflich
Gwyn Jones

NORTH AFRICAN CAMPAIGN. After two years of desert skirmishes among the British, Italians, and Germans, the North African campaign opened on 8 November 1942, when Anglo-American forces under U.S. Gen. Dwight D. Eisenhower landed in French Morocco and Algeria near Casablanca and met bitter French resistance.

An armistice brought the fighting to an end on 11 November, and the French forces soon joined the Allies.

Allied units under British Gen. Kenneth Anderson tried to take Bizerte and Tunis quickly, but Italian and German troops held firm. Field Marshal Erwin Rommel's Italo-German army, defeated at El Alamein, Egypt, in October, retreated across Libya and at the end of the year took defensive positions around Mareth, Tunisia, to halt the pursuing British under Gen. Bernard L. Montgomery. Bad weather brought operations to a close. While the seasoned Axis forces built up strength, the Allies suffered from an inadequate supply line, faulty command arrangements, and American battle inexperience and overconfidence.

In February 1943 the Axis forces, in the Battle of Kasserine Pass, drove the Americans and French back about fifty miles in southern Tunisia. Allied confidence was restored with the arrival of new field commanders, British Gen. Harold Alexander and American Gen. George S. Patton Jr. In March 1943, the Allies attacked and pushed Rommel's army into northern Tunisia. Bizerte and Tunis fell on 7 May, Arnim surrendered, and the last organized Axis resistance in North Africa ended on 13 May, with more than 250,000 prisoners taken. With North Africa secure, the stage was set for operations in Europe.

BIBLIOGRAPHY

Blumenson, Martin. *Kasserine Pass.* Boston: Houghton Mifflin, 1967.

Howe, George F. *Northwest Africa: Seizing the Initiative in the West.* Washington, D.C.: Center of Military History, 1991.

Moorehead, Alan. *The March to Tunis.* New York: Harper and Row, 1967.

Strawson, John. *The Battle for North Africa.* New York: Scribner, 1969.

Martin Blumenson / A. R.

See also **Kasserine Pass, Battle of; World War II.**

NORTH AMERICAN FREE TRADE AGREEMENT. The General Agreement on Tariffs and Trade (GATT), which went into effect in 1948 in the wake of World War II, sought to expand free trade by reducing tariffs between the twenty-three signatory nations. A strong supporter of GATT throughout its history, the United States in 1986 began to urge that GATT move beyond the reduction of trade barriers and that its agenda include foreign investment, services, agriculture, and intellectual property rights.

Increasing competition from Pacific and European countries caused the United States to begin trying to assemble a dollar-dominated block in the American hemisphere. This desire led first to the Free Trade Agreement (FTA) with Canada, effective January 1989, and then to an expanded trilateral agreement with Canada and Mexico, the North American Free Trade Agreement (NAFTA), effective January 1994. Given the earlier agreement between the United States and Canada, NAFTA dealt primarily with restructuring trade between the United States and Mexico and between Mexico and Canada. All tariffs between the United States and Canada would end by the year 1998; those between the United States and Mexico would be eliminated by 2008.

The agreements, however, much like the expanded agenda for GATT, covered more than the elimination of trade barriers and led to divisive debate in all three countries. Concerns among Canadians in 1988 and Mexicans in 1992 reflected a lingering view of the United States as a powerful nation that might yet seek to swallow up or strangle its neighbors. While some critics employed a powerful emotional rhetoric reminiscent of the days when the United States was roundly condemned as the Colossus of the North, others focused on the perceived need to protect Canadian and Mexican sovereignty, which they saw as threatened by expanded U.S. investment in such crucial national resources as oil and in institutions such as banking. Given the unequal status between them and their powerful neighbor, these opponents argued, both Canada and Mexico risked becoming in effect economic colonies of the United States.

In 1988 Canadians voiced many of the same concerns expressed by labor leaders and environmentalists in the United States in the early 1990s. Because Canada was already part of GATT, Canadians questioned the necessity of the FTA and the benefit to Canada of tying itself more closely to the largest debtor nation in the world. They argued that the movement of jobs from Canada to the United States, already a problem because of lower U.S. labor costs, would accelerate and that Canada's higher standards of environmental regulation and social programs would be threatened by U.S. investment and business practices. By far the most emotional issue in all three countries was the effect of NAFTA on employment. While proponents of NAFTA stressed that implementation would create jobs, opponents argued that the accord would lead to job loss. The negotiations commenced and continued during a period of global recession and high unemployment. While the movement of jobs from Canada to the United States and from the United States to Mexico had preceded the FTA and NAFTA negotiations, labor groups in both the United States and Canada were unshakable in their opposition.

As the leaders of both Mexico and the United States sought to assuage the fears of those at home who opposed NAFTA, the fate of the pact had implications beyond the borders of North America in the early 1990s. When President George Bush and Mexican President Carlos Salinas de Gortari announced in June 1990 the possibility of a free trade agreement between Mexico and the United States, Bush also announced the Enterprise for the Americas Initiative, which envisioned a free-trade block stretching from Alaska to Tierra del Fuego. This announcement preceded a dizzying number of new trading alignments within Latin America, including the agreement among

Argentina, Brazil, Paraguay, and Uruguay in March 1991 to establish MERCOSUR, which pledged to integrate their economies by 1995, and numerous framework trade agreements between the United States and its southern neighbors.

The creation of a multinational trading bloc was a political and economic project. By the early 1990s, Latin American leaders had come to see the opportunity to move closer to the United States economically as a way to move their countries politically along a modern path of reform. At stake, then, was more than an economic reordering of the relationship among the three North American countries; there was also a foreign policy objective: strengthening political ties throughout the hemisphere. The U.S. Congress approved NAFTA in November 1993. A complicated and cumbersome document largely unread by proponents and opponents alike, it included concessions from all the parties because the United States, Mexico, and Canada saw in it an opportunity to promote their own economies, and protect the frailest components of those economies.

BIBLIOGRAPHY

Bowker, Marjorie Montgomery. *On Guard for Thee: An Independent Analysis, Based on the Actual Test of the Canada-U.S. Free Trade Agreement.* Hull, Quebec: Voyageur, 1988.

Bulmer-Thomas, Victor, Nikki Craske, and Monica Serrano, eds. *Mexico and the North American Free Trade Agreement: Who Will Benefit?* New York: St. Martin's Press, 1994.

Cavanagh, John, et al., eds. *Trading Freedom: How Free Trade Affects Our Lives, Work, and Environment.* San Francisco: Institute for Food and Development Policy, 1992.

Mary Commager / A. G.

See also **Canada, Relations with; Foreign Investment in the United States; Mexico, Relations with; Tariff; Trade, Foreign.**

NORTH ATLANTIC TREATY ORGANIZATION. The signing of the North Atlantic Treaty on 4 April 1949 marked the end of an American tradition of non-tangling alliances from the years of the early Republic. The treaty reflected Cold War fears of Soviet aggression and linked the United States and Canada on one side of the Atlantic with Iceland, Great Britain, France, Belgium, the Netherlands, Luxembourg, Norway, Denmark, Portugal, and Italy on the other side. (Subsequently, Greece and Turkey in 1952, West Germany in 1955, Spain in 1982, and the Czech Republic, Hungary, and Poland in 1999 would join the alliance.) Western-oriented European governments wanted assurances beyond those implied by the Truman Doctrine (1947) and the Marshall Plan (1948–1951) that the United States would defend them against a Soviet attack. Thus, attention has always been directed at Article 5, in which the signatory members agreed that "an armed attack against one or more of them in Europe or North America shall be considered an attack against them all." If such attack occurred, all would respond as if they were each individually attacked.

But NATO was supposed to be more than merely military and anti-Soviet. Canadian diplomats, led by Escott Reid, argued for positive benefits: for the shared cultural tradition reflected in the waves of emigration from Europe to North America (and elsewhere), and the shared values reaching back to ancient Greece and Rome. As NATO expands into Eastern Europe, this emphasis on cultural tradition and economic exchange is helping the alliance adjust to conditions for which it could not have planned—the collapse of the Soviet Union and the dissolution of its former Eastern European empire in the 1990s.

The years in between the formation of NATO and the collapse of the Soviet Union demonstrated the tensions and stresses one would expect in a relationship among various countries with differing interests, needs, and views, but the alliance met its objective of preventing a Soviet attack, and the rebuilding underpinned by the Marshall Plan revived the economy and society of Western Europe.

There are several periods in the history of NATO. After the outbreak of fighting on the Korean peninsula, NATO became more of a military organization, and a series of American senior officials took command as the Supreme Allied Commander Europe (SACEUR); the first SACEUR was General Dwight D. Eisenhower. To compensate for this American military leadership, the secretary-general of NATO, who chairs the North Atlantic Council, has always been a European. While each of the NATO countries remains responsible for its own defense procurement, NATO has invested more than $3 billion in infrastructure for bases, airfields, pipelines, communications, and depots.

Challenges from Within

The role of West Germany in NATO was one of the early stressors for the alliance. Not unnaturally, the idea of a rearmed Germany caused some concern among Western European nations (and probably for the Soviet Union as well). But by 1954, negotiations had worked out the details of West Germany's participation. When the military occupation of West Germany ended in October 1954, it joined NATO seven months later, which resulted in the Soviet Union forming the Warsaw Pact with Central and Eastern Europe. West Germany became a focal point of NATO defense against possible, highly mechanized attacks through the Fulda Gap and other traditional east-west invasion routes.

After Charles de Gaulle was reelected as president in 1966, France voiced its criticism of the U.S. domination of NATO and of European defense, and sought to follow another path. De Gaulle felt that NATO could subject France to a war based on decisions by non-Frenchmen, which, indeed, was the basis of the theory of collective defense. From 1958 to 1966, France indicated its displeasure and thereafter it withdrew from NATO's military command structure and required NATO forces to leave French soil, but claimed that it remained committed to the North Atlantic Treaty in case of "unprovoked aggression." France continued to meet with NATO staff and kept its forces in West Germany through bilateral agreements with the Bonn government rather than through the Treaty.

Another challenge was the storage and possible use of nuclear weapons, which was considered a necessary evil to deter overwhelming Soviet ground strength in terms of tanks and other mechanized and motorized forces. An initial commitment to massive retaliation matured into a strategy of flexible response, thus retaining choice about the decision to "go nuclear." Typically, nuclear weapons were deployed with a so-called dual-key system, which permitted the United States and the host country to retain veto over their use.

NATO's European members always wanted U.S. armed forces stationed on the continent. At the very least, they would serve as a "trip wire," causing a strong U.S. response in the face of a Soviet attack and presumably high U.S. casualties among this forward-stationed defense force. Similarly, European members wanted U.S. nuclear-armed missiles to counter Soviet advantages in ground forces. The alternative in the case of a Soviet invasion of western Europe, European leaders feared, would be a quick march by Soviet and Warsaw Pact forces to the Rhine and beyond before the United States could send the men and materiel from North America needed for defense.

Outside Challenges

There were outside sources of stress for the alliance as well. The construction of the Berlin Wall was a sober reminder of Soviet power in central Europe. Détente during the Nixon administration challenged the alliance to retain its original purpose. The resurgence of Cold War tensions after the 1979 Soviet intervention in Afghanistan, the election of Ronald Reagan as president in 1980, and the military rearmament in the early 1980s were other challenges. But the greatest challenges were Mikhail Gorbachev and his July 1989 announcement that the Soviet Union would no longer prop up communist governments in Europe, and the collapse of the communist regimes in Poland, East Germany, and throughout Eastern Europe. Indeed, what was the ongoing role of NATO if the major threat, an aggressive and expansive Soviet Union, no longer existed?

In the aftermath of the collapse of the Soviet Union, NATO has changed. It has a new purpose to work with the new regimes in Eastern Europe and seeks to ease tensions and conflicts on its periphery, such as in the Balkans. Thus, NATO is reaching out to its former adversaries, including Russia, and has intervened in the former Yugoslavia to contain the fighting. In the aftermath of the terrorist attacks on 11 September 2001, it invoked Article 5 for the first time and indicated that this attack on America was an attack on all of NATO.

BIBLIOGRAPHY

Baylis, John. *The Diplomacy of Pragmatism: Britain and the Formation of NATO, 1942–1949.* Kent, Ohio: Kent State University Press, 1993.

Brogi, Alessandro. *A Question of Self-Esteem: The United States and the Cold War Choices in France and Italy, 1944–1958.* Westport, Conn.: Praeger, 2002.

Giauque, Jeffrey G. *Grand Designs and Visions of Unity: The Atlantic Powers and the Reorganization of Western Europe, 1955–1963.* Chapel Hill: University of North Carolina Press, 2002.

Kaplan, Lawrence S. *The United States and NATO: The Formative Years.* Lexington: University Press of Kentucky, 1984.

Papacosma, S. Victor, Sean Kay, and Mark Rubin, eds. *NATO after Fifty Years.* Wilmington, Del.: Scholarly Resources, 2001.

Park, William H. *Defending the West: A History of NATO.* Boulder, Colo.: Westview Press, 1986.

Reid, Escott. *Time of Fear and Hope: The Making of the North Atlantic Treaty, 1947–1949.* Toronto: McClelland and Stewart, 1977.

Charles M. Dobbs

See also **Cold War; Foreign Policy.**

NORTH CAROLINA. One of the thirteen states to declare independence from Great Britain in 1776, North Carolina has also been a proprietary British colony, a royal colony, and a state in the Confederacy.

Beginnings

Native Americans have populated North Carolina since about 10,000 B.C.E. After European contact in the 1600s, some thirty tribes numbered about 35,000 people. The largest tribes were the Tuscarora, the Catawba, and the Cherokee. Early European explorers of North Carolina were Giovanni da Verrazzano (1524), Lucas Vasquez de Ayllon (1520 and 1526), Hernando de Soto (1540), Juan Pardo and Hernando Boyano (1566–1567), and Philip Amadas and Arthur Barlowe (1584). Receiving a patent from Queen Elizabeth in 1584, Walter Raleigh dispatched the Ralph Lane Colony to Roanoke Island in 1585, but it returned to England in 1586. In 1587 Raleigh sent a colony under John White to Roanoke Island, but it also failed and became known as the "Lost Colony" because the people disappeared. Virginia sent the first settlers into the Albemarle Sound region of North Carolina in the 1650s.

Proprietary period, 1663–1729. In 1663 Charles II granted eight proprietors a charter for Carolina, intended as a buffer colony between Virginia and Spanish settlements. This charter provided for religious liberty and representative government. Carolina's boundaries extended

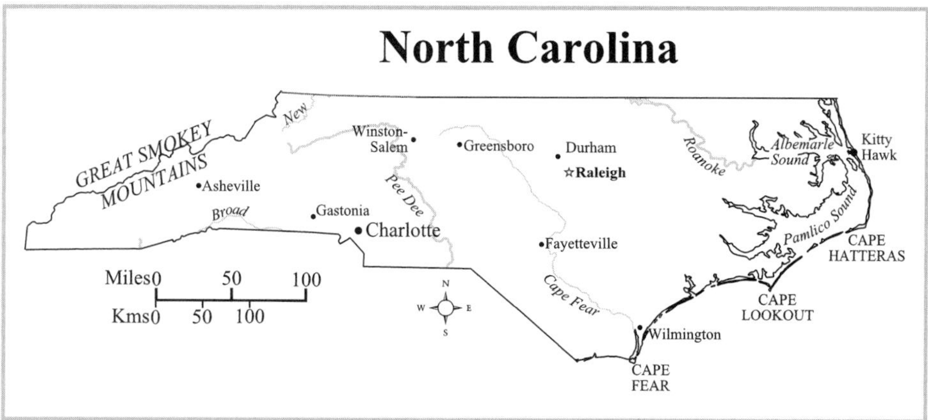

from 29 degrees north to 36 degrees 30 minutes, and from sea to sea. The proprietors sought to establish a feudal society through the Fundamental Constitutions but abandoned the idea by 1700. Instead, the society and government developed as in other colonies, the Assembly being elected by freeholders. In 1711 the proprietors established the separate colonies of North and South Carolina.

North Carolina grew slowly; towns were established at Bath, New Bern, Edenton, Beaufort, and Brunswick from 1705 to1727. New Bern was devastated by the Tuscarora War, 1711–1713. Aided by headrights, colonists arrived from England, Switzerland, the German Palatinate, and France. Slaves also arrived from Africa, and African slavery became a fixed mode of labor. Quakers helped thwart the establishment of the Anglican Church. In 1729 North Carolina became a royal colony; all the proprietors but the earl of Granville sold their interests to the Crown.

Royal colony, 1729–1775. Under royal government North Carolina experienced phenomenal growth. Highland Scots settled the Cape Fear Valley, but most settlers in the Piedmont arrived via the Great Wagon Road from Pennsylvania. They were of Scotch-Irish and German origins and established Presbyterian, Lutheran, Moravian, German Reformed, and Baptist churches. In 1771 Presbyterians founded Queen's College, the first in the colony. The Assembly established the Anglican Church in 1765, but it was never strong. New towns sprang up in the backcountry: Cross Creek (Fayetteville), Hillsborough, Salisbury, and Charlotte. Cherokees siding with the French were defeated in 1761 at the Battle of Echoee. The colonial economy was based on tobacco, foodstuffs, livestock, naval stores, and lumber products.

In government three major conflicts developed, the struggle for power between the governor and the Assembly, the Regulator movement, and opposition to parliamentary taxation. Royal governors used their royal prerogative to demand on occasion that the Assembly do their bidding. The Assembly, however, used its "power of the purse" to control the governor's salary, establish courts, determine a quorum, prevent the appointment of judges for life, and issue bills of credit, all actions the governor was instructed to prohibit.

The Regulator movement was an attempt by backcountry farmers to "regulate" the corrupt actions of county officials. In 1766 Regulators met in Orange County to protest extortionate public fees and corrupt practices. In 1768 they refused to pay taxes, charging the sheriff with embezzlement. While Governor William Tryon ordered Regulators to disband and pay taxes, he also warned county officials against extortion. In 1770 Regulators assaulted local officials at the Orange County courthouse, and Tryon assembled an army and defeated them at Alamance Creek in 1771.

The political issue causing the most conflict was parliamentary taxation. When Parliament passed the Stamp Act in 1765, pamphleteer Maurice Moore argued that colonists could be taxed only with their consent, and they had not consented to the stamp tax. Many towns protested the tax, but in Wilmington the Sons of Liberty forced the stamp master William Houston to resign, leaving no one to enforce the act. HMS *Viper* then seized two ships on Cape Fear because their papers lacked stamps. Armed insurgents, led by Cornelius Harnett and others, boarded the *Viper* and forced the release of the ships.

After the repeal of the Stamp Act, Parliament passed the Townshend Acts (1767), which, among other things, imposed duties on many imported goods. The 1769 Assembly organized an association boycotting British goods until Parliament repealed the taxes. In 1770 Parliament repealed the Townshend Acts but retained the tax on tea, thus leading to the Boston Tea Party. When Parliament ordered the port of Boston closed in 1774, North Carolina sent a shipload of food to help the city. The colony also elected delegates to the First Continental Congress in 1774, which urged nonimportation of British goods.

Locally elected committees of safety enforced the boycott. Supposedly a Charlotte committee of safety adopted a declaration of independence on 20 May 1775. Although corroborating evidence for this event is lacking, the North Carolina flag bears this date.

Revolutionary War and Early Statehood

North Carolina devised a new government after Governor Josiah Martin fled in May 1775. The provincial congress, meeting in Hillsborough, established a provisional government headed by a council of thirteen men and supported by district safety committees. On 12 April 1776 in Halifax the provincial congress urged the Continental Congress to declare independence. This was the first official state action for independence, and this date too is emblazoned on the state flag. The same congress abolished the council of thirteen and created a Council of Safety to govern the state.

Needing a permanent form of government, delegates to the provincial congress in Halifax late in 1776 drafted the first constitution. Conservative delegates wanted a strong executive and protection for property, but radical delegates desired more democratic government, religious freedom, and a strong legislature. The Constitution of 1776 reflected both positions. Conservatives got property and religious qualifications for holding office and a property qualification for voting, while the Radicals got a strong legislature, religious liberty, and the abolition of the established church. The new constitution provided for the separation of powers, but the legislature had preeminent power because it elected the governor and judges.

North Carolina became a battleground in the Revolutionary War. In February 1776 loyalist Scottish Highlanders marched down the Cape Fear Valley to make Wilmington a British base but were defeated at Moore's Creek. The British incited the Cherokees against the colonists in 1776, and General Griffith Rutherford burned their towns. The Cherokees then concluded in 1777 the Treaty of Holston, ceding their lands east of the Blue Ridge. Lord Cornwallis's invasion of North Carolina in late 1780 was blunted by three defeats at Ramsour's Mill, King's Mountain, and Cowpens. Although Cornwallis occupied Wilmington and Hillsborough, he was unable to destroy General Nathanael Greene's army at Guilford Courthouse in March 1781. Cornwallis then abandoned North Carolina for Virginia and defeat at Yorktown.

As an independent state, North Carolina faced many challenges. Industries no longer received British bounties, trade languished, inflation raged, and state government proved weak. Still, much progress was made. Most Tories were pardoned, but much animosity toward them remained. One law confiscating Tory property was declared unconstitutional in the North Carolina Supreme Court decision *Bayard v. Singleton* (1787), the first use of judicial review in one of the United States. The Hillsborough Convention of 1788—called to act on the U.S. Constitution—located a state capital in Wake County. In 1792 the state purchased 1,000 acres of land there and laid off the city of Raleigh. In 1789 the legislature chartered the University of North Carolina, which in 1795 became the first state university to enroll students.

North Carolina sent five delegates to the 1787 Constitutional Convention in Philadelphia, William R. Davie and Hugh Williamson taking active parts. When the new constitution was publicized, eastern planters, merchants, and professionals supported it while western small farmers were opposed. The Hillsborough Convention of 1788 demanded a bill of rights before it would act on ratification. In 1789 Congress proposed a bill of rights and public opinion favored the constitution. The Fayetteville Convention of November 1789 then ratified the constitution.

As in other states, the two-party system that arose around the ideas of Thomas Jefferson and Alexander Hamilton developed in North Carolina as well. The Federalists were at first ascendant, but opposition to Federalist initiatives—especially Jay's Treaty (1794), the Judiciary Act (1801), funding the national debt, assumption of state debts, and the excise tax—emerged and formed the Republican Party. In North Carolina Republicans gained control of the state government, and the Federalist Party declined rapidly after 1800, making North Carolina a one-party state.

Poor Carolina, 1801–1834. Many factors contributed to the state's relative economic and population decline through the 1830s. Although the Republican legislature chartered the state's first two banks in 1804 and created a state bank in 1810, the state lacked capital and a stable currency to support development. The Republican philosophy of the least government being the best government precluded using government for economic development. The lack of cheap transportation also retarded the state. Only one river, the Cape Fear, flowed directly into the ocean; it was navigable up to Wilmington. The state's other main port was Beaufort. The lack of good roads increased the costs of transporting farm products to market and thus discouraged exports. In addition, the lack of an urban culture, little manufacturing except for a few textile mills, emigration to more fertile western lands, and legislative underrepresentation of western counties all hindered development.

Two-party politics and progress, 1837–1861. Following changes in the state constitution made in 1835, the lower house of the legislature came to represent the population and the upper house the amount of taxes paid by county. These constitutional changes ushered in a second era of two-party politics. The Whigs, a new party supporting internal improvements, controlled the governorship 1837 to 1851 and the legislature some of these years. The Whigs supported the state's first railroads, which sped transport, lowered freight costs, and spurred trade and manufacturing. Another Whig contribution was a public school system. In 1839 the legislature enacted a school law allowing counties to establish schools by referendum.

The first school opened in 1840, and by 1850 over 100,000 pupils were enrolled statewide. All of these changes quickened economic activity. The expansion of cotton acreage and the discovery of brightleaf tobacco curing increased farm income by half in the 1850s. Gold mining also flourished and necessitated a branch U.S. mint in Charlotte. Improved transportation greatly enhanced manufacturing, which nearly doubled in value in the 1850s. The leading products by order of value in 1860 were turpentine, flour and meal, tobacco, lumber, and textiles.

During this same antebellum era, religious schools that became Wake Forest University, Duke University, Davidson College, and Guilford College were founded. The federal government, moreover, concluded with the Cherokees the Treaty of New Echota (1835) that led to their later notorious removal and opened their lands to settlement by whites.

Civil War and Reconstruction, 1861–1877

Although North Carolina was not as eager for secession as Deep South states, it followed them into the Confederacy after a state convention overwhelmingly approved secession on 20 May 1861. But state politics during the war reflected North Carolina's ambivalence toward the Confederacy. Zebulon B. Vance, a former Whig Unionist, was elected governor in 1862. He fully supported the war effort, but he fought Jefferson Davis's policies that impinged on civil liberties. In 1864 William W. Holden, a Democratic leader and engineer of Vance's 1862 victory, organized the Peace Party and became its nominee for governor. This party urged North Carolina to rejoin the Union. Vance was reelected, but Holden won favor in the North as a Unionist.

North Carolina furnished a sixth of Confederate troops and suffered high casualties. Wilmington became a major blockade-running port, providing military supplies until it was captured in 1865. The state was also a battleground. Union forces seized the Outer Banks and gained a foothold on the mainland from Plymouth to Beaufort in 1862. In 1865 Sherman's army advanced on Raleigh and secured Joseph E. Johnston's surrender near Durham.

President Andrew Johnson began reconstructing North Carolina by appointing William Holden provisional governor and pardoning many Confederates. Holden called a state convention that voided secession, abolished slavery, and repudiated the state war debt. In the fall elections Jonathan Worth, wartime state treasurer, defeated Holden for the governorship, and many former Confederate officials were elected to Congress. Congress refused to seat these and other delegates sent by governments dominated by former Confederates on the grounds that they were disloyal and freedmen were being mistreated. Indeed, North Carolina was among the states with a "black code" of laws that treated freedmen as a separate class of people, denied basic rights.

Congress and President Johnson became locked in a struggle over Reconstruction policy. Congress wanted full citizenship and civil rights for freedmen, and Johnson opposed this. Congressional Republicans passed over Johnson's veto the Reconstruction acts, which placed the southern states, except Tennessee, under military rule, disfranchised many former Confederates, and required states to revise their constitutions to enfranchise freedmen. When these states were reorganized under their new constitutions, they were required to ratify the Fourteenth Amendment. Then they would regain their seats in Congress.

North Carolina did all that Congress required. William Holden headed the new state Republican Party, which included freedmen, carpetbaggers, and native whites. The Republicans controlled the state convention of 1868 that drafted a more democratic constitution. They also controlled the new state government, and Holden was elected governor.

Opponents of Holden's regime used the issue of "white supremacy" and violence to regain control of state government. The Ku Klux Klan operated in counties with slight Republican majorities. Using murder and intimidation, the Klan suppressed the Republican vote in 1870. Controlling the 1871 legislature, Democrats impeached Holden and removed him from office. The Republican Party still had vitality, for it elected the governor in 1872 and nearly controlled the state convention of 1875 that revised the constitution for Democratic advantage. Finally in 1876 the Democratic Party established white supremacy in state government and used fraud to remain in power.

The New South and Populism, 1877–1901

Young Democratic leaders desired a "New South" of diversified economy and greater wealth for North Carolina. Democrats supported policies under which tobacco manufacturing grew, textile mills expanded, furniture factories arose, and railroads established a 3,800-mile network. Democrats neglected public schools but did charter a black normal school in Fayetteville and an agricultural and mechanical college in Raleigh.

While industry prospered, agriculture languished. Rejecting contract labor, plantation owners adopted sharecropping and the crop-lien system for their labor needs. Tobacco and cotton cultivation were well suited to this system, and overproduction and low prices followed. To address their economic problems, farmers joined the Farmers' Alliance and controlled the 1891 legislature that chartered a female normal college and a black agricultural and mechanical college. Proposing an inflationary monetary policy rejected by the major parties, the Alliance formed the Populist Party in 1892 and fused with the Republicans to control the legislature and elect a Republican governor. The fusionists restored elective local government, secured bipartisan election boards, increased school appropriations, and enhanced railroad regulation. Seizing on the issue of growing numbers of black officeholders, Democrats vowed to restore white supremacy. Using fraud and violence, Democrats controlled the 1899 legislature that proposed a literacy test to disfranchise black voters and a grandfather clause to exempt white voters from the test. Intimidating voters again in 1900, the Democrats secured passage of the literacy test, thus eliminating most black voters and assuring Democratic ascendancy. To win white votes, Democrats began a modern public school system.

Economic Progress, 1901–1929

The great economic expansion of the middle decades of the twentieth century was based partly on the infrastructure developed before 1930. The advent of automobiles led the state to borrow heavily and pave nearly 6,000 miles of roads, thus securing a reputation as a "Good Roads State." Improved roads led to the creation of truck and bus lines and the consolidation of public schools. Streetcar lines flourished from the 1890s to the 1930s, when buses replaced them. Railroads created a 4,600-mile network by 1930. Communications also improved; telephones and radio became common in the 1920s. WBT in Charlotte was the state's first commercial radio station. The Wright brothers first flew at Kill Devil Hill in 1903, and aviation advanced to provide the first air mail in 1927 and the first scheduled passenger service in 1931.

Commercial electrical power generation also spurred economic growth. Companies dammed Piedmont and mountain rivers to make North Carolina a leading hydroelectric power state by 1930. From 1900 to 1930 electrical power helped the state achieve a thirteenfold increase in the value of manufactures. These rapid changes also caused conflict. In the 1920s some legislators introduced bills banning the teaching of evolution in public schools, but they were rejected. Conflict also developed over the stretch-out, a way of forcing textile workers to increase production. Violent textile strikes occurred in Marion and Gastonia in 1929 as employers forcibly suppressed union workers.

Depression and War, 1929–1945

The Great Depression caused economic damage and human suffering. Agricultural prices dropped sharply, forcing tenants from the land and bankrupting many farmers. About 200 banks failed, and the state began stricter regulation. Industrial production declined, causing 25 percent unemployment. Governments and private agencies provided relief and made jobs for the unemployed, but their efforts were inadequate. Unable to pay high property taxes that supported local roads and schools, taxpayers staged a tax revolt. They got the state to pay for all road construction and teachers' pay with a sales tax. Many local governments went bankrupt, and the state henceforth regulated their indebtedness. In 1934 textile workers struck for higher pay but achieved nothing.

New Deal programs provided effective unemployment relief and raised tobacco prices. Despite passage of the Wagner Act in 1935, textile mills blocked union organizing. North Carolina reluctantly provided matching funds for relief programs and social security. Only World War II provided full employment and quickened economic activity. The military established twenty-one training centers in the state, the largest being Fort Bragg, Camp Lejeune, and Cherry Point. Farmers increased production, making North Carolina third in the nation in farm product value. Shipbuilding was one of the major new industries.

Since 1945

North Carolina has eagerly embraced the use of state government to advance the common weal. It has supported a state symphony, an art museum, a zoological park, an arboretum, a residential high school for science and mathematics, a school of the arts, summer schools for gifted students, and an enrichment center for teachers.

Most notable are the state's advances in education. From sixteen disparate state colleges and universities, the state organized in 1971 an excellent university system called the University of North Carolina. The state also constructed an outstanding community college system containing fifty-eight two-year institutions. The system's primary aim is training people for specific jobs. The state has also reformed public schools, providing improved teacher training, standardized tests, experimental charter schools, preschool enrichment, and the grading of each school's performance.

North Carolina has also tackled the problem of low wages—the state ranked forty-fourth in per capita income in 1954. The state recruited industry and helped establish a Research Triangle Park near Raleigh to attract high technology firms, about seventy of them by 2000, when these efforts had raised the state to twenty-ninth place in per capita income.

The recruitment of industry led to greater economic diversification. The old triumvirate of textiles, tobacco, and furniture manufacturing gave way, in order of value, to electrical and electronic equipment, chemicals, and textiles. New industries located mainly in cities, causing a majority of people to move from rural to urban settings. Charlotte, the state's largest city, became a national banking center.

The state also witnessed a revolution in civil rights. In the 1950s African Americans integrated the University of North Carolina and began the integration of public schools. In the 1960s black college students devised the sit-in to integrate Greensboro lunch counters and in Raleigh formed the Student Non-Violent Coordinating Committee to launch sit-ins elsewhere. In Charlotte the NAACP secured the *Swann* decision (1971), which ordered busing to achieve racial balance in public schools.

Since 1972 North Carolina has been evolving as a two-party state. Republicans elected U.S. senators, congressmen, judges, and two governors, but by 2002 they had yet to control the legislature. In every presidential election from 1980 to 2000 the state voted Republican. As politics changed, so did the state's image. Considered a "progressive plutocracy" in the 1940s, the state's image in the early 2000s was cast as a "progressive paradox" or even a "progressive myth."

BIBLIOGRAPHY

Barrett, John G. *The Civil War in North Carolina.* Chapel Hill: University of North Carolina Press, 1963.

Bell, John L., Jr., and Jeffrey J. Crow. *North Carolina: The History of an American State.* 2d ed. Montgomery, Ala.: Clairmont Press, 1998.

Crow, Jeffrey J., et al. *A History of African Americans in North Carolina.* Raleigh, N.C.: Division of Archives and History, 1992.

Durden, Robert F. *The Dukes of Durham, 1865–1929.* Durham, N.C.: Duke University Press, 1975.

Ekirch, A. Roger. *"Poor Carolina": Politics and Society in Colonial North Carolina, 1729–1776.* Chapel Hill: University of North Carolina Press, 1981.

Escott, Paul D. *Many Excellent People: Power and Privilege in North Carolina, 1850–1900.* Chapel Hill: University of North Carolina Press, 1985.

Glass, Brent D. *The Textile Industry in North Carolina: A History.* Raleigh, N.C.: Division of Archives and History, 1992.

Ireland, Robert E. *Entering the Auto Age: The Early Automobile in North Carolina, 1900–1930.* Raleigh, N.C.: Division of Archives and History, 1990.

Lefler, Hugh T., and Albert R. Newsome. *North Carolina: The History of a Southern State.* 3d ed. Chapel Hill: University of North Carolina Press, 1973.

Luebke, Paul. *Tar Heel Politics: Myths and Realities.* Chapel Hill: University of North Carolina Press, 1990.

Powell, William S. *North Carolina through Four Centuries.* Chapel Hill: University of North Carolina Press, 1989.

John L. Bell

See also **Democratic Party; Federalist Party; Hydroelectric Power; Reconstruction; Republicans, Jeffersonian; Two-Party System.**

NORTH DAKOTA, a state with an area of 70,665 square miles, is bounded by the Canadian provinces of Manitoba and Saskatchewan to the north, Montana to the west, and South Dakota to the south. The meandering Red River of the North forms the state's eastern border with Minnesota. The state's topography is as varied as it is beautiful. Pembina, the lowest point at 792 feet above sea level, is situated in North Dakota's northeast corner. To the west, the fertile farms give way to prairies teeming with migratory waterfowl and rolling hills along the Sheyenne, Missouri, and Knife Rivers. In western North Dakota, vast grasslands, plateaus, and multicolored Badlands

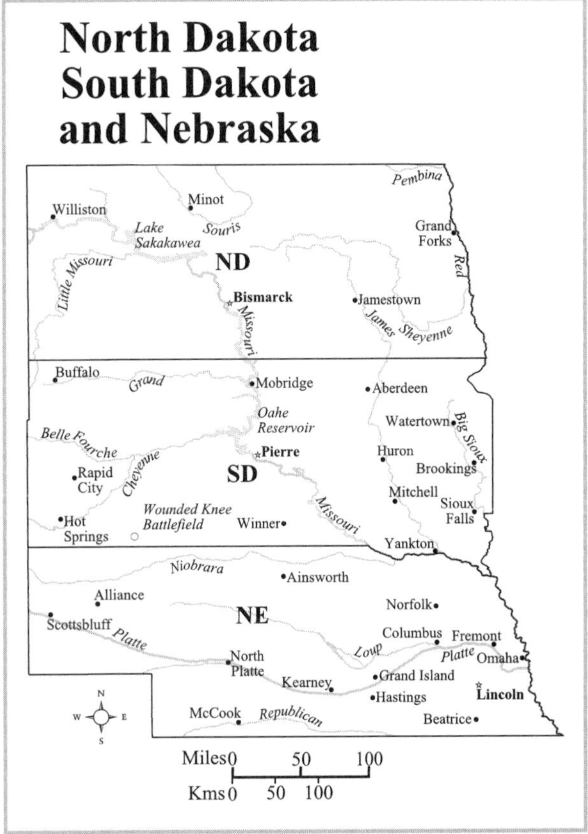

dot the landscape, and the state's highest point, White Butte, rises 3,506 feet above sea level.

Colonial Origins

When Europeans first arrived on the northern Plains during the eighteenth century, they encountered the agricultural Mandan, Hidatsa, and Arikara, who lived in earth lodge villages near the Missouri River. The Chippewa or Ojibway resided to the east in the Turtle and Pembina Mountains. The seminomadic Assiniboine, Cree, Cheyenne, and Dakota or Lakota (called "Sioux" by their enemies) depended upon the bison for their survival. Although the acquisition of the horse transformed these groups into seminomadic buffalo hunters by 1750, they also established commercial ties with traders.

Pierre Gaultier de Varennes, Sieur de La Vérendrye, the first known European to reach present-day North Dakota, visited the region in 1738 during his futile search for a Northwest Passage. The race for colonies, which sparked several armed conflicts, ultimately delayed European settlement of the Northern Plains. In fact, Great Britain, France, and Spain each claimed the Dakotas at some point during the eighteenth century. In 1763, following Britain's victory in the French and Indian War, England acquired France's North American holdings, including the Red River valley, which England later surrendered to the United States in 1818.

From 1762 until 1800, Spain controlled all lands drained by the Missouri and Mississippi Rivers. Napoleon Bonaparte regained this territory for France in 1800, only to sell it to the United States on 2 May 1803. Following Senate approval of the Louisiana Purchase in 1804, President Thomas Jefferson dispatched Meriwether Louis and William Clark to explore the region. The Corps of Discovery's subsequent two-year expedition, much of which was spent in North Dakota at Fort Mandan, revealed a land teaming with abundant game and peaceful natives. Trappers eager to accumulate wealth rushed in. By 1827, the Upper Missouri Outfit monopolized the business. Sadly, the fur trade unleashed a series of devastating epidemics that decimated the region's Natives beginning in 1837.

Dakota Territory and Statehood

Violence erupted across the northern Plains when white settlement increased after the creation on 2 March 1861 of the Dakota Territory, an area initially encompassing the two Dakotas and parts of Montana and Wyoming. The subsequent Homestead Act of 1862, a law offering pioneers 160 acres of free or inexpensive land, accelerated settlement. That same year, Dakota warriors attacked Fort Abercrombie, the first military fort established in present-day North Dakota. General Alfred Sully's subsequent victories at the battles of Whitestone Hill and Killdeer Mountain created conditions fostering white settlement by 1868.

Construction of the westbound Northern Pacific Railway and gold-hungry miners sparked more bloody conflicts during the 1870s. Weakened by disease and hunger, many tribal groups accepted the government's offer of permanent reservations. Lakota warriors, led by Sitting Bull, Red Cloud, and Crazy Horse, remained defiant. Only the destruction of the bison herds forced Sitting Bull, the last holdout, to surrender at Fort Buford in northwestern Dakota Territory in 1881. At the beginning of the twenty-first century, many of the state's 35,228 American Indians lived on one of five reservations: Spirit Lake, Fort Berthold, Standing Rock, Turtle Mountain, and Lake Traverse.

Political Trends

Alexander McKenzie, the Northern Pacific's political agent in northern Dakota, demonstrated the power of outside corporate interests when he conspired with Nehemiah Ordway, the corrupt Republican governor of the Dakota Territory, in 1883 to transfer the territorial capital from Yankton to Bismarck, a town located on the railroad's main line. Hard feelings regarding the relocation motivated residents of southern Dakota Territory to push for the creation of two separate states. On 2 November 1889, President Benjamin Harrison signed legislation admitting both North Dakota and South Dakota into the Union.

Populists, who dominated state politics during the depression years of the early 1890s, fought government corruption. Seeking to strengthen their position, they joined forces with Democrats in 1892 to elect Governor Eli Shortridge. Although defeated by McKenzie's powerful Republican machine in 1894, the reformers had forced the railroads to reduce their rates. When political bosses continued to ignore calls for reform, George Winship, the editor of the *Grand Forks Herald*, founded the Good Government League in 1905. The following year, angry voters elected "Honest" John Burke, the state's first Democratic governor. New movements, particularly the American Society of Equity and the North Dakota Socialist Party, continued to fight outside predatory interests. The progressives' direct appeals to voters tired of corruption produced several changes, including cooperative rural grain elevators, direct primaries, the initiative and referendum, workers' compensation laws, and laws regulating monopolies.

The revolt against out-of-state banks, railroads, and grain interests culminated in Arthur C. Townley's establishment of the Nonpartisan League in 1915. Progressives eager to improve services and to eliminate corruption from government elected Lynn J. Frazier governor in 1918. Frightened conservatives responded by establishing the Independent Voters Association to fight the Nonpartisan League, its candidates, and its proposals. The economic downturn of the 1920s ultimately ended the Nonpartisan League's political power but not its legacy. Despite fierce opposition, reformers created the Bank of North Dakota and the State Mill and Elevator. Remarkably, both state-owned businesses survived into the twenty-first century.

The economic catastrophe of the 1920s and 1930s united citizens in a campaign to eliminate the crooked practices that drove them into bankruptcy. The North Dakota Farmers' Union, established in 1927, became more militant as the depression worsened. William Langer became governor in 1933, and that year he reacted to the farmers' plight by imposing a moratorium on mortgage foreclosure sales. Hoping to drive up commodity prices, Langer also issued an embargo on the shipment of grain and beef from North Dakota. A federal investigation, however, threatened to derail the political maverick's career. The sham trial that followed resulted in the governor's conviction and removal from office in 1934. Langer, whose conviction was overturned following a lengthy legal battle, was reelected governor in 1936 as an independent.

The explosive politics of the Great Depression evolved into a modern political tug-of-war between two parties. The Republicans, led by Fred G. Aandahl and Milton R. Young, dominated the state's post–World War II politics. Liberals, responding to the Republican dominance of the 1940s and 1950s, joined forces. The tactic produced positive results when, in 1958, Quentin N. Burdick became North Dakota's first Democratic congressman. Two years later, a Democrat, William L. Guy, was elected governor, a post Democrats occupied until 1981.

During the 1980s, Republicans reasserted their political clout. After 1986, when Democrats gained control of the state senate for the first time, Republicans piled up impressive electoral victories. By 2000, Republicans once again dominated both branches of the state legislature. Despite the popularity of Republicans, however, North Dakotans, leery of entrusting too much power to one party, subsequently elected an all-Democratic congressional delegation.

Economic and Population Trends

Pacification of the region's Indians, coupled with the completion of new railways, attracted 100,000 new settlers to Dakota Territory between 1879 and 1886. By 1890, North Dakota's population had reached 190,983. Bonanza farms, extensive operations exceeding 3,000 acres, helped popularize North Dakota's bounty. A series of harsh winters, floods, and drought later drove many pioneers away. A second wave of settlers from 1898 to 1915, mostly Scandinavians and Germans, increased the state's resident population to 646,872 by 1920.

A twenty-year depression, compounded by prolonged drought, began in 1921. Hardship and out-migration followed as 40,000 residents fled the state, dubbed "the Too Much Mistake," during the 1930s. Favorable weather conditions and wartime demand for commodities triggered an economic recovery. By 1974 increased global demands produced record-breaking commodity prices. Within two years, however, slumping grain sales and plummeting wheat prices drove many farmers into bankruptcy. Agricultural price supports became a necessary means of survival for many farmers. During the 1990s, weak international demand for American commodities produced even lower prices. The Federal Agricultural Improvement and Reform Act of 1996, which replaced price supports with a fixed and slowly declining subsidy, aggravated the situation. Not surprisingly, the decline of the state's family farms continued.

While North Dakota's reliance on agriculture declined, the state remained a major producer of wheat, sugar beets, barley, sunflower seeds, canola, and flaxseed. The success of producer-owned cooperatives, particularly the Minn-Dak Farmers Cooperative and the Dakota Pasta Growers Association, became encouraging. In addition, the growth of the state's food processing and agricultural equipment manufacturing industries helped revive North Dakota's slumping agricultural economy.

The energy sector, notably coal and oil, has played a critical role in the state's economy. The discovery of high-grade oil near Tioga on 4 April 1951 initiated the state's petroleum industry. The energy crisis of the 1970s revitalized western North Dakota's crude oil operations. A decade later, the oil boom peaked with 52.7 million barrels of crude oil production in 1984. By 1992, production had dropped to 32.9 million barrels. However, international trends, particularly rising energy costs and the uncertain production policies of the Organization of Petroleum Exporting Countries (OPEC), rekindled interest in the nation's ninth largest oil-producing state.

The state's bountiful lignite coal deposits also attracted investors. Following the Arab oil boycott of 1973, corporations built several generating facilities and launched huge strip-mining operations in the state. Exporting two-thirds of its power production, North Dakota became a major supplier of electrical power. The quest for alternative sources of energy also produced the country's first coal-to-synthetic natural gas conversion facility near Beulah in 1983.

North Dakota's industrial structure differs from other states. North Dakota relies heavily upon government employment, with 21 percent of all workers classified as government employees versus just 15 percent nationwide. Unlike other states, North Dakota's manufacturing sector employs a mere 7 percent of the state's workers, half the national average. In addition, agriculture's role in the state economy is five times as large as the national average, with farm production accounting for 7.6 percent of the state's total economic output. When farm-related industries, such as food processing and transportation and distribution of food products, are factored in, this figure rises to 13 percent.

Recognizing the danger of relying too heavily on the boom-and-bust cycles of the state's leading industries, North Dakotans have implemented measures to diversify the state's economy. As a result, the percentage of residents in private nonfarm employment increased 26.8 percent between 1990 and 1998, nearly doubling the national average of 15.7 percent during the same period. Motivated by the success of Fargo's Microsoft Great Plains Business Solutions, politicians also lured information technology businesses to the state by touting North Dakota's affordable utilities, high quality of life, educated workforce, low taxes, and right-to-work laws. The economy also benefited from a booming service sector industry consisting of bank service centers, travel agencies, computer technical support facilities, and health care management companies.

Tourism also became a fast-growing industry. History buffs enjoy the state's abundance of museums, historic trading posts, and military forts. The International Peace Garden and the rugged Badlands also attract visitors. The legalization of casino gambling on the state's American Indian reservations in 1992 and 1993 fueled tremendous growth in amusement and recreation services across the state, and the booming gaming industry brought economic development to the reservation communities. Outdoor enthusiasts, eager to take advantage of the state's unpolluted environment, arrived in growing numbers.

While economic diversification remained central to North Dakota's development, legislators recognized the need to attract new residents. Following a massive influx of Europeans during the 1920s, the state's population peaked at 680,845 in 1930. By 1950, the resident population had dipped to 619,636. In 1970, the state's population reached a modern low of 617,792. The 1980 census counted 652,717 residents, marking the state's first population gain since 1930. The 1990 census, however, enumerated only 638,800 residents, and by 2000 that number had increased to only 642,200 people. North Dakota's Hispanic and American Indian populations increased during the 1990s.

Census numbers also point to the continuing decline of rural North Dakota. While the 1990 census revealed that the state's urban population had eclipsed the rural population, the 2000 census revealed that only six of the state's fifty-three counties gained population during the 1990s. Amazingly half of the counties lost 10 percent of their residents during the decade, a fact attributed to the slumping agricultural economy and out-migration to Fargo, Bismarck, Grand Forks, and Minot.

At the beginning of the twenty-first century, the residents of North Dakota continued to reap the benefits of their reform-minded predecessors, who established a system of government that limited corruption in politics by empowering the people with a direct share in the decision-making process. Although they frequently disagreed, North Dakotans wanted to solve the thorny issues that most threatened their state, including halting the out-migration of young people, promoting rural economic development, and diversifying an economy historically tied to the volatile agriculture and energy sectors.

BIBLIOGRAPHY

Bochert, John R. *America's Northern Heartland.* Minneapolis: University of Minnesota Press, 1987.

Danbom, David B. *Born in the Country: A History of Rural America.* Baltimore: Johns Hopkins University Press, 1995.

———. "North Dakota: The Most Midwestern State." In *Heart Land: Comparative Histories of the Midwestern States.* Edited by James H. Madison. Bloomington: Indiana University Press, 1988.

Howard, Thomas W., ed. *The North Dakota Political Tradition.* Ames: Iowa State University Press, 1981.

Kraenzel, Carl Frederick. *The Great Plains in Transition.* Norman: University of Oklahoma Press, 1955.

Lamar, Howard Roberts. *Dakota Territory, 1861–1889: A Study of Frontier Politics.* Rev. ed. Fargo: North Dakota Institute for Regional Studies, 1997. The definitive history of Dakota Territory politics.

Lindgren, H. Elaine. *Land in Her Own Name: Women as Homesteaders in North Dakota.* Fargo: North Dakota Institute for Regional Studies, 1991.

Newgard, Thomas P., William C. Sherman, and John Guerrero. *African-Americans in North Dakota: Sources and Assessments.* Bismarck, N.Dak.: University of Mary Press, 1994.

Robinson, Elwyn B. *History of North Dakota.* Fargo: North Dakota Institute for Regional Studies, 1995.

Schneider, Mary Jane. *North Dakota Indians: An Introduction.* 2d ed. Dubuque, Iowa: Kendall/Hunt Publishing, 1994.

Tweton, D. Jerome, and Theodore B. Jellif. *North Dakota: The Heritage of a People.* Fargo: North Dakota Institute for Regional Studies, 1976.

Wilkins, Robert P., and Wynona H. Wilkins. *North Dakota: A Bicentennial History.* New York: Norton, 1977.

Jon Brudvig

See also **Dakota Territory; Great Plains; Populism; South Dakota; Tribes: Great Plains.**

NORTH SEA MINE BARRAGE. The North Sea mine barrage was a World War I minefield 230 miles long and more than fifteen miles wide, laid in 1918 between the Orkney Islands off northern Scotland and Norway to blockade German submarines. The mines had long wire antennas that would explode the contents, 300 pounds of TNT, on contact with any metallic object. Altogether 70,263 were laid at a cost of $80 million ($952.8 million in 2002 dollars). The exact number of German U-boats destroyed is unknown but is estimated at seventeen. The effect was perhaps greater in shattering the morale of German submarine crews, thus helping to produce the revolt of German seamen that marked the beginning of the defeat of Germany.

BIBLIOGRAPHY

Mannix, Daniel P. "The Great North Sea Mine Barrage." *American Heritage* 34 (April 1983): 36–48.

Syrett, David. *The Defeat of the German U-Boats,* Columbia: University of South Carolina Press, 1994.

Walter B. Norris/A. R.

See also **Minesweeping; World War I, Navy in.**

NORTH WEST COMPANY. The North West Company, a major fur-trading firm organized in the winter of 1783–1784, was never an incorporated company, as were its chief rivals, the Hudson's Bay Company and the American Fur Company. It resembled a modern holding company, the constituent parts of which were chiefly Montreal firms and partnerships engaged in the fur trade. It came into existence during the American Revolution and ended by coalescing with the Hudson's Bay Company in 1821. In the interim it had reorganized in 1783; added the firm of Gregory, McLeod, and Company, its chief rival, in 1787; split into two factions in the later 1790s; reunited in 1804; joined forces with the American Fur Company temporarily in 1811; been ejected from effective work on the soil of the United States in 1816; and established its posts over much of Canada and the northern United States. Its main line of communication was the difficult canoe route from Montreal, up the Ottawa River, and through Lakes Huron and Superior to its chief inland depot: Grand Portage before 1804 and Fort William thereafter. Beyond Lake Superior, the route to the Pacific was the international boundary waters to Lake of the Woods in Minnesota, the Winnipeg River, Lake Winnipeg, the Saskatchewan River, the Peace River, and the Fraser River. Many lines branched from this main one: south into the Wisconsin, Dakota, Minnesota, and Oregon countries and north to Lake Athabasca and the Mackenzie River area.

The company made unsuccessful attempts to gain access to the interior through Hudson Bay, whose basin was the exclusive trading area of the Hudson's Bay Company. Intense competition between the two companies grew to fever pitch after Thomas Douglas, earl of Selkirk, established his colony in the Red River Valley in 1811, and it led to warfare. Thereafter, but only at the cost of sinking its individuality under the charter rights and acquiring the name of the Hudson's Bay Company, the North West Company got its cheaper transportation route. When this union occurred in 1821, the Scottish, Yankee, English, and French-Canadian employees of the North West Company had behind them nearly fifty years of valorous exploration and trailblazing; they had forced the Hudson's Bay Company to build forts in the interior, and they had developed the voyageur to the acme of his unique serviceability.

BIBLIOGRAPHY

Brown, Jennifer S. H. *Strangers in Blood: Fur Trade Company Families in Indian Country.* Norman: University of Oklahoma Press, 1996.

Keith, Lloyd, ed. *North of Athabasca: Slave Lake and Mackenzie River Documents of the North West Company, 1800–1821.* Ithaca: McGill-Queen's University Press, 2001.

White, Richard. *The Middle Ground: Indians, Empires, and Republics in the Great Lakes Region, 1650–1815.* New York: Cambridge University Press, 1991.

Grace Lee Nute / A. E.

See also **Astoria; Fur Companies; Fur Trade and Trapping; Grand Portage; Indian Trade and Traders; Pacific Fur Company.**

NORTHERN SECURITIES COMPANY V. UNITED STATES, 193 U.S. 197 (1904), began as a contest between competitive railroad trunk lines over control of an intermediate feeder line and ended up as a struggle for supremacy that pitted railroad moguls John Pierpont Morgan and James J. Hill against Edward H. Harriman.

Harriman, who controlled the Union Pacific system, had attempted to wrest from Morgan and Hill a special interest in the Chicago, Burlington, and Quincy, thereby effecting an entrance into Chicago. At first by stealthy moves and then by frenzied bidding culminating in the "Northern Pacific panic" of 1901, Harriman acquired a majority of the voting rights outstanding in Northern Pacific stock. Negotiations ensued for a friendly settlement, and out of them emerged the Northern Securities Company, a massive conglomerate encompassing virtually all the contestants' stock.

Challenged for violation of the Sherman Antitrust Act, the defendants contended that that act did not embrace the mere transfer of proprietary interests in any enterprise from one person to another. However, the Supreme Court upheld the government's contention that the holding company had been used as an illegal device for restraining interstate trade, since its necessary effect was to eliminate competition in transportation service over a large section of the country. The decision gave teeth to the Sherman Antitrust Act and spurred the government's trust-busting efforts.

BIBLIOGRAPHY

Himmelberg, Robert F., ed. *The Monopoly Issue and Antitrust, 1900–1917.* New York: Garland, 1994.

Kolko, Gabriel. *Railroads and Regulation, 1877–1916.* Princeton, N.J.: Princeton University Press, 1965.

McGraw, Thomas K., ed. *Regulation in Perspective.* Boston: Harvard University Press, 1981.

Myron W. Watkins / A. R.

See also **Antitrust Laws; Corporations; Holding Company; Monopoly; Trusts.**

NORTHFIELD BANK ROBBERY. After some days of preliminary scouting, eight men headed by Thomas ("Cole") Younger, a former Confederate guerrilla, rode into Northfield, Minnesota, about noon on 7 September 1876. While three men attempted to hold up the First National Bank, killing teller Joseph Heywood, the remainder engaged townspeople in a wild gun battle, during which two bandits were killed and a bystander was mortally wounded. On 21 September, a posse surrounded four of the gang near Madelia; two men, probably Frank and Jesse James, had escaped. After sharp gunfire in which one bandit was killed, the three Younger brothers, badly wounded, surrendered.

BIBLIOGRAPHY

Appler, Augustus C. *The Younger Brothers.* New York: F. Fell, 1955.

Younger, Cole. *The Story of Cole Younger by Himself.* St. Paul: Minnesota Historical Society Press, 2000.

Willoughby M. Babcock / C. W.

See also **Robberies; Train Robberies; Vigilantes.**

NORTHWEST ANGLE, a projection of land extending north of the forty-ninth parallel on the northern boundary of Minnesota. This 130-square-mile area, separated from the rest of Minnesota by the Lake of the Woods, is the northernmost territory in the contiguous United States. Ignorance of the region's geography caused this curious projection of the international boundary in 1783, when the Definitive Treaty of Peace attempted to fix the United States–Canadian border. Subsequent explorations forced modifications of the line in the Convention of 1818, which were further revised in negotiations conducted in 1824, 1825, and 1842. Boundary surveys continued, however, until a final treaty fixed the boundary in 1925.

BIBLIOGRAPHY

Parsons, John E. *West on the 49th Parallel: Red River to the Rockies, 1872–1876.* New York: Morrow, 1963.

T. C. Blegen / c. w.

See also **Canada, Relations with; Convention of 1818 with England; Surveying; Paris, Treaty of (1783).**

NORTHWEST CONSPIRACY. Military reversals in 1863–1864 led Confederates to promote insurrection in the Northwest. The plan relied on the Sons of Liberty and other Northern sympathizers and called for the liberation of Confederate prisoners from northern prison camps. Insurrectionists would use weapons from federal arsenals to arm themselves and overthrow the governments of Ohio, Indiana, Illinois, and Missouri. With a Northwestern confederacy allied with the pre-existing Confederate states, a dismembered North would be forced to surrender.

Clement L. Vallandigham, supreme commander of the Sons of Liberty, then in Canada, refused to cooperate with Jacob Thompson, Confederate commissioner in Canada. Other, less scrupulous Copperhead (or Peace Democrat) leaders accepted funds and promised cooperation. An uprising planned for 20 July was postponed to 16 August, and again to 29 August, the date of the Democratic National Convention at Chicago. The federal government learned of the plan and reinforced the guard at Camp Douglas, where the first blow was to be struck; the uprising did not take place, although sixty Confederates under Capt. T. H. Hines were present in Chicago.

Abandoning hope of Copperhead assistance, the Confederates proceeded in September and October to create diversions on the Canadian border, most important of which were John Yates Beall's raid to liberate prisoners on Johnson Island in Lake Erie and the raid on Saint Albans, Vermont.

The Northwest conspiracy failed because COPPERHEADS refused to take arms against the federal government and because Copperhead violence would endanger Democratic prospects in the campaign of 1864.

BIBLIOGRAPHY

Klement, Frank L. *The Limits of Dissent: Clement L. Vallandigham and the Civil War.* New York: Fordham University Press, 1998.

———. *Copperheads in the Middle West.* Chicago: University of Chicago Press, 1960.

Charles H. Coleman / T. D.

See also **Canada, Confederate Activities in; Civil War; Knights of the Golden Circle; Sons of Liberty (Civil War).**

NORTHWEST PASSAGE. First navigated during a voyage from 1903 to 1906 by the Norwegian explorer Roald Amundsen in his ship, the *Gjoa*, the Northwest Passage is the sea route that links the North Atlantic Ocean with the North Pacific Ocean. It extends from Baffin Bay, which lies between West Greenland and Baffin Island, to the Bering Strait, which lies between Alaska and Siberia, through the Canadian Arctic Archipelago. Sixteenth- and seventeenth-century explorers hoped to find a shortcut around America to eastern Asia through a passage north of the American continent. However, the passage eluded discovery for centuries because of the intricate geography of the archipelago, along with the obstacle of constant polar ice in the sea.

By the mid-nineteenth century, it had been proven that a Northwest Passage existed, but that it would be very difficult to navigate. After his successful navigation, Amundsen graciously credited British seamen with making his accomplishment possible with their centuries of attempts to locate and navigate the passage, as well as their subsequent maps of the intricate Arctic geography. William Baffin discovered the eastern approach in 1616 in Baffin Bay, and Robert J. Le M. McClure located the passage from the west during a voyage from 1850 to 1854.

BIBLIOGRAPHY

Savours, Ann. *The Search for the North West Passage.* New York: St. Martin's Press, 1999.

Mary Anne Hansen

See also **Polar Exploration.**

NORTHWEST TERRITORY. Part of the vast domain ceded by Great Britain to the United States in the Treaty of Paris (1783), the Northwest Territory encompassed the area west of Pennsylvania, east of the Mississippi River, and north of the Ohio River to the border with British Canada. The "Old Northwest," as the region later came to be known, eventually included the states of Ohio, Indiana, Illinois, Michigan, Wisconsin, and the part of Minnesota east of the Mississippi River. The creation of the Northwest Territory was first implied in the Articles of Confederation (1780), which stipulated that all lands beyond the bounds of the original thirteen states would be owned and administered by the national government.

The establishment of a federal public domain reconciled and negated the competing claims of Massachusetts, Connecticut, Virginia, and New York to lands beyond the Appalachian Mountains. While this cleared the way for confederation, the means for administering these lands was not fully established until 1787, when Congress passed An Ordinance for the Government of the Territory

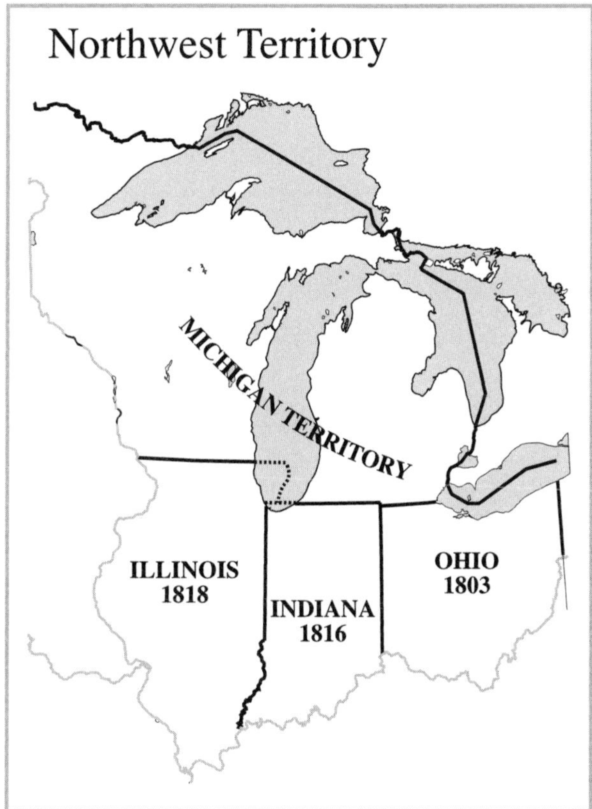

of the United States Northwest of the River Ohio. This Northwest Ordinance provided for the orderly survey of all lands into square sections of 640 acres and established the procedures for their sale to individuals and corporations. Besides the grid pattern of states, counties, towns, farms, and roads that would spread out across the continent, the ordinance also established the methods for creating new states and their admission into the Union "on an equal footing with the original States in all respects whatever."

Although some form of territorial governance continued in the Old Northwest until Minnesota achieved statehood in 1858, the administrative history of the Northwest Territory is fairly brief. The celebrated revolutionary war general Arthur St. Clair established the first territorial government on 15 July 1788. Because of increased migration, Congress in 1800 divided the Northwest Territory for administrative purposes and designated the western portion as the territory of Indiana. The reduced Northwest Territory ceased to exist as an official geopolitical entity in 1803, when the state of Ohio was admitted to the Union and Congress designated the region to the north as the territory of Michigan.

Despite its short duration, the history of the Northwest Territory is marked by some of the most brutal and aggressive warfare in U.S. history. Based on a vision of expanding agricultural settlement and motivated by a desperate need for the revenue that would come from the sale of public lands, federal policy was geared toward the rapid conversion of Indian lands into private property. Native alliances initially took a severe toll on U.S. forces, and at times as much as 80 percent of the entire federal budget went to fighting and removing Indians from their lands. By the end of the short territorial period, Native communities decimated by warfare and disease had moved beyond the bounds of Ohio to areas farther west. The scenario was repeated over the course of three decades, as new states entered the Union and the fertile soils of the Old Northwest were converted into the vast expanse of farms and towns that became a hallmark of the region.

BIBLIOGRAPHY

Cayton, Andrew R. L., and Peter S. Onuf. *The Midwest and the Nation: Rethinking the History of an American Region.* Bloomington: Indiana University Press, 1990.

Rohrbough, Malcolm J. *The Trans-Appalachian Frontier: People, Societies, and Institutions, 1775–1850.* New York: Oxford University Press, 1978.

Mark David Spence

See also **Indian Removal; Territorial Governments; Western Lands.**

NORWEGIAN CHURCHES. Norwegian American churches established in the nineteenth century reflected the Lutheran religious emphases in the homeland. Low-church revivalism, led by Elling Eielsen, a self-taught layman, formed the basis for the Eielsen Synod (1846). This body splintered when the majority organized Hauge's Synod (1876), named in memory of the Norwegian revivalist Hans Nielsen Hauge. Representatives of a more traditional Lutheranism, led by university-trained immigrant clergymen, organized (1853) the Norwegian Synod, which soon formed ties with the German Missouri Synod.

The predestination controversy within the Missouri-influenced Norwegian Synod led to the formation in the 1880s of the Anti-Missourian Brotherhood, which assumed leadership in a union movement that created the United Church (1890). Polity and property disputes in the new body produced the Lutheran Free Church (1897). Negotiations, begun in 1905, brought 98 percent of the Norwegian Lutherans into the Norwegian Lutheran Church of America in 1917. An ultraconservative minority, the Norwegian Synod of the American Lutheran Church, was formed in 1918. The Norwegian Lutheran Church of America was united with the American Lutheran (German background) and the United Evangelical Lutheran (Danish background) churches to form The American Lutheran Church (1960). The Lutheran Free Church joined The American Lutheran Church in 1963. The drift away from an exclusive ethnic identity was all but complete by 1982, when The American Lutheran Church merged with two smaller branches to form the Evangelical Lutheran Church in America (ELCA). With more than 5.2 million baptized members, the ELCA was by 2000 the largest Lutheran church in the United States.

BIBLIOGRAPHY

Nelson, E. Clifford, and Eugene L. Fevold. *The Lutheran Church among Norwegian-Americans: A History of the Evangelical Lutheran Church.* 2 vols. Minneapolis: Augsburg Publishing House, 1960.

E. Clifford Nelson / A. R.

See also **Immigration; Lutheranism; Scandinavian Americans.**

NUCLEAR NON-PROLIFERATION TREATY (1968). Following more than a decade of discussions, on 12 June 1968 the United Nations General Assembly approved the text of a nuclear non-proliferation treaty authored primarily by representatives from the United States and the Soviet Union. On 1 July 1968 the United States, Great Britain, and the Soviet Union signed the treaty, along with fifty-nine other countries. American President Lyndon Johnson submitted the treaty to the U.S. Senate for ratification on 9 July 1968, but after the Soviet invasion of Czechoslovakia on 20–21 August 1968, the Senate was unwilling to approve any treaty with Moscow. As tensions between the superpowers cooled in early 1969, newly inaugurated President Richard Nixon resubmitted the treaty to the Senate. The Senate ratified the treaty on 13 March 1969, and Nixon signed it into law on 24 November 1969. In March 1970, the treaty took effect as international law.

The treaty had three main provisions. First, it prohibited the declared nuclear states (as of 1 January 1967)—the United States, the Soviet Union, Great Britain, France, and the People's Republic of China—from transferring nuclear weapons to nonnuclear states. Nonnuclear states were not allowed to receive or manufacture nuclear weapons. Second, the treaty protected the peaceful uses of nuclear energy by all states. International Atomic Energy Agency safeguards would assure that nuclear energy was not diverted into nuclear weapons. Third, the treaty obligated nuclear weapons states to "pursue negotiations in good faith" for "general and complete disarmament."

Only Israel, India, Pakistan, and Cuba have refused to sign the treaty. They claim that the treaty is unfair because it privileges the nuclear "haves" of the 1960s, while preventing other states from acquiring their own nuclear arsenals. India, in particular, has also accused the United States and other nations of failing to meet their stated obligation to negotiate for "general and complete disarmament." In the twenty-first century the proponents of the treaty will have to seek ways of overcoming these criticisms.

BIBLIOGRAPHY

Bundy, McGeorge. *Danger and Survival: Choices About the Bomb in the First Fifty Years.* New York: Vintage Books, 1990.

Bunn, George. *Arms Control by Committee: Managing Negotiations with the Russians.* Stanford, Calif.: Stanford University Press, 1992.

———. *Extending the Non-proliferation Treaty: Legal Questions Faced by the Parties in 1995.* Washington, D.C.: American Society of International Law, 1994.

Garthoff, Raymond L. *Détente and Confrontation: American-Soviet Relations from Nixon to Reagan.* revised ed. Washington, D.C.: The Brookings Institution, 1994.

Jeremi Suri

See also **Arms Race and Disarmament.**

NUCLEAR POWER refers to the energy produced by fission, when atoms are split, or by fusion, when two nuclei of a light atom are fused to form a single nucleus. The energy produced can be used for weapons or for peaceful purposes. The phrase is also used to designate those nations that have NUCLEAR WEAPONS. The first five nations to declare that they had nuclear weapons were the United States (1945), the former Soviet Union (1949), Great Britain (1952), France (1960), and China (1964), known as the "Big Five." The breakup of the Soviet Union in the early 1990s resulted in the addition of Belarus, Kazakhstan, and Ukraine as nuclear-weapon states because the nuclear missiles and storage sites placed on their territory by the Soviet Union became the property of these newly independent states; all three, however, transferred their weapons to Russia. India conducted its first nuclear test in 1974, followed by Pakistan in 1998. North Korea is believed to have the capacity to develop nuclear weapons within a short time. Others, such as Israel, have likely developed one or more such weapons secretly. Some analysts believe that another group of countries, including Iraq, were trying to develop nuclear weapons at the turn of the twenty-first century.

Nuclear power also refers to plants and industry that generate electric power from nuclear sources. The possibility of using the energy in the atomic nucleus as a power source was widely recognized soon after the discovery of nuclear fission late in 1938, but only the United States was able to devote any significant effort to atomic energy development during World War II. On 2 December 1942 Enrico Fermi and others achieved the first self-sustained chain reaction at Stagg Field at the University of Chicago. This experiment made possible the construction of three large plutonium-producing reactors; each generated about 250,000 kilowatts of energy, but they were not used for electric power production.

Despite the initial popular belief that the use of nuclear power was imminent, technical progress was slow after the war. The U.S. Atomic Energy Commission (AEC), facing extreme shortages of uranium ore, supported only three small reactor projects before 1950. One of these, the Experimental Breeder Reactor No. 1, succeeded in generating a few kilowatts of electric power late in 1951, an accomplishment more symbolic than practical.

Growing industrial interest in nuclear power by 1952, basic revision in atomic energy legislation in 1954, and increasing ore supplies made a more ambitious program possible in the 1950s. The AEC adopted a five-year plan designed to test the feasibility of five different reactor systems. One of these, the pressurized water reactor (PWR)—designed and and built by a joint AEC-Navy team under Rear Adm. H. G. Rickover, at Shippingport, Pennsylvania—produced 60,000 kilowatts of electricity for commercial use before the end of 1957. The AEC's Argonne National Laboratory, at Lemont, Illinois, under Walter H. Zinn, successfully developed the experimental boiling water reactor (EBWR). The PWR and EBWR committed the United States almost exclusively to water-cooled reactors for the next two decades. By the end of 1957, the AEC had seven experimental reactors in operation, and American industry had started nine independent or cooperative projects expected to produce 800,000 kilowatts of electricity by the mid-1960s.

Nuclear Power Scare. On 23 March 1979, the American public's attention was riveted on Three Mile Island in Pennsylvania, where the Edison Nuclear Power Plant experienced a partial core meltdown that resulted in the venting of radioactive vapor. Here, police guard the plant's front gate, with three cooling towers in the background. © AP/Wide World Photos

Nuclear power plants differ from hydroelectric plants—which generate electricity from the force of flowing water—and from coal-, oil-, or gas-fired electric plants, which generate electricity from the heat drawn from burning fossil fuels. Nuclear power plants generate steam to drive electric turbines by circulating liquid through a nuclear reactor. The reactor produces heat through the controlled fission of atomic fuel. Normally the fuel for power reactors is slightly enriched uranium. These differences give nuclear reactors several advantages over power generation using other fuels. Unlike fossil fuels, nuclear fuel does not foul the air and is not dependent on oil imports from unstable parts of the world. Before the environmental effects of radioactive wastes and the safety hazards of nuclear plants became apparent in the 1960s and 1970s, some environmentalists were strong advocates of nuclear power as a "clean" energy source. Others, aware of the rising costs of the world's diminishing coal, oil, and natural gas resources and the limitation on the number of hydroelectric power plants that could be built, believed that nuclear plants could be the key to an independent American energy supply.

The attraction of electricity generated by nuclear power was not limited to the United States. In contrast to the American emphasis on water-cooled reactors, both the United Kingdom and France chose to rely on gas-cooled systems. By 1957 the United Kingdom was building or planning twelve reactors with a capacity of more than 1 million kilowatts; the French were building five reactors totaling more than 350,000 kilowatts. The Soviet Union was planning a 200,000-kilowatt PWR and two smaller boiling-water reactors. By 1966 nuclear power generators were being built or operating in five countries. By 1980 there were a hundred nuclear power plants in the United States.

Technical difficulties prevented any of these national plans from being realized by the early 1960s. In the United States the AEC countered the resulting pessimism by predicting the imminence of economically competitive nuclear power and concentrating resources on the most promising reactor designs—water-cooled reactors for the immediate future and sodium-cooled breeder reactors for later decades in the century. This confidence was fulfilled by early 1964, when an American power company first announced its decision, on the basis of economics alone, to construct a nuclear power plant. Despite a temporary dampening effect of licensing delays and challenges from environmentalists protesting the dumping of radioactive wastes, the trend toward nuclear power accelerated again in the early 1970s. By the fall of 1972, the total nuclear gross generating capacity of all nations outside the Communist bloc had reached 32 million kilowatts. Of this total, the United States provided 13 million electrical kilowatts generated in twenty-eight operating plants. More than a hundred additional plants with a total capacity of more than 116 million kilowatts had been ordered or were under construction in the United States.

A serious accident at Three Mile Island in 1979 proved to be a major turning point for nuclear power in the United States, and no new nuclear generators have been ordered since. All of the increases in nuclear-generated electricity since 1979 have come from existing plants, which have boosted their national capacity factor from under 65 percent in 1970 to 76 percent in 1996.

One of the byproducts of nuclear-power generation is plutonium, a material that can be chemically processed for use in nuclear weapons. The danger of such use by nonnuclear nations led to international safeguards under the 1968 Nuclear Nonproliferation Treaty. In Article III signatory nations agreed to inspections by the International Atomic Energy Agency (IAEA), "with a view to

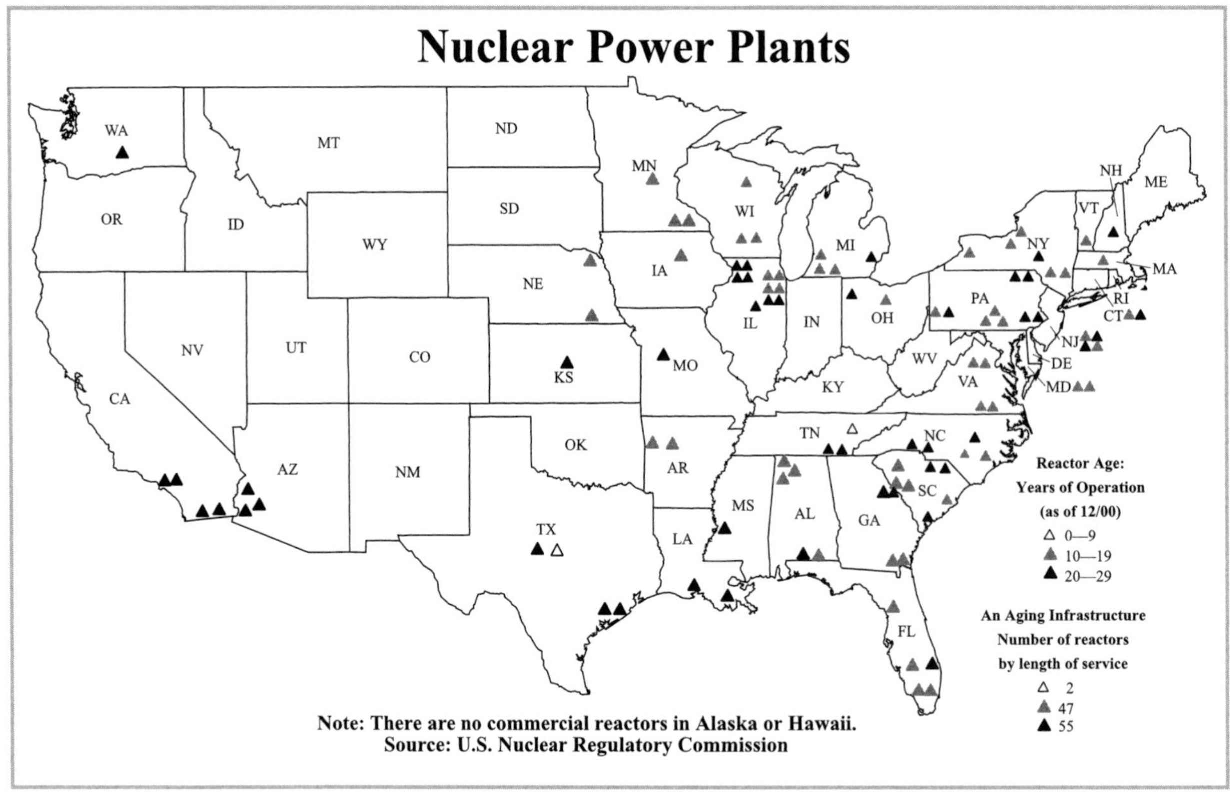

preventing diversion of nuclear energy from peaceful uses to nuclear weapons or other nuclear explosive devices." Most of the world's nuclear and nonnuclear nations signed this treaty. Iraq in 1992 and North Korea in 1994 were subjected to IAEA inspections that proved treaty violations in the former and raised serious suspicions about the latter. Both nations were signatories of the treaty, although North Korea announced its withdrawal some months prior to inspection. Iraq's nuclear-weapon production facilities were discovered as a result of a series of highly intrusive IAEA inspections and were subsequently destroyed by the United Nations.

When Congress passed the Atomic Energy Act of 1954, it approved President Dwight D. Eisenhower's Atoms for Peace program, which included commercial development of nuclear reactors for the purpose of generating electric power. During the 1960s electricity generated by nuclear power contributed 1 to 2 percent of the nation's energy total. Since then that percentage has grown steadily, surpassing the proportion from hydroelectric sources in 1984. By 1990 nuclear power amounted to one-fifth of the nation's total generation of electricity. By 1992 nuclear generation reached 619 billion net kilowatt hours, more than double the amount generated in 1979, the year of the Three Mile Island accident.

In reaction to the 1973 oil embargo, U.S. consumers temporarily used less energy, which diminished the rate of growth in electricity generation. As a result of this and other factors, such as higher construction costs, delays brought on by antinuclear protests, increased operating costs resulting from new federal regulations, and uncertainties about disposal of high-level radioactive waste, no requests for construction of new nuclear power plants have been received by the NUCLEAR REGULATORY COMMISSION since 1978. The level of generation was still rising, however, because plants started in the 1970s had gone on-line, and modernization after 1979 made power plants more efficient. The rising production trend continued until the end of the twentieth century; in the year 2000, for example, 104 commercial nuclear plants in the United States produced 20.5 percent of all electricity consumed in the United States. Nuclear power's future is far from clear, however. The Energy Information Administration projected in 2001 that 27 percent of the nation's nuclear generating capacity then in existence would be retired by 2020, with no construction of new plants anticipated.

BIBLIOGRAPHY

Department of Energy, Energy Information Administration. *Annual Energy Outlook 2002 with Projections to 2020.* Washington, D.C.: Department of Energy, 2001.

Deudney, Daniel, and Christopher Flavin. *Renewable Energy: The Power to Choose.* New York: W.W. Norton, 1983.

Duffy, Robert J. *Nuclear Politics in America: A History and Theory of Government Regulation.* Lawrence: University Press of Kansas, 1997.

Henderson, Harry. *Nuclear Power: A Reference Handbook.* Santa Barbara, Calif.: ABC-CLIO, 2000.

Robert M. Guth
Richard G. Hewlett / c. w.

See also **Nuclear Non-Proliferation Treaty (1978); Nuclear Test Ban Treaty.**

NUCLEAR REGULATORY COMMISSION (NRC), created by the Energy Reorganization Act of 1974, licenses and regulates most commercial nuclear activities in the United States, including nuclear power reactors and the use of radioactive materials in industry, medicine, agriculture, and scientific research. The origins of the NRC trace back to the immediate aftermath of World War II, when its predecessor agency, the Atomic Energy Commission (AEC), was created by the Atomic Energy Act of 1946 to establish and to operate the nation's military and civilian atomic energy programs. A new law, the Atomic Energy Act of 1954, eased the government monopoly on information relating to atomic energy and for the first time allowed the use of the technology for commercial purposes.

The Nuclear Power Debate

The 1954 act assigned the AEC the dual responsibilities of promoting and regulating the commercial applications of nuclear energy. This became a major issue in the late 1960s and early 1970s, when the AEC stood at the center of a major national controversy over nuclear power. At that time, the nuclear industry experienced a boom in which orders for nuclear power plants rapidly increased. The expansion of the industry spawned a corresponding growth in opposition to it. Environmentalists raised a series of objections to nuclear power, which led to highly publicized controversies over thermal pollution, radiation standards, radioactive waste disposal, and reactor safety. Nuclear opponents claimed that the industry and the AEC had not done enough to ensure the safe operation of nuclear plants and that the agency's statutory mandate to encourage nuclear development made it a weak and ineffective regulator. They maintained that the technology was unsafe, unreliable, and unnecessary. Nuclear supporters took sharp issue with that position; they insisted nuclear power was safe (though not risk-free) and essential to meet the energy requirements of the United States. They argued that the benefits of the technology far outweighed its risks.

The Creation of the NRC

Both proponents and critics of nuclear power agreed that the AEC's dual responsibilities for promoting and regulating nuclear power undermined its credibility. In 1974, Congress passed the Energy Reorganization Act, which abolished the AEC and replaced it with the NRC and the Energy Research and Development Administration (which later became a part of the U.S. Department of Energy). The NRC began its existence in January 1975 as the national debate over nuclear power increased in volume and intensity, and within a short time, its policies and procedures became a source of controversy.

The NRC tried to cast off the legacy it inherited from the AEC by stressing that its first priority was safety, but critics were unconvinced. While the nuclear industry complained about the rising costs of building plants and the time the NRC required to review applications, antinuclear activists campaigned against the construction or licensing of nuclear power facilities. Several key issues surrounding the growth of nuclear power attracted widespread media attention and generated a great deal of debate. One was the effectiveness of the NRC's regulations on "safeguards," which were designed to make certain that enriched uranium or plutonium that could be used to make nuclear weapons did not fall into the wrong hands. In response to fears that the expanded use of nuclear power could result in terrorist acquisition of a nuclear weapon, the NRC substantially tightened its requirements for the protection of nuclear fuel and nuclear plants from theft or attacks.

The NRC at the same time was the focal point of controversies over radiation protection standards, the export of nuclear materials to other nations, and the means for estimating the probability of a severe accident in a nuclear power plant. Reactor safety remained a subject of acrimonious dispute, which gained new prominence after a major fire at the Browns Ferry nuclear plants near Decatur, Alabama, in March 1975. In the process of looking for air leaks in an area containing trays of electrical cables that operated the plants' control rooms and safety systems, a technician started a fire. He used a lighted candle to conduct the search, and the open flame ignited the insulation around the cables. The fire raged for seven hours and largely disabled the safety equipment of one of the two affected plants. Nevertheless, the plants were safely shut down without releasing radiation to the environment.

The Three Mile Island Accident

The Browns Ferry fire did not compare in severity or in the attention it commanded with the most serious crisis in the history of nuclear power in the United States. The crisis occurred at Unit 2 of the Three Mile Island nuclear generating station near Harrisburg, Pennsylvania, on 28 March 1979. As a result of a series of mechanical failures and human errors, the accident, researchers later determined, uncovered the reactor's core and melted about half of it. The immediate cause of the accident was a valve that stuck open and allowed large volumes of reactor coolant to escape. The reactor operators misread the signs of a loss-of-coolant accident and for several hours failed to take action to cool the core. Although the plant's emergency core cooling systems began to work according to design, the operating crew decided to reduce the flow from them to a trickle. Even worse, a short time later the operators turned off the large reactor coolant pumps that circulated water through the core. By the time the nature of the accident was recognized and the core was flooded with coolant, the reactor had suffered irreparable damage.

The credibility of the nuclear industry and the NRC fared almost as badly. Uncertainty about the causes of the accident, confusion regarding how to deal with it, conflicting information from government and industry experts, and contradictory appraisals of the level of danger in the days following the accident often made authorities appear deceptive, inept, or both. Press accounts fed public fears and fostered a deepening perception of a technology that was out of control.

Nevertheless, in some ways the Three Mile Island accident produced reassuring information for reactor experts about the design and operation of the safety systems in a large nuclear plant. Despite the substantial degree of core melting, the pressure vessel that held the fuel rods and the containment building that surrounded the reactor, cooling systems, and other equipment were not breached. From all indications, the amount of radioactivity released into the environment as a result of the accident was small.

Those findings were overshadowed by the unsettling disclosures from Three Mile Island. The incident focused attention on possible causes of accidents that the AEC–NRC and the nuclear industry had not considered extensively. Their working assumption had been that the most likely cause of a loss-of-coolant accident would be a break in a large pipe that fed coolant to the core. But the destruction of the core at Three Mile Island resulted not from a large pipe break but from a relatively minor mechanical failure that operator errors drastically compounded. Perhaps the most distressing revelation of Three Mile Island was that an accident so severe could occur at all. Neither the AEC–NRC nor the industry had ever claimed that a major reactor accident was impossible, despite the multiple and redundant safety features built into nuclear plants. But they had regarded it as highly unlikely, to the point of being nearly incredible. The Three Mile Island accident demonstrated vividly that serious consequences could arise from unanticipated events.

The Response to Three Mile Island

The NRC responded to the Three Mile Island accident by reexamining the adequacy of its safety requirements and by imposing new regulations to correct deficiencies. It placed greater emphasis on "human factors" in plant performance by imposing stronger requirements for training, testing, and licensing of plant operators. In cooperation with industry groups, it promoted the increased use of reactor simulators and the careful assessment of control rooms and instrumentation. The NRC also devoted more attention to other problems that had received limited consideration before Three Mile Island. They included the possible effects of small failures that could produce major consequences and the prompt evaluation of malfunctions at operating nuclear plants. The agency expanded its research programs on a number of problems the accident had highlighted. And, in light of the confusion and uncertainty over evacuation of areas surrounding the Three Mile Island plant during the accident, the NRC sought to improve emergency preparedness and planning. Those and other steps it took were intended to reduce the likelihood of a major accident and, in the event that another one occurred, to enhance the ability of the NRC, the utility, and the public to cope with it.

In the immediate aftermath of Three Mile Island, the NRC suspended granting operating licenses for plants in the pipeline until it could assess the causes of the accident. The "licensing pause" ended in 1980, and in the following nine years, the NRC granted full-power operating licenses to more than forty reactors, most of which had received construction permits in the mid-1970s. The NRC had received no new applications for construction permits since 1978, and as more plants were completed and went on line, the agency shifted its focus to regulating operating plants rather than reviewing applications for new ones.

BIBLIOGRAPHY

Balogh, Brian. *Chain Reaction: Expert Debate and Public Participation in American Commercial Nuclear Power, 1945–1975.* New York: Cambridge University Press, 1991.

Duffy, Robert J. *Nuclear Politics in America: A History and Theory of Government Regulation.* Lawrence: University Press of Kansas, 1997.

Walker, J. Samuel. *Containing the Atom: Nuclear Regulation in a Changing Environment, 1963–1971.* Berkeley: University of California Press, 1992.

———. *Permissible Dose: A History of Radiation Protection in the Twentieth Century.* Berkeley: University of California Press, 2000.

Wellock, Thomas Raymond. *Critical Masses: Opposition to Nuclear Power in California, 1958–1978.* Madison: University of Wisconsin Press, 1998.

Winkler, Allan M. *Life Under a Cloud: American Anxiety About the Atom.* New York: Oxford University Press, 1993.

J. Samuel Walker

See also **Energy, Department of; Energy Industry; Energy Research and Development Administration; Nuclear Power; Three Mile Island.**

NUCLEAR TEST BAN TREATY. This international agreement reflected diplomatic attempts to stabilize international relations in the early 1960s as well as public fears of radioactive fallout. Pressures to limit the radioactive fallout from open-air testing of nuclear weapons dated back to 1954. Scientists, journalists, and intellectuals throughout Western Europe and the United States raised awareness about the harmful effects of nuclear radiation. Government leaders, including American president Dwight Eisenhower, recognized a need to respond to growing public fears.

On 10 May 1955, the Soviet Union seized the initiative. Moscow included a ban on nuclear tests as part of a general disarmament proposal. Over time, the Soviet leadership backed away from many elements of this offer. The United States rejected the proposal because it lacked a system of inspections for verifying adherence to the test ban. Eisenhower feared that the Soviet government would take advantage of its closed society to test nuclear weapons in secrecy. The United States suffered from an asymmetry of secrecy—because of America's democratic culture, its leaders could not act with the same secrecy employed by Soviet policymakers.

In 1958, the United States, Great Britain, and the Soviet Union—the three existing nuclear powers—announced unilateral bans on nuclear testing in response to public pressure. Each government sought to show that it was more enlightened than its counterparts. Each government also resumed tests by the end of the decade, fearful that its Cold War adversaries would gain a technical lead in the arms race through additional experiments with nuclear warheads.

In the early 1960s, negotiations for a nuclear test ban gained momentum for reasons beyond the public's fears of radioactive fallout. After years of recurring crises surrounding the status of American-dominated West Berlin—located deep within the territory of communist East Germany—Washington and Moscow sought new mechanisms for stabilizing their relationship. Military rivalry between the superpowers had become too dangerous in a world with huge nuclear arsenals capable of destroying life on the entire planet many times over. The dangers of the Cuban Missile Crisis in October 1962 pushed both American president John F. Kennedy and Soviet premier Nikita Khrushchev to pursue new mechanisms for accommodation.

A nuclear test ban treaty served this purpose. It became an important symbol of amicable relations between Cold War adversaries. The agreement—negotiated during the summer of 1963 in Moscow by President Kennedy's ambassador at large, William Averell Harriman, and the Soviet leadership—recognized the Cold War status quo in Europe. It emphasized the need for restraint instead of continued crisis on this divided continent.

Officially signed by the leaders of the United States, the Soviet Union, and Great Britain on 5 August 1963, the Nuclear Test Ban Treaty prohibited future nuclear tests in the atmosphere, in space, and under water. Due to continued difficulties with verification, the treaty allowed for underground tests. While the signatories continued to explode ever larger warheads beneath the ground, they never again exploded a nuclear weapon in the open air. This greatly reduced radioactive fallout across the globe, and it also helped to lessen the tensions that grew with competing exhibits of nuclear prowess during a prior period of above ground tests.

The initial signatories attempted to convince the leaders of France and China to sign the treaty. The former had recently tested its first nuclear device (on 13 February 1960), and the latter prepared for its first nuclear explosion (on 16 October 1964). Leaders in Washington, London, and Moscow hoped that a global ban on aboveground nuclear tests would prevent France, China, and other states from developing nuclear arsenals of their own. By refusing to sign the treaty, Paris and Beijing indicated that they would not accept continued nuclear domination by the United States, Great Britain, and the Soviet Union. In the subsequent decades other states have followed France and China's lead—including Israel, India, and Pakistan. There have been very few occasions, however, when these states tested nuclear warheads above ground. The nuclear test ban treaty did not prevent further nuclear proliferation, but it slowed this process, stabilized Cold War tensions, and created an international norm against nuclear tests in the open air.

BIBLIOGRAPHY

Beschloss, Michael R. *The Crisis Years: Kennedy and Khrushchev, 1960–1963.* New York: Harper Collins, 1991.

Divine, Robert A. *Blowing on the Wind: The Nuclear Test Ban Debate, 1954–1960.* New York: Oxford University Press, 1978.

Gaddis, John Lewis. *The Long Peace: Inquiries into the History of the Cold War.* New York: Oxford University Press, 1987.

Trachtenberg, Marc. *A Constructed Peace: The Making of the European Settlement, 1945–1963.* Princeton, N.J.: Princeton University Press, 1999.

Wenger, Andreas. *Living With Peril: Eisenhower, Kennedy, and Nuclear Weapons.* New York: Rowman and Littlefield, 1997.

Werner Levi
Jeremi Suri

See also **Arms Race and Disarmament; Treaties with Foreign Nations.**

NUCLEAR WEAPONS derive their energy from the splitting (fission) or combination (fusion) of atomic nuclei. This category of weapons taken together may have finally fulfilled the wish of technologists throughout history for a weapon so terrible that it would make war between great powers obsolete. The twentieth century was the bloodiest in human history, yet no two nations possessing nuclear weapons fought a major war against one another.

The nuclear era began with the MANHATTAN PROJECT, the secret American effort during World War II to construct an atomic bomb. On 6 July 1945 the world's first atomic explosion was created during a test in the New Mexico desert. On 6 and 9 August, respectively, the Japanese cities of Hiroshima and Nagasaki were devastated by atomic bombings, and on 10 August Japan offered to surrender. The wave of celebrations in the United States that followed the end of the war were tinged with an immediate sense of shock at the terrifying power of this new class of weaponry. In a world where the science fiction of

Atomic Bomb. The second test—and the first underwater explosion—at Bikini, an atoll in the Marshall Islands, took place on 25 July 1946. National Archives and Records Administration

H. G. Wells had suddenly become a reality, anything seemed possible, and popular reactions to the bomb varied widely. Many feared that the next world war would result in the literal extinction of humankind, and to witnesses of two world wars in the space of three decades, a third world war seemed a virtual inevitability. Others searched for hope in the new "atomic world," imagining the imminent creation of a world government, the abolition of war, or even a utopia where the atom eradicated disease and provided limitless electrical power. While no such utopia emerged, nuclear energy did eventually fight cancer and generate electricity. No aspect of American society escaped the cultural upheavals of the bomb. By the early 1950s even schoolchildren were instructed by a cartoon turtle that they "must be ready every day, all the time, to do the right thing if the atomic bomb explodes: duck and cover!"

Political, military, and intellectual elites within the United States also grappled with the implications of nuclear weapons. A group of academic nuclear theorists led by Bernard Brodie began developing theories of deterrence for a world where preventing war seemed to be more important than winning one. Military leaders hoped that the American monopoly on nuclear weapons would deter any potential aggressor for the time being, but even optimists did not expect this monopoly to last more than a decade. If war with the Soviet Union did come, and "war through miscalculation" as well as by conscious design was always a fear, planners did not believe that the use of tens or even hundreds of atomic bombs would necessarily bring victory. Expansion of the American nuclear stockpile continued at the maximum possible rate, and following the first Soviet atomic test (years before it was expected) in August 1949, President Harry S. Truman gave permission to proceed with the development of a whole new kind of nuclear weapon, the hydrogen bomb. Unlike an ordinary atomic bomb, no theoretical or even practical limit existed on the terrific energy released by the explosion of one of these new "thermonuclear" weapons. In 1957 the Soviet Union tested the world's first intercontinental ballistic missile (ICBM), and the United States soon followed suit. The potential warning each side might receive of an attack from the other was now reduced from hours to minutes. As a result of these and other technical advances, by the early 1960s political leaders on both sides had reached the conclusion that in any global nuclear war neither superpower could hope to escape unacceptable damage to its homeland.

This realization did not prevent the continuation of the nuclear arms race, however. Each side feared that a technological breakthrough by the other might yield an advantage sufficient to allow a preemptive "first strike" so powerful as to make retaliation impossible. To prevent this, each superpower had to secure its "second strike" capability, thus ensuring the continuation of the deterrent of "Mutual Assured Destruction" or MAD. To this end the United States constructed a "strategic nuclear triad" built around an enormous armada of intercontinental bombers, a force of approximately one thousand land-based ICBMs, and beginning in 1960, a fleet of submarines equipped with nuclear-tipped ballistic missiles. In the 1970s MAD was threatened by the creation by both sides of ICBMs that could deploy multiple warheads, each potentially capable of destroying an enemy missile while it was still in its hardened silo. Another potential threat to MAD was the advent of antiballistic missile (ABM) systems. Both sides had worked on these since the 1950s, but in recognition of the technical difficulty of "hitting a bullet with a bullet" and of the possibly destabilizing nature of a partially effective defense, in May 1972 the two superpowers signed the ABM Treaty, severely curtailing deployment of and future research on such systems. In the 1960s and especially the 1970s nuclear weapons had become so plentiful for both sides that they were deployed in large numbers in a tactical role as well. Relatively small ground units and even individual ships and aircraft were now potential targets of nuclear attack. This raised at least the realistic possibility for the first time in the Cold War of a successful defense of Western Europe against a Soviet ground assault.

The question remained, though, of just how many Europeans might be left after the radioactive smoke had cleared from such a "successful" defense. Advocates of a nuclear freeze swelled in number both in Europe and in the United States, and following the election of President Ronald Reagan in 1981, popular fears of nuclear war grew to a level not seen since the 1950s. Reagan also challenged the prevailing logic of MAD, renewing the ABM debate by calling in March 1983 for the creation of a vast new system of defense against nuclear attack through his "Strategic Defense Initiative" (derided by critics as "Star Wars"). This final round of the arms race was cut short, however, by the collapse of the Soviet economy in the 1980s and in 1991 of the Soviet Union itself.

In the years that followed the end of the Cold War nuclear fears, both public and governmental, rapidly switched from a general nuclear war to the possible acquisition of nuclear weapons by "rogue states," such as Iraq or North Korea, and whether or not to build a limited national missile defense system. After the attacks of 11 September 2001 on the Pentagon and the World Trade Center, nuclear terrorism became the greatest potential nightmare of all.

BIBLIOGRAPHY

Boyer, Paul. *By the Bomb's Early Light: American Thought and Culture at the Dawn of the Atomic Age.* Chapel Hill: University of North Carolina Press, 1994. First published in 1985.

Bundy, McGeorge. *Danger and Survival: Choices about the Bomb in the First Fifty Years.* New York: Random House, 1988. Thoughtful combination of history and memoir.

Carter, Ashton B., John D. Steinbruner, and Charles A. Zraket, eds. *Managing Nuclear Operations.* Washington, D.C.: Brookings Institution, 1987. Standard reference work.

Federation of American Scientists. "United States Nuclear Forces Guide." Available http://www.fas.org.

David Rezelman

See also **Arms Race and Disarmament.**

NULLIFICATION, the theory which holds that a state can suspend, within its boundaries, a federal law, was a deeply held conviction for many "states' rights" advocates in the nineteenth century, and one of the factors that led to the Civil War (1861–1865). Nullification has its roots in the Enlightenment era of the late seventeenth and eighteenth centuries. Political thinkers, such as John Locke, questioned the validity of "divine-right monarchies," and suggested that people had the right to overturn laws, or entire governments, that did not benefit the governed.

The American Revolution (1775–1783), in which Americans declared themselves independent of Great Britain, was a practical extension of Enlightenment political thought. So was the first government of the United States—the Articles of Confederation—which had no strong central government and reserved most major statutory power for the individual states.

However, the Articles were too weak to function adequately, and in 1787 national leaders drafted the Constitution, which created a strong federal government but reserved many rights to the states. Almost immediately, Antifederalists and later Democrat-Republicans charged that the federal government had amassed too much power.

President John Adams, a Federalist, angered Democrat-Republicans when he sought broad protectionist powers with the Alien and Sedition Acts of 1798. In the Virginia and Kentucky Resolutions, James Madison and Thomas Jefferson, both Democrat-Republicans, said that the Alien and Sedition Acts were unconstitutional and that states should nullify them. They reasoned that states had given power to the Constitution by approving it in the ratification process, and they could take that power away if it became abusive. While no state nullified the Alien and Sedition Acts, Jefferson and Madison had sanctioned the idea.

In 1828, nullification nearly split the nation. To help domestic manufactures, Congress enacted a high tariff on imported goods. Southerners, afraid that European states would retaliate with high tariffs on cotton and other southern exports, decried the act as the "Tariff of Abominations" and called for its repeal. Vice President John C. Calhoun, a South Carolinian, penned his "South Carolina Exposition and Protest," in which he invoked the theory of nullification to deal with the tariff.

When Tennessean Andrew Jackson was elected President in 1828, Southerners expected him to back a reduced tariff. Instead, Congress enacted an even higher tariff in 1832. Enraged, Calhoun, now a South Carolina senator more stridently called for nullification.

Spurred by Calhoun's rhetoric, the South Carolina legislature passed an Ordinance of Nullification, making the federal tariff null and void and making it a state offense to collect the tariff after 1 February 1833. Jackson surprised Southerners when he backed congressional passage of a "Force Bill" that authorized federal troops to occupy South Carolina and collect the tariff. In the meantime, Congress also passed a "compromise," or reduced tariff. Pleased with the compromise but shaken by Jackson's threat of force, the South Carolina legislature reconvened in March 1833 and rescinded the Ordinance of Nullification. But to avoid looking cowed by the U.S. Congress, legislators "nullified" the federal Force Bill before they adjourned.

Northern states also dabbled with nullification. In 1814, old line Federalists in New England, angry over Democrat-Republican policies that caused the War of 1812 (1812–1815), sought to nullify federal mandates. And in 1850, some Northern states nullified new fugitive slave laws, part of the Compromise of 1850, that mandated Northern authorities return escaped slaves to the South. Traditionally, though, nullification and states' rights doctrines were the hallmarks of the antebellum South.

BIBLIOGRAPHY

Brinkley, Alan et al. *American History: A Survey*. New York: McGraw-Hill, 1991.

R. Steven Jones

See also **Alien and Sedition Laws.**

NURSING. Prior to the Civil War, nursing in the United States was generally a casual or self-declared occupation practiced as a form of domestic service rather than a skilled craft or a profession. Americans obtained the majority of their health care at home, where family members and friends attended to their needs.

Nursing Reform Leader. Dorothea Dix, pictured here, completely changed the nursing profession during the Civil War, opening the door for women in a field previously dominated by men. She convinced Union officials to name her Superintendent of Female Nurses during the war, and by the war's end she was supervising more than 3,000 female nurses. Working as a volunteer throughout the war, she received no pay. © The Granger Collection Ltd.

Antebellum Nursing

On plantations in the antebellum South black female slaves acted as midwives, provided child care, and performed other nursing duties for both whites and blacks. Male nurses composed the majority of hospital workers in the handful of established marine and charity hospitals of the mid-nineteenth century. Hospital officials often hired former hospital patients who had no formal training in medicine or nursing. The forces that supplanted the untrained nurse did not come into play until the late nineteenth century and early twentieth century. New and centralized technologies fueled the rise of hospital-based care. A greater acceptance of surgical procedures, urbanization, and nurses' own efforts to grapple with social problems culminated in the ascent of the trained nurse.

The idea of nursing—middle-class women managing and supervising the preparation of food, supplies, and linens and administering medications and treatments—gained momentum during the Civil War (1861–1865). Approximately twenty thousand women volunteers worked in military hospitals, but almost none had any hospital or practical training in nursing. Union hospitals hired female nurses to complement the staff of male nurses, convalescent soldiers, and male ward masters responsible for day-to-day supervision. In Confederate hospitals significantly fewer Southern women worked as nurses. Black male slaves bathed and fed patients daily. Catholic nuns played a unique role, nursing wounded soldiers from both the Confederate and Union armies. When the war ended, medical departments dismantled their massive hospital complexes, and most of the female nurses returned to teaching, domestic service, writing, family, and marriage.

Occasionally reformers extolled the benefits of trained nurses and the specific suitability of women for that role, but the goal of a trained nurse attendant languished for more than a decade after the Civil War. The 1880 census revealed that, while over ten thousand nurses were available for hire, fewer than 1 percent were graduates of hospital nursing courses. By 1873 only four schools of nursing existed in the United States: the New England Hospital for Women and Children and Massachusetts General Hospital in Boston, New Haven Hospital in Connecticut, and Bellevue Hospital in New York City. Over the next quarter century Americans witnessed a dramatic increase in the number of nursing schools from slightly over 400 in 1900 to approximately 1,200 by 1910. Among African American women, the number of hospital-trained graduates did not keep pace. Racial quotas in northern nursing schools and outright exclusion from training schools in the South limited their access to training. In 1879 the first African American woman graduated from the New England Hospital for Women and Children in Boston. Hospital schools with the explicit mission of training black nurses to serve the African American community opened their doors in the late nineteenth century: Spelman Seminary in Atlanta (1886), Hampton Institute in Virginia (1891), Providence Hospital in Chicago (1891), and Tuskegee Institute in Alabama (1892).

Nursing Education

By the beginning of the twentieth century middle-class Americans accepted nursing as a worthy albeit demanding vocation for young women. The women who entered nursing schools encountered an unregulated and often exploitative field. Hospital administrators opened nursing programs to avail their hospitals of a cost-effective student labor force. Nursing students practiced their skills as apprentices under the supervision of second- and third-year nursing students. Most schools offered limited courses in basic anatomy, physiology, or biology, and student nurses did not systematically rotate through all medical specialties.

Nursing leaders and educators, aware of the poor formal instruction in most hospital-based programs, pushed for fundamental reforms in nursing education and national legislation governing the licensing and practice of nursing. College-based nursing programs received a welcome endorsement when Columbia University appointed Mary Adelaide Nutting the first full-time professor of nursing in 1907. Nutting and her nursing colleagues established the *American Journal of Nursing* in 1900. Nurses revealed a growing professional awareness when they reorganized several professional nurses' groups under one national organization, the American Nurses Association (ANA), in 1912. That year the National Organization for Public Health Nursing organized its charter. Black graduate nurses, excluded from full representation in the ANA until 1951, established the National Association of Graduate Colored Nurses (NAGCN) in 1908, and Mabel Keaton Staupers served as the organization's first executive director (1934–1946). Although African American nurses grappled with the same professional issues as their white counterparts, racial discrimination and dismal employment opportunities amplified the black nurses' struggles.

Nursing in the Armed Forces

The exegesis of war created a receptive environment for nurses to press their grievances and further their professional goals while providing a crucial service to the nation. When military leaders reluctantly established the Volunteer Hospital Corps for female nurses during the Spanish-American War (1898), nursing leaders insisted on trained applicants from accredited nursing schools. In 1901 the Army Nurse Corps became a permanent service within the Medical Department, and the Navy Nurse Corps followed in 1908. Military medical officials in concert with nursing educators standardized and improved nursing education and established the Army School of Nursing in 1918 to meet the demands of World War I. During World War II the U.S. government agreed to award officer's rank to military nurses. Congressional leaders agreed to subsidize nursing schools and nursing education to attract women to nursing, a boon for all nurses but of special importance to black women. Black nursing leaders vigorously lobbied military officials, who finally agreed to desegregate the Navy Nurse Corps in 1948. Throughout the history of military conflict in the United States, nurses overwhelmingly established their ability to handle the intensity and stresses of wartime nursing, characteristics readily apparent in Korea and Vietnam, where nurses staffed Mobile Army Surgical Hospitals (MASH).

Male nurses did not share equally from the advances in military nursing or the softening of cultural boundaries defining sex-stereotyped roles that came out of the women's movement. Until the mid-twentieth century only a limited number of schools accepted male applicants. State boards of nursing restricted licensure for men, and as far back as the Spanish-American War military officials pointedly refused to accept male applicants in any branch of the Nursing Corps. Nursing remained one of the most thoroughly feminized occupations in the United States with women making up almost 90 percent of all nursing school graduates in 1990.

Nursing in the twenty-first century became a multitiered career. Registered nurses worked in every facet of acute and long-term care; they staffed public, industrial, and community health departments, and they achieved diverse skills and specialization of practice. Nurses who obtain postgraduate degrees enhance their role as providers of health care as nurse practitioners, clinical nurse specialists, nursing educators, and researchers. With degrees in finance and business, nurses have also broadened their job choices as hospital and health-care institution administrators.

BIBLIOGRAPHY

Hines, Darlene Clark. *Black Women in White: Racial Conflict and Cooperation in the Nursing Profession, 1890–1950.* Bloomington: Indiana University Press, 1989.

Kalisch, Philip A., and Beatrice J. Kalisch. *The Advance of American Nursing.* Boston: Little, Brown, 1986.

Maher, Mary Denis. *To Bind Up the Wounds: Catholic Sister Nurses in the U.S. Civil War.* Baton Rouge: Louisiana State University Press, 1999.

Mottus, Jane E. *New York Nightingales: The Emergence of the Nursing Profession at Bellevue and New York Hospital, 1850–1920.* Ann Arbor, Mich.: UMI Research Press, 1981.

Rosenberg, Charles E. *The Care of Strangers: The Rise of America's Hospital System.* Baltimore: Johns Hopkins University Press, 1995.

Schultz, Jane E. "The Inhospitable Hospital: Gender and Professionalism in Civil War Medicine." *Signs* 17, no. 2 (1992): 363–392.

Cecilia S. Miranda

See also **Health Care; Hospitals; Medical Education; Medical Profession.**

NUTRITION AND VITAMINS. Nutritional science was essentially unknown prior to the 1890s, but its origins can be traced to investigations into digestion in the late eighteenth and early nineteenth centuries. One of the most important of these investigations commenced in 1825 when American surgeon William Beaumont (1785–1853) made meticulous notes on the physiological processes of digestion in a live human subject by direct observations through a permanent fistula created by an accidental gunshot wound. His 238 observations, published in 1833, formed the basis for our modern understanding of the gastric processes.

At the same time, European investigations elucidated the principles of nutritional biochemistry. In a classic study by English physician William Prout (1827), foods were classified into what would later be known as carbohydrates, fats, and proteins. Studies into the nature of proteins by the French physiologist François Magendie (1816), Dutch physician Gerrit Jan Mulder (1838), and French agricultural chemist Jean-Baptiste Boussingault (1839) also expanded the understanding of nitrogen-containing foods in nutrition. Michel Eugène Chevreul first chemically described fats (1828), and Boussingault demonstrated the conversion of carbohydrates into fats in experiments with geese and ducks (1845). Knowledge of carbohydrates' role in nutrition was based on the work of Carl Schmidt (1844), H. von Fehling (1849), and Claude Bernard (1856).

While digestion and biochemistry formed the foundation of modern nutritional science, the concept of specific foods as fuel sources for the body was unclear until means for explaining and expressing it could be devised. That was discovered through the application of caloric values to foods and their components (for example, carbohydrates, fats, and sugars).

Nutrition and Calories

A calorie represents the heat energy necessary to raise one gram of water one degree Celsius. Food calories, however, are actually measured in kilocalories (1,000 calories = one kilocalorie) and then converted into whole caloric measures. The calories of any food essentially represent the amount of potential energy it provides. The development of calories as a measure of energy supplied in the food itself grew out of early studies on respiration and combustion by the French chemist Antoine-Laurent Lavoisier in 1777. A series of British investigations furthered this seminal work with research on animal heat by Adair Crawford in 1778, energy metabolism by Edward Smith in 1857, and the sources of muscular power by Edward Frankland in 1866. Through his combustion calorimeter, Frankland was able to determine the heat units of twenty-nine different foods and thus first introduced the quantitative energy concept of foods as they relate to human physiology.

It was an American, Wilbur Olin Atwater (1844–1907), who in 1897 developed a modern calorimeter capable of measuring heat production, energy consumption, and carbon dioxide elimination. By the beginning of the twentieth century, he had developed simplistic nutritional notions that emphasized a diet high in calories. As a result, Atwater recommended that poor and working-class Americans adopt a diet rich in carbohydrates and low on green vegetable "luxuries." The important interplay of caloric intake to comparative nutritional food values would await the discovery and elucidation of vitamins and minerals as essential elements to human health.

Vitamins and Minerals

While the relationship of diet to health had long been noted in the empirical observations of Luigi Cornaro (1467–1566) and Sanctorius (1561–1636), no rationale for it could be established until the discovery of vitamins and the role of minerals in maintaining health. This was accomplished when Casimir Funk (1884–1967) first correlated the etiologies of scurvy, beriberi, pellagra, and rickets to dietary deficiencies. In a landmark 1912 paper, Funk coined the word "vitamine" from "vita" (Latin for life) and "amino" (a group of organic compounds containing a univalent nitrogen radical). When it was subsequently discovered that not all "vitamines" included amines, the "e" was dropped. However spelled, Funk correctly concluded that vitamins in trace amounts could cure and prevent a range of dietary deficiency diseases. Born in Poland, Funk became an American citizen in 1920. While serving as Associate in Biological Chemistry at the College of Physicians and Surgeons in New York City, a translation of his now-classic treatise on *The Vitamines* (a greatly expanded version of his 1912 paper) was issued in 1922. While others during the same period and even earlier were associating specific diseases with diet (that is, Dutch physician Friedrich Bachstrom [1686–1742] first associated the cure for scurvy with the introduction of fresh fruits into the diet, investigations later carried forward by James Lind [1716–1794]; Christiaan Eijkman [1858–1930] in 1896 deduced beriberi from polyneuritis contracted by chickens that were fed white rice; U.S. Public Health Service officer Joseph Goldberger [1874–1929] in 1914 identified pellagra as a nutritional deficiency disease; and English pharmacologist Edward Mellanby [1884–1955] explored the dietary cause of rickets in 1919), Funk's discovery of vitamins' role in health provided the necessary conceptual framework through which virtually all nutritional science would proceed in the modern biochemical era.

The identification of vitamins is roughly based on their order of discovery, although some have been subsequently dropped from the list as not "true" vitamins. While the chemical structures associated with these compounds are gradually replacing the more generic alphabetical vitamin names (A, B_1 B_2, etc.), the public still recognizes the more traditional designations. Much of the pioneer work in elucidating specific vitamins came from the laboratory of Kansas native Elmer V. McCollum (1879–1967). In 1913 McCollum, along with colleague Marguerite Davis, discovered a fat-soluble vitamin A; nine years later he would identify vitamin D. McCollum is also noteworthy for utilizing rats as research subjects rather than the previous practice of using large farm animals. McCollum revolutionized nutritional research with the use of rats, which were smaller, easier, and cheaper to maintain than cows, sheep, and even chickens. Rats' high metabolism rates provided the added bonus of quicker lab results.

While a complete listing of American contributions to vitamin research is impossible here, some major figures are worthy of mention. In 1922 embryologist Herbert Evans (1882–1971), working with Katharine Scott Bishop (1889–1976), discovered vitamin E (α-tocopherol). In 1933 Roger J. Williams (1893–1988), working at the University of Texas at Austin, identified vitamin B_3 (pantothenic acid). Under Williams's direction from 1941 to 1963, the Clayton Foundation Biochemical Institute became the preeminent research center for the discovery and elucidation of vitamins.

Investigators were slower to appreciate the importance of minerals to human health. Eugene Baumann (1846–1896) discovered that the thyroid gland was rich in iodine, a revelation that led Cleveland, Ohio, researcher David Marine (1880–1976) in 1918 to identify iodine deficiency as the chief cause of goiter. Studies in the early twentieth century on the importance of iron, copper, zinc, manganese, and other essential elements in the diet provided a fuller understanding of minerals in human nutrition.

As the 1920s closed, nutrition had come a long way in a comparatively short period of time. A measure of that advance is demonstrated in the founding of the American Society for Nutritional Sciences in 1928.

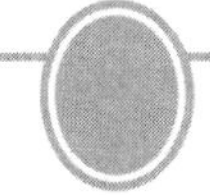

CASIMIR FUNK ON "VITAMINES"

Despite the fact that a number of ideas originated by us are credited to others, it is a source of pleasure to witness the great progress that has been made in vitamine research. In our opinion, the name "Vitamine," proposed by us in 1912, contributed in no small measure to the dissemination of these ideas. The word, "vitamine," served as a catchword which meant something even to the uninitiated, and it was not by mere accident that just at that time, research developed so markedly in this direction. (p. 18)

I regarded it of paramount importance, that the then ruling conception of the necessity of the lipoids or the nuclein substances was substituted by the fundamentally different vitamine theory. At the same time, I must admit that when I chose the name, "vitamine," I was well aware that these substances might later prove not to be of an amine nature. However, it was necessary for me to choose a name that would sound well and serve as a catchword, since I had already at that time no doubt about the importance and the future popularity of the new field. As we noted in the historical part, there was no lack of those who suspected the importance of still other dietary constituents, besides those already known, for the nutrition of animals. These views were unfortunately unknown to me in 1912, since no experimental evidence had appeared in their support. I was, however, the first one to recognize that we had to deal with a new class of chemical substances, a view which I do not need to alter now after eight years. (p. 36)

SOURCE: Casimir Funk, *The Vitamines*, translated from the second German edition by Harry E. Dubin. Baltimore: Williams & Wilkins, 1922.

Vitamins and the American Public

By the 1930s the accumulated knowledge about vitamins sparked unprecedented public interest in nutrition. Nowhere has that been more obvious than in America's fixation with vitamin and mineral supplements. Combining doses of science and pseudoscience with commercial hype, food and drug companies began inundating consumers with assorted vitamin ad campaigns, catapulting vitamin sales from a bit more than $12 million in 1931 to well over $82 million by 1939. In the 1940s and 1950s, patent medicine manufacturers and food producers dazzled health-seeking Americans with an array of "vitamin fortified" products. The fact that individuals can become toxic from fat-soluble vitamins such as vitamin A and that other vitamin supplements taken in large doses are simply eliminated by the body has not dampened a vitamin industry that is a $6.5-billion-dollar a year business. Indeed, one historian has characterized this uniquely American phenomenon as a veritable "vitamania."

None of this, however, should trivialize the importance of vitamins and minerals in the daily diet. Just a few examples include vitamin A (beta-carotene), essential for vision and skin; vitamin B_1 (thiamine), necessary for normal carbohydrate metabolism, the lack of which causes beriberi; vitamin B_2 (riboflavin), important for energy metabolism of fats, proteins, and carbohydrates; vitamin B_3 (niacin), which maintains the nervous system, digestion, and skin, and chronic deficiency of which may result in pellagra; vitamin C (ascorbic acid), crucial for healthy gums, teeth, and bones, and necessary for the prevention of scurvy, which results when vitamin C is chronically absent from the diet; and vitamin D (calciferol), which helps maintain appropriate levels of calcium and phosphorus and severe deficiencies of which can result in rickets.

Nutrition and Public Policy

The importance of vitamins and minerals became painfully evident during the Great Depression, when large numbers of Americans suffered from malnutrition as the result of poor and incomplete diets. The draft during World War II (1939–1945) also revealed large numbers of young men who were unable to meet the military service standards largely due to nutritional factors. These two facts, more than any others, helped move nutrition into the forefront of public awareness and ultimately public policy.

To address these issues, a limited public food program was put into operation from 1939 to 1943 under the auspices of the U.S. Department of Agriculture (USDA). The "War on Poverty" during the 1960s saw this program revisited. An important part of this nutritional revival in American public policy came as the result of a stirring if not disturbing survey, *Hunger in America* (1968). After several hunger marches on Washington and pressure from activist organizations such as The National Council on Hunger and Malnutrition in the U.S., President Richard Nixon convened a conference to examine the problem of hunger and poor nutrition in America. The results of this activity saw the establishment of a national food stamp program in 1974. While food stamps did not eradicate malnutrition in the United States, surveys conducted in 1978–1979 showed that it had largely disappeared as an endemic feature of American poverty.

In the early 1980s, however, the Reagan administration trimmed $12 billion out of various food assistance programs, causing them to shrink by one-third to one-half of their former sizes. With soup kitchens, churches, and other private welfare organizations unable to make up the difference, pressure from beleaguered city leaders beset by problems attendant with these diminished programs caused Congress to vote $9 billion back into food assistance budgets by the end of the decade.

The Food and Nutrition Service (FNS) administers all the dietary assistance programs of the USDA. While the Food Stamp Program remains the cornerstone of this effort, other initiatives to provide good nutrition to Americans include a special supplemental nutrition program for women, infants, and children; child nutrition programs such as the National School Lunch and School Breakfast programs; and a variety of food programs for the elderly. The total cost of all FNS programs in 2000 was $32.6 billion. In 2001 federal food programs provided assistance to approximately 17.3 million Americans.

BIBLIOGRAPHY

Apple, Rima D. *Vitamania: Vitamins in American Culture.* New Brunswick, N.J.: Rutgers University Press, 1996.

Carpenter, Kenneth J., Alfred E. Harper, and Robert E. Olson. "Experiments That Changed Nutritional Thinking." *Journal of Nutrition* 127 (1997, Supplement): 1017S–1053S.

———. "Nutritional Diseases." In *Companion Encyclopedia of the History of Medicine.* Edited by W. F. Bynum and Roy Porter. Vol. 1. London: Routledge, 1993.

Funk, Casimir. *The Vitamines.* Translated by Harry E. Dubin. Baltimore: Williams & Wilkins, 1922.

Mayer, Jan. "National and International Issues in Food Policy." Lowell Lectures (Harvard University, 1989). Updated 14 April 1998. Available from http://www.dce.harvard.edu/pubs/lowell/jmayer.html.

McCollum, Elmer Verner. *A History of Nutrition: The Sequence of Ideas in Nutrition Investigations.* Boston: Houghton Mifflin, 1957. A classic source written by a pioneer in the field.

Todhunter, E. Neige. "Historical Landmarks in Nutrition." In *Present Knowledge in Nutrition.* 5th ed. Washington, D.C.: The Nutrition Foundation, 1984.

U.S. Department of Agriculture. "Food, Nutrition, and Consumer Services." Last updated 14 May 2002. Available at http://www.fns.usda.gov/fns/. [Web source: Last updated 14 May 2002]. Provides current information on all the nutrition programs administered by The Food and Nutrition Service of the USDA.

Michael A. Flannery

OAKLAND. Located on the eastern shore of San Francisco Bay, Oakland is the eighth largest city in California, with a population of 399,484, according to the 2000 census. While the city is racially and ethnically diverse, African Americans constitute its largest group. Oakland is a major industrial center for the state, and boasts extensive port facilities that serve a growing trade with Asia. The city was originally incorporated in 1854, on land carved out of a Spanish-era land grant. The city's fortunes began to rise in 1869 with its selection as the western port terminus of the first transcontinental railroad. By the early twentieth century, Oakland increasingly rivaled San Francisco as the key urban center for the bay area. During World War II, federal investments in shipyards and manufacturing plants sparked economic expansion and attracted large numbers of African Americans seeking industrial employment. In 1962, Oakland's economy was bolstered by extensive harbor renovations, making it the first U.S. port capable of handling containerized shipping. During the same decade, however, the city witnessed growing social tensions, and became the birthplace of the radical Black Panther movement. In the 1980s and 1990s, Oakland had some serious setbacks. Major plant closures shrank the city's industrial base. In addition, the Loma Prieta earthquake in 1989 and wildfires in 1991 caused considerable infrastructure damage.

BIBLIOGRAPHY

Bagwell, Beth. *Oakland: The Story of a City.* Novato, Calif.: Presidio Press, 1982.

Johnson, Marilynn S. *The Second Gold Rush: Oakland and the East Bay in World War II.* Berkeley: University of California Press, 1993.

Eric Fure-Slocum
Daniel J. Johnson

See also **Black Panthers; California; San Francisco.**

OATS, grains of the genus *Avena* of the family Gramineae (grass family) thrive in the moist, temperate regions of the world, though they may be cultivated in a variety of climates. The most widely cultivated is the *Avena sativa,* a cereal grass used for food and fodder. The plant has a flowering and fruiting structure known as inflorescence and is made up of many branches bearing florets that produce the caryopsis or one-seeded fruit. Like most cultivated plants, oats were domesticated from wild varieties at an unknown time. Domestication may have occurred around 2500 B.C., which is recent compared to other common grains.

The wild oat can be traced to western Europe, where it grew as a weed. In northern Europe, as horses were increasingly used as draft animals, oats were grown as feed. Wild oats spread from Europe to other parts of the world and were brought to North America by explorers and settlers who also introduced other grains, such as wheat, rye, barley, and flax, all crops commonly produced by American farms in the twenty-first century. Bartholomew Gosnold planted oats on the Elizabeth Islands in Buzzards Bay about 1600. The Jamestown colonists planted them in 1611. They were grown early in Newfoundland and New Netherland, along with wheat, for beer and for horses, and they spread throughout the English colonies. In the eighteenth century farmers in the Middle Colonies began to use horses instead of oxen and sowed more oats for feed. It was common that as horses became more numerous, oat production increased. George Washington tended several hundred acres of oats at his Mount Vernon farm. Oatmeal became popular during the Civil War, and by the end of the war the demand for oats had increased.

Oats have a high nutritive value but are primarily produced for livestock feed. Their agricultural uses are various. Oats are valuable in crop rotation, and oat straw is used for animal feed and bedding. Those oats produced for human consumption are chiefly rolled oats, flattened kernels with the hulls removed, used as a breakfast food and a baking ingredient. Oat flour, although used in the production of some food, does not contain the glutinous type of protein necessary for making bread. Oat grains are high in carbohydrates and contain about 13 percent protein and 7.5 percent fat. They are a source of calcium, iron, and vitamin B_1. Bran content varies as some or all of the bran is frequently removed and used as a separate food product. Furfural, a chemical used in various types of solvents, is derived from oat hulls.

The Quaker Oats Company, the largest U.S. producer of cereal oats, officially formed in 1901, when the Quaker Mill Company of Ohio incorporated with a large cereal mill in Cedar Rapids, Iowa, and the German Mills American Oatmeal Company of Ohio. In the early twenty-first century the United States was one of the leading oat-producing countries.

BIBLIOGRAPHY

Beeman, Randal S., and James A. Pritchard. *A Green and Permanent Land: Ecology and Agriculture in the Twentieth Century.* Lawrence: University Press of Kansas, 2001.

Heiser, Charles B., Jr. *Seed to Civilization: The Story of Man's Food.* San Francisco: W. H. Freeman, 1973.

Hoffbeck, Steven R. *The Haymakers: A Chronicle of Five Farm Families.* St. Paul: Minnesota Historical Society Press, 2000.

Deirdre Sheets

See also **Agriculture; Cereal Grains.**

OBERLIN COLLEGE. In 1833 the evangelical Protestants John J. Shipherd and Philo P. Stewart founded a utopian community in Northeast Ohio focused on promoting the Oberlin Collegiate Institute to educate ministers to preach salvation to the unchurched West. Named for an Alsatian pastor, John Frederick Oberlin, the school opened in December 1834 as a manual labor institution. While both men and women attended from the beginning, not until 1837 could women pursue the A.B. degree. In 1835 a decision to admit students irrespective of color transformed the fledgling college. With this embrace of interracial education, Oberlin welcomed young men exiled from Lane Theological Seminary for their insistence on conducting ANTISLAVERY revivals. The "Lane rebels" carried with them support from the New York merchant, abolitionist, and evangelical Lewis Tappan, thus ensuring the survival of the college and the recruitment as professor of theology Charles Grandison Finney, the leading evangelical preacher of the time.

Perfectionist radicalism and attendant causes, including the Graham vegetarian diet, female moral reform, temperance, missionary activity, and particularly antislavery activism, permeated early Oberlin. The school officially became Oberlin College in 1850. Although not Garrisonians, Oberlin's abolitionists embraced a "higher law" when, in the Oberlin-Wellington rescue of 1858, students, faculty, and townspeople joined together to free a fugitive captured by bounty hunters. Oberlin students and faculty distinguished themselves in military service during the Civil War, and African American alumni led in the recruitment of Ohio's first troops of color. Men and women graduates played particularly important roles in establishing schools and colleges for freed slaves during Reconstruction.

Oberlin rose to academic prominence in the late nineteenth century. Educational advances included the addition of the Conservatory of Music in 1869, the rise of men's sports, a pioneering women's physical education program, the establishment of laboratory science, the advent of electives, the creation of academic departments, and accreditation as a founding member of the North Central Association of Colleges and Schools in 1895. By 1916 the preparatory department, once the largest part of the institution, closed its doors.

Despite a post-Reconstruction retreat from racial egalitarian principle, at Oberlin in the late nineteenth century, one-third of all African American graduates of predominantly white colleges before 1900 were Oberlin alumni. The college retained many of its other progressive ideals, especially in connecting the developing social sciences and the needs of social reform. In 1890 it appointed its first female professor, although not until 1948 was the first African American appointed to the faculty.

The school's religious orientation, which in 1882 supported the largest college chapter YMCA in the world, spurred Oberlin-trained missionaries to establish schools and churches in Africa and Asia. Although mandatory chapel was eliminated in 1934, later graduates of the theological department and college undergraduates played important roles in the civil rights movement of the 1950s and 1960s. In 1966 the college closed the theological school.

Entering the twenty-first century Oberlin boasted a highly ranked College of Arts and Sciences enrolling 2,200 students and a world-renowned conservatory with 650 students. A pioneering environmental studies program, high academic standards, and social commitment maintain Oberlin's traditions.

BIBLIOGRAPHY

Barnard, John. *From Evangelicalism to Progressivism at Oberlin College, 1866–1917.* Columbus: Ohio State University Press, 1969.

Baumann, Roland M., compiler. *Oberlin History Bibliography: A Partial Listing of Published Titles Bearing on the History of the College and Community Covering the Period 1833 to 1992.* Oberlin, Ohio: Oberlin College, 1992.

Fletcher, Robert Samuel. *A History of Oberlin College from Its Foundation through the Civil War.* 2 vols. Oberlin, Ohio: Oberlin College, 1943.

Carol Lasser

See also **Education, Higher: Denominational Colleges.**

OBERLIN MOVEMENT. This antislavery movement throughout the West began in 1834, when Theodore Dwight Weld, an evangelical abolitionist and protégé of the New York philanthropists Arthur and Lewis Tappan, arrived at the Oberlin Collegiate Institute (now Oberlin College) to lecture and train students as antislavery agents. Weld and his followers had come from Lane Theological Seminary in Cincinnati, which they vacated en masse in 1833 when the school's trustees ordered Weld's antislavery society disbanded. The Oberlin Movement's antislavery agents preached, lectured, and distributed tracts against slavery. The Oberlin Movement helped convert much of Ohio and the Northwest to the antislavery vanguard.

BIBLIOGRAPHY

Abzug, Robert H. *Passionate Liberator: Theodore Dwight Weld and the Dilemma of Reform.* New York: Oxford University Press, 1980.

Timothy M. Roberts

OBERLIN-WELLINGTON RESCUE CASE. The Oberlin-Wellington rescue case grew out of a rescue party's release of a fugitive slave in 1858 in Oberlin, Ohio; the slave had been in the custody of a federal officer at the village of Wellington, nine miles south of Oberlin. The rescuers, mostly citizens of Oberlin and students of the college, were indicted under the Fugitive Slave Act of 1850. From their jail in Cleveland, they published a newspaper, *The Rescuer;* through the barred windows they addressed mass meetings of sympathizers; and in their cells they entertained correspondents of eastern newspapers and deputations from churches and philanthropic societies. The indictments were shortly dismissed, and the rescuers were freed.

Slave Rescue. Thomas Weld, shown here, was one of the founders of Oberlin College and a participant in the Oberlin-Wellington Rescue Case, in which a large group of antislavery advocates rescued a runaway slave from a federal officer in Wellington, Ohio. Group members later faced charges (later dismissed) under the Fugitive Slave Act of 1850. LIBRARY OF CONGRESS

BIBLIOGRAPHY

Shipherd, Jacob R. *History of the Oberlin-Wellington Rescue.* New York: Da Capo Press, 1972.

Gilbert Hobbs Barnes / A. R.

See also **Antislavery; Fugitive Slave Acts.**

OBESITY is defined as having a body mass index (BMI), which is the relationship of mass to height, of 30 or more, or a weight of about 30 pounds over the maximum desirable for the individual's height. Those at least 100 pounds over their ideal weight are regarded as morbidly obese.

Obesity as a health problem was first discussed by Thomas Short (1690?–1772) in *A Discourse Concerning the Causes and Effects of Corpulency. Together with A Method for Its Prevention and Cure* (London, 1727). In 1829, the English physician William Wadd (1776–1829) published his *Comments on Corpulency, Lineaments of Leanness, Mems on Diet and Dietetics.* In 1863, Dr. William Banting (1779–1878) proposed his special "Banting diet" as a treatment for obesity. So-called Bantingism, a diet low in sugar and oily foods, swept across England, making it the first fad diet craze of national proportions. Largely compilations of unscientific speculations and opinions, these early works were supplanted by more systematic studies coming primarily from Germany and France throughout the latter half of the nineteenth century.

The United States did not come into the forefront of obesity research until Hugo Rony's *Obesity and Leanness* (1940). By the 1950s, the National Institutes of Health served as a catalyst for new investigations into the causes and nature of obesity, launching a new era in evaluating this potentially life-threatening condition. Researchers in the early twenty-first century understand obesity as a complex condition that can be approached from one of four different perspectives: behavioral/psychological aspects; physiological factors; cellular bases in the functions of fat cells; and genetic and molecular factors.

This last aspect came to scientists attention in the late twentieth century. In 1992, a specific gene responsible for obesity in mice was discovered and two others were identified shortly thereafter. Since this pathbreaking work, a number of genes thought to be responsible for predisposing humans to obesity have been uncovered. With the advent of new genetically targeted pharmaceuticals, the prospect of developing a "magic bullet" for people in this category might be on the horizon.

Still, the principal cause of obesity for most Americans is a combination of overeating and sedentary lifestyle. The Centers for Disease Control and Prevention

(CDC) has kept data on obesity since 1985 through its Behavioral Risk Factor Surveillance System (BRFSS). The BRFSS reveals an alarming rise in overweight Americans. In 1985, no state had an obese population of 20 percent or more; in 1997, three states reported in that category; by 2000, a staggering 22 states had an obese population of 20 percent or greater. Of even more concern was the rising obesity rate among American children. The CDC reported skyrocketing obesity rates among children ages 12 to 17, from about 4 percent in 1963 to 11 percent by 1994.

As of 2000, 19.8 percent of the total U.S. population was obese. The prevalence of Americans (estimated as high as 47 million) with a metabolic syndrome (high blood pressure, high cholesterol, and high blood sugar and triglycerides) associated with obesity underscored a national need for stricter dietary regimens and more consistent exercise.

BIBLIOGRAPHY

Bray, George A., Claude Bouchard, and W. P. T. James, eds. *Handbook of Obesity.* New York: Marcel Dekker, 1998.

Centers for Disease Control and Prevention. "Health Topic: Obesity/Overweight." Updated 30 May 2002. Available from http://www.cdc.gov/health/obesity.htm.

Pool, Robert. *Fat: Fighting the Obesity Epidemic.* New York: Oxford University Press, 2001.

Michael A. Flannery

See also **Health Food Industry.**

OBJECTIVISM, the philosophy based on writings of novelist and ideologue Ayn Rand (1905–1982), has generated controversy since its organized emergence in the 1950s. Rand, born Alissa Zinovievna Rosenbaum, passed her childhood in volatile St. Petersburg, Russia, where Bolshevik revolutionaries nationalized her family's small business in 1917. After studying history and philosophy at the University of Leningrad, Alissa Rosenbaum obtained a Soviet passport in 1926 and arrived in Chicago for a "visit" with sponsoring relatives. By 1927 she had changed her name to Ayn Rand and found work as a Hollywood scriptwriter. Throughout her life Rand would identify publicly with the self-made geniuses celebrated in her popular though critically censured works.

Beginning with *We the Living* in 1936, Rand's fiction—including *Anthem* (1938), *The Fountainhead* (1943), and *Atlas Shrugged* (1957)—depicts ideal protagonists who refuse to compromise their core principles of egotism, atheism, and rationality to placate religious and socialist opponents. Rand's works of nonfiction—including *The Virtue of Selfishness* (1964), *Capitalism: The Unknown Ideal* (1966), and *The Romantic Manifesto* (1969)—elaborated these core principles, which show the combined influence of (among others) Aristotle and Friedrich Nietzsche. Rand held that both facts and values were "objective" realities, extrinsic and independent of the preferences of the thinker, who can grasp them through a disciplined application of reason. According to Rand, perceptions were truthful if sanctioned by logic, and actions were ethical if they aimed to fulfill the agent's needs as a rational being. Reason, then, was the only correct basis for intellectual and moral judgments: Rand rejected faith, divine revelation, and subjective feeling as false epistemologies. Conscious and individual life, she believed, formed the standard of all values, and "rational selfishness" was a living being's appropriate motive. In addition, Rand advocated laissez-faire capitalism as the only truly moral economic system and argued that art and literature instantiated the deepest values of their creator.

In 1952, Rand's followers, including the psychology student Nathaniel Branden (formerly Nathan Blumenthal) and philosophy student Leonard Peikoff, formed a study group that adopted Rand as its teacher and personal ideal. In 1958, Branden established the Nathaniel Branden Institute, where for ten years he and Rand lectured on objectivist dogma to enthusiastic audiences, mainly of young adults. However, in 1968 the movement divided as Branden—also Rand's lover, by permission of her spouse, Frank O'Connor—revealed his attachment to another woman, prompting Rand to permanently ostracize him from her official circle. After Rand's death in 1982 the objectivist movement split again due to a dispute between Peikoff and the philosopher David Kelley over the boundaries of objectivist doctrine. Today the Ayn Rand Institute, founded by Peikoff in 1985, maintains that the objectivist system is complete as stated by Rand, while neo-objectivists at David Kelley's Objectivist Center (founded in 1990) distance themselves from Rand's "cult of personality," arguing for continued inquiry and reinterpretation. Both groups have yet to establish themselves among academics, who generally are skeptical of objectivists' claims to freethinking and original insight. Meanwhile, the works of Rand and other objectivists continue to sell roughly 400,000 copies each year and inspire equally passionate support and opposition. The Libertarian political movement shows objectivist influence.

BIBLIOGRAPHY

Kelley, David. *The Contested Legacy of Ayn Rand: Truth and Toleration in Objectivism.* New Brunswick, N.J.: Objectivist Center, 2000.

Peikoff, Leonard. *Objectivism: The Philosophy of Ayn Rand.* New York: Dutton, 1991.

Walker, Jeff. *The Ayn Rand Cult.* Chicago: Open Court, 1999.

Rae Sikula Bielakowski

OBSCENITY. *See* **Censorship, Press and Artistic; Pornography.**

OBSERVATORIES, ASTRONOMICAL. The dark-adjusted human eye has a pupil size of only about

College Observatory. Professor Maria Mitchell—the first woman elected to the American Academy of Arts and Sciences, after discovering a comet in 1847 and establishing its orbit—and her class work outside the Vassar College Observatory, 1878. VASSAR COLLEGE LIBRARIES, SPECIAL COLLECTIONS

five millimeters, a biological apparatus with limited light-gathering capability and only for the visual spectrum. By contrast, modern astronomical observatories offer views that are millions of times more powerful and for a wide range both above and below the visible electromagnetic spectrum. These instruments extend human sight even farther by an increasingly complex assortment of measurements and astrophotography.

History of New World Observatories

New World astronomy began with the early observations made and recorded by indigenous peoples, notably evidenced by the stone observatories and calendar inscriptions of the Mayans of Central America, built between A.D. 300 and 900, and the Incas of South America, between A.D. 1200 and 1533, among others. These stone instruments allowed them to predict agricultural seasons as well as such celestial events as lunar and solar eclipses. Early Europeans in the New World used astronomical instruments for navigation and exploration, and Amerigo Vespucci cataloged southern stars from the coast of South America in 1499 and 1501. In time, early English Colonials displayed keen interest in the science of the day, including astronomy. Their observations came in the form of temporary platforms such as the one that David Rittenhouse constructed to view the 1769 transit of Venus.

However, not until the decades following the Revolutionary War (1775–1783) did Americans see a serious observatory, constructed through the efforts of Ferdinand R. Hassler, director of the U.S. Coast Survey, with the support of President John Quincy Adams. Between 1830 and the Civil War (1861–1865), occasional private individuals, such as William Mitchell of Nantucket, Massachusetts, and Lewis M. Rutherfurd in New York City, pursued serious astronomical observations. With an increasing availability of astronomical apparatus, schools began to include practical as well as theoretical astronomy; both private and public funds built some twenty-five observatories complete with refracting telescopes—instruments that use lenses to focus incoming light.

In 1842, the federal Depot of Charts and Instruments founded the U.S. Naval Observatory in Washington, D.C. Congress established the Nautical Almanac Office in 1849 and used the work of the observatory to collect data for both navigators and astronomers. The observatory's primary function was to provide astronomical data for safe navigation at sea, in the air, and in the twentieth century, in space. The facility also provided standardized time for local fire and police stations. By the 1880s, both telegraphs and railroads used the observatory's time. Eventually, Washington's light pollution—that is, excessive light diffracted into the atmosphere and degrading astronomical observations—forced the Naval Observatory to build a second facility in Flagstaff, Arizona, in 1955.

After the Civil War, observatories became a common addition to colleges and universities, which increasingly undertook serious astronomical research. Harvard's Henry Draper became the first to photograph stellar spectra in 1872 and began, with the help of Williamina P. Fleming and others, to develop a catalog of the stars. Nineteenth-century air and light pollution led to a growing number of observatories in rural areas and in the high desert plains and mountains of the American West, as well as in South America and Africa.

The second half of the nineteenth century also saw a movement to build bigger and better telescopes. Alvan Clark and Sons of Cambridgeport, Massachusetts, successfully produced ever larger refractors than any previous ones: 18.5 inches (1863), Dearborn Observatory in Chicago (later relocated to Evanston, Illinois, at Northwestern University); 26 inches (1872), U.S. Naval Observatory; 30 inches (1883), Pulkovo Observatory, near St. Petersburg, Russia; 36 inches (1887), Lick Observatory, near San Jose, California; and 40 inches (1897), Yerkes Observatory, at Williams Bay, Wisconsin. American astronomer Percival Lowell (1855–1916) established the Lowell Observatory in Flagstaff, Arizona, in 1894. Lowell used his facility to make significant observations of the planets and to predict the discovery of Pluto, which astronomers first observed in 1930 from the Lowell Observatory.

Refracting telescopes began to give way to reflecting telescopes; these instruments use mirrors rather than lenses to focus incoming light, allowing for larger construction and more accurate observations and measurements. As a result, the first half of the twentieth century saw the construction of a new generation of large-aperture telescopes: 60 inches (1908), Mount Wilson, California; 100 inches (1918) Mount Wilson; and 200 inches (1948), Palomar Mountain, California.

Hooker Telescope. The 100-inch reflecting telescope—the world's largest from late 1917 to 1948—at Mount Wilson Observatory in Pasadena, Calif.; here in 1929, Edwin Hubble discovered the "red shift" of light emitted by stars and determined that the universe is expanding. © CORBIS

The World's Largest Optical Observatories

Since astronomical observatories tend toward the maxim of "bigger is better," consequent construction has often required increasing collaboration among nations in order to fund the scale of more modern, sophisticated installations. What follows are descriptions of the more noteworthy observatories constructed during the twentieth and early twenty-first centuries.

The Mount Wilson and Palomar observatories were jointly named Hale Observatories in December 1969, in honor of pioneering astronomer George Ellery Hale (1868–1938). The complex focuses on solar observations and studies, and astronomers from around the world use the facility for astrophotography as well as spectroscopic research. The equatorially mounted 60- and 100-inch telescopes on Mount Wilson routinely serve long-exposure celestial photography. The observatory's 60-inch instrument ventured the first measurements of the Milky Way galaxy and determined the distance to M31, the great galaxy in Andromeda. In 1928, the Rockefeller Foundation agreed to fund construction of a 200-inch (or 5.1 meters, since larger telescopes are generally measured in meters) reflecting telescope, which the California Institute of Technology, together with the observatory staff, supervised. World War II (1939–1945) delayed completion of the project, and the great telescope, formally called Hale Telescope, finally saw its dedication twenty years later, in 1948. Because of the encroaching population growth of Los Angeles, Mount Palomar served as the location for later astronomical constructions, although the two facilities continued to operate as one research installation.

Kitt Peak National Observatory, southwest of Tucson, Arizona, began operating in 1960 and is administered by the Association of Universities for Research in Astronomy. The installation contains many telescopes, including the McMath solar telescope, the largest of its type, with a 1.5-meter diameter. The observatory's largest reflecting telescope is a 4-meter instrument completed in 1973. The National Radio Astronomy Observatory operates an 11-meter radio telescope here as well. The facility hosts other telescopes operated by The University of Arizona, the University of Michigan, the Massachusetts Institute of Technology, and Dartmouth College.

Whipple Observatory, located on Mount Hopkins south of Tucson, Arizona, has a number of telescopes, including a ten-meter dish made up of 248 hexagonal-shaped mirrors, installed in 1968. This instrument observes gamma rays from space interacting with the atmosphere. The facility also houses two conventional reflecting telescopes installed in 1970, one with a 1.52-meter mirror and the other with a mirror of twelve inches (30 cm). The largest instrument, completed in the late 1970s, was a multiple-mirror telescope consisting of six 72-inch mirrors with a combined area equivalent to a 4.5-meter mirror. This instrument made both optical and infrared observations of the sky. The six mirrors, however, were replaced in 1997 by a single 6.5-meter mirror.

Mauna Kea Observatory sits atop Hawaii's dormant volcano Mauna Kea and has the nighttime advantage of a minimum of light pollution. Founded in 1967, the observatory operates under the University of Hawaii but houses several internationally sponsored instruments. The United States, Canada, and France sponsor a 3.58-meter optical and infrared reflector, placed in operation in 1979. The United Kingdom and the United States operate a 3.8-meter infrared reflector as well. A 15-meter British-Dutch paraboloid telescope operates in the ultrashort wave band. This instrument, built of 200 individual mirror panels, was completed in 1987. Mauna Kea additionally houses a 3-meter infrared reflector and a 2.24-meter optical and infrared reflector.

Mauna Kea is also home for the Keck Observatory, completed on Mauna Kea in 1990 and housing two of the world's largest optical telescopes. Keck I, completed in 1993, has a ten-meter primary mirror consisting of thirty-six separate hexagonal segments. The telescope produced detailed and significant images of Jupiter when fragments of Comet Shoemaker-Levy 9 bombarded the planet in July 1994. Keck II, completed in 1998, also possesses a similar ten-meter mirror array.

The McDonald Observatory in Fort Davis, Texas, jointly operated by the University of Chicago and the University of Texas, houses the Hobby-Eberly Telescope. The instrument was installed in 1998 with an eleven-meter diameter, making it one of the largest single-mirror telescopes in the world.

One of the most ambitious telescope projects of the late twentieth century occurred as a joint European and Chilean venture atop Chile's Cerro Paranal, where four side-by-side observatories became operational in September 2000. Each of the 8.2-meter telescopes of the ESO Very Large Telescope at Paranal can operate independently or in cooperation through a process known as interferometry, whereby images are made to blend together to create viewing equal to a combined mirror surface of more than 210 square meters.

Nonoptical and Space-Based Telescopes

Of the nonoptical telescopes—that is, those operating outside the visible spectrum of light—the largest is the Very Large Array, which consists of twenty-seven movable radio telescopes constructed on tracks extending some seventeen miles apart, near Socorro, New Mexico. Each parabolic dish is twenty-five meters in diameter, but when the telescopes are spread fully apart, the array can receive signals equivalent to a telescope of seventeen miles in diameter.

Of the space-based observatories, two are particularly prominent. Launched in 1990, the Hubble Space Telescope required corrective optics that astronauts from the space shuttle Endeavor installed in 1993. The instrument's 2.4-meter telescope can study wavelengths from the near-infrared through the ultraviolet. NASA's Chandra X-ray Observatory, launched and deployed by space shuttle Columbia in 1999, is a sophisticated X-ray observatory built to observe X-rays from high-energy regions of the universe, such as the remnants of exploded stars. NASA's premier X-ray observatory was named in honor of the late Indian American Nobel laureate (1983) Subrahmanyan Chandrasekhar, known to the world as Chandra (which means "moon" or "luminous" in Sanskrit). Harvard University and the Smithsonian Institution jointly operate the observatory's research center.

BIBLIOGRAPHY

Barbree, Jay, and Martin Caidin. *A Journey through Time: Exploring the Universe with the Hubble Space Telescope.* New York: Penguin Studio, 1995.

Carroll, Bradley W., et al. *An Introduction to Modern Astrophysics.* Reading, Mass.: Addison-Wesley, 1996.

Chandra X-Ray Observatory Web Site. Home page at http://chandra.harvard.edu/.

Florence, Ronald. *The Perfect Machine: Building the Palomar Telescope.* New York: HarperCollins, 1994.

Kirby-Smith, and Henry Tompkins. *U.S. Observatories: A Directory and Travel Guide.* New York: Van Nostrand Reinhold, 1976.

Tucker, Wallace H., and Karen Tucker. *Revealing the Universe: The Making of the Chandra X-Ray Observatory.* Cambridge, Mass.: Harvard University Press, 2001.

Zeilik, Michael. *Astronomy: The Evolving Universe.* 9th ed. New York: Cambridge University Press, 2002.

Mark Todd

See also **Astronomy; Hubble Space Telescope.**

OCALA PLATFORM. During the 1880s an agricultural depression in the South and Great Plains gave rise to several agrarian lobbying organizations, including the Southern Farmers' Alliance and the National Farmers' Alliance and Industrial Union. Under the leadership of Leonidas Polk and Charles Macune, the two organizations met at Ocala, Florida, in December 1890 to demand government support for the nation's depressed farmers. The Ocala Platform demanded, among other things, the abolition of national banks, a graduated income tax, free and unlimited coinage of silver, the establishment of subtreasuries where farmers could obtain money at less than 2 percent on nonperishable products, and the election of U.S. senators by a direct vote of the people. When neither major party adopted the Ocala demands, the disgruntled farmers turned to direct political action on their own behalf. In July 1892 they organized the Populist Party at Omaha, Nebraska, and nominated James B. Weaver as their presidential candidate. Weaver garnered 1 million votes; carried the states of Colorado, Kansas, Nevada, and Idaho; but finished third in the race. In 1896 the Populist Party fused with the Democratic Party in support of William Jennings Bryan's presidential campaign. Bryan finished a distant second to William McKinley, and the Populist Party soon disbanded.

BIBLIOGRAPHY

Hicks, John D. *The Populist Revolt.* Minneapolis: University of Minnesota Press, 1931.

Goodwyn, Lawrence. *The Populist Moment: A Short History of the Agrarian Revolt in America.* New York: Oxford University Press, 1978.

McMath, Robert C., Jr. *Populist Vanguard: A History of the Southern Farmers' Alliance.* Chapel Hill: University of North Carolina Press, 1975.

W. T. Cash / A. G.

See also **Agriculture; Conventions, Party Nominating; Cooperatives, Farmers'; Farmers' Alliance; Populism.**

OCCUPATIONAL SAFETY AND HEALTH ACT. President Richard Nixon signed the Occupational Safety and Health Act into law on 29 December 1970. Sometimes referred to as the Williams-Steiger Act, after its chief sponsors, Democratic Senator Harrison Williams of New Jersey and Republican Representative William Steiger of Wisconsin, the act is known mostly by its familiar acronym, OSHA. Congress passed OSHA "to assure so far as possible every working man and woman in the Nation safe and healthful working conditions." To meet this lofty goal, Congress created a vast federal bureaucracy empowered to regulate most businesses. OSHA touches nearly every American workplace and has become a landmark in the history of labor, employment, and public health law.

State regulation of workplace safety began as part of the Progressive response to the industrial revolution during the late nineteenth century. Early in the twentieth century, the burgeoning labor movement lobbied successfully for further regulation. Eventually, the federal government became involved in workplace safety during Franklin Roosevelt's presidency. In 1936, as part of Roosevelt's New Deal, Congress passed the Walsh-Healey Public Contracts Act, which allowed the Department of Labor to ban federal contract work done under hazardous conditions. Under the leadership of Frances Perkins, Roosevelt's secretary of labor and the first woman cabinet member, the federal government aggressively asserted its authority to regulate private business.

By the 1960s, however, changes in American industry exposed the ineffectiveness of existing state and federal laws. In 1965, the Public Health Service published an influential report that outlined some of the recently discovered technological dangers, including chemicals linked to cancer. The report called for a major national occupational health effort, criticizing existing federal law as too limited and state programs as uncoordinated and insufficient. The AFL-CIO and other labor organizations urged President Lyndon Johnson to support the report's recommendations.

In 1966, President Johnson directed his secretary of labor, Willard Wirtz, to develop a comprehensive national program to protect workers. In the wake of alarming revelations about cancer among uranium miners, on 23 January 1968, Johnson adopted Secretary Wirtz's plan and urged Congress to act. Congress promptly introduced bills embodying the administration's proposal. Wirtz lobbied vigorously for the bills. He testified that each year 14,500 workers died, 2 million were disabled, and more than 7 million hurt as a result of industrial accidents, and that these numbers were steadily rising. He criticized state, local, and private programs as inadequate and fragmented and federal programs as incomplete. Labor unions, public interest groups, and health professionals supported the bills. Industry representatives opposed them. In part because of this opposition, the bills failed to pass Congress in 1968. They also failed because Vietnam War protest, President Johnson's decision not to run for reelection, riots in the inner cities, and other events diverted congressional and national attention away from worker safety and health.

In 1969, President Nixon also called for the enactment of a federal occupational safety and health law, though his proposal was substantially weaker than the one introduced by his predecessor. Republicans in Congress introduced bills reflecting the administration's proposal, and, sensing that some worker safety law must pass, industry switched its position and supported these bills. Democrats in Congress introduced stronger legislation supported by the labor unions, a nascent environmental movement, and consumer advocates like Ralph Nader.

The most controversial debate centered on the scope of the secretary of labor's authority. Democrats favored bills that gave the secretary power to issue occupational safety and health standards, to conduct inspections and impose sanctions, and to adjudicate appeals. Republicans wanted to establish two independent boards appointed by the president, one with authority to issue the standards and the other with authority to decide enforcement appeals. Republicans claimed they did not want to concentrate too much authority in one person, while Democrats worried that a separation of power would result in a weaker law.

Eventually, Republicans and Democrats worked out a compromise solution. The secretary of labor would create and oversee the Occupational Safety and Health Administration, which would have the power to set standards, conduct inspections, and impose penalties for violators. A separate commission, called the Occupational Safety and Health Review Commission, would adjudicate appeals from businesses fined or otherwise penalized by the secretary of labor. Among other provisions, the compromise bill included a "general duty" clause for all businesses to keep the workplace free of recognized hazards likely to cause death or serious physical harm. In addition, the compromise granted employees the right to file complaints, accompany inspectors, and participate in Review Commission adjudications, and it prohibited reprisals against whistleblowers. Ultimately, the House of Representatives voted 308–60 in support of the compromise bill, and the Senate adopted it on a voice vote without debate.

Soon after its passage, OSHA became a powerful presence in American workplaces. Many businesses deeply resented the government for telling them how to operate, and the act provoked much controversy. Despite this controversy, however, OSHA itself has remained relatively unchanged. It has only been amended once, in 1998, but these amendments were relatively minor.

Administrative rulemaking, however, has kept OSHA current by responding to changing dangers in the American workplace. After first setting standards for worker safety, OSHA shifted its focus to worker health, setting standards to protect workers from the insidious effects of asbestos, cancer-causing chemicals, beryllium, lead, cotton dust, carbon monoxide, dyes, radiation, pesticides, exotic fuels, and other toxins. In setting such standards, OSHA's jurisdiction has steadily expanded. The nature of workplace injuries has also changed, and OSHA has responded, for example, by setting new standards to alleviate repetitive stress disorders like carpal tunnel syndrome.

OSHA's impact on American business has also varied much in response to evolving administrative rulemaking. Under the administration of President Bill Clinton, OSHA attempted to shift from a top-down, command and control system in which the government tells industry what it should do or else, to a partnership between regulators and private businesses. Under a partnership system, businesses that proactively implement comprehensive safety and health programs obtain flexibility and leniency in meeting OSHA standards.

BIBLIOGRAPHY

Levy, JoAnne. "OSHA—What's New at a 'Twenty-Something' Agency: Workplace Environmental Hazards." *Missouri Environmental Law and Policy Review* 1 (Fall 1993): 49.

Mendeloff, John. *Regulating Safety: An Economic and Political Analysis of Safety and Health Policy*. Cambridge, Mass.: MIT Press, 1979. See especially the chapter "Political and Economic Perspectives on the Design of Occupational Safety and Health Policy."

Mintz, Benjamin W. *OSHA: History, Law, and Policy*. Washington, D.C.: Bureau of National Affairs, 1984.

Subcommittee on Labor, Senate Committee on Labor and Public Welfare, Ninety-second Congress, First Session. *Legislative History of the Occupational Safety and Health Act of 1970*. Washington, D.C.: Government Printing Office, 1971.

Shannon C. Petersen

See also **Employers' Liability Laws; Government Regulation of Business; Labor Legislation and Administration.**

OCEANOGRAPHIC SURVEY. Surveys are conducted by the U.S. Navy and civilian government agencies. By their nature, surveys are systematic examinations of the oceans' condition. Although the methods used to conduct these studies have evolved over the last two centuries, expressions such as "sailing in uncharted waters" and "seizing the weather gauge" still attest to their importance.

Early Surveys

All mariners know that accurate information about winds, tides, currents, and ocean bottom depth raise the likelihood of a safe passage. In naval terms, superior "environmental intelligence" can allow one side to gain advantage over the other. In the nation's early years, this knowledge was held by individual seafarers and naval officers, or published, with varying degrees of accuracy, by foreign countries and private commercial operations. In 1807, Congress authorized the creation of a Survey of the Coast to obtain and map basic information about the nation's islands, shoals, and anchorages. The U.S. Navy established the Depot of Charts and Instruments in 1830 to supply accurate nautical charts, books, and navigational instruments to the Navy and American shipping interests. The navy published its first charts in 1837, four maps of the fishing banks off the coast of Massachusetts.

In the 1840s, the practice of oceanographic surveying took a significant step forward on both the naval and civilian sides. Recognizing the need to keep all hydrographic (pertaining to nautical surveys and charts) materials in one place, in 1842 Congress authorized building a central repository for the Depot's collections. The Depot's superintendent, navy officer Matthew Fontaine Maury, made several key advances in the science of hydrography. First, he and his staff reviewed all of the hundreds of ships' logs in their care. By systematically comparing conditions for the same location in different seasons, Maury could suggest navigational routes that maximized speed and safety. The resulting Wind and Current Charts were soon the reference of choice worldwide. Maury also created a template for a standardized log that all navy captains were required to complete for every voyage and to submit to the Depot. Merchant and foreign vessels received copies of Wind and Current

Charts as well in exchange for keeping Maury's logs. Within five years the Depot had received 26 million reports.

Meanwhile, Alexander Dallas Bache took the helm of the U.S. Coast Survey in 1843. Bache raised the level of scientific inquiry in the name of more accurate charts and navigation. His study of the gulf stream, begun in 1845, sought new measures to determine the dynamics of what he suspected was an ever-changing current. For more than a decade, survey ships repeatedly measured temperature at the surface and varying depths, described the bottom depth and character, recorded direction and speed of the currents and the surface and at varying depths, and examined plant and animal life along the way.

Technological Advances

Maury and Bache had laid the groundwork for American scientific exploration of the ocean. Their principle of repeated, systematic observation remains the guiding philosophy; only the tools have changed. In some instances, surveys have supported the deployment of new technologies. For example, entrepreneurs who wanted to set up a telegraph connection across the Atlantic required information about the ocean floor. The resulting survey produced the first published depth chart of the Atlantic Ocean, and in 1858 the first telegraphic messages were sent across the ocean via cable lying on the seabed.

New missions sometimes required new technologies. In the 1870s, Coast Survey officer Charles Sigsbee modified a prototype invented by Sir William Thomson (later Lord Kelvin) to construct a machine that used wire instead of rope to take depth soundings. Sigsbee's sounding machine was used to produce a bathymetric (deep-water depth) chart of the Gulf of Mexico in 1874–1875, the first modern and accurate map of any portion of the deep ocean. Sigsbee and biologist Alexander Agassiz collaborated to replace the rope used to raise and lower equipment with lines made of steel wire. Following this idea, Coast Survey officers developed steel wire lines that allowed vessels to anchor at abyssal depths.

By the 1870s, fish and shellfish stocks showed signs of decline and disputes arose among fishermen over the fairness of some of the new netting and dredging techniques. The Coast Survey worked with the newly created U.S. Fish Commission (1871) to conduct dredging operations of their own to survey fish populations. Coast Survey and Fisheries Commission ships discovered hundreds of marine species on their biological research expeditions crossing the world. In 1878, the Coast Survey merged with the Geodetic (size and shape of the earth) Survey to become the U.S. Coast and Geodetic Survey (C&GS), which began to produce the most complete and accurate maps yet of the United States.

During the last quarter of the nineteenth century, Navy oceanographers turned their attention to Central America, where they assisted in locating suitable sites for a canal linking the Gulf of Mexico and the Pacific Ocean, sparing ships the long and dangerous trip around the tip of South America. Nor had the government given up the idea of a Northwest Passage—a route linking the Atlantic and Pacific via the Arctic Sea. Several expeditions were sent to explore the ice; navy civil engineer Robert Peary reached the North Pole in 1909. The disastrous sinking of the *Titanic* in 1912 also focused new attention on monitoring ice from the polar sea.

During World War I (1914–1918), German submarines posed a new and frightening threat, sinking forty-five U.S. ships while cruising in American waters. American researchers pursued the idea of underwater listening devices as a way to track the U-boats, although the first workable system was not built until after the war. Sonar, the use of sound echoes to locate underwater features and submerged objects, revealed the sea bottom's topography in much greater detail than possible before. In the 1920s, C&GS vessels began to use echo-sounding equipment alongside the traditional wire line to determine accurate values for the velocity of sound in seawater. Survey ships mapped the terrain of the continental shelf, information that would prove valuable for hunting German submarines during World War II (1939–1945). On the eve of World War II, the navy explored the effects of water temperature and salinity on sound transmission underwater, further refining its ability to locate underwater targets.

World War II, and the renewed threat of submarine warfare, spurred more innovative firsts, including deep-sea cameras and electronic navigation systems that used reflected radio waves (radar). Intended originally as a tool in precision aerial bombing, radar was being used by the C&GS to conduct hydrographic surveys by the war's end. Demand for accurate charts had skyrocketed in the wake of Pearl Harbor. The navy's Hydrographic Office dispatched survey ships with onboard printing equipment to accompany the Pacific fleet—43 million charts were printed and issued in one year.

The decades after World War II were notable for collaboration between civilian government agencies, the C&GS, the navy, and academic institutions. One landmark expedition took place in 1955, when the C&GS ship *Pioneer* was engaged by the navy to survey the West Coast out to several hundred miles offshore. The Scripps Institute of Oceanography attached a newly designed tow to the *Pioneer* that would measure magnetic properties of the seabed. The project mapped previously unknown long, magnetic stripes that lay along the ocean floor. This discovery, along with the identification of the Mid-Atlantic Ridge Rift Valley in 1959, and C&GS scientists' studies of underwater earthquakes, ultimately led Princeton University professor Harry H. Hess to outline a theory of plate tectonics in the early 1960s.

The 1960s were a time of rapid advancement in oceanographic surveys. The C&GS built a fleet of new survey ships and spent more than a decade mapping large areas of the North Pacific basin for the Seamap Project. New technical advances included the Deep Tow instrument system, which takes multiple measures of the deep sea environment; multibeam sounding systems, which can take simultaneous readings of a swath of ocean floor to generate a map almost instantly; and the submersible research vessel *Alvin*, which can take scientists to unprecedented ocean depths. Research also focused on the interaction between ocean and atmosphere, which was reflected in the creation of the National Oceanic and Atmospheric Administration (1970) that now encompasses the C&GS as well as the National Weather Service.

Technological advances of the late twentieth century included satellite communication and observation, global positioning, microchip technology, computers small enough to be taken into the field, and more sophisticated modeling techniques. One widely used practical application is the navy's Optimum Track Ship Routing program that uses meteorological and oceanographic data to create a near-real-time forecast of the safest and most efficient passage across the seas. Future surveys are likely to take advantage of microchip technology and satellite communication to obtain large-scale, real-time maps that use remote sensors to transmit data from a vast expanse of ocean. For instance, passive acoustic monitors positioned in the water all over the globe already have been used to detect deep-sea volcanic eruptions and the migratory paths of the blue whale. These technologies, along with even greater computer processing capability, may take oceanographers ever closer to obtaining a pulse of the planet.

BIBLIOGRAPHY

Charts from the U.S. Coast Survey. Available from http://chartmaker.ncd.noaa.gov.

Labaree, Benjamin W., et al. *America and the Sea: A Maritime History.* Mystic, Conn.: Mystic Seaport Museum, 1998.

National Oceanic and Atmospheric Administration. Home page at http://oceanexplorer.noaa.gov.

Naval Oceanographic Office Home page at http://www.navo.navy.mil.

Pinsel, Marc I. *150 Years of Service on the Seas: A Pictorial History of the U.S. Naval Oceanographic Office from 1830 to 1980.* Washington, D.C.: Department of the Navy, Oceanographic Office, 1982.

U.S. Department of Commerce, National Oceanic and Atmospheric Administration. *Discovering Earth's Final Frontier: A U.S. Strategy for Ocean Exploration, The Report of the President's Panel on Ocean Exploration.* Washington, D.C.: October 2000.

Jennifer Maier

See also **Navy, United States; *Titanic,* Sinking of the.**

OCEANOGRAPHY. Although oceanography is a twentieth-century scientific discipline forged from European roots, several American developments in the nineteenth century contributed to its modern formation. First, federal interests in mapping the coastlines, charting seaports, and exploring the vast expanse of the United States inspired the work of the U.S. Coast Survey and the Navy's Depot of Charts and Instruments and the U.S. Exploring Expedition (1838–1842). Second, American educational reformers and intellectuals, with their gaze firmly set upon Europe, embarked on an overhaul of the American university system, adding comprehensive curricula in the sciences to colleges and universities for the first time.

In the nineteenth century, concerns had been voiced about the valuable European North Sea fishery and the cod fishery in New England leading to a new federal agency to investigate this resource. The U.S. Fish Commission gained support in 1871,and centered its activities in a laboratory at Woods Hole (Cape Cod) and on two ships dedicated for open-ocean fisheries work. Thus, when an international meeting was held in 1888 at Plymouth, England, to investigate the collapse of the North Sea fishery and when the International Council for the Exploration of the Sea (ICES) was formed in 1902, American scientists were prepared to participate.

Federal support for oceanography at this time was limited. Indeed, when Alexander Agassiz explored the Pacific and Atlantic at the end of the nineteenth century, he did so aboard Coast Survey and Fish Commission vessels but financed the work with his own personal resources. Thus, by the beginning of the twentieth century, Americans lagged behind the British, Germans, and Scandinavians.

American interests in the sea changed, however, first with the sinking of the *Titanic* (1912), and then from the American experiences in World War I (1914–1918). Both disasters illustrated the need to better understand the oceanic conditions in the North Atlantic and to develop underwater listening devices to protect the country from the new submarine warfare. Lacking a permanent scientific advisory group, President Woodrow Wilson transferred the wartime National Research Council (NRC) to the National Academy of Sciences (NAS) following the war. Continuing its work after 1919, the NRC sponsored research that led in the 1920s to the development and refinement of the sonic depth finder and sonar, acoustical devices that greatly improved navigation and enabled surface ships to detect submarines. With its newfound interest in the sea, the NAS established its Committee on Oceanography in 1927, charged with recommending federal oceanic policy.

By the early twentieth century, Americans already established a research presence alongside the ocean, at marine laboratories on both coastlines. The Marine Biological Laboratory (MBL) enhanced the research objectives of the Fish Commission laboratory at Woods Hole. On the West Coast, William Emerson Ritter established the Scripps Institution of Biological Research in La Jolla (near San Diego) in 1903. But neither Woods Hole nor Scripps had an extensive oceanic research program; indeed, American oceanography was barely in its infancy.

In 1924, Thomas Wayland Vaughan, a geologist, was appointed to direct the Scripps Institution of Oceanography (SIO). Three years later, he was named a member of the NAS's oceanographic committee. By the end of 1927, the committee began to support Vaughan's notion that the country needed "oceanographic stations" scattered along the American Pacific and Atlantic coastlines. Then in 1930, the Rockefeller Foundation announced the establishment of three oceanography centers, Scripps Institution in La Jolla, the Oceanographic Laboratories at the University of Washington, and a large new research center at Woods Hole, Woods Hole Oceanographic Institution (WHOI). Thus, by 1930, the institutional framework for the development of American oceanography was set.

The new scientific field developed rapidly, especially with the infusion of research money from philanthropic, federal, and military sources. The U.S. Navy encouraged developments in marine acoustics and related aspects of physical oceanography as it attempted to develop more sophisticated means to monitor the subsurface environment and to build deterrent devices for submarine warfare. This work led to more sophisticated sonar devices and the invention of hydrophones for submarine sound detection. Geological oceanography received attention especially as it offered a means to direct exploration of shallow oceanic basins for oil. Meteorological research continued at most oceanographic laboratories, attempting to understand the relationship between oceanic currents, open ocean wind patterns, and continental weather.

With the outbreak of World War II (1939–1945), oceanography's centrality to the American war effort was demonstrated once again. Of course, much attention focused on the development of submarine warfare. While at the outset of the war, the Allies lost an inordinate number of vessels, wartime matériel, and manpower to the German submarines, oceanographic developments led to dramatic improvements in submarine detection and, ultimately, to the production of submarines and submarine warfare that exacted an even greater toll from the Germans and Japanese. Not surprisingly, therefore, when the war ended in 1945, the federal government established the Office of Naval Research (ONR), which served to ensure funding for oceanographic centers throughout the United States. In addition, the presence of surplus Navy vessels created a surfeit of oceanic research platforms for American oceanographers.

Following the war, the emergence of the Cold War maintained the U.S. Navy patronage for oceanographic research. In addition to its traditional concerns, the Navy became interested in studying the deep ocean basins. This interest involved an extensive hydrophone system, connected by submarine cables to monitor the movement of Soviet submarines, so the deep basins in the Atlantic and Pacific posed potential problems. These same regions attracted increasing attention from oceanographers in the 1950s and 1960s as ideas of seafloor spreading and continental drift began to be discussed again. The existence of mid-ocean ridges and deep-sea trenches gave these notions added credence, but oceanographers needed new technological tools to investigate the bottom of the sea to validate the mechanism for any movement.

Water sampling, temperature measurements, and bottom sediments were soon the target of many research expeditions. Increasingly, this type of research became more expensive, multidisciplinary, and technological, requiring greater financial resources, larger groups of collaborating researchers, and, in many cases, international cooperation from oceanographic experts scattered worldwide.

With multiple partners, oceanography entered its current phase. Continuing to pursue deep ocean research, oceanographers worked to develop a new technological device, the deep-sea submersible. Following dramatic explorations of the earth's deepest marine trenches in the Trieste, American oceanographers argued for the creation of a highly maneuverable submersible that could withstand the demanding conditions of the oceanic depth. The Navy, too, was interested; after all, the hydrophone network it planned would need to be maintained. Then, the loss of the attack submarine *Thresher* in 1963 underscored the Navy's interests. Working closely with engineers at Woods Hole and other oceanographers with submarine experience, the *Alvin* was commission in 1964 and the era of submersible research in oceanography entered its most dramatic phase.

By the 1970s, the Navy modified submersibles for its own purposes and *Alvin* and its successors were pressed into basic oceanographic research. In the late 1970s, oceanographers soon discovered sea vents adjacent to oceanic ridges worldwide. Even more dramatic, however, were the faunal forms inhabiting these vents. For the first time, luxuriant "gardens" of deep-sea animals, all new to science, were described. Plate tectonics was not just confirmed, but the physical, chemical, and biological aspects of the vents opened a new era for oceanographic research. By the close of the century, new ideas concerning the origin of life, conditions for the emergence of life, sources for the chemical composition of seawater, and deep ocean sources for thermal conductivity created fresh perspectives for oceanographic work. Coupled with exciting extensions of the century-long work to study open-ocean currents, including work on the longitudinal oscillations of large masses of warm and cold water in the central gyres of the oceans that seem to affect the earth's climate, oceanography at the beginning of the twenty-first century promised to maintain its prominent role in scientific research.

BIBLIOGRAPHY

Benson, Keith R., and Philip F. Rehbock, eds. *Oceanographic History: The Pacific and Beyond.* Seattle: University of Washington Press, 2002.

Mills, Eric. *Biological Oceanography, An Early History, 1870–1960.* Ithaca, N.Y.: Cornell University Press, 1989.

Oreskes, Naomi, ed. *Plate Tectonics: An Insider's History of the Modern Theory of the Earth.* Boulder, Colo.: Westview Press, 2001.

Keith R. Benson

See also **Laboratories; Marine Biology; Meteorology; National Academy of Sciences; Submarines.**

OFFICE OF ECONOMIC OPPORTUNITY (OEO) was created in August 1964 by the Economic Opportunity Act. The OEO was part of President Lyndon B. Johnson's social and economic initiatives known as the "Great Society" and the "War on Poverty." The OEO was placed in the executive office of the Johnson administration and its first director was R. Sargent Shriver, who was involved in drafting the Economic Opportunity Act. He served in that position until 1969. When it was created, the OEO coordinated the Job Corps; Neighborhood Youth Corps; work training and study programs; community action agencies including Head Start; adult education; loans for the rural poor and small businesses; work experience programs; and Volunteers in Service to America (VISTA).

Early Years

Although the OEO was placed near the President so he could closely supervise it, the OEO's programs were designed so that they were also subjected to considerable local control. The structure of the OEO and its programs can be traced to the Kennedy administration's Mobilization for Youth program, which was funded by the President's Council as well as by the Ford Foundation and the City of New York. The Mobile Youth Fund organized and coordinated neighborhood councils composed of local officials, service providers, and community members to lower the level of juvenile delinquency. It also enlisted the aid of the school board and city council members. Similar community involvement was the hallmark of OEO programs, which were carried out at the local level by community action agencies.

Community involvement also made the OEO controversial and brought the first political attacks against it. The Economic Opportunity Act required that community action agencies have "maximum feasible participation" in the areas they served. As such, local or state governments, some of which expressed that the federal government had overstepped its boundaries, did not control these agencies. In some major cities, community action agencies were particularly vocal against local officials, who labeled agency members and directors as militants.

These local officials managed to use their political clout in the U.S. Congress to reign in the independence of community action agencies and their directors. As a result, Congress began to redirect funds intended for OEO programs into Congress's own National Emphasis Programs. In 1967, Congress passed the Quie Amendment, which restructured the management of community action agencies. The amendment required that an agency's board of directors select locally elected officials to make up one-third of the board's directors. At least another third of the directors were to be low-income representatives selected by a democratic process, and the balance was to come from the private sector.

Reports of high cost overruns at Job Corps centers and other community action agencies brought further controversy to the OEO. In 1966 and 1967, Congress set spending limits and other restrictions on the Job Corps. In late 1967, Congress passed the Green Amendment, which required that local officials designate community agencies to a particular area. After local officials designated an agency, it could receive funds from the OEO. After months of negotiations, more than 95 percent of the existing agencies were designated. In several large cities, agencies were taken over by the mayor and turned into a public agency.

As originally enacted, the OEO's work programs could be blocked by a state governor's veto. In 1965 the OEO was given the power to override any governor's veto, and the political battle was set to wrest this power from the OEO. In 1967 and 1969, California Senator George Murphy proposed legislation that would enforce a governor's veto on legal aid programs. In 1971, California's governor Ronald Reagan attempted to veto continuation of the California Rural Assistance Program, but his veto was overturned in the courts.

By 1968, there were 1,600 community action agencies covering 2,300 of the nation's 3,300 counties. In that year, the OEO required that many small, single-county agencies merge into larger, multicounty ones, and the overall number of agencies was greatly reduced. By 1969, about 1,000 agencies had been designated under the Green Amendment and recognized by the OEO. Many of these agencies outlasted the OEO.

After the Johnson Administration

The OEO was a product of the Johnson administration, and when Richard M. Nixon became president in 1969, the office's days were numbered. In that same year, R. Sargent Shriver resigned. President Nixon transferred many of the OEO's successful programs to other federal departments such as Labor and Health, Education, and Welfare. During his first term in office, President Nixon continued to have the OEO funded, but he changed its mission. The OEO was just to be the starting ground for new programs, and if they proved to be successful, administration would be turned over to an appropriate federal department.

At the start of his second term in 1973, President Nixon did not request any funds for OEO's Community Action Program division. Congress nevertheless provided these funds. Nixon appointed Howard Philips as director of the OEO and ordered him to dismantle and close the agency, as well as not to send to the community agencies the funds that Congress had allocated. After a series of lawsuits, the Federal District Court in Washington, D.C., ruled that the president could not refuse to spend funds that had been appropriated by Congress. Philips was ordered by the courts to resign because his nomination had not been confirmed by the Senate.

President Gerald Ford finally closed the OEO on 4 January 1975. Supporters of the OEO and its programs, however, reached a compromise with the Ford administration, which replaced the OEO with the Community Services Administration (CSA). All of the OEO's employees were hired by the CSA, which assumed many OEO programs. Other OEO programs, such as Head Start, were transferred to the Department of Health, Education, and Welfare. The Carter administration supported the CSA, but because of pressure from Congress, President Jimmy Carter tightened management control of the CSA and the community action agencies under its aegis.

On 30 September 1981, President Ronald Reagan, who as California's governor had fought the OEO in court, abolished the CSA and the Employment Opportunity Act, which had created the OEO. One thousand CSA employees lost their jobs. Former OEO and CSA programs were transferred to other executive departments. Community action agencies that had been funded by the CSA subsequently received money through Community Services Block Grants.

The legacy of the OEO can be seen in state community action agencies, state economic opportunity offices, and such federal programs as Head Start. Head Start, which is now run by the Department of Health and Human Services, was a key component of President Bill Clinton's social aid programs. Although President George W. Bush's Center for Faith-Based and Community Initiatives was identified with his conservative social policies, its emphasis on community involvement echoes the OEO and its community action programs, which are now regarded as symbolic of 1960s liberalism.

BIBLIOGRAPHY

Andrew, John A. *Lyndon Johnson and the Great Society.* Chicago: Ivan R. Dee, 1998.

Karger, Howard Jacob, and David Stoesz. *American Social Welfare Policy: A Pluralist Approach.* 4th ed. Boston: Allyn and Bacon, 2002.

Trattner, Walter I. *From Poor Law to Welfare State: A History of Social Welfare in America.* 6th ed. New York: The Free Press, 1999.

John Wyzalek

See also **Community Action Program; Great Society; Job Corps; War on Poverty.**

OFFICE OF MANAGEMENT AND BUDGET (OMB), established by executive order in 1971 when President Richard M. Nixon issued his Reorganization Plan 2. The Plan created the OMB as part of the reorganization of the Bureau of the Budget, the agency within the Executive Office of the President responsible since 1939 for the formulation of the national budget. (Prior to 1939 the Budget and Accounting Act of 1921 had placed the Bureau of the Budget in the Treasury Department.) The president selects the director of the OMB, who has cabinet-level status within the federal bureaucracy.

The primary function of the OMB is to assist the president in preparing the national budget and to "supervise and control the administration of the budget." In addition, it has a number of other functions of considerable significance and influence. It is charged with aiding the president in achieving governmental efficiency; advising the president about the potential costs of the administration's legislative program and coordinating the legislative requests of governmental agencies; developing information systems and assembling statistical data; monitoring the performance and efficiency of federal programs; developing programs for recruiting, training, and evaluating career personnel; and coordinating all programs of the executive branch in order to achieve maximum efficiency and efficacy. In short, the reorganization and change in agency title from Bureau of the Budget to Office of Management and Budget reflect a significant expansion of the managerial responsibilities and influence of the agency.

In fulfilling its primary responsibility, the preparation of the national budget, the OMB addresses itself not only to fiscal policy but also to the substantive aims of the administration's policy goals for the fiscal year. During the process of drafting the budget, agencies present their program plans and appropriation requests to the OMB, where its staff examines them in detail. Beginning in the mid-1960s the Bureau of the Budget instituted an evaluation process known as "Planning, Programming, Budgeting" (PPB) for assessing agency programs and appropriation requests. In the PPB process the OMB scrutinizes the efficiency with which the available alternative means, or cost effectiveness, meets the program goals stated in the appropriation requests. The objective of PPB is to achieve the program objectives by choosing the alternative with the optimal cost-benefit ratio.

The Office of Management and Budget, the Department of the Treasury, and the Council of Economic Advisors work together to formulate government fiscal policy and to coordinate the performance of the economy in general with government programs and spending. Once the OMB has evaluated the programs and appropriations of all agencies within the eleven cabinet departments, it prepares the annual budget that the president submits to Congress each January.

During the 1980s and 1990s, critics increasingly attacked the OMB for being a political tool of the administration, in part because it had enormous influence without being accountable to the public and in part because its budget projections were frequently much more optimistic than those coming from the Congressional Budget Office (CBO), founded in 1974. Between 1996 and 1999, however, growth defied the CBO's conservative expectations and generated an enormous surplus more in line with President Bill Clinton's OMB projections. In 1999 the CBO revised its projections to mirror more closely those of the OMB, a move that critics decried for allowing budget projections to drive policy rather than using them simply to forecast actual economic growth.

BIBLIOGRAPHY

Mackenzie, G. Calvin, and Saranna Thornton. *Bucking the Deficit.* Boulder, Colo.: Westview Press, 1996.

Myers, Margaret G. *A Financial History of the United States.* New York: Columbia University Press, 1970.

Wildavsky, Aaron, and Naomi Caiden. *The New Politics of the Budgetary Process.* 3d ed. New York: Longman, 1997.

Stefan J. Kapsch / c. w.

See also **Budget, Federal; Bureaucracy; Council of Economic Advisors; Treasury, Department of the.**

OFFICE OF PRICE ADMINISTRATION (OPA) was the federal agency tasked with establishing price controls on nonagricultural commodities and rationing essential consumer goods during World War II (1939–1945).

The OPA began as the Price Stabilization and Consumer Protection divisions of the Advisory Commission to the Council of National Defense (more commonly known as the National Defense Advisory Commission [NDAC]) created on 29 May 1940 in response to economic pressures from the war in Europe. NDAC's influence was limited, with the Price Stabilization Division setting standards for only basic scrap metals. The Consumer Protection Division's rent-control proposals of 7 January 1941 were universally ignored.

On 11 May 1941, by Executive Order 8734, the Office of Price Administration and Civilian Supply (OPACS) was created from the two NDAC divisions. Leon Henderson, head of the Price Stabilization Division, was appointed as administrator and quickly dubbed in the media as the "Price Czar." Noted economist John Kenneth Galbraith was chosen to direct OPACS's Price Division and served in this function through 1943.

On 28 August 1941, Executive Order 8875 transferred the Civilian Supply group to the Office of Production Management to consolidate the similar efforts of the two entities. OPACS was renamed the Office of Price Administration.

OPA's efforts began in earnest with the outbreak of war on 7 December 1941. Because it had the existing structure to interact with retail outlets and consumers, OPA was delegated the task of rationing. On 27 December 1941 it instituted rationing of rubber tires. Directive Number One of the War Production Board made OPA's rationing role permanent, and by April 1942, rationing had extended to automobiles, sugar, typewriters, and gasoline. By the end of the war, the rationing program also included coffee, shoes, stoves, meats, processed foods, and bicycles.

The Emergency Price Control Act (EPCA) passed on 30 January 1942 provided the legislative basis for OPA to regulate prices, not including agricultural commodities. EPCA also allowed for rent controls. The most prominent result of EPCA was the General Maximum Price Regulation issued by OPA in May 1942. This effectively set the price ceiling at March 1942 levels.

However, EPCA did not address other economic issues beyond price controls. The resulting economic dislocations forced Congress to pass the Stabilization Act on 2 October 1942. This created the Office of Economic Stabilization (OES) that was responsible for controlling wage levels, regulating food prices, and generally stabilizing the cost of living. At this point, any OPA activities that could affect the cost of living had to be coordinated with OES.

The effectiveness of OPA's measures is subject to some debate. While OPA pointed to an overall 31-percent rise in retail prices in World War II compared to a 62-percent rise in World War I (1914–1918), undoubtedly a black market developed in response to price controls. Maintenance of product quality was a constant concern. OPA even colorfully noted in its Twelfth Quarterly Report "a renaissance of cattle rustlers in the West." Reports from OPA's Enforcement Division show that 650,000 investigations were conducted for all of 1943, with 280,000 violations found. In 1944, a total of 338,029 violations were reported, with 205,779 administrative warning letters sent out. Court proceedings were initiated in almost 29,000 cases.

Rationing for gasoline and foodstuffs was discontinued on 15 August 1945. All rationing ended by the end of September 1945. Price controls remained in effect in the hopes of preventing price instability as the war economy converted back to peacetime functions, but they were gradually discontinued through 1947. On 12 December 1946, Executive Order 9809 transferred OPA to the Office of Temporary Controls. While some sugar and rice control programs were transferred to the Department of Agriculture, most other OPA functions were discontinued. OPA was disbanded on 29 May 1947.

BIBLIOGRAPHY

Auerbach, Alfred. *The OPA and Its Pricing Polices.* New York: Fairchild, 1945.

Hirsch, Julius. *Price Control in the War Economy.* New York: Harper and Brothers, 1943.

Thompson, Victor A. *The Regulatory Process in OPA Rationing.* New York: King's Crown Press, 1950.

Wilson, William Jerome, and Mabel Randolph. *OPA Bibliography, 1940–1947.* Washington, D.C.: U.S. Government Printing Office, 1948.

Office of Price Administration. *Quarterly Reports, Volumes 1–22.* Washington, D.C.: U.S. Government Printing Office, 1941–1947. Best source for material on the Office of Price Administration.

Office of Temporary Controls. *The Beginnings of OPA.* Washington, D.C.: U.S. Government Printing Office, 1947.

William G. Hines

See also **World War II.**

OFFICE OF PRICE STABILIZATION also known as the Price Stabilization Board, was the federal agency whose task was to control prices during the Korean War.

The onset of hostilities on 25 June 1950 came as a complete surprise to Americans. Fear of a major conflict with the Soviet Union and still-fresh memories of rationing programs during World War II lead to massive hoarding and panic buying by both consumers and manufacturers. Retail sales for July 1950 increased by 8 percent. After the first month of the war, prices for coffee had increased 9 percent; tin, 26 percent; and rubber, 27 percent. Against this backdrop, on 19 July 1950, in a message to Congress detailing the progress of the war, President Harry Truman asked for limited economic powers to pursue mobilization efforts. This led to the Defense Production Act of 1950, which gave the president the option of imposing rationing and wage and price controls.

Initially, Truman tried to avoid imposing wage and price controls to slow inflation, instead pinning his hopes on credit controls and voluntary compliance. These hopes proved futile. By the end of September 1950, government figures showed that prices for a basket of twenty-eight commodities had increased by 25 percent since the beginning of the war. On 9 September 1951, Executive Order 10161 created the Economic Stabilization Agency (ESA) and Wage Stabilization Board (WSB). The order also allowed for a director of price stabilization under the aegis of the ESA. General Order Number 2 of the ESA formally established the Office of Price Stabilization on 24 January 1951, with Michael DiSalle, mayor of Toledo, as its administrator.

OPS's first act was to announce a price freeze on 26 January 1951. This stopgap measure proved unpopular and unwieldy, and, in many cases, OPS was forced to increase prices. It was not until April 1951 that OPS issued a long-range price control strategy. However, that plan also failed to gather popular support. OPS operations were hampered throughout its existence by the continuous debate over the appropriate level of mobilization and governmental economic control required for an undeclared war. Indeed, Allan Valentine, the first director of ESA, was opposed to establishing price controls. OPS also found many of its efforts undercut by salary rulings of the WSB, especially in the steelworkers' salary dispute of March 1952.

On 6 February 1953, President Dwight Eisenhower's Executive Order 10434 called for the end of all price and wage controls. OPS ended all activities on 30 April 1953 with residual operations passing to ESA.

BIBLIOGRAPHY

Pierpaoli, Paul G., Jr. *Truman and Korea: The Political Culture of the Early Cold War.* Columbia: University of Missouri Press, 1999.

Heller, Francis H., ed. *The Korean War: A Twenty-Five-Year Perspective.* Lawrence: Regents Press of Kansas, 1977.

William G. Hines

See also **Korean War.**

OFFICE OF SCIENTIFIC RESEARCH AND DEVELOPMENT (OSRD) was a federal agency created in 1941 by President Franklin D. Roosevelt to promote research on medicine and weapons technology. In the decades prior to World War II, the federal government had initiated limited research endeavors in the Department of Agriculture, the Bureau of Standards, and other agencies. But the OSRD signaled a greatly expanded federal commitment to science and prepared the way for the even larger science programs of the 1950s. It solidified personal and professional ties between scientists, military leaders, and industry executives. It taught government and military officials the value of basic research for warfare and economic prosperity. It helped consolidate the scientific leadership of key universities such as Harvard, the Massachusetts Institute of Technology (MIT), the University of California at Berkeley, the California Institute of Technology, and the University of Chicago. And by contracting with existing university and industrial laboratories rather than directly hiring or drafting researchers, the OSRD allayed scientists' fears that large-scale public funding would be accompanied by strict government control.

In the spring of 1940 a group of scientists led by engineer and Carnegie Institution of Washington president Vannevar Bush contacted Roosevelt to discuss how the nation's extra-governmental scientific resources might be applied to the national mobilization effort. Roosevelt readily agreed with Bush that the success of the American war effort would depend in large part on scientific research. He created the National Defense Research Committee (NDRC), a civilian agency sustained by his emergency funds, to mediate between the scientific community and military leaders. The research priorities of the NDRC were determined almost entirely by Bush and his colleagues, most notably chemist James B. Conant, the president of Harvard; physicist Karl T. Compton, the president of MIT; and Bell Laboratories head Frank B. Jewett.

Bush pushed for still more authority, including involvement in the military planning of weapons research and the ability to build prototypes of new devices. Roosevelt acceded on 28 June 1941, authorizing the OSRD. The NDRC became a subdivision of the OSRD, alongside a new Committee for Medical Research. As OSRD director, Bush quickly built a close relationship with Roosevelt, meeting with him regularly throughout the war as an informal science adviser. He also gained the confidence of military and congressional leaders, many of whom were more comfortable with his emphasis on private enterprise than with Roosevelt's New Deal liberalism.

Federal support for science increased dramatically under the OSRD, with tangible results. The entire federal budget for science had been around $69 million in 1940, but the OSRD alone spent almost $450 million during its five years of existence. In 1944 the government bankrolled three-fourths of the nation's scientific research. OSRD contractors developed a number of important new devices, including radar and the proximity fuse. The agency also facilitated the mass production of penicillin and oversaw the atomic bomb project before it was transferred to the Army Corps of Engineers' Manhattan District in late 1942.

Hoping to increase the perceived need for a peacetime federal science agency, Bush overrode internal opposition and shut down the OSRD in 1947. Responsibility for federal contracts was transferred to the Office of Naval Research, the National Institutes of Health, the Atomic Energy Commission, and eventually the National Science Foundation.

BIBLIOGRAPHY

Baxter, James Phinney. *Scientists Against Time.* Cambridge, Mass.: MIT Press, 1968 [1946].

Owens, Larry. "The Counterproductive Management of Science in the Second World War: Vannevar Bush and the Office of Scientific Research and Development." *Business History Review* 68 (Winter 1994): 515–576.

Stewart, Irvin. *Organizing Scientific Research for War: The Administrative History of the Office of Scientific Research and Development.* Boston: Little, Brown, 1948.

Zachary, G. Pascal. *Endless Frontier: Vannevar Bush, Engineer of the American Century.* New York: Free Press, 1997.

Andrew Jewett

See also **Manhattan Project; National Science Foundation.**

OFFICE OF STRATEGIC SERVICES. On 13 June 1942, President Franklin D. Roosevelt created the Office of Strategic Services (OSS) to centralize the nation's fragmented and uncoordinated intelligence activities during World War II. An earlier attempt to do so, through the Office of the Coordinator of Information (COI), formed 11 July 1941, had failed to achieve any real success because of unclear lines of authority and bureaucratic jealousies among the various government agencies concerned. As a part of the plan for establishing the OSS, some of the COI functions, such as domestic information activities, became the responsibility of the newly formed Office of War Information. The OSS took on others: the collection and analysis of strategic information and the planning and performance of special operations, particularly in the realms of espionage and sabotage. The Joint Chiefs of Staff were to supervise and direct OSS activities. Col. William J. Donovan became director.

Throughout its existence, the organization of the OSS constantly changed as it grew to an eventual strength of 12,000 personnel. Basically, the OSS consisted of a headquarters and various subordinate offices in and near Washington, D.C., and a series of field units, both in the United States and overseas. Two exceptions were Latin America, where the Federal Bureau of Investigation handled intelligence activities, and the South West Pacific theater, where Gen. Douglas MacArthur refused to accept the OSS.

Three branches of the OSS exemplified the breadth and scope of its operations. The secret intelligence branch dealt with sabotage, spying, demolitions, secret radio communications, and paramilitary functions. The morale operations branch handled the propaganda functions vested in the OSS. The research and analysis office gathered extensive information on all aspects of the areas in which U.S. forces operated. The OSS collected even the most trivial data and used it to further the war effort. All three branches had agents in both enemy and neutral areas.

It is the secret intelligence area from which the OSS gained much of its glamour. Many of its operations were in fact *more* dramatic than the fictionalized accounts found in books and films. In Burma, for example, a small OSS unit of twenty men operated behind Japanese lines with such success that it likely killed or wounded more than 15,000 of the enemy. Beginning in 1943, OSS personnel, along with British and other Allied teams, took part in the Jedburgh operation, which sent hundreds of three-man teams into France and the Low Countries to organize and aid underground forces in advance of the invasion of Europe. In 1944, another group smuggled an Italian inventor out of his German-occupied homeland to the United States, where he was able to produce an effective countermeasure to the torpedo he had designed for the Germans.

The end of World War II brought the demise of the OSS, by an executive order effective 1 October 1945. The departments of state and war split the functions, personnel, and records of the office. It was the experience gained by the OSS that laid the foundation for the Central Intelligence Agency, established in 1947.

BIBLIOGRAPHY

Katz, Barry M. *Foreign Intelligence: Research and Analysis in the Office of Strategic Services, 1942–1945.* Cambridge, Mass.: Harvard University Press, 1989.

Kimball, Warren F., ed. *America Unbound: World War II and the Making of a Superpower.* New York: St. Martin's Press, 1992.

McIntosh, Elizabeth P. *Sisterhood of Spies: The Women of the OSS.* Annapolis, Md.: Naval Institute Press, 1998.

Yu, Maochun. *OSS in China: Prelude to Cold War.* New Haven, Conn.: Yale University Press, 1996.

John E. Jessup Jr. / A. E.

See also **Guerilla Warfare; Intelligence, Military and Strategic; Psychological Warfare; Spies.**

OFFICE TECHNOLOGY consisted mainly of writing implements, paper, and basic furniture in colonial America, and remained so through the first half of the nineteenth century. But as the American industrial revolution accelerated after the Civil War, and as the size of businesses grew, a wave of "efficiency" improvements began to transform office technology.

Mechanizing Correspondence

The typewriter was the best-known icon of office mechanization through much of the twentieth century. It appeared in rudimentary form in 1714 in England, and many variations were produced over the years. However, it began to catch on only after the Civil War, as certain enterprises such as railroads and mail-order catalog businesses began to consolidate. These businesses soon began to try to standardize their office practices, and they sought ways to speed up the production of letters, particularly semistandardized or "form" letters. The Remington typewriter of the early 1870s, produced by the firearm manufacturer of the ame name, was perhaps the earliest commercially successful form of the typewriter.

Typewriting replaced most handwriting for business correspondence between 1875 and the early 1900s. In addition to mechanizing letter writing, the typewriter was at the center of an effort to replace relatively well paid male clerical workers with low-wage women during the same period. Nonetheless, within the limits of women's office work, typists were among the most skilled female workers. As the twentieth century progressed, the desire among women to master typing generated students to fill numerous typing courses, promoted mainly to women, in private business colleges and public schools.

Completing the mechanization of letter writing was the subject of intense interest following the diffusion of the typewriter. By the early 1900s, the phonograph (invented in 1877) was marketed as an adjunct to the typewriter. The Dictaphone Corporation's office phonograph became virtually synonymous with this class of instrument, intended for use by men to record their letters. The company promoted a system whereby Dictaphone records were collected (typically by office boys) and taken to central typing pools, where large numbers of closely supervised women spent their days converting the recordings into typed correspondence. However, the office recorder proved much less successful than the typewriter, and until the latter succumbed to the personal computer it was more common for letters to be dictated to secretaries, who wrote them down on paper in shorthand.

Somewhat more successful, though now made obsolete by the computer, were a wide range of machines which like the phonograph were intended to mechanize further the correspondence process. Where certain businesses used form letters or produced large numbers of slightly customized letters or bills, inventors looked for ways to eliminate as much manual typing as possible. There were numerous attempts to produce automatic typing machines, which could be set up to produce one or a range of semistandardized letters. Some of them relied on a master record resembling a player piano roll. A machine operator then had merely to select phrases from a predetermined list of possibilities, and manually type the addresses and other brief items to complete the job. The most famous of these machines was the Autotypist, introduced in the early 1930s by the American Automatic Typewriter Company. Both the typewriter and these more elaborate letter writing machines were replaced by the word processing machine, discussed below.

Duplicating

A different class of office technology is related to the duplication of documents. Letters written by hand in ink could be duplicated once or twice at the time of their creation simply by pressing them into the pages of a paper copy book, transferring some of the ink to a new sheet. The ink used in the typewriter did not easily allow such methods, but did allow the creation of a few copies using a transfer paper, coated with an ink and wax mixture. Usually called "carbon paper," this transfer paper was invented much earlier but only widely adopted after the diffusion of the typewriter.

For somewhat larger runs of documents, virtually the only viable option until the late nineteenth century was printing. Very small, simplified printing presses were once widely available, even including children's models. While limited, they could be used to print documents. Large businesses often ran their own printing departments in the nineteenth century to handle internal publications and advertisements. The increase in the size of businesses and the pace of transactions stimulated the desire to copy documents more quickly and easily. Among his other accomplishments, Thomas Edison invented one of the technologies that bridged the gap between typewriting and printing in the form of the Mimeograph. Originally, Edison utilized a battery operated "electric pen," which consisted of a tube holding a rapidly oscillating stylus. The pen did not use ink, but "wrote" a series of perforations. The perforated master document was then put in a special press and ink applied to one side. The ink flowing through the tiny holes printed a copy of the original on a clean sheet placed under the stencil. Others found that typewriter keys could also perforate the stencil, and the electric pen faded by 1900. Edison sold his interest in the

Mimeograph, but it remained a successful office technology through the late twentieth century.

Other inventors developed duplicating technologies to fit into even narrower niches. The Mimeograph, it was argued, was not economical for print runs of a few hundred copies or less, so other methods were offered for this purpose. A familiar sight in offices until about the 1980s was the "spirit duplicator" (often confused with the Mimeograph), which used a volatile liquid that produced a distinctive smell. A spirit duplicator master looked much like a sheet of carbon paper. Used with a typewriter or pen, a stencil sheet coated with a waxy ink transferred a reversed facsimile to the master sheet. This master was then inserted in a special rotary press, which coated the master with a duplicating fluid. The fluid partially dissolved the ink, allowing some of it to be transferred to a clean sheet. The process continued until the print was too light to be readable. A number of companies manufactured spirit duplicators, including the "Ditto" machine marketed by the Bell and Howell Corporation.

The last half of the twentieth century saw considerable innovation in office duplication technology. During World War II, there was a surge in governmental document production, resulting in growing sales for an inexpensive form of photographic duplicator called the "Photostat." Ultimately it was a different form of photoduplication that became dominant. An American, Chester Carlson, invented "electro-photography" in 1937, but the process was not commonly used until the 1960s. His process, later called "xerography," exploited the tendency of a sheet of paper to hold a greater static charge in places where it is printed than in places where it is blank. By electrically charging the original, transferring the charge by contact to a metal plate, allowing a powdered ink to adhere to the charged areas of the plate, then transferring the ink to a clean sheet, a reasonable facsimile of the original was produced. The use of the Xerox copier (or similar photocopiers offered by the 1970s) vastly increased the demand for paper in the office.

Telephony, Telegraphy, Fax, and Intercoms

Businesses have long held dear the notion of instantaneous communication. Almost from the inception of practical telegraphy with the opening of Samuel Morse's line from Washington, D.C., to Baltimore in 1843, its primary uses, in addition to government communication, were commercial. The use of the telegraph greatly accelerated the expansion and interconnection of the railroads and became a nearly universal fixture in large businesses after the end of the Civil War. A few of the pioneering telegraph operating companies, such as Western Union, were still in business at the beginning of the twenty-first century, albeit in greatly attenuated form, though telegraph message services have been effectively dead for some years.

The power of the telegraph to overcome geographic separation was so appealing to businesses that many of them took up the use of the telephone immediately after its introduction by Alexander Graham Bell in 1876. For much of the period from the 1870s to the 1920s, the telephone was almost exclusively a business machine, and although the U.S. eventually attained "universal service" to residences as well, the telephone's importance in business operations steadily increased.

The establishment of a nearly complete monopoly on telephone service under the American Telephone and Telegraph Company (AT&T) helped create a seamless national network but also tended to fossilize the telephone technology used in the office. While AT&T was marvelously innovative, little of its effort went into improving the "desk set" telephone, which it preferred to standardize. For this reason, the company successfully resisted innovations such as telephone-based facsimile, answering machines, and other inventions, all of which appeared before 1900. Not until the 1950s did this begin to change, and not until the 1984 breakup of the Bell System were consumers completely free to purchase and install their own equipment. Once this floodgate was open, Americans were presented with a torrent of innovations, the most successful of which are still in use. Facsimile machines were widely adopted in business once their technology was standardized in the early 1980s. Businesses also drove the market in cellular telephones in the 1980s, until their price dropped to the point at which residential customers also began to buy them.

Accounting Machines, Adding Machines, and Computers

A final major category of office technology is the computer. Although today its name hardly describes its usual functions, the computer is derived from machines intended to calculate numbers. Simple mechanical aids to accounting developed in the middle ages gave way to more complex adding machines and calculators in the early nineteenth century. Few of these sold in large numbers in the United States until the introduction of the Felt Company's "Comptometer" in 1885, the Burroughs calculator of 1892, and the Monroe adding machine of 1911. These small calculators were at first unrelated to another class of invention, the statistical tabulating machinery introduced by Herman Hollerith of Washington, D.C., in the 1880s. Used famously to compile the information from the 1890 census, the Hollerith machines retained records in the form of holes in punched paper cards. Hollerith's company eventually grew into the International Business Machines Corporation (IBM), which by the time of World War II was a major manufacturer of office equipment.

World War II would see the transformation of calculating devices and their convergence with punched card tabulating equipment. Prompted mainly by the U.S. government during World War II, engineers and mathematicians built upon the basic mechanical operations of these machines to create the first programmable computers. These machines could be modified relatively easily to perform different series of operations or "programs" and worked with great speed and accuracy. The mechanical elements of computers were soon abandoned in favor of electronic circuits, leading the first electronic computers in the 1940s.

By the early 1950s, when standardized electronic computers were available, large businesses were among the first customers for them. Typically they were used in accounting and billing departments to streamline operations. IBM became the dominant firm in this field and remained so for the next three decades. This company was a leader in the movement to expand the uses of the computer in the office, especially its use in the handling of correspondence. IBM introduced the first "word processing typewriter" around 1964. This consisted of a computer-like device used to control the operation of a modified version of one of the company's Selectric typewriters. Data to be printed was stored on special cards. While not linked to the mainframes, word processing devices and computers ultimately merged with the introduction of the personal computer in the late 1970s. Personal computers became useful to businesses with the introduction of business software programs such as Visicalc accounting software introduced in 1979. Computers today are used not only in dealing with the financial records of companies, but as communication devices, incorporating typing, mail, and increasingly voice and video communication.

BIBLIOGRAPHY

Adler, Michael H. *The Writing Machine: A History of the Typewriter.* London: George Allen and Unwin, Ltd., 1973.

Bruce, Robert V. *Bell.* Ithaca, N.Y.: Cornell University Press, 1973.

Cortada, James W. *Historical Dictionary of Data Processing.* New York: Greenwood Press, 1987.

Millard, Andre. *Edison and the Business of Innovation.* Baltimore: Johns Hopkins, 1990.

Proudfoot, W. B. *The Origins of Stencil Duplicating.* London: Hutchinson, 1972.

Williams, Michael R. *A History of Computing Technology.* Los Alamitos, Calif.: IEEE Computer Society Press, 1997.

Yates, JoAnn. *Control Through Communication.* Baltimore: Johns Hopkins, 1989.

David Morton

See also **Business Machines; Computers and Computer Technology; Fax Machine; Telephone; Typewriter.**

OFFICERS' RESERVE CORPS. Formed in June 1916 by the National Defense Act, the Officers' Reserve Corps (ORC) was originally intended to supply the U.S. armed forces with civilian volunteers who were educated in military leadership and tactics. In 1920, a second National Defense Act created the Organized Reserves, which consisted of both the ORC and an Enlisted Reserve Corps. Early in 1948, the Organized Reserves became the Organized Reserve Corps, which in 1952 became the Army Reserve. Originally, members of the Officers' Reserve Corps served on virtually a voluntary basis, being paid only for the time they served in active duty—two weeks every two to three years. This ended in 1948, when Congress voted to provide ORC members with training pay and retirement benefits with the passage of Public Laws 460 and 810. That same year, women by law were allowed to make up no more than 2 percent of the officer corps.

During the interwar period, the corps saw its membership grow rapidly, reaching 66,000 members in 1921, and 110,000 in 1929. Membership peaked at 191,698 during World War II. Of this number, some 95,000 had graduated from Reserve Officers' Training Corps (ROTC) programs at several hundred colleges and universities. In the 1960s, increased opposition to the Vietnam War in particular and the American military establishment in general led to a decline in both ROTC enrollment and ORC trainees. As membership declined in the 1960s, the ceiling on women officers was removed by acts of Congress in 1967, and higher numbers of African Americans began to enroll in ROTC programs as well. Consequently, both the ROTC and ORC enrollment stabilized beginning in the 1970s.

BIBLIOGRAPHY

Neiberg, Michael S. *Making Citizen-Soldiers: ROTC and the Ideology of American Military Service.* Cambridge, Mass.: Harvard University Press, 2000.

Weigley, Russell Frank. *History of the United States Army.* Bloomington: Indiana University Press, 1984.

John McCarthy

See also **National Guard; Reserve Officers' Training Corps; Women in Military Service.**

OFFSHORE OIL and gas development in the United States since the mid-1970s has responded largely to pressures from two sources: the efforts of the federal government to reduce dependence on foreign oil and efforts by environmentalists and conservationists to reduce energy consumption, especially of fossil fuels.

Aside from the Arab oil embargo of 1973–1974 and the U.S. embargo on Iranian oil, in effect from 1979 to 1981, the trend in the industry has been toward low prices and oversupply of foreign crude oil. It was not until the oil shocks of the 1970s that there was an incentive to expand offshore exploration and production. With the low prices that have prevailed since 1986, expensive and labor-intensive recovery techniques have lost their economic feasibility. Since the 1970s U.S. energy policy has emphasized environmental protection and the conservation of U.S. reserves. The federal government has developed stringent environmental regulations governing the exploration and development of offshore crude-oil fields.

Opposition to offshore drilling is strong, especially in California. As early as 1975, California's State Lands Commission halted drilling in the Santa Barbara Channel, and the National Energy Policy Act of 1992 came close to banning offshore drilling. Federal regulations imposed a leasing moratorium on sections of the Outer Continental Shelf and in the Arctic National Wildlife Refuge. Placing limitations on offshore oil drilling remained a popular political move into the next decade. For instance, in 2000 President Bill Clinton issued an executive order creating New Ocean Conservation Zones and forbidding drilling in such designated areas. In 2002 the federal government under President George W. Bush bought back from various petroleum companies the right to drill for oil in the Gulf of Mexico near Pensacola, Florida. The Bush administration also urged Congress to reopen the Arctic National Wildlife Refuge to oil exploration, but the proposal was stalled by stiff opposition in both houses of Congress and among outraged environmental activists.

BIBLIOGRAPHY

Freudenburg, William R., and Robert Gramling. *Oil in Troubled Waters: Perception, Politics, and the Battle over Offshore Drilling.* Albany: State University of New York Press, 1994.

Gramling, Robert. *Oil on the Edge: Offshore Development, Conflict, Gridlock.* Albany: State University of New York Press, 1996.

Stephen J. Randall/A. E.

See also **Energy Industry; Government Regulation of Business; Louisiana; Petroleum Industry; Petroleum Prospecting and Technology; Tidelands.**

OGDEN V. SAUNDERS, 12 Wheaton 213 (1827), a suit involving the constitutionality of many state bankruptcy laws, was brought before the U.S. Supreme Court by David Bayard Ogden, who sought a discharge in bankruptcy under New York legislation enacted in 1801. In March 1827 the Court by a close division (4 to 3) upheld the validity of the legislation in dispute but restricted its application to the state in which it was enacted. Chief Justice John Marshall gave his only dissenting opinion upon a constitutional question in this important, although not altogether popular, decision.

BIBLIOGRAPHY

Warren, Charles. *Bankruptcy in United States History.* Cambridge, Mass.: Harvard University Press, 1935.

Ray W. Irwin/A. R.

See also **Bankruptcy Laws; Contract Clause; Debt, Imprisonment for; *Fletcher v. Peck*; *Sturges v. Crowninshield*; Supreme Court.**

OHIO. Some 15,000 years ago nomadic hunters known as Paleo-Indians occupied caves and rock cliffs in the Ohio River valley. They gradually disappeared as the mammoths and mastodons they hunted migrated northward with the retreating glacial ice sheets. After 10,000 B.C., archaic Indian peoples lived in Ohio, leaving evidence of their hunting, fishing, and gathering activities. Between 1000 B.C. and 600 A.D. two groups of Mound Builders, the Adena and the Hopewell, both centered in present-day southern Ohio, flourished and left impressive remains in the form of mounds, geometric earthworks, and artifacts (see INDIAN MOUNDS). The Adena, first of the two, built thousands of conical burial mounds and effigy mounds, such as the Great Serpent Mound in Adams County. The Hopewell, appearing after 200 B.C., built geometric earthworks and large hilltop enclosures. The decline of these cultures hundreds of years before the Ohio country was reoccupied by historic Indian tribes in the eighteenth century led to nineteenth-century speculation that the Mound Builders constituted a "lost race." Modern archaeology has dispelled that notion and established a firm, if not yet fully understood, connection between the prehistoric and historic native peoples of the Eastern Woodlands, including Ohio.

Iroquois wars against the Huron and Erie Indians in the seventeenth century caused all tribes largely to abandon the Ohio country for about fifty years, while French explorers, including Robert Cavelier, Sieur de La Salle, explored the region and claimed it for New France. Thought to be the first white man to see the Ohio River, in 1669, La Salle's exploration brought French traders into the area in the early eighteenth century but no permanent French settlements. Various Indian tribes, especially the Shawnee, Miami, Delaware, Ottawa, and Wyandot, as well as British traders, also entered Ohio in the early eighteenth century. British colonial interests and claims in the Ohio Valley, especially those of Virginia, grew stronger by the 1740s and led to the outbreak of war between Britain and France in 1754. Known in North America as the FRENCH AND INDIAN WAR, it found most of the Indians fighting with the French, who enjoyed the initial advantage in the Ohio country. Gradually the British turned the tide in their favor, and the Treaty of Paris in 1763 that ended the war gave them almost total possession of all of mainland North America east of the Mississippi River, including Ohio.

British attempts to limit the westward expansion of settlement across the Appalachian Mountains were mostly unsuccessful, and violence between Indians and white frontier settlers finally led to full-scale war by 1774, when Virginia royal governor Lord Dunmore led an expedition against the Indians along the Ohio River. The American Revolution soon overtook and subsumed these frontier conflicts in the larger struggle between Britain and its American colonies. During the war for American independence the Ohio Indians were allied with the British and fought against American forces entering the region from Pennsylvania, Virginia, and Kentucky. One tragic episode was the massacre at Gnadenhutten in 1782 of ninety-six peaceful Indian men, women, and children, Delawares who had been converted to Christianity by Moravian missionaries.

From Territory to State

In the early 1780s, Virginia, Massachusetts, and Connecticut ceded most of their western land claims to the new national government, and Ohio became part of the Northwest Territory, which also included the later states of Indiana, Illinois, Michigan, and Wisconsin. The Northwest Ordinance of 1787 established a government for the territory with three stages of development leading to eventual statehood. First, a territorial governor and other officials appointed by Congress proclaimed laws and exercised executive authority. General Arthur St. Clair held the office of governor throughout Ohio's territorial period. In 1798 the second stage began when the "free male inhabitants" elected the first territorial legislature, which subsequently wrote the state's first constitution, paving the way for Ohio's admission as the seventeenth state on 1 March 1803. The first permanent white settlement, Marietta, appeared in 1788, and Cincinnati (originally Losantiville) followed later in the same year. Various land companies and speculators, most importantly the Ohio Company of Associates, the Connecticut Land Company, and John Cleves Symmes, began the process of buying and selling Ohio lands, but extensive settlement could not proceed until the threat of Indian attacks was ended.

In the early 1790s, several U.S. military campaigns against the Ohio Indians took place. At first they suffered major defeats, including the loss of more than 600 under the command of St. Clair in November 1791. A new expedition led by General Anthony Wayne, culminating in his victory at the Battle of Fallen Timbers in August 1794, vanquished Indian resistance and led to the GREENVILLE TREATY in 1795. The Indian tribes ceded all of Ohio for white settlement except for the northwest corner; these remaining Indian lands were gradually yielded in subsequent treaties and the last group of Indians left Ohio in 1843.

Territorial governor St. Clair, a Federalist, clashed repeatedly with the emerging Republican party led by Thomas Worthington and Edward Tiffin of Chillicothe over issues of local versus federal control and executive versus legislative authority. With the election of Thomas Jefferson as president in 1800 the national political trend began to favor the interests of Ohio's Jeffersonian Republicans. The new state's boundaries gave political advantage to the mostly Republican Scioto Valley and Chillicothe, the first state capital. Tiffin was elected the first governor and Worthington one of the first pair of U.S. senators. The first state constitution gave the right to vote to all white males regardless of wealth and sharply limited the power of the governor over the legislature. The 1804 "Black Code" denied free blacks in the state the right to vote as well as many other political and civil rights, and although it was partially repealed in 1849, it remained in some form until the close of the Civil War.

Nineteenth-Century Ohio

The peace following the War of 1812 finally ended all threats of Indian or British resistance to American expansion in the lands north and west of the Ohio River, and Ohio's population began to grow rapidly. Cincinnati became the largest city on the Ohio frontier, drawing immigrants from all over the United States as well as from Europe.

Despite the overwhelming predominance of the Republican Party until the late 1820s, Ohio's political leaders divided constantly over regional, economic, and legal issues. The state's economy boomed after the War of 1812. However, the panic of 1819, brought on in part by actions of the Second Bank of the United States in attempting to end excessive local speculative banking practices, caused widespread economic hardship. Some state leaders favored an aggressive program of state aid for internal improvements, especially canals, to boost the economy. Two major canals were completed across the state from Lake Erie to the Ohio River, the Ohio and Erie Canal from Cleveland to Portsmouth in 1832 and the Miami and Erie Canal from Cincinnati to Toledo in 1843. Various branches and feeders connected to the main canal lines at different points in the state. During this same period the National Road was constructed from east to west across the central part of Ohio, stimulating the growth of Columbus, chosen in 1816 to be the permanent site of the state capital because of its central location and the financial support it offered for erecting public buildings. Before the Civil War, Ohio for a time led the nation in the production of corn, wheat, beef, pork, and wool.

By the late 1820s, Ohio's dominant Jeffersonian Republican Party divided and gave way to the spirited competition between Whigs and Democrats that lasted into the 1850s. The Whigs favored government aid for internal improvements, a more highly regulated banking system, and greater development of a public school system. The Democrats emphasized limits on the size and power of government and protection of personal liberty rather than vigorous social reform. They had the greatest appeal to small farmers and artisans and Catholics wary of evangelical Protestant activism in matters such as temperance, Sabbath observance, and public education. The rudiments of a system of public schools began to take shape by the mid-1840s. Denominational competition and town boosterism led to the building of dozens of small private colleges.

The slavery controversy entered Ohio politics in the 1830s as abolitionists did battle with pro-Southern conservatives for the allegiance of the state's citizens. The state became a major center of the UNDERGROUND RAILROAD because of its key location between the South and Canada. Anti-abolitionist mobs in Cincinnati and elsewhere indicated powerful opposition in some quarters, but fear of the political power of Southern slaveowners helped to turn many Ohioans against slavery, or at least its further expansion. This led to third-party activity in the 1840s and early 1850s by the Liberty and then Free Soil parties, which helped to bring about the downfall of the Whigs. This realignment led to the formation of the Republican Party in Ohio in 1854 to oppose the KANSAS-NEBRASKA ACT and repeal of the MISSOURI COMPROMISE. Republicans immediately became the dominant political force in Ohio and largely remained so for the rest of the nineteenth century.

By 1840, Ohio's population had swelled to over 1.5 million, making it the third most populous state in the union, and thousands of Irish and German immigrants in the ensuing decades kept the state's growth at a high level. Industries such as coal, iron, textiles, meatpacking, and agricultural machinery appeared even before the Civil War.

Ohio became one of the main sources of economic strength and manpower for the North during the Civil War. Ohioans who served in the Union Army numbered 350,000, and close to 35,000 died as a result of the conflict. An impressive number of Union military and civilian leaders came from the Buckeye state, including Ulysses S. Grant, William Tecumseh Sherman, Philip Sheridan, James McPherson, William S. Rosecrans, and Rutherford B. Hayes among the generals and Salmon P. Chase and Edwin M. Stanton in Lincoln's cabinet. The only military action that took place in the state was Confederate cavalry leader John Hunt Morgan's daring raid across southern Ohio in the summer of 1863.

As the Ohio economy was transformed during the nineteenth century, state government and politics evolved at a slower pace. A new state constitution in 1851 increased the number of elected offices, but a proposed constitution in 1873 that would have made more significant reforms was rejected. In 1867, Ohio voters rejected black male suffrage, but this became law anyway through the Fifteenth Amendment to the U.S. Constitution ratified in 1870. Large cities such as Cincinnati and Cleveland experienced rule by corrupt local bosses in the late nineteenth century, and the state legislature was increasingly influenced by corporate business interests. However, Ohio contributed seven U.S. presidents in this era, all Republicans, including Grant, Hayes, James A. Garfield, Benjamin Harrison, William McKinley, William Howard Taft, and Warren G. Harding.

The growth of big business in late-nineteenth- and early-twentieth-century Ohio centered on the development of energy resources (coal, natural gas, and oil refining) and industrial manufacturing (steel, rubber, glass, auto parts, and machinery.) The spectacular rise of John D. Rockefeller's STANDARD OIL COMPANY, founded in Cleveland in 1870, characterized the new economic era. Northern Ohio became the most heavily industrialized part of the state, with Cleveland (iron, steel, heavy machinery), Akron (tire and rubber), Toledo (glass, auto parts), and Youngstown (steel) leading the way. But other cities and regions in the state also developed industrially in this period. Cincinnati remained a diversified manufacturing center, and Dayton was home to National Cash Register (NCR) and Delco (part of General Motors). Northwest Ohio experienced a boom in oil and gas production and new railroad lines were built through southeastern Ohio coal fields and throughout the rest of the state. At the beginning of the twentieth century Ohio led the nation in the number of miles of interurban rail track—electric trains that carried both rural and urban passengers between small towns and large cities. By 1900, Cleveland had surpassed Cincinnati to become Ohio's largest and most ethnically diverse city. Seventy-five percent of its residents were first- or second-generation immigrants, many from southern and eastern Europe, and forty different languages were spoken in the city.

Workers' wages and labor conditions varied considerably across Ohio industry, but the size and impersonal conditions of factories bred increasing worker discontent. Some companies tried to counter this with improved employee benefits, but still Ohio workers began to turn toward unions to protect their interests. The Knights of Labor's efforts at mass unionization in the 1870s and 1880s had some success in Ohio, but this approach could not survive the depression of 1893. The American Federation of Labor was founded in Columbus in 1886 but limited its membership to the skilled trades. Hocking Valley coal miners went on strike in 1884, leading to violence, but ultimately the coal operators prevailed. The miners regrouped and in 1890 helped to form the United Mine Workers of America. The radical Industrial Workers of the World (IWW) supported a strike by Akron rubber workers in 1913. That strike also proved unsuccessful due to strong employer opposition, as did a major steel strike in 1919. Ohio industrial workers did not make major gains in union representation and bargaining until the great labor upheavals of the 1930s.

Twentieth-Century Ohio

The beginning of the twentieth century brought continued economic growth and innovation. Orville and Wilbur Wright of Dayton made the first successful flight at Kitty Hawk, North Carolina, on 17 December 1903. Another Daytonian, Charles F. Kettering, developed the self-starting engine for automobiles. Politically the new century found Ohio's large cities in the midst of struggles for progressive reform. Two outstanding mayors, Samuel M. ("Golden Rule") Jones in Toledo, and Tom Johnson in Cleveland, attacked corruption, instituted civil service reform, and generally made their cities healthier, safer, and more efficient for residents. In Columbus the Congregational minister and Social Gospel pioneer Washington Gladden led similar efforts. The progressive impulse spread throughout the state and led to significant actions at the 1912 state constitutional convention. Forty-one constitutional amendments were submitted to the voters, and thirty-three of them were approved on 3 September 1912. They included the power of citizen initiative and referendum in making state laws, home rule charters for cities, the direct primary, a workers compensation system, and greater regulation of natural resources.

Progressive reform continued at the state level under Democratic governor James M. Cox, who served from 1913 to 1915 and 1917 to 1921. He worked to implement the new constitutional provisions against corporate opposition and led the effort to consolidate and modernize rural school districts. However, in the stirred patriotic atmosphere of World War I, Cox advocated a state law, later held unconstitutional, banning the teaching of German in any school below the eighth grade. The Democrats selected Cox to run for president in 1920, with Franklin D. Roosevelt as his running mate, but another Ohioan, Senator Warren G. Harding, swept to victory in a landslide.

After some difficult postwar adjustments, Ohio experienced economic prosperity in the 1920s, especially in industries associated with automobile production or electrical equipment. Large numbers of African Americans from the Deep South and whites from Appalachia migrated north to Ohio cities seeking industrial employment. Blacks in particular were restricted by segregation customs in obtaining housing and the use of public accommodations. Racial and ethnic tensions surfaced in some locations, as did questions relating to the legal enforcement of prohibition. The revived KU KLUX KLAN of the 1920s was very active in several Ohio cities, using its power to elect some public officials. However, by the latter part of the decade it was in decline, weakened by internal scandals and the firm opposition of many religious, racial, and ethnic leaders.

Highly industrialized Ohio was hit hard by the Great Depression of the 1930s. In 1932 an estimated 37 percent of all Ohio workers were unemployed. Industrial unemployment in northern Ohio cities ranged from fifty to eighty percent at its peak. Democrats returned to power in state government and looked to Franklin D. Roosevelt's administration for solutions. Most of the New Deal programs had a significant impact on Ohio, including the largest number of recipients of any state of relief from the WORKS PROGRESS ADMINISTRATION (WPA). Organized labor stirred with the formation of the Congress of Industrial Organizations (CIO) to recruit among industrial workers. Its first major success was the 1936 sit-down strike by Akron's rubber workers. Strikes by steelworkers against Republic, Youngstown Sheet and Tube, and others in 1937 led to more violence and a temporary labor setback. World War II, however, brought union recognition and collective bargaining to the "Little Steel" companies.

Ohio played a key role in America's "arsenal of democracy" during World War II. About one million workers produced goods for the war effort, especially in aircraft, ordnance, and shipbuilding. Some 839,000 Ohioans served in the U.S. military and 23,000 were killed or missing in action. After the war, Ohio's industries worked at full capacity to meet pent-up consumer demand. The Saint Lawrence Seaway, completed in 1959, expanded Great Lakes shipping, and lock and dam improvements on the Ohio River maintained that historic waterway's commercial importance.

Between 1940 and 1960 Ohio's population grew by 40 percent, faster than the national average. However, in the 1970s and 1980s aging plants, high labor and energy costs, and increased foreign competition converged to deal Ohio's industrial economy a severe blow. Most of the large cities lost population and jobs to newer suburbs. The 1990s brought a return to growth, but Ohio's 2000 population of 11,353,000 was only six percent higher than its 1970 level, while the United States overall had grown by thirty-eight percent in that same period. Columbus had replaced Cleveland as the state's largest city.

After 1960, Ohio greatly expanded its system of public higher education, one of the achievements of the long-serving Republican governor James A. Rhodes (1963–1971, 1975–1983). However, he is also remembered for his controversial decision to send National Guard troops to quell student protests at Kent State University in 1970, which led to the death of four students. By the 1960s environmental protection had become a serious issue, as Ohio struggled to undo decades of neglect in this area. In 1997 the state supreme court declared the state's method of funding public schools inequitable and forced the General Assembly to begin to allocate increased funds to poorer districts. Ohio faced its approaching bicentennial in 2003 with both serious needs to be met and a renewed sense of optimism in doing so.

BIBLIOGRAPHY

Bills, Scott L., ed. *Kent State/May 4: Echoes Through a Decade.* Kent, Ohio: Kent State University Press, 1982.

Booth, Stephane E. *Buckeye Women: The History of Ohio's Daughters.* Athens: Ohio University Press, 2001.

Boryczka, Raymond, and Lorin Lee Cary. *No Strength Without Union: An Illustrated History of Ohio Workers, 1803–1980.* Columbus: Ohio Historical Society, 1982.

Brandt, Nat. *The Town That Started the Civil War.* Syracuse, N.Y.: Syracuse University Press, 1990. The antislavery movement in Oberlin, Ohio.

Gerber, David A. *Black Ohio and the Color Line: 1860–1915.* Urbana: University of Illinois Press, 1976.

Grant, H. Roger. *Ohio on the Move: Transportation in the Buckeye State.* Athens: Ohio University Press, 2000.

Havighurst, Walter. *Ohio: A Bicentennial History.* New York: Norton, 1976.

Hurt, R. Douglas. *The Ohio Frontier: Crucible of the Old Northwest, 1720–1830.* Bloomington: Indiana University Press, 1996.

Knepper, George W. *Ohio and Its People.* 2d ed. Kent, Ohio: Kent State University Press, 1997.

Lamis, Alexander P., ed. *Ohio Politics.* Kent, Ohio: Kent State University Press, 1994.

Murdock, Eugene C. *The Buckeye Empire: An Illustrated History of Ohio Enterprise.* Northridge, Calif.: Windsor, 1988.

Shriver, Phillip R., and Clarence E. Wunderlin, eds. *The Documentary Heritage of Ohio.* Athens: Ohio University Press, 2000. A comprehensive collection of primary sources.

John B. Weaver

See also **Cincinnati; Cleveland; Columbus, Ohio; Toledo.**

OHIO COMPANY OF VIRGINIA, a partnership of Virginia gentlemen, a Maryland frontiersman, and a London merchant organized in 1747 to engage in land speculation and trade with the Indians in the territory claimed by VIRGINIA west of the Appalachian Mountains. Early in 1749 the governor of Virginia granted the company's petition for a grant of 500,000 acres of land in the upper OHIO VALLEY. The company sent Christopher Gist on exploring expeditions in 1750 and 1751. After Indians were induced to permit settlement south of the OHIO RIVER at the Treaty of Logstown (1752), a road was opened across the mountains and in 1753, Gist and a number of others settled in what is now Fayette County, Pennsylvania. In the same year the company built a storehouse on the MONONGAHELA RIVER at the site of Brownsville, Pennsylvania. Early in 1754, it began building Fort Prince George at the Forks of the Ohio. The capture of this uncompleted fort by the French in 1754, and the war that ensued, forced the settlers to withdraw. The company's ambition to resume settlement after the fall of Fort Duquesne was frustrated by the prohibition of settlement west of the mountains. The company lost its grant in 1770, and exchanged its claims for two shares in the VANDALIA COLONY. The Ohio Company revealed the intention of England, and also of Virginia, to expand across the mountains into the Ohio Valley; and its activities played a part in bringing on the final contest between the French and the English for control of the interior.

BIBLIOGRAPHY

Bailey, Kenneth P. *The Ohio Company of Virginia.* Glendale, Calif.: Arthur H. Clark Company, 1939.

Hinderaker, Eric. *Elusive Empires: Constructing Colonialism in the Ohio Valley, 1673–1800.* New York: Cambridge University Press, 1997.

McConnell, Michael N. *A Country Between: The Upper Ohio Valley and Its Peoples, 1724–1774.* Lincoln: University of Nebraska Press, 1992.

Solon J. Buck/A. R.

See also **Colonial Charters; Colonial Settlements; Duquesne, Fort; French and Indian War; Land Companies; Land Grants; Land Speculation; Proclamation of 1763; Trading Companies; Trans-Appalachian West.**

OHIO IDEA, the proposal to redeem the Civil War's five-twenty bonds in greenbacks—legal tender that could not be exchanged for gold—rather than in coin (1867–1868). Put forth as an inflationary measure by the *Cincinnati Enquirer,* the proposal was so popular among farmers and manufacturers (groups that depended on easy credit) that both political parties in the Middle West were forced to endorse it, although neither committed itself outright to inflation. Opponents of the measure tended to be investors who wanted to reduce the Civil War's fiscal fluctuations by adopting a noninflationary "hard money" policy.

BIBLIOGRAPHY

Destler, Chester M. "Origin and Character of the Pendleton Plan." *Mississippi Valley Historical Review.* 24, no. 2 (1937): 171–184.

Myers, Margaret G. *A Financial History of the United States.* New York: Columbia University Press, 1970.

Chester M. Destler/C. W.

See also **Greenbacks; Hard Money; Legal Tender.**

OHIO RIVER, the major eastern tributary of the Mississippi River, is also a significant river artery in the north central United States, extending for 981 miles from Pittsburgh, Pennsylvania, to Cairo, Illinois. Formed by the confluence of the Allegheny and Monongahela rivers (325 and almost 130 miles in length, respectively), at the Forks of the Ohio, the river flows northwest from the Keystone State before turning southwest and joining the Mississippi River at Cairo. At Pittsburgh the Ohio is 1,021 feet above sea level, and 322 feet at Cairo. The Falls of the Ohio at Louisville, Kentucky, is a 2.2-mile-long limestone rapids where the river drops 23.9 feet. Canalization around the rapids was completed in 1830, ensuring navigability. Between Pittsburgh and Wheeling, West

Casino Riverboat. The *Argosy,* linked to land by two large ramps, is docked on the Ohio River at Lawrenceburg, Ind., in this 1996 photograph. AP/Wide World Photos

Virginia, the river averages 0.5 miles in width; between Cincinnati, Ohio, and Louisville, 1.1 miles; and from Louisville to Cairo, 1.3 miles.

The Ohio River and its valley have a complex geological history but are young, formed at the end of the Pleistocene epoch, about ten thousand years ago. The valley is narrow and characterized by steep bluffs, and the drainage basin includes about 203,900 square miles and has an annual average flow of 281,000 cubic feet per second. Six major tributaries join the Ohio from the north: the Wabash (Illinois-Indiana border); Muskingum, Miami, Hocking, and Scioto (Ohio); and Beaver (Pennsylvania). From the south the major tributaries are the Great Kanawha and Guyandotte (West Virginia); Big Sandy (West Virginia–Kentucky border); and Licking, Kentucky, Salt, Green, Cumberland, and Tennessee (Kentucky). About 80 percent of the state of Ohio and 85 percent of Kentucky drain into the Ohio-Mississippi system, and there are over 2,900 miles of navigable rivers in the ten-state area of the Ohio River system.

Politically the Ohio River marks the boundaries of five states: Ohio and West Virginia, Ohio and Kentucky, Indiana and Kentucky, and Illinois and Kentucky. In addition to Pittsburgh, the banks of the Ohio serve as the site of five major cities in Ohio (Cincinnati, Gallipolis, Marietta, Portsmouth, and Steubenville); four in Indiana (Madison, New Albany, Evansville, and Mount Vernon); three in West Virginia (Parkersburg, Huntington, and Wheeling); and five in Kentucky (Ashland, Covington, Louisville, Owensboro, and Paducah).

BIBLIOGRAPHY

Banta, Richard E. *The Ohio.* Rivers of America Series 39. New York: Rinehart, 1949; reprinted Lexington: University Press of Kentucky, 1998.

Klein, Benjamin F., and Eleanor Klein, eds. *The Ohio River Handbook and Picture Album.* Cincinnati: Young and Klein, 1969.

Charles C. Kolb

OHIO VALLEY. Since prehistoric times the Ohio River and its tributaries have served as a major conduit for human migration, linking the Atlantic seaboard and Appalachian Mountains and the Mississippi valley. Human occupation in the Ohio valley began over sixteen thousand years ago, and the region was home to a series of cultures: Paleo-Indian (before 9500 B.C.E.), Archaic (9500–3000 B.C.E.), late Archaic–early Woodland (3000–200 B.C.E.), middle Woodland (200 B.C.E.–500 C.E.), late Woodland (500–1600 C.E.), and late Prehistoric (c. 1400–1600). The middle Woodland Hopewell culture, centered in southern Ohio and characterized by earthworks, elaborate burial practices, and long-distance trade, is notable, as is the Fort Ancient culture (1400–1600), located in southern Ohio, northern Kentucky, and eastern Indiana. The valley was occupied by a number of protohistoric and historic Native American societies, some indigenous to the river drainage basin and others who migrated westward, displaced by European colonization in the east. The Native American societies included the Iroquois (especially Seneca, Erie [to 1656], and Mingo) in western Pennsylvania; the Delaware and Seneca in southern Pennsylvania and West Virginia; the Delaware, Miami, Ottawa, Shawnee, Seneca, and Wyandot in Ohio; the Miami in Indiana; and the Delaware and Shawnee in northern Kentucky. The Ohio takes it name from the Iroquois language and means "Great River."

Reputedly the first European to view the Allegheny and Ohio rivers was Robert Cavelier, Sieur de La Salle, in 1669–1670, but the evidence is questionable. Maps of the region frequently were created on the basis of secondhand data, notably Louis Jolliet's (Joliet's) rendition of 1674 and Jean-Baptiste Franquelin's map of 1682, which depicted the Ohio flowing into the Mississippi. The French called the Ohio "La Belle Rivière," and the explorer Pierre Joseph Céloron de Blainville made a historic trip down the Allegheny and Ohio to the Miami River in 1749, placing lead plates at the junctions of major tributaries that claimed the region for France. From 1744 to 1754 traders and land agents from Pennsylvania, such as Joseph Conrad Weiser and George Croghan, came into the Ohio valley, and Christopher Gist explored the region for the Virginia-based Ohio Company in 1750–1751. The strategic significance of the Ohio became evident during the contest between Britain and France for control of the interior of North America in the 1750s. The French built forts on the upper Ohio in Pennsylvania—Presque Isle (Erie), Le Boeuf (Waterford), Venango, and Duquesne at the Forks of the Ohio (Pittsburgh)—precipitating war in 1754. Fort Duquesne was taken by the British in 1758 and was renamed Fort Pitt. The French and Indian War (Seven Years' War) was ended by the Treaty of Paris in 1763, and the British gained control of the Ohio valley.

The American military leader George Rogers Clark led an expedition down the Ohio in 1778 and wrested control of British settlements in what are now Indiana and Illinois. The 1783 Treaty of Paris established the Ohio River as a major American Indian boundary, but Jay's Treaty of 1794 ceded the Ohio valley to the Americans. General Anthony Wayne's victory at Fallen Timbers in 1794 diminished Indian attacks. A majority of settlers entered the Ohio valley through the river's headwaters, and the river became the major transportation route to the west during the first half of the nineteenth century. During the War of 1812 (1812–1815) settlers from the Ohio valley and Atlantic colonies united against the British and Indians. Increased commercial traffic on the Ohio led to the dynamic growth of Pittsburgh, Cincinnati, and Louisville, but the completion of the Erie Canal in 1825 slightly diminished the river as a commercial artery. By the 1840s the Ohio had become a dividing line between free and slave states. Steamboat transportation diminished as railroads became the primary means of transporting raw materials, general cargo, and passengers. Because of shipping accidents a U.S. Coast Guard station was established in Louisville at the treacherous Falls of the Ohio in 1881. Major flood control projects were initiated because of serious floods in 1847, 1884, 1913, and 1937. The river remains a major transportation artery, a distinct sectional dividing line in the United States, and a source of recreation and tourism.

BIBLIOGRAPHY

Banta, Richard E. *The Ohio.* Rivers of America Series 39. New York: Rinehart, 1949; reprinted Lexington: University Press of Kentucky, 1998.

Jakle, John A. *Images of the Ohio Valley: A Historical Geography of Travel, 1740 to 1860.* New York: Oxford University Press, 1977.

Reid, Robert L. *Always a River: The Ohio River and the American Experience.* Bloomington: Indiana University Press, 1991.

Charles C. Kolb

OHIO WARS. Though the Paris Peace Treaty of 1783 officially ended the war between Great Britain and the United States, fighting continued in the Ohio country. Operating under the illusion of conquest, the United States conducted Indian treaties at Fort Stanwix with the Iroquois (1784), at Fort McIntosh with the Wyandots, Ottawas, Delawares, and Ojibwas (1785), and at Fort Finney with a faction of the Shawnees (1786), and through them claimed most of Ohio. Most Ohio Valley Indians rejected these coerced treaties, and with British encouragement continued to resist the Americans. Americans retaliated with raids on Indian towns.

In October 1786, an army of 1,200 Kentucky "volunteers" (many had been impressed) led by Revolutionary War hero George Rogers Clark marched into the Wabash country. Low on provisions, the ill-fated Clark could only garrison Vincennes while hundreds of his men deserted. Meanwhile, his second-in-command, Benjamin Logan, led 790 men on a more devastating raid into western Ohio. They destroyed the Shawnee town of Mackachack, home of chief Moluntha, the Shawnee who had worked hardest to maintain peace with the United States. Logan's men killed over ten Indians, including women, a visiting Ottawa chief, and some delegates from the Iroquois. Against orders, one of Logan's officers murdered Moluntha. Logan's men also destroyed 15,000 bushels of Indian corn, but the attack galvanized, rather than terrorized, Ohio Indians fighting the United States.

Raids and retaliation continued through the late 1780s as white settlers continued to pour into Ohio. In 1789, with the executive powers granted him under the new Constitution, President George Washington authorized a punitive expedition against the Ohio Indians. Led by General Josiah Harmar, a veteran of the Revolution, the army was 2,300 strong, but poorly disciplined. Harmar intended to attack the cluster of Miami towns at Kekionga (now Fort Wayne, Indiana). Harmar did destroy three Indian villages in October of 1790, but ambushes by the Miami war chief Little Turtle and Shawnee war chief Blue Jacket (assisted by British Indian Agent Simon Girty), resulted in 183 Americans killed or missing. Harmar's failure led to his resignation and another American expedition in 1791.

General Arthur St. Clair, also a veteran of the Revolution, took about 1,400 men, a third of them army regulars, to the upper Wabash (near modern Edgerton, Ohio) on 4 November 1791. An attack by some 1,200 Indians under Blue Jacket and Little Turtle routed them, inflicting roughly 900 casualties, including 630 killed. This was the worst defeat an American army ever suffered at the hands of Indians. President Washington and Secretary of War Henry Knox abandoned their conquering pretensions and now sought to negotiate a peace, but the Ohio Indians, flushed with success, refused to end the war until Americans abandoned all of Ohio. This demand was politically and socially unthinkable for the United States, and Washington appointed General "Mad" Anthony Wayne, yet another veteran of the Revolution, to suppress Indians in the Ohio Valley.

Wayne took his time, meticulously training his troops (called "Wayne's Legion") until they were supremely disciplined. With over 2,000 men, Wayne attacked only 500 to 800 Indians led by Blue Jacket and Little Turtle, and a few Canadian militia, at Fallen Timbers (near modern Toledo, Ohio) on 20 August 1794. Wayne suffered about 130 casualties, including forty-four killed, while the Indians lost less than forty men killed. Many of the Indian dead were prominent chiefs and the Indian forces retreated. Wayne's victory, and Great Britain's growing reluctance to support Indian war leaders, proved enough to bring the tribes to the Greenville Treaty council in August of 1795.

The Greenville Treaty gave the United States most of Ohio and ushered in a general peace in the region that lasted until the battle of Tippecanoe in 1811. After Greenville, most of the Indians who remained on reservations in northern Ohio declined to fight against the United States again, and some even served as scouts for America in the War of 1812. There were no large-scale Indian-white military conflicts in Ohio after 1815.

BIBLIOGRAPHY

Kappler, Charles J., ed. *Indian Treaties, 1778–1883.* New York: Interland Publishing, 1972.

Sugden, John. *Blue Jacket: Warrior of the Shawnees.* Lincoln: University of Nebraska Press, 2000.

Sword, Wiley. *President Washington's Indian War: The Struggle for the Old Northwest, 1790–1795.* Norman: University of Oklahoma Press, 1985.

Robert M. Owens

See also **Indian Land Cessions; Indian Policy, U.S., 1775–1830; Indian Treaties.**

OIL CRISES. In 1973–1974 and 1979, the United States experienced shortages of gasoline and other petroleum products because of reduced domestic oil production, greater dependence on imported oil, and political developments in the oil-rich Middle East. Historically, the United States had supplied most of its own oil, but in 1970 U.S. oil production reached full capacity. Imported oil, especially from the Middle East, rose from 19 percent of national consumption in 1967 to 36 percent in 1973. The Arab-Israeli War of 1973 contributed to the first oil crisis. After Egypt and Syria attacked Israel in October and the United States came to Israel's aid, oil ministers from the five Persian Gulf states and Iran banned oil exports to the United States. World oil prices jumped from $5.40 per barrel to more than $17. Retail gasoline prices in the United States increased 40 percent, and consumers often faced long lines at service stations. To conserve gasoline and oil, President Richard M. Nixon reduced the speed limit on national highways to fifty-five miles per hour and encouraged people to carpool and to lower their house thermostats. It was Israeli victories and U.S. arrangement of Arab-Israeli negotiations and not domestic programs, however, that helped end the embargo in March 1974.

The Organization of Petroleum Exporting Countries (OPEC) continued to keep world oil prices high, which slowed the world economy. In 1973–1975, the U.S. gross national product declined by 6 percent and unemployment doubled to 9 percent, but the developing countries that lacked money to pay for expensive oil suffered most. In 1975 Congress established fuel-efficiency standards for U.S. automobiles to reduce energy costs and dependency on foreign oil. President Jimmy Carter urged additional steps. By the late 1970s the United States was exploring both old sources of energy, such as coal, and new ones, including solar, thermal, and wind power, although the new alternatives commanded far fewer resources, public or private, than the former.

A second oil crisis followed the collapse of the government of the shah of Iran and suspension of Iran's oil exports in December 1978. If buyers, including oil companies, manufacturers, and national governments had not panicked, however, this second oil shortage would not have been so severe. Gasoline prices rose, and people again waited in lines at service stations. The worst of the second crisis was over by 1980. In late 1985, a substantial drop in world oil prices gave American consumers a sense that the crisis had ended, but concerns about the increasing U.S. dependence on foreign oil remained in the 1990s.

These worries only increased at the turn of the twenty-first century in response to heightened tensions between Israelis and Palestinians and the American invasion of Afghanistan in retaliation for the terrorist attacks on the United States on 11 September 2001. President George W. Bush pointed to the events of 11 September as evidence to support his claim that the United States needed to develop domestic sources of fossil fuels, especially by drilling for oil in Alaska's Arctic National Wildlife Refuge, in a time of political uncertainty in the Middle East. Although the plan was defeated in Congress the following year, it had revitalized the debate between the petroleum industry and environmentalists over how to reduce dependence on foreign oil: exploration for new deposits of fossil fuel or conservation vs. the increased development of alternative energy sources.

BIBLIOGRAPHY

Bruno, Michael, and Jeffrey D. Sachs. *Economics of Worldwide Stagflation.* Cambridge, Mass.: Harvard University Press, 1985.

Hemmer, Christopher M. *Which Lessons Matter? American Foreign Policy Decision Making in the Middle East, 1979–1987.* Albany: State University of New York Press, 2000.

Ikenberry, G. John. *Reasons of State: Oil Politics and the Capacities of American Government.* Ithaca, N.Y.: Cornell University Press, 1988.

Skeet, Ian. *OPEC: Twenty-Five Years of Prices and Politics.* Cambridge, U.K.: Cambridge University Press, 1988.

Kenneth B. Moss/A. E.

See also **Arab Nations, Relations with; Automobile; Automobile Industry; Energy Research and Development Administration; Offshore Oil; Petroleum Industry; Stagflation;** *and vol. 9:* **Address on Energy Crisis.**

Historic Lucas Gusher. Oil pours out of the top of a derrick in the Spindletop Oil Field near Beaumont, Texas, 1901.

OIL FIELDS. Petroleum results from the decay of fossils and plants. The decayed matter becomes trapped in porous rock, with pools of this greenish-black liquid existing in narrow sandstone belts. The petroleum can bubble to the surface in an "oil seep," but it can also be found several miles below the surface.

The first oil field to be tapped commercially in the United States was near Titusville, Pennsylvania. Small quantities of oil appeared in several seeps along Oil Creek. The first drill was erected over the field in 1859. Two years later, wells in Pennsylvania were producing more than two million barrels of oil annually, and Pennsylvania was responsible for half the world's oil production for the next forty years. Oil fields were located in fourteen states by 1900, including Texas, which sparked the next boom. Drilling started in East Texas in 1866, but large-scale production began in 1901, when a reservoir 1,000 feet under a salt dome named Spindletop was tapped near Beaumont, Texas. This well produced at an initial rate of 100,000 barrels per day, more than all the other producing wells in the United States combined.

Productive oil fields were drilled in northern California as early as 1865, but no major field was discovered until drillers moved south to Los Angeles in 1892. In 1900, California produced four million barrels of oil. A decade later, production had jumped to seventy-seven million barrels annually. Three new fields were discovered in Southern California in the 1920s, making California the nation's leading oil-producing state, supplying one-fourth of the world's needs.

The oil hunt moved offshore as early as 1887, when H. L. Williams built a wharf with a drill 300 feet into the ocean. The first offshore oil well was set in 1932 from an independent platform, but this aspect of the industry did not begin in earnest until 1947, when the Kerr-McGee Corporation struck oil in the Gulf of Mexico off the Louisiana coast. Two years later, forty-four exploratory wells in eleven fields across the Gulf had been drilled. Currently, the Gulf is part of a worldwide triumvirate of offshore fields—the other two are in the Persian Gulf and the North Sea—that provides one-third of the world's oil supply. Severe weather in the North Sea requires the construction of gravity platforms, each of which requires 11,000 work years to construct. A 1,500-foot-high platform owned by Shell Oil in the North Sea and the Great Wall of China are the only two manmade objects that can be seen from the surface of the moon with the naked eye.

The United States' biggest oil field was discovered in Prudhoe Bay, Alaska, in 1968. It is on the Arctic Ocean, 250 miles north of the Arctic Circle. Since 1977, more than 12.8 million barrels of crude have been pumped from nineteen fields in Alaska, most of it shipped through the Alaska Pipeline, built from 1974 to 1977 because tankers could not get through in the winter. The pipeline, which cost $8 billion to build and $210 million annually to maintain, features ten pump stations along 800 miles of pipeline. Today, oil fields are located in thirty-three of the fifty states, with Texas, Louisiana, Alaska, Oklahoma, and California the five largest producers of oil.

BIBLIOGRAPHY

American Petroleum Institute. Web site www.api.org.

Black, Brian. *Petrolia: The Landscape of America's First Oil Boom.* Baltimore: Johns Hopkins University Press, 2000.

Clark, James Anthony, and Michel Thomas Halbouty. *Spindletop: The True Story of the Oil Discovery That Changed the World.* Houston, Tex: Gulf, 1995.

Economides, Michael, and Ronald Oligney. *The Color of Oil: The History, the Money and the Politics of the World's Biggest Business.* Katy, Tex.: Round Oak, 2000.

Pratt, Joseph A., Tyler Priest, and Christopher J., Castaneda. *Offshore Pioneers: Brown and Root and the History of Offshore Oil and Gas.* Houston, Tex.: Gulf, 1997.

T. L. Livermore
Terri Livermore

See also **Offshore Oil; Petroleum Industry; Petroleum Prospecting and Technology.**

Ojibwe Warriors. This engraving shows a war dance; the tribe joined in the so-called Pontiac Rebellion and Tecumseh's resistance to white settlement. LIBRARY OF CONGRESS

OJIBWE reside throughout the western Great Lakes region. The French made the first recorded European contact with the Ojibwe in the early 1600s, in Sault Sainte Marie, at the outlet of Lake Superior. Their name was recorded as the "Outchibous," though its meaning was never given. Consequently, translations range from "Roast Until Puckered Up" to "Those Who Make Pictographs" (a reference to their writing on birch bark).

Further confusion arises from the use of the tribal appellation "Chippewa," though both names should be considered synonymous. Nevertheless, they call themselves the Anishnaabeg, which has been translated as "The Original People" and "Those Who Intend to Do Well." When combined with their linguistic relatives, the Ottawas and the Potawatomis, they are referred to as the Three Fires Confederacy.

Oral tradition of these people places them originally on the Atlantic shore, but they were compelled to travel west to escape some unrecorded disaster. Their migration, directed by elements of the spirit world, was completed when they reached Sault Sainte Marie. There, the three groups split into their current divisions and geographic distribution, with the Potawatomis migrating to the southern Great Lakes region, the Ojibwes spreading across the north, while the Ottawas distributed themselves throughout the central Great Lakes.

While generally enjoying peaceful and productive relations with French fur traders, after the defeat of the French by the British in 1760, the Ojibwes and their Great Lakes Native neighbors joined in the misnamed "Pontiac Rebellion" to resist British control. After the American Revolution, the Ojibwes also resisted American colonists coming into their territory and joined forces with the Shawnee leader Tecumseh and most of the Great Lakes tribes in their struggle to retain control over the "Old Northwest."

After the defeat of Tecumseh and his Native and British allies in the War of 1812, the Ojibwes continued to resist American control until they finally signed a major treaty in 1820 in Sault Sainte Marie. Later, the nineteenth century saw the Ojibwes ceding land all across the Upper Great Lakes. The first of these cessions took place in 1836, when the Chippewas ceded, roughly, the northern third of Michigan's Lower Peninsula, along with the eastern third of the Upper Peninsula. In the U.S., this land cession pattern moved west, culminating in northern Minnesota in 1867. In many of these Upper Great Lakes treaties, the Ojibwes retained hunting rights and "other usual privileges of occupancy" on the ceded lands and adjoining waters, until the land was given over to settlers. This retention of rights to the natural resources of the region has been affirmed since then by U.S. Federal Court decisions.

The Ojibwes of northern Ontario signed two land cession treaties with Canadian authorities in 1850 and incorporated many of the "rights of occupancy" found in the 1836 U.S. treaty. This is not surprising, since there were Ojibwe individuals who signed treaties with both

U.S. and Canadian governments. This pattern of having one person sign treaties with both governments has given the Ojibwes a sense of international sovereignty not enjoyed by many other tribes. The last of the major Ojibwe land cession treaties was not signed until 1923. This treaty with the Canadian government covered a huge expanse of land west of the Georgian Bay and south, along the northern shore of Lake Ontario.

Because of the Removal Act of 1830, the 1836 Michigan treaty contained a clause that said the Ojibwes would be removed "when the Indians wish it." Armed with this language, the Ojibwes and other Anishnaabegs resisted removal, and their resistance resulted in large numbers of Ojibwe-Chippewas remaining in the Upper Great Lakes region. Unlike their U.S. counterparts, the Ojibwes of Canada were not subject to a removal policy. Thus, the Ojibwes remain on their ancestral land throughout the Upper Great Lakes, from Québec in the east to North Dakota in the west, with other reservations scattered as far as Canada's Northwest Territories.

In the United States, the Ojibwes live on twenty-two Reservations in Michigan, Minnesota, Wisconsin, and North Dakota. The 2000 U.S. census showed about 105,000 Ojibwe-Chippewa tribal members, making them the third largest tribe in the United States. Although the numbers are harder to verify, in 2000 about 70,000 Ojibwes lived in Canada on more than 125 reserves.

Ojibwe Mother and Child. This lithograph shows a woman carrying her baby in a cradleboard. Library of Congress

Several Ojibwe tribes in the U.S. operate casinos, which has brought economic prosperity to those tribes able to lure patrons to their remote locations. Some tribes operate casinos in larger Midwest cities, notably the Sault Sainte Marie Tribe of Chippewas, with one in Detroit. In Canada, the Chippewas of Mnjikaning operate Casino Rama in northern Ontario. By agreement with the Ontario government, they contribute sixty-five percent of the casino's revenue to the other 134 First Nations Reserves in Ontario.

Along with their continuing struggle to maintain rights to the natural resources of the region, the Ojibwes also struggle to maintain their sovereign status as "nations" within the context of both U.S. and Canadian society. They assert their treaty rights and, in Canada, their "aboriginal rights," as guaranteed by the Canadian Constitution, including the rights of self-government, self-determination, and cross-border movement and trade. They have also revitalized Ojibwe culture through a renewed interest in their language and religion.

BIBLIOGRAPHY

Clifton, James A., George L. Cornell, and James M. McClurken. *People of the Three Fires: the Ottawa, Potawatomi, and Ojibway of Michigan.* Grand Rapids: Michigan Indian Press, 1986.

Johnston, Basil. *Ojibway Heritage.* Lincoln: University of Nebraska Press, 1990.

Tanner, Helen Hornbeck, et al., eds. *Atlas of Great Lakes Indian History.* Norman: University of Oklahoma Press, 1987.

Phil Bellfy

See also **Indian Removal; Indian Treaties; Pontiac's War.**

OJIBWE LANGUAGE is a Native American tongue that is still spoken by an estimated 60,000 speakers. The language is indigenous to the states of Michigan, Wisconsin, Minnesota, North Dakota, and Montana and the Canadian provinces of Quebec, Ontario, Manitoba, and Saskatchewan. Although dialects vary significantly across the region, this does not pose a significant barrier to communication. Ojibwe is also closely related to Potawatomi and Ottawa and more distantly related to other languages in the Algonquian language family.

Fluency rates for Ojibwe vary from 1 percent in some communities to 100 percent in others. Ojibwe is one of only twenty Native American languages that scholars believe will survive through the twenty-first century. Ojibwe is under pressure in many areas, and tribal governments and schools have been active in trying to revitalize the language. Some immersion programs and schools have been initiated, but it remains to be seen if those endeavors will have the same success that Maori, Blackfeet, or Native Hawaiian efforts have enjoyed.

Okinawa. American troops move ashore from their ships—hundreds of which were targets of Japanese kamikaze pilots during the costly three-month battle for this crucial island. AP/WIDE WORLD PHOTOS

The exact date when the Ojibwe language evolved to its present form is not known. However, linguists believe that Ojibwe is a very ancient language that has been in existence for over 1,000 years. Older variants of Ojibwe (or Proto-Algonquian) date back several thousand years. The Ojibwe people devised a system of writing on birch bark long before contact with Europeans. However, this writing system functioned as mnemonic devices rather than as modern orthography. In 1848, a syllabic orthography was developed for the Ojibwe language that enjoyed widespread success and use, especially in Canada. For many years, the Ojibwe and Cree had one of the highest literacy rates in the world. Other systems were developed over the years, and there is still no single universally accepted orthography. However, the double-vowel system devised by C. E. Fiero in 1945 is now the most widely accepted and used writing system for the Ojibwe language. Unlike most languages of the world, morphological components of Ojibwe are known to everyday speakers. Thus, Ojibwe offers layers of meaning and description that make it a cornerstone of cultural knowledge and a spectacular medium for storytelling.

BIBLIOGRAPHY

Krauss, Michael. "Status of Native Language Endangerment." In *Stabilizing Indigenous Languages.* Edited by Gina Cantoni. Flagstaff: Northern Arizona State University, 1996.

Nichols, John D., and Earl Nyholm. *A Concise Dictionary of Minnesota Ojibwe.* Minneapolis: University of Minnesota Press, 1995.

Treuer, Anton, ed. *Living Our Language: Ojibwe Tales & Oral Histories.* St. Paul: Minnesota Historical Society Press, 2001.

Anton Treuer

See also **Indian Languages.**

OKINAWA lies at the midpoint of the Ryukyu Island chain, located between Japan and Taiwan. A minor Japanese base during most of WORLD WAR II, Okinawa became important when U.S. planners decided to seize it as a staging point for their projected invasion of Japan. The assault began on 1 April 1945. Gen. Mitsuru Ushijima, commanding Japan's 32d Army, allowed Gen. Simon Bolivar Buckner's U.S. 10th Army to storm ashore virtually unopposed. Instead of trying to defend the beaches, Ushijima's troops burrowed into caves and tunnels in a succession of low ridges lying between the beaches and Shuri, the capital. Army and Marine Corps attackers eliminated the dug-in Japanese with "blowtorch" (flamethrower) and "corkscrew" (demolition charge) tactics at heavy cost to themselves.

Driven late in May from their Shuri line, the Japanese retreated to Okinawa's southern tip, where both commanders perished by the battle's end on 21 June. Ushijima died by ritual suicide (*hara-kiri*), and Buckner was killed by one of the last artillery shells fired by the Japanese. Earlier, on the adjacent islet of Ie Shima, the famous war correspondent Ernie Pyle had been killed by a burst fired from a by-passed Japanese machine gun. Equally bitter was the fighting at sea. Japan's air forces hurled more than 4,000 sorties, many by kamikaze suicide planes, at U.S. and British naval forces. In vanquishing 115,000 Japanese defenders, U.S. losses totaled 38 ships of all types sunk and 368 damaged; 4,900 U.S. Navy servicemen died; and U.S. Army and U.S. Marine fatalities numbered 7,900.

BIBLIOGRAPHY

Belote, James H., and William M. Belote, *Typhoon of Steel: The Battle for Okinawa.* New York: Harper and Row, 1970.

Foster, Simon. *Okinawa 1945.* London: Arms and Armour, 1994.

Frank, Benis M. *Okinawa: Capstone to Victory.* New York: Ballantine Books, 1970.

Leckie, Robert. *Okinawa: The Last Battle of World War II.* New York: Viking, 1995.

James H. Belote
William M. Belote/A. R.

See also **Japan, Relations with; World War II, Navy in.**

OKLAHOMA. Few states can boast a motto more appropriate to its history than that of Oklahoma: *Labor Omnia Vincit* (Labor Conquers All Things). Situated in the southern midsection of the United States, the land has provided the environment for development by diverse inhabitants since before its discovery by Europeans in the sixteenth century. A diagonal line drawn across the pan-shaped state from northeast to southwest highlights the difference in geographic regions. The rolling hills of the south and east contain the Ouachita, Arbuckle, Wichita, and Kiamichi Mountains, with forests, substantial rainfall, and diversified agriculture. The drier prairie and plains of the higher elevations in the north and west support wheat production and livestock. Mammoth bones and Clovis culture spearheads uncovered near Anadarko, Oklahoma, predate the more sophisticated artifacts left in ceremonial burial sites by the Mound Builders, who established communities near Spiro, Oklahoma, in the thirteenth century. By the time of European contact, Caddo, Osage, Kiowa, Apache, and Comanche groups traversed the area.

The explorations of Francisco Vásquez de Coronado and Hernando De Soto in 1541 established a Spanish claim to the vast expanse of Louisiana Territory, including what would become Oklahoma. France challenged Spain's control of the region based on the Mississippi River explorations of René-Robert Cavelier, Sieur de La Salle, in 1682. The territory changed hands between these two colonial powers until the United States purchased it from France in 1803. American exploration began almost immediately. Lieutenant James B. Wilkinson secured an alliance for the U.S. government with the Osage Indians and in 1805 to 1806 reported on the navigability of the Arkansas River through northeastern Oklahoma. The government trader George C. Sibley provided the first written description of the northwestern part of the state available to the American public, and promoted interest in the Oklahoma salt plains during his survey of the Santa Fe Trail in 1825 to 1826. The naturalist Thomas Nuttall and Major Stephen H. Long both reported unfavorably on the fertility of the region in similar journeys through the area in 1819 to 1820. Long's official army report labeled the Great Plains as a "Great American Desert," but provided a more comprehensive report of plant and animal life and a more accurate map than any available before. It also delineated the more productive lands in eastern Oklahoma.

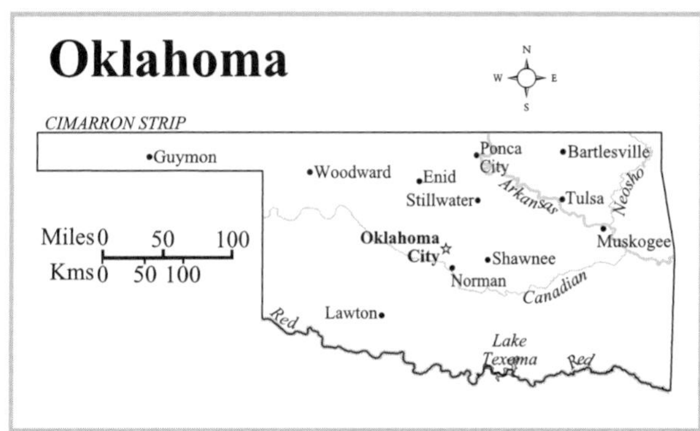

Early Conflicts

From 1817 until 1842, the Cherokee, Choctaw, Chickasaw, Seminole, and Creek Indians of the southeastern states faced increasing pressure by federal and state governments to voluntarily exchange their homelands for new tracts in INDIAN TERRITORY encompassing all of present-day Oklahoma. Violence erupted both within the Indian groups over the issue of land cessions and between the Indians and white intruders. The Cherokee elite, led by Chief John Ross, with the aid of the missionary Samuel Austin Worcester fought removal through the U.S. court system. These actions resulted in two Supreme Court cases with decisions written by Chief Justice John Marshall: *The Cherokee Nation v. Georgia* (1831) and *Worcester v. Georgia* (1832). The latter case upheld the rights of the Cherokee Nation against the state of Georgia. The Indian Removal Act of 1830, however, gave President Andrew Jackson the authority to forcefully move the remaining Indian groups westward. The experiences of the Indians as they were marched overland horrified onlookers. Exposure, starvation, exhaustion, and disease caused a death toll estimated at one-fourth of their populations. For the Cherokees, these hardships became known as the "TRAIL OF TEARS."

Upon arrival in Indian Territory, the Five Tribes recreated themselves into autonomous nations. This period before 1860 has been called the "golden age" in Indian Territory. They formed governments patterned after the U.S. model with executive, legislative, and judicial branches. The Choctaws maintained their law enforcement unit, the Lighthorsemen. The Indians established public school systems for their children and invited American missionaries to build mission stations on their lands. The Cherokee, Choctaw, and Chickasaw nations operated male and female higher education institutions for their youth after 1845 that rivaled educational academies in most states at that time. The Cherokee Sequoyah developed an eighty-six-letter syllabary of the Cherokee language, which allowed the rapid achievement of literacy for the nation and enabled the publication of their newspaper, *The Cherokee Phoenix*, in English and Cherokee. Holding their national land domains in common, Indians built successful stock farms, small service businesses, and cotton plantations. Some, like Robert Love and Joseph Vann, attained considerable wealth. Before removal, many of the Indian–white intermarried elite had adopted the cultural lifestyles of planters in the southern states. They owned slaves, who worked their lands in a variety of labor relationships. These slaves accompanied their Indian masters on the removal journey to Indian Territory and helped to rebuild the comfortable homes and farms of the elite. Prior to the Civil War (1861–1865), approximately 10,000 slaves resided among the Indian people.

The Civil War

The Civil War created the same divisions over slavery and sectional loyalties in Indian Territory as in the adjoining states. The Confederacy sent Commissioner Albert Pike to secure treaties of alliance with the governments of all of the Five Nations in 1861. The Choctaws, Chickasaws, and Cherokees immediately formed mounted rifle regiments. Factions favoring neutrality joined the Creek Chief Opothleyaholo as he led a retreat into Kansas under attack from Confederate Indian forces. The Confederate Cherokee Colonel Stand Watie led his regiment to victory at the Battle of Pea Ridge in Arkansas in 1862. The most significant battle in Indian Territory took place in 1863 when Union troops, loyal Indians, and African American soldiers defeated the Confederate Indian forces at Honey Springs. This allowed the Union to control Fort Gibson and the Texas Road into Indian Territory. Stand Watie continued an effective guerilla campaign against Union supply lines in Indian Territory for the remainder of the war. Promoted to Brigadier General, Watie was the last Confederate general to surrender in 1865.

The Civil War battles, destruction of property, lawless pillaging, and foraging for supplies devastated Indian Territory. More than 10,000 died from wounds, exposure, and disease. Indian and black refugees in Kansas and Texas returned to find their homes, schools, and churches vandalized or destroyed. Fields were burned, fences were torn down, and thousands of livestock were stolen. The Indian governments were in disarray, and the federal government now held them accountable for their alliance with the Confederacy. Reconstruction treaties with each of the Five Nations in 1865 to 1866 exacted a high price that would eventually lead to the dissolution of Indian Territory. The government ordered the Indian nations to abolish slavery and to incorporate the Indian freedmen into their respective nations as citizens. The agreements also included acceptance of sizable land reductions, a railroad right-of-way through Indian Territory, and a future unified government for Indian Territory. The Choctaw leader Allen Wright suggested the Choctaw word *Oklahoma*, meaning "the land of the red people," for the name of the new territory.

The federal government used the large tracts of land in the western half of the territory taken from the Five Nations to create reservations for a variety of Plains Indian groups. Approximately 30,000 Plains Indians were militarily disarmed, stripped of their leaders and horse herds, and forcefully confined to lands designated for them. African American military units, the Ninth and Tenth Cavalries, commanded by Benjamin Grierson, earned the respect of the Plains Indians, who gave them the name "Buffalo Soldiers." These units built Fort Sill (Lawton, Oklahoma) and policed the boundaries of the Indian lands. Conditions on the reservations deteriorated when Congress decreased appropriations and failed to honor treaty obligations made to the Plains people. Out of desperation, raiding parties left the reservation lands. Frequent skirmishes, known as the Red River War, between the military and the Indians occurred in 1874 to 1875. The most violent encounter actually occurred some years before, in 1868 near Washita in western Oklahoma. There, General George A. Custer led an attack that resulted in the deaths of the peaceful Cheyenne Chief Black Kettle, a village of approximately one hundred men, women, and children, and several hundred ponies. The Apache leader Geronimo surrendered in 1886 and remained a prisoner of war at Fort Sill until his death. One by one, the Plains Indian groups settled on their lands. By statehood, Oklahoma had become the home of sixty-seven different Indian groups.

The Reconstruction treaty alterations in the sovereignty status of the Five Nations opened the territory for exploitation. The demand for beef on Indian reservations and in eastern cities led Texas ranchers to drive herds of cattle along the East and the West Shawnee Trails and the Chisholm Trail (near present Interstate Highway 35) through Indian Territory to Kansas railheads. African Americans fleeing the South joined white citizens illegally invading the territory to take advantage of the rich farmlands. Coal deposits in the Choctaw lands created a demand for workers with mining experience. White intermarried businessmen, such as J. J. McAlester, recruited immigrants from European countries in order to develop the mineral assets. The Missouri, Kansas and Texas, Friscoe, Rock Island, and Santa Fe Railroads hired construction crews to build lines that crisscrossed the territory connecting small communities. After the turn of the century, the discovery of substantial oil deposits created instant boomtowns. Large-scale producers, such as the Glen Pool wells, increased Indian Territory production between 1904 and 1907 from one million to approximately forty-five million barrels a year. This economic development acquainted thousands of non-Indians with the potential value of these Indian lands.

Not all immigrants to Indian Territory were law-abiding citizens. The closest district court administered law enforcement for Indian Territory from Fort Smith, Arkansas, through Judge Isaac C. Parker, known as the "Hanging Judge." The territory became a haven for drifters, con men, whiskey peddlers, and hardened criminals such as the Doolin Gang, the Daltons, Jesse James, the Younger clan, Ned Christie, and the most famous female outlaw, Belle Starr. The large area of land, rough terrain, and Indian–white confrontations made maintaining order and tracking criminals more difficult for the marshals, including Bill Tilghman, Heck Thomas, and the African American Bass Reeves, who served more than thirty years in Indian Territory.

Changes in Oklahoma

Interest group pressure increased in the 1870s through the 1880s for the opening of sizable tracts of land in Indian Territory that had not been specifically assigned to Indian groups. Charles C. Carpenter, David Payne, and William L. Couch led expeditions of homesteaders called "boomers" into the Indian lands to establish colonies, defy government regulations, and open the lands to white settlement. Congress attached the Springer Amendment to the Indian Appropriations Bill in 1889 providing for the opening of the Unassigned Lands. President Benjamin Harrison issued a proclamation that declared the lands available for settlement on 22 April 1889. On that date, approximately 50,000 people participated in the land run to secure quarter sections. Some home seekers sneaked onto the lands illegally prior to the opening and became known as "Sooners." The 1887 Dawes Act (or General Allotment Act) provided for the abolition of tribal governments, the survey of Indian lands, and the division of reservation land into 160-acre homesteads. Between 1891 and 1895, there were four more land runs for additional areas that were added to Oklahoma Territory, which had been created on 2 May 1890. Land run disputes proved so difficult that the last western lands were added by lottery and sealed auction bids. The area controlled by the Five Nations was originally exempt, and for seventeen years the twin territories, Oklahoma Territory and Indian Territory, existed side by side. But the Curtis Act of 1898 ended the independence of the Five Nations, and in spite of rigorous opposition, they, too, were forced to enroll for allotments.

Economic development and increased population led to demands for statehood. The combined population of the twin territories around 1900 approached 750,000. African American promoters, among them E. P. McCabe, recruited black migrants from the South to establish all-black communities, such as Boley, Langston, and Clearview, where freedom from race discrimination and economic uplift could be enjoyed. Approximately twenty-seven such all-black towns developed in the twin territories, leading to the speculation that Oklahoma might be made into a state exclusively for African Americans. The Indian population in Indian Territory, now outnumbered four to one by whites, hoped for the creation of two states, while the white population lobbied for a combination of the territories into a single state. Between 1889 and 1906, Congress entertained thirty-one bills for either single or joint statehood. Congress rejected an Indian state to be called Sequoyah in 1905, and President Theodore Roosevelt signed the Oklahoma Enabling Act creating one state in 1906. A constitutional convention dominated by delegates from the Democratic Party met in Guthrie in 1906 to 1907 to complete a constitution. A coalition of reformers and business and agricultural interests led by William Murray, Pete Hanraty, Charles Haskell, and Kate Barnard produced a 250,000-word document that included major Progressive Era protective measures. On 16 November 1907, Roosevelt signed the proclamation bringing Oklahoma into the union as the forty-sixth state. Oklahoma comprises seventy-seven counties with a land area of 68,667 square miles. The capitol at Guthrie was relocated to Oklahoma City after a vote of the electorate in 1910.

As the territorial days waned, popular interest in the "old Wild West" increased across the nation. Three famous Wild West shows originated in Oklahoma and provided working experience for future Hollywood and rodeo cowboy stars. Zach Mulhall created a show from his ranch near Guthrie that toured from 1900 through 1915 showcasing the talents of his daughter, Lucille. President Theodore Roosevelt invited Lucille to ride in his inaugural parade, and her performances across the United States led to what is believed to be the first use of the word "cowgirl." Mulhall's show included a young trick roper from Claremore, Oklahoma, named Will Rogers, who became Oklahoma's favorite son and a nationally celebrated performer, comedian, and political commentator in the 1920s and 1930s. Gordon "Pawnee Bill" Lillie featured his wife, May Lillie, in his show, and the Miller Brothers' 101 Ranch near Ponca City, Oklahoma, produced a popular show that toured until the Great Depression. Famous cowboys from Oklahoma included Bill Pickett, Tom Mix, and Gene Autry. Informal local rodeo competitions testing a variety of cowboy skills developed into more than one hundred rodeos yearly in Oklahoma involving events at the high school, the intercollegiate, and the professional levels.

Republican Party appointees dominated territorial politics in Oklahoma, with only a single Democratic governor, William C. Renfrow (1893–1897). The opposite has been true since statehood. Only three Republicans have been elected governor of the state. The first, Henry Bellmon, served from 1963 to 1967 and again from 1987 to 1991. Oklahoma politics since the 1950s, however, has followed a pattern of Democrat leadership in the state, but support for Republican national presidential candidates. Lyndon Johnson, in 1964, was the only Democrat to win Oklahoma's presidential vote in the last third of the twentieth century. From 1968 through the end of the twentieth century, a majority of U.S. Senate seats also went to the Republicans. Following the reports from the year 2000 census, Oklahoma dropped from six seats in the House of Representatives to five. A dome and a statue of a Native American titled "The Guardian" for the capitol building were completed in 2002. The dome had been planned for the state capitol building, originally completed in 1917, but had been abandoned because of financial commitments during World War I (1914–1918).

Oklahoma's economic development most often followed cycles of boom and bust. The state benefited from the national demands for increased production of oil and agricultural products during World War I, but the 1920s and 1930s proved to be economically and politically challenging. Two governors in the 1920s, John Walton and Henry Johnston, were impeached and removed from office. Longstanding racial tensions erupted into a race riot in Tulsa in 1921 that left the African American section of the city a burned ruin and hundreds dead or missing. Ku Klux Klan activity and smoldering Oklahoma Socialist Party discontent underscored worsening economic conditions. By the 1930s, the majority of Oklahoma farms were operated by tenant farmers, and western Oklahoma experienced the devastation of the DUST BOWL. The state treasury had a $5 million deficit, the oil market was depressed, and mass unemployment, bank failures, and foreclosures threatened the state. Thousands of impoverished Oklahomans, referred to negatively as "Okies," joined migrants from other states making their way west in search of work. The census reported a decline in the state population between 1930 and 1940 by approximately 60,000.

Boom and bust continued to mark the state's economic progress through the 1980s. World War II (1939–1945) demands for petroleum, coal, food, and cotton, as well as substantial government spending for military installations, brought a return of prosperity to the state. Following the war, Oklahoma ranked fourth in the nation in the production of petroleum and natural gas, and continued to rely on this industry and cattle and agriculture for economic growth. The Arab oil embargo and grain sales to the Soviet Union in the 1970s pushed per capita income to national levels. The 1980s produced a massive readjustment as oil prices plummeted from a high of $42 per barrel to just over $10. Wheat prices declined dramatically as well. This major downturn in primary business investments affected every sector of the state's economy and led to a determined effort to diversify economic activities through recruitment of manufacturing and technology. Trade, services, public administration, and manufacturing top the list as largest employers in the state. Cooperative planning efforts between state government and Oklahoma's forty-three colleges and universities led to innovations such as the National Weather Center. State per capita personal income increased 46 percent from 1990 to 2000.

Oklahoma, its history, and its people gained renewed national interest following the bombing of the Alfred P. Murrah Federal Building in Oklahoma City on 19 April 1995 by Timothy McVeigh and Terry Nichols. A national memorial now stands at the site of the tragedy, which killed 168 people. The state's population grew by 9.7 percent between 1990 and 2000 to reach 3,450,654. In 2000 Oklahoma had a larger Native American population, 273,230, than any other state in the union. The Hispanic population was the fastest growing group in the state, more than doubling in size from 86,160 in 1990 to 179,304 in 2000. Since 1950, more Oklahomans have lived in the cities than in rural areas. At the beginning of the twenty-first century Oklahoma City (506,132) ranked first in size, followed by Tulsa (393,049) and Norman (95,694).

BIBLIOGRAPHY

Baird, W. David, and Danney Goble. *The Story of Oklahoma.* Norman: University of Oklahoma Press, 1994.

Gibson, Arrell Morgan. *Oklahoma, A History of Five Centuries.* Norman: University of Oklahoma Press, 1965.

Joyce, Davis D., ed. *An Oklahoma I Had Never Seen Before: Alternative Views of Oklahoma History.* Norman: University of Oklahoma Press, 1994.

Morgan, David R., Robert E. England, and George G. Humphreys. *Oklahoma Politics and Policies: Governing the Sooner State.* Lincoln: University of Nebraska Press, 1991.

Reese, Linda Williams. *Women of Oklahoma, 1890–1920.* Norman: University of Oklahoma Press, 1997.

Stein, Howard F., and Robert F. Hill, eds. *The Culture of Oklahoma.* Norman: University of Oklahoma Press, 1993.

Thompson, John. *Closing the Frontier: Radical Response in Oklahoma, 1889–1923.* Norman: University of Oklahoma Press, 1986.

Wickett, Murray R. *Contested Territory: Whites, Native Americans and African Americans in Oklahoma, 1865–1907.* Baton Rouge: Louisiana State University Press, 2000.

Linda W. Reese

See also **Chisholm Trail; Dust Bowl; Indian Policy, U.S.: 1830–1900; Indian Policy, U.S.: 1900–2000; Sequoyah, Proposed State of; Tulsa.**

OKLAHOMA CITY, capital of the state of Oklahoma, achieved national prominence after the bombing of the Alfred P. Murrah Federal Building on 19 April 1995 by American terrorists Timothy McVeigh and Terry Nichols, resulting in the deaths of 168 people and injuring more than 500. A national memorial now stands at the site of the tragedy. Before this event, the city's history

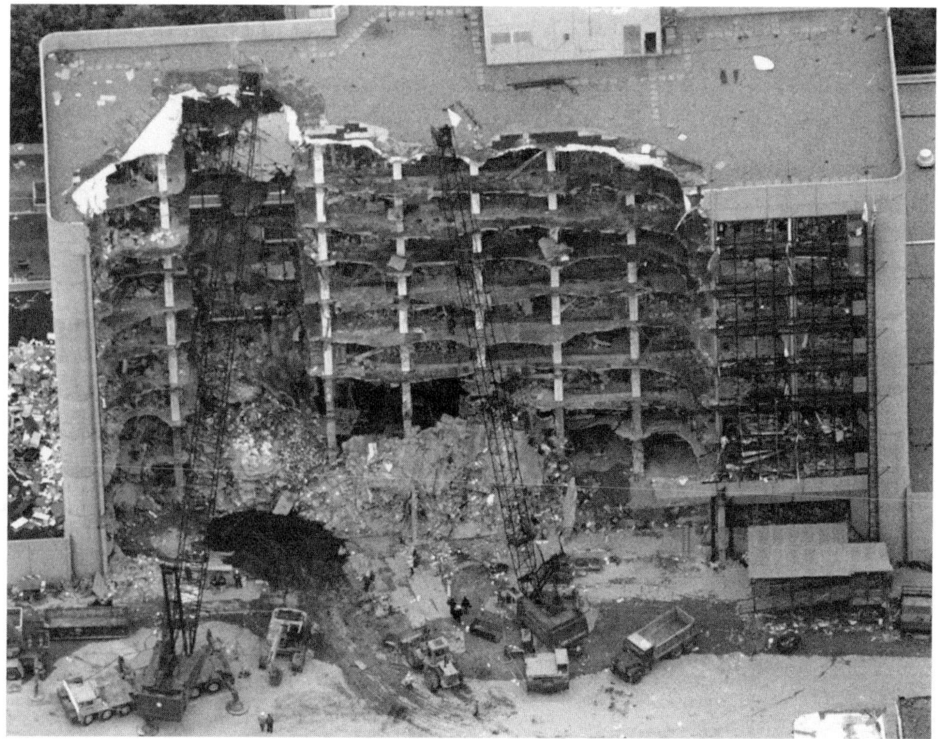

Domestic Terrorism. On 19 April 1995, Americans turned on their morning news to find that terrorists had used explosives to nearly destroy the Alfred P. Murrah Federal Building in Oklahoma City, Oklahoma (photo shows building after the bombing). While international terrorists were the first suspects, the bomber turned out to be Timothy McVeigh, a decorated ex-soldier, who held strong antigovernment views and wished to seek revenge for the government's actions against the Branch Davidian cult movement on the same date in 1993, in which eighty people were killed. McVeigh was convicted of the bombing and put to death on 11 June 2001. © AP/Wide World Photos

rested upon its Western and Native American heritage and its instant creation when ten thousand settlers established a town on the site following the 22 April 1889 land run. By 1910, local business leaders forced the transfer of the state capital from its previous location in Guthrie to Oklahoma City. The 1928 discovery of petroleum in the area spurred the city's growth. In politics, early domination by the Democrats changed to a Republican majority in the 1970s. Politics, business, and oil directed the boom-and-bust economy until the 1990s, when the city embarked on an ambitious urban revitalization plan known as MAPS (Metropolitan Area Projects) to establish the city as a diversified regional cultural, residential, educational, service, and manufacturing center. The population increased 14 percent between the 1990 and 2000 censuses to 506,000. In 2000, the city's population was 68 percent white, 15 percent African American, 3.5 percent Native American, and 10 percent Hispanic (a minority doubling in size since 1990). Oklahoma City identifies itself with the heartland of the nation.

BIBLIOGRAPHY

Faulk, Odie B. *Oklahoma City: A Centennial Portrait.* Northridge, Calif.: Windsor Publications, 1988.

Linda Reese

OKLAHOMA CITY BOMBING (19 April 1995), a devastating act of domestic terrorism, in which political extremist Timothy McVeigh bombed the Alfred P. Murrah Federal Building in Oklahoma City. McVeigh's truck bomb, made of fertilizer and diesel fuel, killed 168 people, including 19 children, and injured more than 500 others. Television coverage burned the catastrophe into the nation's psyche with chilling images of bodies being removed from the rubble. The mass murderer turned out to be a 27-year-old decorated U.S. Army veteran of the Persian Gulf War with extreme antigovernment views. McVeigh's motive was to avenge a bloody 19 April 1993 federal raid on the Branch Davidian sect in Waco, Tex., in which some 80 people died. The Federal Bureau of

Investigation tracked McVeigh down through the Ryder rental truck that exploded in Oklahoma City. An accomplice, Terry Nichols, was implicated through a receipt for fertilizer and a getaway map linked to the blast. The FBI also searched unsuccessfully for an unidentified "John Doe" suspect whom eyewitnesses placed at the crime scene. This phantom suspect, and the trials of McVeigh and Nichols—both of whom pleaded not guilty—fueled theories of a larger conspiracy. But prosecutors maintained the men acted alone, and both were convicted. McVeigh was sentenced to death, and eventually admitted he carried out the strike. Nichols was sentenced to life in prison for his role. Just five days before McVeigh was scheduled to die, his case took a final dramatic turn. The FBI admitted it had withheld 3,135 documents from McVeigh's lawyers. The execution was briefly postponed. But on 11 June 2001, in Terre Haute, Ind., McVeigh was put to death by lethal injection. Through a grant of special permission by the U.S. Attorney General, victims and survivors watched the execution on closed-circuit television in Oklahoma City.

BIBLIOGRAPHY

Linenthal, Edward T. *The Unfinished Bombing: Oklahoma City in American Memory.* New York: Oxford University Press, 2001.

Serrano, Richard. *One of Ours: Timothy McVeigh and the Oklahoma City Bombing.* New York: Norton, 1998.

Margaret Roberts

See also **Terrorism; Waco Siege.**

OLD AGE. Attitudes toward and the treatment of old people have varied substantially in different societies and historical periods. In some preliterate cultures, elders were valued as custodians of wisdom and teachers of survival skills. In others, they were considered a liability and even abandoned when they could not keep up with nomadic groups or were a drain on a subsistence economy. Native American tribes respected elders, and among early colonial settlers such as the Puritans, elders were revered as evolved spiritual persons. However, in the United States, as in Europe, the industrial revolution and reliance on science and up-to-date education meant that older workers were often considered obsolete. And the rise of individualism and mobility rather than family and community meant that older people were apt to live alone.

Increasing Life Expectancy

Because twentieth-century advances in public health increased longevity, the number of old people increased tremendously as a proportion of the population in many developed countries, including the United States. In 1776, the average American lived to age thirty-five and in 1876 to age forty. In 1900, only one in twenty-five Americans was sixty-five or older. In 2000, 35 million Americans sixty-five or older represented 12.7 percent of the U.S. population, or about one in every eight Americans. As the U.S. Bureau of the Census reports, during the twentieth century the population under age sixty-five tripled, but the population over age sixty-five increased by a factor of eleven. The fastest-growing category of Americans is those aged eighty-five or older. In 2050, there will be 18.2 million Americans over eighty-five. More U.S. residents were also reaching age 100. In 2000, there were 68,000 people 100 or more, but in 2050, 834,000 people are expected to reach that age.

Life expectancy at age 65 increased by only 2.4 years between 1900 and 1960, but it grew 3.5 years between 1960 and 2000. People reaching 65 in 2000 had, on average, an additional life expectancy of 17.9 years, or 19.2 years for females and 16.3 years for males. The gender gap meant that over age 65 there were about 140 women for every 100 men, and over age 85, there were about 240 women for every 100 men. Baby boomers, the 76 million Americans born between 1946 and 1964, will begin to get social security benefits starting in 2011. By 2030, there will be about 70 million elders in the United States.

Public and Private Assistance

The increase in longevity and the growing aged population resulted in many government programs. The Social Security Act of 1935, passed during Franklin Roosevelt's presidency during the Great Depression, was a retirement insurance plan designed to provide retirees with some income and also to encourage them to leave the workforce to make room for younger workers. In 1965, Congress passed the Older Americans Act, which set up the Administration on Aging (AOA) as part of the Department of Health, Education, and Welfare, now the Department of Health and Human Services. In 1972, the Older Americans Act was amended to set up Supplemental Security Income (SSI) for those without sufficient social security eligibility. The 1973 amendments to the Older Americans Act set up state and area agencies on aging and local service providers to dispense information and operate programs. As of 2002, more than 2,500 information and assistance programs across the country helped older Americans and caregivers through nearly 14 million contacts annually. Available programs included adult day care, community senior centers, congregate and home-delivered meals, consumer protection, elder abuse prevention, energy assistance, financial services, health insurance, counseling, home health care, home repair and modification, homemaker/chore services, housing options, legal assistance, pension counseling, respite services, reverse mortgages, SSI and food stamps, and transportation services.

The growth in the aged population and in the programs available to it have expanded the professions serving the old. Many new occupations arose, such as care managers for elders and lawyers working in elder law. Two of the leading organizations for professionals in aging, the American Society on Aging and the National Council on

Aging, had their historic first joint conference in 2001, attended by 4,000 professionals.

Medicare, federal health insurance for seniors, was established in 1965, with Part A covering hospitalization for all social security recipients and the optional Part B covering other medical services. Medicare picks up 45 percent of an elder's health care costs but does not cover long-term care, although some private insurance does in part. Many senior citizens purchased so-called "Medigap" private insurance to supplement Medicare. The issue of financing Medicare and social security provoked much discussion and political activity in the late twentieth and early twenty-first centuries. To lower costs, in 2000 the age at which social security became available was raised to sixty-seven for those born after 1960.

These government programs have been supported, supplemented, and criticized by senior-citizen advocacy groups. The American Association of Retired Persons (AARP), founded in 1958, advocates for older Americans and is the largest voluntary association in the world, with 35 million members. It provides discounts and services for members, who must be fifty or older. In an article entitled "'Long Goodbye' to Benefits" in its July/August 2001 *Bulletin*, AARP protested employers nationwide for cutting health insurance benefits to retirees. Families USA, another advocacy organization, also protested Medicare cuts and other benefit losses to elders.

As older Americans required more costly services, some resentment arose among those still in the workforce, and intergenerational programs began to combat "ageism." Benefits from the government and other sources were particularly crucial for older people with low incomes, a disproportionate number of whom were women. The poverty rate was nearly 12 percent for older women, compared to 7 percent for older men. Older people who lived alone were more likely to be poor, and most American widows did live alone. In 1999, 45 percent of women over sixty-five were widows. Older women's median income was $10,943 in 1999, while for older men it was $19,079.

Medicare cuts in the late twentieth and early twenty-first centuries resulted in the closing of many nursing homes because costs exceeded reimbursement, according to the nursing home industry. New alternatives also reduced the number of seniors in nursing homes. The May 2001 issue of *U.S. News and World Report* stated that nursing home residents numbered just 1.5 million in the United States. About 800,000 elders lived in assisted-living facilities with private apartments and staff to provide some care, while 625,000 lived in continuing-care retirement communities that offered all levels of care from independent living to full care. In addition, some 6 million chronically ill and disabled elderly people received various levels of care at home. Another 1.5 million seniors living in independent apartments received simpler services such as prepared dinners, *U.S. News and World Report* found.

Many of the alternatives to nursing homes were very expensive and little was covered by the government. Some low-income elders lived in subsidized housing, but long waiting lists for these apartments were common. The assisted-living industry was not well regulated, and abuses occurred.

Diversity

The racial and cultural diversity of the aged population also grew. By 2000, the elder Hispanic population was one of the fastest growing. In 1990, 5.6 percent of the Hispanic population was sixty-five or older, but demographers expected that the percentage would be 14.1 by 2020. In the Asian American and Pacific Islander populations, demographers expected the greatest increase of those over sixty-five—358 percent. Demographers also estimated that the number of African American elders would increase 102 percent by 2020. African American life expectancy in 2000 was only 70.2 years, compared to an average life expectancy of 76.5 years for all elders. This discrepancy is largely because more than 68 percent of old African Americans are poor, marginally poor, or economically vulnerable.

The Administration on Aging's budget under Title 6 of the Older Americans Act provided grants and aid to American Indians, Alaska Natives, and Native Hawaiian elders, and those older persons received nearly 3 million congregate and home-delivered meals annually.

Diversity in sexual orientation is also significant. The AOA estimates that between 1.75 and 3.5 million Americans aged sixty and over are lesbian, gay, bisexual, or transgendered, and that number will enlarge with the aging population's growth.

Retirement

Mandatory retirement was a greatly contested issue in the late twentieth century. In 1967, the Age Discrimination in Employment Act was passed. In 1978, due to the advocacy of the Gray Panthers and other organizations, the act was amended to raise the age of mandatory retirement from sixty-five to seventy for most occupations.

The options for activities after retirement increased along with the aging population. Millions of elders began attending special college programs or taking regular college courses. Many travel programs served elders of means, and corporations generally geared up to serve an aging market. Elderhostel sponsored learning vacations all over the world for older people, as well as sponsoring service programs in which elders volunteer. Many retirees volunteered in their communities, worked part-time, or started small businesses. A wealth of advice books were published on such topics as how to have a good old age, and some employers provided retirement counseling for those who left the workforce. Lifestyles became very different for the healthy old as creative pursuits expanded horizons.

BIBLIOGRAPHY

Atchley, Robert C. *Social Forces and Aging*. 9th ed. Belmont, Calif.: Wadsworth, 2000.

Dychtwald, Ken. *Healthy Aging: Challenges and Solutions*. Gaithersburg, Md.: Aspen, 1999.

Jacobs, Ruth Harriet. *Be an Outrageous Older Woman*. New York: HayerPerennial, 1997.

Shapiro, Joseph P. "Growing Old in a Good Home." *U.S. News and World Report*, 21 May 2000, 56–61.

U.S. Administration on Aging. *The Many Faces of Aging*. Washington, D.C.: 2001. Available at http://www.aoa.dhhs.gov.

Ruth Harriet Jacobs

See also **American Association of Retired Persons; Gray Panthers; Life Expectancy; Medicare and Medicaid; Retirement; Retirement Plans;** *and vol. 9:* **The New American Poverty.**

OLD HICKORY. During the WAR OF 1812, General Andrew Jackson's endurance and strength inspired his soldiers to give him the nickname "Old Hickory." He was affectionately known by this name among his friends and followers for the rest of his life. The nickname also featured prominently in Jackson's successful campaign for the presidency in 1828.

BIBLIOGRAPHY

Hickey, Donald R. *The War of 1812: A Forgotten Conflict*. Urbana: University of Illinois Press, 1989.

Remini, Robert V. *Andrew Jackson and the Course of American Empire, 1767–1821*. New York: Harper and Row, 1984.

P. Orman Ray / A. R.

See also **Cherokee Wars; Corrupt Bargain; Frontier Defense.**

"OLD IRONSIDES." *See* ***Constitution.***

OLD NORTH CHURCH is the more common name for Christ Church in Boston. Erected in 1723, it was the second Episcopal church established in Boston and is the oldest church edifice in the city. The bells in its tower, cast in 1744 in England, were probably the first to peal in North America. The Old North Church has earned its greatest fame as the location where, on the night of 18 April 1775, a Boston patriot placed the two signal lights that indicated to Paul Revere that the British were approaching Lexington by sea and not by land.

BIBLIOGRAPHY

Fischer, David Hackett. *Paul Revere's Ride*. New York: Oxford University Press, 1994.

Alvin F. Harlow / A. E.

Old North Church. The bell tower where two signal lights were placed on the night of 18 April 1775, setting Paul Revere (and others) off on the legendary ride at the outset of the American Revolution. © CORBIS-BETTMANN

See also **Lexington and Concord, Battles of; Revere's Ride; Revolution, American: Military History.**

OLD NORTHWEST. *See* **Northwest Territory.**

OLIVE BRANCH PETITION. In May 1775 John Jay and John Dickinson moved in the Second Continental Congress for a humble petition to George III, which, when adopted on 5 July 1775, became known as the Olive Branch Petition. A fundamentally conservative document, it acknowledged the colonists' duty as loyal subjects of the king but asked for cessation of hostilities in order to schedule negotiations in which they could air their grievances. Dickinson, its primary author, meant the petition, even if it failed in its primary purpose to appease the king and his ministers, to fire the colonists' morale with proof that they were truly fighting an unjust system. Delivered by Arthur Lee and Richard Penn to the court in London, the very existence of the petition so infuriated George III that he refused to read it.

BIBLIOGRAPHY

Flower, Milton E. *John Dickinson: Conservative Revolutionary*. Charlottesville: University Press of Virginia, 1983.

Jacobson, David E. *John Dickinson and the Revolution in Pennsylvania, 1764–1776.* Berkeley: University of California Press, 1965.

Margaret D. Sankey

See also **Revolution, American: Diplomatic Aspects.**

OLNEY COROLLARY. On 20 July 1895, during a dispute between Great Britain and Venezuela over the latter's boundary with British Guiana, Secretary of State Richard Olney told the British to submit to arbitration. "The United States is practically sovereign on this continent," he wrote, "and its fiat is law upon the subjects to which it confines its interposition." After a brief war scare, the British agreed to an arbitration process that gave them nine-tenths of the disputed land. Venezuela was not consulted. Olney's claim to supremacy in the Western Hemisphere was the broadest interpretation to date of the MONROE DOCTRINE, which rejected European interference in the Americas.

BIBLIOGRAPHY

Braveboy-Wagner, Jacqueline Anne. *The Venezuela-Guyana Border Dispute: Britain's Colonial Legacy in Latin America.* Boulder, Colo.: Westview Press, 1984.

Eggert, Gerald G. *Richard Olney: Evolution of a Statesman.* University Park: Pennsylvania State University Press, 1974.

Max Paul Friedman

See also **Latin America, Relations with.**

OLNEY-PAUNCEFOTE TREATY. The Olney-Pauncefote Treaty was an accord resulting from Anglo-American arbitration. It was drafted primarily by Secretary of State Richard Olney and Sir Julian Pauncefote, British ambassador to the United States. The United States and the United Kingdom had considered such a treaty for some years when, in January 1896, the British prime minister, Robert Gascoyne-Cecil, Lord Salisbury, suggested it anew. Salisbury proposed one of limited terms whereas Olney believed in giving arbitration the greatest possible scope and in making the awards securely binding. The treaty he and Pauncefote drew up during 1896 made pecuniary and most other nonterritorial disputes completely arbitrable. Territorial disputes and any "disputed questions of principle of grave importance" were arbitrable subject to an appeal to a court of six, and if more than one of the six dissented, the award was not to be binding. Parliament promptly ratified the treaty. President Grover Cleveland sent it to the Senate on 11 January 1897 with his strong approval, but it remained suspended until the Republican administration came into office. Then, although President William McKinley and Secretary of State John Hay earnestly supported it, ratification failed.

BIBLIOGRAPHY

Bentley, Michael. *Lord Salisbury's World: Conservative Environments in Late-Victorian Britain.* Cambridge, U.K.: Cambridge University Press, 2001.

Wright, L. R. *Julian Pauncefote and British Imperial Policy, 1855–1889.* Lanham, Md.: University Press of America, 2002.

Allan Nevins/A. E.

See also **Foreign Policy; Great Britain, Relations with; International Law.**

OLYMPIC GAMES, AMERICAN PARTICIPATION IN. The modern Olympic Games are a quadrennial sports event open to athletes of all nations. Except for the Moscow Games of 1980, American athletes have participated in all editions of the modern games.

Origins and Organization of the Games

The Olympic Games originated in ancient Greece, where the first recorded games were held in Olympia in 776 B.C. Similar games were held in Corinth, Delphi, and Nemea. The Roman emperor Theodosius outlawed the games as pagan (they were held in honor of Zeus) in A.D. 393. The French baron Pierre de Coubertin revived the games, starting in Athens, Greece, in 1896. Chamonix, France, hosted the first Winter Olympics in 1924. (Since 1994, the Winter Olympics have been held two years after the Summer Olympics.)

U.S. host cities have been St. Louis (1904), Los Angeles (1932, 1984), and Atlanta (1996) for the Summer Olympics, and Lake Placid, New York (1932, 1980), Squaw Valley, California (1960), and Salt Lake City, Utah (2002), for the Winter Olympics. The United States Olympic Committee (USOC), headquartered in Colorado Springs, Colorado, is in charge of selecting, training, transporting, and housing the American delegation to the games and of selecting the U.S. cities that will bid to host the games, while the International Olympic Committee (IOC) in Lausanne, Switzerland, chooses the host city and determines the program of the games and the rules of amateurism.

U.S. Athletic Records in the Games

From 1896 through the Summer Olympics of 2000, U.S. athletes won a total of 2,268 medals (930 gold, 714 silver, 624 bronze). While medals are not officially tallied by national origins (until 1908, athletes were not even part of a national team and the original charter of the Olympic movement specifically required that they compete as individuals), the United States won more gold medals than any other nation, including the Soviet Union (526), Germany (407), Italy (187), and France (181). Most (2,004) of these medals were won during the Summer Olympics (825 gold, 632 silver, 547 bronze). With 154 medals (59 gold, 55 silver, 40 bronze), the United States ranked fourth in the Winter Olympics in 1996, behind Germany (96 gold medals), the Soviet Union (86), and Norway (83).

The United States added 13 medals to that total (6 gold, 3 silver, 4 bronze) at the 1998 Nagano Winter Olympics. Sports in which the United States has traditionally reaped more medals than any other nation have been track and field (298 gold medals from 1896 to 2000), basketball (16), boxing (47), diving (47), and swimming (191). On the other hand, American athletes have usually performed poorly in cycling, fencing, handball, judo, and winter sports.

American athletes James B. Connolly (triple jump, 1896) and Charles Jewtraw (500-meter speed skating, 1924) received the first gold medals ever attributed in the first Summer and Winter Olympics, respectively. Eddie Eagan is the only U.S. athlete to win gold medals in both the Summer and Winter Olympics (light heavyweight gold, 1920; four-man bobsled gold, 1928). Starting in 1983, the USOC created a Hall of Fame for the greatest American Olympians. Individual inductees from 1983 to 1992 are listed here, with the year and event in which the athletes won a gold medal in parentheses:

Boxing: Floyd Patterson (middleweight, 1952), Cassius Clay (later Muhammed Ali) (light heavyweight, 1960), Joe Frazier (heavyweight, 1964), George Foreman (super heavyweight, 1968), Ray Charles "Sugar Ray" Leonard (light welterweight, 1976)

Cycling: Connie Carpenter-Phinney (road race, 1984)

Diving: Sammy Lee (platform, 1948, 1952), Patricia McCormick (platform, springboard, 1952; platform, springboard, 1956), Maxine "Micki" King (springboard, 1972), Greg Louganis (platform, springboard, 1984; platform, springboard, 1988)

Figure skating: Dick Button (1948, 1952), Tenley Albright (1956), Peggy Fleming-Jenkins (1968), Dorothy Hamill (1976), Scott Hamilton (1984)

Gymnastics: Bart Conner (parallel bars, team event, 1984), Mary Lou Retton (all-around, 1984), Peter Vidmar (pommel horse, team event, 1984)

Rowing: John "Jack" B. Skelly Sr. (single and double sculls, 1920; double sculls, 1924)

Skiing: Phil Mahre (alpine skiing [slalom], 1984)

Speed skating: Eric Heiden (500-, 1,000-, 1,500-, 5,000- and 10,000-meter races, 1980)

Swimming: Duke Paoa Kahanamoku (3 gold medals, 1912, 1920), Johnny Weismuller (5 gold medals, 1924, 1928), Helene Madison (3 gold medals, 1932), Don Schollander (5 gold medals, 1964, 1968), Donna de Varona (2 gold medals, 1964), Debbie Meyer (three gold medals, 1968), Mark Spitz (9 gold medals, 1968, 1972, including 7 gold medals and seven world records in 1972), Shirley Babashoff (2 gold medals, 1972, 1976), John Naber (4 gold medals, 1976), Tracy Caulkins (3 gold medals, 1984)

Track and field: Alvin Kraenzlein (60-meter dash, 110- and 200-meter hurdles, long jump, 1900), Ray Ewry (eight gold medals in jumps, 1900, 1904, 1908), Mel Sheppard (800- and 1,500-meter races, 1,600-meter medley relay, 1908; 1,600-meter relay, 1912), Jim Thorpe (decathlon and pentathlon, 1912), Charley Paddock (100-meter dash and 400-meter relay, 1920), Frank Wykoff (400-meter relay, 1928, 1932, 1936), Mildred "Babe" Didrikson (javelin, 80-meter hurdles, 1932), James Cleveland "Jesse" Owens (100- and 200-meter dash, 400-meter relay, long jump, 1936), William Harrison Dillard (100-meter dash, 1948; 110-meter hurdles, 1952; 400-meter relay, 1948, 1952), Bob Mathias (decathlon, 1948, 1952), Malvin "Mal" Whitfield (800 meter, 1948, 1952; 1,600-meter relay, 1948), William Parry O'Brien (shot put, 1952, 1956), Bob Richards (pole vault, 1952, 1956), Lee Calhoun (110-meter hurdles, 1956, 1960), Milton Campbell (decathlon, 1956), Glenn Davis (400-meter hurdles, 1956, 1960; 1,600-meter relay, 1960), Bobby Joe Morrow (100- and 200-meter dash, 400-meter relay, 1956), Al Oerter (discus, 1956, 1960, 1964, 1968), Ralph Boston (long jump, 1960), Rafer Johnson (decathlon, 1960), Wilma Rudolph (100-meter, 200-meter, 400-meter relay, 1960), Billy Mills (10,000 meter, 1964), Wyomia Tyus (100-meter dash, 1964; 100-meter dash and 400-meter relay, 1968), Bob Beamon (long jump, 1968), Willie D. Davenport (110-meter hurdles, 1968), Lee Evans (400-meter dash and 1,600-meter relay, 1968), Richard "Dick" Fosbury (high jump, 1968), Bill Toomey (decathlon, 1968), Frank Shorter (marathon, 1972), Bruce Jenner (decathlon, 1976), Edwin Moses (400-meter hurdles, 1976, 1984), Fred Carlton "Carl" Lewis (9 gold medals: 100- and 200-meter dash, 400-meter relay, long jump, 1984; 100-meter dash, long jump, 1988; 400-meter relay, long jump, 1992; long jump, 1996)

Weightlifting: John Davis (super heavyweight, 1948, 1952), Tamio "Tommy" Kono (lightweight, 1952; light heavyweight, 1956)

Wrestling: Dan Gable (lightweight, 1972)

Track and field and swimming were again the big U.S. medal earners at the 2000 Sydney Summer Olympics. In track and field, Maurice Greene won two gold medals (100-meter dash, 400-meter relay). Michael Johnson, after winning the 200- and 400-meter dash in Atlanta in 1996, won two more gold medals (400-meter dash, 1,600-meter relay). Marion Jones won five medals, three of them gold (100- and 200-meter dash, 1,600-meter relay). In the swimming events, Lenny Krayzelburg won three gold medals (100- and 200-meter backstroke, 400-meter medley relay) and the women's team captured three gold medals in relays (400-meter medley, 400-meter freestyle, 800-meter freestyle). The men's basketball team, even though less dominating than its predecessors, won its third straight gold medal by defeating France (85–75), while the women's team earned its second straight gold medal when it defeated Australia (76–54). In super heavyweight Greco-Roman wrestling, Rulon Gardner beat heavily favored Alexandre Kareline of Russia.

The Political and Economic Importance of the Games

The 1896 Athens Olympic Games attracted only 245 athletes (including 13 Americans) from fourteen countries competing for nine titles. The first games ever held on American soil, the 1904 St. Louis Summer Olympics, were ancillary to the Louisiana Purchase Exhibition. Only thirteen countries sent athletes to the then-remote location (Olympics founder Coubertin did not even attend), and American athletes, the only participants to many competitions, won 80 percent of the gold medals. Such a lopsided result was never repeated. More than one million tickets were sold for the 1932 Los Angeles Summer Olympics, and ten million for the 1996 Olympics in Atlanta, where ten thousand athletes from 197 countries shared the 271 gold medals awarded in twenty-six different sports ranging from archery to table tennis and badminton. The growth of the games paralleled that of the American public's interest in them. Many sports like track and field, amateur skating, and gymnastics attract television audiences much larger than those sports usually garner in non-Olympic events. The Olympic Games are the most closely followed international sports competition in the United States. They also appeal to sections of the American population, such as women, who have a limited interest in other sports events.

Given the Olympics' popularity among American consumers, the economic value of the games reached great heights in the late twentieth century. The commercial success of the 1984 Los Angeles Summer Olympics, which netted a profit of $223 million with no government help, is widely credited for ushering in the era of gigantic games dominated by corporate and television sponsorship. (*Time* magazine chose Los Angeles organizing committee president Peter Ueberroth for its Man of the Year award.) Even when the Olympics are held outside the United States, American companies provide almost half of the budget. NBC television paid $450 million for television rights (half of the $900 million worldwide rights) to broadcast the 1996 Olympics. Seven of the ten worldwide corporate sponsors for the 2002 and 2004 games are American: Coca Cola, John Hancock, Kodak, McDonald's, Time-Sports Illustrated, Visa, and Xerox. The reputation of the IOC and of the U.S. Olympic movement were tarnished when it was learned that the Salt Lake City bid committee had awarded lavish gifts to IOC members to obtain the Winter Olympics of 2002.

The Olympic Games were not isolated from outside political events; world wars forced the cancellation of the 1916, 1940, and 1944 games. African American sprinter Jesse Owens's four track-and-field medals in the 1936 Berlin games undermined the Nazis' claim to racial Aryan superiority. (Ironically, segregation was still the rule in Owens's home state of Alabama, where he had picked cotton as a child.) At the 1968 Mexico games, Tommie Smith and John Carlos won the gold and bronze medals for the 200-meter dash and then raised their gloved fists in a "black power" salute while the U.S. national anthem was being played during the awards ceremony. Both Smith and Carlos were banned from the U.S. team and expelled from the Olympic village, but their protest remains as one of the most vivid images in civil rights and Olympic history.

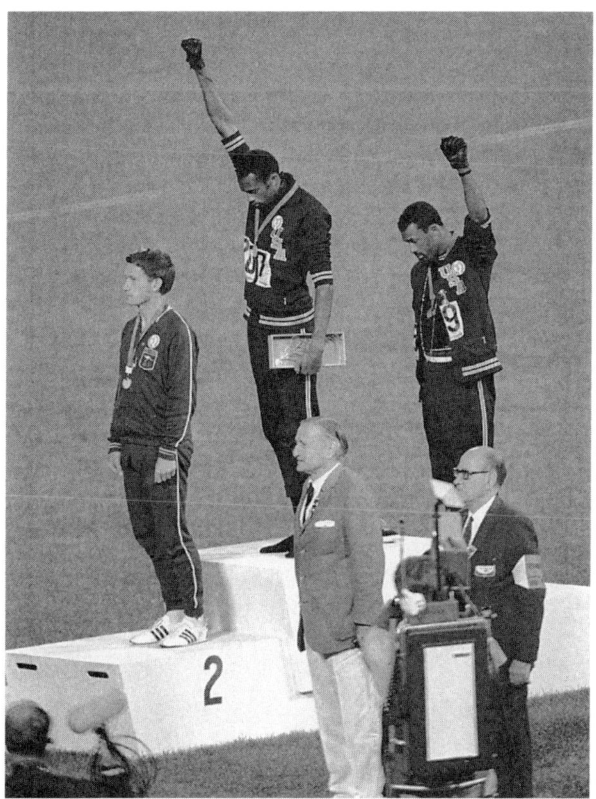

Olympic Protest. Tommie Smith (*center*) and John Carlos (*right*) extend their fists in a "black power" salute (the silver medalist is Peter Norman, a white Australian) during the playing of "The Star-Spangled Banner" at the 1968 games. AP/ Wide World Photos

The political use of Olympic results reached a climax during the Cold War as both the United States and the Soviet Union tried to prove their superiority in stadiums as well as in more conventional venues. In order to protest the December 1979 Soviet invasion of Afghanistan, President Jimmy Carter decided that his country's athletes would boycott the 1980 Moscow Summer Olympics unless the Soviets withdrew by February 1980. The Soviets refused (they remained in Afghanistan until 1988), and U.S. athletes who tried nevertheless to attend the games were threatened with loss of citizenship. At Carter's urging, many U.S. allies refused to go to the Moscow games, which only eighty nations attended, twelve less than in Montreal (1976), and forty-one less than in Munich (1972).

The 1980 Lake Placid Winter Olympics saw a politically charged final in the men's ice hockey event, when the American team won a 4–3 upset victory over the heavily favored Soviets. (Soviet teams had won the previous four gold medals in the discipline.) Four years later, the Soviet Union and fourteen other Eastern bloc countries (all except Rumania) boycotted the 1984 Los Angeles Summer Olympics. In the absence of such sports powerhouses as the Soviet Union and East Germany, the United States won a total of 174 medals (83 gold), more than its three closest rivals combined (West Germany, Romania, and Canada, which won a total of 156 medals, 47 of them gold).

The United States was not directly affected by the capture and death of eleven Israeli athletes during the 1972 Munich games, but another terrorist attack marred the Atlanta Summer Olympics twenty-four years later. On 27 July 1996, a bomb exploded in the Centennial Olympic Park, killing one person on the spot and injuring 111.

BIBLIOGRAPHY

Greenspan, Bud. *100 Greatest Moments in Olympic History.* Los Angeles: General Publishing Group, 1995.

Guttmann, Allen. *The Olympics: A History of the Modern Games.* Urbana: University of Illinois Press, 1992.

Wallechinsky, David. *The Complete Book of the Olympics.* Woodstock, N.Y.: Overlook Press, 2000.

Young, David C. *The Modern Olympics: A Struggle for Revival.* Baltimore: Johns Hopkins University Press, 1996.

Philippe R. Girard

See also **Sports.**

OMNIBUS BILL, an attempt at a comprehensive adjustment of the territorial question reported on 8 May 1850 by the special Senate Committee of Thirteen. On 17 June the senators made popular sovereignty the criterion for Utah's statehood bid. President Zachary Taylor and radicals on both sides prevented the bill's adoption. On 31 July, the sections relating to California, New Mexico, and Texas were stricken, and on the following day the Senate adopted the Utah bill. Later legislation included substantially the ground of the originally proposed compromise.

BIBLIOGRAPHY

Holt, Michael F. *The Political Crisis of the 1850s.* New York: Wiley, 1978.

Arthur C. Cole / A. R.

See also **Compromise of 1850; Nashville Convention; Popular Sovereignty; Slavery; States' Rights.**

OÑATE EXPLORATIONS AND SETTLEMENTS. In 1598, the Spanish explorer Juan de Oñate left Chihuahua, Mexico, with an expeditionary force of almost five hundred soldiers and colonists to conquer and colonize a new Mexico along the Rio Grande. In April 1598, near present-day El Paso, Texas, Oñate declared dominion over the land and its inhabitants in the name of King Philip II of Spain before continuing north along the Rio Grande to the pueblo of Ohke. There, north of modern-day Santa Fe, New Mexico, he established a capital and renamed the town San Juan. Shortly thereafter, however, he moved the capital to nearby Yúngé, displaced its Pueblo residents, and renamed it San Gabriel.

After establishing the colony, Oñate explored the surrounding lands and subjugated the Pueblo people. In September 1598, he sent an expedition into eastern New Mexico via the Canadian River to hunt buffalo. In October, Oñate explored the pueblos to the southeast and west of San Gabriel. In June 1601, he led an expedition east along the Pecos, Canadian, and Arkansas Rivers to the Quivira settlement in modern-day Kansas. In 1604, after two failed attempts, Oñate discovered a route to the Pacific via the Gila and Colorado Rivers. Although not the first Spaniard to explore these areas, Oñate established the first Spanish settlement in the Southwest. At the urging of the king, in 1608 Oñate resigned his post as governor of the new territory.

BIBLIOGRAPHY

Hammond, George P., and Agapito Rey. *Don Juan de Oñate: Colonizer of New Mexico, 1595–1628.* Albuquerque: University of New Mexico Press, 1953.

Simmons, Marc. *The Last Conquistador: Juan de Oñate and the Settling of the Far Southwest.* Norman: University of Oklahoma Press, 1991.

Spicer, Edward Holland. *Cycles of Conquest.* Tucson: University of Arizona Press, 1962.

Weber, David J. *The Spanish Frontier in North America.* New Haven, Conn.: Yale University Press, 1992.

Jennifer L. Bertolet

See also **Conquistadores; Exploration of America, Early; Explorations and Expeditions: Spanish.**

ONEIDA COLONY, established in 1848 between Syracuse and Utica, in NEW YORK STATE, was America's most radical experiment in social and religious thinking. From literal concepts of perfectionism and Bible communism, the colony advanced into new forms of social relationships: economic communism, the rejection of monogamy for complex marriage, the practice of an elementary form of birth control (*coitus reservatus*), and the eugenic breeding of stirpicultural children. John Humphrey Noyes, leader of the group, was a capable and shrewd Yankee whose sincere primitive Christianity expressed itself in radically modern terms. His fellow workers, having experienced profound religious conversions, followed him

John Humphrey Noyes. The founder and leader (until he left for Canada in 1879) of the utopian Oneida Colony in upstate New York. ARCHIVE PHOTOS, INC.

into a communal life that rejected the evils of competitive economics while it preserved the methods of modern industry, believing that socialism is ahead of and not behind society.

From the inception of the colony the property grew to about 600 acres of well-cultivated land, with shoe, tailoring, and machine shops, the latter producing commercially successful traps and flatware among other items; canning and silk factories; and great central buildings and houses for employees. The group also formed a branch colony in Wallingford, Connecticut. Assets had reached more than $550,000 when communism was dropped. Health was above the average, women held a high place, children were excellently trained, work was fair and changeable, and entertainment was constant.

In 1879, forced by social pressure from without and the dissatisfaction of the young within, monogamy was adopted, and within a year communism was replaced by joint-stock ownership. In its new form, Oneida continued its commercial success, but as a conventional company. During the twentieth century, the Oneida Company was noted for its production of fine silver and stainless steel flatware.

BIBLIOGRAPHY

DeMaria, Richard. *Communal Love at Oneida: A Perfectionist Vision of Authority, Property, and Sexual Order.* New York: E. Mellen Press, 1978.

Klaw, Spencer. *Without Sin: The Life and Death of the Oneida Community.* New York: Allen Lane, 1993.

Thomas, Robert D. *The Man Who Would be Perfect: John Humphrey Noyes and the Utopian Impulse.* Philadelphia: University of Pennsylvania Press, 1977.

Allan Macdonald / A. R.

See also **Birth Control Movement; Family; Polygamy; Radicals and Radicalism; Sexuality; Socialist Movement; Utopian Communities.**

ONIONS, apparently native to Asia, were unknown to the American Indians. Early colonists first brought them to America. Wethersfield, Connecticut, soon became a noted onion-growing center. Records show that Wethersfield was shipping onions as early as 1710. A century later it was sending out a million bunches annually. Nonetheless, as onion culture spread to all parts of the country, Wethersfield lost its preeminence. Soon after 1900 extensive production of Bermuda onions began in Texas, California, and Louisiana. By 2002 Idaho, Oregon, Washington, and California had come to lead the United States in onion production. In that year the American onion crop was worth between $3 billion and $4 billion retail.

BIBLIOGRAPHY

Benes, Peter. *Two Towns, Concord and Wethersfield: A Comparative Exhibition of Regional Culture, 1635–1850.* Concord, Mass.: Concord Antiquarian Museum, 1982.

Main, Jackson Turner. *Society and Economy in Colonial Connecticut.* Princeton, N.J.: Princeton University Press, 1985.

Alvin F. Harlow / A. E.

See also **Agriculture; Food and Cuisines.**

ONONDAGA, a reservation of 7,300 acres just south of Syracuse, New York, is both the geographic and the political center of the Iroquois Confederacy in New York State. The community is also the religious center of the *Gaiwiio*, the traditional religion of the IROQUOIS founded in 1799–1800 by Handsome Lake, the Seneca prophet, who is buried there.

Originally centered in and around Onondaga Lake, Onondaga before the American Revolution was 12 million acres, extending north to Lake Ontario and south to the Susquehanna River. Ten of the Onondaga villages were destroyed by an American army in 1779. The reservation was established in 1788 by the Onondaga–New York State Treaty of Fort Schuyler, an accord that set aside a tract of one hundred square miles. In a series of state treaties from 1793 to 1822, all negotiated in violation of federal law, Onondaga was reduced in size.

The Onondagas, "fire keepers" and "wampum keepers" of the Iroquois Confederacy, convene Grand Councils on the reservation. Their fourteen chiefs include the *Tadodaho* or spiritual leader who presides at the Grand Councils. During the second half of the twentieth century, the reservation became the center of Iroquois political activism. At the beginning of the twenty-first century, approximately 1,600 enrolled Onondagas lived in New York State.

BIBLIOGRAPHY

Blau, Harold, Jack Campisi, and Elisabeth Tooker. "Onondaga." *Handbook of North American Indians.* Edited by William C. Sturtevant et al. Volume 15: *Northeast,* edited by Bruce G. Trigger. Washington. D.C.: Smithsonian Institution, 1978.

Hauptman, Laurence M. *Conspiracy of Interests: Iroquois Dispossession and the Rise of New York State.* Syracuse, N.Y.: Syracuse University Press, 1986.

———. *The Iroquois Struggle for Survival.* Syracuse, N.Y.: Syracuse University Press, 1986.

———. *Formulating American Indian Policy in New York State, 1970–1986.* Albany: State University of New York Press, 1988.

———. *The Iroquois and the New Deal.* Syracuse, N.Y.: Syracuse University Press, 1999.

Vecsey, Christopher, and William A. Starna, eds. *Iroquois Land Claims.* Syracuse, N.Y.: Syracuse University Press, 1988.

Laurence M. Hauptman

OPEN DOOR POLICY was a foreign policy initiative enunciated formally by Secretary of State John Hay in his Open Door notes of 1899 and 1900. The first note was issued on 6 September 1899 to Great Britain, Germany, and Russia, with notes following to Japan, France, and Italy. The initial note requested that the various governments ensure that equal commercial opportunity be allowed and that no nation with a sphere of influence use that power to benefit its own nationals. Although Hay's initial note did not receive unqualified and complete support, the secretary of state followed it up with a second note on 20 March 1900 that asserted that all nations had assented. With these statements, the United States formally declared its intentions to support American commercial interests in China.

The American idea of the open door was constituted by three interrelated doctrines: equality of commercial opportunity, territorial integrity, and administrative integrity. The Open Door policy emerged from two major cycles of American expansionist history. The first, a maritime cycle, gained impetus from the new commercial thrust of the mid-nineteenth century and blended into the new cycle of industrial and financial capitalism that emerged toward the end of the century and continued into the 1930s. Thereafter, its vitality ebbed away as political and economic forces posed a new power structure and national reorganization in the Far East.

First Cycle of Expansionism

The first cycle of open door activity developed through the mid-nineteenth-century interaction of the expansion of American continental and maritime frontiers. The construction of the transcontinental railroads gave rise to the idea of an American transportation bridge to China. The powers behind the lush China trade, headquartered in the mid-Atlantic and New England coastal cities, established commercial positions on the north Pacific Coast and in Hawaii in order to transfer furs and sandalwood as items in trade with the Chinese. The resulting expansion of maritime commerce was coordinated with a variety of commercial interests, including American investment in whaling; the great interest in the exploration of the Pacific Ocean and historic concern for the development of a short route from the Atlantic to the Pacific across Central America; a growing American diplomatic, naval, and missionary focus on eastern Asia; the opening of China to American trade on the heels of the British victory in the Anglo-Chinese War of 1839–1842 via the Cushing Treaty of 1844; and the push into the Pacific led by Secretary of State William H. Seward that culminated in the purchase of Alaska in 1867 and the Burlingame Treaty of 1868.

Throughout this period, the United States adapted British commercial policy to its own ends by supporting the notion of free and open competition for trade in international markets, while denouncing British colonial acquisitions and preferential trade positions. The European subjection of China by force and the imposition of the resulting treaty system gave American maritime interests an opportunity to flourish without a parallel colonial responsibility or imperial illusion. The expansionist thrust of this cycle of mercantile exchange and trade reached its peak with the onset of the Spanish-American War and the great debate over the annexation of Hawaii and the Philippines during the pivotal year of President William McKinley's administration, 1898.

Second Cycle of Expansionism

The second cycle of expansionist development sprang from the advent of industrial capitalism and the requirements of commercial American agriculture for export markets, bringing together a peculiarly complex mixture of farm and factory interests that had traditionally clashed over domestic economy policy and legislation. A mutually advantageous worldview of political economy was welded as both interests prepared to move into and expand the China market. As the increasing commercialization of American agriculture led to a need for greater outlets for American grain and cotton manufactured goods, China also was becoming a potential consumer of American heavy-industry products, including railroad equipment, and of oil products. At the same time, outlets were needed for the investment of growing American fortunes, and it was thought that the modernization of China through expansion of communication and transportation would in turn increase the demand for products of American economic growth.

Critics of Hay's policy assert that the open door formula "was already an old and hackneyed one at the turn of the century," that its "principles were not clear and precise," and that it could not "usefully be made the basis of a foreign policy." It may well be that American announcements on behalf of China's territorial integrity did create an erroneous "impression of a community of outlook among nations which did not really exist." But it was a foreign policy expressive of national ambition and protective of American interests, actual and potential. The policy was stimulated by international rivalry at the end of the nineteenth century for control of ports, territories, spheres of influence, and economic advantage at the expense of a weak China. It was manipulated through the influence of British nationals in the Imperial Maritime Customs Service (established by the foreign treaty system) who were intent on protecting their vested administrative interests even at the expense of their own country's position in China. And the policy was a time-honored tactic that attempted to strengthen the American position in China by cloaking its claims in the dress of international morality on behalf of China's territorial and political independence while simultaneously protecting the interests of the powers in maintaining the trade and political positions already acquired there. Dealing as Hay did from American bias in developing a position of power without admitting the power of an already existing ambition in China, the tactic of the open door served well to initiate a chain of open door claims that steadily expanded up to World War I and beyond.

Although Hay's Open Door notes are conventionally interpreted as an attempt to bluff the European and Japanese powers into accepting the American position in China, the notes actually announced the decision of the United States to press its interests on its own behalf.

From that time forward the United States involved itself in the international rivalries in Manchuria as well as in China proper. At first the United States was anti-Russian in Manchuria. But then, determined to extend American railroad, mining, and commercial privileges there, the United States became anti-Japanese after the Russo-Japanese War of 1905, although it was not able to make a definitive commitment of national resources and energy. Influenced by the caution of President Theodore Roosevelt, in the Taft-Katsura Agreement of 1905 and the Root-Takahira Agreement of 1908, the United States recognized Japan's growing power in eastern Asia in return for stated open door principles and respect for American territorial legitimacy in the Far East. In 1909 and 1913, during the administration of President William Howard Taft, the United States attempted to move into Manchuria and China proper via open door proposals on behalf of American railroad and banking investment interests and in so doing made overtures of cooperation with the European powers as well as Russia and Japan. This was evident in the creation of the American Banking Group, which joined an international consortium to direct foreign investments in China. During President Woodrow Wilson's administrations, the United States veered from side to side. It forced the withdrawal of the American Banking Group from the consortium in 1913, attempted to protect its stake in China by opposing Japan's Twenty-One Demands on China in 1915, and then attempted to appease Japan's ambitions in Manchuria by recognizing the Japanese stake there in the Lansing-Ishii Agreement of 1917.

Five years later, at the Washington Armament Conference negotiations, the open door outlook was embedded in the details of the Nine-Power Treaty, which called for territorial and administrative integrity of China and equality of trade opportunity without special privileges for any nation. Additional efforts that emerged from the conference to ensure the Open Door policy of territorial and administrative integrity included plans for the abolition of extraterritoriality; the creation of a new tariff system, the removal of foreign troops and postal services, and the integrity of the railway system.

During the period 1929–1933, Manchuria came to the forefront of American open door concerns with the invocation of the Kellogg-Briand Pact of 1928 against Japan's use of force in Manchuria. By 1931, Secretary of State Henry L. Stimson had established the continuity of American policy by linking the principles of the Kellogg-Briand Pact with those expressed in the Nine-Power Treaty of 1922. A year later, in 1932, Stimson made history by articulating his nonrecognition doctrine regarding Japan's conquest of Manchuria and the establishment of the puppet state of Manchukuo.

From that point onward, throughout the 1930s and on to World War II, the United States, led by Secretary of State Cordell Hull, maintained growing opposition to Japan's aggrandizement in the sphere of China and the enlargement of Japan's ambitions throughout Southeast Asia. The United States continued to be influenced by the concepts that the Open Door notes outlined and expanded its use of the doctrine beyond China.

BIBLIOGRAPHY

Cohen, Warren I. *America's Response to China: A History of Sino-American Relations.* 3d ed. New York: Columbia University Press, 1990. The original edition was published in 1971.

Fairbank, John K. *The United States and China.* 4th ed. Cambridge, Mass.: Harvard University Press, 1983. The original edition was published in 1948.

Israel, Jerry. *Progressivism and the Open Door: America and China, 1905–1921.* Pittsburgh, Pa.: University of Pittsburgh Press, 1971.

Kennan, George. *American Diplomacy 1900–1950.* Exp. edition. Chicago: University of Chicago Press, 1984. The original edition was published in 1951.

Williams, William A. *The Shaping of American Diplomacy.* 2d ed. Chicago: Rand McNally, 1970.

David R. Buck

See also **China, Relations with; China Trade.**

OPEN-MARKET OPERATIONS are the purchase and sale of government securities and other assets by central banks. Along with reserve requirements, discount-window operations, and moral suasion, they constitute the instruments of monetary policy. When the U.S. central bank—the Federal Reserve System—was established in 1913, discount-window operations were considered the principal instrument of monetary policy. Open-market operations were simply used by the twelve regional banks in the Federal Reserve System to acquire interest-earning assets. In the mid-1920s, frustrated with competing against each other to purchase securities, the regional banks established the Open-Market Investment Committee (OIC), under the control of the Federal Reserve Bank of New York (FRBNY), to coordinate their open-market operations. The OIC then became involved in futile attempts to salvage the gold standard, which was abandoned in September 1931.

Both the efforts to salvage the gold standard and a tendency to subordinate open-market operations to the interests of the large banks prompted the OIC to conduct contractionary open-market operations in the midst of the Great Depression. In response to the public outrage that ensued, the government changed the Federal Reserve's structure, placing control of open-market operations in the Federal Open Market Committee (FOMC). The FRBNY was still represented on the FOMC, but its influence was counterbalanced by the seven members of the Federal Reserve Board in Washington, D.C., particularly its chair, who dominates decisions regarding the use of open-market operations.

In the 1940s the FOMC conducted open-market operations to maintain a fixed interest-rate structure, ranging from 3/8 percent on Treasury bills to 2.5 percent on government bonds. The March 1951 Treasury–Federal Reserve Accord freed the FOMC to use open-market operations to stabilize the economy on a noninflationary growth path. Ample evidence suggests the FOMC has not pursued this goal in good faith. But even if it did, it remains questionable that such stabilization can be achieved by means of open-market operations.

In the late 1950s the FOMC implemented a "bills only" policy (that is, it only purchased and sold Treasury bills). Except for Operation Twist in the early 1960s, when the FOMC bought government bonds to offset its sales of Treasury bills, this policy has remained in effect. During the 1960s the FOMC used open-market operations to target the level of the federal funds rate (FFR). In February 1970 it began to target the rate of growth of monetary aggregates, accomplished by setting target ranges for the FFR. So long as the FFR remained in the targeted range, the FOMC tried to target a particular rate of growth of monetary aggregates.

In the 1970s the target ranges for the FFR were narrow (for example, 0.5 percent). But in October 1979 the FOMC started to set such broad ranges for the FFR that it effectively abandoned efforts to control the FFR in favor of concentrating on control of the rate of growth of monetary aggregates, especially M_2 (a monetary aggregate, composed of currency in circulation, demand deposits, and large time deposits). The result was wild fluctuations not only in interest rates but also in the rate of growth of the monetary aggregates. In the late 1980s the FOMC acknowledged the failure of its efforts to target the rate of growth of monetary aggregates and returned to using open-market operations to target specific levels of the FFR.

BIBLIOGRAPHY

D'Arista, Jane W. *Federal Reserve Structure and the Development of Monetary Policy, 1915–1935.* Washington, D.C.: Government Printing Office, 1971.

Dickens, Edwin. "U.S. Monetary Policy in the 1950s: A Radical Political Economic Approach." *Review of Radical Political Economics* 27, no. 4 (1995): 83–111.

———. "Bank Influence and the Failure of U.S. Monetary Policy during the 1953–1954 Recession." *International Review of Applied Economics* 12, no. 2, (1998): 221–233.

Edwin Dickens

See also **Federal Reserve System.**

OPERA performance in America has predominantly consisted of works imported from Europe. The earliest operas heard were English ballad operas brought over from London in the 1730s. French opera flourished in New Orleans from the 1790s through the nineteenth century. Italian opera was more popular in the north, first heard in English adaptations and then introduced in the original language in 1825. After the 1850s, German opera, particularly that of Richard Wagner, became more prevalent until it dominated the repertory toward the turn of the century. Twentieth-century audiences enjoyed a wide variety of foreign works in many languages as well as a growing number of American operas, particularly after the 1960s.

Early opera performances were typically produced by touring companies in temporary quarters until such institutions as the Metropolitan Opera (established 1883) were founded. The twentieth century saw the development of organizations including the San Francisco Opera (1923), the New York City Opera (1944), the Lyric Opera of Chicago (1954), and dozens of other regional companies, as well as summer festivals and opera workshops. Radio broadcasts since 1921 and television brought opera to a growing audience.

Tabor Grand Opera House. A 1908 photograph by Louis Charles McClure of Denver's opulent opera house, built by the silver millionaire Horace A. W. Tabor in 1881 and, after serving many other uses, demolished in 1964. LIBRARY OF CONGRESS

Opera composed by Americans prior to the twentieth century adhered to the style of imported works popular at the time, as illustrated by Andrew Barton's ballad opera, *The Disappointment* (1767), or the first grand opera, William Henry Fry's *Leonora* (1845), composed in the style of Vincenzo Bellini or Gaetano Donizetti. A number of operas acquired an American identity through plot or setting and often include indigenous musical elements, such as jazz and spirituals in George Gershwin's *Porgy and Bess* (1935) or Appalachian folk style in Carlisle Floyd's *Susannah* (1956). Virgil Thomson's *Four Saints in Three Acts* (1934) exhibited a new musical style modeling the inflections of American speech. Many other composers did not attempt to develop a dramatic or musical style identifiable as "American" but pursued a variety of individual, even eclectic, approaches to opera on a wide variety of subjects.

BIBLIOGRAPHY

Dizikes, John. *Opera in America: A Cultural History.* New Haven, Conn.: Yale University Press, 1993.

Kirk, Elise K. *American Opera.* Urbana: University of Illinois Press, 2001.

Sadie, Stanley, ed. *The New Grove Dictionary of Opera.* 4 vols. New York: Grove's Dictionaries of Music, 1992.

Sadie, Stanley, and H. Wiley Hitchcock, eds. *The New Grove Dictionary of American Music.* 4 vols. New York: Grove's Dictionaries of Music, 1986.

Martina B. Bishopp

See also **Music: Classical.**

OPERATION DIXIE. In early July 1944, the U.S. Army Observer Group (renamed the Yenan Observer Group in July 1945) left Chongqing (Chungking), the temporary capital of Nationalist China, to journey to Yan'an (Yenan), the headquarters of the Chinese communist movement, seeking to use communist guerrillas in the war against Japan. The operation was dubbed the Dixie Mission because it was entering "rebel territory." Led by Colonel David D. Barrett, the group's number fluctuated between one and two dozen junior military observers, technicians, embassy officials, and operators of the Office of Strategic Services. Efforts proved abortive, for by January 1945 communist and American hostilities had grown, and U.S. involvement on behalf of Chiang Kai-shek had deepened.

BIBLIOGRAPHY

Barrett, David D. *Dixie Mission: The United States Army Observer Group in Yenan, 1944.* Berkeley: Center for Chinese Studies, University of California, 1970.

Carter, Carolle J. "Mission to Yenan: The OSS and the Dixie Mission." In *The Secrets War: The Office of Strategic Services in World War II.* Edited by George C. Chalou. Washington, D.C.: National Archives and Records Administration, 1992.

Justus D. Doenecke

See also **China, Relations with; China, U.S. Armed Forces in; World War II.**

OPERATION RESCUE, founded in 1986, became known as one of the most militant groups opposing a woman's right to abortion as established in the 1973 Supreme Court case ROE V. WADE. Like other antiabortion groups, Operation Rescue asserted that life begins at conception, and therefore, abortion is murder of a living being. The founder, Randall Terry, became a national icon in 1988 when he organized 1,200 demonstrators to "rescue" babies by blocking access to abortion clinics in Atlanta, Georgia, during the Democratic National Convention. Insisting that the PRO-LIFE MOVEMENT needed to become more active in halting abortions, Terry also inspired violent crimes by antiabortionists. Though Operation Rescue was not directly linked to major crimes, in the early 1990s, its radicalization of the movement led to the murders of doctors who performed abortions in Florida, Kansas, and Massachusetts. Another antiabortion organization, the National Right to Life Committee, disavowed use of direct-action tactics, underscoring that the vast majority of people opposing abortion did not subscribe to Operation Rescue's methods.

By the 1990s, Operation Rescue had become associated with fundamentalist Christian religiosity and conservative social values. The group had branches across the country. In 1999, the national umbrella organization changed its name to Operation Save America and was led by Reverend Philip "Flip" Benham after 1994. Also in 1994, Congress passed the Freedom of Access to Clinic

Entrances Act, which protects people offering or seeking reproductive health service from violence, threats, or intimidation. The act was used against Operation Rescue in numerous federal civil lawsuits that the organization continued to fight in the early 2000s.

BIBLIOGRAPHY

Craig, Barbara Hinkson, and David M. O'Brien. *Abortion and American Politics.* Chatham, N.J.: Chatham House Publishers, 1993.

Faux, Marian. *Crusaders: Voices from the Abortion Front.* New York: Carol Publishing Group, 1990.

Tatalovich, Raymond. *The Politics of Abortion in the United States and Canada.* Armonk, N.Y.: M. E. Sharpe, 1997.

Eric S. Yellin

See also **Abortion.**

OPTIONS EXCHANGES. An options exchange is an organized securities exchange that provides a location and framework for trading standardized option contracts. It handles its trades much as a stock exchange handles trading in stocks and bonds. Until 1973, with the opening of the Chicago Board Options Exchange (CBOE), all options were traded through a limited number of specialized firms. Today, among the options exchanges in the United States are the American Stock Exchange, CBOE, the Chicago Board of Trade, the Chicago Mercantile Exchange, Mid-America Commodity Exchange, the Pacific Exchange, the Philadelphia Stock Exchange, and the International Securities Exchange.

BIBLIOGRAPHY

Goodman, Jordan E. *Everyone's Money Book.* 3d ed. Chicago: Dearborn Financial Publishing, 1998.

Kaufman, Perry. *Trading Systems and Methods.* 3d ed. New York: Wiley, 1998.

Meg Greene Malvasi

ORATORY. Although Indian orators like Pontiac and Red Jacket had stirred their people to action, eloquence among colonists lay dormant until the Revolution aroused Samuel Adams, James Otis, and Patrick Henry. In Henry's great speeches on the "Parson's Cause" (1763), on the Stamp Act (1765), and in the "Liberty or Death" speech (1775), he left his mark upon U.S. history. John Randolph's invective reigned in Congress until Henry Clay, John Calhoun, and Daniel Webster emerged in times of crisis. Clay was remarkable for frequent and fluent remarks; Calhoun for subject mastery and logical presentation; Webster for magnificent voice, memory, and presence. In the middle period, eminent speakers included John Quincy Adams, Thomas Hart Benton, Thomas Corwin, Seargent Smith Prentiss, Robert Toombs, and William Yancey. Stephen A. Douglas's sonorous voice and superb confidence matched Abraham Lincoln's admirable directness in their debates (1858), the apogee of this style of political campaigning. Lincoln's inaugural addresses are the best of their kind.

Except for Charles Sumner, Albert J. Beveridge, and the elder Robert La Follette, the greatest orators since the Civil War have not been in Congress. Wendell Phillips achieved popular success in unpopular causes. George W. Curtis fought for civic reform; Robert G. Ingersoll defended agnosticism; and Henry W. Grady championed the "New South" (1886). The greatest pulpit orators have been Henry Ward Beecher, Phillips Brooks, and Harry Emerson Fosdick. Foremost among legal advocates have been William Pinkney, Rufus Choate, and Clarence Darrow. The Populist orators anticipated William Jennings Bryan, Theodore Roosevelt, and Woodrow Wilson as molders of public opinion, effective phrasemakers, and persuasive moralists. Franklin D. Roosevelt, whose clarity of expression suffused his first inaugural address (1933) and "fireside chats," remained unrivaled among U.S. public figures during his lifetime. Since World War II, the emphasis on oratory has declined, although a few notable orators, such as civil rights leader Martin Luther King Jr., have appeared. King's speech "I Have a Dream" (1963) caused many Americans to give their support to him and to his movement.

BIBLIOGRAPHY

Gustafson, Sandra M. *Eloquence Is Power.* Chapel Hill: University of North Carolina Press, 2000.

Mann, Barbara Alice, ed. *Native American Speakers of the Eastern Woodlands.* Westport, Conn.: Greenwood Press, 2001.

Warren, James Perrin. *Culture of Eloquence.* University Park: Pennsylvania State University Press, 1999.

Harvey L. Carter / c. w.

See also **Civil Rights Movement; Cross of Gold Speech; "Give Me Liberty or Give Me Death!"; Indian Oratory; Lincoln-Douglas Debates; March on Washington; Parson's Cause; South, the: The New South; Stamp Act; Webster-Hayne Debate.**

ORDER OF AMERICAN KNIGHTS. *See* **Knights of the Golden Circle.**

ORDINANCES OF 1784, 1785, AND 1787. In a series of ordinances enacted between 1784 and 1787, the Confederation Congress established the framework for the privatization of the national domain and for the expansion of the union. In compliance with conditions set forth in land cessions of the regions north and west of the Ohio River by Virginia (1 March 1784) and other states, Congress determined that public lands would be sold for the benefit of the United States as a whole and that settlements would eventually be formed into new states.

The first ordinance for territorial government, approved by Congress on 23 April 1784, invited settlers to form temporary governments that would adopt the "constitution and laws" of one of the existing states. When the new "state" gained a population of twenty thousand free inhabitants, it would be entitled to draft its own constitution and claim admission to the union "on an equal footing with the . . . original states." The 1784 ordinance stipulated the boundaries of sixteen new states, including ten north of the Ohio River that were given fanciful names by the committee chair, Thomas Jefferson. But none of its provisions could be implemented until public land sales opened the way for legal settlement.

The outlines of congressional land policy were sketched in a companion ordinance proposed to Congress on 30 April 1784 by Jefferson and Hugh Williamson of North Carolina. Under the proposed scheme, prior to settlement, the national domain would be surveyed and divided into the now familiar grid system. The ordinance, eventually adopted by Congress on 20 May1785, incorporated the prior survey principle, dividing the national domain into townships of six square miles each. Beginning with seven ranges running north from the Ohio River to Lake Erie; when the first surveys were completed, the townships would be sold in fractional units at a dollar per acre. Sluggish land sales made Congress receptive to the overtures of land companies, most notably the Ohio Company, which purchased 1.5 million acres of land west of the seven ranges at the much-reduced price of a million dollars in depreciated continental certificates. Despite these and future modifications, Congress successfully established its authority over land distribution, extending the survey system throughout the national domain.

Implementation of congressional land policy precipitated changes in territorial government and led to the formation of new states. The new land system and a military presence capable of driving off illegal squatters and defending settlements against the Ohio Indians (who resisted encroachments on their ancestral lands) called for a much stronger and more elaborate "temporary" government. The greatest pressure to revise the 1784 ordinance came from prospective settlers themselves. Because their first concerns were with law and order and secure land titles, they pressed Congress to set up a court system under its own authority before providing for territorial self-government. It was no coincidence that the Ohio Company purchase was completed on 14 July 1787, the day after the Northwest Ordinance was enacted.

On 13 July 1786, Congress made the key move in abandoning the 1784 ordinance by adopting the report of a new committee on western government headed by James Monroe of Virginia. Monroe urged Congress to create a "colonial" system for the Northwest and, based on his own observations of the region's potential, concluded that it should ultimately be divided into "not more than five nor less than three" new states. On 13 July 1787, these principles were incorporated into the "Northwest Ordinance" to regulate the territorial government.

In the first stage of territorial government prescribed by the new ordinance, Congress would govern through the appointment of a governor, a secretary, and three judges. The governor appointed all subordinate civil officers, as "he shall find necessary for the preservation of peace and good order." Settlers would gain legislative representation in the second stage, once there were five thousand free adult males in the territory, and admission to the union was guaranteed when "any of the said States shall have sixty thousand free inhabitants." The ordinance also provided for the inheritance of estates as well as "articles of compact," guaranteeing settlers' legal rights and civil liberties and securing the status of the new territories and their successor states in the union. The most famous compact article, the sixth, provided that "there shall never be Slavery nor involuntary Servitude in the said territory."

Responding to settlers' demands, Congress eventually dispensed with "colonial" rule in the first stage, and the ban on slavery was quietly dropped in federal territories south of the Ohio (beginning with the Southwest Territory in 1790). Nor were other specific provisions of the ordinance, including the new state boundaries sketched out in the fifth compact article, faithfully observed in practice. Nonetheless, the Northwest Ordinance assumed a quasi-constitutional status in the developing territorial system, particularly in the new states in the Old Northwest.

BIBLIOGRAPHY

Eblen, Jack Ericson. *The First and Second United States Empires: Governors and Territorial Governments, 1784–1912.* Pittsburgh: University of Pittsburgh Press, 1968.

Onuf, Peter S. *Statehood and Union: A History of the Northwest Ordinance.* Bloomington: Indiana University Press, 1987.

Philbrick, Francis S. *The Laws of Illinois Territory, 1809–1818.* Springfield: Illinois State Historical Library, 1950.

Peter S. Onuf

See also **Land Policy; Northwest Territory; Ohio Company of Virginia.**

ORDNANCE originally referred to military firearms: gun tubes, ammunition, and auxiliary equipment supporting the immediate firing process. Since about 1890, however, technical revolutions in weaponry have continually broadened the meaning of the term, and in America it now stands for all types of weapons and weapons systems.

Army Ordnance

In the United States the manufacture of ordnance has traditionally been a federal concern. In 1794 Congress authorized the establishment of arsenals for the development and manufacture of ordnance at Springfield, Massachusetts, and at Harpers Ferry, Virginia. In 1812 Congress created a U.S. Army Ordnance Department to operate them. A major achievement during this early period was the introduction by Eli Whitney of interchangeable parts for mass-produced firearms.

In the nineteenth century five more arsenals were added to satisfy the army's demand for small arms, powder, shot, and cannon. Although CIVIL WAR needs sent arsenal and private ordnance production soaring, this hyperactivity ended abruptly in 1865. The navy had been given an Ordnance Bureau in 1842 but continued to rely heavily on army and civilian producers.

During the early twentieth century the pace of ordnance development accelerated rapidly and was accompanied by a growing gap between the designer-manufacturer and the user. Until 1917, the Ordnance Department, under Maj. Gen. William B. Crozier, dominated the army's weapons acquisition process; after 1917 and between the two world wars, the combat arms determined their own needs, and the department devoted itself to planning industrial mobilization. But the growing cost and sophistication of ordnance were making the centralization of procurement a necessity.

Another new factor was the increasing importance of private industry. WORLD WAR I had shown the importance of private ordnance-producing resources, or at least the need to be able to mobilize those resources quickly, but the United States abandoned its policy of restricting peacetime ordnance production to federal arsenals with great reluctance. On 16 June 1938 the Educational Orders Act authorized the immediate placement of ordnance contracts with civilian firms in order to strengthen outside procurement procedures and ease a future transition to a wartime economy. In WORLD WAR II private arms production dwarfed governmental efforts, especially in weapons carriers and auxiliary equipment; at the same time, as ordnance continued to grow more complex, public and private defense production became more integrated.

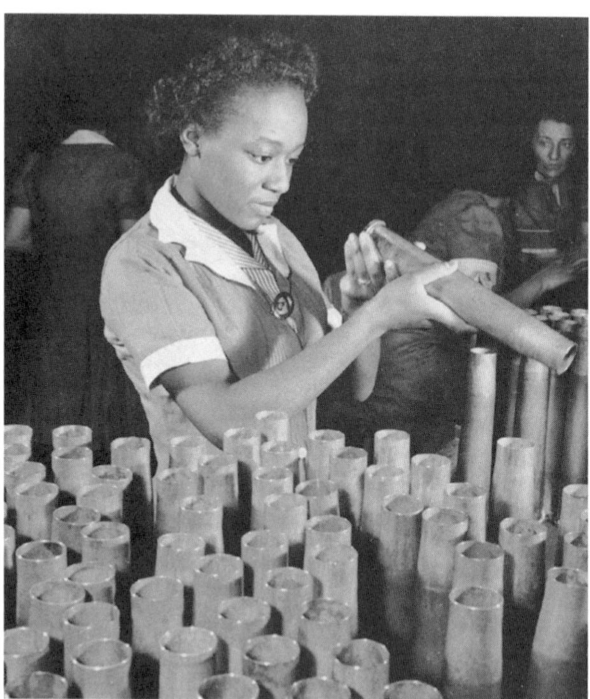

Women in the Workforce. With the majority of able-bodied men (especially Caucasians) serving in the armed forces during World War II, women and minorities (and even minority women, such as the woman shown here inspecting an artillery shell) were called upon to work in the munitions factories producing the ordnance needed to fight the Axis powers. NATIONAL ARCHIVES AND RECORDS ADMINISTRATION

From 1945 to 1973, worldwide commitments forced the United States to remain in a state of semimobilization and made dependence on arsenal production alone impractical. Ordnance was increasingly discussed in terms of weapons systems, which bore little resemblance to the firearms of 1860 or even 1917, and the army soon joined the naval and air arms in their dependence on private industry for a great proportion of their ordnance and ordnance-supporting equipment. In recognition of these trends, President John F. Kennedy's defense reorganizations of 1961–1963 placed the three service staffs on a functional basis, established three large matériel commands, and continued the centralization of the ordnance selection process. The manufacture of ordnance had become one of America's largest enterprises and demanded constant executive attention. Even after the end of the Cold War in the early 1990s, the United States remained the largest weapons manufacturer in the world.

Naval Ordnance

Naval ordnance includes all the weapons and their control systems used by naval forces. These can be classed by type (guns, mines, torpedoes, depth charges, bombs, rockets, or missiles); by warheads (conventional or nuclear); by launching platform (surface, airborne, or underwater); or by targets (submarine, air, or surface).

Until the mid-nineteenth century, U.S. Navy ships were armed with carriage-mounted, muzzle-loading, smooth-bore cannons, principally of iron, firing solid shot at point-blank range. At the time of the Civil War, pivot mounts, turrets, rifled guns, and explosive projectiles were in use. By WORLD WAR I, directors, rangekeepers (computers), and breech-loading steel guns were in use. By WORLD WAR II, radar and automatic controls had been added. Battleship sixteen-inch guns were capable of firing 2,700-pound armor-piercing projectiles at ranges up to twenty miles; proximity fuses for use against aircraft were developed; and bombardment rockets were also added.

Moored mines, contact-activated or controlled from the shore, were used in the Civil War. Starting in World War II, additional sensors were developed (magnetic, pressure, and acoustic). Preceded by spar-mounted "torpedoes" of the Civil War, self-propelled torpedoes were introduced into the U.S. Navy in the latter part of the

Naval Ordnance. Including all weapon systems and their controls, naval ordnance became increasingly sophisticated with each twentieth-century war. Here, as part of the unprecedented U.S. military buildup during World War II, seamen load gun belt cartridges into an SBD-3 aircraft at the Naval Air Station in Norfolk, Virginia. NATIONAL ARCHIVES AND RECORDS ADMINISTRATION

nineteenth century. Homing torpedoes first appeared in World War II. World War I aircraft were armed with MACHINE GUNS and crude bombs. Gyroscopic bombsights and aircraft rockets were in use in World War II.

Introduced in combat against Japanese ships in 1945, the first homing missile was the Bat, an air-launched, antiship, radar-homing, glider bomb. Since then a variety of ship, air, and submarine guided missiles have been developed. The first of the navy's long-range ballistic missiles, introduced in 1960, was the submerged-launched, 1,200-mile Polaris, made possible by solid propellants, inertial guidance, small thermonuclear warheads, and sophisticated fire-control and navigational systems. Its successor, the Poseidon, has a 2,500-nautical-mile range and was later equipped with multiple warheads. The Trident missile system, with greater range and improved capabilities, was developed in the mid-1970s. At the height of the COLD WAR, in the early 1980s, the navy introduced Los Angeles-class nuclear submarines to the fleet. The collapse of the Soviet Union removed the navy's only major international rival, but naval innovation continued unabated. In 1989 the navy began construction on new Seawolf-class attack submarines, designed to be more than ten times quieter than LA-class submarines.

BIBLIOGRAPHY

Battison, Edwin. *Muskets to Mass Production: The Men and the Times That Shaped American Manufacturing.* Windsor, Vt.: American Precision Museum, 1976.

Freedman, Norman. *Submarine Design and Development.* Annapolis, Md.: Naval Institute Press, 1984.

Green, Constance M. *Eli Whitney and the Birth of American Technology.* Boston: Little Brown, 1956.

Hogg, Oliver F. G. *Artillery: Its Origin, Heyday, and Decline.* Hamden, Conn.: Archon Books, 1970.

Peck, Taylor. *Round Shot to Rockets: A History of the Washington Navy Yard and U.S. Naval Gun Factory.* Annapolis, Md.: United States Naval Institute, 1949.

Jeffrey J. Clarke
Edwin B. Hooper/A. G.

See also **Aircraft Armament; Artillery; Chemical and Biological Warfare; Missiles, Military; Munitions; Rifle, Recoilless; Torpedo Warfare.**

OREGON. The word Oregon first appeared in print as the name of a great river flowing westward from the Great Lakes into the Pacific in Jonathan Carver's *Travels Through the Interior Parts of North America in the Years 1766, 1767, and 1768* (1778). The word's origin is uncertain. It may have been a misreading of the word *Ouisconsin* on an early map or it may derive from the word *ooligan*, an Indian word for the smelt, a fish widely traded in the western parts of North America.

Originally much larger than the state of Oregon, Oregon Country ran from the present-day Oregon-California border to today's Alaska-Canada border and ran westward from the crest of the Rocky Mountains to the Pacific Ocean.

Oregon Indians

Humans have lived in this region for at least 14,000 years. The first people probably came by a land bridge from Siberia over to Alaska, and then filtered southward to the Pacific Northwest. Over time, they separated into three major cultural groupings. Along the coast of modern Oregon lived Salishan, Penutian, and Athapaskan speakers. In the plateau region of central and eastern Oregon were Sahaptian speakers. In the southeast were the Northern Paiutes. Although Oregon Indians were divided by area and language, they shared certain characteristics. All of them hunted, foraged, fished, and traded; and, unusual for North American Indians, they did not practice agriculture. Salmon was the staple food for most Oregon Indians. It was also an important article of trade, the basis for an important religious ceremony, and served as a motif in their art. The Indians' religion was animism, a belief

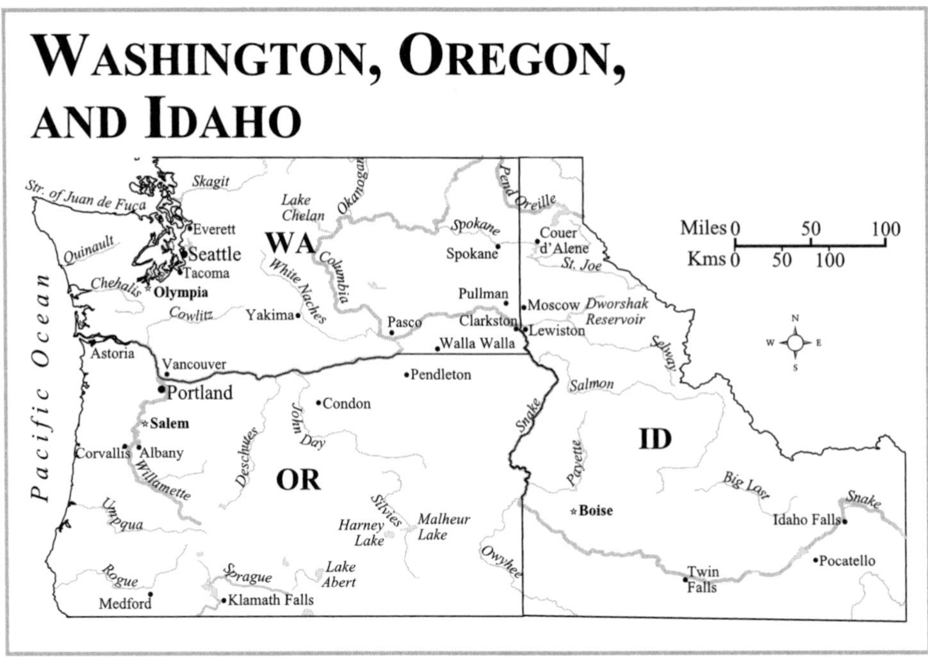

that natural beings or objects have supernatural spirits. Political and social life was based upon village-clan groups rather than on tribes.

Maritime Explorers

The first white explorers came to Oregon by sea. Spain sent the first documented explorer, Juan Cabrillo, in 1542. After Cabrillo's death, his second in command, Bartolomé Ferrelo, reached the southwestern coast in 1543 looking for a passageway between the Pacific and Atlantic oceans, the NORTHWEST PASSAGE. The Englishman Francis Drake may have seen the Oregon coast just north of the forty-second parallel in 1579. After another Spanish expedition in 1603 that reached perhaps as far north as forty-three degrees, maritime exploration ended for over 170 years.

It resumed in 1774 when Spain sent Juan Pérez to forestall an anticipated Russian advance into the Oregon Country from their base in Alaska. In 1775, Bruno de Heceta discovered what would later be named the Columbia River, though he did not enter it. In 1776, the British government sent James Cook to the Northwest to search for the Northwest Passage and to claim the land for Great Britain. Cook reached Oregon, but like his predecessors, he did not land. After Cook's death in Hawaii, his men reached China and discovered a profitable market for the sea otter furs they had acquired from the Indians of Vancouver Island. News of this sent the first British businessman, James Hanna, to Oregon in 1785 to trade for furs with the Indians.

The Fur Trade and Lewis and Clark

The first American citizen to reach Oregon was a fur trader, Robert Gray, whose ship arrived in 1788. Gray returned in 1792 and on 12 May entered the Columbia River, which he named for his ship. A short time later, a British naval officer, George Vancouver, entered the Columbia River and sent a party, commanded by William Broughton, approximately 120 miles upriver, that helped establish a British claim to the Oregon Country. In 1793, Alexander Mackenzie, a fur trader for the North West Company, reached the Pacific at the mouth of the Bella Coola River in modern British Columbia, initiating overland exploration to the Northwest Coast. In 1804, President Thomas Jefferson sent Lewis and Clark to lead the first American overland expedition. The objectives of this expedition were to find the best route between the waters of the Columbia and Missouri Rivers for the purpose of the fur trade; to inventory the flora and fauna; to make commercial arrangements with the Indians; and to strengthen the American claim to Oregon first established by Robert Gray. On 16 October 1805, the expedition first entered the Oregon Country at the junction of the Snake and Columbia rivers. They spent from 25 December 1805 to 23 March 1806 at Fort Clatsop, near present-day Seaside, Oregon.

After the Lewis and Clark expedition, fur traders came to the region. In 1805, the Canadian North West Company established a post in what is now British Columbia. John Jacob Astor's Pacific Fur Company, the first American inland fur trading company, established its headquarters at Fort Astoria in 1811 at the mouth of the Columbia River.

The Question of Sovereignty

By the early nineteenth century, ownership of the Oregon Country was disputed among Spain, Britain, Russia, and the United States. In 1818, Britain and the United States made a joint occupation agreement that postponed the question of sovereignty, but allowed each country to govern its own citizens. (At this time there were no American citizens living in Oregon.) Spain relinquished its claims to Oregon in 1819; and Russia gave up its claims to the area to the United States and Britain, respectively, in 1824 and 1825. In 1827, the joint occupation treaty was renewed.

The Missionaries

American missionaries arrived in the region in the 1830s. Methodist missionaries, under the leadership of Jason Lee, arrived in 1834 to Christianize and civilize the Indians of the Willamette Valley. They settled near today's Salem, Oregon, and moved the mission headquarters there in 1841. By the 1830s, however, the Indians in the Willamette Valley had been decimated by disease and their numbers were greatly reduced. In 1836, Dr. Marcus Whitman led a party sent by the Presbyterians, Congregationalists, and Dutch Reformed churches to the Oregon country. It included Narcissa Whitman and Eliza Spalding, the first white women to settle in Oregon. Their first mission stations were at Lapwai, in present-day Idaho, and Waiilatpu, near present-day Walla Walla, Washington. In 1837, Cayuse Indians destroyed the Whitman mission. In 1838, the Roman Catholics sent their first missionaries, Modeste Demers and Francis Blanchet, who set up their initial stations on the Cowlitz River in present-day Washington State and at St. Paul near the Willamette River in Oregon.

The Pioneer Generation

Fur traders and missionaries publicized Oregon to the American public. In the early 1840s, large numbers of pioneers began to come over the Oregon Trail to the Willamette Valley. Most of them came from the farms of the Middle West. They left home to escape harsh weather and frequent sickness, to flee the national depression that began in 1837, or simply for the sake of adventure. Most came, though, for a better material life on the rich soils of the Willamette Valley. A minority of Oregon emigrants of the pre-Civil War era were young businessmen who came from Northeastern cities to pursue mercantile careers in the urban areas of Oregon. Chinese immigrants began to come to the southern Oregon gold fields in the 1850s, and there were a few African Americans in Oregon before the Civil War.

The presence of these new settlers was a factor in the making of the Oregon Treaty of 1846, which was negotiated by President James K. Polk. This agreement divided the Oregon Country at the forty-ninth parallel, with Great Britain obtaining the land to the north. In local government, the American settlers comprised the principal group creating the Provisional Government of 1843, which guaranteed squatters' land claims, and law and order, until the Treaty of 1846 decided the sovereignty question. In 1848, Congress created the Territory of Oregon. Joseph Lane was its first governor. In 1853, the Territory of Washington was split off from Oregon. On 14 February 1859, Oregon became the thirty-third state. The provisions of its constitution, such as the separation of powers, were similar to those of the Midwestern states.

Before the Civil War, Oregon's political life was largely based upon local issues. The Democrats were the majority party, but Whigs and Republicans also had many supporters. The major national issue was whether slavery should extend to the federal territories. In the presidential election of 1860, Oregonians favored the Republican Abraham Lincoln who opposed the expansion of slavery into the territories. When the Civil War came, there were no battles in Oregon and few Oregonians fought in the eastern theaters.

During the pioneer era, most Oregonians were farmers. Some towns sprang up and one major city, Portland. Oregonians exported WHEAT, cattle, and lumber to California in return for gold. In cultural life, churches, schools, and colleges were begun. Indian wars broke out in the 1850s when gold miners going to Southern Oregon caused the Rogue River War (1855–1856). In other parts of Oregon, white farmers encroached on Indian lands resulting in the Indians being placed on reservations. In 1855, the Warm Springs Reservation was created in Central Oregon for the Wasco, Walla Walla, and later the Paiutes.

Economics and Politics

In the 1880s, Oregon became more integrated into the national economy with the arrival of the Northern Pacific and Union Pacific transcontinental railroads. Some local industry developed, but wheat and lumber were the basis of the economy. Wheat farmers benefited from the re-

Oregon Log Train, c. 1880. Along with wheat farming, the lumber industry played an important role in the early development of the state.

Abigail Scott Duniway. An autographed portrait of the leading suffragist in Oregon, who waged a four-decade struggle in her state and nationwide for women's rights. © CORBIS

duction in transportation costs the railroad brought, as well as from mechanization and cheap land. Lumber exports also gained from low railroad rates, from mechanical inventions such as double circular saws, and from building booms in California, on the East Coast, and overseas. Cattlemen ran their stock on the open ranges of eastern Oregon and sheepherders competed with them for this pasturage. The salmon canning industry began on the Columbia River in 1867. By the beginning of the twentieth century, its effects were felt in reduced salmon runs.

After the Civil War, the Democrat and Republican parties as well as a few third parties grappled with several issues. The most important issue was the regulation of the railroads, especially the Southern Pacific Railroad. Critics of the railroads charged that rates were too high and service inadequate. This worked to corrupt the political system, as legislators were bribed. The first political opponent of the railroads was the Oregon State Grange, organized in 1873. It worked for railroad regulation with little success, except for the creation of a railroad commission in 1887 that had investigative but not regulatory powers.

Abigail Scott Duniway led the fight for woman's suffrage. In 1871, she began a newspaper in Portland called *The New Northwest.* Duniway also worked for a woman's suffrage constitutional amendment. Although the amendment was defeated in 1874, Duniway persevered and the amendment was passed in 1912.

In the late nineteenth century, Oregon's population became more ethnically diverse. The African American population rose as the railroads created economic opportunities for black migrants. They worked in the car shops, roundhouses, and yards in Portland, Roseburg, and La Grande. They also worked as Pullman and dining car employees and as teamsters and porters around the railroad stations. Chinese immigrants worked as farm laborers, salmon canners, construction workers, and domestic servants. Japanese immigrants were employed as farmers, truck gardeners, and railroad tracklayers. Asian immigrants, both Chinese and Japanese, were victims of widespread discrimination. In contrast to Asians and blacks, immigrants from Great Britain, Germany, and the Nordic lands were welcomed and assimilated easily.

Industry in the Twentieth Century

In the twentieth century, agriculture, lumber, cattle, sheep, and fishing were the most productive sectors of the economy until the rise of the technology and tourist industries. The first attempt to attract tourists was the Columbia River Scenic Highway built from 1913 to 1922. In the 1940s, technology companies such as Electro Scientific Industries and Tektronix were founded in Portland. In later years, other homegrown technology companies were started, and imports from other states, such as Intel and Hewlett-Packard, and from other nations, such as Epson and Fujitsu, established themselves in Oregon.

The Progressive Movement and After

Oregon's politics in the past century went through progressive and conservative phases. William S. U'Ren led the Progressive movement. It was caused by a variety of discontents: farmers and businessmen still concerned about the monopolistic power of the railroad; industrial workers desiring improved wages, hours, and working conditions; citizens frustrated with corruption in state and municipal politics; and those fearful of the social problems of growing urban areas. Progressivism was not based on a third party, but had both Democrat and Republican supporters, who effected many changes. In 1902, Oregon adopted the initiative and referendum. Other reforms followed: the direct primary (1904), the recall (1908), the presidential preference primary (1910), and woman's suffrage (1912). Progressives also passed social and economic legislation, including a ten-hour day for women in factories and laundries (1903) upheld by the Supreme Court in *Muller vs. Oregon* (1908). Taxes were raised on public utilities and public carriers (1906), an eight-hour day was adopted for public works projects (1912), and an eight-hour day was set for women workers in certain occupations (1914). In 1903, Oregon obtained a child labor law and a state board of health. A workman's compensation law was established in 1913; prohibition was enacted in 1914; and Oregon passed the nation's first gasoline tax in 1919.

The most contentious political development in the 1920s was the rise of the KU KLUX KLAN. The group helped enact an initiative requiring parents to send their children to public rather than private or parochial schools. Passed in 1922, the law was declared unconstitutional by the Supreme Court in 1925. Soon after this decision, the Klan faded away. The majority of Oregonians voted for Franklin Roosevelt in 1932, 1936, and 1940, but they elected conservative or moderate, mainly Republican, governors, state legislators, congressmen, and senators.

Environmental Legislation

After the close of World War II, Oregon became a two-party state. In the 1960s, it captured national attention with a series of environmental laws: the Willamette River Park System Act (1967) and the Willamette Greenway Act (1973), a revision of its predecessor. An unprecedented system of statewide land use was enacted (1969, 1973). In 1970, the Oregon Scenic Water Ways Act was passed, as was an act in 1975 that banned the use of fluorocarbons in aerosol spray cans. During the 1980s and 1990s, Oregon politics became more conservative as voters became less willing to spend tax dollars. In 1990, Ballot Measure 5, a property tax limitation, was adopted as a constitutional amendment, which had the effect of crippling state services, such as higher education. Oregon's governors from the late 1980s to the early 2000s were all Democrats: Neil Goldschmidt (1987–1991), Barbara Roberts (1991–1995), and John Kitzhaber (1995–2003), but they accomplished little because of Republican strength in the state legislature. On the national level, Senator Bob Packwood (1969–1995) was a proponent of tax simplification, while Senator Mark O. Hatfield (1967–1996) was best known for championing a noninterventionist foreign policy in Vietnam and opposing a federal constitutional amendment to balance the national budget. Senator Wayne Morse (1945–1969) was an advocate for organized labor and an early opponent of the Vietnam War.

A More Diverse Population

Oregon's population became more diverse in the twentieth century. Many immigrants came from southern, eastern, and central Europe. Japanese immigrants suffered from the prejudice of white Oregonians, and were placed in internment camps during the Second World War. At the conclusion of the war, some returned to Oregon.

Native Americans were affected by changes in national policy. The Wheeler-Howard Act in 1934 permitted Indians to reorganize into tribes, but the Termination Policy in 1953 then broke up many of the remaining tribes. Beginning in the 1980s, some Native Americans obtained tribal recognition again. The African American presence increased greatly during World War II, when many blacks came to Oregon to work in the shipyards. They built upon existing community institutions and gained their first member of the state legislature in 1973 and their first statewide office holder in 1993. Oregon's Hispanic population also grew. For much of the century Hispanics worked as migratory farm workers, but by the end of the century most had settled into permanent residences in towns and cities. In the 2000 census 86.6% of Oregonians were white, 8% Hispanic, 3% Asian, 1.6% African American, and 1.3% American Indian.

Late Twentieth-Century Cultural Developments

In cultural life, support of public libraries and bookstores was above the national average, and Oregonians gained distinction in literature. Don Berry published a trilogy of historical novels about the pioneer era including *Trask* (1960), *Moontrap* (1962), and *To Build a Ship* (1963), while Ken Kesey received acclaim for *One Flew Over the Cuckoo's Nest* (1962) and *Sometimes A Great Notion* (1964); both were made into motion pictures. Ursula Le Guin was one of the world's most distinguished authors of science fantasy. Craig Lesley's works included *Winterkill* (1984) and *River Song* (1989) and Molly Gloss wrote *The Jump-Off Creek* (1989) and *Wild Life* (2000). In architecture, Pietro Belluschi founded the Northwest Style, which uses regional materials to construct churches and residences that fit their natural surroundings.

BIBLIOGRAPHY

Abbott, Carl. *Portland: Planning, Politics, and Growth in a Twentieth-Century City.* Lincoln: University of Nebraska Press, 1983.

Carey, Charles H. *General History of Oregon Through Early Statehood.* 3rd ed. Portland, Ore.: Binfords & Mort, 1971.

Clark, Malcolm, Jr. *Eden Seekers: The Settlement of Oregon, 1818–1862.* Boston: Houghton-Mifflin, 1981.

Dodds, Gordon B. *Oregon: A Bicentennial History.* New York: W.W. Norton, 1977.

———. *The American Northwest: A History of Oregon and Washington.* Arlington Heights, Ill.: Forum Press, 1986.

Johansen, Dorothy O. *Empire of the Columbia: A History of the Pacific Northwest.* 2d ed. New York: Harper & Row, 1967.

MacColl, E. Kimbark. *Merchants, Money and Power: The Portland Establishment, 1843–1913.* Portland, Ore.: The Georgian Press, 1988.

MacColl, E. Kimbark. *The Growth of a City: Power and Politics in Portland, Oregon, 1915 to 1950.* Portland, Ore.: The Georgian Press, 1979.

Merk, Frederick. *The Oregon Question: Essays in Anglo-American Diplomacy and Politics.* Cambridge, Mass.: Harvard University Press, 1967.

Morison, Dorothy Nafus. *Outpost: John McLoughlin and the Far Northwest.* Portland: Oregon Historical Society Press, 1999.

Robbins, William G. *Landscapes of Promise: The Oregon Story, 1800–1940.* Seattle: University of Washington Press, 1997.

Walth, Brent. *Fire at Eden's Gate: Tom McCall & The Oregon Story.* Portland: Oregon Historical Society Press, 1994.

Gordon B. Dodds

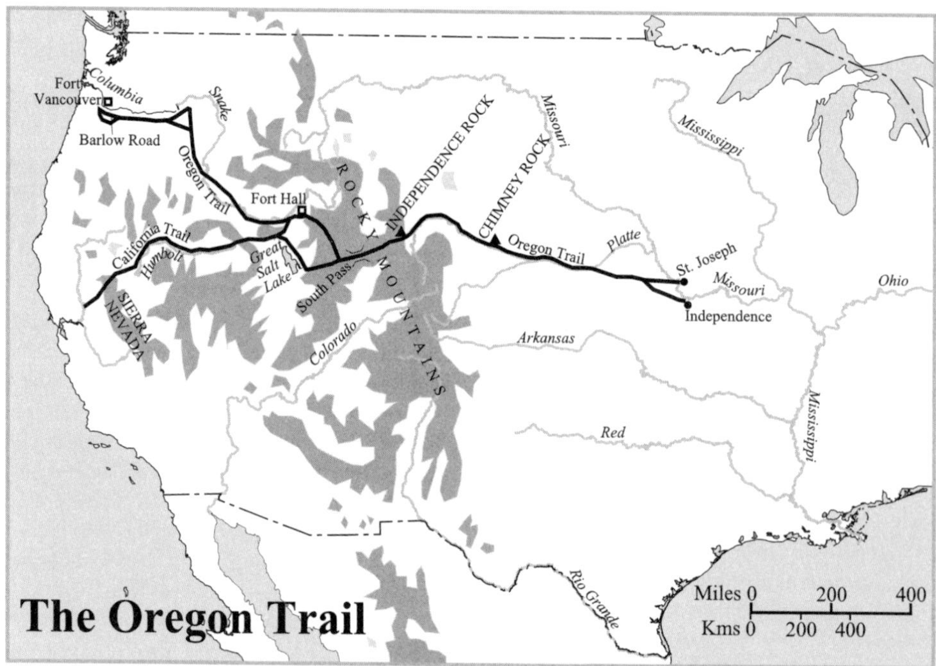

See also **Columbia River Exploration and Settlement; Fur Trade and Trapping; Joint Occupation; Lumber Industry; Pacific Northwest; Tribes: Northwestern;** *and vol. 9:* **Women in Industry (Brandeis Brief).**

OREGON SYSTEM. The "Oregon System" refers to the use of INITIATIVE and REFERENDUM, populist lawmaking tools. The former allows citizens to *initiate* state legislation, while the latter *refers* laws passed by the legislature to the people for approval.

By the 1890s direct democracy had become a major goal of the Populist movement, which aimed to counter corrupt influences in politics that could supersede the will of the voting public. In 1894 William S. U'Ren became chair of the Oregon convention of the People's Party, the electoral project of the Populists. He used his party to create the Oregon Direct Legislation League and widened that coalition until his plan passed the state legislature in 1901. The voters approved it by an eleven-to-one margin the next year.

The results were extraordinary. In 1908 U'Ren proposed an initiative that made Oregon the first state in the nation to popularly elect U.S. senators. In 1910 another initiative in Oregon created the nation's first presidential primary. Then, in 1912 Oregon women won by initiative the right to vote, thanks to hardworking suffragists led by Abigail Scott Dunaway. In 1914 initiatives established prohibition and banished the death penalty in Oregon.

Most of the states to establish the "Oregon System" did so by the end of the 1910s. Thus, the strong residual populist influence on politics in the far West during that era determined the locale of most states that still used the initiative and referendum system in the early 2000s. Seventeen of twenty-three direct-democracy states were west of the Mississippi River.

BIBLIOGRAPHY

Schmidt, David D. *Citizen Lawmakers: The Ballot Initiative Revolution.* Philadelphia: Temple University Press, 1989.

Adam Hodges

OREGON TRAIL, one of several routes traveled in the mid-nineteenth century by pioneers seeking to settle in the western territories. Over a period of about thirty years, roughly 1830 to 1860, some 300,000 Americans crowded these overland trails. The Oregon Trail was first traveled in the early 1840s. Only some 5,000 or so had made it to Oregon Territory by 1845, with another 3,000 making their way to California three years later. This trickle would turn into a flood in the following decade.

The Oregon Trail totaled some 2,000 miles. The Oregon and California Trails followed the same path for almost half of this journey, so overlanders headed to either destination faced many of the same natural obstacles. Departing from the small towns of Independence or St. Joseph, Missouri, or Council Bluffs, Iowa, miles of open plains initially greeted the travelers. The trail followed first the Missouri and then the Platte River. The water of the Platte was too dirty to drink, not deep enough to float a barge, and so broad that it left great mud flats and quicksand in the way of the unsuspecting settler. As the Rocky Mountains neared, the overlanders shifted to the north side of the Platte, and then maneuvered to cross the Continental Divide at the South Pass, low enough, broad

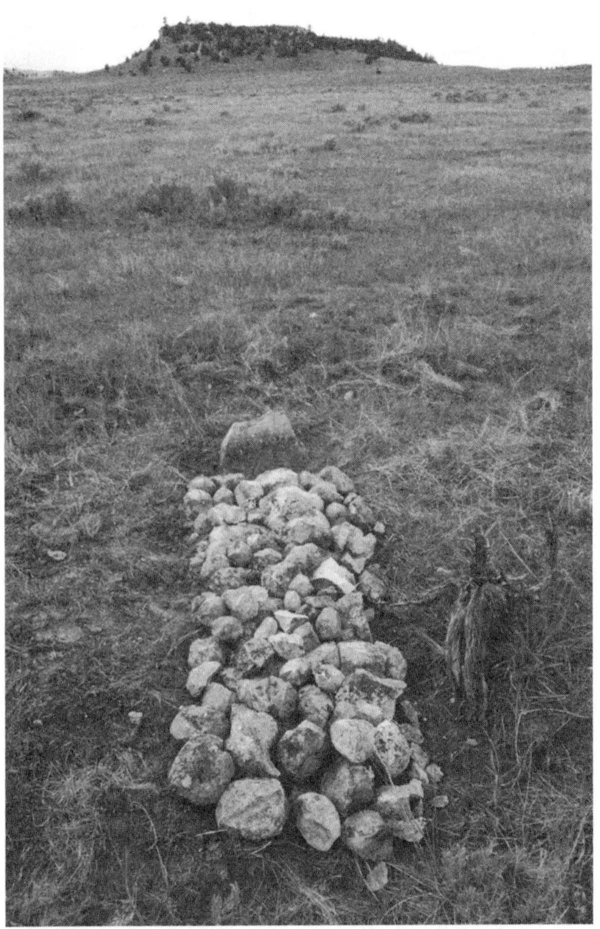

Oregon Trail. This photograph by James L. Amos shows a pile of stones marking a pioneer's grave near Guernsey, Wyo.—one of the countless settlers who never made it to the West. © CORBIS

enough, and safe enough for wagon transit. At this halfway point, the Oregon and California Trails diverged, the former heading north. Settlers bound for Oregon Country shadowed the Snake River and faced one last mountain obstacle, the Blue Mountains. The Willamette Valley awaited those sturdy enough to complete this passage and some finished their travels on a reasonably safe boat ride down the Columbia River.

It took six to seven months to travel the complete length of the Oregon Trail. Ideally, those making this journey departed in May to arrive before November and the first heavy snowfalls. However, those leaving too early risked getting mired in mud, and those leaving too late confronted snow at the end of their travels, a dangerous and foreboding prospect. The overlanders traveled in wagon trains, in groups ranging from ten to one hundred wagons. As the trails became better known and well-traveled, most wagoneers preferred smaller trains. Smaller wagon trains moved more quickly and were delayed less often due to internal arguments. When disputes did arise they might be settled by vote or, especially in larger wagon trains, according to a written constitution. On the trail, hardships and dangers proved numerous and discouraging. Accidents, such as drowning, ax wounds, shootings, or being run over by wagons or trampled by livestock, claimed many victims. Sickness, especially cholera from poor drinking water, weakened countless travelers, eventually killing some. Despite the obstacles, people made the journey for economic reasons. The depression of 1837, the most severe of its day, pushed those contemplating a move west to do so sooner rather than later. California's gold rush, starting in 1848, did much to fuel travel west via the overland trails. Fertile land and the potential for wealth from trapping drew people to the Northwest.

Migrants to the West were farmers as well as storekeepers, clerks, saloonkeepers, former soldiers, and other adventurers. They came from all over the United States, including the Upper South, the Midwest, and the Northeast. Because of the difficulty of the journey, most fell between the ages of ten and forty.

Much folklore grew up around the overlanders and their journey. Perhaps the biggest legend of all concerns the danger posed to the migrants by Native Americans. In fact, Native Americans aided, directed, and even accompanied the overlanders. Deaths at the hands of Plains Indians probably numbered only in the hundreds, almost certainly not reaching the several thousands reported in legend. Most Indians sought to profit from the wagoneers by imposing either a toll to cross a river, a fee for guidance down an uncertain road, or by offering an exchange of goods for renewed provisions. Horses often acted as currency.

With the completion of the transcontinental railroad in 1869, the wagon era came to a close. Yet a change in mode of transportation did little to detract from the accomplishment of those who toughed it out on the Oregon Trail and other trails. These pioneers had opened a land and settled it all in one motion.

BIBLIOGRAPHY

Billington, Ray Allen. *The Far Western Frontier, 1830–1860.* London: Harper and Row, 1956.

Unruh, John D., Jr. *The Plains Across: The Overland Emigrants and the Trans-Mississippi West, 1840–1860.* Urbana: University of Illinois, 1979.

Matthew J. Flynn

See also **California Trail; Wagon Trains;** *and vol. 9:* **The Oregon Trail.**

OREGON TREATY OF 1846. This agreement set the boundary between the United States and Canada at the 49th parallel west of the Rocky Mountains, veering around Vancouver Island and then proceeding through the Strait of San Juan de Fuca. The Oregon Treaty settled the dispute between the United States and Great Britain over the area in Oregon located between the Columbia River and the 49th parallel. In 1818, both countries had agreed to a joint occupation of Oregon, and this agreement had been renewed by treaty in 1827.

Elected in 1844 on an expansionist platform that included the acquisition of the entire Oregon Territory, which extended to 54 degrees, 40 minutes to the north, President James K. Polk had to satisfy the demands of his countrymen for the region. After a compromise proposal was rejected in July 1845, Polk acquired congressional authority in December to abrogate the 1827 treaty. On 15 June 1846, the Senate ratified a treaty that established the boundary at the 49th parallel. Deteriorating relations with Mexico and favorable public opinion made the compromise acceptable to the United States, while Britain was likewise interested in a peaceful solution because it had more pressing domestic and foreign issues to consider.

BIBLIOGRAPHY

Bergeron, Paul B. *The Presidency of James K. Polk.* Lawrence. University Press of Kansas. 1987.

Jones, Howard. *Crucible of Power: A History of American Foreign Relations to 1913.* Wilmington, Del.: Scholarly Resources, 2002.

Ronda, James P. *Astoria and Empire.* Lincoln: University of Nebraska Press, 1990.

Gregory Moore

ORGANIC FARMING coalesced as a movement in the United States in the 1940s with the work of J. I. Rodale of Emmaus, Pennsylvania, who followed the British agricultural botanist Sir Albert Howard in the belief that healthy soil produces healthy people. Beginning in 1942, Rodale published *Rodale's Organic Gardening*, a magazine dedicated to organic gardening and farming, which drew subscribers ranging from home gardeners to truck farmers. Spurning synthetic fertilizers, he advocated natural soil-builders, such as composted organic materials and ground rock. He and his disciples reacted against synthetic pesticides such as DDT, and livestock antibiotics such as penicillin, which were just finding their way onto farms and into farm produce. After the publication of Rachel Carson's *Silent Spring* (1962), many Americans became concerned with human health and permanence. Thus, organic farming found many adherents in the late 1960s and the 1970s among both antitechnology members of the counterculture and environmentally concerned consumers. Synthetic agricultural chemicals, which had become a staple in U.S. agriculture in the post–World War II period, increasingly came under attack as scientists recognized many of them as carcinogenic. The back-to-basics philosophy of the environmental movement boosted the popularity of organic agriculture as a healthy alternative to the seemingly apocalyptic results of high technology.

For decades the U.S. Department of Agriculture (USDA) had advocated use of synthetic agricultural chemicals while bemoaning the loss of humus and topsoil. Responding to environmental concerns, petroleum shortages, and rampant inflation in the 1970s, the USDA began to advocate research into conversion of urban and industrial organic wastes into composted soil-builders that farmers could use to increase fertility and restore soil structure. The Organic Foods Production Act of 1990 called for federally funded pilot projects to help introduce organic techniques as supplements to chemical-intensive agriculture. Advocates maintained that organic farming would support family farms by lowering costs, increasing yields, and raising quality, as well as by helping farmers to conserve soil and other natural farm resources. By the mid-1980s organic techniques such as low-till and no-till farming, in which farmers leave crop residues in fields to increase humus and to decrease water and wind erosion, were common practice among cereal farmers in the Midwest.

Public awareness of these issues continued to grow. In the late 1980s a widely publicized controversy erupted over Alar, a chemical sprayed on apples and other produce to enhance color and prolong shelf life, which had been linked to cancer in laboratory studies. The Environmental Protection Agency attempted to reconcile 1950s legislation prohibiting carcinogenic pesticide residues on food with the highly sensitive measuring devices of the 1990s. Projects such as Biosphere 1 and 2 experimented with a sustainable lifestyle in a closed ecosystem. Organic farmers hoped to tap into the antichemical sentiment that drove these activities by selling produce labeled "organically grown" in supermarkets. Initially organic farming was an attempt to preserve "good farming" practices in the face of a rapidly changing agriculture. By the 1990s organic farming techniques had gained wide acceptance as a result of environmental regulation, rising energy prices, and consumer demand.

BIBLIOGRAPHY

Hays, Samuel P. *Beauty, Health, and Permanence: Environmental Politics in the United States, 1955–1985.* New York: Cambridge University Press, 1987.

Wolf, Ray, ed. *Organic Farming: Yesterday's and Tomorrow's Agriculture.* Emmaus, Pa.: Rodale Press, 1977.

Dennis Williams / c. w.

See also **Agriculture; Agriculture, Department of; Cancer; Gardening; Hydroponics; Soil.**

ORGANIZATION FOR ECONOMIC COOPERATION AND DEVELOPMENT (OECD), headquartered in Paris, aims to stimulate economic growth. Originally a twenty-nation association, by 2002 the OECD counted among its members Australia, Austria, Belgium, Canada, the Czech Republic, Denmark, Finland, France, Germany, Greece, Hungary, Iceland, Ireland, Italy, Japan, Korea, Luxembourg, Mexico, The Netherlands, New Zealand, Norway, Poland, Portugal, the Slovak Republic, Spain, Sweden, Switzerland, Turkey, the United Kingdom, and the United States. In addition, the OECD maintains relationships with seventy other countries.

The OECD began its existence on 30 September 1961, when it replaced the Organization for European Economic Cooperation (OEEC), originally organized in 1948 to administer the Marshall Plan and the cooperative efforts for European recovery from the economic disaster of WORLD WAR II. The United States was not a member of OEEC. Its membership in OECD was a major step forward for the United States in economic internationalism.

The stated purpose of OECD is to achieve economic growth in member countries, to contribute to economic expansion, and to increase the expansion of world trade. Broadly speaking, the objective is to foster the free international flow of payments, services, capital, human resources, and scientific developments. Likewise, OECD is concerned with developments in industry and agriculture, the use of nuclear energy for peaceful purposes, and environmental problems. The OECD gathers and disseminates information about numerous economic indicators in its member countries, and about the issues that affect those economies.

The late 1990s witnessed the beginnings of an explosion of protest over the free flow of capital and the lack of regulation of global corporations. Though the World Trade Organization and the INTERNATIONAL MONETARY FUND have been at the center of the protests, the OECD has also come under fire for supporting those institutions. Protests met the OECD's proposed Multilateral Agreement on Investment (MAI) in October 1998, forcing the convention on the agreement to close early and prompting several countries to suggest moving the MAI to the bailiwick of the World Trade Organization.

BIBLIOGRAPHY

Organisation for Economic Cooperation and Development. *OECD; History, Aims, Structure.* Paris: Organisation for Economic Cooperation and Development, Information Service, 1971.

Taylor, Annie, and Caroline Thomas, eds. *Global Trade and Gobal Social Issues.* New York: Routledge, 1999.

Thomas Robson Hay / D. B.

See also **General Agreement on Tariffs and Trade; North American Free Trade Agreement; Trade Agreements; Trade, Foreign.**

ORGANIZATION OF AFRO-AMERICAN UNITY (OAAU) was founded by Malcolm X after his departure from the NATION OF ISLAM. The Organization of Afro-American Unity was inspired by the Organization of African Unity, which drew together the fifty-two nations of Africa to discuss and solve pressing problems pertinent to the continent. The OAAU sought to build independent institutions in the African American community and to support black participation in mainstream politics. The OAAU was the clearest indication that Malcolm X, or as he had renamed himself in 1964, El-Hajj Malik El-Shabazz, was moving politically in a new direction. Although he considered himself a black nationalist, there were some indications he was moving toward socialism. His assassination in February 1965 in the Audubon Ballroom left those matters unclear. The demise of the OAAU came shortly after Malcolm's death.

BIBLIOGRAPHY

Perry, Bruce. *Malcolm: The Life of A Man Who Changed Black America.* Tarrytown, N.Y.: Station Hill, 1991.

Charles Pete Banner-Haley

See also **Black Nationalism; Civil Rights Movement.**

ORGANIZATION OF AMERICAN STATES (OAS; Organización de Los Estados Americanos) was established in 1948 following the Ninth International Conference of American States in Bogota, Colombia. The OAS succeeded the Union of American Republics and its secretariat, the Pan American Union, which had been set up in 1910. Twenty-one governments participated in the establishment of the OAS and ratified their membership in the organization in the 1950s. They were Argentina, Bolivia, Brazil, Chile, Colombia, Costa Rica, Cuba, the Dominican Republic, Ecuador, El Salvador, Guatemala, Haiti, Honduras, Mexico, Nicaragua, Panama, Paraguay, Peru, the United States of America, Uruguay, and Venezuela.

In 1962, because of its pro-Soviet leanings in the Cold War, the Cuban government was formally prevented from participating in OAS meetings and activities. However, the OAS charter had no provision by which a government could be expelled. This meant that Cuba retained its status as a de jure member. The former British Caribbean colonies of Barbados, Jamaica, and Trinidad and Tobago joined the OAS in the 1960s. They were followed in the 1970s and 1980s by the additional former British Caribbean colonies of Dominica, Saint Lucia, Antigua and Barbuda, the Bahamas, Saint Kitts and Nevis, and Saint Vincent and the Grenadines, as well as by Suriname, formerly a Dutch colony. In the 1990s Canada and the former British colonies of Belize and Guyana joined the OAS.

The primary activity of the OAS, following its establishment in the early years of the Cold War, has been around issues of conflict resolution and collective security. Changes in orientation or emphasis over time are reflected in the four formal amendments to the Charter of the Organization of American States (COAS) since it was written in 1948. The first amendments, the 1967 Protocol of Buenos Aires, resulted from the desire of a number of governments in Latin America to enhance the social and economic provisions of the charter and weaken those provisions related to political and security questions, with which the United States was most concerned. In the 1970s the OAS also began to try to play a greater role in the protection of human rights. While not involving any changes to the COAS, this inclination led to the establishment of the Inter-American Court of Human Rights in 1978.

The second set of amendments to COAS, the Protocol of Cartagena de Indias of 1985, involved a reaffirmation of the principle of nonintervention and the amplification of the role of the organization's secretary-general in negotiating peace settlements. This restatement of nonintervention was a response on the part of a number of members to the Falklands-Malvinas War in 1982, the U.S. invasion of Grenada in 1983, and U.S. activities directed at the government of Nicaragua in the 1980s. With the end of the Cold War, the OAS began also to place more emphasis on promoting democracy. For example, the Protocol of Washington in 1992 involved amending the original charter to strengthen the ability of the OAS to suspend a member country when its democratically elected government was "overthrown by force." The Protocol of Managua of 1993 involved a fourth series of amendments, which were aimed at enhancing the OAS's role in regional economic integration and development. This protocol led to the creation of the Inter-American Council for Integral Development (IACID) in 1996.

BIBLIOGRAPHY

Sheinin, David. *The Organization of American States.* New Brunswick, N.J.: Transaction Publishers, 1996.

Stoetzer, O. Carlos. *The Organization of American States.* 2d ed. New York: Praeger, 1993.

Thomas, Christopher R., and Juliana T. Magloire. *Regionalism versus Multilateralism: The Organization of American States in a Global Changing Environment.* Boston: Kluwer Academic Publishers, 2000.

Mark T. Berger

See also **Contra Aid; Cuba, Relations with; Grenada Invasion; Latin America, Relations with; Nicaragua, Relations with.**

ORGANIZED CRIME. *See* **Crime, Organized.**

ORGANIZED CRIME CONTROL ACT. The purpose of this 1970 act was to eliminate organized crime "by establishing new penal prohibitions and by providing enhanced sanctions and new remedies to deal with the unlawful activities of those engaged in organized crime." As the title suggests, lawmakers sought to provide enhanced and novel legal tools for law enforcement. Because the level of violence and crime had continued to rise in post–World War II America, there were many who criticized existing laws related to personal safety and the security of property. McCarthyism, the Kefauver Hearings, civil rights demonstrations, Vietnam War protests, and liberal court rulings gave Americans a sense that state and local governments could no longer enforce laws against sophisticated criminals. Congress, therefore, expanded the federal government's role in preventing crime and punishing criminals by passing a series of laws.

In a response to concerns about increased street and gang crime, Congress passed the Juvenile Delinquency and Youth Offenses Control Act of 1961, which earmarked $10 million annually to fund community crime-control efforts and to train local officials to work with juvenile delinquents and gangs. The Omnibus Crime Control and Safe Streets Act, passed seven years later, authorized over $100 million, with $50 million to assist law enforcement agencies in riot control and fighting organized crime. The bill also outlawed interstate trade in handguns, raised the minimum age for handgun purchases to twenty-one, and established a national gun licensing system. The Gun Control Act of 1968 extended these restrictions to cover rifles, shotguns, and ammunition.

The Organized Crime Control Act of 1970, signed into law by Richard Nixon, was the major statute that gave the federal government new and sweeping ways to combat organized crime. Title I grants greater powers to grand juries and permits detention of unmanageable witnesses by authorizing special grand juries to sit for up to thirty-six months while investigating organized criminal activity. Title II weakened the witness immunity laws. Title III gives courts the ability to detain uncooperative witnesses for up to eighteen months. Title IV allows witnesses to be tried for perjury, based solely on contradictions in their testimony. Title V authorizes the Attorney General to form a witness protection program for cooperative federal and state witnesses and their families. Title VIII makes it a federal crime to protect an illegal gambling business by obstructing state law or to use income from organized criminal activity to run a business engaged in interstate commerce. Title IX—known as The Racketeer Influenced and Corrupt Organizations Act, or RICO—has been called the most sweeping criminal statute ever passed by Congress. This section covers twenty-four types of federal crimes and eight state felonies. It provides for a $20,000 fine, twenty years in prison, asset forfeiture, and civil damage suites. Title XI, modeled after the Gun Control Act of 1968, includes sections known as the Explosives Control Act and establishes certain types of bombing and arson as federal crimes and contains provisions for strict industry regulation.

Because of its comprehensiveness, the Organized Crime Control Act laid the foundation for additional legislation passed during the latter quarter of the twentieth century. Efforts toward reducing criminal activity have included a number of far-reaching programs, such as community action networks, larger police forces, tougher sentencing, limits on gun ownership, and new definitions of criminal activity. Congress built on the original law by passing the Omnibus Crime Control Act of 1970 and a major anticrime package in 1984. Congress continued with legislation such as the Brady Handgun Violence Prevention Act in 1993 and the Omnibus Crime Control Act and Safe Streets Act of 1994. These acts ban nineteen types of assault weapons, allow judges to waive minimum sentences for nonviolent, first-time drug offenders, and expand the number of federal capital crimes. Congress approved additional penalties for "hate crimes," federal offenses against victims based on race, religion, ethnicity, gender, disability, or sexual orientation, and instituted the "three strikes and you're out" policy that mandated life imprisonment for criminals convicted of three violent felonies.

BIBLIOGRAPHY

Blakey, G. Robert. "Racketeer Influenced and Corrupt Organization Act (RICO)." *The Encyclopedia of the United States Congress* 3, 1659 (1995).

Brookings Institute. "Government's Fifty Greatest Endeavors: Reduce Crime." Available from http://www.brook.edu/dybdocroot/gs/cps/50ge/endeavors/crime.htm.

Friedman, Joel M. et al. "Fighting Organized Crime: Special Responses to a Special Problem (Symposium-perspectives on organized crime)." *Rutgers Law Journal* 16, no. 439 (1985).

James F. Adomanis

See also **Crime, Organized; RICO.**

ORIGINAL PACKAGE DOCTRINE for determining the point at which goods pass from federal control over interstate commerce to state control over local commerce was first enunciated by the SUPREME COURT in *Brown v. Maryland* (1827). Merchandise brought into the state "in the original form or package in which it was imported," ruled the Court, clearly fell under federal jurisdiction. *Leisy v. Hardin* (135 U.S. 100 [1890]) clarified that goods in interstate shipment have not "arrived" for purposes of regulation by the state until they have been delivered into the hands of the consignee, and the original package has been broken.

BIBLIOGRAPHY

Corwin, Edward S. *The Commerce Power Versus States' Rights.* Princeton, N.J.: Princeton University Press; London: H. Milford, Oxford University Press, 1936.

W. Brooke Graves/A. R.

See also ***Brown v. Maryland*; Commerce Clause; Interstate Commerce Laws; Trade, Domestic.**

ORISKANY, BATTLE OF (6 August 1777). The British threefold battle plan of 1777 included the advance of Lt. Col. Barry St. Leger across New York from Fort Oswego to meet generals John Burgoyne and William Howe in Albany. On 3 August, St. Leger, with an army of approximately 1,200 Tories and Mohawks approached Fort Stanwix on the Mohawk River. Gen. Nicholas Herkimer and his 800 militiamen hoped to surprise the British force with a rear attack, but scouts discovered the ambush and the advancing Americans were themselves set upon by a British detachment under Sir John Johnson about two miles west of Oriskany Creek. When the main force from Fort Stanwix finally arrived, the Tories retreated. St. Leger, unable to force the surrender of the fort, on 22 August retreated to Oswego.

BIBLIOGRAPHY

Peckham, Howard H. *The Toll of Independence.* Chicago: University of Chicago Press, 1974.

Scott, John A. *Fort Stanwix and Oriskany.* Rome, N.Y.: Rome Sentinel Company, 1927.

A. C. Flick/A. R.

See also **Indians in the Revolution; Revolution, American: Military History.**

ORLEANS, TERRITORY OF. The Territory of Orleans was so called only during the period of American territorial government. The region, now the state of Louisiana, was first claimed by France in 1682. Jean Baptiste Le Moyne, then governor of Louisiana, founded New Orleans in 1718 and made it the capital in 1722. Louisiana was ceded to Spain in 1762, returned to France in 1800, and sold to the United States in 1803 as part of the Louisiana Purchase. The Territory of Orleans, approved 26 March 1804, included most of the present state of Louisiana. William Claiborne was governor throughout the territorial period. The state of Louisiana was admitted 30 April 1812.

BIBLIOGRAPHY

Conrad, Glenn R., ed. *The French Experience in Louisiana.* Lafayette: University of Southwestern Louisiana, 1995.

Din, Gilbert C., ed. *The Spanish Presence in Louisiana, 1763–1803.* Lafayette: University of Southwestern Louisiana, 1996.

Edgar B. Nixon/H. S.

See also **Louisiana; Louisiana Purchase; New Orleans.**

ORNITHOLOGY, the branch of natural history that deals with the systematic study of birds, began in America in the eighteenth century. The British naturalist Mark Catesby was the first individual to thoroughly document the flora and fauna of the New World. His illustrated, two-volume work, *Natural History of Carolina, Florida, and the Bahama Islands* (1731–1743), included descriptions of more than a hundred North American birds.

Roseate Spoonbill. London engraver Robert Havell Jr. turned John James Audubon's drawings and watercolors into aquatints, like this one from 1836, for Audubon's monumental *Birds of America*. © ACADEMY OF NATURAL SCIENCES OF PHILADELPHIA/CORBIS

Early Studies

In the period surrounding the Revolutionary War, Philadelphia served as an important center for American natural history. A pivotal figure here was William Bartram, whose *Travels through North and South Carolina, Georgia, East and West Florida* (1791) contained a list of 215 avian species. Bartram's exuberant descriptions of the southeastern landscape inspired many Americans to embrace the study of natural history and to regularly visit his home for guidance. They also patronized the Philadelphia museum of Charles Willson Peale, the American artist and naturalist who used a combination of European taxidermy methods and his own techniques to preserve specimens, thereby making possible the creation of permanent bird skin collections. The Scottish immigrant Alexander Wilson frequented both locations, and at Bartram's persistent urging, began an ambitious project to describe and illustrate every North American bird species. Wilson spent nearly a decade scouring the countryside to find the material needed for his multivolume *American Ornithology* (1808–1814), which treated more than 264 species, including forty-eight that were new to science.

Wilson's book was soon eclipsed by John James Audubon's masterful *Birds of America* (1827–1838), which contained 435 hand-colored, life-sized engravings. Audubon was a brilliant artist, though he sometimes sacrificed scientific accuracy for aesthetic effect. Nevertheless, his reputation as America's foremost bird illustrator remains secure, his exquisite drawings continue to be widely reproduced, and his name has been permanently memorialized in the National Audubon Society.

Institutionalization

The generation of ornithologists that followed Wilson and Audubon were more technical in orientation, and as a result, their publications became less accessible to the general public. Increasingly, American ornithology began to coalesce into a scientific discipline unified by the goal of providing a precise inventory of the nation's birds. State natural history surveys, western exploring expeditions, and individual collectors provided the raw material for this enterprise. By the middle of the nineteenth century, the Academy of Natural Sciences in Philadelphia, the Museum of Comparative Zoology at Harvard, the Smithsonian Institution in Washington, and other public and private museums were amassing the large study collections ornithologists needed to conduct their taxonomic research. Later in the century, these pioneering institutions were joined by the American Museum of Natural History in New York, the Field Columbian Museum of Chicago, and the Carnegie Museum in Pittsburgh. Curatorships at these and other museums provided most of the few paid positions available to ornithologists until the early twentieth century.

The establishment of societies devoted to bird study marked another important stage in the institutionalization of American ornithology. In 1873 a small group of ornithologists associated with William Brewster, of Cambridge, Massachusetts, established the first bird study organization in the United States: the Nuttall Ornithological Club. A decade later this society became the springboard for the creation of the American Ornithologists' Union (AOU), an organization dominated by technically oriented ornithologists. By 1900, there were dozens of ornithological societies in the United States, including not only the Nuttall Club and the AOU, but also the Wilson Ornithological Club, the Cooper Ornithological Club, and the Delaware Valley Ornithological Club. Many of these organizations remain active today.

Throughout the second half of the nineteenth century, scientific ornithologists continued their struggle to produce a single authoritative inventory of the continent's avifauna, down to the level of species and subspecies (the latter are those geographic races delimited by small average morphological differences in specimens). A smaller number of economic ornithologists, on the other hand, studied the diets of birds. Through stomach content analysis and observation, they began to document the role that birds, especially songbirds, played in the control of insect pests. Their data became important in the wildlife conservation movement that emerged at the end of the nineteenth century.

Birdwatching and the Audubon Movement

Ornithologists played a crucial role in the movement to gain protection for birds, especially from commercial hunting for food and the millinery trade. In 1905, a series of state Audubon societies joined in a loose confederation, the National Association of Audubon Societies for the Protection of Wild Birds and Animals (later renamed the National Audubon Society). Audubon societies lobbied for bird protection laws, promoted the establishment of bird sanctuaries, and developed public education campaigns stressing the beauty and economic utility of birds.

The beginning of birdwatching also dates from this period. While the transcendental writer Henry David Thoreau might have been the first American to devote considerable time observing birds in the wild, few followed his lead until the beginning of the twentieth century. By then, the development of inexpensive field glasses, the publication of the first portable field guides, a decline in the average work week, the diffusion of romantic sensibilities, and the prodding of Audubon officials enticed the public to embrace birdwatching as an important leisure activity. The publication of Roger Tory Peterson's *Field Guide to the Birds* (1934) provided further impetus for this hobby, which today tens of millions of Americans regularly enjoy.

Recent Trends

During the first half of the twentieth century, scientific ornithology finally began to broaden from its previous preoccupation with the classification and description of North American birds. The development of graduate programs in ornithology, ecology, and evolutionary biology played an important role in diversifying ornithological research. By the 1920s and 1930s, Cornell, Berkeley, and Michigan had active graduate programs in these areas, and the number continued to rise into the middle of the twentieth century. University-trained ornithologists were more likely to pursue ecological, behavioral, and physiological studies than their largely self-trained nineteenth-century counterparts. They found employment in a variety of positions, ranging from museum curators and researchers to conservationists and wildlife managers. Those ornithologists who remained interested in the classification of birds have become increasingly global in orientation, and they often conduct their research using the latest scientific techniques. Both of these trends are exemplified in the research of Charles Sibley and Jon Ahlquist, who in the1970s and 1980s used DNA hybridization to produce a new classification of the birds of the world. Because birds have been so thoroughly studied, ornithologists have also played an important role in documenting the biodiversity crisis—the worldwide decline of wildlife brought on by human-induced changes to the biosphere.

BIBLIOGRAPHY

Allen, Elsa G., *The History of American Ornithology before Audubon.* Transactions of the American Philosophical Society, n.s. 41, no. 3. Philadelphia: American Philosophical Society, 1951.

Barrow, Mark V., Jr. *A Passion for Birds: American Ornithology after Audubon.* Princeton, N.J.: Princeton University Press, 1998.

Davis, William E., and Jerome A. Jackson, ed., *Contributions to the History of North American Ornithology.* 2 vols. Cambridge, Mass.: Nuttall Ornithological Club, 1995–2000.

Gibbons, Felton, and Deborah Strom. *Neighbors to the Birds: A History of Birdwatching in America.* New York: Norton, 1988.

Mark V. Barrow Jr.

See also **Audubon Society.**

ORTHODOX CHURCHES are among the oldest Christian groups in existence. Originating in the eastern part of the Roman Empire, they have held tenaciously to the classical theological definitions of the first seven ecumenical councils, held between A.D. 325 and 787. The major work of these councils consisted of defining the doctrines of the Trinity and the two natures in Christ,

Russian Orthodox Church. An early-twentieth-century photograph of the Church (now Cathedral) of the Holy Ascension, built in 1824 (and renovated and enlarged much later) on Unalaska, one of the Aleutian Islands. Library of Congress

and in determining the possibility of representing Christ in an image or icon. Eastern Orthodox churches see their bishops as symbols of the unity of the church but do not recognize any single bishop as having authority over all the churches.

The eastern branch of Christianity began to separate from the western branch shortly after the fall of Rome in the fifth century. While early Western theology developed along eschatological (doctrines dealing with death, resurrection, and judgment) and moral lines, reflecting the influence of Aristotle and Augustine, the theology of the East moved in a mystical direction. The schism came during a ninth-century dispute between Pope Nicholas I and Photius, archbishop of Constantinople. Nicholas refused to recognize the election of Photius and excommunicated him (A.D. 863). After further disagreements over the interpretation of the Nicene Creed, in 1054 mutual anathemas (condemnation, excommunication) were pronounced, further deepening the split. These anathemas were rescinded (abolished) in 1965 by Pope Paul IV and Patriarch Athenagoras.

The tenth century was the great age of the expansion of Orthodoxy into Eastern Europe—for which saints Cyril and Methodius prepared the way by translating both the Orthodox scriptures and liturgical books into the Slavic language in the previous century. In 988, the spread of Orthodoxy was completed when the Russians entered the Byzantine ecclesiastical fold. After the fall of Constantinople to the Turks in 1453, Moscow became the chief protector of the Orthodox faith. As the nations of Eastern Europe became independent in the nineteenth century, their churches also became independent national churches with full rights of self-government.

Although the first American Orthodox churches were the nineteenth-century Russian missions in Alaska, Orthodoxy in the United States grew most rapidly during the heavy immigration from Eastern Europe at the end of the nineteenth and beginning of the twentieth centuries. The American history of these churches has been a story of division and controversy, as Old World issues have been perpetuated. Since the mid-twentieth century, there have been signs that this period of controversy is drawing to a close. The patriarch of Moscow healed some of the schisms among the American Russian Orthodox church in 1970 and declared the American church to be autocephalous (self-governing); since then, the various Greek churches, now organized as the Orthodox Church in America, have moved toward a greater degree of unity and centralization. Many of the Eastern Orthodox churches in the United States have been active in the ecumenical movement and have joined both the National Council of Churches and the World Council of Churches.

During the early 1980s and 1990s, the American church refocused its efforts on coping with the growth of its membership and, by the year 2000, numbered more than one million. Meanwhile, as church leaders in Constantinople, Moscow, and Serbia established new ties with the Orthodox Church in America, the concept of a global mission emerged as a central unifying theme. In the late 1990s, the church organized a number of humanitarian efforts in the war-ravaged former Yugoslavia and the Caucasus region of Russia.

BIBLIOGRAPHY

Attwater, Donald. *The Christian Churches of the East.* Milwaukee, Wis.: Bruce Publishing, 1947; Tenbury Well, U.K.: Tomas Moore Books, 1961.

Bogolepov, Aleksandr A. *Toward an American Orthodox Church: The Establishment of an Autocephalous Orthodox Church.* New York: Morehouse-Barlow, 1963; Crestwood, N.Y.: St. Vladimir's Seminary Press, 2001.

Counelis, James S. *Inheritance and Change in Orthodox Christianity.* Scranton, Pa.: University of Scranton Press, 1995.

Glenn T. Miller / A. R.

See also **Religion and Religious Affiliation; Russian and Soviet Americans.**

OSAGE. Originally part of a large Dhegian-Siouxan speaking body of Indians, the Osages lived on the lower Ohio River. Attacks from aggressive tribes to the east drove the group west of the Mississippi River in the early seventeenth century. By about 1650, the Dhegians comprised five autonomous tribes: Quapaws, Kansas, Omahas, Poncas, and Osages. The Osages inhabited a region that straddled the plains and the woodlands of western Missouri. Culturally adaptable, the Osages kept old practices when useful, and adopted new ones when necessary. Osage women continued to plant crops in the spring, but men increasingly hunted deer and buffalo commercially on the plains during summer and fall.

The Osages organized themselves into two patrilineal groupings, or moieties, one symbolizing the sky and peace, the other focusing on the earth and war. Each moiety originally had seven, and later twelve, clans. Some clans had animal names, and some were named after nat-

Osage. A group of tribal members poses on the steps of the U.S. Capitol in Washington, D.C., 1920, several years after the discovery of oil on Osage land. Library of Congress ural phenomena or plants. Villages had two hereditary chiefs, one from each moiety. Osage parents arranged their children's marriages, with the bride and groom always from opposite moieties, and the new couple lived in the lodge of the groom's father. Over time, however, the custom changed, and the couple would live with the bride's family. The Osages believed in an all-powerful life force *Wa-kon-da* and prayed at dawn each day for its support. Religious ceremonies required the participation of all clans.

The French made contact with the Osages in 1673 and began trading, particularly in guns. The Osages needed firearms to fend off attacks from old enemies like the Sauks, Fox, Potawatomis, Kickapoos, and Illinois, and put great energy into commercial hunting and trading livestock and slaves in order to buy them. Further, they used their geographic location to block tribes to the west, the Wichitas, Kansas, Pawnees, Caddos, and Quapaws, from joining the arms race. The Osage were able to control the region between the Missouri and Red Rivers through their superior firepower and great numbers—for much of the eighteenth century, the Osages could muster about one thousand warriors.

By the eighteenth century, the tribe had split into three bands: the Little Osages along the Missouri River, the Arkansas along the Verdigris River, and the Great Osages on the upper Osage River. By the 1830s, there were at least five bands. American expansion in the early nineteenth century moved more than sixty thousand already displaced eastern Indians (Chickasaws, Cherokees, Delawares, and others) west of the Mississippi, overrunning the Osages. In 1839, a treaty with the U.S. government forced the Osages to remove to Kansas. Wisely, the Osages made peace with the Comanches and Kiowas and leapt into the prosperous trade in buffalo hides.

White settlers, especially after the Homestead Act of 1862, encroached on Osage lands, and, by 1870, the tribe had ceded its remaining territory in Kansas. Proceeds from the sale of Osage lands went into a government trust fund and the purchase of a 1.5 million acre reservation from the Cherokees in the Indian Territory (Oklahoma). The decades after 1870 saw the dissolution of the old political forms; pressure from "civilizing" missionaries; and increased tension between full-blooded and mixed-blood Osages. The Osage Allotment Act of 1906 divided oil revenues from their Oklahoma fields among the 2,229 members of the tribe, with the provision that no new headrights be issued. Oil revenues peaked at about $31,000 per headright in 1981. The 1990 census showed 9,527 people who identified themselves as Osage.

BIBLIOGRAPHY

Rollings, Willard H. *The Osage: An Ethnohistorical Study of Hegemony on the Prairie-Plains.* Columbia: University of Missouri Press, 1995.

Sturtevant, William C., and Raymond J. DeMallie, eds. *Handbook of North American Indians: Plains.* Washington, D.C.: Smithsonian Institution, 2001.

Robert M. Owens

See also **Cherokee; Illinois (Indians); Indian Removal; Indian Reservations; Indian Territory; Tribes: Great Plains.**

OSAGE ORANGE (*Maclura pomifera*) is a relatively small, unusually twisted, and frequently multitrunked tree with a small natural range in northern Texas, southeastern Oklahoma, and neighboring parts of Arkansas that roughly coincides with the historical home of the Osage Indians. Because they and other native groups used its wood to make bows, French explorers called the tree "bois d'arc," and it is still sometimes referred to colloquially as "bodarc" or "bodock." The range of the Osage orange expanded dramatically between 1840 and 1880 when, before the development of barbed wire, it was seen as the best and cheapest way to control livestock on the Great Plains. When planted close together and appropriately pruned, its branches and spiny thorns make a nearly impenetrable hedge able to turn away any animal larger than a bird or a rabbit. While it remains common in Illinois, Iowa, Missouri, Kansas, and Nebraska and present even in many eastern states, Osage orange fell from general use as cheaper fencing materials became available in the late nineteenth century.

BIBLIOGRAPHY

Petrides, George A. *A Field Guide to Western Trees.* Boston: Houghton-Mifflin, 1998.

Webb, Walter Prescott. *The Great Plains.* Boston: Ginn and Co., 1931.

Michael Sherfy

See also **Barbed Wire.**

OSBORN V. BANK OF THE UNITED STATES, (9 Wheaton 738 [1824]), a SUPREME COURT decision upholding a circuit court ruling against the taxing by a state of branches of the second BANK OF THE UNITED STATES. In February 1819, the Ohio legislature levied a tax of $50,000 on each state branch of the second bank. Chief Justice John Marshall's opinion, following the precedent of *McCulloch v. Maryland* (1819), held the Ohio law unconstitutional. Despite passing a law withdrawing the protection of state laws from the Bank of the United States, the Ohio legislature made no attempt to nullify the Supreme Court decision.

BIBLIOGRAPHY

White, G. Edward. *The Marshall Court and Cultural Change, 1815–1835.* New York: Macmillan, 1988.

Eugene H. Roseboom / A. R.

See also **Banking: State Banks; *Cohens v. Virginia*; Implied Powers; Judiciary Act of 1789; *McCulloch v. Maryland*; Ohio; Taxation.**

OSLO ACCORDS. *See* **Israeli-Palestinian Peace Accord.**

OSTEND MANIFESTO. Southern desires to expand slave territory led to this foreign policy debacle in 1854. Even though U.S. victory in the Mexican-American War, 1846–1848, annexed California and the Southwest to the nation, it brought little prospect for new slave territory. Eager to permanently add slave states and increase their representation in Congress, southerners wanted Spanish-held Cuba.

In 1854, William Marcy, secretary of state under President Franklin Pierce, bowed to southern pressure and instructed James Buchanan, John Mason, and Pierre Soulé, ambassadors to England, France, and Spain, respectively, to meet in a convenient place to discuss further U.S. attempts to acquire Cuba. They met in Ostend, Belgium, and crafted the so-called Ostend Manifesto. It said that Cuba was vital to U.S. domestic interests. Further, if Spain would not sell Cuba, the United States had no choice but to take it by force. The document caused a diplomatic firestorm, reinforcing foreign fears of aggressive American expansion. Pierce and Marcy tried to distance the administration from the manifesto, but to no avail. Domestically, the document was one of several events leading to the Civil War, helping convince old Whigs and new Republicans that a Democrat-controlled "slave power" ran the country.

BIBLIOGRAPHY

Connell-Smith, Gordon. *The United States and Latin America: A Historical Analysis of Inter-American Relations.* London: Heinemann Educational, 1974.

Gara, Larry. *The Presidency of Franklin Pierce.* Lawrence: University of Kansas, 1991.

Plank, John, ed. *Cuba and the United States: Long-Range Perspectives.* Washington, D.C.: Brookings Institute, 1967.

Schoultz, Lars. *Beneath the United States: A History of U.S. Policy toward Latin America.* Cambridge, Mass.: Harvard University Press, 1998.

Smith, Elbert B. *The Presidency of James Buchanan.* Lawrence: University of Kansas, 1975.

R. Steven Jones

See also **Cuba, Relations with; South, the: The Antebellum South.**

OSTEOPATHY is a system of medicine in which the structure and functions of the body are given equal importance and advocates the body's natural ability to heal itself under the right conditions. Focusing on the "rule of artery," osteopaths manipulate body joints in an effort to improve circulation. The frontier physician Andrew Taylor Still (1828–1917) developed the system in 1874 while living in Kansas. As Still's system of treatment evolved, he attempted to present his methods to the faculty of Baker University in Kansas but was turned away. Without the support of the medical community or any patients, Still made his living as an itinerant doctor until his popularity grew enough for him to establish an infirmary. He settled in Kirksville, Missouri, in 1889. Just three years later, Still opened the American School of Osteopathy (later renamed Kirksville College of Osteopathic Medicine); the school was chartered a year later. The first graduating class of seventeen men and five women studied under Still, his sons, and other doctors. Dr. James Littlejohn and Dr. William Smith—Smith, the first to be awarded the Doctor of Osteopathy (D.O.) degree, from Scotland—played important roles in the growth of the school and popularity of osteopathy. In 1897, the American Association for the Advancement of Osteopathy, later called the American Osteopathy Association, and the Associated Colleges of Osteopathy were formed. Once organized into professional associations, osteopaths began to formalize educational and professional standards. In 1905, a three-year course of study was developed; in 1915, the course was increased to four years. As the profession grew, it received recognition from governmental departments as well as the Department of Defense, which granted officer rank to osteopathic doctor volunteers. By the close of the 1970s, Doctors of Osteopathy held full practice rights in all fifty states. In 1982, more than twenty thousand doctors of osteopathy were practicing in the United States.

BIBLIOGRAPHY

Wardwell, Walter I. *Chiropractic: History and Evolution of a New Profession.* St. Louis, Mo.: Mosby-Year Book, 1992.

Lisa A. Ennis

OTTAWA. The Ottawa are an Algonquin tribe closely related to the Ojibway (Chippewa) and the Potawatomi, which together form the Three Fires Confederacy. Their name, by most accounts, means "traders," which reflects their role as the intermediaries between the Ojibway to the north and the Potawatomi to the south. Their involvement in the European fur trade was a natural extension of their tribal role within the confederacy.

At the time of contact, the Ottawa resided on Manitoulin Island and on the Bruce Peninsula along the eastern shore of Lake Huron. During the early post-contact era, they took up residence in northern Michigan, notably along the eastern shore of Lake Michigan. As did most area tribes, the Ottawa vigorously fought to maintain their grip on their homeland and way of life, most notably through the actions of Pontiac, who lead an uprising against the British in 1763.

While most Ottawa still live in Michigan, others were removed to Kansas and Oklahoma during the early nineteenth century. Still others have returned to the islands of the North Channel of Lake Huron and the Georgian Bay. Also, because of early French trade policies and later U.S. Removal efforts, many Ottawa now live on Walpole Island on the north end of Lake St. Clair. While early estimates of their numbers are clouded by their often being counted as Ojibway, estimates in the early twenty-first century put their numbers at about 15,000, with two-thirds of those resident in what is now the United States (mostly in Michigan) with the rest living in Canada.

BIBLIOGRAPHY

McClurken, James M. *Gah-baeh-Jhagwah-buk: The Way It Happened, a Visual Cultural History of the Little Traverse Bay Bands of Odawa.* East Lansing: Michigan State University Museum, 1991.

White, Richard. *The Middle Ground: Indians, Empires, and Republics in the Great Lakes Region, 1650–1815.* New York: Cambridge University Press, 1991.

Phil Bellfy

See also **Great Lakes; Indian Trade and Traders; Tribes: Northeastern.**

"OUR FEDERAL UNION! IT MUST BE PRESERVED!" was President Andrew Jackson's volunteer toast delivered at the annual Democratic Jefferson Day dinner on 13 April 1830 in response to the South Carolina senator Robert Hayne's pronullification speech. Hayne's speech and the toasts that followed were intended to display a united front for states' rights within the party. Jackson became aware of the plan before the dinner, and he decided to pronounce finally his position on nullification and win back the initiative. To the attendees' shock, Jackson, often identified with states' rights, declared his opposition to nullification and proclaimed his belief in a supreme, perpetual Union. This episode foreshadowed Jackson's successful confrontation with the South Carolina nullifiers, led by Vice President John C. Calhoun, in 1832–1833.

BIBLIOGRAPHY

Freehling, William W. *Prelude to Civil War: The Nullification Controversy in South Carolina, 1816–1836.* New York: Harper and Row, 1966.

———. *The Road to Disunion.* Vol. 1: *Secessionists at Bay, 1776–1854.* New York: Oxford University Press, 1990.

Remini, Robert V. *Andrew Jackson.* New York: HarperPerennial, 1999.

Watson, Harry L. *Liberty and Power: The Politics of Jacksonian America.* New York: Hill and Wang, 1990.

Aaron J. Palmer

See also **Nullification; Secession; Sectionalism; States' Rights.**

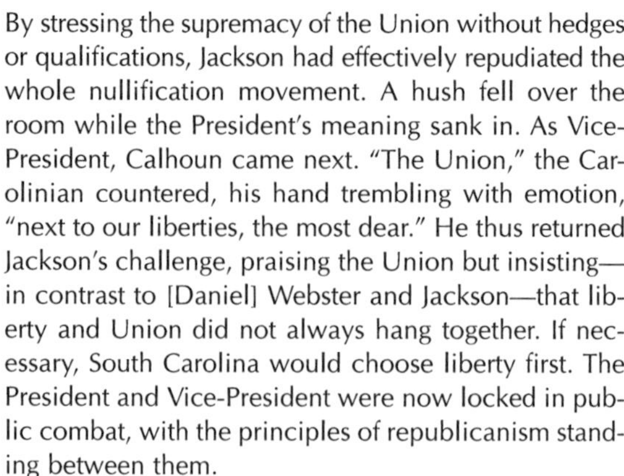

By stressing the supremacy of the Union without hedges or qualifications, Jackson had effectively repudiated the whole nullification movement. A hush fell over the room while the President's meaning sank in. As Vice-President, Calhoun came next. "The Union," the Carolinian countered, his hand trembling with emotion, "next to our liberties, the most dear." He thus returned Jackson's challenge, praising the Union but insisting—in contrast to [Daniel] Webster and Jackson—that liberty and Union did not always hang together. If necessary, South Carolina would choose liberty first. The President and Vice-President were now locked in public combat, with the principles of republicanism standing between them.

SOURCE: Watson, *Liberty and Power,* p. 121.

OVERLAND COMPANIES, or wagon trains, traveled from the Missouri River to California or Oregon. Beginning in 1839, most traveling groups were families. During the gold rush, single men joined joint-stock companies, paying $300 to $500 for passage. Groups organized prior to starting, sometimes with written constitutions and bylaws. Once underway, overlanders might join another group for various reasons. After 1850, eastbound companies were not uncommon. Initially, companies hired experienced mountain men as guides. After 1850 the routes were well worn, guidebooks were available, and experienced travelers were willing to guide others. Over a quarter of a million emigrants passed over the trails in two decades.

BIBLIOGRAPHY

Unruh, John D., Jr. *The Plains Across: The Overland Emigrants and the Trans-Mississippi West, 1840–60.* Urbana: University of Illinois Press, 1993.

Laurie Winn Carlson

See also **Oregon Trail; Westward Migration.**

OVERLAND TRAIL. Established and owned by the "Stagecoach King," Ben Holladay, the Overland Trail was a variation of the Oregon Trail. In 1862, Holladay and his Overland Stage Company were directed by the U.S. Post Office to move from the established route through Wyoming that followed the North Platte River to a different route following the South Platte. The new route had the advantage of being shorter, but it was also chosen in an effort to avoid Indian attacks that had been occurring on the Oregon Trail.

The route of the Overland Trail followed the southern bank of the South Platte River to Latham, near today's Greeley, Colorado, then went up along the Cache le Poudre River, crossed the Laramie Plains, traveled through Bridger's Pass, and rejoined the Oregon Trail at Fort Bridger. The western route out of Latham was also known as the Cherokee Trail.

While the Oregon Trail may have been more popular, the Overland Trail was not simply a detour. From 1862 to 1868, it was the only route upon which the federal government would permit travel and it served as the main highway to the west in those years. Holladay owned the Overland Stage Company until 1866 when, realizing the Transcontinental Railroad would end the need for stagecoach travel, he sold it to Wells Fargo.

BIBLIOGRAPHY

Faragher, John M. *Women and Men on the Overland Trail.* 2d ed., New Haven, Conn.: Yale University Press, 2001. The original edition was published in 1979.

Gregory Moore

See also **Cherokee Trail; Oregon Trail; Westward Migration.**

OVERSEER AND DRIVER. If the slaveholders were to be believed, their overseers were a low-bred class of scoundrels whose management of the southern slaves swung erratically from violent abuse to lackadaisical incompetence. The truth was more complicated. Overseers were the middlemen of the antebellum South's plantation hierarchy. As such they occupied an impossible position. The masters expected them to produce profitable crops while maintaining a contented workforce of slaves—slaves who had little reason to work hard to improve the efficiency of the plantation. It would have required a prodigy to balance these competing pressures to the complete satisfaction of both the master and the slaves. Few overseers were prodigies.

No one knows for sure how many overseers there were in 1860, but the best estimates are that the number of overseers was roughly equal to the number of plantations with thirty or more slaves. These men were a varied lot. Some were the sons of planters who served their fathers as overseers, learning the art of plantation management before striking out on their own. Others, perhaps the largest number, were semiprofessional managers hoping one day to set up their own agricultural operations. And still others lived up to the worst reputation of their class: violent men, often drunkards, unable to hold steady jobs, who moved repeatedly from plantation to plantation. But the average overseer rarely lasted in any master's service for more than a few years. The best moved on to other things. The worst were fired. And even the merely competent rarely satisfied an employer for long. A bad

Crossing the Platte. A woodcut by Albert Bierstadt, published in *Harper's Weekly* on 13 August 1859, of settlers moving their covered wagons across the river as Indians smoke nearby; the safer Overland Trail was established soon afterward. © CORBIS

crop year, sickly slaves, or the untenable contradictions of the job itself ensured that few overseers lasted long on any one plantation.

Drivers were another story. They were slaves appointed by masters to positions of authority on the plantation. Where masters were resident, black drivers often replaced overseers. On larger plantations, especially in the Lower South, black drivers worked under the supervision of white overseers. The drivers' jobs were manifold, but they were expected above all to maintain discipline in the fields and order in the quarters.

Like overseers, drivers were subjected to competing pressures that demanded both technical skill and a strong measure of self-confidence. But the pressures on drivers were different in important ways. Drivers were a part of the slave community, but they were especially favored by the master. To maintain the goodwill of the master without losing the respect of one's fellow slaves was no small achievement. Yet the evidence suggests that the drivers often succeeded where the overseers failed. They were chosen for their intelligence and abilities; they often understood how to manage a plantation more effectively than the overseers. Accordingly, drivers often held their positions for decades. The masters came to rely on the drivers for their competence; the slaves came to expect the drivers to moderate some of the harshness of the regime.

BIBLIOGRAPHY

Scarborough, William Kauffman. *The Overseer: Plantation Management in the Old South.* Baton Rouge: Louisiana State University Press, 1966.

Van Deburg, William L. *The Slave Drivers: Black Agricultural Labor Supervisors in the Antebellum South.* Westport, Conn.: Greenwood Press, 1979.

James Oakes

See also **Plantation System of the South; Slavery.**

OXEN, used from the time of early settlements in America as draft animals and for plowing. Their slow pace was counterbalanced on rough, muddy pioneer roads by strength and endurance far superior to the horse. They were a favorite of loggers and early canal and railroad builders. In an 1805 test on the Middlesex Canal in Massachusetts, one yoke of oxen drew 800 tons of timber, but at only one mile per hour, too slow to be permitted on the towpath. Nineteenth-century small farmers in the South prized "steers" for general use, and still used them, although rarely, as late as the 1920s.

Oxen drew many wagons in all the great westward migrations—to the Ohio country, Tennessee, Kentucky, the prairie states, and finally in 1848–1849 on the long treks over plains and mountains to Oregon and California. Next, Western freighters employed oxen in enormous numbers, often using six, eight, or ten yoke of oxen to pull large loaded wagons—often hooked together and drawn over rough trails. Rigs of this sort, traveling together for safety, were known in western parlance as "bull trains." The freighting firm of Russell, Majors and Waddell, while they were hauling supplies for the army from the Missouri River to Utah in 1857–1858, are said to have worked 40,000 oxen. When the gold rush to the Black Hills (South Dakota) began in 1875, one company, freighting from Yankton to Deadwood, made use of 4,000 oxen at the height of the rush.

BIBLIOGRAPHY

Faragher, John Mack. *Women and Men on the Overland Trail.* New Haven, Conn.: Yale University Press, 1979.

Harlow, Alvin F. *Old Waybills.* New York: D. Appleton-Century Co., 1934.

Alvin F. Harlow / c. w.

See also **Gold Mines and Mining; Mule Skinner; Pack Trains; Wagon Trains.**

OXFORD MOVEMENT. The Oxford Movement was a religious revival in the Church of England (1833) that emphasized the church's Catholic heritage in doctrine, polity, and worship. In America the movement found congenial soil among Episcopalians already influenced by the high churchmanship of Bishop John H. Hobart of New York (1775–1830). Opposition by those who believed the movement endangered the protestantism of the church reached an apex during the 1840s. Several high-profile conversions to Roman Catholicism increased party tension. Although the matter was settled by the 1874 canon, which prevented liturgical practices inconsistent with the church's doctrines, the movement exercised a permanent influence on the liturgy of the Episcopal church.

BIBLIOGRAPHY

Chadwick, Owen. *The Spirit of the Oxford Movement: Tractarian Essays.* Cambridge, U.K.: Cambridge University Press, 1990.

Mullin, Robert Bruce. *Episcopal Vision/American Reality: High Church Theology and Social Thought in Evangelical America.* New Haven, Conn.: Yale University Press, 1986.

Massey H. Shepherd Jr. / a. r.

See also **Episcopalianism; Religious Thought and Writings.**

OZETTE was the largest of five Makah towns at the Pacific corner of Washington State, the ancient home of the unique Chimakum language. About a thousand years ago, Nootkan speakers from southern Vancouver Island moved across the Strait of Juan de Fuca to become the Makahs.

Near a seal rookery and offshore reef, Ozette had a population of 200 in fifteen houses in 1870. Its size dwindled as Deah (modern Neah Bay) became the hub of the Makahs' federal agency and school.

Ozette has earned a special place as the "American Pompeii" because a massive mudslide buried at least four shed-roof houses and a beached whale about A.D. 1500. These crushed dwellings provided details about construction, from their leveled floor to their standing framework of posts, beams, and side bunks for attaching removable wall planks. Inside, risers served as beds, seating, storage, and shelter (for ill-fated puppies). Families lived in each house by rank, with nobles in the back, commoners along the sides, and slaves exposed at the doorway.

Between 1970 and 1981, using garden hoses to wash away dirt, archaeologists and Makahs exposed 50,000 artifacts and a million plant fibers, including 6,000 weaving fragments of baskets, clothing, mats, and cordage. Thanks to quickly devised special preservation techniques, these remains are now proudly displayed in a tribal museum at Neah Bay.

BIBLIOGRAPHY

Wessen, Gary. "Prehistory of the Ocean Coast of Washington." In *Handbook of North American Indians*. Edited by William C. Sturtevant. Volume 7: *Northwest Coast*, edited by Wayne Suttles. Washington, D.C.: Smithsonian Institution, 1990.

Jay Miller

See also **Tribes: Northwestern.**

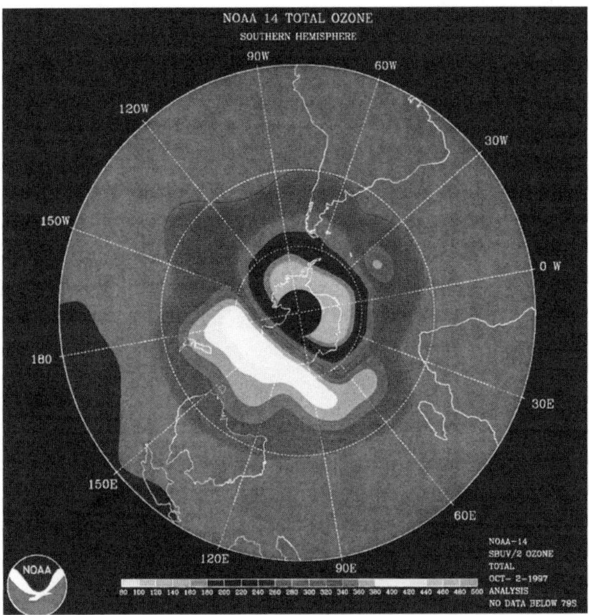

Ozone Hole. An enhanced graphic showing a large area of severe thinning in the ozone layer at the South Pole, 1997—one of a multitude of large-scale environmental changes since the mid-twentieth century, widely attributed to man-made causes and predicted to lead to eventual ecological crises. AP/Wide World Photos/National Oceanic and Atmospheric Administration

OZONE DEPLETION became a serious concern in the 1980s and has prompted international agreements and changes in manufacturing processes in an attempt to slow depletion and minimize health and environmental problems. Ozone is a denser form of oxygen that shields the Earth from excessive ultraviolet radiation from the sun; without it, the earth's inhabitants and environment are exposed to damaging UV-B rays. Scientists detected substantial seasonal fluctuations in stratospheric ozone levels over Antarctica as early as the 1950s. In the 1970s the chemists Sherwood Rowland and Mario Molina of the University of California (in findings later confirmed by the National Academy of Sciences) blamed the lower wintertime level of ozone over Antarctica on the rapidly increasing use of chlorofluorocarbons (CFCs) as refrigerants and as propellants in aerosol cans and in the manufacture of plastic foam products. CFC molecules deplete the ozone layer because they migrate to the stratosphere, collect over the Antarctic ice cap during the cold winter months, and become fixed on polar stratospheric clouds, isolated from the normal atmospheric circulation. When sunlight returns to Antarctica in early spring, its ultraviolet rays trigger a chemical reaction that releases a chlorine-oxide free radical, which precipitates another reaction that breaks up the oxygen molecules that form the ozone layer. A world that has been producing and releasing into the atmosphere 1 million tons of CFCs per year has seen CFC levels in the atmosphere rise from 0.8 parts per billion by volume in 1950 to at least 4 parts per billion at the close of the century.

In 1985 the discovery of an ozone "hole" over wintertime Antarctica prompted international action. In 1987 all major industrial nations signed the Montreal Protocol, agreeing to deadlines for ending the use of CFCs; eighty nations signed amendments calling for the almost total elimination of CFCs, methyl chloroform, and carbon tetrachloride by 1996. By the 1990s, 173 countries, including the United States, had signed.

However, the danger is far from over. Alarm bells rang in October 2000, when for the first time ever, a major ozone hole opened over a populated city: Punta Arenas, Chile. Not all countries and industries are complying with the ban on ozone-depleting substances; for instance, U.S. companies have been fighting efforts to cut use of methyl bromides, claiming that scientists exaggerate their effects on the ozone layer. Furthermore, a black market in CFCs is thriving. Many nations lack the resources to monitor production of ozone-depleting chemicals, and some consumers in more industrialized nations buy smuggled-in compounds to avoid retrofitting the many appliances made before the CFC-phaseout. Without major cuts in CFC and methyl bromide emissions, continuing thinning of the ozone layer may bring quadrupled levels of skin cancer by 2100, increases in cataracts, suppression of the immune system, and increasing rates of non-Hodgkin's lymphoma. Scientific findings in the early 2000s suggest far-reaching ecological disruption may also ensue, including genetic mutations and accelerated species extinctions.

BIBLIOGRAPHY

Cogan, Douglas G. *Stones in a Glass House: CFCs and Ozone Depletion.* Washington, D.C.: Investor Responsibility Research Center, 1988.

de Gruijl, Frank R., and Jan C. van der Leun. "Environment and Health: 3. Ozone Depletion and Ultraviolet Radiation." *Canadian Medical Association Journal* 163 (2000): 851–855.

Grundmann, Reiner. *Transnational Environmental Policy: The Ozone Layer.* New York: Routledge, 2001.

Rowland, F. Sherwood. "Stratospheric Ozone in the Twenty-First Century: The Chlorofluorocarbon Problem." *Environmental Science and Technology* 25 (1991): 622–628.

Nancy M. Gordon / D. B.

See also **Chemical Industry; Climate; Environmental Movement; Epidemics and Public Health.**

PACIFIC FUR COMPANY, organized by John Jacob Astor in 1810, was the western subsidiary of his American Fur Company and the lynchpin in his plan to control the American fur market. Astor supplied capital up to $400,000 and was to bear all losses for the first five years. He retained 50 percent of the stock and prorated the remainder among several field partners. The firm was to ship sea otter and beaver pelts from Astoria, at the mouth of the Columbia River in Oregon, to Canton, China. There, furs would be exchanged for Chinese goods, which Astor's ships would then deliver to the United States. The wreck of two of the ships, unfortunate management in the field, and the War of 1812 resulted in the failure of the Pacific Fur Company, and Astoria and its equipment were sold by the field partners, at a great sacrifice, to the North West Company.

BIBLIOGRAPHY

Karamanski, Theodore J. *Fur Trade and Exploration: Opening the Far Northwest, 1821–1852.* Norman: University of Oklahoma Press, 1983.

Lavender, David. *The Fist in the Wilderness.* Albuquerque: University of New Mexico Press, 1979 [1964].

Robert Moulton Gatke / T. D.

See also **Astoria; Fur Companies; Fur Trade and Trapping.**

PACIFIC ISLANDERS do not form one distinctive ethnic group, but come from across Micronesia, Melanesia, and Polynesia. Pacific Islanders come from the islands of Hawaii, the U.S. insular territories of American Samoa, Guam, and the Northern Mariana Islands, as well as the Freely Associated States of Micronesia and the tiny nations of the Marshall Islands and Palau. Other places of origin outside of U.S. affiliation include Fiji, Tahiti, the Solomon Islands, and Tonga.

In the 2000 census, 874,000 people, or 0.3 percent of the U.S. population, identified themselves as Pacific Islanders, either exclusively or in combination with other groups. Of this total, native Hawaiians, Samoans, and Guamanians-Chamorros accounted for 74 percent of the respondents. The majority of Pacific Islanders were born in Hawaii. Honolulu, New York, Los Angeles, San Diego, and Phoenix were the largest population centers, with groups of Pacific Islanders also found in Utah, Texas, and Washington.

Pacific Islanders had the highest proportion of people reporting more than one race. Ethnic identification may be situational; for example, a person might be a Samoan living in Hawaii, but may also have Tongan, Maori, and European ancestors, and yet ultimately be identified as Hawaiian when on the mainland. In this sense, Pacific Islander is an inclusive designation, and mixed ancestry is as definitive as pure ancestry. The Pacific Islander has a larger household than average, which often includes extended family members. Language and culture, closely linked to family and tradition, are the keystones to retaining Pacific Islander identity when living in the United States.

Migration of Pacific Islanders has occurred in response to shrinking economic opportunities in their homelands or to the changing status of the island nations and their relationship to the United States. Although only 16 percent of those who identify themselves as Pacific Islanders were actually born on the islands, they continue to maintain close economic and political ties to their homeland communities.

The first of the islands to come under U.S. authority was American Samoa, in 1872. It remained under the authority of the U.S. Navy until 1951, when it was transferred into the administration of the U.S. Department of the Interior. After World War II (1939–1945) the United Nations granted the United States trusteeships of the small island nations of Micronesia, known as the Trust Territory of the Pacific Islands. These trusteeships began to be dissolved in the 1970s, a process that was concluded in 1994. The fluidity of the compacts with the United States allowed large numbers of Pacific Islanders to migrate to Guam and Hawaii, where they had a significant impact on the local economies.

Hawaii was annexed in 1898 and became a state in 1959. In the 1990s a movement for Hawaiian sovereignty grew, which had popular support among native Hawaiians, but has not succeeded in legal challenges to the status of the islands. The sovereignty movement brought to attention the means by which Hawaii had been acquired, and in 1993, President William Jefferson Clinton signed a congressional resolution apologizing for the overthrow of the Kingdom of Hawaii one hundred years earlier. Similar movements have appeared in Guam, but remain outside the mainstream.

BIBLIOGRAPHY

Spickhard Paul R., and Rowena Fong. "Pacific Islander Americans and Multiethnicity: A Vision of America's Future?" *Social Forces* 73 (1995): 1365–1383.

Statistics Site. Office of Insular Affairs. Home page at http://www.pacificweb.org/.

White House Initiative on Asian Americans and Pacific Islanders. Home page at http://www.aapi.gov/.

Denise Rosenblatt

See also **Guam; Hawaii; Marshall Islands; Samoa, American.**

PACIFIC NORTHWEST is the region of the United States that comprises the northern coast of California, all of Oregon and Washington, and (according to some) the western part of Idaho. The region is known for its active volcanic peaks, such as Mount St. Helens in Washington. Spain, Russia, and Great Britain all had an early interest in the area. Meriweather Lewis and William Clark explored the region in the early 1800s, but it was not until the 1840s, after the Oregon Trail had been established, that settlers arrived in significant numbers. In 1846, the United States and England agreed that the 49th parallel would be the dividing line between the American Pacific Northwest and the British territory of Canada. Large coniferous forests supported the development of a variety of timber-related industries, including shipbuilding and later lumber and paper. Significant precipitation, along with two major rivers, the Columbia and the Snake, gave rise to various hydroelectric projects. Fishing, particularly for salmon, has long been an economic mainstay of the region; the aerospace and high technology industries dominate its economy in the twenty-first century. The region's exceptional natural beauty has attracted people with a strong environmental awareness and a tendency toward conservation rather than commercial exploitation.

BIBLIOGRAPHY

Muir, John. *Northwest Passages: From the Pen of John Muir in California, Oregon, Washington, and Alaska.* Palo Alto, Calif.: Tioga, 1988.

Weiss, Michael Arthur. "Bringing Natural History to the People: Three Pioneers of the Pacific Northwest Frontier." Master's thesis, University of Oregon, Eugene, 1989.

Christine E. Hoffman

See also **Columbia River Exploration and Settlement; Mount St. Helens; Oregon; Snake River; Washington, State of.**

PACIFIC RIM, a region comprising the countries and regions bordering the Pacifc Ocean, particularly (but not exclusively) the small nations of eastern Asia. Geologically, the region, dominated by the vast expanse of ocean between America to the east and Asia to the west, contains four-fifths of the world's seismic activity. It is its economic activity, however, that has given the geological term currency in international business and in world politics, especially with regard to Asia. Asian economies went from producing just 4 percent of the world's overall economic output in the 1960s to 25 percent in the 1990s. By the early 1990s U.S. exports to Asia exceeded those to Europe; transpacific trade had at last become more important than the transatlantic. The region's economic growth was led not only by Japan but also by the "little dragons" of Singapore, Hong Kong, South Korea, and Taiwan, as well the "tigers" of Southeast Asia, particularly Indonesia, Malaysia, and Thailand.

Adding to the importance of this region was the increasing involvement of the People's Republic of China in international trade as it reluctantly began to open its market of 1.2 billion consumers to outside trade and capitalist incentives after the conclusion of the Cold War in 1991. To mark this shift, in 1989 China joined eleven other Pacific Rim nations in forming the Asia-Pacific Economic Cooperation (APEC). In 1994 APEC signed an accord to achieve "free and open trade and investment" in the region among its industrialized members while giving its developing nations until the year 2020 to comply. The hope was that the agreement would transform the region into the world's largest free-trade area, though there was much doubt about this after the global economic slowdown of the late 1990s. Since its inception in 1989, APEC has grown from an informal dialogue of a dozen Pacific Rim economies to a major regional institution with twenty-one members. The United States works closely with APEC and sees it as an important part of the nation's engagement in the Asia-Pacific region. It has become America's primary vehicle for advancing both economic cooperation and investment liberalization in the region.

In the opening years of the twenty-first century, APEC member economies were: Australia, Brunei, Canada, Chile, China, Hong Kong, Indonesia, Japan, Republic of Korea, Malaysia, Mexico, New Zealand, Papua New Guinea, Peru, Philippines, Russia, Singapore, Chinese Taipei, Thailand, United States, and Vietnam.

BIBLIOGRAPHY

Besher, Alexander, ed. *The Pacific Rim Almanac.* New York: Harper Perennial, 1991.

West, Philip, et al., eds. *The Pacific Rim and the Western World.* Boulder, Colo.: Westview Press, 1987.

Joseph M. Siracusa

See also **Australia and New Zealand, Relations with; Canada, Relations with; Chile, Relations with; China, Relations with; Japan, Relations with; Korea, Relations with; Mexico, Relations with; Philippines; Russia, Relations with; Vietnam, Relations with.**

PACIFISM. Four unique types of pacifism have entered American life and politics: (1) conscientious objection to war, resulting in personal refusal to participate in war or military service; (2) opposition to and renunciation of all forms of violence; (3) a strategy of nonviolent action to overcome specific injustices or to bring about radical change in the social order; and (4) a "positive testimony" to a way of life based on conviction of the power of love to govern human relationships.

Conscientious objection to war was a central doctrine of the "historic peace churches" (BRETHREN, MENNONITES, and QUAKERS), which held war to be in fundamental contradiction to their religious faiths. In prerevolutionary Pennsylvania, Quakers tried with some success to apply their pacifist convictions in the colony that William Penn had established as a "holy experiment," a colony where they could live at peace with each other and with all persons, including their Indian neighbors. The American Revolution, however, split the Quakers on the issue of political pacifism and led to their permanent withdrawal from politics as an organized religious body. This development returned pacifism to the individual for decision—on refusing to fight, pay taxes for military purposes, or in other ways to support the war "system."

The number of objectors and the form of their objection varied with the moral appeal of each war, reaching a climax of opposition to U.S. military action in Vietnam and Cambodia in the late 1960s. Probably one out of five of those of draft age during this period were exempted from military service because of conscientious objection (although many of these were ostensibly deferred for other reasons, because local draft boards did not wish to acknowledge such claims formally). An unprecedented, though unspecified, number of draftees were discharged from military service or were absent without leave (AWOL) because of objections after induction. In addition, a substantial number were imprisoned because they refused to fight or to be inducted.

During this time pacifist ranks reached out to most denominations, and many of the country's religious leaders were included. Also, persons whose objection to war stemmed from humanitarian or philosophical convictions rather than religious training and belief—the criterion for conscientious objection specified in the Selective Training and Service Act of 1940—were legitimized by a succession of SUPREME COURT decisions. Meanwhile, pacifists in the twentieth century had again sought political means to prevent war and keep the United States out of war. They were a principal force in the American peace movement and were often at odds with those who urged a collective-security system with international military sanctions as the most effective approach to maintaining peace.

The second form of pacifism abjures violence in any form and sees violence operating not only in outright war but also through social institutions that permit human exploitation and discrimination and that rely on repression and force to maintain "law and order." Consequently, the major goal of such pacifists has been social reform. The core of the American antislavery movement was largely pacifist. For example, in the 1750s John Woolman preached to his fellow Quakers that slavery was incompatible with their professed respect for "that of God in every man." Social pacifism also infused the struggle for prison reform, the fight against capital punishment, the championing of women's rights, efforts to improve care of the mentally ill and retarded, and the securing of civil rights for all minorities.

Social-reform pacifists were in direct conflict with those who insisted that effective action demanded violence. They found themselves denounced as soft-headed dupes, if not outright lackeys, of the entrenched oppressors. To such charges pacifists responded with the third pattern—a strategy of nonviolent direct action. Modeled on Mahatma Gandhi's philosophy of civil disobedience (*satyagraha*), sit-ins (put to an early test by some unions in the industrial conflicts of the 1930s), marches (which achieved dramatic impact with the "stride toward freedom" from Selma to Montgomery, Alabama, of Martin Luther King Jr., who called for an end to racial discrimination), vigils (usually conducted by smaller groups with a strong religious motif), and boycotts (as notably organized by César E. Chavez, 1965–1970, on behalf of grape pickers striking against California growers) became expressions of nonviolent protest. These actions were characterized by extraordinary self-discipline, even when met by violent counteraction.

Pacifist influence was fractured by a succession of violent events. The assassination of King silenced the most effective spokesperson for nonviolence at a time when militants among blacks and others in the civil rights movement were clamoring for confrontation by force. Later, a sense of helplessness swept over the peace movement when President Richard M. Nixon moved to extend the war into Cambodia and substituted massive, electronically controlled bombing and mining for the presence of most American draftees in Vietnam. But backlash against the civil rights and peace movements demonstrated that a wide base of nonpacifist values existed throughout America. The collapse of the George S. McGovern campaign for the presidency in 1972 seemed to bury the hopes for effective political expression of pacifist concerns, leaving a vacuum of disillusionment that militants eagerly sought to fill.

Two influences combined to generate a fourth type of pacifism. Many conscientious objectors became increasingly troubled by the essentially negative posture of their position. They wanted not simply to protest wars and injustice, but also to create the conditions for a human community. Second, a growing number felt that societies in general and American society in particular were past reforming and that peace would have to be sought within a small group of kindred souls. Both influences moved toward a definition of pacifism as a total philosophy of life and toward experimentation with human relationships in which love would replace violence. These two expressions of pacifism, however, differed in focus. The first emphasized an outward "testimony" by which the principles of cooperative community could be demonstrated to others as a viable way of life. This was the original intent of the Civilian Public Service program, which had been organized voluntarily by the historic peace churches to offer an alternative to military service during World War II. Conscientious-objector units worked, with commendable efficacy, on conservation and park projects, in fire fighting and disaster relief, in mental health hospitals and schools for retarded children, and as "guinea pigs" for medical research. The effectiveness of the testimony-by-work approach was seriously undermined, however, by Selective Service control and the inescapable consciousness that the testifiers were in fact conscripts, not volunteers.

The second approach rejected society in favor of a commune of persons willing to live simply on a sharealike basis, as independently as possible from the requirements of the so-called system (including fixed employment). The new communes followed the long tradition in America of experimental communities devoted to the ideal of self-sufficient and harmonious living. In the mid-1970s pacifism in America seemed to have returned to its pristine base of individual conviction. But the activism of the 1960s had imparted both a commitment to conscientious objection to war and a sensitivity to social injustice that encompassed a much broader swath of American life than ever before. Indeed, events of the late twentieth and early twenty-first century revealed a broad spectrum of Americans ready to protest what they saw as injust wars, at home and abroad.

Citizens organized beginning in the 1980s to protest the civil-liberties violations, injuries, and deaths, and high imprisonment rates wrought by the war on drugs launched in the early 1980s by the administration of President Ronald Reagan. The police became increasingly militarized, using tactics of war rather than domestic law enforcement. The 1990s saw more traditional antiwar protests over the Persian Gulf War. After Iraq's leader, Saddam Hussein, invaded Kuwait in 1991, the United States launched a war to push Iraq back out. The United States government sent some 500,000 troops to the region and dropped huge numbers of bombs on Iraq, killing tens of thousands of Iraqis and destroying much of the nation's infrastructure. A significant protest movement against the Persian Gulf War, and the economic sanctions that followed, developed in the United States.

Pacifism became a much more dangerous position to hold publicly in the United States after 11 September 2001, when Islamic terrorists flew planes into the World Trade Center and the Pentagon, killing thousands and shattering Americans' sense of safety. President George W. Bush launched a "war on terrorism," which involved both sending military personnel around the globe and restricting privacy rights and other civil liberties at home. Citizens across the political spectrum, who had been shocked and horrified by the events of 11 September, nonetheless found themselves ill at ease over a "war" with no clear ending point and with an alarming tendency to rationalize the curbing of domestic civil liberties.

BIBLIOGRAPHY

Birnbaum, Jonathan, and Clarence Taylor, eds. *Civil Rights since 1787: A Reader on the Black Struggle.* New York: New York University Press, 2000.

Bush, Perry. *Two Kingdoms, Two Loyalties: Mennonite Pacifism in Modern America.* Baltimore: Johns Hopkins University Press, 1998.

Early, Frances H. *A World without War: How U.S. Feminists and Pacifists Resisted World War I.* Syracuse, N.Y.: Syracuse University Press, 1997.

Hawkley, Louise, and James C. Juhnke, eds. *Nonviolent America: History through the Eyes of Peace.* North Newton, Kan.: Bethel College, 1993.

Kammen, Michael, ed. *Contested Values: Democracy and Diversity in American Culture.* New York: St. Martin's Press, 1995.

Klejment, Anne, and Nancy L. Roberts, eds. *American Catholic Pacifism: The Influence of Dorothy Day and the Catholic Worker Movement.* Westport, Conn.: Praeger, 1996.

Schlabach, Theron F., and Richard T. Hughes, eds. *Proclaim Peace: Christian Pacifism from Unexpected Quarters.* Urbana: University of Illinois Press, 1997.

Tracy, James. *Direct Action: Radical Pacifism from the Union Eight to the Chicago Seven.* Chicago: University of Chicago Press, 1996.

Philip E. Jacob/D. B.

See also **Antiwar Movements; Civil Rights Movement; King, Martin Luther, Assassination; Missiles, Military; Persian Gulf Syndrome; Persian Gulf War of 1991; Shakers; United Farm Workers Union of America; Utopian Communities; Youth Movements;** *and vol. 9:* **Peace and Bread in Time of War.**

PACK TRAINS were a means by which raw materials and consumer goods were transported across the Allegheny Mountains. After crops were harvested in autumn, entrepreneurs in rural areas organized caravans of packhorses, each horse laden with pelts, whiskey, and other goods for barter. The main Pennsylvania trails were the Kittanning, along the Allegheny River, and the Raystown Path, from the Ohio to the eastern cities. The pack trains returned with salt, iron, sugar, and perhaps some urban "luxuries" such as crockery. From its communal beginnings, packing became a professional vocation. As waterborne traffic on the Allegheny and Ohio Rivers became safer and more efficient in the early nineteenth century, the pack trains waned.

BIBLIOGRAPHY

James T. Lemon, "Urbanization and the Development of Eighteenth-Century Southeastern Pennsylvania and Adjacent Delaware." *William and Mary Quarterly* 24 (1967): 501–542.

E. Douglas Branch / A. R.

See also **Rural Life; Wagoners of the Alleghenies.**

PACKAGING. Even before modern mass packaging, merchants sold goods in crocks, barrels, or bottles or wrapped in paper, fabric, or leaves. Some of the earliest prepackaged, prelabeled items were patent medicines and tobacco products. However, most products before the late nineteenth century were sold loose from bulk containers.

The history of modern mass-produced, prepackaged products parallels the rise of complex industrial organization and standardized, large-scale production processes beginning in the late nineteenth century. Industry began to use packages as a way to sell a visually distinctive national brand—promoting it in the new mass-media advertising outlets—to consumers who increasingly shopped not in dry goods stores but in large, well-stocked department stores and supermarkets. Thus, innovation in industrial organization, production processes, and advertising media evolved synergistically with innovations in packaging technologies and processes. This was particularly true in the food industry, where the rise of mason jar–steam pressure packing (1870s), tin can manufacturing machinery (early 1900s), and the paper carton enabled more products to be sold on a wider scale and advertised by brand. General Foods and many other large, multinational corporations arose from the merger of many smaller companies whose brands had become known to consumers through their distinctive packaging. Along with new packaging techniques came new forms of food preservation, such as freezing and pasteurization. Later, the rise of aseptic and shrink-wrap technologies, along with new preservation technologies, paralleled the rise of the globalized fresh food economy.

In tandem with the rise of packaging technologies was the development of product design and labeling. American package design lagged behind that of the European manufacturers, but by the 1920s, the United States began to draw heavily from the European Beaux Arts movement to create a more modern-looking package that sold the product. Increasingly efficient packaging machinery also became more sophisticated in terms of meeting advanced design requirements, including the development of flexographic printing and other forms of advanced lithography.

Along with the development of modern packaging design came consumer demands for greater information about the nature of the goods within. From the beginning, manufacturers made unsubstantiated claims on packages and associated advertisements. In response, the pure food consumer movement lobbied for the legislation that created labeling criteria for ingredients and additives. Concerns over nutrition also led to the establishment of nutritional information on food packages. Over time, packages displayed more third-party certifications of quality and purity, such as awards from international expositions. Increasing consumer concern led to a proliferation of certifications on packages, from industrial standards of manufacture to parent association approvals.

Public concern moved to the question of packaging itself. Environmental movements led to the establishment of recycled packaging as well as demands for "source reduction" in the packaging system. Nevertheless, these trends are often counteracted by demands for convenience and safety.

BIBLIOGRAPHY

Chandler, Alfred. *Strategy and Structure: Chapters in the History of the American Industrial Enterprise.* Boston: MIT Press, 1962.

Heller, Steven. "Commercial Modern: American Design Style, 1925–1933." *Print* 49 (1995): 58–69.

Levenstein, Harvey A. *Revolution at the Table: The Transformation of the American Diet.* New York: Oxford University Press, 1988.

E. Melanie DuPuis

See also **Advertising; Recycling.**

PACKERS AND STOCKYARDS ACT. The Packers and Stockyards Act, passed in August 1921 after several years of controversy, made it unlawful for packers to manipulate prices, to create a monopoly, or to award favors to any person or locality. The legal regulation of stockyards attempted to guarantee nondiscriminatory services, reasonable rates, open schedules, and fair charges. Administration of the law was the responsibility of the secretary of agriculture, who heard complaints, held hearings, and issued "cease and desist" orders. The bill was a significant part of the agrarian legislation of the early 1920s.

BIBLIOGRAPHY

Ruttan, Vernon W., comp. *Agricultural Policy in an Affluent Society.* New York: Norton, 1969.

Thomas S. Barclay / C. W.

See also **Antitrust Laws; Meatpacking; Monopoly; Packers' Agreement.**

PACKERS' AGREEMENT. The federal government's investigation into the meatpacking industry begun in 1917 resulted in the exposure of monopoly and a variety of unfair practices within the industry. Public opinion forced the larger packers in 1920 to agree voluntarily with the government to sell all holdings in public stockyards, stockyard railroads, cold storage warehouses, and terminals; dispose of their interests in all market newspapers; give up the selling of all products unrelated to the meat industry; abandon the use of all transportation facilities for the carrying of any but their own products; and submit to a federal injunction forbidding monopoly.

BIBLIOGRAPHY

Colver, William B. "Federal Trade Commission and the Meat Packing Industry." *Annals of the American Academy of Political and Social Science*, 1919.

Ernest S. Osgood/c. w.

See also **Antitrust Laws; Meatpacking; Monopoly.**

PACKETS, SAILING. The packet ship was the predecessor of the twentieth-century ocean liner. Packet ships sailed between American and European ports on regular schedules.

The first packet company, the Black Ball Line, began operations in 1818, with four ships offering a monthly service between New York and Liverpool. By the mid-1820s packets were sailing from American and British ports each week. For the next decade they carried most of the passengers, high-valued freight, and mail that passed between the Old World and the New.

The typical packet ship was about two hundred feet long, with three masts and a bluff-bowed hull that, though lacking the speed and grace of the later clipper ship, could plow through the worst North Atlantic seas with reasonable speed and stability. In good weather a packet could make two hundred miles a day.

By the late 1830s steamships were beginning to attract lucrative cargoes and wealthy passengers, leaving the sailing vessels to people who could afford nothing faster. In the mid-nineteenth century millions of working-class immigrants from western Europe came to the United States, most of them on board packet ships. Eventually the steamers took over the passenger trade entirely, relegating the packet lines to the hauling of nonperishable freight. The last of the packets sailed in 1881.

BIBLIOGRAPHY

Albion, Robert G. *Square-Riggers On Schedule: The New York Sailing Packets to England, France, and the Cotton Ports.* Hamden, Conn.: Archon, 1965.

Cutler, Carl C. *Queens of the Western Ocean: The Story of America's Mail and Passenger Sailing Lines.* Annapolis, Md.: Naval Institute Press, 1961.

Lubbock, Basil. *The Western Ocean Packets.* New York: Dover, 1988.

John A. Tilley

See also **Shipping, Ocean.**

PAINTING. *See* **Art: Painting.**

PAIRING, a practice whereby two members of Congress of opposing parties who plan to be absent agree that, during a specified period, they will refrain from voting in person but will permit their names to be recorded on opposite sides of each question, thereby not affecting the vote. It was first used in the House of Representatives as early as 1824 and was first openly avowed in 1840, but pairing was not officially recognized in the House rules until 1880. Pairing is also permitted in the Senate, and is customary, though not universal, in state legislatures.

BIBLIOGRAPHY

Fenno, Richard. *The United States Senate: A Bicameral Perspective.* Washington, D.C.: American Enterprise Institute for Public Policy Research, 1982.

Mason, Paul. *Manual of Procedure for Legislative and Other Government Bodies.* New York: 1953.

P. Orman Ray/A. G.

See also **Blocs; Majority Rule; Reed Rules; Rules of the House.**

PAIUTE. The Northern and Southern Paiute Indians of northern Arizona, Utah, Nevada, Oregon, and eastern California live in the southern and northwestern portions of the Great Basin. They have migrated seasonally throughout these arid lands for thousands of years. The Northern Paiutes speak the Western Numic branch of the Shoshonean division of the Uto-Aztecan language family, while the Southern Paiutes speak the related Southern Numic branch. Organized in small family bands, Paiute communities evolved in intimate contact with the fragile ecologies of the Great Basin. They harvested pine nuts, berries, seeds, and grasses in the spring, summer, and fall, and consumed stored foods with game, fish, and fowl throughout the year. Using the precious resources of the Great Basin for all aspects of their lives, Paiute communities have creatively adapted to their changing environments, imbuing their ecological and human geographies with deep philosophical and spiritual meaning.

Northern and Southern Paiutes numbered approximately eight thousand in the early nineteenth century, when they came into contact with intruding Europeans and other Native groups. Living in northern Arizona and southern Utah, Southern Paiute communities became incorporated into the political economy of colonial New Mexico in the late 1700s. Unlike the Utes to their east, Southern Paiutes had difficulty incorporating horses into their spare ecologies, and when Spanish traders, missionaries, and traders ventured into their territories, they often noted the effects of Ute and Spanish slaving on Paiute communities. Unsure of the exact sociopolitical distinctions among these non-equestrian Paiute bands, Spanish, Mexican, and early American officials often failed to identify them consistently.

Northern Paiutes generally lived in more concentrated communities in California's Owens Valley, Ne-

Paiute. This 1873 photograph by John K. Hillers shows a Southern Paiute hunter in Utah; a century later, Paiute communities there had to wage a long struggle to restore federal recognition of their tribal status. NATIONAL ARCHIVES AND RECORDS ADMINISTRATION

vada's Pyramid and Walker Lakes, and along the Humboldt and Truckee Rivers in Nevada. Northern Paiutes also faced the challenges of conquest, but unlike the Southern Paiutes they negotiated treaties that established extensive reservations at Pyramid Lake and Walker River. Many of these treaties came at the end of wars, including the 1860 Paiute War north of Virginia City, Nevada. Smaller Northern Paiute groups in Oregon and California often migrated to neighboring Indian communities for survival, and many Western Shoshone, Wasco, and other Indian groups throughout the region have welcomed Paiute families into their communities. Indeed, throughout the twentieth century Western Shoshones and Northern Paiutes have lived together throughout Nevada, particularly in federally recognized urban Indian communities, known as colonies.

Several prominent Paiute leaders, artists, and intellectuals have achieved worldwide fame. In the nineteenth century, Sarah Winnemucca Hopkins compiled her family and communities' struggles in her acclaimed autobiography, *Life Among the Piutes,* while a Walker River Paiute, Jack Wilson, also known as Wovoka, initiated the pan-Indian spiritual movement known as the Ghost Dance that prophesized the end of white supremacy and the return of Indian lands and the deceased.

Over a dozen Paiute communities with over eleven thousand members in 1990 extend from Warm Springs, Oregon, through northern, central, and southern Nevada, eastern California, and into southern Utah. Several Utah Paiute communities lost federal recognition in the 1950s as part of the federal government's termination program, which "terminated" over a hundred Indian tribes' federally recognized status, handing Indian affairs from the federal to the state government of Utah. This termination policy ended Paiute eligibility for federal funding for education, health care, and governance and was subsequently repealed under the Paiute Indian Tribe of Utah Restoration Act of 1980.

BIBLIOGRAPHY

Knack, Martha C. *Boundaries Between: The Southern Paiutes, 1775–1995.* Lincoln: University of Nebraska Press.

Knack, Martha C., and Omer C. Stewart, *As Long as the River Shall Run: An Ethnohistory of Pyramid Lake Indian Reservation.* Reprint, Reno: University of Nevada Press, 1999.

Sturtevant, William C., gen. ed. *Handbook of North American Indians.* Vol. 11, *Great Basin.* Edited by William L. D'Azevedo. Washington, D.C.: Smithsonian Institution, 1986.

Ned Blackhawk

See also **Indian Economic Life; Indian Land Cessions; Indian Policy, U.S.: 1830–1900, 1900–2000; Indian Reservations; Indian Treaties; Wars with Indian Nations: Later Nineteenth Century (1840–1900).**

PAKISTAN. *See* **India and Pakistan, Relations with.**

PALESTINIAN AMERICANS. *See* **Arab Americans.**

PALIMONY, a term derived from *alimony,* is legal action upholding oral agreements to share property and earnings acquired while an unmarried couple shared an abode. In 1976 Michelle Triola Marvin sued the actor Lee Marvin, claiming she abandoned her singing career to serve as his companion, cook, and confidante and that, in return, he agreed to share his earnings. She sued Marvin for close to $2 million for "services" as his "wife" and for loss of her career under the theory that the couple had an oral contract. She won $104,000. The legal basis of palimony suits where states allow them is an oral contract for services, other than sexual, provided during cohabitation.

BIBLIOGRAPHY

DiFonzo, J. Herbie. *Beneath the Fault Line.* Charlottesville: University Press of Virginia, 1997.

Paul Finkelman / c. w.

See also **Divorce and Marital Separation; Marriage.**

PALMER RAIDS. The Palmer Raids (1919–1920) involved mass arrests and deportation of radicals at the height of the post–World War I era red scare. Attorney General A. Mitchell Palmer encouraged the raids in the hope that they would advance his presidential ambitions. Ultimately, the extra-constitutional nature of this action destroyed Palmer's political career. He was viewed not as a savior but rather a threat to the civil rights and liberties of all Americans. J. Edgar Hoover, the chief of the Justice Department's Radical (later General Intelligence) Division who actually organized the raids, went on to a forty-eight-year career as director of the Federal Bureau of Investigation (FBI) (originally called the Bureau of Investigation). The other principal, Anthony Caminetti of the Department of Labor's Immigration Bureau, remained an obscure bureaucrat.

A wave of strikes, race riots, and anarchist bombings in eight cities provided the context for the Palmer Raids. One of those bombs partly destroyed the attorney general's own home in Washington, D.C. From February 1917 to November 1919, federal agents deported sixty aliens of some 600 arrested as ANARCHISTS. More raids followed over the next two months, the most notable being the 249 persons, including Emma Goldman, deported on December 21 aboard a single "Red Ark," the *Buford.* The most ambitious raids occurred on January 2, 1920, with lesser efforts continuing over the next few days. In all, Hoover utilized 579 agents from the Bureau of Investigation and vigilantes from the recently disbanded American Protective League to orchestrate massive raids against communists in twenty-three states. At least 4,000 and perhaps as many as 6,000 persons from thirty-three cities were arrested. Most were Communist Party members or suspected members. About 300 were members of the Communist Labor Party. Among the abuses documented by the American Civil Liberties Union and such prominent attorneys as Zechariah Chafee Jr., Roscoe Pound, and Felix Frankfurter were abuses of due process, illegal search and seizure, and indiscriminate arrests, use of *agents provocateurs*, and torture.

BIBLIOGRAPHY

Hoyt, Edwin P. *The Palmer Raids, 1919–1920: An Attempt to Suppress Dissent.* New York: Seabury Press, 1969.

Preston, William. *Aliens and Dissenters: Federal Suppression of Radicals, 1903–1933.* New York: Harper & Row, 1966.

Schmidt, Regin. *Red Scare: FBI and the Origins of Anticommunism in the United States, 1919–1943.* Copenhagen: Museum Tusculanum Press/University of Copenhagen, 2000.

Kenneth O'Reilly

See also **Anticommunism; Deportation; Radicals and Radicalism.**

PALSGRAF V. LONG ISLAND RAILROAD COMPANY, 248 NY 339, 162 N.E. 99 (1928), is one of the most debated tort cases of the twentieth century. The case began in 1927 with an incident at a Long Island Railroad (LIRR) loading platform. Seeing a man running to catch a departing train, two railroad guards reached down to lift him up. In the process, the man dropped a package containing fireworks, which exploded. Either the explosion or an ensuing rush of people at the platform knocked over a nearby scale, injuring Helen Palsgraf.

Palsgraf won $6,000 in a suit against the LIRR. The case went through three appeals, finally ending up in the New York Court of Appeals. Chief Justice Benjamin Cardozo (a future U.S. Supreme Court justice) wrote a majority opinion that reversed the original court decision. Cardozo argued that negligence is a matter of "relation." He said that the LIRR guards may have been negligent toward the man they helped aboard by not foreseeing injury to him or his package, but they were not negligent toward Palsgraf because she stood too far away in relation to the initial incident.

Justice William Andrews wrote a dissenting opinion, arguing that Palsgraf was closely related to the incident. Had there been no explosion, Palsgraf would not have been injured. Andrews argued that justices should consider a wider base of liability when considering tort cases.

BIBLIOGRAPHY

White, G. Edward. *Tort Law in America: An Intellectual History.* New York: Oxford University Press, 1980.

R. Steven Jones

PAMPHLETEERING was a means of propagating new or controversial ideas through the distribution of inexpensive and easily produced tracts or pamphlets. Because the pamphlets were brief and written in a popular style, they enjoyed tremendous circulation. Read aloud in taverns, churches, and town meetings, pamphlets became a significant means of mass communication and an essential vehicle for carrying on political debates in colonial America.

Pamphleteering had its roots in English practice, particularly during the religious controversies and political contests of the commonwealth period. Sermons, often with a political tinge, were distributed as pamphlets in colonial America. During the revolutionary period, figures such as James Otis, Stephen Hopkins, and John Dickinson debated the issue of taxation by Parliament through pamphlets. When military conflict broke out, patriots and loyalists alike engaged in pamphlet wars to justify their political choices. The most renowned pamphleteer of the American Revolution was Thomas Paine. His *Common Sense* was one of the strongest and most effective arguments for independence, and *The Crisis* papers were a powerful buttress to the morale of the patriot cause.

Americans continued to engage in pamphlet debates over issues that confronted the new government, especially the question of adopting the CONSTITUTION OF THE

UNITED STATES. Although newspapers were the forum for some of these debates—as was the case with the *Federalist Papers*—political opponents also used pamphlets to promote their points of view. Federalist pamphleteers included John Jay, Noah Webster, Pelatiah Webster, Tench Coxe, and David Ramsay. Representing the ANTIFEDERALISTS, Elbridge Gerry, George Mason, Melancthon Smith, Richard Henry Lee, Luther Martin, and James Iredell produced pamphlets in opposition.

The proliferation of newspapers in the early national period made pamphlet warfare less common, but some writers still used pamphlets to express their positions. Religious enthusiasts, reform groups, and propagators of utopian societies or economic panaceas often found the pamphlet an effective tool. Campaigns flooded the country with pamphlets to augment the circulation of newspapers or to make political attacks. Toward the end of the nineteenth century, socialists and populists used pamphlets to gain converts, and a free silver advocate produced the notorious *Coin's Financial School*. Propagandists during WORLD WAR I, especially pacifists, utilized the pamphlet to sustain morale or refute criticism. After World War I pamphlet use declined. Increasingly, government organizations, religious groups, and learned societies continued to use pamphlets more often for informational purposes than for the propagation of controversial positions.

BIBLIOGRAPHY

Adams, Thomas R. *The British Pamphlet Press and the American Controversy, 1764–1783.* Worcester, Mass.: American Antiquarian Society, 1979.

Bailyn, Bernard, and Jane N. Garrett, eds. *Pamphlets of the American Revolution, 1750–1776.* Cambridge: The Belknap Press of the Harvard University Press, 1965.

Bailyn, Bernard, and John B. Hench, eds. *The Press and the American Revolution.* Boston: Northeastern University Press, 1981.

Silbey, Joel H., ed. *The American Party Battle: Election Campaign Pamphlets, 1828–1876.* Cambridge: Harvard University Press, 1999.

Wakelyn, Jon L. *Southern Pamphlets on Secession, November 1860–April 1861.* Chapel Hill: University of North Carolina Press, 1996.

Milton W. Hamilton / S. B.

See also **Committee on Public Information; *Common Sense*; "Taxation without Representation"; Propaganda; Revolution, American: Political History; Stamp Act.**

PAN AM FLIGHT 103, a U.S. passenger jet, was destroyed by a terrorist bomb on 21 December 1988, over Lockerbie, Scotland, killing 259 passengers and crew and 11 residents. Among the passengers were thirty-five foreign-study students from Syracuse University. The incident ignited a protracted effort to bring the suspected perpetrators to trial and marked a shift from hijacking to sabotage in terrorism against Western targets. The air-

Pan Am Flight 103. A portion of the wreckage left after a terrorist bomb blew up the jet over Lockerbie, Scotland, on 21 December 1988. © CORBIS

craft was traveling from London's Heathrow Airport to New York when it was destroyed by a plastic explosive hidden in a Toshiba radio cassette player that was inside an unaccompanied suitcase apparently transferred from another airline. Relatives of the dead blamed U.S. authorities for failing to make public a warning of a terrorist attack on a flight originating in Frankfurt, Germany. Groups of relatives filed civil litigation against Pan Am, and later against Libya, in U.S. courts.

Early speculation focused on Iran's threat to retaliate for the U.S. downing of an Iranian passenger jet in the Persian Gulf in July 1988, and on a German cell of the Popular Front for the Liberation of Palestine–General Command, which was found to be packing plastic explosives into Toshiba radio cassette players. In November 1991, however, the United States and Scotland indicted two Libyans, Abdel Baset Ali al-Megrahi and Lamen Khalifa Fhimah, for the bombing of Pan Am Flight 103. Their ostensible motive was revenge for the U.S. bombing of Libya in 1986, during which the adopted daughter of Moammar Qadhafi, Libya's leader, was killed. In 1992, for the first time in its history, the United Nations Security Council ordered one country, Libya, to surrender its own nationals to another country. When Libya refused, citing the lack of an extradition treaty with either the U.S. or the U.K., the Security Council imposed an air, arms, and oil equipment embargo on the country. Libya challenged the Council's actions by bringing still unresolved litigation against both countries in the International Court of Justice.

The Council's sanctions were suspended in April 1999 when Libya voluntarily turned over its two nationals to an ad hoc Scottish Court in the Netherlands. After a nine-month trial, on 31 January 2001, a panel of three Scottish judges found al-Megrahi guilty and sentenced him to life imprisonment (20 years minimum) in Scotland; they found Fhimah not guilty. Many relatives of the victims questioned whether the trial adequately answered who had originally ordered the attack and what their motive was. U.S. media were similarly skeptical of the trial's outcome. Megrahi's conviction was upheld on appeal in March 2002, while civil litigation against Libya was pending.

BIBLIOGRAPHY

Cox, Matthew, and Tom Foster. *Their Darkest Day: The Tragedy of Pan Am 103 and Its Legacy of Hope.* New York: Grove Weidenfeld, 1992.

Wallis, Rodney. *Lockerbie: The Story and the Lessons.* Westport, Conn.: Praeger, 2001.

Donna E. Arzt
Bruce J. Evensen

See also **Terrorism.**

PAN-AFRICANISM. Although the term "Pan-Africanism" has occasionally been applied to the struggle for the political unification of the continent of Africa, the concept has more to do with race than with geography. In its eighteenth-century origins, it overlapped the concept of black nationalism, the idea that a modern nation-state with distinct geographical boundaries should be established in Africa as a center of racial unity and identity. Because it ignored or sought to override political, cultural, and economic differences in the heritages of a broadly defined "racial group," the movement always flourished more successfully in the realms of ideological romanticism and ethnic sentimentalism than in the domain of practical politics.

Pan-Africanism, which is as much a passion as a way of thinking, is more successfully defined in terms of its rhetorical manifestations than by its nominal characteristics. The term has always communicated various, sometimes contradictory ideas to the diverse individuals who professed to be Pan-Africanists. Some scholars refer to Pan-Africanism as a "macronationalism," a term applied to ideologies or movements among widely dispersed peoples who claim a common ancestry—in this case "black African," although Pan-Africanists often reject that term, insisting that Africans are by definition black, or, as they prefer to say, "Africoid." Like all nationalistic and macronationalistic movements, Pan-Africanism possesses a fundamentally religious quality.

Origins and Early Developments

The roots of Pan-Africanism are traceable to the late eighteenth-century writings of westernized Africans expressing the pain and resentment of humiliating encounters with slavery, colonialism, and white supremacy. In 1787 a group of twelve Africans living in England drafted a letter of appreciation to the British philanthropist Granville Sharp for his efforts toward abolition of the international slave trade. One of the drafters, Olaudah Equiano, had traveled widely in Britain's Atlantic empire as a ship's steward, and eventually published his *Interesting Narrative*, revealing emotional commitments to the universal improvement of the African condition. Ottobah Cugoano, one of Equiano's associates, also issued a pamphlet denouncing slavery, significantly "addressed to the sons of Africa," in 1791.

A group of enslaved Africans petitioned the General Court of Massachusetts at the onset of the American Revolution for the right to the same treatment as white indentured servants, who were able to work their way out of bondage. They were aware that their counterparts in Spanish colonies sometimes had that right, and they expressed the hope of eventual repatriation in Africa once free. In the late eighteenth century, a few African Americans pledged themselves to the universalistic doctrines of Freemasonry, but did so in segregated institutions, thus illustrating Pan-Africanism's ideological paradox—a commitment to the universal solidarity of all humanity, but a special solidarity with African populations in Africa and the Caribbean. This sense of solidarity was animated by the Haitian revolution, which, like the American and French Revolutions, enlisted Enlightenment ideals in support of its bloody nationalistic objectives.

In the early 1800s, two free African entrepreneurs in the maritime professions, Paul Cuffe, a sea captain, and James Forten, a sail maker, took steps to establish a West African trading company, and actually settled a few people

Edward Wilmot Blyden. The most prominent advocate in the late nineteenth and early twentieth centuries of what subsequently came to be called Pan-Africanism. LIBRARY OF CONGRESS

in the British colony of Sierra Leone. In 1820 the slave conspiracy planned in South Carolina by Denmark Vesey, putatively a native of the Danish West Indies, aimed at creating an empire of emancipated Africans throughout the American South and the Caribbean. Vesey's conspiracy influenced another South Carolinian, David Walker, who published his *Appeal, in Four Articles, Together with a Preamble, to the Colored Citizens of the World* (1829), an example of Pan-African sentiment, as its title declares. The Convention of the Free People of Color, meeting in 1831, likewise demonstrated a hemispheric Pan-Africanism as it considered a plan for a college in New Haven, Connecticut, arguing that a seaport location would facilitate communication with the West Indies.

Early Pan-Africanism disassociated itself from the West African colony of Liberia, established by the white-controlled American Society for Colonizing the Free People of Color. Some African Americans were willing to cooperate with the liberal abolitionist wing of that group by the mid–nineteenth century, however. By that time, the term "African Movement" was used by a black organization known as the African Civilization Society, established in 1858 and dedicated to "the civilization and christianization of Africa, and of the descendants of African ancestors in any portion of the earth, wherever dispersed." The organization's leader, Henry Highland Garnet, resuscitated the idea of a Caribbean empire, reminiscent of that envisioned by Denmark Vesey thirty years earlier. He also encouraged selective and voluntary migration to Africa, where, he believed, a new nation-state was destined to emerge as "a grand center of Negro nationality."

In 1859, Martin Delany, one of Garnet's associates, published a serialized work of fiction, *Blake, or the Huts of America*, presenting his dreams for an African nation, a Caribbean empire, and global unity among all African peoples. Under the nominal auspices of the African Civilization Society, Delany made a tour of West Africa and negotiated a treaty with the king of Abbeokuta. In the course of this pilgrimage he visited the missionary Alexander Crummell, the son of a West African father and an African American mother, born in New York and educated at Cambridge University in England. Crummell had migrated to Liberia in 1853 and published his first book, *The Future of Africa* (1862), an extensive contemporary defense of Liberian nationalism, calling on African Americans to accept responsibility for uplift of the entire continent. His associate Edward Wilmot Blyden, a native of the Danish West Indies, became the most prominent advocate of Pan-Africanism until his death in 1912. Blyden's publications included occasional reflections on what he called "the African personality," an amorphous expression of racial romanticism that was recycled more than once in the twentieth century. After the Civil War, Blyden, Crummell, Delany, and younger African Americans cooperated intermittently with the Civilization Society.

W. E. B. Du Bois. Among his many achievements over a long career was the organization of six Pan-African conferences between 1919 and 1945. LIBRARY OF CONGRESS

Pan-Africanism in the Twentieth Century

In 1900, Henry Sylvester Williams, a Trinidad barrister, organized in London the first meeting of Africans and Africans of the diaspora under the banner of Pan-Africanism, a term that appeared in related correspondence, although the meeting officially came to be known as the London Conference. Williams was apparently the first person to apply the term "Pan-Africanism" to what had earlier been called "the African movement." Alexander Walters and W. E. B. Du Bois were among the principal promoters of the conference in the United States. In 1919, Du Bois still used the term "African Movement" to denote "the redemption of Africa . . . , the centralization of race effort and the recognition of a racial fount." Later, Du Bois preferred the term "Pan-African," which he applied to a series of six conferences that he convened in the capitals of European colonial empires from 1919 to 1945.

African intellectuals meanwhile became increasingly prominent in the movement for black world solidarity. The Gold Coast intellectual Joseph Ephraim Casely Hayford cooperated with Booker T. Washington, founder of Tuskegee Institute in Alabama, to organize a series of conferences on Africa. Heartened by the victory of Ethiopian troops over an Italian army at Adowa in 1896, Hayford published the novel *Ethiopia Unbound* in 1911, dedicated "to the sons of Ethiopia the world wide over." That same year, Mojola Agbebe, a Yoruba from Lagos, addressed the First Universal Races Conference in London, which was attended by Blyden and Du Bois.

The Pan-African sentiment of highly literate intellectuals was not disassociated from the consciousness of the masses. The historian Edwin S. Redeye found evidence that black peasants in the South were aware of such leadership figures as Blyden. The cultural historian Miles Mark Fisher has insisted that folk songs and folklore gave evidence of a continuing identification with Africa among the masses. Working people in the Midwest subscribed to an emigration project led by the Barbadian Orishatukeh Faduma and the Gold Coast chief Alfred C. Sam during World War I, although most of the migrants soon returned to the United States. In 1916, the year following the exodus led by Sam and Faduma, Marcus Garvey arrived in the United States from Jamaica to organize an immensely popular international movement for "Universal Negro Improvement." Garvey denied, with indignation, any linkage or continuity between Sam's movement and his own, and although his program contained a back-to-Africa component, his goal was to develop the international commercial and political interests of African peoples everywhere.

William H. Ferris, a collaborator with Garvey and an associate of Faduma, drew on his broad knowledge of African leadership on four continents to produce his magnum opus, *The African Abroad or His Evolution in Western Civilization, Tracing His Development Under Caucasian Milieu* (1913). Ferris was a member of the American Negro Academy, an organization with Pan-African membership, presided over by Alexander Crummell and including among its active and corresponding members Du Bois, Casely Hayford, Faduma, Edward W. Blyden, and other African and Caribbean intellectuals. Ferris and the formerly enslaved autodidact John Edward Bruce were a bridge between the American Negro Academy and the Garvey movement.

The Pan-African conferences, including that of 1900 and those organized by Du Bois in 1919, 1921, 1923, and 1927, were the forerunners of another, held in Manchester, England, in 1945, which focused on the promotion of African independence from European colonialism. The Pan-African Congress that met in Ghana in 1958 was no longer dominated by Americans and West Indians. African independence had been achieved in most of the former European colonies, and the movement focused on the political unification of the continent.

Although many of Pan-Africanism's twenty-first-century American adherents still thought of a movement for achievable economic and political goals, the ideology, for better or for worse, was not dominated by such concerns. Pan-Africanism had merged with "Afrocentrism," a semireligious movement, existing mainly on the sentiment level, among the many people who identified emotionally with black Africa and believed their own interests to be tied inextricably to its fortunes.

BIBLIOGRAPHY

Geiss, Imanuel. *The Pan-African Movement.* Translated by Ann Keep. London: Methuen, 1974.

Langley, J. Ayodele. *Pan-Africanism and Nationalists in West Africa, 1900–1945: A Study in Ideology and Social Classes.* Oxford: Oxford University Press, 1973.

Makonnen, Ras. *Pan-Africanism from Within.* Nairobi, Kenya: Oxford, 1973.

Mazrui, Ali A. *The African Condition.* London: Oxford, 1980.

Padmore, George. *Pan-Africanism or Communism? The Coming Struggle for Africa.* London: Dennis Dobson, 1956.

Wilson J. Moses

See also **Africa, Relations with; Black Nationalism; Liberia, Relations with.**

PAN-AMERICAN EXPOSITION. The Pan-American Exposition, held at Buffalo, New York, was the scene of the assassination of President William McKinley after the delivery of his Pan-American speech in the fair's Temple of Music on 6 September 1901. The fair was designed to show the progress of a century in the New World and to promote commercial and social interests; its cost was almost $2.5 million. The New York State Building, an imitation of the Parthenon in Greece, now houses the Buffalo Historical Society. The exposition presented a comprehensive picture of the beauties and possibilities of modern electricity.

Frank Monaghan / T. G.

See also **Assassination Attempts; Assassinations, Political; Capital Punishment; Terrorism; Violence.**

PAN-AMERICAN UNION. The Pan-American Union was the secretariat of the Union of American Republics from 1910 to 1948. The Union of American Republics succeeded the International Union of American States (1890–1910) and preceded the ORGANIZATION OF AMERICAN STATES (OAS) (1948–).

The International Union of American States was founded following the first International Conference of American States in Washington, D.C. (2 October 1889–19 April 1890), attended by representatives from Argentina, Bolivia, Brazil, Chile, Colombia, Costa Rica, Ecuador, El Salvador, Guatemala, Haiti, Honduras, Mexico, Nicaragua, Paraguay, Peru, Uruguay, Venezuela, and of course, the United States. From 1890 to 1910 the International Union of American States more or less operated as a branch of, and was based in, the U.S. Department of State. When it was reorganized as the Union of American Republics with the Pan-American Union as its secretariat, it was moved to the new Pan-American Union Building on Constitution Avenue and 17th Street NW in Washington, D.C.

Following the formative meeting in Buenos Aires, Argentina, in 1910, the Pan-American Union organized inter-American conferences in Santiago, Chile, in 1923; Havana, Cuba, in 1928; Montevideo, Uruguay, in 1933; and Lima, Peru, in 1938. The Pan-American Union also organized the meeting in Bogota, Colombia, in 1948 that led to the founding of the Organization of American States (OAS). In 1951 the Pan-American Union was officially renamed the Secretariat of the OAS.

BIBLIOGRAPHY

Gilderhus, Mark T. *Pan American Visions: Woodrow Wilson in the Western Hemisphere, 1913–1921.* Tucson: University of Arizona Press, 1986.

Inman, Samuel Guy. *Inter-American Conferences, 1826–1954: History and Problems.* Edited by Harold Eugene Davis. Washington, D.C.: The University Press, 1965.

Mark T. Berger

See also **Latin America, Relations with.**

PANAMA CANAL. In 1513, the Spanish explorer Vasco Núñez de Balboa crossed the Isthmus of Panama and sighted the Pacific Ocean. From that point forward, the Spanish and then the Dutch, French, British, and Americans would seek to create a path between the seas that would shorten the trip from the Atlantic to the Pacific without traveling around Cape Horn. It would take nearly four centuries to accomplish the goal.

Early Plans and Construction of the Canal

Once Colombia won independence from Spain, European and American interest in the canal began in earnest as Panama remained a province of Colombia. In 1829, Simón Bolívar commissioned a British engineer, John Lloyd, to study building a canal across Panama. With a positive report, the Colombians threw open the bidding in 1834, promising 100,000 acres of land and revenues for fifty years.

In the mid-1830s, President Andrew Jackson sent Charles Biddle to Central America. He negotiated with Bogotá to build a road to the navigable Chagres River and import two steamships to conduct trade across the isthmus. For his work, Bogotá promised 140,000 acres, an additional 750,000 at fifty cents an acre, and a fifty-year lease. All Biddle's efforts were for naught, however, as Jackson lost interest when a rival Dutch plan in Nicaragua failed.

Despite the initial setback, interest in the canal remained high. By the late 1840s, British and U.S. officials decided to negotiate for a "great highway" across Central America, to be open to all nations. Sir Henry Bulwer and U.S. Secretary of State John Clayton signed the Clayton-Bulwer Treaty on 19 April 1850. Both promised never to monopolize or fortify the proposed canal and agreed that neither would colonize any new part of Central America. While little happened during the next forty years to advance construction of a waterway outside of the creation of railroads and steamship enterprises, people still dreamed about a trans-isthmian canal. The great French engineer Ferdinand de Lesseps, builder of the Suez Canal, won a concession from the Colombian government to construct a canal in Panama in the 1880s. His French Canal Company failed miserably, but his successors retained the concession and asked $109 million for it.

In 1898, the war with Spain renewed interest when the U.S. Pacific Fleet had to travel around South America to Cuba. In 1901, the new president, Theodore Roosevelt, soon addressed a major obstacle, the Clayton-Bulwer Treaty. In November of that year, after tedious negotiations, Secretary of State John Hay and the British ambassador to Washington, Lord Pauncefote, signed an agreement that superseded the Clayton-Bulwer Treaty and permitted the United States to build and fortify a Central American canal.

With the British out of the way, Roosevelt made construction of the canal a priority, announcing his intention to make "the dirt fly" in Central America. As Roosevelt had taken office in September 1901, a commission had recommended a Nicaraguan canal. Working on the recommendation, in January 1902 the House of Representatives voted 308–2 to pursue the Nicaraguan canal. The French company, now called the New Panama Canal Company and led by Philippe Bunau-Varilla, swung into action. It hired a high-powered American lobbyist, William Cromwell, who had personal access to the White House. Cromwell and Bunau-Varilla succeeded, and in June 1902, Congress passed the Spooner Act, a measure that allowed Roosevelt to negotiate for the right of way in Panama.

Secretary of State Hay immediately set about the task of coming to an agreement with the Colombians. In January 1903, he and a Colombian diplomat, Tomás Herrán, signed an accord. The treaty granted the United States the right to build a canal zone six miles wide. In return, the United States promised a payment of $10 million and annual payments of $250,000 after nine years, with the lease renewable in perpetuity. Immediately Bogotá expressed reservations and told Herrán to wait for new instructions. The U.S. Senate refused to delay and approved the treaty in March 1903.

Problems resulted when the Colombians balked at the original agreement. The Colombian congress unanimously rejected the Hay-Herrán Treaty in August 1903. In response, Cromwell and Bunau-Varilla began formulating plans for Panama's secession from Colombia and for American ownership of the canal. Plotting from the New York Waldorf-Astoria Hotel during the summer of 1903, the group planted newspaper stories about Panama's plan to rebel and grant the United States sover-

Panama Canal Failure. A dynamited hilltop, 1886, part of the French effort in the 1880s to cut across the Isthmus of Panama. NATIONAL ARCHIVES AND RECORDS ADMINISTRATION

eignty over the Canal Zone. They also gathered money for bribes of Colombian officials and organized a small army.

The Panamanians launched their rebellion on 3 November 1903. By the end of that day the rebels had formed a provisional government and unveiled a constitution, one written in New York. The presence of the USS *Nashville* and the use of bribes allowed a successful revolution. In one day and with only one death, the new Republic of Panama was born.

Washington immediately extended diplomatic recognition. Within several days, Bunau-Varilla (who had received permission from the provisional government to represent Panama) began negotiations. On 18 November, the two parties signed the Hay–Bunau-Varilla Treaty. It gave the United States a ten-mile strip of land, all the rights to construct and administer a canal, and the right to protect the canal. In return, the Panamanians received $10 million and an annual rent of $250,000. Washington also promised to maintain Panama's independence.

Despite some criticisms of the agreement, Roosevelt pressed the Senate for ratification, urging it to follow the example of the Panamanian Congress. After spirited debate, on 23 February 1904 the Senate voted 66–14 to accept it. Immediately Washington purchased the assets of the New Panama Canal Company for $40 million. The Panamanians received their money and American engineers quickly set to work.

The canal took a decade to complete. It was a technological marvel, composed of a series of six locks that linked various waterways. Under the supervision of the engineers John F. Stevens (1905–1907) and Lieutenant Colonel George W. Goethels (1907–1914), the Canal Commission completed the construction with substantial assistance from workers imported from the Caribbean islands and southern United States, in numbers exceeding 44,000 in 1913. Employing heavy machinery—and benefiting from new techniques to reduce yellow fever and other tropical diseases in an effort led by Dr. William Crawford Gorgas—the laborers created a new society within the newly independent Panama. The canal opened for commerce on 15 August 1914. The United States now had major new support for its economic and military growth as the water route from New York City to San Francisco shrank from 13,165 miles to 5,300.

Panama Canal Zone, 1914–1979

For nearly forty years, the Panama Canal Zone operated under various acts of Congress with executive supervision.

Panama Canal Success. This photograph by Archie W. French shows construction work on one of the six huge locks, completed by 1914 after years of labor. LIBRARY OF CONGRESS

In 1950, Congress passed the Thompson Act, which created the Panama Canal Company, operated under the auspices of a board of directors. A governor of the Canal Zone, appointed by the U.S. president, monitored the day-to-day operations of the zone and used revenues to make improvements and maintain the canal. In addition, the U.S. military maintained bases in the Canal Zone to protect the important strategic site.

Throughout the period, Panamanian nationalists clamored for more beneficial terms than those in the 1903 treaty. A 1936 agreement increased the annuity paid by the U.S. government to Panamanians, and a 1942 treaty transferred various civil works projects to the Panamanian government and promised additional infrastructure development. Additional revisions occurred in the 1950s, including the flying of the Panamanian flag in the Canal Zone as the United States tried to address issues of sovereignty.

Despite compromises, tensions continued to mount. In January 1964, the most serious confrontation over the canal developed. American high school students, supported by their parents, refused to raise the Panamanian flag at the Canal Zone's Balboa High School. Panamanians marched to show their flag near the school. As they neared, an American mob attacked them, tearing the flag. The news quickly spread, and thirty thousand Panamanians descended on the main avenue approaching the Canal Zone. Snipers poured hundreds of rounds into the U.S. positions, and U.S. troops fired back. Riots erupted as Panamanians destroyed American businesses.

Panama's President Roberto Chiari suspended diplomatic relations, and hard-liners in Congress urged President Lyndon Johnson to respond with force. However, Johnson chose to negotiate and dispatched Thomas Mann and Secretary of the Army Cyrus Vance to mediate the dispute, which Johnson blamed on the communists.

After four days of fighting and looting, the Panamanian National Guard reestablished order. Four Americans died and eighty-five were wounded. Twenty-four Panamanians died and more than two hundred were wounded. The fighting caused more than $2 million in damage, much of it to American businesses.

While blaming the communists, most American policymakers could not ignore the animosity that provoked the confrontation. In the aftermath, the Chiari government and the Johnson administration opened negotiations to address Panama's grievances. Ultimately Washington agreed to terminate the 1903 treaty in return for granting U.S. control and operation of the canal until 1999. Despite strong public criticism, Johnson submitted the treaty to the Senate in 1967. It languished there as Johnson's attentions focused on Vietnam and internal events in Panama sabotaged acceptance. It would take another Democratic president, more than a decade later, to push through Johnson's original ideas.

The Panama Canal Treaty

In 1977, President Jimmy Carter took control of the White House. One of his first goals regarding Latin America was the settlement of the Canal Zone debates. Carter believed that a treaty would have a positive impact on U.S.–Latin American relations. Carter and Secretary of State Cyrus Vance built on negotiations begun by Johnson and continued by Henry Kissinger during the presidencies of Richard Nixon and Gerald Ford. The Carter administration pushed hard for a treaty, dealing closely with Panamanian dictator Omar Torrijos, who had controlled the country since 1968. Tense negotiations headed by Ellsworth Bunker and Sol Linowitz continued for nearly a year.

Finally, on 11 August 1977, the parties held a press conference in Panama and unveiled the treaty. It had several parts, starting with the process of returning the canal to Panama by 31 December 1999. Second, the treaty guaranteed the rights of American workers in the Canal Zone through their retirement. Third, it provided the United States with a permanent right to defend the canal's neutrality. Last, Washington increased payment for its use of the canal from $2.3 million to $40 million annually and promised additional economic and military assistance.

The announcement of the treaty stirred debates in both countries. Since the treaty required approval by the Panamanian people (as outlined in their constitution) and confirmation by a two-thirds vote of the U.S. Senate, victory appeared far away in April 1977. In Panama, Torrijos pushed through the plebiscite in Panama, although not without opposition. In the United States, the Senate began deliberations in the summer of 1978. President Carter and his staff pushed hard, winning the support of diverse groups including the Pentagon (which believed the canal had outlived its tactical purpose) and the Catholic Church along with distinguished diplomats including Kissinger. Over time, Carter won the backing of important senators from both parties including Senate Majority Leader Robert Byrd (D-West Virginia) and Senate Minority Leader Howard Baker (R-Tennessee). With promises of compromise and pork barrel projects, the pro-treaty group moved forward.

Throughout the summer the foes battled on the floor of the Senate and in public forums. Carter secured an extra promise from Torrijos guaranteeing the right of the United States to defend the Canal Zone after 2000, which won additional votes. In March 1978, the Senate approved the neutrality part of the treaty 68–32. By mid-April, they approved the other part of the treaty, outlining administration through 2000, by the same vote. Carter, the Senate leadership, and pro-treaty forces enjoyed a major victory. The president emphasized that the treaty symbolized the efforts by the United States to create not only positive relations with Panama but with other Third World countries. The goal was partnerships based on mutual respect.

Relinquishing U.S. Control, 1979–1999

The process of turning over the canal began in October 1979, as Carter's term was ending. The Panamanians gained control over the former Canal Zone, and the Panama Canal Commission, composed of Americans and

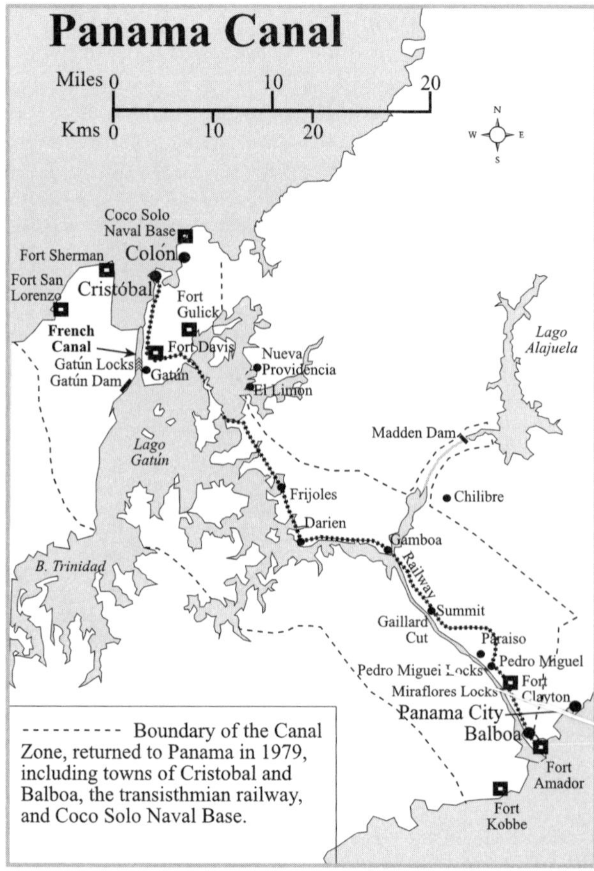

Panamanians, began the process of overseeing the transition. In the summer of 1980 a Committee on the Environment and a Coordinating Committee began working to implement sections of the treaty.

During the 1980s, the Panama Canal remained an issue of concern to the United States. Some thought that the election of Ronald Reagan might mean that the treaty would be overturned as he had been one of its leading critics during the presidential debates. But in fact the movement toward transition continued unabated during his two terms. More Panamanians became integrated into the Canal Zone as policemen and pilots, and American employees there gradually were weaned off their ties to the U.S. government.

Furthermore, the presence of the left-wing Sandinistas in Nicaragua in the 1980s and possible threats in the Caribbean led Americans to continue to view the Canal Zone and its defense installations as vital to U.S. national security. This made them fearful of provoking a confrontation in Panama. Reagan administration officials worked with General Manuel Noriega, who had replaced Torrijo after his death in a mysterious plane crash. Noriega allowed the contras—right-wing foes of the Sandinista government who were supported by the Reagan administration—to train in his country. While rumors had swirled for many years about Noriega's ties to the drug trade, U.S.

leaders ignored them. In fact, the Drug Enforcement Agency (DEA) and Attorney General Edwin Meese sent letters of commendation to the Panamanian dictator. Noriega also regularly received U.S. dignitaries, including Vice President George H. W. Bush, to discuss policy issues.

By the middle of the 1980s, problems began to develop. As the Iran-Contra scandal blossomed and Reagan's credibility suffered, the tales of Noriega's drug ties became more prominent. Senator John Kerry (D-Massachusetts) held hearings in the Senate Foreign Relations Committee's Subcommittee on Terrorism, Narcotics, and International Operations that further substantiated published reports about Noriega's drug trafficking and money laundering.

When George H. W. Bush took office as president in 1989, he began concerted efforts to deal with Noriega, building on some late efforts by Reagan. The problem became more complicated when a Miami grand jury indicted Noriega on drug charges in 1988. Tensions heightened in early 1989 when Noriega overturned an election. Critics jumped on Bush's failure to do anything. Even when an opportunity presented itself in the form of a coup by disenchanted Panamanians, he did nothing. Soon after, Noriega defiantly declared a "state of war" between Panama and the United States, often brandishing a machete at mass anti-American rallies. With relations deteriorating, Panamanians killed an off-duty marine, and the Panamanian Defense Forces beat an American officer and threatened to rape his wife. Bush concluded that he had enough.

On 20 December, the United States attacked Panama with more than twenty thousand men. Code-named Operation Just Cause, the Pentagon employed all the latest weaponry including Stealth bombers. Hundreds of Panamanian civilians perished in the cross fire between the Panamanian Defense Forces and U.S. troops (twenty-three Americans died). The fighting inflicted more than $1 billion of damage in Panama City, especially in the poorest areas, where thousands found themselves homeless. Noriega evaded capture for fifteen days, but on 3 January 1990 he finally left his sanctuary in the papal nunciature (papal diplomatic mission headed by a nuncio), and DEA agents immediately put him on a plane to Miami.

In the aftermath of Operation Just Cause, the United States installed in office the legally elected president, Guillermo Endara. Washington poured more money into the country, but unemployment and poverty remained high. In 1994, one of Noriega's cronies, Ernesto Pérez Balladares, won the presidency. As for Noriega, an American jury sentenced him to forty years in jail without parole. Most observers concluded that despite Noriega's removal, the invasion accomplished little in stopping the drug trade and in fact created more animosity toward the United States.

In the aftermath of the invasion, despite calls from some Americans for a total renegotiation of the Panama Canal Treaty, it moved forward. In September 1990, Gilberto Guardia Fabréga became the Panama Canal Commission administrator, the first Panamanian in such a high position. Throughout the 1990s, the process continued. In 1997, the Panama Canal Authority was created, the final step toward removing any U.S. government control. In September 1998, Albert Alemán Zubieta became the first administrator of the Panama Canal Authority. Soon after, Panama's legislative assembly created the Canal Authority's budget for its first fiscal year of 2000.

All of these steps led to great fanfare for the celebration of 14 December 1999. Foreign dignitaries attended the ceremony where the United States completely relinquished its claim to the canal. Former president Jimmy Carter signed for the United States while Panamanian President Mireya Moscoso represented the new owners. Officially, on 31 December 1999, the Panama Canal became the possession of the nation of Panama.

BIBLIOGRAPHY

Collin, Richard H. *Theodore Roosevelt's Caribbean: The Panama Canal, the Monroe Doctrine, and the Latin American Context.* Baton Rouge: Louisiana State University Press, 1990.

Conniff, Michael L. *Black Labor on a White Canal: Panama, 1904–1981.* Pittsburgh, Pa.: University of Pittsburgh Press, 1985.

———. *Panama and the United States: The Forced Alliance.* Athens: University of Georgia Press, 1992.

Dinges, John. *Our Man in Panama: The Shrewd Rise and Brutal Fall of Manuel Noriega.* New York: Random House, 1990. Rev. ed., New York: Times Books, 1991.

Furlong, William L., and Margaret E. Scranton. *The Dynamics of Foreign Policymaking: The President, the Congress, and the Panama Canal Treaties.* Boulder, Colo.: Westview Press, 1984.

Hogan, J. Michael. *The Panama Canal in American Politics: Domestic Advocacy and the Evolution of Policy.* Carbondale: Southern Illinois University Press, 1986.

LaFeber, Walter. *The Panama Canal: The Crisis in Historical Perspective.* New York: Oxford University Press, 1978. Updated ed., New York: Oxford University Press, 1989.

Leonard, Thomas M. *Panama, the Canal, and the United States: A Guide to Issues and References.* Claremont, Calif.: Regina Books, 1993.

Major, John. *Prize Possession: The United States and the Panama Canal, 1903–1979.* Cambridge and New York: Cambridge University Press, 1993.

McCullough, David G. *The Path between the Seas: The Creation of the Panama Canal, 1870–1914.* New York: Simon and Schuster, 1977.

Moffett, George D., 3d. *The Limits of Victory: The Ratification of the Panama Canal Treaties.* Ithaca, N.Y.: Cornell University Press, 1985.

Scranton, Margaret E. *The Noriega Years: U.S.-Panamanian Relations, 1981–1990.* Boulder, Colo.: Lynne Rienner, 1991.

Kyle Longley

See also **Panama Canal Treaty; Panama Invasion; Panama Revolution.**

PANAMA CANAL TREATY (1977). In January 1964, twenty-one Panamanians died in severe riots in their home country, where waves of demonstrators were a recurring phenomenon. They demanded U.S. withdrawal from the isthmus where the United States had had the mandate to exercise "all the rights, power, and authority" of a sovereign state since President Theodore Roosevelt orchestrated the 1903 Hay–Bunau-Varilla Treaty. The Panama Canal Zone, and the Southern Command of U.S. troops there, came to symbolize "yankee" domination of Central America.

In December 1964, President Lyndon B. Johnson promised negotiations to abrogate the 1903 treaty, and by June 1967 a draft treaty had been initialed. Strong resistance in both countries doomed its prospects. President Richard Nixon resumed discussions in 1970, and four years later Secretary of State Henry Kissinger signed an agreement of principles with Panamanian foreign minister Juan Antonio Tack. The Watergate scandal and the weak presidency of Gerald Ford jeopardized implementation.

President Jimmy Carter, wanting to foster goodwill in Latin America, resumed negotiations and finalized two treaties based on the 1967 principles. The Canal Treaty prescribed twenty-two years for control to gradually pass to Panama. The Neutrality Treaty required Panama to keep the canal open and accessible. A "statement of understanding" permitted the United States to defend the canal "against any aggression or threat" but not to intervene in Panama's domestic affairs.

The signing ceremony with Panama's ruler, Colonel Omar Torrijos Herrera, was held on 7 September 1977 in the presence of Western Hemisphere leaders. Approval in Panama was secured by a plebiscite on 23 October 1977. In the United States, ratification took two years after strong opposition from the Republican presidential candidate Ronald Reagan and Senator Dennis DeConcini of Arizona, who opposed the closing of the Southern Command, other U.S. bases, and a surrender of territory and influence.

Carter personally secured the requisite two-thirds majority for the 1978 ratification of these treaties in the Senate, both by a 68 to 32 margin. Carter ceded control and sovereignty to Panamanians in an attempt to reverse the legacy of U.S. domination by endorsing equality, self-government, and territorial integrity. DeConcini attached an amendment to the Neutrality Treaty—which was approved on 16 March—that gave the United States the right to use force if necessary to keep the canal open. The Democratic leadership of the Senate introduced an amendment to the Canal Treaty—approved on 18 April—that negated any U.S. right to intervene in Panama's internal affairs. Enabling legislation for the two treaties passed the House and Senate in September 1979, and both treaties went into effect on 1 October 1979.

In the 1980s, Panama's ruler, General Manuel Noriega, a former American ally, became increasingly independent and provocative toward the United States. He was also involved in drug trafficking and money laundering. On 20 December 1989, President George H. W. Bush ordered Operation Just Cause, which restored a duly-elected Panamanian, Guillermo Endara, as president but made the country a de facto American protectorate for several years. The United States ousted and captured Noriega just days before an independent Panamanian, Gilberto Guardia Fabréga, was to oversee the Panama Canal Commission for the first time. Ten years later, at noon on 31 December 1999, the U.S. presence ended in the Canal Zone, and Panama assumed full and total sovereignty.

BIBLIOGRAPHY

Rumage, Sarah. "Panama and the Myth of Humanitarian Intervention in U.S. Foreign Policy: Neither Legal Nor Moral, Neither Just Nor Right." *Arizona Journal of International and Comparative Law* 10 (1993): 1–76.

Itai Sneh

See also **Panama Canal; Panama Invasion; Panama Revolution.**

PANAMA INVASION (1989). The invasion of Panama by U.S. forces in December 1989 was designed in part to end the rule of General Manuel Antonio Noriega. A graduate of the Peruvian Military Academy in 1962, he had supported Colonel Omar Torrijos Herrera, the ruler of Panama, during an attempted coup against the latter in 1969. Noriega soon became head of the Panamanian military intelligence service and served Torrijos for a decade as chief of security. Two years after Torrijos's death in an airplane crash in 1981, Noriega became commander of the Guardia Nacional, renamed the Panama Defense Forces (PDF). Torrijos and subsequently Noriega aided the U.S.-sponsored Contras with arms and supplies in their struggle against the Sandinista regime in Nicaragua. American officials excused the corrupt and brutal nature of Noriega's regime on the grounds that he supported the U.S. effort to stop communist penetration of Latin America. Noriega's involvement with the Medellín drug cartel in the 1980s and the emergence of Panama as a money-laundering site proved far more lucrative than receiving U.S. support because of assistance to the Contras.

In 1987 a feud between Noriega and his chief of staff, Roberto Diaz Herrera, led to Diaz's publicly charging Noriega with crimes and encouraged Panamanian opponents to demand Noriega's resignation. Noriega responded with arrests and brutality. Secret negotiations between Panamanian and U.S. representatives designed to facilitate Noriega's departure broke down. The U.S. Justice Department filed indictments against Noriega in federal court; soon afterward the U.S. government imposed a series of economic sanctions. The United States sent additional military forces to the Canal Zone in Panama, recalled its ambassador, and encouraged PDF officers to overthrow Noriega. An attempted coup in 1989 failed and led to executions. The media criticized President George

Bush and Secretary of Defense Richard Cheney for failing to provide more support to the coup leaders. The U.S. military drew up plans for an invasion, which began when a U.S. serviceman died from gunfire outside PDF headquarters on 16 December 1989.

Operation Just Cause began on 20 December and lasted through 24 December. The PDF numbered 5,000, augmented by 8,000 paramilitary troops organized in "dignity battalions." The 13,000 U.S. troops stationed in Panama were reinforced by an additional 9,000. Fighting centered around Noriega's headquarters in Panama City. Noriega took refuge with the papal nuncio (the Vatican's representative in Panama) but surrendered on 3 January 1990. Twenty-three U.S. soldiers were killed during the invasion. Panamanian deaths—military and civilian—exceeded 500. U.S. public opinion supported the operation but many foreign governments did not. A new civilian regime took control in Panama and the country experienced severe economic problems and a troubled security situation for months afterward. Noriega became a federal prisoner in Miami on 4 January 1990; he was tried and convicted in April 1992 of cocaine smuggling and given a life sentence. Political and economic stability remained an elusive commodity in Panama; nationalist resentment against the United States surged. Under the terms of the Panama Canal Treaty negotiated by the Carter administration in the 1970s, Panama regained control of the Canal Zone in 1999, a historic transfer of power that at least partially assuaged anti-Americanism in Panama.

BIBLIOGRAPHY

Bush, George, and Brent Scowcroft. *A World Transformed.* New York: Knopf, 1998.

Flanagan Jr., Edward. *Battle for Panama: Inside Operation Just Cause.* Washington, D.C.: Brassey's, 1993.

Parmet, Herbert S. *George Bush: The Life of a Lone Star Yankee.* New York: Scribner, 1997.

Woodward, Bob. *The Commanders.* New York: Simon and Schuster, 1991.

Richard W. Turk/A. G.

See also **Contra Aid; Defense, Department of; Defense, National; Grenada Invasion; Mexico, Punitive Expedition into; Nicaragua, Relations with; Panama Canal; Unconditional Surrender.**

PANAMA REFINING COMPANY V. RYAN (293 U.S. 388 [1935]). The National Industrial Recovery Act of 1933, among other delegations of power, authorized the president to limit the transportation in interstate and foreign commerce of oil to the production level permitted by the state from which the oil was shipped. The Supreme Court, in *Panama Refining Company v. Ryan*, known as the "Hot Oil" case, invalidated this provision by declaring that Congress had delegated essential legislative power to the president. Shortly afterward, Congress passed an act that preserved this system of regulating oil shipments while avoiding such broad delegation of power.

BIBLIOGRAPHY

Cushman, Barry. *Rethinking the New Deal Court: The Structure of a Constitutional Revolution.* New York: Oxford University Press, 1998.

P. Orman Ray/A. R.

See also **Delegation of Powers; National Recovery Administration.**

PANAMA REVOLUTION. After winning independence from Spain in 1821, Colombia faced secessionist moves by its province of Panama, separated by impassable jungle from the rest of the country. Throughout the nineteenth century, Panamanian nationalists rebelled against rule by distant Bogotá. As the prospect of a transisthmian canal began to seem real, they heightened their struggle, hoping for control over this major potential source of revenue.

On 3 November 1903, after the Colombian senate voted to reject a treaty that would have given the United States broad control over a canal, Panamanians launched a revolt. They were led by two groups: officials of the Panama Railroad, held by the French-owned New Panama Canal Company, which sought to benefit financially from selling the rights to build a canal; and leaders of the oligarchy, who hoped for political control of the area once free from Colombia's rule. The rebels were quickly victorious, aided by the presence of American warships sent to intimidate Colombia. On 6 November, President Theodore Roosevelt recognized the new Panamanian regime led by Manuel Amador, who had previously visited the United States seeking promises of assistance. The new government quickly signed a treaty granting all concessions sought by Roosevelt, permitting construction of the Panama Canal.

BIBLIOGRAPHY

Farnsworth, David N., and James W. McKenney. *U.S.-Panama Relations, 1903–1978: A Study in Linkage Politics.* Boulder, Colo.: Westview Press, 1983.

LaFeber, Walter. *The Panama Canal: The Crisis in Historical Perspective.* Updated ed. New York: Oxford University Press, 1989.

Major, John. *Prize Possession: The United States and the Panama Canal, 1903–1979.* Cambridge: Cambridge University Press, 1993.

Max Paul Friedman

See also **Panama Canal; Panama Canal Treaty.**

***PANAY* INCIDENT.** Japanese aircraft, engaged in fighting Chinese forces, bombed and strafed the U.S. gunboat *Panay* and three Standard Oil supply ships in the Yangtze River near Nanking on 12 December 1937. Several crew members were killed in the attack, which sank the *Panay*, and a number of other Americans were wounded. Reaction in the United States was mixed. Several prominent naval officers called for war with Japan, and Secretary of State Cordell Hull demanded full redress. President Franklin D. Roosevelt considered economic sanctions against the Japanese, or even a blockade. Many in Congress and among the American public, however, were less interested in the attack itself than in knowing what U.S. ships were doing in China in the first place. The incident led to calls for stronger measures to maintain American neutrality, in particular a proposal to require a nationwide referendum before the country could declare war. Roosevelt could not afford to ignore public opinion, and soon backed away from any effort at retaliation. When after a few days the Japanese apologized, offered to pay all damages, and pledged to safeguard the rights of Americans in China in the future, the president let the matter drop.

BIBLIOGRAPHY

Dallek, Robert. *Franklin D. Roosevelt and American Foreign Policy, 1932–1945.* New York: Oxford University Press, 1979.

Koginos, Manny T. *The Panay Incident: Prelude to War.* Lafayette, Ind.: Purdue University Studies, 1967.

John E. Moser
Oscar Osburn Winther

See also **China, U.S. Armed Forces in; Japan, Relations with.**

PANHANDLE. A panhandle, as the name implies, is a long, usually narrow, tract of land appended to the main area of a state. Many such areas exist in the United States. WEST VIRGINIA's panhandle extends northward between PENNSYLVANIA and OHIO. OKLAHOMA's panhandle, a long strip about twenty-five miles wide, lies between TEXAS on the south and COLORADO and KANSAS on the north. The Texas panhandle, a large, nearly square area, includes the northern portion of the state.

The term *panhandle* also applies to the portion of IDAHO between WASHINGTON and MONTANA; the western extension of NEBRASKA north of Colorado; the northwestern corner of Pennsylvania along Lake Erie; and the long western extension of FLORIDA.

BIBLIOGRAPHY

Rand McNally and Company. *Atlas of American History.* Chicago: Houghton Mifflin, 1999.

Erwin N. Griswold / c. w.

See also **Geography.**

PANICS. *See* **Financial Panics.**

PANTON, LESLIE AND COMPANY began trading with the Native peoples of the American Southeast during the Revolution. Scottish Loyalists William Panton, John Leslie, and Thomas Forbes fled to Florida, and after the 1783 Treaty of Paris gave the territory back to Spain, the firm was allowed to continue to operate out of St. Augustine and Pensacola. In 1785, Spain granted the company the exclusive right to trade with the Creeks, and in 1788 Spain broadened the grant to include the Choctaws and Chickasaws. The firm supplied the tribes with munitions, rum, and other assorted goods in exchange for deerskins, furs, bear oil, honey, and foodstuffs. The company expanded its reach as far as the Bahamas, Texas, Louisiana, and Yucatán, and it continued to trade as John Forbes and Company until 1847. These prominent traders were able to survive and profit in a violent and volatile setting during a period of massive, rapid historical change. Their papers, scattered in archives throughout Great Britain, the United States, Spain, and Latin America, detail their commercial exploits and open the world of late-eighteenth and early nineteenth-century Native Americans to interested researchers.

BIBLIOGRAPHY

Coker, William S., and Thomas D. Watson. *Indian Traders of the Southeastern Spanish Borderlands: Panton, Leslie & Company and John Forbes & Company, 1783–1847.* Pensacola: University of West Florida Press, 1986. The foreword by J. Leitch Wright, Jr. eloquently describes the activities and importance of the company.

Matthew Holt Jennings

See also **Indian Trade and Traders.**

PAPAL STATES, DIPLOMATIC SERVICE TO. The United States maintained diplomatic ties to the papal states from 1797 to 1867. Congress established a consulate in Rome in 1797 to facilitate commercial and legal transactions between Americans and the papal states. In 1848, Congress approved President James K. Polk's proposal to raise the consulate to a ministry. This action was designed to affirm the reformist Pope Pius IX, improve commercial prospects in Rome, gain influence in other Catholic states, and please the burgeoning Catholic vote at home.

Formal diplomatic relations lasted less than two decades. Tension mounted when the U.S. chargé d'affaires Nicholas Browne celebrated the republic created in the 1848 revolution as a triumph of liberty over papacy. Congress terminated the mission to Rome in 1867. As the Italian unification movement challenged papal authority, liberals regretted U.S. recognition of the nondemocratic papal government, and the minuscule level of commerce provided no rationale for continuing to fund a mission.

BIBLIOGRAPHY

Schreiner, Mary Naomi. "A Study of the Relations of the American Government with the Papal States from 1797 to 1867." Master's thesis, St. John College, 1950.

Stock, Leo Francis, ed. *United States Ministers to the Papal States: Instructions and Despatches, 1848–1868.* Washington, D.C.: Catholic University Press, 1933.

Peter L. Hahn

See also **Catholicism.**

PAPER AND PULP INDUSTRY. With origins in China over 2,000 years ago, the paper and pulp industry produces the different kinds of paper used for printing, bags, signs, cardboard, and more. William Rittenhouse, a German immigrant, introduced the industry to colonial America in 1690. Coming from a family of papermakers, Rittenhouse settled near Philadelphia, built a log mill, and began making paper. The Rittenhouse family continued to operate the mill until 1820. The *American Weekly Mercury,* Philadelphia's first newspaper, was founded by Andrew Bradford, the son of one of Rittenhouse's partners, and was printed on Rittenhouse paper.

During the pre-Revolutionary years, the industry spread slowly. The papermaking process was long and complicated. Cloth rags were balled and kept wet for six to eight weeks, turning the rags into pulp. The rags that did not rot were then put in bowls and pounded by levers attached to an axle turned either by hand or by water power. Once the substance was made batter-like, the vat man dipped a mold with a screened bottom into the vat to collect a layer of the pulp and drained excess water. He then passed the mold to the coucher, who skillfully turned the mold over on a piece of felt. The two did this until they had 144 sheets each, separated by felt. Workers using a large wooden screw press, which removed the remaining water and compacted the rag fibers, then pressed the 144 sheets. The pages were separated by a layman and hung to dry. Once dry, the sheets were dipped into a mixture of boiled animal hides to reduce the absorbency of the porous paper. They were pressed and dried again, and the last step was to polish the paper with agate or soapstone.

This time-consuming and labor-intensive process, combined with the scarcity of rags, made paper a valuable and expensive commodity. While Philadelphia and the surrounding area remained the center of papermaking in the colonies, the demand for paper required importation.

When the colonies declared their independence and the importation of paper stopped, drastic measures were taken. Paper was rationed, interest-free loans were awarded to those opening mills, and papermakers were even exempt from military service. As a result, a number of new mills were opened during and in the years immediately following the Revolution. At the end of the war, an estimated 80 mills were in operation, and by 1810 that number leaped to almost 200 mills, producing 425,000 reams and an annual income of over $1 million.

After the Revolution, entrepreneurs began addressing the two main problems in papermaking: the long process and the scarcity of rags. A French veteran of the Revolutionary War developed the first paper machine around 1799, but Thomas Gilpin of Delaware is credited with inventing the first machine in America in 1816. Around the same time another man, John Ames from Springfield, Massachusetts, also invented a machine that, like Gilpin's, used a cylinder washer and finisher. The various machines, operated by fewer workers, were fed pulp and made larger and longer sheets of paper. Experiments using plant fibers sought to alleviate the problem of rag shortages, but the only fiber used commercially was straw.

With science and technology addressing the issues of time, labor, and raw material, papermaking continued to grow. Before the Civil War, the U.S. had approximately 440 mills, with the bulk of them in New York, Massachusetts, Pennsylvania, and Connecticut. The Civil War and the depression of 1873, however, meant losses for all industries. The remaining papermakers organized themselves into trade presses and organizations. The International Paper Company, formed in 1898, represented twenty mills from five states. It grew to control 90 percent of newsprint and own 1 million acres of timberland in the U.S. and 1.6 million acres in Canada.

In 1866, Frederick Wuertzbach traveled to Germany to purchase a new machine that used water to grind wood into pulp. Developed by Heinrich Voelter, the machine offered papermakers an abundant raw material with which to replace rags. The first paper made from wood pulp was made 8 March 1867 at the Smith Paper Company. While wood pulp did not produce paper of such high quality as rag pulp, and initially met with some resistance, wood pulp became the primary material for paper.

As the industry gradually accepted wood pulp, it shifted geographically to areas with large forests, first to the Northeast and then to the South. Science and technology continued to find ways to make quality paper from different kinds of timber. In the South, Dr. Charles Herty, a chemist and professor, developed new techniques for using Georgia's high-resin pine for wood pulp.

From the onset of World War I until the Great Depression, the paper industry boomed. The wartime demand for paper gave workers the leverage, sometimes through strikes, to lobby for better working conditions and salaries. During the depression the government stepped in to help the paper industry, largely through the National Recovery Administration. Franklin Roosevelt's New Deal was good for the industry, but it opened the door to increased governmental control. At the start of World War II the industry was producing approximately 6 million tons of paperboard. The demands of the war, however, meant shortages in just about every area of life, including pulpwood as well as the labor to harvest trees and work in mills. Further challenges came in the environmental movements of the 1970s, as concern grew about forest lands and the disposal of hazardous waste from chemicals used to bleach, dye, and make pulp.

Despite war shortages and other challenges, the industry grew throughout the twentieth century. The United States remains the largest consumer of paper products in the world, with a 1995 per capita consumption of 736 pounds. Of the 555 U.S. facilities, approximately half produce both paper and pulp, and the industry employs over 200,000 people.

BIBLIOGRAPHY

Smith, David C. *History of Papermaking in the United States (1691–1969).* New York: Lockwood, 1970.

Wilkinson, Norman B. *Papermaking in America.* Greenville, Del.: Hagley Museum, 1975.

Lisa A. Ennis

PARAMILITARY GROUPS. *See* **Militia Movement; Minutemen.**

PARAPSYCHOLOGY, a term denoting the organized experimental study of purported "psychic" abilities, such as telepathy (the knowledge of human thoughts without sensory communication), clairvoyance (the knowledge of physical objects without sensory aid), psychokinesis (the ability to influence an object physically without contact with it), and precognition (the knowledge of future events). The term, originally German, found its way into English in the 1930s and has supplanted the older term "psychical research" in America and to a degree in Great Britain.

Organized psychical research came into being in the United States in 1885, at the height of popular interest in spiritualism, with the founding of the American Society for Psychical Research. The most prominent American supporter of psychical research at this time was William James, although most American psychologists were, and are, hostile to the subject. Many famous mediums were studied, the most noteworthy being Leonora E. Piper, extensively investigated by James himself. The three principal leaders of American psychical research in its early years were Richard Hodgson, James Hervey Hyslop, and Walter Franklin Prince.

Funds and fellowships for the conduct of psychical research were established in three American universities—Harvard, Stanford, and Clark—in the first two decades of the twentieth century, but the work done there was greatly overshadowed by the work done in the early 1930s by Joseph Banks Rhine with associates in the Psychology Department of Duke University. Rhine ran thousands of tests with Duke students, some of whom achieved striking extra-chance results in card guessing. The results were published in 1934 in *Extra-Sensory Perception;* the methods described there soon became standard experimental procedure, and Rhine's term ESP (extrasensory perception) has become a common label for psychic abilities. Rhine established the *Journal of Parapsychology* in 1937, and in the 1940s he carried his investigations at his laboratory at Duke into the fields of psychokinesis and precognition.

Parapsychology aroused controversy and hostility in scientific and academic quarters; objections were made both to its experimental and statistical methods and to its philosophical implications. Fifty years after university studies began, the subject was still not yet well established academically and had not yet developed a clear professional structure and status. In the popular mind, and to some degree in the field, the connections with spiritualism and the occult remained close. Scientific clarity seemed an especially distant goal in the 1970s and 1980s, as parapsychology merged with popular curiosity in UFO and alien abduction lore, witchcraft, and New Age alternative religions and concepts of holistic health. But the revival of interest in occultism created a wide information network, and during these decades, research in parapsychology was being pursued at various academic centers, including the University of Virginia, the City University of New York, and Maimonides Hospital in New York City, as well as at the American Society for Psychical Research and at private foundations in Durham, North Carolina, and elsewhere. This later experimental work was broadly diversified, with researchers attempting to bring physiology, psychiatry, and studies of animal behavior to bear on parapsychology.

BIBLIOGRAPHY

Beloff, John. *Parapsychology: A Concise History.* London: Athlone Press, 1993.

Griffin, David R. *Parapsychology, Philosophy, and Spirituality: A Postmodern Exploration.* Albany: State University of New York Press, 1997.

Seymour H. Mauskopf
Michael R. McVaugh / A. R.

See also **Mysticism; New Age Movement.**

PARATROOPS, trained and equipped with parachutes, jump behind enemy lines from aircraft. They usually fight in conjunction with an amphibious landing, a large-scale ground offensive, or as highly mobile reinforcements. As light infantry these troops lack heavy weapons and cannot remain in the field long without heavy aerial resupply or contact with ground forces.

The French first used paratroops during World War I. German success with paratroops early in World War II spurred the formation of American airborne divisions. American paratroops participated in combat on all fronts. There were two airborne operations by U.S.

Paratroopers. Private Ira Hayes, shown here in full gear while standing in the open doorway of an aircraft during World War II, is one of the most famous paratroopers of all-time. A full-blooded Pima Indian, Hayes is one of the six U.S. marines in the famous photograph by Joe Rosenthal that shows the soldiers straining to plant the American flag on the rocky slopes of a small peak on the island of Iwo Jima. NATIONAL ARCHIVES AND RECORDS ADMINISTRATION

troops during the KOREAN WAR and one during the VIETNAM WAR.

BIBLIOGRAPHY

Breuer, William B. *Geronimo!: American Paratroopers in World War II.* New York: St. Martin's Press, 1989.

Warner Stark / A. E.

See also **D Day; Normandy Invasion; Sicilian Campaign.**

PARIS CONFERENCES. During 1946 the United States participated in two lengthy international conferences in Paris that sought to draft a postwar European settlement. The Council of Foreign Ministers, made up of representatives from the United States, the Soviet Union, Great Britain, and France, met from 25 April to 16 May and from 15 June to 12 July in an effort to agree on peace treaties for the former Axis satellites, Finland, Bulgaria, Romania, Hungary, and Italy. After extended argument, the participants reached compromise agreements that allowed the convening of the Paris Peace Conference on 29 July 1946; the parley was composed of the twenty-one nations that had been at war with Germany. Concluding on 15 October, this conference recommended modifications in the draft peace treaties to the Big Four, but the essential elements of the treaties had been hammered out in the preliminary foreign ministers meetings.

The Paris conferences of 1946 significantly heated the simmering tensions between the United States and the Soviet Union. The bitterness and acrimony that marked the foreign ministers' efforts to agree on relatively minor matters—such as the Italian-Yugoslav boundary, Italian reparations, disposition of the Italian colonies, and rules for the international navigation of the Danube—indicated that agreement on the far more complex German peace treaty was some distance away. Furthermore, each nation used these public forums as a means of ratcheting up the confrontational public rhetoric. Final provisions of the satellite peace treaties were agreed to at the New York foreign ministers meeting on 4 November–12 December 1946, and the treaties were signed by the United States in Washington, D.C., on 20 January 1947 and by the other powers at Paris on 10 February.

Another Big Four foreign ministers conference was held at Paris from 23 May to 20 June 1949. This conference dealt mainly with the German problem, which revolved largely around the Big Four's inability to agree on terms for a peace treaty for that country. The meeting at Paris had been agreed to by the United States, Great Britain, and France in return for Soviet agreement to drop the blockade of Berlin, which had been begun in 1948 in protest against the Western powers' decision to create an independent West Germany. At the conference the West rejected a Soviet plan for German reunification, and the Soviets turned down a Western proposal for extension of the new West German constitution to East Germany.

In 1959 the heads of state of the United States, Great Britain, France, and the Soviet Union agreed to hold a summit conference in Paris in May 1960 to discuss the mutual reduction of tensions. This conference had been agreed to as an outcome of Premier Nikita S. Khrushchev's determination to sign a peace treaty with the East Germans that would have impaired Western access rights to Berlin. Plans for the conference went awry two weeks before its opening when an American reconnaissance aircraft (the U-2) was shot down over the Soviet Union. When President Dwight D. Eisenhower refused to disavow responsibility or apologize for the flight, Khrushchev dramatically refused to participate in the summit conference and canceled an invitation for Eisenhower to visit the Soviet Union.

The longest series of negotiations at Paris in which the United States participated was the talks regarding the settlement of the VIETNAM WAR, which began in 1968 and did not end until 1973. Following President Lyndon B.

Johnson's agreement to restrict the bombing of North Vietnam and his withdrawal from the presidential campaign in March 1968, the North Vietnamese agreed to meet with the Americans at Paris to discuss a settlement of the war. The talks were later broadened to include the contending parties in South Vietnam: the South Vietnamese government and the National Liberation Front. In 1969 Henry Kissinger, then the special adviser for national security affairs to President Richard M. Nixon, began secret meetings at Paris with the North Vietnamese politburo member Le Duc Tho. These meetings were made public early in 1972, and by the fall of that year had brought the two sides close to agreement. Differences of interpretation arose that led to a temporary suspension of the talks in December 1972, before the peace settlement of 1973.

BIBLIOGRAPHY

Beschloss, Michael R. *MAYDAY: Eisenhower, Khruschev, and the U-2 Affair.* New York: Harper and Row, 1986.

Gaddis, John Lewis. *The United States and the Origins of the Cold War, 1941–1947.* New York: Columbia University Press, 2000.

John Lewis Gaddis / T. G.

See also **Cold War; Germany, American Occupation of; Germany, Relations with; Russia, Relations with.**

PARIS, TREATY OF (1763). The Paris Treaty of 1763, forged among Great Britain, France, and Spain, brought to an end the French and Indian War. At the war's close Britain had achieved military supremacy over the French in North America. The terms of the treaty reflected Britain's dominant position: France ceded all of Canada to Great Britain, the British advanced the boundary of their continental colonies westward to the Mississippi River, and the British received full navigation rights to the river. Cuba, conquered by the British, was returned to Spain, which in return ceded East Florida and West Florida to Britain. As compensation for its losses, Spain received from France by the Treaty of Fontainebleau (1762) all the territory west of the Mississippi River and the island and city of New Orleans. France retained only the islands of Saint Pierre and Miquelon off the south coast of Newfoundland, together with the privilege of fishing and drying fish along the northern and western coasts of Newfoundland, as provided in the Treaty of Utrecht (1713). In the West Indies, Great Britain retained the islands of Saint Vincent, Tobago, and Dominica; Saint Lucia, Martinique, and Guadeloupe were returned to France. The Treaty of Paris left only two great colonial empires in the Western Hemisphere, the British and the Spanish.

BIBLIOGRAPHY

Anderson, Fred. *Crucible of War: The Seven Years' War and the Fate of Empire in British North America, 1754–1766.* New York: Vintage Books, 2001.

Gipson, Lawrence H. *The British Empire before the American Revolution.* New York, 1936.

Max Savelle / T. G.

See also **Canada, Relations with; Canadian-American Waterways; France, Relations with; French and Indian War.**

PARIS, TREATY OF (1783). This treaty between Great Britain and the United States, signed in Paris on 3 September 1783, marked the consummation of American independence. At the same time, Great Britain also signed peace treaties with France, an ally of the United States, and Spain, an ally of France; it had signed a treaty with the Netherlands the previous day. More important, the treaty is rightly considered the greatest triumph in the history of American diplomacy.

To secure its independence, the new United States had entered into an alliance with France (after the tremendous victory over Burgoyne at Saratoga in October 1777), and France, in turn, had agreed to an alliance with Spain. While America had achieved its goal—since Britain had, in principle, accepted the idea of American independence—Spain had not gained its objective, the recapture of Gibraltar. And, given these entangling alliances, the conflict dragged on, though the fighting had largely ended in North America.

There were other issues as well. Spain, for example, also wanted to limit the size of the new United States well east of the Mississippi River, to protect Spanish holdings along the Gulf Coast in the area that became Florida and Texas. Britain also wanted to limit the size of the United States, to protect its position in Canada and with the Native American tribes. France wanted to weaken its traditional opponent, Britain, as much as possible, which required a stronger United States to compete with Britain in North America.

America's diplomats John Adams, Benjamin Franklin, John Jay, and Henry Laurens engaged in a shrewd negotiation. Beginning in March 1782 (Cornwallis had surrendered at Yorktown on 19 October 1781), they opened negotiations first with the government of Prime Minister Charles Rockingham and later with the government of the earl of Shelburne, Sir William Petty. They achieved success with a preliminary, conditional treaty, signed on 30 November 1782, which would not take effect until Britain reached a settlement with France, and France delayed until Britain and Spain achieved a settlement. Again, Spain wanted Gibraltar, which the British were not willing to return.

The conditional British-American treaty fixed the boundaries of the United States to the northeast and northwest, established the Mississippi River as the west-

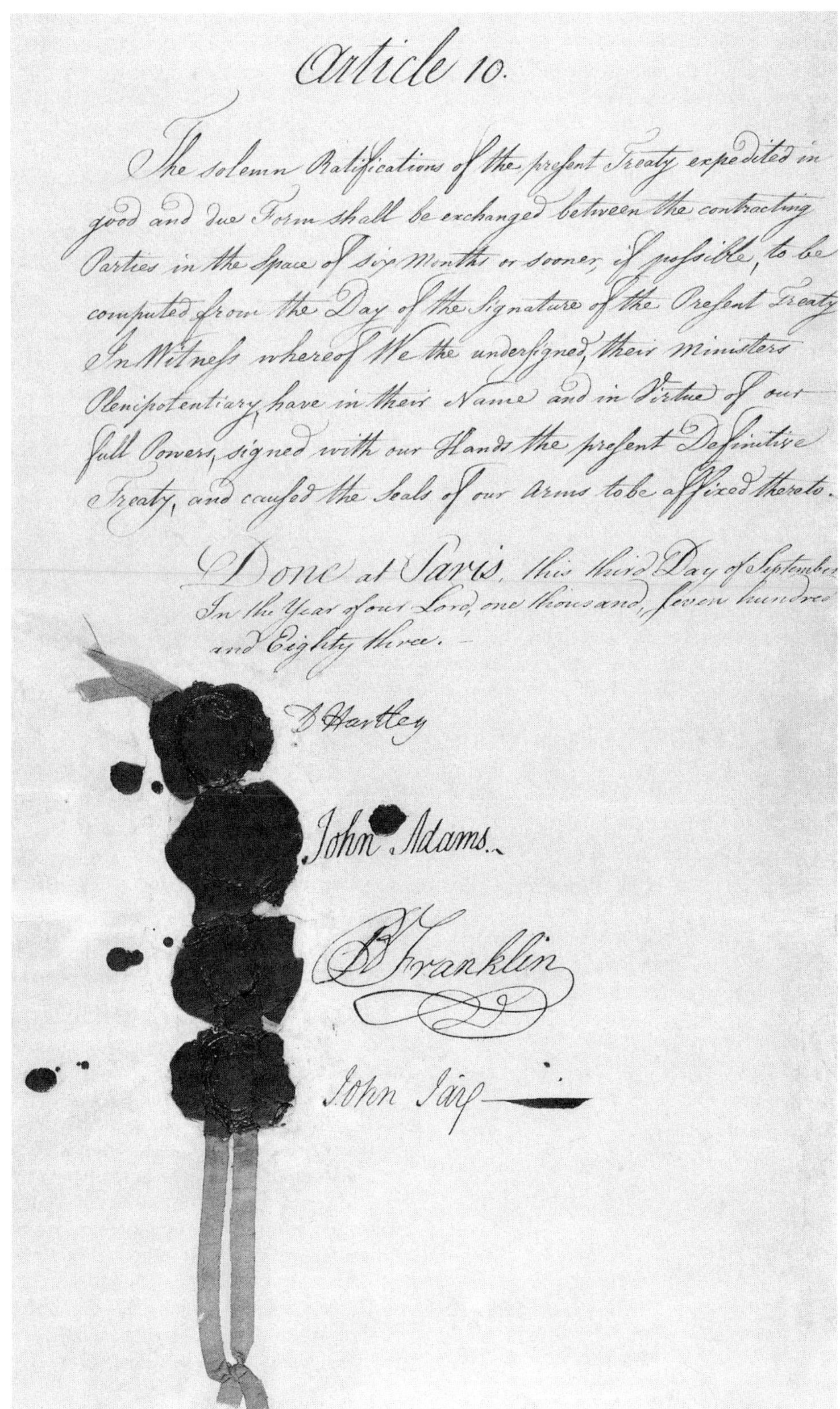

Article 10.

The solemn Ratification of the present Treaty expedited in good and due Form shall be exchanged between the contracting Parties in the Space of Six Months or sooner if possible, to be computed from the Day of the Signature of the Present Treaty. In Witness whereof We the undersigned their Ministers Plenipotentiary have in their Name and in Virtue of our full Powers, signed with our Hands the present Definitive Treaty, and caused the Seals of our Arms to be affixed thereto.

Done at Paris, this third Day of September In the Year of our Lord, one thousand, seven hundred and Eighty three. –

D Hartley

John Adams.

B Franklin

John Jay

Treaty of Paris. The historic treaty, formally ending the American Revolution and establishing the borders of the United States of America, bears the signatures and seals of David Hartley, for Great Britain, and of the American negotiators John Adams, Benjamin Franklin, and John Jay, 3 September 1783. © CORBIS ern boundary (a great and grand achievement) and secured navigation along the Mississippi for British and American citizens (although the entrance to the Gulf of Mexico flowed through Spanish-controlled New Orleans); the treaty also granted Americans fishing rights off Newfoundland's Grand Banks and the right to cure fish in uninhabited parts of nearby landfall, but not in Newfoundland itself. The treaty also committed the U.S. government to guarantee repayment of debts to British creditors and to improve the treatment of American Loyalists, including the restitution of property seized during the revolutionary fighting.

While these negotiations were taking place, the British stiffened their position after learning that Spain's long siege of Gibraltar had failed. John Jay, in particular, had great fear that France and its minister Charles Gravier, Comte de Vergennes, might seek a separate peace with Britain, at America's expense, to satisfy France's ally Spain. There were the typical machinations associated with such important diplomatic maneuverings. But Benjamin Franklin, though sick with gout, managed to imply to Vergennes that further French opposition to the treaty he had helped negotiate with Britain could drive America back into British arms; he also wrote to Vergennes that the Americans and French would not want the British to see them divided, and thus France should support what the United States had achieved in its separate negotiation. For Vergennes, this helped him out of a difficult situation, since he could not tie France's foreign policy to Spain's longtime quest to regain Gibraltar. Vergennes was able to use America's initiative to convince the Spanish to sign its treaty.

And, thus, on 3 September 1783, this intricate conflict came to a close and the United States achieved its independence and, by gaining land between the Appalachian Mountains and the Mississippi River, laid the ground for what would become a vast country.

BIBLIOGRAPHY

Bemis, Samuel Flagg. *The Diplomacy of the American Revolution.* Westport, Conn.: Greenwood Press, 1983.

Dull, Jonathan R. *A Diplomatic History of the American Revolution.* New Haven, Conn.: Yale University Press, 1985.

Hutson, James H. *John Adams and the Diplomacy of the American Revolution.* Lexington: University Press of Kentucky, 1980.

Kaplan, Lawrence S. *Colonies into Nation: American Diplomacy, 1763–1801.* New York: Macmillan, 1972.

Charles M. Dobbs

See also **Revolution, Diplomacy of the.**

PARIS, TREATY OF (1898). The Paris Treaty of 1898 terminated the Spanish-American War. Under its terms Spain relinquished all authority over Cuba and ceded to the United States Puerto Rico, the Philippine Islands, and Guam in exchange for $20 million as the estimated value of public works and nonmilitary improvements in the Philippines. Hostilities had been suspended 12 August, and on 1 October the five U.S. commissioners, headed by former Secretary of State William R. Day, opened negotiations with the Spanish commissioners in Paris. The most difficult questions encountered were the disposition of the Philippines, which Spain was reluctant to relinquish, and of the $400 million Spanish debt charged against Cuba, which the Spanish wished assumed by either Cuba or the United States. Eventually Spain yielded on both points. An attempt by the U.S. commissioners to secure the island of Kusaie in the Carolines was blocked by Germany, which had opened negotiations for the purchase of these islands. The treaty was signed 10 December. The Senate, after bitter debate over the adoption of an imperialistic policy, exemplified in the annexation of the Philippines, consented to ratification by a close vote on 6 February 1899. The United States subsequently fought a three-year war to suppress the Filipino independence movement.

BIBLIOGRAPHY

Beisner, Robert L. *Twelve against Empire: The Anti-Imperialists, 1898–1900.* Chicago: Imprint Publications, 1992.

Pratt, Julius W. *Expansionists of 1898: The Acquisition of Hawaii and the Spanish Islands.* New York: P. Smith, 1951.

Julius W. Pratt / T. G.

See also **Philippine Insurrection; Philippines; Spain, Relations with; Spanish-American War; Treaties with Foreign Nations.**

"PARITY" IN NAVAL DEFENSE. "Parity" was the philosophy behind the naval armament treaties adopted at the Washington Conference of 1921 and 1922. The United States agreed to reduce its capital-ship and aircraft carrier tonnage until it equaled that of the British fleet and was five-thirds the size of Japan's navy. Restrictions on Asian naval bases gave Japan near parity with Britain and America for Pacific operations. Japan consented to withdraw from northern China and to sign the Nine-Power Treaty that guaranteed Chinese political and territorial integrity. In 1936 the United States, Great Britain, and Japan failed to renew the limitation treaties when American and British delegates refused Japanese demands for naval parity in the Far East.

BIBLIOGRAPHY

Fanning, Richard W. *Peace and Disarmament: Naval Rivalry and Arms Control, 1922–1933.* Lexington: University Press of Kentucky, 1995.

Dudley W. Knox / E. M.

See also **London Naval Treaties; Warships; Washington Naval Conference.**

PARLIAMENT, BRITISH. Although not the oldest legislative body in history, the British Parliament has been the model, both positive and negative, for the legislative branches of most Western countries, including the Congress of the United States of America.

The Anglo-Saxons had a legislative assembly called the witenagemot, but this institution was suppressed by the Norman invasion of 1066. The genesis of the House of Lords occurred in the thirteenth century, with the Curia Regis, the king's feudal council, more commonly called the great council, to which he summoned his tenants in chief, the great barons, and the great prelates, to serve primarily as a judicial and executive body.

The House of Commons originated in the thirteenth century in the occasional convocation of representatives of other social classes of the state—knights and burgesses—usually to report the consent of the counties and towns to taxes imposed by the king. Its meetings were often held in conjunction with a meeting of the great council, for in the early thirteenth century there was no constitutional difference between the two bodies; the formalization of Parliament as a distinct organ of government took at least another century to complete.

During the Barons' War, Simon de Montfort summoned representatives of the counties, towns, and lesser clergy in an attempt to gain support from the middle classes. His famous Parliament of 1265 included two representative burgesses from each borough and four knights from each shire, admitted, at least theoretically, to full standing with the great council. Although Edward I's so-called Model Parliament of 1295 (which contained prelates, magnates, two knights from each county, two burgesses from each town, and representatives of the lower clergy) seemed to formalize a representative principle of composition, great irregularities of membership in fact continued well into the fourteenth century.

The division of Parliament into two houses did not coalesce until the fourteenth century. Before the middle of the century the clerical representatives withdrew to their own convocations, leaving only two estates in Parliament. The knights of the shires, who, as a minor landholding aristocracy, might have associated themselves with the great barons in the House of Lords, nevertheless felt their true interest to lie with the burgesses, and with the burgesses developed that corporate sense that marked the House of Commons by the end of the century.

The Growth of Parliamentary Sovereignty

The constitutional position of Parliament was at first undifferentiated from that of the great council. Large assemblies were called only occasionally, to support the king's requests for revenue and other important matters of policy, but not to legislate or consent to taxation in the modern sense.

In the fourteenth century, Parliament began to gain greater control over grants of revenue to the king. From Parliament's judicial authority (derived, through the Lords, from the judicial powers of the great council) to consider petitions for the redress of grievances and to submit such petitions to the king, developed the practice of withholding financial supplies until the king accepted and acted on the petitions. Statute legislation arose as the petition form was gradually replaced by the drafting of bills sent to the king and ultimately enacted by Commons, Lords, and king together. Impeachment of the king's ministers, another means for securing control over administrative policy, also derived from Parliament's judicial authority and was first used late in the fourteenth century.

In the fourteenth century, through these devices, Parliament wielded wide administrative and legislative powers. In addition, a strong self-consciousness on the part of its members led to claims of parliamentary privilege, notably freedom from arrest and freedom of debate. However, with the growth of a stronger monarchy under the Yorkists and especially under the Tudors, Parliament became essentially an instrument of the monarch's will.

The House of Lords with its chancellor and the House of Commons with its speaker appeared in their modern form in the sixteenth century The English Reformation greatly increased the powers of Parliament because it was through the nominal agency of Parliament that the Church of England was established. Yet throughout the Tudor period Parliament's legislative supremacy was challenged by the Crown's legislative authority through the privy council, a descendant of part of the old feudal council.

With the accession (1603) of the Stuart kings, inept in their dealings with Parliament after the wily Tudors, Parliament was able to exercise its claims, drawing on precedents established but not exploited over the preceding 200 years. In the course of the English civil war, Parliament voiced demands not only for collateral power but for actual sovereignty. Although under Oliver Cromwell and the Protectorate, parliamentary authority was reduced to a mere travesty, the Restoration brought Parliament back into power—secure in its claims to legislative supremacy, to full authority over taxation and expenditures, and to a voice in public policy through partial control (by impeachment) over the king's choice of ministers. Charles II set about learning to manage Parliament, rather than opposing or circumventing it. James II's refusal to do so led to the Glorious Revolution of 1688, which permanently affirmed parliamentary sovereignty and forced William III to accept great limitations on the powers of the Crown. During the reign of Queen Anne even the royal veto on legislation disappeared.

The Ascendancy of Commons

Despite a general division into Whig and Tory parties toward the end of the seventeenth century, political groupings in Parliament were more inclined to form about a particular personality or issue. Although members had considerable freedom to make temporary political alliances without regard to their constituencies, control over members was exercised by the ministry and the Crown through patronage, which rested on the purchase of parliamentary seats and tight control over a narrow electorate. As members were paid no salaries, private wealth and liberal patronage were prerequisites to a seat in Commons; as a result, Parliament represented only the propertied upper classes, and private legislation took precedence over public acts throughout the eighteenth century. The parliamentary skills of Sir Robert Walpole, in many respects the first prime minister, both signified and contributed to the growing importance of Commons. The Crown retained the theoretical power to appoint a ministry of its choice, but the resignation (1782) of George III's minister Lord North established, once and for all, a tendency that had developed gradually since the Glorious Revolution—that the prime minister could not function without the support and confidence of the House of Commons.

The part played by Parliament in the administration of the colonies before 1763 was very small, for North America was regarded as an appurtenance of the Crown and governed by ordinances of the privy council. Only in matters of combined domestic and colonial interest, or involving the welfare of the empire as a whole, did Parliament legislate for the colonies, as in the Molasses Act of 1733, designed to promote trade between New England and the British West Indies and to benefit West Indian planters.

Not until the firm establishment of the principle of parliamentary supremacy in England, concurrent with the close of the French and Indian War (1763), did Parliament seriously set itself to the direction of colonial affairs (see COLONIAL POLICY, BRITISH). It quickly made itself odious to Americans by asserting its authority in regard to colonial taxation and appropriation, which the assemblies had long looked upon as their exclusive domain. Americans felt that Parliament had no right to assume powers that the Crown had formerly been unable to make good, and the uncompromising attitude of the ministry of George Grenville concerning the STAMP ACT (1765) precipitated a crisis in which colonial opinion everywhere stiffened against Parliament. Two years later, the passage of the TOWNSHEND ACTS widened the breach, and in 1773 the resolution of the British prime minister, Frederick, Lord North, to "try the issue [of taxation] in America" led directly to the Revolution.

BIBLIOGRAPHY

Bank, Dina Citron. *How Things Get Done.* 2d rev. ed. Columbia: University of South Carolina Press, 1979.

Cruikshanks, E. *Parliamentary History.* 4 vols. 1985.

Jones, Ossie Garfield. *Parliamentary Procedure at a Glance.* Enl. and rev. ed. New York: Hawthorn, 1971.

Mackenzie, Kenneth R. *The English Parliament.* Harmondsworth, U.K.: Penguin, 1950, repr. 1963.

Namier, Lewis, and John Brooke. *The House of Commons, 1754–1790.* Published for the History of Parliament Trust. New York: Oxford University Press, 1964.

Pollard, A. F. *The Evolution of Parliament.* 2d ed. rev. London: 1964.

Sayles, G. O. *The King's Parliament of England.* New York: Norton, 1974.

Ryan, M. Stanley. *Parliamentary Procedure: Essential Principles.* New York: Cornwall, 1985.

Jon Roland

See also **Colonial Policy, British.**

PARSON'S CAUSE, refers to conflict over ministers' salaries in the 1750s and 1760s. Ministers' salaries had been fixed (1748) at 17,200 pounds of tobacco a year, and laws in 1755 and 1758 sought to limit price fluctuations by allowing payment in paper money at twopence per pound. Because tobacco sold for sixpence a pound, ministers assailed the law, obtaining a royal veto in 1759. In court battles in the 1760s, Patrick Henry defended Virginia against claims for back wages, assailing vetoes of laws for the public good and securing a jury award of one penny damages. After a series of further setbacks, the ministers ceased their agitation after 1767.

BIBLIOGRAPHY

Christie, I. R. *Crisis of Empire.* New York: Norton, 1966.

O. M. Dickerson/c. w.

See also **Legal Tender; Royal Disallowance; Tobacco as Money.**

PASSAMAQUODDY/PENOBSCOT. The Passamaquoddies and Penobscots, residents of eastern and central Maine, respectively, were among the first Native Americans contacted by Europeans. Both groups had fluid social organizations, spoke related Algonquian languages, and lived in small villages or seasonal family band camps while relying on hunting, fishing, and gathering for subsistence. They were never organized as tribes but were perceived as such by English colonials and later state and federal officials. In 2002, most Penobscots resided on Indian Island in the Penobscot River, while the Passamaquoddies were divided between Pleasant Point on Passamaquoddy Bay and Indian Township near the St. Croix River.

The Passamaquoddies and Penobscots avoided European domination throughout most of the colonial period due to their strategic location and their remoteness

Spearing a Porpoise. This print by M. J. Bruns shows two Passamaquoddy fishermen off the coast of Maine. North Wind Picture Archives

from English settlements. Catholic conversion and French intermarriage fostered friendly relations, but French influence has often been exaggerated. The six wars occurring between 1677 and 1760 were each caused locally by a combination of English insistence on sovereignty, disputes concerning subsistence or land, and indiscriminate mutual retaliation. These conflicts resulted in the decline and migration of Native populations and the merging of refugees into Penobscot and Passamaquoddy villages.

After supporting the American Revolution, these Indians were administered by Massachusetts (Maine after 1820), contrary to federal law. State authorities forced them to make large land cessions in 1794, 1796, 1818, and 1833. Significantly, each group has had a nonvoting representative to the state legislature since the early 1800s. Maine was the last state to grant reservation Indians voting rights (1954), but it created the first state Department of Indian Affairs (1965). In the late 1960s, the Passamaquoddies and Penobscots initiated the Maine Indian Land Claims, arguing that state treaties violated the Indian Nonintercourse Act of 1790. Several favorable court rulings prompted a $81.5 million settlement in 1980 and provided the foundation for other suits by eastern tribes.

BIBLIOGRAPHY

Brodeur, Paul. *Restitution: The Land Claims of the Mashpee, Passamaquoddy, and Penobscot Indians of New England.* Boston: Northeastern University Press, 1985.

Ghere, David. "Abenaki Factionalism, Emigration, and Social Continuity in Northern New England, 1725–1765." Ph.D. diss., University of Maine, 1988.

Morrison, Kenneth M. *The Embattled Northeast: The Elusive Ideal of Alliance in Abenaki-Euramerican Relations.* Berkeley: University of California Press, 1984.

David Ghere

See also **Tribes: Northeastern.**

PASSES, MOUNTAIN. Two mountain chains traverse America from north to south, the Appalachians and Rockies, and both formed barriers to westward movement. Early hunters in search of pelts and pioneers who coveted western lands met the difficulty by finding natural outlets through the mountains. Early trails were, when possible, water trails, so the Mohawk and the Ohio Rivers were the key routes to the Great Lakes and the Mississippi Valley. The Iroquois and French barred the Mohawk route on the north, and the Cherokees and other confederate tribes blocked routes through the lowlands south of the Appalachians. Accordingly, the confluence of the Allegheny and Monongahela Rivers at Pittsburgh and the breaks in the mountain ridges in the corner between Virginia and North Carolina leading into Kentucky were the points of easiest passage. Such gaps in the Appalachians were frequently the result of troughs cut through the mountain slopes by rivers seeking an outlet to the Ohio or the Atlantic Ocean. The Virginia coast range is low, but early maps show only three passes into the Shenandoah Valley: Williams, Ashby, and Vestal Gaps, all in Fairfax County.

The most important pass in the Kentucky approach was the Cumberland Gap, which led by way of the Holston and Clinch Rivers in eastern Tennessee over and through the mountains and then along the Kentucky River and its tributaries to the Falls of the Ohio. This was known as Boone's Wilderness Road. Early travelers also noted Flower Gap, from tidewater to the sources of Little River; Blue Ridge Gap, another passage from tidewater to the Shenandoah Valley; and Moccasin Gap, between the north fork of the Holston and Clinch Rivers.

Those headed west encountered Chester's Gap in the Blue Ridge Mountains on the Virginia road by Braddock's Road to Pittsburgh. They crossed Miller's Run Gap on the Forbes Road, running west from Philadelphia to Pittsburgh, northwest of the present site of Ligonier, in Westmoreland County, Pa.

The Rockies, because of their uninterrupted length and great height, offered a more serious problem. For the most part, early Spanish missionaries at the south and fur traders, emigrants, and army explorers at the north and center unlocked their secrets. Spaniards made the earliest approaches in the south when pushing into California from New Mexico. After Mexico revolted and American trade with Santa Fe began, fur trappers thrust westward from Taos and Santa Fe to San Diego and Los Angeles. The river valleys unlocking the southern route to the West were the Gila and the Colorado. The Colorado trail, known as the Spanish Trail, went north from Taos, crossed the Wasatch Mountains and Mojave Desert, and entered California by the Cajon Pass. The Gila route was the shorter trail from Santa Fe, going west across the mountains and, by way of Warner's Pass, eventually reaching San Diego.

By following the Arkansas River west to Pueblo, Colo., and crossing the mountains by a choice of three or four different passes, the Williams or Sandy Hill, the Roubideau or Mosca, and the Sangre de Cristo or Music Passes, travelers could reach Taos by turning south or California by turning northwest on a route traced by John C. Frémont. This route crossed the Great Basin of Utah and Nevada and surmounted the Sierra Nevada passes in California. The most important of these passes were the Walker, the Carson, the Virginia, the Frémont, the Sonora, the Donner, and the Truckee. After travelers had scaled the eastern escarpment, there still remained mountain folds in the Sierra Nevada that impeded progress to the coast. The Tehachapi Pass into San Joaquin Valley crossed one such fold.

The central approach to the Rockies was by way of the Platte River, which sends fingers high up into the mountains. The most important pass in the entire Rocky Mountain chain, South Pass, was on this route. It has easy grades, and many travelers bound for California used it by turning south at Fort Hall, Idaho.

Of all river approaches, the Missouri was the most effective and was the route that Meriwether Lewis and William Clark used. They crossed the Rockies by Lemhi, Clark, and Gibbon Passes. Other useful passes of the Northwest were the Nez Perce and Lo Lo through the Bitterroot Mountains on the Montana and Idaho border. The Bozeman Pass offered access from the valley of the Gallatin River to that of the Yellowstone River. For traveling south from Oregon to California the Siskiyou Pass proved useful.

Important passes in the midcontinental region were the Union, crossing the Wind River Mountains in southwestern Wyoming; Cochetope Pass over the San Juan Mountains in southwestern Colorado, used by Frémont and others in passing from Colorado to Utah; and Muddy Pass, two degrees south of South Pass, which was useful in crossing the Atlantic and Pacific divides from Platte headwaters. Bridger's Pass, discovered in the early days of the fur trade, crossed the divide south of South Pass and saved distance on the California route; for this reason, it was used by the Pony Express.

BIBLIOGRAPHY

Carnes, Mark C., and John A. Garraty et al. *Mapping America's Past: A Historical Atlas.* New York: Henry Holt, 1996.

Earle, Carville. *Geographical Inquiry and American Historical Problems.* Stanford, Calif.: Stanford University Press, 1992.

Meinig, D. W. *The Shaping of America: A Geographical Perspective on 500 Years of History.* New Haven, Conn.: Yale University Press, 1986.

Nevins, Allan. *Frémont: Pathmarker of the West.* Lincoln: University of Nebraska Press, 1992.

Carl L. Cannon / A. E.

See also **Cumberland Gap; Frémont Explorations; Oregon Trail; Pony Express; Roads; Rocky Mountains; South Pass; Western Exploration; Westward Migration.**

PASSPORTS issued to United States citizens provide proof of identity abroad and request, in the name of the secretary of state, that the holder be permitted to travel "without delay or hindrance" and, if necessary, be given "all lawful aid and protection." The earliest surviving passport issued by U.S. diplomatic officials dates to 1788. Until 1856, officials such as governors and mayors, as well as the U.S. Department of State, issued passports. After

1856, however, issuance was confined to the Department of State. Except for the Civil War period, passports were not required of foreign travelers to the United States until 1918. The requirement was made permanent in 1921. Under the Internal Security Act of 1950, passports could not be issued to members of communist organizations or to those whose activities abroad would violate the laws of the United States. The provision debarring U.S. communists from obtaining passports was revoked in 1964. Formerly, issuance was deemed to be at the absolute discretion of the Department of State, but in 1958 the Supreme Court recognized that the "right to travel" constituted a liberty of which a law-abiding citizen could not be deprived. As the twenty-first century began, plans were afoot to replace passports with a system whereby software would translate the pattern of a person's iris into a passport number.

BIBLIOGRAPHY

Borchard, Edwin Montefiore. *The Diplomatic Protection of Citizens Abroad.* New York: Banks Law Publishing, 1928.

Freedom to Travel: Report of the Special Committee to Study Passport Procedures of the Association of the Bar of the City of New York New York: Dodd, Mead, 1958.

Stuart, Graham H. *American Diplomatic and Consular Practice.* 2d ed. New York: Appleton-Century-Crofts, 1952.

Robert Garland

See also **State, Department of.**

PATCO STRIKE. *See* **Air Traffic Controllers Strike.**

PATENTS AND U.S. PATENT OFFICE. Some system for encouraging invention and industrial growth by granting monopolies has existed since the colonial period; the early system ultimately evolved into the twentieth century's patent system. The valuable patent monopoly has always been subject to detailed requirements to ensure that the privilege was granted only in appropriate instances and endured only for a limited time. The rare colonial approval of monopolies for the purchase, production, and sale of commodities derived from the British Crown's authority to grant such monopolies in the national interest. The Crown's authority was restricted in scope by *Darcy v. Allin* (1602), which invalidated the patent of Queen Elizabeth I for the manufacture of playing cards because she had failed to show that the process was an invention; the monopoly was therefore not considered to be in the national interest. Common law rules prohibiting such anticompetitive practices as engrossing, regrating, and forestalling served as the backdrop for the 1624 Statute of Monopolies, which authorized monopolies only to "the true and first inventor" of a new manufacturing process. The monopolies were limited to fourteen years, presumably an adequate period to train apprentices in the new technology and receive the deserved monetary benefits.

Early America

Against this background, the General Court of Massachusetts Bay Colony granted monopolies for stated periods, with the objective of encouraging domestic industry. Benefits to inventors or innovators took the form of monopolies or monetary grants for each sale of the patented item. Since the Articles of Confederation made no mention of patents, individual states continued the precedent established in colonial Massachusetts. Maryland, for example, granted patents to James Rumsey for his steamboat and to Oliver Evans for his milling machinery.

In 1790, Congress passed the first patent law under the power provided in Article I, section 8 of the newly ratified Constitution. Congress was empowered "to promote the Progress of Science and useful Arts, by securing for limited Times to . . . Inventors the exclusive Rights to their . . . Discoveries." This act federalized the patent power, so that states no longer granted patents. The act provided that petitions for patents would be forwarded to the secretaries of state and war and to the attorney general, and that any two members of this patent board could approve a fourteen-year patent. The attorney general was then to submit the approved patent for the president's signature. Thomas Jefferson, the secretary of state and a notable inventor himself, played the leading role in this procedure. Because of his abhorrence of monopoly, he strictly applied the rule of novelty and usefulness to each application. Only three patents were approved in 1790.

Objections to delays in processing petitions and the narrow interpretation of the 1790 act led to passage in 1793 of a new law that eliminated the board and created an administrative structure for examining the merits of petitions. The secretary of state was to register the patents and appoint a board of arbiters when two or more petitioners claimed the same invention. The courts would handle disputes about the validity of the petitioners' claims. There was concern that the courts were excessively occupied with patent litigation and not well qualified to adjudicate disputes about claims of priority and technical questions. This caused Secretary of State James Madison to establish the Patent Office in 1802. It was administered by William Thornton, who in September 1814 saved the patent files from destruction by British troops.

The Nineteenth Century

Senator John Ruggles of Maine, a persistent critic of the 1793 legislation, led a successful effort to adopt a completely revised patent law; the new legislation was signed on 4 July 1836. The law created the Office of Commissioner of Patents within the Department of State. This legislation, which is the foundation of the modern patent system, gave the Patent Office responsibility for examining petitions and ruling on the validity of the claims for an invention, its usefulness, and its workability. The fourteen-year monopoly could be extended for an additional seven years if a special board (later, the commissioner of patents) found that the patentee had encountered unusual problems in producing and marketing the device. In 1861, Congress reserved such grants to itself. To give the patentee additional time for producing and marketing new products, Congress increased the monopoly period to seventeen years.

Congress codified and modified the various patent laws again in 1870 and gave the Patent Office the power to register trademarks. This trademark registration statute was held unconstitutional in 1879, on the ground that trademarks were neither copyrightable writings nor patentable discoveries, and so were outside the scope of Article I, section 8 of the Constitution. Trademark laws were subsequently passed under the authority of the commerce clause, and the Patent Office continued to administer the trademark registration process. The 1870 act moved responsibility for administering the copyright laws, some of which had been in the Patent Office, to the Library of Congress. It also sanctioned the procedures for adjudicating interferences (contests by patent claimants as to coverage or priority) by establishing the Office of the Examiner of Interferences.

Reforming the Patent System

In the ensuing decades, the Patent Office—which had been transferred to the Department of the Interior when the latter was created in 1849 and was later moved to the Department of Commerce in 1925—developed its present basic organization and essential procedures. Executive and managerial authority were vested in the commissioner of patents, one or more assistant commissioners, and an office of administration. A registry office registered patent applications and assignments of approved patents, published and distributed patent specifications, and organized a scientific and technical library. The chief operating function of examining the claims was delegated to several patent examining divisions. Separate units processed trademark applications. Boards with important staff functions, such as the Trademark Trial and Appeal Board, the Board of Patent Interferences, and the Board of Appeals, began adjudicating appeals to review examiners' findings with regard to utility and design patents, along with trademark disputes. In the Plant Patent Act of 1930, Congress extended patent protection to asexually reproduced plants, renewing an interest in promoting agriculture that went back to an 1839 program, administered by the Patent Office, of collecting and distributing seeds and information of interest to farmers.

The statute governing patents was substantially revised again in 1952. The new act codified rules that had previously been established by court decisions. Significantly, the requirement that inventive developments be "nonobvious" was codified for the first time in the 1952 revision. The nonobviousness requirement represents the important substantive difference between a new development and a new development that qualifies as an invention. In 1970, patent protection for plants grown from seeds was embodied in the Plant Variety Protection Act, and in the 1980 case of *Diamond v. Chakrabarty* (447 U.S. 303), the U.S. Supreme Court held that ordinary utility patents could be sought for genetically altered microorganisms. This decision laid the groundwork for the important role that patent law plays in the biotechnology industry. The decision was controversial at the time, and remained so at the turn of the twenty-first century.

Legislative modifications continued throughout the rest of the twentieth century. Perhaps the most important was legislation in 1982 to create the U.S. Court of Appeals for the Federal Circuit. This circuit court has exclusive appellate jurisdiction over patent disputes, and its decisions have been important in unifying patent law doctrine. Another particularly important change, effective in 1995 as a result of the adoption of the Uruguay Round Agreement of the General Agreement on Tariffs and Trade, altered the term of patents from seventeen years from issuance to twenty years from filing.

Patents and New Technology

The late twentieth century saw the patent law system struggle with the question of how to accommodate computer software. After some early indications that the Patent Office regarded software as unpatentable, the system ultimately accepted the idea of software patents. This decision was controversial as a matter of policy, with many arguing that patent law protection was both unnecessary and unsuitable. Critics also questioned the capacity of the Patent Office to engage in meaningful evaluation of applications in the field of software technology.

Although the patent system has long played a significant role in the history of American science and technology, it has been the subject of considerable adverse criticism. Critics, as in the 1938 hearings of the Temporary National Economic Committee, claimed that the patent system fostered undesirable monopolies by creating producers who, by superior technology protected by patents, could corner large parts of the market. Later, after the *Chakrabarty* decision ruled that a genetically modified microorganism was patentable, critics pointed to the possible unfortunate effects, both ethical and practical, of allowing patents on "life." Critics have also accused the system of suppressing inventions to delay change. Patent advocates, on the other hand, who probably outnumber the critics, have called attention to the virtues of a reward system that is proportional to an invention's public value. They also point to the availability of antitrust law when companies become too dominant in an industry. Supporters also emphasize the importance of Patent Office publications in disseminating specifications and drawings of inventions, and to the economic significance of the U.S. technology system in the global economy—a system that relies importantly on patents. Since the founding of

Thomas Edison's laboratory in 1876, most significant inventions have been developed by institutional research sponsored by the federal government, universities, and private companies, and the incentive of the patent system has played a crucial role in stimulating investment in that research.

BIBLIOGRAPHY

Campbell, Levin H. *The Patent System of the United States, So Far as It Relates to the Granting of Patents: A History.* Washington, D.C.: McGill and Wallace, 1891.

Chisum, Donald S., and Michael A. Jacobs. *Understanding Intellectual Property Law.* New York: Matthew Bender, 1992.

Halpern, Sheldon W., Craig Allen Nard, and Kenneth L. Port. *Fundamentals of United States Intellectual Property Law: Copyright, Patent, and Trademark.* Boston: Kluwer Law International, 1999.

Meyer H. Fishbein
John A. Kidwell

See also **Copyright; Intellectual Property; Trademarks.**

PATERSON SILK STRIKE began on 23 January 1913, when 800 workers walked off their jobs in the "Silk City" of Paterson in northern New Jersey. They were joined within two weeks by nearly 24,000 additional workers at more than one hundred of Paterson's mills. Manufacturers instigated the six-month strike when new machinery enabled them to double the number of looms per worker, from two to four. Factory operatives averaged twelve-hour days, and feared the machines would increase their workloads and create pay cuts and unemployment. Workers set aside differences in language, religion, ethnicity, and skill levels to unite behind the Industrial Workers of the World (IWW). Victorious at a similar strike in Lawrence, Massachusetts, in 1912, the IWW sent William Haywood and Elizabeth Gurley Flynn to coordinate the Paterson strike. Unfortunately for the workers, the new machinery allowed mill owners to increase operations elsewhere and maintain profits. Manufacturers initiated numerous acts of violence, and their influence with local politicians and police led to the arrest of more than 2,000 largely peaceful strikers. At least one worker was killed by the mill owners' private guards, who were never brought to trial. In a last-ditch attempt to win financial and public support, New York radicals Walter Lippman, Max Eastman, Mabel Dodge, and John Reed staged the "Paterson Strike Pageant" at Madison Square Garden. The strike's theatrical dramatization earned rave reviews, but little money. Skilled ribbon weavers were the first to break ranks and accept the mill owners' terms, returning to work on 18 July, and most of the remaining strikers returned to work, defeated, on 28 July, with a few holding out until 25 August.

BIBLIOGRAPHY

Dubofsky, Melvyn. *We Shall Be All: A History of the Industrial Workers of the World.* 2d ed. Urbana: University of Illinois Press, 1988.

Golin, Steve. *The Fragile Bridge: Paterson Silk Strike, 1913.* Philadelphia: Temple University Press, 1988.

Tripp, Anne Huber. *The I.W.W. and the Paterson Silk Strike of 1913.* Urbana: University of Illinois Press, 1987.

John Cashman

See also **Strikes.**

PATIENTS' RIGHTS, a movement that grew out of the push for individual rights of the 1960s and 1970s, gave rise to the idea of a set of rights for protection of medical patients and succeeded in having those rights enacted into law in many states. Although medical and hospital patients in most states were beneficiaries of common-law rights well before the 1960s, these protections consisted only of the right to not be treated without consent, the confidentiality of statements made to a physician during treatment, the right to damages in event of malpractice, and, to some extent, the confidentiality of a patient's hospital records. In 1973 an advance in patients' rights occurred when the American Hospital Association (AHA) approved a bill of rights for adoption by member HOSPITALS. It promised patients considerate and respectful care, the right to know hospital rules and regulations relating to patient conduct, the right to know the identity of the physician in charge of care, sufficient information to enable patients to make informed decisions with respect to their treatment, the right to obtain information concerning diagnosis and treatment as well as prognosis if medically advisable, the right not to be a subject of experiment, the confidentiality of clinical records, and the right to receive an explanation of the hospital bill.

Although the AHA represented almost all of the 5,300 nonprofit, general, and investor-owned hospitals in the United States in the 1990s, the bill of rights adopted by most of the association's members was of little or no legal value because it was voluntary. Nonetheless, it established public awareness of patients' rights and set the stage for a second advance that took place between 1975 and 1985, when one-third of the states enacted patients' rights statutes. Although these statutes varied, they all incorporated the AHA pledges and generally went beyond them to guarantee the right to prompt emergency attention, the right to examine one's clinical chart during the course of treatment and to obtain a copy of it, the right, within limits, to privacy during the hospital stay, the right to receive an itemized bill, and the right to receive information about financial assistance and free care. The most important aspect of these statutes was that they were enforceable. California, Colorado, Illinois, Maryland, Massachusetts, Michigan, Minnesota, New York, Pennsylvania, and Rhode Island were some of the states that enacted statutes. In most instances the statutes also applied to nursing homes. The right to refuse treatment extended to psychiatric patients if they were competent. By the 1990s federal law required hospitals and nursing homes to advise patients of their right to refuse care and their right to execute living wills or to name proxies if they become unable to make life-and-death treatment decisions.

BIBLIOGRAPHY

Annas, George J. *The Rights of Patients: The Basic ACLU Guide to Patient Rights.* Totowa, N.J.: Humana Press, 1992.

Huttmann, Barbara. *The Patient's Advocate.* New York: Penguin, 1981.

Ziegenfuss, James T. *Patients' Rights and Organizational Models: Sociotechnical Systems Research on Mental Health Programs.* Washington, D.C.: University Press of America, 1983.

Jack Handler / A. E.

See also **Death and Dying; Euthanasia; Health Care; Medicine and Surgery; Mental Illness.**

PATRONAGE, POLITICAL, is often defined as public office awarded in payment for political support. Examples abound: John Adams famously appointed the midnight judges to continue Federalist policies and thwart the Republicans. Democrat William Clinton appointed Republican William Cohen secretary of defense to lessen opposition from the Republican Congress. And politicians who need votes appoint someone who can bring them in, as did John F. Kennedy when he chose Lyndon Johnson to be his running mate. However, this narrow definition of patronage fails to capture its essence in U.S. history. American patronage politics can be best understood as a distinct organizational form of government.

Politicians must promise benefits to the voting public in order to win elections. In theory, those who promise the most benefits at the least cost (to the public) garner the most votes. For some governments (whether local, state, or federal) it is most efficient to provide general benefits—such as roads or schools—that are equally available to all members of a constituency; civil service governments tend to dominate in this circumstance. For other governments, particularly when the population of voters is heterogeneous and isolated (that is, different voters want different things), it works better to provide specific benefits to individuals; this is most conducive to patronage governments.

Whatever their formal job description (trash collector in Richard Daley's Chicago, land office manager on Andrew Jackson's frontier), patronage workers are appointed to government payrolls by elected officials primarily to design, effect, and monitor exchanges between voters and government. Patronage workers interview voters to determine what governmental promises appeal, relay their patron's message to influence votes, and deliver direct, personally tailored benefits in payment for votes. Civil service workers, in contrast, are hired based on merit and paid to produce or provide general benefits (such as housing for those formulaically prequalified). The political tasks of interviewing voters and relaying politicians' messages are accomplished outside of and paid for independently of government, using polling firms, think tanks, and impersonal media (broadcast, news, and mail).

This distinctive American patronage came to state and then to federal government before it came to cities. Voters who moved west began to want government's help keyed to their new locations, such as the removal of Indians or cheap water transport. Sending patronage workers to find out what these scattered voters wanted and to relay candidates' messages proved a winning campaign strategy for gubernatorial candidate Martin Van Buren as settlement spread west in New York, and then for presidential candidate Andrew Jackson as population spread west in the nation. The federal government adopted patronage with the election of Jackson in 1828, and it only began to abandon it for a bureaucratic form of government mass-producing goods and services when faster mail, the telegraph, and railroads promised speeded commerce. Patronage employees lost value to federal politicians as newspapers' growing circulation let politicians communicate directly with the public. While patronage waned at the federal level (by 1901, 44 percent of federal employees were civil servants), it waxed in large old cities rapidly filling with immigrants with heterogeneous wants and needs. Urban political regimes that efficiently insured the poor against the hardships of the new industrial life (for example, matching relief to individual family size and circumstance) ruled the large industrial cities, while scientific city managers administered smaller, homogeneous midwestern farm cities. With the halt to immigration in World War I, the heterogeneity of the industrial urban electorate diminished. At the same time, the Progressives began to worry that the immigrants' excesses would endanger the cities' brave new manufacturing world. These developments and the sudden jump in the perceived need for governmental largesse with the coming of the Depression empowered the federal government in 1933 to supplant (patronage) city welfare with (general) federal assistance programs. To block any return to patronage, Progressives allied with the federal government to demand qualifications tests for state and local governmental jobs. Now, all large cities and most states claim to hire on merit.

BIBLIOGRAPHY

Bridges, Amy. *A City in the Republic: Antebellum New York and the Origins of Machine Politics.* Cambridge: Cambridge University Press, 1984.

Breton, Albert. *Competitive Governments: An Economic Theory of Politics and Public Finance.* New York: Cambridge University Press, 1996.

Johnson, Ronald N., and Gary D. Libecap. *The Federal Civil Service System and the Problem of Bureaucracy: The Economics and Politics of Institutional Change.* Chicago: University of Chicago Press, 1994.

Joseph D. Reid

See also **Appointing Power; Civil Service; Machine, Political; Political Parties; Spoils System.**

PATRONS OF HUSBANDRY was founded as a farmers' lodge on 4 December 1867, in Washington, D.C. It served as the vehicle through which the Granger movement operated. It had a secret ritual like the Masons and admitted both men and women to membership. Each local unit was known as a "Grange." In 1876 the order reached its peak membership of 858,050, but by 1880 the collapse of the Granger movement had reduced this figure to 124,420. Thereafter, by abandoning business and politics for its original program of social and educational reforms, the order began a slow and steady growth. By 1934, the Patrons of Husbandry again claimed over 800,000 members, mainly in New England, the North Central states, and the Pacific Northwest. By 1974, membership had declined to about 600,000. Of late years it has not hesitated to support legislation, both state and national, deemed of benefit to farmers. In the early twenty-first century, the Grange and the Patrons of Husbandry actively supported movements to diversify the crops of tobacco farmers into other marketable products. They also encouraged use of the money pending from tobacco class action settlements to ease dislocation in tobacco farming.

BIBLIOGRAPHY

Nordin, Dennis S. *Rich Harvest: A History of the Grange, 1867–1900.* Jackson: University Press of Mississippi, 1974.

Wiest, Edward. *Agricultural Organization in the United States.* Lexington: University of Kentucky Press, 1923.

John D. Hicks/H. S.

See also **Granger Movement.**

PATROONS. On 7 June 1629, the directorate of the Dutch West India Company granted a charter of freedoms and exemptions which provided for the grant of great estates, called patroonships, to those members of the company who were able to found, in what is now New York, settlements of fifty persons within four years after giving notice of their intentions. The patroon, after extinguishing the Indian title by purchase, was to hold the land as a "perpetual fief of inheritance" with the fruits, plants, minerals, rivers, and springs thereof. Before the end of January 1630, five patroonships had been registered, only one of which, that of Kiliaen van Rensselaer, was successful. The difficulties of transportation across the Atlantic Ocean, lack of cooperation from the company, quarrels with the authorities at New Amsterdam, Indian troubles, and the difficulties of management from 3,000 miles away were all factors in their failure. In 1640, the revised charter reduced the size of future patroonships, but the same factors contributed to prevent the success of these smaller grants. At the close of Dutch rule in 1644, the company had repurchased all but two of the patroonships. Thereafter, the English colonial governments of New York rewarded influential political supporters with large land grants that some families used to create manors with large numbers of rent-paying tenants. By 1750, these New York patroons formed a landed elite whose wealth was second only to the Carolina rice planters.

BIBLIOGRAPHY

Flick, Alexander C., ed. *History of the State of New York.* Volume 1. New York: Columbia University Press, 1933.

Huston, Reeve. *Land and Freedom: Rural Society, Popular Protest, and Party Politics in Antebellum New York.* New York: Oxford University Press, 2000.

Kim, Sung Bok. *Landlord and Tenant in Colonial New York: Manorial Society, 1664–1775.* Chapel Hill: University of North Carolina Press, 1978.

A. C. Flick/C. P.

See also **Land Grants; Land Policy; New Netherland; New York State.**

PATTERNS OF CULTURE, an anthropological work published in 1934 that became one of the most widely read pieces of social science ever written in the United States. Its author, Ruth Benedict, did no fieldwork, but wrote evocatively about cultural diversity. She helped persuade a generation of Americans that members of their own society were generally too quick to judge negatively the values and practices of people different from themselves. *Patterns of Culture* did more than any other work to popularize "cultural relativism," the notion that the "good" is not absolute and universal, but relative to a particular culture.

Benedict made her arguments by describing the different ways of living found in the Zuni and Kwakiutl peoples of North America and the Dobu people of the East Indies. Benedict presented each case as an integrated cultural unit—a way of life that made sense within its own terms even if foreign to readers whose culture was that of the United States. Benedict wrote idealistically of an "arc of culture," a virtually infinite inventory of possibilities for human life, from which each society had in effect selected a set of specific elements in order to create their own way of life. In her most widely quoted construction, Benedict quoted an elderly Indian to the effect that at the start of the world, the creator had given to each of the world's peoples a "cup" from which to drink "from the river of life." That his tribe was in decline showed that their cup was now "broken."

Yet Benedict was not only evocative and descriptive, but openly didactic as well. She urged her readers to adopt more tolerant, generous attitudes toward peoples whose values and practices were different from their own. *Patterns of Culture* was later criticized by anthropologists and philosophers for begging difficult questions in evaluation, and for representing cultures as too autonomous and internally harmonious.

Paving America. To help lift America out of the Great Depression, President Franklin D. Roosevelt created the Works Progress Administration (WPA), which employed millions. One major WPA effort was the Road Construction Project, which paved thousands of roads and repaved thousands of additional roads, as shown here. It is estimated that WPA workers built more than 650,000 miles of roads throughout the United States.

BIBLIOGRAPHY

David A. Hollinger. "Cultural Relativism." In *Cambridge History of Science*. Vol. 7, *Social Sciences*. Edited by Dorothy Ross and Theodore M. Porter. New York: Cambridge University Press, 2002.

David A. Hollinger

See also **Anthropology and Ethnology.**

PAVING. All the earliest paving in America seems to have been done with cobblestones. The first mention of paving is found in a court record in New Amsterdam in 1655, a reference to repairs of the paving in Pearl Street. Brouwer Street was paved with cobbles in 1658 and thereafter called Stone Street, even to the present time. Several other short New York streets were paved before 1700. In Boston, State and Washington Streets were cobble paved in the seventeenth century. In 1719, it was said that some citizens of Philadelphia laid stone to the middle of the street in front of their own property, but the city was notorious for muddy thoroughfares for many decades thereafter. Alongside some city streets very narrow brick or slab stone sidewalks were laid as early as 1700. Some macadamizing with broken stone or gravel and some cobble paving were done in the eighteenth century, but even in 1800 most city streets were still given over to dust or mud. In fact, some downtown business streets in New York were quagmires as late as 1850, and in Chicago streets remained dirty and muddy long after that.

In 1832, what is said to have been the first granite or Belgian block pavement in America was laid in New York. That city also introduced wood paving in 1835, laid in hexagonal blocks, a technique said to be Russian in origin. Later, cities lay square blocks. Although wooden paving was easy on horses, and the clumping of their hoofs was muffled on impact, wet weather caused the wood to swell and become uneven. When Chicago burned in 1871, the weather had been so dry that even the wooden paving burned. In New Orleans, built on soft alluvial soil, many streets were surfaced with thick wooden planks laid crosswise—some streets until well into the twentieth century.

With the coming of the automobile and the decline of horse transportation, wood paving in urban centers declined. The first brick street paving was laid in Charleston, West Virginia, in 1870. New York first tried laying asphalt in 1877 and pronounced it a failure, though the

Pawnee. Tribal members outside (and atop) lodges in Nebraska in 1873, not long before the forced removal of the tribe south to a reservation in present-day Oklahoma. NATIONAL ARCHIVES AND RECORDS ADMINISTRATION

technique quickly became popular. After 1900, asphalt paving began slowly to be replaced by concrete, which for some years had been vying with sawed Bedford stone in popularity for sidewalks. Various mixtures of crushed stone with tar, bitumen, asphalt, and cement were developed for streets and roads as the automobile era dawned, but for the main highways, concrete came to be the only material considered. Glass paving bricks were announced in 1905 but never came into use, and rubber paving was tried in 1923.

By 1970 the surface paving of streets in most major cities was a bituminous mixture from either asphalts (petroleum products) or tars (coal products). Modern roads require several layers of pavement to support heavy vehicles moving at high speeds. Modern paving engineers design highways and interstates with three distinct layers, which includes the roadbed, base course, and wearing course, the latter being either asphalt or concrete.

BIBLIOGRAPHY

Hart, Virginia. *The Story of American Roads.* New York: Sloane, 1950.

Lewis, Tom. *Divided Highways: Building the Interstate Highways, Transforming American Life.* New York: Viking, 1997.

Seely, Bruce Edsall. *Building the American Highway System: Engineers as Policy Makers.* Philadelphia: Temple University Press, 1987.

Alvin F. Harlow / H. S.

See also **City Planning; Interstate Highway System; Roads.**

PAWNEE. Archeological investigations in Nebraska have revealed that pottery, tool, and implement types found in the Lower Loup Phase beginning between the 1500s and 1600s indicate a distinct grouping of people. Similarities were discovered between Lower Loup artifact types and cultural patterns found in later eighteenth-century historic Pawnee sites. Information in European colonial and later American sources indicated that the Pawnees lived and hunted in a region now located in Nebraska and parts of Kansas. The Pawnees' first contact with non-Indians occurred in the seventeenth century, when the French traded with tribes along the Missouri River tributaries. Later the Spanish considered the Pawnees subjects of the Spanish crown. Next, in the early 1800s American explorers and treaty makers came. United States treaties resulted in tribal land cessions, placed the tribe on a Nebraska reservation, and reduced its traditional territory, until 1875, when the tribe faced forced removal to a reservation in Indian Territory. Estimates indicate a population of between 10,000 and 20,000 in the 1800s, dropping to less than 700 by 1906. The rapid decline resulted from intertribal warfare, disease, and hunger caused by improvident government policies.

The sacred was all-encompassing in Pawnee life. The seasonal round of subsistence activities, including crop growing, gathering, and biannual bison hunting, called for ceremonies in which hide-wrapped sacred bundles containing powerful objects were used ritually to secure success in each endeavor. Harvest and success in war and hunting called for particular tribal ceremonies. Important in Pawnee religion was the belief in Tirawahut, an abstraction described as all-powerful in the universe. Certain sky constellations, Mother Corn, the buffalo, and all things in nature had sacred connotations. A few sacred bundles belong to the Pawnees now, but their use and ceremonies are mostly forgotten. Today, tribal members may belong to local Christian churches or the Native American Church.

The Pawnee tribe historically was governed by a council composed of chiefs from each of the four bands, the Chaui, Pitahawirata, Kitkahahki, and Skidi, that once lived in separate locations and villages. After land cessions they were compelled to live together on reservations. Later in Oklahoma, after passage of the 1936 Oklahoma Welfare Act, a Business Council and the Nasharo (Chiefs) Council became governing bodies.

Important historical events include loss of tribal land resulting from forced cessions and the Allotment Act of 1896; use of Pawnee warriors as United States scouts in the 1860s and 1870s; forced removal to Indian Territory, away from sacred places and tribal graves; deaths of leading chiefs, ceremonial leaders, and tribal members that initiated loss of sovereignty and culture; the ongoing yearly visit between the Caddoan-speaking Wichitas and Pawnees, stemming from an ancient friendship; the leadership of Pawnees in the Native American Rights Fund and repatriation issues; and the selection of Kevin Gover as recent head of the Bureau of Indian Affairs.

United States legislation in the second half of the twentieth century benefited the Pawnees by providing for grants to educate doctors, lawyers, teachers, and other professionals; health benefits; and greater tribal autonomy and decision making, including government-funded, tribal-managed programs. These programs include a tribal court, a tax commission, tribal law enforcement, repatriation of tribal remains and artifacts, substance abuse programs, after-school tutoring, cultural retention programs with language classes, and others that improve the conditions and status of the people. All these programs provide employment for tribal members. Others are employed locally or in other cities and states.

The tribe numbers approximately 2,500, most of whom live away from the old Oklahoma reservation area. Many return for the four-day Pawnee Homecoming sponsored by the Pawnee Veterans' Association. A few older ceremonies survive and other feasts and tribal dances bring the people together as Pawnees.

BIBLIOGRAPHY

Blaine, Martha Royce. *Pawnee Passage: 1870–1875.* Norman: University of Oklahoma Press, 1990.

———. *Some Things Are Not Forgotten: A Pawnee Family Remembers.* Lincoln: University of Nebraska Press, 1997.

Hyde, George E. *Pawnee Indians.* Norman: University of Oklahoma Press, 1974.

Weltfish, Gene. *The Lost Universe: Pawnee Life and Culture.* Lincoln: University of Nebraska Press, 1977.

Martha Royce Blaine

See also **Tribes: Great Plains.**

PAXTON BOYS. In late 1763, a posse from Paxton, Pennsylvania, frustrated by an assembly influenced by Quakers and its subsequent failure to protect frontier settlements against Pontiac's War, killed twenty peaceful Conestoga Indians in Lancaster County. They also threatened a group of Indians converted to the Moravian Brethren, who took refuge in Philadelphia. A large band of angry Paxton Boys marched on the capital to demand protection and protest the Quaker assembly. President Benjamin Franklin stepped in to negotiate the crisis, convincing the mob to return home and assuring increased protection.

BIBLIOGRAPHY

Dunbar, John Raine, ed. *The Paxton Papers.* The Hague: Nijhoff, 1957.

Merrell, James H. *Into the American Woods: Negotiators on the Pennsylvania Frontier.* New York: Norton, 2000.

Vaughan, Alden T. *Roots of American Racism: Essays on the Colonial Experience.* New York: Oxford University Press, 1995.

Julian P. Boyd/H. S.

See also **Moravian Brethren; Pontiac's War; Quakers.**

PEABODY FUND, the pioneer educational foundation in the United States, was established in 1867 by George Peabody, a native of Massachusetts, who subsequently became a banker in London. He gave $2 million to encourage and assist educational efforts in the U.S. South, to help the region recover from the ravages of the Civil War. To administer the fund he named sixteen men of distinction from the North and the South. The fund greatly assisted general education and teacher training for both whites and blacks in the states that had formed the Confederacy and in West Virginia. Dissolved in 1914, during its lifetime the Peabody Fund distributed about $3.65 million.

BIBLIOGRAPHY

Dillingham, George A. *The Foundation of the Peabody Tradition.* Lanham, Md.: University Press of America, 1989.

Edgar W. Knight/D. B.

See also **Civil War; Education; Education, African American; Philanthropy; Reconstruction; South, the: The New South; Teacher Training.**

PEACE COMMISSION (1867). The 1867 Peace Commission was an attempt to bring peace to western lands by creating reservations for Indian tribes, enabling white settlers to claim former Indian territories and railroads to continue to lay tracks toward the Pacific, thus fulfilling the doctrine of Manifest Destiny. In 1867, under the leadership of Major Joel Elliot, the U.S. government signed treaties with the Cheyennes, Plains Apaches, Comanches, Arapahos, and Kiowas. Three major reservations were established in present-day South Dakota, Oklahoma, and Arizona. Later that year, a second series of treaties was signed that governed the southern plains. In addition to reservation land, the tribes were to receive food, blankets, farming implements, homes, and clothing.

The Peace Commission failed to end conflict between western nations' territorial claims and U.S. expansionism. From 1860 to 1890 reservation lands came under extreme pressure from white settlers, leading to increased conflict, while the U.S. army failed to distribute promised annuities. Tribal leaders had agreed to reservations in an attempt to preserve their way of life and to avoid further bloodshed but were not entirely able to compel their people to move onto them. War parties composed mostly of young men opposed to reservation life continued to counter white settlers with violent opposition; the settlers, meanwhile, ignored the provisions of the conference and continued to encroach on Indian lands.

BIBLIOGRAPHY

Brown, Dee. *Bury My Heart at Wounded Knee*. New York: Bantam, 1970.

———. *The American West*. New York: Scribners, 1994.

Nabokov, Peter, ed. *Native American Testimony*. New York: Penguin Books, 1978.

Deirdre Sheets

See also **Indian Removal; Indian Reservations.**

PEACE CONFERENCES are those international conferences in which the United States has participated in an effort to establish procedures for settling international disputes without resort to war. A wide range of tactics has been employed at one time or another in pursuit of this goal, and these have enjoyed varying degrees of success.

Arbitration

Arbitration—that is, the voluntary submission of a dispute to an impartial body for a decision that the disputants agree in advance to accept—is the oldest method by which U.S. diplomats have sought to alleviate international tensions. The first arbitration agreement in which the United States participated was written into Jay's Treaty of 1794 with Great Britain. The Treaty of Ghent of 1814, also with Great Britain, established arbitration boards to handle conflicts over boundaries arising out of the settlement. The most notable nineteenth-century example of arbitration in which the United States was involved was the Treaty of Washington of 1871, in which Great Britain and the United States agreed to submit to an arbitration commission claims arising from the raids of the *Alabama* and other British-built Confederate warships on Union vessels during the American Civil War.

By the turn of the century, considerable sentiment had built up in favor of having the United States sign with other nations bilateral treaties providing for the automatic submission of certain classes of disputes to arbitration. Secretary of State Elihu Root negotiated a series of twenty-four such agreements in 1908 and 1909, of which the Senate ratified all but three. Secretary of State William Jennings Bryan renewed some of the Root treaties in 1913 and 1914 and negotiated others.

These agreements had little practical effect. The tendency of arbitration boards to resolve conflicts by merely splitting the difference between disputants made American diplomats reluctant to employ the procedure for the settlement of significant territorial or financial issues. Disputes involving vital interests were regularly excluded from arbitration treaties, and the Senate insisted on the right to reject the use of arbitration in each case. As a result, arbitration was employed only rarely as a means of settling international disputes, and then only in situations of minor significance.

Mediation

The use of mediation in the resolution of international conflicts has been less frequent, but overall it has proved more effective where tried. The United States accepted Russian mediation in setting up negotiations with Great Britain leading to a settlement of the War of 1812. In general, however, a sense of American exceptionalism led the country more often to serve as mediator in the disputes of others than to accept foreign mediation over crises in which the United States was directly involved. American diplomats rejected British attempts to mediate the two most important U.S. conflicts of the nineteenth century, the Mexican War of 1846–1848 and the Civil War. On the other hand, the United States has, with varying degrees of success, employed mediation in its relations with Latin America. The United States successfully mediated an end to the struggle between Spain and the Latin American countries of Chile, Peru, Ecuador, and Bolivia in 1869, but failed in several efforts between 1879 and 1884 to mediate the War of the Pacific between Chile, Peru, and Bolivia. President Theodore Roosevelt also employed mediation successfully in two important situations: settlement of the Russo-Japanese War in 1905 and resolution of the first Morocco crisis at the Algeciras Conference of 1906. President Woodrow Wilson made several efforts to mediate World War I between 1914 and 1916, none of which was successful.

International Organization

World War I marked a shift away from both arbitration and mediation as means of defusing international crises but saw the rise of international organizations for that purpose. An unwillingness to enter into binding overseas commitments led Americans to avoid participation in such organizations, so that throughout the nineteenth century the country only associated itself with such innocuous international arrangements as the Universal Postal Union and the Geneva Convention on the treatment of the wounded in warfare. One partial exception was American membership in the Commercial Union of the American Republics (later the Pan-American Union) in 1889, but its primary function was the facilitation of trade, not the peaceful resolution of disputes. In the early twentieth century, the United States participated regularly in conferences devoted to humanizing the rules of warfare—the most significant of which were the Hague Conferences of 1899 and 1907—but these produced no significant action to prevent war.

American involvement in World War I greatly increased U.S. interest in the possibility of creating an international organization to prevent war. Wilson had endorsed this concept as early as 1916, and, following the Allied victory in 1918, he devoted great effort toward the establishment of such an organization as part of the peace settlement. The result was the League of Nations, an international organization of states whose members were obliged, in the words of Article X of the covenant, "to respect and preserve as against external aggression the territorial integrity and existing political independence of all Members of the League." Article XVI required members to apply economic and, if necessary, military sanctions against aggressors. Wilson himself did not see this as an ironclad commitment to resist aggression anywhere at any time, but many Americans, including a substantial portion of the Senate, did. Because of this, and because Wilson refused to accept reservations making clear the nonbinding nature of the commitment, the Senate refused to approve U.S. membership in the League of Nations.

Nonetheless, the United States did not exclude itself from other international peacekeeping efforts in the interwar period. The United States called the Washington Naval Conference of 1921–1922, which imposed limitations on the construction of certain classes of warships, and participated in conferences at Geneva (1927 and between 1932 and 1934) and at London (1930), which attempted, generally without success, to extend the disarmament agreements reached at Washington, D.C. Secretary of State Frank B. Kellogg was a prime mover behind the multilateral Kellogg-Briand Pact of 1928 (Pact of Paris), the signatories of which renounced the use of war as an instrument of national policy except in cases of self-defense. The question of U.S. membership in the Permanent Court of International Justice, established by the League of Nations in 1920, was also widely debated during the period, although because of the Senate's refusal to accept membership without reservations, the United States never joined.

World War II revived interest in the possibility of creating an international structure to maintain peace. Convinced that the United States had made a great mistake by refusing membership in the League of Nations, State Department planners began working, even before the United States entered the war, to create a new international organization to safeguard peace in the postwar period. President Franklin D. Roosevelt and Secretary of State Cordell Hull carefully sought to avoid Wilson's mistakes by consulting Congress at every step of this process. Their efforts paid off when the Senate endorsed U.S. membership in the United Nations in July 1945, by a vote of eighty-nine to two.

The United Nations resembled the League of Nations in its structure, but unlike the league, it did not require member nations automatically to apply sanctions against aggressors. The General Assembly, in which all members had one vote, could only recommend action. The Security Council could take action but only with the approval of its five permanent members: the United States, Great Britain, the Soviet Union, France, and China, each of which had the right of veto. In the end, the United Nations could be effective only if the great powers were in agreement; in disputes between the great powers themselves the world organization could do little.

At the insistence of the United States, a provision was inserted into the UN charter allowing members to create regional security organizations outside the framework of the world organization. As tensions between the United States and the Soviet Union intensified, revealing the limitations of the United Nations as a peacekeeping agency, the U.S. government began looking toward the formation of such organizations as a means of promoting security; it was a prime mover in the establishment of the Organization of American States in 1948, the North Atlantic Treaty Organization in 1949, the Southeast Asia Treaty Organization in 1954, and the Central Treaty Organization in 1959. The relative ineffectiveness of the latter two, together with a general feeling that the United States had become overcommitted, caused the U.S. government to deemphasize the role of regional security organizations by the mid-1960s. American interest in the United Nations also remained low, partly because of the continuing inability of that organization to deal effectively with conflicts involving the great powers and partly because of the decreasing influence of the United States in the world body as a result of the proliferation of new member-states in Asia and Africa.

Peace Negotiations since the 1960s

After the Cuban missile crisis of 1962, the United States relied with increasing frequency on direct negotiations with its principal adversary, the Soviet Union, as a means of relaxing international tensions. The 1970s saw a series of U.S.-Soviet summit meetings aimed at ending the arms race and solving pressing international problems such as the Vietnam War. After President Richard M. Nixon's visit to China in 1972, this tactic was applied more and more to relations with this country as well. Direct negotiations bore fruit in the form of arms-control agreements such as the 1971 Anti-Ballistic Missile (ABM) Treaty and the 1987 Intermediate-Range Nuclear Forces (INF) Treaty, both with the Soviet Union. They also led to the establishment of full diplomatic relations with China in 1979. Despite a brief escalation of tensions with the Soviet Union in the early 1980s, this general policy of détente dominated U.S. foreign policy through the end of the Cold War.

The 1970s also saw a renewal of interest among American diplomats in mediation, particularly in the Middle East. In 1974, Secretary of State Henry Kissinger enjoyed some success in mediating differences between Egypt and Israel following the 1973 Yom Kippur War. President Jimmy Carter continued this process in the Camp David Accords, signed in 1978, in which Egypt granted diplomatic recognition to Israel.

But while the end of the Cold War might have been expected to offer new opportunities for the United States, as the only remaining global superpower, to mediate international disputes, the actual results were mixed. Attempts by President Bill Clinton to mediate between Israel and the Palestinians, despite promising starts in Washington, D.C. (1993), and at the Wye River Plantation in Maryland (1998), had little practical effect. American mediation of a war in the Balkans was more successful, leading in 1995 to an agreement among the governments of Serbia, Bosnia, and Croatia in Dayton, Ohio. However, it failed to bring lasting peace to the peninsula, which erupted in bloodshed once again over Kosovo in 1999.

Finally, the post–Cold War era brought with it a new willingness to rely on international organizations such as the United Nations, as improved relations with Russia and China permitted the Security Council occasionally to align in favor of action against so-called "rogue states" such as Iraq in the 1990s. This also led to increased U.S. involvement in multilateral peacekeeping missions dispatched to various locations in Africa and the Middle East. The purpose of the North Atlantic Treaty Organization in the post–Cold War world also broadened to include peacekeeping operations in Europe, specifically, intervention against Serbia in crises over Bosnia and Kosovo. A further sign of NATO's changing mission was the expansion of the organization in 1999 to include several eastern European countries that had previously been allied with the Soviet Union. At the start of the twenty-first century, therefore, direct negotiations and international organization remained the most common and overall the most effective mechanisms for the resolution of disputes between nations.

BIBLIOGRAPHY

Diehl, Paul F. *International Peacekeeping*. Baltimore: Johns Hopkins University Press, 1994.

Dunne, Michael. *The United States and the World Court, 1920–1935*. New York: St. Martin's Press, 1988.

Kaplan, Lawrence S. *The Long Entanglement: NATO's First Fifty Years*. Westport, Conn.: Greenwood, 1999.

Kuehl, Warren F. *Seeking World Order: The United States and International Organization to 1920*. Nashville, Tenn.: Vanderbilt University Press, 1969.

Leopold, Richard W. *The Growth of American Foreign Policy: A History*. New York: Knopf, 1962.

Mecham, J. Lloyd. *The United States and Inter-American Security, 1889–1960*. Austin: University of Texas Press, 1961.

Ostrower, Gary B. *The United Nations and the United States*. New York: Twayne, 1998.

Stromberg, Roland N. *Collective Security and American Foreign Policy: From the League of Nations to NATO*. New York: Praeger, 1963.

Weihmiller, Gordon R. *U.S.-Soviet Summits: An Account of East-West Diplomacy at the Top, 1955–1985*. Lanham, Md.: University Press of America, 1986.

Zacher, Mark W. *International Conflicts and Collective Security, 1946–1977*. Westport, Conn.: Greenwood, 1979.

John Lewis Gaddis
John E. Moser

See also **Arbitration; Hague Peace Conferences; League of Nations; North Atlantic Treaty Organization; United Nations Conference; Washington Naval Conference;** *and vol. 9:* **The Fourteen Points.**

PEACE CORPS. Created in 1961 by President John F. Kennedy, the Peace Corps has been an enduring U.S. federal government program to provide trained volunteers to help developing nations alleviate poverty, illiteracy, and disease.

The Peace Corps' inception was both a product of the Cold War struggle and a reaction to the growing spirit of humanitarian activism evident throughout the Western world by the beginning of the 1960s, a spirit that had manifested itself in volunteer humanitarian programs already implemented in Canada, Australia, Britain, France, and Japan. The proposal to create a similar U.S. program had first been placed on the national political agenda by Democratic candidates during the 1950s, notably by Adlai E. Stevenson in his failed presidential campaigns of 1952 and 1956. During the course of the 1960 campaign, Kennedy, the Democratic Party's new candidate, adopted the proposal and it became one of Kennedy's signature campaign issues, largely due to its appeal to young liberals.

Once in office, Kennedy continued to challenge Americans to contribute to national and international public service, calling in his inaugural address of 20 January 1961 for Americans to form a "grand and global alliance" to fight tyranny, poverty, and disease. On 1 March 1961, he temporarily established the Peace Corps by Executive Order 10924 under the auspices of the Department of State and appointed his brother-in-law, R. Sargent Shriver Jr., to act as the Corps' first director at a token salary of one dollar per year. In September 1961, shortly after Congress formally endorsed the Peace Corps by making it a permanent program, the first volunteers left to teach English in Ghana, the first black African nation to achieve independence (in 1957) and whose government had since become an outspoken advocate of anticolonialism. Contingents of volunteers soon followed to Tanzania and India. By the turn of the century, the Peace Corps had sent over 163,000 American volunteers to over 135 nations.

Since its inception the primary missions of the Peace Corps have remained unchanged. The aim of the Peace Corps was not direct intervention to cure poverty per se; rather, it was to provide technical assistance to developing nations to make progress toward sustainable self-sufficiency. The Peace Corps' objectives reflect a mix of altruistic idealism and enlightened national self-interest. As President Kennedy explained the idealistic sentiment, "To those people in the huts and villages of half the globe struggling to break the bonds of mass misery, we pledge our best efforts to help them help themselves." In tandem with this offer of technical assistance, the Corps also aims to foster better mutual understanding. Ideally a reciprocal process, a large part of the objective was to promote the American way of life so as to negate the appeal of communism to third world countries.

In order to retain the support of young liberals, from whose ranks most new recruits have traditionally been drawn, Shriver had striven to preserve the Corps' integrity by shielding it from bureaucratic politics. By the beginning of the 1970s, however, amidst rampant protest and cynicism about American foreign policy exacerbated by the Vietnam War, the Corps' bureaucratic independence came under political attack. In 1971 President Richard Nixon combined the Peace Corps with several other federal volunteer programs under a new agency called *ACTION*. In 1979, however, President Jimmy Carter reversed this by reestablishing the Peace Corps' autonomy, and in 1981 Congress passed legislation to make it an independent federal agency for the first time. With the end of the Cold War, Peace Corps volunteers were dispatched to former Soviet bloc countries struggling with new independence, such as Hungary, Poland, Latvia, Estonia, and Lithuania, and in 1995, in a move to supplement the primary mission of the Peace Corps, a Crisis Corps was established to mount short-term humanitarian relief efforts.

Typically serving for a period of two years, Peace Corps volunteers are invited by host nations to assist in a variety of roles of the host nation's choice. Most Peace Corps volunteers have contributed in the field of education (particularly teaching English), but the work ranges across community development, agriculture, health care, and public works. Prior to their service, volunteers receive intensive, specialized training, and once on location they are actively encouraged to assist where possible but refrain from involvement in the host nation's domestic politics.

Throughout its existence, the Peace Corps has weathered charges of cultural imperialism and persistent questioning of its self-proclaimed altruism. Critics have often suggested that it was in fact a front for the Central Intelligence Agency. Nevertheless, since its inception the Peace Corps has proved remarkably resilient to the political tides of Washington and has arguably even enjoyed qualified success in fulfilling its mission.

BIBLIOGRAPHY

Hoffman, Elizabeth Cobbs. *All You Need Is Love: The Peace Corps and the Spirit of the 1960s.* Cambridge, Mass.: Harvard University Press, 1998.

Rice, Gerald T. *The Bold Experiment: JFK's Peace Corps.* Notre Dame, Ind.: University of Notre Dame Press, 1985.

David G. Coleman

PEACE MOVEMENT OF 1864. In an effort to end the Civil War through a negotiated peace settlement, Horace Greeley of the *New York Tribune* and Confederate commissioners James P. Holcombe, Clement C. Clay, and Jacob Thompson met at Niagara Falls, Canada, in July 1864. The Confederate representatives insisted on complete southern independence, whereas Greeley presented President Abraham Lincoln's terms of reunion and emancipation. Efforts continued throughout the summer and fall without result.

Lincoln's message to Congress in December stipulated Confederate surrender as the only basis for peace. Visits to Davis by Francis P. Blair Sr. in January 1865, led to the abortive Hampton Roads Conference in February.

BIBLIOGRAPHY

Neely, Mark E., Jr. *The Fate of Liberty: Abraham Lincoln and Civil Liberties.* New York: Oxford University Press, 1991.

Silbey, Joel H. *A Respectable Minority: The Democratic Party in the Civil War Era, 1860–1868.* New York: Norton, 1977.

Charles H. Coleman / A. G.

See also **Civil War; Confederate States of America; Copperheads; Democratic Party; Hampton Roads Conference.**

PEACE MOVEMENTS. Aspects of peace culture existed in North America before European colonialism and settlement. The Iroquois had modes of mediation, as did the Quakers later on. William Penn's peace plans preceded organized political movements for peace, which were very much a post-Enlightenment, post-industrial phenomenon. Immigrant peace sects such as the Amish, Hutterians, and many others had religious peace doctrines, often refusing military service and leading nonviolent lives. Nevertheless these groups did not constitute social movements in the way that the term is used in the social sciences: mobilized public groups that take action for social change.

Such peace movements emerged as a response to the Napoleonic wars of the early nineteenth century as the members of various economic and social classes engaged in political debate and publication. Usually taking the form of specific organizations (for example, labor or peace societies), these groups in the United States were often initially linked to similar groups in Europe. Although the first local peace society was formed in New York in 1815 by David L. Dodge, expanded in 1828 into the American Peace Society by W. Ladd (both were reformist, liberal pressure groups that opposed standing armies and supported worldwide peace), firmly establishing a starting date or founding leaders is difficult. The United States has never had a single mass movement or an overarching, unified peace organization.

Not until the later decades of the nineteenth century did broad-based social and political mass movements concerned with peace arise. Earlier, individuals like Ladd, Dodge, the itinerant blacksmith Elihu Burritt (who had popular backing and a broader base as well as an English branch for his League [1846]), and later Alfred Love, who formed The Universal Peace Movement in 1866, and William Lloyd Garrison, as well as individual peace prophets like Henry David Thoreau were the main promulgators of the peace message, the latter introducing ideas of civil disobedience. Churches espousing pacifism, such as the Society of Friends (QUAKERS), MENNONITES, and the Church of the Brethren, were already well established and utopian societies with pacifist views grew in the mid-nineteenth century. Although all these elements were often informally in touch with one another, they did not constitute a true social movement (compare the abolitionist movement).

U.S. peace movements, like those of other industrialized democracies, were composed of overlapping groups, organizations, and individuals that formed temporary coalitions and alliances. The peace movement did not have a single unifying principle, although opposition to war appears to be an obvious one; however, such opposition was often based on isolationism, national chauvinism, economic self-interest—motivations that had little to do with peace. The various peace groups, rooted in a variety of traditions, methods, and ideologies, regularly disagreed—especially on the issue of PACIFISM or about ideologies such as socialism, communism, feminism, or religious doctrines.

Not until about 1900 did several parallel social movements against war and militarism and for pacific internationalism emerge. These included organizations such as the American Union Against Militarism, the Emergency Peace Federation, and the Women's Peace Party, all formed after 1914 to keep the United States out of the European maelstrom. Together with socialist and syndicalist agitation, this represents the first genuine peak of mass peace and antiwar movement activity (1900–1915). Yet with the exception of Jane Addams (who was a key founder of the Women's International League for Peace and Freedom in 1920) and Eugene Debs, head of the Socialist Party, there were no prominent founders of the movement, although Randolph Bourne, Norman Thomas, and Emma Goldman were important critics of war. Out of this activity emerged such organizations as the interdenominational Fellowship of Reconciliation and the largely secular War Resisters League. This activity also spawned the U.S. Communist Party with its ever-shifting peace fronts; the Communist Party's relationship with the peace movement was problematic and often disruptive, though undoubtedly individuals held genuine antimilitarist views. A. J. Muste, who later became a major pacifist leader, was an active Trotskyist in the interwar years.

Ebb and Flow

Like many major social movements, peace movements worldwide are cyclical, often responding to the build up to, conduct of, and aftermath of major wars. In addition, peace movements have tried to forestall war and stop or decelerate arms races. Before 1917 and 1936, the United States had several peace groups working to prevent war or American entry into war. American women helped organize an international women's conference in The Hague in 1915 to try to promote an armistice to end World War I, and by 1936 the League against War and Fascism had a large and stable base, especially on U.S. college campuses. After 1940, however, the U.S. peace movement experienced a long and dramatic decline, with both internationalists and pacifists becoming isolated.

Peace movements have also tried to prevent U.S. entry into wars on other continents and have worked to achieve ceasefires or armistices. Additionally, peace movements have been involved in trying to bring about reconciliation and, especially at the end of the world wars, the establishment of institutions, such as the United Nations, that would provide a venue for settlement of conflict and differences between nations that did not involve going to war. The peace movement in the United States was influenced in character and organization by the late entry of the United States into World Wars I and II and its early ventures in Indochina.

Peaks of peace activity can be seen in U.S. history. The first stretched from the late nineteenth century to the United States' entry into World War I; the second was in the early 1920s, fueled by disillusionment with the outcome of the "war to end wars" and associated with the failure of the LEAGUE OF NATIONS and other international organizations; the third came in the 1930s in response to the accelerating arms race. The fourth, beginning in the late 1950s was concerned mainly with nuclear weapons and served as the base for the fifth, which arose in the mid-1960s in response to the escalation of U.S. involvement in Vietnam. The antiwar peace movement of the 1960s and 1970s included massive demonstrations and mass draft refusal with many young men emigrating to

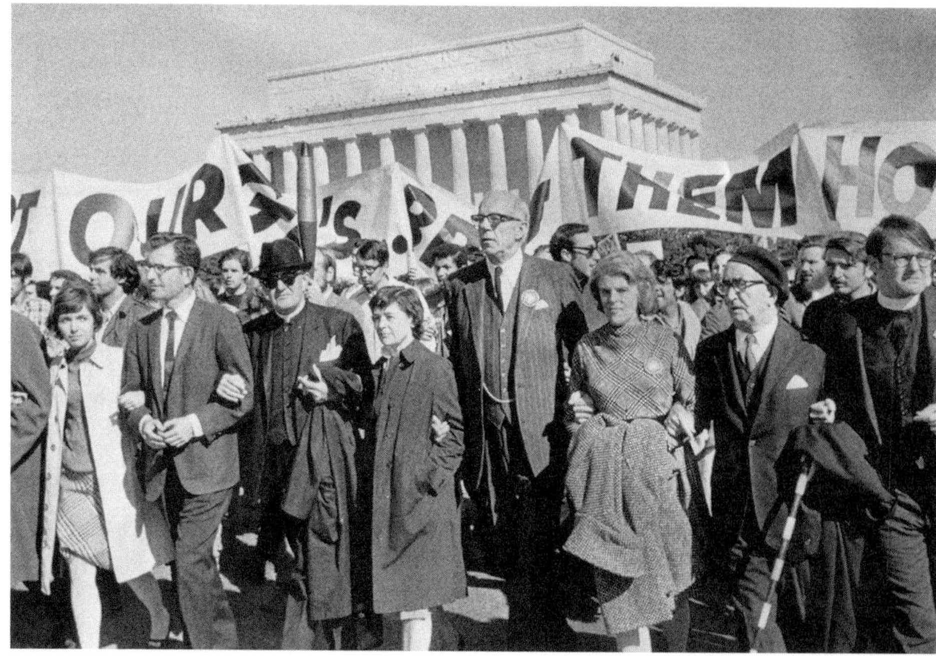

March for Peace. Dr. Benjamin Spock *(fourth from right)*, the famous baby doctor, and thousands of other demonstrators from 150 organizations protesting the Vietnam War begin a two-mile march from the Lincoln Memorial to the Pentagon, 21 October 1967, ending in an overnight vigil, some provocations and violent reactions, and hundreds of arrests. © BETTMANN/CORBIS

Canada and other countries to avoid the draft. The sixth peak of peace activity came after 1979 and focused on preventing nuclear war; it also included feminist and ecological concerns from the mid-1970s to the mid-1980s. At first nuclear energy was a key issue; but by November 1982 the campaign to stop the nuclear arms race had organized strong local groups and could mount large demonstrations and get referenda on local ballots. This coalition formed the "Nuclear Freeze" campaign, led by Randall Forsberg and Randy Kehler; prominent spokespersons were Benjamin Spock and Helen Caldecott. It was at this time that distinctive women's peace movements emerged. Since this final peak, the peace movement continued episodic patterns, and overlapped with the antiglobalization movement of the 1990's and beyond.

At all times the interaction between U.S. and European peace movements was important. From Burritt's League of Universal Brotherhood (1846), which sponsored two European congresses (1848 and 1853) to the Hague Appeal of 2000, peace movement members in the United States have supplied financing and strongly influenced European movements and meetings. American industrialist Andrew Carnegie's gift of the Peace Palace at The Hague as the seat for the International Courts of Justice symbolized the continuing role and influence of the United States. Equally significant was the importation of peace ideologies and strategies into the United States with the migrations of the later years of the nineteenth century.

Post–World War II

At times in the post–World War II years, when peace movements could have given significant support to Eleanor Roosevelt and Ralph Bunche in their work with the newly established UNITED NATIONS, the movements became isolated and were stigmatized as "Red Communist" or traitorously pacifist. Often, as in 1918, peace movement leaders were imprisoned. After 1940, many peace movements found that their organizational supports had evaporated. However, a viable remnant in the form of small organizations and key activists, speakers, and organizers remained. Termed the "prophetic peace minorities," they resurfaced in key roles at the start of each new phase of peace activity, sometimes as initiators.

In the mid-twentieth century, small pacifist groups raised the issue of nuclear weapons and conducted nonviolent direct action at military bases; these groups also engaged in peace marches in Cuba and Moscow and sailed into nuclear testing areas. These groups tended to be strongly reinforced by the Japanese movement in the early 1950s and, after 1959, by their European counterparts. The emergence of the opposition to the Vietnam War after 1965 strongly influenced the rise of similar radical (often student based) movements in Europe and the rest of the world. In 1979, however, as opposition to the development of a neutron bomb and to placement of intermediate nuclear weapons in European nations grew in Europe, the peace movement in the United States again lagged that of Europe; the character of the U.S. movement was much more moderate, endorsing gradualism and shunning unilateralist policies.

Peace Movement Defined

What then defines the peace movements, given their individualistic and largely discontinuous character? Peace movements appear to be independent of states or governments, they are autonomous groupings of civil society, and though nonaligned with any nation's foreign policy, they are not necessarily neutral in conflicts. In addition, their methods are actively nonviolent. What then are their goals?

Peace movements have tended to coalesce around goals related to preventing or stopping specific wars, abolishing certain weapons or weapons systems, or opposing military conscription. Peace movements have always had a pacifist dimension, opposing all war. They have also had a radical, socialist, or liberal dimension that critiqued the links of capitalism to imperialism and militarism. Often there was a commitment to refusing to participate in specific wars. The political left—anarchist, syndicalist, social democrat, Marxist—has often taken an antiwar and antimilitarist stances, often in alliance with more traditional peace groups.

Until World War I, refusing military service was motivated primarily by religious belief, but the reasons for conscientious objection grew more secular in the years after 1917. Conscientious objection on nonreligious grounds evolved during and after World War II; by 1970, pacifism was a major force within American society in general. Peace movements, however, had found a new religious constituency: Roman Catholic peace activity following the 1970 papal encyclical, *Pacem in Terris*, ranged from opposing death squads and intervention in Latin America to actively opposing nuclear weapons. The Roman Catholic group, Pax Christi, evolved from a tiny pressure group in 1960 to a significant part of the overall peace movement.

From World War I onward radical pacifists used the social gospel to advance political change. Also inspired by Gandhi's use of nonviolence, active pacifists such as A. J. Muste and Bayard Rustin engaged in direct action against military bases, racial injustice, and civil defense, advocated for Civil Rights and the nonviolent transformation of a militarized and often unjust society, and supported positive peace (for example, racial justice).

At times radical pacifists adopted anticapitalist and anti-imperialist positions. In the 1960s, socialist critiques reemerged in the New Left in organizations like the Student Peace Union and the Students for a Democratic Society. At times large peace coalitions were infiltrated, manipulated, or even led by members of left-wing political groups. At other times, in the two decades before 1917, for example, socialist agitation against militarism was largely separate from other peace activity. (Such isolation left socialists very vulnerable to repression; the International Workers of the World and the Socialist Party under Eugene Debs were savagely suppressed.) In the 1920s and 1930s communists and Trotskyists often practiced "entrism" (covert participation) in peace organizations, moving peace alliances into an antifascist or later even isolationist or pro-Soviet position. After 1946, pro-Soviet "peace fronts" helped stigmatize the rest of peace movements. Thus, the massive 1950 Stockholm Peace appeal, which involved millions of noncommunists, was made less effective by its support of the Soviet Union.

By the early 1960s, however, growing political nonalignment, or a "third way" position, in peace coalitions allowed transnational linkages with other independent movements to grow. After 1959 these linkages were encouraged by A. J. Muste, Dave Dellinger, and *Liberation* Magazine. By the 1980s, these coalitions included groups opposed to communist regimes in Russia and Eastern Europe.

Boundaries

Boundaries of the peace movement are hard to establish. It has played a key role in disseminating the theory and methods of nonviolent action and conflict transformation; many peace movements were broadly programmatic and its members participated in community organizing and civil rights campaigns. The American Civil Liberties Union emerged from the defense of the freedom of conscience and speech during and prior to World War I. Much of the inspiration for the civil rights movement came from peace leaders and activists from World War II and the decade following.

What kind of relationship to have with oppressive governments and violent liberation movements has always vexed peace movements. Pacifists have been divided on the issue of just wars. Although at moments of mass peace mobilization those in disagreement have joined together in large demonstrations or days of action, the ideological differences remain. Some peace lobbying groups prefer educational or pressure group work and conferences as methods to achieve peace.

Success and Failure

What criteria can we use to assess the successes and failures of the American peace movements? While few stated goals have been achieved, their support has significantly aided international peace organizations. Cultural dimensions of peace have entered mainstream culture, not so much politically as in music, literature, art, theater, and film. The growth of peace research, peace studies, and peace education in schools, colleges, and universities since the 1970s has started to legitimate the interdisciplinary fields of peace and conflict studies as an area of inquiry and pedagogy. More peace programs exist in the United States than anywhere else in the world; most of them reflect concerns of the early 1970s (Vietnam) and early 1980s (nuclear war). Without a peace movement such programs almost certainly would not have been developed. In the 1950s, for example, a "conspiracy of silence" and censorship surrounded the nature of nuclear war—peace groups took on the role of public education. The peace movement has also brought to light and into question U.S. military or paramilitary intervention in various parts of the world.

As for specific impact on government policy, domestic successes include the expansion of the legal right for individuals to declare conscientious objection to participating in war and the humane treatment of conscientious objectors. They also include the signing of a partial, atmospheric nuclear test ban treaty of 1963,the decision to end the ground and then air wars in Vietnam, the suspension of the peace time draft, and the increasing reluctance to incur casualties in combat by the United States.

Over the years the peace movement has accumulated ideas, organizations, and traditions while rarely having more than 10 percent of the public supporting its positions. The peace movement, however, has succeeded in weaving its ideas, symbolism, and styles of action into American culture. Following the acts of global terrorism in the late twentieth and early twenty-first centuries, a transnational peace strategy may begin to make sense to a far wider constituency.

Such traditions as religious pacifism and conscientious objection, Gandhian nonviolence, liberal and socialist internationalism, and anticonscriptionism have been enhanced by the special role of women's peace activity, conflict resolution, mediation, and dispute settlement as well as a growing belief in international law, justice, and arbitration through transnational bodies and nongovernmental organizations. All these have become an accepted, if sometimes contested, part of normal political life in America even if they are often minority positions. The peace movements of the past one hundred and fifty years have made this transformation and evolution possible.

BIBLIOGRAPHY

Brock, Peter, and Nigel Young. *Pacifism in the Twentieth Century.* Syracuse, N.Y.: Syracuse University Press, 1999.

Chatfield, Charles. *The American Peace Movement: Ideals and Activism.* New York: Twayne, 1992.

DeBenedetti, Charles. *The Peace Reform American History.* Bloomington: Indiana University Press, 1980.

Peterson, H. C., and Gilbert Fite. *Opponents of War, 1917–1918.* Madison: University of Wisconsin Press, 1957.

Wittner, Lawrence S. *Rebels against War: The American Peace Movement, 1933–1983.* Philadelphia: Temple University Press, 1984.

Nigel J. Young

See also **Antiwar Movements; Arms Race and Disarmament; Conscientious Objectors; Peace Conferences; Utopian Communities; Women and the Peace Movement;** *and vol. 9:* **Peace and Bread in Time of War; Statement by Committee Seeking Peace with Freedom in Vietnam.**

PEACEKEEPING MISSIONS. Traditionally handled by the United Nations, peacekeeping missions are instances of intervention in civil or international disputes for the purpose of upholding the peace or of encouraging peaceful settlement of existing conflicts. The United States has, on several occasions, pursued peacekeeping operations independent of the UN.

The first United Nations peacekeeping mission was deployed to the Middle East in 1948 in an attempt to bring an end to the war between Arab nations and the new state of Israel; a second was dispatched in the following year to Kashmir, which was the object of war between India and Pakistan. In both of these early interventions, the forces sent by the UN were very small and unarmed.

The peacekeeping role of the United Nations changed dramatically in the 1950s with the establishment of an armed force—the so-called "Blue Helmets"—to keep belligerents separated and promote peaceful resolution of disputes. The Blue Helmets were first dispatched to the Middle East in response to the Suez Crisis of 1956.

Before the 1990s, the Blue Helmets were used relatively infrequently because of the decision-making structure of the United Nations during the Cold War. Any decision to send a peacekeeping mission required the unanimous approval of the five permanent members of the UN Security Council, thus any proposed intervention was likely to run into opposition from either the United States or the Soviet Union. Therefore, even as late as 1991 the UN had deployed only eleven peacekeeping missions, involving approximately 11,000 Blue Helmets.

The end of the Cold War changed deployment of peacekeeping missions dramatically. The great powers now were able to reach consensus much more easily. The number and scope of peacekeeping missions jumped almost immediately, so that by 1994 76,600 Blue Helmets were involved in seventeen interventions around the world. Indeed, between 1990 and 2000 the Security Council authorized no fewer than thirty-six missions—twice as many as it had in the previous forty years.

The involvement of the United States in UN peacekeeping missions was extremely limited during the Cold War. In fact, troops from any of the great powers were intentionally excluded from such missions for fear that they would be incapable of impartiality. However, the United States frequently played a supporting role by setting up supply and communications systems and providing military hardware to the Blue Helmets.

When the United States did involve itself directly in peacekeeping efforts, it did so independently of the UN. For example, in the early 1980s a Multinational Force (MNF) made up of French, Italian, and American troops was deployed to Lebanon to serve as a buffer between the Israelis and the Palestinian Liberation Organization. Ordinarily this would have been a matter for UN concern, but Israel was unwilling to involve that organization, which had a few years earlier passed a resolution equating Zionism with racism. The MNF did little to bring about an end to Middle East tensions, and public support in the

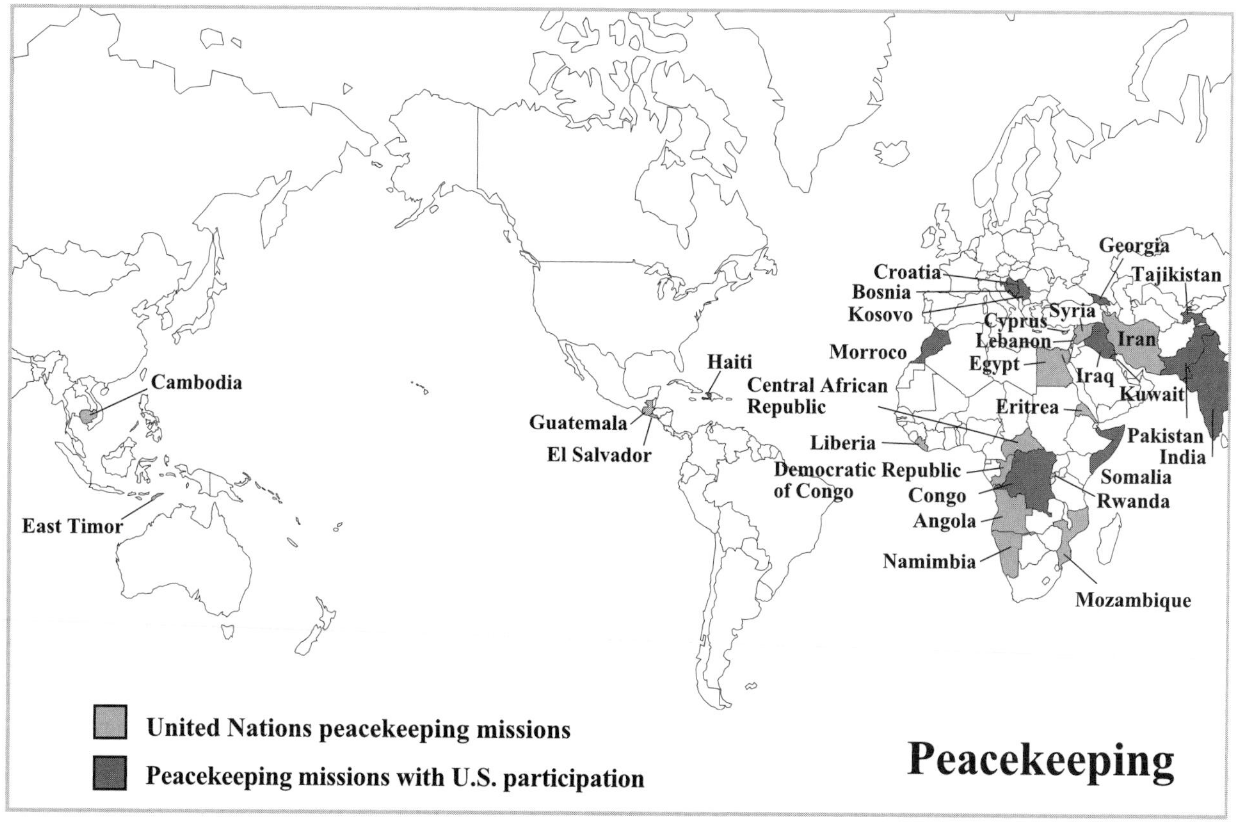

United States for its mission plummeted after 1983, when 241 American marines were killed in a terrorist attack. The mission was terminated soon afterward.

The end of the Cold War also brought with it greater opportunity for the United States to participate in UN peacekeeping missions. In December 1992 President George H. W. Bush sent 28,000 American soldiers to Somalia, and Bush's successor, Bill Clinton, placed several thousand of these under UN command. However, it was in Somalia that the Blue Helmets for the first time abandoned their traditional role as impartial peacekeepers and became actively involved in military action against local warlords. The results proved costly to UN forces in general, but in particular to the Americans, when two Black Hawk helicopters and eighteen U.S. soldiers were lost in a firefight in the Somali capital of Mogadishu in October 1993.

After the debacle at Mogadishu, American interest in participating in UN peacekeeping missions dropped sharply. The Republican Party called for legislation making it illegal for American troops to be placed under UN command, and the Clinton administration bowed to the pressure. In May 1994 the president issued a directive instructing that in the future U.S. soldiers could only submit to UN command if some tangible national interest were at stake. As a result, in the summer of 2001 only 677 Americans were serving in UN peacekeeping operations (2.1 percent of the over thirty-two thousand peacekeepers worldwide), and these were in advisory and observatory roles.

However, the United States did not withdraw altogether from peacekeeping efforts. In 1993 the U.S. Army established an agency called the Peacekeeping Institute, dedicated to preparing the American military for participation in such missions. In the 1990s, American forces were deployed to a number of locations for peacekeeping purposes, among them Bosnia, Haiti, and Kosovo. While these missions sometimes operated in conjunction with UN forces, they remained independent of that body and were commanded by American officers.

BIBLIOGRAPHY

Coulon, Jocelyn. *Soldiers of Diplomacy: The United Nations, Peacekeeping, and the New World Order.* Toronto: University of Toronto Press, 1994.

Diehl, Paul F. *International Peacekeeping.* Baltimore: Johns Hopkins University Press, 1993.

John E. Moser

PEARL HARBOR is located on the island of Oahu, HAWAII. The U.S. naval base at Pearl Harbor and the sup-

Pearl Harbor. A sailor is rescued from a burning oil slick near the battleships USS *West Virginia (foreground)*—which soon sank but was refloated and eventually returned to wartime service—and USS *Tennessee*, which was also damaged in the Japanese attack on the U.S. naval base on Oahu. © Hulton-Getty/Liaison Agency

porting army forts and airfields grew in strategic importance during the 1930s as diplomatic relations with Japan deteriorated. On 7 December 1941, Pearl Harbor entered into history as the location of the infamous surprise attack by the Japanese navy on the United States.

Admiral Isoroku Yamamoto selected Commander Minoru Genda to develop the plan to destroy the U.S. fleet and give Japan time to conquer the Philippine Islands, Malaya, and the Dutch East Indies. Vice Admiral Chuichi Nagumo commanded the First Air Fleet, consisting of six aircraft carriers *(Akagi, Kaga, Soryu, Hiryu, Shokaku,* and *Zuikaku)* carrying 400 Kate torpedo bombers, Val dive-bombers, and Zero fighters.

The U.S. Pacific Fleet was under the command of Admiral Husband E. Kimmel. Major General Walter C. Short commanded U.S. Army forces, which consisted of the Twenty-fifth Infantry Division, Coast Artillery batteries, and the U.S. Army Air Forces in Hawaii.

The U.S. Army and Navy intelligence services had broken the Japanese diplomatic code, and messages had been sent to both commanders that the Japanese might be planning offensive military operations in the Pacific. Even so there was no warning specifically indicating that the American forces in Hawaii were a target. These warnings would result in many years of charges and counter-charges about who was "at fault" for the disaster that occurred.

The Pacific Fleet's primary striking power was in its three aircraft carriers *(Lexington, Saratoga,* and *Enterprise)* and eight battleships *(Pennsylvania, Arizona, Maryland, Tennessee, West Virginia, California, Oklahoma,* and *Nevada).* On the morning of 7 December the *Saratoga* was undergoing refitting in California, and the *Lexington* and *Enterprise,* with their escorts of fast cruisers and destroyers, were returning from delivering Marine Corps Wildcat fighters to the islands of Midway and Wake.

The initial contact with the Japanese came when the destroyer *Ward* sighted and fired upon one of five mini-submarines that were attempting to penetrate the harbor in order to attack the battleships in coordination with the aerial assault. At dawn, Commander Mitsuo Fuchida led the first wave of Japanese aircraft, consisting of 133 torpedo, dive, and horizontal bombers and Zeros. Although radar operators located at Opana Point detected the flight, their commander interpreted the signals they received as an indication that a flight of B-17 bombers was arriving as planned from California.

The air forces defending Oahu consisted of ninety-nine P-40 and thirty-nine P-36 fighters, along with twelve B-17, thirty-three obsolete B-18, and six A-20 bombers. The bombers were stationed at Hickam Airfield, next to Pearl Harbor, while the fighters were at Wheeler Field with four squadrons dispersed for training at Bellows and

Haleiwa fields. The navy had sixty-nine PBY flying boats stationed at Kaneohe.

The Japanese struck Wheeler Field at 7:52 A.M., destroying most of the fighters that were lined up in the center of the airfield as protection against sabotage. The main force of torpedo, dive, and horizontal bombers struck the battleships anchored alongside Ford Island at 7:55. The initial torpedo runs ripped out the sides of the *West Virginia*, *Oklahoma*, and *Utah*. Two later runs capsized and sank the *California*. Meanwhile, a bomb detonated in the forward ammunition magazine of the *Arizona*, destroying the ship and killing approximately 1,200 of her crew. Dive and horizontal bombers struck the *California*, *Maryland*, and *Tennessee*, with the *Maryland* sinking on an even keel. Other bombers and fighters then attacked the aircraft at Ford Island, Hickam Field, and Kaneohe. Less than a dozen P-40s and P-36s from Haleiwa and Bellows fields managed to take off to defend Oahu. Their pilots shot down thirteen Japanese aircraft.

The 170 aircraft of the second wave arrived over Pearl Harbor at 8:55 A.M. The dive-bombers focused on the *Nevada* as it started to leave the harbor. Receiving multiple bomb and torpedo hits, the ship's captain beached her rather than risk being sunk in the channel entrance. Other bombers struck the *Pennsylvania*, which had escaped damage during the first wave, and the cruisers and destroyers, which had until then been ignored. Other elements of the Japanese force struck Ewa, Bellows, and Wheeler fields, destroying the remaining aircraft there.

The Japanese lost twenty-nine aircraft, five minisubmarines, and sixty-five personnel. Declining to launch a third strike to destroy the harbor's oil storage tanks, submarines, and maintenance facilities, Admiral Nagumo turned his force back to Japan after the second wave returned shortly after noon.

Approximately 2,500 American sailors and soldiers died in the attack. Another 1,176 were wounded. Every aircraft was either destroyed or damaged, but not all were damaged beyond repair. Of the ninety-four warships in the harbor, all eight battleships were sunk or severely damaged. Two destroyers were sunk, and several other destroyers and cruisers were damaged.

In the aftermath of the attack, Admiral Kimmel and Major General Short were both relieved of command and forced into early retirement because of their lack of judgment, especially in light of the warnings they had received. The argument over who was "really responsible" for the debacle, however, continues.

BIBLIOGRAPHY

Clausen, Henry C., and Bruce Lee. *Pearl Harbor: Final Judgement.* New York: Crown, 1992.

Lord, Walter. *Day of Infamy.* New York: Henry Holt, 1957; 60th anniversary ed., 2001.

Prange, Gordon W., with Donald M. Goldstein and Katherine V. Dillon. *At Dawn We Slept: The Untold Story of Pearl Harbor.* New York: McGraw-Hill, 1981. 60th anniversary ed., New York: Penguin, 2001.

Prange, Gordon W., with Donald M. Goldstein and Katherine V. Dillon. *December 7, 1941: The Day the Japanese Attacked Pearl Harbor.* New York: McGraw-Hill, 1988.

Frank R. Shirer

See also **World War II; World War II, Air War Against Japan; World War II, Navy in;** *and vol. 9:* **War against Japan.**

PECULIAR INSTITUTION was a euphemistic term that white southerners used for slavery. John C. Calhoun defended the "peculiar labor" of the South in 1828 and the "peculiar domestick institution" in 1830. The term came into general use in the 1830s when the abolitionist followers of William Lloyd Garrison began to attack slavery. Its implicit message was that slavery in the U.S. South was different from the very harsh slave systems existing in other countries and that southern slavery had no impact on those living in northern states.

BIBLIOGRAPHY

Freehling, William W. *The Road to Disunion: Secessionists at Bay, 1776–1854.* New York: Oxford University Press, 1990.

Kolchin, Peter. *American Slavery: 1619–1877.* New York: Hill and Wang, 1993.

Fletcher M. Green / C. P.

See also **Sectionalism; Slavery; South, the: The Antebellum South.**

PEDDLERS. Also known as hawkers or chapmen, peddlers were itinerant merchants who roamed the country when its interior markets were still underdeveloped and extremely diffuse. Beginning in the colonial period, such men—frequently of New England origin—traveled from farm to farm with their trunks strapped on their backs or, as roads improved, in wagons. Trunk peddlers who sold smaller items like combs, pins, cheap jewelry, knives and woodenware, knitted goods, and books (Parson Mason Weems of Virginia, Washington's biographer, was an itinerant bookseller) usually tended to be "on their own hooks"—independent entrepreneurs who owned their stock. Most were willing to barter their wares in exchange for farm products from their cash-strapped and isolated rural customers (many early Indian fur traders were in this sense little more than peddlers), then carry those goods for resale at a cash profit in country stores and town markets.

Beginning in the late eighteenth century many peddlers, especially in the burgeoning tinware trade, were "staked" by small northern manufactories who paid them a percentage of sales, sometimes even a flat wage. The importance of these "Yankee peddling companies" as a primitive but effective distribution system for durable goods is demonstrated by the wooden shelf-clock industry

Peddlers. A Syrian street peddler sells food on the streets of early–twentieth-century New York. While such street peddlers were and still are common in large cities, America was home to another type of peddler in the nineteenth century. Often called "Yankee peddlers" because they sold goods manufactured in the North, these peddlers went door-to-door selling items such as everyday household goods, clocks, furniture, and even medical supplies. In some parts of the rural South, peddlers still existed in the twentieth century, but they were a dying breed. © CORBIS

of early-nineteenth-century Connecticut. Mass production processes perfected by Eli Terry allowed thousands of clocks to be manufactured annually by a single workshop, increases that would have been of little use without the marketing prowess of the Yankee peddler to transport, explain, and sell (often "on time") the luxury items. The folklore surrounding the fictional Sam Slick attests to the ubiquity of the antebellum clock peddler; by the 1840s one traveler to the frontier South remarked that "in every cabin where there was not a chair to sit on there was sure to be a Connecticut clock."

The character of Sam Slick also underscores the outsider status of the Yankee peddler (who began to be supplanted in the late 1830s by large numbers of German Jewish emigrants), which made them targets of suspicion and hostility, especially in the South. Men resented peddlers' intrusions into the household (particularly seductive sales pitches directed to their wives); established merchants complained about the threat peddlers ostensibly presented to local trade. Fears of abolitionist-fueled slave insurrections led to widespread attempts to regulate "foreign" itinerant merchants through onerous licensing fees in the 1830s, although such legislation had antecedents in the colonial era.

Anti-peddler laws were also promulgated in many northern states during the mid-nineteenth century, and such legislation—along with the rise of wholesale distribution networks (and, later in the century, corporate "TRAVELING SALESMEN")—led to the decline of rural peddling in the North by the Civil War. But peddling persisted well into the twentieth century in pockets of the rural South, notably under the auspices of the W. T. Rawleigh Company and the J. R. Watkins Medical Company. Peddlers who sold goods, such as furniture, on installment credit also remained common in the immigrant communities of northern cities through the 1920s.

BIBLIOGRAPHY

Jaffee, David. "Peddlers of Progress and the Transformation of the Rural North, 1760–1860." *Journal of American History* 78, no. 2 (September 1991): 511–535.

Jones, Lu Ann. "Gender, Race, and Itinerant Commerce in the Rural New South." *Journal of Southern History* 66, no. 2 (May 2000): 297–320.

Rainer, Joseph T. "The Honorable Fraternity of Moving Merchants: Yankee Peddlers in the Old South, 1800–1860." (Ph.D. diss., College of William and Mary, 2000.)

Scott P. Marler

See also **Clock and Watch Industry; Colonial Commerce.**

PELELIU. The site of an important Japanese air base during World War II. Some American war planners viewed the Palaus Island chain as a stepping-stone on the way back to the Philippines; others thought it should be bypassed. The decision was made in mid-1944 to seize three of the southern Palaus. First to be invaded was Peleliu. The U.S. First Marine Division, under Gen. William H. Rupertus, landed early on 15 September 1944. The 10,000-strong Japanese force, strongly entrenched in the island's central ridge system, fought back stubbornly. It took over two months and the addition of an entire regiment to subdue the last Japanese defenders. While nearly 2,000 Americans died in taking Peleliu, some questioned its value. Airfields on Peleliu, it was discovered, could not support the Philippine invasion in the manner expected.

BIBLIOGRAPHY

Hallas, James H. *The Devil's Anvil: The Assault on Peleliu.* Westport, Conn.: Praeger, 1994.

Ross, Bill D. *Peleliu: Tragic Triumph: The Untold Story of the Pacific War's Forgotten Battle.* New York, Random House, 1991.

Stanley L. Falk / A. R.

See also **Japan, Relations with; Philippine Sea, Battle of the; World War II; World War II, Air War Against Japan; World War II, Navy in.**

PENDERGAST MACHINE. From 1890 to 1939 a Democratic political organization called the Pendergast machine dominated politics in Kansas City, Mo. From the time of his appointment to a county judgeship in 1922 until his election to the U.S. Senate in 1934, Harry S. Truman, a Missouri Democrat, was a beneficiary of the vote-getting ability of the machine, but he avoided involvement in the machine's corruption. Throughout the

1930s Thomas Pendergast, the machine's boss, controlled enough votes to direct state politics, but the machine came to an end when he went to prison for tax fraud in 1939.

BIBLIOGRAPHY

Dorsett, Lyle W. *The Pendergast Machine.* New York: Oxford University Press, 1968.

McCullough, David. *Truman.* New York: Simon and Schuster, 1992.

Lyle W. Dorsett/A. G.

See also **Democratic Party; Kansas City; Machine, Political; Missouri.**

PENDLETON ACT (16 January 1883), the federal government's central civil service law, was written by Dorman B. Eaton, sponsored by Sen. George H. Pendleton of Ohio, and forced through Congress by public opinion. The act aimed to reform the spoils system by eliminating many political appointments in favor of jobs only awarded to candidates who met predetermined uniform standards of merit. It reestablished a Civil Service Commission to prepare rules for a limited classified civil service, which the president could expand at discretion. Competitive examinations determined the qualifications of applicants, while appointments were apportioned among the states according to population.

BIBLIOGRAPHY

Fish, Carl Russell. *The Civil Service and the Patronage.* New York: Russell and Russell, 1963.

Chester McA. Destler/C. W.

See also **Civil Service; Patronage, Political; Spoils System.**

PENINSULAR CAMPAIGN (1862), an advance against Richmond, began on 4 April 1862, when Maj. Gen. George B. McClellan departed from Fortress Monroe with his Union army of approximately 100,000 to attack the Confederate capital by way of the peninsula formed by the York and James Rivers. McClellan had counted on a larger force and aid from the navy on the James River. The administration withheld 45,000 troops to protect Washington, D.C., and the navy was unable to help because of the menace of the *Merrimack* and Confederate shore batteries.

The campaign unfolded in three phases. The early Union advance was marked by Confederate resistance behind entrenchments across the peninsula from Yorktown. On 5 April McClellan besieged Yorktown, which was evacuated on 3 May. He then pushed slowly forward, fighting at Williamsburg on 5 May, reaching and straddling the Chickahominy River on 20 May and facing a strengthened Confederate force under Gen. Joseph E. Johnston.

Help expected from Union Gen. Irvin McDowell's 40,000 men was lost to McClellan in May when Confederate Gen. T. J. ("Stonewall") Jackson's Shenandoah Valley campaign scattered or immobilized the Union armies before Washington. The first phase of the campaign ended with the indecisive two-day Battle of Fair Oaks (or Battle of Seven Pines), 31 May and 1 June. Johnston was wounded on 1 June and Robert E. Lee succeeded to his command.

After Fair Oaks came the second phase, three weeks without fighting, marked by Confederate Gen. J. E. B. Stuart's spectacular cavalry raid around the Union army, from 11 to 13 June.

McClellan, reinforced, intended to retake the offensive, but Lee forestalled him and opened the third phase of the campaign by attacking the Union right at Mechanicsville on 26 June. This began the Seven Days' Battles, during which McClellan changed his base to the James River, fending off waves of Confederate attacks as the Union Army retreated to its base at Harrison's Landing. With the appointment on 11 July of Gen. Henry W. Halleck to command all land forces of the United States, the Army of the Potomac began its withdrawal from the peninsula.

Union casualties in the campaign were approximately 15,000, with 1,700 killed; Confederate losses were about 20,000, with 3,400 killed. The Union forces greatly outnumbered the Confederate at the start of the campaign; toward its close the opposing forces were nearly equal.

BIBLIOGRAPHY

Catton, Bruce. *The Army of the Potomac.* Volume 1: *Mr. Lincoln's Army.* Garden City, N.Y.: Doubleday 1951.

Martin, David G. *The Peninsula Campaign, March–July 1862.* Conshohocken, Pa.: Combined Books, 1992.

Sears, Stephen W. *To the Gates of Richmond: The Peninsula Campaign.* New York: Ticknor and Fields, 1992.

Webb, Alexander Stewart. *The Peninsula: McClellan's Campaign of 1862.* New York: Scribners 1881.

Edwin H. Blanchard/A. R.

See also **Civil War; Seven Days' Battles.**

PENNSYLVANIA. The geography of Pennsylvania is complex, and the physical differences among the commonwealth's different regions have helped shape its history. Early colonists would have first encountered the coastal plain in what is now southeast Pennsylvania, along the Delaware River. This area is flat and fertile. Beyond the coastal plain is the Piedmont region, which covers most of southeastern Pennsylvania, and is very productive farmland. In the middle of Pennsylvania are the Appalachian Ridge and the Great Valley, the latter consisting of many small valleys that also provide good farmland. In the far northwest is the Lake Erie Lowland, the sandy soil of which has proven good for growing tubers such as potatoes and other vegetables.

Early History

The earliest human remains in the state indicate that a nomadic people archaeologists call Paleo-Indians began passing through Pennsylvania between 12,000 and 10,000 B.C. They hunted with spears, pursuing large game such as bison, and they may have trapped smaller game. Around A.D. 1000, modern Native Americans settled Pennsylvania, favoring the lowlands over the rough central plateau. They used bows and arrows more often than spears for hunting. They introduced the wigwam, a domed hut made of branches overlaid with tree bark or animal skins, and lived in small communities consisting of a few families.

By the time European colonists arrived, the Native Americans had developed the longhouse, a big structure made of branches and bark that housed several families. The longhouse was very important to the development of sophisticated Native American communities because it encouraged large groups of people to live and cooperate together.

European Settlement

When the first Europeans visited the area that is now Pennsylvania, the Native Americans of the region lived in a settled, complex mix of cultures. In the far east of Pennsylvania, on both sides of the Delaware River, lived the Leni-Lenapes (variously translated "the Original People," "the True People," and "the Real People"; they were also known as the Delawares). They sold their lands to English colonists and drifted westward.

In a large region around the Susquehanna River lived the Susquehannocks, a culturally Iroquois tribe that valued its independence. At the time Europeans arrived in their territory, the Susquehannocks were being exterminated by the Iroquois Confederacy, which came close to killing all the Susquehannocks by 1675. The few survivors of the Susquehannocks joined the Conestoga tribe. South of Pennsylvania were the Shawnees, who began migrating in the 1690s into the region formerly occupied by the Susquehannocks. Under pressure from colonists, they slowly migrated westward. Along the shore of Lake Erie lived the Erie tribe. During the era of colonial settlement, many other tribes lived in or moved through Pennsylvania, including the Munsees and the Mingos, who lived on the Allegheny Plateau. The Mahicans were driven out of their homes in New York by the Iroquois Confederacy and fled south, eventually joining the Leni-Lenapes in their westward migration.

Both England and the Netherlands claimed what are now Pennsylvania and Delaware by the end of the first decade of the seventeenth century, with English explorers having visited the area as early as 1497. In 1608, England's John Smith traveled up the Susquehanna River, where he met some of the Susquehannock tribe. In 1609, Henry Hudson, sailing for the Dutch, sailed into what would be named Delaware Bay a year later, when Virginia's Samuel Argall sailed into it and named it for Thomas West, lord De La Warr, then the governor of Virginia. In the late 1630s, Swedes settled near the mouth of the Delaware River, and in 1643 they moved their settlement to Tinicum Island, which was near where PHILADELPHIA would eventually be established.

The Dutch of New Amsterdam were unhappy with the Swedes' move into territory that they wanted for themselves. In 1647, they established a trading post in what is now Pennsylvania, part of a planned southward movement in which they hoped to claim the territories all the way to Virginia. By then, the Swedes were calling their small colony "New Sweden" and were establishing trading relationships with the local Native Americans. The Dutch governor Peter Stuyvesant had armed parties move downriver in 1655, seizing the Swedish colony on Tinicum. He declared the region to be part of New Amsterdam. In 1664, England blunted the Dutch colony's ambitions by seizing the area east of the Susquehanna River in the name of the duke of York, the brother of Charles II. The Dutch regained control from 1673 through 1674, but were driven out by the English. In 1676, the duke of York declared the region to be under English law.

William Penn the elder had been a close friend and an admiral in service to Charles II of England. He had loaned Charles II £16,000, which became due to his heirs when he died. His son, William Penn the younger, had converted to Quakerism and been imprisoned for not honoring the Church of England. William Penn told the king that instead of repayment of the £16,000 owed to his father, he wanted a land grant in North America where he could establish a home for the QUAKERS. Wiping out the debt and getting rid of some of the troublesome Quakers seemed a good deal to Charles II, particularly since the area Penn wanted was considered to be of little value. The Charter of Pennsylvania—named by the king for young Penn's father—was granted 4 March 1681, and William Penn was named the territory's proprietor, meaning the land actually belonged to him. Any governor of Pennsylvania would actually serve Penn.

William Penn wanted Pennsylvania to be a place where people would not be jailed or otherwise persecuted for their religious beliefs, and he published advertisements urging oppressed people to move there. He drew up the First Frame of Government as the colony's first constitution. He sent his cousin William Markham to Pennsylvania in April 1681 as his deputy. Penn arrived on the ship *Welcome* in the colony in October 1682. He picked the site for Philadelphia, "city of brotherly love," which was to be the capital city, and drew up a street plan for the city, with all avenues straight and meeting at right angles. On 4 December 1682, he summoned the first General Assembly, which became the colony's legislative body. On 7 December, the General Assembly enacted the Great Law, which was a statement of civil rights for the people of Pennsylvania. In 1683, the second General As-

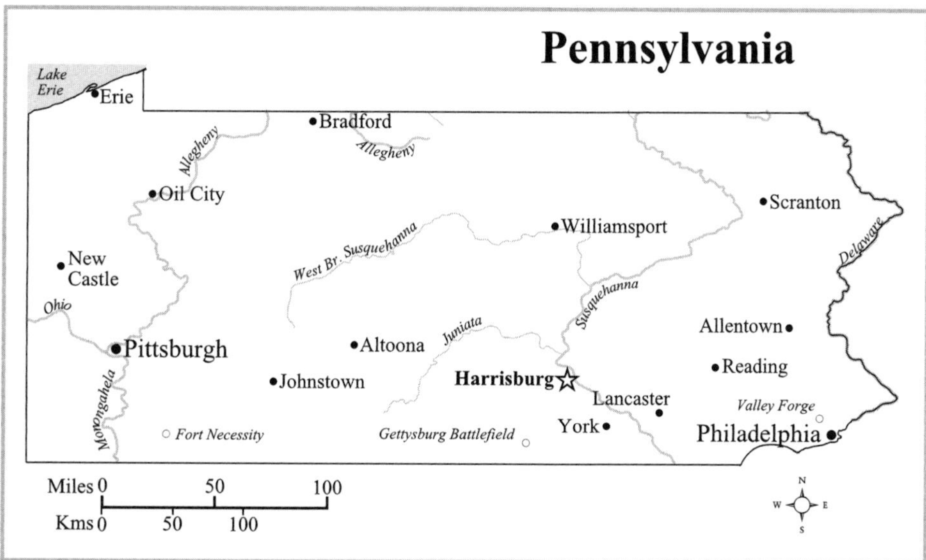

sembly adopted a Second Frame of Government, which more plainly laid out what form Pennsylvania's government would take.

Pennsylvania was the twelfth of the original thirteen American colonies to be founded, but it quickly grew to be the second most populous after Virginia. Quakers, Mennonites, Amish, Presbyterians, and Roman Catholics from Great Britain, Germany, Ireland, Sweden, and the Netherlands flocked to Pennsylvania, where they could worship in peace. Although the Quakers and many other colonists opposed slavery, Pennsylvania had about 4,000 slaves by 1730. However, thousands of African Americans were free in Pennsylvania, and they began founding their own Christian churches. Jews, too, found homes in Pennsylvania, adding to the cosmopolitan atmosphere of Philadelphia and other cities. In the first half of the eighteenth century, Philadelphia was the second most populous English-speaking city in the world after London, although German, Swedish, and other languages were often spoken as well. In the farms of the Piedmont region, the dialect Pennsylvania Dutch evolved out of German (the word "Dutch" coming from *Deutsche*, the German word for the German language).

Revolution

In the 1750s, France made a strong bid to control western Pennsylvania by erecting and manning a series of forts in the frontier. An allied army of French and Native American forces ambushed a British army at Monongahela in 1755, destroying it. The French built Fort Duquesne at the site of modern-day Pittsburgh, and Pennsylvania might have lost about one-third of its territory had not combined British and colonial forces led by General John Forbes recaptured the area and seized the fort. In the early 1760s, Chief Pontiac of the Ottawas formed a coalition of tribes and tried to force colonists out of the western frontier; he was defeated in the Battle of Bushy Run by colonial forces led by Colonel Henry Bouquet in August 1763.

Although Philadelphia had not been the center of revolutionary fervor, in the 1770s it seemed the logical place for representatives of the rebellious colonies to meet, in part because it was a city open to peaceful divergence of opinions. It had become known as the "Athens of America," and was chosen to be the new nation's capital when the Continental Congress declared independence from Britain on 4 July 1776. By then, Pennsylvania had already renounced allegiance to England. On 28 September 1776, the state convention wrote a new state constitution, which included a "Declaration of Rights," intended to protect individual civil liberties.

For nine months in 1777, the British occupied Philadelphia, a severe blow to the young nation. From December 1777 to June 1778, the Continental Army camped in Valley Forge. The army lost about one-fourth of its troops to exposure and starvation, yet by June it was able to force the British to abandon Philadelphia, where the Continental Congress thereafter met. Native American allies of the British raided western Pennsylvania, killing farmers and burning hamlets, but in 1779 expeditions led by Daniel Brodhead and John Sullivan against the Iroquois Confederacy drove the Native American forces away.

In 1779, the government of Pennsylvania officially seized all lands owned by Penn family members. In 1780, while the Revolutionary War (1775–1783) was still underway, Pennsylvania's legislature passed a law providing for the "gradual abolition of slavery." Anyone born within Pennsylvania's borders was automatically free, regardless of ancestry.

On 17 September 1787, the Constitutional Convention, meeting in Philadelphia, offered a new national constitution for ratification by the American states. On 12 December 1787, Pennsylvania became the second state to ratify it. The new nation needed funds and therefore levied taxes. One tax was on whiskey, which resulted in Pennsylvanians creating one of the first major challenges to federal authority. Farmers in the Allegheny Plateau found shipping their grain to markets in the east to be very expensive because of numerous hills and valleys in their region, so they made whiskey at home; the new tax on whiskey forced them to stop making their own and to lose money shipping grain to whiskey makers in the east. In 1791, they rebelled, chasing away tax collectors. By 1794, they were a threat to the security of the Commonwealth of Pennsylvania. President George Washington raised an army of 13,000 troops, which marched on the rebels. Fighting was brief, one man was killed, the WHISKEY REBELLION leaders were jailed (but soon released), and the new federal government had made its point.

Philadelphia served as America's capital from 1790 to 1800, when the capital moved to Washington, D.C. The state capital moved to Lancaster in 1799, and then to Harrisburg in 1812.

Industry and Labor

Pennsylvania created "Donation Lands," territory it gave for free to Revolutionary War veterans. This helped to spread the state's population westward. Presbyterian Irish immigrants seemed to have a preference for frontier lands, and as Pennsylvania became more populous, they moved westward. In the 1840s, a potato famine impelled a great migration of Irish to America, and many of them settled in Pennsylvania. Yet, Pennsylvania's traditionally open attitude was changing for the worse. In 1838, a mob burned down Pennsylvania Hall soon after its construction as a meeting place for antislavery activists and others. In the same year, African American citizens had their right to vote taken away. In 1844, there were riots in Kensington against Roman Catholics.

A state constitutional convention was called in 1837, and the new 1838 constitution established three years as a governor's term of office and added new constitutional offices. Although it seemed to enhance the voice of voters in governmental affairs by increasing the powers of the legislature while curtailing those of the governor, it included outrages such as denying black Americans the vote. Even so, a staunch abolitionist, David Wilmot, was elected to the U.S. Congress, where he fought in 1846 to make the new state of Texas a free state. Wilmot reflected the anxiety of many Pennsylvanians over the issue of slavery. Pennsylvania had a law that made capturing fugitive slaves and sending them back to slavery kidnapping, but in 1842 the U.S. Supreme Court in *Prigg v. Pennsylvania* overturned the law, opening the way for the bounty hunting of escaped slaves in free states. In defiance, Pennsylvania made it illegal to use its jails to hold fugitive slaves. The federal Fugitive Slave Law of 1850 was meant to be a compromise between antislavery and proslavery forces in the United States, but it resulted in riots in Pennsylvania against its implementation; the Christiana Riot of 1851 against slave hunters was notorious for its violence.

In 1860, the Republicans, composed of antislavery groups encompassing disaffected Democrats and remnants of the Whigs, as well as Independents, won control of Pennsylvania's government. The Pennsylvanian James Buchanan was elected president of the United States in 1856, serving from 1857 to 1861. He tried to forge compromises between slave and free states, but the pending creation of more free states in America's western frontier spawned a revolt in his Democratic Party; the rebels ran a candidate of their own, splitting the Democratic vote and throwing the election to Abraham Lincoln. Among Buchanan's last acts as president was to send reinforcements to army posts in slave states.

During the Civil War (1861–1865), Confederate cavalry sometimes raided towns in Pennsylvania, and in June 1863, General Robert E. Lee tried to separate the Union's supply lines by driving toward Harrisburg. Pennsylvania was a major supplier of raw materials for the Union, and arms and other supplies moved through it south to the Army of the Potomac and west to armies led by Ulysses S. Grant. By taking control of central Pennsylvania, the Confederates could cut off Washington, D.C., from supply and threaten New England. The Union could be forced to sue for peace. The Union General George Meade had stationed infantry on high ground in Gettysburg, just in case Lee moved his men in that direction, and the citizens of Harrisburg fortified their city, burning a bridge between them and Lee's army. The two armies met at Gettysburg. After three days of relentless combat from 1 to 3 July, Lee retreated while trying to hold together his nearly shattered army. It was in Gettysburg that Lincoln made his famous address that declared America a nation "of the people."

After the Civil War, Pennsylvania became more industrialized, becoming a major source of COAL and petroleum. In 1874, the state created a new constitution, which set the office of governor to one four-year term. Women's rights came to the fore in political debates. In some areas, Pennsylvania was a leader in women's rights. In 1850, the Women's Medical College was founded in Philadelphia, and other women's colleges were created. The National Woman Suffrage Association was organized in Philadelphia in 1868. Yet, efforts to extend the right to vote to women failed; as late as 1915, a state constitutional amendment passed by the Assembly was voted down in a general election. On the other hand, in August 1920, Pennsylvania was the seventh state to ratify the Nineteenth Amendment to the U.S. Constitution, which gave women the right to vote.

Another difficult area involved labor disputes. The industries of coal mining and steel production became dominant in the state, employing hundreds of thousands of people. As early as the 1840s, Pennsylvania passed laws to protect workers, but abuses persisted. The secretive MOLLY MAGUIRES (named for a similar organization in Ireland whose members dressed in women's clothes as a disguise) organized coal miners in Pennsylvania. They terrorized owners, bosses, and foremen, sometimes murdering them. In 1877, the Molly Maguire organization was broken by private investigators hired by mine and railroad owners; several members of the group were convicted of murder.

In 1902, a coal strike created severe hardships for miners and those whose jobs depended on coal. President Theodore Roosevelt's intervention in the strike helped owners and union members to reach a peaceful agreement and set the precedent for presidential intercession in labor disputes. Laws slowly brought relief to workers. Whereas workers in some factories had to work ten hours a day, seven days a week in 1900, in the 1920s the government mandated eight-hour days, five days a week. Pennsylvania was fertile ground for the growth of unions, among the most powerful of which was the United Mine Workers.

Pennsylvania produced about 50 percent of America's steel in the first half of the twentieth century and was home to other industries as well. It maintained a strong farming culture and developed a powerful food processing industry. The Hershey Chocolate Company was started in 1894 as a subsidiary of Milton S. Hershey's Lancaster Caramel Company. The forerunner of the H. J. Heinz Company was founded in 1869 and built model factories that were well ventilated, spacious, and full of light. Railroads were also important, and George Westinghouse got his start by designing safety equipment for trains. Road building became an important source of income for workers during the depression of the 1930s, and in 1940, the Pennsylvania Turnpike was opened. Pennsylvania was a pioneer in communications, with the nation's first commercial radio station, KDKA of Pittsburgh, beginning broadcasting on 2 November 1920. The first all-movie theater opened on 19 June 1905 in Pittsburgh.

Modern Era

The economy of Pennsylvania did fairly well during World War II (1939–1945) because of demand for steel and coal, but after the war it had many problems. Steel strikes in 1952 were damaging to the nation's economy, inspiring President Harry S. Truman to try to nationalize the steel industry. Another steel strike in 1959 brought the intervention of President Dwight D. Eisenhower and inspired new federal laws restricting union activities. In the 1970s, union strength in Pennsylvania waned, in part because Pennsylvania's coal was high in sulfur and thus too polluting to meet the standards of the federal Clean Air Act of 1970. In 1957, America's first commercial nuclear power plant opened in Shippingport. In March 1979, the Three Mile Island nuclear power plant had an accident, during which a small amount of radioactive gas was released into the atmosphere. This was another blow to the state economy.

In 1968, the Commonwealth of Pennsylvania created yet another new constitution. This one allowed governors to seek reelection and modified some offices of the executive branch. There had been race riots in Philadelphia in 1964, and thus many Pennsylvanians took it as a good sign of racial harmony when W. Wilson Goode, an African American, was elected mayor of that city in 1983.

By 2000, Pennsylvania had a population of 12,281,054, although its population growth was one of the lowest in the United States, probably because of a large population of retirees. There were about 500,000 more women than men in the commonwealth. Although Pennsylvania was founded by Quakers, only about 15,000 lived in the state. The production of aluminum, the manufacturing of helicopters and small airplanes, and the processing of food were all major industries. Even so, big industries such as steel had declined markedly, with steel production dwindling to about 8 percent of national production. On the other hand, Pennsylvania's numerous scenic wonders, its mix of cultures, and its cosmopolitan cities drew tourists by the millions. Agriculture became the backbone of Pennsylvania's economy, marking a shift to farming after many decades of industrial growth, with over 51,000 farms. The Amish, still using farming techniques from the eighteenth century, had some of the most productive farms in the commonwealth.

BIBLIOGRAPHY

Beers, Paul B. *Pennsylvania Politics Today and Yesterday: The Tolerable Accommodation.* University Park: Pennsylvania State University Press, 1980.

Forrey, William C. *History of Pennsylvania's State Parks.* Harrisburg: Bureau of State Parks, Department of Environmental Resources, Commonwealth of Pennsylvania, 1984.

Fradin, Dennis B. *The Pennsylvania Colony.* Chicago: Children's Press, 1988.

Heinrichs, Ann. *Pennsylvania.* New York: Children's Press, 2000.

Kent, Donald H. *History of Pennsylvania Purchases from the Indians.* New York: Garland, 1974.

Klein, Philip S., and Ari Hoogenboom. *A History of Pennsylvania.* 2d and enl. ed. University Park: Pennsylvania State University Press, 1980.

Stevens, Sylvester K. *Pennsylvania, Birthplace of a Nation.* New York: Random House, 1964.

Wills, Charles A. *A Historical Album of Pennsylvania.* Brookfield, Conn.: Milbrook Press, 1996.

Kirk H. Beetz

See also **Christiana Fugitive Affair; Coal Mining and Organized Labor; Duquesne, Fort; Great Law of Pennsylvania; Pennsylvania, Invasion of.**

PENNSYLVANIA GERMANS comprise several religious communities rooted in sixteenth-century Anabaptism, a Protestant movement emphasizing adult baptism, nonviolence, separation from "worldly" society, and communal self-sufficiency. Between 1700 and 1840, three to five thousand Mennonites and Brethren and one thousand Amish emigrated from the German Palatine and Switzerland to Pennsylvania. They established agrarian settlements in Lancaster County that have maintained their language and *Ordnung* (religious and social customs). "Old Order" Amish and Mennonite populations increased dramatically in the twentieth century, in 2000 numbering some fifty thousand in Pennsylvania. They have continued to avoid motorized vehicles, public utilities, and government services, as their economic base shifts from farming to small enterprises. Their distinctive folk art, music, manufactured products, and efficient farming techniques are widely appreciated.

BIBLIOGRAPHY

Kraybill, Donald B. and Carl F. Bowman. *On the Backroad to Heaven: Old Order Hutterites, Mennonites, Amish, and Brethren.* Baltimore: Johns Hopkins University Press, 2001.

Yoder, Paton. *Tradition and Transition: Amish Mennonites and Old Order Amish, 1800–1900.* Scottsdale, Pa.: Herald Press, 1991.

Jane Weiss

See also **Amish; German Americans; Mennonites; Pennsylvania.**

PENNSYLVANIA, INVASION OF (1863). The Confederate victory at Chancellorsville, Virginia, early in May 1863 forced General Robert E. Lee to rethink his battle plans. Lee divided his army into three corps under generals James Longstreet, Richard S. Ewell, and A. P. Hill. He was preparing his army for a tactical gamble: an offensive on northern soil that would free Virginia from the danger of invasion, demoralize the enemy, and turn the tide of northern public opinion for a peaceable settlement.

Between Lee and Pennsylvania stood Union General Joseph Hooker's army on the Rappahannock River. Lee approached Hooker in early June, forcing him northward so as to keep him between Lee and Washington, D.C. On 23 June, Confederate General J. E. B. Stuart and his cavalry dashed into Maryland, and rejoined Lee in Pennsylvania on 2 July. In retrospect it was a fatal detachment. The Confederate army was well into Pennsylvania when Lee learned that Hooker's replacement—General George C. Meade—was in pursuit; on 29 June Lee ordered a concentration of his scattered army. The absence of Stuart's cavalry deprived Lee of exact knowledge of enemy movements and position. As a result, Hill's troops inadvertently and accidentally brought on the three-day battle at Gettysburg that ended in Confederate defeat.

The wounded Confederate army retreated slowly, its progress impeded by driving rain and floods. Meade pursued overcautiously, and by the time he reached a decision to attack, the Potomac River had fallen sufficiently to permit Lee's army to cross over into Virginia during 13 and 14 July. On 8 August, Lee, assuming complete responsibility for the failure of the campaign, asked President Davis to select someone else to command the army. Davis refused.

BIBLIOGRAPHY

Hattaway, Herman, and Archer Jones. *How the North Won.* Urbana: University of Illinois Press, 1983.

Large, George R. *Battle of Gettysburg: The Official History by the Gettysburg National Military Park Commission.* Shippensburg, Pa.: Burd Street Press, 1999.

McPherson, James M. *Battle Cry of Freedom.* New York: Oxford University Press, 1988.

Palmer, Michael A. *Lee Moves North.* New York: Wiley, 1998.

Thomas Robson Hay / A. R.

See also **Civil War; Gettysburg, Battle of; Pickett's Charge.**

PENNSYLVANIA TROOPS, MUTINIES OF. On 1 January 1781, Pennsylvania troops stationed at Morristown, New Jersey, mutinied. They killed or wounded several officers, and demanded that the Continental Congress furnish back pay, food and clothing, and adjust enlistment terms. On 11 January, the troops met with Joseph Reed, president of the Supreme Executive Council of Pennsylvania and agreed to a modified list of demands.

On 13 June 1783, some Pennsylvania troops in Philadelphia presented a memorial demanding pay due them. Congress, then sitting in Philadelphia, did not resolve the issue and on 21 June the soldiers held a public demonstration. Hearing of the approach of troops however, they dispersed or surrendered.

BIBLIOGRAPHY

Carp, E. Wayne. *To Starve the Army at Pleasure: Continental Army Administration and American Political Culture, 1775–1783.* Chapel Hill: University of North Carolina Press, 1984.

Neimeyer, Charles Patrick. *America Goes to War: A Social History of the Continental Army.* New York: New York University Press, 1996.

Royster, Charles. *A Revolutionary People at War: The Continental Army and American Character, 1775–1783.* Chapel Hill: University of North Carolina Press, 1979.

Thomas Robson Hay / T. D.

See also **Newburgh Addresses; Revolution, American: Military History.**

PENOBSCOT. *See* **Passamaquoddy/Penobscot.**

PENOBSCOT EXPEDITION (1779), an attempt by Massachusetts to dislodge the British from Bagaduce (now Castine), on the Penobscot peninsula of Maine, which they had occupied in June 1779. Nineteen armed vessels with more than 2,000 men, commanded by Capt.

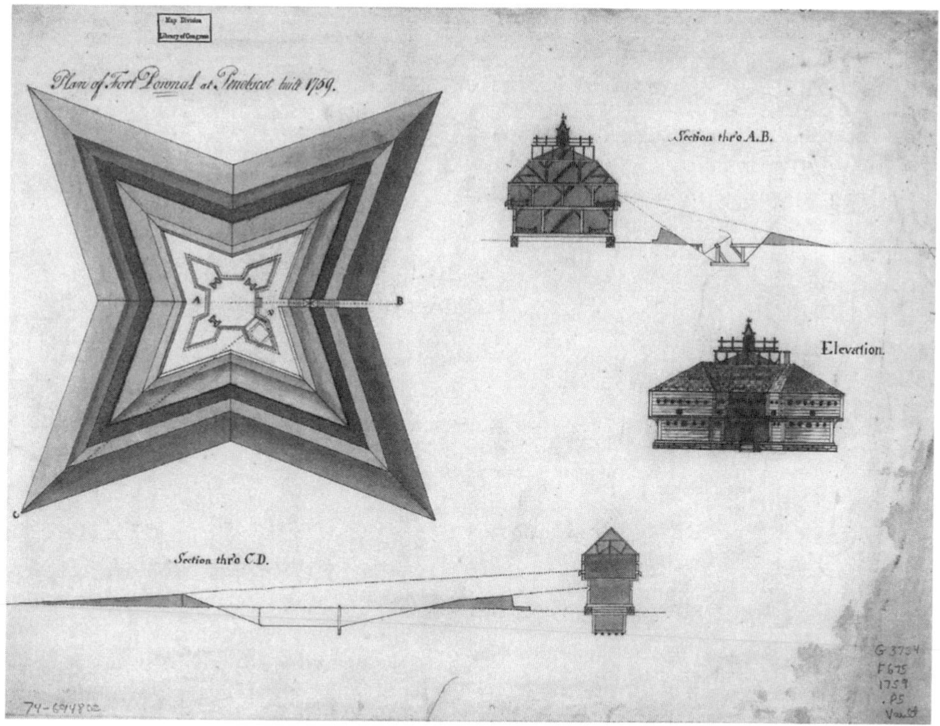

Penobscot Fort. A plan of Fort Pownal, which the British built at the mouth of the Penobscot River in 1759, during the French and Indian War. LIBRARY OF CONGRESS

Dudley Saltonstall, together with twenty-four transports carrying about 900 militia under Gen. Solomon Lovell, with Paul Revere as chief of artillery, arrived at Penobscot Bay on 25 July 1779. Lovell's forces made a courageous landing, but Saltonstall failed to cooperate. When British naval reinforcements arrived on 13 August Saltonstall hardly attempted a defense and lost nearly all his vessels, most of them being burned by their crews to prevent capture. Ill-conceived, ill-planned, and worse executed, the expedition cost Massachusetts £1,739,000 in inflated currency and nearly its whole trading fleet.

BIBLIOGRAPHY

Cayford, John E. *The Penobscot Expedition: Being an Account of the Largest American Naval Engagement of the Revolutionary War.* Orrington, Maine: C & H, 1976.

Fowler, William M. *Rebels under Sail: The American Navy during the Revolution.* New York: Scribners, 1976.

Robert E. Moody/A. R.

See also **Maine; Penobscot Region; Revolution, American: Military History.**

PENOBSCOT REGION is located on Maine's mid-coast and includes the Penobscot Bay and the Penobscot River, Maine's largest, as well as numerous islands, towns, and rivers. Vikings are thought to have visited the area in the tenth century, but there is no proof of this. Europeans first visited in the late 1400s and early 1500s, in search of a northwest passage to the Far East. After hearing of the abundant sea life, European fishermen followed. Despite the very cold winters, by the 1620s fishermen began to spend winters in the area, recognizing winter as the best season for fishing. They also discovered that the coastal areas were not nearly as harsh in winter as inland areas. Explorers and traders came and went; the fishermen were the first to establish the first permanent European settlements in Maine. British and French interests argued and fought over ownership to the region. The French established the Pentagoet trading post in 1613, in what is now Castine; the British built a post there in 1626, but the French drove them out. The ABENAKI Confederacy of Indians formed an alliance with the French against the encroaching British, resulting in nearly a century of bloodshed. British colonists did not settle into the region in large numbers until after the war. The population of the islands and coastal areas grew rapidly after the Revolutionary War. As colonists came, the Indians were pushed out. All of the Indian reservations were placed outside the region, except the Penobscot Reservation, established in the 1830s on Indian Island in the Penobscot River.

The British also fought with Americans, in an effort to keep them from shipping lumber and other resources down the coast. Americans feared the British would control shipping from Maine to Massachusetts, so in 1779 they planned an attack, the PENOBSCOT EXPEDITION. Paul Revere commanded the land artillery under Solomon Lovell, and Dudley Saltonstall commanded the fleet. Twenty-one armed vessels and twenty-four unarmed transport vessels headed from Boston to Castine. Twenty-one ships with 900 men anchored off Castine on 25 July 1779. A few days later, 500 men converged on Castine near the British fort. The British prepared to surrender, but the Americans did not attack immediately. By the time they did, British reinforcements had arrived, and the Americans fled up the Penobscot River only to be trapped. Rather than give up their boats to the British, the Americans burned seventeen of their ships and fled home through the woods.

With all the warfare, the area became stagnant until the end of the American Revolution. Maine became a major shipbuilding center for the United States, leading the country and world in ocean commerce from 1835 to 1857, when a depression hit. Maine also exported many of its natural resources, such as granite, ice, lime, and wood to build the cities on the eastern seaboard. Although the region still flourishes economically, a very small percentage of jobs are in commercial fishing. The area has become a tourist haven in the summer, with many jobs in the service industry. The three counties comprising the region, Waldo, Hancock, and Knox, have a total population of about 128,000, with about 11.7 percent of the population living below the poverty level.

BIBLIOGRAPHY:

Banks, Ronald F., ed. *A History of Maine: A Collection of Readings on the History of Maine, 1600–1976.* Dubuque, Iowa: Kendall/Hunt Publishing, 1976.

Duncan, Roger F. *Coastal Maine: A Maritime History.* New York: Norton, 1992.

Shain, Charles, and Samuella D. Shain, eds. *Growing Up in Maine: Recollections of Childhood from the 1780s to the 1920s.* Camden, Maine: Down East Books, 1991.

Mary Anne Hansen

See also **Maine; Passamaquoddy/Penobscot; Shipbuilding.**

PENSION ACT, ARREARS OF (1879), the most significant and costly piece of pension legislation of the post–Civil War period. The act provided that all soldiers' pensions commence from the date of discharge, not from the date the pension law was passed, forcing states to retroactively pay arrears at the same rate of the original pension. Pushed by a well-organized veterans' lobby, it received only eight negative votes, excluding the southern congressmen and senators, most of whom abstained. Within two years, President Chester A. Arthur had placed the cost at $250 million. In the twentieth century, the principle of public support for veterans would figure importantly in calls for further expansion of the federal welfare apparatus.

BIBLIOGRAPHY

Kelly, Patrick J. *Creating a National Home: Building the Veterans' Welfare State, 1860–1900.* Cambridge, Mass.: Harvard University Press, 1997.

McConnell, Stuart C. *Glorious Contentment: The Grand Army of the Republic, 1865–1900.* Chapel Hill: University of North Carolina Press, 1992.

John W. Oliver / A. R.

See also **Grand Army of the Republic; Surplus, Federal; Veterans' Organizations; Welfare System.**

PENSION PLANS are used to fund retirement programs and may involve employers, the government, or both. Created to provide payments to workers or their families upon retirement, they also provide benefits in the event of death or disability. Self-employed persons generally have individual arrangements. Funding for pension programs may include employee contributions supplemented by matching funds from the employer, deferred profit-sharing programs, stock purchase programs, or employee savings. Social security, a federal pension program established in 1935, may supplement employer and private pension plans.

Different pension plans exist for federal, state, and local government employees; military personnel; and public school teachers. An individual may enhance a pension plan through individual retirement accounts (IRAs) or 401(k) programs or through programs such as the Teachers Insurance and Annuity Association College Retirement Equities Fund (TIAA-CREF). Tax deferments allow retirement contributions to be funded with tax-free dollars, while retirement savings accounts may accumulate interest while delaying tax payments on their growth until funds are withdrawn, promising a larger income at retirement.

Military Pensions

Congress established the General Law pension system in 1862 to provide payments for veterans who had been disabled as a direct result of military service. Payments were determined by the degree of disability as determined by a local medical board. This was usually based on the ability to perform manual labor.

The federal government created a more general pension plan for Union Army veterans in 1890. Although originally designed to assist disabled veterans, it included the beginnings of a collective disability and old-age program for Union veterans of the Civil War. This law provided a pension regardless of whether the condition was caused by military service. Although the law did not recognize old age as a basis for receiving a pension, the Pension Bureau instructed doctors to authorize pensions for applicants over age sixty-five, unless the individual appeared exceptionally vigorous. One effect seems to have been the encouragement for more men to retire, so that, by the early twentieth century, retired Union Army veterans outnumbered nonveteran retirees.

By 1900, this program grew to the extent that it took up nearly 30 percent of the federal budget. Housed in its own building, the pension program provided benefits to veterans as well as their widows and dependant children. Almost a third of those between fifty-five and fifty-nine received pension payments, as did about 20 percent of those between sixty and sixty-five; 15 percent of those aged sixty-five to sixty-nine; and a bit less than ten percent of those seventy or older. The pension program seems to have contributed to these veterans' political power, and they made benefits an important issue in the early twentieth century. Not unlike today's senior citizens, they were well organized and lobbied Congress effectively, despite their small numbers. They tended to support high tariffs and campaigned to have the additional funds directed into the pension fund.

Private Pensions

In the final quarter of the nineteenth century, private pension plans were developed because of employees' growing desire for status, security, and higher salaries combined with management's needs for loyal, dedicated, and productive employees. Partly an expression of welfare capitalism, these early plans were also the result of a belief that benevolent and generous programs, such as pensions, could help create the durable, industrious, and devoted workforce management wanted.

The initial private pension plans were developed by the railroads. The American Express Company established the first one in 1875, followed five years later by the Baltimore and Ohio Railroad (B&O). In 1900, the Pennsylvania Railroad offered its employees a plan. Although these plans arose primarily from a desire to retain employees, they also reflected growing concerns about unions, the welfare of workers, and a wish to display corporate benevolence toward employees. The pension plan created by the B&O had a provision for old-age protection that would serve as an example for future plans, as it allowed employees to retire at sixty-five or, if they were disabled, at age sixty. Another interesting aspect of the plan was its treatment of old age as a disabling illness, providing retirees the same benefits as those who had suffered long-term disabilities. A unique feature of the Pennsylvania Railroad plan was the establishment of corporate control over the plan's administration, setting a precedent for the evolution of modern personnel administration. Other railroads that adopted pension plans soon copied this feature.

Despite the pioneering efforts of the railroads, few other corporations offered any sort of pension plan by 1900. Undoubtedly, the long-term commitment required by such plans discouraged many companies from offering them. Profit-sharing plans were more popular, since the entire workforce could benefit from them, and occasionally, a firm might tie a pension program to its profit sharing plan.

Government Pensions

Although the federal government had established age as a basis for making pensions available to veterans of the Union Army in 1890, it would be another thirty years before a retirement and pension program was established for government employees. As with the private sector, government's interest in pension plans was related to efficiency and security. Generally speaking, civil service employees tended to hold on to their jobs because of the security they offered, but the late nineteenth century saw aging within the bureaucracy become a problem. Many civil service workers were Union Army veterans, who were unlikely to be removed from their jobs for political reasons. These men stayed on in their positions, contributing to an aging and increasingly inefficient bureaucracy. By the beginning of the twentieth century, there was a growing interest in a retirement and pension policy for civil service employees, leading to the creation of the United States Civil Service Retirement Association (USCSRA) in 1900. This association spent several years collecting data and investigating methods by which a federal retirement policy could be established and funded.

These efforts drew the support of the administrations of Theodore Roosevelt and William Howard Taft. Roosevelt established the Keep Commission to investigate the question. The commission's final report offered statistical evidence that, as workers age, they become less efficient.

Taft furthered the movement with the formation of the Commission on Economy and Efficiency, which recommended a plan for civil service retirement. Taft endorsed the plan, and its call for compulsory retirement at age seventy and the creation of an employee financed pension fund. The USCSRA supported this recommendation, but action was prevented by a new group, the National Association of Civil Service Employees (NACSE), which favored a government-funded program.

The debate continued into the Wilson Administration. Political concerns led Woodrow Wilson to withhold support for the issue until 1918, when he responded favorably to a proposed retirement bill. Southern Democratic opposition, however, helped delay passage of the bill until 1920. Civil service employees were now able to retire at age seventy, while others could retire as early as age sixty-two. Funding came from a small salary deduction. An amended law passed in 1926 increased the benefit package, after it became apparent that the original benefits provided in the 1920 law were inadequate.

The problems of unemployment and poverty among the elderly during the Great Depression led to the enactment of the Social Security Act. From the beginning of the New Deal, President Franklin D. Roosevelt's administration wanted a federally sponsored program that would furnish social insurance for the elderly and unemployed. The bill, passed in 1935, would develop into one of the most far-reaching and complex laws Congress had ever enacted. The object of social security was to create a system of insurance rather than welfare. While the law was originally designed to target a small group of people truly in need and unable to support themselves, the program has expanded to assist the elderly, the disabled, and the survivors of those whose payroll deductions contributed to the federal funds that are paid out. The key feature of the program linked benefits to those payroll deductions. This served to create a sense among contributors that they had a vested interest in the program and the right to collect benefits and pensions as promised under the law.

Current Pension Trends

Even so, the present concept of retirement did not emerge until the late 1960s or early 1970s. Prior to this, the Social Security Act had been amended several times to allow more and more workers into the system, but no significant improvement in retirement benefits had taken place, and the concept of social security as supplemental retirement income had not been challenged. But, continued high poverty rates among senior citizens added credibility to their complaints that the benefits were no longer sufficient. Between 1965 and 1975, benefit levels were increased five times, and in 1972, they were indexed in relation to the Consumer Price Index.

A reorganization of private pension plans also occurred in the 1970s. Noteworthy was the passage of the Employee Retirement Income Security Act (ERISA), which legalized vesting plans while giving workers some protection against the loss of benefits. Inflation also led private plans to provide automatic benefit increases to offset the rising cost of living. Additionally, because of increased participation, private plans began to encourage early retirement and offered greater benefits to those who took this option, instead of the reduced benefits that had been common before.

By 2000, there were growing concerns about the future of Social Security, primarily because of the program's expansion during the last decades of the twentieth century. By 2030, the number of persons eligible to receive benefits may double, while the number of those paying into the system will increase by only 20 percent. This has led to talk of privatizing social security or implementing reforms such as taxing all wage earners or allowing a semi-private government agency to oversee and manage the program's investments to assure adequate funding for future beneficiaries. Another suggestion is to raise the retirement age to sixty-seven or seventy. Similarly, owing to an increasing number of major bankruptcies, by the early 2000s, the private sector was increasingly concerned about the well-being of corporate pension programs. In addition to this, the government was experiencing increasing pressure to take more significant steps to protect private pension plans as well as to assure the continued functioning of the social security system.

BIBLIOGRAPHY

Costa, Dora L. *The Evolution of Retirement: An American Economic History, 1880–1900.* Chicago: University of Chicago Press, 1998.

Graebner, William. *A History of Retirement: The Meaning and Function of an American Institution, 1885–1978.* New Haven, Conn.: Yale University Press, 1980.

Haber, Carole, and Brian Gratton. *Old Age and the Search for Security: An American Social History.* Bloomington: Indiana University Press, 1993.

Sass, Steven A. *The Promise of Private Pensions: The First Hundred Years.* Cambridge, Mass.: Harvard University Press, 1997.

Schieber, Sylvester J. *The Real Deal: The History and Future of Social Security.* New Haven, Conn.: Yale University Press, 1999.

Gregory Moore

See also **Retirement.**

PENSIONS, MILITARY AND NAVAL. The United States has granted pensions to participants in all its wars and to members of the regular army and navy in peacetime. They include: (1) pensions for injuries incurred in the service or to dependents of those whose death was caused by the service; (2) qualified service pensions for service of specified length combined with some other qualification, such as age, disability, or indigence; and (3) pensions for service alone. Since World War II even the reserve components of the services have a retirement schedule.

The systems grew haphazardly. Before 1817 American wars were fought mainly by volunteer armies. Pensions were offered as inducements to enlistment in colonial wars and in the Revolution. Early federal enactments granting pensions to persons who had served in the Revolution provided only for disabilities incurred in the service. The first service pension law was enacted in 1818, and the first pensions for widows of soldiers of the Revolution were granted in 1836.

A separate system for the regular army and navy was established in 1790. The acts raising troops for the War of 1812 and the Mexican-American War promised the volunteers the same pensions as the regulars, and acts increasing these pensions before 1862 applied alike to the army and navy, the War of 1812, and the Mexican-American War. The first service pension was granted for the War of 1812 in 1871, and for the Mexican-American War in 1887.

Two innovations appeared during the Civil War. First, the "general laws" of 1862, providing uniform pensions on account of death or disability of service origin for both regulars and volunteers of the armed forces, applied to future wars. Second, certain specific disabilities were pensioned in 1864 at higher rates than under the general laws.

A combination of political factors, including patriotism, the soldier vote, veterans lobbies, and pension attorneys, led to the establishment in the United States of the most generous pension system in the world. President Grover Cleveland's vetoes of private pension bills and of the Dependent Pension Bill of 1887 made the subject an issue in the election of 1888. The act of 1890 gave a qualified service pension to Civil War veterans who, from any cause, were incapacitated for performing manual labor. In 1904 an administrative order made age above sixty-two years a pensionable disability under this act. The first Civil War pension for service alone was enacted in 1920. At the beginning of the Spanish-American War, volunteers and state militia were specifically granted the same pensions as regulars. In 1920 a qualified service pension was given to all above sixty-two years of age.

The philosophy of veteran treatment was transformed by World War I and its aftermath. Subsequently the able-bodied veteran shared immediate and substantial benefits with his less fortunate comrades-in-arms. The new policy began during the war with enactments of a liberal life insurance program and a $60 discharge allowance. Thereafter, benefits progressively grew, largely through the persistent, indefatigable efforts of the American Legion, organized in 1919, almost simultaneously with the federal Veterans Bureau, created to oversee the traditional caretaking of casualties. Able-bodied veterans were soon lobbying for what was called the Bonus Bill, predicated on $1 per day for domestic service and $1.25 per day for overseas service. In 1924 Congress passed the bill over President Calvin Coolidge's veto. Sums exceeding claims of $50 were paid in life insurance certificates maturing in 1945, when the principal was to be paid. Compound interest and an adjustment scale made an average claim of $400 worth $1,000 at maturity. The depression came, and veterans organizations militated for preferential treatment. In 1931 Congress overrode President Herbert Hoover's veto to authorize veteran borrowing from the Treasury of amounts up to 50 percent of their certificates. The next year the Bonus Expeditionary Force marched on Washington, D.C., in a futile effort to force premature, lump-sum payment. In 1935 President Franklin D. Roosevelt's veto of a bill for such payment was sustained. In 1936 his veto was overridden and the then enormous sum of $2.491 billion was disbursed. It was an omen. From the Revolution to 1930 all federal disbursements to veterans totaled about $15 billion, a sum that by 1973 would cover only a year and a half of Veterans Administration (VA) commitments.

Established in 1930, the VA expanded rapidly in scope and complexity, originally befriending 4.6 million veterans, 3.7 percent of the U.S. population. By 1971 veterans numbered 28.3 million, a sizable 13.7 percent of the citizenry. It was estimated that they had about 97.6 million relatives, making 47 percent of the U.S. population actual or potential beneficiaries of the VA.

The major benefits provided by the VA are medical care, insurance, education and training, loans, and guardianship of minors and incompetents. Some 60 percent of the budget goes to compensation and pensions, the former to recompense veterans for the loss of earning power because of injury or disease arising from military service. Pensions recognize an obligation to give aid when necessary for non-service-connected disease or death. Some 20 percent of the VA budget goes for medical programs. In 1972 the VA maintained 166 hospitals and 298 other facilities, such as nursing homes and clinics, serving 912,342 inpatients. After World War II, GI bills of rights gave education or training to nearly 16 million veterans, besides their dependents. For World War II service, such benefits expired on 25 July 1956; for service in Korea, on 31 January 1965; and service after the Korean War generally provided an eligibility of eight years from the day of release from active duty. The first GI bill was generous, covering up to forty-eight school months all the costs of tuition, fees, and study materials and providing living allowances of a monthly $65–160, scaled to the number of a veteran's dependents.

By 1972 the VA had a staff of 182,546 people, almost exactly ten times the size of the regular army at the outbreak of the Civil War, underscoring the great expansion in veteran benefits since then. By the end of the 1990s, the annual fiscal 1999 VA budget was over $40 billion.

BIBLIOGRAPHY

Daniels, Roger. *The Bonus March: An Episode of the Great Depression.* Westport, Conn.: Greenwood, 1971.

McConnell, Stuart C. *Glorious Contentment: The Grand Army of the Republic, 1865–1900.* Chapel Hill: University of North Carolina Press, 1992.

Donald L. McMurry
R. W. Daly/A. G.

See also **Army, United States; Bonus Army; Bonuses, Military; Defense, Department of; Demobilization; Pension Plans; Soldiers' Home; Veterans Affairs, Department of.**

PENTAGON, situated in Arlington, Virginia, across the Potomac River from the nation's capital, is the home of America's defense establishment and symbolizes the country's warmaking capability and its projection abroad. In June 1941, the War Department moved into its new War Department Building, but the rapid growth of the armed forces in the months before Pearl Harbor had already made the structure inadequate. To meet the demand for office and storage space, Brigadier General Brehon B. Somervell, chief of the construction division in the quartermaster general's office, advanced the idea of a single building to house the expanding department. The Arlington site was selected for its accessibility to Washington and the availability of land already owned by the government. Discussions over location, size, and shape, some of which involved President Franklin Roosevelt, eventually produced a five-sided structure with five floors and floor space of more than six million square feet. The

Pentagon. A 1990 aerial view of the distinctive home of the Department of Defense. © CORBIS

pentagonal shape, the idea of architect G. Edwin Bergstrom, was adapted from army forts that were similarly shaped, thus giving the Pentagon the image of a fortress. It consists of five concentric pentagonal rings connected by perpendicular corridors. The building is 71 feet high and each outer side is 921.6 feet long. It covers 28.7 acres and rests on a site of 280 acres with parking for 9,500 vehicles. The final cost of what is the largest office building in the world was $50 million, with additional costs of roads and external buildings raising the total to $85 million.

Construction of the Pentagon began in September 1941 and took sixteen months to complete, utilizing as many as 15,000 workers on site. It has a slab-and-beam reinforced concrete framework with a limestone facade. Its style is "stripped classicism," a synthesis of classical and modern styles similar to that of other government buildings built at that time. Architects were Bergstrom and David J. Witmer. Supervising construction for the army were Somervell, Colonel Leslie R. Groves, and Captain Clarence Renshaw. The primary building company was John McShain, Inc. The Pentagon officially opened in January 1943 and reached its highest occupancy of 33,000 employees that year and again in 1952 during the Korean War. Since the reorganization of the military establishment in 1947, the Pentagon has become the home of the Department of Defense, including its secretary, the Departments of the Army, Navy, and Air Force, the Joint Chiefs of Staff, and the war room of the National Military Command System. It was the scene of several antiwar protests during the Vietnam era. On 11 September 2001, terrorists hijacked an American Airlines plane and crashed it into the west wing of the Pentagon, killing 189 people.

BIBLIOGRAPHY

Goldberg, Alfred. *The Pentagon: The First Fifty Years.* Washington, D.C.: Historical Office, Office of the Secretary of Defense, 1992.

Ronald L. Heinemann

See also **Defense, Department of; Defense, National; War Department.**

PENTAGON PAPERS. Popularly known as the Pentagon Papers, the "History of U.S. Decision-Making Process on Vietnam Policy" is a forty-seven volume, 7,000-page, 2.5 million-word study that traces the involvement of the United States in Vietnam from World War II to 1968. Four thousand pages of the study consist of republished government documents; the balance comprises historical studies prepared by thirty-six civilian and military analysts and focused on particular events. Secretary of Defense Robert S. McNamara commissioned the study in 1967 during the administration of President Lyndon B. Johnson. The Vietnam War had sparked serious dissent within the United States, and U.S. foreign policy was dominated by Cold War thinking that emphasized the importance of containing the spread of communism. Directed by Leslie H. Gelb, the study was completed shortly before Richard M. Nixon was sworn in as president in January 1969. The fifteen copies made were classified "top secret sensitive."

The first volumes of the study reviewed U.S. policy toward Indochina during and immediately following World War II, as well as the U.S. involvement in the Franco–Viet Minh War between 1950 and 1954, the Geneva Conference of 1954, and the origins of insurgency from 1954 to 1960. Most of the study, however, was devoted to the years following the election of President John F. Kennedy in 1960. It included detailed reviews of the overthrow of Ngo Dinh Diem; the Tonkin Gulf episode; the decision to begin and expand the air war against North Vietnam; the decision to deploy U.S. ground forces in Vietnam; the buildup of those forces; the strategy for the use of troops; and the history of the war's diplomacy from 1964 to 1968.

As a history, the Pentagon Papers had shortcomings. The staff did not collect White House documents or conduct interviews, and the Central Intelligence Agency as well as other branches of government withheld documents. Because the historical studies were based solely on the collected documents, the subjects analyzed were narrowly conceived and treated.

Believing that the public disclosure of the Pentagon Papers might shorten the war in Vietnam, Daniel Ellsberg, a defense department consultant working at the Rand Corporation, made the study available to the *New York Times* reporter Neil Sheehan in early 1971. On 13 June 1971 the *New York Times* published the first of a ten-part series on the Pentagon Papers under a headline that read: "VIETNAM ARCHIVE: PENTAGON STUDY TRACES 3 DECADES OF GROWING U.S. INVOLVEMENT." The opening paragraph of that first article sounded a theme that many thought distilled the salient meaning of this government study: the U.S. government had through successive administrations misled the American public about "a sense of commitment to a non-Communist Vietnam, a readiness to fight the North to protect the South, and an ultimate frustration with this effort."

Initially the Pentagon Papers drew little public attention or comment, but when the United States obtained a temporary restraining order barring the *New York Times* from publishing its fourth installment, the dry and tedious study captured national attention. The government initiated litigation premised on the claim that further publication would endanger national security at a time when U.S. combat troops were fighting a land war in Vietnam, and proceeded frantically through all three levels of the federal courts. Eventually the *Washington Post* and other newspapers became involved. On 30 June 1971, in *New York Times Co. v. United States*, 403 U.S. 713, the United States Supreme Court, by a vote of 6 to 3, denied the government's request for a prior restraint on the ground that the government's evidence fell short of what the constitution required. The outcome was widely hailed as a landmark in the history of free press.

The United States criminally prosecuted Ellsberg and Anthony J. Russo, who had helped in photocopying the study, mainly on charges of espionage, but in 1973 U.S. District Judge William M. Byrne dismissed the charges because of government misconduct. There is no evidence that the public disclosure of the Pentagon Papers injured national security as the government contended it would. The disclosure had no discernible impact on the course of the war, did not appreciably reignite the antiwar movement within the United States, and did not result in the commencement of war-crimes prosecution against high-level U.S. officials.

The entire Pentagon Papers episode was, however, a critical turning point for the Nixon administration, which located within the White House a group that became known as the "Plumbers Unit." Ostensibly charged with investigating the improper disclosure ("leaks") of classified information, in the fall of 1971 this group burglarized the office of Ellsberg's psychiatrist in search of information about Ellsberg and his accomplices. Nine months later it broke into the headquarters of the Democratic Party at the Watergate building complex in Washington, D.C. Thus, the Pentagon Papers indirectly led to the Watergate scandal, which caused Nixon to resign the presidency on 9 August 1974.

BIBLIOGRAPHY

Herring, George C., ed. *The Secret Diplomacy of the Vietnam War: The Negotiating Volumes of the Pentagon Papers.* Austin: University of Texas Press, 1983.

The Pentagon Papers: The Defense Department History of United States Decision-Making on Vietnam. 4 vols. Boston: Beacon Press, 1971.

Rudenstine, David. *The Day the Presses Stopped: A History of the Pentagon Papers Case.* Berkeley: University of California Press, 1996.

Sheehan, Neil, et al. *The Pentagon Papers: As Published by the* New York Times, *Based on Investigative Reporting by Neil Sheehan.* New York: Bantam, 1971.

Ungar, Sanford J. *The Papers and the Papers: An Account of the Legal and Political Battle over the Pentagon Papers.* New York: Columbia University Press, 1989.

David Rudenstine

See also **Cold War; *New York Times;* Nixon, Resignation of; Vietnam War; Watergate;** *and vol. 9:* **Excerpt from the Pentagon Papers.**

PENTECOSTAL CHURCHES emerged from the teachings fostered by the National Holiness Association in the late nineteenth century. Holiness churches within the Methodist tradition emphasized John Wesley's teaching of a "second blessing" or sanctification experience following conversion. Beginning in the 1890s, independent Pentecostals began to take note of the teaching of Benjamin Irvin of the Fire–Baptized Holiness Church who formulated the notion of a post-sanctification baptism of the Holy Spirit (or third blessing). This teaching was given a new force when the black preacher William J. Seymour presided over the Asuza Street revival. Seymour had been taught that, while the sanctification experience cleansed the believer, baptism with the Holy Spirit brought power for service; the only evidence for this was provided by the gift of tongues (or glossolalia) recorded in the Acts of the Apostles. At 312 Azusa Street in Los Angeles, he led an interracial revival that began in 1906 and would last until 1909. The style of worship, with much weeping and speaking in tongues and without a choir or recognized order of service, would characterize the worship style of the later Pentecostal denominations. The two denominations that drew most from the Azusa experience were the Church of God in Christ, founded by C. H. Mason in 1897, and the Church of God (Cleveland, Tennessee) established in 1906 by A. J. Tomlinson. Mason attended the Asuza revival in 1907 as the leader of the largest African American Pentecostal grouping in the world. Tomlinson helped establish the concept of speaking in tongues as a central tenet of Pentecostal teaching. Both Southern groups helped add to the holiness doctrine of sanctification the idea of a "baptism of fire" and the vibrant tradition of Pentecostal hostility to jewelry, lodges, life insurance, and medicine.

Doctrinal Controversies

The early stress on glossolalia as an essential ingredient provoked hostility from former Baptists entering the movement, who did not share the Wesleyan heritage of their ex-Methodist brethren. In 1908, William H. Durham sought to deny the Wesleyan idea of a residue of sin following conversion, instead considering sanctification to be analogous with conversion. Durham's notion of the "finished work" gained ground with independent churches newly established in urban areas to care for migrants from

Pentecostal Church of God. Russell Lee's photograph of a church in Lejunior, Ky., attended mostly by coal-mining families, shows congregants handling serpents, 15 September 1946. NATIONAL ARCHIVES AND RECORDS ADMINISTRATION

the rural South. In 1914, E. N. Bell and H. G. Rogers helped to establish the Assemblies of God, a largely white body, which espoused the "finished work" doctrine and adopted a congregational polity. The Assemblies of God were also forced to confront a challenge from members who argued there was only one personality in the Trinity—Jesus Christ—and that new birth, sanctification, and the gift of tongues all occurred at the same moment. The Assemblies of God issued a Trinitarian doctrinal statement in 1916, at which point their Unitarian-inclined members left to later merge with the Pentecostal Assemblies of the World in 1917.

The Racial Divide

Racial divisions have characterized the Pentecostal movement throughout its history. Although the early churches were racially integrated, only the Pentecostal Assemblies of the World enjoyed much interracial comity. In the Church of God (Cleveland, Tennessee) and the Pentecostal Holiness Church, southern culture and black demands for independence led to effective segregation. Nevertheless, the style of Pentecostal worship and its reputation as a faith of the downtrodden meant that Pentecostalism did exercise allure for African Americans. By 1990, the Church of God in Christ had become the fifth-largest denomination in the United States. Black Pentecostals were excluded from the transdenominational Pentecostal Fellowship of North America (PFNA), when it was founded in 1948, and only gradually did white Pentecostals come to see a value in the civil rights movement. In 1994, the PFNA was dissolved and then replaced by the Pentecostal and Charismatic Churches of North America, in which the black churches enjoyed full standing.

A New Legitimacy

Pentecostal churches have faced problems gaining acceptance in wider society. Early associations with the more dramatic aspects of "holy rollerism" provoked violence against them. Over time, as many working-class Pentecostals gained a foothold in middle-class society, this prejudice waned. They steadily entered the evangelical mainstream and played a part in the formation of the National Association of Evangelicals (the conservative counterpart to the Federal Council of Churches) in 1943. The establishment of an educational system, of which the crown jewel was Oral Roberts University in Tulsa, Oklahoma, also conferred legitimacy. Even more important for social legitimation was the phenomenon of neo-Pentecostal manifestations within the mainstream Protestant and Roman Catholic churches, which accepted the Pentecostal experience as a release of grace given and received at a water baptism. Today, Pentecostals have passed from a subculture into the mainstream of American life. Pentecostal televangelists like Pat Robertson have wielded great influence in American society. In 1995, Brownsville Assemblies of God Church was the scene of a mass revival, which caught world attention and had by 1997 attracted 1.6 million attendees and 100,000 responses to altar calls.

Pentecostals Today

There are a vast variety of Pentecostal groups in the United States today. The three largest are the Assemblies of God with 2,574,531 members in 1999, the Church of God in Christ with 5,499,875 members in 1991, and the Pentecostal Assemblies of the World with 1,500,000 members in 1998. Groups with over 100,000 members are the Church of God (Cleveland, Tennessee) with 870,039 in 1999, the Full Gospel Fellowship of Churches and Ministers International with 325,000 in 2000, the International Church of the Foursquare Gospel with 253,412 in 1999, the International Pentecostal Holiness Church with 185,431 in 1999, and the Pentecostal Church of God with 105,200 in 1999. Smaller groups include the Apostolic Faith Mission Church of God with 10,651 in 1999, the Apostolic Overcoming Holy Church of God with 10,714 in 2000, the Church of God of Prophecy with 75,112 in 1999, the Full Gospel Assemblies International with 52,500 in 1998, and the Pentecostal Free Will Baptist Church with 28,000 in 1998.

BIBLIOGRAPHY

Anderson, Robert Mapes. *Vision of the Disinherited: The Making of American Pentecostalism.* New York: Oxford University Press, 1979.

Cox, Harvey. *Fire from Heaven: The Rise of Pentecostal Spirituality and the Reshaping of Religion in the Twenty-First Century.* Reading, Mass.: Addison-Wesley, 1995.

Crews, Mickey. *The Church of God: A Social History.* Knoxville: University of Tennessee Press, 1990.

Synan, Vinson. *The Holiness-Pentecostal Tradition: Charismatic Movements in the Twentieth Century.* Grand Rapids, Mich.: W. B. Eerdmans, 1997.

Wacker, Grant. *Heaven Below: Early Pentecostals and American Culture.* Cambridge, Mass.: Harvard University Press, 2001.

Jeremy Bonner

See also **Discrimination: Religion; Religion and Religious Affiliation; Religious Thought and Writings.**

PEONAGE is involuntary servitude, under which a debtor is forced to make payment to a master through labor. It differs from slavery, serfdom, and contract labor by both the necessary element of indebtedness and the indefinite term of service. Prior to 1800, the system was prevalent in Spanish America, especially Mexico and Guatemala. While not wholly confined to blacks in the United States, peonage developed in the South after the abolition of slavery in 1865, just as it had in the Southwest following its acquisition from Mexico. An employer paid fines imposed for a petty crime in exchange for work by the sentenced person. And when agricultural laborers and tenants were advanced cash and supplies, any attempt to leave was interpreted as having obtained credit under false pretenses, which, under state law, was a criminal offense.

Peonage did not lose its legal sanction until 1910, when the U.S. Supreme Court declared such state laws to be in violation of the Thirteenth and Fourteenth amendments (*Bailey v. Alabama*, 219 U.S. 219). In spite of the laws, as late as 1960, sharecroppers in the Deep South were pressured to pay off old debts or taxes through peonage. Peonage is interpreted in the Constitution (Title 18, U.S.C., Section 1581), as holding a person in debt servitude. This practice, though illegal, is being found again in the U.S. in relation to the smuggling of illegal immigrants into the country. The immigrants are then placed in garment "sweat shops" or other small businesses to work off their transportation debt. The current law states that those found enforcing peonage on another can be fined or imprisoned up to ten years.

BIBLIOGRAPHY

Daniel, Pete. *The Shadow of Slavery: Peonage in the South, 1901–1969.* Urbana: University of Illinois Press, 1990.

Packard, Jerrold M. *American Nightmare: The History of Jim Crow.* New York: St. Martin's Press, 2002.

Karen Rae Mehaffey
Rupert B. Vance

See also **Sharecroppers.**

PEQUOT WAR (1636–1637). Tensions between English settlers and Pequot Indians, who inhabited southeastern New England and had made enemies among many other Indian tribes, developed by the early 1630s. These tensions escalated when Pequots killed English colonists and traders in 1633 and 1636. After the murder of an English captain on Block Island in 1636, both sides began to prepare for further hostilities. While English troops arrived to strengthen Saybrook Fort, located at the mouth of the Connecticut River, some Pequot Indians attacked Wethersfield further north, killing nine. This event led the general court of the recently settled river towns—Windsor, Hartford, and Wethersfield—to declare war on the Pequot Indians in May 1637.

Under English and Mohegan command, white and Indian troops allied against the Pequot and courted support from the Narragansett Indians. After a two-day march, the party surprised and burned the Pequot fort near present-day Mystic. Only seven Indians escaped the slaughter. English forces attacked a second Pequot stronghold two miles away the same night.

In response, hundreds of Pequot Indians decided to flee the area rather than stay and fight. The English and their allies pursued them and caught up with the group in Sasqua Swamp, near present-day Southport, Conn. The ensuing battle resulted in the capture of about 180 Pequots. The Pequots' Indian enemies adopted many of the captives into their own tribes and killed many of those who initially escaped. The war decimated the Pequot tribe as a formal political unit until the twentieth century, when Pequot descendants reorganized in southern New England.

BIBLIOGRAPHY

Kupperman, Karen Ordahl. *Indians and English: Facing Off in Early America.* Ithaca, N.Y.: Cornell University Press, 2000.

Nobles, Gregory H. *American Frontiers: Cultural Encounters and Continental Conquest.* New York: Hill and Wang, 1997.

George Matthew Dutcher/s. b.

See also **Colonial Settlements; Colonial Wars; Frontier; Indian Warfare; New England Colonies; Tribes: Northeastern.**

PEQUOTS, an Eastern Algonquian-speaking people, were located in what is now southeastern Connecticut when the Dutch began trading with them in the early 1600s. When the English replaced the Dutch after 1630, they sought control of trade and land and came into conflict with the Pequots in 1636. In 1637 the English and Indian allies attacked a Pequot village and killed some 600 Pequots. The war ended in 1638 when captured Pequots were sold as slaves or given to the English allies, the Mohegans and Narragansetts. The tribe's lands and name were taken away.

But the Pequots did not disappear. Instead, two tribes emerged, one at Noank and later Mashantucket, and the other at Paucatuck and later in Stonington. The two tribes continue to occupy their colonial-state reservations, although in the nineteenth century Connecticut passed laws reducing their acreage. The tribes have continuously governed their affairs, maintained their independence, and supported their members. In 1976, the Mashantucket Pequots filed a lawsuit to recover the land lost by state

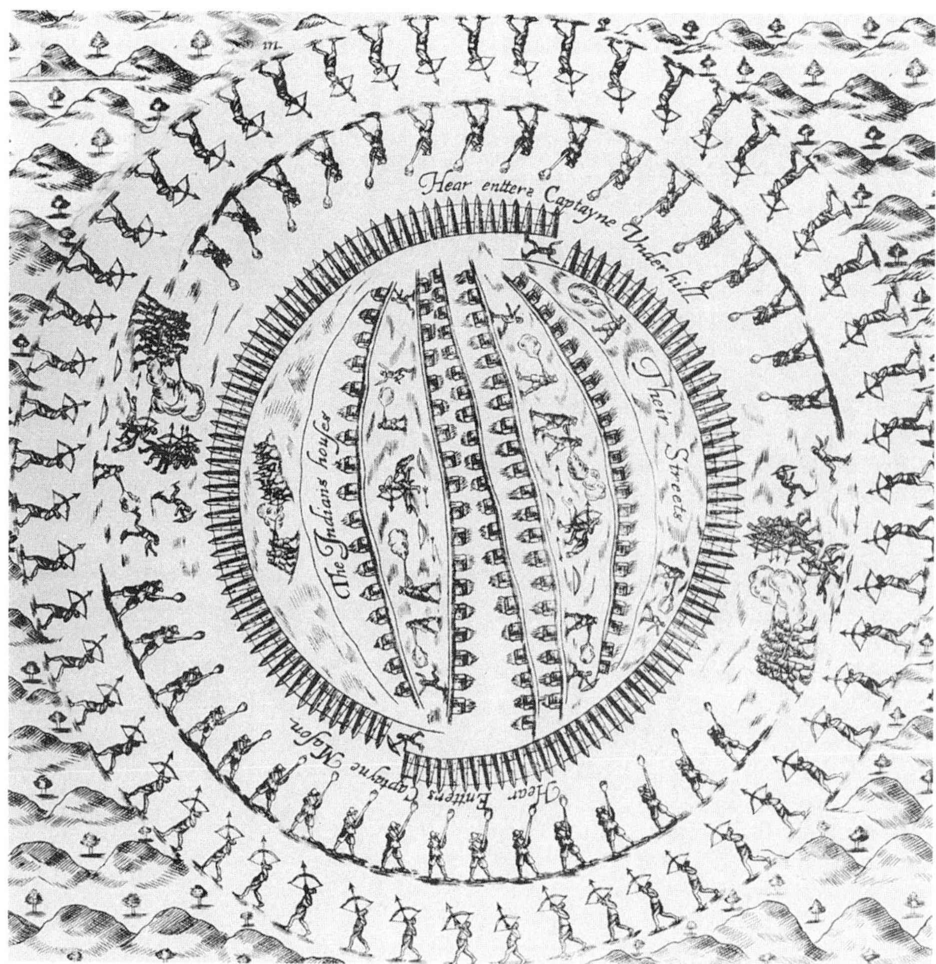

Massacre at Mystic. This woodcut, first published in 1638 in Captain John Underhill's book *Newes from America*, depicts the encirclement of the stockaded Pequot village (in present-day Groton, Conn.) by Major John Mason's Connecticut militia and his Indian allies on 26 May 1637. Nearly all of about 600 trapped Pequot men, women, and children were killed, many of them burned alive. LIBRARY OF CONGRESS

action, and in 1983 they were federally recognized and their land claim settled. The other Pequot community also filed a land suit, then split into two groups, each petitioning for federal recognition.

BIBLIOGRAPHY

Campisi, Jack. "The Emergence of the Mashantucket Pequot Tribe, 1637–1975." In *The Pequots in Southern New England: The Fall and Rise of an American Indian Nation.* Edited by Laurence M. Hauptman and James D. Wherry. Norman: University of Oklahoma Press, 1990.

Conkey, Laura E., Ethel Boissevain, and Ives Goddard. "Indians of Southern New England and Long Island: Late Period." In *Handbook of North American Indians.* Edited by William C. Sturtevant et al. Vol. 15: *Northeast,* edited by Bruce G. Trigger. Washington, D.C.: Smithsonian Institution, 1978.

Jack Campisi

See also **Tribes: Northeastern; Wars with Indian Nations.**

PERMANENT COURT OF ARBITRATION.

See **International Court of Justice.**

PERRY-ELLIOTT CONTROVERSY. At the Battle of Lake Erie (10 September 1813), a major engagement of the War of 1812, Jesse D. Elliott, commander of the *Niagara,* did not move his ship to support the *Lawrence,* commanded by Oliver Hazard Perry, until the *Lawrence* was practically destroyed. This inaction led to a long running feud. In 1818, Elliott challenged Perry to a duel, and Perry pressed charges against Elliott for his conduct during the engagement. President James Monroe did not pursue the charges but the controversy raged on.

In 1839 James Fenimore Cooper was violently attacked by Perry's supporters for failing to criticize Elliott in his *History of the Navy of the United States of America.* Cooper not only won two libel suits, but based his *Battle of Lake Erie* (1843) on the controversy surrounding the two men. Although another libel suit was also won by Cooper, his 1839 history was excluded for a time from the school libraries of New York State.

BIBLIOGRAPHY

Dillon, Richard. *We Have Met the Enemy: Oliver Hazard Perry, Wilderness Commodore.* New York: McGraw–Hill, 1978.

Mills, James Cooke. *Oliver Hazard Perry and the Battle of Lake Erie.* Detroit, Mich.: J. Phelps, 1913.

Walter B. Norris/T. D.

See also **Lake Erie, Battle of; Literature; War of 1812.**

PERRY'S EXPEDITION TO JAPAN. America's interest in Japan was part of its larger interest in China and in opening ports and expanding trade in Northeast Asia. The Tokugawa Shogunate in Japan, by contrast, had tried for more than 200 years to isolate Japan and to limit contact with the outside world.

In 1852, Matthew Calbraith Perry, who commanded the U.S. East India Squadron, received orders from President Millard Fillmore to travel to Japan, meet with its leader, and open diplomatic and trading relations. This included obtaining permission for U.S. vessels to secure coal, provisions, and fresh water; arranging for the protection of shipwrecked American sailors and cargoes; and, most importantly, opening Japanese ports to U.S. trade.

Perry entered Edo (present-day Tokyo) Bay with four ships, two of which were coal-burning steam ships, in July 1853. The black smoke from the steamers caused the Japanese to refer to the small fleet as "black ships." Perry sought to present a letter to the Emperor, but he was commanded to leave. He returned in February 1854 with eight ships—one-third of the U.S. Navy—and on 31 March 1854, he signed the Treaty of Kanagawa, which opened Japan to trade and provided for care of shipwrecked Americans. Still, the Japanese conceded little. They did not grant full commercial relations or extraterritorial rights, which gave the imperialist powers control over their own citizens in Japan, and the ports they opened were far from the center of the country, thus isolating American sailors from the Japanese people.

Perry's and America's motives were obvious, the Japanese' were less so. Japanese leaders saw China being battered by the British and French and the spread of the so-called unequal treaty system granting the Western power extensive rights and privileges in China; there also were powers in Japan, rich daimyo, or feudal lords, in the southwest, who wanted to reform Japan to resist foreign encroachments. Perry and America seemed the lesser of evils, and so Perry met with limited success. His visit became part of a larger discussion in Japan about how to meet the threat of the modern West, which ultimately resulted in the Meiji Restoration in 1868.

BIBLIOGRAPHY

Blumberg, Rhoda. *Commodore Perry in the land of the Shogun.* New York: Lothrop, Lee and Shepard, 1985.

Dulles, Foster Rhea. *Yankees and Samurai; America's Role in the Emergence of Modern Japan.* New York: Harper & Row, 1965.

Schroeder, John H. *Matthew Calbraith Perry: Antebellum Sailor and Diplomat.* Annapolis, Md.: Naval Institute Press, 2001.

Wiley, Peter Booth. *Yankees in the Land of the Gods: Commodore Perry and the Opening of Japan.* New York: Viking Press, 1990.

Charles M. Dobbs

See also **Japan, Relations with.**

PERRYVILLE, BATTLE OF (8 October 1862). After Confederate Gen. Braxton Bragg had attended the inauguration of the secessionist governor of Kentucky, he gathered his scattered army to form a junction with reinforcements, commanded by Gen. Edmund Kirby-Smith, coming from Cumberland Gap. On 8 October 1862, Bragg's army was drawn up in battle array near Perryville. Union troops under Gen. Don Carlos Buell, marching from Louisville, unexpectedly encountered the Confederate force. A bloody battle followed. The Confederates retained possession of the battlefield, but withdrew eastward during the night to join Kirby-Smith and then southward the following day to protect Knoxville, Tenn.

BIBLIOGRAPHY

Hattaway, Herman, and Archer Jones, *How the North Won: A Military History of the Civil War.* Urbana: University of Illinois, 1983.

McWhiney, Grady. *Braxton Bragg and Confederate Defeat.* New York: Columbia University Press, 1969.

Thomas Robson Hay/A. R.

See also **Civil War; Cumberland, Army of the; Cumberland Gap; Morgan's Raids.**

PERSIAN GULF SYNDROME refers to the controversial "disease" or cluster of symptoms reported by numerous American and British Gulf War veterans. About 700,000 U.S. citizens, including military and nonmilitary personnel, took part in the Gulf War to oust Iraqi forces from Kuwait, an operation that lasted from 16 January to 28 February of 1991. Although the war was short-lived, by 1993 some veterans began to speak out about mysterious symptoms such as headaches, chronic fatigue, cardiovascular and respiratory illness, skin rashes, and muscle pain. Studies of about 4,000 reported cases of the disease were undertaken throughout the 1990s; some estimate that the United States government funded over 150 different projects at a cost of nearly $150 million. No clear diagnosis has been made; researchers have hypothesized that the syndrome may have multiple origins stemming from the variety of chemicals soldiers could potentially have been exposed to, such as fumes from oil fires, destroyed Iraqi biological and chemical weapons (including Sarin and mustard gas), depleted uranium sources, and medical vaccines. A study by the NIH in 2000 concluded that no clear link has been shown between chemicals, medicines and other materials, and the syndrome. Nonetheless, in the early 2000s Senator Kay Bailey Hutchison and former presidential candidate Ross Perot continued to press for more funding for research, while many Gulf War veterans decried the official "cover-up" and the tendency of military leaders to downplay the physical and mental consequences of war.

BIBLIOGRAPHY

"Desperately Seeking a Syndrome." *Nature* 407 (19 October 2000): 819.

Hersh, Seymour. *Against All Enemies: Gulf War Syndrome: The War between American Ailing Veterans and Their Government.* New York: Ballantine, 1998.

J. G. Whitesides

See also **Persian Gulf War; Veterans Affairs, Department of; Veterans' Organizations.**

PERSIAN GULF WAR. The invasion of Kuwait by 140,000 Iraqi troops and 1,800 tanks on 2 August 1990, eventually led to U.S. involvement in war in the Persian Gulf region. Instead of repaying billions of dollars of loans received from Kuwait during the eight-year war between Iran and Iraq (1980–1988), Iraqi dictator Saddam Hussein resurrected old territorial claims and annexed Kuwait as his country's nineteenth province.

President George H. W. Bush feared that Saddam might next invade Saudi Arabia and thus control 40 percent of the world's oil. Bush organized an international coalition of forty-three nations, thirty of which sent military or medical units to liberate Kuwait, and he personally lobbied United Nations Security Council members. By November the UN had imposed economic sanctions and passed twelve separate resolutions demanding that the Iraqis withdraw. Bush initially sent 200,000 U.S. troops as part of a multinational peacekeeping force to defend Saudi Arabia (Operation Desert Shield), describing the mission as "defensive." On November 8, Bush expanded the U.S. expeditionary force to more than 500,000 to "ensure that the coalition has an adequate offensive military option." Contingents from other allied countries brought the troop level to 675,000. UN Security Council Resolution 678 commanded Iraq to evacuate Kuwait by 15 January 1991, or else face military attack.

What Saddam Hussein had hoped to contain as an isolated regional quarrel provoked an unprecedented alliance that included not only the United States and most members of the North Atlantic Treaty Organization (NATO) but also Iraq's former military patron, the Soviet Union, and several Arab states, including Egypt and Syria. The Iraqi dictator must have found Washington's outraged reaction especially puzzling in view of recent efforts by the administrations of Presidents Ronald Reagan and Bush to befriend Iraq. Off-the-books U.S. arms transfers to Iraq were kept from Congress from 1982 to 1987, in violation of the law. Washington had supplied intelligence data to Baghdad during the Iran-Iraq war, and Bush had blocked congressional attempts to deny agricultural credits to Iraq because of human rights abuses. The Bush administration had also winked at secret and illegal bank loans that Iraq had used to purchase $5 billion in Western technology for its burgeoning nuclear and chemical weapons programs. Assistant Secretary of State John H. Kelly told Congress in early 1990 that Saddam Hussein acted as "a force of moderation" in the Middle East. Only a week before the invasion Ambassador April Glaspie informed Saddam Hussein that Washington had no "opinion on inter-Arab disputes such as your border dispute with Kuwait."

Bush and his advisers, without informing Congress or the American people, apparently decided early in August to use military force to expel Saddam Hussein from Kuwait. "It must be done as massively and decisively as possible," advised General Colin Powell, chairman of the Joint Chiefs of Staff. "Choose your target, decide on your objective, and try to crush it." The president, however, described the initial deployments as defensive, even after General H. Norman Schwarzkopf had begun to plan offensive operations. Bush did not announce the offensive buildup until after the November midterm elections, all the while expanding U.S. goals from defending Saudi Arabia, to liberating Kuwait, to crippling Iraq's war economy, even to stopping Saddam Hussein from acquiring nuclear weapons. UN sanctions cut off 90 percent of Iraq's imports and 97 percent of its exports. Secretary of State James Baker did meet with Iraqi Foreign Minister Tariq Azziz in early January 1991, but Iraq refused to consider withdrawal from Kuwait unless the United States forced Israel to relinquish its occupied territories. Bush and Baker vetoed this linkage, as well as any Arab solution whereby Iraq would retain parts of Kuwait. Iraq's aggression, which the president likened to Adolf Hitler's, should gain no reward.

Although Bush claimed he had the constitutional authority to order U.S. troops into combat under the UN resolution, he reluctantly requested congressional authorization, which was followed by a four-day debate. Senator Joseph R. Biden of Delaware declared that "none [of Iraq's] actions justify the deaths of our sons and daughters." Senator George Mitchell of Maine cited the risks: "An unknown number of casualties and deaths, billions of dollars spent, a greatly disrupted oil supply and oil price increases, a war possibly widened to Israel, Turkey or other allies, the possible long-term American occupation of Iraq, increased instability in the Persian Gulf region, long-lasting Arab enmity against the United States, a possible return to isolationism at home." Senator Robert Dole of Kansas scorned the critics, saying that Saddam Hussein "may think he's going to be rescued, maybe by Congress." On 12 January, after Congress defeated a resolution to continue sanctions, a majority in both houses approved Bush's request to use force under UN auspices. Virtually every Republican voted for war; two-thirds of House Democrats and forty-five of fifty-six Democratic senators cast negative votes. Those few Democratic senators voting for war (among them Tennessee's Al Gore and Joseph Lieberman of Connecticut) provided the necessary margin.

Operation Desert Storm began with a spectacular aerial bombardment of Iraq and Kuwait on 16 January 1991. For five weeks satellite television coverage via Cable News Network enabled Americans to watch "smart" bombs hitting Iraqi targets and U.S. Patriot missiles intercepting Iraqi Scud missiles. President Bush and Secretary Baker kept the coalition intact, persuading Israel not to retaliate after Iraqi Scud missile attacks on its territory and keeping Soviet Premier Mikhail Gorbachev advised as allied bombs devastated Russia's erstwhile client. On 24 February General Schwarzkopf sent hundreds of thousands of allied troops into Kuwait and eastern Iraq. Notwithstanding Saddam's warning that Americans would sustain thousands of casualties in the "mother of all battles," Iraq's largely conscript army put up little resistance. By 26 February Iraqi forces had retreated from Kuwait, blowing up as many as 800 oil wells as they did so. Allied aircraft flew hundreds of sorties against what became known as the "highway of death," from Kuwait City to Basra. After only 100 hours of fighting on the ground, Iraq accepted a UN-imposed cease-fire. Iraq's military casualties numbered more than 25,000 dead and 300,000 wounded; U.S. forces suffered only 148 battle deaths (35 from friendly fire), 145 nonbattle deaths, and 467 wounded (out of a coalition total of 240 dead and 776 wounded). An exultant President Bush proclaimed, "By God, we've kicked the Vietnam syndrome."

The war itself initially cost $1 million per day for the first three months, not including the ongoing expense of keeping an encampment of 300,000 allied troops in Saudi Arabia, Iraq, and Kuwait. The overall cost of the war was estimated to be $54 billion; $7.3 billion paid by the United States, with another $11 billion from Germany and $13 billion from Japan, and the remainder ($23 billion) from Arab nations. For the first time in the twentieth century, the United States could not afford to finance its own participation in a war.

Bush chose not to send U.S. forces to Baghdad to capture Saddam Hussein, despite his earlier designation of the Iraqi leader as public enemy number one. Attempts during the fighting to target Saddam had failed, and Bush undoubtedly hoped that the Iraqi military or disgruntled associates in the Ba'ath party would oust the Iraqi leader. When Kurds in northern Iraq and Shi'ites in the south rebelled, Bush did little to help. As General Powell stated: "If you want to go in and stop the killing of Shi'ites, that's a mission I understand. But to what purpose? If the Shi'ites continue to rise up, do we then support them for the overthrow of Baghdad and the partition of the country?" Powell opposed "trying to sort out two thousand years of Mesopotamian history." Bush, ever wary of a Mideast quagmire, backed away: "We are not going to permit this to drag on in terms of significant U.S. presence à la Korea." Saddam used his remaining tanks and helicopters to crush these domestic rebellions, sending streams of Kurdish refugees fleeing toward the Turkish border. Public pressure persuaded President Bush to send thousands of U.S. troops to northern Iraq, where the UN designated a security zone and set up makeshift tent cities. Saddam's survival left a sour taste in Washington, and created a situation that Lawrence Freedman and Efraim Karsh have compared to "an exasperating endgame in chess, when the winning player never seems to trap the other's king even though the final result is inevitable."

Under Security Council Resolution 687, Iraq had to accept the inviolability of the boundary with Kuwait (to be demarcated by an international commission), accept the presence of UN peacekeepers on its borders, disclose all chemical, biological, and nuclear weapons including missiles, and cooperate in their destruction. What allied bombs had missed, UN inspectors did not. Saddam Hussein's scientists and engineers had built more than twenty nuclear facilities linked to a large-scale Iraqi Manhattan Project. Air attacks had only inconvenienced efforts to build a bomb. Inspectors also found and destroyed more than a hundred Scud missiles, seventy tons of nerve gas, and 400 tons of mustard gas. By the fall of 1992 the head of the UN inspection team rated Iraq's capacity for mass destruction "at zero."

Results from the war included the restoration of Kuwait, lower oil prices, resumption of peace negotiations between Israel and the Arabs, and at least a temporary revival of faith in the United Nations. Improved relations with Iran and Syria brought an end to Western hostage-taking in Beirut. Firefighters extinguished the last of the blazing oil wells ignited by the retreating Iraqis in November 1991, but only after the suffocating smoke had spread across an area twice the size of Alaska and caused long-term environmental damage. An estimated 200,000 civilians died, largely from disease and malnutrition. Millions of barrels of oil befouled the Persian Gulf, killing more than 30,000 sea birds. Finally, an undetermined but large and growing number of U.S. veterans of the Persian Gulf War found themselves plagued with various medical conditions, referred to as "Gulf War Syndrome" and thought to be the result of exposure to various toxic gases and radioactive exposure from ammunition.

BIBLIOGRAPHY

DeCosse, David E., ed. *But Was It Just?: Reflections on the Morality of the Persian Gulf War.* New York: Doubleday, 1992.

Ederton, L. Benjamin and Michael J. Mazarr, eds. *Turning Point: the Gulf War and U.S. Military Strategy*. Boulder, Colo.: Westview Press, 1994.

El-Baz, Farouk, and R. M. Makharita, eds. *The Gulf War and the Environment*. New York: Gordon and Breach Science Publishers, 1994.

Greenberg, Bradley S., and Walter Gantz, eds. *Desert Storm and the Mass Media*. Cresskill, N.J.: Hampton Press, 1993.

Head, William Head, and Earl H. Tilford, Jr., eds. *The Eagle in the Desert: Looking Back on U.S. Involvement in the Persian Gulf War*. Westport, Conn.: Praeger, 1996.

Ursano, Robert J., and Ann E. Norwood, eds. *Emotional Aftermath of the Persian Gulf War: Veterans, Families, Communities, and Nations*. Washington, D.C.: American Psychiatric Press, 1996.

J. Garry Clifford/D. B.

See also **Air Pollution; Arab Nations, Relations with; Iraqgate; Oil Crises; Persian Gulf Syndrome; United Nations; War Casualties; War Costs;** *and vol. 9:* **Address to the Nation: Allied Military Action in the Persian Gulf; Gulf War Letter; Gulf War Story.**

PERSONAL ADS, solicitations for employment, financial assistance, friendship, romance, or lost family members, debuted in American newspapers by the late eighteenth century. The use of personal ads increased in the nineteenth century as populations became more migratory. The *Boston Pilot* carried advertisements from Irish immigrants seeking elusive family members, while in other papers a westward-bound man might solicit a wife with means. Personal ads reveal much about the mores and styles of their journals' readers, from the freewheeling sexual revelations of the *Village Voice* to the bourgeois aspirations and preoccupations of more recent personal columns in the *New York Times*. Since the personal computer revolution, personals have proliferated in various formats on the Internet.

BIBLIOGRAPHY

Harkison, Judy. "'A Chorus of Groans,' Notes Sherlock Holmes." *Smithsonian*, 18, no. 6 (September 1987): 196.

Mott, Frank Luther. *American Journalism: A History, 1690–1960*. 3d ed., New York: Macmillan, 1962.

John J. Byrne
Mina Carson

PERSONAL LIBERTY LAWS. Federal laws of 1793 and 1850 allowed for the arrest and removal of alleged fugitive slaves with only minimal evidence presented by the master or master's agent claiming a person as a fugitive. Many northern states adopted various laws, generally known as "personal liberty laws," that were designed to prevent the kidnapping of free blacks as well as to provide a fair process for the return of actual fugitives. The kidnapping of a number of free black children in Philadelphia, some of whom were never returned to their families, led to the passage of Pennsylvania's 1826 law. Most of the early state laws required clearer evidence that the person arrested was actually a fugitive slave. The laws also gave alleged fugitives greater procedural rights. Pennsylvania's law of 1826, for example, required that anyone removing a black from the state as a fugitive slave first obtain a certificate of removal from a state judge, justice of the peace, or alderman. Other laws, like Vermont's act of 1840, specifically guaranteed that an alleged fugitive be given a jury trial. While these laws provided protection for free blacks and procedural rights for actual fugitives, they also contained language and provisions that allowed claimants to turn to the states for enforcement of the fugitive slave law. Under these laws, for example, state officials could issue arrest warrants for fugitives and incarcerate them during a trial to determine their status.

In *Prigg v. Commonwealth of Pennsylvania* (1842), Justice Joseph Story of the U.S. Supreme Court found unconstitutional any state laws that slowed down the removal process or in any way interfered with the return of fugitive slaves. Story asserted:

> We have not the slightest hesitation in holding, that, under and in virtue of the Constitution, the owner of a slave is clothed with entire authority, in every state in the Union, to seize and recapture his slave, whenever he can do it without any breach of the peace, or any illegal violence. In this sense, and to this extent this clause of the Constitution may properly be said to execute itself; and to require no aid from legislation, state or national.

Following this decision, some northern states adopted new personal liberty laws, withdrawing all of their support for the enforcement of the Fugitive Slave Laws. Under these laws, state officers were prohibited from helping to enforce the law, and state facilities, such as jails, were closed to slave catchers.

Partially in response to these new personal liberty laws, Congress passed the Fugitive Slave Law of 1850. This law created a mechanism for national enforcement, including, if necessary, the use of U.S. marshals, state militias, and federal troops to return fugitive slaves to their masters. At least nine states responded to this law with new personal liberty laws, closing state facilities to slave catchers and denying any state or local support for the return of fugitive slaves. These laws helped undermine the effectiveness of the new law.

BIBLIOGRAPHY

Morris, Thomas D. *Free Men All: The Personal Liberty Laws of the North, 1780–1861*. Baltimore: Johns Hopkins University Press, 1974.

Paul Finkelman

See also **Fugitive Slave Acts.**

PERSONNEL ADMINISTRATOR OF MASSACHUSETTS V. FEENEY, 442 U.S. 256 (1979), a Supreme Court case that considered whether a Massachusetts law giving veterans a lifetime preference in filling open civil service positions discriminated against women in violation of the equal protection clause of the Fourteenth Amendment. Helen B. Feeney was a civil servant who received higher grades on civil service examinations than male veterans. Because of the preference law, however, males repeatedly were promoted over her. Twice the federal district court declared the law unconstitutional. The state of Massachusetts, supported by the solicitor general of the United States, appealed to the Supreme Court. The Court in a seven-to-two decision sustained the law.

A basic question was whether the effect of the preference classification was "purposeful discrimination." It was generally agreed that the statute disproportionately affected women. Until 1967 there had been a 2 percent quota on women in the military. Male nonveterans, however, suffered from this preferred treatment as much as female nonveterans. Because it distinguished between veterans and nonveterans, not between women and men, the Court detected no discriminatory purpose in the statute. The opinion raised the standard for proving gender discrimination by obliging plantiffs to prove that the legislature that drafted the statute in question specifically intended the law to achieve the foreseeable discriminatory outcome.

BIBLIOGRAPHY

Hoff, Joan. *Law, Gender, and Injustice: A Legal History of U.S. Women.* New York: New York University Press, 1991.

Rosenblum, Bruce E. "Discriminatory Purpose and Disproportionate Impact: An Assessment after *Feeney.*" *Columbia Law Review* 79 (November 1979).

Tony Freyer/A. R.

See also **Civil Service; Equal Protection of the Law; Discrimination: Sex; Women in Military Service; Women's Rights Movement: The Twentieth Century.**

PESTICIDES. *See* **Insecticides and Herbicides.**

PET BANKS. An attempt by President Andrew Jackson to eliminate the Bank of the United States resulted in the rise of seven "pet banks," state banks that received deposits of federal money on 1 October 1833. Use of the pet banks contributed to a national financial panic that year. By the end of 1836, there were ninety-one of these "pet banks," so called by those opposing Jackson's fiscal policy. These banks issued notes far in excess of their ability to cover them with gold and silver coin, and many of the notes were issued for highly speculative ventures, particularly in stocks and land.

BIBLIOGRAPHY

Hammond, Bray. *Banks and Politics in America, from the Revolution to the Civil War.* Princeton, N.J.: Princeton University Press, 1957.

Remini, Robert. *Andrew Jackson.* New York: Twayne, 1966.

T. L. Livermore
Terri Livermore

See also **Bank of the United States.**

"PETER PRINCIPLE" is an idea first formulated by Canadian author Laurence J. Peter (1919–1990) in his best-selling book *The Peter Principle: Why Things Always Go Wrong* (1969). The central thesis of Peter's satirical commentary on business bureaucracies is that "in a hierarchy, every employee tends to rise to his level of incompetence." According to Peter, work is accomplished only by those employees who have not yet reached their level of incompetence. In this way, organizations and businesses can still function. The result is that stagnant companies are more likely to have incompetent employees at many levels of their organization, whereas growing companies who add new positions and employees can forestall the Peter Principle as long as growth continues.

BIBLIOGRAPHY

Peter, Laurence J., and Raymond Hull. *The Peter Principle: Why Things Always Go Wrong.* New York: Buccaneer Books, 1996.

Meg Greene Malvasi

PETERSBURG, SIEGE OF (1864–1865). Repulsed by the Confederate forces of Gen. Robert E. Lee at Cold Harbor (3 June 1864), Gen. Ulysses S. Grant decided to approach Richmond, Va., from the south, through Petersburg. Crossing the James River at Wyanoke Neck on 14 June, his leading corps attacked Petersburg on 15 June. After three days of fighting, the federal troops captured the eastern defenses. Lee's army then arrived, occupied a shorter line nearer the city, and turned away the last assaults.

While waging siege operations on the eastern front, Grant pushed his left flank southwestward to envelop Petersburg and cut the railways leading south. Defeated at the Battle of the Crater, 30 July, Union forces finally succeeded in cutting the Weldon Railroad in late August. In September Grant extended his right flank across the James and captured Fort Harrison, eight miles south of Richmond, compelling Lee to move much of his army north of the James. The Confederates retreated until Lee decisively halted Grant's advance on 27 October, and field operations virtually ceased during the winter.

Foreseeing that when spring came his attenuated line would be broken by superior numbers, Lee, on 25 March 1865, assaulted Fort Stedman. The attack failed and

Siege of Petersburg. From 15 June 1864 until 2 April 1865, Union troops laid siege to the city of Petersburg, Virginia, just to the south of the Confederate capital of Richmond. The city finally fell after the Union troops cut off the last railroad and won the final battle on 2 April, shown in this Currier and Ives print. LIBRARY OF CONGRESS

Grant countered on 29 March by sending Gen. Philip Sheridan, with heavy cavalry and infantry forces, to Dinwiddie Courthouse to destroy the Southside Railroad. Initially defeated on 31 March by divisions led by Gen. George Edward Pickett, Sheridan received reinforcements and on 1 April routed Pickett at Five Forks, rendering the railroad indefensible. Lee evacuated Petersburg and Richmond on 2 April and retreated westward.

BIBLIOGRAPHY

Davis, William C. *Death in the Trenches: Grant at Petersburg.* Alexandria, Va.: Time-Life Books, 1986.

Linderman, Gerald F. *Embattled Courage: The Experience of Combat in the American Civil War.* New York: Free Press, 1987.

Sommers, Richard J. *Richmond Redeemed: The Siege at Petersburg.* Garden City, N.Y.: Doubleday, 1981.

Joseph Mills Hanson / A. R.

See also **Civil War; Cold Harbor, Battle of; Richmond Campaigns.**

PETITION AND REMONSTRANCE OF NEW NETHERLAND, documents drawn up by a group of Dutch colonists to protest the government of that colony. In 1647, in order to induce the colonists to contribute to the expenses of the government, Peter Stuyvesant had permitted the election of a board known as the Nine Men. In spite of Stuyvesant's objections, in July 1649, this board penned two documents of protest to the home government. The petition was a short, concise statement of the condition of the province, with suggested remedies. The remonstrance was a long essay that gave in more detail and in historic perspective the facts and grievances upon which the petitioners based their appeal for changes. The colonists especially resented the autocratic proceedings and personal characters of the governor and his councillors. They questioned the expenditure of public funds and severely criticized the administration of justice. They asked for more farmers as colonists and for concessions in trading rights. Although the Amsterdam Chamber of the DUTCH WEST INDIA COMPANY granted a new charter with enlarged trading rights, the arbitrary powers of the governor remained untouched, and Stuyvesant continued his autocratic course until April 1652, when the Amsterdam Chamber instructed him to give NEW AMSTERDAM a "burgher government."

BIBLIOGRAPHY

Nooter, Eric, and Patricia U. Bonomi, eds. *Colonial Dutch Studies: An Interdisciplinary Approach.* New York: New York University Press, 1988.

Rink, Oliver A. *Holland on the Hudson: An Economic and Social History of Dutch New York*. Ithaca, N.Y.: Cornell University Press; Cooperstown: New York State Historical Association, 1986.

A. C. Flick/A. E.

See also **New Netherland.**

PETITION, RIGHT OF, is both a political ideal and a constitutional doctrine. As a political ideal it reflects the democratic notion that the officials of government must hear and respond to complaints brought by citizens. As a constitutional doctrine, it is enshrined in the text of the First Amendment, although it is not an absolute right.

Its English roots are in the ancient custom of subjects petitioning the king directly for redress for wrongs done either by officials or by other subjects. Magna Charta's article 16 (1215) required a form of petition, which influenced later imaginations, but that article was omitted from the final version of Magna Charta confirmed by Edward I in 1297. Even so, subjects continued to seek privileges and immunities from the Crown, petitioning the monarch directly. Many petitions were claims for property unlawfully held by the monarch, and royal ministers referred such claims by writ to various courts, usually the Exchequer. Parliament also petitioned the king, both for privileges for Parliament or its members and for royal policy in various matters. Most famously, the Petition of Right (1628) confirmed the freedoms of the subject from arbitrary arrest, trials by military commissions, and taxation by any but Parliament.

Parliament too was petitioned by individuals, as well as towns, grand juries, churches, and other entities. A Commonwealth statute (1648) proclaimed "it is the Right and Privilege of the Subjects of England, to present unto the Parliament their just Grievances, by Way of Petition, in a due Manner; and they shall be always ready to receive such Petitions."

Despite these assurances, both king and Parliament imprisoned inconvenient petitioners. Immunity to petition the king was confirmed by William and Mary's assent to the Declaration of Rights (1689). Parliament, however, was another matter, arresting petitioners from the grand jury of Kent in 1701 and prompting an outcry led by pamphleteer Daniel Dafoe. The Kentishmen were released, and throughout the 1700s, petitioning meetings and riots remained essentially immune from state interference.

Similarly, the English colonies in North America protected petitions. The Body of Liberties of the Massachusetts Bay Colony (1642) gave a universal liberty to " move any lawful, seasonable or material Question, or to present any necessary Motion, Complaint, Petition, Bill or Information" to any public meeting or court. Although the colony of New York prosecuted two petitioners, most colonies adopted liberties similar to those of Massachusetts, and much colonial legislation was passed in response to such petitions. Indeed, the American Declaration of Independence was drafted in the form of a petition, and one of its bases for independence was the claim that "We have Petitioned for Redress in the most humble terms: Our repeated Petitions have been answered only by repeated injury." Most of the first state constitutions contained a right to petition the government, although some qualified this right, requiring it to be exercised peaceably.

The failure of the Constitution of 1789 to provide a right of petition was one of the objections raised by Antifederalists. Following both debate and amendment of James Madison's draft clause, the third proposed article of amendment provided that "Congress shall make no law . . . abridging . . . the right of the people . . . to petition the Government for a redress of grievances." As ratified, this became and remains the sixth clause of the First Amendment.

The first test of the article followed adoption of the Alien and Sedition Acts (1798). Numerous petitions were presented to Congress, demanding their repeal. A New York assemblyman, Jedediah Peck, was arrested for sedition for acts including promoting such a petition. He was later released under popular pressure, and after the act expired in 1801, Thomas Jefferson's administration paid the fines of all arrested under them.

Although many petitions were brought to Congress in the nineteenth century, the right to petition first began to figure in the federal courts as a collateral element in litigation over other conduct. In *Crandall v. Nevada* (1867), the U.S. Supreme Court declared a right to interstate travel free of a travel tax, because travel was necessary to exercise the right to petition the federal government. In *United States v. Cruikshank* (1876), although the Court limited the application of a Reconstruction statute protecting assemblies, it did allow protection of assemblies for the purpose of petitioning, noting the "very idea of a government, republican in form, implies a right on the part of its citizens to meet peaceably for consultation in respect to public affairs and to petition for a redress of grievances."

In the twentieth century, however, the Court began to limit the right to petition. In *Thomas v. Collins* (1945), the Supreme Court held that the nature and scope of the freedom to petition was inseparable from the First Amendment freedoms of speech, press, and assembly. On this basis, the Court in 1961 limited protection for lawsuits or other petitions that might otherwise violate antitrust laws, holding in *Eastern Railroad Conference v. Noerr Motor Freight* that a petition that served an ulterior motive would be subject to antitrust limits. Similarly, in *McDonald v. Smith* (1985), the Court held that the limits on the exercise of the freedoms of speech, press, and assembly also apply to petitions; thus one who wrote to the president to complain of a candidate for executive appointment could still be sued for libel under the standards of *New York Times v. Sullivan* (1964). In the years since McDonald, many cases involving petitions—such as testimony before legislatures, writings to executives, and lawsuit complaints or testimony—have been considered by the Supreme Court to be exercises not of a right to petition but a right to free speech. Most cases since 1985 in which a right to petition has been argued have been decided by lower federal courts.

Despite such limits, the right of petition was a valuable tool in the struggle for the protection of civil rights in the 1960s. Courts protected not only marches and rallies but petition drives and voter registration programs as acts necessary to the petition of government.

In the twenty-first century, the right to petition is protected as a component of political expression, but the petition must be on a matter of public, not private or personal, concern. It is subject to federal and state laws protecting peace and order, as well as to reasonable, minimal restrictions of time, place, and manner, including requirements that the petition be written and not oral. Therefore, it also does not give a right to personally contact any given official. The employment of lobbyists is protected by the right; however, requirements that the lobbyists be registered do not violate the right. Petitions presented to the federal courts are subject to the rules of standing, in which the petitioner must prove personal harm from the issue petitioned.

Beyond the constitutional right as it is protected by the courts, the democratic ideal persists. Ideally any citizen or group of citizens may petition a legislature, executive, agency, or court, and all petitions must be heard and acted upon by officials without regard to the influence or wealth of their source.

BIBLIOGRAPHY

Higginson, Stephen A. "Note, A Short History of the Right to Petition Government for the Redress of Grievances." *Yale Law Journal* 96 (1986): 142.

Lawson, Gary, and Guy Seidman. "Downsizing the Right to Petition." *Northwestern University Law Review* 93 (1999): 739–767.

Mark, Gregory A. "The Vestigial Constitution: The History and Significance of the Right to Petition." *Fordham Law Review* 66 (1998): 2153–2232.

Pfander, James E. "Sovereign Immunity and the Right to Petition: Toward a First Amendment Right to Pursue Judicial Claims Against the Government." *Northwestern University Law Review* 91 (1997): 899–1014.

Smith, Norman B. "'Shall Make No Law Abridging . . .': An Analysis of the Neglected, But Nearly Absolute, Right of Petition." *University of Cincinnati Law Review* 54 (1986): 1153.

Steve Sheppard

See also **Bill of Rights in U.S. Constitution; Magna Carta.**

PETROCHEMICAL INDUSTRY. This industry and the products it makes play an enormous role in our daily lives. Imagine life without gasoline, cosmetics, fertilizers, detergents, synthetic fabrics, asphalt, and plastics. All of these products—and many more—are made from petrochemicals—chemicals derived from petroleum or natural gas.

Crude oil, or petroleum fresh out of the ground, has been used sporadically throughout history. Many hundreds of years ago, Native Americans used crude oil for fuel and medicine. But the start of the oil industry as it is known today can be traced back to 1859. In that year, retired railroad conductor Edwin L. Drake drilled a well near Titusville, Pennsylvania. The well, powered by an old steam engine, soon produced oil and sparked an oil boom. By the 1860s, wooden derricks covered the hills of western Pennsylvania. In 1865, the first successful oil pipeline was built from an oil field near Titusville to a railroad station five miles away. From there, railcars transported oil to refineries on the Atlantic coast.

The business of refining oil was largely the domain of John D. Rockefeller. The New York–born industrialist financed his first refinery in 1862. He then went on to buy out competitors, and, along with his brother, William, and several associates, he created Standard Oil Company. By 1878, Rockefeller controlled 90 percent of the oil refineries in the United States.

Drilling for oil quickly spread beyond Pennsylvania. By 1900, Texas, California, and Oklahoma had taken the lead in oil production, and eleven other states had active oil deposits. Annual U.S. oil production climbed from two thousand barrels in 1859 to 64 million barrels in 1900. Other countries were also getting into the oil business. Russia was producing slightly more than the United States around the beginning of the twentieth century. Smaller producers included Italy, Canada, Poland, Peru, Venezuela, Mexico, and Argentina. The first major oil discovery in the Middle East occurred in Iran in 1908. Prospectors struck oil in Iraq in 1927 and in Saudi Arabia in 1938.

The Petrochemical Industry Soars

Kerosene, a fuel for heating and cooking, was the primary product of the petroleum industry in the 1800s. Rockefeller and other refinery owners considered gasoline a useless byproduct of the distillation process. But all of that changed around 1900 when electric lights began to replace kerosene lamps, and automobiles came on the scene. New petroleum fuels were also needed to power the ships and airplanes used in World War I. After the war, an increasing number of farmers began to operate tractors and other equipment powered by oil. The growing demand for petrochemicals and the availability of petroleum and natural gas caused the industry to quickly expand in the 1920s and 1930s. Many chemical companies, including Dow and Monsanto, joined the industry. In 1925, annual crude oil production surpassed a billion barrels.

During World War II, vast amounts of oil were produced and made into fuels and lubricants. The United

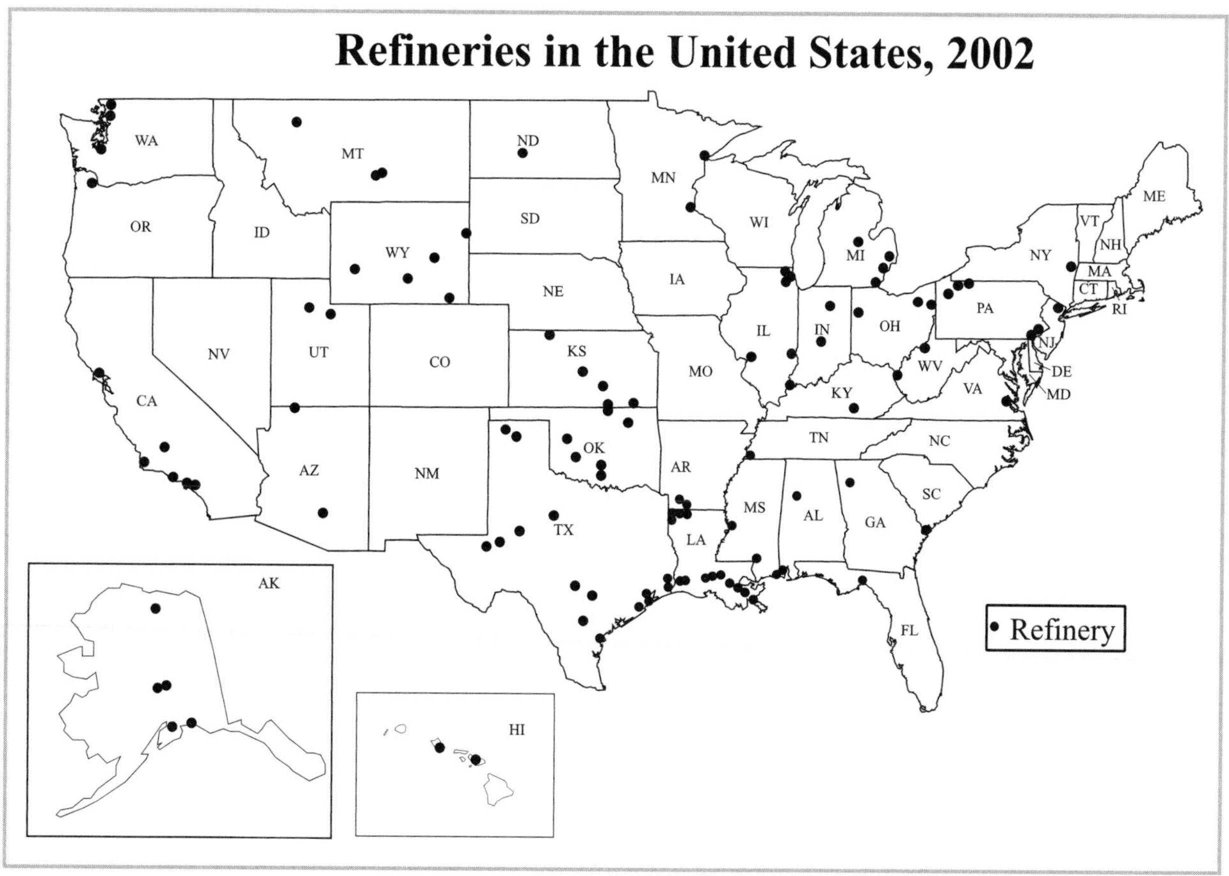

States supplied more than 80 percent of the aviation gasoline used by the Allies during the war. American oil refineries also manufactured synthetic rubber, toluene (an ingredient in TNT), medicinal oils, and other key military supplies.

Plastics: A Petrochemical Gold Mine

The demand for petroleum products became even greater after World War II. Petroleum use in the United States went from about 1.75 billion barrels in 1946 to almost 2.5 billion barrels in 1950. By the early 1950s, petroleum had replaced coal as the country's chief fuel. And plastic was the primary reason.

Originally, most plastics were made from the resins of plant matter. But it wasn't long before plastics were developed from petrochemicals. The packaging industry, the leading user of plastics, accounts for about one-third of total U.S. production. The building industry ranks second, which uses plastic to make insulation, molding, pipes, roofing, siding, and frames for doors and windows. Other industries, including automobile and truck manufacturing, also rely heavily on plastics.

The United States was hardly alone in its rising use of petroleum products. Throughout the world, increased industrialization and rapid population growth created new and greater demands for oil. By the late 1950s, petrochemicals became one of the largest industries, and control over the sources and transportation of oil became a major national and international political issue.

The Petrochemical Industry Slowdown

The environmental movement, spawned in the 1960s and 1970s, led Americans to be wary of industries that pollute—and the petrochemical industry was seen as a primary suspect. A backlash against the industry contributed to a slowdown. Around the same time, other events also led to lean times within the industry, including the buildup of European and Japanese petrochemical industries, a demand for natural gas that exceeded the supply, the 1979 OPEC (Organization of the Petroleum Exporting Countries) crisis, and an economic recession in the United States. These events led many chemical companies to abandon the petrochemical industry altogether.

Slowed but not stopped, the petrochemical industry in the 1980s and 1990s was largely restructured, as individual production plants were purchased or refinanced and chemical companies reformed. Major petrochemical companies, such as Shell and Mobil, became involved in mergers in an effort to strengthen their positions in the marketplace.

The Geography of Petrochemicals

By the last decade of the twentieth century, there were almost a million oil wells in more than one hundred countries producing more than 20 billion barrels per year. Most experts give Saudi Arabia credit for having the largest original oil endowment of any country, and the Middle East as a whole is believed to have about 41 percent of the world's total oil reserve. North America is a distant second. Because of the large deposits in Russia, Eastern Europe is also well endowed with oil. Most of Western Europe's oil lies below the North Sea. Many believe that an estimated 77 percent of the world's total recoverable oil has already been discovered. If so, the remaining 23 percent, mostly located in smaller fields or in more difficult environments, may be more expensive to find and to recover.

BIBLIOGRAPHY

Burdick, Donald L., and William L. Leffler. *Petrochemicals in Nontechnical Language*. Tulsa, Okla.: PennWell, 2001.

Deffeyes, Kenneth S. *Hubbert's Peak: The Impending World Oil Shortage*. Princeton, N.J.: Princeton University Press, 2001.

Fenichell, Stephen. *Plastic: The Making of a Synthetic Century*. New York: HarperBusiness, 1996.

Garverick, Linda, ed. *Corrosion in the Petrochemical Industry*. Materials Park, Ohio: ASM International, 2000.

Henderson, Wayne, and Scott Benjamin. *Standard Oil: The First 125 Years*. Osceola, Wis.: Motorbooks International, 1996.

Meikle, Jeffrey L. *American Plastic: A Cultural History*. New Brunswick, N.J.: Rutgers University Press, 1997.

Spitz, Peter H. *Petrochemicals: The Rise Of An Industry*. Hoboken, N.J.: Wiley InterScience, 1988.

Lynda DeWitt

See also **Environmental Movement; Environmental Protection Agency; Kerosine Oil; Midcontinent Oil Region; Offshore Oil; Oil Crises; Oil Fields; Standard Oil Company; Wildcat Oil Drilling.**

PETROGRAPHY deals with the systematic description of rocks. The term is sometimes loosely used as synonymous with "petrology," which, being the broad science of rocks, is concerned not only with precise description but also with understanding the origin (petrogenesis), modification (metamorphism), and ultimate decay of rocks. Petrography as a science began with a technique invented in 1828 by the Scottish physicist William Nicolfor producing polarized light by cutting a crystal of Iceland spar (calcite) into a special prism, which is still known as the Nicol prism. The addition of two such prisms to the ordinary microscope converted the instrument into a polarizing, or petrographic, microscope. By means of transmitted light and Nicol prisms, it became possible to deduce the internal crystallographic character of even very tiny mineral grains, thereby greatly advancing the specific knowledge of a rock's constituents.

But it was a later development that truly laid the foundations of petrography. This was a technique, perfected in the late 1840s by Henry C. Sorby in England and others, whereby a slice of rock was affixed to a microscope slide and then ground so thin that light could be transmitted through mineral grains that otherwise appeared opaque. The position of adjoining grains was not disturbed, thus permitting analysis of rock texture. Thin-section petrography became the standard method of rock study—and since textural details contribute greatly to a knowledge of the sequence of crystallization of the various mineral constituents in a rock, petrography ranges into petrogenesis and thus into petrology.

It was in Europe, principally in Germany, that petrography burgeoned in the last half of the nineteenth century, and American geologists went to Germany for their introduction to this new science. For example, Florence Bascom, the first woman to be hired by the U.S. Geological Survey, studied with Victor Goldschmidt in Heidelberg, Germany, and returned to make major contributions to the nascent study of petrography in America. Her dissertation at Johns Hopkins, completed in 1893, showed that rocks previously thought of as sediments were actually metamorphosed lava flows. This period also coincided with the exploration of the western United States. Notable among the early surveys was the U.S. Geological Exploration of the fortieth parallel under the direction of Clarence King, who became the first director of the U.S. Geological Survey in 1878. The sixth volume of the report of the exploration, *Microscopical Petrography* (1876), was at King's invitation prepared by Ferdinand Zirkel of Leipzig, at the time acknowledged as one of the two leading petrographers in the world. This publication, in a sense, introduced petrography to the United States.

Subsequent monographs and other publications of the U.S. Geological Survey, as well as some of the state surveys, were replete with beautifully lithographed plates of distinctive rock types as seen in thin sections. Many of these became collector's items, for they are models of scientific accuracy and artistic merit. Many new and interesting rock types were discovered using petrographic methods, and because names of rocks commonly reflect the geography of a type of locality, some exotic names have resulted: for example, shonkinite, from the Shonkin Sag, Montana; ouachitite, from the Ouachita Mountains, Arkansas; and uncompahgrite, from Uncompahgre Peak, Colorado.

Descriptions of rocks are not confined to thin-section studies. One of the earliest members of the U.S. Geological Survey, George F. Becker, recognized that to understand rock minerals properly, it would be necessary to synthesize them from chemically pure components. This awareness led to the establishment of the Geophysical Laboratory of the Carnegie Institution in 1907, of which Arthur L. Day was first director. Chemical principles were applied in investigating sequences and stability ranges of rock minerals, and in parallel studies improved methods of accurate chemical analyses of rocks were developed. Working with colleagues at the Geological Survey, Henry S. Washington, a chemist at the Geophysical Laboratory, brought out *The Quantitative Classification of Igneous Rocks* in 1903, a work that had worldwide impact on petrography and petrology. This was followed in 1917 by *Chemical Analyses of Igneous Rocks,* U.S. Geological Survey Professional Paper 99, perhaps still the largest compendium of chemical analyses of rocks ever brought together. Each analysis, of which there are several thousand, was converted to the author's special classification—a classification still in use, along with the more conventional mineralogical and textural classifications.

Meantime, the physicochemical studies of rock-forming minerals at the laboratory were leading to new interpretations of the origin of rocks, culminating with *The Evolution of the Igneous Rocks* in 1928 by Norman L. Bowen—a publication that has perhaps had wider influence in petrology than any other emanating from America.

Until the 1920s, when the National Research Council first established a committee on sedimentation, petrographers were concerned chiefly with igneous and metamorphic rocks, for it was these two categories (sometimes grouped as the crystalline rocks) that contained the widest variety of minerals, presented the best-formed crystals, and occurred in the most interesting combinations. Sedimentary rocks, by contrast, appeared relatively uniform and monotonous. Recognition of the economic importance of sediments (especially for their hydrocarbon content) led to an upsurge in sedimentary petrography. Many new authoritative works were published dealing with the special types of petrographic investigations that are appropriate for sediments.

Some of the most exciting developments in petrography involve the sample of moon rocks collected by U.S. astronauts during the first moon mission in 1969. Never before had so many and such highly sophisticated methods of petrographic study been so thoroughly applied: X-ray studies of many kinds, electron microprobes, spectrographic and isotopic analyses, and a host of other advanced techniques, together with the classic petrographic studies. The studies are aided by the fact that since the moon is without atmosphere and apparently without water, moon rocks are not subject to the types of decay that affect most rocks on the earth's surface and tend to obscure thin-section observations and to contaminate (or at least render difficult) chemical studies. Petrographers may well look to the rock formations of the moon and other celestial bodies for new revelations in the field of microscopic petrography.

BIBLIOGRAPHY

Drake, Ellen T., and William M. Jordan, eds. *Geologists and Ideas: A History of North American Geology.* Boulder, Colo.: Geological Society of America, 1985.

Horowitz, Alan S. *Introductory Petrography of Fossils.* New York: Springer-Verlag, 1971.

Milner, Henry B. *Sedimentary Petrography.* New York: MacMillan, 1962.

Stanton, R. L. *Ore Petrology.* New York: McGraw-Hill, 1972.

Turner, Francis J. *Metamorphic Petrology.* New York: McGraw-Hill, 1981.

Williams, Howel, Francis J. Turner, and Charles M. Gilbert. *Petrography: An Introduction to the Study of Rocks in Thin Sections.* San Francisco: Freeman, 1982.

Ian Campbell/A. R.

See also **Geological Survey, U.S.; Geology; Moon Landing; Paleontology.**

PETROLEUM INDUSTRY. Petroleum, Latin for "rock oil," fuels 60 percent of all energy humans use. It also provides the raw material for synthetic cloth, plastics, paint, ink, tires, drugs and medicines, and many other products.

Crude oil can be separated into many different parts called fractions, each of which boils at a different temperature. As crude oil is boiled, the different fractions vaporize and rise to various levels of the distillation tower, also called a still. Thinner oils boil at lower temperatures and consequently reach the top of the tower before they condense. The heavier oils, which boil at higher temperatures, do not reach as high before condensing. The lightest vapors, from the thinnest oils, produce liquefied gases, propane and butane, and petrochemicals. Petrochemicals can be changed into a variety of products: plastics, clothes fabrics, paints, laundry detergent, food additives, lawn chemicals, and more than 6,000 other everyday products. The middle vapors result in gasoline, kerosene, and diesel fuel, as well as jet fuel (a form of kerosene). Next come the fractions that make home heating oil and fuel for ships and factories. The heaviest oil produces lubricating oil and grease, which can also be turned into items such as candle wax. At the very bottom of the distillation tower is the leftover sludge, also called bitumen, which is used in the asphalt that makes roads and roofing.

At the beginning of the twenty-first century, 1.5 million people in the United States were employed in the petroleum industry, which fueled 97 percent of American transportation. Oil provided 38 percent of the country's energy, while natural gas, which is either mixed with the crude oil or lying as a separate layer on top of it, accounted for 24 percent.

Petroleum's Commercial Beginnings

Although people knew of oil prior to 1850 and even had some uses for it, primarily as lamp fuel, it was not a sought-after commodity. Oil bubbled to the surface in "seeps," and several of these could be found along Oil Creek near Titusville, Pennsylvania. No one was able to collect enough oil to make it an economically sound venture. Titusville resident Joel Angier transacted the first petroleum lease in 1853 when he leased a portion of an Oil Creek seep from a local saw mill. Although Angier's collection, like those before him, was not economically viable, enough of his oil made it to commercial centers to pique interest in its use and begin theories regarding its extraction. Downstream, farmer Hamilton McClintock gathered enough oil from another seep to produce twenty or thirty forty-two-gallon barrels in a season. His was the largest oil operation of its day, and it set the standard for measurement of oil. Although forty-two-gallon barrels are no longer used, this is still the measurement used for oil production. McClintock fielded some interest from an investment group from New York and Connecticut, but his $7,000 asking price was deemed too exorbitant.

Another group, the Pennsylvania Rock Oil Company of New York, later renamed the Seneca Oil Company, purchased Angier's seep for $5,000. Company principals George H. Bissell and Jonathan G. Eveleth hired Benjamin Silliman Jr., a professor of chemistry at Yale, to analyze the crude oil from their seep. Silliman produced an 1855 report that determined crude oil could be separated into fractions, each with a use. His report emphasized that one of the fractions could be useful as a high-quality illuminant. This report enabled Bissell to get additional financing for his oil venture. The Seneca Oil Company hired Edwin Drake to extract the oil. His first attempt produced ten gallons of crude a day, which was not enough to provide a return on the investment. Drake attempted to increase production by opening more springs and trying to mine the oil, but neither met with success. He eventually settled on drilling. He hired salt well driller Billy Smith, who drilled to a depth of 69.5 feet on 27 August 1859. The next day Smith looked into the well and saw crude oil rising up in it. Reports claim this well's productivity ranged anywhere from ten to forty barrels per day, a minimum of a 400-fold increase in production. This discovery of a method for extracting larger quantities of oil generated the first oil boom. People inundated Pennsylvania, leasing the flats around Oil Creek. By 1861, the commonwealth's wells were producing more than 2 million barrels annually, accounting for half the world's oil production.

Oil Refinery. Early cracking stills—distillation towers with heat added for better and more fine-tuned production of different petroleum products—at a Sinclair facility. © BETTMANN/CORBIS

Birth of the Modern Oil Industry

In 1900, worldwide crude oil production stood at nearly 150 million barrels. Illuminants served as the primary product of the oil industry, but new inventions such as the automobile and the airplane used petroleum as fuel. Gasoline was also used as an industrial solvent. Initially a barrel of oil yielded eleven gallons of gasoline. Refining began in 1850, when James Young of England patented the first oil refining process. Samuel Kier founded the first commercial refining process in the United States in the 1860s. In 1913, refineries achieved their first major technological breakthrough, adding heat to the oil molecules, thereby "cracking" heavier molecules of hydrocarbons into lighter molecules. By the 1960s, a barrel of oil yielded more than 21 gallons of gasoline, nearly double the production of the first two decades of the twentieth century. Catalytic cracking in 1936 produced a higher octane fuel as well as the lighter gases that provided the first step in producing five major products: synthetic rubber, plastics, textiles, detergents, and agricultural chemicals.

While Pennsylvania was initially the biggest oil producing state, that didn't stop people from hunting elsewhere. Independent oil prospectors, known as wildcatters, as well as oil companies, discovered oil in Ohio, Indiana, Illinois, Oklahoma, Kansas, California, and Texas. Often oil was discovered by people drilling for water, as happened with the Corsicana field in Texas. Pennsylvania oilman John Galey and his partner, James Guffy, came to Texas at the behest of Anthony Lucas, an engineer and salt miner working for Patillo Higgins, who believed oil could be found under salt domes. In particular, Higgins was eyeing Spindletop, a hill whose elevation had increased over the centuries as the salt continued to rise under the surface. Galey had drilled to 1,020 feet by 10 January 1901. When the drill was pulled out to change equipment, mud began to bubble up the hole, and the drill pipe was shoved out of the hole with tremendous force. Mud followed by natural gas followed by oil shot out of the ground to a height of more than 150 feet, the first "gusher" experienced by the oil industry. The Lucas gusher produced at an initial rate of 100,000 barrels per day, more than all the other producing wells in the United States combined. In a matter of months the population of nearby Beaumont, Texas, swelled five times, to 50,000 residents, and more than 100 different oil companies put wells on Spindletop. The find was instrumental in creating several large oil companies such as Gulf, Amoco, and Humble, which became part of Standard Oil. It also gave rise to a new drilling technique, since drilling through several hundred feet of sand had proved problematical. Driller Curt Hamill pumped mud rather than water down the drill hole to keep the rotary drill bit cool and to flush out the cuttings. The mud stuck to the sides of the hole and prevented the sand from caving. Since then, mud has been used in almost every drill hole around the world.

While companies retrieved $50 million in oil from the salt dome, they had invested $80 million. Consequently, the site was familiarly known as "Swindletop." It served to usher in the modern age of oil, causing the industry to realize that tremendous potential existed for the vast amounts of this natural resource that had barely been tapped. It became the fuel of choice for transportation, everything from ships and trains to cars and planes. Worldwide oil production in 1925 stood at 1 billion barrels and doubled fifteen years later.

Transportation of Oil

Horses served as the primary means of transporting machinery to the oil field, as well as carrying the product to refineries, in the early Pennsylvania oil fields. By 1865 horses had been supplanted by the newly completed rail line, and tank cars, originally two open tubs, were developed for rail transport. The first pipeline was developed in 1863, when Samuel Van Syckle pumped crude through five miles of a two-inch pipe from the Pithole field in western Pennsylvania to a railroad terminal. In the 1870s a six-inch pipeline ran from oil fields to Williamsport, Pennsylvania, 130 miles away. Ten years later pipelines ran from Pennsylvania to Cleveland, Buffalo, and New York City. At the end of the twentieth century, the United States had over 1 million miles of oil pipeline in use. Most pipelines were buried, with the exception to the 800-mile trans-Alaska pipeline, built partially above ground in the 1970s to prevent damaging the fragile permafrost.

The California oil boom in the 1920s gave rise to yet another industry, that of the oil tanker. Removed from the industrial centers in the East, California looked overseas for its market. The first tanker, the *George Loomis*, took its maiden voyage in 1896. From that beginning, petroleum and petroleum products now account for nearly half the world's seaborne trade. The materials are hauled on supertankers, the largest ships ever built, a quarter mile long and half a million tons in weight, shipping 1 million barrels of oil.

The Politics of Oil

Attempts to control the oil industry began as early as the 1870s, when the newly-formed Standard Oil Company, established by brothers John D. and William Rockefeller, sought to gain a monopoly in the industry. They made generous profit offers to companies that merged with them and threatened those that didn't. Early success was recognized in the rapid rise of Standard Oil's market share, from 10 percent in 1872 to 95 percent by 1880, but Standard Oil couldn't control the rapid pace of discovery and development of new fields over the next two decades. By the time the U.S. Supreme Court dissolved the Standard Oil Company into 34 separate companies for violating the Sherman Antitrust Act of 1911, Standard's market share had dropped to 65 percent.

By 1925 the United States was supplying 71 percent of the world's oil. Increased production in Oklahoma and East Texas in the wake of the Great Depression, between 1929 and 1932, caused an oil glut, dropping the price of oil to a low of 10 cents per barrel. This resulted in the Interstate Oil Compact of 1935, followed by the Connally "Hot Oil" Act, which prohibited interstate shipment of oil produced in violation of state conservation laws. The intent was to coordinate the conservation of crude oil production in the United States, and was the first attempt by the federal government to control the supply and demand of the industry. The government stepped in again in 1942, rationing civilian petroleum supplies during World War II. In 1945, the last year of the war, one-third of domestically produced petroleum was going to the war effort.

Continual expansion of offshore drilling gave rise to the 1953 U.S. Submerged Lands Act, which determined that the federal government's ownership of land extends three miles from the coastline. That same year Congress passed the Outer Continental Shelf Lands Act, which provided federal jurisdiction over the shelf and authorized the secretary of the interior to lease those lands for mineral development.

Domestic production of crude oil doubled after the war, but demand tripled. The United States accounted for over half the world's oil production in 1950, but Americans were also using all they produced and more, for the first time becoming a net importer of oil. Thirty years previously the United States had imported only 2 percent of its total petroleum. Now imports accounted for 17 percent of the total. Thirty years after that, in 1980, the United States was importing 45 percent of its petroleum. By 2002 the United States was importing 56 percent of its petroleum, and that figure was projected to grow to 65 percent by the year 2020.

Government regulation of the oil industry reached a pinnacle of invasiveness in the 1970s, as the government sought to reduce import dependency, encourage domestic production, and stabilize prices. These actions were largely a result of an embargo of oil exports by the Persian Gulf nations of the Middle East. Reacting to the United States' support for Israel in the 1973 Arab-Israeli war, the

Organization of Petroleum Exporting Countries (OPEC) nations withheld their oil exports, driving the cost of petroleum from $5 per barrel in the late 1960s to $35per barrel in 1981.

At the same time, domestic oil production declined from 9.6 million barrels a day in 1970 to 8.6 million barrels in 1980. To address the demand and supply issue, President Richard Nixon created what amounted to a paradoxical energy policy: to restrict imports and reduce reliance on foreign oil, while at the same time encouraging imports to protect domestic reserves and encourage lower prices for domestic use. He first imposed price controls on oil in 1971 and then, two years later, abolished the import quotas established twenty years earlier by the Eisenhower administration. Nixon's 1973 "Project Independence" was a plan to make the United States self-sufficient in oil by 1985 by increasing domestic supplies, developing alternative energy sources, and conserving resources. His successor, Gerald Ford, continued a program to reduce reliance on foreign oil through reduction of demand and increased domestic production. Ford focused on transporting oil from Alaska and leasing the outer continental shelf for drilling. He also established the Strategic Petroleum Reserve, a federal storage of oil. By 2002 the reserve stood at 578 million barrels of crude, equal to a fifty-three-day supply of imports. President Jimmy Carter created a National Energy Plan in 1977. He wanted to increase taxes to reduce demand, impose price controls, and shift consumption from imported to domestic sources. He also wanted to direct the nation toward nuclear energy. Despite the attempts of three administrations to reduce national dependence on foreign oil, all of these policies had little impact on oil imports. American imports from OPEC continued to increase throughout the 1970s. By the beginning of the twenty-first century OPEC provided 42 percent of the United States' imported oil and 24 percent of the total oil used in the United States. The 1979 revolution in Iran curtailed U.S. supply from that country and drove prices to unprecedented levels for three years. The Iranian political situation eventually stabilized by 1982, and the oil crisis abated for the first time in over a decade.

The American political policy toward oil under presidents Ronald Reagan and George H. W. Bush adhered to a free-market philosophy. Reagan abandoned conservation and alternative energy initiatives and deregulated oil prices, policies continued by Bush. One result of these policies was an increase in imports from the Middle East, and by 1990 the Persian Gulf states were supplying 600 million of America's 2.2 billion imported barrels annually. President Reagan also signed Proclamation 5030 in 1983, establishing the "U.S. exclusive economic zone," claiming U.S. rights 200 nautical miles off national coastlines, in an effort to expand the search for oil.

A rift in OPEC in the mid-1980s over market share helped cause a collapse of oil prices. Prices plummeted to as low as $10 per barrel, down from a high of $31. While a boon for consumers, this caused a severe recession in regions of the United States where much of the industry revolved around petroleum. In 1983 Texas, Alaska, Louisiana, and California accounted for three quarters of domestic oil production. Along with Oklahoma, these states are still the top oil producers in the nation.

The George H. W. Bush administration developed a comprehensive national energy policy when the Gulf War of 1991 caused concern over the security of the long-term oil supply. However, the legislation passed by Congress in 1992 did not really address oil and gas, focusing instead on electric utility reform, nuclear power, and increased funding for research and development of alternative fuels. During the 1990s the Clinton administration generally adopted a "status quo" approach to energy, with some exceptions. Clinton suggested the use of tax incentives to spur conservation and alternative fuels, while also encouraging modest tax breaks to increase domestic production. Clinton tightened pollution-reducing regulations on the petroleum industry. Additionally, he closed off several areas of the United States to oil production, supported the ban on drilling in the Arctic National Wildlife Refuge (ANWR), and signed the Kyoto Protocol, a worldwide attempt to limit the production of greenhouse gases. In contrast to the Clinton administration, Congress sought to end restrictions on Alaska North Slope exports and the lift the ban on drilling in the ANWR. Toward the same end, Congress also implemented royalty relief for projects in the Gulf of Mexico. Royalty relief was intended to provide incentives for development, production increases, and the encouragement of marginal production. Deepwater Gulf drilling leases more than tripled between 1995 and 1997.

In 2000 the George W. Bush administration indicated a shift in U.S. energy policy. Like those before him, Bush intended to increase domestic production and decrease consumption. His conservation program proposed to study options for greater fuel efficiency from automobiles and create tax incentives for purchasing hybrid cars that run on gas and electricity. More significantly, to increase production, Bush wanted to review, with the objective of easing, pollution control regulations that may adversely impact the distribution of gasoline. He was seeking to open the ANWR to drilling, despite the Senate's rejection of such drilling in April 2002. Incidents such as the 1989 spill by the *Exxon Valdez*, which ran aground on Bligh Reef off the Alaskan shore, and the intent to drill in the ANWR brought opposition to the continued search for oil. The *Exxon Valdez* spilled 10.8 million gallons of oil into Prince William Sound in Alaska, contaminating 1,500 miles of coastline—the largest oil spill in North America.

Demand and Supply

Despite the conservation efforts of repeated administrations, national demand for petroleum products continued to increase. As the twenty-first century began, the United

States was using 19.5 million barrels of petroleum per day—an average of three gallons per person. This usage rate meant America's entire production of oil comprised only half its total consumption. The other 50 percent came from all over the globe, half of it from other nations in the Western hemisphere, 21 percent of it from the Middle East, 18 percent from Africa, and the rest from elsewhere. Canada is the United States' largest supplier, followed in order by Saudi Arabia, Venezuela, and Mexico. The United States uses more than one-quarter of the world's oil production each year. Initially, when oil was extracted and refined for widespread commercial use in the United States in the 1860s, national oil reserves increased as new fields were discovered and better techniques for extracting and refining the oil were implemented. However, the amount of available reserves plateaued in the 1960s and a decline began in 1968. The discoveries in Alaska temporarily alleviated the decline, but the daily output continued to drop from 9.6 million barrels daily in 1970 to nearly 6 million barrels per day in 2002.

The hunt for oil continues. While Drake's original well came in at 69.5 feet, current U.S. holes are on average one mile deep, and at least one is seven miles in depth. Once natural pressure quits forcing the flow of oil up the well, an assembly of pipes and valves called a Christmas tree is used to pump additional oil out. Carbon dioxide and other gases, water or chemicals are injected into the well to maintain pressure and increase production. U.S. fields are among the world's oldest continually producing fields. By 2002, the Earth had yielded 160 billion barrels of oil, with an estimated 330 billion barrels left in the ground. Some estimates suggest that at current production rates the world's proven oil reserves will last until 2050.

BIBLIOGRAPHY

Ball, Max W. *This Fascinating Oil Business.* Indianapolis: Bobbs-Merrill, 1965.

Conoway, Charles F. *The Petroleum Industry: A Non-Technical Guide.* Tulsa, Okla.: PennWell, 1999.

Deffeyes, Kenneth S. *Hubbert's Peak: The Impending World Oil Shortage.* Princeton: Princeton University Press, 2001.

Doran, Charles F. *Myth, Oil, and Politics: Introduction to the Political Economy of Petroleum.* New York: Free Press, 1977.

Economides, Michael, and Oligney, Ronald. *The Color of Oil: The History, the Money, and the Politics of the World's Biggest Business.* Katy, Texas: Round Oak Publishing Company, 2000.

Levy, Walter J. *Oil Strategy and Politics, 1941–1981.* Boulder, Colorado: Westview Press, 1982.

Yergin, Daniel. *The Prize: The Epic Quest for Oil, Money, and Power.* New York: Simon and Schuster, 1991.

T. L. Livermore
Terri Livermore
Michael Valdez

See also **Energy Industry; Energy, Renewable; Kerosine Oil; Petrochemical Industry; Petroleum Prospecting and Technology; Standard Oil Company.**

PETROLEUM PROSPECTING AND TECHNOLOGY. Residents of North America knew what oil was and where to find it long before they had enough uses to make extracting it a viable concern. Evidence suggests Native Americans and early European settlers skimmed oil seeps, where oil surfaces of its own accord, and used the viscous liquid for medicinal purposes as a purge and balm, for lamp fuel, and for machinery lubrication. Spanish explorers used it to waterproof their boats and boots.

Not until 1859, near Titusville, Pennsylvania, did oil extraction become economically feasible, launching an industrial explosion. Area residents already knew how to collect oil from a seep by damming the nearby stream and skimming the resulting pool. The largest operation produced twenty to thirty barrels of oil in a season, not enough to be cost effective.

Principals of the Seneca Oil Company believed that oil, if extracted in enough quantity, could be sold primarily as a high-quality illuminant. Edwin Drake, hired by Seneca to extract the oil, borrowed the concept of drilling from salt drillers. To get through the unconsolidated gravel in the flats around Oil Creek, he invented the drive pipe, made of cast iron with ten-foot joints that protected the upper hole as it was created. Tools could then be lowered through the pipe to work on the shale bedrock. Drake's well came in on 27 August 1859, and this discovery of the means by which to extract large quantities of oil touched off the first oil boom.

Through the latter half of the nineteenth century, the search for oil expanded. However, the primary method of finding oil required locating surface evidence, including oil seeps, paraffin dirt (soil with petroleum elements), and sulfurous gases. People drilling for salt and water also occasionally discovered oil.

Despite growth in the number of wells and some drilling enhancements, the oil industry did not really burgeon until the early 1900s. The invention of the automobile catapulted gasoline into the industry's leading seller. Ships and trains that had previously run on coal began to switch to oil. The Santa Fe Railroad went from one oil-driven locomotive in 1901 to 227 in 1904. Petroleum also served as the fuel source for airplanes. By then, many of the obvious oil locations had been drilled and finding oil had become more difficult. Oil prospectors had to develop prospecting methods beyond the obvious. At the turn of the century, Patillo Higgins was convinced that a salt dome, Spindletop, near Beaumont, Texas, harbored crude oil beneath it. Higgins' recognition that a specific geological structure may harbor oil was one of the first geologic contributions to prospecting. Higgins was proved correct about salt domes when Spindletop began producing oil in 1901 in what was then the single largest producing well. Despite his success, however, geology still played a limited role in petroleum prospecting. The first geologist was not hired by an oil company until 1911. It wasn't until 1913, when Charles Gould of the Oklahoma Geological Survey wrote a paper outlining the

Oil Rig. Shell Oil Company's thirty-one-story-high Mars rig—the deepest oil-producing platform in the world at the time, able to reach down more than three thousand feet—on 12 March 1996, before being towed from Ingleside, Texas, to the Gulf of Mexico 130 miles southeast of New Orleans. AP/ WIDE WORLD PHOTOS

relationship between rock structure and oil and gas, that petroleum prospecting began to really explore the uses of geology. By 1915 oil companies were hiring most of the geology graduates at the University of Oklahoma.

Geologists began determining likely deposit areas based on surface ground and underlying rock. The search for salt domes saw the introduction of the torsion balance, one of the earliest geophysical instruments used in petroleum prospecting. The torsion balance measures the density of rock beneath the earth's surface by measuring the gravitational field. The gravitational force varies according to differences in mass distribution at the earth's surface. Salt domes are associated with light gravity. The Nash Dome, in Brazoria County, Texas, discovered with a torsion balance in 1924, hosted the first oil uncovered by geophysical means. Pendulums were also used to record variations in the earth's gravity. Gravity meters superceded pendulums, although those were not very effective until the mid-1930s.

Geology is the driving force in petroleum prospecting. Geologists gather information above ground to determine what lies underneath. They look for evidence of source rock, reservoir rock, and structural traps. Oil typically exists in nonmagnetic rock, near salt, and in faults and folds in the earth's crust. Geologists trail magnetometers during aerial surveys to measure magnetism over a large area. Field balances are used in the surface to measure magnetism in a specific location. Geologists also use sophisticated equipment to send sound waves into the earth, analyzing the wave return to determine the type and depth of different rock layers. This allows them to locate the porous rock strata in which petroleum most likely resides. "Sniffers," high-tech devices that act like a "nose" are also used to detect traces of hydrocarbon gases that escape from below-surface oil deposits. To analyze the rock fragments brought to the surface with the mud during drilling, geologists create "mud logs."

Despite technological advances in prospecting, drilling is still the only method to confirm oil's existence. The search for oil is still speculative. Wells drilled more than a mile from existing production, known as wildcat wells, have a one in ten chance of success. Wells drilled in unproven frontiers, "rank wildcat wells," have a one in forty chance of success.

BIBLIOGRAPHY

Conoway, Charles F. *The Petroleum Industry: A Non-Technical Guide.* Tulsa, Okla.:PennWell, 1999.

Economides, Michael, and Oligney, Ronald. *The Color of Oil: The History, the Money, and the Politics of the World's Biggest Business.* Katy, Texas: Round Oak, 2000.

Owen, Edgar Wesley. *Trek of the Oil Finders: A History of Exploration for Petroleum.* Tulsa, Okla.: American Association of Petroleum Geologists, 1975.

Stoneley, Robert. *Introduction to Petroleum Exploration for Non-Geologists.* New York: Oxford University Press, 1995.

Terri Livermore
T. L. Livermore

See also **Energy Industry; Energy, Renewable; Kerosine Oil; Petrochemical Industry; Petroleum Industry.**

PEW MEMORIAL TRUST, the largest of the seven Pew Charitable Trusts, is a private general-purpose foundation created in 1948 by the family of the Sun Oil Company founder Joseph Newton Pew (1848–1912). Six additional trusts were created over the next three decades, all managed together with coordinated grant-making programs. Based in Philadelphia, the Pew Charitable Trusts are among the nation's top ten foundations, with assets around $5 billion and annual grants of over $200 million. The trusts' program areas include culture, education, environment, health issues, public policy, and religion, and each gives annually between $20 and $50 million.

In the early years the Pew Memorial Trust's most active voice was the donor and trustee J. Howard Pew (1882–1971). His political and economic convictions were based on the notion of the indivisibility of freedom, that political, religious, and "industrial freedom" were linked. Under his leadership the trusts supported a wide variety of conservative political and religious interests, including Billy Graham Crusades, the journal *Christianity Today,* and a number of Christian colleges and seminaries, including Grove City College in Grove City, Pennsylvania. It was also active in support of African American higher education. In the 1970s and 1980s the Pew Charitable Trusts began actively supporting conservative think tanks, such as the American Enterprise Institution, that contributed to the social and economic policies of the Reagan administration. It now supports a broad range of programs in education, the environment, health care, and religion.

BIBLIOGRAPHY

Pew Charitable Trusts. Home page at http://www.pewtrusts.com/.

Smith, James Allen. *The Idea Brokers: Think Tanks and the Rise of the New Policy Elite.* New York: Free Press, 1991.

Fred W. Beuttler

See also **Philanthropy.**

PEWTER. *See* **Metalwork.**

PHARMACEUTICAL INDUSTRY. Production of substances for the prevention or treatment of disease or other human ailments began in the American colonies as an unspecialized craft. By the mid-twentieth century, however, it was largely the province of a few specialized corporate enterprises that depended on a flow of creative product developments from well-financed research laboratories. In the colonial period, physicians of limited training and even the keepers of general stores often compounded and distributed medicinal materials, but by about 1800, pharmaceutical production and distribution began to emerge as a specialized area of commerce.

During the second half of the nineteenth century, the character of production of pharmaceutical preparations again changed substantially. The large military demand during the Civil War encouraged large-scale, specialized, and mechanized production. The rapid growth and dispersion of the population in the late 1800s stimulated further entry of manufacturers into the field, many of whom were trained pharmacists or physicians. Around 1900 many new substances joined the pharmacopoeia, which reflected the influence of scientific work. Leadership in both scientific and commercial development came from Germany, Switzerland, and France. In the early twentieth century, a few American companies introduced research facilities, but they enjoyed only limited success competing against German and Swiss companies.

The two world wars did much to change the character and role of the American industry. The large military market and American and Allied civilian markets, cut off from the German suppliers, became the domain of American companies. Moreover, American patents held by German firms became available to American companies. The new therapeutic approaches that emerged during the first third of the century, including the development of chemicals that specifically attack disease-causing agents without harming the human host and the identification of vitamins and hormones, changed the general character of the pharmacopoeia. One of the most important new developments, antibiotics, was the product of British research from the late 1920s to the early 1940s, but leading American companies introduced commercial production of the first antibiotic, penicillin, during World War II. After the war, the leading companies introduced a number of important new antibiotics, which helped to place the American industry in a position of international leadership in innovation and sales.

About two dozen corporations came to dominate the industry. The drug industry grew rapidly and began to produce a host of new products that were effective in the prevention, treatment, and eradication of many deadly diseases. Drug therapy became important, widespread, and generally cost effective. The drug industry in the late twentieth century was a large, highly profitable, socially important, and politically powerful entity. As a result of these successes and some widely publicized failures, drug company activities became highly politicized.

The largest and most sophisticated multinational drug companies combined research and development with an elaborate network for distribution of information and products. The industry became increasingly international. Worldwide production doubled between 1975 and 1990, reaching $150 billion. Market growth proved nearly as robust. Debate continued in the early twenty-first century about the extent and appropriateness of the high profits of the industry, which were well above the average for all manufacturing industries as well as for Fortune 500 companies.

By the end of the 1980s, public concern over the cost of health care and growing interest in health care reform had increased markedly. This concern politicized federal agency and industry decisions. Drugmakers typically offered price breaks to hospitals and health maintenance organizations, but pharmacists often faced huge markups. In the early 1990s, retail pharmacists and others brought price-discrimination suits against drug manufacturers. Analysts doubted the pharmacists would prevail in court because they suspected that the real intent behind such suits may have been to keep pressure on Washington to include some limits on differential pricing practices as part of health care reform.

Conservatives and industry spokespeople argued against government interference in the market, particularly through price controls. They claimed that without high profits, there would be little innovation. Liberals and consumer advocates pointed to the monopoly benefits of patent protection, evidence of oligopolistic behavior, and extensive government subsidization of research costs to back their claims that there should be price controls or profit limits set by the government.

Pricing decisions have always taken place within the context of patent laws, and in industrial countries, patent protection usually lasts sixteen to twenty years from the date of application. During this period, the company has exclusive marketing rights. Once the patent expires, a drug is much less profitable. Even when prices are high, companies may claim products are cost-effective by pointing to the cost of alternative methods such as surgery and other treatments. Since the 1950s, debate over pharmaceutical profits has been tied to the question of whether high profitability is the result of monopoly or oligopoly. It is doubtful that any firm enjoys monopolistic status, but evidence suggests that some enjoy considerable market power.

The largely cordial relationship between government and the drug industry began to change in 1959 with the Kefauver hearings. Questions emerged about research practices, drug safety and effectiveness, and price disparities between brand-name drugs and generic equivalents. The Thalidomide disaster, widely publicized in 1961, heightened public concern. Such events led to a more complex approval process and stricter manufacturing guidelines in the attempt to ensure both the safety and efficacy of drugs.

Drug manufacturers have complained about such regulations as lengthy approval processes by claiming that they prevent marketing of potentially beneficial drugs. Many new drugs, however, are often essentially equivalent to existing drugs and are not necessarily more effective. The industry has often benefited from government policies. Pharmaceutical manufacturers have rightly noted that research and development is risky and expensive, but university laboratories, small companies, and the National Institutes of Health (NIH) bear much of the risk associated with the research and development of new drugs. These organizations do much of the initial screening of compounds for possible therapeutic efficacy. Once they discover a promising compound, they can sell or license it to the large drug companies. Furthermore, the government provides roughly half of all U.S. health-related research money, largely through the NIH. The NIH conducts drug-related research, and when promising compounds appear, companies bid for a license to market them. The industry benefits from a variety of tax breaks, including Section 936 of the U.S. Internal Revenue Code. Intended to promote economic development in Puerto Rico, Section 936 allows U.S. industries partial tax exemption on profits from operations in Puerto Rico and other U.S. possessions. Consumer advocates and policy-makers continue to debate these and other issues as they address the rising costs of health care.

BIBLIOGRAPHY

Abraham, John. *Science, Politics, and the Pharmaceutical Industry: Controversy and Bias in Drug Regulation.* New York: St. Martin's Press, 1995.

Blackett, Tom, and Rebecca Robins, ed. *Brand Medicine: The Role of Branding in the Pharmaceutical Industry.* New York: St. Martin's Press, 2001.

Gambardella, Alfonso. *Science and Innovation: The US Pharmaceutical Industry during the 1980s.* Cambridge, U.K.: Cambridge University Press, 1995.

Harris, Michael R., and Mark Parascandola. *Medicines: The Inside Story.* Madison, Wis.: American Institute of the History of Pharmacy, 1996.

Kaplan, Steven N., ed. *Mergers and Productivity.* Chicago: University of Chicago Press, 2000.

Schweitzer, Stuart O. *Pharmaceutical Economics and Policy.* New York: Oxford University Press, 1997.

Swann, John Patrick. *Academic Scientists and the Pharmaceutical Industry: Cooperative Research in Twentieth-Century America.* Baltimore: Johns Hopkins University Press, 1988.

Weatherall, Miles. *In Search of a Cure: A History of Pharmaceutical Discovery.* Oxford: Oxford University Press, 1990.

Reese V. Jenkins / A. E.

See also **Acquired Immune Deficiency Syndrome (AIDS); Biochemistry; Chemical Industry; Clinical Research; Food and Drug Administration; Health and Human Services, Department of; Health Care; Medicine and Surgery; Medicine, Military; Pharmacy; Pure Food and Drug Movement.**

PHARMACY. There were but few who could claim any prior pharmaceutical training in all the colonies in the seventeenth century. By the end of the eighteenth century, however, and far into the nineteenth, four types of practitioners of pharmacy were identifiable. First was the physician who compounded and dispensed his own medicines and often kept a "Doctor's shop." Second was the apothecary who, like his English model, not only compounded and dispensed drugs, but also diagnosed and prescribed. Third was the druggist, later also to be called a pharmacist. The term "druggist" was originally applied to wholesalers but subsequently described one who compounded medicines in shops in which a major concern was pharmaceuticals and related items. Fourth was the merchant who took on a supply of drugs; many eventually evolved into pharmacists.

The Drugstore

The nineteenth-century American drugstore carried a full line of simples (mainly crude vegetable drugs) and chemicals with which pharmacists compounded and dispensed medicines, with or without a prescription. They were artisans who spread their own plasters and prepared pills, powders, tinctures, ointments, syrups, conserves, medicated waters, and perfumes. Economic necessity forced them to handle such commodities as confections, tobacco, paints, glass, groceries, spices, and liquor. They were thus commonly also merchants, and pharmacists often differed among themselves as to whether theirs was a trade or a profession.

By the mid-nineteenth century this artisanal role of pharmacists had begun to diminish. A pharmaceutical industry was providing medicines that pharmacists had previously made entirely by hand. There was a burgeoning growth of proprietary ("patent") medicines, flamboyantly advertised, with which pharmacists had to deal. Economic competition from department stores, groceries, and chain stores added to the pressure. Late in the century the competition—including that among pharmacists, for the "cut-rate" pharmacy shop had become ubiquitous—led to a number of plans to fix prices, but both these plans and the fair trade statutes of the mid-twentieth century fell afoul of federal antitrust laws.

One peculiarly American development was the drugstore soda fountain, which was an outcome of the pharmacist's knowledge of flavors and carbonated water. The pharmacist Elias Durand operated a soda fountain in his Philadelphia shop as early as 1825. American soft drinks, the colas particularly, had their beginnings in the drugstore. The soda fountain was not to disappear from the drugstore until the mid-twentieth century, when it gave way to more profitable alternative uses for the space.

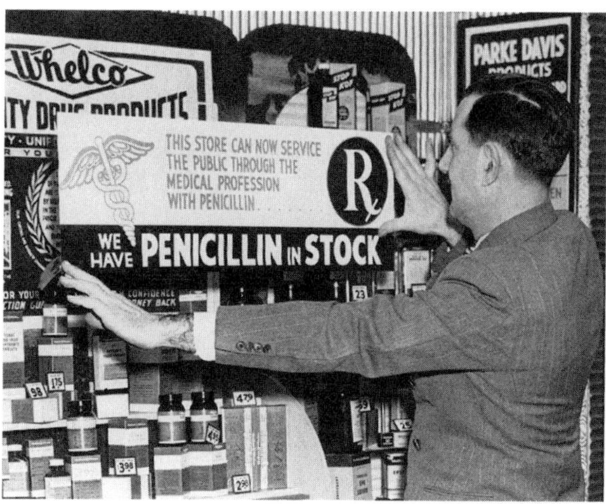

"We Have Penicillin in Stock." Manager Dave Tarlow of a Whalen's Drug Store in New York City notifies the public that the new wonder drug is now available (though only to those with a prescription), 16 March 1945. © BETTMANN/CORBIS

Science and Technology

The great scientific and technological advances in the medical and biological sciences in the late nineteenth century transformed pharmacy in a number of ways. First, the old *materia medica*—still showing evidence of ancient lineage—increasingly gave way to new medications based on a better scientific understanding of the etiology of diseases and of the mechanisms of drug action. These medications were the products of synthetic and medicinal chemistry, new powerful tools. Second, in the twentieth century these new medications were largely the discoveries and innovations of the rapidly developing pharmaceutical industry and, moreover, were the products of research and manufacture that the individual pharmacist could not duplicate. This meant that the compounding of medicines by the pharmacist gave way to the dispensing of medications completely prepared by industry. By the 1970s only one percent of prescriptions required some combination or manipulation of ingredients. Third, the sciences gave impetus to the separation of pharmaceutical practice from medical practice.

Pharmacy Law

The training of the pharmacist was accomplished largely through the apprenticeship system and, in the absence of legal restrictions—a concomitant of Jacksonian democracy—it was possible for any persons to set themselves up as pharmacists. The first laws providing for the examination and licensing of pharmacists in an American jurisdiction were passed in Louisiana, where the Franco-Spanish tradition in pharmacy prevailed in regulations of the Territory of Orleans in 1808 and of the state in 1816. The few other such attempts before the Civil War, in three southern states and a few localities, were, in the prevailing democratic milieu, ineffectual.

Rhode Island passed the first modern state law for the examining and licensing of pharmacists in 1870. Pressure for such laws came from the American Pharmaceutical Association, founded in 1852, and from state and territorial pharmaceutical associations (of which there were forty-five and two, respectively, by 1900). As a consequence, forty-seven states had such laws by the end of the century. This legislation established state boards of pharmacy, composed originally of pharmacists. The boards, among other powers, examined candidates and imposed educational requirements that became more advanced as the colleges of pharmacy increased the depth and length of the pharmacy curricula. Following standards and accreditation requirements developed by the American Association of Colleges of Pharmacy (founded in 1900) and by the American Council on Pharmaceutical Education (founded in 1932), these curricula increased from two- and three-year Graduate in Pharmacy (Ph.G.) and Pharmaceutical Chemist (Ph.C.) programs, to four- and five-year baccalaureate programs, and to six-year Doctor of Pharmacy (Pharm.D.) programs. In 1999 over 45 percent of all the pharmacy graduates in the country received the Pharm.D. degree as their first professional degree.

Under the American constitutional system it was state law that regulated pharmacy and imposed restrictions on the sales of poisons and abortifacients. The federal government first became involved in the regulation of pharmacy with the Pure Food and Drug Act of 1906. That legislation and its principal amendments (1912, 1938, 1952, and 1962) and the Harrison Narcotic Act of 1914 set the stage for what became the very close federal involvement in the control of drugs. "Legend drugs," requiring a physician's prescription, and a list of "controlled dangerous substances" made the pharmacist subject to federal, as well as state, authority.

Pharmaceutical Education

Pharmaceutical education began in the United States with the founding of the Philadelphia College of Pharmacy (now the University of the Sciences in Philadelphia) in

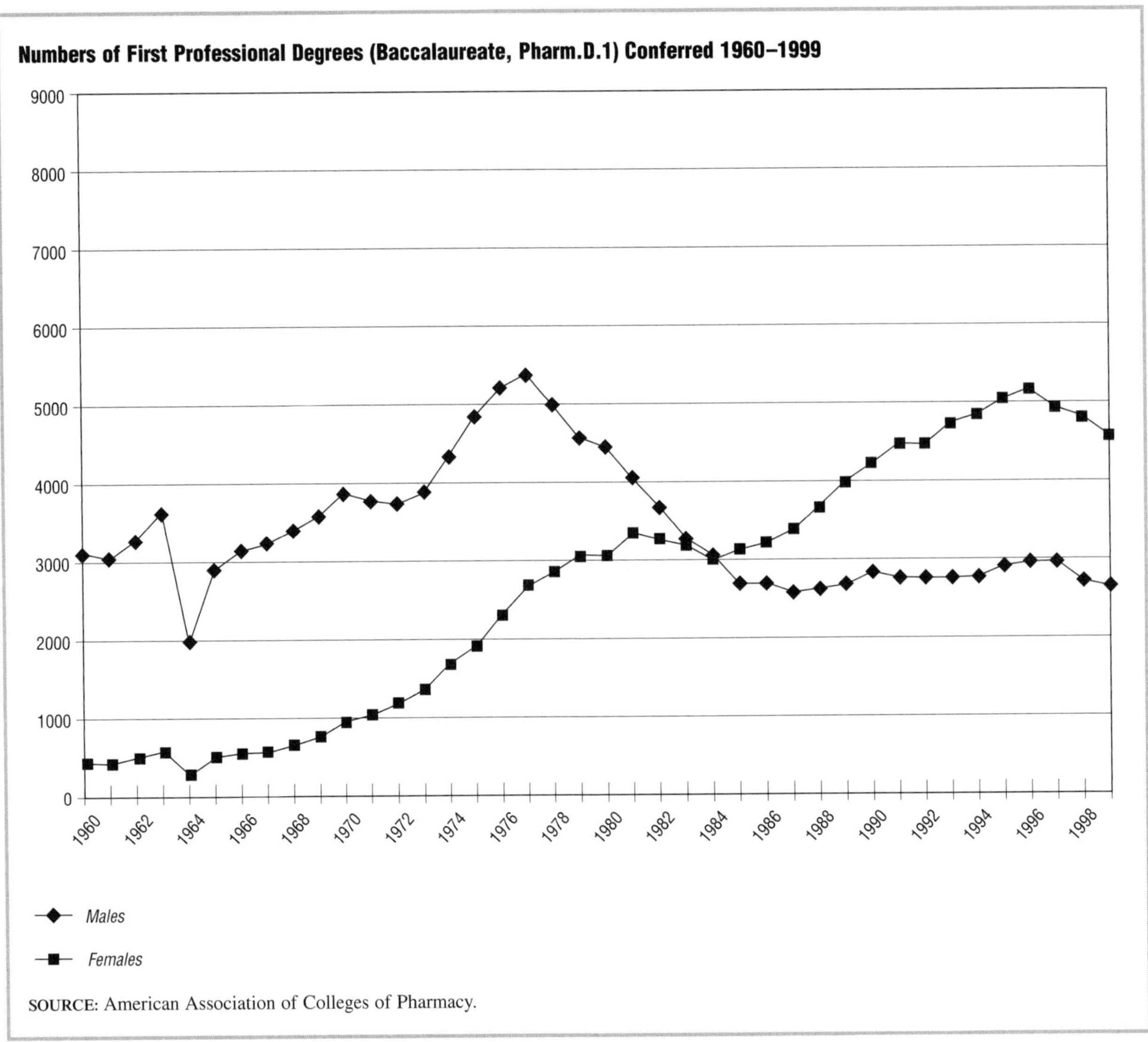

SOURCE: American Association of Colleges of Pharmacy.

1821. The term "college" was intended at first to suggest only a society rather than a school, but the Philadelphia College offered lectures almost from the start. Local societies of pharmacy, also calling themselves colleges, were formed in Boston, New York City, Baltimore, Cincinnati, Chicago, and St. Louis, and all of them sooner or later engaged in pharmaceutical instruction. By 1900 about sixty programs were or had been in operation. The program of instruction in these institutions, especially in the good number that were private and proprietary, was indeed meager, consisting mainly of a series of lectures in the evening in rented rooms.

In 1868 the University of Michigan embarked upon a full program of scientific training in pharmacy, eventually developing a full-time, day program of two years. The University of Wisconsin followed suit in 1883 and nine years later it pioneered in offering a four-year program leading to a bachelor's degree. As noted, the length and the curricular requirements took off from there, reflecting new developments in the pharmaceutical sciences and the changing professional role of the pharmacist, both in and beyond the drugstore. The curriculum changes demanded by the doctorate included more attention to the humanities and emphasized clinical pharmacy and relatively new sciences like pharmacokinetics and pharmacotherapeutics. Externship programs in community, industrial, hospital, and clinical pharmacy became part of the curriculum.

The Changing Role of the Pharmacist

The plethora of new and complex medicines that industry was providing, along with the increasing demands for prescription drugs as the population aged, meant that pharmacists who dealt directly with the patient needed to be more than just artisans who compounded or dispensed drugs. Limited in their freedom of activity by the introduction of Medicaid and Medicare, the new managed care systems, and computerization, pharmacists found that their choice of drugs and their prices were no longer under their control. The pharmacist assumed a new, consultative role in health-care delivery that demanded knowledge of the drugs and their action in the body and the monitoring of the drug regimen of the patients.

The responsibility of the pharmacist in providing correct and effective medication and in preventing errors was evident in the great expansion of pharmacists into the health field beyond the drugstore. Hospital pharmacy goes back in the United States to before the Revolution; by 1942 hospital pharmacists had become so significant a part of the heath-care community that they formed the American Society of Hospital Pharmacists. As the twentieth century progressed, the practice of clinical pharmacy developed. In clinical pharmacy the pharmacist is responsible in a hospital situation for cooperating with the physician in monitoring the prescribed medications. Clinical and consulting pharmacists also are involved in other institutions, such as nursing homes and assisted living quarters. In recognition of the broader role of clinical and consultative pharmacy, the American Society of Hospital Pharmacists became the American Society of Health-System Pharmacists in 1995.

Demographics and Infrastructure

The demography of pharmacy personnel changed quite rapidly in the late twentieth century. Beginning in 1985, more than half of each year's pharmaceutical degree recipients were women. In 1999 women graduates made up 63.5 percent of the total. The ethnicity of personnel was also changing. The percentage of white graduates fell from 86 percent in 1979 to 64 percent in 1999, while the percentage of Asian, Native Hawaiian, and Pacific Islanders rose from under 4 percent to over 18 percent in the same period. African Americans rose from 3.6 percent to 5.6 percent; Hispanics and Latinos declined from 3.8 percent to 3.7 percent.

The last decade of the twentieth century saw a drop in the total number of drugstore outlets from 58,642 in 1990 to 53,105 in 1999. The decline, however, was only among independent pharmacies. They went from 31,879 to 20,649, a decrease of 11,230 units in the decade. Chain stores, supermarket units, and mass merchandiser units all increased in number. One factor in the decline of independent pharmacies was the development of Pharmacy Benefit Management organizations (PBMs) and the accompanying growth of mail-order prescription services.

At the end of the twentieth century the National Community Pharmacists Association (founded as the National Association of Retail Druggists in 1898) still had a membership of 25,000. The American Society of Health-System Pharmacists had an equal number of members. Pharmacy had developed in two directions.

BIBLIOGRAPHY

Cowen, David L., and William H. Helfand. *Pharmacy: An Illustrated History.* New York: Abrams, 1990.

Higby, Gregory J. *In Service to American Pharmacy: The Professional Life of William Procter, Jr.* Tuscaloosa: University Alabama Press, 1992.

Nona, Daniel A. "A Brief History of the Present—As Told by Accreditation Standards for Pharmaceutical Education." *Journal of the American Pharmaceutical Association* 40 no. 5 suppl. 1 (2000).

Ozick, Cynthia. "A Drugstore Eden." In *Quarrel & Quandary: Essays by Cynthia Ozick.* New York: Knopf, 2000.

Sonnedecker, Glenn. *Kremers and Urdang's History of Pharmacy.* 4th ed. Philadelphia: Lippincott, 1976.

David L. Cowen

See also **Food and Drug Administration; Hospitals; Medicine and Surgery; Pure Food and Drug Movement.**

PHI BETA KAPPA SOCIETY, a collegiate honors society. It is the oldest and generally considered the most prestigious undergraduate honors society in the United States. Taking its name from the initials of the Greek motto "Philosophia Biou Kubernetes" (Love of wisdom, the guide of life), the organization was founded on 5 December 1776 at the College of William and Mary in Williamsburg, Virginia. Phi Beta Kappa was originally created as a secret social and literary organization, complete with an elaborate initiation process and an oath of secrecy. The original society at William and Mary was only active for four years, until the school was forced to shut down because of the approach of the British army during the Revolutionary War. Two chapters, at Harvard and Yale, had been set up a year earlier, and it was these that would mold the character of the organization. In 1831 the Harvard chapter became the first to abolish the secrecy requirements, in the face of anti-Masonic sentiments, and other chapters soon followed. The year 1883 saw the founding of the United Chapters of Phi Beta Kappa, unifying the twenty-five chapters and 14,000 members. The first women were admitted to Phi Beta Kappa at the University of Vermont in 1875. The name of the national organization was changed to Phi Beta Kappa Society in 1988. In 2000 living membership was more than 500,000 at about 250 chapters.

BIBLIOGRAPHY

Current, Richard N. *Phi Beta Kappa in American Life: The First Two Hundred Years.* New York: Oxford University Press, 1990.

Voorhees, Oscar M. *The History of Phi Beta Kappa.* New York: Crown, 1945.

Eli Moses Diner

See also **Secret Societies.**

PHILADELPHIA. Founded in 1682, Philadelphia has throughout its long history been notable for its religious and ethnic diversity, importance as a center of trade

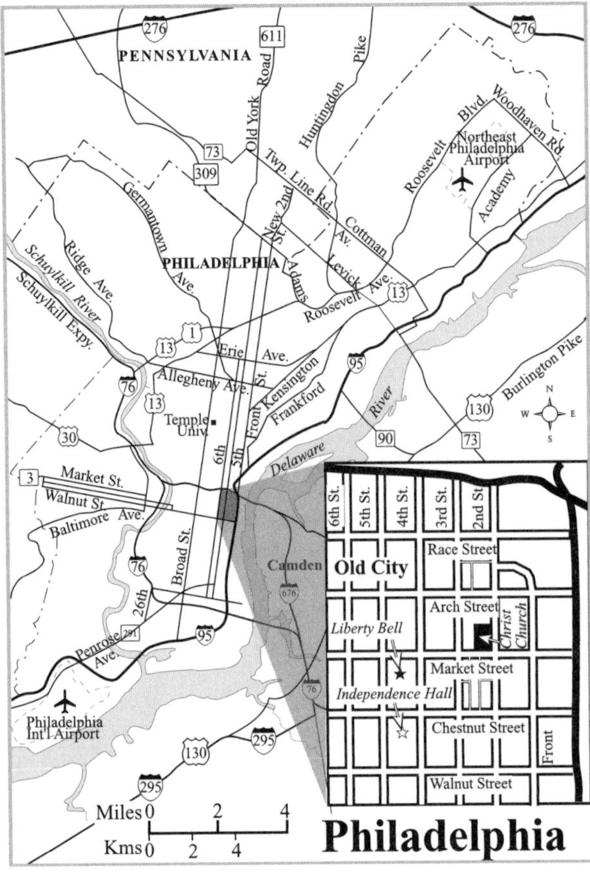

and commerce, and role in perpetuating learning and the arts. Although many have quipped that its moniker as the City of Brotherly Love is something of a misnomer—Philadelphia sports fans once famously booed Santa Claus at halftime of a professional football game—its significance in American history is undeniable.

During the colonial period, Philadelphia embodied its founder William Penn's ethos of religious pluralism and tolerance. By the mid-eighteenth century, Philadelphia was home to more religious denominations than any other American city, featuring vibrant Quaker, Anglican, Presbyterian, Baptist, Lutheran, Catholic, and Moravian congregations, among others. Philadelphia was also early America's most cosmopolitan city, with significant numbers of Swede, German, and Scottish settlers in addition to its English majority. Colonial Philadelphia was home to several notable intellectual institutions, including the Library Company (the oldest lending library in America), the American Philosophical Society (the oldest scientific association in America), and the College of Philadelphia (later the University of Pennsylvania), the only nondenominational college in colonial America. In 1776, Philadelphia was the largest city in colonial British America with 28,400 residents. Its pivotal role in the Revolutionary and early national eras testifies to its status as early America's first city; it served as the site for the Continental Congress from 1774 through 1783, for the Constitutional Convention in 1787, and as the new nation's capital from 1790 to 1800. Perhaps the two most important founding documents in American history, the Declaration of Independence and the Constitution, were written in the City of Brotherly Love. It continued as an important intellectual and cultural center through the early nineteenth century; the Philadelphia Academy of the Fine Arts, founded in 1805, was the new nation's first art school.

The early nineteenth century saw New York eclipse Philadelphia as the United States' largest and most significant commercial city. Despite Philadelphia's financial significance—it was home to both the First and Second Bank of the United States—the rapid settlement of upstate New York and the consequent expansion of New York City's hinterland fueled its growth at Philadelphia's expense. Despite this economic change, Philadelphia continued to be a center of religious and ethnic diversity during the antebellum era. Home to one of the largest free African American populations in the United States, Philadelphia also played a pivotal role in black religious life. Fighting racial discrimination in the city's churches, the minister Richard Allen culminated a long struggle for independence with the organization of the African Methodist Episcopal Church, the nation's first black religious denomination. Perhaps because of its religious diversity, Philadelphia was also the site of fierce and often violent conflict. The 1840s and 1850s saw nativist Protestants incite riots against local German and, especially, Irish Catholic immigrants; in 1844, nativists even burned several Catholic churches to the ground. Antebellum Philadelphia continued to be a significant commercial and industrial center, a leader in the textile, shipbuilding, and locomotive industries. The city expanded, and its population reached 565,529 by the eve of the Civil War—the second largest city in the United States. By the time of the city's Centennial Exposition in 1876, Philadelphia was one of the largest cities in both Europe and America, surpassed only by New York, London, and Paris.

Although during the Gilded and Progressive Eras Philadelphia continued to be an important cultural and educational center, the city began to decline economically in the twentieth century. The city's economy, based mainly on light manufacturing, metal products, textiles, food products, and chemical industries, as well as the largest refining operations on the east coast, began to stagnate during this period. Nevertheless, the city maintained a world-class stature in the arts through institutions like the Academy of the Fine Arts (where artists and teachers like Thomas Eakins had helped build an American art movement in the late nineteenth century), The Philadelphia Orchestra (founded in 1900), and the Philadelphia Museum of Art (founded in 1928). The city was by then also home to more than a dozen colleges and universities and six medical schools.

Despite a brief upturn around World War II—largely the result of wartime military production and the efforts of reform mayors like Joseph S. Clark Jr. and Richardson

Philadelphia. This 1790 engraving shows *(left to right)* the Episcopal Academy, Congress Hall (where Congress met, 1790–1800), the State House (now Independence Hall), Philosophical Hall, the Library Company (America's oldest subscription library), and Carpenters' Hall (where the First Continental Congress met). THE LIBRARY COMPANY OF PHILADELPHIA

Dilworth after the war—the city suffered from the same urban decline that afflicted most American industrial cities in the twentieth century. In an effort to attract middle-class and upper-class residents back to Philadelphia, the city made pioneering efforts at urban renewal and revitalized certain neighborhoods, but failed to stem the tide out of the city as a whole. Philadelphia's population began to drop in the postwar period. Following a high of 2,072,000 residents in 1950, the city's population had declined by more than 18 percent by 1980, losing nearly 300,000 residents from 1970 to 1980 alone.

Most of this change was the result of "white flight" to the region's rapidly growing suburbs; the city's minority population reached 40 percent during this period. Racial and political tensions accompanied these economic and demographic changes, epitomized by Frank L. Rizzo. A former police chief who served two terms as mayor in the 1970s, Rizzo was extremely popular among Philadelphia's white ethnic population for his aggressive efforts against crime, while the city's African Americans felt he pandered to white fears through his blatant efforts to link crime and race. In the 1980s, W. Wilson Goode, the city's first African American mayor, won acclaim for handling race relations well but received criticism for alleged administrative incompetence. Under Edward G. Rendell's mayoral administration in the 1990s, the city's fortunes improved somewhat. Following near-bankruptcy in 1991, Rendell was able to put the city on firmer financial footing and largely stem the flow of jobs and residents out of the city to the suburbs. Despite Rendell's success, in 2002 it was still uncertain whether his administration marked a temporary aberration in Philadelphia's history or a true revitalization for one of the United States' oldest, most historically significant, and culturally important cities.

BIBLIOGRAPHY

Bissinger, Buzz. *A Prayer for the City*. New York: Random House, 1997.

Nash, Gary B. *First City: Philadelphia and the Forging of Historical Memory*. Philadelphia: University of Pennsylvania Press, 2001.

Warner, Sam Bass, Jr. *The Private City: Philadelphia in Three Periods of Its Growth*. 2d ed. Philadelphia: University of Pennsylvania Press, 1987.

Weigley, Russell F., ed. *Philadelphia: A 300-Year History*. New York: Norton, 1982.

John Smolenski

See also **Pennsylvania.**

PHILADELPHIA CORDWAINERS' CASE. In the fall of 1805 the journeymen cordwainers of Philadelphia went on strike to enforce their demands for the wage scale prevailing at New York and Baltimore and for a discontinuance of the rebate of wages for export work. Eight union leaders were then arrested on a charge of criminal conspiracy. Agreeing with the prosecution that "a conspiracy of workmen to raise their wages" was criminal at common law, the Court found the defendants guilty and fined them a token $8.00. The strike was broken, and an important precedent was set for the criminal prosecution of labor union activities which had multiplied with the rise of wholesale manufacturers. This was the first of six criminal conspiracy cases brought against union shoemakers in this period; four of the cases were decided against the journeymen.

BIBLIOGRAPHY

Forbath, William E. *Law and the Shaping of the American Labor Movement.* Cambridge, Mass.: Harvard University Press, 1991.

Steinfeld, Robert J. "The Philadelphia Cordwainer's Case of 1806." In *Labor Law in America: Historical and Critical Essays.* Edited by Christopher Tomlins and Andrew J. King. Baltimore: Johns Hopkins University, 1992.

*Richard B. Morris/*A. R.

See also **Industrial Revolution; Labor; Restraint of Trade; Scab; Strikes; Wages and Hours of Labor, Regulation of.**

PHILADELPHIA PLAN. On 25 June 1941 President Franklin D. Roosevelt issued Executive Order 8802, which declared that the policy of the government was to encourage full participation in national defense programs by all U.S. citizens, regardless of race, creed, color, or national origin. It established a Fair Employment Practice Committee (FEPC) with no funds, a limited staff, and no direct enforcement power. It was limited primarily to making recommendations to federal agencies and the president. Its significance was more symbolic than substantive, but it was the first government-wide administrative effort to establish a national policy of nondiscriminatory employment. It inspired continued efforts for the enactment of a federal FEPC law, and every president since has issued a similar executive order or kept his predecessor's. There was early success in the enactment of state FEPC laws, but Congress did not act until the Civil Rights Act of 1964, which implicitly approved John F. Kennedy's Executive Order 10925, issued in 1961. The order imposed on contractors (and their subcontractors) doing $10,000 or more of business with the federal government for the first time an obligation to engage in affirmative action to ensure equality of employment opportunity. The obligation was undefined; President Lyndon Johnson retained the Kennedy concepts in Executive Order 11246 (25 September 1965), and it remains in effect today.

The Philadelphia Plan itself—a local construction industry initiative of senior Philadelphia officials that was declared illegal in 1968 by U.S. Comptroller General opinion—is but an obscure historical footnote in this continued effort to help eradicate employment discrimination by executive orders. The plan likely would have passed into obscurity after the 1968 election of Richard Nixon. But an early embarrassment over affirmative action in the textile industry indirectly led to the issuance of the Philadelphia Plan Revised in 1969 to repair the administration's civil rights image. Limited to construction, the Philadelphia Plan included for the first time obligations overtly specifying goals and timetables. Thus began the thirty-year-long debate over affirmative action versus quotas.

In preparing the plan, the Department of Labor had conducted hearings and gathered statistical information to establish that minority participation in the six trades (ironworkers, plumbers and pipe fitters, steam fitters, sheet-metal workers, electrical workers, and elevator-construction workers) was approximately 1 percent despite the fact that minorities were 30 percent of the construction industry in the area. In comparable skills trades, excluding laborers, minority representation was approximately 12 percent. There were jobs available and training to increase the pool of minorities. Against this factual backdrop, the plan mandated "good faith effort" to reach goals ranging from 5 to 9 percent in the first year, 9 to 15 percent in the second year, 14 to 20 percent in the third year, and 19 to 26 percent in the final year of the plan. At the highest ranges of the final year, the goal was less than the minority representation in the Philadelphia construction industry. If the contractors were able to reach the even lowest threshold of the ranges for each year, they would be in compliance. And the operative enforcement standard was "good faith effort" to reach the goals, not whether they were achieved.

Opponents of the plan sued in a federal district court in Pennsylvania in March 1970 and lost. Expecting victory, the Labor Department had issued Order No. 4 applying the Philadelphia Plan concept to nonconstruction contractors employing more than fifty employees with federal contracts of at least $50,000. After revisions, the order was published in the *Federal Register.* Multiple efforts to get federal legislation to restrict the utilization of the Philadelphia Plan and related rules failed. Instead, in 1992, Congress amended the Civil Rights Act of 1964 by adding Section 718, giving statutory support to affirmative action plans.

Despite periodic attempts since 1970 to convince Congress and presidents to prohibit affirmative action programs, provisions for all federally assisted construction contracts and hometown or imposed plans that explicitly refer to the Philadelphia Plan remain in place. The published rules and regulations of the Office of Federal Contract Compliance of the U.S. Department of Labor are contained in the *Code of Federal Regulations* of 2001 and also provide for goals and timetables for females, Vietnam-era veterans, and individuals with disabilities.

Prior to the Revised Philadelphia Plan, affirmative action under the executive order EO 11246 was largely hortatory. By 2001 it had substance and had spread throughout all U.S. business and industry. U.S. Supreme Court cases on affirmative action have included admission to university and professional schools, diversity in the media, contract set-asides, and a few employment cases, but none addressing the president's executive order EO 11246. Attacking any manifestation of affirmative action seems to have become a cottage industry for a conservative segment of society. Ironically, the main impetus for affirmative action was the Nixon administration's contribution to the civil rights arsenal. Meanwhile, if advertising is the measure, corporate America has decided that demographics are destiny and diversity is good business.

BIBLIOGRAPHY

Book 3, "Employment." In *Commission on Civil Rights Report.* Washington, D.C.: U.S. Government Printing Office, 1961.

Code of Federal Regulations. Title 41, chapters 1–100, "Public Contracts and Property Management." July 1, 2000. Chapter 60, Office of Federal Contract Compliance Programs, Equal Employment Opportunity, Department of Labor. Washington, D.C.: U.S. Government Printing Office, 2000. Part 60-4 regarding construction contractors included provisions for hometown plans as well as imposed plans. However, the rules specified that after its effective date "all solicitation of construction contracts shall include the notice specified in the regulation in lieu of the hometown and imposed plans, including the Philadelphia Plan." Thus the rules, published in the volumes of the *Federal Register* as of July 1, 2000, provide for updating goals and timetables, as applicable, in imposed or hometown plans. The rules also contain affirmative action and nondiscrimination for special disabled veterans and veterans of the Vietnam era and individuals with disabilities. In 41 CFR Part 60-20, the rules include goals and timetables for females, sex discrimination guidelines, and specifically require affirmative action to recruit women to apply for jobs from which they have previously been excluded.

Graham, Hugh Davis. *The Civil Rights Era: Origins and Development of National Policy.* Oxford and New York: Oxford University Press, 1990.

Jones, James E., Jr. "The Rise and Fall of Affirmative Action." In *Race in America: The Struggle for Equality.* Herbert Hill and James E. Jones, Jr., eds. Madison: University of Wisconsin Press, 1993.

Millenson, Debra A. "W(h)ither Affirmative Action: The Future of Executive Order 11246." *University of Memphis Law Review* 29 (1999): 679–737.

Norgren, Paul H., and Samuel Hill. *Toward Fair Employment.* New York and London: Columbia University Press, 1964.

James E. Jones Jr.

See also **Affirmative Action; Discrimination.**

PHILADELPHIA RIOTS. On 6 to 8 May and 5 to 8 July 1844, riots in Philadelphia climaxed the first phase of American nativistic agitation. Protestant nativists, their passions inflamed by antipapal propagandists, began systematic attacks on Irish Catholics and foreigners. During the actual rioting, Philadelphia resembled a war-torn city: cannon were mounted in the public squares, Catholic churches were burned, and hundreds of immigrants' homes were sacked by mobs. A score of persons was killed and nearly 100 wounded before militia ended the mob rule. Public reaction against this violence contributed to the downfall of the American Republican Party and sent the whole nativistic movement into temporary eclipse.

BIBLIOGRAPHY

Billington, Ray Allen. *The Protestant Crusade, 1800–1860: A Study of the Origins of American Nativism.* New York: Rinehart, 1938.

Feldberg, Michael. *The Philadelphia Riots of 1844: A Study of Ethnic Conflict.* Westport, Conn.: Greenwood Press, 1975.

———. *The Turbulent Era: Riot and Disorder in Jacksonian America.* New York: Oxford University Press, 1980.

Ray Allen Billington / A. R.

See also **Anti-Catholicism; Catholicism; Nativism; Philadelphia; Riots, Urban.**

PHILANTHROPY. Philanthropy is private action for the public good. Americans like to think of themselves as a generous people, although much of their generosity stems from their distinctive political culture, which encourages and even requires public-private partnerships. The development of a "third sector" of private, nonprofit organizations results primarily from the separation of church and state, a political arrangement that has given rise to hundreds of thousands of voluntary organizations, all seeking their own vision of the public good.

A distinction can be made between philanthropy and charity. The word "charity" derives from the Latin "caritas," meaning unconditional love. Charity often refers to short-term relief, while philanthropy is normally applied to attempts at investigating and reforming underlying causes. While most giving in America is in the form of small contributions, much of it for religious purposes, a significant development has been the creation of large philanthropic foundations, which contributed over $27 billion in 2000. While this constitutes less than 10 percent of total voluntary contributions, it is heavily concentrated, and thus has great impact. There are around fifty thousand foundations in the United States, with assets of around $450 billion, although one-third of this sum is held by the top twenty-five foundations.

Philanthopy in the Colonial Period

Philanthropy, wrote Rockefeller Foundation director Warren Weaver, "is not a modern invention," for "concern for one's fellow men extends back to ancient times." Private gifts for community purposes were not uncommon in the classical period, the most famous being Plato's gift of productive land as an endowment for his academy. Early Christians were commanded to give to the poor beyond their ability. Gifts of property were common in the Christian era, and were used to establish monasteries, hospitals, colleges, and other semi-public institutions. In the Middle Ages the church had primary responsibility for religious, cultural, service, and educational activities; thus, the seizure of the monasteries during the early phase of the English Reformation created practical problems. Queen Elizabeth sought a middle way between Catholic and Puritan purposes. Toward the end of her reign Parliament passed two major laws that shaped colonial philanthropic efforts.

The most famous was the Elizabethan Poor Law of 1601, which made church parishes "overseers of the poor" and established the principle of local responsibility for indigent populations. The Statute of Charitable Uses, passed the same year, provided for church supervision of charitable bequests, such as "lands, tenements, rents, annuities, profits, inheritances," and listed legitimate objects of charity, including poor relief, education in "free schools" and universities, medical treatment, and care of widows and orphans.

The Puritans who came to New England in 1630 had a different theoretical basis for philanthropic activity. The first governor of Massachusetts Bay, John Winthrop, imagined in his lay sermon, "A Model of Christian Charity," a "city upon a hill," a divinely ordered society of rich and poor with reciprocal duties. "We must be knit together in this work as one man," Winthrop urged, so that "every man afford his help to another in every want or distress." The "care of the public" must supersede any private gain. Political enforcement through taxation, however, did not limit private gifts. Thus, John Harvard donated his personal library to the new colony's college.

The revocation of the Massachusetts charter after England's revolution of 1688 meant that government policy was no longer under the complete control of Puritan social theory. In this new context, cleric Cotton Mather, in his *Bonifacius: Essays to Do Good* (1710), urged congregations to develop voluntary organizations for social reform. Doing good was not a means of salvation, but rather an obligation to God and sound social policy, although Mather was careful to point out that giving wisely was better than giving generously.

Philanthropy in the middle colonies originated from a dissenting religious tradition and developed in the context of religious diversity. In 1681 Quaker William Penn established his colony as a "holy experiment" for religious refugees. Heavily influenced by Mather's *Bonifacius*, Benjamin Franklin introduced a secular spirit and self-help tradition into American philanthropy. His Junto, established in 1727, was a group of middling artisans who organized themselves for social purposes, and helped establish a free library, town watch, and fire company in Philadelphia. Franklin was instrumental in forming a voluntary militia to help defend the officially pacifist Quaker colony during the French and Indian War, and he established numerous other Philadelphia institutions, such as the American Philosophical Society, the Pennsylvania Hospital, and the University of Pennsylvania. These efforts were later jointly funded by taxation and private contributions. Many Philadelphians continued this tradition of civic philanthropy, including Benjamin Rush, who founded the Philadelphia Dispensary in the 1780s, the first free medical clinic in America.

The Great Awakening of the 1740s provided a major impetus to making philanthropy more a mass movement rather than a strictly upper-class phenomenon. New revivalist congregations needed voluntary support from their members, which not only required individual giving but also weakened support for established churches. Itinerant English evangelist George Whitefield preached throughout the colonies and encouraged giving for an orphanage in Georgia; one of the first colonywide fund-raising drives, it moved beyond the localism of the poor laws.

A New Order for the Ages: Revolutionary Disestablishment

While important, colonial philanthropy was not significantly different from its historical antecedents. Far more profound were the fundamental changes that occurred between the Revolution and the passage of the Bill of Rights in 1791. The idea of limited government, combined with the separation of church and state, created a distinctive political tradition that not only allowed for voluntary activity, but in fact required it. Revolutionary ideology, which considered strong governments as destructive of liberty, opposed centralized power along with government support for charitable and cultural activities. Beyond a vague provision for "the general welfare," the Constitution severely restricted federal authority, leaving whole areas of the common good, such as education, health, and poor relief, to either the states or private effort. Constitutional theory encouraged this devolution of power, not only through federalism and representation, but also by acknowledging freedoms of religion, speech, and assembly. In his *Federalist* essays, James Madison argued that numerous competing factions and interests were the best means of preserving liberty and of providing for various definitions of the public good. Thomas Jefferson's Virginia Statute of Religious Freedom (1786), the precedent for the First Amendment, withdrew all governmental funding for religious activities, mandating a voluntary system of religious and charitable giving.

The status of nonreligious institutions, however, was at this point unclear. Jeffersonian democrats insisted that institutions that claimed to serve the public interest should be under state legislative control. This argument was rejected in the *Dartmouth College Case* (1819), in which the U.S. Supreme Court upheld the independence and autonomy of "eleemosynary," or nonprofit, corporations. Relying upon the right of contract, Chief Justice John Marshall established the legal rights of all corporations by protecting their trustees from legislative interference.

This case opened the way for numerous private charitable organizations to pursue benevolent and philanthropic goals. Visiting in the 1830s, Alexis de Tocqueville observed in *Democracy in America*, "an immense assemblage of associations" for countless political, civic, and charitable causes:

> Americans make associations to give entertainments, to found seminaries, to build inns, to construct churches, to diffuse books, to send missionaries to the antipodes; . . . Wherever at the head of some new undertaking you see the government in France, or a man of rank in England, in the United States you will be sure to find an association.

These voluntary organizations competed against each other for contributions and acceptance. Occasionally they worked together in a so-called "benevolent empire" for moral improvement and social reform. Many had explicitly political aims, such as the abolition of slavery, while others concerned themselves with charitable activities.

Education and research relied heavily upon philanthropy. Before the Civil War hundreds of colleges were founded, mostly by religious denominations through private contributions, since Congress refused to establish any national university. One of the most famous philanthropic gifts was that of James Smithson, a British chemist who gave around $500,000 for "an establishment for the increase and diffusion of knowledge among men." After a decade of debate, Congress finally created the Smithsonian Institution in 1846. Smithson's gift encouraged others in support of scientific research and public education, such as that of Abbot Lawrence for naturalist Louis Agassiz's laboratory at Harvard, Peter Cooper for the establishment of Cooper Union, and the founding of public libraries in Boston and New York.

During the Civil War both sides supported their respective war efforts through voluntarism. In the North the Christian Commission donated food, clothing, religious literature, and other supplies to troops, while the rival U.S. Sanitary Commission concentrated on coordinating local relief agencies, improving their administration, and reducing disease in military camps and hospitals. Funds were raised through "sanitary fairs" throughout the country that spread the voluntary spirit. Without compensation or accreditation, Clara Barton organized nursing care for wounded soldiers. She formed the American Red Cross in 1881 and served as its first president until 1904. Abolition societies pressured President Abraham Lincoln for emancipation and after the war, worked to establish the Freedmen's Bureau with federal funding. Other organizations flooded the postwar South with teachers and schools. Gen. Samuel Armstrong founded the Hampton Institute in Virginia and George Peabody established a fund for the "strickened South."

The Rise of Scientific Philanthropy

The rapid industrialization of American society in the late nineteenth century, combined with increased immigration, led to a series of social problems on a scale hitherto unimagined. Local- and religious-based philanthropy continued, of course, but urban conditions frequently overwhelmed traditional voluntarism. The social settlement house movement, exemplified by the founding of Hull House by Jane Addams in Chicago during 1889, sought to alleviate some of the worst conditions and encouraged the development of social science–based investigation of urban poverty.

That same year, steel magnate Andrew Carnegie published his essay "Wealth," in which he urged its "proper administration . . . so that the ties of brotherhood may still bind together the rich and poor in harmonious relationship." Carnegie chastised "indiscriminate charity" as morally destructive, instead calling for support for institutions of self-help, such as universities, libraries, and museums. The man of wealth was to be "the mere agent and trustee for his poorer brethren . . . doing for them better than they would or could do for themselves." Carnegie implemented his "gospel of wealth" at first through gifts of libraries to communities that promised to support them. After selling his steel interests, however, he concentrated on establishing permanent institutions and foundations.

Carnegie's businesslike approach fit well with a progressive belief in scientific investigation. After experimenting with various institutional forms, three major philanthropists—Carnegie, John D. Rockefeller, and Margaret Olivia Sage—created a new type of institution between 1907 and 1913, the general purpose foundation. Differing from the British model of a charitable trust, which restricted trustees to the specific wishes of donors, the American foundation often was established with broad purposes, much like a business corporation, thus giving enormous discretion to trustees and staff. Eschewing charity, these institutions followed Rockefeller's advice to focus upon attacking underlying conditions. "Money," he said, "is a feeble offering without the study behind it which will make its expenditure effective."

While founding private organizations, Carnegie, Rockefeller, and Sage each assumed that their creations would work closely with government, providing research and a sort of venture capital for public programs. Often philanthropy filled gaps in government policy, as when southern states refused to fund the construction of black schools. Rockefeller's General Education Board and the Julius Rosenwald Fund assisted in the construction of thousands of schools in the South. Another model was provided by the Rockefeller Sanitary Commission, which concentrated on a public health campaign to eradicate hookworm, work later taken over by state and local governments.

In their early decades, foundations concentrated on the advancement of formal knowledge. Much of this effort focused on the basic medical sciences and the strengthening of university departments and medical schools. For example, the Carnegie-funded *Report on Medical Education in the United States and Canada* (1910), by Abraham Flexner, profoundly transformed medical training, especially after the General Education Board began heavily supporting medical schools on the Flexner model. As one Rockefeller Foundation staff member described it, the goal was to "make the peaks higher" and to develop research infrastructures in basic academic disciplines.

The business-corporate model also rationalized charities, especially after the formation of the Cleveland Foundation in 1914. Initially consisting of local charities, such community foundations coordinated the distribution of funds in a given locality, as through Community Chests, and also offered modest donors the professional administration of funds.

Philanthropy and the Voluntary State

In the 1920s Carnegie and Rockefeller philanthropies, along with the Russell Sage Foundation, began emphasizing the importance of the social sciences, especially in their relation to government policy formation. Foundation money helped create a number of institutions, such as the National Bureau of Economic Research, the Social Science Research Council, and the Brookings Institution, and also strengthened university departments of sociology, economics, and public administration.

The emergence of Herbert Hoover as secretary of commerce and later as president increased the reliance of government upon private foundations in policy development. A network of university social scientists, supported by foundations, provided the expertise necessary for government programs, resulting in what might be called a voluntary state. Even before the Depression, Hoover sought expert advice on business cycles, old age pensions, unemployment insurance, and health care, which led to the publication of the monumental report, *Recent Social Trends* (1933). Many New Deal programs, such as Social Security, relied upon this type of research. One controversial program was the Carnegie Corporation support for studies on race relations, especially Gunnar Myrdal's *An American Dilemma* (1944), which was significant in shaping the *Brown v. Board of Education* (1954) decision that barred segregation.

This public-private partnership existed also in international matters. The Senate's refusal to approve American membership in the League of Nations led to an increased involvement of philanthropy overseas. Rockefeller philanthropy had supported basic medical research in China, and after World War I that backing was expanded to research programs in Europe and Asia. Also created were various International Houses on major university campuses, along with scholarly exchange programs to encourage greater understanding.

The economic upheavals of the 1930s depressed foundation endowments and also forced a change in federal tax policy, as inheritance taxes became permanent in 1935. Henry Ford, Eli Lilly, and Robert Wood Johnson each created new foundations to shelter their wealth. The new tax laws also allowed for-profit companies to give to charity, and later to form their own foundations, which they did increasingly after the 1950s.

Philanthropy during the American Century

As World War II approached, foundations helped in establishing preparedness, which included encouraging many refugee scholars, including Albert Einstein, to flee Europe. Foundations funded special programs, as in science and language training, that were critical to the war effort. After World War II, philanthropy became increasingly tied to American foreign policy, especially in the Cold War. The Ford Foundation, joined by the Rockefeller Foundation and the Carnegie philanthropies, became increasingly involved in international affairs, developing university-based area studies programs and various cultural activities that were indirectly anti-communist.

Foundations came under attack in the early 1950s, most significantly by two congressional committees. In 1952 the Cox Committee examined whether foundations were undermining the exiting capitalistic structure. Two years later the more McCarthyite-like Reece Committee investigated whether they were subversive. Foundations responded by increasing their public visibility and accountability and by moving closer to the political mainstream. One result of congressional scrutiny was the largest single grant in history, the Ford Foundation's gift of over $550 million in 1955 for private universities, medical schools, and hospitals. While relatively unimaginative, this gift helped offset the massive governmental funding of public universities.

The developing world was an area of significant philanthropic activity in the 1950s and 1960s. One major focus was on plant genetics, with the goal of increasing food production. Started initially by the Rockefeller Foundation in Mexico, such agricultural research was drastically expanded with Ford Foundation support in the 1960s, leading to the Green Revolution. The research targeted cereal grains such as rice, and resulted in dramatically increased food supplies. India even became a food exporter for the first time. Philanthropies also expanded studies in human genetics and family planning, which helped reduce population growth.

Foundations resumed major political engagement in the 1960s. Nelson Rockefeller, with significant support from the Rockefeller Brothers Fund, commissioned a series of policy studies in the late 1950s that became the basis of numerous initiatives in the Kennedy administration. The Rockefeller Foundation president, Dean Rusk, joined the administration as secretary of state and the president of the Carnegie Corporation, John Gardner, served as secretary of Health, Education and Welfare under President Lyndon Johnson. Gardner left in 1968 to form the citizens' lobby Common Cause, and later, Independent Sector to promote nonprofit organizations. McGeorge Bundy, the dean at Harvard, became Kennedy and Johnson's national security adviser, and left government to head the Ford Foundation. Under its public affairs director, Paul Ylvisaker, Ford began increasingly to address civil rights issues, supporting the Gray Areas Program in inner cities, funding voter registration drives, and backing the controversial Community Action Programs. Other philanthropic efforts included grants to explore Head Start programs and public television.

The increased visibility of foundation philanthropy led to new congressional investigations, such as one led by the populist U.S. representative Wright Patman starting in 1961. An indirect result was the Tax Reform Act of 1969, which restricted political activity, increased reporting requirements, and forced a payout percentage of foundation assets. Foundation reaction was generally supportive, and John D. Rockefeller III initiated the Filer Commission on

Private Philanthropy and Public Needs in 1973 to help strengthen and increase philanthropic effectiveness.

In response to the perceived leftward tilt of many mainstream foundations, more conservative foundations, such as the Olin Foundation, the Pew Charitable Trusts, and the Bradley Foundation, began developing strategies for a revival of conservatism. The presidential victory of Ronald Reagan in 1980 resulted in part from the strategic policy support of conservative foundations. By the 1980s there had emerged blocks of foundations that supported various sides of the policy spectrum. Reagan's partial dismantling of the social safety net increased the pressures on nonprofits and private philanthropy to make up for the decline in federal social spending. Also bringing attention to the role of private philanthropy was President George H. W. Bush's call for "a thousand points of light"—although Republicans have at least rhetorically favored small contributors over professional foundations. Democrats have relied upon their own philanthropic allies to fund the studies necessary for the continuation of favorite policies, as when the Robert Wood Johnson Foundation supported Hillary Clinton's health care reform initiatives in the mid-1990s.

While the vast majority of philanthropy is devoted to domestic matters, the end of the Cold War led to an expanded international effort on the part of American foundations. The rise of Mikhail Gorbachev stemmed in part from Carnegie Corporation support in the 1980s, and soon after the fall of the Soviet Union, the Ford Foundation established an office in Moscow. Financier George Soros formed the Open Society Fund to create the private Central European University and to encourage democratic pluralism in eastern Europe. In 1997 media mogul Ted Turner pledged a billion dollars to the United Nations over a ten-year period, the largest gift in history, in part to encourage others of the newly rich to donate more to philanthropic causes.

The Future of Philanthropy

After almost a century of criticism from the left, the right, and populists on all sides, what is significant is that philanthropy has become an accepted part of American political culture. Despite all the political involvement of foundation philanthropy in controversial policy areas, there have not been any congressional investigations for over thirty years. In the coming decades, philanthropy will become of increasing importance, as the passing of the World War II generation will lead to the greatest transfer of wealth in history, in the trillions of dollars. Much of that will be turned over to philanthropic foundations, which will continue America's distinctive tradition of encouraging private expenditures for public purposes.

BIBLIOGRAPHY

Arnove, Robert F. ed. *Philanthropy and Cultural Imperialism: The Foundations at Home and Abroad.* Boston: G. K. Hall, 1980.

Bremner, Robert H. *American Philanthropy.* 2d ed. Chicago: University of Chicago Press, 1988.

The Chronicle on Philanthropy. Available at http://philanthropy.com. A biweekly publication that is an essential starting point for current philanthropic activity.

Dowie, Mark. *American Foundations: An Investigative History.* Cambridge, Mass.: MIT Press, 2001.

The Foundation Center. Available at http://fndcenter.org. Basic research on the largest foundations can be found here.

Hall, Peter Dobkin. *Inventing the Nonprofit Sector and Other Essays on Philanthropy, Voluntarism, and Nonprofit Organizations.* Baltimore: Johns Hopkins University Press, 1992.

Hammack, David, ed. *Making the Nonprofit Sector in the United States.* Bloomington: Indiana University Press, 1998.

Karl, Barry D. "Foundations and Public Policy." In *Encyclopedia of the United States in the Twentieth Century.* Vol. 1. Edited by Stanley Kutler. New York: Scribners, 1996.

Kiger, Joseph C. *Philanthropic Foundations in the Twentieth Century.* Westport, Conn.: Greenwood Press, 2000. Kiger was the research director of the Cox Committee.

Lagemann, Ellen Condliffe, ed. *Philanthropic Foundations: New Scholarship, New Possibilities.* Bloomington: Indiana University Press, 1999.

O'Connell, Brian, ed. *America's Voluntary Spirit: A Book of Readings.* New York: The Foundation Center, 1983.

Fred W. Beuttler

See also **Carnegie Corporation of New York; Carnegie Foundation for the Advancement of Teaching; Carnegie Institution in Washington; Charity Organization Movement; Dartmouth College Case; Rockefeller Foundation; Sanitary Commission, United States.**

PHILIPPINE INSURRECTION. More usually called the Philippine-American War or the Philippine War, the Philippine Insurrection (1899–1902) was America's first conflict of the twentieth century. On 1 May 1898, at the beginning of the SPANISH-AMERICAN WAR Commodore George Dewey sank the Spanish fleet in Manila Bay, PHILIPPINES. Believing they would be given independence by America, Filipino forces under Emilio Aguinaldo, who had been fighting the Spanish since 1896, laid siege to Manila and occupied the rest of the archipelago, destroyed Spanish control, and declared independence as a democratic republic on 12 June 1898.

U.S. volunteer troops under Generals George M. Anderson and Wesley M. Merritt, later replaced by General Elwell S. Otis, occupied Manila. Tensions rose as Filipinos requested a voice in peace negotiations between the United States and Spain. However, President William McKinley declined to recognize the Philippine government or its independence nor assure Filipinos that their nation would not be given back to Spain.

With the signing of the Treaty of Paris on 10 December 1898, Spain ceded the Philippines to the United States. American troops were ordered to occupy the entire archipelago. Talks between Otis, who demanded unconditional submission of the Filipinos, and Aguinaldo, who demanded a promise of future independence, were unfruitful and eventually broke down.

Hostilities erupted on 4 February 1899 in the outskirts of Manila. While American troops were initially outnumbered twelve thousand to twenty-five thousand, they had better discipline and organization and the advantage of surprise. The Filipinos also lacked experience of conventional warfare and weapons expertise.

Some thirty major engagements between U.S. and Filipino troops occurred in the next ten months. In November 1899, with Aguinaldo in hiding, the Filipino army was officially disbanded, and the war moved into a guerrilla phase. Lasting until 1902, the guerrilla war was marked by atrocities on both sides.

Otis, who had believed that Filipinos ought to be American subjects, was replaced by the more objective General Arthur MacArthur (father of Douglas MacArthur). Military action was accompanied by a "hearts and minds" campaign that included education, fiscal reform, and civil construction projects.

Hoping that a victory by William Jennings Bryan in the 1900 U.S. presidential election would lead to independence, Filipinos continued fighting. Bryan lost to McKinley, a blow to insurgent morale. This, and a forceful campaign by MacArthur with seventy thousand men, led to an increasing number of surrenders and captures of Filipino forces in 1900 and 1901.

In March 1901 Major Fredrick S. Funston entered Aguinaldo's headquarters under false colors and captured him. William Howard Taft, later to be president of the United States, was appointed as civilian governor, and MacArthur was replaced by General Adna R. Chaffee.

By the end of 1901, organized resistance in the Christianized part of the country continued in two provinces, Batangas and the island of Samar. Resistance in Batangas was ended by General James Franklin Bell, who introduced a *reconcentrado* policy to separate the population from the guerrillas. Samar was pacified by five thousand U.S. marines in a punitive expedition following the killing of forty-eight men of the Ninth Infantry regiment in Balangiga, southern Samar, the worst American loss of the war. With the surrender of Filipino General Miguel Malvar in Luzon and the capture of General Vicente Lukban in Samar, Filipino forces lost centralized leadership and were unable to recover.

President Theodore Roosevelt announced a formal end to hostilities in the Philippines on 4 July 1902. Unrest (which continued until 1913) arose again in Samar in 1904 with the emergence of the religious extremists, the Pulahanes. Conflict with the Muslims of Mindanao began in 1902 and was never entirely resolved; it is not usually considered part of the Philippine-American War.

Some 130,000 American troops were employed in the Philippine Insurrection. In 2,811 formal engagements and many more unconventional engagements, U.S. losses amounted to some four thousand with another twenty-nine hundred wounded in action. Estimates of Filipino dead, directly and indirectly due to the war, range from two hundred thousand to 1 million. The war led to bitter recriminations within the United States, particularly by the Anti-Imperialist League, supported by Mark Twain and Andrew Carnegie. Many were shocked by a Senate inquiry into the war and resultant courts martial of General Jacob Smith, Lieutenant Waller T. Waller, and other officers.

Philippine independence was finally recognized in 1946. Permanent U.S. Navy and Air Force bases were maintained in the Philippines until 1992 and played a critical role in conflicts such as Vietnam and Korea and in projecting American influence into the Asia-Pacific region.

The Philippines is America's oldest and most militarily active ally in southeast Asia.

BIBLIOGRAPHY

Agoncillo, Teodoro. *The History of the Filipino People.* Quezon City, Philippines: R.P. Barcia, 1974.

Gates, John M. *Schoolbooks and Krags, The United States Army and The Philippines. 1898–1902.* Westport, Conn.: Greenwood, 1973.

Gleek, Lewis L. *The American Half-Century, 1896–1946.* Rev. ed. Quezon City, Philippines: New Day Publishers, 1998.

Linn, Brian McAllister. *The Philippine War, 1899–1902.* Lawrence: University of Kansas, 2000.

Taylor, John R. M. *The Philippine Insurrection Against the United States.* Pasay City, Philippines: Eugenio Lopez Foundation, 1971.

Robert D. Couttie

See also **Anti-Imperialists.**

PHILIPPINE SEA, BATTLE OF THE (19–20 June 1944). During the offensive against Japan in the central Pacific beginning in November 1943, the Fifth Fleet of the U.S. Pacific Fleet, led by Adm. Raymond A. Spruance, assaulted strategically important Saipan in the Mariana Islands in June. Japan's undertrained pilots were quickly shot down by seasoned American navy airmen; Japan's sea command fared little better. In June 1944, two Japanese heavy carriers sank from torpedoes from the American submarines *Albacore* and *Cavalla*, and a third fell prey to American planes as it tried to escape westward. The Japanese fleet surrendered control of the Marianas and the central Pacific to the U.S. Navy; from these islands, long-range bombers reached Tokyo in November 1944.

BIBLIOGRAPHY

Lockwood, Charles A. *Battles of the Philippine Sea.* New York: Crowell, 1967.

Miller, Nathan. *The Naval Air War, 1939–1945.* Annapolis, Md.: Naval Institute Press, 1991.

Smith, Robert Ross. *The Approach to the Philippines.* Washington, D.C.: Center of Military History, U.S. Army, 1996.

Y'Blood, William T. *Red Sun Setting: The Battle of the Philippine Sea.* Annapolis, Md.: Naval Institute Press, 1981.

Clark G. Reynolds/A. R.

See also **Aircraft Carriers and Naval Aircraft; Japan, Relations with; World War II; World War II, Air War Against Japan; World War II, Navy in.**

PHILIPPINES. Discovered by Ferdinand Magellan in 1521, the Philippine Islands were occupied by Spain from 1565 to 1898. This occupation was continuous, other than for a brief partial occupation by Great Britain from 1762 to 1764. As a result of the Spanish-American War, possession of the islands was assumed by the United States in 1898.

The Colonial Years

Spanish occupation introduced Christianity and western ideas in general to the Filipino people, while restricting the influence of Islam, primarily in Mindanao and nearby regions. After the United States assumed control of the islands, there was a greater focus on educational, commercial, and agricultural development of the Philippines, along with the introduction of democratic principles. Agitation for independence, which began under Spanish rule, continued in the Philippines under American control.

American interest in the Philippines was largely the result of a desire to expand the nation's economic influence into the Pacific and Asia. When the closing of the frontier seemed imminent by the 1890s, many Americans looked to Asia and the Pacific as golden opportunities to expand American trade and avoid future economic depressions like those of the past twenty-five years. American ambitions for trade, investment opportunities, and territory in East Asia, particularly China, were threatened by competition among the other great powers—England, France, Russia, Germany, and Japan. The Philippines were attractive because they could provide a military and commercial base from which the United States could protect its interests in China. As American relations with Spain deteriorated over the crisis in Cuba, the McKinley Administration saw an opportunity to deal with the situations in Asia and the Caribbean simultaneously.

On 1 May 1898, following the outbreak of war with Spain, Commodore George Dewey destroyed the aging Spanish fleet in Manila Bay. An American expeditionary force arrived in Manila seven months later, and Spain formally surrendered the city. After an armistice in August 1898, peace negotiations in Paris resulted in a treaty in December 1898 that ceded the Philippines to the United States in return for $20 million.

The acquisition of the Philippines gave rise to a protracted and bitter debate. Expansion into the Caribbean fit neatly into American perceptions of being the preeminent power in the Western hemisphere, but assuming control of a large, heavily populated territory thousands of miles away was a different and disquieting challenge. McKinley publicly claimed he had been opposed to acquiring the islands, but a night of reflection and prayer supposedly led him to conclude there was no alternative but to keep them. McKinley understood the Philippines would give the United States an Asian presence and make it easier to guard American interests there. Even so, McKinley was reluctant to assume responsibility for governing the islands, since there was a strong Filipino revolutionary army that had been fighting the Spanish and planned to govern the country. The president authorized Philippine acquisition, however, because he was concerned that another great power might seize the islands; because of the need to protect American commercial interests in Asia; and because he was convinced that the Filipinos could not govern themselves. While imperialists such as Theodore Roosevelt applauded the decision and justified the move on the grounds that the United States had an obligation to teach the Filipinos self-government, others justified the action on the basis that the islands would be the American equivalent of Hong Kong, allowing the country to exploit trading opportunities throughout Asia and the East Indies. Many Republicans also recognized the political benefits of expansion, since it was a victorious war fought under a Republican administration.

But there was fierce opposition to acquisition of the Philippines. While the Senate debated ratification of the treaty, a strong anti-imperialist movement began to develop, which included some of the nation's most prominent citizens, including Andrew Carnegie and Mark Twain. One anti-imperialist argument centered on the morality of imperialism, suggesting that it was a violation of an American commitment to human freedom. Others opposed it on racial grounds, fearing the admission of "inferior" Asian races into America. Some voiced concerns about cheap labor and cheap sugar flooding the domestic market, and the resources the country would have to expend to defend the new territories. Nevertheless, the Senate ratified the Treaty of Paris on 6 February 1899, and the reelection of McKinley in 1900 seemed to indicate that the nation as a whole favored imperialism and the acquisition of the Philippines.

The country soon found itself embroiled in a much more difficult conflict than the one recently concluded with Spain. Filipino insurgents had been in rebellion against Spain before the Spanish-American War, and when the United States supplanted Spain, the revolutionaries directed their resistance against the new rulers. Generally ignored today, the Philippine War (1899–1901) was one of the bloodiest in American history. Some 200,000 American soldiers took part, and with 4,300 deaths, the United States suffered nearly ten times the fatalities of the Spanish-American War. The number of Filipinos who were killed remains uncertain but estimates range upward of fifty thousand. Led by Emilio Aguinaldo, the rebels harassed the American occupation forces for more than three years. The guerrilla tactics used by the Filipinos prompted an increase in brutality on the part of American soldiers, who came to view the enemy as subhuman and who justified increasingly vicious and savage tactics to suppress the insurrection. Although the war continued into 1902, the capture of Aguinaldo in 1901 signaled the turning point. Aguinaldo encouraged his supporters to stop fighting and proclaimed his allegiance to the United States, causing the rebellion to begin losing momentum. Although some fighting continued over the next four or five years, the United States had secured the islands.

At first, the military assumed responsibility for governing the Philippines. Then, during the summer of 1901, administrative authority was transferred to William Howard Taft, the first civilian governor of the territory. Taft promptly announced the intention of the United States to prepare the Filipinos for independence, and he permitted a good deal of local autonomy during his term of service. Taft established the Philippines Commission to serve as a legislative body, and a program of education was begun as well. American soldiers served as teachers until trained teachers could arrive from the United States.

American rule brought the construction of roadways, sanitary facilities and schools. Commerce, trade, and agriculture were given additional attention, and, in August 1907, the United States created the Philippine Assembly. Filipinos were given a majority of seats on the Philippine Commission under President Woodrow Wilson and gained greater autonomy during the administration of Francis Burton Harrison, the governor general from 1913 to 1921. The Jones Act of 1916 permitted the establishment of an elective senate and house of representatives to replace the Philippine Commission and Assembly. In 1934, the Tydings-McDuffie Act mandated a ten-year transition to full independence for the Philippines.

As president, Theodore Roosevelt had referred to the Philippines as the Achilles heel of America in Asia and the Pacific, recognizing that the islands could be a tempting prize for another power such as Japan. With the Lansing-Ishii Agreement of 1917, the Wilson administration secured Japanese assurances that they had no ambitions regarding those islands. The Tydings-McDuffie Act, which promised the Philippines independence in ten years, can be further construed as an admission of American vulnerability there.

As population and economic pressures began to squeeze Japan in the late 1920s and early 1930s, that nation embarked on a program of expansion that led to war with China in 1937. That war had reached an impasse by 1941, leading the Japanese to decide on a southern strategy to secure the resources and markets of Southeast Asia and the East Indies. The United States had thus far given China limited support against Japan, but when Japan seized French Indochina in July 1941, the Roosevelt Administration placed a trade embargo on the Japanese. For the Japanese, this meant restoring good relations with the United States or proceeding with plans to secure the resources to the south. American efforts to get Japan out of China were unsuccessful, and the United States was unwilling to accept anything less. From the Japanese perspective, it seemed that the only option was to consider war with the United States. The location of the Philippine Islands further strengthened the possibility of war from Japan's point of view. The Philippines would make it easy for the United States to interdict shipments of vital raw materials from the East Indies. Therefore, to assure those materials would arrive safely in Japan, the Philippines would have to be taken as well, making war with the United States all the more unavoidable.

Ten hours after the attack on Pearl Harbor, Japanese warplanes struck American air bases in Manila, destroying the small air force of General Douglas MacArthur while it was still on the ground. Perhaps more from ego than sensible military judgment, MacArthur fought the Japanese invaders with an inadequate army, suffering the loss of most of his forces. American and Filipino forces on Corregidor Island held out until 6 May 1942; the captured survivors were led on the infamous "death march" to prison camps. MacArthur, meanwhile, had escaped to Australia after promising to return to liberate the Philippines. Japan set up a puppet government in October 1943, with Jose Laurel as president.

In October 1944, MacArthur did return to the Philippines, along with 200,000 American troops. A combination of bad weather and fanatical Japanese defenders slowed the progress of the invasion, although the American navy decisively defeated the Japanese navy at Leyte Gulf. In February 1945, MacArthur fought a terribly destructive battle for Manila that cost the lives of more than a hundred thousand Filipino civilians. The Philippines were finally liberated on 5 July 1945.

Independence and the Struggle for Autonomy

One year later, 4 July 1946, the United States formally granted the Philippine Islands their independence, with Manuel Roxas as the new nation's first president. This was the first time an imperial power had ever voluntarily relinquished its possession of a colony. Independence, however, did not mean an end to Philippine dependence on the United States, nor was the U.S. willing to cut its ties completely. Concerned about the ability of the Philippines to recover from the ravages of the war, and with the growing exigencies of the Cold War, the United States soon incorporated the islands into its expanding military and economic fold. On 17 March 1947, the United States concluded an agreement with the Philippines that gave the United States leases on military bases there for ninety-nine years. The United States also monitored the Filipino government, often urging reforms that would end corruption and mismanagement. The Philippines would remain an important location for American air force and naval bases until the early 1990s. American loans, foreign aid, and trade agreements helped support the Philippine economy. A security pact between the United States and the Philippines was signed on 30 August 1951.

The war in Vietnam and continued American presence in the Philippines led to anti-American protests and riots in Manila and elsewhere in the late 1960s and early 1970s. These contributed to the autocracy of Ferdinand Marcos, who, in his second term as president, declared martial law and established a dictatorship in 1972. Although American investments and economic interests in the islands had fallen behind those of the Japanese and Taiwanese, the importance of the American military bases there led the Nixon and Ford administrations to keep silent about the end of democracy in the Philippines.

Increasing criticism of the government in the mid-1970s led to greater repression by Marcos; the policy of the United States was to turn a blind eye in that direction. Unwilling to risk talks about the military bases, the administration of Jimmy Carter carefully avoided criticizing the human rights record of Marcos, despite killings by the Philippine military and the imprisonment of thousands. The Carter administration reached a new accord regarding American military bases with the Marcos regime in 1979, and American economic support continued as well.

Growing unrest in the Philippines created a problem for the Reagan administration. Despite Marcos's repressive regime, Reagan liked the Philippine leader personally, having met him first in 1969, and continued to support him because of the Cold War. But the 1983 assassination of Benigno Aquino, Marcos's chief political opponent, made it clear that American strategic and economic interests were in jeopardy. A significant American financial commitment remained in place, while strategic interests dictated keeping Clark Air Field and the Subic Bay Naval Station, both of which were under leases granted by Marcos and due to expire in 1991. Marcos was pressured to implement badly needed reforms, but the Filipino leader continued his repressive ways. This led to more protests, the revival of a communist insurgency by a Maoist group called the Nationalist People's Army, and renewed attacks by Muslim guerillas.

Marcos tried to win back American support by staging elections in February 1986, which he intended to control. The opposition candidate was Aquino's widow, Corazon, and her calls for reform drew widespread support. Relying on massive election fraud, Marcos claimed victory, which was at first upheld by the Reagan White House. But the fraudulent nature of the election was so obvious that the administration had to back off from its support of Marcos when it became evident that any attempt by Marcos to stay in power would result in civil war. Reagan began to urge Marcos to step aside. Marcos finally gave in to American pressure and fled to Hawaii on an American Air Force transport. Corazon Aquino became president of the Philippines.

Although she reestablished democratic institutions, Aquino could not solve the economic problems of her country. Nor could she win the support of the military and the Filipino elite, halt the rampant corruption, or stem the communist insurgency that had now spread to nearly every province. She did implement some political and economic reforms, survived more than a half dozen coup attempts, and supported the 1992 election of her successor, General Fidel Ramos, one of the early defectors from Marcos. Ramos attempted to revitalize the economy, eliminate corruption, and attract foreign investors.

American strategic influence in the Philippines began to diminish in the 1990s. American financial aid stopped almost completely, partly because of domestic economic woes in the first part of the decade. Clark Air Force Base was abandoned after it was destroyed by a volcanic eruption, and, when no agreement on acceptable financial compensation could be reached, the Philippine Senate refused to renew the lease on the naval base at Subic Bay. These actions gave the country greater autonomy, while reflecting its lessened importance in American foreign policy.

A twenty-four-year insurrection led by the Moro National Liberation Front came to an end in 1996, with the signing of a peace accord that would grant the movement greater independence in many of that island's provinces. However, a splinter group, the militant Moro Islamic Liberation Front, rejected the agreement and continued to resist the government.

Joseph Estrada, a popular, though politically inexperienced motion picture actor, replaced Ramos as president in 1996. Elected on promises that he would revive the economy, Estrada headed a corrupt administration. Impeached in 2000 and brought to trial on charges of taking bribes from gambling syndicates, Estrada and his supporters tried to block the prosecutor's access to his financial records in order to delay or end his trial. This led to mass demonstrations that forced Estrada to resign in January 2001. His successor, Gloria Arroyo, promised to wipe out poverty and corruption and refused to grant Estrada amnesty for his alleged crimes. The Arroyo regime struggled to establish its political qualifications, revitalize the country, and deal with Islamic rebel groups, such as the Abu Sayyaf separatists. Just one of many Muslim separatist groups that have been fighting for independence for thirty years or more in Mindanao, the group has been accused of associations with the Al Qaeda network. As of 2002, the Philippine army was still fighting these rebels with assistance from the United States.

BIBLIOGRAPHY

Gleeck, Lewis Jr. *General History of the Philippines: The American Half-Century*. Quezon City, R.P.: Garcia. 1984.

Golay, Frank. *Face of Empire: United States-Philippine Relations, 1898–1946*. Madison, Wis.: Center for Southeast Asian Studies, 1997.

Hahn, Emily. *The Islands: America's Imperial Adventure in the Philippines.* New York: Coward, McCann and Geoghegan. 1981.

Karnow, Stanley. *In Our Image: America's Empire in the Philippines.* New York: Ballantine, 1990.

McFerson, Hazel M. ed. *Mixed Blessing: The Impact of the American Colonial Experience on Politics and Society in the Philippines.* Westport, Conn.: Greenwood Press. 2002.

Roth, Russell. *Muddy Glory: America's "Indian Wars" in the Philippines, 1898–1935.* West Hanover, Conn.: Christopher, 1981.

Stanley, Peter W. *A Nation in the Making: The Philippines and the United States, 1899–1921.* Cambridge, Mass.: Harvard University Press, 1974.

Welch, Richard E., Jr. *Response to Imperialism: The United States and the Philippine-American War, 1899–1902.* Chapel Hill, N.C.: The University of North Carolina Press, 1979.

Gregory Moore

See also **Imperialism;** *and vol. 9:* **Anti-imperialist League Platform.**

PHILOSOPHY in America has encompassed more or less systematic writing about the point of our existence and our ability to understand the world of which we are a part. These concerns are recognizable in the questions that thinkers have asked in successive eras and in the connections between the questions of one era and another. In the eighteenth and nineteenth centuries, theologians asked: What was the individual's relation to an inscrutable God? How could human autonomy be preserved, if the deity were omnipotent? After the English naturalist Charles Darwin published his *Origin of Species* in 1859, philosophers asked: How could human freedom and our sense of the world's design be compatible with our status as biological entities? Early in the twentieth century academic thinkers wanted to know: If we were biological organisms, enmeshed in a causal universe, how could we come to have knowledge of this universe? How could mind escape the limits set by causal mechanisms? By the second half of the twentieth century, professional philosophers often assumed that we were of the natural world but simultaneously presupposed that knowledge demanded a transcendence of the natural. They then asked: How was knowledge possible? What were the alternatives to having knowledge?

Much philosophical exchange existed across national boundaries, and it is not clear that anything unique characterizes American thought. Nonetheless, standard features of philosophy in this country stand out. In the period before the Revolutionary War, thinkers often looked at the "new learning" of Europe with distaste, and the greater religious coloration of American thought resulted from self-conscious attempts to purge thinking of the evils of the Old World. In the nineteenth century the close association of thinkers in Scotland and America revealed both their dislike of England and their sense of inferiority as its intellectual provinces. In the twentieth century the strength and freedom of the United States, especially in the period of Nazi dominance, made America an attractive destination for European intellectuals and dramatically altered philosophy at home. During the period of the Vietnam War suspicion of the United States also affected thought.

From the middle of the eighteenth century American thinkers have been attracted to idealism, that speculative view that existence is essentially mental. The position of the German philosopher Immanuel Kant, that the physical world did not transcend consciousness, or of objective or absolute idealism, that the world was an aspect of an absolute mind, has repeatedly been formulated as a viable option. Thinkers have also enunciated communitarian idealism—that one or another aggregate of finite minds defines reality. But there has been a long circuitous march from a religious to a secular vision of the universe. In America this march has taken a longer time than in other Western cultures. One might presume that the march would diminish the role of the mental, a term often a step away from the spiritual or religious. But despite the growing emphasis on the nonreligious, the deference to one or another kind of idealism has meant in America that realism—the view that physical objects at least exist independently of mind—has often been on the defensive, although a constant option. The eccentric journey away from religion has meant the relatively slow growth of what is often thought to be realism's cousin, materialism—that monistic position opposed to idealism, stipulating that the mental world can be reduced to the physical. More to the point, idealism and a defense of science have often coincided. Philosophers have regularly conceded that scientific investigation could easily but erroneously combine with materialism, but they have usually argued that only some sort of idealism can preserve scientific priorities. The varieties of idealism have also been characterized by a strong voluntaristic component: the will, volition, and the propensity to act have been crucial in defining the mental or the conscious.

The Era of Jonathan Edwards

In the eighteenth and most of the nineteenth century, people in America known formally as philosophers were part of a wider dialogue that had three major components. Most important were parish ministers, primarily in New England, who wrote on theology and participated in a conversation that embraced a religious elite in England and Scotland, and later Germany. These clerics expounded varieties of Calvinist Protestantism. Jonathan Edwards (1703–1758) was the most influential and talented member of this ministerial group, which later included Horace Bushnell (1802–1876) and Ralph Waldo Emerson (1803–1882). But the latter two lived at a time when such thinkers were deserting their congregations and turning away from traditional Protestant doctrine.

The second major component of American speculative thought was located in the seminaries that grew up in the Northeast, the South, and the old Midwest throughout the nineteenth century. These institutions, often independent entities not connected to American colleges, were—aside from law and medical schools—the only places where an aspiring young man could receive instruction beyond what an undergraduate received; they arose to train a professional ministry. The specialists in theology at these centers gradually took over the role played by the more erudite ministry. Leonard Woods (1774–1854) of Andover Theological Seminary, Henry Ware (1764–1845) of the Harvard Divinity School, Nathaniel William Taylor (1786–1858) of the Yale Divinity School, Charles Hodge (1797–1878) of the Princeton Theological Seminary, and Edwards Amasa Park (1808–1900) of Andover belong to this cadre. Among these institutions Yale was primary.

The divinity school theologians had the major power base in the nineteenth century. They trained the ministers and controlled much learned publication. Their outlook tended to be more narrow and sectarian than that of those speculators who were not professors of divinity, but it is difficult to argue that they were not the intellectual equals of those outside the divinity schools.

A final group were actually known as philosophers; they were the holders of chairs in mental, moral, or intellectual philosophy in the American colleges of the nineteenth century. Their function was to support theoretically the more clearly religious concerns of the divinity school theologians and the most serious ministers on the hustings. The philosophers were inevitably ministers and committed Protestants themselves, but in addition to showing that reason was congruent with faith, they also wrote on the grounds of the social order and politics and commented on the affairs of the world. Frequently the presidents of their institutions, they had captive student audiences and easy access to publication. Worthies here include Francis Bowen (1811–1890) of Harvard, James McCosh (1811–1894) of the College of New Jersey (Princeton), and Noah Porter (1811–1892) of Yale, again the leading educator of philosophical students.

This philosophical component of the speculative tradition was provincial. Until after the Civil War, the American college was a small, sleepy institution, peripheral to the life of the nation. It leaders, including philosophers, participated in the shaping of public discourse but were generally undistinguished. Their libraries were inadequate, their education mediocre, and the literary culture in which they lived sentimental and unsophisticated. Europe barely recognized these philosophers, except when they went there to study. Yet the philosophers found senior partners in transatlantic conversations and were on an intellectual par with American clergymen and divinity school theologians.

The intersecting dialogues among amateurs, divinity school theologians, and college philosophers focused on the ideas of Edwards, expressed in works like his *Religious Affections* (1746) and *Freedom of the Will* (1754). His ruminations on the moral responsibility of the solitary person confronting a sometimes angry, at least mysterious, deity controlled subsequent thinking, which tended to emphasize a priori deliberation about the fate of the individual soul. Indeed, the founding fathers of the Revolutionary and Constitutional period—men like Benjamin Franklin (1706–1790), Thomas Jefferson (1743–1826), James Madison (1751–1836), Alexander Hamilton (1755–1804), and John Adams (1735–1826)—were rarely considered philosophers. They had denigrated the study of theology, made politics primary, and grounded their thought in history and experience.

William James. The most influential of the philosophical pragmatists associated with Harvard University. ARCHIVE PHOTOS, INC.

Pragmatism

In the last third of the nineteenth century the work of Darwin dealt a body blow to the religious orientation of American speculative endeavors. The primacy of divinity schools in the scholarly world ended, and the explicit Christian thought that governed intellectual life all but disappeared. At the same time, in the space of thirty years, many old American colleges were transformed into large,

Clarence Irving Lewis. A member of the Harvard branch of pragmatism who in the 1920s led a divergence from pragmatic assumptions, based in part on his interest in symbolic logic. AP/Wide World Photos

internationally recognized centers of learning, while new public and private universities commanded national attention. Students who a generation earlier would have sought "graduate" training in Europe, especially Germany, or in an American seminary, would by 1900 attend a postbaccalaureate program in an American university to obtain the Ph.D., the doctoral degree. Many of these students now found in philosophy what previously had been sought in the ministry or theological education. Those who, in the nineteenth century, had been a creative force outside the system of the divinity schools and the colleges, vanished as professional philosophers took their place.

Among the first generation of university thinkers from 1865 to 1895, philosophical idealism was the consensus. At the end of the nineteenth century, one form of idealism—pragmatism—came to dominate the discourse of these thinkers. Pragmatism won out not only because its proponents were competent and well placed but also because they showed the philosophy's compatibility with the natural and social sciences and with human effort in the modern, secular world. A rich and ambiguous set of commitments, pragmatism associated mind with action and investigated the problems of knowledge through the practices of inquiry, tinting the physical world with intelligence and a modest teleology. Knowledge of the world was ascertainable, but the pragmatists did not define it as the intuitive grasp of a preexisting external object. Knowledge was rather our ability to adjust to an only semihospitable environment. Beliefs were modes of action and true if they survived; experience competitively tested them. The pragmatists used Darwinian concepts in the service of philosophy. Nonetheless, at another level, pragmatism's use of Darwin permitted the reinstatement, in a chastened fashion, of beliefs that were religious if not Protestant. Pragmatists emphasized the way that ideas actually established themselves in communities of investigators and what their acceptance meant. If beliefs about the spiritual prospered, they were also true. In part, the world was what human beings collectively made of it. When most influential, pragmatism was a form of communitarian idealism.

There were two main variants of pragmatism. One was associated with Harvard University in Cambridge, Massachusetts (a tradition that eventually extended to the end of the twentieth century). It included Charles Peirce (1839–1914), William James (1842–1910), Josiah Royce (1855–1916), and later C. I. Lewis (1883–1964), Nelson Goodman (1906–1998), W. V. Quine (1908–2000), Thomas Kuhn (1922–1996), and Hilary Putnam (1926–). This group of thinkers made mathematics, logic, and the physical sciences the model of inquiry, although William James, the most influential of them, famously held that science and religion were similarly justified and could each be defended.

The second variant of pragmatism was called "instrumentalism" by its leading light, John Dewey (1859–1952). Dewey's vision inspired a school of thinkers at the University of Chicago, where he taught in the 1890s, and shaped the intellectual life of New York City and its universities—New York University, City College of New York, the New School for Social Research, and Columbia—after he moved to Columbia in 1904. Instrumentalism in Chicago and New York took the social sciences as the model of inquiry and, especially in the person of Dewey, was far more interested in social and political issues than the pragmatism of Harvard.

While the philosophers in this period wrote for their own learned journals, they also contributed to the leading non-religious journals of opinion such as *The Nation* and *The New Republic.* Through the first third of the twentieth century, philosophy rationalized the work of the scholarly disciplines that promised solutions to the problems of life for which religion had previously offered only consolation. Public speaking went from ministerial exhortation to normative social-science reformism. This mix of the popular and the professorial in what is called the "golden age" of philosophy in America extended from the 1890s until Dewey's retirement in 1929. It gave philosophy its greatest influence and public import and produced a series of notable works—among them Peirce's essays in the *Popular Science Monthly* of 1877–1878, James's *Pragmatism* (1907), and Dewey's *Quest for Certainty* (1929).

Professional Philosophy

Although variants of pragmatism were never absent from discussion, in the second third of the twentieth century a number of vigorous academics conducted a refined epistemological critique of the empirical bases of knowledge. Pragmatic assumptions were called into question. C. I. Lewis of Harvard in *Mind and the World-Order* (1929) and Wilfrid Sellars (1912–1989) of the University of Pittsburgh in "Empiricism and the Philosophy of Mind" (1956) were regarded as the preeminent writers in this area. The intellectual migration from Europe caused by the rise of totalitarianism in the 1930s contributed to this argument when a uniquely stringent empiricism, logical positivism, made an impact on the debate after World War II. The United States became known for its "analytic philosophy," which emphasized clarity and precision of thought, often using logic and the foundations of mathematics to make its points, denigrating much "normative" reasoning in the areas of social and moral philosophy, and presupposing an apolitical sensibility. Leading philosophers in the United States were secular in their commitments, but in a culture still oriented to Judeo-Christian belief, they turned away from the civic sphere.

John Dewey. The educator and philosophical leader of "instrumentalism," a variant of pragmatism, focusing primarily on social and political issues.

These developments gave American thought worldwide honor in circles of scholars, but came at great cost to the public presence of philosophy and even to its audience in the academy. In contrast to what philosophy had been, both in and outside the university, during the period of James, Royce, and Dewey, philosophy after World War II had narrow concerns; it became a complex and arcane area of study in the university system. The 1960s accentuated the new academic status of philosophy. The radicalism and spirit of rebellion surrounding the Vietnam War condemned professional thought as irrelevant.

In the last quarter of the century a cacophony of voices competed for attention in the world of philosophy. A most influential movement still had a connection to Cambridge, originating in the "pragmatic analysis" developed after World War II by Goodman and Quine. This movement was often materialistic in its premises but also skeptical of all claims to knowledge, including scientific ones. The pragmatic analysts had an uneasy connection to an extraordinary publication of 1962, Kuhn's *Structure of Scientific Revolutions*. Although Kuhn's work was ambiguous, it soon justified a much more romantic attack on the objectivity of science and on the pursuit of analytic philosophy itself. The publications of Richard Rorty (1931–) in the last twenty years of the century, especially *Philosophy and the Mirror of Nature* (1979), gave a deeper philosophical justification for these ideas, as many philosophers in philosophy departments rejected straitened approaches to their field without being able to assert a compelling vision of another sort. Moreover, scholars in other disciplines—most importantly in English departments—claimed that traditional philosophy had reached a dead end. These nondisciplinary philosophers challenged philosophers for the right to do philosophy. These developments took American philosophy from the high point of achievement and public influence of the "classic" pragmatists to a confused and less potent role at the end of the twentieth century.

BIBLIOGRAPHY

Brent, Joseph. *Charles Sanders Peirce: A Life*. Rev. ed. Bloomington: Indiana University Press, 1998.

Clendenning, John. *The Life and Thought of Josiah Royce*. Rev. ed. Nashville, Tenn.: Vanderbilt University Press, 1999.

Feigl, Herbert, and Wilfrid Sellars, eds. *Readings in Philosophical Analysis*. New York: Appleton-Century-Crofts, 1949.

Kuklick, Bruce. *Philosophy in America: An Intellectual and Cultural History, 1720–2000*. Oxford: Oxford University Press, 2002. A comprehensive survey.

Miller, Perry. *Jonathan Edwards*. New York: William Sloane Associates, 1949. The first and still the most influential of modern works on Edwards.

Muelder, Walter G., Laurence Sears, and Anne V. Schlabach, eds. *The Development of American Philosophy: A Book of Readings*. 2d ed. Boston: Houghton Mifflin, 1960.

Perry, Ralph. *The Thought and Character of William James.* 2 vols. Boston: Little, Brown, 1935. Still the authoritative work.

Rorty, Richard, M., ed. *The Linguistic Turn: Essays in Philosophical Method.* Chicago: University of Chicago Press, 1992.

Simon, Linda. *Genuine Reality: A Life of William James.* New York: Harcourt, Brace, 1998. The most recent of many biographies.

Stuhr, John J. ed. *Pragmatism and Classical American Philosophy: Essential Readings and Interpretative Essays.* 2d ed. New York: Oxford University Press, 2000.

Westbrook, Robert B. *John Dewey and American Democracy.* Ithaca, N.Y.: Cornell University, Press, 1991.

Bruce Kuklick

See also **Existentialism; Positivism; Post-structuralism; Pragmatism; Religious Thought and Writings; Transcendentalism.**

PHOENIX. In 1867, pioneers entered the Salt River valley in central Arizona and admired the remains of the ancient canal system of the Hohokam, a people who had lived in the area prior to 1400. Homesteading the land, clearing out old irrigation ditches, planting crops, and negotiating supply contracts with nearby military posts and mining camps, the pioneers created an economic base for their community. Realizing that they were revitalizing the land of an ancient people, the settlers in 1870 named the town site Phoenix, a fitting symbol of life rising anew from the remains of the past. Growth was slow but steady, and by 1900, the valley center contained a population of 5,444 and offered an impressive array of urban goods, services, and amenities. By then it was a railroad hub, the seat of Maricopa County, and the territorial capital.

Phoenix leaders, taking advantage of the National Reclamation Act of 1902, supported the federal government in the construction of Roosevelt Dam, completed in 1911. Water management projects brought vital stability to the area, allowed irrigation control, and assured agricultural prosperity. Local promoters also encouraged campaigns to attract new residents and visitors to the Valley of the Sun, emphasizing the opportunities and the amenities available, especially the mild winter climate. By 1930, the city had become a regional urban center of 48,118. The Great Depression retarded progress, but the central Arizona oasis recorded a population of 65,414 in 1940.

During the 1930s, the federal government helped to alleviate distress in the city and the valley through New Deal programs, and during and after World War II, the relationship between Washington and the Phoenix area grew stronger as the Arizona capital became a major military and manufacturing center. By 1955, manufacturing had become the city's number-one source of income, with farming and tourism in second and third places. Major firms in the 1950s included Motorola, General Electric, Goodyear Aircraft, Kaiser Aircraft and Electronics, AiResearch, and Sperry Rand.

Phoenix. A bird's-eye view, c. 1908—just four years before the capital of Arizona Territory became the capital of the forty-eighth state. LIBRARY OF CONGRESS

Business initiative, sunny days, and modern technology prevailed in the popular desert hub. Especially appealing were new attractions such as air conditioning. As in other Sun Belt cities, the mass production of air conditioners in the 1950s and the consequent age of refrigeration attracted not only manufacturers but also more residents and tourists. Throughout the years, the winning combination of opportunities and amenities continued to attract newcomers; occasional downturns occurred, but overall, Phoenix boomed. Economic enterprise and the Phoenix lifestyle drew more people to the area. By 2000, more than a million people lived in Phoenix, and it had become the sixth largest city in the nation.

BIBLIOGRAPHY

Luckingham, Bradford. *The Urban Southwest: A Profile History of Albuquerque, El Paso, Phoenix, and Tucson.* El Paso: Texas Western, 1982.

———. *Phoenix: The History of a Southwestern Metropolis.* Tucson: University of Arizona Press, 1989.

———. *Minorities in Phoenix: A Profile of Mexican American, Chinese American, and African American Communities, 1860–1992.* Tucson: University of Arizona Press, 1994.

Bradford Luckingham

See also **Arizona; Sun Belt.**

PHOTOGRAPHIC INDUSTRY. In 1839 the Frenchman Louis J. M. Daguerre introduced in Paris the first commercial photographic process, the daguerreotype. This novel process used a camera to produce unique positive images on silvered plates. Because of the perishability of the photosensitive materials and the complexity of the process, the practice of daguerreotypy, which soon became popular in the United States, was restricted to technically oriented persons who produced their own photosensitive materials at the site of the picture-taking. Daguerreotypists obtained the optical apparatus from small optical instrument makers and chemical supplies from chemical manufacturers. Within a decade the number of professional daguerreotypists and specialized photographic supply houses had multiplied in the larger cities.

During the mid-1850s a variety of wet collodion processes replaced the daguerreotype. Fluid collodion served as carrier for the photosensitive halogen salts. The photographer flowed the salted collodion onto glass for direct positive images in the ambrotype process, onto japanned iron plates for direct positive images in the tintype process, and onto glass for the popular negative-positive process. The perishability of the photosensitive negative and positive materials confined their production to professional photographers.

The tintype became the most successful—and most distinctively American—style of photograph during this period. Small tintype medals of the presidential candidates widely distributed in the campaign of 1860 first brought national recognition, but the tremendous popularity of the tintype occurred during the Civil War, when itinerant photographers made prodigious numbers of small tintypes in oval cutout mounts, known as "gems."

Changing technology influenced many of the small producers of supplies for the photographer: for example, the Scovill Manufacturing Company of Waterbury, Conn., the principal American producer of unsensitized daguerreotype plates, shifted its product line. While small producers of such new photographic supplies as tintype plates and unsensitized print paper did emerge in the 1860s and 1870s, the most powerful firms in the industry were the Anthony and the Scovill companies, which dominated the jobbing function in photographic supplies and in producing photographic papers, chemicals, cameras, and albums.

In the early 1880s dry gelatin supplanted wet collodion as the carrier of photosensitive salts on negative glass plates, which preserved the photosensitivity of the halogen salts for many months. This change permitted centralized factory production of photosensitive materials for the first time. The industry's traditional marketing and production companies did not take the lead in producing plates and papers, allowing new firms to seize production leadership—Cramer, Seed, and Hammer in Saint Louis; American Aristotype in Jamestown, N.Y.; Eastman in Rochester, N.Y.; Stanley in Boston; and Nepera Chemical in Yonkers, N.Y. The technical complexities still deterred most people from practicing photography.

In 1884 George Eastman, despairing of the intense price competition in the dry-plate market, sought with William H. Walker, a Rochester camera maker, to develop an alternative to dry plates. Improving substantially on Leon Warnerke's commercially unsuccessful system, they introduced in 1885 a roll-film system. In 1888 he addressed the enormously large and previously untapped mass amateur market by isolating the technical complexities from picture taking. He added to the company's established production of photosensitive materials by designing a simple-to-operate, highly portable roll-film camera, the Kodak, and by providing factory service that included the unloading and reloading of the camera with film and the developing and printing of the pictures. With a highly successful advertising campaign featuring the slogan "You press the button—we do the rest," Eastman inaugurated photography for novices and revolutionized the industry. During the next decade the company introduced numerous improvements, including a Celluloid base for film and daylight-loading film cartridges. The company's tight patent control on the film system and its policy of continuous innovation helped it establish and maintain market dominance.

As Eastman Kodak grew in size, it sought to broaden and strengthen its nonamateur product line by acquiring, during the decade from 1898 to 1908, a number of photographic-paper, plate-camera, and dry-plate companies. Despite a number of large competitors—including Ansco, Defender, Cramer, and Hammer in the United States; Ilford in Britain; and AGFA in Germany—Eastman Kodak held a substantial market share at home and abroad by 1910 and maintained it by emphasizing product quality, innovations, and patents. In recognition of the increasing importance of chemistry and physics to the industry, Eastman established in 1912 the Eastman Kodak Research Laboratory, directed by the British photochemist C. E. Kenneth Mees. Within a decade of its founding the laboratory began to have a direct influence on the output of the Eastman Kodak production lines.

The introduction of the roll-film system stimulated the development of cinematographic apparatus. Early in the twentieth century, concurrent with the rapid growth of amateur photography, an American cinematographic industry began to emerge, with innovators in projection equipment assuming the initial leadership. At the end of the first decade of the century a number of firms producing apparatus and commercial films combined their patents and other assets to form the Motion Picture Patents Company. It sought to limit competition in the motion picture industry, but adverse court decisions in an antitrust suit and a series of product and marketing innovations brought the organization's demise within a decade. Large new corporations that integrated production, distribution, and exhibition functions emerged by 1920 as the new leaders of the cinematographic industry. These included Paramount, Fox, and Loew. The introduction of sound films in the late 1920s altered this structure somewhat as the innovators, Warner and RKO, joined the small group of leaders.

Meanwhile, the rapidly growing demand for raw cine film greatly stimulated Eastman Kodak's film production, where the production of cine film substantially exceeded the production for still photography after 1910. Although the company carefully avoided entry into the professional cine field, the territory of its largest customers, it introduced home movie equipment with nonflammable film in the early 1920s. In the late 1920s the company developed and introduced a series of color processes for motion pictures. During the middle 1940s the motion picture industry enjoyed its greatest success, but soon the introduction of television inaugurated a quarter-century of decline. In response the industry introduced spectaculars; three-dimensional and widescreen productions; new exhibition methods, such as drive-in and shopping-center theaters to replace the giant downtown movie palaces of an earlier era; and, later, low-budget, sensational movies featuring sexuality and violence.

In still photography between World War I and World War II the German industry began to compete with the American. German camera makers, influenced by cinematography, introduced in the early 1920s small 35-mm cameras that appealed to journalists and serious amateur photographers. Also, in the late 1920s Ansco, which had faltered since its founding because of limited capital and technical resources, sold its assets to the I. G. Farben-Industrie and became the American outlet for the research-oriented German photographic industry. During World War II the U.S. government assumed ownership and operation of the firm, and the government relinquished ownership only in 1965, when the firm became a public corporation, General Aniline and Film (GAF).

Professional photographers were typically in the forefront of technology and trends. To compensate for the disappearance of skilled portraiture and documentation in the wake of the 35-mm revolution, photographers turned to publishing and advertising. Their favorite camera was a 2-inch format equipped with motor drives, multiple lenses, and sophisticated lighting devices. Fine-art photographers devoted considerable energy to experimenting with equipment, format, film, and paper, and their subjects tended toward the eclectic. Beginning in the late 1940s, they attempted to capture "private realities," a quest drawing inspiration from Eastern religious philosophies, psychoanalytic theory, and abstract expressionist painting. Its popularity in the United States stemmed from the postwar economic boom, the ability of former military personnel to attend art schools at federal expense, and the founding of the Institute of Design, the Western Hemisphere's version of the Bauhaus, which advocated a "new vision" of interpreting common places in personal ways.

The straight tradition popularized by Edward Weston remained the dominant but far from the only style in professional photography in the late twentieth century. A gifted photographer, educator, and author, Minor White encouraged his followers to reveal "things for what they are." His advocacy of the "equivalent image" produced a cultlike following from the 1960s into the 1990s. With large-format cameras, White's followers photographed such natural phenomena as gnarled trees, tumultuous ocean waves, and dew-tinged leaves and petals. Photographers like Walter Chappell and Paul Caponigro struggled to evoke the mystic divinity of nature itself.

Photographers took to the streets in the 1950s and 1960s using handheld units to frame reality with sardonic or ironic twists. Like the painter Andy Warhol, they opted for the vernacular and emblems of popular culture. Modern masters like William Klein, Garry Winogrand, and William Wegman chose human (and in Wegman's case, canine) interaction among artifacts, whereas Elliott Erwitt, who began capturing everyday scenes from around the world in the late 1940s, preferred symbols largely free of human encroachment.

Within the American photographic industry, five developments in the post–World War II period were of particular importance. First, Eastman Kodak, as a result of its research and development, successfully introduced and promoted color-print photography. Second, Japan, manufacturer of high-quality miniature cameras for the serious amateur photographer, developed a dominant influence in that specialized sector of the market. Third, in 1948 the Polaroid Corporation introduced a new system of photography that produced finished prints direct from the camera that was well-protected by a system of patents. Fourth, Eastman Kodak, in response to the Polaroid challenge, introduced a series of Instamatic camera systems that further simplified negative-positive picture-taking. Fifth, electronic cameras, introduced in the early to mid-1990s, became increasingly sophisticated and easy to use, producing high-resolution photos and spelling the end of film photographic processes in certain quarters, notably news coverage. In 1987, for example, United Press International and Associated Press, the largest news wire services in the United States, began transmitting pictures electronically. Four of these five developments reflect the importance of the research-and-development strategies and of the mass amateur-market emphasis of the American industry in its maintenance of international dominance despite the competitive efforts of German and Japanese firms.

Combined, these developments made photography increasingly easy for unskilled practitioners at the end of the twentieth century. Affordable 35-mm compact automatics and high-quality digital cameras had become widely available. Photographic images in silver, color dyes, and printers' ink, along with sophisticated home computers capable of processing and manipulating digital images, had spread around the world. Innovations in moving film made faraway events accessible through simultaneous broadcast. These technological improvements in cameras and in their supporting infrastructures have undergirded the achievements of all photographers since the 1970s. The single-lens reflex camera became smaller and more reliable, with large-format cameras revamped to fit the computer age. In 1972 the Polaroid camera was improved with the SX-70 system, which was in turn supplanted by the 600 system, featuring automatic focus, electronic flash, and battery together with high-speed color film. In the last quarter of the twentieth century both black-and-white and color-positive-and-negative film vastly improved in speed and resolution. Infrared film sensitive to light invisible to the human eye had wide use in science. In the 1990s both AGFA and Ilford marketed wide-latitude film that joined dye couplers with silver halides to form images.

Still-picture versions of camcorders or video cameras (which themselves gained wide use as observation and surveillance tools in prisons, hospitals, courts, schools, and banks and were employed to help diagnose injuries and perform such surgery as laparoscopy) came into being, and digital cameras enabled photographers to store pictures on computer chips, which can be downloaded and tinkered with on a personal computer, obviating the need for the darkroom. Digital imaging and computer manipulation of photos led to the use of faked and "enhanced" pictures in magazines, on television, and in newspapers. A 1994 *Time* magazine cover featured a digitally altered image of O. J. Simpson's mug shot, taken when he was arrested for the murder of his former wife and one of her friends. Among applications by the scientific community was the use in 1994 of digital image processing of conventional photographs to reveal detailed views of the sun's corona during an eclipse.

The high cost of digital cameras through the mid- to late-1990s delayed their widespread use, but a rapid drop in prices in the late 1990s and early 2000s, coupled with a rapid increase in the memory and resolution capabilities of affordable digital cameras, created a booming market for amateur digital cameras and to industry predictions that they were poised to do to the traditional silver halide photography market what camcorders did to Super-8 home movies.

BIBLIOGRAPHY

Collins, Douglas. *The Story of Kodak.* New York: Abrams, 1990.

Jeffrey, Ian. *Photography: A Concise History.* New York: Oxford University Press, 1981.

Jenkins, Reese V. *Images and Enterprise: Technology and the American Photographic Industry, 1839–1925.* Baltimore: Johns Hopkins University Press, 1975.

Marder, William. *Anthony: The Man, the Company, the Cameras.* Plantation, Fla.: Pine Ridge, 1982.

Newhall, Beaumont. *The History of Photography: From 1839 to the Present.* 5th ed. New York: Museum of Modern Art, 1982.

Newhall, Nancy Wynne. *From Adams to Stieglitz: Pioneers of Modern Photography.* New York: Aperture, 1989.

Peeler, David P. *The Illuminating Mind in American Photography: Stieglitz, Strand, Weston, Adams.* Rochester, N.Y.: University of Rochester Press, 2001.

Taft, Robert. *Photography and the American Scene: A Social History, 1839–1889.* New York: Dover Publications, 1964.

Willsberger, Johann. *The History of Photography: Cameras, Pictures, Photographers.* Garden City, N.Y.: Doubleday, 1977.

Evelyn S. Cooper
Reese V. Jenkins
Robert Taft / c. w.

See also **Art: Photography; Brady Photographs; Digital Technology; Film; Photography, Military; Videocassette Recorder (VCR).**

PHOTOGRAPHY. *See* **Art: Photography.**

PHOTOGRAPHY, MILITARY. Since its invention in 1839 photography has come to have an increasing number of military uses. Both still and motion-picture photography document combat, provide military intelligence and topographic data, aid military training, and help in mapping terrain. The first recorded use of photography for military subjects was a series of daguerreotypes of the Mexican-American War of 1846–1848. Popular journals used the daguerreotypes, taken during battlefield lulls, to illustrate their accounts of the action. During the Crimean War (1854–1856) the Englishman Roger Fenton became the first person to photograph battlefield scenes under fire. Because of bulky equipment and slow photographic materials, he could photograph only landscapes and portraits.

Most photographs from the American Civil War, such as those of Mathew Brady and his assistants, were

Military Photography. High-speed processing equipment and sequence cameras are just two of the innovations in military photography between World War I and World War II. Here, Marine Sergeant Grace L. Wyman practices aerial photography at the United States Marine Corps Air Station at Cherry Point, North Carolina. NATIONAL ARCHIVES AND RECORDS ADMINISTRATION taken for a primarily civilian audience, although Union forces attempted on at least one occasion, in 1862, to take aerial photographs from a balloon. Because of technical limitations, photography principally captured images of the battlefield dead and ruins; few pictures depicted actual battles. Photography in the Spanish-American War of 1898 also had the primary aim of informing the general public.

World War I witnessed military recognition of the utility and technological improvements of photography. In 1915 the British at Neuve-Chapelle, France, used aerial photographs to prepare trench maps of enemy lines. By the end of the war each of the rival powers was taking thousands of aerial photographs daily for intelligence purposes, and the art of photo interpretation became an important intelligence skill. Although the limitations of aircraft restricted the uses of aerial photography, new high-speed shutters, improved lenses, and light-sensitive materials led to great advances in the actual aerial photographs. Photography also took on new military roles unrelated to the battlefield itself, as both sides began to use films for training and indoctrination and for home-front information and propaganda.

Between the world wars military specialists—notably Gen. George W. Goddard—facilitated the further technical advancement of military photography. The development of lenses with longer focal lengths, high-speed processing equipment, sequence cameras, and infrared and color films made photography more flexible and useful for the military. Motion pictures also came to be used, principally for training and documentary purposes. An example of the peacetime, defensive use of military photography is to be found in the sophisticated photography during high-altitude reconnaissance flights over Cuba in 1962, which detected the preparations for the arrival and installation in Cuba of Soviet nuclear missiles.

Photography from satellites circling the earth is one of the latest technological advances to be put to military use. The United States launched its first satellite, Explorer 1, only four months after the Soviet Union launched Sputnik on 4 October 1957. The technology developed rapidly, and by 2000, over 2,200 satellites, many of them military, circled the Earth. In addition to spy satellites that provide a number of different types of photographic images for military consumption, the military has also used satellites since 1986 as part of the Global Positioning System (GPS), which allows users to pinpoint their location anywhere on the globe. Most GPS receivers, which have been commercially available since 1990, provide a location within fifteen meters of one's actual location; licensed military users, however, can accurately gain their precise position to within one meter or less.

BIBLIOGRAPHY

Goddard, George W. *Overview: A Life-Long Adventure in Aerial Photography.* Garden City, N.Y.: Doubleday, 1969.

Newhall, Beaumont. *The History of Photography from 1839 to the Present.* New York: Museum of Modern Art, 1982.

Steinberg, Gerald M. *Satellite Reconnaissance: The Role of Informal Bargaining.* New York: Praeger, 1983.

Richard A. Hunt / c. w.

See also **Balloons; Brady Photographs; Intelligence, Military and Strategic; Maps and Mapmaking; Photographic Industry; Space Program.**

PHRENOLOGY in antebellum America became a significant influence on the thought of major reformers and literary figures. Perhaps more importantly, it also served as a practical system of psychological diagnosis, prognosis, and counseling that had a major impact on the lives of many individuals. Its roots lay in the late-eighteenth-century claims of the Germans Franz Josef Gall (1758–1828) and Johann Christoph Spurzheim (1776–1832), who argued that the brain is the organ of the mind and that specific mental faculties are located in specific parts of the brain. Many contemporaneous philosophers and physiologists made similar assertions. The phrenologists went further, however, and argued that the strength of each faculty determines the physical size and shape of the specific part of the brain in which it is localized and that the shape of the brain itself determines the shape of the skull that surrounds it.

Phrenology Diagram. This study of the human head was published in Kentucky in 1843. © CORBIS

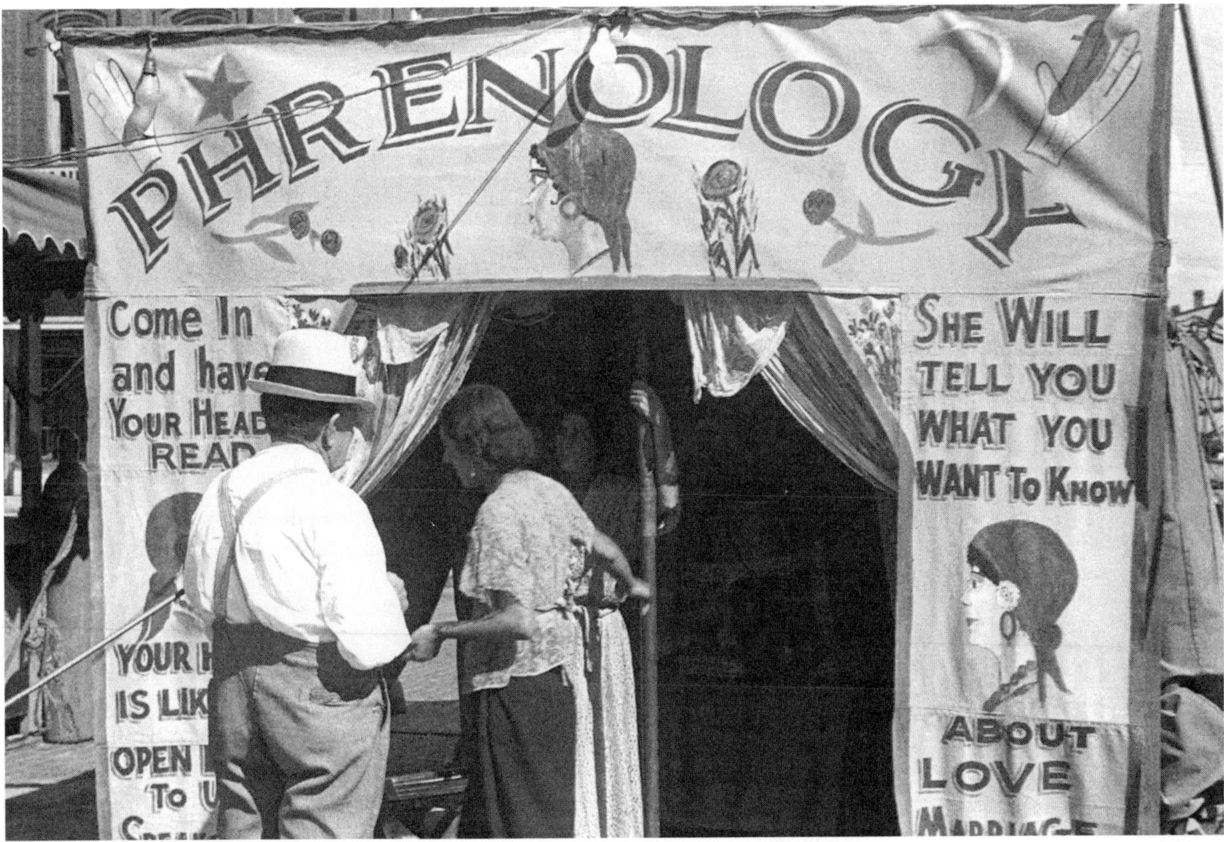

Phrenology Booth. The artist Ben Shahn's photograph, taken in 1938, shows an attraction sponsored by a home for veterans of World War I at a summertime fair in London, Ohio. © CORBIS

European phrenological discourse largely revolved around further claims for the broad philosophical and social import of the science, and early American interest in phrenology developed similarly. Although the first American to advance phrenology was, apparently, the Kentuckian Charles Caldwell (1772–1853) of Transylvania University, Americans responded more fully to lecture tours of Spurzheim himself in 1832 and of the Scottish phrenologist George Combe (1788–1858) in the late 1830s. Many were impressed by phrenology's congruence with the "faculty psychology" of Scottish commonsense realism, the prevalent mental philosophy of the period, which emphasized an individual's specific psychological traits. Such considerations excited political and social reformers, including the Protestant clergyman Henry Ward Beecher, the newspaper editor Horace Greeley, the abolitionist and suffragist Sarah M. Grimké, Samuel Gridley Howe (who advocated for the blind and the "feebleminded"), and the educator Horace Mann. They were attracted to phrenology's concern for "self-knowledge" and "self-improvement" and grew to believe that they could use phrenological insights to promote their causes. Scholars have argued that these beliefs helped shape such individually focused reform movements as care for the insane, convict rehabilitation, sex education, temperance, vegetarianism, and women's rights. Literary figures also looked to phrenological insights about character and temperament, and critics have found phrenological influences in the works of such dissimilar authors as Nathaniel Hawthorne, Herman Melville, Edgar Allan Poe, Mark Twain, and Walt Whitman.

Other antebellum Americans—especially economically and socially striving white middle-class men and women—took phrenology's implications for the individual more personally. Many thus came to believe that an informed phrenological examination by a skilled observer of a person's skull could reveal much about his or her character and mental abilities, and could serve as the basis of expert guidance about an individual's prospects and behavior. As early as 1836, practical phrenologists—most notably the Fowler brothers, Orson Squire (1809–1887) and Lorenzo Niles (1811–1896); their sister, Charlotte Fowler Wells (1814–1901); and her husband, Samuel Robert Wells (1820–1875)—established thriving consulting practices in major American cities that offered premarital, career, and other forms of advice. The New York–based firm of Fowler and Wells also sold phrenological publications and plaster casts of phrenological skulls, and published (in addition to dozens of books and pamphlets) the *American Phrenological Journal and Miscellany* from 1838 through 1911.

Itinerant phrenologists provided similar psychological services for rural America, and residents of many smaller cities and towns looked forward to their regular visits. Such stopovers often included free (or low-cost) public lectures to illustrate their science's value. But they emphasized private appointments for phrenological character readings. One especially active itinerant phrenologist was Nelson Sizer (1812–1897), who alternately worked with the Fowlers in New York and traveled through New England and the Middle Atlantic states. His memoir, *Forty Years in Phrenology* (1882), provides many significant insights into the science and its practice.

Many reformers' and literary figures' interest in phrenology began to wane by the 1850s. Although some observers claim this decline can be traced to growing mainstream medical and scientific criticisms of phrenology, it more likely stems from the reorienting of reform efforts away from the use of moral suasion to promote individual "self-enlightenment" (about which phrenology claimed to have something to say) to attempts to pass laws prohibiting or requiring specific behaviors. (Archetypically, temperance yielded to prohibition.) This decline had (at least initially) little impact on the Fowlers or the itinerant phrenologists, who continued through the 1880s and after to provide individual psychological guidance. After all, many scholars agree that the phrenologists derived their character readings less from their studies of their clients' skull shapes than from their sensitivity to all aspects of an individual's behavior, language, dress, and "body language" during their examinations. (In this way, Author Conan Doyle's Sherlock Holmes later emulated their practice.) The phrenologists hinted as much in private and emphasized the positive "spin" they gave to their readings to enhance their impact. Phrenological advice remained sought after by Americans for many years; a phrenological vocational guidance bureau operated in Minneapolis during the 1930s. Historians of psychology even argue that phrenology's emphasis upon the practical helped shape the scientific interests of the first academically trained American psychologists. These men and women abandoned their German teachers' overriding interests with "the mind" to emphasize mental function and ability and life in the world—just the concerns that the phrenologists stressed—and these concerns have dominated American psychology since the 1880s.

BIBLIOGRAPHY

Davies, John D. *Phrenology: Fad and Science: A Nineteenth-Century American Crusade.* New Haven, Conn.: Yale University Press, 1955.

Fowler, Orson S. *The Practical Phrenologist: A Compendium of Phreno-Organic Science.* Boston: O. S. Fowler, 1869.

Sizer, Nelson. *Forty Years in Phrenology; Embracing Recollections of History, Anecdote, and Experience.* New York: Fowler and Wells, 1882.

Sokal, Michael M. "Practical Phrenology as Psychological Counseling in the 19th-Century United States." In *The Transformation of Psychology: Influences of 19th-Century Philosophy, Technology, and Natural Science.* Edited by Christopher D. Green, Marlene Shore, and Thomas Teo. Washington, D.C.: American Psychological Association, 2001.

Stern, Madeleine B. *Heads and Headlines: The Phrenological Fowlers.* Norman: University of Oklahoma Press, 1971.

Michael M. Sokal

See also **Psychiatry; Psychology; Self-Help Movement.**

PHYSICIAN ASSISTANTS (PAs) are persons trained, certified, and licensed to take medical histories, conduct physical examinations, and diagnose and treat medical problems under the supervision of physicians. In the mid-1990s there were more than 20,000 PAs practicing in the United States in such areas as primary care, internal medicine, surgery, geriatrics, psychiatry, and pediatrics.

Eugene A. Stead, chairman of the Department of Medicine at Duke University in the mid-1960s, created this new profession. A 1959 Surgeon General's report indicated that the nation faced a shortage of medical personnel, particularly among such traditionally underserved populations as the rural and inner-city poor and elderly. Stead's idea was that medical corpsmen returning from Vietnam, with their experience treating illness and injury, could be quickly trained to work in health care. In 1965 four medical corpsman entered the first PA program under Stead's direction at Duke; thirty years later there were fifty-eight such programs throughout the United States.

The American Medical Association officially recognized the profession in 1971 and began developing requirements for PA certification. PA training has not changed a great deal since. Most programs require two years and include intensive clinical rotations under physician supervision. Physician supervision continues throughout the careers of PAs, making them "dependent practitioners" along with nurses. PAs see patients with routine and minor complaints, freeing physicians to see more serious cases, and providing continuity for regular patients in settings with medical residents and interns, whose positions turn over rapidly. All states except Mississippi license and regulate PA practice and most allow PAs to write prescriptions. The American Academy of Physician Assistants claims six jobs for every graduating PA and the Department of Labor projects a 44 percent increase between 1990 and 2005. PAs are no longer an experiment but an important part of mainstream medical care.

BIBLIOGRAPHY

American Academy of Physician Assistants. *Physician Assistants: Statistics and Trends.* Alexandria, Va.: American Academy of Physician Assistants, 1997.

Schafft, Gretchen Engle, and James F. Cawley. *The Physician Assistant in a Changing Health Care Environment.* Rockville, Md.: Aspen Publishers, 1987.

Susan Andrew / T. D.

See also **Health Maintenance Organizations; Hospitals; Medical Profession; Medicine and Surgery; Nursing.**

PHYSICS

This entry includes 4 subentries:

OVERVIEW

From the colonial period through the early nineteenth century, physics, which was then a branch of natural philosophy, was practiced by only a few Americans, virtually none of whom earned his living primarily in research. Some, like John Winthrop at Harvard, were college professors who were expected and encouraged only to teach. Others were gentlemanly amateurs with private laboratories. The physics of that day ranged from astronomy and navigation to pneumatics, hydrostatics, mechanics, and optics. In virtually all these subjects Americans followed the intellectual lead of Europeans, especially the British. As well as the practitioners of other sciences, they were also inspired by the English philosopher Francis Bacon, who had urged scholars to study the facts of nature and had taught that knowledge led to power. Thus, American physicists emphasized the accumulation of experimental facts rather than mathematical theorizing, and they made no distinction between abstract and practical research, or what a later generation would call pure and applied science. The archetypal American physicist was Benjamin Franklin, the retired printer, man of affairs, and deist, who was celebrated for his practical lightning rod as well as for his speculative and experimental contributions to electrical science.

Nineteenth Century

From the Jacksonian era through the Civil War, American physics became more specialized, with its subject matter narrowing to geophysics, meteorology, and such topics of physics proper as the older mechanics and the newer heat, light, electricity, and magnetism. The leading American physicist of the period was Joseph Henry, who discovered electromagnetic induction while teaching at the Albany Academy in Albany, New York. Later he became a professor at Princeton and then the first secretary of the Smithsonian Institution. Imbibing the nationalism of the day, Henry worked to advance the study of physics and, indeed, of all science in America. With Henry's support, Alexander Dallas Bache, Franklin's great-grandson and the director of the U.S. Coast Survey, enlarged the scope of that agency to include studies in the geodesy and geophysics of the entire continent. In the 1850s the survey was the largest single employer of physicists in the country. Henry also channeled part of the Smithsonian's income into fundamental research, including research in meteorology. During Henry's lifetime, American physics became more professional; the gentlemanly amateur was gradually superseded by the college-trained physicist who was employed on a college faculty or by the government.

In the quarter-century after the Civil War, many physicists set themselves increasingly apart from utilitarian concerns and embraced the new ethic of "pure" science. At the same time, the reform of higher education gave physics a considerable boost by permitting students to major in the sciences, making laboratory work a standard part of the curriculum, creating programs of graduate studies, and establishing the advancement of knowledge, at least nominally, as an important function of the university and its professors. Between 1865 and 1890 the number of physicists in the United States doubled, to about 150. The profession included Albert A. Michelson, the first American to win the Nobel Prize in physics (1907), who measured the speed of light with unprecedented accuracy and invented the Michelson interferometer during his famed ether drift experiment in 1881. During the late 1870s and the 1880s, Henry A. Rowland won an international reputation for his invention of the Rowland spectral grating and for his painstakingly accurate determinations of the value of the ohm and of the mechanical equivalent of heat. Generally, American physics remained predominantly experimental, with the notable exception of the brilliant theorist Josiah Willard Gibbs of Yale, an authority in thermodynamics and statistical mechanics.

Professionalization by the Early-Twentieth Century

In 1893 Edward L. Nichols of Cornell University inaugurated the *Physical Review*, the first journal devoted to the discipline in the United States. Six years later Arthur Gordon Webster of Clark University helped found the American Physical Society, which in 1913 assumed publication of the *Review*. After the turn of the century, a sharp rise in electrical engineering enrollments created an increased demand for college teachers of physics. Employment opportunities for physicists rose elsewhere also. Some of the major corporations, notably General Electric Company and American Telephone and Telegraph Company, opened industrial research laboratories; and the federal government established the National Bureau of Standards, whose charter permitted it to enter a wide area of physical research. Before World War I, the graduation of physics Ph.D.s climbed steadily, reaching 23 in 1914, when membership in the American Physical Society was close to 700.

Americans had not been responsible for any of the key discoveries of the 1890s—X rays, radioactivity, and the electron—that introduced the age of atomic studies.

Felix Bloch. A professor at Stanford University and a recipient of the 1952 Nobel Prize in physics for the discovery of nuclear magnetic resonance, used in studying solids and liquids. AP/WIDE WORLD PHOTOS

Like many of their colleagues in Europe, the older American members of the profession were disturbed by the development in the early twentieth century of the quantum theory of radiation and the theory of relativity. But the younger scientists turned to the new atomic research fields, although not immediately to the new theories, with growing interest and enthusiasm. At the University of Chicago, Robert A. Millikan demonstrated that all electrons are identically charged particles (1909) and then more accurately measured the electronic charge (1913). Richard Tolman of the University of Illinois and Gilbert N. Lewis of the Massachusetts Institute of Technology delivered the first American paper on the theory of relativity (1908). By the beginning of World War I, modernist physicists like Millikan were moving into the front rank of the profession, which was focusing increasingly, at its meetings and in its publications, on the physics of the quantized atom.

During the war, physicists worked for the military in various ways, most notably in the development of systems and devices for the detection of submarines and for the location of artillery. Their success in this area helped bolster the argument that physics, like chemistry, could produce practical and, hence, economically valuable results. Partly in recognition of that fact, industrial research laboratories hired more physicists in the 1920s. Moreover, the funding for physical research rose considerably in both state and private universities. During the 1920s about 650 Americans received doctorates in physics; a number of them received postdoctoral fellowships from the International Education Board of the Rockefeller Foundation and from the National Research Council. After studying with the leading physicists in the United States and Europe, where the revolution in quantum mechanics was proceeding apace, many of these young scientists were well prepared for the pursuit of theoretical research.

World Class Physics by the 1930s

By the end of the 1920s the United States had more than 2,300 physicists, including a small but significant influx of Europeans, including Paul Epstein, Fritz Zwicky, Samuel Goudsmit, and George Uhlenbeck, who had joined American university faculties. During that decade, Nobel Prizes in physics were awarded to Millikan (1923), director of the Norman Bridge Laboratory of Physics (1921) and chief executive at the California Institute of Technology, and to Arthur H. Compton (1927) of the University of Chicago for his quantum interpretation of the collision of X rays and electrons. At the Bell Telephone Laboratories, Clinton J. Davisson performed the research in electron diffraction for which he became a Nobel laureate in 1937. By the early 1930s the American physics profession compared favorably in experimental achievement with its counterparts in Europe; and in theoretical studies its potential, although not yet its accomplishment, had also reached the first rank.

During the 1930s the interest of physicists shifted from the atom to the nucleus and to what were later called elementary particles. In 1932, while conducting research for which they later won Nobel Prizes, Carl Anderson of the California Institute of Technology identified the positron in cosmic rays and, at the University of California at Berkeley, Ernest O. Lawrence successfully accelerated protons to one million volts of energy with his new cyclotron. Despite the depression, which at first reduced the funds available for physics research, U.S. physicists managed to construct cyclotrons, arguing that the exploration of the nucleus might yield the secret of atomic energy or that the radioactive products of cyclotron bombardment might be medically useful, especially in the treatment of cancer. All the while, more Americans earned Ph.D.s in physics, and the profession was further enriched by such refugees from the Soviet Union as George Gamow, and from Nazi Europe as Albert Einstein, Hans Bethe, Felix Bloch, Victor Weisskopf, Enrico Fermi, Emilio Segrè, Leo Szilard, Eugene Wigner, and Edward Teller. By the end of the 1930s, the American physics profession, with more than 3,500 members, led the world in both theoretical and experimental research.

During World War II, physicists, mobilized primarily under the Office of Scientific Research and Development, contributed decisively to the development of microwave radar, the proximity fuse, and solid-fuel rockets. They also worked on the atomic bomb in various laboratories of the Manhattan Project, notably Los Alamos, New Mexico, which was directed by J. Robert Oppenheimer. Equally important, physicists began advising the military how best to use the new weapons tactically and, in some cases, strategically.

After World War II, American physicists became prominent figures in the government's strategic advisory councils, and they played a central role in the debates over nuclear and thermonuclear weapons programs in the 1950s and 1960s. Recognized as indispensable to the national defense and welfare, physics and physicists received massive governmental support in the postwar decades, notably from the National Science Foundation, the Atomic Energy Commission, and the Office of Naval Research. Thus, the profession expanded rapidly, totaling more than 32,000 by 1972. About half of all American physicists were employed in industry, most of the rest in universities and colleges, and the remainder in federal laboratories.

Big Science

Many academic physicists did their research in groups organized around large, highly energetic particle accelerators, notably those at the Stanford Linear Accelerator Center and the Fermi National Accelerator Laboratory (Illinois). The large teams of scientists and engineers involved, the giant machines constructed, and the huge budgets required reflected a new style of research in peacetime, appropriately called Big Science. With these accelerators, American physicists were among the world's leaders in uncovering experimental data about elementary particles, one of the central fields of postwar physics. New particles were discovered by Emilio Segrè, Owen Chamberlain, Burton Richter, Samuel Ting, and Martin Perl, among others, while the necessary detection apparatus, such as bubble and spark chambers, were devised by Donald Glaser, Luis Alvarez, and others. Theoretical understanding included the work of Murray Gell-Mann, Steven Weinberg, and Sheldon Glashow in particle physics, Julian Schwinger, Richard P. Feynman, and Freeman Dyson in quantum electrodynamics, and Tsung Dao Lee and Chen Ning Yang in the nonconservation of parity. I. I. Rabi, Otto Stern, and others measured nuclear properties to unprecedented accuracy, while Maria Goeppert-Mayer advanced the shell model of the nucleus.

Charles H. Townes in the early 1960s played a major role in the development of the laser, an optical device useful both for research and several applications. These latter included bar-code readers in stores, compact disk players, and an X-ray laser, built in 1984 as a component of the now-defunct Strategic Defense Initiative, to destroy enemy missiles.

Meanwhile, physicists, notably at Princeton University, developed the tokamak, a donut-shaped magnetic enclosure in which ionized matter could be contained and heated to the very high temperatures necessary for nuclear fusion to take place. By 1991 they sustained fusion for two seconds, a step on the path to creating an energy machine similar to the fission reactor. Lasers were also being used in the attempt to achieve controlled nuclear fusion.

John Bardeen, Leon Cooper, and Robert Schrieffer in the early 1970s developed a theory of superconductivity to explain the phenomenon where, at very low temperatures, electrical resistance ceases. Physicists soon discovered that a combination of the elements niobium and germanium became superconducting at 22.3 K, about 2 degrees higher than the previous record, and in the late 1980s and 1990s scientists found yet other combinations with much higher (but still very cold) temperatures—above 120 K—that still lacked electrical resistance. Commercial applications, with great savings in electricity, were promising, but not near.

Other American physicists pursued such important fields as astrophysics and relativity, while in applied physics, William Shockley, John Bardeen, and Walter Brattain invented the transistor. This device, widely used in electronic products, made computers—and the information age—possible. It is an example of the way in which the products of physics research have helped to mold modern society. A measure of the quality of research in this country is the record that, from the time the Nobel Prize in Physics was initiated in 1901 to the year 2001, more than seventy American physicists won or shared this honor.

In the last half of the twentieth century physicists came out of their ivory towers to voice concerns about political issues with technical components. Veterans of the Manhattan Project in 1945–1946 created the influential *Bulletin of the Atomic Scientists* and formed the Federation of American Scientists to lobby for civilian control of atomic energy domestically and United Nations control of weapons internationally. During the intolerance of the McCarthy period of the 1950s, many physicists were held up to public scorn as communists or fellow travelers, or even feared as spies for the Kremlin. The President's Science Advisory Committee, formed in reaction to the Soviet Union's launch of Sputnik (1957), was initially dominated by physicists—whose understanding of the fundamentals of nature enabled them to advise knowingly on projects in other fields, such as missile technology.

The nation's principal organization of physicists, the American Physical Society, like many other professional groups, departed from its traditional role of publishing a journal and holding meetings. It began to lobby for financial support from a congress that contained few members with scientific credentials, and to issue reports on such controversial subjects as nuclear reactor safety, the Strategic Defense Initiative, and the alleged danger to health of electrical power lines. Some physicists participated in the long series of Pugwash Conferences on Science and World Affairs, meeting with foreign colleagues to help solve problems caused mostly by the arms race. Others created the Council for a Livable World, a political action committee whose goal was to help elect senators who supported arms control efforts. Still others joined the Union of Concerned Scientists, an organization that documented the danger of many nuclear reactors and the flaws of many weapons systems. The community of physicists had come of age, not only in producing world-class physics but in contributing to the economic and political health of society, often from a socially responsible perspective.

BIBLIOGRAPHY

Childs, Herbert. *An American Genius: The Life of Ernest Orlando Lawrence.* New York: Dutton, 1968.

Coben, Stanley. "The Scientific Establishment and the Transmission of Quantum Mechanics to the United States, 1919–1932." *American Historical Review* 76 (1971): 442–466.

Kevles, Daniel J. "On the Flaws of American Physics: A Social and Institutional Analysis." *In Nineteenth-Century American Science.* Edited by George H. Daniels. Evanston, Ill.: Northwestern University Press, 1972.

———. *The Physicists: The History of a Scientific Community in Modern America.* Cambridge, Mass.: Harvard University Press, 1995.

National Research Council, Physics Survey Committee. *Physics in Perspective.* Washington, D.C.: National Academy of Sciences, 1973.

Reingold, Nathan. "Joseph Henry." In *Dictionary of Scientific Biography.* Volume 6. Edited by Charles C. Gillispie. New York: Scribners, 1972.

Tobey, Ronald. *The American Ideology of National Science, 1919–1930.* Pittsburgh, Pa.: University of Pittsburgh Press, 1973.

Lawrence Badash, Owen Gingerich, Daniel J. Kevles, S. S. Schweber

See also **Laboratories; Laser Technology; Manhattan Project; National Academy of Sciences; National Bureau of Standards; National Science Foundation; Radar; Rockets; Sheffield Scientific School; Strategic Defense Initiative.**

High-Energy Physics

High-energy physics, also known as particle physics, studies the constitution, properties, and interactions of elementary particles—the basic units of matter and energy, such as electrons, protons, neutrons, still smaller particles, and photons—as revealed through experiments using particle accelerators, which impart high velocities to charged particles. This extension of nuclear physics to higher energies grew in the 1950s. Earlier generations of accelerators, or "atom smashers," such as the cyclotron, reached the range of millions of electron volts (MeV), allowing fast-moving charged particles to crash into targeted particles and the ensuing nuclear reactions to be observed. (Particles must collide with the nucleus of the target matter in order to be observed.) Immediately after World War II, Vladimir I. Veksler in the Soviet Union and Edwin McMillan at Berkeley independently devised the synchrotron principle, which adjusts a magnetic field in step with the relativistic mass increase experienced by particles traveling near the velocity of light. In this way more energy could be imparted to the projectiles. Since the moving particle's wavelength decreases as its energy increases, at high energies it provides greater resolution to determine the shape and structure of the target particles. By the 1970s large accelerators could attain hundreds of millions or even several billion electron volts (GeV) and were used to produce numerous elementary particles for study. Cosmic rays provide another source of high-energy particles, but machines offer a greater concentration under controlled circumstances, and are generally preferred.

Theoretical physics kept pace in understanding these particles, which compose the atomic nucleus, and their interactions. By the early 1960s physicists knew that in addition to the protons, neutrons, and electrons that had been used to explain atomic nuclei for several decades, there was a confusing number of additional particles that had been found using electron and proton accelerators. A pattern in the structure of the nucleus was discerned by Murray Gell-Mann at the California Institute of Technology and by the Israeli Yuval Ne'eman. Gaps in the pattern were noticed, predictions of a new particle were made, and the particle (the so-called Omega-minus) was promptly discovered. To explain the pattern, Gell-Mann devised a theoretical scheme, called the eightfold way, that attempted to classify the relationship between strongly interacting particles in the nucleus. He postulated the existence of some underlying but unobserved elementary particles that he called "quarks."

Quarks carry electrical charges equal to either one-third or two-thirds of the charge of an electron or proton. Gell-Mann postulated several different kinds of quarks, giving them idiosyncratic names such as "up" (with a charge of plus two-thirds), "down" (with a charge of minus one-third), and "strange." Protons and neutrons are clusters of three quarks. Protons are made of two up quarks and a single down quark, so the total charge is plus one. Neutrons are made of one up quark and two down quarks, so the total charge is zero.

Another group of particles, the mesons, are made up of quarks and antiquarks (identical to quarks in mass, but opposite in electric and magnetic properties). These more massive particles, such as the ones found independently by Burton Richter at the Stanford Linear Accelerator and Samuel C. C. Ting at Brookhaven National Laboratory in 1974, fit into the picture as being made from charm quarks. The masses of these particles, like the spectrum of the hydrogen atom used by Niels Bohr many decades earlier to elucidate the quantum structure of the outer parts of atoms, now provided a numerical key for understanding the inner structure of the atom. Six different "flavors" of quarks are required to account for these heavy particles, and they come in pairs: up-down, charm-strange, and top-bottom. The first member of each pair has an electrical charge of two-thirds and the second of minus one-third.

Meanwhile, Sheldon Lee Glashow at Harvard University, Steven Weinberg at the Massachusetts Institute of Technology, and Abdus Salam at Imperial College in London in 1968 independently proposed a theory that linked two of the fundamental forces in nature, electromagnetism and the so-called weak nuclear force. Their proposal, known as quantum field theory, involved the notion of quarks and required the existence of three massive particles to "carry" the weak force: two charged particles (W+ and W−) and one neutral particle (Z). These particles are short-lived, massive versions of the massless photons that carry ordinary light. All of these particles are called bosons, or more precisely, gauge bosons, because the theory explaining them is called a gauge theory. The name boson, which comes about for purely historical reasons, refers to a type of symmetry in which labels of the particles can be interchanged according to rules suggested by quantum mechanics, and the resulting forces (and gauge bosons) are found as a consequence of the symmetry requirements. By 1972 indirect evidence for the existence of the Z particle was found in Geneva at the European Organization for Nuclear Research (CERN). It was not until 1983 that the Z particle itself was found, also at CERN, and close on the heels of this discovery came the detection of the W particle.

In the United States, accelerator construction and use was supported primarily by the Atomic Energy Commission, by its successor, the Department of Energy, and by the National Science Foundation. One of the nation's principal machines, the Stanford Linear Accelerator fires particles down its two-mile length. Most other machines, such as those at CERN, Brookhaven (New York), KEK (Japan), and DESY (Germany) are circular or oval in shape. To increase energies still more, beams traveling in opposite directions are led to meet in "colliders," thereby doubling the energy of collision. In early 1987 the Tevatron proton-antiproton accelerator at the Fermi National Accelerator Laboratory (Fermilab) in Illinois came into operation, a machine in the trillion electron volt range. Having narrowly missed out on some of the earlier discoveries, Fermilab scientists were particularly keen to find evidence for the postulated top quark, the only one of the quarks not yet measured and a particle so massive that only the most powerful accelerators could produce enough energy to find it. Their search at last succeeded in 1995.

The Standard Model

By the closing decades of the twentieth century, along with the quarks and bosons, a third type of particle completed the roster: the lepton, of which the electron, positron, and a group of neutrinos are the best known examples. The leptons and quarks provide the building blocks for atoms. The gauge bosons interact with the leptons and quarks, and in the act of being emitted or absorbed, some of the gauge bosons transform one kind of quark or lepton into another. In the standard model, a common mechanism underlies the electromagnetic, weak, and strong interactions. Each is mediated by the exchange of a gauge boson. The gauge bosons of the strong and weak interactions carry electrical charges, whereas the photon, which carries the electromagnetic interactions, is electrically neutral.

In its simplest formulation, the standard model of the strong, weak, and electromagnetic interactions, although aesthetically beautiful, does not agree with all the known characteristics of the weak interactions, nor can it account for the experimentally derived masses of the quarks. High-energy physicists hoped that the SUPERCONDUCTING SUPER COLLIDER (SSC), a machine with a fifty-mile circumference that was under construction in Texas in the late 1980s, would provide data to extend and correct the standard model. They were greatly disappointed when Congress cut off funding for this expensive atom smasher.

The standard model is one of the great achievements of the human intellect. It will be remembered—together with general relativity, quantum mechanics, and the unraveling of the genetic code—as one of the outstanding intellectual advances of the twentieth century. It is not, however, the "final theory," because too many constants still must be empirically determined. A particularly interesting development since the 1970s is the joining of particle physics with the astrophysics of the earliest stages of the universe. The "Big Bang" may provide the laboratory for exploration of the grand unified theories (GUTs) at temperatures and energies that are and will remain inaccessible in terrestrial laboratories. Also of profound significance will be an understanding of the so-called dark matter that comprises most of the mass of the universe.

In acknowledgment of the importance of the subject, experimental and theoretical high-energy physics research was recognized with a host of Nobel Prizes, many of them to American scientists. With the demise of the SSC, however, the field's future is likely to lie in machines built by associations of several nations.

BIBLIOGRAPHY

Brown, Laurie M., and Lillian Hoddeson, eds. *The Birth of Particle Physics.* New York: Cambridge University Press, 1983.

Close, Frank, Michael Marten, and Christine Sutton. *The Particle Explosion.* New York: Oxford University Press, 1987.

Taubes, Gary. *Nobel Dreams: Power, Deceit, and the Ultimate Experiment.* New York: Random House, 1986.

Weinberg, Steven. *Dreams of a Final Theory.* New York: Pantheon Books, 1992.

Lawrence Badash
Owen Gingerich
S. S. Schweber

See also **Energy, Department of.**

NUCLEAR PHYSICS

The age-old goal of physicists has been to understand the nature of matter and energy. Nowhere during the twentieth century were the boundaries of such knowledge further extended than in the field of nuclear physics. From an obscure corner of submicroscopic particle research, nuclear physics became the most prominent and fruitful area of physical investigation because of its fundamental insights and its applications.

Discovery of the Nucleus

In the first decade of the twentieth century J. J. Thomson's discovery of the electron at Cambridge University's Cavendish Laboratory changed the concept of the atom as a solid, homogeneous entity—a "billiard ball"—to one of a sphere of positive electrification studded throughout with negative electrons. This "plum pudding" atomic model, with a different number of electrons for each element, could not account for the large-angle scattering seen when alpha particles from naturally decaying radioactive sources were allowed to strike target materials. Thomson argued that the alpha particles suffered a series of small deflections in their encounters with the target atoms, resulting in some cases in a sizable deviation from their initial path. But between 1909 and 1911 in the Manchester laboratory of Thomson's former pupil Ernest Rutherford, Hans Geiger and Ernest Marsden produced scattering data that showed too many alpha particles were bent through angles too large for such an explanation to be valid.

Instead of a series of small deflections, Rutherford suggested early in 1911 that large-angle scattering could occur in a single encounter between an alpha particle and a target atom if the mass of the atom were concentrated in a tiny volume. While the atomic diameter was of the order of 10^{-8} centimeters, this atomic core (or nucleus), containing virtually the atom's entire mass, measured only about 10^{-12} centimeters. The atom, therefore, consisted largely of empty space, with electrons circulating about the central nucleus. When an alpha-particle projectile closely approached a target nucleus, it encountered concentrated electrostatic repulsion sufficient to deflect it more than just a few degrees from its path.

The Danish physicist Niels Bohr absorbed these concepts while visiting Rutherford's laboratory and in 1913 gave mathematical formulation to the rules by which the orbital electrons behaved. The order and arrangement of these electrons were seen to be responsible for the chemical properties exhibited by different elements. Pursuit of this field led to modern atomic physics, including its quantum mechanical explanation, and bore fruit earlier than did studies in nuclear physics. Radioactivity was recognized as a nuclear phenomenon, and the emission of alpha particles, known by then to be nuclei of helium atoms; beta particles, long recognized as electrons; and gamma rays, an electromagnetic radiation, reopened the question of whether atoms were constructed from fundamental building blocks. The work in 1913 of Henry G. J. Moseley, another former student of Rutherford's, showed that an element's position in the periodic table (its atomic number), and not its atomic weight, determined its characteristics. Moreover, he established that the number of positive charges on the nucleus (equal to its atomic number) was balanced by an equal number of orbital electrons. Since atomic weights (A) were (except for hydrogen) higher than atomic numbers (Z), the atom's nuclear mass was considered to be composed of A positively charged particles, called protons, and A − Z electrons to neutralize enough protons for a net nuclear charge of Z.

Early Nuclear Transmutations

In 1919 Rutherford announced another major discovery. Radioactivity had long been understood as a process of transmutation from one type of atom into another, occurring spontaneously. Neither temperature, nor pressure, nor chemical combination could alter the rate of decay of a given radioelement or change the identity of its daughter product. Now, however, Rutherford showed that he could deliberately cause transmutations. His were not among the elements at the high end of the periodic table, where natural radioactivity is commonly found, but were among the lighter elements. By allowing energetic alpha particles (^4_2He) from decaying radium C′ to fall upon nitrogen molecules, he observed the production of hydrogen nuclei, or protons (^1_1H), and an oxygen isotope. The reaction may be written as

$$^4_2He + ^{14}_7N \rightarrow ^1_1H + ^{17}_8O,$$

where the superscript represents the atomic weight and the subscript the atomic number, or charge.

During the first half of the 1920s Rutherford, now at Cambridge, where he had succeeded Thomson, was able to effect transmutations in many of the lighter elements. (In this work he was assisted primarily by James Chadwick.) But elements heavier than potassium would not yield to the alpha particles from their strongest radioactive source. The greater nuclear charge on the heavier elements repelled the alpha particles, preventing an approach close enough for transmutation. This finding suggested that projectile particles of energies or velocities higher than those found in naturally decaying radioelements were required to overcome the potential barriers of target nuclei. Consequently, various means of accelerating particles were devised.

The Neutron

In 1920 William D. Harkins, a physical chemist at the University of Chicago, conceived that the existence of a neutron would simplify certain problems in the construction of nuclei. In the same year, Rutherford (on the basis of incorrectly interpreted experimental evidence) also postulated the existence of such a neutral particle, the mass of which was comparable to that of the proton. Throughout the 1920s he, and especially Chadwick, searched unsuccessfully for this particle. In 1931 in Germany Walther Bothe and H. Becker detected, when beryllium was bombarded by alpha particles, a penetrating radiation, which they concluded consisted of energetic gamma rays. In France, Irène Curie and her husband, Frédéric Joliot, placed paraffin in the path of this radiation and detected protons ejected from that hydrogenous compound. They, too, believed that gamma rays were being produced and that these somehow transferred sufficient energy to the hydrogen atoms to break their chemical bonds. Chadwick learned of this work early in 1932 and immediately recognized that beryllium was yielding not gamma rays but the long-elusive neutron and that this particle was encountering protons of similar mass, transferring much of its kinetic energy and momentum to them at the time of collision. Since the neutron is uncharged, it is not repelled by atomic nuclei. Consequently, it can enter easily into reactions when it finds itself near a nucleus; otherwise it travels great distances through matter, suffering no electrostatic attractions or repulsions.

Quantum Mechanics Applied to the Nucleus

Werner Heisenberg, in Leipzig, renowned for his articulation of quantum mechanics and its application to atomic physics, in 1932 applied his mathematical techniques to nuclear physics, successfully explaining that atomic nuclei are composed not of protons and electrons but of protons and neutrons. For a given element, Z protons furnish the positive charge, while $A-Z$ neutrons bring the total mass up to the atomic weight A. Radioactive beta decay, formerly a strong argument for the existence of electrons in the nucleus, was now interpreted differently: the beta particles were formed only at the instant of decay, as a neutron changed into a proton. The reverse reaction could occur also, with the emission of a positive electron, or positron, as a proton changed into a neutron. This reaction was predicted by the Cambridge University theoretician P. A. M. Dirac and was experimentally detected in 1932 by Carl D. Anderson of the California Institute of Technology in cloud-chamber track photographs of cosmic-ray interactions. Two years later the Joliot-Curies noted the same result in certain radioactive decay patterns. The "fundamental" particles now consisted of the proton and neutron—nucleons (nuclear particles) with atomic masses of about 1—and of the electron and positron, with masses of about 1/1,840 of a nucleon.

The existence of yet another particle, the neutrino, was first suggested in 1931 by Wolfgang Pauli of Zurich in an address before the American Physical Society. When a nucleus is transmuted and beta particles emitted, there are specific changes in energy. Yet, unlike the case of alpha decay, beta particles exhibited a continuous energy distribution, with only the maximum energy seen as that of the reaction. The difference between the energy of a given beta particle and the maximum was thought to be carried off by a neutrino, the properties of which—very small or zero mass and no charge—accounted for the difficulty of detecting it. In 1934 Enrico Fermi presented a quantitative theory of beta decay incorporating Pauli's hypothesis. Gamma radiation, following either alpha or beta decay, was interpreted as being emitted from the daughter nucleus as it went from an excited level to its ground state.

Further Understanding Provided by the Neutron

The neutron, the greatest of these keys to an understanding of the nucleus, helped to clarify other physical problems besides nuclear charge and weight. In 1913 Kasimir Fajans in Karlsruhe and Frederick Soddy in Glasgow had fit the numerous radioelements into the periodic table, showing that in several cases more than one radioelement must be placed in the same box. Mesothorium I, thorium X, and actinium X, for example, all were chemically identical to radium; that is, they were isotopes. This finding meant they each had 88 protons but had, respectively, 140, 136, and 135 neutrons. Also, in the pre–World War I period Thomson showed that nonradioactive elements exist in isotopic forms—neon, for example, has atomic weights of 20 and 22. His colleague F. W. Aston perfected the mass spectrograph, with which during the 1920s he accurately measured the masses of numerous atomic species. It was revealed that these masses were generally close to, but were not exactly, whole numbers. The difference was termed the "packing effect" by Harkins and E. D. Wilson as early as 1915, and the "packing fraction" by Aston in 1927. After 1932 it was also learned that atomic masses were not the sums of Z proton masses and $A-Z$ neutron masses, and the difference was termed the "mass defect." The concept of nuclear building blocks (protons and neutrons) was retained; however, it was seen that a certain amount of mass was converted into a nuclear binding energy to overcome the mutual repulsion of the protons. This binding energy is of the order of a million times greater than the energies binding atoms in compounds or in stable crystals, which indicates why nuclear reactions involve so much more energy than chemical reactions.

The existence of deuterium, a hydrogen isotope of mass 2 (^2_1H), present in ordinary (mass 1) hydrogen to the extent of about 1 part in 4,500, was suggested in 1931 by Raymond T. Birge and Donald H. Menzel at the University of California at Berkeley and shortly thereafter was confirmed by Harold C. Urey and George M. Murphy at Columbia University, in collaboration with Ferdinand G. Brickwedde of the National Bureau of Standards. The heavy-hydrogen atom's nucleus, called the deuteron, proved to be exceptionally useful: it entered into some nuclear reactions more readily than did the proton.

Shortly after their discovery in 1932, neutrons were used as projectiles to effect nuclear transmutations by Norman Feather in England and Harkins, David Gans, and Henry W. Newson at Chicago. Two years later the Joliot-Curies reported the discovery of yet another process of transmutation: artificial radioactivity. A target not normally radioactive was bombarded with alpha particles and continued to exhibit nuclear changes even after the projectile beam was stopped. Such bombardment has permitted the production of about 1,100 nuclear species beyond the 320 or so found occurring in nature.

Nuclear Fission, Fusion, and Nuclear Weapons

During the mid-1930s, Fermi and his colleagues in Rome were most successful in causing transmutations with neutrons, particularly after they discovered the greater likelihood of the reactions occurring when the neutrons' velocities were reduced by prior collisions. When uranium, the heaviest known element, was bombarded with neutrons, several beta-particle ($_{-1}^{0}e$)-emitting substances were produced, which Fermi reasoned must be artificial elements beyond uranium in the periodic table. The reaction may be expressed as

$$_{0}^{1}n + {}_{92}^{238}U \rightarrow {}_{92}^{239}U \rightarrow {}_{93}^{239}X + {}_{-1}^{0}e,$$

with a possible subsequent decay of

$$_{93}^{239}X \rightarrow {}_{94}^{239}Y + {}_{-1}^{0}e.$$

But radiochemical analyses of the trace amounts of new substances placed them in unexpected groupings in the periodic table, and, even worse, Otto Hahn and Fritz Strassmann, in Berlin toward the end of 1938, were unable to separate them chemically from elements found in the middle part of the periodic table. It seemed that the so-called transuranium elements had chemical properties identical to barium, lanthanum, and cerium. Hahn's longtime colleague Lise Meitner, then a refugee in Sweden, and her nephew Otto R. Frisch, at that time in Bohr's Copenhagen laboratory, in 1938 saw that the neutrons were not adhering to the uranium nuclei, followed by beta decay, but were causing the uranium nuclei to split (fission) into two roughly equal particles. They recognized that these fission fragments suffered beta decay in their movement toward conditions of greater internal stability.

With the accurate atomic-mass values then available, it was apparent that in fission a considerable amount of mass is converted into energy; that is, the mass of the neutron plus uranium is greater than that of the fragments. The potential for utilizing such energy was widely recognized in 1939, assuming that additional neutrons were released in the fission process and that at least one of the neutrons would rupture another uranium nucleus in a chain reaction. The United States, Great Britain, Canada, France, the Soviet Union, Germany, and Japan all made efforts in this direction during World War II. A controlled chain reaction was first produced in Fermi's "pile," or "reactor," in 1942 at the University of Chicago, and an uncontrolled or explosive chain reaction was first tested under the direction of J. Robert Oppenheimer in 1945 in New Mexico. Among the scientific feats of the atomic-bomb project was the production at Berkeley in 1940–1941 of the first man-made transuranium elements, neptunium and plutonium, by teams under Edwin M. McMillan and Glenn Seaborg, respectively. A weapon involving the fission of the uranium isotope 235 was employed against Hiroshima, and another using plutonium (element 94, the "Y" above) nuclei destroyed Nagasaki.

Like the fission of heavy elements, the joining together (fusion) of light elements is also a process in which mass is converted into energy. This reaction, experimentally studied as early as 1934 by Rutherford and his colleagues and theoretically treated in 1938 by George Gamow and Edward Teller, both then at George Washington University, has not been controlled successfully for appreciable periods of time (preventing its use as a reactor); but its uncontrolled form is represented in the HYDROGEN BOMB, first tested in 1952.

Particle Accelerators

The growth of "big science," measured by its cost and influence, is manifest not only in weaponry and power-producing reactors but also in huge particle-accelerating machines. Alpha particles from naturally decaying radioelements carry a kinetic energy of between about 4 and 10 million electron volts (MeV). But, as only one projectile in several hundred thousand is likely to come close enough to a target nucleus to affect it, reactions occur relatively infrequently, even with concentrated radioactive sources. Cosmic radiation, which possesses far greater energy, has an even lower probability of interacting with a target nucleus. Means were sought for furnishing a copious supply of charged particles that could be accelerated to energies sufficient to overcome the nuclear electrostatic repulsion. This feat would both shorten the time of experiments and increase the number of reactions. Since electrical technology had little or no previous application in the range of hundreds of thousands or millions of volts, these were pioneering efforts in engineering as well as in physics. In the late 1920s Charles C. Lauritsen and H. R. Crane at the California Institute of Technology succeeded with a cascade transformer in putting 700,000 volts across an X-ray tube. Merle A. Tuve, at the Carnegie Institution of Washington, in 1930 produced protons in a vacuum tube with energies of more than a million volts. The next year, at Princeton, Robert J. Van de Graaff built the first of his electrostatic generators, with a maximum potential of about 1.5 million volts. In 1932 Ernest O. Lawrence and his associates at Berkeley constructed a magnetic resonance device, called a cyclotron because a magnetic field bent the charged particles in a circular path. The novelty of this machine lay in its ability to impart high energies to particles in a series of steps, during each revolution, thereby avoiding the need for great voltages across the terminals, as in other accelerators. The cyclotron soon exceeded the energies of other machines and became the most commonly used "atom smasher."

Although Americans excelled in the mechanical ability that could produce such a variety of machines, they were only beginning to develop theoretical and experimental research to use them. They also lacked the driving force of Rutherford. Since 1929 John D. Cockcroft and E. T. S. Walton had been building and rebuilding, testing and calibrating their voltage multiplier in the Cavendish Laboratory. Rutherford finally insisted that they perform a real experiment on it. The Russian George Gamow and, independently, Edward U. Condon at Princeton with R. W. Gurney of England, had applied quantum mechanics to consideration of the nucleus. Gamow concluded that particles need not surmount the potential energy barrier of about 25 MeV, for an element of high atomic number, to penetrate into or escape from the nucleus; instead these particles could "tunnel" through the barrier at far lower energies. The lower the energy, the less likely it was that tunneling would occur, yet an abundant supply of projectiles might produce enough reactions to be recorded. With protons accelerated to only 125,000 volts, Cockcroft and Walton, in 1932, found lithium disintegrated into two alpha particles in the reaction

$$^{1}_{1}H + ^{7}_{3}Li \rightarrow ^{4}_{2}He + ^{4}_{2}He.$$

Not only was this the first completely artificial transmutation (Rutherford's transmutation in 1919 had used alpha-particle projectiles from naturally decaying radioelements), but the two also measured the products' range, and therefore energy, combined with a precise value of the mass lost in the reaction, and verified for the first time Albert Einstein's famous $E = mc^2$ equation.

The United States continued to pioneer machine construction, often with medical and biological financial support: Donald W. Kerst of the University of Illinois built a circular electron accelerator, called a betatron, in 1940, and Luis W. Alvarez of Berkeley designed a linear proton accelerator in 1946. D. W. Fry in England perfected a linear electron accelerator (1946), as did W. W. Hansen at Stanford. Since particles traveling at velocities near that of light experience a relativistic mass increase, the synchrotron principle, which uses a varying magnetic field or radio frequency to control the particle orbits, was developed independently in 1945 by Vladimir I. Veksler in the Soviet Union and by McMillan at Berkeley. By the 1970s, large accelerators could attain hundreds of millions, or even several billion, electron volts and were used to produce numerous elementary particles. Below this realm of high-energy or particle physics, recognized as a separate field since the early 1950s, nuclear physics research continued in the more modest MeV range.

Nuclear Structure

With these methods of inducing nuclear reactions and the measurements of the masses and energies involved, questions arose about what actually occurs during a transmutation. Traditional instruments—electroscopes, electrometers, scintillating screens, electrical counters—and even the more modern electronic devices were of limited value. Visual evidence was most desirable. At Chicago in 1923 Harkins attempted unsuccessfully to photograph cloud-chamber tracks of Rutherford's 1919 transmutation of nitrogen. In 1921 Rutherford's pupil P. M. S. Blackett examined 400,000 tracks and found that 8 exhibited a Y-shaped fork, indicating that the alpha-particle projectile was absorbed by the nitrogen target into a compound nucleus, which immediately became an isotope of oxygen by the emission of a proton. The three branches of the Y consisted of the incident alpha and the two products, the initially neutral and slow-moving nitrogen having no track. Had the now-discredited alternative explanation of the process been true, namely, that the alpha particle merely bounced off the nitrogen nucleus, which then decayed according to the reaction

$$^{4}_{2}He + ^{14}_{7}N \rightarrow ^{4}_{2}He + ^{1}_{1}H + ^{13}_{6}C,$$

a track of four branches would have been seen.

Experimental work by Harkins and Gans in 1935 and theoretical contributions by Bohr the next year clearly established the compound nucleus as the intermediate stage in most medium-energy nuclear reactions. Alvarez designed a velocity selector for monoenergetic neutrons that allowed greater precision in reaction calculations, while Gregory Breit at the University of Wisconsin and the Hungarian refugee Eugene P. Wigner at Princeton in 1936 published a formula that explained the theory of preferential absorption of neutrons (their cross sections): If the neutrons have an energy such that a compound nucleus can be formed at or near one of its permitted energy levels, there is a high probability that these neutrons will be captured.

It was recognized that the forces holding nucleons together are stronger than electrostatic, gravitational, and weak interaction (beta particle–neutrino) forces and that they operate over shorter ranges, namely, the nuclear dimension of 10^{-12} centimeters. In 1936 Bohr made an analogy between nuclear forces and those within a drop of liquid. Both are short range, acting strongly on those nucleons/molecules in their immediate neighborhood but having no influence on those further away in the nucleus/drop. The total energy and volume of a nucleus/drop are directly proportional to the number of constituent nucleons/molecules, and any excess energy of a constituent is rapidly shared among the others. This liquid-drop model of the nucleus, which meshed well with Bohr's understanding of the compound-nucleus stage during reactions, treated the energy states of the nucleus as a whole. Its great success, discovered by Bohr in collaboration with John A. Wheeler of Princeton (1939), in explaining fission as a deformation of the spherical drop into a dumbbell shape that breaks apart at the narrow connection, assured its wide acceptance for a number of years.

The strongest opposition to this liquid-drop interpretation came from proponents of the nuclear-shell model, who felt that nucleons retain much of their individuality—that, for example, they move within their own well-defined orbits. In 1932 James H. Bartlett of the University of Illinois, by analogy to the grouping of orbital electrons, suggested that protons and neutrons in nuclei also form into shells. This idea was developed in France and Germany, where it was shown in 1937 that data on magnetic moments of nuclei conform to a shell-model interpretation.

To explain the very fine splitting (hyperfine structure) of lines in the optical spectra of some elements—spectra produced largely by the extranuclear electrons—several European physicists in the 1920s had suggested that atomic nuclei possess mechanical and magnetic moments relating to their rotation and configuration. From the 1930s on, a number of techniques were developed for measuring such nuclear moments—including the radio-frequency resonance method of Columbia University's I. I. Rabi—and from the resulting data certain regularities appeared. For example, nuclei with an odd number of particles have half units of spin and nuclei with an even number of particles have integer units of spin, while nuclei with an even number of protons and an even number of neutrons have zero spin. Evidence such as this suggested some sort of organization of the nucleons.

With the shell model overshadowed by the success of the liquid-drop model, and with much basic research interrupted by World War II, it was not until 1949 that Maria Goeppert Mayer at the University of Chicago and O. Haxel, J. H. D. Jensen, and H. E. Suess in Germany showed the success of the shell model in explaining the so-called magic numbers of nucleons: 2, 8, 20, 28, 50, 82, and 126. Elements having these numbers of nucleons, known to be unusually stable, were assumed to have closed shells in the nucleus. Lead 208, for example, is "doubly magic," having 82 protons and 126 neutrons. More recent interpretations, incorporating features of both liquid-drop and shell models, are called the "collective" and "unified" models.

Aside from the question of the structure of the nucleus, after it was recognized that similarly charged particles were confined in a tiny volume, the problem existed of explaining the nature of the short-range forces that overcame their electrical repulsion. In 1935 Hideki Yukawa in Japan reasoned that just as electrical force is transmitted between charged bodies in an electromagnetic field by a particle called a photon, there might be an analogous nuclear-field particle. Accordingly, the meson, as it was called (with a predicted mass about 200 times that of the electron), was soon found in cosmic rays by Carl D. Anderson and Seth H. Neddermeyer. The existence of this particle was confirmed by 1938. But in 1947 Fermi, Teller, and Victor F. Weisskopf in the United States concluded that this mu meson, or muon, did not interact with matter in the necessary way to serve as a field particle; and S. Sakata and T. Inoue in Japan, and independently Hans A. Bethe at Cornell and Robert E. Marshak at the University of Rochester, suggested that yet another meson existed. Within the same year, Cecil F. Powell and G. P. S. Occhialini in Bristol, England, found the pi meson, or pion—a particle slightly heavier than the muon into which it decays and one that meets field-particle requirements—in cosmic-ray tracks. Neutrons and protons were thought to interact through the continual transfer of positive, negative, and neutral pions between them.

Wider Significance of Nuclear Physics

In addition to the profound insights to nature revealed by basic research in nuclear physics, and the awesome applications to power sources and weapons, the subject also contributed to important questions in other fields. Early in the twentieth century, Bertram B. Boltwood, a radiochemist at Yale, devised a radioactive dating technique to measure the age of the earth's oldest rocks, at one time a subject considered the domain of geologists. These procedures were refined, largely by British geologist Arthur Holmes and later by geochemist Claire Patterson at the California Institute of Technology, as data on isotopic concentrations were better appreciated and better measured, leading to an estimation of the earth's antiquity at several billion years. Measuring a shorter time scale with unprecedented accuracy, chemist Willard Libby at the University of Chicago developed a method of dating artifacts of anthropological age using the carbon 14 isotope. Nuclear physics informed yet another subject of long-standing fascination to humanity: What keeps stars shining over enormous periods of time? Just before World War II, Hans Bethe of Cornell conceived the carbon cycle of nuclear reactions and calculated the energy output of each step. And shortly after the war, Gamow extended the range of nuclear physics to the entire universe, answering the cosmological question of origin with the "Big Bang," and detailing the nuclear reactions that occurred over the next several hundred million years.

The Profession

Although nuclear physics is sometimes said to have been born during the early 1930s—a period of many remarkable discoveries—it can more appropriately be dated from 1911 or 1919. What is true of the 1930s is that by this time nuclear physics was clearly defined as a major field. The percentage of nuclear-physics papers published in *Physical Review* rose dramatically; other measures of the field's prominence included research funds directed to it, the number of doctoral degrees awarded, and the number of fellowships tendered by such patrons as the Rockefeller Foundation. Although they were by no means the only scientists fashioning the subject in the United States, Lawrence at Berkeley and Oppenheimer at the California Institute of Technology and Berkeley were dominating figures in building American schools of experimental and theoretical research, respectively. This domestic activity was immeasurably enriched in the 1930s by the stream of refugee physicists from totalitarian Europe—men such as Bethe, Fermi, Leo Szilard, Wigner, Teller, Weisskopf, James Franck, Gamow, Emilio Segrè, and, of course, Einstein. Prominent Europeans had earlier taught at the summer schools for theoretical physics held at several American universities; now many came permanently.

Much of this domestic and foreign talent was mobilized during World War II for the development of radar, the proximity fuse, and most notably the MANHATTAN PROJECT, which produced the first atomic bombs. So stunning was the news of Hiroshima's and Nagasaki's obliteration that nuclear physicists were regarded with a measure of awe. In the opinion of most people nuclear physics was the most exciting, meaningful, and fearful area of science, and its usefulness brought considerable government support. American domination of nuclear physics in the postwar decades resulted, therefore, from a combination of the wartime concentration of research in the United States and the simultaneous disruptions in

Europe, and from another combination of rising domestic abilities and exceptional foreign talent, financed by a government that had seen (at least for a while) that basic research was applicable to national needs.

In the postwar period, the U.S. Atomic Energy Commission and then the Department of Energy supported most research in this field. It was conducted in universities and in several national laboratories, such as those at Los Alamos, Livermore, Berkeley, Brookhaven, Argonne, and Oak Ridge. With the most fashionable side of the subject now called high-energy or particle physics, ever more energetic particle accelerators were constructed, seeking to produce reactions at high energies that would reveal new particles and their interactions. Their size and cost, however, led to dwindling support. By the end of the twentieth century, the nation's two most significant machines were at the Stanford Linear Accelerator Center and the Fermi National Accelerator Laboratory. A larger machine of the next generation, the Superconducting Super Collider, was authorized by Congress and then cancelled when its fifty-mile-long tunnel was but a quarter excavated, because of its escalating, multi-billion-dollar price tag. Consequently, the research front will be at accelerator centers run by groups of nations for the foreseeable future.

BIBLIOGRAPHY

Glasstone, Samuel. *Sourcebook on Atomic Energy.* 3d ed. Princeton, N.J.: Van Nostrand, 1967.

Livingston, M. Stanley. *Particle Accelerators: A Brief History.* Cambridge, Mass.: Harvard University Press, 1969.

Stuewer, Roger, ed. *Nuclear Physics in Retrospect: Proceedings of a Symposium on the 1930s.* Minneapolis: University of Minnesota Press, 1979.

Weiner, Charles, ed. *Exploring the History of Nuclear Physics.* New York: American Institute of Physics, 1972. Proceedings of the institute's conferences of 1967 and 1969.

Weisskopf, Victor F. *Physics in the Twentieth Century: Selected Essays.* Cambridge, Mass.: MIT Press, 1972.

Lawrence Badash

See also **Energy, Department of; Physics, High-Energy Physics.**

Solid-State Physics

Solid-state is the branch of research that deals with properties of condensed matter—originally solids such as crystals and metals, later extended to liquids and more exotic forms of matter. The multitude of properties studied and the variety of materials that can be explored give this field enormous scope.

Modern solid-state physics relies on the concepts and techniques of twentieth-century atomic theory, in which a material substance is seen as an aggregate of atoms obeying the laws of quantum mechanics. Earlier concepts had failed to explain the most obvious characteristics of most materials. A few features of a metal could be explained by assuming that electrons moved freely within it, like a gas, but that did not lead far. Materials technology was built largely on age-old craft traditions.

The Rise of Solid-State Theory

Discoveries in the first quarter of the twentieth century opened the way to answers. The work began with a puzzle: experiments found that for most simple solids, as the temperature is lowered toward absolute zero, adding even an infinitesimally small amount of heat produces a large change in temperature. The classical model of a solid made up of vibrating atoms could not explain this. In 1907, Albert Einstein reworked the model using the radical new idea that energy comes in tiny, discrete "quantum" packets. The qualitative success of Einstein's theory, as refined by other physicists, helped confirm the new quantum theory and pointed to its uses for explaining solid-state phenomena.

In 1912, scientists in Munich discovered an experimental method of "seeing" the internal arrangement of atoms in solids. They sent X rays through crystals and produced patterns, which they interpreted as the result of the scattering of the X rays by atoms arranged in a lattice. By the late 1920s, X-ray studies had revealed most of the basic information about how atoms are arranged in simple crystals.

The theories that attempted to explain solids still contained crippling problems. Solutions became available only after a complete theory of quantum mechanics was invented, in 1925 and 1926, by the German physicist Werner Heisenberg and the Austrian physicist Erwin Schrödinger, building on work by the Danish physicist Niels Bohr. A quantum statistics that could be applied to the particles in condensed matter was invented in 1926 by the Italian physicist Enrico Fermi and the British physicist P. A. M. Dirac.

The next few years were a remarkably productive period as the new conceptual and mathematical tools were applied to the study of solids and liquids. Many leading physicists were involved in this work—Germans, Austrians, Russians, French, British, and a few Americans, notably John Van Vleck and John Slater. Between 1928 and 1931, Felix Bloch, Rudolf Peierls, Alan Wilson, and others developed a powerful concept of energy bands separated by gaps to describe the energy distribution of the swarm of electrons in a crystal. This concept explained why metals conduct electricity and heat while insulators do not, and why the electrical conductivity of a class of materials called semiconductors varies with temperature. Another breakthrough came in 1933 when Eugene Wigner and his student Frederick Seitz at Princeton University developed a simple approximate method for computing the energy bands of sodium and other real solids. By 1934, some of the most dramatic properties of solids, such as magnetism, had received qualitative (if not quantitative) explanation.

But the models of the new theory remained idealizations, applicable only to perfect materials. Physicists could not extend the results, for the available materials contained far too many impurities and physical imperfections. Most practically important characteristics (such as the strength of an alloy) were far beyond the theorists' reach. In the mid-1930s, many theorists turned their attention to fields such as nuclear physics, which offered greater opportunities for making exciting intellectual contributions.

Yet a broader base was being laid for future progress. Established scientists and engineers, particularly in the United States, were avidly studying the new quantum theory of solids. It also became a standard topic in the graduate studies of the next generation. Meanwhile, leaders in universities, industrial labs, and philanthropies were deliberately striving to upgrade American research in all fields of physics. Their efforts were reinforced by the talents of more than 100 European physicists who immigrated to the United States between 1933 and 1941 as a result of the political upheavals in Europe.

Dynamic Growth in World War II and After

Military-oriented research during World War II (1939–1945) created many new techniques that would be useful for the study of solids. For example, Manhattan Project scientists studied neutrons, and in the postwar period these neutral subatomic particles were found to be effective probes of solids, especially in exploring magnetic properties. The fervent wartime development of microwave radar also brought a variety of new techniques useful for studying solids, such as microwave spectroscopy, in which radiation is tuned to coincide with natural vibrational or rotational frequencies of atoms and molecules within a magnetic field. The Collins liquefier, developed just after the war at the MASSACHUSETTS INSTITUTE OF TECHNOLOGY, made it possible for laboratories to get bulk liquid helium and study materials under the simplified conditions that prevail at extremely low temperatures. Methods were also developed during the war for producing single crystals in significant quantities. The production of pure crystals of the elements silicon and germanium, which found wartime use in microwave devices, became so highly developed that an enormous number of postwar studies used these semiconductors as prototypes for the study of solid-state phenomena in general.

Thus, by the late 1940s a seemingly mature field of solid-state physics was growing in scope and also in terms of the number of physicists attracted to the field. By 1947 solid-state physics had become a large enough field to justify establishing a separate division for it within the American Physical Society.

In the postwar period solid-state physics became even more closely tied to practical applications, which then stimulated new interest in the field and increased its funding. The development of the transistor offers a striking example. In January 1945, the Bell Telephone Laboratories in New Jersey officially authorized a group to do fundamental research on solids. William B. Shockley, one of the group's two leaders, believed that such research could lead to the invention of a solid-state amplifier. Members of a small semiconductor subgroup led by Shockley directed their attention to silicon and germanium, whose properties had been closely studied during the wartime radar program. In December 1947, two members of the group, the theorist John Bardeen and the experimentalist Walter Brattain, working closely together, invented the first transistor.

The transistor rectifies and amplifies electrical signals more rapidly and reliably than the more cumbersome, fragile, and costly vacuum tube. It rapidly found practical application. Among the first to take an interest were military agencies, driven by Cold War concerns to fund advanced research as well as development in all fields of physics. Commercial interests promptly followed; the first "transistorized" radio went on the market in 1954, and the term "solid-state" was soon popularized by advertisers' tags. Transistorized devices revolutionized communications, control apparatus, and data processing. The explosive growth of commercial and national security applications led to wide popular interest, and swift increases in funding for every kind of research. By 1960, there were roughly 2,000 solid-state physicists in the United States, making up one-fifth of all American physicists. Here, as in most fields of science since the war, more significant work had been done in the United States than in the rest of the world put together. As other countries recovered economically, they began to catch up.

Unlike most fields of physics at that time, in solid-state about half of the U.S. specialists worked in industry. Universities did not want to be left out, and starting in 1960 they established "materials science" centers with the aid of Department of Defense funding. As the name implied, the field was reaching past solid-state physicists to include chemists, engineers, and others in an interdisciplinary spirit.

Throughout the 1950s and 1960s, theory, technique, and applications of solid-state physics all advanced rapidly. The long list of achievements includes a theory for the details of atomic movements inside crystals, understanding of how impurities and imperfections cause optical properties and affect crystal growth, quantitative determination of such properties as electrical resistivity, and a more complete theory for the phase transitions between different states of matter. The biggest theoretical breakthrough of the period was an explanation of superconductivity in 1957 by Bardeen and two other American physicists, Leon N. Cooper and J. Robert Schrieffer. Their theory led the way to explanations of a whole series of so-called cooperative phenomena (which also include superfluidity, phase transitions, and tunneling) in which particles and sound-wave quanta move in unison, giving rise to strongly modified and sometimes astonishing properties. Theorists were further stimulated in 1972 when scientists at Cornell University, deploying ingenious new techniques to reach extremely low temperatures, discovered that Helium-3 could become a superfluid with remarkable properties.

Meanwhile, many other important techniques were developed, such as the Josephson effect. In 1962, the young British physicist Brian D. Josephson proposed that a supercurrent can "tunnel" through a thin barrier separating two superconductors. This led to important devices such as the SQUID (Superconducting Quantum Interference Device), which can probe the surface structures of solids and can even map faint magnetic fields that reflect human brain activity. Still more versatile were techniques to create entirely new, artificially structured materials. With vapors or beams of molecules, physicists could build up a surface molecule by molecule like layers of paint.

The list of applications continued to grow rapidly. By the mid-1970s, in addition to countless varieties of electronic diodes and transistors, there were, for example, solid-state lasers employed in such diverse applications as weaponry, welding, and eye surgery; magnetic bubble memories used in computers to store information in thin crystals; and improved understanding of processes in areas ranging from photography to metallurgy. In 1955, Shockley had established a semiconductor firm in California near Stanford University, creating a nucleus for what was later dubbed Silicon Valley—a hive of entrepreneurial capital, technical expertise, and innovation, but only one of many locales from Europe to Japan that thrived on solid-state physics. The creation of entire industries in turn stimulated interest in the specialty, now virtually a field of its own. In 1970 when the American Physical Society split up its massive flagship journal, the *Physical Review*, into manageable sections, the largest was devoted entirely to solids. But it was the "B" section, for in terms of intellectual prestige, solid-state physics had always taken second place behind fields such as nuclear and particle physics, which were called more "fundamental."

Condensed Matter from Stars to Supermarkets

To advance their status, and to emphasize their interest in ever more diverse materials, practitioners renamed the field; in 1978 the American Physical Society's division changed its name from "Solid State" to "Condensed Matter." The condensed-matter physicists were rapidly improving their understanding and control of the behavior of fluids and semidisordered materials like glasses. Theoretical studies of condensed matter began to range as far afield as the interiors of neutron stars, and even the entire universe in the moment following the Big Bang. Meanwhile, theory had become a real help to traditional solid-state technologies like metallurgy and inspired entire new classes of composite materials.

Experiment and theory, seemingly mature, continued to produce surprises. One spectacular advance, pointing to a future technology of submicroscopic machinery, was the development in the early 1980s of scanning microscopes. These could detect individual atoms on a surface, or nudge them into preferred configurations. Another discovery at that time was the Quantum Hall Effect: jumps of conductivity that allowed fundamental measurements with extraordinary precision. Later, a startling discovery at Bell Laboratories—using semiconductor crystals of unprecedented quality—revealed a new state of matter: a Quantum Hall Effect experiment showed highly correlated "quasiparticles" carrying only fractions of an electron's charge.

For research that could be considered fundamental, attention increasingly turned toward condensed matter systems with quantized entities such as cooperatively interacting swarms of electrons, seen especially at very low temperatures. The physics community was galvanized in 1986 when scientists at IBM's Zurich laboratory announced their discovery of superconductivity in a ceramic material, at temperatures higher than any previous superconductor. The established way of studying solids had been to pursue the simplest possible systems, but this showed that more complex structures could display startling new properties all their own. The study of "high-temperature" superconductivity has led to new concepts and techniques as well as hosts of new materials, including ones that superconduct at temperatures an order of magnitude higher than anything known before 1986. Many novel applications for microelectronics have grown from this field. Equally fascinating was the creation in the 1990s of microscopic clouds of "Bose-Einstein condensed" gases, in which the atoms behave collectively as a single quantum entity.

Most of this work depended on electronic computers: the field was advancing with the aid of its own applications. With new theoretical ideas and techniques developed in the 1960s, calculations of electronic structures became routine during the 1970s. In the 1980s, numerical simulations began to approach the power of experiment itself. This was most visible where the study of chaos and nonequilibrium phenomena, as in the phase transition of a melting solid, brought new understanding of many phenomena. There was steady progress in unraveling the old, great puzzle of fluids—turbulence—although here much remained unsolved. Studies of disorder also led to improved materials and new devices, such as the liquid crystal displays that turned up in items on supermarket shelves. Magnetism was studied with special intensity because of its importance in computer memories.

Physicists also cooperated with chemists to study polymers, and edged toward the study of proteins and other biological substances. Spider silk still beat anything a physicist could make. But the discovery that carbon atoms could be assembled in spheres (as in buckminsterfullerene) and tubes held hopes for fantastic new materials.

Some research problems now required big, expensive facilities. Ever since the 1950s, neutron beams from nuclear reactors had been useful to some research teams. A larger step toward "big science" came with the construction of machines resembling the accelerators of high-energy physics that emitted beams of high-intensity radiation to probe matter. The National Synchrotron Light Source, starting up in 1982 in Brookhaven, New York, was followed by a half-dozen more in the United States and abroad. Yet most condensed-matter research continued to be done by small, intimate groups in one or two rooms.

In the 1990s the steep long-term rise of funding for basic research in the field leveled off. Military support waned with the Cold War, while intensified commercial competition impelled industrial leaders like Bell Labs to emphasize research with near-term benefits. The community continued to grow gradually along with other fields of research, no longer among the fastest. By 2001 the American Physical Society division had some 5,000 members, largely from industry; as a fraction of the Society's membership, they had declined to one-eighth. This was still more than any other specialty, and represented much more high-level research in the field than any other country could muster.

The field's impact on day-to-day living continued to grow. The applications of condensed-matter physics were most conspicuous in information processing and communications, but had also become integral to warfare, health care, power generation, education, travel, finance, politics, and entertainment.

BIBLIOGRAPHY

Hoddeson, Lillian, et al, eds. *Out of the Crystal Maze: Chapters from the History of Solid-State Physics.* New York: Oxford University Press, 1992. Extended essays by professional historians (some are highly technical).

Hoddeson, Lillian, and Vicki Daitch. *True Genius: The Life and Science of John Bardeen.* Washington, D.C.: The Joseph Henry Press, 2002. Includes an overview of solid-state physics for the general reader.

Kittel, Charles. *Introduction to Solid-State Physics.* New York: Wiley, 1953. In five editions to 1976, the classic graduate-student textbook.

Mott, Sir Nevill, ed. *The Beginnings of Solid-State Physics. A Symposium.* London: The Royal Society; Great Neck, N.Y.: Scholium International, 1980. Reminiscences by pioneers of the 1930s–1960s.

National Research Council, Solid-State Sciences Panel. *Research in Solid-State Sciences: Opportunities and Relevance to National Needs.* Washington, D.C.: National Academy of Sciences, 1968. The state of U.S. physics fields has been reviewed at intervals by panels of leading physicists. Later reviews, by the National Academy of Sciences, are:

National Research Council, Physics Survey Committee. *Physics in Perspective.* Vol. II, part A, *The Core Subfields of Physics.* Washington, D.C.: National Academy of Sciences, 1973. See "Physics of Condensed Matter," pp. 445–558.

National Research Council, Physics Survey Committee, Panel on Condensed-Matter Physics. *Condensed-Matter Physics.* In series, *Physics Through the 1990s.* Washington, D.C.: National Academy Press, 1986.

National Research Council, Committee on Condensed-Matter and Materials Physics. *Condensed-Matter and Materials Physics: Basic Research for Tomorrow's Technology.* In series, *Physics in a New Era.* Washington, D.C.: National Academy Press, 1999.

Riordan, Michael, and Lillian Hoddeson. *Crystal Fire: The Birth of the Information Age.* New York: Norton, 1997. For the general reader.

Weart, Spencer R., and Melba Phillips, eds. *History of Physics.* New York: American Institute of Physics, 1985. Includes readable articles on aspects of the history by P. Anderson, P. Ewald, L. Hoddeson, C. S. Smith.

Lillian Hoddeson
Spencer Weart

PHYSIOLOGY can be traced back to Greek natural philosophy, yet in our age it has emerged as a sophisticated experimental science with numerous subspecialties. After distinction from its origins in the older discipline of anatomy, physiology encompassed study of physical and chemical functions in the tissues and organs of all living matter. Dynamic boundaries of the field are evident in that neuroscience, pharmacology, biophysics, endocrinology, and other scientific and medical specialties have roots in physiology. Given that plant physiology came to be defined as a specialization of botany, however, "physiology" today connotes the study of life-sustaining body functions and structures of animals, especially humans.

Development of Physiology in the United States

Scientific physiology in the United States developed slowly at first. Medical schools in the late eighteenth and early nineteenth centuries taught classes in physiology—then called the "institutes of medicine"—with no laboratory work being done. The earliest physiology professorship was founded in 1789 at the College of Philadelphia. Robley Dunglison, once a physician to Thomas Jefferson and one of a few full-time medical teachers at the time, wrote the subject's first comprehensive American textbook, *Human Physiology*, in 1832. William Beaumont (1785–1853) published a classic work on digestive function in 1833, given his opportunity to observe the subject in nineteen-year-old Alexis St. Martin, whose abdomen was blown open in a shotgun accident.

Prior to the Civil War (1861–1865), American physiologists were amateurs who tended to earn their livelihood through medical practice or teaching. Significant change in that state of affairs resulted from work by two pioneers of American physiology, John C. Dalton Jr. (1825–1889) and S. Weir Mitchell (1825–1914). As did many of their medical colleagues, Dalton and Mitchell traveled to Europe for postgraduate work, particularly in Paris, where they studied with physiologist Claude Bernard, famous for his carbohydrate metabolism research. Returning to the United States around 1851, Dalton eschewed a promising medical career, accepted a New York medical college professor's chair, and there became America's first professional physiologist. Like his French mentor, Dalton was a strong proponent of experimental physiology and favored vivisection in his teaching, a practice that later placed him in controversy with early animal rights activists. Mitchell returned from Paris at the same time, settling in Philadelphia, where he failed in two significant efforts to secure a physiology professorship, due in part, as he saw it, to his expressed enthusiasm for the sort of experimental approach to the science he had learned in Europe. After serving as a surgeon in the Civil War, Mitchell's career turned toward excellent work in the study and treatment of neurological disorders, but he retained his devotion to physiology and eventually helped to found the science's first professional society.

Dalton and Mitchell's love for experimental physiology found fruition and institutional support in Henry P. Bowditch (1840–1911) and H. Newell Martin (1848–1896). Bowditch had studied in the prominent German school of physiology under Carl Ludwig, a master laboratory technician. As he returned to the United States in 1871, a reform movement in higher education fortunately called for more emphasis on experimentation, and Bowditch established America's first full-fledged physiology lab as a professor at the Harvard Medical School. Martin, a postgrad student in the prestigious British physiology school, was recruited by newly formed and well-endowed Johns Hopkins University, where he accepted a biology professorship and established a state-of-the-art physiology laboratory in 1876. In turn, Martin developed a mammalian heart preparation that led to important cardiac physiology discoveries. Fellowships allowed Martin to attract a bright cohort of students at Johns Hopkins, and, along with Bowditch and his students at Harvard, they founded physiology as an experimental research-based science in the United States.

Bowditch and Martin mentored a generation of physiologists who were eager, willing, and able to further the science, despite few gainful employment opportunities. They established new labs at the University of Michigan, Yale University, and Columbia University. Their professionalization of physiology coincided with medical education reforms calling for increased emphasis on experimental science and research. Thus the new physiology gained more than a foothold in medical schools; it became the preeminent discipline, leading to America's international prominence in biomedical science that has continued into the twenty-first century. In 1887, Bowditch and Martin heralded their scientific establishment to the world by founding the American Physiological Society (APS). Another original APS member, Johns Hopkins–educated William Howell, published his landmark *American Textbook of Physiology* in 1896. That was followed by initial circulation of the APS's prestigious *American Journal of Physiology* (AJP) in 1898.

Despite animal physiology's enhanced position, however, experimental biologists were not willing to concede the field. Replete with antagonism toward their counterparts in the 1880s, the biologists proposed a broader notion of physiology, combining the study of plants, zoology, microorganisms, and embryology toward a unified theory of life. These general physiologists, as they came to be known, found a leader in Charles Otis Whitman, who established a school for the broader science at the University of Chicago. The general physiology movement lost momentum around 1893, however, lacking broad institutional support and firm disciplinary structure. Although the Chicago school remained a haven for general physiologists, the medically oriented stream of animal physiology maintained power enough to define the term.

American Physiology in the Twentieth Century

Burgeoning into the twentieth century as well, American physiology achieved international ascendance during World War I (1914–1918). Progress in German and English labs was profoundly stifled by the war, while American physiologists continued their work in relative isolation. Even as new research continued, practical physiology was applied to submarine and aviation adaptation, troop nutrition, poison gas effects, munitions factory worker fatigue, wound shock, and other areas. Physiology continued to stimulate the medical field. Harvey W. Cushing, for example, a former student of Bowditch who also worked in the Johns Hopkins physiology lab, pioneered the practice of brain surgery. By all indications, including publications in the AJP and American research citations in international journals, American physiology was excellent.

Four physiologists stood out during the early to mid-twentieth century. Foremost among them was Walter B. Cannon (1871–1945), another former student of and eventual successor to Bowditch at Harvard. Among his achievements, Cannon used the new X-ray technology to advance understanding of digestive processes; he explained adrenal gland functions in response to emotional stress; and his classic work, *The Wisdom of the Body*, introduced a profound physiological principle, homeostasis. Not to forget the influence of his *Textbook*, William Howell (1860–1945) at Johns Hopkins did important heart research, described the pituitary gland, made momentous blood coagulation discoveries, and presided over the International Physiological Congress, which met in the United States in 1929. A. J. Carlson (1875–1956) at the University of Chicago was prolific in cardiac and gastric physiology research. Joseph Erlanger at Washington University in St. Louis, along with Herbert Gasser, won the 1944 Nobel Prize for research in nerve action, which incorporated valve amplification and introduced cathode ray tube technology, thus heralding the electronic age of physiological research.

A disciplinary orientation had developed in twentieth-century American physiology, emphasizing the study of intrinsic and extrinsic function, integration, and regulation of body systems over their structures. A talented national field of scientists operating in well-funded programs thus undertook the study of metabolism, reproduction, muscular contractility, cardiopulmonary transport, regulation (for example, homeostasis), and how information is passed through the nervous system. This trend toward functional specialization, facilitated by advances in microscopy, imaging, and other technology, allowed physiological analysis to intensify from the level of entire bodies to specific organs, down to cells, and eventually to molecules. After many practical applications during World War II (1939–1945), American physiology expertise continued to gain during the Cold War, finding novel uses in the space program and especially in medical surgery. Latter twentieth century Americans enjoyed increased and enhanced life spans, if also rising health care costs. The heart and other vital organs, for example, could now be restored and even replaced; sexual function was demythologized; mental illness was treated with new drugs and lesser side effects; and nutritional information lowered cholesterol counts—all advances stemming from physiology research. Now given a vast array of subdisciplines, the specialization trend has separated the close association of physiology with medicine, although benefits to well-being are still claimed as justification for experimental research funding.

American physiology retains its world-class status achieved early in the twentieth century, evidenced by tens of Nobel Prizes in physiology and medicine awarded to U.S. citizens over the past thirty years. The work of Nobel winners Robert C. Gallo, Michael Bishop, and Harold E. Varmus, for example, led to the identification of retroviruses, which has proved invaluable in combating AIDS and even cancer. The simultaneous rise of sports and obesity in the United States has stimulated popular interest in exercise physiology. Aided by supercomputer technology and other American innovations, explosive recent discoveries in genetics, a field intimately related to physiology, promise monumental benefits, and moral controversies, to humankind. From its professional foundation in the latter nineteenth century to its status as a mature, expanding science in the new millennium, American study of animal body functions and structure (that is, physiology) promises further life-enhancing and perhaps even life-creating discoveries.

BIBLIOGRAPHY

The American Physiological Society. Home page at http://www.the-aps.org/.

Fye, Bruce W. *The Development of American Physiology: Scientific Medicine in the Nineteenth Century.* Baltimore: Johns Hopkins University Press, 1987.

Geison, Gerald L. *Physiology in the American Context, 1850–1940.* Baltimore: Williams and Wilkins, 1987.

Ronald S. Rasmus

See also **Laboratories; Medical Research; Medicine and Surgery.**

PICKETING, said the U.S. Supreme Court in 1941, is "the workingman's means of communication." The nonviolent competitive tactics of workers in labor disputes with employers have traditionally been limited to the strike, the secondary boycott, and the picket line. To get the employer or other entity being picketed to accede to their demands, picketers seek to impede deliveries and services; to cause employees to refuse to cross the line to work; to muster consumer sympathy to withhold patronage; and to be a "rallyround" symbol for the picketers and other workers. Their objective may be either to get recognition as the bargainers for employees or to gain economic demands.

Picketing has promoted interests other than those of workers, notably in protests against racial discrimination. For instance, African Americans in the first half of the twentieth century launched "Don't Buy Where You Can't Work" pickets against employers who practiced racial discrimination when hiring. But its history is very strongly linked to public policy regulatory of labor-management disputes. Very few states have comprehensive statutes governing labor disputes. At common law, state courts have been divided over the legality of picketing. Most have held it to be an unjustified infliction of economic harm. Some, as in California, in *Messner v. Journeymen Barbers* (1960), have refused to take sides in these competitive situations. They have reasoned that risks of loss among competitors should not be abated by courts, absent statutory regulation, since hardship does not make less legitimate the objectives of a union seeking organization, or of a nonunion shop resisting it, or of nonunion workers who may either join or resist. A number of courts, without statutory standards, enjoin picketing to forestall economic hardship, even though a decree merely shifts the loss from one competitor (the employer) to another (the union). Federal law is mostly statutory; it regulates picketing in terms of purposes and effects under the NATIONAL LABOR RELATIONS ACT of 1935, as amended in 1947 and 1959, and usually preempts state law.

In 1940 the Supreme Court added a constitutional dimension to the existing common law and to statutory law. In *Thornhill v. Alabama* it declared that picketing is a right of communication under the First and Fourteenth amendments, although regulation is available to curb numbers, threats, obstruction, fraud, misrepresentation, or violence. Still, the Court has had trouble in reconciling the conduct of patrolling with what, rather artificially, it has termed "pure speech"—oral communication, in contrast to overall communicative conduct—and in balancing regulatory policies against the communication values inherent in picketing. *Teamsters v. Vogt* (1957) seemed to strip constitutional insulation from picketers, leaving them open to sweeping injunctions, excepting only outright prohibition. But *Food Employees v. Logan Valley Plaza* (1968) cautioned that controls, improper for "pure speech" but proper for picketing because of the intermingling of protected speech and unprotected conduct, must still be applied to avoid impairment of the speech elements.

The conditions under which picketing is judged legally acceptable change according to the composition of judges, and the political bent of the current presidential administration. The National Labor Relations Board in the 1990s and early twenty-first century ruled rather narrowly on which pickets were acceptable. Pickets are best understood in the broader context of labor history (see cross-references).

BIBLIOGRAPHY

Brecher, Jeremy. *Strike!* Revised and updated ed. Boston: South End Press, 1997.

Gould, William B. *Labored Relations: Law, Politics, and the NLRB—a Memoir.* Cambridge, Mass.: MIT Press, 2000.

Gross, James A. *Broken Promise: The Subversion of U.S. Labor Relations Policy, 1947–1994.* Philadelphia: Temple University Press, 1995.

Edgar A. Jones Jr. / D. B.

See also **American Federation of Labor-Congress of Industrial Organizations; Class Conflict; Labor; Labor, Department of; Lockout; National Labor Relations Act; Strikes.**

PICKETT'S CHARGE (3 July 1863), more properly the Pickett-Pettigrew charge, was the culminating event of the Battle of Gettysburg. Repulsed on 1 and 2 July, Confederate Gen. Robert E. Lee assaulted the Union center with divisions under George Edward Pickett, J. J. Pettigrew, and William Pender. After a preliminary bombardment, 15,000 men advanced eastward from Seminary Ridge to a "little clump of trees" on the front of the Second Corps along Cemetery Ridge. The assault carried the column of attack to the Union position but failed when the Union forces closed in from three sides. The Confederates, retreating under heavy fire, lost about 6,000 men, including three of Pickett's brigade commanders and most of his field officers.

Pickett's Charge. Together with Gen. J. J. Pettigrew, Gen. George Edward Pickett led Confederate troops in a final charge against Union lines at the Battle of Gettysburg on 3 July 1863. Pickett prepared his troops in full view of the Union position, so the attack came as no surprise. The Union soldiers buckled and nearly broke, but eventually they held the line, inflicting more than 6,000 Confederate casualties.

BIBLIOGRAPHY

Gordon, Lesley J. *General George E. Pickett in Life and Legend.* Chapel Hill: University of North Carolina Press, 1998.

Reardon, Carol. *Pickett's Charge in History and Memory.* Chapel Hill: University of North Carolina Press, 1997.

Douglas Southall Freeman / A. R.

See also **Civil War; Gettysburg, Battle of; Pennsylvania, Invasion of.**

PIECES OF EIGHT, Spanish silver coins of eight reals (eight bits), first authorized in 1497. Also known as pesos and Spanish dollars, they were minted in enormous quantities and soon became recognized as a reliable medium of exchange in the European colonies of North America. Subsidiary coins—four reals (half dollar, four bits) and two reals (quarter dollar, two bits)—were also minted. In 1728, Spain began coinage of the milled dollar to replace the piece of eight. The Coinage Act of 1792 made the dollar the new nation's official currency and fixed it at approximately the same weight of silver as the Spanish peso.

BIBLIOGRAPHY

Brock, Leslie V. *The Currency of the American Colonies, 1700–1764: A Study in Colonial Finance and Imperial Relations.* New York: Arno Press, 1975.

McCusker, John J. *Money and Exchange in Europe and America, 1600–1775.* Chapel Hill: University of North Carolina Press, 1978.

Walter Prichard / A. R.

See also **Currency and Coinage; Doubloon; Money; Proclamation Money; Spanish and Spanish American Influence.**

PIECEWORK is a system of labor in which payment is based on the actual number of pieces produced rather than hours worked, regardless of how long it takes. Piecework has had a place in many societies. In ancient systems, laborers bartered their amount of production for an amount of payment—often in the form of food. In England, prior to the Industrial Revolution, the textile industry relied on work done in homes on a piecework basis. In America, similar systems began in homes and with the use of convict labor and then became an established method of payment used in factory labor.

Advocates of the piecework system say that the hardest and most able workers are rewarded for their results while others are compensated fairly. Those opposed to piecework consider it an abusive and unnecessarily competitive system in which workers toil for long hours without adequate compensation and in which inferior products are produced as quantity is stressed over quality.

According to a 1949 amendment to the Fair Labor Standards Act of 1938, pieceworkers must be paid at least minimum wage. This law, however, is not absolute and many workers still earn significantly less than the minimum wage. Labor advocates have long been opposed to piecework. In his 1906 novel, *The Jungle*, about the working conditions in the Chicago stockyards, Upton Sinclair described a common abuse of the system

> In piecework they would reduce the time, requiring the same work in a shorter time, and paying the same wages; and then, after the workers had accustomed themselves to this new speed, they would reduce the rate of payment to correspond with the reduction in time! (Ch. 11, pg. 1)

Although the piecework system has been employed in a variety of types of factory and sweatshop labor, it is commonly associated with the textile industry. Piecework is also commonly employed by technology industries.

BIBLIOGRAPHY

Dubofsky, Melvyn, and Foster R. Dulles. *Labor in America: A History.* Wheeling, Ill.: Harlan Davidson, 1999.

Gorn, Elliott J. *Mother Jones: The Most Dangerous Woman in America.* New York: Hill and Wang, 2001.

Rutherford, F. James, and A. Ahlgren. *Science for All Americans.* New York: Oxford University Press, 1990.

Sinclair, Upton. *The Jungle.* New York: Signet Classic, 2001.

Deirdre Sheets

See also **Textiles.**

PIEDMONT REGION. A "foothill" region, 500 to 1500 feet in elevation, that extends from New Jersey to Alabama. It is composed of deeply weathered, mostly metamorphic rocks, the soils are acidic, and the original forest was deciduous hardwoods. The contact with the Coastal Plain on the eastern side is marked by a fall zone with navigable streams to the coast and entrepôt cities, such as Philadelphia, Washington, D.C., Richmond, Virginia, Columbia, South Carolina, and Columbus, Georgia. The northern portion was marked by diversified agriculture and manufacturing. From Virginia south, the area nearest the fall zone, the lower Piedmont, was a slave plantation economy with tobacco grown to the north and cotton to the south. The area nearest the Blue Ridge Mountains to the west, or upper Piedmont, featured cotton and tobacco yeomanry. Soil erosion was rampant from early times, but was curtailed starting in the 1930s, and most old agricultural fields are now in pine forests. Manufacturing became important in the late nineteenth century and has continued.

Blacksmith's Shop, Hell's Half Acre. This June 1936 photograph by Carl Mydans shows a building in the Plantation Piedmont agricultural demonstration project, near Eatonton, Ga. LIBRARY OF CONGRESS

BIBLIOGRAPHY

Aiken, Charles S. *The Cotton Plantation South since the Civil War.* Baltimore: Johns Hopkins University Press, 1998.

Coggeshall, John M. *Carolina Piedmont Country.* Jackson: University Press of Mississippi, 1996.

Gray, L. C. *History of Agriculture in the Southern United States to 1860.* 2 vols. Gloucester, Mass.: Peter Smith, 1958.

Trimble, Stanley W. *Man-Induced Soil Erosion on the Southern Piedmont, 1700–1970.* Ankeny, Iowa: Soil Conservation Society of America, 1974.

Stanley W. Trimble

See also **Fall Line.**

PIERCE V. SOCIETY OF SISTERS, 268 U.S. 510 (1925). Also known as the Oregon Parochial School Case, *Pierce v. Society of the Sisters of the Holy Names of Jesus and Mary* was decided in 1925 by the Supreme Court. At issue was the Oregon Compulsory Education Act of 1922, a voter initiative mandating public school attendance for children eight through sixteen. Though never enforced, the law threatened to destroy existing private schools, which were deemed a threat to community morals and safety. Like many education regulations of the period, it was at least in part the product of anti-Catholic and anti-immigrant sentiment.

Pierce was brought by the Society of Sisters and the Hill Military Academy against Governor Walter M. Pierce. The Court was unsympathetic to the law, as was the district court that had previously considered it. Justice McReynolds, in a unanimous decision, found it in violation of economic and noneconomic liberties guaranteed by the Fourteenth Amendment (property owners' right to be free of unreasonable power; parents' right to make educational decisions for their children). This was one of the first state police power regulations invalidated for violating a noneconomic constitutional guarantee. It has since become a symbol of so-called substantive due process jurisprudence. In the early 2000s the case was cited approvingly in privacy, parental rights, and free exercise decisions; advocates of school choice found it useful when defending their position.

JUSTICE JAMES C. MCREYNOLDS, FROM THE *PIERCE* OPINION:

"The fundamental theory of liberty upon which all governments in this Union repose excludes any general power of the state to standardize its children by forcing them to accept instruction from public teachers only. The child is not the mere creature of the state; those who nurture him and direct his destiny have the right, coupled with the high duty, to recognize and prepare him for additional obligations."

BIBLIOGRAPHY

Carter, Stephen L. "Parents, Religion, and Schools: Reflections on *Pierce*, Seventy Years Later." *Seton Hall Law Review* 27 (1997): 1194.

Fraser, James W. *Between Church and State: Religion and Public Education in a Multicultural America.* New York: St. Martin's Press, 1999.

Kimberly A. Hendrickson

See also **Education, Parental Choice in.**

PIETISM. The name given to the renewal movement in German Protestantism that flourished in the late seventeenth and early eighteenth centuries, Pietism aimed to combat growing formalism in the Lutheran Church. The father of the movement was Philipp Jakob Spener, the senior Lutheran minister in Frankfurt am Main, who began *collegia pietatis*, small lay groups formed to promote bible study and prayer. He stressed the Christian behavior in daily life, urged lay members to play a larger role in church work, and promoted reform of theological education. His younger protégé, August Hermann Francke, established near the University of Halle a massive complex of institutions (including an orphanage, several schools, and bible and mission societies) that became the principal pietistic center.

In the American colonies the influence of churchly Pietism was exerted chiefly through the German Lutherans and the Moravians. Heinrich Melchior Mühlenberg was sent to North America in 1742 by the church fathers at Halle to bring the troubled Lutheran congregations into order and to counter the proselytizing efforts of Count Nikolaus Ludwig von Zinzendorf, leader of the Moravian Church. Mühlenberg succeeded in organizing the Lutheran parishes and is thus referred to as the patriarch of the Lutheran Church in America. The American Moravians were the most pietistic of all the colonial religious bodies and were especially adept at creating religious music. In addition, various movements were influenced by Radical Pietism, which advocated separation

Philipp Jakob Spener. The German founder of Pietism, which opposed orthodox dogma in the Lutheran Church, in the late seventeenth century. LIBRARY OF CONGRESS

from state churches. These included the Brethren (nicknamed Dunkers), who arrived in 1719, and the communitarian Ephrata Society that broke from them, led by Conrad Beissel. Later communal bodies of similar orientation were the Harmonists, the Separatists of Zoar, and the Amana Colonies. Pietism was from the beginning strongly missionary in emphasis and for that reason had large significance in colonial America and later church development.

BIBLIOGRAPHY

Pitzer, Donald R., ed. *America's Communal Utopias.* Chapel Hill: University of North Carolina Press, 1997.

Stoeffler, F. Ernest, ed. *Continental Pietism and Early American Christianity.* Grand Rapids, Mich.: Eerdmans, 1976.

Donald F. Durnbaugh
William W. Sweet

See also **Religion and Religious Affiliation.**

PIGS. *See* **Hogs; Livestock Industry.**

PIKE, ZEBULON, EXPEDITIONS OF. The acquisition of Louisiana in 1803 and President Thomas Jefferson's interest in asserting control over the region led to a series of expeditions funded by the U.S. government to establish the borders of the nation, negotiate proper relations with Native American tribes and settlers, and acquire pertinent scientific information. Lieutenant Zebulon Pike led two expeditions, one in 1805 and 1806 to search for the headwaters of the MISSISSIPPI RIVER and another in 1806 and 1807 to determine the source of the Arkansas and Red Rivers in the southern reaches of the Louisiana Purchase.

Zebulon Pike. The leader of two important expeditions from 1805 to 1807 that had some military, scientific, and political success, he is best remembered today for the mountain peak named after him. LIBRARY OF CONGRESS

On 9 August 1805, Pike left St. Louis with twenty men for a two-thousand-mile trek into present-day Minnesota to locate the source of the Mississippi River. This nine-month expedition provided important geographical data, located and identified the major Indian nations of Minnesota Territory, and asserted U.S. dominion over the region to all settlers, especially some British and French traders who inhabited the area. Pike erroneously concluded that Cass Lake in Minnesota Territory was the source of the Mississippi River and the party returned to St. Louis on 30 April 1806. His error was corrected in 1832 when Lake Itasca was identified as the headwater of the Mississippi River.

Pike's second expedition was directed to explore the Arkansas and Red Rivers, probe the northern boundaries of New Spain, identify the economic potential of the area, and negotiate peaceful terms with the Indian population. Departing St. Louis on 15 July 1806, the expedition traveled up the ARKANSAS RIVER. The group sighted Grand Peak (labeled PIKES PEAK by cartographers), Colorado, in November 1806. After an unsuccessful attempt to reach the top of the mountain, Pike predicted that "no one would ever reach the summit." Turning south in search of the Red River, Pike and his group crossed the Sangre de Cristo Mountains into Spanish territory near Santa Fe and were promptly arrested. Zebulon Pike was closely interrogated by Spanish soldiers who believed that he was mapping the region of northern Mexico to satisfy the expansionist objectives of the United States as expressed in the purchase of Louisiana. Relieved of all maps and journals, Pike and his men were released on 1 July 1807, at Natchitoches, Louisiana, a border town between New Spain and the United States.

Pike's explorations between 1805 and 1807 failed to achieve their stated objectives: identification of the headwaters of the Mississippi River in the case of the first expedition, and the location of the source of the Arkansas River in the second expedition. Furthermore, Pike's foray into northern Mexico and his close association with General James Wilkinson, who provided the commission for both expeditions, have raised questions about his role in the Burr Conspiracy.

Despite failed objectives and intrigue, Pike's expeditions provided important geographic information, opened relations with Indian nations, highlighted the challenges of arid regions, and generated national interest in the

American Southwest. Pike's narrative, *An Account of Expeditions to the Sources of the Mississippi and through Western Parts of Louisiana* (1810), supplements the *Journals of Lewis and Clark* and provides a sweeping account of government-sponsored exploration in the early nineteenth century.

BIBLIOGRAPHY

Pike, Zebulon. *The Expeditions of Zebulon Montgomery Pike*. Edited by Elliott Coues. New York: Dover, 1987.

Scheuerman, Richard, and Arthur Ellis, eds. *The Expeditions of Lewis and Clark and Zebulon Pike: North American Journeys of Discovery*. Madison, Wisc.: Demco Publishers, 2001.

James T. Carroll

See also **Explorations and Expeditions: U.S.; Western Exploration.**

PIKES PEAK, standing 14,110 feet in the Rocky Mountains in El Paso County, Colorado, was first attempted in November 1806 by Lt. Zebulon M. Pike. Pike failed to summit because of heavy snow. Popular usage by trappers and others of the name "Pikes Peak" led to an official name. Pikes Peak is of historical significance as a landmark of early traders and trappers and as the name of the region now known as Colorado. The discovery of gold in 1858 brought large numbers to the region. Thousands who crossed the Plains with the slogan "Pikes Peak or Bust" opened up various mining camps near Pikes Peak or settled in the valleys of Colorado.

BIBLIOGRAPHY

Hollon, Eugene W. *The Lost Pathfinder: Zebulon Montgomery Pike*. Norman: University of Oklahoma Press, 1949.

Montgomery, M. R. *Jefferson and the Gun-Men: How the West Was Almost Lost*. New York: Crown Publishers, 2000.

Terrell, John Upton. *Zebulon Pike: The Life and Times of an Adventurer*. New York: Weybright and Talley, 1968.

Malcolm G. Wyer / H. S.

See also **Colorado; Pikes Peak Gold Rush.**

PIKES PEAK GOLD RUSH. In 1858, an expedition led by William G. Russell, comprised of miners from the goldfields of Georgia and California, followed reports of gold to Ralston Creek, near present day Denver. Discouraged after a few days of unsuccessful searching, most of these prospectors returned home. The remnant of the Russell party discovered some placer gold in Cherry Creek and other tributaries of the South Platte in July of 1858. Word of these finds brought new hopefuls to the region. Exaggerated stories of the reputed goldfields circulated in the nation's press during the winter of 1858–1859. Although seventy-five miles from the site of the discoveries, Pikes Peak was the best-known landmark, and the region adopted the name. The meager amount of dust found in 1858 hardly warranted so much excitement. But the country, suffering from the recent panic of 1857, grasped at any hope of rehabilitation. Merchants and newspapers in Missouri River towns, with an eye to spring outfitting, spread stories to encourage miners. The directed publicity created a great flood of goldseekers who traveled across the Plains in the spring. The Leavenworth and Pikes Peak Express, the first stage line to Denver, was established in 1859 as a result of these expeditions. Many early arrivals, finding that creeks were not yellow with gold, turned back. When John H. Gregory found rich gold veins near present-day Central City in 1859, an estimated 100,000 persons set out for the gold region, though only half of them reached the mountains.

BIBLIOGRAPHY

Barney, Libeus. *Letters of the Pike's Peak Gold Rush: or, Early Day Letters from Auraria*. San Jose, Calif.: Talisman Press, 1959.

King, Joseph E. *A Mine to Make a Mine: Financing the Colorado Mining Industry, 1859–1902*. College Station: Texas A&M University Press, 1977.

Leonard, Stephen J., and Thomas J. Noel. *Denver: Mining Camp to Metropolis*. Niwot: University Press of Colorado, 1990.

LeRoy R. Hafen / H. S.

See also **Colorado; Denver; Gold Mines and Mining.**

PILGRIMS. At the turn of the seventeenth century, a small group of English separatists sought to practice their religion free from the persecution of Henry VIII. By 1609, the congregation settled near Leiden, Holland. Soon dissatisfied, a small group of them sailed from Plymouth, England, aboard the Mayflower on 16 September 1620, carrying a charter for what would become the first permanent English settlement in North America. These Pilgrims arrived in Provincetown Harbor on Massachusetts Bay on 21 November and soon settled in neighboring Plymouth Harbor. Half the residents died in the first

Pilgrims. This 1856 engraving, created to illustrate a banknote, shows the Pilgrims arriving at Plymouth, with the *Mayflower* in the background. LIBRARY OF CONGRESS

harsh winter, yet the colony grew, and in 1691, was absorbed by the Massachusetts Bay Colony.

BIBLIOGRAPHY

Abrams, Ann Uhry. *The Pilgrims and Pocahontas: Rival Myths of American Origins.* Boulder, Colo.: Westview Press, 1999.

Bradford, William. *Of Plymouth Plantation, 1620–1647: The Complete Text.* New York: Knopf, 1963.

Dillon, Francis. *The Pilgrims.* Garden City, N.Y.: Doubleday, 1975.

Barbara Schwarz Wachal

See also **Massachusetts Bay Colony; *Mayflower*; Plymouth Colony; Religious Liberty;** *and vol. 9:* **The Mayflower Compact.**

PILLORY, a device for publicly punishing petty offenders. The pillory consisted of a frame with holes in which the head and hands of the standing prisoner were locked. This device was not as common in the American colonies as were the more merciful stocks, in which the prisoner sat, fastened by the hands and feet. But one or the other probably existed in every town in which a court sat. Offenders sentenced to the pillory typically included perjurers, forgers, counterfeiters, and blasphemers. Judges based their decisions to use the pillory (and other forms of punishment) on both local tradition and precedent in English criminal law.

BIBLIOGRAPHY

Pestritto, Ronald J. *Founding the Criminal Law: Punishment and Political Thought in the Origins of America.* DeKalb: Northern Illinois University Press, 2000.

Clifford K. Shipton / S. B.

See also **Crime; Ducking Stool; Manners and Etiquette; Prisons and Prison Reform; Punishment; Stocks.**

PILLOW, FORT, MASSACRE AT (12 April 1864). Fifteen hundred Confederate cavalry under Gen. Nathan B. Forrest approached Fort Pillow, Tenn., on the morning of 12 April 1864. Forrest warned the Union garrison of 557 men (295 white and 262 black) that unless they surrendered, he could "not be responsible for [their] fate." When the Union force refused, the Confederates attacked and drove the defenders out of the fort. Forrest took prisoner 168 white and 58 black troops. Surviving Union witnesses testified before federal authorities that on Forrest's orders, Confederates massacred several hundred prisoners. All 262 blacks garrisoned at the fort were slain, most after they had ceased to resist.

BIBLIOGRAPHY

Cornish, Dudley Taylor. *The Sable Arm: Black Troops in the Union Army, 1861–1865.* Lawrence: University Press of Kansas, 1987.

MacAluso, Gregory J. *The Fort Pillow Massacre.* New York: Vantage Press, 1989.

John D. Milligan / A. R.

See also **Civil War; Military Service and Minorities: African Americans; War, Laws of.**

PIMA. *See* **Akimel O'odham and Tohono O'odham.**

PINCKNEY PLAN, the details of more than thirty provisions for a new constitution, was introduced by Charles Pinckney at the Constitutional Convention on May 29, 1787. Pinckney is credited with the notion of the separation of church and state; he is remembered for his stand on religious freedom. Pinckney is said to have coined the phrase, "the legislature of the United States shall pass no law on the subject of religion," though this wording does not appear until the First Amendment of the Bill of Rights (1789). Although Pinckney's original plan was lost, the details have been reconstructed from convention records.

BIBLIOGRAPHY

McLaughlin, Andrew C., ed. "Documents: Sketch of Pinckney's Plan for a Constitution, 1787." *American Historical Review* 9, no. 4 (1904): 735–747.

Stokes, Anson Phelps, and Leo Pfeffer. *Church and State in the United States.* Vol. 1. New York: Harper and Brothers, 1964.

U.S. House. *Documents Illustrative of the Formation of the Union of the American States.* 69th Cong., 1st sess., 1927 H. Doc. 398.

Mary Anne Hansen

See also **Church and State, Separation of; Constitution of the United States; Religious Liberty.**

PINCKNEY'S TREATY of 1795, also known as the Treaty of San Lorenzo, between the United States and the Spanish Empire, established the thirty-first parallel as the border between the United States and Spanish West Florida. Spain had ceded that area in 1763 to Great Britain, which had moved the boundary from the thirty-first parallel to a line north of the thirty-second parallel. When the British gave Florida back to Spain after the War of Independence, this boundary was disputed. In addition to meeting the American position on this issue, Spain allowed the United States free navigation of the Mississippi River to the Gulf of Mexico and granted it the right to deposit goods in New Orleans. This was of vital importance to the farmers and merchants who lived in Kentucky and Tennessee and to the settlers of the Ohio Valley, who now could ship their harvests and goods on the waterways to the eastern seaboard of the United States, to Europe, or to other areas. Additionally, both nations agreed not to incite attacks by Native Americans against the other nation. Signed at San Lorenzo El Real on 27 October 1795, the "Treaty of Friendship, Limits, and Navigation Between Spain and the United States" was negotiated by Thomas Pinckney, minister to Great Britain, who had been sent to Spain as envoy extraordinaire.

BIBLIOGRAPHY

Bemis, Samuel Flagg. *Pinckney's Treaty: America's Advantage from Europe's Distress, 1783–1800.* New Haven: Yale University Press, 1960.

Michael Wala

See also **Spain, Relations with.**

PINE TREE FLAG, a colonial flag of Massachusetts, used as early as 1700 and declared the state's official navy flag in 1776. Also one of the earliest symbols of the union of the thirteen colonies, the pine tree was incorporated into the flags of the American revolutionary forces from 1775 to 1777 in various ways, often with the motto "An Appeal to Heaven," and sometimes with the rattlesnake flag of the southern colonies with its motto, "Don't tread on me." The six armed vessels that George Washington commissioned in 1775 flew a pine tree flag, as did two American floating batteries that attacked Boston in September 1775.

BIBLIOGRAPHY

Crouthers, David D. *Flags of American History.* Maplewood, N.J.: C. S. Hammond, 1962.

Guenter, Scot M. *The American Flag, 1777–1924: Cultural Shifts from Creation to Codification.* Rutherford, N.J.: Fairleigh Dickinson University Press, 1990.

Stanley R. Pillsbury/D. B.

See also **Flags; Massachusetts; Revolution, American: Military History; State Emblems, Nicknames, Mottos, and Songs.**

PINE TREE SHILLING. In response to the dearth of hard currency, Massachusetts established a mint in June 1652. The following year, it issued a crude silver coin about the size of a modern half-dollar but weighing only one-third as much. On the obverse, between two beaded circles, was MASATHVSETS IN.; within the inner circle was a pine tree, from which the coin got its name. On the reverse was NEWENGLAND. AN. DOM. between two beaded circles and 1652, XII, within the inner one. The Roman numerals indicated the number of pence in a shilling. The mint closed in 1684.

BIBLIOGRAPHY

McCusker, John J. *Money and Exchange in Europe and America, 1600–1775: A Handbook.* Chapel Hill: University of North Carolina Press, 1978.

Newman, Eric P., and Richard G. Doty, eds. *Studies on Money in Early America.* New York: American Numismatic Society, 1976.

Thomas L. Harris/A. R.

See also **Colonial Commerce; Currency and Coinage; Massachusetts; Proclamation Money.**

PINKERTON AGENCY. Founded in Chicago in 1850 by Scottish-born Allan Pinkerton, the Pinkerton National Detective Agency was America's first professional private investigation company. When in 1861 the Pinkertons foiled a plot to assassinate president-elect Abraham Lincoln, a grateful Lincoln charged Pinkerton with establishing a secret service, thus catapulting the agency into the national spotlight.

Among its many notable assignments, the Pinkerton Agency, under the stewardship of Pinkerton, his sons, or his grandsons, was called upon to secure the return of Thomas Gainsborough's *Duchess of Devonshire* to its rightful owners, to protect the Hope diamond, and to ensure the safe delivery of the manuscript of the Gettysburg Address. By the 1870s, Pinkerton branches were established in several major U.S. cities, and all were equipped with Allan Pinkerton's innovative methods for criminal detection, some of them useful (such as rogues galleries of known malfeasants complete with photographs and personal histories, a rarity at the time) and some of them peculiarities of their age (such as phrenology). Although many of his agencies vehemently disagreed, Pinkerton also insisted on violating social tradition by hiring female operatives.

Avowedly antilabor in his later years, Allan Pinkerton was not averse to playing the role of strikebreaker. In 1877, the Pinkertons were hired by the president of the Pennsylvania and Reading Coal and Iron Company to infiltrate and destroy the radical, violent labor group called the Molly Maguires. The resulting trial led to the hanging executions of some nineteen so-called Mollies, most of them young men, a few of them probably innocent. When Pinkerton guards took part in a steelworkers strike in Homestead, Pennsylvania, in 1892, several participants on both sides were killed. While many working people were appalled by the murder of foremen and mine bosses and the dynamiting of private property, many also learned to hate and resent the Pinkertons as a dangerous enemy to the goals of organized labor.

The Pinkerton Agency was the forerunner of the modern Federal Bureau of Investigation and Interpol. At the height of its power, it was connected not only to every major law enforcement agency in the United States but had cultivated contacts with those in England and Europe as well. The agency is still in operation today, with branch offices in some thirty-two countries.

BIBLIOGRAPHY

Barber, James, and Frederick Voss. *We Never Sleep: The First Fifty Years of the Pinkertons.* Washington: Smithsonian Institute Press, 1981.

Horan, James D. *The Pinkertons, The Detective Dynasty That Made History.* New York: Crown Publishers, Inc., 1968.

Horan, James, and Howard Swiggett. *The Pinkerton Story.* New York: G. P. Putnam's Sons, 1951.

Morn, Frank. *"The Eye That Never Sleeps": A History of The Pinkerton National Detective Agency.* Bloomington: Indiana University Press, 1982.

Wormser, Richard. *Pinkerton: America's First Private Eye.* New York: Walker and Company, 1990.

Jason Philip Miller

See also **Crime; Molly Maguires.**

PIONEERS. The term "pioneer" now encompasses nearly all endeavors or persons that are first in any new movement: geographic, intellectual, scientific, or cultural. Historically, however, "pioneer" refers to nineteenth-century American frontier settlers. The American frontier consisted of several enterprises: the mining frontier, the logging frontier, the farming frontier, and others. Migrating into the American West, pioneers kept their own culture and superimposed it on the established Indian or Hispanic cultures. Most settled in communities in which social control through voluntary organizations and gendered roles maintained economic and social stability. While some pioneers were bound together by religion, such as Mormon communities, most were linked through self-interest. Many migrants relocated with friends and family, establishing themselves as a community in rural areas, or as a separate community within a larger urban area, such as the Chinese in San Francisco. Occasionally, individuals broke away from initial communities to create new settlements, but usually did so with others of similar backgrounds, reinforcing cultural identity and group connectedness.

Unmarried individuals, usually male, were likely to seek urban areas, mining camps, or cattle towns, where they could market their labor. Males outnumbered females throughout the pioneer period in the West, except

African American Pioneers. This photograph shows a sod house and "exodusters" in Nicodemus, Kans., the first settlement (now a National Historic Site) founded by blacks migrating to the "promised land" of Kansas from Kentucky starting in 1877; it later failed—but was never completely abandoned—after the railroad bypassed it. DENVER PUBLIC LIBRARY–WESTERN COLLECTION in rural areas marked by family farms. Single males with few assets created anxiety in communities where there were few institutions that could ameliorate discontent or disruption. Communities established churches, schools, and voluntary organizations as mechanisms to counter the rise of prostitution, and saloons as gathering places for unattached laborers.

BIBLIOGRAPHY

White, Richard. *"It's Your Misfortune and None of My Own": A History of the American West*. Norman: University of Oklahoma Press, 1991.

Laurie Winn Carlson

See also **Frontier; West, American;** *and vol. 9:* **Across the Plains to California in 1852; The Oregon Trail; A Pioneer Woman's Letter Home, c. 1856.**

PIPELINES, EARLY. The first oil pipelines eliminated the risk, expense, and uncertainty of boat and wagon transportation, increasing efficiency. However, they also prompted labor protest, business failures, rate wars, and monopolization. The first pipeline proposal was defeated in 1861 by opposition from the teamsters, workers who transported the oil and who saw their occupation threatened. In 1862 the first successful pipeline, one thousand feet long, began operations at Tarr Farm in Oil Creek, Pennsylvania. It was operated by Barrows and Company. In 1865 Samuel Van Syckle built a 5.25-mile pipeline from Pithole, Pennsylvania, that could carry eighty-one barrels of oil an hour, the equivalent of three hundred teams working ten hours. Disgruntled teamsters cut the line in several places, but Van Syckle managed to complete that line and another. Other businesses followed suit.

Although the pipelines reduced the cost of shipping oil to the uniform rate of $1.00 per barrel, they proved to be monopolies of the worst sort, keeping their prices just below the teamsters' to eliminate teaming, yet high enough so that producers derived little benefit. Teamsters left the fields in droves, and those who remained made threats and even set fire to some tanks. Eventually, the teamsters reduced their rates, but to no avail. Van Syckle's partners suffered financial failure not long after completing their line. It was bought and combined with another in 1867 to form the first great pipeline company, the Allegheny Transportation Company. During the next few years, short pipelines multiplied, crossing and paralleling one another in every direction. Competition was keen, and ruinous rate wars ensued, soon resulting in the consolidation of the lines.

BIBLIOGRAPHY

Boatright, Mody Coggin, and William A. Owens. *Tales From the Derrick Floor: A People's History of the Oil Industry*. Garden City, N.Y.: Doubleday, 1970.

Giddens, Paul H. *The Birth of the Oil Industry*. Use and Abuse of America's Natural Resources Series. 1938. Reprint, New York: Arno Press, 1972.

Miller, Ernest C. *Pennsylvania's Oil Industry*. 3d ed. Pennsylvania History Studies, no. 4. Gettysburg: Pennsylvania Historical Association, 1974.

Paul H. Giddens/D. B.

See also **Petroleum Industry; Petroleum Prospecting and Technology.**

PIRACY. From the early seventeenth century to the early nineteenth century, the Atlantic and Gulf coasts witnessed extensive acts of piracy against nations engaging in shipping and trade. From New England's earliest settlement, its shipping suffered from coastal piracy. In 1653 Massachusetts made piracy punishable by death, and governors sometimes sent out armed ships to attack offshore pirates. At the same time, however, colonial governors granted "privateering" commissions to sea desperadoes.

The Navigation Acts, passed by Great Britain between 1650 and 1696, halted all foreign ships from trading in the American colonies; this led to colonial smuggling and eventually to piracy. Colonial merchants and settlers bought pirates' stolen goods and thus obtained necessary commodities at a cheap price. New York, Philadelphia, and Newport, Rhode Island, were rivals in this scandalous trade, with Boston, Virginia, and the Carolinas also buying stolen goods. When Richard Coote, earl of Bellomont, became governor of New York and New England in 1697, he was ordered to "suppress the prevailing piracy" causing "so much distress along the coast." Coote found general colonial connivance with pirates, however, especially in New York, Rhode Island, and Philadelphia. One New York merchant secured $500,000 in seven years through promotion of piracy.

Piracy reached a peak during the period 1705–1725, and particularly between 1721 and 1724, when terror reigned on the New England coast. English men-of-war ended this peril, but after the American Revolution piratical attacks on U.S. ships by French "privateers" led to an undeclared war between France and the United States and contributed to the creation of the U.S. Navy. Piratical operations of English men-of-war on U.S. coasts and the high seas, including the impressment of American seamen, hastened the War of 1812. The period 1805–1825 witnessed a resurgence of piracy, which led to the expansion of the U.S. Navy, which was active suppressing piracy and convoying ships. More than three thousand instances of piracy were recorded between 1814 and 1824, half of them on U.S. shipping.

Beginning in 1805 the navy began warring on pirates on the Louisiana and Gulf coasts, a region long plagued by piracy. The Barataria pirates were driven out in 1814, and the Aury-Laffite pirates were purged from Galveston, Texas, in 1817. From 1816 to 1824 the United States faced the perplexing problem of dealing with the piratical "privateers" of the new Latin American republics. Congress finally was so angered by these freebooters' depredations that in 1819 it passed an act prescribing the death penalty for piracy.

The Spaniards of Cuba and Puerto Rico sent out pirates who captured American ships, murdered their crews, and nearly brought on a war between the United States and the two Spanish colonies. Congress denounced this piracy in 1822, and in 1823 and 1824 it dispatched a strong naval squadron to suppress the pirates. By 1827 piracy had ended on all U.S. coasts.

BIBLIOGRAPHY

Bromley, John S. *Corsairs and Navies, 1660–1760.* History Series. London: Hambledon Press, 1987.

Lane, Kris E. *Pillaging the Empire: Piracy in the Americas, 1500–1750.* Armonk, N.Y.: Sharpe, 1998.

Marley, David. *Pirates and Privateers of the Americas.* Santa Barbara, Calif.: ABC-CLIO, 1994.

Swanson, Carl E. *Predators and Prizes: American Privateering and Imperial Warfare, 1739–1748.* Studies in Maritime History. Columbia: University of South Carolina Press, 1991.

Honor Sachs
George Wycherley

See also **France, Quasi-War with; Navigation Acts; Privateers and Privateering; War of 1812.**

PIT, the popular name for trading floors of commodity exchanges, is most often applied to that of the Board of Trade of the City of Chicago, the largest exchange in the United States. The Pit records world opinion on the price of key commodities and promotes a liquid market by providing opportunities to make contracts for future delivery ("futures") and to protect buyers against price changes ("hedges").

Founded on 3 April 1848, the Board of Trade was organized in 1850 under a general statute and incorporated by a special legislative act on 18 February 1859. The Board of Trade is governed by a board of directors; an appointed professional serves as president.

BIBLIOGRAPHY

Cowing, Cedric B. *Populists, Plungers, and Progressives: A Social History of Stock and Commodity Speculation: 1890–1936.* Princeton, N.J.: Princeton University Press, 1965.

Benjamin F. Shambaugh / c. w.

See also **Commodity Exchanges; Exchanges.**

PITHOLE, in northwest Pennsylvania, was a boomtown spawned in the wake of the first oil well drilled in the area (1859). In 1865 the United States Petroleum Company hit a gusher near Pithole Creek. News of the strike precipitated an oil stampede. Leases sold for fabulous sums, more wells were drilled, and a city of 15,000 people arose in a whirl of speculation. By December 1866, the wells had run dry and Pithole's population had fallen to less than 2,000. The discovery of kerosene as an effective replacement for whale lamp oil drove this frantic quest for oil. Important technologies such as pipeline systems and refining techniques were first developed at this time.

BIBLIOGRAPHY

Giddens, Paul H. *The Birth of the Oil Industry.* New York: Arno Press, 1972.

Yergin, Daniel. *The Prize: The Epic Quest for Oil, Money, and Power.* New York: Simon and Schuster, 1992.

Paul H. Giddens
Jennifer Lane Maier

See also **Petrochemical Industry; Petroleum Industry; Wildcat Oil Drilling.**

PITTSBURGH. Once described by the writer Lincoln Steffens as "hell with the lid off," Pittsburgh has transformed from an acrid industrial and manufacturing city into a nationally renowned center for health care, high technology, robotics, and education. The "smoky city," historically known for its steel production, has been beautified and revitalized, with few remnants remaining from its dark past. Pittsburgh sits at the intersection of the Monongahela, Allegheny, and Ohio Rivers. The first inhabitants were Native American tribes, later joined by

Pittsburgh. This photograph shows a steel plant along the Monongahela River, emblematic of the city until the latter part of the twentieth century. Library of Congress

European settlers pushing westward. The French and British fought to control the waterway. The French ousted a British garrison in 1754 and built Fort Duquesne, which in turn was taken by the British in 1758 and renamed Fort Pitt.

As a port city, Pittsburgh grew rapidly in the 1800s and the discovery of coal guaranteed its place as an industrial hotbed. The Civil War solidified Pittsburgh's reputation as the "Iron City" since it supplied most of the iron for the Union army. Spurred on by a steady flow of immigrant labor, other industries also developed, including oil, glass, and other metals. Important business leaders built their empires in Pittsburgh, such as Andrew Carnegie, Henry Clay Frick, Henry J. Heinz, and Andrew W. Mellon. Years of relying on heavy industry gave Pittsburgh a bad reputation in the twentieth century. Downtown, the streetlights often burned all day to offset the heavy smoke from the plants. After World War II, however, foreign competitors decimated the city's industrial base, and Pittsburgh came to symbolize the nation's Rustbelt.

A revitalization effort that began after World War II was implemented with renewed vigor. Civic leaders supported the rebirth of the city through a series of "Renaissance" programs. In 1977, Mayor Richard Caliguiri began the Renaissance II program, which resulted in the building of several distinctive skyscrapers in the downtown Golden Triangle and a neighborhood revitalization effort citywide. Later, several important cultural institutions were built to resurrect the downtown cultural life. In 2001, Heinz Field debuted, a new football stadium for the Steelers, while Pirates baseball was played at the new PNC Park. Pittsburgh's three rivers remain the largest inland port in the nation, while the Pittsburgh International Airport serves more than 20 million passengers annually. The Pittsburgh metropolitan area in 2002 encompassed a six-county region of western Pennsylvania that covered over 4,500 square miles and included a population of about 2.5 million.

BIBLIOGRAPHY

Hays, Samuel P., ed. *City at the Point: Essays on the Social History of Pittsburgh.* Pittsburgh: University of Pittsburgh Press, 1991.

Lubove, Roy. *Twentieth-Century Pittsburgh: The Post-Steel Era.* Pittsburgh: University of Pittsburgh Press, 1996.

Bob Batchelor

See also **Duquesne, Fort; Iron and Steel Industry; Pennsylvania.**

PLAN OF 1776, a model set of articles for treaties that the United States would negotiate with foreign powers. John Adams, Benjamin Franklin, John Dickinson, and Robert Morris drew it up. The plan remains significant because of its definition of neutrality rights, otherwise known as freedom of the seas. The committee selected from eighteenth-century European treaties definitions of neutral rights that would appeal to small-navied powers, such as the doctrine of free ships, free goods. It also restricted the category of contraband to a carefully defined list of arms, munitions, and implements of war, not including foodstuffs or naval stores.

BIBLIOGRAPHY

Dull, Jonathan R. *A Diplomatic History of the American Revolution.* New Haven: Yale University Press, 1985.

Hutson, James H. *John Adams and the Diplomacy of the American Revolution.* Lexington: University Press of Kentucky, 1980.

Samuel Flagg Bemis / A. E.

See also **Contraband of War; Foreign Policy; Freedom of the Seas; International Law; Neutral Rights; Neutrality; Treaties with Foreign Nations.**

PLANK ROADS, introduced into the United States from Canada about 1837, were first constructed in New York and later in Pennsylvania, South Carolina, Illinois, Ohio, Wisconsin, and Michigan. Builders created thousands of miles of plank roads at a mileage cost of $1,000 to $2,400. To create a plank road, builders first provided good drainage by digging ditches on either side. Next they laid planks, three or four inches thick and eight feet long, at right angles to stringers, which rested lengthwise on the roadbed. Portable sawmills set up in neighboring forests prepared the planks. For a time, plank roads successfully competed with railroads, but paved roads eventually replaced them.

BIBLIOGRAPHY

Majewski, John, Christopher Baer, and Daniel B. Klein. "Responding to Relative Decline: The Plank Road Boom of Antebellum New York." *Journal of Economic History* 53, no. 1 (March 1993): 106–122.

Taylor, George Rogers. *The Transportation Revolution, 1815–1860.* The Economic History of the United States, vol. 4. New York: Rinehart, 1951.

Charles B. Swaney / A. E.

See also **Roads; Transportation and Travel;** *and picture (overleaf).*

PLANNED PARENTHOOD OF SOUTHEASTERN PENNSYLVANIA V. CASEY, 505 U.S 833 (1992), is best known for what it did not do—overrule *Roe v. Wade* (1973). By 1992 five associate justices had been appointed to the Supreme Court by Presidents Ronald Reagan and George H. W. Bush, both of whom pledged to select judges committed to overturning *Roe,* which had legalized abortion. Reagan had named William Rehnquist, one of the original dissenters in *Roe,* as chief justice in 1986. *Webster v. Reproductive Health Services*

THE MAIL CARRIER OF 100 YEARS AGO.

Plank Roads. An early mail carrier rides on a plank road in this lithograph. © CORBIS

(1989) and *Rust v. Sullivan* (1991) had upheld laws limiting access to abortion and seemed indicators of doctrinal shifts. The Pennsylvania Abortion Control Act at issue in *Casey* did not ban abortion, but the Court upheld all of the restrictions on abortion imposed by Pennsylvania except mandatory notification of the husband. These included a twenty-four-hour waiting period, informed consent of one parent for pregnant teenagers, reporting requirements, and a state-scripted warning against the medical procedure.

As a result of *Casey*, restrictions on abortion would no longer be judged by a strict-scrutiny standard requiring a "compelling state interest," as did restrictions on other constitutional rights. Instead, an "undue burden" standard was substituted, allowing states to place restrictions on abortion unless they posed "substantial obstacles" to the woman's right of privacy recognized in *Roe*. Justices Sandra Day O'Connor, Anthony Kennedy, and David Souter, all appointed by either Reagan or Bush, concurred that "the reservations any of us may have in reaffirming the central holding of *Roe* are out-weighed by the expectation of individual liberty." Hence, *Casey* represented a victory for centrist judicial politics.

BIBLIOGRAPHY

Craig, Barbara Hinkson, and David M. O'Brien. *Abortion and American Politics*. Chatham, N.J.: Chatham House, 1993.

Judith A. Baer / A. R.

See also **Abortion; Pro-Choice Movement; Pro-Life Movement; *Rust v. Sullivan*; *Webster v. Reproductive Health Services*.**

PLANS OF UNION, COLONIAL, were proposed by both the crown and the colonies throughout the colonial period, to promote a stable power structure (especially with regard to arbitration of trade and boundary disputes), to exercise greater control on the part of the crown over colonial assemblies, and to foster increased collaboration between colonies in the name of common interests. Each of the plans proposed a governing structure for the American colonies, whether crown appointed, popularly generated, or some combination of the two.

There was no effective union in colonial America until the Revolution; the colonies, each established separately—the result of corporate, proprietary, and royal interests—struggled with multiple agendas and intercolonial jealousies. There were, however, interests that united two or more of the colonies at a time, which resulted in diverse plans for union. Prime among the issues prompting plans for union was that of military defense against Native Americans and the protection of lands claimed by the British. Plans of union also addressed competition with Dutch and French trading interests in North America, in some instances related to competing trade agreements with Native Americans.

Frontier defense prompted several of the most prominent plans. The first known proposed union was the United Colonies of New England, a loose confederation including Massachusetts, Plymouth, Connecticut, and New Haven, formed in 1643 for the purpose of uniting in common defense against Indians. (Attempts by the confederated commission to mediate boundary and trade disputes failed, largely because it was not sufficiently empowered to take action on those issues.) Similarly, in 1689, New York, Massachusetts, Plymouth, and Connecticut entered into a temporary military league, the Intercolonial Congress, to provide for frontier defense. The crown also proposed a union for common defense in 1698, to be administered by the earl of Bellomont, commissioned as governor of Massachusetts, New York, and New Hampshire. Colonial representatives proposed several plans in the early eighteenth century to the Board of Trade.

Notorious among the crown-instituted plans was the DOMINION OF NEW ENGLAND (1686), which revoked the charters of Connecticut and Rhode Island, and merged them with Massachusetts Bay and Plymouth. These colonies, with the addition of New York and New Jersey in 1688, were joined in a royal dominion under one governor, Sir Edmund Andros, who was empowered to abolish all legislative assemblies.

Plans of union varied greatly with regard to the level of detail and proposed structures of governance. Several organized the colonies under a governor or director general appointed by the crown, assisted by an advisory council composed of an equal number of representatives from each of the colonies; others recommended the formation of an intercolonial assembly or congress. The ALBANY PLAN was drafted by Benjamin Franklin and presented at a meeting in Albany, New York, in 1754, attended by representatives from seven colonies. Among the most detailed plans, it proposed a crown-appointed president-general and an intercolonial council with membership apportioned according to both wealth and population. Although accepted by the Albany Congress, the plan was rejected by the state legislatures and the crown.

The divergent interests that hobbled early plans for colonial union presaged the conflicts between colonies over the structure of a federal government in the creation of the Articles of Confederation and the Constitution.

BIBLIOGRAPHY

Craven, Wesley Frank. *The Colonies in Transition, 1660–1713.* New York: Harper and Row, 1968.

Dickerson, Oliver Morton. *American Colonial Government: A Study of the British Board of Trade in its Relation to the American Colonies.* New York: Russell and Russell, 1962. The original edition was published in 1939.

Jennings, Francis. *Empire of Fortune: Crowns, Colonies, and Tribes in the Seven Years' War in America.* New York: Norton, 1988.

Johnson, Richard R. *Adjustment to Empire: The New England Colonies, 1675–1715.* New Brunswick, N.J.: Rutgers University Press, 1981.

Leslie J. Lindenauer

See also **Frontier Defense; New England Colonies.**

PLANTATION SYSTEM OF THE SOUTH.

William Bradford, governor of the Plymouth colony in Massachusetts, invoked the standard English usage of his day when he entitled his remarkable history of the colony *Of Plymouth Plantation.* In the seventeenth century, the process of settling colonies was commonly known as "transplantation," and individual settlements went by such names as the Jamestown plantation or, in the case of the Massachusetts Pilgrims, the Plymouth plantation. Yet by the end of the colonial period, the generic term for English settlements had given way to a new definition. A "plantation" referred to a large-scale agricultural operation on which slaves were put to work systematically producing marketable crops such as rice, tobacco, sugar, and COTTON. In fact, the link between plantations and SLAVERY had been forged over several centuries, long before William Bradford and other English settlers ever dreamed of establishing colonies in Massachusetts and Virginia.

The cotton plantations of the Old South were the lineal descendents of the sugar plantations established by Europeans in the eastern Mediterranean around 1100 A.D. For the next 750 years, sugar plantations would spread westward across the Mediterranean, darting out into the Atlantic islands hugging the west coast of Africa, then across the ocean to Brazil before jumping from one Caribbean island to another over the course of the seventeenth, eighteenth, and nineteenth centuries. Not until the first half of the nineteenth century did a permanent sugar-plantation economy reach the North American mainland in the parishes of southern Louisiana. Yet long before then, sugar plantations had established the precedent for the slave society that came into existence in the eighteenth century in the southern colonies of British North America.

All of these plantations shared certain crucial features. Unlike feudal manors, plantation lands were owned outright, as absolute property, by the masters. This had two important consequences. First, it gave plantation owners an incentive to rationalize their operations to make them more productive. Thus plantations from the beginning were organized to produce as large a volume of marketable staples as possible. Second, absolute property precluded the use of serfs, who would have had some claim to rights in the land. Thus plantations early on tapped into another source of labor, slavery, which had survived along the Mediterranean margins of southern Europe, where feudalism had not taken hold. As the plantations spread from the Levant to Cyprus to Sicily, and then out into the Atlantic, owners grew increasingly dependent on African slaves as their source of labor. Thus the spread of the sugar plantations occasioned the growth of the Atlantic SLAVE TRADE. By the time the English colonists at Jamestown discovered that they could grow tobacco for profit, they already knew how to build rationally organized plantations based on private property and slave labor.

Tobacco and Rice Plantations

Not all plantations were alike. In the eighteenth century, two very different systems of plantation agriculture developed in the southern colonies. In Virginia and Maryland, in the region bordering on Chesapeake Bay, and therefore known as "the Chesapeake," tobacco plantations flourished with slaves organized into gangs. In the lowcountry district of South Carolina and Georgia, slaves on rice plantations were put to work under a "task" system. The different crops and their distinctive patterns of labor organization gave rise to several other important distinctions as well.

Tobacco was the first plantation crop in North America. English settlers in the Chesapeake region recognized tobacco's profitable potential in the early seventeenth century. They built their first plantations using the labor of British indentured servants rather than African slaves. But in the late 1600s the market for English servants dried up, and Virginia planters turned instead to slavery. By 1720 a full-scale plantation system was in place throughout the Chesapeake, grounded on the labor of slaves and oriented toward the production of tobacco. By the standards of Brazilian and Caribbean sugar plantations, however, Chesapeake tobacco plantations were modest in size. They reached their peak efficiency with perhaps twenty or thirty slaves, whereas sugar plantations were most efficient when they had at least fifty slaves.

The rice plantations of lowcountry South Carolina and Georgia more closely approximated the sugar plantations. It took at least thirty slaves to set up a rice plantation. Because rice crops needed constant irrigation, they could only be established in coastal lowlands. Yet because rice cultivation was not a particularly delicate process, it did not require intensive oversight from masters and overseers. Hence rice slaves worked on a "task" system by which each slave was assigned a specific task to complete on his or her own each day. The higher capital investment required of rice plantations, plus the reduced amount of labor supervision, made rice plantations far more profitable than tobacco plantations. And over the course of the eighteenth century, technological improvements doubled rice's profitability. This was true despite the fact that lowcountry rice plantations were famously unhealthy for the slaves, who suffered terrible rates of sickness and death and who were barely able to maintain a natural rate of reproduction.

So it was that tobacco, not rice, set the pattern that would be followed by the great nineteenth-century cotton plantations. On tobacco plantations, as on the wheat plantations that replaced many of them in the second half of the eighteenth century, slaves worked in gangs under the direct supervision of the master or his overseer. Tobacco, unlike rice, required extensive and careful cultivation, and it was this need for direct supervision that explains why tobacco tended to produce smaller plantations than did rice. Because tobacco could be grown inland, plantations could expand westward as eastern soils became exhausted. Away from the unhealthy climate of the lowcountry, slaves on tobacco plantations were less sickly, and they were able to achieve a relatively robust rate of natural population increase.

Cotton and Sugar Plantations

These characteristics of the tobacco plantation economy were reproduced, beginning in the late eighteenth century, on the short-staple cotton plantations for which the antebellum South became famous. Eli Whitney's invention of the cotton gin in the 1790s made the growth of the cotton kingdom possible. Spreading first southward from Virginia into the upcountry regions of South Carolina and Georgia, the cotton plantations soon began expanding into Alabama, Mississippi, Louisiana, and finally, Texas.

Like their tobacco-producing predecessors, cotton plantations were rationalized business enterprises oriented toward the cultivation of marketable staples sold primarily to the northern and European market. Slaves were organized in gangs, their work supervised directly by a hierarchy of masters, overseers, and on larger plantations, slave drivers. The cycle of cotton growing made it efficient for planters to cultivate foodstuffs—primarily corn and pork—of sufficient nutrition and in sufficient quantities to maintain a relatively healthy slave labor force. And because cotton, like tobacco, was not grown in swampy lowlands, the slave population was able to grow on its own, without infusions from the Atlantic slave trade.

The natural growth of the slave population was one of the sources of the cotton-plantation economy's profitability. But the growth of the antebellum sugar plantations in southern Louisiana suggests that slave plantations could be profitable even when they were deadly to the slaves. Even more than rice, sugar plantations required huge capital investments and were therefore most efficient with very large numbers of slave laborers. Because they were established long after Brazilian and Caribbean sugar plantations, Louisiana's sugar plantations benefited from the technological advances of their predecessors. Thus by investing in the most advanced milling machinery, and by putting larger numbers of slaves to work at an inhumanly grueling pace, the sugar planters of southern Louisiana reaped huge profits from a slave population that actually died off at the rate of nearly 14 percent every decade. Thus the plantation system could be profitable even when it literally killed off its own workers.

Indeed, the famed inefficiencies commonly associated with slave—as opposed to free—labor never seemed to appear in the Old South. A highly efficient interstate slave trade compensated for the absence of a free labor market, moving tens of thousands of slaves across the South every decade; it allowed planters to sell their surplus slaves without difficulty or to purchase more slaves with similar ease. In addition, a highly rationalized pattern of plantation organization kept the slaves busy and productive throughout the year, even in the winter months after the crops had been harvested. Finally, a network of rivers, roadways, and eventually rail lines moved the cotton swiftly and efficiently from plantation to market, a trade facilitated by an elaborate network of "factors" who served as both middlemen and creditors to the plantation system. For all of these reasons, cotton plantations thwarted classical political economy's confident predictions of slavery's imminent demise. Instead, cotton plantations flourished, so much so that their relentless expansion farther and farther west helped provoke the sectional crisis that led to the Civil War.

Because the Civil War resulted in the death of slavery, it would make sense to terminate the history of the plantation system at the same point. But just as seventeenth-century tobacco plantations flourished with indentured servants rather than slaves, nineteenth-century cotton plantations persisted in the face of slavery's demise. What changed, of course, was the labor system upon which the plantation economy was based. Once the slaves became free laborers, planters were forced for the first time to negotiate contracts with their former slaves. As this contract system evolved in the years after the Civil War, cotton planters abandoned the gang system. In its place a "sharecropping" system emerged in which individual families contracted to work a plot of land on a larger plantation in return for yearly wages in the form of a share of the final crop.

Sharecropping physically transformed the layout of cotton plantations across the South. Where slaves once lived together in quarters, freed people now lived in their own cabins working on their own plots. Sharecropping similarly altered the marketing system for cotton plantations. Because sharecropping families now made their own consumption decisions, they established their own relations with merchants and creditors across the South. Thus the number of merchants proliferated and a merchant class took on newfound significance to the plantation system. The planter-merchant alliance of the postwar plantations persisted well into the twentieth century. In the meantime, huge plantations based on gangs of wage laborers reappeared in the newly settled cotton-growing areas of the Mississippi. Only after the successive shocks of the persistent drought and severe economic depression did a weakened plantation system finally succumb to the modernizing incentives created by the New Deal in the 1930s. Only then, after hundreds of years of vigorous life, did the southern plantation die its final death.

BIBLIOGRAPHY

Curtin, Philip D. *The Rise and Fall of the Plantation Complex: Essays in Atlantic History.* Cambridge, U.K., and New York: Cambridge University Press, 1990.

Dusinberre, William. *Them Dark Days: Slavery in the American Rice Swamps.* New York: Oxford University Press, 1996.

Eltis, David. *The Rise of African Slavery in the Americas.* Cambridge, U.K., and New York: Cambridge University Press, 2000.

Fogel, Robert William, ed. *Without Consent or Contract: The Rise and Fall of American Slavery.* New York: Norton, 1989.

Genovese, Eugene D. *The Political Economy of Slavery: Studies in the Economy and Society of the Slave South.* 2d ed. Middletown, Conn.: Wesleyan University Press, 1989. The original edition was published in 1965.

Morgan, Philip D. *Slave Counterpoint: Black Culture in the Eighteenth-Century Chesapeake and Lowcountry.* Chapel Hill: University of North Carolina Press, 1998.

Oakes, James. *The Ruling Race: A History of American Slaveholders.* New York: Knopf, 1982.

Phillips, Ulrich Bonnell. *American Negro Slavery: A Survey of the Supply, Employment, and Control of Negro Labor As Determined by the Plantation Regime.* New York: D. Appleton, 1918. Reprint, Baton Rouge: Louisiana State University Press, 1966.

Ransom, Roger L., and Richard Sutch. *One Kind of Freedom: The Economic Consequences of Emancipation.* 2d ed. Cambridge, U.K., and New York: Cambridge University Press, 2001. The original edition was published in 1977.

Smith, Mark. *Mastered By the Clock: Time, Slavery, and Freedom in the American South.* Chapel Hill: University of North Carolina Press, 1997.

Tadman, Michael. *Speculators and Slaves: Masters, Traders, and Slaves in the Old South.* Madison: University of Wisconsin Press, 1989. Reprint, 1996.

Woodman, Harold D. *New South, New Law: The Legal Foundations of Credit and Labor Relations in the Postbellum Agricultural South.* Baton Rouge: Louisiana State University Press, 1995.

James Oakes

See also **Rice Culture and Trade; South, the: The Antebellum South; Sugar Industry; Tobacco Industry;** *and vol. 9:* **Letter Describing Plantation Life in South Carolina.**

PLASTICS. Perhaps the most prevalent manufactured material in society today is plastics. About 200 billion pounds of plastics are produced annually in the world, 90 billion pounds in the United States alone. In the 1967 movie *The Graduate*, the title character, played by Dustin Hoffman, was offered one word of advice for future success: "plastics." It is difficult to imagine society without plastics. Plastics come in innumerable forms, types, and items. They can take the form of adhesives, casting resins, coating compounds, laminates, or molded plastics. They are formed through extrusion, injection, compression, blowing, transfer (fusing), or by a vacuum. There are thermoplastics of nylon, polyester, polyethylene, polypropylene, polyvinyl chloride, polystyrene, and many other substances. There are also thermoset plastics, made of phenols, urea-formaldehydes, melamines, or epoxies. A single object may involve many different types of plastics. For example, the plastics in a car include phenolic and glass (fiberglass), acetal, nylon, polypropylene, fluorocarbon, polyethylene, acrylic, butyrate, and melamine. Plastic can be a natural substance or a synthetic one. In other words, "plastics" can mean any number of different substances and products.

History

Resin is the key to plastics. Until the mid-nineteenth century, societies used natural plastic materials such as amber, sealing wax, shellac, or animal horns. These materials could be softened and molded. When cooled, they retained the new shape. Sealing wax was used to close documents with a personal mark. Items made from animal horns included buttons, cups, hornbooks, and lantern windows. Shellac (a gutta-percha molded plastic) was often used for lamination and for phonograph records (until vinyl was introduced).

In the mid-nineteenth century, the organic chemical industry began, which led to a study of the chemical makeup of materials and many man-made products. Early plastics were created from cellulose wood fibers treated with nitrate. A German, Christian Friedrich Schönbein, was one of the first to develop cellulose nitrate plastics in 1846. Later, in England, Alexander Parkes developed Parkesine, a pressure-molded collodoin (cellulose nitrate in ethanol). He displayed many Parkesine objects at the 1862 London International Exhibition. However, as happened with so many inventions from Europe, it was the Americans who developed them as commercial successes. John Wesley Hyatt and his brother created the Celluloid Manufacturing Company in Newark, New Jersey, in 1872; this company became the renowned Celanese Corporation of America, renamed CelaneseAG in1999. Hyatt used camphor as a plasticizer with cellulose, which proved safer and, therefore, more commercially viable. Camphor is still used as a natural plasticizer. Hyatt also introduced injection molding, extrusion molding (forcing molten plastics through an opening), and blow molding (like glass blowing). His work in celluloid made possible motion picture film for Thomas Edison, photographic film for George Eastman, and other products such as collars, eyeglass frames, and side curtains for automobiles. The great disadvantage of celluloid nitrate was its flammability. However, by World War I (1914–1918) the Tennessee Eastman Corporation had developed cellulose fibers mixed with acetate, which proved much less flammable and was used widely on airplane wings.

Leo Baekeland, a Belgian who came to the United States in 1889, developed the first commercial synthetic resin and the first thermoset resin in the early 1900s. He created a substance from phenolics (found in coal tar) and formaldehyde to impregnate fibrous sheets. His new synthetic was called Bakelite, which became the foremost name in plastics.

The work of Hermann Staudinger in Zurich in the 1920s was critical in explaining how the plastic molecules, polymers, were created. Once his work was accepted in the 1930s, the plastics industry developed rapidly with diversified products for commercial uses. In the 1930s the new plastics materials included urea resins, acrylics, and polyethylene in 1931; vinyl resins in 1933; melamine, fiberglass, and styrene in 1937; Teflon and epoxy in 1938; and nylon in 1939. After World War II (1939–1945), society entered the "Plastics Age."

What Are Plastics?

Plastics are inexpensive substances that are soft and malleable during manufacturing and are fabricated into lightweight, tough, rigid or flexible, clear or opaque, corrosive-resistant objects. There are some inorganic substances that conform to this definition—concrete, mortar, and plaster of Paris for example. However, as we think of them, plastics are organic substances made up of huge molecules called polymers. The organic material generally used is coal, oil, natural gas, or wood. Plastics have a high molecular weight; for instance, the molecular weight of oxygen is 32, and that of a polymer is between 10,000 and 500,000. Chemicals are used to distill and modify the organic substance. Chemicals found in plastics include carbon, hydrogen, oxygen, and nitrogen. Chlorine, fluorine, sulfur, or silicon may also be present. To make the polymers more flexible or tougher, a plasticizer is added. There are many different plasticizers, and it is important to use the right one in the right amount for the particular substance or object desired. If the wrong plasticizer is used, the polymer loses its plasticity in a short time. In the early days of the plastics industry, this happened often with raincoats, handbags, curtains, and other objects, which soon became brittle and cracked.

There are two types of plastics—thermoplastics and thermoset plastics. Thermoplastics are formed from long linear chains of molecules (polymers). These polymers can be softened and when cooled regain a solid state. These plastics can be first formed as sheets, pellets, films, tubes, rods, or fibers. These forms can then be reheated and molded into other shapes. For example, nylon thread can be made into fabric. The various chemical and molecular properties of thermoplastics determine whether they are called nylon, polyester, polypropylene, polystyrene, polyethylene, polyvinyl chloride (PVC), or other names.

Thermoset plastics are different. These polymers are formed from two directions and produce three-dimensional networks of molecules, not linear chains. Such substances cannot be remelted. They are formed through compression molding or casting. Thermoset plastics include phenolic laminates (the original Bakelite), urethane, melamine, epoxy, acrylic, silicone, fluorocarbons, and others.

Uses of Plastics

Plastics are prolific and have many advantages over other heavier, easily corroded, breakable, or more expensive materials. A home provides a good example of the ubiquity and versatility of plastics. The house may use vinyl concrete, vinyl siding, vinyl window frames, vinyl wallpaper, and vinyl venetian blinds. These are long lasting and require little upkeep. The wiring in the house could be polyethylene with epoxy coating. The insulation may be silicone or polystyrene. The house will also have polyvinyl chloride pipes. The outdoor furniture is likely to be molded PVC. Windows may be acrylic and so, too, the sofa. Seat cushions and pillows will likely be made with urea-formaldehyde foam; the carpets, nylon. The tables and cabinets may be polyurethane. Dishes may be melamine, which is easily dyed, durable, and very scratch resistant. The family car is also likely to be melamine coated. Pots and pans often use Teflon, a fluorocarbon invented in 1943. Serving dishes may be the acrylic Lu-

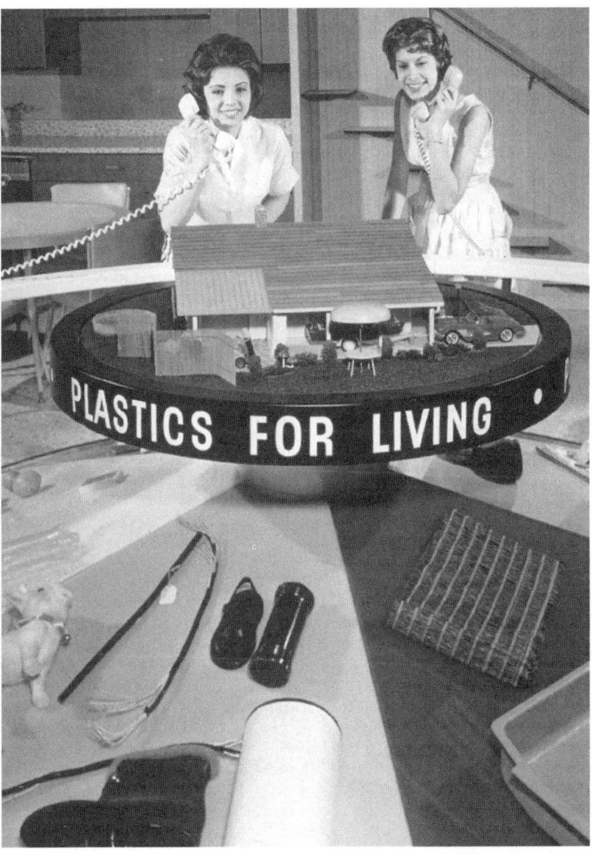

Plastics. Plastics for Living, a display by B. F. Goodrich at the National Plastics Exposition at the New York Coliseum, with a sampling from the world of plastics, 1963. GETTY IMAGES

cite, and small windows may be of another acrylic, Plexiglas. Clothing may also be of plastics, including nylon stockings and nylon underwear. In the late 1960s, clothing often was all polyester; today, polyester fibers are often mixed with natural fibers such as wool or cotton for a more natural look. The home's air ducts are also likely to be polyester, and if there is a boat, it is most likely fiberglass, made from polyester and glass fiber mix. The glass fibers reinforce the plastics and allow for repairs. Foods in a home, especially meats, are packaged in Styrofoam, made from polystyrene, as are some carry-out containers. Polystyrenes are thermoplastics that are easily molded, rigid, and good insulators.

The five most prevalent plastics are all thermoplastics and account for 90 percent of the plastics of the early twenty-first century. These include polyethylene, used in all types of bags, diaper liners, agricultural covers, and milk and juice jugs; polyethylene terephthalate (PET), used principally for soda bottles and videotapes; polystyrene, used as clear packaging, as a foam (Styrofoam), or for furniture, toys, utensils, and dishes; polypropylene, used for battery cases, crates, film, molded car parts, appliances, fish nets, and wire coating; and polyvinyl chloride, used as a flexible substance in film, hoses, rainwear, and wall coverings, or as a rigid substance in pipes, buildings, and credit cards. The most prevalent thermoset plastics are phenolics, used with formaldehyde and fillers in plywood, fiberglass, and circuit boards; and urea resins, used in polyurethane foam fillers.

The uses of plastics are always expanding and new polymers are being created. One example of thermoset plastics whose uses are expanding is silicone. It is an oxygen-based, and not the usual carbon-based, substance. Because it is highly resistant to ozone, chemicals, sunlight, and aging, it has a wide variety of uses, such as polishes, insulation, waterproofing, adhesives, and implants. Two very versatile thermoplastics are polyethylene and polycarbonate. Polyethylene is used for toys, electronic devices, wires, and milk carton coatings. Polyethylene is also now used widely in medical procedures, for example, to replace aortas or as prosthetic devices. Polycarbonates are fairly new polymers that are formed from bonding oxygen and silicon. Polycarbonates are easy to use yet highly rigid and very corrosive resistant. They have replaced phenol laminates in spacecraft, automobiles, and ships.

Disadvantages of Plastics

Though plastics are ubiquitous and versatile, they also have several disadvantages. The original plastic, cellulose nitrate, was highly flammable; celluloid acetate lessened that danger. Later plastics have included flame retardants, which delay the outbreak of flames but not the decomposition before reaching flammable temperatures. Because of the flame retardants, plastics produce thick, dense smoke that is acrid from the chemicals, especially carbon monoxide. In some of the most disastrous fires, more people suffocated from the plastics smoke and soot than died from the flames. Also, once plastic does flame, it burns faster and hotter than natural substances.

Decomposition is another issue. Because plastics are made from long chains of molecules that receive high heat to set or mold them, decomposition can emerge as weaknesses in the chain. When thermoplastics are remolded, weaknesses can increase. Some plastics also decompose more rapidly than others, especially the less expensive plastics such as PVC and urethane foam. Some critics claim that the phthalate plasticizers used in PVC create low-level toxicity. The urethane foam cushions begin to break down fairly quickly, leaving bits of foam and dust. Leaving plastics exposed to sunlight and heat also causes decomposition and cracking. As plastics decompose, they release chemicals such as carbon monoxide, chlorine, and benzene into the air. For example, the "office worker's illness" is caused by decomposing polymers of the air ducts, furniture, and equipment, and too little fresh air.

Future

Another problem with plastics is waste disposal. In the United States alone, some 60 billion pounds of plastics are discarded annually and over 90 percent of the waste is not yet recycled. Thermoset plastics cannot be reused; neither can some thermoplastics because of impurities (including disposable diapers, food packaging, and trash bags). Nevertheless, in the United States and Europe plastics recycling has become a major industry, tripling in the United States since 1990. Recycled bottles alone have grown from 411 million pounds in 1990 to 1,511 million pounds in 2000. There are over 1,400 products made from recycled plastics, most of the same items as new synthetic plastics—furniture, packaging, household items—but also new items such as lumber and posts.

Composting is a principal method of recycling plastics. Synthetic plastics may decompose through photodegradation, oxidation, or hydrolysis—naturally or chemically. Success in composting depends on the environment and the chemicals used in the plastics. Some, such as the polyolefins, are hydrophobic (water-resistant) and thus highly resistant to biodegradation.

The newest research and development in plastics is in bioplastics, biodegradable plastics whose components are principally derived from renewable raw materials. This often means a return to many of the natural polymers used in the nineteenth century, with late-twentieth- or twenty-first-century technology added. In 1941 Henry Ford produced a prototype Ford made of soybean plastics. Due to war needs and the rise of synthetic plastics, the work was abandoned, but such innovation is typical of today's research and development. Bioplastics are already used in a wide variety of products including all types of bags, packaging, fishnet and lines, pet toys, wall coverings, razors, and golf tees.

Starch is a prolific raw material that makes a good plastic. It is now used in many fast-food containers and for the "peanuts" used in shipping. The water solubility of starch is both an advantage for decomposition and a limitation, which technology may overcome. For example, some eating utensils are now made of 55 percent cornstarch and 45 percent poly(lactic acid), which is insoluble in water but biodegradable in seawater. Poly(lactic acid) is a polyester synthesized from lactic acid. It shows solid commercial production growth and is used, for example, in compost bags, agricultural films, fibers, and bone repair. Cellulose is another bioplastic from the past. It is contained in 40 percent of organic matter and thus is renewable. Its limitation is that it is not thermoplastic, though it can be made into films.

Though bioplastics have limitations such as tensile strength, solubility, and cost, they produce less toxicity to humans and the environment and are based on renewable resources. Improved technology may overcome the limitations.

BIBLIOGRAPHY

Hooper, Rodney. *Plastics for the Home Craftsman.* London: Evans Brothers, 1953.

Simonds, Herbert R., and James M. Church. *A Concise Guide to Plastics.* New York: Reinhold Publishing Company, 1963.

Stevens, E. S. *Green Plastics: An Introduction to the New Science of Biodegradable Plastics.* Princeton, N.J.: Princeton University Press, 2002.

Wallace, Deborah. *In the Mouth of the Dragon.* Garden City Park, N.Y.: Avery Publishing Group, 1990.

Diane Nagel Palmer

See also **Building Materials; Carpet Manufacture; Industrial Research; Manufacturing; Textiles.**

PLATFORM, PARTY. A party platform is a political party's statement of governmental principle and policy. Some historians consider the Virginia and Kentucky Resolutions of 1798–1799 the first party platform; others point to the list of resolutions the "young men" of the National Republican Party adopted on 11 May 1832. No major party adopted a platform in 1836, but since 1840, party platforms have been a regular feature of national political campaigns. Platforms are not binding. Nevertheless, they have shaped many state and national elections. They also reflect the changing issues, controversies, and visions that have constituted American political discourse.

In the nineteenth century, when candidates were silent and parties reigned, campaigns more frequently stood by party platforms. The nominees' brief acceptance letters bound the nominee to the platform while accepting the party's nomination. As a result, the committee that drafted the platform and presented it to the convention was critical in setting the party agenda and determining national debate. Conventions took the platform seriously—as evidenced by the many clashes over principles and wording.

During the antebellum slavery debates—as during other national conflicts—platforms, like the major parties themselves, alternated between offering clear, potentially polarizing statements and flaccid compromises. The 1852 Whig platform, for example, avoided commenting on slavery directly. By contrast, the Republican platform of 1860 was blunt, branding "the recent reopening of the African slave trade . . . a crime against humanity." Similarly, in 1892, the Democratic platform endorsed the "use of both gold and silver as the standard money of the country" vaguely. Four years later, after the pro-silver forces overran the Democratic Convention, the platform demanded "the free and unlimited coinage of both silver and gold at the present legal ratio of 16 to 1."

By contrast, third parties' platforms have more consistently featured sharp rhetoric and clear positions, be it the antislavery Free Soil Party of 1848, the agrarian Populist Party of 1892, the reforming Progressive Party of 1912, or the segregationist Dixiecrat Party of 1948. Over the years, the major parties have adopted various third-party planks, once deemed radical.

After the Civil War (1861–1865), more active nominees deviated from the platforms more frequently. Remarkably, even in the modern age of weak parties and independent candidates, parties still struggle in drafting the platforms. In 1964, black Republican delegates, infuriated by the defeat of a civil rights amendment in the party's education plank, marched in protest. In the late twentieth century, women's rights, affirmative action, and abortion provoked bitter platform fights.

The media view a party's platform as an indicator of the party's tone—and as a potential source of conflict between the candidate and the party. Delegates and voters still recognize the platform as an essential first step in transforming ideas into laws, and in determining the party's trajectory. Scholars estimate that platform amendments of winning parties have been enacted into law at least 50 percent of the time. Furthermore, where competing platforms agree—and disagree—continues to reflect points of consensus and conflict in the American political system.

BIBLIOGRAPHY

Polsby, Nelson W., and Aaron Wildavsky. *Presidential Elections: Contemporary Strategies of American Electoral Politics.* 8th ed. New York: Free Press, 1991.

Troy, Gil. *See How They Ran: The Changing Role of the Presidential Candidate.* Cambridge, Mass.: Harvard University Press, 1991, 1996.

Gil Troy

See also **Elections, Presidential; Political Parties;** *and vol. 9:* **American Party Platform.**

PLATT AMENDMENT, a rider attached to the army appropriations bill of 1901. It made Cuba essentially a protectorate of the United States until 1934. The amendment began as a series of eight articles drafted by Secretary of War Elihu Root in 1901 as guidelines for United States–Cuba relations. Congress passed the amendment, sponsored by Senator Orville Hitchcock Platt of Connecticut, in an attempt to address the relations between Cuba and the United States in the shadow of the U.S. occupation of postwar Cuba. After Spanish troops left Cuba in 1898 at the end of the Spanish-American War, the United States occupied Cuba until the provisions of the amendment were incorporated into the Cuban constitution in 1902. The Cuban convention was resistant to passage, and it was only under the threat of continued U.S. occupation that it agreed to accept the amendment, on 13 June 1901. On 22 May 1903, the articles were written into a formal treaty. The terms of the amendment allowed the United States "the right to intervene for the preservation of Cuban independence, the maintenance of a government adequate for the protection of life, property, and individual liberty." The amendment also permitted the United States to lease lands for the establishment of a naval base in Cuba. The amendment was abrogated on 28 May 1934.

BIBLIOGRAPHY

Pérez, Louis A., Jr. *Cuba under the Platt Amendment, 1902–1934.* Pittsburgh: University of Pittsburgh Press, 1986.

Suchlicki, Jaime. *Cuba: From Columbus to Castro and Beyond.* Washington, D.C.: Brassey's, 2002.

Shira M. Diner

See also **Cuba, Relations with; Spanish-American War.**

PLEA BARGAIN. Plea bargaining is the process of negotiation between the parties in a criminal case involving the defendant's agreement to plead guilty in return for the prosecutor's concession reducing either the sentence or the seriousness of the charge. Typically, more than 75 percent of criminal cases end in guilty pleas, almost all resulting from plea bargaining. In federal courts, virtually all defendants who plead guilty qualify for a 20 percent reduction in the length of their sentence.

Prosecutors benefit from plea bargaining by eliminating the risk of an acquittal and saving on the costs associated with the time and elaborate procedures a trial entails. Some plea bargains also obligate the defendant to provide information or other cooperation to law enforcement. Defendants benefit by reducing the uncertainty associated with trial and avoiding harsher punishment. In some plea bargains, the defendant must bear a degree of risk because the judge, who typically is not a part of the negotiation, still decides what sentence the defendant receives. In these cases, the benefit to the defendant is the likelihood that the judge will accept the prosecutor's recommendation that a charge be dismissed or that the defendant receive a lighter sentence.

The U.S. Supreme Court has recognized that plea bargaining is an important component of our judicial system and that it is legitimate for prosecutors to use their power to persuade defendants to plead guilty. Plea bargaining is constitutional so long as prosecutors perform all the terms of the agreement and do not threaten defendants with charges unsupported by probable cause.

BIBLIOGRAPHY

Supreme Court Cases

Blackledge v. Allison, 431 U.S. 63 (1977).

Bordenkircher v. Hayes, 434 U.S. 357 (1978).

Brady v. United States, 397 U.S. 742 (1970).

Santobello v. New York, 404 U.S. 257 (1971).

Federal Laws

United States Sentencing Guidelines, 18 United States Code Appendix, §3E1.1.

Rossman, David. *Criminal Law Advocacy*, Vol. 2. *Guilty Pleas.* New York: Matthew Bender, 1999.

David Rossman

See also **Jury Trial.**

PLEDGE OF ALLEGIANCE. The Pledge of Allegiance developed as part of a promotional campaign in the 1890s by the editors of *The Youth's Companion*, a popular weekly magazine published in Boston. Its purpose was to encourage patriotic education by placing the flag in the public schools and standardizing a flag salute. The original version, called "The Youth's Companion Flag Pledge," was published on 8 September 1892 and read "I pledge allegiance to my Flag and ["to" added here the following month] the Republic for which it stands: one Nation, indivisible, with Liberty and Justice for all." The Pledge was a collaboration between James P. Upham, a junior partner of the magazine's publishing company, and his assistant, Francis M. Bellamy, a Baptist minister whose socialist ideas had lost him his pulpit. Disagreement persists over who should be considered its author, but two research teams—one by the United States Flag Association in 1939 and another by the Library of Congress in 1957—gave Bellamy the honor. The widespread popularity of the Pledge began with its central place in the nationwide school ceremonies associated with the first Columbus Day celebration, held in conjunction with the dedication on 19 October 1892 of the Chicago World's Columbian Exposition, marking the four-hundredth anniversary of Columbus's landing. National Flag Conferences in 1923 and 1924 agreed that the words "my flag" should be specified as "the flag of the United States" (and soon after "of America"). Congress eventually adopted the Pledge as part of an official flag code in 1942.

In 1935, members of the JEHOVAH'S WITNESSES began challenging regulations requiring compulsory recitation of the Pledge, insisting that the ceremony of allegiance contravened biblical injunctions opposing worship of a graven image. While the 1940 *Gobitis* case was unsuccessful before the U.S. Supreme Court, that body reversed its decision in *West Virginia Board of Education v. Barnette* (1943) when it ruled that citizens could not be forced to confess their loyalty. In 1953, the House of Representatives, at the urging of the Knights of Columbus, introduced a resolution to add the words "under God" to the Pledge. President Dwight D. Eisenhower supported this revision and signed it into law on FLAG DAY, 14 June 1954. Dissenters (including a 2002 California court of appeals) argued that the change violated the First Amendment clause that "Congress shall make no law respecting an establishment of religion." The Pledge has long been widely memorized by school children and plays a prominent role in naturalization ceremonies. Its thirty-one words read: "I pledge allegiance to the flag of the United States of America and to the republic for which it stands—one nation, under God, indivisible—with liberty and justice for all."

BIBLIOGRAPHY

Baer, John W. *The Pledge of Allegiance, A Centennial History, 1892–1992.* Annapolis, Md.: Free State Press, 1992.

Brandt, Nat. "To the Flag." *American Heritage* 22, no. 4 (June 1971): 72–75, 104.

Rydell, Robert W. "The Pledge of Allegiance and the Construction of the Modern American Nation." *Rendezvous* 30, no. 2 (Spring 1996): 13–26.

Timothy Marr

See also **Flag of the United States; Flags; Loyalty Oaths.**

PLESSY V. FERGUSON, 163 U.S. 537 (1896). African American activists and eighteen black members of the Louisiana state legislature of 1890 organized to defeat a bill requiring racial segregation on railroads by trading votes with white Democrats on the issue of a state lottery. When the "equal, but separate" law passed, the lawyer and editor Louis A. Martinet marshaled much of the group to test the law's constitutionality. They hired the white Reconstruction judge and popular novelist Albion W. Tourgee as the organization's lawyer, and recruited Homer Plessy to board a railroad car reserved for whites. Arrested by arrangement with the railroad company, which wished to avoid the expense of maintaining separate cars for patrons of each race, Plessy was arraigned before Orleans Parish Criminal Court Judge John H. Ferguson.

Tourgee argued that segregation contravened the Thirteenth and Fourteenth Amendments, because it was a "badge of servitude" intended not to separate the races (black nurses could travel with white employers) but purely to emphasize the blacks' subordinate status. It was also arbitrary and unreasonable, because it allowed mere railroad conductors to determine a person's race, and because race had nothing to do with transportation.

After Judge Ferguson and the racist Louisiana Supreme Court rejected or sidestepped these arguments, Tourgee appealed to a U.S. Supreme Court, which was undergoing an unusually high personnel turnover, adding five new justices during the four years that *Plessy* was pending. Different appointments might have led to a different decision. As it was, the Louisiana law was upheld seven to one, with four of the positive votes coming from members of the more racist Democratic Party.

The arguments—between justices Henry Billings Brown of Michigan for the majority and John Marshall Harlan of Kentucky in dissent—came down to three basic points. First, Brown thought racial separation and social inequality natural and unalterable by statutory or constitutional law, while former slaveholder Harlan pointed out that it was Louisiana law, not custom, that imposed segregation here. Stealing a phrase from Tourgee's brief, Harlan announced that "Our Constitution is color-blind." Second, the justices disagreed on whether the separate car law had an invidious purpose, the northerner denying it, but the southerner knowing better. Third, Brown ruled that the legislature's imposition of segregation was "reasonable," citing laws and lower court decisions from other states that supported his position. He deliberately ignored, however, the fact that nearly every northern state had passed laws prohibiting racial segregation in schools and public accommodations. In response, Harlan criticized "reasonableness" as merely another name for a judge's personal values, agreed with Tourgee that the law was arbitrary, and predicted that the *Plessy* decision would stimulate racial hatred and conflict. Thus, the disagreements between Brown and Harlan turned more on facts and armchair social psychology than on precedent or public opinion.

The terms of the argument between Brown and Harlan insured that the campaign of the National Association for the Advancement of Colored People to overturn *Plessy*, which led to *Brown v. Board of Education* (1954), would spotlight testimony by professional social psychologists and focus on social facts.

BIBLIOGRAPHY

Klarman, Michael J. "The Plessy Era." *The Supreme Court Review* (1998): 303–414.

Lofgren, Charles A. *The Plessy Case: A Legal-Historical Interpretation.* New York: Oxford University Press, 1987.

Thomas, Brook, ed. *Plessy v. Ferguson: A Brief History with Documents.* Boston: Bedford Books, 1997.

J. Morgan Kousser

See also ***Brown v. Board of Education of Topeka;*** **Desegregation; Segregation.**

PLOESTI OIL FIELDS, AIR RAIDS ON (1941–1944). Refineries located near Ploesti, Romania, provided one-third of the oil supply of the Axis forces in World War II, making the oil fields a crucial Allied target. Minor air attacks by the Russians in 1941 and the United States in 1942 were ineffective. The Germans, anticipating further strikes, increased their defenses.

By mid-1943 a force was available for a one-time attack. Three U.S. Liberator groups based in England joined Major General Lewis H. Brereton's two Ninth Air Force groups in Libya. Brereton planned a low-level attack; this unusual strategy required special flight training over a simulated Ploesti site constructed in the desert. At dawn on 1 August, 177 aircraft were airborne on a 2,300-mile mission. Simultaneous treetop strikes were planned against eight refineries. Fierce battles ensued in the developing inferno of the target area. Fifty-four aircraft were lost and fifty-five damaged by defending guns, fighters, airships, and bombs. Refinery production was reduced by about one-half.

Major General Nathan F. Twining's Fifteenth Air Force, based in Italy, struck the oil fields again in April 1944, opening a successful high-altitude campaign that continued until 19 August. Bomber crews dreaded meeting Ploesti's defenses, which included flak guns, German fighters, and smoke screens. Campaign bomber sorties numbered 5,287, with a 3.6 percent loss. The British contributed 900 night sorties. Combined with attacks on German refineries by other forces, the campaign deprived the Germans of a sizable quantity of the fuel essential for war.

BIBLIOGRAPHY

Dugan, James, and Carroll Stewart. *Ploesti: The Great Ground-Air Battle of 1 August 1943.* New York: Random House, 1962.

Sweetman, John. *Ploesti: Oil Strike.* New York: Ballantine, 1974.

Leon W. Johnson / A. R.

See also **Air Power, Strategic; World War II, Air War against Germany.**

PLUMB PLAN, a system of public ownership of railroads to replace the Railway Administration after World War I, proposed by Glenn E. Plumb, counsel for the organized railway employees, and considered in Congress in 1919 as the Sims Bill. It called for the government to purchase railroad properties at fair values, subject to judicial review. A quasi-public corporation representing the government, operators, and classified employees would then operate the railroads. Improvements would be financed by federal and local funds, with profits used to retire the public bonds, reduce rates, and increase railway wages. The bill failed, and in December, President Woodrow Wilson called for the return of railroads to private operation.

BIBLIOGRAPHY

Kerr, K. Austin. *American Railroad Politics, 1914–1920: Rates, Wages, and Efficiency.* Pittsburgh, Pa.: University of Pittsburgh Press, 1968.

Plumb, Glenn E., and William G. Roylance. *Industrial Democracy: A Plan for Its Achievement.* New York: B. W. Huebsch, 1923.

Martin P. Claussen / A. R.

See also **Government Ownership; Railroad Administration, U.S.; Railroad Mediation Acts; Railroads; World War I, Economic Mobilization for.**

PLUMBING. Plumbing is the system that supplies, distributes, uses, and removes water from a building. Among the components used in the system are pipes, fittings, sinks, basins, faucets, valves, drains, toilets, and tubs. In colonial America, water used for cleaning or cooking was typically brought into a building by bucket and the wastewater was later removed in the same way. Elimination, for the most part, tended to take place outside in a privy or outhouse. Although there were rare isolated examples of indoor toilets and running water based on or using English and European technology, it was not until the mid-nineteenth century that there were an appreciable number of plumbing installations. For many households they amounted to nothing more than a hand pump and kitchen sink. For a far smaller number it also might be hot and cold running water and what early on became known as the bathroom. During the 1840s and 1850s, the major elements of the bath were in place and consisted simply of a water closet or toilet and a "bathtub." Light washing still took place at the bedroom washstand with its basin, water pitcher, and slop jar or bucket. It was not until the 1860s that these items began to be replaced gradually by basins, faucets, and running water installed in the bathroom.

The Evolution of Bathroom Fixtures

Those who attempted to bring plumbing indoors faced technical as well as attitudinal challenges. Decisions on how wastewater was removed required as much concern as those made to ensure an adequate water supply. But equally vexing was the prevailing miasma theory of disease, which held that illnesses stemmed from "bad air" that was readily identifiable by its offensive odor. This led to a distrust of early indoor plumbing that tended to leak and a deadly fear of the sewer gas that accompanied the leaks. It is no wonder then that many individuals maintained a strong belief that elimination was best taken care of out of doors.

Of the components that were part of plumbing, the development of a reliable and trouble-free water closet posed the most problems. A number had been invented by the middle of the nineteenth century, but all had shortcomings. The most common complaints were that they were troublesome to flush and were easily clogged. Perhaps the most offensive of the lot was the pan water closet. It was so named for the waste-collecting sheet metal pan that was designed to close off and seal the bottom of the closet bowl. When the unit was flushed the pan tipped aside, opening the drain at the same time water rinsed the bowl and the pan. The operating mechanism was intricate and because of its location easily became fouled; it also required regular attention. The most serious deficiency common to nearly all toilets of the time was the poor seal they provided between the bathroom and the soil pipe that carried away waste.

The introduction of the first water-retaining traps or seals in the 1850s, and the common use of "U"-shaped traps in the 1870s, were major steps forward. The design of the trap ensured that enough water remained in it to effectively block the passage of sewer gas back through the plumbing fixtures. During the 1870s vent pipes were introduced. They not only carried sewer gas out of the system, but also broke the suction created by movement of liquid in the pipes and eliminated the possibility of siphoning water that sealed the traps.

One of the most important improvements was the development of the siphon toilet, patented in 1890. This greatly simplified yet highly efficient glazed earthenware toilet had no moving parts to get out of order and flushed perfectly every time. Its operation, a combination of a slight vacuum created by siphonic action and a large volume of water, made it self-cleansing. Furthermore, the possibility of leaking sewer gas was eliminated by its interior design. Water that remained in it after flushing provided a perfect seal between the bathroom and the sewer.

Plumbing. Pictured here is a plumbing supply store in Brockton, Mass., in 1941. LIBRARY OF CONGRESS

The Securing and Disposing of Water

Several of the nation's larger cities were providing water to their residents during the first decade of the nineteenth century, but only infrequently was water actually brought into homes. City-provided water was used in large part to fight fires and flush streets. Household water was most likely taken from a tap located outside of the house or a common hydrant. For those not connected to city mains, and even some who were, there were still other ways to obtain water. If a stream was not near by, there was rain runoff from a roof. It could be collected in one or more tanks located in out-of-the-way places in a house and feed the plumbing system through gravity.

Types of Pipe

Several types of pipe were used during the nineteenth century. With little or no knowledge of its possible long-term harmful effects, lead pipe was widely used. Its low price and the ease with which it could be formed and joined made it the material of choice for many installations. Iron, brass, and copper pipe were used as well. It was not unusual for a structure to be plumbed with several types of pipe, each used where it was most suited. But by the early twentieth century there was a move away from lead piping. The basic elements of domestic plumbing, in both the kitchen and bathroom, were in place by the 1890s. Changes since that time have been primarily aesthetic and in the materials used. During the second half of the twentieth century, tubs and basins that previously had been made of glazed ceramic or enameled iron, and much of the pipe manufactured in the United States as well, were being made of plastic.

Plumbing—from fixtures to vent pipes—in high-rise buildings and skyscrapers duplicated that used in other structures, but with the addition of several unique features. As gravity-fed city mains generally lift water no more than five or six stories, electrically operated pumps raise it to elevated storage tanks beyond that point. Water levels in the tanks are maintained automatically. Water is supplied from them throughout the structure by gravity, air pressure, or booster pumps. Likewise, gravity removes waste water by way of drainage pipes.

Beginning in the 1950s plastic pipe, most notably that made of polyvinyl chloride, has been used in ever increasing amounts. In the following decades, other plastics were introduced into pipe manufacture. However, by the last years of the century a number of plastic-pipe failures had occurred. Problems were attributed to defective manufacture and, in some cases, a chemical reaction taking place between the material used to make the pipe and chlorine in the water that it carried. These events led to class action lawsuits and a general reevaluation of the use of this inexpensive and easily worked alternative piping material.

Federal Regulation

Where plumbing had been a mostly locally regulated matter for most of its history, the federal government became involved in the early 1990s. Until the 1950s, toilets generally used five or more gallons per flush (GPF). During the decades that followed, the plumbing industry reduced the standard volume for toilet flush tanks to 3.5 gallons. A further reduction in volume resulted from the Energy Policy Act of 1992, which in the name of conservation mandated that all new toilets made in the United States must use no more than 1.6 GPF. The same legislation also regulated the flow in shower heads and faucets. Although the first low-flow toilets proved unsatisfactory and were met with public disapproval, redesigned equipment employing new technology has removed most objections.

BIBLIOGRAPHY

Elliott, Cecil D. *Technics and Architecture: The Development of Materials and Systems for Buildings.* Cambridge, Mass.: MIT Press, 1992.

Ierley, Merritt. *The Comforts of Home: The American House and the Evolution of Modern Convenience.* New York: Clarkson Potter, 1999.

Ogle, Maureen. *All the Modern Conveniences: American Household Plumbing, 1840–1890.* Baltimore: Johns Hopkins University Press, 1996.

William E. Worthington Jr.

See also **Housing; Sanitation, Environmental.**

PLURALISM is both a doctrine and the label for a commonsense perception. As a doctrine, pluralism holds that multiplicity is a virtue in ideas and institutions; hence pluralism rejects unity as the measure of intellectual and institutional development. As a label, pluralism describes the cultural diversity and interest-group politics that characterize American life. Pluralist doctrine implies a commitment to difference often unacknowledged in uses of the label. In early-twentieth-century debates about immigration and national identity, doctrine and label converged. Their union was short-lived, however, as the cultural pluralism that emerged from these debates upheld a collectivist vision of American life anathema to liberal individuality. Over the course of the twentieth century, social scientists enlisted the term to describe a range of social and political developments. The triumph of multiculturalism at the century's end revived pluralism's association with ethnicity and culture, though few contemporary multiculturalists endorse the racial essentialism and ethnic separatism that distinguished cultural pluralism.

Early Commonsense Perceptions of Pluralism

Americans perceived the fact of pluralism long before they delineated pluralist doctrine. From colonial times, but especially after the Revolutionary War (1775–1783), American writers trumpeted the egalitarianism and religious and ethnic diversity of the New World to bemused European audiences. None exceeded in enthusiasm French immigrant farmer J. Hector St. John de Crèvecoeur. "What, then, is the American, this new man," Crèvecoeur demanded in *Letters from an American Farmer and Sketches of Eighteenth-Century America* (1782):

> "He is either an European or the descendant of an European; hence that strange mixture of blood, which you will find in no other country. I could point out to you a family whose grandfather was an Englishman, whose wife was Dutch, whose son married a French woman, and whose present four sons have now four wives of different nations. He is an American, who, leaving behind him all his ancient prejudices and manners, receives new ones from the new mode of life he has embraced, the new government he obeys, and the new rank he holds." (pp. 69–70)

Two generations later, Herman Melville boasted in *Redburn* (1849) that one could not "spill a drop of American blood without spilling the blood of the whole world." (p. 238) In a similar vein, Ralph Waldo Emerson proclaimed America an "asylum of all nations" and predicted that "the energy of Irish, Germans, Swedes, Poles & Cossacks, & all the European tribes,—of the Africans, & of the Polynesians" would combine on American soil to forge "a new race, a new religion, a new State, a new literature" to rival modern Europe's. (*Journals and Miscellaneous Notebooks*, pp. 299–300) Emerson's paean to American exceptionalism was unusual in including non-Westerners in the mix; most denied the presence in the New World of slaves, Indians, and other "undesirables," elisions that suggest an enduring characteristic of pluralist discourse, namely its tendency to fix and maintain intellectual and social boundaries. But Emerson followed convention in regarding national homogeneity as a requisite of politics and culture. Neither he, Melville, nor Crèvecoeur was pluralist in the sense of wanting to preserve diversity for diversity's sake. All three regarded ethnic diversity as a defining but not enduring quality of American life. All expected *pluribus* to yield ineluctably to *unum.*

Indeed, unity was America's burden in its first century of national life. Only after the Civil War (1861–1865) did Americans possess sufficient national consciousness to abide a flirtation with genuine difference. Which is not to say that most, let alone many, Americans embraced pluralism either before or after the Civil War. The majority probably concurred with John Jay, who, in *Federalist 2*, counted ethnic and cultural homogeneity among the blessings Providence bestowed on the thirteen states. No asylum for European refugees, Jay's America was home to a vigorous "people descended from the same ancestors, speaking the same language, professing the same religion, attached to the same principles of government, [and] very similar in manners and customs . . ." (p. 38). This America seems to have little in common with that of the literary bards. But from a pluralist perspective, the product of all these visions is more or less the same: cultural homogeneity in the service of national unity; *unum*, though with a different face.

Two other frequently cited pluralist texts from the late eighteenth century, James Madison's *Federalist 10* and Thomas Jefferson's commentary on religious toleration, similarly aimed not to promote diversity for its own sake, but to neutralize political and social divisions in the name of civic order. Witness Madison, whose reputation as a pluralist stems from his conception of republican politics as an arena of competing factions. Madison cannot be said to have valued faction in its own right. He regarded factionalism as a mortal disease conducive to overbearing majorities and corrosive of the public good. Had it been possible, Madison would have expunged faction from politics. But "the latent causes of faction" were "sown in the nature of man," he recognized, hence there could be no eradicating faction without extinguishing liberty—a remedy "worse than the disease." Rather, he would mitigate faction's toxin by delineating a model of federal republicanism designed to propel individuals out of the ruts of local self-interest and into more amplitudinous state and national coalitions. "Extend the sphere" of government, he maintained, "and you take in a greater variety of parties and interests; you make it less probable that a majority of the whole will have a common motive to invade the rights of other citizens . . ." (pp. 77, 84). Concern for individual and minority rights likewise motivated Jefferson's defense of religious toleration in *Notes on the State of Virginia.* Jefferson viewed faith as a matter of private conscience and therefore beyond government jurisdiction. States that insisted on imposing an official religion invited social discord; by contrast, states that exercised religious tolerance enjoyed unrivaled prosperity. A self-described Christian who eschewed institutional religion, Jefferson appears to have been indifferent about the long-term fate of the world's faiths. He even suggests that given peace, prosperity, and the free play of reason, belief will converge on "the true religion," a proposition anathema to pluralist doctrine (p. 256).

Toward a Doctrine of Pluralism in the Late Nineteenth Century

Arguments on behalf of pluralism drew sustenance from the romantic reaction to the Enlightenment. Where Enlightenment thinkers tended to regard the world as governed by universal laws, Romantic critics insisted that human understanding of the world differs across cultures and that these differences make life meaningful. The German philosopher J. G. Herder argued for a world composed of distinct, language- and descent-based cultures, irreproducible, incommensurable, and of fundamentally equal value. Herder regarded culture as the repository of wisdom and expression; the sine qua non of human flourishing, culture was at once the source and foundation of individual agency. Writing at the end of the eighteenth century and thus well in advance of German unification, Herder said little about how different national cultures might interact across state boundaries and nothing at all about the challenge countries such as the United States faced in forging national solidarity amid ethnic diversity. For the generation of American intellectuals who took up that challenge a century later, and who were determined to effect solidarity without sacrificing cultural diversity, Herder's anthropology was inspiring but insufficient. They wanted a theory capable of reconciling the one and the many. They believed they found that theory in the pluralism of the American philosopher William James.

James engaged the problem of pluralism in the 1870s and 1880s not to vindicate cultural diversity but to vanquish "monism" in metaphysics and epistemology. Heirs to Enlightenment rationalism, nineteenth-century monists posited a single cosmos governed by a set of universal and objective laws. By the early 1870s, James had grown disenchanted with an account of the world that did not jibe with commonsense experience. In 1896, he identified the monism/pluralism distinction as "perhaps the most pregnant of all the differences in philosophy. Prima facie the world is a pluralism," James wrote; "as we find it, its unity seems to be that of any collection; and our higher thinking consists chiefly of an effort to redeem it from that first crude form." James devoted the last years of his life to elucidating this distinction. In *A Pluralistic Universe*, he likened pluralism's world to a "federal republic" of sensations in which:

> "Everything you can think of, however vast or inclusive, has on the pluralistic view a genuinely 'external' environment of some sort or amount. Things are 'with' one another in many ways, but nothing includes everything, or dominates over everything. The word 'and' trails along after every sentence. Something always escapes. 'Ever not quite' has to be said of the best attempts made anywhere in the universe at attaining all-inclusiveness." (pp. 321–322)

James's pluralism appears at first glance to offer little aid to Progressive Era thinkers struggling with the problem of ethnic diversity. But look what happens when we inject Herder's culture into the preceding quote in place of James's amorphous "things." We get a federated republic of cultures in which cultures are with one another in many ways, but no one culture encompasses every other, or dominates over every other and from which something always escapes.

This is the move carried out by two of James's disciples at Harvard University, sociologist W. E. B. Du Bois and philosopher Horace Kallen, to counter Anglo American nativism at the turn of the twentieth century. Du Bois would one day despair over the seemingly dim prospect of African Americans flourishing in America, but he insisted that the salvation of African Americans could only come in the United States. He delivered this message in two early and cogent essays, "The Conservation of Races" and "Strivings of the Negro People," both of which appeared in 1897, but of which only the latter, reissued in 1903 as chapter one of *The Souls of Black Folk*, garnered widespread attention. "Strivings" introduced Du Bois's potent imagery of the Veil and expressed his yearning "to be a co-worker in the kingdom of culture, to escape both death and isolation, and to husband and use his best powers." "Conservation" posed the dilemma that underlay that aspiration, and which has confronted members of every race and ethnic group that has had to weigh the cultural cost of pledging allegiance to American institutions and, by implication, to the dominant Anglo-American minority. "What after all am I," Du Bois demanded? "Am I an American or am I a Negro? Can I be both? Or is it my duty to cease to be a Negro as soon as possible and be an American?" (p. 11) According to Du Bois's melding of Herder and James, there could be but one answer to this query: race was irrelevant as a function of citizenship; ethno-racial diversity was essential to national vitality.

Cultural pluralism achieved full elaboration in the work of Kallen. In the winter of 1915, Kallen published a two-part essay in *The Nation* entitled "Democracy Versus the Melting Pot" in which he repudiated the conventional wisdom, given new life in nativist broadsides, that cultural homogeneity was a requisite of effective politics. Not so, Kallen maintained. The nation's political principles were culturally neutral, hence in no need of cultural buttress. Kallen wanted government to do for ethnic groups what it had long done for individuals: to underwrite their pursuit of happiness. The product would be a "federated republic"—a phrase borrowed from James—of wholesome ethnic groups, each contributing its respective genius to the nation. Kallen's pluralism cut against the grain of American liberalism. Rather than challenging the racist premise of Anglo American nativism, Kallen recapitulated it, making race the bulwark of selfhood at the expense of individual agency. Nativists erred, his argument went, not by conflating culture and race, but by exalting one culture above all others. Kallen's would-be allies in the battle against Anglo American nativism recoiled from the communalism, racial essentialism, and ethnic separatism this vision implied; over the course of the next few years Randolph Bourne and Alain Locke, both friends of Kallen, produced apologies for ethnic diversity markedly more mindful of the imperative of individual agency. Moreover, Kallen's cultural pluralism assumed a degree of economic and political parity between ethnic groups demonstrably absent in Progressive Era America. His defense of cultural pluralism could only have come from a member of a few select immigrant communities, among them, Jews, whose assimilation in America afforded them the luxury to address culture independent of power.

The Legacy of Cultural Pluralism in the Twentieth Century

Kallen did not coin the term "cultural pluralism" until 1924, nine years after his essay in *The Nation.* By 1924, the heyday of cultural pluralism had past, at least for most liberal intellectuals. The publication of Kallen's *Culture and Democracy in the United States* coincided with the passing of the Johnson-Reed Immigration Act, restricting immigration on the basis of national origin. Together with wartime jingoism, postwar reaction, and the persecution of African Americans, the immigration legislation soured American intellectuals on the prospects of cultural differentiation as a medium of progressive reform. In the face of white, racist, cultural retrenchment, assimilation seemed a safer and more realistic means of achieving social and political integration. Kallen himself seems to have become discomfited by the essentialism and separatism undergirding cultural pluralism. He said very little about pluralism over the next three decades. When he finally returned to the subject in 1956, he appeared less confident that pluralism alone could serve as an animating source of national solidarity. A universalist ideology rooted in an increasingly conventional understanding of the so-called American creed now accompanied his cultural advocacy. In this, Kallen joined company with many Cold War liberals concerned to distinguish the United States from its totalitarian rivals. Liberals landed on culture diversity as the nation's signal characteristic: we were a pluralist country committed to liberty of groups and individuals, they totalitarian regimes devoted to eradicating diversity in the name of national aggrandizement. Later scholarship demolished the myths latent in Cold War ideology. More interesting from a pluralist perspective is Kallen's contribution to the process by which the doctrine of cultural pluralism he had helped establish came more and more to resemble the label. In the name of pluralism, America would demonstrate its openness to difference by assimilating it.

Writers still genuinely committed to cultural diversity had to reckon with this assimilationist consensus. Sociologists Robert M. MacIver and Robin M. Williams worried lest undue emphasis on group differences alienate the assimilated public on whose sympathy de facto pluralism relied. Anticipating the response of white Americans to 1960s cultural nationalism, they exhorted advocates of pluralism to eschew rhetorical provocation for political bridge building across ethnic and racial divides. Stewart G. and Mildred Wiese Cole regarded cultural diversity primarily as a problem of democratic governance. Too much separatism would breed mutual suspicion and forestall social and political cooperation, they warned; too much assimilation would erode the individual and group integrity on which political empowerment relied. Meanwhile, Gordon Allport endorsed a choice-based approach to cultural affiliation. Some members of cultural communities would inevitably perpetuate core characteristics; others would just as surely drift from the core. There was little one could do about it in any case, short of intolerable coercion.

MacIver, Williams, Allport, and the Coles exposed the tension in American liberalism between individual agency and group identity, one destined to mount in the last several decades of the twentieth century. There were many catalysts of the renewed interest in cultural diversity: the exodus in the 1950s of African Americans from the deep South; the Immigration Act of 1965, ending restrictions on immigration based on national origin; student protest against alleged U.S. imperialism around the world; the radicalization of the civil rights movement. In "black power," particularly, we can chart pluralism's continuing evolution as the means to a political, rather than cultural, end. For the point of black power, activist Stokely Carmichael insisted repeatedly to audiences disinclined to listen, was not to celebrate black culture as an end in itself, but to foster racial solidarity sufficient to galvanize African Americans into a political force capable of negotiating independently with the white political parties. Only as an independent political force, Carmichael argued, did African Americans stand a chance of addressing the structural racism and inequality that endured in the wake of vaunted civil rights victories. Every African American of voting age who assimilated into white politics decreased the likelihood of black success. Carmichael's logic was very different from the early Kallen and had different ramifications for the members of racial and ethnic groups. For the early Kallen, culture was literally the end of human aspiration; perpetuating culture is what individuals did. For Carmichael, by contrast, culture was the means to economic and political justice; race-based commitment now, choice the payoff of the promised land.

Carmichael and black power have become a symbol of much that went wrong with late-twentieth-century cultural politics. By basing his political movement on color, he merely recapitulated the racism of the enemy, thereby ensuring his own defeat. So went the argument of a host of progressive intellectuals who recognized that the gravest threat to individuality at the end of the twentieth century stemmed from economic injustice spawned by racism, yet who rejected arguments like those of Du Bois and Carmichael that only race could vanquish racism. With great cogency, starting in the 1970s scholars John Higham, Steven Steinberg, and David A. Hollinger, along with many others, have upheld choice, agency, right of exit, and revocable consent as the route beyond racism. They argue that only individuals who insist they are more than members of a single race will ever be recognized as such by a still-racist society.

Political Pluralism in the Twentieth Century

Just as reformers were becoming wary of pluralism as a tool for cultural analysis, political theorists adopted the term to describe American politics. In this, the theorists followed the lead of Arthur F. Bentley, an independent scholar whose *Process of Government* (1908) is credited with establishing pluralism as a concept in political analysis despite never using the term. Like Madison (whom, curiously, Bentley does not cite), Bentley set out to explain the remarkable functioning of a government beholden to special interests. He began by revising Madison's psychology. Faction—interest, to Bentley—was not the product of some innate selfishness in mankind to be overcome by virtue; rather, interest was the mechanism by which men acted. Thus, government could not be distinguished from interest; government consisted of the ceaseless collision of interests themselves. This was no less true of despotism than of democracy, though democracy differed from despotism by promoting a broader plurality of interests. Bentley's political theory promoted an ideal of government free of exclusions. Although he acknowledged that government often seemed the province of particular ("private") interests, his insistence that "no interest group has meaning except with reference to other interest groups" led him to attribute influence to even the most dispossessed classes.

> "The lowest of despised classes," he wrote, "deprived of rights to the protection of property and even life, will still be found to be a factor in the government, if only we can sweep the whole field, and measure the caste in its true degree or power, direct or represented, in its potentiality of harm to the higher castes, and in its identification with them for some important purposes, however deeply hidden from ordinary view. No slaves, not the worst abused of all, but help to form the government." (p. 271)

Writing in the 1950s and 1960s, Robert A. Dahl recapitulated and amplified Bentley's argument. Dahl's *Preface to a Democratic Theory* (1956) attributed the success of the American political system to the endless, decentralized interest-group haggling it encouraged. Despite its shortcomings, the system maintained "a high probability that any active and legitimate group will make itself heard effectively at some stage in the process of decision"—"no mean thing in a political system" (p. 150). Dahl's *Pluralist Democracy in the United States: Conflict and Consensus* (1967) invoked the term "pluralism" itself to describe what he had earlier hypothesized: a decentralized system of government with multiple centers of power each contested by a broad range of interests. Here, as in Bentley, were Madison's factions without the toxin.

BIBLIOGRAPHY

Allport, Gordon W. *The Nature of Prejudice.* Garden City, N.Y.: Doubleday, 1958 [1954].

Bentley, A. F. *The Process of Government.* Cambridge, Mass.: Harvard University Press, 1967 [1908].

Bourne, Randolph. "Trans-National America." In *War and the Intellectuals: Collected Essays, 1915–1919.* Edited by Carl Resak. New York: Harper and Row, 1964.

Cole, Stewart G., and Mildred Wiese Cole. *Minorities and the American Promise: The Conflict of Principle and Practice.* New York: Harper and Bros., 1954.

Dahl, Robert A. *A Preface to Democratic Theory.* Chicago: University of Chicago Press, 1956.

———. *Pluralist Democracy in the United States: Conflict and Consent.* Chicago: Rand McNally, 1967.

de Crèvecoeur, J. Hector St. John. *Letters from an American Farmer and Sketches of Eighteenth-Century America.* New York: Penguin Books, 1981 [1782].

Du Bois, W. E. B. "Strivings of the Negro People." *Atlantic Monthly* 80 (August 1897): 194–198.

———. "Conservation of Races." *American Negro Academy Occasional Papers* 2 (1897): 5–15.

Emerson, Ralph Waldo. *The Journals and Miscellaneous Notebooks of Ralph Waldo Emerson.* Volume 9. Edited by Ralph H. Orth and Alfred R. Ferguson. Cambridge, Mass.: Harvard University Press, 1971.

Hamilton, Alexander, James Madison, and John Jay. *The Federalist Papers.* Edited by Clinton Rossiter. New York: Mentor, 1961.

Herder, Johann Gottfried. *J. G. Herder on Social and Political Culture.* Translated and edited by F. M. Barnard. Cambridge, U.K.: Cambridge University Press, 1969.

Higham, John. *Send These to Me: Jews and Other Immigrants in Urban America.* Baltimore: Atheneum, 1974.

Hollinger, David. *Postethnic America: Beyond Multiculturalism.* 2d. ed. New York: Basic Books, 2000.

James William. *The Will to Believe and Other Essays in Popular Philosophy.* New York: Dover, 1956 [1897].

———. *Talks to Teachers on Psychology and to Students on Some of Life's Ideals.* New York: Norton, 1958 [1899].

Jefferson, Thomas. "Notes on the State of Virginia." In *The Life and Selected Writings of Thomas Jefferson.* Edited by Adrienne Koch and William Peden. New York: The Modern Library, 1993.

Kallen, Horace. *Culture and Democracy in the United States.* New Brunswick, N.J.: Transaction, 1998 [1924].

Katkin, Wendy F., and Ned Landsman, eds. *Beyond Pluralism: The Conception of Groups and Group Identities in America.* Urbana: University of Illinois Press, 1998.

Locke, Alain Leroy. *Race Contacts and Interracial Relations.* Edited by Jeffrey C. Stewart. Washington, D.C.: Howard University Press, 1992 [1916].

MacIver, Robert M. *Civilization and Group Relationships.* New York: Institute for Religious Studies, 1945.

Melville, Herman. *Redburn.* New York: Penguin Books, 1986 [1849].

Sollors, Werner. *Beyond Ethnicity: Consent and Descent in American Culture.* New York: Oxford University Press, 1986.

Steinberg, Stephen. *The Ethnic Myth: Race, Ethnicity, and Class in America.* New York: Athaeneum, 1981.

Williams, Robin M., Jr. *The Reduction of Intergroup Tensions: A Survey of Research Problems of Ethnic, Racial, and Religious Group Relations.* New York: Social Science Research Council Bulletin 57, 1947.

Jonathan M. Hansen

See also ***Federalist Papers;*** **Multiculturalism; Nativism; Political Theory;** ***Souls of Black Folk, The.***

PLYMOUTH COLONY (or Plantation), the second permanent English settlement in North America, was founded in 1620 by settlers including a group of religious dissenters commonly referred to as the Pilgrims. Though theologically very similar to the Puritans who later founded the MASSACHUSETTS BAY COLONY, the Pilgrims believed that the Church of England could not be reformed. Rather than attempting to purify the church, the Pilgrims desired a total separation.

Settlement, Founding, and Growth

One hundred and twenty-five Pilgrims, some of whom founded Plymouth, first departed England in 1608. English authorities had forced the Pilgrims to halt Separatist worship at Scrooby Manor (their residence in Nottinghamshire, England). Thus, seeking freedom of worship, they left for Holland, first passing through Amsterdam and then settling in Leyden. The Pilgrims did indeed enjoy freedom of worship in Leyden but found Holland an imperfect refuge. Most being farmers, the Pilgrims had difficulty prospering in urban Holland. More importantly, the Pilgrims feared their children were growing up in a morally degenerate atmosphere and were adopting Dutch customs and language. Seeing little chance for establishing a separate, godly society in Holland, and fearing the country's conquest by Catholic Spain, which would surely bring the horrors of the Inquisition, the Pilgrims needed a place where they would be left to worship and live as they chose.

Virginia offered such an opportunity. By 1620 the Virginia Company was in deep financial difficulty. One of many measures designed to shore up the company's financial situation was selling special patents to settlers who desired to establish private plantations within Virginia. Though under Virginia's general domain, the Pilgrims would be allowed to govern themselves. Thomas Weston and a group of London merchants who wanted to enter the colonial trade financed the Pilgrims' expedition. The two parties came to agreement in July 1620, with the Pilgrims and merchants being equal partners.

The Pilgrims sold most of their possessions in Leyden and purchased a ship—the *Speedwell*—to take them to Southampton, England. Weston hired another ship—the *Mayflower*—to join the *Speedwell* on the voyage to America. On 22 July 1620 a group of about thirty Pilgrims left Delfshaven, Holland, and arrived in Southampton by month's end. They met the *Mayflower*, which carried about seventy non-Separatists hired by Weston to journey to America as laborers. After a great deal of trouble with the *Speedwell*, the ship had to be abandoned, and only the *Mayflower* left Plymouth, England, for America on 16 September 1620. The overcrowded and poorly provisioned ship carried 101 people (35 from Leyden, 66 from London/Southampton) on a sixty-five day passage. The travelers sighted Cape Cod in November and quickly realized they were not arriving in Virginia. Prevented from turning south by the rocky coast and failing winds, the voyagers agreed to settle in the north. Exploring parties were sent into Plymouth harbor in the first weeks of December, and the *Mayflower* finally dropped anchor there on 26 December 1620. The weary, sickly passengers gradually came ashore to build what would become Plymouth Colony.

The winter was not particularly harsh, but the voyage left the passengers malnourished and susceptible to disease. Half of the passengers died during the first winter, but the surviving colonists, greatly aided by a plundered supply of Indian corn, were still able to establish a stable settlement. The 1617–1619 contagion brought by English fishermen and traders had greatly weakened the local Indian populace, so the Pilgrims initially faced little threat from native peoples. Plymouth town was, in fact, conveniently built on cleared area that had once been an Indian cornfield. The colonists built two rows of plank houses with enclosed gardens on "Leyden Street." Eventually the governor's house and a wooden stockade were erected. At the hill's summit, the settlers built a flat house to serve as the meeting or worship house.

Migration from England allowed the colony to grow, albeit slowly. In 1624 Plymouth Colony's population stood at 124. By 1637 it reached 549. By 1643 settlers had founded nine additional towns. Compared to its neighbor Massachusetts Bay, Plymouth Colony grew very modestly, reaching a population of only about 7,000 by 1691.

Government and Politics

Since the Pilgrims did not settle in Virginia, their patent was worthless, and they established Plymouth without any legal underpinning. Needing to formulate some kind of legal frame for the colony's government, the Pilgrims crafted the Mayflower Compact, in which the signers agreed to institute colonial self-government. The ship's free adult men signed the compact on 11 November 1620 before the settlers went ashore. They agreed to establish a civil government based upon congregational church compact government, in which freemen elected the governor and his assistants, just as congregational church members chose their own ministers.

As the colonists spread out and founded new towns, the system needed modification. Having meetings of all freemen (most adult men) in Plymouth town to elect officials became impractical. Starting in 1638, assemblies of freemen in individual towns chose deputies for a "General Court." William Bradford dominated political life in Plymouth for a generation, being elected thirty times between 1621 and 1656, but the governor's power lessened as the General Court became a true representative assembly. The General Court became a powerful legislature, with sole authority to levy taxes, declare war, and define voter qualifications. Plymouth, however, never received a legal charter from the crown, and based its existence as a self-governing entity entirely on the Mayflower Compact and the two patents issued by the Council for New England in 1621 and 1630, the latter defining the colony's physical boundaries.

Economy and Society

Plymouth was intended for family settlement and commerce, not staple production or resource extraction like many other colonies. The Pilgrims, bound together by their faith and social covenant, envisioned building a self-sustaining agricultural community that would be a refuge for Separatist dissenters. Thus life in Plymouth revolved around family and religion. Every person had a place and set of duties according to his or her position within the colony and family, and was expected to live according to God's law. Those who did not, or those who openly challenged Separatist religious doctrine, were severely punished or driven from the colony entirely.

Small, family farms remained at the heart of Plymouth's economy throughout its history. Land was divided fairly evenly, with each colonist initially receiving 100 acres of land, with 1,500 acres reserved for common use. Apart from home plots, acreage was initially assigned on a yearly basis. When Pilgrim leaders broke with their London merchant partners in 1627, every man was assigned a permanent, private allotment. The venture's assets and debts were divided among the Pilgrim colonists, with single men receiving one share (twenty acres and livestock) and heads of families receiving one share per family member. Farming proved productive enough to make the colony essentially self-sufficient in food production by 1624. The fur trade (initially run by government monopoly) proved very profitable, and allowed the colony to pay off its debt to the London merchants.

Indian Relations

The colonists were extremely vulnerable during the first winter, and could have been annihilated had the Indians attacked. The first face-to-face meeting, however, was peaceful. In March 1620 an English-speaking Wampanoag—Samoset—approached Plymouth, and provided useful information about local geography and peoples. On 22 March 1621 Pilgrim leaders met with the Wampanoag chief Massasoit, who was in need of allies, and agreed to a mutual defense treaty. By the late 1630s, however, the New England colonies (especially Massachusetts) were rapidly expanding, and Indian tribes were increasingly encroached upon. English encroachments in the Connecticut River valley led to the bloody Pequot War in 1637. Plymouth officially condemned Massachusetts's harsh actions against the Pequots, but still joined with that colony and Connecticut in forming the New England Confederation in 1643. The three colonies allied for mutual defense in the wake of massive, rumored Indian conspiracies, but were undoubtedly defending their often aggressive expansion at the Indians' expense.

The last great Indian war in seventeenth-century New England—King Philip's or Metacom's War—was a terrible, bloody affair, resulting in attacks on fifty-two English towns. Metacom (called King Philip by the English) was Massasoit's son, and formed a confederation of Indians to destroy English power. His efforts became intensely focused after he was forced to sign a humiliating treaty with Plymouth in 1671. Plymouth's execution of three Wampanoag Indians in 1675 sparked the war, which started with an attack on several Plymouth villages on 25 June 1675. Intercolonial military cooperation prevented Metacom's immediate victory, but disease and food shortages ultimately prevented him from winning a war of attrition. By the summer of 1676, English forces had rounded up and executed the Indian leaders, selling hundreds more into slavery in the West Indies.

Plymouth's Demise

Metacom's War piqued the crown's already growing interest in the New England colonies, and thereafter it set out to bring them directly under royal control. Massachusetts's charter was revoked in 1684, and in 1686 James II consolidated all of New England, plus New York and New Jersey, into one viceroyalty known as the "Dominion of New England." Assemblies were abolished, the mercantile Navigation Acts enforced, and Puritan domination was broken. Hope for self-government was revived in 1688–1689, when Protestant English parliamentarians drove the Catholic James II from power. William III and Mary II (both Protestants) succeeded James by act of Parliament. Massachusetts's leaders followed suit and ousted the Dominion's governor. The new monarchs had no great interest in consolidating the colonies, and thus left the Dominion for dead. The crown issued a new charter for Massachusetts in 1691, but denied the Puritans exclusive government control. Plymouth, by now wholly overshadowed by Massachusetts, failed to obtain its own charter, and was absorbed by Massachusetts in 1691, thus ending the colony's seventy-year history as an independent province.

BIBLIOGRAPHY

Bradford, William. *History of Plymouth Plantation, 1620–1647.* Edited by Samuel Eliot Morison. New York: Russell and Russell, 1968.

Deetz, James, and Patricia Scott Deetz. *The Times of Their Lives: Life, Love, and Death in Plymouth Colony.* New York: W. H. Freeman, 2000.

Demos, John. *A Little Commonwealth: Family Life in Plymouth Colony.* 2d ed. Oxford: Oxford University Press, 2000.

Johnson, Richard R. *Adjustment to Empire: The New England Colonies, 1675–1715.* New Brunswick, N.J.: Rutgers University Press, 1981.

Langdon, George D. *Pilgrim Colony: A History of New Plymouth, 1620–1691.* New Haven, Conn.: Yale University Press, 1966.

Miller, Perry. *The New England Mind: The Seventeenth Century.* Cambridge, Mass.: Harvard University Press, 1954.

Nash, Gary. *Red, White, and Black: The Peoples of Early North America.* 4th ed. Upper Saddle River, N.J.: Prentice Hall, 2000.

Shurtleff, Nathaniel B., and David Pulsifer, eds. *Records of the Colony of New Plymouth in New England.* 12 vols. 1855. Reprint, New York: AMS Press, 1968.

Vaughan, Alden T. *New England Frontier: Puritans and Indians, 1620–1675.* 3d ed. Norman: University of Oklahoma Press, 1995.

Aaron J. Palmer

See also **Dominion of New England; King Philip's War; New England Confederation; Pequot War; Puritans and Puritanism; Separatists, Puritan Pilgrims;** *and vol. 9:* **The Mayflower Compact.**

PLYMOUTH ROCK. Plymouth Rock is the stone upon which the Pilgrims were said to have stepped when the MAYFLOWER arrived in Plymouth harbor on 21 December 1620. Identified in 1741 by Thomas Faunce, who was born in Plymouth, Massachusetts, in 1650, the massive rock was moved to the Town Square in 1774. Geologists classify it as an erratic glacial boulder of Dedham granite. Placed under an ornate portico in 1880, it was moved for the Tercentenary celebration in 1921 under an elaborate granite canopy on the hill overlooking Plymouth harbor. Although no evidence supports its legend, Plymouth Rock is a national icon that attracts countless tourists each year.

BIBLIOGRAPHY

Seelye, John. *Memory's Nation: The Place of Plymouth Rock.* Chapel Hill: University of North Carolina Press, 1998.

Peter C. Holloran

See also **Plymouth Colony.**

PLYMOUTH, VIRGINIA COMPANY OF (1606–1620), one of two companies incorporated in the first Virginia charter in 1606. In 1605 a group of men representing the City of London and the outports of Bristol, Plymouth, and Exeter petitioned for a charter to plant colonies in America. Although the petitioners were men

Sir John Popham. The lord chief justice in England, and one of the two leaders of the Plymouth Company, until his death in 1607.

bound by the ties of relationship, friendship, or common interest, the rivalry between London and the outports was such that the leaders wished to proceed with the project under separate companies. The charter of 1606 therefore created two companies, the Virginia Company of London and the Virginia Company of Plymouth. The London Company had permission to establish a colony in southern Virginia between thirty-four and forty-one degrees north latitude (i.e., from present-day South Carolina to New York), to be called the First Colony of Virginia. The Plymouth Company would establish the Second Colony of Virginia, to be located farther north, between thirty-eight and forty-five degrees north latitude (i.e., from Chesapeake Bay to what is now northernmost Maine). The overlapping area was to be a neutral zone in which the settlements could not come within one hundred miles of each other.

The Plymouth Company, like the London Company, was to be under the jurisdiction of the royal council for Virginia, but it had its own resident council of thirteen to govern its projected plantation. To what extent the company could control the trade of its colony was not made clear in the charter. The leaders of the Plymouth Company were Sir John Popham and Sir Ferdinando Gorges.

The Plymouth Company sent its first expedition in the summer of 1606 to seek a desirable site for a plantation. The vessel was captured en route by the Spanish near Puerto Rico, where it had been driven by adverse winds, and the men were carried off as prisoners to Spain. Only a few made their way back to Plymouth.

A second vessel, dispatched in the autumn of 1606, reached the coast of Maine in safety. It returned with such glowing accounts that in May 1607 the company sent out two ships carrying settlers, the *Gift of God* and the *Mary and John*. They began a plantation near the mouth of the Sagadahoc (now Kennebec) River and built Fort St. George, but the colony did not prosper. Gorges ascribed its failure to lack of food and to "childish factions." The cold winter, the loss of the storehouse and many dwellings to fire, and the consequent shortage of supplies weakened the planters' interest. The death of some of the men whom Gorges had left in charge of the settlement—including the governor, George Popham, a nephew of Sir John—discouraged the company in England from pushing the enterprise further. However, some of the company's members continued their interest in the fisheries and sent out several expeditions to fish and trade with the Indians. Profits from these activities were sufficient to convince men like Gorges of the region's potential and thus to pave the way for reorganizing the project in 1620 under a new company, the Council for New England.

BIBLIOGRAPHY

Greene, Jack P. *Pursuits of Happiness: The Social Development of Early Modern British Colonies and the Formation of American Culture.* Chapel Hill: University of North Carolina Press, 1988.

Viola F. Barnes/A. R.

See also **Colonial Charters; Land Patents; Trading Companies.**

POCKET VETO,

an indirect veto by which a U.S. president negates legislation without affording Congress an opportunity for repassage by an overriding vote. The Constitution provides that measures presented by Congress to the president within ten days of adjournment and not returned by him before adjournment fail to become law. They are said to have been pocket vetoed. First employed by President James Madison, the pocket veto has been used by every president since Benjamin Harrison. Controversy over the practice has focused on the definition of "adjournment": presidential usage has included brief recesses, whereas congressional critics have argued that the term intends only lengthy adjournments.

BIBLIOGRAPHY

Jones, Charles O. *The Presidency in a Separated System.* Washington, D.C.: Brookings Institution, 1994.

Neustadt, Richard. *Presidential Power and the Modern Presidency: The Politics of Leadership from Roosevelt to Reagan.* New York: Free Press, 1990.

Schlesinger Jr., Arthur M. *The Imperial Presidency.* Boston: Houghton Mifflin, 1973.

Taft, William Howard. *The Presidency: Its Duties, Its Powers, Its Opportunities, and Its Limitations.* New York: Scribner, 1916.

Tugwell, Rexford G., and Thomas E. Cronin, eds. *The Presidency Reappraised.* New York: Praeger, 1974.

Norman C. Thomas/A. G.

See also **Connecticut Compromise; Constitution of the United States; Delegation of Powers; Implied Powers; President, U.S.**

POET LAUREATE, a position created in 1937 for the purpose of raising Americans' consciousness of and appreciation for the reading and writing of poetry. The librarian of Congress, in consultation with poetry experts and critics, appoints the poet laureate for a one-year term. Serving from October to May, the poet laureate receives a stipend of $35,000 funded by a gift trust. Although the appointee is encouraged to pursue his or her own projects while in residence at the Library of Congress, the laureate's duties also include giving a lecture and a poetry reading. The poet laureate also customarily introduces participants in the library's annual poetry series, which dates back to the 1940s. In addition, those holding the position often use the forum to bring their own artistic and educational concerns to the fore.

Joseph Auslander served as the nation's first poet laureate; other notable laureates have included Allen Tate, Robert Penn Warren, Elizabeth Bishop, Robert Frost, James Dickey, Richard Wilbur, and Robert Pinsky.

BIBLIOGRAPHY

McGuire, William. *Poetry's Catbird Seat: The Consultantship in Poetry in the English Language at the Library of Congress, 1937–1987.* Washington, D.C.: Library of Congress, 1988.

Barbara Schwarz Wachal

See also **Library of Congress; Literature.**

POINT FOUR was a foreign aid program to assist the poor in so-called underdeveloped countries. In his second inaugural address in 1949, President Harry S. Truman called for this "bold new program" as part of an overall effort to promote peace and freedom. Inviting other nations to participate, he called for the program to be a "worldwide effort" for the achievement of "peace, plenty, and freedom" through technical assistance, private foreign investment, and greater production. In the first phase of the Cold War, and in the wake of the TRUMAN DOCTRINE, the MARSHALL PLAN, and the creation of the NORTH ATLANTIC TREATY ORGANIZATION, Point Four was designed as an offer to the emerging nations to decide against communism—to become neutral or non-aligned. Although Truman stood behind this sweeping but ill-defined program, almost half a year had passed before he asked Congress for the initial appropriations of $45 million. It then took Congress until the end of May 1950 to pass Point Four as the Act for International Development. For the first year, only $29.9 million were appropriated. Without stable conditions, trade agreements, and guarantees, businesses were reluctant to invest, particularly in those countries needing foreign capital the most. In 1952 and 1953, the Technical Cooperation Administration, which implemented Point Four, received a little more than $300 million to provide technical assistance. By 1954, Point Four was overseen by the Foreign Operations Administration and its budget had reached $400 million. Hundreds of Point Four technicians visited dozens of impoverished nations, and thousands of students from these countries were invited to study in the United States. Like the Marshall Plan, Point Four was directed by the United States and not through the United Nations. This led to criticisms of undue American influence in the internal affairs of developing nations. The ambitious ideals proclaimed by Truman clashed with the realities of the Cold War and the Korean War (1950–1953), and they were largely incompatible with the profit orientation of private business.

BIBLIOGRAPHY

Bingham, Jonathan B. *Shirt-sleeve Diplomacy: Point 4 in Action.* New York: John Doyle, 1954.

Michael Wala

See also **Cold War; Foreign Aid.**

POLAR EXPLORATION

Origins of North Polar Exploration

The first explorers of the North Polar region, the Arctic, probably crossed from northeastern Asia to northwestern North America more than 100,000 years ago, exploring the north as well as lands to the south. Exactly when the Inuit (Eskimos) took up residence in the Arctic is not known, although both they and the Vikings arrived in Greenland about a thousand years ago, which means they did not completely circle the Arctic until historical times.

The Vikings explored much of the north Atlantic beginning in the 800s. It was they who pioneered the first part of what became known as the "Northeast Passage," sailing north of Norway and to the northern coast of what is now Russia. In 1527, after European explorers had begun to show that the New World was composed of huge landmasses that blocked east-to-west passage from Europe to eastern Asia, England's Robert Thorne urged King Henry VIII to send an expedition to the North Pole, arguing that it would allow passage directly from England to Asia. The king did not act on Thorne's suggestion, but Thorne's idea that the North Pole would be in open water persisted into the 1800s.

In the late 1500s, explorers tried to find a Northwest Passage north of North America, or a Northeast Passage north of Asia. Willem Barents of the Netherlands tried to find a Northeast Passage in 1594 and 1595, discovering the Barents Sea, but in 1596 he and commanders Jacob van Heemskerck and Jan Corneliszoon Rijp took two ships to 79°49′ N, and discovered Bear Island, the island of Svalbard (part of an archipelago), and a wall of ice. From 1607 to 1611, Henry Hudson made four voyages from England to find a northern passage to eastern Asia, at first trying to find a Northeast Passage and then trying to find a Northwest Passage. His discoveries included the huge Hudson's Bay, and he laid the foundation for future expeditions by mapping much of the northern extremities of Scandinavia and North America.

During the eighteenth century two divergent views of the North Pole would develop. Whalers held the view that an ice sheet covered the Arctic Ocean; others, most of whom had never been to the Arctic, held that there was a wall of ice along the northern Atlantic, north of which was an open sea. England's Captain James Cook's last mission was to sail to the northern Pacific and there find an entry created by warm currents through the wall of ice to the open Arctic sea. He was killed in Hawaii before he could discover that there was no such entry.

The First to Reach the North Pole

The early expeditions to the Arctic had been motivated by money; a short route through northern waters would have meant immense wealth for the explorers and their governments. Once it became clear that the route was nonexistent, exploration of the North Pole became a matter of scientific interest and adventure. On 25 March 1827, a British expedition led by William Edward Parry sailed to the Seven Islands, beyond Spitsbergen, and used human powered sledges. They made it to 82°36′52″N but discovered that the ice pack flowed southward, and they were unable to go farther north without running out of supplies. American explorer Elisha Kent Kane sailed in 1853 along Greenland's coast and, in 1854, mapped undiscovered areas of northern Greenland.

Crucial to reaching the North Pole was Charles Francis Hall's 1871 English expedition aboard the ship Polaris. He followed Kane's route in the hope of penetrating farther north, perhaps all the way to the North Pole. He and his crew made it to 82°11′ N, where he died, probably murdered by arsenic. Even so, he had shown a way to get near the North Pole by ship.

From 1881 to 1884, the United States funded a scientific mission to the edge of the Arctic to collect meteorological data and to explore Greenland, which helped scientists better understand the flow of the northern ice and the patterns of Arctic weather.

The great controversy over who was first to reach the North Pole began in 1908, when American explorer Frederick Albert Cook claimed he reached the North Pole on foot with three Inuit companions on 21 April 1908. In 1909, another American explorer, Robert Edwin Peary claimed he reached the North Pole by foot on 6 April 1909. Cook's claim fell apart when it was discovered that he had written a best selling book about climbing to the top of Mt. McKinley that was mostly lies; he barely made it halfway. Further, he failed to sight land that he should have seen on his path north. And his Inuit companions said they and Cook had not ventured more than a couple of days north from their base camp. On the other hand, Peary's data was sound; a review of his data in 1998 by the National Geographic Society showed that he passed at least within five miles of the North Pole.

On 9 May 1926, American naval officer Richard Evelyn Byrd flew over the North Pole in an airplane. There were claims in the 1970s that he missed the North Pole by many miles, perhaps falsifying his records, but the weight of evidence supports his claims.

The Modern Era of North Polar Exploration

On 4 August 1958, the nuclear-powered submarine Nautilus reached the North Pole underwater. On 12 August 1958, another American nuclear submarine, the Skate, broke through about fifteen feet of ice and surfaced at the North Pole. On 29 April 1978, the Japanese explorer Naomi Uemura reached the North Pole using sled dogs, becoming the first person to make a solo journey to the pole and back safely. More important was the Soviet Union's nuclear-powered icebreaker Arktika, which reached the North Pole on 17 August 1977, the first ship to make it all the way to the pole. These ships opened the Northeast Passage that had been sought for four hundred years, making the natural resources of Siberia available for export. By the 1990s, Russia had converted a few of its enormous icebreakers into tourist ships and took tourists to the North Pole in comfort.

Origins of South Polar Exploration

The first person to see Antarctica may have been Hui-te-Rangiora, a Polynesian who, in A.D. 650, sailed south from New Zealand, seeing a "white land." Europeans had long suspected a South Polar continent—not because of scientific evidence, but because of a theory that the earth had to be in balance, and without a southern continent it would be unbalanced. Thus mapmakers would describe a southern continent without knowing of anyone who had seen it. In 1519, the crew of Ferdinand Magellan's epic around-the-world voyage thought Tierra del Fuego was the tip of a southern continent, but in 1578, Francis Drake disproved this when he sailed south of Tierra del Fuego.

On 17 January 1773, English ships commanded by James Cook became the first to cross the Antarctic Circle, at 66°33′S. In February 1819, English captain William Smith sailed south of latitude 62°S and discovered the South Shetland Islands. British naval officers ridiculed his report. In October 1819, he and his crew sailed south again, discovering George Island, where they landed, claiming it for England. South Seas sealers, however, were willing to believe Smith's claims, and during the next few years they visited the islands Smith had discovered, slaughtering seals by the hundreds of thousands—almost every seal in the region. In 1820, the Royal Navy's Edward

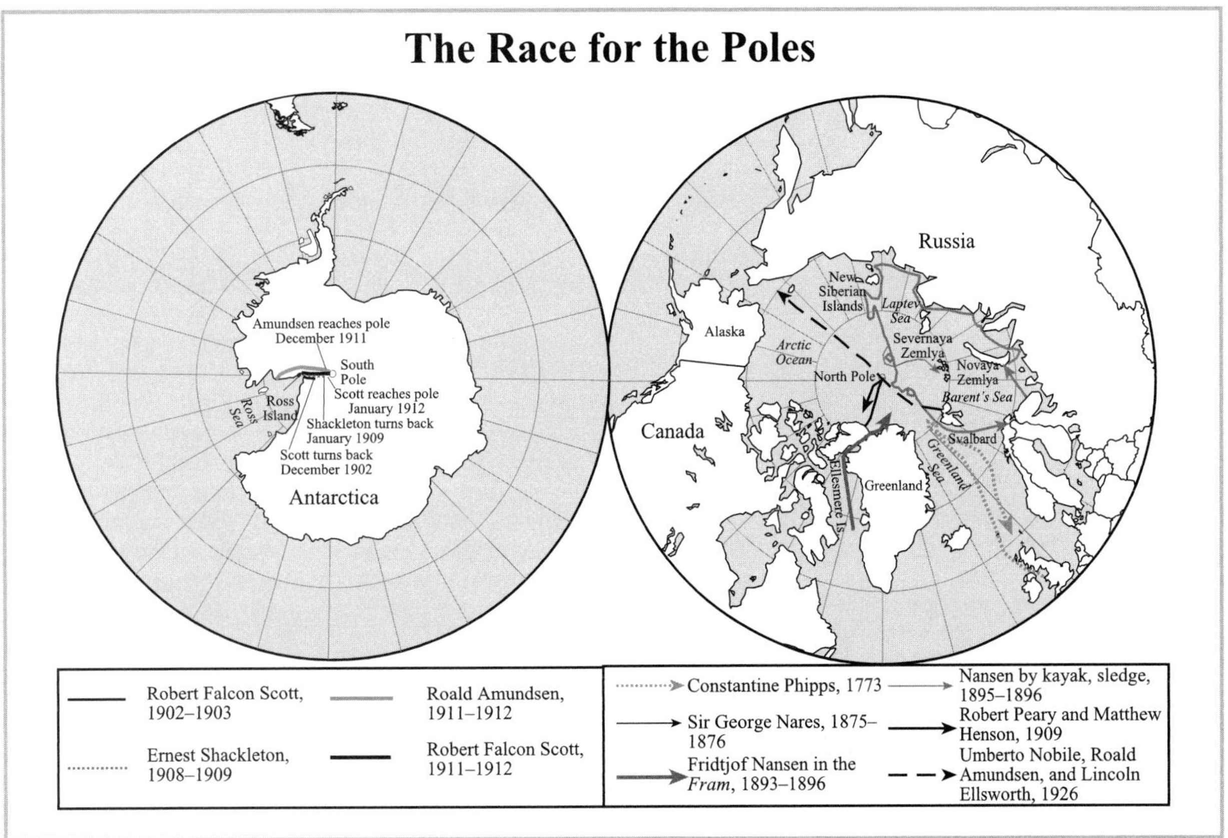

Bransfield, guided by Smith, was among the first to see the Antarctic Peninsula. In November 1820, nineteen-year-old American Nathaniel Palmer was sent south from a sealer to search for land and saw the Antarctic Peninsula.

The First to Reach the South Pole

On 7 February 1821, the sealer Cecilia, captained by John Davis, landed the first men on Antarctica, along the Danco Coast near Hughes Bay. In 1831, England mounted an expedition to determine the size of Antarctica and whether it was land or mostly water. Led by John Biscoe, the expedition circumnavigated Antarctica and proved it was land.

The United States Exploring Expedition of 1840 was the first overseas scientific enterprise sponsored by the United States government. Under the command of Lieutenant Charles Wilkes, the expedition charted twelve hundred miles of Antarctica's coastline, proving that the South Polar region was a landmass big enough to be called a continent. In January 1840, English ships commanded by James Clark Ross, discovered Victoria Land, Ross Island, Mt. Erebus, the Ross Sea, and the Ross Ice Shelf.

In November 1892, Captain Carl Larsen landed his ship Jason on Seymour Island and discovered petrified wood, which showed that Antarctica had once had a much more temperate climate. In 1899, English-Norwegian adventurer Carsten Borchgrevink landed at Cape Adare. Living in prefabricated huts, he and his crew became the first to spend a winter on Antarctica, use sled dogs there, and explore the Ross Ice Shelf.

From 1901 to 1904, an expedition led by Englishman Robert Falcon Scott camped at McMurdo Sound and mapped much of the interior of Antarctica. In November 1902, Scott, Ernest Shackleton, and Edwin Wilson crossed the Ross Ice Shelf in an effort to reach the South Pole, but they stopped at 82°33′S and returned suffering from malnutrition, scurvy, and snow blindness. Once back in Britain, Scott began to form plans for another scientific expedition to Antarctica. In 1911, he and an extraordinarily well-equipped expedition set up camp on Ross Island.

Meanwhile an expedition led by Norwegian Roald Amundsen set up camp in the Bay of Whales on the Ross Ice Shelf. He sailed on a ship that had been used successfully to ride Arctic ice floes, the Fram. It had an egg-shaped hull that rode up on top of ice floes rather than being crushed when ice floes pressed upon it. Amundsen set off with four men on skis to the South Pole and reached it 14 December 1911, pitched a tent, planted a flag, left Scott a note, and departed for his base camp. He and his companions all returned safely.

Scott, on the other hand, and four others, Birdie Bowers, Edgar Evans, Titus Oates, and Edward Wilson, arrived at the South Pole on 18 January 1912. Scott was determined to continue his expedition's scientific studies, even though two of his men were very sick, and he got them lost for about a day looking for fossils. Whereas Amundsen had placed many small depots of supplies along his route, Scott had placed only big ones spaced farther apart. Evans died on 18 February. About a day's travel from one food supply, he and his men were trapped in their tents by a storm. Oates, on the verge of losing his legs to frostbite, staggered out into the storm, never to be seen again. Scott and the others froze to death.

On 28 November 1929, Richard Evelyn Byrd duplicated his North Polar feat by being the first to fly, with three companions, over the South Pole. In November 1935, another American, Lincoln Ellsworth, became the first to fly across Antarctica, from one side to the other, landing near Byrd's base, Little America. In 1958, an expedition led by Vivian Fuchs crossed Antarctica from the Weddell Sea to the Ross Sea via the South Pole in ninety-nine days, covering 2,158 miles.

The Modern Era of South Polar Exploration

The Antarctic Treaty, signed in Washington, D.C., in 1961, declared that Antarctica was international land and that it would be used only for "peaceful" purposes. Even so, various countries have tried to lay tacit claim to large regions of the continent. Argentina and Chile have nearly gone to war over claims to Antarctic islands. By the beginning of the twenty-first century, the United States had the largest presence in Antarctica, including a base at the South Pole, although the base was drifting away from the pole at thirty-two feet per year.

In 1981, the scientist Joseph Farman—a leader of the British Antarctic Survey based in Halley Bay close to the Weddell Sea—discovered that the ozone layer thinned over Antarctica during the winter. Eventually, it was shown that the "hole in the ozone" broke up into "bubbles" that would float north, sometimes over populated areas. The hole grew larger every winter, encompassing nearly the whole continent by 1989. Although Farman's findings were at first ridiculed, the nations of the world eventually agreed to eliminate CFC use by 2000. CFCs are widely believed to have caused the ozone hole.

BIBLIOGRAPHY

Bertrand, Kenneth J. *Americans in Antarctica, 1775–1948.* New York: American Geographical Society, 1971.

Heacox, Kim. *Antarctica: The Last Continent.* Washington, D.C.: National Geographic Society, 1998.

Herbert, Wally. *The Noose of Laurels: The Discovery of the North Pole.* London: Hodder and Stoughton, 1989.

Holland, Clive, ed. *Farthest North: Endurance and Adventure in the Quest for the North Pole.* New York: Carroll and Graf, 1999.

Huntford, Roland. *The Last Place on Earth.* New York: Atheneum, 1986.

Kirwan, Laurence Patrick. *A History of Polar Exploration.* New York: Norton, 1960.

Mountfield, David. *A History of Polar Exploration.* New York: Dial Press, 1974.

Porter, Nancy. *Alone on the Ice: The Story of Admiral Richard Byrd.* Videocassette. Boston: WGBH, 1999.

Rodgers, Eugene. *Beyond the Barrier: The Story of Byrd's First Expedition to Antarctica.* Annapolis, Md.: Naval Institute Press, 1990.

Kirk H. Beetz

See also **Greely's Arctic Expedition; Wilkes Expedition.**

POLICE agencies in the United States are oriented toward local control. Their counterparts in other industrialized countries, by contrast, are usually part of a centralized national police force. As a result of the focus on independent local control, there are some 20,000 different police agencies in the U.S. (not including the wide variety of specialized federal forces), financed and managed by states, counties, and municipalities. The lack of a centralized national system has led to problems of jurisdiction, information sharing, and even basic ideology. But the overriding fear of a national force and the abuse of its power has long been a hallmark of the American system of law.

Police Organization

Metropolitan police agencies in the U.S. were originally organized on a military model, and their development in the second half of the nineteenth century was strongly influenced by Robert Peel's Metropolitan Police Force of London, founded in 1829. The British system used an organization of constables and watchmen who patrolled the streets and often charged fees for their services. Early law enforcement efforts in the U.S. were loosely organized, as there was no perceived need for full-time, professional forces, and watchmen were usually volunteers. By the middle of the eighteenth century, however, large metropolitan areas such as New York, Philadelphia, Boston, and Chicago had created permanent fulltime police forces. Professional, fulltime state police forces were not commonplace in the U.S. until the twentieth century.

Because most U.S. police agencies have been created and funded by the local communities, and because they were created at different times, there are many variations in how the agencies are organized and financed. In general, city police are funded by the municipality and headed by a police chief, either appointed by the mayor or elected. Counties employ patrolmen and sheriffs, who usually answer to an elected county official. State police agencies, which have broader jurisdiction, assist in statewide investigations and are responsible for traffic law enforcement in areas outside municipalities. Local law enforcement agencies also have a variety of specialized units, including those for transit, parks, ports, housing, and schools.

Federal police agencies mostly developed later, although the United States Treasury established the U.S.

Mint Police in 1792. The Treasury Department oversees other specialized police agencies as well, including the U.S. Customs Service, the Internal Revenue Service; the Bureau of Alcohol, Tobacco, and Firearms; and the Secret Service. The Justice Department law enforcement agency was established in 1870 and includes the Drug Enforcement Agency, the Federal Bureau of Investigation, the Immigration and Naturalization Service, and the U.S. Marshals (in charge of guarding and transporting federal prisoners, among other duties). In addition, other federal agencies have been established for specific law enforcement. These include the U.S. Park Police, the Border Patrol, the National Security Agency, and the Federal Trade Commission. The executive branch directs most federal agencies, with oversight by the legislative and judicial branches.

According to the U.S. Department of Justice's Bureau of Justice Statistics, in 1996 there were 922,200 full-time, local police personnel, of whom 663,535 had arrest powers. Steady increases for the last two decades indicate a 2001 estimate of around 1,000,000 local law enforcement employees across the country, about a quarter of them women and minorities. Statistics from 1997 show that, on average, local police officers were required to have 1,100 hours of training (sheriffs averaged 900 hours), and, by 2000, more than thirty-seven percent of local police agencies were required to have some college education. In 2000, there were 88,496 federal officers, about thirty-one for every 100,000 people (in Washington, D.C., the ratio was 1,397 federal officers for every 100,000 residents). The majority of federal officers are in Texas; California; Washington, D.C.; New York; and Florida.

History of Police Forces

Permanent police forces were created in metropolitan areas such as New York (1853) and Philadelphia (1856) to handle the increase of population and the social problems that came with urban industrialization. Police officers were uniformed, making them easily identifiable on the street, which in turn expanded their duties beyond mere law enforcement; policemen gave directions, took in lost children, assisted the indigent, enforced health codes, and, with the emergence of the automobile, directed traffic and enforced the rules of the road. Police reform in the late nineteenth century made police officers civil servants, providing a salary and doing away with the earlier system of fees for services. As a result, police officers were more inclined to help all victims of crime, not just those who could afford the fees. In 1906, in an effort to end nepotism and favoritism, San Francisco established a system of hiring based on scores from civil service tests, a practice that became the national standard.

The twentieth century brought scientific research and technology to the world of policing. New techniques in identifying physical characteristics (such as fingerprints, first used in the early 1900s) meant police agencies spent more energy on criminal investigations, crime prevention, and other specialized tasks. Between the 1920s and 1940s, most large cities had special juvenile crime divisions; in the 1920s and 1930s, there was an expansion of traffic divisions; in the 1940s and 1950s, police agencies created public relations positions; the 1950s brought the first telephoto transmissions of documents, photographs, and fingerprints; and since the 1970s, police agencies have worked toward computerized data collecting, sharing, and analysis. By the end of the twentieth century, metropolitan police forces had specialized units for dealing with exigencies such as bombs, hostage situations, crowd control, underwater rescue, and terrorism.

Forensic science advanced evidence gathering and analysis in the last decades of the twentieth century, but smaller, rural police forces seldom had the resources or training to take advantage of scientific advancements. Whereas the results of DNA testing were usually considered reliable, such tests could take months without the necessary resources or trained personnel to conduct them. As of 2001 there were still several states with no uniform system of preserving crime scenes and gathering evidence.

Issues in Policing

Because police officers are authorized to use physical force, including deadly force, concerns over the abuse of power have long been a central and justified concern. The ethnic and racial makeup of early police agencies usually mirrored those who held political power, with nonwhites and women generally barred from employment as regular officers. Not until the 1960s did women and minorities became visible as police officers. By 2000, the Justice Department estimated that women and minorities represent around twenty-two percent of the nation's local police force.

Historically, the minority populations of urban areas have experienced strained relations with the police. In the 1850s, so-called nativist movements fought the inclusion of immigrants on police forces in Chicago and New York. Although police squads protected black residents from white mobs during the 1940s and 1950s, the 1960s brought race riots, including those in Chicago after the assassination of Martin Luther King Jr., which left nine people dead, and the 1965 riots in the Los Angeles neighborhood of Watts, which left four dead. Riots broke out in Los Angeles in 1992 after the not-guilty verdict in the case against four white police officers who had been videotaped beating Rodney King, an African American. New York had also notorious abuse scandals in the late 1990s, including the police torture of the Haitian immigrant Abner Louima in 1997 and the shooting death in 1999 of the West African immigrant Amadou Diallo. Such high-profile cases have spurred a reexamination of police policies and the way internal investigations are conducted.

Although abuse of power by police officers is a legitimate concern, according to a 1999 review of police agency statistics, police officers use force in only 0.2 percent of their interactions with the public, the majority involving physical force without the use of a weapon.

Police Agencies in the Future

Social science has aided police work just as forensic science has. Most modern metropolitan police forces have adapted to the diverse needs of their communities, with specialized units and creative alternatives to traditional police methods. One of the strongest trends has been toward community policing, an attempt to make police officers more familiar to the residents and merchants of a neighborhood. Community involvement in policing has also influenced the investigation and rectification of police abuse and corruption, with the public demanding a greater role. Fears of "racial profiling," the alleged tendency of police officers to target minority groups, has spawned efforts to educate police about the cultural differences between ethnic and racial groups.

Police reform has been slow, because discussions generally take place at the national level, whereas new policies are drafted by local departments. This situation will almost certainly evolve as the need for interagency cooperation increases, and as federal police agencies work in concert with local agencies to form a national computer database for gathering information and sharing intelligence.

BIBLIOGRAPHY

Dulaney, W. Marvin. *Black Police in America.* Bloomington: Indiana University Press, 1996.

Riley, Gail Blasser. *Miranda v. Arizona: Rights of the Accused.* Hillside, N.J.: Enslow, 1994.

U.S. Department of Justice. Home Page available from http://www.usdoj.gov/.

Vila, Brian, ed. *The Role of Police in American Society: A Documentary History.* Westport, Conn.: Greenwood Press, 1999.

Woods, Gerald. *The Police in Los Angeles: Reform and Professionalization.* New York: Garland, 1993.

Paul Hehn

See also **Boston Police Strike; Los Angeles Riots; *Miranda v. Arizona;* Police Brutality; Police Power.**

POLICE BRUTALITY. Police brutality is the use of any force exceeding that reasonably necessary to accomplish a lawful police purpose. Although no reliable measure of its incidence exists—let alone one charting change chronologically—its history is undeniably long. The shifting nature and definition of police brutality, however, reflect larger political, demographic, and economic changes.

Much police brutality in the nineteenth and early twentieth centuries was officially sanctioned, aimed at undermining labor actions or controlling working-class leisure. Some scholars have argued, however, that local police often sympathized with workers, obliging industrialists to call upon state or private police to forcibly regulate discontented laborers. For example, the Pennsylvania state militia, not members of the local police force, killed twenty during the 1877 Pittsburgh railroad strike; between 1869 and 1892, private Pinkerton officers were involved in brutally breaking seventy-seven strikes.

Rodney King. An image from a videotape showing police brutality against a motorist, which led to a trial of four Los Angeles police officers and then—after their acquittal in April 1992—days of extensive rioting, causing more than fifty deaths and $1 billion in damage. AP/Wide World Photos

Progressive era reform efforts to professionalize crime control paradoxically distanced local police from the communities they served, thus eroding important social checks on abuse. Local officers, for example, beat hundreds at a 1930 labor rally in New York City, while Chicago police killed ten strikers in the Republic Steel Memorial Day Massacre of 1937. Less dramatic, but equally revealing, Dallas police formally charged less than five percent of the 8,526 people they arrested "on suspicion" in 1930.

The waves of labor migration after 1917—most prominently, African Americans moving from the rural South to the urban North—racialized police brutality, leading to three major eras of riots stemming from conflict between police and minority groups: 1917–1919, 1943, and 1964–1968. Both the civil rights movement and subsequent urban unrest laid bare the flaws in a model of police professionalism that focused narrowly on fighting crime while ignoring the needs of the communities, especially poor communities, being policed.

Some observers, relying on findings that an officer's race is unrelated to the propensity to use force, assert racial animosity alone cannot account for brutal actions by the police. Such scholarship holds that brutality under the guise of "quality-of-life" policing serves economic elites by paving the way for urban gentrification. The accelerating reorganization of post-industrial urban economies around financial, cultural, and high-tech activities has not only decimated employment prospects for low skilled (and often minority) workers, but also required their displacement as a new knowledge-professional class seeks fresh neighborhoods in which to play and live.

Despite early enthusiasm, civilian review boards—able neither to investigate nor control departmental policies—have often proved disappointing, leaving critics to view legislation as the last best hope.

BIBLIOGRAPHY

Friedman, Lawrence. *Crime and Punishment in American History.* New York: Basic Books, 1993.

Garland, David. *The Culture of Control: Crime and Social Order in Contemporary Society.* Chicago: University of Chicago Press, 2001.

Websdale, Neil. *Policing the Poor: From Slave Plantation to Public Housing.* Boston: Northeastern University Press, 2001.

Gregory Fritz Umbach

POLICE POWER is the authority of government to regulate "health, safety, welfare, and morals." In U.S. constitutional law, it is the plenary power of government to regulate any matter affecting its citizens so long as it is not barred by the Constitution.

Derived from *polis,* Greek for city-state, "police" was a common eighteenth-century concept. Adam Smith lectured that police comprehended attention to roads, security, and "cheapness or plenty." In book four of his *Commentaries on the Laws of England* (4 vols., 1765–1769), William Blackstone defined public police and economy as "due regulation and domestic order of the kingdom," enforcing "the rules of propriety, good neighbourhood, and good manners." Samuel Johnson's *Dictionary of the English Language* (2 vols., 1755) defined police as "the regulation of a country or a city, so far as regards the inhabitants." Thus, Joseph Galloway's *Plan of a Proposed Union between Great Britain and the Colonies* (1774) specified that "each colony shall retain its present whatsoever."

The U.S. Constitution does not employ the term "police" but divides the powers of domestic regulation, delegating some to the central government, particularly in Article I, section 8, and reserving all others to the states in the Tenth Amendment. Still, in Federalist 34, Hamilton described the police of a nation-state to include support of its agencies and the encouragement of agriculture and manufactures.

John Marshall, the chief justice of the U.S. Supreme Court, described the power of a state to regulate gunpowder as a police power in *Brown v. Maryland* (1827). Yet Massachusetts chief justice Lemuel Shaw most influentially framed the definition of police power in *Commonwealth v. Alger* (1851) as a state power vested in the Legislature by the constitution, to make, ordain, and establish all manner of wholesome and reasonable laws, statutes, and ordinances, either with penalties or without, not repugnant to the constitution, as they shall judge to be for the good and welfare of the commonwealth, and of the subjects of the same. This formula was widely adopted and encompassed arguments over governmental powers and their limits, past and future.

The U.S. Supreme Court expanded the doctrine throughout the nineteenth century into an inalienable power that the state could not divest, although the states could be flexible in its exercise. Likewise, the scope of the police power increased as states legislated over contracts, employment relationships, and the use of property. In 1911, Justice Oliver Wendell Holmes could declare "the police power extends to all the great public needs." New Deal courts and scholars expanded the police powers from regulation alone to include the governmental provision of services, particularly by the national government, using the commerce clause to underpin a federal police power.

Conflicts over the exercise of police power usually arise as arguments of limits on a state or the federal government, arising either from conflicts between that state and the national government or from limits protecting individual rights to property, contract, speech, or other civil rights. These limits may be either in state or federal constitutions. Notorious conflicts arose, initially, over the regulation of property and commerce. (Compare *Dartmouth College v. Woodward* [1819], in which the U.S. Supreme Court ruled that states could not alter college charters, and *Willson v.Black Bird Creek Marsh College,* in which the Court determined that states may dam a navigable creek.) In the late 1800s labor laws were the source of contention (see *Lochner v. New York* [1905], where the Supreme Court overturned state labor laws), while in the early twentieth century it was the powers of the regulatory state. (See *Nebbia v. New York* [1934], allowing any state regulations as a "reasonable exertion of governmental authority" if not "arbitrary or discriminatory" and *West Coast Hotel Co. v. Parrish* [1937], upholding state labor laws.) There are recurrent disputes over the definition and enforcement of civil rights. (Compare *Dred Scott v. Sanford* [1857], where the Court ruled that state law defines slaves and citizens, with its *Heart of Atlanta Motel v. United States* [1964] determination that Congress may ban racial discrimination in public accommodations, with *Bowers v. Hardwick* [1986], where the Court declared that states may ban homosexual conduct.)

BIBLIOGRAPHY

Cooley, Thomas M. *A Treatise on the Constitutional Limitations Which Rest upon the Legislative Power of the States of the American Union.* 1871. 2 vols. Boston: Little, Brown, 1927.

Freund, Ernst. *The Police Power: Public Policy and Constitutional Rights.* Chicago: Callaghan and Company, 1904.

Novak, William J. *The People's Welfare: Law and Regulation in Nineteenth-Century America.* Chapel Hill: University of North Carolina Press, 1996.

Stephen M. Sheppard

See also **Eminent Domain.**

POLIOMYELITIS, or infantile paralysis, was one of the most feared diseases of the twentieth century, especially for its ability to cripple children and adolescents. The disease is caused by one of three strains of intestinal virus that under certain conditions invades and damages or destroys the anterior horn cells of the spinal cord. Paralysis is caused when damaged or destroyed nerves can no longer enervate muscles. The virus is commonly spread through contaminated fecal material. Before modern sanitation the poliovirus was constantly present, and most individuals were infected as young children, thereby gaining protective antibodies. Epidemics occurred when modern sanitation interrupted virus circulation for several years, creating a large susceptible population. In epidemics, perhaps as many as 90 to 95 percent of those infected had inapparent cases and a flu-like illness with no paralysis. Four to eight percent of those infected had an abortive case with mild symptoms. Less than 2 percent of all infections reached the central nervous system and caused paralysis. Polio killed when the muscles involved in breathing were paralyzed, but the disease was rarely fatal.

The first sizable polio epidemic in the United States occurred in Vermont in 1894. Recurrent epidemics in Europe and North America sparked research on the disease, and in 1908 the Vienna immunologist Karl Landsteiner discovered the poliovirus. Simon Flexner, the director of the Rockefeller Institute for Medical Research in New York, soon isolated the virus in the United States and discovered polio antibodies in patients.

In 1916, New York and the Northeast experienced the nation's most severe polio epidemic, with 27,000 cases and 6,000 deaths. In New York City alone there were 8,928 cases and 2,407 deaths. This epidemic puzzled physicians and frightened citizens. Polio struck both infants and adults, individuals living in clean, sanitary conditions and those living in filth, the wealthy and the poor. Lacking effective cures and vaccines, public health officials conducted a campaign to clean up the city and eradicate the flies believed to carry the disease. Polio patients were quarantined in their homes or removed, sometimes forcibly, to hastily established isolation hospitals. For the next four decades epidemics of poliomyelitis struck some part of the nation every year.

In 1921, Franklin D. Roosevelt, who later served as governor of New York and president of the United States, developed polio while vacationing at the family home. Seeking to regain the use of his paralyzed legs, he discovered the therapeutic effects of warm mineral water at a failing resort in Warm Springs, Georgia. In 1926 he purchased the resort and, with the help of his law partner, Basil O'Connor, turned it into a model facility for polio rehabilitation, although Roosevelt himself never walked unaided.

During the 1920s and 1930s, scientists and physicians sought to better understand the disease and to find a cure or vaccine. The researchers James D. Trask, John R. Paul, and Dorothy Horstmann of the Yale University Poliomyelitis Study Unit confirmed polio's character as an intestinal disease when they isolated the virus in water supplies and sewage during epidemics. Australian scientists in 1931 discovered that there were at least two different strains of poliovirus. Scientists ultimately discovered a third strain and placed the poliovirus in the family of enteroviruses. In 1935 two American physicians, Maurice Brodie in New York and John A. Kolmer in Philadelphia, developed and tested polio vaccines. These vaccines, however, proved ineffective and may actually have caused cases of the disease.

Polio rehabilitation also advanced in the 1930s, especially at the Georgia Warm Springs Foundation established by Roosevelt. The President's Birthday Ball Commission began raising funds in 1934 to support rehabilitation and research and was succeeded in 1938 by the National Foundation for Infantile Paralysis headed by Basil O'Connor. The National Foundation's March of Dimes campaign raised over $600 million between 1938 and 1962. About 60 percent of this money assisted individuals with hospital and doctor bills, and about 11 percent was spent on grants to scientists. The iron lung, a large canister-shaped respirator that "breathed" for patients with paralyzed respiratory muscles was developed in the 1930s. In the 1940s, Elizabeth Kenny, an Australian nurse, introduced her unorthodox ideas for treating polio paralysis. In place of immobility and casts to prevent the contraction of paralyzed limbs, Kenny applied hot packs to sooth paralyzed muscles and movement in order to maintain flexibility and retrain paralyzed muscles. Although many doctors rejected her theories about the causes of polio paralysis, her therapeutic practices soon became commonplace.

In the late 1940s, John F. Enders, Thomas H. Weller, and Frederick C. Robbins, physicians at Harvard funded by the National Foundation, first grew poliovirus on tissue culture outside the body, necessary for a successful vaccine. They won the Nobel Prize in 1954 for their discovery. The National Foundation also funded a typing program to identify all the possible strains of the virus in anticipation of producing a vaccine against every variant.

This research occurred against the background of an increasing incidence of epidemics in the late 1940s and early 1950s. Nine of the ten worst years for polio occurred between 1945 and 1955, and the epidemic of 1952 was second only to 1916 in its severity. The improved sanitation of the postwar years, the move to the suburbs, and the baby boom ensured that many children and even adolescents were vulnerable. Those years were marked by summers of fear when parents kept their children out of swimming pools and movie theaters and warned them against drinking from water fountains. The fund-raising of the March of Dimes, the information disseminated by the National Foundation, and the heartbreaking personal narratives that appeared in popular magazines kept polio in the forefront of the nation's consciousness. The specter of the crippling paralysis of polio threatened the postwar American Dream of healthy, happy children.

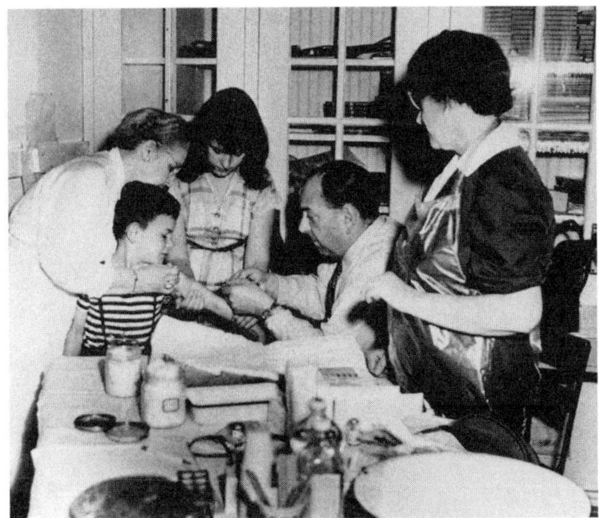

Polio Vaccine. A child receives the Salk vaccine, which was later replaced by the oral Sabin vaccine. AP/Wide World Photos

The fund-raising efforts of the March of Dimes and the laboratory work of the physicians came together in the 1950s. Jonas Salk, a University of Pittsburgh physician, applied lessons he had learned working on influenza vaccine and developed a successful killed virus vaccine that could be mass produced. By the early 1950s he was conducting preliminary trials of the vaccine. In 1954 the National Foundation arranged for a large-scale field trial of the Salk vaccine conducted by Dr. Thomas Francis Jr. of the University of Michigan. Over 1.8 million children were enrolled as "polio pioneers" in the trial. On 12 April 1955, Francis announced that the Salk vaccine was both safe and effective in protecting vaccinated children from polio. The U.S. government licensed the vaccine the same day. Basil O'Connor had already ordered millions of doses from pharmaceutical companies in order to begin a mass vaccination immediately. Unfortunately, a few weeks later, a bad batch of vaccine produced by Cutter Laboratories resulted in more than 200 cases of vaccine-associated poliomyelitis, including eleven deaths. This was an isolated episode, and the vaccination of America's children soon continued. Even as many children were protected by the Salk vaccine, Albert Sabin, also supported by the National Foundation, worked on an attenuated poliovirus vaccine. An attenuated vaccine, in which the virus was live but significantly weakened, had several advantages. It induced a stronger, longer lasting immune response; immunity was achieved more quickly; and it could be given orally instead of being injected. After field trials in the United States, the Soviet Union, and elsewhere, the Sabin vaccine was licensed for use in 1962. These two vaccines virtually eliminated poliomyelitis in the United States by the early 1960s. Since then only a handful of cases have occurred annually, usually in new immigrants or as vaccine-associated cases.

The survivors of the postwar polio epidemics often spent long periods in rehabilitation hospitals before being fitted with braces, wheelchairs, and respirators that allowed them to return to families, school, and work. Because of the barriers they faced in attempting to live and work, polio survivors were often in the forefront of the disability rights movement that emerged in the 1970s. Activists like Ed Roberts, who was one of the founders of the Independent Living Movement, insisted that individuals with disabilities had a right to accessible living and working environments. In the 1980s, many polio survivors began experiencing increased pain, muscle weakness and even paralysis that physicians eventually identified as post-polio syndrome, an apparent effect of the overuse of nerves and muscles to compensate for the destruction caused by the initial infection. The oral polio vaccine also came under attack in the United States for causing eight to ten cases of polio every year. In 2000 the federal government recommended returning to a safer Salk-type killed virus. The Sabin vaccine, however, remained in use overseas as the World Health Organization tried to eradicate the poliovirus worldwide. Thus in the twenty-first century, poliomyelitis, which was so feared in the twentieth century, may become only the second infectious disease, after smallpox, to be eliminated as a threat to humans.

BIBLIOGRAPHY

Black, Kathryn. *In the Shadow of Polio: A Personal and Social History.* Reading, Mass.: Addison-Wesley, 1996.

Gould, Tony. *A Summer Plague: Polio and Its Survivors.* New Haven: Yale University Press, 1995.

Paul, John R. *A History of Poliomyelitis.* New Haven: Yale University Press, 1971.

Rogers, Naomi. *Dirt and Disease: Polio Before FDR.* New Brunswick: Rutgers University Press, 1990.

Seavey, Nina Gilden, Jane S. Smith, and Paul Wagner. *A Paralyzing Fear: The Triumph Over Polio in America.* New York: TV Books, 1998.

Smith, Jane S. *Patenting the Sun: Polio and the Salk Vaccine.* New York: William Morrow, 1990.

Daniel J. Wilson

See also **Epidemics and Public Health; March of Dimes; Medical Research.**

POLISH AMERICANS. By the mid-1700s Poland, once one of the largest and among the most powerful states in Europe, had succumbed to its own decentralized political structure and its neighbors' ambitions. By century's end, Prussia, Russia, and Austria had conquered and partitioned the country, thrusting each partition onto its own separate path from semifeudal agrarianism to modernized, commercial agriculture.

Early Immigration

Polish society was neither static nor self-contained. In 1608, a few itinerant Polish artisans became America's

Polish American Immigrants. A woman and her three sons arrive in New York in 1948, part of a wave of immigrants fleeing the aftermath of war and the establishment of Communist dictatorship. © UPI/CORBIS-BETTMANN

first Polish settlers when they joined the Jamestown colony. Recruited to produce soap, tar, and pitch, they left their mark on Virginia political history by resisting a 1619 attempt by the House of Burgesses to disenfranchise them. Protestant "Polanders" also had settled in colonial New Amsterdam and in Pennsylvania. The American Revolution also benefited from a few talented Polish nobles of democratic sympathies, like General Casimir Pulaski ("Father of the American Cavalry"), who was slain at the Battle of Savannah (1779), and General Thaddeus Kościuszko, a military engineer whose fortifications contributed decisively to the American victory at the Battle of Saratoga (1777). Kościuszko also wrote the first U.S. army artillery manual. Kościuszko's will, eventually superseded, bequeathed his American estate to free and educate African American slaves. Although numerically insignificant, these early Polish arrivals established later Polish immigrants' claims to authenticity as Americans.

Polish settlement in the United States became numerically noteworthy only after the 1830s, when scattered veterans of a succession of failed Polish insurrections against foreign rule fled to the United States during Europe's "Springtime of Nations." Even then, this "Great Emigration" only numbered a thousand or so individuals who dispersed widely and assimilated easily, although it did establish the first Polish American periodicals, literary societies, and the political groups that laid the groundwork for a Polish nationalist movement in the United States. Nationalist aspirations knit Poles together at home and abroad, but concurrently raised divisive issues. Although the majority of their inhabitants were Roman Catholics and ethnic Poles, the Polish partitions contained sizeable ethnic minorities—Jews, Ukrainians, and Germans. Polish nationalists debated whether Polish identity would be pluralistic, civic, and secular, or based on ethnicity and religion.

Years of Mass Migration

With the gradual capitalist transformation and "modernization" of the Polish countryside after the 1850s, Polish immigration to the United States (and elsewhere) increased. Author and Nobel laureate Henryk Sienkiewicz (1905) remarked that Poles came "in search of bread and freedom," but the majority probably came more for economic reasons. The Polish mass migration "for bread" (*za chlebem*) brought about 2.5 million ethnic Poles (including regional subgroups like the Kashubes and the Górale, or Tatra highlanders) to the United States from the 1850 to 1920. (This figure includes 434,000 "German Poles" from the German-held Polish partition, who came primarily from 1850 to 1900; 800,000 "Austrian Poles" from the Austrian-held Polish partition, who arrived between 1880 and 1920; and 805,000 "Russian Poles" from the Russian-held Polish partition, who immigrated from 1890 to 1920). Up to 30 percent of the Austrian and Russian Poles did not remain in the United States, returning to their land of origin. Although the immigrants included Poles of all classes, most had rural, typically peasant, backgrounds, were young, disproportionately male, and unmarried. Immigrant Poles entered many occupations including farming (a mere 10 percent), shopkeeping, the professions, skilled labor, and the arts; but fully 80 percent took semiskilled and unskilled jobs in mass production and heavy industry—coal mining, oil refining, steelmaking, meatpacking, and textiles, electrical goods, and auto manufacture.

Community Building

Rural Panna Maria, Texas, generally is recognized as the first Polish settlement (1854) of the era of the peasant mass migration, but most Poles settled in northeastern and midwestern towns and cities. (Chicago had the second largest Polish population of any city; only Warsaw boasted greater numbers of Poles.) Polish immigrants concentrated in the industrial belt that extended from Boston to Philadelphia and westward across New York and Pennsylvania, through Pittsburgh, northern Ohio, and northern Indiana, to Chicago and Milwaukee. Social dislocations they experienced were amply documented in William I. Thomas and Florian Znaniecki, *The Polish Peasant in Europe and America* (1918–1920), the classic work of the "Chicago school" of sociology. Nevertheless, the Polish immigrant community—"Polonia" (Latin for Poland), as these enclaves individually and collectively were known—became vital centers of immigrant social life, with immigrant small businesses, press, theater, and a network of athletic, cultural, political, and fraternal benevolent associations. The heart of Polonia, however, was its Polish Roman Catholic parishes, (peaking at over 800 in the 1930s). With many established by the Polish Resurrectionist order, these parishes (with their parochial schools and teaching nuns like the Felicians) provided cradle-to-grave social services, encapsulated immigrant spiritual and aesthetic life (best merged, perhaps, in images of Our Lady of Częstochowa, Poland's "Black Madonna") and (with the largest numbering over 40,000 parishioners) gave rise to Polonia's first great leaders, priests like Chicago's Rev. Wincenty Barzyński, C.R.

Religious and Political Affairs

During the years of mass migration, Polonia's main rival fraternal organizations, the secularist Polish National Alliance (1880) and the religionist Polish Roman Catholic Union (1873), argued and then compromised on Polish American ethnic identity: Polish and Roman Catholic. The linkage of Roman Catholicism and Polishness (*Polskość*) increasingly influenced nationalist politics in Poland into the twentieth century. Insurrectionary veteran Rev. Joseph Dąbrowski established a Polish Roman Catholic seminary in Detroit in 1883 to provide a patriotic ethnic clergy, while other Poles, led by Rev. Wenceslaus Kruszka, argued for representation and equality within the heavily Irish church hierarchy, succeeding modestly with the consecration of Paul Rhode as the first Polish American Roman Catholic bishop (1908). Immigrant religious participation was not without contention. Between the 1890s and 1920s, immigrant lay-trusteeism and Polish nationalism produced the most important schism yet to rock American Roman Catholicism, climaxing in the 1904 founding of the Polish National Catholic Church by Scranton, Pennsylvania, priest Francis Hodur. Following World War I, the Polish nationalist movement also achieved its central goal, as pianist Ignacy Jan Paderewski and others won the support of the administration of President Woodrow Wilson for the reestablishment of a united, sovereign, independent Poland. Poland came into being again in 1918, with its existence confirmed by the Treaty of Versailles (1919).

Involved in the Progressive Era's labor movement and radical politics (a Polish anarchist, Leon Czolgosz, assassinated President William McKinley in 1901), Polish workers played a key role in the 1930s and 1940s in the rise of the United Automobile Workers (UAW) and other mass production unions associated with the Congress of Industrial Organizations. In the heroic 1935–1937 period, Poles and other Slavs were fully a quarter of the membership. Polish Americans overwhelmingly supported President Franklin Delano Roosevelt and the Democratic Party in the 1930s, a loyalty shaken by the Yalta Agreement (1945) which, after World War II, stripped Poland of territory, left it a Soviet satellite, and gave rise to fifty years of Polish American anticommunism championed by Polonia's new umbrella political body, the Polish American Congress (1944).

Post–World War II Migration

After World War II, new waves of immigrants from Poland reshaped the Polish presence in the United States. Between 1945 and 1956, over 190,000 political exiles and displaced persons came to the United States. From 1965 to 1990, about 178,000 entered after the liberalization of Polish migration policies (1956), political crackdowns in Poland (1968), and passage of the Immigration and Naturalization Act of 1965. During the same period roughly 957,000 nonimmigrant temporary visitors came, many of whom stayed and obtained work. Between 1983 and 1990, about 35,000 entered; these were political refugees from

Polish American Craftsman. In this photograph by George Pickow, an artisan makes designs for a Catholic church's stained-glass windows, c. 1950. © HULTON GETTY/LIAISON AGENCY

the Solidarity (*Solidarność*) movement, the Polish trade union movement and democratization campaign. Census figures for 2000 estimate the Polish American population (persons either from Poland or identifying Polish as a principal ancestry) at about 9 million, or about 3.3 percent of the national total. The states with the largest Polish American population are New York (958,893), Illinois (946,241), and Michigan (900,335). Other states with sizeable Polish American populations include Pennsylvania, New Jersey, Massachusetts, Ohio, Wisconsin, California, and Florida. The large Polish American presence in California and Florida resulted from late-twentieth-century secondary migrations.

Contemporary Polish America

As an ethnic group, Polish Americans experienced mixed fortunes in America after World War II. With a high rate of home ownership, older urban Polonias tended to remain in place despite changing urban racial composition. Nonetheless suburban out-migration, intermarriage, language loss, assimilation, and upward mobility have undercut ethnic group numbers and identification. Polish Americans have moved into managerial, professional, and technical occupations, while the mass marketing of such traditional Polish food items like *pączki* (doughnuts) and *pierogi* (filled dumplings) symbolized their cultural "arrival." The white ethnic revival of the late 1960s heightened ethnic consciousness for some Polish Americans who also felt considerable ethnic pride when Karol Cardinal Wojtyła became the first Polish pope, John Paul II (1978), and Solidarity leader Lech Wałęsa led a nonviolent revolution for democracy in Poland in the early 1980s. Polish Americans who have attained national recognition in contemporary American culture include television actress Loretta Swit (*M*A*S*H*), athletic figures like basketball coach Mike Krzyzewski and baseball star Stan "The Man" Musial, homemaking doyenne Martha Stewart (neé Kostyra), and émigré Nobel laureate Czesław Miłosz.

Despite such successes, Polish Americans continue to score low in "social status" rankings owing to persistent anti-Polish stereotyping, particularly in the media, which has inspired antidefamation campaigns. Contemporary Polish American politics also have focused on cultural survival issues, Polish membership in NATO (achieved in 1999), relations with post-socialist Poland, and improvement in Polish-Jewish relations, historically a difficult issue. In postwar national politics, Polish American visibility peaked when Maine Senator Edmund Muskie (Marciszewski) won the Democratic Party vice presidential nomination (1968) and Zbigniew Brzezinski was named as President Jimmy Carter's national security adviser (1976); but "realigned" Polish American voters increasingly voted for Republican candidates after 1968. In the opening years of the twenty-first century, the most prominent Polish-American political figure was Senator Barbara Mikulski (D., Md.).

Besides the older fraternal associations, the principal Polish American organizations today include the Polish American Congress, the Polish Institute of Arts and Sciences of America and the Kościuszko Foundation (both in New York City), the Polish Museum of America (Chicago), the Polish American Historical Association, the American Council for Polish Culture, the Polish American Journal (Buffalo, N.Y.), the Polish Genealogical Society of America, and St. Mary's College of Ave Maria University (Orchard Lake, Michigan). Contemporary Polish American writers include Anthony Bukoski, Stuart Dybek, Gary Gildner, Leslie Pietrzyk, and Suzanne Strempek Shea.

BIBLIOGRAPHY

Bukowczyk, John J. *And My Children Did Not Know Me: A History of the Polish Americans.* Bloomington: Indiana University Press, 1987.

Bukowczyk, John J., ed. *Polish Americans and Their History: Community, Culture, and Politics.* Pittsburgh: University of Pittsburgh Press, 1996.

Davies, Norman. *God's Playground: A History of Poland.* 2 vols. New York: Columbia University Press, 1984.

Greene, Victor. "Poles." In *Harvard Encyclopedia of American Ethnic Groups,* edited by Stephan Thernstrom. Cambridge, Mass.: Belknap Press of Harvard University Press, 1980.

Gladsky, Thomas S. *Princes, Peasants, and Other Polish Selves: Ethnicity in American Literature.* Amherst: University of Massachusetts Press, 1992.

Pula, James S. *Polish Americans: An Ethnic Community.* New York: Twayne, 1995.

Silverman, Deborah Anders. *Polish-American Folklore.* Urbana: University of Illinois Press, 2000.

John J. Bukowczyk

See also **American Federation of Labor–Congress of Industrial Organizations; Immigration Act of 1965; United Automobile Works of America; Yalta Conference.**

POLITICAL ACTION COMMITTEES, (PACs), groups that collect contributions from their members or politically like-minded citizens, represent a single interest group, and use their funds to influence the legislative and executive branches of government. PACs attempt to gain support for their interests by contributing to political campaigns, hoping their favors will be returned once candidates reach office. Because federal-level political campaigns cost so much during the late twentieth century, candidates who eschewed PAC money could not compete with those who accepted PAC donations, unless they were independently wealthy.

The origin of PACs can be traced to the American labor movement and the Congress of Industrial Organizations (CIO). The first PAC was formed during World War II, after Congress prohibited the assets of organized labor from being used for political purposes. The CIO created a separate political fund in 1943 to receive and spend voluntary contributions, calling it the Political Action Committee. A PAC called the Committee on Political Education (COPE) was formed in 1955 after the CIO merged with the American Federation of Labor. Other PACs, such as the American Medical Political Action Committee (AMPAC) and the Business-Industry Political Action Committee (BIPAC), were formed during the 1950s and 1960s, but it was not until the reform legislation of the 1970s that the number of PACs began to increase significantly.

Although labor unions formed PACs during the 1940s, corporations were not allowed to support candidates until the Federal Election Campaign Act (FECA) of 1971, which allowed corporations to use their money to set up PACs. FECA was amended in 1974 and 1976, giving trade associations and corporations a new role in politics. As a result, FECA changed its guidelines for raising political money, sparking a tremendous growth in the number of PACs and the amount of money spent to influence the political system. Even though revisions in FECA set limits on the amount of money PACs could contribute to individual candidates and political campaigns ($5,000) and set a $1,000 limit on individual contributions per candidate per election, PACs were able to get around these limitations and still influence the political system.

Observers argued for reform of the election process, insisting that PAC money should be eliminated or at least severely limited. Even when there were legal limits, individuals and groups circumvented them by giving so-called soft money to political parties instead of directly to candidates. Officially, soft money was to be used for maintaining the parties themselves, but parties managed to pass on some of the cash to candidates. Gifts of soft money tended to obligate party managers to PACs and their political goals. The existence of PACs after the 1970s ran up the tab on elections to such an extent that congressional elections routinely involved millions of dollars in campaign expenditures. By 1988 the number of PACs had increased to approximately 4,200, with $132 million in contributions, primarily to incumbents. This increase raised public criticism of PACs and led to congressional proposals to eliminate them in 1991 and 1992, but no significant action was taken.

During 1997 and 1998 some 4,600 PACs raised approximately $503 million and spent about $471 million, contributing $220 million to federal candidates, some of whom would run for election in future years. As in the past, incumbents received most of the PAC money, with Republican candidates receiving slightly more than Democratic candidates. PACs spent money to support favored candidates, but they also spent a lesser amount toward the defeat of candidates they opposed.

BIBLIOGRAPHY

Bennett, W. Lance. *The Governing Crisis: Media, Money, and Marketing in American Elections.* New York: St. Martin's Press, 1992.

Sorauf, Frank J. *Money in American Elections.* Glenview, Ill.: Scott, Foresman/Little, Brown College Division, 1988.

Stirton, Ian. "FEC Releases Information on PAC Activity for 1997–98." Federal Election Commission, U.S. Government. Available from http://www.fec.gov/press/pacye98.htm.

Wertheimer, Fred, and Susan Weiss Manes. "Campaign Finance Reform: A Key to Restoring the Health of Our Democracy." *Columbia Law Review* 94, no. 4 (May 1994): 1126–1159.

Alan Chartock / A. G.

See also **Corruption, Political; Election Laws; Elections.**

POLITICAL CARTOONS are art forms portraying government programs, policies, and personalities in humorous ways. Although occasionally used to elicit praise, political cartoons more often employ satire and parody to criticize opponents during election campaigns. Political cartoons also manipulate well-known cultural symbols to enhance the cartoon's comments about newsworthy situations. Political cartoons are the legitimate offspring of graffiti, and they retain the salacity and naughtiness of their parent. Political cartoons have become more pervasive with advances in communications technology.

The modern history of the political cartoon began in Great Britain in 1735. The passage of "Hogarth's Act" (8 George II c13) extended copyright and protection to the satires on current events reproduced by the new copper engraving plates. The works of William Hogarth (1697–1764) and other satirists on British politics and the Parliament drew immediate crowds to the bars, taverns, and coffeehouses throughout the colonial American cities of

Political Cartoon. This lithograph, published on 20 December 1890, attacks Indian agents as greedy political appointees who starved Indians into rebellion; by then, white fears about the Ghost Dance movement had peaked, Sitting Bull had just been killed, and a band of Sioux was on the run, only days away from tragedy at Wounded Knee, S.D. LIBRARY OF CONGRESS

Philadelphia, Boston, and New York. Benjamin Franklin drew and published the first political cartoon in the American colonies. In 1747, his woodcut leaflet "Plain Truth" displayed a kneeling man praying to Hercules who is sitting on a cloud. Franklin's allegory of "Heaven helps him who helps himself" told the American colonists to defend themselves against the Indians without British help. His 1754 cartoon of a snake chopped into pieces, each piece labeled with a colony's name, advised the colonies to "join or die," that is, to unite against their common foes. American folklore always asserted a cut-up snake could rejoin its parts and live. Thus, Franklin made classics, mythology, and folklore into staples of the American political cartoon.

Satirical posters, leaflets, and banners quickly became an integral part of American political life, especially during the election campaigns. Most of these early efforts remained anonymous. Exceptions included Elkanah Tilsdale's "The Gerry-mander" (1812), the infamous winged dragon shaped from Massachusetts townships grouped for electoral advantage. Edward William Clay (1799–1857) drew cartoons extolling President Andrew Jackson in his fights with the U.S. Bank. George Caleb Bingham (1811–1879) painted effective parade banners of Henry Clay for Whig Party rallies in Missouri in 1844. The Currier and Ives Company used the new lithographic print process to churn out cartoon handbills by their chief draftsman Louis Maurer (1832–1932) for any party or candidate willing to pay for them from 1835 until 1907.

Political cartoons from New York City magazines spread their candidates' messages across the nation. *Frank Leslie's Illustrated* (1855–1891) published caricatures of Abraham Lincoln by Frank Bellew (1828–1888) that became almost as famous as Harper's Weekly (1857–1916), and Thomas Nast (1840–1902) later made cartoons of local political boss Thurlow Tweed. When Tweed fled the country to avoid prosecution, Spanish police identified him from Nast's caricatures. After the Civil War, New York City humor magazines continued to lampoon political figures. *Puck* (1877–1918) supplied pro–Democratic Party cartoons by Joseph Keppler (1838–1894) while *The Judge* (1881–1939) and Bernard Gillam (1856–1896) provided the Republican Party. Created for a literate clientele, such periodicals referenced Shakespeare and the classics to a higher degree than anyone had previously done.

Political cartoons appeared in daily newspapers as early as the 1860 presidential election. Walt McDougall began routine daily front-page cartoons for William Randolph Hearst's *New York World* with the half-page "The Royal Feast of Belshazzar, Blaine, and the Money Kings" on 30 October 1884. Republican James G. Blaine lost the 1884 presidential election to Democrat Grover Cleveland because he lost New York's electoral votes. Such cartoons also supposedly enhanced circulation, but photographs and banner headlines quickly took over the front page of newspapers, moving the political cartoon to the editorial page. Many unemployed sketch artists then reinvented themselves as "editorial" cartoonists. By 1900, American newspapers employed around 500 of these new editorial cartoonists.

Editorial cartoons widened the genre's horizons by including seemingly nonpolitical cultural themes. They also turned bland because of owners' desires for profits and the establishment of the Pulitzer Prize for editorial cartoons in 1922. The Columbia University School of Journalism invariably chose inoffensive cartoons with subtle and universal messages for the Pulitzer. Until 1967, the school awarded the prize for single cartoons, resulting in three-time winners: Rollin Kirby (1875–1952) for the *New York World* and Edmund Duffy (1899–1962) for the *Baltimore Sun*. Eight others won twice. After 1967, the school conferred the Pulitzer only for a cartoonist's body of work. Gary Trudeau won in 1975 for his cartoon strip "Doonesbury," which most newspapers quickly moved to the editorial section. Cartoonists generally agreed with the Pulitzer's choices for recipients despite its methods for selecting cartoons.

Liberal-minded European American males dominated the ranks of political cartoonists from Franklin's time through the early twenty-first century. Late-twentieth-century giants indicative of this trend included Herbert Block ("Herblock") and Pat Oliphant. The historical list of women and racial minority editorial cartoonists is short. Edwina Dumm became the first regularly employed female editorial cartoonist in 1915 for the Columbus, Ohio *Daily Monitor*. In 1991, Barbara Brandon (Universal Press Syndicate) became the first black female cartoonist nationally syndicated in the mainstream press. In 1992, Signe Wilkinson of the *Philadelphia Daily News* became the first woman to win the Pulitzer. In 2002, Daryl Cagle's exhaustive Web site for editorial cartoonists listed only a dozen women out of 350 working cartoonists. Black male Oliver W. Harrington (1912–1995) drew regularly for *Amsterdam News* (New York City) in the 1930s and as an independent contributor thereafter. Michael Ramirez of the *Los Angeles Times* and Lalo Alcaraz of *L.A. Weekly* represent the growing Hispanic population. Political conservatives are equally as scarce. In 2002, only thirty-two of an estimated 350 employed editorial cartoonists regarded themselves as conservative.

In the twenty-first century, the Internet returned the genre to its visceral roots. Internet cartoonists excoriated both candidates for office and political issues in ways not seen in a century. Local party groups on the Internet and suburban newspapers distributed political cartoons by free-lance conservative cartoonists such as Jim Huber. Internet sites produced more daily political cartoons than newspapers do editorial cartoons.

BIBLIOGRAPHY

"Daryl Cagle's Professional Cartoonists Index." Available from http://cagle.slate.msn.com

Hess, Steven, and Sandy Northrop. *Drawn and Quartered: The History of American Political Cartoons.* Montgomery, Ala.: Elliott and Clark, 1996.

Press, Charles. *The Political Cartoon.* Rutherford, N.J.: Fairleigh Dickinson University Press, 1981.

Bill Olbrich

See also **Magazines; Newspapers.**

POLITICAL CORRECTNESS. Originally used by old-guard communists to mean toeing the party line, the term "politically correct" was resurrected in the 1970s and early 1980s by rightist writers and activists, who used it in an ironic sense to mock the Left's tendency toward dogmatic adherence to "progressive" behavior and speech.

The term entered general use in the late 1980s, when neoconservatives adopted "political correctness" as a disparaging name for what they believed was rigid adherence to multicultural ideals on college campuses. Allan Bloom's *The Closing of the American Mind* (1987) and Dinesh D'Souza's *Illiberal Education* (1992) became best-sellers indicting academic political correctness. They argued that academic extremists had corrupted higher education through, among other things, affirmative action in admissions, speech codes, and the substitution in the undergraduate curriculum of recent literature by women and minorities for the classics of Western civilization. Proponents of multiculturalism defended expansion of the curriculum and greater diversity within the undergraduate student body as a means of strengthening democracy. They also argued that conservatives often distorted the views of academic liberals, invented widespread oppression from isolated incidents, and used charges of political correctness to silence their opponents.

In the 1990s the use and meaning of the term continued to expand. "Politically correct" appeared on T-shirts and sports pages and in television show names, newspaper headlines, book titles, comic strips, and ordinary conversations. "P.C." became a label attached to a wide range of liberal positions, including environmentalism, feminism, and, in particular, use of inclusive, inoffensive terminology related to various groups. Rooted in dissatisfaction with university policies and fear of cultural change, charges of political correctness became a popular way to attack liberal activists and their causes.

BIBLIOGRAPHY

Berman, Paul, ed. *Debating P.C.: The Controversy Over Political Correctness on College Campuses.* New York: Dell, 1992.

Bloom, Allan. *The Closing of the American Mind: How Higher Education has Failed Democracy and Impoverished the Souls of Today's Students.* New York: Simon and Schuster, 1987.

D'Souza, Dinesh. *Illiberal Education: The Politics of Race and Sex on Campus.* New York: Vintage Books, 1992.

Levine, Lawrence W. *The Opening of the American Mind: Canons, Culture, and History.* Boston: Beacon Press, 1996.

Wilson, John K. *The Myth of Political Correctness: The Conservative Attack on Higher Education.* Durham, N.C.: Duke University Press, 1995.

Patrick Allitt / C. P.

See also **Academic Freedom; Manners and Etiquette; Multiculturalism.**

POLITICAL EXILES TO THE UNITED STATES. America has been envisioned by some as a haven for religious and political exiles since the earliest settlement attempts in what is now Florida by French Huguenots in the sixteenth century. Though these early refugee colonies did not survive, English Puritans established successful colonies in Massachusetts, while Charles I of England chartered a viable Catholic colony in Maryland. As political dissidents and others were banished in increasing numbers from the French and Spanish empires, the British colonies in North America became used as a place to relieve the pressures caused by those thought to be subversive. By the end of the seventeenth century, England actively promoted its colonies as a refuge for the oppressed of its rivals. English officials encouraged the migration to North America of Protestant settlers from France, Spain, and elsewhere by promising free land, religious freedom, naturalization, and a general regime of the "rights of Englishmen." Though such policies were clearly based on British self-interest, and were obviously contradicted by the maintenance of slavery, involuntary servitude, and other oppressive practices, the idea of British North America as a haven for the oppressed and an asylum for dissidents gradually took powerful hold.

During the Revolutionary War, many American patriots enthusiastically endorsed Thomas Paine's ringing call, in *Common Sense* (1776), to "prepare in time an asylum for mankind." The Revolutionary War, however, also revealed deep contradictions in the ideal of America as a haven for those with dissident political views. Ideological conformity became a powerful part of the emerging national character, as newly formed governments sought to exclude and banish monarchists and others whose principles were deemed too dangerous to tolerate. Quaker pacifists, for example, were interned in Virginia, while laws in Georgia prohibited the entry of Scottish immigrants, who were believed to support monarchy.

Throughout the 1790s, the tensions between a vision of America as a haven and a nation that sustained political conformity became stronger. The first Naturalization Act, passed in 1790, required immigrants to take an oath to support the Constitution. Federalists became increasingly concerned about Jacobin and "Wild Irish" ideas arriving with new immigrants, while Republicans worried about the aristocratic leaning of refugees from the successful uprising in St. Domingue led by Toussaint L'Ouverture. The Federalist-sponsored Alien and Sedition Acts of 1798, inspired by fears of French influence in U.S. affairs, constituted a decisive, though temporary, rejection of the asylum principle in favor of a desire to exclude and deport European radicals.

With the ascendance to the presidency of Thomas Jefferson in 1800, the immediate threats posed by the 1798 sedition and deportation laws passed. Jefferson, however, was ambivalent about the United States as an open country for political exiles. Indeed, in his *Notes on the State of Virginia* (1782), he had worried that immigrants from monarchies would "bring with them the principles of the governments they leave." Still, the general Republican view, as Jefferson expressed it in "A Republican Farmer" during the election campaign of 1800, was a return to the conception of the United States as a place where "every oppressed man . . . would find an asylum from tyranny." In his first Annual Message to Congress in 1801, Jefferson, supporting a restoration of more open immigration policies, asked, "shall oppressed humanity find no asylum on this globe?"

During the War of 1812, however, U.S. policies toward political exiles hardened again. Over 10,000 British aliens were forced to register with U.S. marshals. As "alien enemies," British nationals faced mandatory relocation and other restrictions. After the war, and until the late nineteenth century, America remained open to virtually all European immigrants, including many political exiles from Germany, Poland, Hungary, and Russia.

The late nineteenth century witnessed the development of harsh, race-based exclusion and deportation laws aimed at Chinese laborers and other non-European immigrants. These laws eroded the general openness that had characterized U.S. immigration law and led to ideological exclusion laws in the early twentieth century. The government began to focus increasingly on so-called "subversive" ideas such as anarchism and socialism. The 1903 Immigration Act mandated the exclusion of "anarchists, or persons who believe in or advocate the overthrow by force or violence of the Government of the United States or of all governments or of all forms of law, or the assassination of public officials." This was the first law since 1798 to bar newcomers based on their opinions. The immigration acts from 1917 up to 1952 expanded the ideological exclusions of the 1903 Act and authorized DEPORTATION for "subversive" advocacy without a time limit after entry. The so-called PALMER RAIDS, led by Attorney General A. Mitchell Palmer in 1919 through 1920, resulted in the arrest of thousands and the ultimate deportation of some 500 aliens on political grounds.

By the mid-twentieth century, the developing idea of a refugee as a person having special rights to protection began to contradict the exclusion of immigrants based on their political opinions. Ad hoc provisions for various persons and groups, however, proved inadequate to deal with the massive persecutions and displacements caused by World War II. After the war, it became clear that the problem of millions of "displaced persons" across Europe was a humanitarian crisis. The U.S. government began to take the problem of political exiles and refugees more seriously as a matter of law and policy at this time. The 1948 Displaced Persons Act authorized approximately 200,000 persons to enter the United States over a two-year period. A 1950 amendment, the "Act of June 16, 1950," permitted 400,000 more refugees to enter the United States.

The most important current protections for political exiles in the United States derive from international law. In 1951, the United Nations adopted the Convention Relating to the Status of Refugees. Article 1 of the Refugee Convention specifically defined the term "refugee" to include any person who had been considered a refugee under certain specific prior laws or who, "As a result of events occurring before 1 January 1951 and owing to well-founded fear of being persecuted for reasons of race, religion, nationality, membership in a particular social group, or political opinion, is outside of the country of his nationality and is unable to or, owing to such fear, is unwilling to avail himself of the protection of that country." The definition also protected certain persons who had no nationality or had multiple nationalities.

The Convention included provisions for civil rights for refugees in Contracting States and protections against the expulsion of refugees lawfully in their territory "save on grounds of national security or public order." Article 33 specifically prohibited the expulsion or return of a refugee in any manner whatsoever to the frontiers of territories where his life or freedom would be threatened" on account of one of the grounds listed above. Article 34 provided that the Contracting States "shall as far as possible facilitate the assimilation and naturalization of refugees." Protections under the Convention, however, were denied to persons who had committed various types of crimes, especially war crimes, or who had been "guilty of acts contrary to the purposes and principles of the United Nations."

The United States did not become a party to the Convention until 1968, when it acceded to a 1967 Protocol. Thus, through the 1950s and 1960s, U.S. actions for refugees and political exiles remained largely discretionary and ad hoc. Such measures tended to be strongly biased in favor of those fleeing Communist regimes. For example, the 1953 Refugee Relief Act authorized the admission of 200,000 refugees from Communist countries. In 1965, amendments to the 1952 Immigration and Nationality Act allocated 10,200 visas each year to refugees. However, the definition of refugee was limited to those who had fled "from any Communist or Communist-dominated country or area," from "any country within the general areas of the Middle East," or those who were "uprooted by catastrophic natural calamity." As a result, throughout the 1970s, refugee admissions to the United States were highly ideologically biased in favor of those fleeing the Soviet Union and other Communist regimes. For example, hundreds of thousands of Cubans have been admitted to the United States under so-called "parole power" and more than 500,000 Cuban immigrants have become lawful permanent residents as a result of the Cuban Adjustment Act of 1966. Over 100,000 refugees from Vietnam were admitted to the United States by special laws in the mid-1970s.

The Refugee Act of 1980 sought to regularize U.S. law relating to political exiles and refugees and to bring it into compliance with international law. It removed the ideological requirement of flight from a Communist country. The Act contains a definition of the term "refugee" that is derived from that of the 1951 United Nations Convention. By the beginning of the twenty-first century some 70,000 to 100,000 refugees were being authorized for admission per year. Since the passage of the Act, more than one million refugees have obtained permanent resident status.

Political exiles who seek to enter the United States still face a complicated, and in some respects a contradictory, legal regime. Certain ideological grounds of exclusion still exist. Thus, U.S. immigration laws still ban, among others, "any alien who . . . seeks to enter the United States to engage . . . in any activity a purpose of which is the opposition to, or the control or overthrow of, the Government of the United States by force, violence, or other unlawful means." Members of the Palestine Liberation Organization are specifically banned, as are certain immigrants who were members of a Communist "or any other Totalitarian" party. Still, U.S. asylum and refugee laws continue to protect and provide a safe harbor for thousands of political exiles every year.

BIBLIOGRAPHY

Baseler, Marilyn C. *"Asylum for Mankind": America, 1607–1800.* Ithaca, N.Y.: Cornell University Press, 1998.

Goodwin-Gill, Guy S. *The Refugee in International Law.* Oxford: Clarendon Press, 1983.

Legomsky, Stephen H. *Immigration and Refugee Law and Policy,* 3rd ed. New York: Foundation Press, 2002.

Musalo, Karen, Jennifer Moore, and Richard Boswell. *Refugee Law and Policy: Cases and Materials.* Durham, N.C.: Carolina Academic Press, 1997.

Daniel Kanstroom

See also **Alien and Sedition Laws; Aliens, Rights of; Chinese Exclusion Act; Immigration Restriction;** *and vol. 9:* **Maya in Exile: Guatemalans in Florida**

POLITICAL PARTIES, along with other political organizations (such as Political Action Committees, or PACs) have the ability to increase the political effectiveness of individuals by bringing them into an aggregate. The importance and distinctiveness of parties as political organizations spring from their domination of electoral politics. Candidates are identified solely by party affiliation on the ballots and, although many candidates in the United States now use television advertisements that omit this information, the party label is still the principal cue for the voter at the polls.

The relationship of the parties to mass electoral politics is apparent in their evolution. Originally, political parties were legislative caucuses and elite nominating organizations. They assumed their modern form with the expansion of the male suffrage in the first half of the nineteenth century, when the parties first gained broad support in the electorate and a network of constituency-based local parties. Thus, they became instruments for organizing and representing the expanding electorates. By the latter half of the century, in fact, they had become instruments by which the new masses of voters wrested control of cities from old patrician and economic elites.

Origin and Development of American Political Parties

The origin and development of the American political parties stand entirely apart from the U.S. Constitution. Nowhere in it are they mentioned or even anticipated. Throughout American history they have been instruments of the democratization of the Constitution as well as a result of that process. The parties and their system of loyalty transformed the electoral college and the entire process of electing an American president into something approaching a majoritarian decision.

Scholars have identified five party systems that arose out of what political scientist V. O. Key called "critical elections," or periods of political realignment. Political participation rose suddenly, after a decline, and key components of a national coalition rearranged themselves. For example, the realignment of 1896 ushered in a generation of Republican dominance of politics in all areas except the South. Newly arrived immigrants affiliated for the first time with the GOP ("Grand Old Party," as the Republican Party is known), because the Republicans addressed themselves to the interests of urban workers by sponsoring protectionism. The Democrats, under William Jennings Bryan, addressed themselves to agrarian issues at the expense of urban interests.

The first party system, of Federalists and Democratic Republicans, took on the character of a mass-based party system after the election of 1800 which featured a dramatic rise in turnout that eventually included the majority of adult white males in most states. This "Revolution of 1800," as well as the first party system collapsed in the 1820s; the Jacksonian, or second party system, followed the critical election of 1828, with two parties that were competitive in every state of the Union, the Whigs and the Democrats. The third party system followed the 1860 election and continued for a generation after the Civil War. In this period, Democrats and Republicans achieved the highest rates of turnout ever recorded in American elections. This party system was driven by deep sectional, religious, ethnic, and racial antagonism. The election of 1896 promoted Republican dominance of American politics until 1932. With the exception of the Wilson years in the White House (1913–1921), the Democrats spent most of this time deeply divided between the agrarian and the urban wings of the party. The fifth party system, following the election of Franklin D. Roosevelt in 1932, was the model by which Key developed his notion of critical elections. Republicans and Democrats, while retaining some of their sectional and religious differences, primarily appealed to different voters on the basis of their socioeconomic classes rather than their regional or religious backgrounds. Thus for the first time, African Americans, who had always voted for the party of Lincoln, now found their economic interests better addressed by the New Deal Democrats and they altered their party loyalties accordingly. The fifth party system endured until the 1960s, when the Democratic coalition, forged in the New Deal, of labor, immigrants, small farmers, Catholics, Jews, African Americans, and white southerners began to break down. In the chaotic politics of the 1960s, southern whites, Catholics, and labor felt increasingly alienated from what they saw as the "cultural" politics of the 1970s: inclusive politics emphasizing the interests of women, African Americans, and Latinos. During this period, these groups became a swing coalition altering their partisan preferences from election to election, becoming Democrats for Nixon, Democrats for Carter, Reagan Democrats, and Clinton Democrats. The result of this large swing component in the electorate has been what some political scientists call "de-alignment," or the detachment of voter identification from consistent party loyalty.

American parties are also marked by a distinctive, three-part character that sets them apart from other political organizations. They are composed of an identifiable set of committees and activists (the party organization), a group of public officeholders and would-be officeholders (the party in the government), and a large contingent of loyalists who consider themselves to be members of the party (the party in the electorate). Ordinary usage recognizes any of the three sectors as the party, and, as in parties elsewhere, American party organizations and parties in government have contested for supremacy in the party and for control of its symbols and decisions. It is peculiar to the American party system that party organizations have rarely subjected the party's officeholders to even the mildest forms of direction or sanctions.

Special Characteristics of American Parties

While the development of American parties was similar to that of parties in other Western democracies and for most of the same reasons, the American party system has always had special characteristics. In form it has long been marked by considerable decentralization, by nonbureaucratic, skeletal organizations, and by the persistence of only two competitive parties. That is to say, the American parties have always been loose confederations of state and local party organizations. Never have they developed the strong national executives or committees that parties elsewhere have. Nor have they developed the membership organizations common in the twentieth century in other countries. Largely without formal memberships or career bureaucracies, they have been staffed at most levels—except perhaps within the classic urban machine—by only a few party functionaries investing only limited time and energy in the business of the party. Along with the British parties and few others, the American parties have remained two in number. The parliamentary systems in English-speaking democracies have opted for a first-past-the-post system of elections, except in Ireland. This kind of system creates strong incentives for a two-party system to maximize the vote.

Related to these formal organizational characteristics has been the parties' chief functional trait: the pragmatic, almost issueless majoritarianism through which they piece together electoral majorities through strategies of compromise and accommodation. They have been much less involved in the business of doctrine or ideology than similar parties elsewhere. Platforms have revealed only modest differences between the two parties. Periodically one finds movements and candidates within the parties who have been intensely programmatic, but, until the presidency of Ronald Reagan, their records of success, even when they have captured their party's presidential nominations, have not been good.

The American parties have found their major role as nominators and electors of candidates for public office. They waxed in the nineteenth century in their ability to confer the party label on candidates, first in party caucuses and then in the more widely consultative conventions that Jacksonian Democracy favored. Especially during the prevailing one-partyism of so much of American politics at the end of the nineteenth century, the excesses of party power in those nominations led to the advent of the direct primary in the years between 1900 and World War I. By the 1970s, party control of nominations was limited to some degree by primary laws in every state. In several states, to be sure, the primary law left some nominations to party conventions; in others in which it did not, the parties devised ways (especially in preprimary endorsements) of affecting the primary-election outcomes. The quadrennial national conventions at which the parties choose their presidential candidates remain an important but increasingly vestigial remnant of the party's once unchallenged control of nominations.

Control of nominations has shifted away from the party organization to the party in government; the same is true of the control of election campaigns. The vigorous political organizations of the late nineteenth century and early twentieth century controlled, even monopolized, the major election resources. Its army of workers publicized the candidates, raised their own campaign funds, and recruited their own workers. And they have been able to find sources of campaign experience other than the party organization—the opinion pollsters, the political public relations firms, the mass media. Just as the primary ended the party organization's monopoly of nominations, the rise of the new campaign expertise threatens its control of the election campaign.

Nonetheless, most American officeholders reach office on the ticket of one of the major American parties. American presidents and governors are party leaders, and in the early part of the twentieth century all state legislatures (except the nonpartisan legislature of Nebraska) were organized along party lines. Beginning in the 1990s, moreover, Congress and, to a lesser extent, the state legislatures began to adopt a more assertive form of partisanship. Beginning with the Republican Party's Contract with America in the 1990s, the House and Senate leadership put into effect an ideologically oriented public policy. In the Contract with America, in budget negotiations with the White House, and with the impeachment of President Bill Clinton, "party votes" roll calls—in which the majority of one party opposed a majority of the other—began to increase, after a decline that had lasted for almost all of the twentieth century.

American presidents, on the other hand, have found it necessary to be less partisan than their congressional colleagues. Building majority support for a president's program, to be successful, has in recent years required votes from the opposition party. Ronald Reagan achieved his legislative successes with the help of the Boll Weevils, the conservative Democrats from the Deep South and Texas who supported his tax-cutting policy. Bill Clinton relied on moderate Republicans not only for assistance in getting his budget bills passed, but also for his very survival in the Senate trial after his impeachment. Despite the president's less partisan approach, it is the president's record that most reflects on the party. The power of the political party has been joined to the power of the presidency. As coalitions led by the executive, American parties find their governing role conditioned above all by the American separation of powers. That role contrasts sharply with the role of the cohesive parties that support cabinets in the parliaments of most other Western democracies.

BIBLIOGRAPHY

Broder, David. *The Party's Over: The Failure of Politics in America.* New York: Harper, 1972.

Chambers, William Nisbet, and Walter Dean Burnham. *American Party Systems: Stages of Political Development.* New York: Oxford University Press, 1975.

Formisano, Ronald P. *The Birth of Mass Political Parties: Michigan, 1827–1861.* Princeton: Princeton University Press, 1971.

Key, V. O. *Politics, Parties, and Pressure Groups.* 5th ed. New York: Crowell, 1965.

Ladd, Everett Carl. American Political Parties: Social Change and Political Response. New York: Norton, 1970.

Sorauf, Frank J. *Political Parties in the American System.* Boston: Little, Brown, 1964.

Shafer, Byron E. *The End of Realignment?: Interpreting American Electoral Eras.* Madison: University of Wisconsin Press, 1991.

Andrew W. Robertson

See also **Caucus; Convention of 1800; Conventions, Party Nominating; Primary, Direct; Platform, Party; Two-Party System.**

POLITICAL SCANDALS. Scandals are events committed by particular individuals that create public concern, indignation, and outrage. While misbehavior by movie stars or rock stars produces little public outcry, political leaders are a different matter. Historical context complicates the situation. Public norms change. What is happening in the nation can influence the impact of a political scandal and its consequences. Since scandal means a damaged reputation or even imprisonment in extreme cases, public officials suppress or manipulate information given to the media and employ spokespeople who try to spin the issue out of existence. But cable television news programs and tabloids are eager to feed the public's hunger for bad news, and scandals do happen. At best Americans are ambivalent about government. Many Americans distrust government since it is the most powerful institution in the society; hence the potential for scandal is great. History gives us several examples.

Sources of Scandals

Although the political culture changes, two sources of scandal are constant. First, government at all levels has vast resources, from taxing power to franchises, endless contracts, and material resources. Many officials have discretionary power over their use and distribution. The use of political office for personal financial gain was impressive in the nineteenth century—from land schemes to the Crédit Mobilier, from corrupt federal agents in places such as the Bureau of Indian Affairs to the post office Star Route scandals in the Gilded Age.

Preferential treatment is a staple element in political scandals. In the 1950s the Federal Communication Commission improperly awarded television licenses on the basis of personal friendship. Money has often been the means of gaining political influence, and in the twentieth century campaign funds were the preferred method of influence rather than the kind of straight cash payments that forced Vice President Spiro T. Agnew to resign in 1973.

Sex is another contributor to political scandal. It has been used for material gain or to get preferential treatment, but more often sexual misconduct has allowed a politician's opponents to take the high moral ground. From Alexander Hamilton's confession of his affair with Maria Reynolds during George Washington's administration to Congressman Gary Condit's liaison with a legislative intern at the turn of the twenty-first century, the political consequences have varied but the incidents are interesting. Andrew Jackson's marriage to Rachel before her divorce was final and the ostracizing of Peggy Eaton during the Jackson administration, which eventually led to Vice President John Calhoun's resignation, were nineteenth-century examples. Grover Cleveland and Warren G. Harding were both accused of fathering illegitimate children. With the rise of feminism, sexual harassment became a feature of scandal, as Senator Robert Packwood discovered in the 1990s. Women were not hesitant about revealing their roles in sexual scandals while they "worked" for political and financial leverage. Paula Jones and Monica Lewinsky used their positions effectively regarding William Jefferson Clinton. All of these events have their moments in politics with advantages and disadvantages gained and lost, seriously damaging the fabric of governance.

Reform

In the early twentieth century progressive legislation regarding the direct election of United States senators, closer regulation of campaign expenditures and their use, and the general idealism of domestic reform all contributed to the hope of clean government guided by men of integrity. For some Americans, the United States' entry into World War I suggested a new beginning for a virtuous domestic society and a moral world order, but the hope was not realized. President Warren Harding's appointment of his friends and supporters, the Ohio Gang, to his cabinet led to several scandals, the largest being the Teapot Dome scandal, when Harding's secretary of the interior made a fortune off of government oil contracts. The scandals spawned only modest reforms, and the political fallout for the Republicans was minor, since they retained the presidency until the Great Depression gave Franklin Roosevelt victory in 1932. No major scandal touched Roosevelt's New Deal. During World War II, Harry Truman's senate committee investigating war contracts was generally successful in keeping scandal to a minimum.

The influence-peddling incidents in the Truman and Eisenhower White House were minor. The probe into influence peddling by the congressional aide Bobby Baker did not touch President Lyndon Johnson. The Watergate affair was different, and its consequences shaped politics and the public's perception of government for the remainder of the century and into the future.

Significance of Watergate

Watergate had unique repercussions in that Richard Nixon resigned as president, and its scope was extensive, including criminal behavior, cover-up, illegal political contributions, and the compromising of the FBI. Eventually the many investigations involved all three branches of the federal government and television covered it all. Television was present at the Alger Hiss case and the Army-McCarthy hearings, but those situations were issues of national security. Joseph McCarthy's methods provided the scandal in that case.

The historical significance of Watergate was how it became the "model" for future revelations of misdeeds. Every circumstance would have a "gate" attached to it, and everyone wanted to be in the spotlight investigating or defending. All investigations would become political grist for the mills of partisanship, and it was all on television. The tragic result was a rise in public cynicism as people guilty of serious crimes eventually went unpunished.

The Iran-Contra affair involved many misdeeds: misuse of federal funds, corruption of the CIA, direct violation of the law and a congressional resolution, the wanton destruction of government documents, and a systematic cover-up from President Reagan to other members of the administration. The illegal selling of arms to Iran to underwrite the Reagan administration's subversion of the Nicaraguan government on behalf of the Contra rebels was at least as big a scandal as Watergate. Oliver North and John Poindexter never went to prison because their limited testimony before Congress prevented their being charged with criminal behavior, as Lawrence Walsh, the independent counsel, warned at the time. The important point for all concerned was that the spectacle was on television.

Scandals and rumors of scandals marked the Clinton presidency. Clinton served the same function for conservatives as Richard Nixon did for liberals. The essence of Whitewater, a land deal in which Bill and Hilary Clinton took part fifteen years before he became president, was a synthetic event that existed in the minds of their political enemies. To be sure, the Clinton administration provided much material for scandal—the behavior of cabinet members, personnel issues in the White House, the suicide of Vince Foster, and so on. The conviction of Clinton's business associates in the savings and loan scandals did not help the president's image. The wildest of rumors and charges whirled through the Internet as political forces used scandal rather than ideology in an attempted discrediting of the Clinton era. Congressional scandals also abounded in that era. The scandals leading to Representatives James Wright's and Newt Gingrich's loss of power and position had a major impact on the political makeup of Congress in the last part of the twentieth century.

BIBLIOGRAPHY

Kutler, Stanley I. *The Wars of Watergate: The Last Crisis of Richard Nixon.* New York: Knopf, 1990. A detailed, first-rate analysis.

Markovits, Andrei S., and Mark Silverstein, eds. *The Politics of Scandal: Power and Process in Liberal Democracies.* New York: Holmes and Meier, 1988.

Thompson, Dennis F. *Ethics in Congress: From Individual to Institutional Corruption.* Washington, D.C.: Brookings Institution, 1995. Effectively explores the context of congressional misdeeds.

Uslaner, Eric M. *The Decline of Comity in Congress.* Ann Arbor: University of Michigan Press, 1993. A good account of a major consequence of the post-Watergate years.

Walsh, Lawrence E. *Firewall: The Iran-Contra Conspiracy and Cover-Up.* New York: Norton, 1997. An inside account of the scandal.

Williams, Robert. *Political Scandals in the USA.* Edinburgh: Keele University Press, 1998. A brief and insightful history of Watergate and later scandals.

Donald K. Pickens

See also **Abscam Scandal; Baker, Bobby, Case; Clinton Scandals; Corruption, Political; Iran-Contra Affair; Teapot Dome Oil Scandal; Watergate;** *and vol. 9:* **Nixon's Watergate Investigation Address.**

POLITICAL SCIENCE. In 1968, the eminent political scientist David Easton wrote: "Political Science in mid-twentieth century is a discipline in search of its identity. Through the efforts to solve this identity crisis it has begun to show evidence of emerging as an autonomous and independent discipline with a systematic structure of its own." However, the search for identity has been characteristic of political science from its inception on the American scene. Initially, the discipline was confronted with the task of demarcating its intellectual boundaries and severing its organizational ties from other academic fields, particularly history. Subsequently, debate arose over goals, methods, and appropriate subject matter as political scientists tried to resolve the often conflicting objectives of its four main scholarly traditions: (1) legalism, or constitutionalism; (2) activism and reform; (3) philosophy, or the history of political ideas; and (4) science. By the late twentieth century, the discipline had evolved through four periods outlined by Albert Somit and Joseph Tanenhaus in their informative work *The Development of American Political Science: From Burgess to Behavioralism* (1967). The four periods are the formative (1880–1903), the emergent (1903–1921), the middle years (1921–1945), and disciplinary maturity (1945–1990).

The Formative Period, 1880–1903

Before 1880, the teaching of political science was almost nonexistent. Francis Lieber, generally considered the first American political scientist, held a chair of history and political economy at South Carolina College (being the second incumbent) in 1835–1856. In 1858, he became professor of political science at Columbia College. Johns Hopkins University inaugurated the study of history and politics in 1876; but not until 1880, when John W. Burgess established the School of Political Science at Columbia University, did political science achieve an independent status with an explicit set of goals for learning, teaching, and research. Burgess, like Lieber, had been trained in Germany and sought to implement the rigor of his graduate training and the advances of German Staatswissenschaft ("political science") in the United States. Under his leadership, the Columbia school became the formative institution of the discipline, emphasizing graduate education that drew on an undifferentiated mix of politi-

Francis Lieber. Nineteenth-century educator, editor (of the first *Encyclopaedia Americana*), prolific author, and theorist: the German-trained father of political science in the United States. LIBRARY OF CONGRESS

cal science, history, economics, geography, and sociology to develop theories.

The discipline grew rapidly in the formative years 1880–1903. Burgess, Theodore Woolsey, Woodrow Wilson, Frank J. Goodnow, and Herbert Baxter Adams brought fame and direction to the field with their pioneering works. Columbia began publication of the *Political Science Quarterly* in 1886; Johns Hopkins published the *Johns Hopkins Studies in Historical and Political Science* (1882). New departments were formed and the first American Ph.D.s were awarded.

As with any new discipline, a lively debate ensued about the intellectual boundaries of political science, particularly as those boundaries related to history. There were those who envisioned the distinction in the words of Edward A. Freeman: "History is past politics and politics present history." Others eschewed the connection with history, arguing that law, economics, and sociology were more relevant to the discipline. Methods of study were also debated. Early advocates of a scientific approach argued with scholars who contended that the subject matter did not lend itself to the methods of the natural sciences. During this period, political scientists combined a strict research orientation with willingness to take an active part in public affairs. They dealt with current political issues in their scholarship, and took on the function of educating college students for citizenship and public affairs.

The Emergent Period, 1903–1921

With the establishment of the American Political Science Association (APSA) in 1903, political science asserted its independence as a discipline. More important, the formation of an association provided a vehicle through which to pursue recognized common interests effectively. Annual conventions fostered a lively exchange of ideas and continued organizational development. In 1906, the association launched the *American Political Science Review*, which soon became the leading professional journal in the discipline, containing notes about personnel in the profession as well as scholarly articles; in 1912, it had 287 subscribers, and by 1932, it had 580.

Growth continued at a rapid pace throughout the period. The association's membership rose from 200 to 1,500. In a canvass of university programs prior to 1914, it was determined that 38 institutions had separate political science departments and that an additional 225 had departments that combined political science with other disciplines, most frequently with history or history and economics. It is estimated that the annual output of Ph.D.s rose from between six and ten to between eighteen and twenty. The increase in domestically trained Ph.D.s Americanized the profession, whereas previously the majority of new professionals had earned their degrees at German and French institutions. Concomitantly, undergraduate instruction came to focus more on American government and less on comparative and European government and politics. Original research and reviews in the journals emphasized American materials.

While taking steps toward securing their discipline, political scientists were not reflective respecting the intellectual content of their field. Political scientists mostly studied political structures and processes using available official sources and records; their analyses were routine descriptions. The forward-looking and iconoclastic Arthur F. Bentley complained in his *Process of Government* (1908; p. 162) that "We have a dead political science." He, along with Henry Jones Ford and Jesse Macy, agitated for an empirical study of contemporary political events instead of mere perusal of dry historical documents.

The Middle Years, 1921–1945

The intellectual complacency of the second era was interrupted in 1921 with the publication of Charles E. Merriam's "The Present State of the Study of Politics" in the *American Political Science Review*. Impressed with statistics and the rigor of psychology, Merriam called for "a new science of politics" characterized by the formulation of testable hypotheses (provable by means of precise evidence) to complement the dominant historical-comparative and legalistic approaches. The discipline, according to Thomas Reid, should become more "policy-oriented." Merriam was joined in his effort by William B.

Munro and G. E. G. Catlin—the three being considered the era's leading proponents of the "new science" movement. Merriam's work led to the formation of the APSA's Committee on Political Research, and to three national conferences on the science of politics. With Wesley C. Mitchell, Merriam was instrumental in creating the Social Science Research Council in 1923.

William Yandell Elliott, Edward S. Corwin, and Charles A. Beard, all opponents of "scientism," quickly moved to challenge its advocates. They questioned the existence of rigorous determinist laws and the possibility of scientific objectivity in the study of politics. They were concerned with the propriety of the participation of "scientists" in citizenship education and public affairs, endeavors that made objectivity difficult. The "scientists" responded by urging, in principle, that research become more important than civic education. However, the Great Depression and World War II made it difficult to contest the significance of civic responsibility. Thus, when the APSA president William Anderson pronounced in 1943 that the preservation of democracy and "direct service to government" were the foremost obligations of political science, he was representing the prevailing view of American political scientists.

The discipline continued to grow. The APSA doubled its membership. The number of Ph.D.s awarded annually increased from thirty-five in 1925 to eighty in 1940; the number of universities granting degrees expanded. On the basis of efforts made in 1925 and 1934 to rate the quality of the various departments, California, Chicago, Columbia, Harvard, Illinois, Michigan, Princeton, and Wisconsin ranked as the leaders.

Disciplinary Maturity, 1945–1990

The postwar world stage changed the priorities for the nation. The stark realities of the military and ideological struggle of American capitalism and democracy versus Soviet communism shaped the environment in which political scientists worked. Political science retained its fascination with American democracy and continued to be characterized by disciplinary disunity, which gave it strength through diversity and debate. Four major developments are evident during the Cold War period. Most obvious is the steadily increasing emphasis on mathematical models, making it difficult for nonspecialists to read political science journals by the late twentieth century. Second is the development of the "behaviorist" method in the 1950s and 1960s. Third is behaviorism's eclipse by "positive political theory" in the 1970s and 1980s. Fourth is the development of the field of comparative politics and area studies. Gradual evolution is evident in the subfields structuring the discipline, with "political philosophy and psychology," "government of the U.S. and dependencies," "American state and local government," "foreign and comparative government," "international organization, politics, and law," and "U.S. public administration," shaping political science in 1950; and with "political theory," "American government," "comparative politics," "international relations," and "public policy" shaping it in 1990. An increased interest in issues of gender and race relations added ethnic studies and the feminist perspective into professional studies and undergraduate curricula.

The development of political science between 1945 and the late 1960s was dramatic, although this growth subsequently leveled off. The APSA more than tripled in size as a membership of 4,000 in 1946 grew to 14,000 in 1966; in 1974 the APSA had 12,250 members, in 1990 it had 10,975 members, and by 2002 it had 13,715. More than 500 independent political science departments were in existence; all major U.S. universities had developed competitive political science programs. By the mid-1970s, more than 300 Ph.D.s were awarded annually over seventy-five departments offering doctoral programs. There were at least twelve major professional journals. The careers of Henry A. Kissinger (secretary of state in 1973–1977) and Joseph S. Nye Jr. (deputy undersecretary of state, 1977–1979, and later dean of Harvard's Kennedy School of Government) demonstrate that a career as a political scientist could serve as a vehicle for prominent public office, and vice versa.

Behaviorism

Behaviorism is best viewed as a broad-based effort to impose standards of scientific rigor, relying on empirical evidence, on theory building, in contrast to the legalistic case-study approach in vogue in the 1940s and 1950s. Harold Lasswell, Gabriel Almond, David Truman, Robert Dahl, Herbert Simon, and David Easton, the movement's leading figures, each contributed his unique view of how this goal could be achieved. *The Political System* (1953) by Easton and *Political Behavior* (1956) by Heinz Eulau and others exemplified the movement's new approach to a theory-guided empirical science of politics. Data gathered from public-opinion polls, initiated in 1935, and from social surveys were central to the movement. In 1946, the University of Michigan established a leading research program, the Survey Research Center, which undertook field studies of voting behavior and amassed data. It also created in 1962 the Inter-University Consortium for Political and Social Research (ICPSR), which was designed to share precious data among its twenty-one-member community. By the 1980s, this consortium incorporated more than 270 colleges and universities, both in the United States and abroad. Statistics, as presented to political scientists in V. O. Key Jr.'s *A Primer of Statistics for Political Scientists* (1954), became an indispensable tool for analysis. Quantitative analysis became integral to graduate curriculum in political science, over time replacing the long-standing requirement of knowledge of two foreign languages.

The behavioral movement was informed by the logical positivist philosophy of Karl R. Popper, Hans Reichenbach, and Bertrand Russell, who emphasized cumulative scientific knowledge based on empirical testing of

Hannah Arendt. One of the European émigrés who reshaped political theory after World War II; she is perhaps best known for *Origins of Totalitarianism* (1951) and her concept of "the banality of evil" as applied to Nazi war crimes. © BETTMANN/CORBIS

hypotheses. Although the method still exists in political science, it dissipated as a distinct intellectual movement in the early 1970s as Thomas Kuhn's *Structure of Scientific Revolutions* (1962) signaled a defeat for logical positivism by questioning its assumption of cumulative, fact-based scientific knowledge. As well, the social unrest over the war in Vietnam raised consciousness among political scientists that behaviorism could be perceived as amoral and irrelevant to the normative concerns governing human lives.

Positive Political Theory

From their initial enunciation in the 1950s, behaviorism and positive political theory, or rational choice theory, as it is also referred to, shared practitioners and research goals. Both drew strength from broad interdisciplinary support, which ranged throughout the social sciences for behavioralism and was found in economics, psychology, sociology, philosophy, mathematics, and public policy, as well as in political science, in the case of rational choice theory. Both emphasized general theory based on empirical tests. However, the two movements deviated in their precise method: behaviorism used data concerning human behavior to build and test theory; rational choice theory made deductive models of human interactions based on the assumption that individuals are self-interested rational actors.

Positive political theory was pioneered by William H. Riker, who built the powerful political science department at the University of Rochester and served as its chair from 1963 to 1977. Riker was not alone in his initiative to formulate a science of politics based on deductive models of rational self-interested action subject to empirical tests. He built his theory using John von Neumann and Oskar Morgenstern's game theory, Duncan Black and Kenneth J. Arrow's mathematical analyses of voting, and Anthony Downs's economic theory of democracy. He also benefited from the work of other early advocates of the rational choice approach—Vincent Ostrom, James M. Buchanan, Gordon Tullock, and Mancur Olson, who together formed the Public Choice Society in 1967 and immediately thereafter established the journal *Public Choice.* These scholars turned the conventional study of politics upside down by considering politicians to be self-interested actors seeking to win office as opposed to officials serving the public. From its humble origins, rational choice theory became established as a disciplinary standard not just across the United States, but also worldwide by 1990. By 1987, 35 percent of the articles published in the *American Political Science Review* adopted the rational choice approach. The method's stellar success was due to its attraction of adherents, its interdisciplinary dynamism, its promise to deliver scientific results, its overlapping boundaries with the public policy, and its assumption of individualism shared with American philosophy of capitalist democracy.

Area Studies

While both behaviorism and positive political theory exemplify the commitment to scientific rigor hoped for by Charles Merriam, the Cold War development of area studies had a less direct relationship to its predecessors. Prior to World War II, Americans had been inwardly focused; during this earlier era, "comparative politics" signified contrasting European parliamentary-style democracy with the American presidential model. However, with the rise of Adolf Hitler's Germany and Joseph Stalin's Soviet Union in the 1930s and 1940s, it became evident that democracy needed to be assessed in comparison to fascism and totalitarianism. As the world broke into the two camps of Eastern communism and Western democracy in the 1950s and 1960s, and American political leaders required detailed knowledge of Eastern bloc nations and of Southeast Asia, political science departments and specialized institutes responded to this need. These undertakings were generously funded by the National Defense Education Act (NDEA); from 1958 to 1973 the NDEA Title IV provided $68.5 million to the approximately 100 language and area centers. By 1973, these centers had produced 35,500 B.A.s, 14,700 M.A.s, and over 5,000 Ph.D.s.

Area studies focused on questions of modernization and industrialization and strove to understand the differing developmental logic of non-Western cultures; they embraced diverse methods for understanding native languages and native cultures and remained skeptical of approaches to comparative politics adopting universalizing assumptions. Lucian W. Pye, Robert E. Ward, and Samuel P. Huntington championed the approach, with Huntington's *Clash of Civilizations* (1996) epitomizing the perspective afforded by the field.

Political Theory

During the Cold War period, the study of political theory continued to include the great books of Plato, Aristotle, Machiavelli, Thomas Hobbes, John Locke, and Karl Marx, but it was reshaped by the influx of European émigrés. Leo Strauss, Herbert Marcuse, Hannah Arendt, and Theodore Adorno stirred the imagination of American theorists through their perspectives developed under the duress of the Nazi occupation of much of Europe. Political theory, with its emphasis on timeless works and its input from European theorists, became international in scope during the Cold War period. Thus, European scholars such as Jürgen Habermas and J. G. A. Pocock were as germane to scholarly discussions as were the American theorists John Rawls and Robert Nozick. Emigrant scholars published in *Social Research*, and newfound interest in political theory among indigenous scholars was reflected in the more recently established journals *Philosophy and Public Affairs* (1971) and *Political Theory* (1973). Whereas much American political science saw the world from the perspective of the United States, political theory retained a critical edge: it was skeptical of social science methods boasting of objectivity, and of what might be regarded as a collusion between American political science and American democracy and capitalism.

General Political Science

Independently from well-defined movements, the mainstay of political science, American political institutions, political behavior, comparative politics, and international relations were pursued throughout this period by numerous methods. For example, a 1987 study found that the 262 political scientists contributing to legislative research adopted the following approaches in significant proportions: behavioral analysis; case studies; "new institutionalist"; organizational theory; historiography; positive political theory; democratic theory; and other approaches, including policy studies. Not necessarily representing a single school, prominent political scientists central to the field included Richard F. Fenno Jr., Nelson Polsby, Warren E. Miller, Harold Guetzkow, Donald R. Mathews, Samuel J. Eldersveld, Dwaine Marvick, Philip E. Converse, Donald E. Stokes, and Joseph LaPalombara.

Since 1990

In the 1990s, disciplinary divisions existed over the efficacy and merits of the rational choice approach to politics, with many American political science departments divided into camps for and against. In leading centers for rational choice, including Rochester, Carnegie Mellon, California Institute of Technology, and George Washington, as many as half of the faculty adopted this method of study. Disciplinary controversy culminated in the publication of Donald P. Green and Ian Shapiro's *Pathologies of Rational Choice Theory* (1994), and the responding issue of *Critical Review* (winter-spring 1995). Whereas the future of this disciplinary strife remains unclear, it is clear that the rational choice theory has an ascendant position across the social sciences and in the spheres of business, law, and public policy.

American political science continues to question its identity, and to reflect on appropriate research methodology; methodological pluralism continues to reign. The field's continued self-examination reflects three independent axes. One embodies the two extremes of particular and localized studies versus universalizing analyses; a second is defined by the extremes of considering either groups or individuals as the key to analysis; and a third is represented by the belief that a normative stance is unavoidable at one extreme, and by a firm commitment to the possibility of objectivity at the other extreme. In the midst of the numerous topics and methods structuring political science, one certainty is that it is no longer possible for a single individual to master the entire field.

BIBLIOGRAPHY

Almond, Gabriel A. *A Discipline Divided: Schools and Sects in Political Science.* Newbury Park, Calif.: Sage Publications, 1990.

Amadae, S. M., and Bruce Bueno de Mesquita. "The Rochester School: The Origins of Positive Political Theory." *Annual Review of Political Science* 2 (1999): 269–295.

Collini, Stefan, Donald Winch, and John Burrow. *That Noble Science of Politics: A Study in Nineteenth-Century Intellectual History.* Cambridge, U.K.: Cambridge University Press, 1983.

Crick, Bernard. *The American Science of Politics: Its Origins and Conditions.* Berkeley: University of California Press, 1959.

Crotty, William, ed. *Political Science: Looking to the Future.* 4 vols. Evanston, Ill.: Northwestern University Press, 1991.

Farr, James, and Raymond Seidelman, eds. *Discipline and History: Political Science in the United States.* Ann Arbor: University of Michigan Press, 1993.

Finifter, Ada W. *Political Science: The State of the Discipline.* Washington, D.C.: American Political Science Association, 1983.

———. *Political Science: The State of the Discipline II.* Washington, D.C.: American Political Science Association, 1993.

Pye, Lucian W., ed. *Political Science and Area Studies: Rivals or Partners?* Bloomington: Indiana University Press, 1975.

Ricci, David. *The Tragedy of Political Science: Politics, Scholarship, and Democracy.* New Haven, Conn.: Yale University Press, 1984.

Seidelman, Raymond, and Edward J. Harpham. *Disenchanted Realists: Political Science and the American Crisis, 1884–1984.* Albany: State University of New York Press, 1985.

Somit, Albert, and Joseph Tanenhaus. *The Development of American Political Science: From Burgess to Behavioralism.* Enlarged ed. New York: Irvington Publishers, 1982.

S. M. Amadae

See also **Behaviorism; Economics; Philosophy; Political Theory; Statistics.**

POLITICAL SUBDIVISIONS are local governments created by the states to help fulfill their obligations. Political subdivisions include counties, cities, towns, villages, and special districts such as school districts, water districts, park districts, and airport districts. In the late 1990s, there were almost 90,000 political subdivisions in the United States.

American colonists brought the tradition of counties with them from England and kept them for administrative purposes after the Revolution. Only Connecticut and Rhode Island do not having working county governments. Typically, the whole territory of a state is covered by counties, which perform a range of governmental functions such as tax collection, highway construction, and law enforcement. There are about 3,000 counties in the United States.

Unlike counties, which are involuntary, cities, towns, and villages are formed by their residents, usually based on common interests. In the seventeenth and eighteenth centuries, clusters of people established cities for protection and for commercial, political, and religious infrastructure. In the nineteenth century, cities became convenient mechanisms for the delivery of public services such as water and garbage collection.

Incorporation can serve other purposes as well. People create new cities to inflate land values—common in the frontier West—dodge taxes, or exclude unwanted inhabitants. For example, when church groups planned to build public housing in the unincorporated area of Black Jack, Missouri, in 1969, residents petitioned to become a city and promptly zoned out apartment buildings.

State governments establish the procedures and requirements for requesting city charters, such as dictating a minimum population. They also determine which functions city governments can perform. Beginning in the late nineteenth century, cities won HOME RULE from the states, which gave them considerably more authority over their own affairs. But, while modern cities provide services, ranging from police protection and recycling, to elevator inspection, they nevertheless remain divisions of the state and operate under state law.

Like cities, special districts are voluntary. They usually provide the services that a city or county might offer. While one city might run its own fire, water, and parks departments, another might get those services from three separate special districts. They enjoy many of the powers given to cities, including eminent domain and the authority to tax, but they are comparatively free of bureaucracy and, therefore, much easier to create and control. They are also less accountable to the public; turnout in district elections tends to be extremely low. Because special districts can operate with less visibility, some have been made to serve private interests. For example, Walt Disney World Resort in Orlando, Florida, is also the Reedy Creek Improvement District. Walt Disney influenced the creation of the special district in 1967 to prevent surrounding localities from interfering with the construction of his theme park.

Special districts first became popular during the New Deal, when local governments on the verge of default used them to circumvent debt limits. The number of special districts has more than doubled since then, reaching almost 50,000 by the late 1990s.

BIBLIOGRAPHY

Berman, David R. *County Governments in an Era of Change.* Westport, Conn.: Greenwood Press, 1993.

———. *State and Local Politics.* Armonk, N.Y.: M. E. Sharpe, 2000.

Burns, Nancy. *The Formation of American Local Governments: Private Values in Public Institutions.* New York: Oxford University Press, 1994.

Jeremy Derfner

See also **Local Government.**

POLITICAL THEORY. The term "political theory" is used in both narrow and broad senses, but the two are not easily separated. In the narrowest sense, it refers to that branch of the academic discipline of "political science" that concerns itself with the theoretical analysis of political institutions and practices. This analysis generally relies upon the normative use of certain abstract concepts believed to be central both to the understanding of political behavior and to the formulation of sound public policy—concepts such as liberty, rights, citizenship, sovereignty, legitimacy, justice, representation, the state, federalism, equality, constitutionalism, and law. But even when one starts within this relatively narrow understanding, "political theory" ends up sprawling out over an enormous amount of territory, running the gamut from the broadly philosophical works of Plato, Aristotle, Locke, Rousseau, and Rawls, which treat political theory as one element in a comprehensive inquiry into the nature of the human person, to a more narrowly gauged technical professional literature, grounded in the careful empirical and historical analysis of existing societies, and directed toward the solution of specific problems.

In its broader sense, then, "political theory" can refer to any serious and systematic reflections upon the political aspects of human existence, particularly when such reflections are pitched at a sufficiently high level of abstraction to shed light on a wide range of times, places, and circumstances. Sometimes it concerns itself with mapping out in detail the mechanisms by which particular political systems actually operate; other times it inquires into how those systems ought to operate, and what ends they ought to subserve. Generally, however, when it is at its best, political theory finds itself doing all of these things at the same time. Perhaps such multiplicity reflects the porousness and diffuseness of the field, many of whose practitioners do not even agree about what its proper objects are or should be. But it also reflects the deeper lineage of political science itself, as a discipline rooted in canonical works such as Aristotle's *Politics*, which combine inquiry into the specific forms of political life with a more general normative and philosophical account of both the natural and human worlds. Political theory, perhaps more than any other aspect of political science, has found it hard to sustain the Weberian distinction between facts and values, since it must perforce deal with them both.

Modern political science, however, beginning with such figures as Machiavelli and Hobbes, set out to move things in the opposite direction. It sought to make the subject of politics more "scientific" precisely by freeing it from its teleological moorings in moral philosophy, abandoning such formative goals as the cultivation of moral virtue in the citizenry, and instead focusing upon the value-neutral, quantitative study of observable political behavior, with a view toward the usefulness of such knowledge in promoting equilibrium and stability. The definition of politics offered in 1953 by David Easton: "the behaviors or set of interactions through which authoritative allocations (or binding decisions) are made and implemented for a society," can be taken to typify the behaviorist, functionalist, and scientistic strains that came to dominate American political science for most of the twentieth century. That dominance has reached a pinnacle of sorts in the current reign of "rational choice" theory, which exceeds all its predecessors in setting the production of precise (and experimentally testable) mathematical models for political behavior as the only goal worthy of political science.

In the resulting intellectual environment, political theory, as a "soft" practice with at least one foot in the traditional concerns of philosophy and the other humanities, has been put on the defensive and increasingly pushed to the edges of the field. Instead, the dominant tone continues to be set by empirical work that makes claims of "hard" scientific precision and is able to propound the kind of detailed research agendas that more readily attract the support of deep-pocketed funding agencies. Even under such adverse circumstances, however, the reflective voice of political theory has continued to be heard and cultivated by such thoughtful scholars as Sheldon Wolin, Charles Taylor, Michael Sandel, Jean Bethke Elshtain, Harvey Mansfield, William Connolly, Peter Berkowitz, Nancy Rosenblum, George Kateb, Michael Walzer, and many others who work to perpetuate the discipline's humanistic traditions.

The fact that a higher status is accorded the "harder" and more "useful" social sciences is nothing new in American history. It accords well with certain established propensities. Alexis de Tocqueville claimed in 1840 that Americans were "addicted" to "practical science," while indifferent to any "theoretical science" that could not promise some concrete payoff. The historian Daniel Boorstin went even further in 1953, asserting that the United States was "one of the most spectacularly lopsided cultures in all of history," because the amazing vitality of its political institutions was equaled by "the amazing poverty and inarticulateness of [its] theorizing about politics." What is more, Boorstin seemed to think this unreflectiveness should be considered a virtue, part of "the genius of American politics," a built-in protection against the destructive force of revolutionary ideologies such as Nazism and Communism.

Such observations greatly exaggerated matters, but also had more than a grain of truth in them. The documentary basis of American political thought was a patchwork of disparate pieces, composed in response to very particular audiences and circumstances—Thomas Paine's *Common Sense*; the Declaration of Independence; Jefferson's *Notes on the State of Virginia*; the debates over the ratification of the Constitution, including the newspaper articles making up *The Federalist*; Washington's *Farewell Address*; the Adams-Jefferson correspondence; the Webster-Hayne debates; the writings of John C. Calhoun; the Lincoln-Douglas debates; the speeches of Lincoln; and the like. Most were produced in the white heat of political exigency; none was the product of systematic and detached reflection on a par with the great treatises of European political thought. Considered by the loftiest standards of political theory, the American political tradition might seem a bit scrappy.

One would have a hard time, however, producing just one historical example of an equally durable government based on more weighty foundational treatises. True, the American political tradition can point to no Rousseaus or Hegels. But what it does have is a rich tradition of intelligent debate on certain recurrent themes, a political midrash devoted to the endless reconsideration of such matters as the proper locus of sovereignty, the separation and division of powers, the meaning of federalism, the sources of political authority, the proper place of religion in public life, and the rights and responsibilities of individuals. Such debates presume a high degree of prior agreement about certain first principles, notably the natural rights of individuals and the desirability of republican institutions. Once one moves beyond these desiderata, however, the debates quickly ensue. Even *The Federalist*, rightly praised for its perspicacious blend of theoretical, historical, and prudential wisdom, cannot stand alone as a complete expression of America's political philosophy. Even the Constitution itself, the principal object of Americans' political veneration, began life as the revision of a previous effort, was itself the object of several compromises, and has to be read "as amended" by the Bill of Rights—a remarkable fact that suggests an institutionalization of debate was incorporated into the very beginnings of the new nation's history.

The profession of political science has been a participant in these public debates, but never their moderator or ringmaster. In that sense, the original hopes of the discipline's American founders have never been realized. John W. Burgess of Columbia University, arguably the discipline's American founding father, and his Progressive-era successors, sought to devise a neutral and transpartisan "science" of administration. Although their vision has influenced the debate, and altered the structure of some American political institutions, it has never carried the day and is now widely held in disrepute by a public that distrusts all claims of disinterestedness. One suspects that even the fairy dust of rational-choice theory will not change this and provide the long-sought breakthrough that will render Americans' debates over ideology and values—and therefore the work of political theory itself—obsolete.

Such a mixed outcome well befits the appropriate role of intellect in a democracy, where even the most accomplished experts must learn to be persuasive to the wider public. It also suggests that political science will have a bright future and a contribution to make to American political discourse, precisely to the extent that it is willing to look beyond the scientistic dreams at its disciplinary origins and make more room for the deeper themes that have always animated serious political reflection.

BIBLIOGRAPHY

Ceasar, James W. *Liberal Democracy and Political Science.* Baltimore: Johns Hopkins University Press, 1990.

Crick, Bernard. *The American Science of Politics: Its Origins and Conditions.* Berkeley: University of California Press, 1964.

Kloppenberg, James T. *The Virtues of Liberalism.* New York: Oxford University Press, 1998.

McDonald, Forrest. *Novus Ordo Seclorum: The Intellectual Origins of the Constitution.* Lawrence: University Press of Kansas, 1985.

Ross, Dorothy. *The Origins of American Social Science.* New York: Cambridge University Press, 1992.

Somit, Albert, and Tanenhaus, Joseph. *The Development of American Political Science: From Burgess to Behavioralism.* New York: Irvington Publishers, 1982.

Strauss, Leo. *Natural Right and History.* Rev. ed. Chicago: University of Chicago Press, 1999.

Wood, Gordon S. *The Creation of the American Republic, 1776–1787.* Rev. ed. Chapel Hill: University of North Carolina, 1998.

Wilfred M. McClay

See also ***Democracy in America*** **(Tocqueville);** ***Federalist Papers*****; Liberalism; Locke's Political Philosophy.**

POLK DOCTRINE. In 1844, James K. Polk, the Democratic candidate for the U.S. presidency, campaigned on expansionism, reaffirming the Monroe Doctrine and advocating "reoccupying" Oregon and "reannexing" Texas. He also set out to acquire California. As president, in his first annual message to Congress in December 1845, he declared the United States opposed to "any European interference" in the Americas, even "by voluntary transfer." In 1848, Polk reinforced that view to prevent Yucatán from seceding from Mexico and joining a European nation. Latin American nations viewed the Polk Doctrine as encroaching on their sovereignty, but Polk defended it, claiming the United States would prevent European domination of weak American nations.

BIBLIOGRAPHY

Mahin, Dean B. *Olive Branch and Sword: The United States and Mexico, 1845–1848.* Jefferson, N.C.: McFarland, 1997.

Laurie Winn Carlson

See also **Latin America, Relations with; Monroe Doctrine.**

POLL TAX. A tax levied on each person within a particular class (for example, adult male) rather than on his property or income is called a poll, head, or capitation tax. Poll taxes were employed in all the American colonies at one period or another. It was Virginia's only direct tax for years, and before the Revolution Maryland had practically no other direct tax. Poll taxes continued to be levied by most states through the nineteenth century and well into the twentieth. In 1923 thirty-eight states permitted or required the collection of poll taxes. The amount of the tax varied from one to five dollars, and the proceeds were often allocated to specific public facilities, such as state schools or roads.

For many years states (five states as late as 1962) used the poll tax as a means of discouraging blacks from registering to vote by making the payment of the tax a prerequisite to the exercise of the right to vote.

In 1964 the Twenty-fourth Amendment to the Constitution was ratified, nullifying all state laws requiring payment of a poll tax as a condition "to vote in any [federal] primary or other [federal] election."

BIBLIOGRAPHY

Perman, Michael. *Struggle for Mastery: Disfranchisement in the South, 1888–1908.* Chapel Hill: University of North Carolina Press, 2001.

Weisbrot, Robert. *Freedom Bound: A History of America's Civil Rights Movement.* New York: W. W. Norton, 1991.

Woodward, C. Vann. *The Origins of the New South, 1877–1913.* Baton Rouge: Louisiana State University Press, 1951.

Eric L. Chase
Harold W. Chase/A. G.

See also **Ballot; Civil Rights Act of 1957; Literacy Test; Primary, White; Suffrage, Colonial; Suffrage, Exclusion from the.**

POLLING is a form of surveying conducted by the canvassing or questioning of a universe. A universe can consist of a particular group, such as steel workers, or can rely on a more general population, such as a political survey of public opinion in an election year. Polling dates back to 1824 in the United States, when two newspapers, the Harrisburg *Pennsylvanian* and the Raleigh *Star,* attempted to predict the presidential election by use of "show votes." By the twentieth century, polls would be taken by magazines, such as *Farm Journal* (1912) and *Literary Digest* (1916). However, these polls were mostly local in scope. The first major national poll was conducted during World War I, and asked participants whether or not the United States should become involved in the war.

In 1936, the process of polling would change forever. George H. Gallup, founder of the American Institute of Public Opinion (1935), had issued a challenge to *Literary Digest,* claiming that he could more accurately predict the outcome of that year's presidential election. At the time, this seemed foolhardy, for the *Literary Digest* had correctly predicted every presidential election correctly since 1916. Confident in his methods, Gallup had developed a system of interviewing based on quota samples, which employed a relatively small number of people to mathematically determine the views of the public at large. He came up with fifty-four different questions, and considered each question demographically, with such key determinants as age, sex, income, and region. The *Literary Digest,* meanwhile, had conducted an old-fashioned straw poll, based on telephone and car buyer lists. In the past, such lists had been serviceable, but in 1936, during the depression, they proved to be heavily biased in favor of the Republican candidate, Alfred M. Landon. For this reason, the *Literary Digest,* having predicted a landslide victory for Landon, was upstaged by the audacious Gallup, who correctly predicted another victory for Franklin D. Roosevelt. Other, lesser-known forecasters, such as Elmo Roper and Archibald Crossley, had also predicted Franklin's victory using similar sampling methods.

However, even Gallup would be proven wrong in the presidential election of 1948. In that year, all major pollsters predicted the Republican candidate, Thomas E. Dewey of New York, would defeat Harry S. Truman, the current president. Gallup had used the same sampling techniques as before, but had made a terrible mistake by concluding his poll weeks before Election Day. Furthermore, Gallup had made the incorrect assumption that the "undecided" votes would split in much the same way as the "decided" ones. This would prove untrue, as most of the "undecideds" either voted for Truman or did not vote at all.

Gallup would learn from his mistakes and recover ever stronger after the election. He improved his sampling techniques, taking into account a greater number of influences, and reanalyzing the effects of the inner city and other regions, which, to his undoing, his interviewers had neglected in 1948. Gallup also made certain that polling was done consistently, a process known as tracking, and that the likelihood of a person actually voting was now also taken into consideration.

With these improvements, Gallup's organization was able to accurately predict future elections. Between 1952 and 2000, the Gallup poll, as it came to be known, achieved an average accuracy of just over 2 percent deviation in presidential elections. In the controversial 2000 election between Al Gore and George W. Bush, Gallup's final preelection prediction had the race as a "statistical dead heat," meaning that the candidates were locked within a range of error of plus or minus 3 percent.

Gallup also introduced polling to social issues. He conducted polls on such complicated topics as the Vietnam War and education. He felt that polls gave the people a voice, and that they were therefore an important aspect of democracy.

Many, however, criticize polling, claiming that it has a "bandwagon effect" on voters, and too much control over politicians. Yet polling continues to play an important role in the political process.

Polling techniques are also extensively used in industry to conduct market research. Companies use sampling in order to determine what products consumers are willing to buy. Such techniques may include random sampling, in which everyone is a potential candidate for an interview; stratified sampling, in which sampling candidates are divided into nonoverlapping groups; quota sampling, random sampling subject to demographic controls; and cluster sampling, in which "clusters," or groups, are selected from various sectors of the population, such as the middle class or working class.

BIBLIOGRAPHY

Chaffee, S. H. "George Gallup and Ralph Nafziger: Pioneers of Audience Research." *Mass Communication and Society* 3 (2000): 317–327.

Marchand, Roland. *Advertising the American Dream.* Berkeley and Los Angeles: University of California Press, 1985.

David Burner
Ross Rosenfield

See also **Elections, Presidential; Marketing Research; Public Opinion; Statistics.**

POLLOCK V. FARMERS' LOAN AND TRUST COMPANY, 157 U.S. 429 (1895), was a case in which the Supreme Court ruled that the income tax provision of the Gorman-Wilson tariff (1894) was unconstitutional because it was a direct tax and hence subject to the requirement of apportionment among the states according to population. In a prior hearing, only the tax on real estate income had been declared unconstitutional, and the Court was divided evenly, four to four, regarding other forms of income. On a rehearing, the Court decided five to four against the income tax on personal property because one justice, probably David J. Brewer, reversed his earlier decision and opposed the income tax, and another, Howell E. Jackson, who had not participated in the earlier hearing, voted with the minority in the rehearing. This decision inspired a popular attack on "judicial usurpation," resulting in the Democratic income tax plank of 1896 and leading ultimately to the passage of the Sixteenth Amendment (1913).

BIBLIOGRAPHY

Paul, Randolph E. *Taxation in the United States.* Boston: Little, Brown, 1954.

Harvey Wish / A. R.

See also **Income Tax Cases; *Springer v. United States*; Taxation.**

POLLUTION. *See* **Air Pollution; Noise Pollution; Water Pollution.**

POLYGAMY is defined as having more than one wife or husband at the same time, usually a man with several wives. Polygamy differs from bigamy in that the wives and children of the polygamist generally form one family. Often in a polygamous marriage, a man marries sisters or the daughter of a wife. The bigamist, on the other hand, keeps his plural marriages a secret and marries the next woman without the other wife's knowledge.

Throughout history many societies have condoned or accepted plural marriages, another term for polygamy. References to its acceptance are in the Bible, the Koran, and other religious texts. Plural marriage is still legal in many Muslim countries, as a practice in accordance with the Koran. However, most modern Muslim families do not practice polygamy, often for financial reasons. Although accepted elsewhere, polygamy has not been a generally accepted practice in the United States. It is illegal in every state and is a federal crime as well.

Nevertheless, the definition and discussion of polygamy is not that simple. Throughout U.S. history, several groups have practiced "free love," which some consider polygamy. In the mid-1800s, during the Second Great Awakening, the Oneida Perfectionists, followers of John Humphrey Noyes, lived together as one family, sharing property, housing, production, and children. They claimed that because there was no marriage in heaven, on earth all men were married to all women. Men and women could have a relationship with whomever they chose. However, Noyes became the arbiter of which men and women could procreate, a situation termed a complex marriage. Although expelled from Putney, Vermont, the Oneida Perfectionists settled peacefully in Oneida, New York. In 1880 the group voted to disband themselves and form a company, Oneida Ltd., which still exists and is famous for its silverware.

Another group, the Church of Jesus Christ of Latter-day Saints, popularly known as Mormons, originated in 1830 in Palmyra, New York. The original leader, Joseph Smith, and his followers believed in polygamy. Persecuted for their beliefs, the Mormons fled to Illinois, where Joseph Smith and his brother were lynched in 1844. Seeking refuge, Brigham Young led the majority of Mormons west to the Great Salt Lake to establish the State of Deseret.

Relatively few Mormons, usually church leaders, practiced polygamy. Polygamy was not a federal crime until passage of the Morrill Act in 1862. Mormon leaders unsuccessfully challenged this act, charging that banning polygamy violated First Amendment rights to freedom of religion. To achieve statehood in 1896, the Utah constitution and the Mormon church had to renounce the practice of plural marriage.

Since then even fewer Mormons have practiced polygamy. As of 2002, in Utah, with a population of 2.5 million, somewhere between 20,000 and 40,000 people lived in polygamous situations. The financial burden was evident; in the areas where most polygamous families lived, roughly one-third lived on welfare.

Occasionally, a case of polygamy received national attention. In 2000–2001, Tom Green of Utah confessed on two national television shows that he had five wives and some twenty-five children. Consequently, he was tried for bigamy, welfare fraud, nonsupport, and child rape (for allegedly marrying his thirteen-year-old daughter). Green had divorced each wife before marrying another, yet he continued to live with them all; hence, they were common law marriages. The case was the first major prosecution in over fifty years and received a great deal of media coverage. Green was convicted and sentenced to five years in jail.

In keeping with the open cultural mores of the late twentieth century, some groups still advocated polygamy, usually on secular grounds. They argued that plural marriage avoids bigamy and adultery. Other groups stated that the high American divorce rate results in a form of "serial polygamy," as distinguished from "simultaneous polygamy." Still other groups, generally formed by former plural marriage wives, fought against the practice of polygamy on the grounds that it inappropriately and unduly subjugated women to the power of a particular man.

BIBLIOGRAPHY

Altman, Irwin. *Polygamous Families in Contemporary Society.* New York: Cambridge University Press, 1996.

Foster, Lawrence. *Religion and Sexuality: The Shakers, the Mormons, and the Oneida Community.* Urbana: University of Illinois Press, 1984.

Foster, Lawrence. *Women, Family, and Utopia: Communal Experiments of the Shakers, the Oneida Community, and the Mormons.* Syracuse, N.Y.: Syracuse University Press, 1991.

Gordon, Sarah Barringer. *The Mormon Question: Polygamy and the Constitutional Conflict in Nineteenth Century America.* Chapel Hill: University of North Carolina Press, 2002.

Kilbride, Philip. *Plural Marriage for Our Times.* Westport, Connecticut: Bergin and Garvey, 1994.

Klaw, Spencer. *Without Sin: Life and Death of the Oneida Community.* New York: Penguin Books, 1993.

Litchman, Kristin Embry. *All is Well.* New York: Delacorte Press, 1998.

Diane Nagel Palmer

See also **Latter-day Saints, Church of Jesus Christ of; Mormon War; Oneida Colony.**

PONTIAC'S WAR. By 1700, waves of epidemics and devastating Iroquois raids in the Great Lakes region had subsided and a lasting peace was forged between a constellation of Algonquian Indian communities and the French. With outposts at Detroit and Sault Ste. Marie, French fur traders and missionaries traveled throughout the region, linking Indian communities with French political, economic, and religious centers in Montreal and Quebec City. This precariously maintained but shared Algonquian-French world collapsed in the mid-1700s during the French and Indian War (1754–1763). Ceding their extensive North American empire to Britain, French imperial officials in 1763 left behind French, Indian, and métis (mixed-blooded) citizens and allies.

As the French influence in the Great Lakes waned, Indian leaders throughout the region grew increasingly concerned. Few could imagine a world without French trade goods or markets for their furs. As the British attempted to take control of the region, Indian leaders became incensed at their failure to follow existing trading, political, and social protocols. British commanders, such as General Jeffrey Amherst at Detroit, refused to offer credit and gifts to Indian leaders while British settlers often refused to even visit Indian encampments, practices at odds with the intimate ties that had been forged between Indians and the French.

Several prominent Indian leaders attempted to unite the region's diverse Indian populations together to resist British domination. From a religious perspective, several prophets—including Neolin, the Delaware Prophet—called for the abandonment of Indian dependence on European goods and a return to older cultural values and practices. One Ottawa chief, Pontiac, became particularly influenced by Neolin's vision and began organizing the region's warrior societies to repel the British. By late June 1763, Pontiac and his forces had sacked every British fort west of Niagara, taking eight out of ten. The two most strategic posts, at Fort Pitt and Fort Detroit, held out. As Pontiac's forces lay siege to Detroit, British reinforcements arrived to relieve the fort, and after more than a year of war, Pontiac withdrew in November 1763.

Having negotiated a peace with British leaders in 1766, Pontiac was unable to unite again the region's diverse Indian populations against the British and was killed in 1769 by a rival warrior. Having initially brought together most of the region's groups against the British, Pontiac ironically succeeded in gaining what most Indian communities desperately needed: goods, markets, and allies. Struggling to feed and clothe themselves during the war, many Great Lakes communities found their new postwar ties with the British comparable with their previous relations with the French. British leaders now offered gifts and credit to Indian leaders at forts and trading outposts throughout the region, and British leaders in Canada and New York welcomed Indian guests as allies. Equally important, British officials also attempted to keep colonial settlers out of Indian lands, recognizing the legitimacy of Indian claims to the Ohio Valley and Great Lakes. While Pontiac's War with the British did not drive the British out, it ultimately forged more than a generation of shared ties between British and Indian communities in the region.

BIBLIOGRAPHY

Anderson, Fred. *Crucible of War: The Seven Years' War and the Fate of Empire in British North America, 1759–1766.* New York: Knopf, 2000.

White, Richard. *The Middle Ground: Indians, Empires, and Republics in the Great Lakes Region, 1650–1815.* New York: Cambridge University Press, 1991.

Ned Blackhawk

See also **French and Indian War; Indian Policy, Colonial; Indian Trade and Traders; Indian Treaties, Colonial; Wars with Indian Nations: Colonial Era to 1783.**

PONY EXPRESS. The Pony Express officially lasted from 3 April 1860 to 26 October 1861, although a few scattered runs were made through November. At first, mail was carried once a week; after June 1860 it was carried twice a week. It operated as a private enterprise, but beginning on 1 July 1860, it was a subcontracted mail route of the U.S. Post Office Department. Prior to the Pony Express, mail could take weeks, even months to arrive from the eastern to the Pacific states. Most was carried by water. Those who wanted their mail in less than two months had only one option, John Butterfield's Overland Mail stagecoach service. Butterfield's stages used the Southern Route between Tipton, Missouri, and San Francisco, California. At its swiftest, mail traveled this route in twenty-four days. Westerners demanded faster mail service. The Central Overland California and Pikes Peak Express Company (COC&PP) freighting firm stepped up to the challenge. The owners, William Russell, Alexander Majors, and William Waddell, proposed a relay system of

The Mochila

Mochila is the Spanish term for knapsack, although the *mochilas* used by pony express riders did not resemble knapsacks. Made of leather, with four pockets, or cantinas, the *mochilas* carried the mail. Three of the cantinas were locked. The keys were held by stationmasters at each end of the route and at the home stations where riders handed off the mail. The *mochila* was easy to slip on or off a saddle, and when riders changed horses, they just grabbed the *mochila* and swung it over the saddle of the new horse. Riders sat on the *mochila*-covered saddle. Openings cut into the leather allowed it to fit over the saddle horn and cantle.

horses to carry the mail across the then less accessible 1,966-mile-long Central Route between St. Joseph, Missouri, and Sacramento, California. They boasted of cutting mail delivery time down to ten days. Russell anticipated that the resulting publicity from a successful, showy service would help him secure a lucrative mail contract over that route.

The Pony Express used an intricate relay system of riders and horses to carry the mail over a route that passed through the present states of Kansas, Nebraska, Colorado, Wyoming, Utah, Nevada and California. Riders carried the mail across the Plains, along the valley of the Platte River, across the Great Plateau, through the Rockies, into the valley of the Great Salt Lake, through the alkali deserts of Nevada, then over the Sierra Nevada and into the Sacramento Valley. Russell and his partners bought four hundred horses and hired riders and stationmasters. Stations were placed approximately ten miles apart. Where they did not previously exist, the company built and stocked them.

Riders were assigned seventy-five-mile-long portions of the trail and kept a speedy pace by switching horses at each station. Riders carried letters and telegrams as well as newspapers printed on special lightweight paper. Mail was wrapped in oiled silk for protection and placed in the pockets of a specially designed saddle cover called a *mochila*. When horse or rider switches were made, the mochila was whipped off of one saddle and tossed onto the next one.

The price of a letter was $5 per half-ounce at first, and reduced to $1 per half-ounce on 1 July 1861. The fastest delivery time recorded for the Pony Express was seven days and seventeen hours, conveying Abraham Lincoln's inaugural address. Russell, Majors, and Waddell lost $30 on every letter they carried. By the time they sold their assets for debts, employees joked that the company's initials stood for "Clean Out of Cash and Poor Pay." In March 1861, the Pony Express became the property of the Butterfield Overland Express and Wells, Fargo. On 1 July 1861, Butterfield's Overland Mail line was moved from the Southern to the Central Route.

Although a financial failure, the Pony Express successfully filled the communication gap before the com-

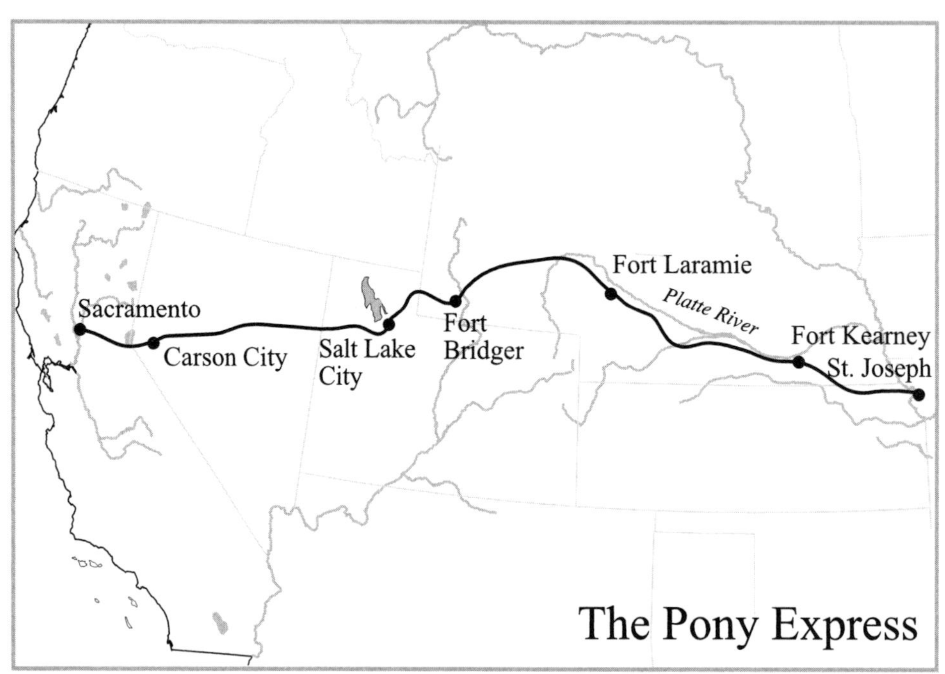

Pony Express. This photograph shows one of the riders (with his *mochila* on the horse behind him) for the surprisingly short-lived mail delivery service in the West, which has endured only in legend since 1861. National Archives and Records Administration

pletion of the telegraph, provided westerners with speedier access to family and friends in the East, improved contact between western military outposts, proved the Central Route was passable year round, and paved the way for permanent transportation systems along its route.

BIBLIOGRAPHY

Bloss, Roy S. *Pony Express, the Great Gamble.* Berkeley: Howell-North, 1959.

Bradley, Glenn Danford. *The Story of the Pony Express.* 2d ed. San Francisco: Hesperian House, 1960.

Chapman, Arthur. *The Pony Express: the Record of a Romantic Adventure in Business.* New York: Cooper Square, 1971.

Settle, Raymond W. *The Pony Express: Heroic Effort, Tragic End.* San Rafael, Calif.: Pony Express History and Art Gallery, 1959.

Nancy A. Pope

See also **Mail, Overland, and Stagecoaches; Mail, Southern Overland.**

POOLS, RAILROAD, agreements between railroads to divide competitive business, sometimes by dividing traffic but usually by dividing income. The Chicago-Omaha pool, dating from 1870, divided business among three railroads, effectively squelching competition from other carriers. Equally effective was the cattle eveners' pool, formed in 1875 to equalize traffic in livestock between Chicago and New York. Section 5 of the Interstate Commerce Act of 1887 and the Sherman Antitrust Act of 1890 outlawed pools, but the practice continued in modified forms. The Transportation Act of 1920 provided for legal pooling agreements when approved by the Interstate Commerce Commission, but the railroads rarely made use of this privilege. They had found other methods better suited to their needs.

BIBLIOGRAPHY

Hoogenboom, Ari, and Olive Hoogenboom. *A History of the ICC: From Panacea to Palliative.* The Norton Essays in American History. New York: Norton, 1976.

Kerr, K. Austin. *American Railroad Politics, 1914–1920: Rates, Wages, and Efficiency.* Pittsburgh, Pa.: University of Pittsburgh Press, 1968.

Ulen, Thomas S. "Cartels and Regulation: Late Nineteenth Century Railroad Collusion and the Creation of the Interstate Commerce Commission." Ph.D. diss., Stanford University, 1979.

Harvey Walker / a. r.

See also **Antitrust Laws; Interstate Commerce Commission; Railroad Rate Law.**

POOR RICHARD'S ALMANAC (1732–1796), published by Benjamin Franklin, contained Franklin's pithy sayings and moral prescriptions in addition to the usual almanac information on the weather, tides, and medicinal remedies. Each edition saw increased sales; the almanac was second only to the Bible in popularity among colonial readers, with annual sales reaching ten thousand copies. Franklin likely ceased to write for the almanac after 1748, when he began to devote most of his time and energy to public affairs. He continued as its editor and publisher until 1757, and the almanac was published until 1796. In 1758 Franklin collected the best of his contributions to the almanac in *Father Abraham's Speech*, better known as *The Way to Wealth.*

BIBLIOGRAPHY

Brands, H. W. *The First American: The Life and Times of Benjamin Franklin.* New York: Doubleday, 2000.

Clark, Ronald W. *Benjamin Franklin: A Biography.* New York: Random House, 1983.

E. H. O'Neill / s. b.

See also **Almanacs;** *and vol. 9:* **Maxims from Poor Richard's Almanack.**

POOR WHITES, a term applied, frequently in scorn, to the lowest social class of white people in the South. Before the Civil War most early writers and travelers were interested only in the aristocracy and slaves and tended to dismiss almost all others as "poor whites." In the 1930s scholars began to draw a clearer distinction between what they thought were the comparatively few genuine poor whites in the antebellum period and the much greater numbers of artisans, yeoman farmers, and self-respecting mountaineers.

Whatever their numbers, the poor whites were a degraded class. Slaveless and usually located in isolated areas of poor soil such as the sandhills at the fall line or the "pine barrens" from the Carolinas to Mississippi, they became the victims of a vicious circle. A combination of malnutrition and disease deprived them of the energy necessary to rise out of the poverty that produced the very conditions that held them down. They thus became objects of contempt, as they lived in squalor, subsisted largely on a miserable fare of coarse cornmeal, sweet potatoes, beans or peas, and a little meat, and gave birth to numerous progeny afflicted like themselves with pellagra, malaria, tuberculosis, hookworm, and other chronic diseases.

An early theory that these agricultural slum dwellers were the descendants of English criminals, debtors, and the lowest class of indentured servants brought over in the colonial period is no longer given credence; nevertheless, their ignorance and lack of ambition made them despised even by the slaves. Disdaining manual labor, the men supported themselves primarily by hunting and fishing, while their gaunt wives attempted to supplement their diet from small gardens.

After the Civil War the term took on a more elastic meaning as the rapid spread of sharecropping and farm tenancy engulfed even many of the formerly independent yeomanry in poverty. During the almost continuous agricultural depression that ran from the 1870s through the 1930s great numbers of southerners found themselves vulnerable to derision as "poor whites." The virtual eradication of hookworm, malaria, and pellagra in the twentieth century, however, plus the spread of compulsory education, the post–World War II agricultural revival, and urbanization eventually eliminated many of the problems plaguing these people and their numbers have declined. Nevertheless, poverty rates among both whites and blacks in the South remain the highest in the nation.

BIBLIOGRAPHY

Newby, I. A. *Plain Folk in the New South: Social Change and Cultural Persistence, 1880–1915.* Baton Rouge: Louisiana State University Press, 1989.

Owsley, Frank Lawrence. *Plain Folk of the Old South.* Baton Rouge: Louisiana State University, 1949.

Reed, John Shelton. *Southerners: The Social Psychology of Sectionalism.* Chapel Hill: University of North Carolina Press, 1983.

Wright, Gavin. *Old South, New South: Revolutions in the Southern Economy since the Civil War.* New York: Basic Books, 1986.

Robert W. Twyman / A. G.

See also **Backcountry and Backwoods; Black Belt; Cotton; Feuds, Appalachian Mountain; Lower South; Mason-Dixon Line; Natchez Trace.**

POP ART refers to the paintings, sculpture, assemblages, and collages of a small, yet influential, group of artists from the late 1950s to the late 1960s. Unlike abstract expressionism, pop art incorporated a wide range of media, imagery, and subject matter hitherto excluded from the realm of fine art. Pop artists cared little about creating unique art objects; they preferred to borrow their subject matter and techniques from the mass media, often transforming widely familiar photographs, icons, and styles into ironic visual artifacts. Such is the case in two of the most recognizable works of American pop art: Andy Warhol's *Campbell Soup Can* (1964), a gigantic silkscreen of the iconic red-and-white can, and Roy Lichtenstein's *Whaam!* (1963), one of his many paintings rendered in the style of a comic book image.

American pop art emerged from a number of converging interests both in the United States and abroad. As early as 1913, Marcel Duchamp introduced "ready-made" objects into a fine-art context. Similarly Robert Rauschenberg's "combine-paintings" and Jasper John's flag paintings of the mid-1950s are frequently cited as examples of proto-pop. However, the term "pop art" originated in Britain, where it had reached print by 1957. In the strictest sense, pop art was born in a series of discussions at London's Institute of Contemporary Arts by the Independent Group, a loose coalition of artists and critics fascinated with postwar American popular culture. The 1956 "This Is Tomorrow" exhibition at the Whitechapel Art Gallery introduced many of the conventions of pop art. Its most famous work, Richard Hamilton's collage *Just What Is It That Makes Today's Homes So Different, So Appealing?* (1956), uses consumerist imagery from magazines, advertisements, and comic books to parody media representations of the American dream.

By the early 1960s, American pop artists were drawing upon many of the same sources as their British counterparts. Between 1960 and 1961, Andy Warhol, Roy Lichtenstein, and Mel Ramos each produced a series of paintings based on comic book characters. James Rosenquist's early work juxtaposed billboard images in an attempt to reproduce the sensual overload characteristic of American culture. As the decade progressed, and a sense of group identity took hold, pop artists strove even further to challenge long-held beliefs within the art community. The work of such artists as Tom Wesselmann, Ed Ruscha, Claes Oldenburg, and Jim Dine introduced even greater levels of depersonalization, irony, even vulgarity, into American fine art.

Andy Warhol. One of the leading figures of pop art, with his appropriation of the label for Brillo soap pads; he was also a popular culture icon, avant-garde filmmaker, and backer of Lou Reed's seminal proto-punk band, the Velvet Underground, and of assorted happenings at the Warhol "Factory" in Manhattan. AP/Wide World Photos

Not surprisingly, older critics were often hostile toward pop art. Despite the social critique found in much pop art, it quickly found a home in many of America's premiere collections and galleries. Several pop artists willingly indulged the media's appetite for bright, attention-grabbing art. Andy Warhol's sales skyrocketed in the late-1960s as he churned out highly recognizable silk screens of celebrities and consumer products. By the decade's end, however, the movement itself was becoming obsolete. Although pop art was rapidly succeeded by other artistic trends, its emphasis on literalism, familiar imagery, and mechanical methods of production would have a tremendous influence on the art of the following three decades.

BIBLIOGRAPHY

Alloway, Lawrence. *American Pop Art.* New York: Collier Books, 1974.

Crow, Thomas E. *The Rise of the Sixties: American and European Art in the Era of Dissent 1955–1969.* London: George Weidenfield and Nicolson, 1996.

Livingstone, Marco. *Pop Art: A Continuing History.* New York: Thames and Hudson, 2000.

John M. Kinder

POPHAM COLONY. *See* **Sagadahoc, Colony at.**

POPULAR SOVEREIGNTY. A broad political principle originally advanced by members of the English Parliament in the 1640s as they sought to limit the divine right of kings and asserted the right of self-government, popular sovereignty acquired a new, albeit ambiguous, meaning between 1847 and 1860. In August 1846, Pennsylvania Democratic Congressman David Wilmot argued that language forever banning slavery in any territory acquired from Mexico should be added to a Mexican-American War appropriations bill. His Wilmot Proviso raised the complex question of whether or not Congress possessed the power to prohibit slavery in the western territories. The United States soon acquired some 500,000 square miles of land from Mexico, and leading Democrats, including presidential contender Lewis Cass of Michigan, felt compelled to respond to Wilmot.

In a December 1847 letter to his Tennessee political supporter, A. O. P. Nicholson, Senator Cass argued that the Wilmot Proviso was unconstitutional because the federal government lacked authority to interfere with slavery in states or territories. Cass declared that the actual settlers of a new territory should decide whether or not to permit slavery. As chairman of the Senate Committee on Territories, Illinois Democratic Senator Stephen A. Douglas defended this view of popular sovereignty for the next decade. Like Cass, Douglas believed that slavery was a local matter. By embracing popular sovereignty, these prominent western Democrats and their supporters hoped to advance their own political interests, preserve the national Democratic Party, and alleviate sectional tensions.

Seeking to placate both pro- and antislavery men within their party, Cass and Douglas never specified precisely when the residents of a new territory would decide whether or not to permit slavery. Thus popular sovereignty as loosely defined in the published Nicholson letter and in later pronouncements by Cass and Douglas initially reassured Southern Democrats who assumed that slavery would be permitted at least until a territory drafted a constitution and pursued statehood. Northern Democrats, in contrast, could assure their constituents that a territorial legislature might prohibit slavery at any time prior to statehood.

Cass, Douglas, and other moderate Democrats enjoyed some political successes. In 1848 Cass won the Democratic presidential nomination, but the votes cast for the new Free Soil Party cost him the White House.

Douglas engineered the Compromise of 1850, including federal nonintervention on the question of slavery for the new Utah and New Mexico territories.

In 1854, however, when Douglas backed a bill to organize the Kansas and Nebraska territories on the principle of popular sovereignty, he was stunned by the storm of protest from Northern voters. Antislavery Northerners formed the new Republican Party to prevent the extension of slavery. Douglas denied that the Supreme Court's 1857 Dred Scott decision negated popular sovereignty. When Douglas articulated his Freeport Doctrine in 1858 in debates with Abraham Lincoln, he fanned Southern fears that territorial legislatures would fail to pass the local laws necessary to support slavery. By 1860 many Southerners became convinced that popular or "squatter" sovereignty would not meet their needs. In that year's presidential election, a sectionally divided Democratic Party enabled Lincoln to defeat Douglas. Support for popular sovereignty tarnished the reputations of Lewis Cass and Stephen A. Douglas during and after their lifetimes because these pragmatic politicians did not treat slavery as a moral issue.

BIBLIOGRAPHY

Johannsen, Robert W. *Stephen A. Douglas.* New York: Oxford University Press, 1973.

Klunder, Willard Carl. *Lewis Cass and the Politics of Moderation.* Kent, Ohio: Kent State University Press, 1996.

Julienne L. Wood

See also **Dred Scott Case; Freeport Doctrine; Territorial Governments; Wilmot Proviso.**

POPULATION. *See* **Demography and Demographic Trends.**

POPULISM arose in the late 1880s and 1890s as a movement of farmers, laborers, and other reformers protesting the inequities of American life. The late nineteenth century was an era of rapid innovations in telecommunications, steam transport, industrial organization, and global trade. The Populists believed that these changes unfairly benefited the leaders of industry and finance, and impoverished the men and women of the farms and workshops that produced the nation's wealth. Because of this belief, scholars have often described Populism as an expression of the resistance of tradition-bound small producers to the modernizing ethos of progress. Yet many late-nineteenth century farmers and laborers showed as much commitment to the ideals of progress as any other group of Americans. Instead of rejecting change, the Populists sought to put their own stamp on the technical and market revolutions. Farmers, mechanics, and other ordinary citizens were confident that they could collectively shape commerce and government to serve their own interests. Therein lay the significance of the Populist movement.

After the Civil War (1861–1865), the combination of Indian removal and railroad expansion opened up vast areas of the trans-Mississippi West to wheat and other staple-crop farming. In the South, too, cotton growing expanded into new territory. The global market for American cereals and fibers, however, failed to keep pace with the rapid growth of American agriculture, which placed a steady downward pressure on market prices. Between 1870 and 1890, the wholesale index of farm products in the United States declined from 112 to 71. For many farmers, their highly mortgaged and indebted farms offered scant prospects of sustainability, much less of prosperity.

Farmers' Alliances

Reform-minded farmers resorted to organization. In the upper Midwest, they affiliated with the Northwestern Farmers' Alliance led by Milton George, and with the Illinois-based Farmers' Mutual Benefit Association. The National Farmers' Alliance and Industrial Union, or Southern Alliance, represented the largest and most influential farm organization. Originating in Texas, the Southern Alliance organized farmers from Georgia to California, and from the Dakotas to New Mexico. By 1890, it claimed over 1,200,000 members in twenty-seven states.

Charles Macune, the president of the Southern Alliance, believed that farmers had to organize as a business interest on a par with other commercial interests. Accordingly, farmers' organizations lobbied to raise the position of agriculture in the national economy. They sought diffusion of commercial, scientific, and technical knowledge. They advocated cooperative business principles and experimented with large-scale incorporated enterprises to regulate cotton and other agricultural markets. They also pressed for an expanded government role in the farm economy. They took the federal postal system as a model of potential reform, and demanded postal savings banks, a postal telegraph, and nationalized railways. Macune also proposed a subtreasury system that would provide low-interest federal loans on staple crops to be stored in federal warehouses.

Farm reformers also sought rural education. They campaigned for public schools and colleges. At the same time, the Alliance movement itself was to serve as "the most powerful and complete educator of modern times." The Alliances created an extensive system of literature networks, lecture circuits, and adult education across much of rural America. Farmwomen took part in this educational work in numbers then unmatched by any secular mobilization of women in American history. Roughly one out of four Alliance members was female. Their ranks included the famous orator Mary Lease, the editor Annie Diggs of Kansas, Marion Todd of Illinois, and Bettie Gay of Texas. Women often joined the rural reform movement in pursuit of female suffrage and temperance. They also sought to ease the burdens of rural labor and realize a more independent, modern life.

The Alliance movement organized along strict racial lines. Many rural reformers advocated Chinese exclusion, and the Southern Alliance enforced a "whites only" rule. Although blacks joined their own Colored Farmers' Alliance, the white and black Alliances were very separate and unequal. In part, this reflected the gap between white Alliance members, who tended to be middling farmers with property, and black Alliance members, who tended to be poor renters working white owners' land as tenants or sharecroppers. It also reflected the commitment of the white Alliance to segregation and white supremacy.

The People's Party

The Alliance movement originally embraced a policy of nonpartisanship, which meant effecting reform by supporting sympathetic candidates within both the Democratic and the Republican Parties. Many reformers, however, grew discontent with this policy, convinced that the existing parties were too bound by graft and corruption to challenge corporate privilege. Such discontent provided the impulse for a third party. After a series of preliminary meetings, farm, labor, and other reform groups held the founding convention of the People's Party of the U.S.A., also known as the Populist Party. in Omaha, Nebraska, in July 1892. The Populist platform contained the fundamental Alliance demands regarding money, transportation, and land. This included the subtreasury plan, an expanded national currency and the coinage of silver to stimulate the economy and provide debt relief, a graduated income tax, government ownership of the telegraph, telephones, and railroads, and the prohibition of speculative land ownership by railroad corporations and foreign investors. The People's Party also favored the adoption of the secret ballot, direct election of Senators, legislation by referendum, and other measures to break the corrupting influence of corporate lobbyists over the political process.

Populist efforts to win the support of the labor movement produced mixed results. Most urban wage earners, especially in the Northeast, where Populism had only minimal organization, showed little interest in the third party. The Populists, who were mainly native-born and Protestant, never succeeded in appealing to large numbers of Catholic and immigrant workers. Nonetheless, especially with the onset of a severe economic depression in 1893, significant sections of the labor movement looked to Populism for answers. In Chicago and other cities, socialists and trade unionists made political agreements with the People's Party.

More importantly, miners and railroad workers—two of the largest and most dynamic forces in the labor movement—shared much in common with the rural Populists. They, too, sought systematic organization as a counterbalance to corporate power. They, too, believed in government intervention in the form of regulation and mandatory arbitration, and they believed in public ownership as the ultimate means to restrain the corporations. Mine workers provided the main support for the People's Party in several Midwestern and Rocky Mountain states. Many railroad employees also joined the third-party effort. The Populists supported the railroad workers in the great Pullman strike during the summer of 1894. After the suppression of the strike by federal authorities, the imprisoned leader of the railroad workers, Eugene V. Debs, emerged as one of the most highly regarded champions of the People's Party. Jobless workers also looked to the Populists. Jacob Coxey, a People's Party candidate from Ohio, led the "Industrial Armies" on a march to Washington to demand a federal "Good Roads" bill to provide jobs for the unemployed.

Populism also provided a meeting ground for the nation's nonconformists, iconoclasts, and free thinkers. It attracted advocates of every type of social and mental innovation. Of these, the most influential were the adherents of the economic panacea movements, such as the Single Tax leagues inspired by the tax doctrines of Henry George, and the Nationalist clubs that pursued the state-capitalist utopia sketched in Edward Bellamy's novel *Looking Backward* (1888). The People's Party also embraced religious nonconformists. Populists were often raised in Protestant homes and held strong religious beliefs. Yet many reformers abandoned ideas of traditional piety in favor of a social gospel more fitting to the demands of secular reform. Other Populists embraced agnosticism, spiritualism, mental science, and other belief systems that they considered to be more suitable to a scientific age.

Fusion and Decline

The People's Party stirred deep anxiety among upper- and middle-class Americans. The political establishment attacked the Populists as "cranks and heretics" who threatened to subvert the republic with "anarchy and lawlessness." Nevertheless, Populism scored a number of electoral victories. William A. Peffer of the Kansas People's Party gained a seat in the U.S. Senate in 1890. In the 1892 presidential election, the Populist candidate James B. Weaver of Iowa carried six states with twenty-two electoral votes. That same November, the Populists elected two governors, Davis Waite of Colorado and Lorenzo D. Lewelling of Kansas. Populists in the U.S. Congress included Thomas E. Watson of Georgia, Marion Cannon of California, and "Sockless Jerry" Simpson of Kansas.

These modest achievements, however, only underscored the formidable institutional obstacles facing a third party that attempted to crack the winner-take-all, two-party system. Populism struggled to present itself as a viable political alternative. By 1896, many supporters of the People's Party favored electoral combination, or fusion, with one of the dominant parties. Fusion led to the election that fall of seven senators and thirty-two congressmen supported by the Populists. Fusion also led to Populist endorsement of the 1896 Democratic presidential candidate, Nebraska Congressman William Jennings Bryan. The Democratic-Populist Bryan campaign focused on the single issue of coining silver, leaving aside the more substantial Populist reforms. Bryan's defeat at the polls delivered a mortal blow to the Populist cause. Although the People's Party did not formally disband until the beginning of the new century, it lost political credibility. The Populist experiment had run its course.

BIBLIOGRAPHY

Ayers, Edward L. *The Promise of the New South: Life after Reconstruction.* New York: Oxford University Press, 1992.

Barthelme, Marion K. *Women in the Texas Populist Movement: Letters to the Southern Mercury.* College Station: Texas A&M University Press, 1997.

Goodwyn, Lawrence. *Democratic Promise: The Populist Moment in America.* New York: Oxford University Press, 1976.

Hicks, John D. *The Populist Revolt: A History of the Farmers' Alliance and the People's Party.* Minneapolis: University of Minnesota Press, 1931. Reprint, Westport, Conn.: Greenwood Press, 1981.

Larson, Robert W. *Populism in the Mountain West.* Albuquerque: University of New Mexico Press, 1986.

McMath, Robert C., Jr. *American Populism: A Social History, 1877–1896.* New York: Hill and Wang, 1993.

Ostler, Jeffrey. *Prairie Populism: The Fate of Agrarian Radicalism in Kansas, Nebraska, and Iowa, 1880–1892.* Lawrence: University Press of Kansas, 1993.

Charles Postel

See also **Farmers' Alliance; Machine, Political; Political Parties; Third Parties.**

PORCELAIN. Benjamin Franklin viewed the domestic manufacture of porcelain as an important step toward economic independence from England, and it ultimately became intimately linked with the industrialization of the nation. However, its production in the United States was never as crucial as stoneware and redware production.

Porcelain, first made in China during the Tang dynasty (618–907 A.D.), remained a Chinese secret sought by the West for many hundreds of years. It was not until 1708 and 1709, after the German ceramist Johann Friedrich Böttger had discovered its secret, kaolin, that true hard-paste porcelain was produced outside of China. In 1738, Andrew Duché of Savannah, Georgia, made the first recorded piece of porcelain in North America, "a small teacup . . . very near transparent."

Around 1825 some twenty skilled craftsmen from England and France were employed to make porcelain for the Jersey Porcelain and Earthenware Company in Jersey City, New Jersey. Other ventures followed in Philadelphia. In 1853, when the Crystal Palace Exhibition of the Industry of All Nations was held in New York City, work by the Haviland Brothers, who had a china shop there, was much praised. By the mid-1860s, Parian ware, a type of porcelain having the appearance of marble, became so popular that no fashionable Victorian parlor would be without a piece or two. Ott and Brewer of Trenton, New Jersey, sold a wide line of Parian ware. From the 1880s on, Belleek, a light, marvelously thin, ivory-colored porcelain variant of Parian, named after its Irish town of origin, became the greatest American ceramics success story.

After the influential Centennial Exhibition in Philadelphia, art pottery became a serious business in America. Porcelain, while a minor branch of the industry, had its champions in M. Louise McLaughlin (1847–1939) and especially Adelaide Alsop Robineau (1865–1929). By the 1930s, porcelain found wide application in industry and began to be studied at colleges, universities, and art schools such as Cranbrook. An intense interest in porcelain continues.

BIBLIOGRAPHY

American Ceramics: The Collection of Everson Museum of Art. New York: Rizzoli, 1989.

Frelinghuysen, Alice Cooney. *American Porcelain, 1770–1920.* New York: The Metropolitan Museum of Art, 1989.

See also **Art: Pottery and Ceramics.**

PORK BARREL. Pork barrel politics consist of trying to obtain appropriations for one's own district. Politicians consider fighting for their constituents' best interests virtuous, but fiscal conservatives, claiming the practice has led to unnecessary investments at taxpayers' expense, use the term in a derogatory manner. "Pork barrel" originally referred to American slaves' rushed attempts to obtain some of the pork given to them as a group in large barrels. The term entered the political vocabulary after the Civil War. Harbor and river improvements were classic examples of pork, later surpassed by defense contracts and highway construction.

BIBLIOGRAPHY

Ferejohn, John A. *Pork Barrel Politics: Rivers and Harbors Legislation, 1947–1968.* Stanford, Calif.: Stanford University Press, 1974.

Philippe R. Girard

See also **Conservatism; Interstate Highway System; Veto, Line-Item.**

PORNOGRAPHY. The definition of pornography, loosely understood as written or visual images intended to excite sexually, has been notoriously slippery, and Americans have never all agreed on the boundaries of what is pornography, and on the extent to which it should be regulated. In the 1990s, hard-core pornography was widely accessible and often depicted nonconsensual sexual intercourse in violent graphic images, whereas at the beginning of the twentieth century that which was merely "immoral" or "sensational," such as a hazy drawing of a seminude woman, was viewed as pornographic. Thus, historically a far broader range of literature and visual images was subject to legal governmental regulation, from erotic photographs to literary classics. A provision of the 1842 Tariff Act restricted "obscene" pictures and prints from entering the United States. The government became more interested in pornography during the Civil War, when soldiers began trading and collecting French postcards of pictures of nude and seminude women. The U.S. postmaster general in 1865 received a limited right to confiscate "obscene" materials in the mail. The Comstock laws of 1873 went further by making it illegal to sell or distribute through the mail a multitude of images in literature and art, as well as information on birth control or abortion.

From the 1870s through the mid-1930s, legal regulation of printed material and motion pictures was at its most restrictive. During this era the Supreme Court did not use arguments based on free speech and the First Amendment to challenge or modify obscenity laws and postal restrictions on literature or visual images. Until 1957 the Court accepted with only slight modification the British 1867 definition of "obscenity," which based censorship rulings on whether the written or spoken word (or visual representation) was intended to "deprave and corrupt those whose minds are open to such immoral influences, and into whose hands such a publication might fall." In effect, the Supreme Court upheld a definition of obscenity that created a standard for culture based on the lowest common denominator of acceptability—one that would not impair the moral development of children.

Before 1933 some novels that are now regarded as classics could not be distributed in the United States. The situation changed dramatically for literature in that year when federal judge John M. Woolsey, ruled that Irish author James Joyce's *Ulysses* was not obscene, arguing that the work should be taken as a whole, and prosecutors could not quote passages out of context as proof a book was obscene. On its first case against motion pictures in 1915, the Supreme Court ruled that the movie industry was a profit-inspired business, not an art form, and therefore subject to regulation. This allowed censorship by review boards before distribution of movies to the public by any state or local government that deemed it necessary or desirable. Beginning in 1934 the movie industry practiced rigorous self-regulation, through the Motion Picture Association of America and its Production Code, trying to avoid federal censorship.

At the turn of the century, censorship was popularly viewed as a device for social change. Groups such as the Woman's Christian Temperance Union joined vice societies to advocate censorship of literature and art. The American public has continued to support laws restricting the access of youth to pornographic films, as well as harsh action against anyone who creates or distributes child pornography. Like earlier reformers, Americans in the 1990s argued that censorship was necessary to protect children and family values. With *Miller v. California*, however, which was decided by the Supreme Court in 1973, the only adult pornography subject to governmental regulation became that which an "average person" deemed was without literary, artistic, political, or scientific value. The so-called LAPS test was weakened in 1987 when the Court in *Pope v. Illinois* ruled that because community views varied, "reasonable person" should be substituted for "average person." Combinations of sex and violence soon began permeating not only low-budget pornographic films but mass-distributed movies, videos, and magazines, making violent portraits of adult sex readily available. By the 1990s pornographic materials were a $10 billion operation in the United States alone.

Late-twentieth-century adherents of the women's movement had divided opinions about pornography. Because of increasing violence against women, some feminists believed that pornography, especially images depicting violence against women or nonconsensual sex, are often harmful to female actors and, more broadly, to all women. This belief in the danger of pornography is based on the assumption that male viewers watch and read pornography as if it were a manual or an instruction guide to behavior, including relations between the sexes. Although the most extreme antipornography activists asserted that men learn to rape by watching and reading pornography, no study has proven a direct link; however, many researchers have indicated that pornography diminishes male sensitivity to women's legal rights including the right to withhold consent to sex. Feminists Catharine MacKinnon and Andrea Dworkin oppose pornography both as "injurious speech," because it condones and encourages violence against women, and as a violation of women's civil rights. In the 1980s they successfully lobbied for ordinances in Minneapolis, Bellingham (Washington State), and Indianapolis. All were subsequently ruled unconstitutional on First Amendment grounds.

Anticensorship feminists who focus on the First Amendment argue that pornography should remain a protected form of speech. Rejecting the idea that people respond to pornographic movies or books by trying to emulate the characters, they argue that pornography may serve as a safety valve, preventing violence against women by serving as a form of fantasy and as "safe sex." Some anticensorship feminists also doubt the efficacy of censorship and dislike its tendency to be used against such political minorities as homosexuals. They suggest that pornography's most objectionable images could be counteracted if feminist women and men produced their own pornography that challenged patriarchal and/or heterosexual notions about women's place in society. Anticensorship feminists point out that violence against women was a problem before pornography became as available and graphic as it has since the 1960s and conclude that banning pornography would probably not solve the physical abuse of women.

In the early twenty-first century, advances in computer technology raised new challenges regarding the definition and control of pornography. Pornography proliferated on the internet, and computer imaging technology sometimes made it difficult to distinguish which images depicted acts between real people, and which were simply computer-generated. Whereas anticensorship laws generally protected people who wished to post or download sexually graphic images, using or creating child pornography was generally not protected, because it depicted illegal acts between legal minors. But debate arose over computer-generated images of children engaged in sexual acts: some argued that because no actual children were involved in making the images, they should be legal; others argued that the difficulty in distinguishing between "real" and computer-generated images made this course of action dangerous. Continuing advances in computer and communication technology are likely to prompt further debates over the definition and distribution of pornography.

BIBLIOGRAPHY

Assiter, Alison, and Avedon Carol, eds. *Bad Girls and Dirty Pictures: The Challenge to Reclaim Feminism.* Boulder, Colo.: Pluto Press, 1993.

Baird, Robert M., and Stuart E. Rosenbaum, eds. *Pornography: Private Right or Public Menace?* Amherst, N.Y.: Prometheus Books, 1998.

Cate, Fred H. *The Internet and the First Amendment: Schools and Sexually Explicit Expression.* Bloomington, Ind.: Phi Delta Kappa Educational Foundation, 1998.

Cornell, Drucilla, ed. *Feminism and Pornography.* New York: Oxford University Press, 2000.

Stan, Adele M., ed. *Debating Sexual Correctness: Pornography, Sexual Harassment, Date Rape, and the Politics of Sexual Equality.* New York: Delta, 1995.

Alison M. Parker/D. B.

See also **Censorship, Press and Artistic; Convention on the Elimination of All Forms of Discrimination Against Women; Internet; Music Television; Violence Against Women Act; Women's Rights Movement: The Twentieth Century.**

PORNOGRAPHY COMMISSION. There have been two presidential commissions charged with investigating the explicit depictions of sex and sexuality that some call PORNOGRAPHY—even though "pornography" (unlike "obscenity") is not a legal term.

In 1970 President Richard Nixon appointed the President's Commission on Obscenity and Pornography, also known as the Lockhart Commission. The commission's eighteen members spent over $2 million reviewing the extant research, interviewing experts, and also funding a survey of its own. The final report concluded that there was no evidence demonstrating any significant social harm from pornography depicting consenting adults, and recommended that existing obscenity laws should be repealed. President Nixon refused to accept either the report or the commission's conclusions.

President Ronald Reagan charged Attorney General Edwin Meese in 1985 with forming a commission to investigate the effects of pornography. The Meese Commission was given a budget of $500,000—in real dollars about one-sixteenth of the Lockhart Commission's funding. Unable to afford research of its own, the commission held hearings to interview invited witnesses in six major cities. The commission's final report said that pornography contributed significantly both to sexual violence and to societal discrimination against women, although critics charged that the commission's membership and witness list were both selected to make such conclusions foregone.

BIBLIOGRAPHY

Donnerstein, Edward, Daniel Linz, and Steven Penrod. *The Question of Pornography: Research Findings and Policy Implications.* New York: Free Press, 1987.

Hawkins, Gordon, and Franklin E. Zimring. *Pornography in a Free Society.* Cambridge, U.K., and New York: Cambridge University Press, 1988.

J. Justin Gustainis

PORT AUTHORITIES. These forms of special-purpose government are utilized in the United States and in other countries. In the early 2000s special-purpose governments were the fastest growing type of local government in the nation (municipalities were second). Port authorities are tax-free corporations funded by user fees and/or proceeds from tax-free bonds. Their function is typically legally limited to the financing, construction, and operation of facilities and projects involving rivers, lakes, oceans, and other waterways, such as canals, harbors, docks, wharves, and terminals. One hundred fourteen U.S. metropolitan areas had port authorities with varying levels of function and authority in 1987. The oldest port authority in the United States is likely that of Portland, Oregon, established in 1917. The most well-known port authority in the United States is the Port Authority of New York and New Jersey, established in 1921. It is exceptional because it serves two different states and because the actions of its governing body may be vetoed by the governors of New York and New Jersey. Sometimes port authority activities have been controversial, for instance over the question of whether port authority autonomy fosters growth and development inconsistent with public goals.

BIBLIOGRAPHY

Foster, Kathryn A. *The Political Economy of Special-Purpose Government.* Washington, D.C.: Georgetown University Press, 1997.

Mitchell, Jerry, ed. *Public Authorities and Public Policy: The Business of Government.* New York: Greenwood Press, 1992.

Timothy M. Roberts

PORT AUTHORITY OF NEW YORK AND NEW JERSEY. The Port Authority of New York and New Jersey is a self-supporting, interstate, corporate organization of New York and New Jersey. It was created in 1921 to protect and promote the commerce of New York Harbor and to develop terminal and transportation facilities in the New York metropolitan area.

The Port of New York Authority, as it was originally called (the name changed in 1972), was created by the joint efforts of Governor Alfred E. Smith of New York and Governor Walter Edge of New Jersey with a view to solving the problems caused by the artificial New York-New Jersey boundary line down the middle of the Hudson River, which split the natural unity of the port. Because it was an interstate treaty, approval of Congress was required. By the compact of organization, the Port Authority is permitted "to purchase, construct, lease and/or operate any terminal or transportation facility" and "to make charges for the use thereof." Its sphere of jurisdiction extends over a twenty-five-mile radius from lower Manhattan. Jurisdiction may be extended beyond this limit if approved by the governors and legislatures of both New York and New Jersey. A twelve-person Board of Commissioners governs the Port Authority. The New York and New Jersey governors appoint six members each, subject to the approval of their respective state senates. The commissioners appoint an executive director who manages the day-to-day operations of the Port Authority. The leadership of J. Austin Tobin, executive director of the Port Authority from 1946 to 1972, is widely credited for making it a powerhouse on planning and economic development issues within the region and the largest organization of its type in the nation. Tobin's success depended on his ability, with a minimum of political controversy, to use revenue from the Port Authority's bridges and tolls to finance economic development projects that expanded the organization's power.

In addition to running many of the region's bridges and roadways, the scope of the Port Authority's work includes the construction and management of infrastructure for mass transit and marine and aviation industries, as well as the development of office and industrial real estate. Among the facilities built, owned, and operated by the Port Authority are the George Washington Bridge (1931); the Goethals Bridge between Staten Island and Elizabeth, New Jersey (1928); the Lincoln Tunnel (1937); the Port Authority Bus Terminal (1950); and the George Washington Bridge Bus Station (1963). The Port Authority owns and operates major marine facilities in Elizabeth, New Jersey, and Brooklyn, New York, as well as industrial parks in Elizabeth and the Bronx, New York. The Port Authority operates the region's major airports (Kennedy, La Guardia, and Newark), all owned by municipal governments. Perhaps the most prominent Port Authority facility was the World Trade Center, two 110-story office towers in lower Manhattan that opened in 1973 and dominated New York City skyline as a symbol of U.S. economic power until they were destroyed in a terrorist attack on 11 September 2001. The site of the towers, dubbed "Ground Zero" in the aftermath of the attack, became hallowed ground in memory of the many office workers and New York City fire and police officers who died there.

In 2000, the Port Authority's cumulative investment in facilities and infrastructure totaled $35 billion. Its budget totaled $4.6 billion, and it employed 7,200.

BIBLIOGRAPHY

Doig, Jamison W. *Empire on the Hudson: Entrepreneurial Vision and Political Power at the Port of New York Authority.* New York: Columbia University Press, 2001.

Richard M. Flanagan

See also **Airports, Siting and Financing of; George Washington Bridge; Lincoln Tunnel; New York City; 9/11 Attack; Transportation and Travel; World Trade Center; World Trade Center Bombing, 1993.**

PORT ROYAL. Port Royal, Nova Scotia, at the site of present-day Annapolis Royal on the southeastern shore of the Annapolis Basin, was variously under the control of France and England throughout the seventeenth century. Pierre du Guast established the earliest settlement of Port Royal in 1605. Though alternately destroyed or taken by the British over the course of the seventeenth century, Port Royal remained the most important French outpost in Acadia, and became the seat of French government there in 1684. The town's strategic location made it desirable as a launch site for French attacks on British colonial soil. After several battles during which the region changed hands, Acadia was ceded to the British in the Treaty of Utrecht, and Port Royal was renamed Annapolis Royal. Once the British designated Halifax as the seat of their government in Acadia in 1749, Annapolis Royal lost both its strategic and governmental importance.

Port Royal enjoyed a renewed prominence in the eighteenth century, as a destination for some of the thousands of Loyalists who fled the United States in the wake of the American Revolution. Among those who settled in Nova Scotia were enslaved Africans who fought in the service of the British on the promise that they would gain their freedom. Thousands of freed slaves who were promised farms by the British journeyed north, only to confront bitter cold and near starvation. On receiving a petition describing the plight of the 102 freed black families in Annapolis Royal and 100 families in New Brunswick, the British Secretary of State ordered that, if the petition proved true, the province must either finally compensate the families or send them to Sierra Leone. In January of

1792, more than one thousand black Loyalists departed Nova Scotia, bound for Sierra Leone.

BIBLIOGRAPHY

Hodges, Graham Russell. *The Black Loyalist Directory: African Americans in Exile after the American Revolution.* New York: Garland, 1996.

Quarles, Benjamin. *The Negro in the American Revolution.* Chapel Hill: University of North Carolina Press, 1961.

Robert E. Moody
Leslie J. Lindenauer

PORTAGES AND WATER ROUTES. Foremost among the factors that governed the exploration and settlement of the United States and Canada were the mountain ranges and the river systems—the former an obstacle, the latter an aid to travel. For more than a century the Allegheny Mountains barred the British from the interior. By contrast, the French, who secured a foothold at the mouth of the St. Lawrence River, found ready access to the interior along that waterway. By the Richelieu River–Lake Champlain route, they could pass southward to the Hudson River, while numerous tributaries of the Ottawa and St. Lawrence Rivers pointed the way to Hudson Bay.

Over the eastern half of primitive America stretched a forest that only winding rivers and narrow trails penetrated. Wherever rivers ran, boats could travel. Nevertheless, travel by water was subject to interruption, either by rapids, shallows, waterfalls, or portages. At heavily traveled portages, people frequently maintained horses or oxen and carts for hauling boats across the portage.

French explorer Samuel de Champlain opened the Ottawa River route to the upper Great Lakes. From Lake Erie, travelers could reach the Ohio River by numerous routes: the Lake Chautauqua Portage to the Allegheny, the Presque Isle–Allegheny Portage, or the Maumee–Miami and the Maumee–Wabash portages. From Lake Huron access was open to Lake Superior by the St. Marys River or to Lake Michigan by the Straits of Mackinac. From Lake Superior, travelers could pass by numerous river-and-portage routes to Hudson Bay, to the Mississippi River system, or to the great river systems that drained the vast interior plain of Canada into the Arctic Ocean. From Lake Michigan many routes led to the Mississippi system; from the St. Joseph access was open to the Wabash and Ohio Rivers.

With access to the Mississippi system, the heart of the continent lay open to the traveler. The encirclement of the English by the French precipitated the French and Indian War, which ended in the conquest of New France and the division of its territory between England and Spain. However, the waterways retained their importance as highways of trade and travel to the end of the wilderness period. At places where a break in transportation occurred—such as Chicago—forts and, later, cities were established. Places like Detroit and Mackinac Island owed their importance to their strategic location at central points of travel.

Compared with modern standards, wilderness travel was at best laborious and time-consuming. If some rivers were deep and placid, others were swift and beset with shoals and rapids. Portage conditions, too, varied widely from place to place, or even at the same place under different seasonal conditions. For instance, in 1749 Pierre de Céloron de Blainville spent five days of arduous toil traversing the ten-mile portage from Lake Erie to Lake Chautauqua and spent two weeks reaching the Allegheny at Warren, Pennsylvania. Travelers' adherence to the waterways under such difficult circumstances supplies striking evidence of the still greater obstacles encountered by land.

BIBLIOGRAPHY

Dunnigan, Brian Leigh. *Frontier Metropolis: Picturing Early Detroit, 1701–1838.* Detroit, Mich.: Wayne State University Press, 2001.

Eccles, W. J. *The French in North America, 1500–1783.* East Lansing: Michigan State University Press, 1998.

Skaggs, David Curtis, and Larry L. Nelson, eds. *The Sixty Years' War for the Great Lakes, 1754–1814.* East Lansing: Michigan State University Press, 2001.

Spinney, Robert G. *City of Big Shoulders: A History of Chicago.* DeKalb: Northern Illinois University Press, 2000.

M. M. Quaife / A. E.

See also **Fox-Wisconsin Waterway; Grand Portage; Niagara, Carrying Place of.**

PORTLAND, the largest city in OREGON, located at the confluence of the Willamette and Columbia Rivers, is named for Portland, Maine. Incorporated in 1851, the city has depended on trade throughout its history. The city tapped the wheat belt of the surrounding country to supply the California gold miners, then provided supplies to the miners of Idaho and Montana in the 1860s, as it did for Alaska miners at the end of the nineteenth century. After the Civil War, the city drew the Columbia River and railroad wheat traffic of eastern Oregon and southeastern Washington. It profited from shipbuilding during World War I and World War II.

During the 1970s, 1980s, and 1990s the city enjoyed substantial revitalization and earned a reputation for livability. Neighborhoods were preserved, a light rail transit system developed, reinvestment attracted to the downtown, and new suburban development contained within an urban growth boundary. The area's principal employers in the 1990s were wholesaling and transportation, services, and manufacturing, particularly a substantial electronics industry. Portland in the nineteenth century attracted many Chinese and Scandinavian immigrants; in the late twentieth century it experienced growth in Asian American and Hispanic residents. The city of Portland recorded a population of 529,121 in 2000, and the six-county metropolitan area recorded 1,913,009 residents.

BIBLIOGRAPHY

Abbott, Carl. *Portland: Planning, Politics, and Growth in a Twentieth-Century City.* Lincoln: University of Nebraska Press, 1983.

———. *Greater Portland: Urban Life and Landscape in the Pacific Northwest.* Philadelphia: University of Pennsylvania Press, 2001.

MacColl, E. Kimbark. *Merchants, Money, and Power: The Portland Establishment, 1843–1913.* Portland, Ore.: Georgian Press, 1976.

Carl Abbott
Gordon B. Dodds

PORTSMOUTH, TREATY OF. Russia and Japan accepted President Roosevelt's offer to help end the Russo-Japanese War of 1904–1905 and agreed to meet with him and Governor John McLane in Portsmouth, New Hampshire. Russia agreed after losing major naval and land battles. Japan, which had begun the war with a surprise attack on Port Arthur in Manchuria, agreed after running out of money to finance the war.

On 10 August 1905, the Japanese presented twelve terms. They negotiated daily, but by 19 August, they had reached an impasse. Roosevelt worked to reach compromises on war reparations by Russia to Japan, returning captured Japanese vessels, curtailment of Russia's Pacific navy, and Russia's buying back half of Sakhalin Island for $40,000,000. Russia's envoys were under strict orders not to authorize any kind of payment.

From 20–30 August, Roosevelt persuaded the Japanese to forego reparations and Russia's purchase of southern Sakhalin. Russia agreed to allow Japan to occupy the southern half of Sakhalin and to leave Korea. Both agreed to return Manchuria to China, to restrict their activities in China, and to divide the fisheries they had claimed. The Treaty of Portsmouth was signed on 5 September 1905. In 1906, President Roosevelt was awarded the Nobel Peace Prize for his role in the negotiations.

BIBLIOGRAPHY

Russo-Japanese War Research Society. Available at http://www.russojapan.com.

Westwood, J. N. *Russia against Japan 1904–1905: A New Look at the Russo-Japanese War.* Albany: State University of New York Press, 1986.

Kirk H. Beetz

POSITIVISM, an empiricist philosophy that emerged in early nineteenth-century Europe, and whose chief exponent was Auguste Comte, the French philosopher of science. Once the secretary of utopian socialist Claude Henri de Saint-Simon (1760–1825), Comte articulated his own grand system in a series of lectures subsequently published as the *Cours de philosophie positive* (1830–1842). Extending the insights of Francis Bacon, David Hume, Immanuel Kant, and others, this philosophical tour de force laid out the component parts of positivism: an empiricist epistemology, an inductive method, a hierarchical classification of the sciences, and an elaborate philosophy of history. Like other empiricists, Comte restricted knowledge to data gained only through sensory perception and rejected any consideration of first or ultimate causes. In the "law of the three stages," Comte claimed to have discovered the law of historical development that revealed human society progressing from the primitive theological stage (where deities were invoked to explain natural phenomenon), to the philosophical stage (where reified ideas were employed in causal explanation), to, ultimately, the thoroughly empirical positive stage. Comte's hierarchy of the sciences built upon this "science of history"; he believed that each field of study had attained the positive level at a different time. Comte ranked mathematics first (as the most general and independent), then astronomy, physics, chemistry, biology, and, finally, sociology, the "queen of the sciences." The latter, truly a science of society, was the last to attain the positive method.

Because he held that the social instability of nineteenth-century Europe was rooted in intellectual chaos, Comte developed a detailed social blueprint founded upon his empiricist philosophy in the *Système de politique positive* (1851–1854). Comte's so-called "second system" included an institutionalized religion of humanity headed by a priestly scientific class. He believed that worship was an essential part of human nature but that religion had been mistakenly based on theology, rather than on positive science. Accordingly, Comte identified a host of secular scientific saints in his church's calendar and offered himself as the first "Supreme Pontiff of Humanity."

European Followers and Critics

Comparatively few European intellectuals embraced all of Comte's controversial social and religious ideas. Yet, by the 1870s, some sort of positivism was accepted by a broad spectrum of thoroughly naturalistic thinkers. At one pole stood Comte's few orthodox disciples such as Pierre Lafitte and (in England) Richard Congreve. Nearer the center of the spectrum were those who broke with the official cult but who shared many of Comte's social and political concerns and who believed that the empiricist epistemology and philosophy of history did have social ramifications. One could include in this group G. H. Lewes (and his wife, the author George Eliot) and Frederic Harrison. Finally, there emerged a more generic school of positivists at the other end of the spectrum who, like John Stuart Mill, had been profoundly influenced by the theory and method of the *Cours* but were repelled by the *Système*, which Mill dismissed as despotic. Another generic positivist, T. H. Huxley, who combined positivist empiricism with evolutionary theory, aptly characterized Comte's religion of humanity as "Catholicism without Christianity."

Still, even these critics shared Comte's thoroughly naturalistic assumptions and his hostility to theology, and, like Comte, they attempted to employ a strict empiricism in their methodology.

American Positivists

All three of these points along the positivist spectrum had representatives in Gilded Age America, although historians have often ignored the first two groups. English émigré Henry Edger embraced orthodox positivism in 1854 and corresponded with Comte, who soon appointed Edger "Apostle to America." Edger settled in a small perfectionist commune on Long Island known as Modern Times. From there, he sought converts in neighboring New York City. A tiny clique of sectarian Comtists coalesced around the *New York World* editor David G. Croly in 1868, but it soon broke away from Edger and official Comtism and fractured further as the years passed.

Arguably, the major American thinker most influenced by Comte's *Cours* and some of the French philosopher's social ideals was Lester Frank Ward (1841–1913). Indebted to the political principles of the American Whigs, Ward used Comte's ideas to articulate the first naturalistic critique of William Graham Sumner's political economy. Drawing upon Comte's interventionism, Ward stressed that the mind was a key "social factor" that laissez-faire systems—like that proposed by Sumner—had overlooked or misunderstood. Social science, properly applied, could enable humanity to control the human environment and thereby ensure social progress; it was neither unnatural nor unscientific for the state to intervene in the private economy.

The other American advocates of a more generic positivism during the late nineteenth century included John William Draper, Chauncey Wright, and Henry Adams. Draper, president of the medical faculty at New York University and a popular author, read Comte in 1856 and adopted a modified form of Comte's "law of the three stages" in his work; he had even visited Croly's New York group during the 1860s. Wright, a philosopher of science and a mathematician, was one of Mill's most important American followers; he rejected any sort of metaphysical argument and attacked Herbert Spencer as not being an authentic positivist in terms of method. Adams encountered Comte by reading Mill's influential essay *Auguste Comte and Positivism.* He wrote in his autobiographical *Education* that by the late 1860s, he had decided to become "a Comteist [sic], within the limits of evolution" (p. 926).

By the 1890s, grand theorists such as Comte and Spencer and their monistic systems were decidedly out of favor both in the emerging social science disciplines and in academic philosophy. "At the end of the nineteenth century," notes Maurice Mandelbaum, "the earlier systematic form of positivism had to all intents and purposes lost its hold upon the major streams of thought. What had once seemed to be the philosophic import of the physical sciences no longer carried the same conviction" (Mandelbaum, p. 19). Although Ward finally obtained an academic appointment at Brown University in 1906, his approach had by then begun to look decidedly outmoded. Other, younger pioneering sociologists such as Albion Small at the University of Chicago and Edward A. Ross, first at Stanford and then at Wisconsin, moved away from a reductionistic explanatory method. Yet their meliorism and interest in social control also evidenced their early reading of Ward and, indirectly, the impact of Comtean assumptions. In the final pages of *Social Control* (1901), Ross portrayed the sociologist as a sort of priestly technocrat who would carefully guard the secret of social control but would "address himself to those who administer the moral capital of society—to teachers, clergymen, editors, lawmakers, and judges, who wield the instruments of control" (p. 441). The historian Robert Bannister describes American sociology growing into two distinct types of scientism in the early twentieth century and explains this development as a bifurcation of "the legacy of Comtean positivism: the one [branch] adopting the emphasis on quantification as the route to positive knowledge, and the other, Comte's utopian program without the mumbo jumbo of the Religion of Humanity" (Bannister, p. 6).

Meanwhile, Charles S. Peirce and William James in philosophy softened positivism's harsh rejection of religious experience by the close of the nineteenth century. They both recognized the limitations of science in a way that some of their critics feared would open the door to metaphysics. James poked fun at the "block universe" of Spencer and, by implication, at the pretensions of all-inclusive systems. James and John Dewey were both influenced by the neo-Kantian revival in philosophy and came to stress the dynamic organizing function of the mind. Pragmatism may have been influenced by positivism but much of its approach diverged from Comte's assumptions.

On a more popular level, the journalist Herbert Croly, son of orthodox positivist David Croly, blended German idealism and a Comtean concern for social order and coordinated social progress. In *Promise of American Life* (1909), Croly called upon Americans to leave behind the provincial negative-state liberalism of the Jeffersonian tradition and embrace a more coherent national life. As Croly biographer David Levy has shown, Croly's organicist understanding of society owed much to his father's positivism. In a 1918 article supporting the establishment of a school of social research (which later became the New School), Croly referred to Ward and explained in Comtean terms that "the work of understanding social processes is entangled inextricably with the effort to modify them" (Croly, quoted by Harp, p. 201).

A New Variant

By the 1920s a new stream, styling itself logical positivism, emerged in Vienna. It represented a more radical sort of empiricism that stressed the principle of verification. Logical positivists dismissed arguments as metaphysical unless they could be verified on the basis of convention or with reference to empirical phenomenon. They called upon philosophy to be as precise a discipline as mathematics. In 1935, Rudolf Carnap came to the United States from Europe and joined the University of Chicago the following year, thereby becoming one of the key American proponents of this variety of positivism, especially after World War II. Aspects of this movement proved to have a long-lasting impact upon American academia in general.

Positivism shaped the intellectual discourse of the late nineteenth century. Combined with Darwinism, it contributed significantly to the secularization of Anglo-American thought, to the undermining of classical political economy, and to bolstering the cultural authority of science. While varieties of philosophical idealism weakened its appeal by the end of the nineteenth century, it continued to influence the methodology of philosophy and of the social sciences well into the post–World War II era. In particular, its hostility to metaphysics marked American philosophy and social science until the end of the twentieth century.

BIBLIOGRAPHY

Adams, Henry. *Writings of Henry Adams.* New York: Norton, 1986.

Bannister, Robert C. *Sociology and Scientism: The American Quest for Objectivity, 1880–1940.* Chapel Hill: University of North Carolina Press, 1987.

Cashdollar, Charles D. *The Transformation of Theology, 1830–1890: Positivism and Protestant Thought in Britain and America.* Princeton, N.J.: Princeton University Press, 1989.

Harp, Gillis J. *Positivist Republic: Auguste Comte and the Reconstruction of American Liberalism, 1865–1920.* University Park: Pennsylvania State University Press, 1995.

Hawkins, Richmond L. *Auguste Comte and the United States, 1816–1853.* Cambridge, Mass.: Harvard University Press, 1936.

———. *Positivism in the United States, 1853–1861.* Cambridge, Mass.: Harvard University Press, 1938.

Kent, Christopher. *Brains and Numbers: Elitism, Comtism, and Democracy in Mid-Victorian England.* Toronto: University of Toronto Press, 1978.

Levy, David W. *Herbert Croly of the New Republic: The Life and Thought of an American Progressive.* Princeton, N.J.: Princeton University Press, 1985.

Mandelbaum, Maurice. *History, Man, and Reason: A Study in Nineteenth-Century Thought.* Baltimore: Johns Hopkins University Press, 1971.

Ross, Dorothy R. *The Origins of American Social Science.* Cambridge: Cambridge University Press, 1991.

Schneider, Robert Edward. *Positivism in the United States: The Apostleship of Henry Edger.* Rosario, Argentina, 1946.

Gillis J. Harp

See also **Economics; Philosophy; Pragmatism; Science and Religion, Relations of; Sociology.**

POST ROADS. Mail routes between New York and Boston took shape in the late seventeenth century. These roads traced routes that became great highways and are still known as the post roads. The Continental Congress began creating post roads during the revolutionary war. To designate a highway as a post road gave the government the monopoly of carrying mail over it; on other roads, anybody might carry the mail. At first the mail was conveyed on horseback. Later, stagecoaches carried both mail and passengers; the inns that served them became noted and prosperous hostelries. In 1787 connecting stretches of road reaching as far north as Portsmouth and Concord, N.H., as far south as Augusta, Ga., and as far west as Pittsburgh, Penn., were declared post roads. Between 1790 and 1829 successive acts of Congress increased the post-road mileage from 1,875 to 114,780. Steamboat captains also carried letters and collected the fees for them, until in 1823 all navigable waters were declared to be post roads, which checked the practice. Private letter-carrying companies after 1842 did much house-to-house mail business in the larger cities; but the postmaster general circumvented them in 1860 by declaring all the streets of New York, Boston, and Philadelphia to be post roads. The Rural Post Roads Act of 1916 provided federal aid to the states for the construction of rural post roads. The term "rural post road" was construed, with certain limitations, to mean any public road over which the U.S. mails were then, or thereafter might be, transported.

BIBLIOGRAPHY

John, Richard R. *Spreading the News: The American Postal System from Franklin to Morse.* Cambridge, Mass.: Harvard University Press, 1995.

Alvin F. Harlow / A. R.

See also **Postal Service, United States; Rural Free Delivery; Stagecoach Travel; Taverns and Saloons.**

POSTAL SERVICE, U.S. In many ways the U.S. Postal Service is the federal government agency most intimately involved on a daily basis with its citizens. It was and is a truly nationalizing service, connecting Americans to one another irrespective of state lines and geographic distance. However, in its earliest years its ineffectuality undermined the new nation's ability to fight the American Revolution and hampered efforts at creating a national polity in the years immediately following independence.

Benjamin Franklin was deputy postmaster of Philadelphia from 1737 until 1753, when he was appointed deputy postmaster of the colonies. At the Second Continental Congress, Franklin headed the committee that established an American national postal service and in 1775 became the first postmaster general.

The postal service languished during the Revolution. Afterward, as delegate to the Confederation Congress in the 1780s, Franklin continued to press the weak federal government to pay more attention to developing a postal service worthy of the name. He died in 1790, living just long enough to see his pleas and early efforts attended to by the strong federal government created under the Constitution of 1783. Under President George Washington, a strong Post Office department became a national priority in 1789. In September of that year Samuel Osgood was named postmaster-general; at the time there were fewer than eighty post offices in the United States. The Post Office was initially placed in the department of the Treasury. Under the nationalizing influence of the new Constitution, the number of local post offices with full-time or part-time postmasters increased dramatically. By 1800 there were well over eight hundred post offices in the United States.

As was true of so much of the federal government's operations in the Federalist decade, the Post Office department was quickly politicized, and remained so through the Age of Jackson. The Federalist Party built its organization in the 1790s around federal government employees in the states. The party also introduced politically oriented partisan newspapers everywhere in America, as did the opposition, the Jeffersonian Republicans. But the Federalists were in control, and they conjoined both sources of party support by naming many among its host of new printer-publishers as local postmasters. It was a natural marriage: Postmasters in villages, towns, and cities across America were the earliest recipients of national and international news; they not only were able to use the new postal routes being established to expedite delivery of their own newspapers, they could impede the opposition as well. They were able to frank (send without postal fee) their weekly papers to subscribers in many instances. At the same time it was very much in the political interests of the national government to designate local roads as post roads, thus providing subsidies for the building, extension, or improvement of key routes connecting the nations' states and localities. It was under these conditions that the more-than-eightfold growth in the size of the U.S. postal service took place.

Isaiah Thomas is a prime example of a printer-postmaster. After Benjamin Franklin, he was the most eminent representative of this eighteenth-century type. Appointed postmaster of Worcester, Massachusetts, in 1775, Thomas was the publisher and editor of *The Massachusetts Spy*. The *Spy* was a staunchly Federalist weekly sheet reaching readers throughout the Berkshires in western Massachusetts. The printer combined his operation with running the local post office, his stationer's shop, and his book publishing business. The Berkshires was an area crucial to the Federalist Party interests, for it was the locale of Shays's Rebellion, an uprising against national economic policies perceived to be unfair to farmers that roiled American society to its core from 1786 through 1787.

As postmaster, Thomas's value to the Federalist Party increased immeasurably. Not only was the printer assured of early receipt of foreign and domestic news via incoming exchanged newspapers, he knew that as postmaster he could frank at least part of the heavy mail generated by his newspaper as well as the paper's delivery through the Berkshires along newly upgraded post roads that he had designated. For Thomas and the *Spy* it was a marriage of business, politics, and government made in heaven and writ large, a grass roots part of national postal operations that extended through the Age of Jackson and beyond.

The Jeffersonian Republicans who took power in 1801 continued this path of postal politicization; as the nation grew in the early nineteenth century, so did the number of postal routes and postmasters who counted themselves partisan printers of newspapers. Among the earliest postmasters-general were prominent national political figures like Timothy Pickering (served 1791–1795), a Federalist, and Gideon Granger (1801–1814), a Jeffersonian Republican.

In the Age of Jackson (1824–1850), the U.S. population greatly increased along the eastern seaboard with the arrival of vast numbers of immigrants from Europe, and in the West as Americans moved into the Ohio Valley and beyond and into the Southwest as far as Texas. The Post Office kept pace. John McLean served as the postmaster general from 1823 to 1829, and he maintained the department's partisan character even as he effectively presided over its rapid expansion. Beginning in 1829 with William T. Barry, the postmaster-general was added to the president's cabinet, although the Post Office did not become officially established as an executive department until 1872 (it was removed from the cabinet in 1971 and renamed the U.S. Postal Service). By the time Andrew Jackson was elected president (with McLean's support) in 1828, there were more than three thousand post offices across America. McLean was rewarded with an appointment to the U.S. Supreme Court, a position he held until the Civil War. Jackson's "spoils system" of course included the Post Office department. One of Jackson's closest advisors, Amos Kendall, served as postmaster general from 1835 to 1840. A former newspaper printer and local postmaster, Kendall was not only a member of Jackson's cabinet, he also ranked high among the handful of political advisor's that made up Old Hickory's "kitchen cabinet." The political eminence of the postmaster-general reflected the importance of the U.S. Post Office department to the administration's political operations.

Among other political meddling, Kendall introduced a dangerous precedent when he banned Abolitionist tracts from the mail. It was the first of many instances when the U.S. Post Office involved itself in efforts to draw its own line in the sand between the national interest as the postmaster-general saw it and Constitutional protections of freedom of speech and the press. Other instances followed: supposedly "obscene" literature was banned periodically between 1868 and 1959, subject to postal enforcement. It included material that was generally agreed to be obscenity as well as material that was or came to be acknowledged as significant literature, such as works by Henry Miller, Leo Tolstoy, and many others. In 1918 the Post Office seized and burned issues of the *Little Review* containing chapters of James Joyce's *Ulysses.* During World War I several newspapers and magazines were banned from the mail under the terms of the Espionage Act of 1917. Birth control information also fell victim to Post Office censorship.

By the middle of the nineteenth century the U.S. Post Office had become a great unifier for the nation, maybe its most important in a rapidly expanding and diversifying republic. The mail got through efficiently and cheaply, helped by large infusions of federal money. In an age of slow travel, the Post Office linked most Americans to each other across the spreading population. Technology mingled with age-old means of transportation to get the mail through. By 1845, for example, the newly developed steamship was employed to deliver the mails both along the American coast and on inland rivers that could accommodate deep-draft vessels. In 1845 the Postal Act provided subsidies to American steamship companies that carried the mail to Europe, and lowered postage rates domestically to five cents for distances up to three hundred miles. In a nation rapidly expanding westward, the stimulus to commerce was incalculable, and connections were made possible among increasingly separated families as young sons and daughters and arriving immigrants alike moved west.

When even the new technology would not suffice, the Post Office turned to the saddle horse, the simplest and oldest means of rapid transit. Scheduled overland service was introduced in 1858 to carry the mail west. In April 1860 the Pony Express was introduced as a private enterprise, opening a route from St. Joseph, Missouri, to Sacramento, California, more than 1900 miles. The trip was made in just over ten days, with horses being changed at 157 stations along the way, every seven to twenty miles, depending on the terrain. One of Buffalo Bill Cody's first jobs was as a Pony Express rider on the Mormon Trail route in the early 1860s. He rode from his native Iowa on a route that ended in Salt Lake City, Utah. In July 1861 the Pony Express was contracted by the Post Office to deliver the mail, but it soon passed into history with the introduction of the transcontinental telegraph in October 1861.

Following the Civil War, the transcontinental railroads did a better, cheaper, and faster job of delivering the mail. Postal cars were a fixture on the cross-country railways from the late nineteenth century on. The service expanded, and the cars came to carry all sorts of insured or bonded valuables as well as stamped mail. Like the Pony Express, the rolling post offices of the railway systems made their way into mainstream American culture, usually as the targets of daring train robbers.

The Post Office adopted the use of stamps in 1847 and made prepayment of mail via stamps mandatory in 1855. Money orders were added as a service in 1864 and free daily urban delivery to the home was introduced at the same time. Rural free delivery was added on an experimental basis in 1896 and became permanent in 1902. Postal savings banks were introduced in 1911. The Post Office played an increasing part in American daily life as the twentieth century opened. Technology made this expansion possible. Railway post offices made the sorting of mail in transit an art form; machines to post mark and cancel stamps were in every post office, no matter how small; and conveyor belts and pneumatic tubes moved the mails in all of the large cities of America by World War I. Registered letters and parcel post deliveries were in place by the same time, no matter how rural the locale.

Another aspect of postal operations had some interesting by-products. A few people became rich off of U.S. Post Office errors. A handful of upside-down airmail stamps of the 1920s became collector's items. Stamp collectors swamped post offices in 1962 to buy the commemorative stamp issued to honor Dag Hammarskjöld, late secretary-general of the United Nations, when it was found to have been printed with its yellow background inverted; however, the postmaster-general ordered a new printing of the stamp with the "error" intentionally repeated, destroying the collector value of the original misprinting. Dozens of other stamp-plating errors, large and small, drew would-be collectors. Tens of thousands of children were encouraged to pore over stamp albums looking for gold.

The introduction of airmail was part of Post Office lore. Even before Charles A. Lindbergh popularized single-engine long-distance travel in 1927, the U.S. Post Office had introduced airmail. As a direct outgrowth of the mystique of the single-engine fighter planes of World War I, the postal service began delivering small amounts of mail by air in 1918. The first airmail service carried letters costing six cents between New York City and Washington, D.C. By 1920, again with New York as the hub, airmail service to San Francisco got underway, almost Pony Express-like in its relay system. Technology played its part, as airplanes improved dramatically and radio guidance beacons aided navigation. Government largesse also had a role, as it had with the post roads, the Pony Express, and railroad subventions. The Air Commerce Act of 1926 introduced government support of private airlines with contracts for carrying the mail and subsidies for building new airports. The Post Office was in the air all over the map before Lindbergh made his landing outside Paris.

James A. Farley, a long-time associate of Franklin Roosevelt, and the chief architect of Roosevelt's victory in the 1932 presidential election, was rewarded with the office of postmaster-general in the New Deal administration. He gave new visibility to the department and renewed its association with American politics, an association that had weakened in the wake of two generations of civil service reform beginning in the late nineteenth century.

Farley's political clout was in evidence in another crucial way. A long-time proponent of putting people back to work in the wake of the Great Depression, as postmaster-general with access to the president he was able to tap into the deep funding available for the Public Works Administration. Under Farley's aegis, hundreds of new post offices were built in villages, towns, and cities across America. Many of these are architectural gems. They grace the town squares of towns and the civic centers of large cities alike. Many are Art Deco in design, others are Greek Revival. Designed by otherwise unemployed architects and built by dedicated craftsmen, stonemasons, masons, and plumbers as well as tens of thousands of unskilled laborers, these buildings stand as prized examples of what public funding can do when both the will and the need are present.

Many of these local post offices were built with disproportionately large rotundas. These were meant to symbolize Post Office service, but they were also backdrops for life-size murals painted by out-of-work artists. Here Farley utilized his authority to tap into the funding of the Works Projects Administration (WPA). Many of the frescoes that were painted in the 1930s and 1940s are now considered significant works of art. Ben Shahn, for example, worked for the WPA from 1933 to 1943. Perhaps his best Post Office mural is the thirteen-panel one in the central post office in the Bronx, New York, depicting urban and rural working class life in America.

By the end of the twentieth century the ritual of the familiar daily mail delivery had deepened America's attachment to its Post Office. It was a daily connection of virtually all Americans to their federal government. Many aspects of American culture symbolized that attachment. In the "Blondie" comic strip, Blondie and Dagwood's postman, usually arriving a couple of times a week followed by a neighborhood dog, was introduced to Chic Young's seven-day-a-week comic strip in 1932. Similarly, Norman Rockwell's *Saturday Evening Post* covers featured more than one kindly postman (or a small post office) from the 1930s through the 1950s. A late-eighteenth-century printer's post office and a nineteenth-century country post office in a West Virginia country store were fully restored as part of the Smithsonian's National Museum of American History in Washington, D.C. The rural mail carrier in a red-white-and-blue jeep and the bag-toting urban postal worker both became welcome sights across the American landscape.

High-technology postal sorting systems in cavernous regional postal centers, with the alienating effects of sophisticated equipment and attendant depersonalization, have taken their toll on the mail delivery system. Competing with the homey images from the past are those beginning in the 1980s of mail workers "going postal," a synonym for violence in the workplace. Although challenged by competition from private delivery companies as well as the advent of instant electronic means of communication, the Post Office remains the most ubiquitous of federal agencies in a federal establishment that often seems very distant from the day-to-day concerns of Americans.

BIBLIOGRAPHY

Israel, Fred L., ed. *U.S. Postal Service.* New York: Chelsea House, 1986.

Marling, Karal Ann. *Wall-to-Wall America. A Cultural History of Post Office Murals in the Great Depression.* Minneapolis: University of Minnesota Press, 1982.

Prince, Carl E. *The Federalists and the Origins of the U.S. Civil Service.* New York: New York University Press, 1978.

U.S. Postal Service. *History of the United States Postal Service, 1775–1993.* Washington, D.C.: U.S. Government Printing Office, 1993.

Carl E. Prince

See also **Courier Services; Direct Mail; Pony Express; Rural Free Delivery.**

POSTMODERNISM. In the 1970s, "postmodernism" became a descriptive reference for certain changes occurring in American social, intellectual, and cultural life. The term had an elusive quality about it, and scholarly efforts to give it greater precision abounded. Postmodernism also yielded a critical literature as intellectuals pondered its political and ideological significance. Like "modernism," "postmodernism" conveyed different notions in the different categories in which the word was used. Examining the postmodern phenomenon in those categories does, however, suggest parallel meanings that paint a larger picture of American life in the late twentieth century. Causal interconnections are by no means self-evident, but common themes and motifs do appear.

Economic Affiliation

Postmodernism concurs with the emergence of postindustrialism. In the mid-1970s, the United States became, statistically, a service economy, with more workers employed in that category than in industrial jobs. Long-standing landmarks of the industrial era—steel, automobiles—declined and service businesses—hotels, travel agencies, restaurants, medical and health care organizations, sports, health clubs, real estate—provided the growth sectors of the American economy. These outlets serviced the greater leisure and discretionary time available to many Americans. Family patterns and gender roles were changing and greater personal choice produced a "lifestyle" revolution. Postindustrialism also connoted an "information age." Communications, the television medium, research and development, and the dissemination of knowledge in all forms attained higher prominence and importance. By the century's end personal computers had become common household items and computer functions proved indispensable to virtually every business function in the postindustrial economy. The information age, with its ever-accelerating pace, compelled Americans to process data and symbols in a new sensory environment.

Social critics perceived the change. The futurist Alvin Toffler's *Future Shock*, a best-selling book of 1970, described the new "feel" of the "super industrial economy." The rapid pace of change, the accelerated mobility of the business world, the "throwaway society" of the consumer market, Tofler asserted, all created the transient and impermanent sense of life in the new era. Human relations became more ad hoc as older social structures dissolved, Toffler believed. Christopher Lasch, in *The Culture of Narcissism* (1979) lamented the triumph of a hedonistic culture. Reflecting on the "political crisis of capitalism," Lasch recounted the emergence of a "therapeutic sensibility" and Americans' pervasive quest for psychic well-being. According to Lasch, Americans knew only the overwhelming present of the capitalist marketplace; self-preoccupation, indiscriminate hedonism, and anarchic individualism had become the normative social impulses of American life.

Postmodern Intellect

Impermanence, PLURALISM, dissolution, and the decay of authority constituted thematic emphases in the intellectual dimensions of postmodernism. The major influence, in the fields of language and literary theory, came heavily from the French. In the late 1960s, American students began to hear of thinkers like Ferdinand de Saussure, Roland Barthes, Jacques Lacan, Jacques Derrida, and others. They provided the leads in the redirection in American literary studies, "the linguistic turn" that would have influence in many academic disciplines. Influenced by the German philosophers Friedrich Nietzsche and Martin Heidegger, the French thinkers sought to deflate the pretensions of the logocentric, or word-focused, culture of Western civilization. Literary and intellectual texts, they asserted, always, when under close examination, yield both multiple and contradictory meanings. They "deconstruct" themselves. They do not produce truth systems; they confront us only with an endless chain of signifiers. Meaning always recedes, and eludes the reader. Western thinking, the poststructuralists maintained, had always been a quest for metaphysical comfort—a quest for the Absolute. But the efforts, they asserted, collapse from their very excesses. Poststructuralists such as those associated with the Yale School of academics in the 1970s deprived literary texts of subject authority ("the disappearance of the author"), coherence (texts are "de-centered"), and social reference ("there is nothing outside the text"). On the other hand, in poststructuralism, loss of authority also signified the positive alternative of reading as personal freedom ("re-creation"); Barthes wrote of the "pleasure of the text." In the Yale School, Geoffrey Hartman urged that the very indeterminacy of language empowered a creative criticism that broke the shackles of univocal meaning.

Postmodernism in its poststructuralist mode challenged the European and American left. In France, it replaced a Marxism that had dominated in the universities into the 1960s. In the United States, a sustained attack came from the literary scholar Frank Lentricchia in his 1980 book *After the New Criticism*. Leftist scholars, and particularly Marxists, had long insisted that literature, like all culture, reflected the hegemony of the dominant classes in capitalism; thus it always had a social connection and a historical foundation. Lentricchia saw in the American poststructuralists merely a formalist and hermetic approach to literature, depriving it of social and political context. "Pleasures of the text" conveyed to Lentricchia only the habits of aesthetic indulgence in bourgeois appropriations of culture, in short, a familiar recourse to hedonism. The linguistic turn to this extent, he believed, registered the most damning aspects of American capitalist culture, dissevering literature from the class struggle and rendering it a decorative and therapeutic device that invites us to take our pleasure as we like it.

In philosophy, Richard Rorty moved in a similar postmodernist direction. His *Philosophy and the Mirror of Nature* (1979) sought, like the poststructuralists, to deflate the pretensions of his discipline. Western thinking, he insisted, had gone awry in its long-standing efforts to secure a foundational epistemology, to make mind the mirror of nature. Rorty faulted the ahistorical character of this quest. Philosophy became defensive, he charged, freezing reality in privileged forms or essences. Appealing to the American pragmatist John Dewey, Rorty wished to return philosophy to the problematical aspects of ordinary life. In this era of "post-" and "neo-" labeling, Rorty called for a "post-Philosophy" that abandons pursuit of the conditioning groundwork of all thinking; instead, philosophy should be a form of hermeneutics. Post-Philosophy, for Rorty, had a relaxed and playful manner; it becomes an aspect of conversation, rooted in social and historical conditions. Here, too, a therapeutic quality stands out: philosophy helps us cope.

Postmodernism had a major social voice in the brilliant writings of the French thinker Michel Foucault. Though a voice of the political left, Foucault represents the postmodernist diminution of Marxism. To many poststructuralists like Foucault, Marxism conveyed traditional Western habits of logocentrism and notions of totality, from Hegel and onto "Western" Marxist humanism in the twentieth century. Foucault added to textual analysis the ingredient of power and saw language systems and intellectual discourse as vehicles of control. Foucault, however, read society like poststructuralists read literary texts, as decentered systems. In contrast to Marxists, he described power not as hegemony but as multiplicities, localities of activities, spaces, in which resistance and subversion are always at work. Foucault faulted Marxism as an intellectual residual of nineteenth-century ideology. Postmodernists like the French critic Jean-François Lyotard, in his influential book *The Post-Modern Condition* (1979), distrusted all holistic theorizing and "metanarratives." Absolutism in thought, he believed, led to totalitarianism in the political realm, the Gulag.

Postmodernist Arts

Postmodernism had specific references to the visual arts and redefined trends in painting and architecture. In the 1960s the reign of modernism in painting weakened. Nonrepresentational forms, of which the most often highlighted was abstract expressionism, gave way to stark contrasts, as in pop art. New styles proliferated: photorealism, pattern and decorative art, high-tech art. Although some new genres—such as feminist and performance art—often suggested a subversive intent, generally commentators saw that postmodernism took painting away from the critical edge and alienated mood of modernism. They found in the newer varieties a relaxed posture. And against the arctic purity of modernism, its successor forms invited a sensual indulgence, not only in the marketplace of suburban America, but also in older art forms obscured or discredited by the modernist imperium. Museums sponsored revivals and retrospective exhibits of all kinds.

Architecture saw a similar shift. Sleek, glass rectangular skyscrapers, born of the severe rationalism of the Bauhaus school decades previously, had long dominated the main streets of America's large cities. Revolting against this restrictive formalism of modernist architecture, Robert Venturi led a postmodernist protest. His book *Learning from Las Vegas* (1972) celebrated the "ordinary and ugly" buildings of that American playground. Then in 1978, Philip Johnson, a noted practitioner of modernism, surprised the critics in revealing his design for the new AT&T building in New York City. Johnson affixed to the top of the slender rectangular slab a 30-foot-high pediment, broken in the center by a circular opening, an orbiculum that capped the building with a stylistic crown. It looked to some like the crest of an old grandfather clock. Almost overnight, it seemed, Johnson's "Chippendale" effect gave architects a license to appropriate freely from any and all older mannerisms. Postmodernist architecture signified a pervasive and playful eclecticism.

These directions raised more critical voices, mostly on the cultural left. The Marxist scholar Fredric Jameson provided the most trenchant attack in his *Postmodernism: or, the Cultural Logic of Late Capitalism* (1991). Everywhere postmodernism signified to Jameson the loss of critical distance, the triumph of "kitsch," the collapse of all signs and symbols under the global marketplace of international capitalism. Under postmodernism, he said, historicity dissolved. The past presented itself only as commodifiable pastiche. Postmodernism, in Jameson's account, meant the flattening out of all historically conditioned realities that constitute the vehicle of social reconstruction. It leaves only the reign of simulacra, the therapeutic salve, the pseudo-reality of a dehumanized civilization.

Postmodernist culture reflected the proliferating diversity of American life in the late twentieth century. It fostered a mood of acceptance and democratic tolerance. Some resented its anti-elitism and found it meretricious and too comfortable with the commercial nexus. The postmodernist era brought a politics of diversity and group identity—in women's rights, gay liberation, black, Indian, and Chicano ethnic movements. Here, too, postmodernism broke down prevailing norms and idealizations of American life. Some saw in the effects a healthy, democratic tolerance. Others wondered whether there remained any unifying force or any center in American life.

BIBLIOGRAPHY

Bertens, Hans. *The Idea of the Postmodern: A History*. London: Routledge, 1995.

Hoeveler, J. David, Jr. *The Postmodernist Turn: American Thought and Culture in the 1970s*. New York: Twayne Publishers, 1996.

Kellner, Douglas, ed. *Postmodernism: Jameson Critique*. Washington, D.C.: Maisonneuve Press, 1989.

Silverman, Hugh J., ed. *Postmodernism: Philosophy and the Arts*. New York: Routledge, 1990.

J. David Hoeveler

See also **Post-structuralism.**

POST-STRUCTURALISM is an eclectic school of thought that significantly influenced literary and cultural theory in the 1970s and 1980s. It emerged as a reaction against the claims of 1960s French structuralism to scientific rigor, objectivity, and universal validity. Structuralism convinced many theorists that the key to understanding culture lay in the linguistic systemization of interrelationships in language. Building on the theories of the Swiss linguist Ferdinand de Saussure, the French anthropologist Claude Lévi-Strauss, and Russian Formalism, the structuralists found the clue to literary and cultural analysis in the phoneme, a unit of sound meaningful only because of its differences from other phonemes. Phonemes exemplify the elements in a cultural system that derive meaning from relations and contrasts with other elements. Structuralists determine meaning not by correlation to external reality but by analyzing its functions within a self-contained, culturally constructed code. Linguistic meaning is often established through binary opposition, or the contrast of opposites, such as cold versus hot and nature versus culture. A critic who understands the underlying rules or "language" determining individual utterances will understand meaningful combinations and distinctions.

Post-structuralism was in part a reaction to structuralism's claim to comprehensive and objective exploration of every cultural phenomenon. This countermovement denied the objectivity of linguistic and cultural codes, language, and categories of conceptualization. It emphasized the instability of meanings, categories, and the inability of any universal system of rules to explain reality. The result was a radically nonhierarchical plurality of indeterminate meanings. Central to post-structuralist thought is Jacques Derrida's deconstructionism. Influential among literary critics at Yale University in the 1970s and 1980s, deconstructionism indicts the Western tradition of thought for ignoring the limitless instability and incoherence of language. The dominant Western logocentric tradition sought a transcendent center or primal guarantee for all meanings. Logocentric thinking, common since Plato, attempts to repress the contingency and instability of meaning. Thus, any privileging of some terms as central to truth is denied as being merely arbitrary. For example, consider male over female and white over black. In the United States, literary critics used post-structuralist analysis to challenge the boundary between criticism of literature's subjectivity and objectivity, while elevating figurative language and interpretation. For post-structuralists there is no God, Truth, or Beauty, only gods, truths, and beauties. In the early 1990s, post-structuralism underwent an intense critique from a range of social critics. Aside from the obscurantism of the movement, it seemed ahistorical, dogmatic, willfully nihilistic, and unable to provide a critique of moral and social injustice. Perhaps a part of the hedonistic flight from social responsibility of previous years, the movement seemed to slow down. The trend away from post-structuralism has continued into the twenty-first century, as the gradual tapering off of publications on the topic from its height in the mid-1980s clearly indicates.

BIBLIOGRAPHY

Caputo, John D., ed. *Deconstruction in a Nutshell: A Conversation with Jacques Derrida.* New York: Fordham University Press, 1997.

Kearney, Richard, ed. *Dialogues with Contemporary Thinkers.* Manchester: Manchester University Press, 1984.

Mouffe, Chantal, ed. *Deconstruction and Pragmatism.* New York: Routledge, 1996.

Raman, Selden, and Peter Widdowson, eds. *A Reader's Guide to Contemporary Literary Theory.* 3d ed. Lexington: University Press of Kentucky, 1993.

Alfred L. Castle / A. E.

See also **Anthropology and Ethnology; Assimilation; Linguistics; Philosophy.**

POST-TRAUMATIC STRESS DISORDER (PTSD) is a psychological condition, affecting people who have experienced an event that involves actual or threatened death or serious injury to themselves, witnessing of horrifying events and feeling unable to escape or alter them, or learning about the violent death or serious injury of a family member or close associate. PTSD can occur at any age, and symptoms usually manifest within three months but might be delayed by years. Features of PTSD include intrusive memories or thoughts about the event, efforts to avoid thinking about the event, a general numbing of emotional responsiveness, and a constantly heightened level of arousal. A diagnosis of PTSD requires that symptoms have been present for at least a month and hamper normal functioning in social and work settings. Dissociation, a sense of detachment from the reality of one's surroundings, is a way people often cope with repeated trauma. PTSD, as the explanation for "hysteria," emerged in the research of French psychologist Pierre Janet and, early in his career, that of Sigmund Freud. During World War I, PTSD, called combat neurosis, shell shock, or battle fatigue, was common in soldiers. The American psychiatrist Abram Kardiner developed this concept in his book *The Traumatic Neuroses of War* (1941). PTSD became an official diagnosis of the American Psychological Association in 1980, due largely to the symptoms of Vietnam veterans. The revival of the feminist movement in the late 1960s led to heightened awareness of domestic violence and abuse as a cause of PTSD.

BIBLIOGRAPHY

Herman, Judith Lewis. *Trauma and Recovery.* Reprint, New York: Basic Books, 1997.

Livesley, W. John. *The DSM-IV Personality Disorders.* New York: Guilford Press, 1995.

William Ira Bennett
Lisa A. Ennis

POTASH (potassium carbonate) and soda (sodium carbonate) have been used from the dawn of history in bleaching textiles, making glass, and, from about A.D. 500, in making soap. Soda was principally obtained by leaching the ashes of sea plants, and potash from the ashes of land plants. In their uses, potash and soda were largely but not entirely interchangeable. Indeed, before the mid-eighteenth century, people only vaguely differentiated between the two.

With the advent of gunpowder at the end of the Middle Ages, potash found a new use for which soda could not substitute: the manufacture of saltpeter. Thus, the increasing demand for glass, soap, textiles, and gunpowder in sixteenth- and seventeenth-century Europe accelerated the decimation of the forests from which producers obtained potash. In 1608 the first settlers in Virginia established a "glass house," and the first cargo to Britain included potash. Britain obtained most of its potash from Russia, but a potash crisis in about 1750 led Parliament to remit the duty and led the Society of Arts of London to offer premiums for the production of potash in America.

Potash-making became a major industry in British North America. Great Britain was always the most important market. The American potash industry followed the woodsman's ax across the country. After about 1820, New York replaced New England as the most important source; by 1840 the center was in Ohio. Potash production was always a by-product industry, following from the need to clear land for agriculture.

By 1850, potash had gained popularity as a fertilizer, but forests available for indiscriminate burning were becoming ever scarcer. Fortunately, deep drilling for common salt at Stassfurt, Germany, revealed strata of potassium salts, and in 1861 production of this mineral potash began. The United States, having decimated its forests, joined most of the rest of the world in dependency on German potash. The dependency still existed when WORLD WAR I cut off this source of supply. Frantic efforts produced some domestic potash, notably from the complex brines of some western saline lakes. The United States surmounted the wartime urgency, but the shortage directed attention to reports of oil drilling that had brought up potash salts. These clues led to large deposits near Carlsbad, NEW MEXICO. After 1931 a number of mines there supplied about 90 percent of the domestic requirement of potash. Some 95 percent of this production became fertilizer.

BIBLIOGRAPHY

Godfrey, Eleanor Smith. *The Development of English Glassmaking, 1560–1640.* Chapel Hill: University of North Carolina Press, 1975.

Hall, Bert S. *Weapons and Warfare in Renaissance Europe: Gunpowder, Technology, and Tactics.* Baltimore: Johns Hopkins University Press, 1997.

Hoffman, Ronald, et al., eds. *The Economy of Early America: The Revolutionary Period, 1763–1790.* Charlottesville: University Press of Virginia, 1988.

McCusker, John J., and Russell R. Menard. *The Economy of British America, 1607–1789.* Chapel Hill: University of North Carolina Press, 1985.

Robert P. Multhauf/A. E.

See also **Bounties, Commercial; Chemical Industry; Enumerated Commodities; Fertilizers; Geological Survey, U.S.; Industries, Colonial.**

POTATOES. The so-called Irish potato, a native of the Andes, was introduced into England in the sixteenth century. A ship is known to have carried potatoes from England to Bermuda in 1613, and in 1621 the governor of Bermuda sent to Governor Francis Wyatt of Virginia two large chests filled with plants and fruits then unknown to the colony, among them potatoes, which were planted and grown in the settlements along the James River. In 1622 a Virginia bark brought about twenty thousand pounds of potatoes from Bermuda to Virginia. Their cultivation did not spread widely, however, until a party of Scotch-Irish immigrants brought potatoes with them to Rockingham County, New Hampshire, in 1719. Because of this introduction and because potatoes had become a major crop in Ireland by the end of the seventeenth century, "Irish" became a permanent part of the potato's name.

The Swedish botanist Peter Kalm found potatoes being grown at Albany in 1749. Thomas Jefferson wrote of cultivating potatoes, "both the long [sweet?] and the round [Irish?]." Decades later, the Navaho Indians of the Southwest were found to be planting a small, wild variety common in some parts of Mexico. The Irish potato came to be a daily item on the American dinner table—especially in the northern states as an accompaniment for meats—and a major food crop in many states during the nineteenth century. Aroostook, the large, northernmost county of Maine, began extensive potato growing, and in 1935 that county's potatoes produced half of the agricultural income of Maine. Aroostook homemakers are said to have been the first, or among the first, to make starch for their white garments by soaking potato pulp in water and then drying it. Starch sheds began to appear along the streams, and eventually Aroostook produced 90 percent of the nation's potato starch. The use of this starch declined greatly in the twentieth century, and industrial alcohol appeared as a new means of saving the culls and the surplus.

Sweet potatoes (botanically, wholly unrelated to the Irish tuber) were being cultivated by the Amerindians before the arrival of Christopher Columbus, who, with the other members of his party, ate these potatoes and esteemed them highly. Because they were best grown in the South, and because they gave an enormous yield (200 to 400 bushels per acre), they became a favorite vegetable in that region, although they remained unknown to the table in large areas of the North. To the southern poor, sweet potatoes inevitably accompanied opossum meat, although they were also served with fresh pork and other meats; the sweet potato has often been the main item in the diet of some poor families, especially in winter. The cultivation of sweet potatoes spread to California and gradually crept up the Atlantic coast as far as New Jersey.

By 1999 annual U.S. production of Irish potatoes had reached 478 million hundredweight; production of sweet potatoes in the same year totaled nearly 12 million hundredweight.

BIBLIOGRAPHY

Salaman, Redcliffe N. *The History and Social Influence of the Potato.* Revised ed. New York: Cambridge University Press, 1985. The original edition was published in 1949.

Zuckerman, Larry. *The Potato: How the Humble Spud Changed the Western World.* Boston: Faber and Faber, 1998.

Alvin F. Harlow/C. W.

See also **Agriculture; Agriculture, American Indian.**

POTAWATOMI. Closely allied with the Ottawas and Ojibwes, the Potawatomis occupied a broad homeland; from southern Wisconsin it stretched across northern Illinois, northern Indiana, and southern Michigan, to Detroit. From the seventeenth century onward, the Potawatomis were close allies of the French, and often assisted them in their colonial wars with the British. During the American Revolution, the easternmost Potawatomi bands supported the British, while Potawatomis from Wisconsin and Illinois were neutral or assisted the Americans. In

Potawatomi Farm. Pisehedwin, a Potawatomi, and other Indians are photographed at his Kansas farm, 1877. NATIONAL ARCHIVES AND RECORDS ADMINISTRATION

the post-Revolutionary period, Potawatomis joined the Indian coalition that resisted the American occupation of Ohio and participated in the border warfare of the 1790s. Many Potawatomis later became followers of Tecumseh and the Shawnee Prophet and fought with the British during the War of 1812.

After the War of 1812, many Potawatomis, both men and women, were prosperous traders in the Midwest. During the 1830s, part of the tribe was removed to Iowa and Kansas, and in the decade that followed, consolidated on a reservation near Topeka, Kansas. After the Civil War, the Citizen Band moved to Oklahoma, where they maintained tribal offices in Shawnee. The Prairie Band, a more traditional community, continues to occupy a reservation near in Mayetta, Kansas. Since 1913, the Forest Band has resided on a reservation in Forest County, Wisconsin. Other Potawatomis maintain reservation communities in Michigan and southern Ontario.

BIBLIOGRAPHY

Clifton, James. *The Prairie People: Continuity and Change in Potawatomi Indian Culture, 1665–1965.* Lawrence: The Regents Press of Kansas, 1977.

Edmunds, R. David. *The Potawatomis: Keepers of the Fire.* Norman: University of Oklahoma Press, 1978.

———. *Kinsmen through Time: An Annotated Bibliography of Potawatomis History.* Metuchen, N.J.: Scarecrow Press, 1987.

Sleeper-Smith, Susan. *Indian Woman and French Men: Rethinking Cultural Encounters in the Western Great Lakes.* Amherst: University of Massachusetts Press, 2001.

R. David Edmunds

See also **Pottawatomie Massacre; Tribes: Prairie; Wars with Indian Nations, Colonial Era to 1783; Wars with Indian Nations, Early Nineteenth Century (1783–1840).**

POTOMAC RIVER drains the eastern slopes of the central ALLEGHENY MOUNTAINS into Chesapeake Bay. Two main streams, the East and West Branches, unite to form the upper Potomac, which is joined by the Shenandoah River at Harpers Ferry. A freshwater river for 287 miles, the Potomac below Washington, D.C., is a tidal estuary 125 miles long and between two and eight miles in width. The region, especially the lower portion, was home to many Native Americans. Spaniards probably reached the Potomac estuary before 1570, and it was mapped by Captain John Smith in 1608 at the time of initial English settlement in Virginia. Agents of George Calvert probably explored the upper Potomac. After the founding of Maryland in 1634, the Potomac was the early passageway for the colony. Owing to Great Falls above Washington, rapids at Harpers Ferry, and Indian problems, the upper Potomac was long unimportant. In the 1720s, Tidewater Virginians, Germans, and Scots-Irish crossed it into the SHENANDOAH VALLEY, and about 1740 Thomas Cresap, a militant Marylander, settled at Oldtown above the junction of the South Branch in western Maryland. Slowly, the Potomac Valley became a pathway to the Ohio Valley, used by the OHIO COMPANY OF VIRGINIA, by George Washington, and by General Edward Braddock. Later enterprises using the route were the Patowmack Company of 1785, the CUMBERLAND ROAD of 1807 (later extended westward as the National Road), the Baltimore and Ohio Railroad of 1827, and the Chesapeake and Ohio Canal

Potomac River. This July 1865 photograph by James Gardner shows the confluence of the Potomac River and the smaller Shenandoah River at Harpers Ferry, W.Va. NATIONAL ARCHIVES AND RECORDS ADMINISTRATION

Company of 1828. The canal competed with roads and railroads until the early 1900s. The Potomac formed the effective eastern border between the Union and the Confederacy and was the scene of many campaigns and crossings including Antietam.

BIBLIOGRAPHY

Gutheim, Frederick A. *The Potomac.* New York: Rinehart, 1949. One of the excellent *Rivers of America* series.

Potter, Stephen R. *Commoners, Tribute, and Chiefs: The Development of Algonquin Culture in the Potomac Valley.* Charlottesville: University Press of Virginia, 1993.

Sanderlin, Walter S. *The Great National Project: A History of the Chesapeake and Ohio Canal.* Baltimore: Johns Hopkins Press, 1946.

Alfred P. James
Stanley W. Trimble

POTSDAM CONFERENCE took place in a suburb of Berlin from 17 July to 2 August 1945. President Harry S. Truman, Marshal Joseph Stalin, and Prime Minister Winston Churchill (replaced at midpoint by the newly elected Clement Attlee) met to reach accord on postwar Germany and the Pacific war. The "big three" confirmed a decision, made at Yalta, to divide Germany into British, American, Russian, and French occupation zones. They pledged to treat Germany as a single economic unit while allowing each of the four occupying commanders to veto any decision. Germany was slated for total disarmament, demilitarization, the trial of war criminals, and denazification. Other provisions included reparations (with the final sum unspecified); the forced return of 6.5 million Germans from Poland, Czechoslovakia, and Hungary in an "orderly and humane manner"; and the temporary retention of the Oder-Neisse boundary. The Council of Foreign Ministers, a body composed of the United States, Great Britain, France, and Russia, was entrusted with preparing peace terms for Italy, Romania, Bulgaria, Austria, Hungary, and Finland. On 14 July, having been informed of the successful atomic tests at Alamogordo, New Mexico, three days before, Truman told an unsurprised Stalin, "We have perfected a very powerful explosive which we are going to use against the Japanese and we think it will end the war."

As Russia had not yet declared war on Japan, the Potsdam Declaration of 26 July 1945 was signed only by the United States and Great Britain, though with China's concurrence. It threatened the "utter devastation of the Japanese homeland" unless Japan accepted "uncondi-

Potsdam Conference. The leaders seated at the table, separated by four advisers to either side, are President Harry S. Truman (*bottom, left of center*), the soon-to-be-replaced Prime Minister Winston Churchill (*upper left*), and Marshal Joseph Stalin (*upper right*). NATIONAL ARCHIVES AND RECORDS ADMINISTRATION

tional surrender." Specific terms included total disarmament, the destruction of its "war-making power," the limitation of Japan's sovereignty to its home islands, stern justice to "all war criminals," the establishment of "fundamental human rights," the payment of "just reparations in kind," and the limitation of its economy to peacetime undertakings.

BIBLIOGRAPHY

Feis, Herbert. *Between War and Peace: The Potsdam Conference.* Princeton, N.J.: Princeton University Press, 1960.

Gormly, James L. *From Potsdam to the Cold War: Big Three Diplomacy, 1945–1947.* Wilmington, Del.: Scholarly Resources, 1990.

Mee, Charles L., Jr. *Meeting at Potsdam.* New York: M. Evans, 1975.

Justus D. Doenecke

See also **Germany, American Occupation of; Japan, Relations with; World War II; Yalta Conference.**

POTTAWATOMIE MASSACRE, the murder by free-state men of five proslavery settlers near Dutch Henry's Crossing at Pottawatomie Creek, Franklin County, Kansas, on the night of 24–25 May 1856. The principal facts became known almost immediately. John Brown, four of his sons, and three other men were accused of the murders. Although warrants were issued, only one suspect, James Townsley, was arrested. The case never went to trial. Some proslavery newspapers gave fairly accurate statements of the facts but were confused in attributing motives; the free-state press misrepresented both. Brown's first biographer, James Redpath, denied Brown's presence at the murder and prior knowledge of the events. Only after Townsley's statement was published in December 1879 did the Brown family and friends (with a few exceptions) admit the truth. From that date, the Brown controversy centered on motives and justification rather than denial, but with little success in establishing either.

The primary political issue in the spring of 1856, just before the massacre, was enforcement of the so-called bogus laws. In various parts of the territory, threats were made against the courts and enforcement officers. Significantly, all but one of the Pottawatomie victims either were members of the Franklin County grand jury or were otherwise associated with the 21–22 April court session. These facts place the massacre in the category of political assassination, designed to prevent enforcement of law by resorting to terror.

BIBLIOGRAPHY

Oates, Stephen B. *To Purge This Land with Blood: A Biography of John Brown.* New York: Harper and Row, 1970. 2d ed., Amherst: University of Massachusetts Press, 1984.

Potter, David M. *The Impending Crisis, 1848–1861.* Completed and edited by Don E. Fehrenbacher. New York: Harper and Row, 1976.

James C. Malin / c. w.

See also **Antislavery; Border War; Kansas-Nebraska Act.**

POVERTY. While aspects of poverty in the United States have changed significantly since colonial times, debates about how best to alleviate this condition continue to revolve around issues of morality as well as economics. In eighteenth- and early-nineteenth-century America, most people worked throughout their lives at a succession of unstable jobs, under unhealthy conditions. Widows, immigrants, the ill, and the elderly generally had few sources of support outside their own poor families. Townships and counties resorted to such drastic solutions as auctioning off poor local residents to local farmers. Indigent nonresidents would simply be sent out of town. The primary form of public assistance, known as "outdoor relief," consisted of food, fuel, or small amounts of money. Poorhouses were founded to serve the indigent more cheaply than outdoor relief while discouraging them from applying for further public assistance. Especially in the North, poorhouses attempted to improve their residents' personal habits. Supervised work, such as farming, weaving, and furniture building, was required; alcohol was forbidden.

Poorhouses became notorious for overcrowding, filth, disease, and corrupt management. Reformers also increasingly criticized outdoor relief for demoralizing the poor and attracting idlers and drunks. By the Civil War (1861–1865), private relief associations run by evangelical Protestants, immigrant groups, and upper-class women's groups had begun to assume a more bureaucratic form. The Charity Organization Society, founded in Buffalo, New York, in 1877 (chapters were established in most U.S. cities by 1892) attempted to systematize relief by sending volunteers to investigate the circumstances of each applicant and advise them on how to live a respectable life. Handouts were to be given only in cases of extreme need. This approach, known as "scientific charity," proved impractical. Yet elements of its method evolved into the caseworker system of social welfare agencies.

At the end of the nineteenth century, one-fifth to one-quarter of the poorhouse population was long-term—primarily elderly people, along with the mentally ill and the chronically sick. Most inmates—out-of-work men, or women giving birth to illegitimate children—stayed only for a week or two at a time. Poor children were generally separated from their parents and moved into orphan asylums. Increasingly, the able-bodied homeless slept on police station floors and in the new shelters (municipal houses or wayfarers' lodges) that began to open around the turn of the century.

Defining Poverty Levels

Attempts to define poverty levels in the United States have long been arbitrary and controversial. From about 1899 to 1946, poverty minimum subsistence levels were based on "standard budgets"—goods and services a family of a certain size would need to live at a certain level. In his 1904 book *Poverty Social Worker,* Robert Hunter set one of the first national poverty line figures: below $460 annually for a five-person family in the North; below $300 for the same size family in the South. A study commissioned by the Congressional Joint Committee on the Economic Report in 1949 determined the poverty line to be $1,000 for farm families and $2,000 for nonfarm families.

In 1965, the federal government adopted landmark poverty thresholds, devised by economist Molly Orshansky, that took into account household sizes and types (such as elderly or nonelderly). Specifying an amount of money adequate for a family might be fraught with difficulties, Orshansky wrote, but it was possible to determine a level that was clearly insufficient. She based her figures on information from the Department of Agriculture, using the "economy" food plan—the cheapest of the four standard food plans, intended for "temporary or emergency use when funds are low"—and a survey showing that families of three or more people spent about one-third of their after-tax income on food. Lacking minimum-need standards for other household necessities (such as housing, clothing, and transportation), Orshansky simply multiplied these food costs by three to determine minimum family budgets.

In 1969, the thresholds began to be indexed to the Consumer Price Index rather than the cost of the economy food plan. The weighted average poverty thresholds established by the U.S. Census Bureau for 2001 range from $8,494 for an individual 65 or older to $39,413 for a family of nine people or more with one related child under eighteen.

This measurement of poverty has been widely criticized. It does not account for noncash government benefits, such as free school lunches or food stamps, and it fails to account for geographic differences in the cost of living. Critics also believe the thresholds do not properly reflect the overall rise in U.S. income since the 1960s.

Who Are the Poor?

Measurements of the extent of poverty in the United States depend, of course, on how it is defined. Poverty is a relative term; it must be understood differently for an affluent postindustrial culture than for a developing country. As the economist John Kenneth Galbraith wrote, "People are poverty-stricken when their income, even if adequate for survival, falls markedly behind that of the community."

In his groundbreaking 1962 book *The Other America: Poverty in the United States,* Michael Harrington called attention to a group of between 40 million and 50 million

Americans (20 to 25 percent of the population at that time) living without adequate nutrition, housing, medical care, and education—people deprived of the standard of living shared by the rest of society. Harrington derived his figures from several sources, including a late-1950s survey by sociologist Robert J. Lampman and family budget levels from the Bureau of Labor Statistics.

In 2000, 11.3 percent of the population—31.1 million people—were considered poor, continuing a decline in poverty that began during the economic boom of the mid-1990s, when the poor accounted for 14.5 percent of the population. Before then, the last major decline occurred between 1960, when the rate was 22.2 percent, and 1973 (11.1 percent).

As of 2002, child poverty rates also had fallen since their peak in 1993. Yet more than 11 million children—16.2 percent of all Americans 18 years old or younger—were living in poverty, about the same number recorded in 1980. This group included 17 percent of all children under the age of six. About 5 million children were living in extreme poverty, in families with incomes less than half of the poverty line. Among African Americans, the childhood poverty rate was 30 percent; among Latino families it was 28 percent.

The enormity of this continuing problem cannot be overstressed. The infant mortality rate is more than 50 percent higher in poor families. Children growing up in poverty are more likely to drop out of high school and become parents in their teens, more likely to have junk food diets that predispose them to childhood obesity and diabetes, more likely to suffer chronic health conditions and mental retardation, and more likely to lack positive role models for academic and job success. Thirty-five percent of single-parent families live in poverty, more than twice the national average. Teenagers in poor families are more likely than other teens to be single parents. Poor single parents attempting to join the workforce are seriously hampered by the need to find affordable quality health care and child care (which can consume more than 20 percent of a poor working mother's income).

Another way to look at poverty by the numbers is to see how total income is shared in the United States and whether the poor are closing the gap between themselves and the rest of society. Harrington noted that the increase in the share of personal income earned by the poorest one-fifth of the population between 1935 and 1945 was reversed between 1945 and 1958. The poor increased their share in the late 1960s, only to see these gains reversed once more, beginning in the 1980s.

In 1968, the Citizens Board of Inquiry Into Hunger and Malnutrition in America estimated that 14 million Americans were going hungry. Nearly thirty years later, the U.S. Department of Agriculture reported that nearly 35 million Americans were unable to supply their families with sufficient amounts of food. Other poverty markers include lack of education: The poverty rate for high school dropouts is three times the rate for those who have a high school diploma.

In 1960, the federal Commission on Rural Poverty report, *The People Left Behind*, found that nearly one-third of rural Americans lived in poverty. Their homes were substandard, their access to health care was rare, and their education—particularly among the children of black field workers—was minimal. By the late 1990s, the percentage of poor rural Americans declined to 16 percent, partly due to mechanization and closure of coal mines in Appalachia, which caused workers to migrate to urban areas. Electricity and plumbing are now standard, but isolated rural residents have fewer child care options and social and educational services than their urban peers.

The nearly 9 million rural poor—one-fifth of the poor population—are 55 percent white, 32 percent black, and 8 percent Hispanic. Migrant field workers from Mexico and Central America, who struggle to support families on substandard pay, generally live in crowded, makeshift housing. Native Americans are also hard hit by poverty; more than a quarter of the population lives below the poverty line. On reservations, the unemployment rate is three times the average for rest of the U.S. population, with high levels of alcoholism and tuberculosis as well.

While the stereotype of the poor is of a group that goes from cradle to grave without improving its lot, there is substantial movement in and out of poverty. About one-third of the poor in any given year will not be among the poor the following year. Only 12 percent of the poor remain poor for five or more years. A national study in the 1990s found that more than half of these "poverty spells" lasted one year or less. The reasons people slide into poverty include divorce, job loss, and incomes that do not keep pace with the cost of living, especially in low-wage occupations.

Other common misconceptions about the poor are not borne out by the figures. While poverty rates are greater among blacks and Hispanics than among other ethnic groups, non-Hispanic whites comprise 48 percent of the poor, African Americans account for 22.1 percent, and Hispanics, 22 percent. Less than half (42 percent) of the poor live in central cities, and less than 25 percent live in inner-city ghettos. Surprisingly, more than one-third (36 percent) of the poor live in the suburbs.

Official poverty figures do not include the homeless (or people in institutions—jails, mental institutions, foster care, nursing homes), but the best estimates put the homeless population at anywhere from 500,000 to more than 800,000. The ranks of the homeless swelled when enlightened social policy of the 1970s—deinstitutionalizing the mentally ill with the goal of reintegrating them into society—fell afoul of budget cutbacks and lack of community follow-through in the 1980s.

There are many economic and social reasons poverty remains a major problem in the United States. As American companies have opened manufacturing plants abroad, where labor is cheaper and lower benefit standards are the norm, well-paying, often unionized, jobs for blue-collar workers have disappeared from American cities. Other jobs have moved to the car-dependent suburbs, out of reach to a population largely dependent on public transportation. Meanwhile, the expanding service sector is split between high-paying professional employment in business and technology, and low-wage service industry jobs (janitors, maids, fast-food and retail workers). While one person is employed in about 60 percent of poor families, minimum-wage jobs—often lacking health and other benefits—do not pay enough to keep families from poverty. With little or no accumulated wealth, the poor and their families have no savings to fall back on if they lose a job or have unanticipated expenses.

The Welfare System

The foundation of the welfare system and the government's only program of mass public assistance—the Aid to Families with Dependent Children (AFDC)—was established during the Great Depression as part of the 1935 Economic Security Act. The federal government paid half the cost of the program for the families of needy children and established broad guidelines. State governments picked up the rest of the cost, set payment levels, and administered the program. Food Stamps (Food and Nutritional Assistance) also originated during the New Deal, as a means of supplementing farm income with coupons that could be redeemed for food.

Social programs in the United States tend to operate in thirty-year cycles. The "rediscovery" of poverty after the Great Depression began with the publication of such influential books as John Kenneth Galbraith's *The Affluent Society* (1958) and Michael Harrington's *The Other America: Poverty in the United States* (1962), in which he argued that the poor—in particular, children, the elderly, and nonwhites, increasingly isolated in urban ghettos—had become invisible to the middle-class white majority. Although President John F. Kennedy's support of antipoverty proposals was cut short by his assassination, President Lyndon B. Johnson announced a "War on Poverty" in his 1964 inaugural speech. The success of Johnson's Great Society program—which included urban renewal and a broadscale fight against poverty, disease, and lack of access to education and housing—was greatly helped by relatively low unemployment and inflation, a federal budget surplus, the growing civil rights movement, and an increasing level of public confidence in sociological studies. Certain aspects of these social programs were enhanced in the 1970s, under the administration of President Richard Nixon.

In 1967, the Kerner Commission, appointed by President Johnson to study the causes of the riots that swept American inner cities that year, recommended that the federal government establish "uniform national standards" of welfare aid "at least as high as the annual 'poverty level' of income" (which was then $3,335 for an urban family of four). The commission also advised that states be required to participate in the Unemployed Parents program of the AFDC and that welfare mothers of young children no longer be required to work.

AFDC cash benefits were pegged to the number of children in the family, which caused some critics to believe that women on welfare were having more children to boost the amount of their checks, or separating from the father of their children in order to qualify for this benefit. (However, while the proportion of mother-only households increased during the years of the program, the real value of the payments decreased.) About one-third of AFDC recipients were found to remain in the program for six or more years. The Family Support Act of 1988 expanded AFDC benefits to families with two unemployed parents and required absent parents to pay child support. Eight years later, however, AFDC was eliminated and replaced by block grants to states, which administer their own programs.

President Kennedy revived the food stamp program in 1961; nine years later, Congress set a minimum benefit level for food stamps—which were now free—and offered them at a low cost to families over the poverty line; eligibility was broadened later in the 1970s. All funds for the program, administered by state welfare agencies, are provided by the federal government.

Under Medicaid, established in 1965, the federal government pays matching funds to states to cover a portion of medical expenses for low-income elderly, blind, and disabled persons, and for members of low-income families with dependent children. States have considerable latitude in setting eligibility, benefits, and payments to service providers. In 1963, a physician had never examined 20 percent of Americans below the poverty level; in 1970, this number fell to 8 percent. Prenatal visits by pregnant women increased dramatically, which contributed to an overall drop in infant mortality of 33 percent (50 percent in some poor areas) between 1965 and 1972.

Initiated in 1972, Supplemental Security Income (SSI) gives cash benefits to elderly, blind, and disabled persons in order to bring their income to federally established minimum levels. The program is administered by the Social Security Administration, with some benefits supplemented by individual states.

Beginning in the 1970s, Section 8 Low-Income Housing—administered by the Department of Housing and Urban Development (HUD)—initiated payments to private developers who set aside apartments at below-market rates for low-income families. Now known as the Housing Choice Voucher Program, it accounts for more than half of federal funds spent on housing for the poor; low-rent public housing accounts for another 25 percent. Only about 19 percent of the poor receive housing benefits, however, compared with about 40 percent receiving cash benefits from AFDC and SSI. The Earned Income Tax Credit (EITC), expanded under the administrations

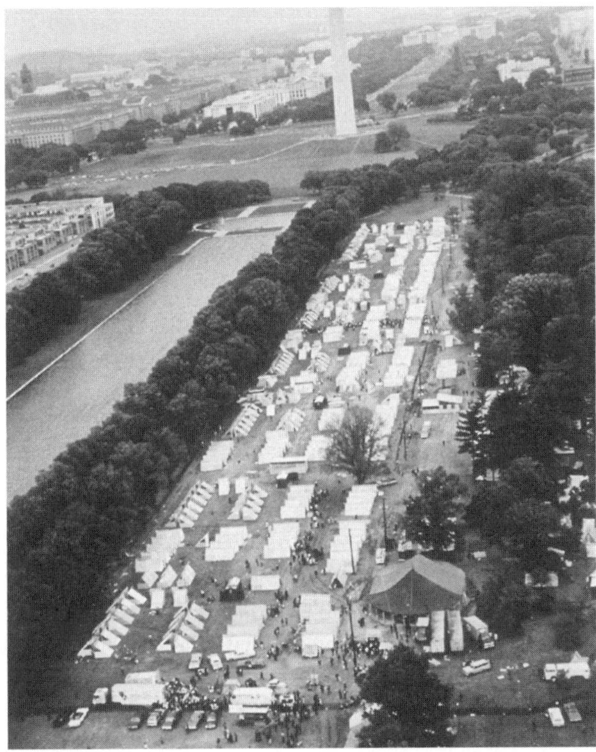

Resurrection City. After the assassination of Martin Luther King Jr. on 4 April 1968, his planned Poor People's March on Washington, D.C., instead became this rain-soaked encampment near the Lincoln Memorial and a series of poorly attended, ineffective antipoverty rallies, lasting from 13 May to 24 June before fading away as police took down the tents. © CORBIS

of Presidents Ronald Reagan, George Bush, and Bill Clinton, gives workers a tax break based on their earned income, adjusted gross income, and the number of children they have. In 2001, the income of recipients with no qualifying children had to be less than $10,710; with two or more qualifying children, the income limit was $32,121. This program was appealing to policymakers because it rewards workers (benefits increase with increased income), helps families with children, and works through the tax code, with no need for a separate bureaucracy.

Other social programs have increased the availability of services to the poor, including day care for children, health care, work-training, special programs for agricultural workers, and free legal assistance. While Social Security, instituted in 1935, is not based on need—it is based on the amount of Social Security tax paid on wages—this entitlement, with its substantial monthly payments, has played a huge role in keeping the elderly from poverty.

The Welfare Backlash

Beginning in the mid-1970s, the phenomenon of the "inner city" as a cauldron of joblessness, major crime, drug addiction, teenage pregnancy, and welfare dependency began to make headlines. For more than a decade, liberals had decried the low level of benefits welfare clients received while conservatives argued that welfare breeds dependency. Increasingly, welfare applicants were the offspring of welfare families. Tabloid stories of "welfare queens" using their government stipend to buy Cadillacs only inflamed the debate. Many agreed that welfare served to tide people over when they hit bottom but created a subclass of citizens with little dignity or self-respect.

During the Reagan administration, many social programs were reduced in scope or eliminated. The self-perpetuating nature of poverty noted by influential sociologist Oscar Lewis—who coined the phrase "the culture of poverty"—was seized upon by conservatives eager to end welfare. Lewis's sympathetic description of the way six-year-old slum children in South America had become so accustomed to a hopeless view of the world that they seem unlikely to be able to escape from poverty was intended to shift attention from individual poverty victims to the culture of impoverished communities. But conservatives used his views to argue that the children of ghetto families lack a work ethic. This sentiment was exacerbated during the 1980s by lack of income growth among middle-class wage earners, which made many leery of "handouts" going to a group often perceived as undeserving. (In fact, nearly half the income the poor received came from wages; welfare accounted for only 25 percent of the total.)

By the 1992 presidential campaign, Bill Clinton was promising to "end welfare as we know it." The Personal Responsibility and Work Opportunity Reconciliation Act of 1996 officially ended the entitlement status of welfare and (as revised in 1997) denied assistance to newly arrived legal emigrants. The goal of this program was to reduce the welfare rolls, increase the number of working poor, and reduce out-of-wedlock births.

AFDC was replaced by Temporary Assistance for Needy Families (TANF), a $16.5 billion block grant program to the states to fund "welfare-to-work" programs. Unlike AFDC, which supplied federal matching funds of one to four dollars for every dollar in state appropriations, TANF's block grants are not tied to state expenditures. The new rules require that 50 percent of able-bodied adults receiving assistance be cut off after two years, and that 80 percent of each state's welfare recipients receive no more than five years of aid in a lifetime. Adults who do not have children under age six must work at least 30 hours per week to receive food stamps; unmarried teenage mothers receiving welfare benefits must attend school and live with an adult.

The burden on former welfare recipients has been significant. Finding and keeping even a temporary, low-paid job is generally a daunting undertaking for someone with a shaky or nonexistent job history, few skills, and little experience with the schedules and social skills working people take for granted. People new to the job market often must find the money for child care and transportation to work. Cut off from Medicaid benefits after one year and usually uninsured at work, this population has become even more vulnerable to health crises.

Changing Views of the Poor

The prevailing nineteenth-century view of the poor, whether religious or sectarian, rested on the assumption that weak moral fiber was to blame for their situation. In the twentieth century, thinking about poverty shifted to a greater emphasis on social and environmental factors. Robert Hunter, author of *Poverty* (1904), boldly declared that most of the poor "are bred of miserable and unjust social conditions. . . ." In *Democracy and Social Ethics* (1902), Jane Addams—cofounder of Hull House, which offered community services to the poor in Chicago—questioned the reformers' insistence on thrift and hard work as specific virtues for the poor, because the rich were not held to the same standards. The best way to ensure virtuous behavior on the part of the poor, she wrote, was to push for shorter hours, better wages (including a level of pay for women that would keep them from turning to prostitution), restrictions on child labor, and alternatives to the temptations of the saloon.

Yet overreliance on government handouts continued to be seen as a moral issue even in the midst of the Great Depression, when New Deal policies were created to promote economic recovery, not specifically to eliminate poverty. In 1935, President Franklin D. Roosevelt said, "Continued dependence upon relief induces a spiritual and moral disintegration fundamentally destructive to the national fiber."

In the 1960s, the reigning belief was that behavior associated with the ghetto was due not to ingrained cultural characteristics, but rather to segregation and a history of limited opportunities that—coupled with bitter personal experiences—made the prospect of a better life through hard work seem unrealistic. Urban field studies undertaken in the late 1960s were interpreted in light of this point of view.

Black ghettos were once home to middle-class as well as lower-class African Americans. As William Julius Wilson has pointed out, this social geography offered young people a range of role models and job contacts. By the 1970s, the growth of suburbs and civil rights legislation had enabled middle-class African Americans to move out of the inner city. Without an adequate tax base to fund good schools and other city services or middle-class incomes to support banks, shops, and other services, neighborhoods declined. High-density housing projects built in the 1950s to replace old slums tore apart the tight-knit fabric of communities and created an apathetic culture that became the festering center of unemployment, drug addiction, and crime. The inner-city population is also a particularly youthful one, and the fourteen- to twenty-five-year-old group is statistically more likely to commit crime, be welfare dependent, and have out-of-wedlock births.

One of the most controversial documents of the 1960s was "The Negro Family: The Case for National Action," by Daniel Patrick Moynihan, a white paper issued by the Department of Labor in 1965. Moynihan wrote that the instability of black families was a primary cause of poverty, and that welfare policies should encourage intact families and work as a means of integrating these families into the mainstream. Critics took Moynihan to task for blaming the poor rather than advocating societal change.

Another influential book, *Regulating the Poor: The Functions of Public Welfare*, by Frances Fox Piven and Richard A. Cloward (1971), proposed that welfare recipients should not be encouraged to work at a menial job just to bring in some money and avoid idleness—they should hold out for jobs that pay a living wage—and that welfare is necessary to the economic survival of women, whose jobs traditionally pay less than men's.

Charles Murray's book *Losing Ground: American Social Policy, 1950–1980*, published in 1984, was one of several prominent studies that decried liberal social policies for creating a welfare-dependent population during the 1970s. In Murray's view, the federal government should withdraw from the welfare business, and the poor—except for the truly deserving, whose needs would be served by private charity and local government—should take responsibility for their own lives. Murray's critics say the economic downturn was responsible for increased unemployment, which in turn made more people poor during the 1970s. Also to blame, they say, was a decline in real wages—the actual purchasing power of income—and the effect of baby boomers entering the job market. Critics maintain that the poverty rate would have risen even farther had Great Society programs not been in place.

BIBLIOGRAPHY

Bane, Mary Jo, and David T. Ellwood. *Welfare Realities: From Rhetoric to Reform.* Cambridge, Mass.: Harvard University Press, 1994.

Blank, Rebecca M. *It Takes a Nation: A New Agenda for Fighting Poverty.* Princeton, N.J.: Princeton University Press, 1997.

Citro, Constance F., and Robert T. Michael. *Measuring Poverty: A New Approach.* Washington, D.C.: National Academy Press, 1995.

Copeland, Warren R. *And the Poor Get Welfare: The Ethics of Poverty in the United States.* Nashville, Tenn.: Abington Press, 1994.

Danziger, Sheldon H., et al. *Confronting Poverty: Prescriptions for Change.* Cambridge, Mass.: Harvard University Press, 1994.

Duncan, Cynthia M. *Worlds Apart: Why Poverty Persists in Rural America.* New Haven, Conn.: Yale University Press, 1999.

Edin, Kathryn, and Laura Lein. *Making Ends Meet: How Single Mothers Survive Welfare and Low-Wage Work.* New York: Russell Sage Foundation, 1997.

Harrington, Michael. *The Other America: Poverty in the United States.* New York: Macmillan. 1962.

Jencks, Christopher. *Rethinking Social Policy: Race, Poverty, and the Underclass.* Cambridge, Mass.: Harvard University Press, 1992.

———, and Paul E. Peterson, eds. *The Urban Underclass.* Washington, D.C.: Brookings Institute, 1991.

Katz, Michael B. *In the Shadow of the Poorhouse: A Social History of Welfare in America.* New York: Basic Books, 1996.

Lavelle, Robert, et al. *America's New War on Poverty: A Reader for Action.* San Francisco: KQED Books, 1995.

Moynihan, Daniel P. *Maximum Feasible Misunderstanding: Community Action in the War on Poverty.* New York: The Free Press, 1969.

Murray, Charles. *Losing Ground: American Social Policy, 1950–1980.* New York: Basic Books, 1984.

O'Hare, William P. *A New Look at Poverty in America.* Washington, D.C.: Populations Reference Bureau, Inc., vol. 51, no. 2, Sept. 1996.

Schwartz, Joel. *Fighting Poverty with Virtue: Moral Reform and America's Urban Poor, 1825–2000.* Bloomington: Indiana University Press, 2000.

Schwarz, John E., and Thomas J. Volgy. *The Forgotten Americans.* New York: Norton, 1992.

Wilson, William Julius. *The Truly Disadvantaged: The Inner City, the Underclass, and Public Policy.* Chicago: University of Chicago Press, 1987.

Cathy Curtis

See also **Urban Redevelopment; Urbanization;** *and vol. 9:* **The New American Poverty; In the Slums, 1890.**

POVERTY POINT, in northeastern Louisiana, is the most striking example of prehistoric Archaic culture in the southeastern United States. In addition to typical Archaic stone projectile points, grooved stone axes, adzes, celts, tubular pipes, and steatite and sandstone vessels, the site also contains some of the most impressive aboriginal earthworks and mounds in North America. A series of six concentric artificial ridges forming a "C" shape was constructed between 1300 and 200 B.C. on an ancient alluvial fan in a former channel of the Arkansas River. The largest of these earth ridges is more than twelve hundred meters across. Gaps between the ridges allowed access to a central plaza. Archaeologists are still unsure whether Poverty Point's population lived at the site or gathered at the mounds for ceremonial purposes only, living instead in scattered sites nearby.

A twenty-three-meter-high earth mound, shaped like a bird with outspread wings, was constructed immediately outside the settlement in a position seven degrees south of due west. The purpose of this large mound, whose base is two hundred meters across, remains a mystery. Another mound, uncompleted but probably planned in a shape similar to that of the first, is located two kilometers north of the ridges, at about seven degrees west of true north. Conical burial mounds and a small amount of fiber-tempered pottery indicate an advanced, transitional character for the population.

Archaeologists have long wondered how a site of this size could exist without signs of intensive agriculture. The site's occupants may have cultivated local plants such as squash, sunflowers, and sumpweed, but there is no sign that they grew maize, the staple of later concentrated populations, and it is probable that they lived primarily from hunting, fishing, and gathering. The site had clear trade connections to other related sites throughout the Southeast. Figurines of clay representing nude females, pendants of hard stones representing birds' heads, small bead buttons, stone blades struck from prepared cores, and petaloid greenstone celts are among artifacts that suggest contact with Mesoamerica, but such contact is fiercely debated. In spite of extensive research, much of this remarkable site and the people associated with it remains a mystery.

BIBLIOGRAPHY

Byrd, Kathleen M., ed. *The Poverty Point Culture: Local Manifestations, Subsistence Practices, and Trade Networks.* Geoscience and Man, vol. 29. Baton Rouge: Geoscience Publications, Louisiana State University, 1991.

Guy Gibbon / J. H.

See also **Archaeology and Prehistory of North America; Indian Mounds; National Park System.**

POWELL CASE (*Powell v. McCormack*, 395 U.S. 486, 1969). In 1967 Adam Clayton Powell Jr., a veteran member of the U.S. House of Representatives, was denied membership in the House for alleged financial misconduct before his reelection in 1966. Powell challenged the House's decision in U.S. courts. At issue was whether the House could deny membership on any grounds other than those stipulated in the Constitution, namely, age, citizenship, and residence. In 1969 in *Powell v. McCormack* the Supreme Court ruled in Powell's favor, declaring that the House had exceeded its constitutional authority. The Powell case demonstrated the need for an external check to guarantee the people's right to a representative of their choice.

BIBLIOGRAPHY

Dionisopoulos, P. A. *Rebellion, Racism, and Representation: The Adam Clayton Powell Case and Its Antecedents.* Dekalb: Northern Illinois University Press, 1970.

Hamilton, Charles V. *Adam Clayton Powell Jr.: The Political Biography of an American Dilemma.* New York: Atheneum and Maxwell Macmillan International, 1991.

P. Allan Dionisopoulos / A. R.

See also **Congress, United States; Constitution of the United States.**

POWELL EXPEDITIONS. *See* **Colorado River Explorations.**

POWER OF POSITIVE THINKING, THE, a book that headed the nonfiction best-seller list for two years and sold two million copies in the 1950s, tried to reconcile liberal Protestantism to the affluent society and to psychoanalysis. Its author, Norman Vincent Peale (1898–1993), the minister of the prestigious Marble Collegiate Church on Fifth Avenue in New York City, assured his readers that material success was a defensible Christian goal and that achieving it was largely a matter of cultivating the right mental attitude. In the tradition of mind cure, New Thought, and the "gospel of success," he regarded God more as a benign power working from within the individual than as the divine judge of earlier American Protestantism.

Peale, with his partner Smiley Blanton, ran a religious and psychoanalytical clinic at his church and published the inspirational magazine *Guideposts.* He also traveled and broadcast widely, specializing in success-oriented addresses to groups of businessmen. *The Power of Positive Thinking* (1952) capitalized on the success of his earlier *Guide to Confident Living* (1948). It included "how to" passages on overcoming anxiety and succeeding in business, and inspirational tales that conformed to the middle-class and anticommunist orthodoxies of the moment. Characteristic chapter headings are "Expect the Best and Get It," "Inflow of New Thoughts Can Remake You," and even "How to Get People to Like You." Just as it contradicted Freud's militant atheism, so it lacked the painful drama of Freud's psychological works. Instead, it declared blandly that "you can have peace of mind, improved health, and a never-ceasing flow of energy."

Peale capitalized on the book's success, despite sharp criticism from all points on the religious spectrum—from evangelical Protestants for his loose interpretation of scripture, and from the neo-orthodox for what looked to them like his too-easy embrace of materialism and the consumer way of life.

BIBLIOGRAPHY

George, Carol. *God's Salesman: Norman Vincent Peale and the Power of Positive Thinking.* New York: Oxford University Press, 1993.

Meyer, Donald. *The Positive Thinkers: Religion as Pop Psychology from Mary Baker Eddy to Oral Roberts.* New York: Pantheon, 1980.

Patrick N. Allitt

See also **Psychology; Self-Help Movement.**

POWHATAN CONFEDERACY, a paramount chiefdom in the coastal plain of Virginia, named for its leader at the time of English colonization. Powhatan had inherited the leadership of a group of six tribes in the sixteenth century and expanded his authority to more than thirty tribes by 1607. Much of this expansion was by conquest. The Powhatans had a system of dual leadership with a "peace chief" responsible for internal affairs and a "war chief" for external affairs, including warfare. There was also a powerful council, which included priests and other advisers. Powhatan led the confederacy from before 1607 to 1617; after that the war chief Opechancanough was most visible, although a brother, Itoyatin, succeeded Powhatan as peace chief.

The region of the Powhatan Confederacy was called Tsenacommacah. Its core lay in the area between the James and Mattaponi Rivers in the inner coastal plain; other territories, each with its own chief and villages, were predominantly east of this area. All of these constituent chiefdoms paid tribute to Powhatan as paramount chief. To the north and south were other groups not part of the confederacy but culturally and linguistically similar. The geographic fall line running through modern Richmond, Virginia, constituted a western boundary across which were other groups speaking different languages; relatively little is known of those people.

The Powhatans lived in villages, many fortified, that could have over a thousand inhabitants, although most were a few hundred or smaller. The daily lives of villagers included farming, fishing, hunting, and gathering wild resources. Paralleling their political organization, Powhatan cosmology featured two powerful deities and a number of lesser spiritual powers. Powhatan males bonded with these *manitus* through the *huskanaw*, a vision-quest ritual, and their lives were shaped by the particular *manitu* with whom they shared a personal connection. Chiefs, priests, and curers had access to the most powerful *manitus*, but most Powhatans could personally draw on the spiritual realm; women had an innate spirituality related to their reproductive capacity.

The Powhatans were vital to the English Virginia colony in its early years. Cultural differences precluded understanding, and each saw the other as inferior, but for some years the Jamestown colony survived on food traded (or stolen) from the Powhatans. In the winter of 1607–1608, Powhatan attempted to adopt the English colony through the well-known ritual in which Powhatan's daughter Pocahontas symbolically saved Captain John Smith; in October 1608, the English tried to crown Powhatan as subordinate to their king.

Although the Powhatans tolerated the English for their desirable goods, throughout the first half of the seventeenth century they had to attempt violent corrections for what they saw as inappropriate actions by the colonists. The colonists also responded with violence to what they considered inappropriate actions by the Powhatans. The marriage of Pocahontas and John Rolfe in 1614 brought a measure of peace to the area, but Pocahontas died in early 1617 while visiting England. Led by Opechancanough, the Powhatans conducted large-scale at-

Pocahontas. The illustration on this package of tobacco, c. 1860, depicts the apocryphal tale of the Indian maiden who saved Captain John Smith by appealing to her father, Powhatan, the leader of his eponymous confederacy. Library of Congress

tacks on the colony in 1622 and again in 1644; after the latter, Opechancanough was captured and killed. The 1646 treaty was signed by "king of the Indians" Necotowance, but by then Virginia was firmly controlled by the English and the Powhatans were dependent "tributary Indians" confined to designated reservations.

Through the eighteenth and nineteenth centuries, descendants of the Powhatan Indians remained in eastern Virginia, but they were relatively invisible—except for the descendants of Pocahontas, who were a proud part of white society. In the late nineteenth century, the Powhatans began the long struggle for recognition. The anthropologist Frank Speck promoted their cause beginning in 1919, and opposed racist policies directed against them. He aided a revival of the "Powhatan Confederacy" in the 1920s; another was attempted around 1970. While these reorganized confederacies did not last, individual tribes continued both on the two surviving reservations and in several other communities. Although they lacked federal recognition in the twenty-first century, most were recognized by the state of Virginia.

BIBLIOGRAPHY

Gleach, Frederic W. *Powhatan's World and Colonial Virginia: A Conflict of Cultures.* Lincoln: University of Nebraska Press, 1997.

Rountree, Helen C. *The Powhatan Indians of Virginia: Their Traditional Culture.* Norman: University of Oklahoma Press, 1989.

———. *Pocahontas's People: The Powhatan Indians of Virginia through Four Centuries.* Norman: University of Oklahoma Press, 1990.

Speck, Frank G. *Chapters on the Ethnology of the Powhatan Tribes of Virginia.* New York: Heye Foundation, 1928.

Frederic W. Gleach

See also **Indian Political Life.**

***POWHATAN* INCIDENT.** When the Civil War began, President Abraham Lincoln determined not to give up the two remaining federal forts in southern territory—Fort Sumter at Charleston, South Carolina, and Fort Pickens at Pensacola, Florida. The administration ordered relief expeditions to both forts, but Secretary of State William H. Seward, in an attempt to maintain his supremacy in Lincoln's cabinet, secretly ordered the warship *Powhatan* to Fort Pickens instead of Fort Sumter. Although Lincoln eventually countermanded Seward's order, the ship was already on its way to Fort Pickens. The Pickens expedition was successful, but without the *Powhatan*'s firepower, the relief of Sumter failed.

BIBLIOGRAPHY

Current, Richard Nelson. *Lincoln and the First Shot.* Philadelphia: Lippincott, 1963.

Potter, David Morris. *Lincoln and His Party in the Secession Crisis.* Baton Rouge: Louisiana State University Press, 1995.

Thomas Robson Hay / t. g.

See also **"Alabama"; Confederate States of America; Executive Orders; Federal Government; South, the: The Antebellum South.**

POWWOW, a Native American gathering centered around dance. In post–World War II America, "powwow," derived from the Narragansett word for "shaman," became the term for the Plains Indians social dance that spread to all fifty states, Canada, and Europe. Held indoors or outdoors, powwows typically occur as Saturday afternoon or evening single events, three-day weekend events, or week-long annual events. Powwows vary regionally and attract Native Americans, non-Indian hobbyists, and tourists who travel to rural and urban tribal, intertribal, and hobbyist venues to socialize in and around the circular powwow arena. Powwows commemorate Indian culture and entertain.

Powwows originated in Oklahoma in the mid-nineteenth century, when intertribal warfare transformed into visiting and dancing networks that expanded through common experiences in boarding schools, Wild West shows, the peyote religion, and the Ghost Dance. The most popular powwow dance, the war dance, evolved from the War Dance Complex of the Southeastern Ceremonial Complex (A.D. 800–1500) and was aboriginal to the Caddoan-speaking Pawnees and the Dhegihan Omahas, Poncas, and Osages. From these groups the war dance diffused in the 1860s to the northern Plains tribes, where it became the Omaha dance or grass dance. In the early 1880s, the war dance appeared in western Oklahoma as the Crow dance or the Ohomo dance. By the mid-twentieth century, the Oklahoma or southern Plains variant of the war dance became the straight dance.

Heightened involvement in tourism and contest dancing in the early 1920s compelled western Oklahoma tribes to transform the war dance into the fast-paced, colorful fancy dance, which became the main attraction of powwows. A typical Oklahoma-influenced powwow features several dance styles: gourd dance, round dance, fancy dance, straight dance, traditional dance, two-step dance, women's fancy shawl and jingle dress dances, and perhaps hoop dance or shield dance. Singers in Oklahoma prefer a southern drum, whereas northern Plains singers maintain a northern drum style.

BIBLIOGRAPHY

Galloway, Patricia, ed. *The Southeastern Ceremonial Complex: Artifacts and Analysis.* Lincoln: University of Nebraska Press, 1989.

Kavanaugh, Thomas W. "Powwows." In *Encyclopedia of North American Indians.* Edited by Frederick E. Hoxie. Boston: Houghton Mifflin, 1996.

Powers, William K. *War Dance: Plains Indian Musical Performance.* Tucson: University of Arizona Press, 1990.

Benjamin R. Kracht

See also **Ghost Dance; Indian Dance; Indian Social Life; Sun Dance.**

PRAGMATISM is the name given to a worldwide philosophic movement that was most important in the United States in the late nineteenth century and early twentieth century. Two centers of "classic" pragmatism existed in the United States. The one at the University of Chicago was led by John Dewey, who later taught at Columbia University in New York City, and included James H. Tufts, George Herbert Mead, and Addison W. Moore. The other had its nucleus at Harvard University and included Charles S. Peirce, William James, and Josiah Royce. Later in the twentieth century Harvard continued to be an influential stronghold of academic pragmatism, while New York City's intellectual life reflected Dewey's concerns. At the end of the twentieth century an important revival of pragmatism took place in scholarly disciplines outside of PHILOSOPHY.

Pragmatism arose as the most sophisticated attempt to reconcile science and religion in the wake of the widespread acceptance of Darwinian biology. The early pragmatists argued that the truth of an idea lay primarily in its ability satisfactorily to orient individuals to the world of which they were a part but also in its consistency with other ideas and its aesthetic appeal. Ideas were plans of action and would be deemed true if action in accordance

Charles Sanders Peirce. The first major formulator of what he called pragmatism, in 1878, and a leader of its advocates at Harvard University (as well as an important early thinker in such fields as psychology and semiotics); he later split away from his colleague William James.

with them "worked" in the long run. The pragmatists rejected what later became known as "representationalism," the belief that a true idea corresponded to its object. Truth was not a connection something mental had to something outside the mind but instead characterized a way of behaving. For the pragmatists, philosophers should not look for answers to speculative problems by cogitation in the library; rather, the practices of communities of inquirers should be explored. Accordingly the pragmatists accepted the findings and methods of the sciences and urged that their methods be applied in all areas of study. But they also thought that religious ideas, for example, belief in the existence of God and in a benign universe, might be justified if they had survival value.

William James. The best known of the philosophical pragmatists associated with Harvard University, who based the model of inquiry on what is scientifically verifiable. LIBRARY OF CONGRESS

Pragmatism at Harvard

In "How to Make Our Ideas Clear," published in *Popular Science Monthly* in 1878, Peirce originally expressed these views in connection with the meaning of the concepts of the physical sciences. James's exposition was vigorously and forcefully popular, especially in his collected essays *Pragmatism* (1907). For James the chief virtue of the pragmatic account of truth was that it made philosophy concrete. James's position reflected his early interest in physiology and psychology, and he elaborated his insights in a long argument with his Harvard colleague Royce, who formulated a less-individualistic doctrine called "absolute pragmatism." Counting the emotional benefits of holding a belief to be true as part of the meaning of truth, James defended heartfelt spiritual creeds, and Peirce, calling his own views "pragmaticism," dissociated himself from James's nontechnical theorizing. James had an international reputation, and his support assisted in the promulgation of his ideas by F. C. Schiller in England, Henri Bergson in France, and Giovanni Papini in Italy.

Pragmatism at Chicago and Columbia

Steeped in the cultural thought of German idealism, Dewey used his version of pragmatism, called "instrumentalism," to attack educational, social, and political problems, as in *The School and Society* (1899) and *Liberalism and Social Action* (1935). Throughout Dewey's long and prolific career he was involved in controversy and led many liberal intellectual causes. His beliefs about "experimentalism" and the use of the "method of intelligence" in social life became the theoretical underpinning of the social sciences in the American university that often tilted against the status quo. A crude form of pragmatism became widely known as the rationale behind reformist politics: the political pragmatist was the liberal who restricted progressive goals to what was obtainable practically, to programs that could succeed.

A second period of pragmatism was under way when Dewey retired from teaching in 1929. In New York City a version of his system was propagated first of all by a younger group of "Columbia naturalists," including Ernest Nagel, John Herman Randall, and Herbert Schneider. For these thinkers intelligence grew out of a "natural" biological realm that yet provided an adequate locus for a moral and political life valuing humanism, social democracy, and internationalism. The naturalists also included among their allies Morris Cohen of the City College of New York, who sent generations of students to Columbia for graduate study; Dewey's student Sidney Hook, who articulately defended his mentor's ideas and pragmatism's public role from his position at New York University; and Alvin Johnson, director of the New School for Social Research, who presided over an expansion of instrumentalist ideas in sociology and political science.

Later Pragmatisms

At Harvard the second period of pragmatism made Cambridge, Massachusetts, the premier place to study professional philosophy. A student of Royce and James, C. I. Lewis developed an epistemological system called "conceptual pragmatism." In his influential book of 1929, *Mind and the World-Order*, Lewis argued that the various frameworks of ideas by means of which people gained knowledge about the world were chosen on the basis of their practical value, but he emphasized the primacy of the hard sciences in obtaining knowledge. Over the next fifty years Lewis's academic writing was central to the

George Herbert Mead. One of the leading adherents of pragmatism at the University of Chicago, along with John Dewey; Mead focused extensively on the mind and the development of language. LIBRARY OF CONGRESS

"pragmatic analysts," the most significant group of American philosophers, Nelson Goodman, Willard Quine, and Hilary Putnam, all of whom subsequently taught at Harvard. These scholars and a host of lesser figures focused on logic and the philosophy of science. They intimated that humans lived in a Darwinian universe bereft of purpose and best explored by physics. At the same time they acknowledged that people selected conceptual structures with communal human purposes in mind and that often alternative structures were equally legitimate in accounting for the flux of experience and for attempts to navigate experience. A crucial explanation of these tension-laden concerns was laid out in Quine's celebrated essay, "Two Dogmas of Empiricism," published in the *Philosophical Review* in 1951.

The Revival of Pragmatism

In the last quarter of the twentieth century pragmatic ideas remained alive in the work of the pragmatic analysts but had neither the religious nor social dimension of the more publicly accessible views of James or Dewey. In the discipline of philosophy in the United States classic pragmatism was considered an old-fashioned and unrefined philosophical commitment. Nonetheless at the end of the century a large-scale pragmatic renewal depended on the arguments of the analysts but also resurrected the concerns of classic figures.

These developments began with the extraordinary publication of *The Structure of Scientific Revolutions* in 1962 by Thomas Kuhn, who had studied at Harvard and been influenced by Quine. Kuhn's thesis, that succeeding scientific worldviews were not progressive but incommensurable and thus to some degree relative, was ignored or patronized by many philosophers. Nonetheless his best-selling cross-disciplinary book was widely adopted by social scientists in a variety of disciplines, by departments of literature and the humanities generally, and by historians. It became common for many Kuhn-tinged thinkers to assert that *The Structure of Scientific Revolutions* had proved beyond doubt that no ideas could be proved true.

In 1979, using the ideas of Quine and Kuhn, Richard Rorty published *Philosophy and the Mirror of Nature*, which gave some philosophical support to Kuhn's relativistic ideas. But Rorty also linked them to the classic pragmatists, urging that human beings had different "discourses" available to them to attain whatever ends they might have, but no one discourse, including that of natural science, was privileged above the others. All were to be justified by their ability to lead expeditiously to the achievement of goals. Critics argued that such a "linguistic" pragmatism was less robust in its public implications than that of James and Dewey, a charge that Rorty both accepted in his commitment to private concerns and rebutted in writings that promoted the political side of his pragmatism. Rorty had an impact within the discipline of philosophy, but he was more connected to programs in humanities and comparative literature and was most generously read outside of the discipline of philosophy. He in any event had led the way to a revitalized pragmatic movement that regarded the classic thinkers as engaged in debates relevant to the twenty-first–century world.

BIBLIOGRAPHY

Kloppenberg, James T. *Uncertain Victory: Social Democracy and Progressivism in European and American Thought, 1870–1920.* New York: Oxford University Press, 1986. Puts pragmatism in an international context.

Kuklick, Bruce. *A History of Philosophy in America, 1720–2000.* Oxford and New York: Clarendon Press, 2001. Most recent synthesis with a large section on pragmatism.

Perry, Ralph Barton. *The Thought and Character of William James.* 2 vols. Boston: Little, Brown, 1935. The outstanding philosophical biography.

Stuhr, John J., ed. *Pragmatism and Classical American Philosophy: Essential Readings and Interpretive Essays.* 2d ed. New York: Oxford University Press, 2000.

Thayer, H. S. *Meaning and Action: A Critical History of Pragmatism.* Indianapolis, Ind.: Bobbs-Merrill, 1968. A standard treatment.

Westbrook, Robert B. *John Dewey and American Democracy.* Ithaca, N.Y.: Cornell University Press, 1991. An excellent account of classic pragmatism.

Bruce Kuklick

PRAIRIE is a major North American biome, or ecological region. It extends from central Canada to the Mexican border and from the eastern flank of the Rocky Mountains to Indiana. Its topography ranges from rolling hills to the flatlands of former glacial lake bottoms. Its climate is characterized by relatively low annual precipitation (twenty to forty inches per year) and a high rate of evapotranspiration. This topography and climate contributed to the dominance of grasses, the subdomination of broadleaf plants, and sparse forest cover.

The region was originally sparsely populated by Native Americans who settled in greater numbers after the arrival of the horse. European Americans began settling the region in earnest only after the arrival of the railroads in the 1870s. The primary economic activity has been and continues to be AGRICULTURE, with livestock production and grain production dominating. This activity has resulted in the loss of over 99 percent of the original prairie. Today the region is home to more than 33.5 million people. Concerns about the ecological region include the continuing loss of virgin prairie, topsoil erosion, and groundwater contamination and depletion.

BIBLIOGRAPHY

Risser, Paul G. "Grasslands." In *Physiological Ecology of North American Plant Communities.* Edited by Brian Chabot and Harold A. Mooney. New York: Chapman and Hall, 1985.

Polly Fry

PRAIRIE DU CHIEN, INDIAN TREATY AT. This treaty was signed 19 August 1825 by members of the Dakota (Sioux), Chippewa, Sauk, Fox, Potawatomi, Ho-Chunk (Winnebago), and Iowa nations in an effort to end long-standing conflicts between the Dakotas and the Chippewas and their respective allies. In 1824 a deputation to Washington requested that the federal government help establish new tribal boundaries. During the treaty gathering at Prairie Du Chien, General William Clark of St. Louis and Governor Lewis Cass of Michigan Territory mediated among more than one thousand tribal

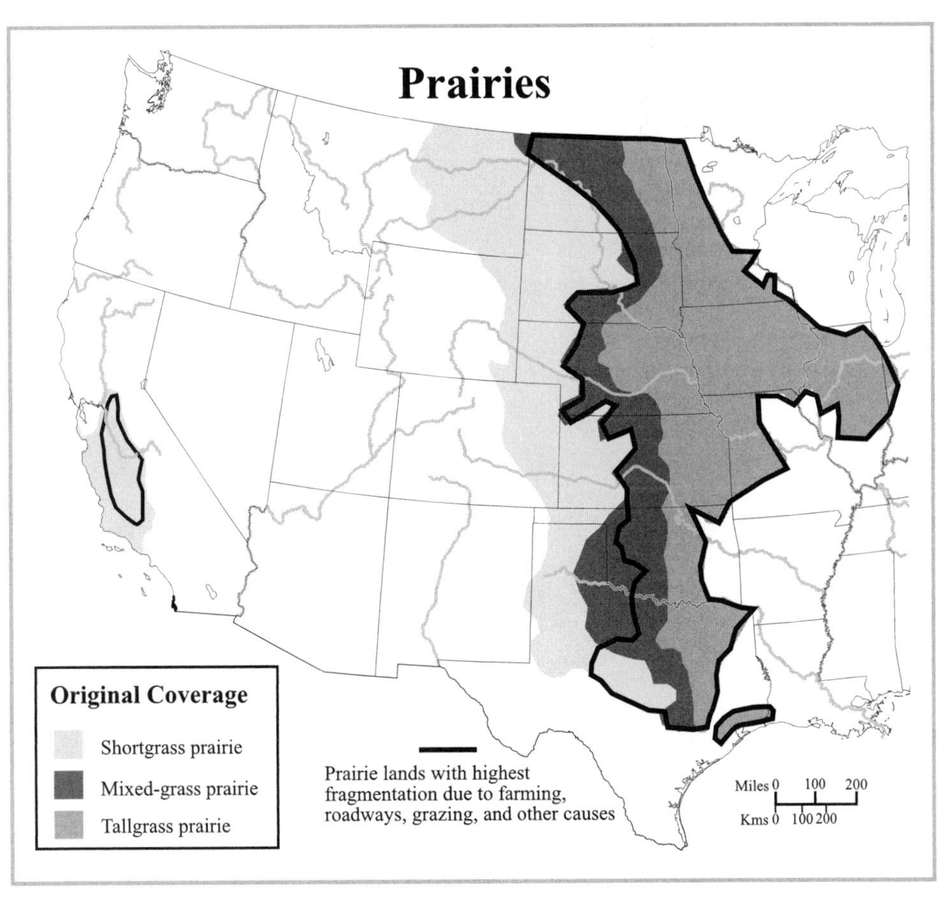

leaders. The treaty, one of few not to include land cessions, reduced, but did not eliminate, conflict in the region.

BIBLIOGRAPHY

Prucha, Francis Paul. *American Indian Treaties: The History of a Political Anomaly.* Berkeley: University of California Press, 1994.

Scanlan, Peter Lawrence. *Prairie du Chien: French, British, American.* Reprint. Menasha, Wis.: Banta, 1985. The original edition was published in 1937.

Louise Phelps Kellogg / J. H.

See also **Indian Treaties.**

PRAIRIE SCHOONER, a wagon used for long-distance travel and freight transport in the nineteenth century. The wagon was made with six or seven arching wooden bows supporting a canvas cover. Seen from a distance, the vehicle so resembled a ship at sea as to suggest the name. Mormons, California gold-seekers, emigrants to Oregon, freighters operating on the GREAT PLAINS, and settlers seeking homesteads all used the schooner after it was brought into common use in the Santa Fe trade soon after 1821. It was not only the chief means for the transportation of goods, but it also provided a home for pioneer families as they journeyed west in search of land.

BIBLIOGRAPHY

Dunbar, Seymour. *History of Travel in America.* Indianapolis, Ind.: Bobbs-Merrill, 1915.

Winther, Oscar Osborn. *The Transportation Frontier: Trans-Mississippi West, 1865–1890.* New York: Holt, Rinehart and Winston, 1964.

Edward Everett Dale / F. H.

See also **Conestoga Wagon; Oregon Trail; Transportation and Travel; Wagon Trains.**

Prairie Schooner. Covered wagons such as this one in Asheville, N.C., being lighter and easier to pull than the older Conestoga wagons, were better suited for migration to the West by nineteenth-century pioneer families. © CORBIS

PRAYING TOWNS. The term "Praying Towns" generally refers to the Christian Indian communities set up by the MASSACHUSETTS BAY COLONY between 1651 and 1674, although similar settlements were created at Lorette, near Quebec by the French, at Mashpee in Plymouth Colony, and on Martha's Vineyard. The Reverend John Eliot and other Puritan leaders believed that these towns would allow them to isolate and manage potential converts in order to completely change Native ways. Natives who went to live in the towns gained material assistance, education, and deeper connections to the colonists and their god. Natick was the first praying town, followed by six others in a north-south arc west of Boston. Residents were required to follow a legal code designed to force them into English social and political patterns. Christian Indians led each town, although Eliot and Bay Colony officials supervised their actions. In 1674 this program (and Puritan influence) was extended to seven additional Nipmuc towns farther west, alarming other Native and colonial leaders and contributing to the tensions that resulted in King Philip's War. After the war, four of the towns—Natick, Hassanamisco, Chabanakongkomun, and Punkapog—became, until Plymouth and the islands were added in 1692, the only Indian villages in the Bay Colony. They survived into the nineteenth century, gradually becoming networks of scattered families as non-Indians moved into the villages and the Indians moved to nearby cities and towns.

BIBLIOGRAPHY

Axtell, James. *The Invasion Within: The Contest of Cultures in Colonial North America.* New York: Oxford University Press, 1985.

Mandell, Daniel. *Behind the Frontier: Indians in Eighteenth-Century Eastern Massachusetts.* Lincoln: University of Nebraska Press, 1996.

Daniel R. Mandell

See also vol. 9: **A Dialogue between Piumbukhou and His Unconverted Relatives.**

PREFERENTIAL VOTING, a method of voting under which the voter expresses a first choice, second choice, and sometimes third and further choices among the candidates nominated. It is frequently used as a substitute for primary elections. It is one feature of the Hare system of PROPORTIONAL REPRESENTATION and is also used in several different forms for majority elections of individual officials. The major consequence of preferential voting is that minority constituencies exercise a larger role in elections than in a system of simple MAJORITY RULE. In the United States preferential voting systems make up only a minuscule fraction of elections.

BIBLIOGRAPHY

Bybee, Keith J. *Mistaken Identity: The Supreme Court and the Politics of Minority Representation.* Princeton, N.J.: Princeton University Press, 1998.

Guinier, Lani. *The Tyranny of the Majority: Fundamental Fairness and Representative Democracy.* New York: Free Press, 1994.

Powell Jr., G. Bingham. *Elections as Instruments of Democracy: Majoritarian and Proportional Visions.* New Haven, Conn.: Yale University Press, 2000.

Richie, Robert. *Reflecting All of Us: The Case for Proportional Representation.* Boston: Beacon, 1999.

George H. Hallett Jr. / A. G.

See also **Election Laws; Elections.**

PREGNANCY DISCRIMINATION ACT (PDA), a 1978 amendment to Title VII of the Civil Rights Act of 1964, prohibits workplace discrimination on the basis of pregnancy. The impetus for the act was a 1976 Supreme Court decision, *General Electric v. Gilbert,* in which the Court held that denial of benefits for pregnancy-related disability was not discrimination based on sex. This holding echoed past management decisions by which married women faced job discrimination and pregnant women were routinely fired. By 1977, women made up more than 45 percent of the labor force, but only one-quarter had insurance plans that allowed sick leave for pregnancy-related illness. Reaction to the *Gilbert* decision was swift. Women's organizations, feminists, labor and civil rights advocates, and some right-to-life groups formed a coalition known as the Campaign to End Discrimination Against Pregnant Workers to seek legislative relief from the Court's decision. Legislation to amend Title VII and overturn *Gilbert* was introduced in Congress in 1977 and passed, as the Pregnancy Discrimination Act, one year later.

The PDA prohibits discrimination against pregnant women in all areas of employment, including hiring, firing, seniority rights, job security, and receipt of fringe benefits. The most controversial features of the bill have been those requiring employers who offer health insurance and temporary disability plans to give coverage to women for pregnancy, childbirth, and related conditions. Although by 1977 many major corporations were already providing such benefits, business associations argued that pregnancy was a "voluntary condition," not an illness, and that the bill would raise insurance costs. The PDA does not, however, require employers who do not offer health insurance or disability benefits at all to adopt such plans, and Title VII applies only to employers with fifteen or more employees. These provisions leave many female workers unprotected by the act.

Although all major feminist organizations supported the 1978 amendment to Title VII, feminists in 2002 remained divided on how to apply the act. At issue was the language in the act that says employers cannot treat pregnancy "more or less" favorably than other disabilities. Some feminists argued that gender equality requires identical treatment of women and men without regard to pregnancy. This "equal treatment" group said that the PDA prohibits treatment of pregnant workers in a way that favors them over workers with other kinds of temporary disabilities. Other feminists argued that the only way to ensure equal opportunity for women is through pregnancy-specific benefits ensuring that pregnant women are not disadvantaged because of real biological difference from men. This "special treatment" group said that the PDA permits justifiably favorable treatment of pregnant workers.

Some states have enacted legislation that gives pregnant women benefits not available to other workers. The Supreme Court upheld one such statute in *California Federal Savings and Loan Association v. Guerra* (1987). In that case, the Court held that the California statute requiring unpaid maternity leave and guaranteed job reinstatement was not preempted by the PDA, because the purposes of the state law were not inconsistent with those of the PDA or Title VII.

BIBLIOGRAPHY

Gelb, Joyce, and Marian Lief Palley. *Women and Public Policies.* 2d ed., rev. and exp. Princeton, N.J.: Princeton University Press, 1987. Rev. ed., Charlottesville: University Press of Virginia, 1996.

Hoff, Joan. *Law, Gender, and Injustice: A Legal History of U.S. Women.* New York: New York University Press, 1991.

Vogel, Lise. *Mothers on the Job: Maternity Policy in the U.S. Workplace.* New Brunswick, N.J.: Rutgers University Press, 1993.

Weisberg, D. Kelly, ed. *Feminist Legal Theory: Foundations.* Philadelphia: Temple University Press, 1993.

Graham Russell Hodges / C. P.

See also ***Automobile Workers v. Johnson Controls, Inc.*****; Family and Medical Leave Act;** ***General Electric Company v. Gilbert*****; Women's Equity Action League; Women's Rights Movement: The Twentieth Century.**

PREPAREDNESS, a campaign designed to strengthen U.S. military forces after the outbreak of World War I. The movement began in 1914 and gathered momentum steadily as the danger of American involvement in the European struggle grew. In 1914 and 1915 Theodore Roosevelt, along with members of two newly formed organizations, the National Security League and the League to Enforce Peace, rallied popular support behind military preparation. Initially, President Woodrow Wilson's administration was cool to the preparedness agitation, and many of the movement's leaders, particularly Roosevelt, openly criticized the president's inaction.

As time passed, however, Wilson apparently decided that preparedness fit well with his demand that warring nations respect American rights. Wilson became a strong advocate of larger armaments after the Germans began their submarine warfare in February 1915. In December 1915 the administration presented Congress with a comprehensive national defense plan, which lawmakers enacted as the National Defense Act of 3 June 1916 and the Naval Appropriations Act of 29 August.

Although both statutes called for an unprecedented increase in the nation's armed forces, neither proved to be particularly effective. As a result, the material achievement of Roosevelt and other advocates of American military preparation was small compared to the tremendous national war effort of 1917 and 1918. Yet, the preparedness campaign readied the nation psychologically for the ordeal that lay ahead and specifically paved the way for the federal government's institution of compulsory service.

BIBLIOGRAPHY

Ferrell, Robert H. *Woodrow Wilson and World War I, 1917–1921.* New York: Harper and Row, 1985.

Keegan, John. *The First World War.* New York: Knopf, 1999.

Kennedy, David M. *Over Here: The First World War and American Society.* New York: Oxford University Press, 1980.

Eric J. Morser
C. P. Stacey

See also **American Legion; Defense, National; Mobilization.**

PRESBYTERIANISM is a form of church government that locates church authority in pastors and elders who serve in the local congregation and in regional and national assemblies. It is also part of the Reformed branch of the Protestant Reformation as distinguished from Lutheranism and Anglicanism. As such, Presbyterianism is the Anglophone world's equivalent for Reformed and traces its roots back to the church reforms of John Calvin (1509–1564). Presbyterianism moreover is bound up with the peculiar character of the Church of England and the complicated relations between Crown, Parliament, and bishops. Although the Presbyterian creed, the Westminster Standards, originated at the instigation of Parliament during the English Civil War of the 1640s, Presbyterianism succeeded principally in Scotland and Northern Ireland, the Old World breeding grounds for Presbyterianism in North America.

The Westminster Standards constitute arguably the most comprehensive and detailed creedal statement of Calvinism. Yet the institutional development of Presbyterianism in the New World depended on more than doctrine. Especially significant was the political situation out of which the varieties of Presbyterianism emerged. Three distinct expressions of Presbyterianism took root in the United States after the eighteenth century. Two, the Covenanters and the Seceders, reflect particular circumstances of Scottish Presbyterian history. The third and mainstream branch of American Presbyterianism developed independently of Scottish politics.

Mainstream Presbyterianism

The oldest Presbyterian body in North America, the mainstream branch, originated in 1706 with the founding of the Presbytery of Philadelphia under the leadership of Francis Makemie (1658–1708). Born and educated in Northern Ireland, he migrated to the mid-Atlantic colonies, pastoring Scotch-Irish immigrants in Maryland, Delaware, and Pennsylvania. At its founding, the first presbytery consisted of four Scotch-Irish pastors and three pastors from New England. The composition of this body was significant for two reasons. The first concerned a tension between Scotch-Irish Presbyterianism and New England Puritanism that eventually resulted in the division between Old Side and New Side Presbyterians from 1741 to 1758. The controversy focused largely on the revivals of George Whitefield, with the Scotch-Irish (Old Side) cautious and the New Englanders (New Side) supportive. The second notable feature of the first Presbytery was its formal autonomy from Scottish Presbyterianism, which thus made it a church that grew as American society developed.

The uniquely American attributes of mainstream Presbyterianism were readily evident at the time of American independence. The only clergyman who signed the Declaration of Independence was John Witherspoon, a Scottish American Presbyterian minister and the president of the College of New Jersey. Likewise, other mainstream Presbyterian clergy ardently supported the American Revolution. Furthermore, just after the ratification of the U.S. Constitution, the mainstream Presbyterian denomination held its first general assembly in 1789, calling itself the Presbyterian Church in the United States of America (PCUSA).

Covenanters and Seceders

If Old World norms imposed few constraints upon mainstream Presbyterianism, Scottish church history created some barriers for the other two streams of Presbyterianism in the New World. The chief religious ideal of the oldest of these groups, Covenanters, was to preserve the autonomy of the church from interference by the state. This outlook achieved notable expression in the National Covenant of 1638 and the Solemn League and Covenant of 1643. The Covenanters' first congregation in North America took shape in 1742 in Lancaster County, Pennsylvania. By 1782 the Covenanters had established enough congregations to form a presbytery, and in 1809 they became the Reformed Presbyterian Church of North America (RPCNA). Among this church's distinguishing features was the prohibition against members voting or holding office in American politics because Jesus Christ was not acknowledged as Lord by the Constitution.

A further development in Scotland contributed to a third branch of American Presbyterianism. In 1733 the Seceders withdrew from the Scottish Kirk to protest lay patronage, with debates about Enlightenment closely in the background, and formed the Associate Synod. Some of these Presbyterians migrated to the colonies in the first half of the eighteenth century and in 1753 formed an associate presbytery. By 1782 this body joined with Scotch-

Irish Presbyterians from New York to form the Associate Reformed Presbyterian Church (ARPC), though some New York congregations remained separate. During the nineteenth century some Seceders were absorbed into the mainstream Presbyterian Church, while others joined with Associate Presbyterians to form the United Presbyterian Church of North America (UPCNA). This left the Synod of the Carolinas to carry on the Associate Reformed Presbyterian name alone. By the end of the nineteenth century, mainstream Presbyterianism accounted for 967,900 members (80 percent in the North, 20 percent in the South) and was the most American branch with respect to its worship and attitudes toward government. The Covenanters in the Reformed Presbyterian Church of North America were the smallest of the three branches with 4,600 members but were also the denomination most clearly stamped with Old World convictions. The Seceders accounted for two denominations, the UPCNA and the ARPC with 94,400 and 8,500 members respectively, and shared with the Covenanters the practice of exclusive psalmody while following the mainstream branch in attitudes toward government.

New Denominations

Because of its character as the most American of the Presbyterian groups, the mainstream church regularly experienced divisions and mergers based to some extent on the degree of the church's acculturation. In 1810 the Cumberland Presbyterian Church (CPC), which had 164,900 members by 1900, emerged as a separate denomination when its leaders favored American notions of autonomy over Presbyterian teaching on predestination. Mainstream Presbyterians also divided in 1837 between the Old School and New School denominations over the issues of revivalism and social reform, with the former adopting a conservative stance. This division doubled in the aftermath of the Civil War, with Old School and New School bodies existing in the North and the South. After the war, both sides reunited in the South (1867) and the North (1869), but the PCUSA (northern) and PCUS (southern) remained separate.

Even so, the reunion of Old School and New School Presbyterians launched ecumenical activities that set the pattern for twentieth-century developments. To unify Christians and to pool resources against infidelity, mainstream Presbyterians led in forming the Pan Presbyterian Alliance (1880) and the Federal Council of Churches (1908). In 1906 the PCUSA also incorporated a majority of the Cumberland Presbyterian Church, though a sizable minority remained separate. One exception to the trend of consolidation was the formation in 1874 of the Cumberland Presbyterian Church of America (CPCA), which had 12,900 members in 1900 and was an African American denomination that reflected the autonomy of blacks after emancipation. In 1936 the Orthodox Presbyterian Church (OPC) separated from the PCUSA in the aftermath of the fundamentalist controversy because of perceived compromises involved in ecumenical efforts. In turn, controversies among conservatives generated two other denominations, the Bible Presbyterian Synod (BPS) in 1937 and the Evangelical Presbyterian Church (EPC) in 1961. A similar dispute about cooperation and the church's relationship to society occurred in the South in 1972, when the Presbyterian Church in America (PCA) left the PCUS in opposition to the apparent softening of historic Presbyterianism. These conservative departures made possible the 1983 reunion of the northern and southern Presbyterian mainstream churches into the PCUSA. Not all in the mainstream welcomed the merger, and some concerned about theological pluralism formed the Evangelical Presbyterian Church (EPC) in 1981. A different denomination from the conservative one of the same name formed in 1961, which two decades later was called the Reformed Presbyterian Church, Evangelical Synod. By the end of the twentieth century, the mainstream branch of Presbyterianism accounted for 3,079,500 members spread over six denominations: PCUSA 2,631,400; PCA 267,000; CPC 87,800; EPC 56,500; OPC 21,000; CPCA 15,100; BPS 10,000.

The Covenanter and Seceder traditions were not immune to trends in the mainstream. The ARPC upheld the Seceder tradition and was strong in the South with 38,900 members. The UPCNA, however, merged in 1958 with the (northern) PCUSA. The Covenanter tradition of exclusive psalmody and insistence upon a constitutional amendment continued to find vigorous expression in the RPCNA, with 5,700 members by the end of the twentieth century; another wing of the Covenanters, the New Lights, who became a separate denomination in 1833, when they revoked prohibitions on participation in civil affairs, merged with the UPCNA in the late nineteenth century, and the rest joined the Evangelical Presbyterian Church in 1965 to form the Reformed Presbyterian Church, Evangelical Synod. In 1983 this body joined the Presbyterian Church in America to become the second largest Presbyterian denomination.

Presbyterian Influence

Although Presbyterianism maintains a reputation of respectability and social prominence, its influence on American culture has been limited. Presbyterianism's largest influence on American life has been through the institutions of higher education it founded, especially Princeton University and Princeton Theological Seminary. Several Presbyterians have been prominent in American politics, among them President Woodrow Wilson and John Foster Dulles, secretary of state under President Dwight Eisenhower. Presbyterianism was also a vital part of the Protestant establishment that flourished between 1880 and 1960. As much as the mainstream Presbyterian tradition has adapted to American realities, however, it has not competed well against evangelical and charismatic Protestants, whose forms of devotion dovetail with American individualism and egalitarianism. Since the decline of the Protestant establishment and the resurgence of evangelical Protestantism after 1960, Presbyterianism's role in American life has waned.

BIBLIOGRAPHY

Fiske, William Lyons. *The Scottish High Church Tradition in America: An Essay in Scotch-Irish Ethnoreligious History*. Lanham, Md.: University Press of America, 1995.

Hutchinson, George P. *The History behind the Reformed Presbyterian Church, Evangelical Synod.* Cherry Hill, N.J.: Mack Publishing, 1974.

Loetscher, Lefferts A. *The Broadening Church: A Study of Theological Issues in the Presbyterian Church since 1869*. Philadelphia: University of Pennsylvania Press, 1954.

Longfield, Bradley J. *The Presbyterian Controversy: Fundamentalists, Modernists, and Moderates.* New York: Oxford University Press, 1991.

Marsden, George M. *The Evangelical Mind and the New School Presbyterian Experience: A Case Study of Thought and Theology in Nineteenth-Century America.* New Haven, Conn.: Yale University Press, 1970.

Thompson, Ernest Trice. *Presbyterians in the South.* 3 vols. Richmond, Va.: John Knox Press, 1963–1973.

Thompson, Robert Ellis. *A History of the Presbyterian Churches in the United States.* New York: Christian Literature Company, 1895.

Trinterud, Leonard J. *The Forming of an American Tradition: A Re-Examination of Colonial Presbyterianism.* Philadelphia: Westminster Press, 1949.

D. G. Hart

See also **Protestantism; Religion and Religious Affiliation; Scotch-Irish.**

PRESERVATION MOVEMENT. The effort to protect and maintain buildings and spaces of historic value gained enough support in the 1920s to earn the title "preservation movement." Concerned with historic preservation, rather than wilderness preservation, this movement gained even broader support after World War II, as a booming economy, sprawling development, and rapid cultural changes convinced many in the United States that vigorous steps had to be taken to preserve the nation's cultural heritage.

Important antecedents to the broader movement reflected the desire of individuals to protect sites of historic and patriotic significance. These included George Washington's headquarters in Newburgh, New York, successfully protected in 1850, and Washington's estate at Mount Vernon, protected by a private group, the Mount Vernon Ladies' Association of the Union in 1858. The federal government took an important step in 1906 with the passage of the Antiquities Act, which allowed the president to create national monuments, both of historic and prehistoric value.

In the 1920s automobile travel began its dramatic transformation of the American landscape, as the building of roads, gas stations, parking lots, and billboards announced the arrival of a new driving culture. The automobile provided two different impetuses for preservation, first by threatening known landscapes with demolition, and second by providing great mobility for tourists seeking historical landmarks. Some regions in the nation, fearing a coming homogenization of American culture, set out to preserve sites that revealed their distinct heritages. This effort was particularly strong in New England, where the Society for the Preservation of New England Antiquities, created in 1910, and numerous local, amateur efforts helped create a region steeped in its history and its historical image.

Perhaps the most famous case of historic preservation began in 1926, when W. A. R. Goodwin, a professor at William and Mary College, started the long process of preserving and restoring Williamsburg, Virginia. Goodwin won the support of John D. Rockefeller Jr., whose great wealth and interest in American history combined to create Historic Williamsburg. Eventually Rockefeller spent nearly $100 million in restoring 173 acres and creating an historical tourist destination. Combined with other regional historic sites—the Jamestown settlement and the Yorktown battleground, both controlled by the federal government—preservation in the Williamsburg area has emphasized the importance of national memory, instilling patriotism, and the celebration of the national past. In recent decades, Williamsburg has also been the focus of great debate, especially concerning first the absence of slavery from this colonial representation and then its painful presence. The debate heightened awareness of the power of historic sites to shape national self-conception.

In 1935 the preservation movement received greater support from the federal government with the passage of the Historic Sites Act, which authorized the purchase of historic places and their administration by the National Park Service. With a professional staff of historians, architects, and archaeologists, the National Park Service suddenly became a central preservation institution, protecting places as various as the Theodore Roosevelt birthplace in New York and the Fort Union Trading Post in North Dakota.

The postwar movement gained strength with the 1949 organization of the private National Trust for Historic Preservation. Founded to provide "leadership, education and advocacy to save America's diverse historic places and revitalize our communities," as its mission statement reads, the National Trust has been an important information clearinghouse, particularly through its magazine, *Preservation.* Preservation of urban architecture gained considerable popular support after the demolition of New York City's monumental Pennsylvania Station. The demolition of Penn Station—destroyed in 1964 to make way for Madison Square Garden and a large office tower—symbolized for many the tremendous loss that could come from rapid economic development. In partial response to the destruction of Penn Station, New York created the Landmarks Preservation Commission (1965) to help prevent further destruction of architecture with historical value, especially the city's other great railroad terminal, Grand Central. The loss of Penn Station undoubtedly aided the passage of the National Historic Preservation Act of 1966, which reaffirmed the federal government's role in preserving the nation's historic sites, particularly through strengthening the National Park Service program, expansion of the National Register for Historic Places, and support for the National Trust.

As interest in historic preservation grew, so too did the list of places worthy of preservation. Moving well beyond the movement's early focus on patriotic sites, such as battlefields and presidential homes, the postwar movement sought to protect even the mundane, believing that such sites gave witness to a broader cultural heritage. Entire neighborhoods gained attention from preservationists, as the character of urban space changed rapidly, particularly as older buildings gave way to surface parking and entire neighborhoods faced removal in the interest of highway building or "urban renewal."

Clearly historic preservation gained considerable popular support in the 1960s and in subsequent decades. Still, preservationists found themselves in continuous battle with development. By the 1980s suburban sprawl began encroaching on already protected landmarks, including Civil War battlefields, and the pace of change threatened to remove or obscure visible reminders of the nation's past. On the other hand, heightened environmental concern contributed to a growing realization of what might be lost through economic development, further broadening the appeal of historic preservation. In another effort to widen the scope of the movement, many activists called for the preservation of urban landscapes, not just buildings, and by the 1970s historic city spaces had gained landmark status, through both local and national legislation offering support for the protection and restoration of urban historic places. Perhaps most famously, New York's Central Park experienced a renewal in the 1980s, as private and public efforts combined to re-create the park using the original plans and visions of its creators, Frederick Law Olmsted and Calvert Vaux.

In the 1990s the historic preservation movement was as strong as ever, with activists working through local, regional, and national organizations and with the support of various levels of government. Still, the pace of physical change in the American landscape, dictated by economic growth, required continuous vigilance in the effort to preserve places of historic value.

BIBLIOGRAPHY

Alanen, Arnold R., and Robert Z. Melnick, eds. *Preserving Cultural Landscapes in America.* Baltimore: Johns Hopkins University Press, 2000.

Holleran, Michael. *Boston's "Changeful Times": Origins of Preservation and Planning in America.* Baltimore: Johns Hopkins University Press, 1998.

Hosmer, Charles B., Jr. *Preservation Comes of Age: From Williamsburg to the National Trust, 1926–1949.* Charlottesville: University Press of Virginia, 1981.

Murtagh, William. *Keeping Time: The History and Theory of Preservation in America.* 2d rev. ed. New York: John Wiley, 1997.

David Stradling

See also **Antiquities Act; Automobile; Central Park; Mount Vernon; National Trust for Historic Preservation; Williamsburg, Colonial.**

PRESIDENT, U.S. The president of the United States is by far the best known politician both within the United States and around the world. Americans who struggle to recall the name of their representative, senator, or governor almost certainly know the name of the president. Citizens of other countries from Iraq to China, Australia to Russia, are generally familiar with the president's name and photograph and have an opinion on his performance in office. The fame that U.S. presidents enjoy today is appropriate, for the person who holds that office is at the center of both American politics and world affairs. Yet the president is not all-powerful at home or abroad. U.S. presidents are often frustrated overseas (for example, in their attempts to bring peace to the Middle East or Northern Ireland), and domestically it is well to remember that, as the political scientist Charles O. Jones has emphasized, the United States does not have a presidential system of government in the sense that presidents are free to make and implement policy.

Powers of the Office

The Constitution, as is well known, created a system of checks and balances to prevent tyrannical government. The political scientist Richard Neustadt correctly noted that the Constitution did not create a system of separated powers favored by theorists such as Montesquieu, in which legislative, judicial, and executive powers were kept separate from one another. Rather, the Constitution gave pieces of all these powers to all branches of government. The power to oversee the departments and agencies of the federal government is given to Congress and the courts as well as to the president; Congress as well as the president is involved in foreign policy through Congress's powers to block the appointment of ambassadors and decide whether to accept or reject treaties, and through its general power of the purse through which it decides how much, if at all, to fund policies proposed by the president and his officers.

The Constitution is also particularly brief and ambiguous in describing the powers of the president. The president is given the rights to nominate ambassadors and other officers of the United States and to require their opinions in writing, to veto legislation (subject to override by a two-thirds majority), to report on the state of the union, to negotiate treaties, and to be commander in chief. The Constitution therefore provides a mixture of both precise and ambiguous powers to the president. There was no doubt from the earliest years of the republic that the power to veto legislation provided presidents with an enormously valuable bargaining chip in the legislative process. In the case of other Constitutional grants of power, it has taken many years of practice and interpretation to define what they mean. At the time the Constitution was written, the role of the British king as commander in chief had become merely ceremonial and honorific. Yet by the late twentieth century, U.S. presidents had successfully asserted that this title empowered them to order American forces into battle even if Congress had not used its undoubted constitutional right to decide whether or not to declare war. In the Cold War nuclear era, the implications were sobering. On a less dramatic level, the question of which officers and officials of the United States the president can not only appoint but dismiss is similarly ambiguous in the Constitution. The matter was not fully settled by the Supreme Court until the twentieth century; for example, the president can fire the Attorney General or the Secretary of State, but cannot fire members of independent regulatory commissions or independent counsels. In important respects, therefore, the powers of the president have accumulated over the centuries rather than invariably originating unambiguously from the Constitution.

The Constitution gave the president one enormous advantage compared with the other two branches of government, namely the singularity of the office. Power in Congress is widely fragmented between two chambers and among numerous committees, subcommittees, and part leaders. Individual legislators are hesitant to grant much of their own power to anyone. The president in contrast enjoys a solitary splendor. As Alexander Hamilton recognized in the *Federalist Papers*, the president is much better placed to act with speed and dispatch in making decisions than the fragmented Congress. The president's bargaining position with Congress is also enhanced by its divisions and his singularity.

Presidents enjoy one important advantage because of a constitutional practice rather than the Constitution as such. The president is uniquely positioned to claim to be the person who can speak for the United States and the national interest, particularly during crises and emergencies. This reflects the fact that, contrary to the plan for electing the president set out in the Constitution, the president is in practice elected directly by the people voting state by state. Thus the president can claim with some plausibility to be the only politician to have been elected by all the people, in contrast to legislators elected by a single state or district. Yet all these Constitutional advantages must be set against the constraints the Constitution provides and that we have discussed above. The most obvious are worth reiterating. Presidents cannot legislate without Congress. Presidents cannot even implement established policies unless Congress, which has the power of the purse, provides the funding. The contrast with a prime minister who can rely on a disciplined parliamentary majority (as is generally the case in Great Britain) is striking.

The Presidency in the Political System

The Constitution therefore confers both opportunities and constraints upon the president. As we have seen, American presidents share all their powers with other branches of government. Presidents can achieve their policy goals only by winning the support of other political actors. The nature of American politics makes the challenge all the greater. Political parties in the United States are famously (or notoriously) less disciplined than parties in parliamentary systems; the president's unofficial role as leader of his party nationally does not automatically result in legislators from that party supporting one of the president's bills in Congress, particularly if their constituents' interests or opinions conflict with it. Attempts by even the most prestigious presidents to punish members of their own party who have failed to support them (such as Roosevelt in the 1930s) have harmed presidents more than the objects of their wrath. American political parties historically have not coalesced around explicit ideologies to which presidents can appeal for support. It is true that in the late twentieth century the parties in Congress achieved much greater cohesion than in the past, with much larger proportions of legislators voting with their party much more often than in previous years. Yet, as President Clinton experienced when his proposal for national health insurance failed in a Congress controlled by his own Democratic Party without even a formal vote being taken, higher party unity scores do not necessarily result in support for a particular presidential proposal from his own party. As Richard Neustadt argued, the power of the president is the power to persuade.

Fortunately for presidents, they enjoy a number of advantages not enumerated in the Constitution to help them in their attempts to persuade. Particularly in times of acute crisis, such as the beginning of a war, the president's dual role as head of state as well as head of government causes a "rally effect" in which the public and other politicians unite in support of the nation's leader. Presidents can reward support with government contracts for the legislator's constituency, appointments for friends, or support for the legislator's own favorite proposal. Most importantly, presidents have the ability to "go public" in the words of Samuel Kernell, appealing to the public for support over the heads of other politicians. The rise of the electronic media, first radio and then television, has enabled presidents to establish a direct, almost personal relationship with voters that skilled presidents such as Ronald Reagan or Bill Clinton have used to good effect. It is probably advisable for presidents to use this tactic on a limited number of important issues lest it lose its impact. If used wisely, it can be decisive.

The degree to which presidents are successful in persuading other politicians to follow their lead has varied significantly. Three different cycles can be distinguished. First, success varies over the course of a presidency. Even those presidents regarded as the most successful in gaining support from Congress have found that toward the end of their presidencies their success has faltered. Both Franklin Roosevelt and Lyndon Johnson experienced dramatic success in obtaining legislation from Congress only to experience subsequent periods of frustration and failure. Second, a president's success may be influenced by reactions to events that occurred under his predecessors. Gerald Ford and Jimmy Carter both suffered from the belief that under their predecessors an overly powerful "imperial presidency" had developed. Ronald Reagan benefited from a fear that under Carter and Ford the presidency had become "imperiled, not imperial." Third, there have been longer-term historical variations. The unimposing presidents that James Bryce had in mind when he discussed the office in his magisterial book, *The American Commonwealth*, gave way to the strong presidencies of Theodore Roosevelt and (after William Howard Taft) Woodrow Wilson. The uninspiring presidents after Wilson were followed by the strong leadership of Franklin Roosevelt and Harry Truman.

The Office

The Constitution talks of the president, but in the modern era, at least, the presidency is not merely the president but a sizable political institution employing over 1,500 people. By way of contrast, the Executive Office contained less than half that number (703) in 1943 when Roosevelt had a world war to run. Some of these people are civil servants, notably in the Office of Management and Budget that constructs the president's budget and monitors the regulations that agencies and departments develop. Around 400 are members of the White House staff, a group of political appointees whose role and power varies from the relatively mundane (arranging travel, answering correspondence) to the extremely important (writing speeches, advising on policy issues.)

The growth in the size of the Executive Office might be seen as reflecting merely the growth in the responsibilities of governments in all advanced industrialized economies and in the international role of the United States. It is important to note, however, that new functions or responsibilities of American government could have been entrusted to established departments such as State or the Treasury. After all, American presidents are given far more freedom to make political appointments to the top positions in government departments than most democratic heads of government enjoy, and the number of such political appointees continues to grow. Newly elected presidents in the United States can make about 5,000 political appointments; a British prime minister in a country with admittedly only about one-fifth of the U.S. population can make fewer than two hundred.

All modern presidents have felt, however, that they needed their own staffers to advise them from within the White House rather than relying on the cabinet secretaries. In part this results from the fact that issues do not correspond to departmental boundaries; a foreign policy crisis will almost certainly involve the Department of Defense, the Treasury, and the Department of Justice as well as the State Department. It also reflects, however, presidents' suspicions about the responsiveness of the civil service in government departments and the commitment of cabinet secretaries to the president's agenda. After all, many political appointments are made more for political reasons (ensuring that there are enough women or minorities in the president's appointments) rather than because those selected are known to have a clear commitment to the president's policy preferences. Indeed, often presidents must make appointments to positions in policy fields that they have rarely thought about, and they have no clear preferences until a problem develops. Moreover, political appointees in departments must operate in a political setting in which many influences upon them—powerful congressional committees, the opinions of the permanent bureaucracy, interest groups—can pull them away from the president's priorities and policy positions.

Unlike the leaders of most advanced democracies, American presidents are presented with the challenge of constructing the core executive for themselves. British prime ministers used to walk through the front door of 10 Downing Street to take charge of a prime ministership that was ready to use and with key officials (who are permanent civil servants) in place. U.S. presidents arrive to find that their predecessor has removed all key files and computer discs. A number of obvious dangers lie in wait for the new president in constructing his or her administration. Some presidents (Johnson, Nixon) are said to have created a severely hierarchical structure for the White House staff that screened out and sheltered them from bad news or contrary opinions that they needed to hear. Others (Carter for most of his administration, Clinton for periods of his) have been criticized for allowing too much access to them by too many of their staff, resulting in incoherent decision making and excessive demands on their time, down to, in Carter's case, allegedly deciding on who could use the White House tennis courts. Reagan claimed that members of his Executive Office, notably Lieutenant Colonel Oliver North of the National Security Council staff, had organized the illegal sale of weapons to Iran and transfer of the proceeds to right-wing rebels in Nicaragua. In short, the Executive Office, if organized ineffectively, can harm presidents as well as helping them. An appropriate structure for the White House staff and the Executive Office in general will avoid these dangers. It will also, however, take into account the styles and personalities of the incumbent; an appropriate structure for one president may be inappropriate for another.

The Presidency and the World

Presidents of the United States are elected only by Americans, but their policies and performance matter to people throughout the world. Although the end of the Cold War meant that presidents were no longer as obviously leaders of a mighty "Western" coalition, the dominant position of the United States in the world has compelled U.S. presidents to accept a role of global leadership. Post–Cold War presidents Bill Clinton and George W. Bush came into office determined to be more domestically oriented than their predecessors but were unable to escape the demands of world leadership. Global issues ranging from climate change to trade, from bringing peace to the Balkans to combating international terrorism against the United States, from countering the Iraqi invasion of Kuwait to settling disputes with the European Union over the use of growth hormones in beef cattle, have regularly forced themselves onto the agendas of the post–Cold War presidents.

Leaders in other countries are as much a part of the attentive audience for presidents as, for example, representatives in Congress. The annual meeting of the leaders of major advanced industrialized nations known as the G8 brings presidents (and more extensively, their staffs) into regular dialogue with foreign counterparts. Certain foreign leaders (the British prime minister, the Russian president) expect to speak with the U.S. president regularly and informally on major global issues. Almost all foreign heads of government prize the publicity and prestige that a visit to the White House brings. Foreign leaders know that, given the extent of American economic, diplomatic, and military power, a decision not to become involved in a problem that concerns them is as much a policy decision on the part of the American president as a decision to become involved. Presidents frequently find themselves practicing what Robert Putnam termed the "two level game" of balancing the sometimes conflicting, sometimes coinciding demands of global politics on the one hand and domestic politics on the other.

The Presidency in a New Century

The history of the U.S. presidency has been a history of expansion. The institution has grown in terms of the number of people it employs, in terms of the range of policy problems for which presidents are held accountable, and in terms of the international responsibilities of its incumbent. In spite of the misleading adage that "all politics is local," Americans feel that through the medium of television they have a closer connection with the president than with any other politician. Yet all the prominence and responsibilities that befall a modern president must still be handled within the framework established by an eighteenth-century document, the Constitution, that created not a presidential system of government but a system of separated institutions sharing the powers of government. The president, whose international prominence is so great, must always remember that at home, success depends on the ability to persuade other politicians to cooperate.

BIBLIOGRAPHY

Burke, John P. *The Intuitional Presidency: Organizing and Managing the White House from FDR to Clinton.* Baltimore and London: Johns Hopkins University Press, 2000.

Edwards, George C. *At the Margins: Presidential Leadership of Congress.* New Haven, Conn.: Yale University Press, 1969.

Greenstein, Fred I. *The Hidden Hand Presidency; Eisenhower as Leader.* New York: Basic Books, 1982.

Hart, John. *The Presidential Branch.* New York: Pergamon, 1987.

Rockman, Bert A. *The Leadership Question: The Presidency and the American System.* New York: Praeger, 1984.

Schlesinger, Arthur M., Jr. *The Imperial Presidency.* Boston: Houghton Mifflin, 1973.

Skowronek, Stephen S. *The Politics Presidents Make: Leadership from John Adams to George Bush.* Cambridge, Mass.: Belkap Press, 1993.

Graham Wilson

See also **Congress, United States; Constitution of the United States.**

PRESIDENTS AND SUBPOENAS. Courts have the general power to issue subpoenas compelling individuals to appear before them. Courts can also compel those served with subpoenas to produce certain materials relevant to a pending trial. Early in American history, courts became the forum in which it was decided whether the president of the United States would be exempt from such court orders. In the 1800 federal Circuit Court case of *United States v. Cooper,* Thomas Cooper, who had published a number of articles highly critical of President John Adams, was charged with violating the Sedition Act of 1798. Cooper, a scientist and lawyer who had recently come to the United States from England and who represented himself in court, asked one of the presiding judges, United States Supreme Court Justice Samuel Chase, to subpoena President Adams so that the president could answer for what he claimed were the injustices of the Sedition Act. Justice Chase refused Cooper's request to subpoena the president, but went on to charge the jury and said, "Now, gentlemen, the motives of the president, in his official capacity, are not a subject of inquiry with you. Shall we say to the president, you are not fit for the government of this country?" Justice Chase did, however, agree to Cooper's requests to subpoena members of Congress. Cooper was nevertheless convicted, paid a large fine, and spent six months in prison. This case appears to have been the first in which a president could possibly have been subpoenaed, and it was determined that America's chief executive is generally immune from such court orders.

This issue was revisited in the case of *United States v. Burr* (1807). Chief Justice John Marshall presided over this case, which was heard in the Circuit Court of the United States. Marshall allowed a subpoena *duces tecum* to be issued for certain documents in the possession of

President Thomas Jefferson that were relevant to the proceedings against Burr. Jefferson responded cordially, referring in repeated letters to the "request" of the court, and did provide certain documents, but refused to produce other relevant materials or to appear in person. Jefferson claimed that the pressing duties of the presidency made it impossible for him to travel outside the seat of government in Washington to attend trials. Jefferson wrote that, "To comply with such calls would leave the nation without an executive branch, whose agency nevertheless is understood to be so constantly necessary that it is the sole branch which the constitution requires to be always in function." This set a longstanding precedent that a sitting president of the United States could not be forced to appear in court or produce materials relevant to a trial through the use of a subpoena. Based on this principle, presidents also refused to comply with requests from Congress to testify before various committees. The practice came to be known as "claiming executive privilege," although such a privilege is nowhere explicitly stated in the Constitution.

The issue lay largely dormant until the nation arrived at the constitutional crisis that resulted from the Watergate affair and President Richard M. Nixon's involvement in that and other activities. Testimony before the Senate about the 17 June 1972 break-in at the Democratic National Committee headquarters, located in the Watergate Office Building in Washington, D.C., made it clear that there were tape recordings made in the Oval Office that were relevant to the congressional investigation. Congressional committees and two special prosecutors demanded that President Nixon turn over the tapes. Subpoenas were then issued demanding, among other things, that Nixon personally testify and give the tapes in question to the federal District Court prosecuting the cases against those directly involved with the burglary and the subsequent cover-up. Following in Jefferson's steps in the *Burr* case, Nixon complied to an extent with these subpoenas, releasing some materials that had clearly been altered and edited, but claiming that other materials were protected by executive privilege.

In *United States v. Nixon* (1974), the Supreme Court of the United States, citing many landmark cases, including Chief Justice Marshall's opinions *Marbury v. Madison* (1803) and *United States v. Burr*, said that it was incumbent on the High Court to balance between the president's need for confidentiality in executing his constitutional duties, on the one hand, and "the fundamental demands of due process of law in the fair administration of criminal justice," on the other. The Court's unanimous opinion delivered by Chief Justice Warren E. Burger was careful to give great credence to the president's need for complete candor and objectivity from his advisors. The justices also recognized the need for a great degree of confidentiality for the internal deliberations of the executive branch of government. Chief Justice Burger agreed that, if military or diplomatic secrets were at stake, the Court might reach a different conclusion. However, given that President Nixon's claims were based on a blanket statement of executive privilege without claiming that any state secrets were at stake, the constitutional duty of the courts is to guarantee due process of law, something that Nixon's actions were gravely impairing, according to the Court. The justices ruled that President Nixon had to comply with the subpoena *duces tecum* issued by Chief Judge John J. Sirica of the United States District Court for the District of Columbia. Nixon immediately prepared to turn over the subpoenaed materials to Chief Judge Sirica.

Presidents since Nixon have continued to claim that the special place the presidency holds under America's constitutional system demands that much of its internal deliberations remain secret and privileged. When faced with investigations, special prosecutors, subpoenas, and impeachment proceedings, President William J. Clinton, for example, claimed that much of what went on in the Oval Office was protected by executive privilege and executive immunity, and that he and his aides should not have to respond to subpoenas. As was the case with President Nixon, President Clinton eventually accepted his and his office's place under the rule of law. Since *United States v. Nixon*, executive branch claims of immunity from the normal processes of the American legal system have been tempered by the fact that the constitutional demands of due process of law and justice are likely to outweigh claims of executive immunity from subpoenas.

BIBLIOGRAPHY

Ball, Howard. *"We Have a duty": The Supreme Court and the Watergate Tapes Litigation.* New York: Greenwood Press, 1990.

Berger, Raoul. *Executive Privilege: A Constitutional Myth.* Cambridge, Mass.: Harvard University Press, 1974.

Melanson, Philip H. *Secrecy Wars: National Security, Privacy, and the Public's Right to Know.* Washington, D.C.: Brassey's, 2001.

Moynihan, Daniel P. *Secrecy: The American Experience.* New Haven, Conn.: Yale University Press, 1998.

Rozell, Mark J. *Executive Privilege: The Dilemma of Secrecy and Democratic Accountability.* Baltimore: Johns Hopkins University Press, 1994.

Akiba J. Covitz
Esa Lianne Sferra
Meredith L. Stewart

PRESIDENTS, INTERMENT OF. Beginning with George Washington, presidents have traditionally decided their own places of interment. When Washington died in 1799, Congress attempted to have him buried beneath the Capitol Rotunda, but before his death, Washington directed his family to bury him at his estate at Mount Vernon, Virginia, a wish with which the family complied. In death, as in life, Washington set a precedent that his successors would follow. From John Adams and Thomas Jefferson in 1826 to Richard Nixon in 1994, the great majority of presidents have chosen to be buried in their home states, and, in many cases, on their own family property or on the grounds of their presidential library. The handful of exceptions include Ulysses Grant, who is buried in Manhattan, New York; Woodrow Wilson, who is buried at the National Cathedral in Washington, D.C.; and John Kennedy, who is buried at ARLINGTON NATIONAL CEMETERY. Although several presidents have lain in state at the Capitol, none has been buried there. Washington's National Cathedral, completed in the early twentieth century, was originally intended as a final resting place for American leaders on the model of Westminster Abbey in London. As of the beginning of the twenty-first century, however, Wilson is the only president interred there.

BIBLIOGRAPHY

Hyland, Pat. *Presidential Libraries and Museums: An Illustrated Guide.* Washington D.C.: Congressional Quarterly, Inc., 1995.

Lamb, Brian, and C-SPAN Staff. *Who's Buried in Grant's Tomb? A Tour of Presidential Gravesites.* Baltimore: Johns Hopkins University Press, 2000.

Anthony J. Gaughan

PRESIDIO. The Presidio was a Spanish institution established primarily to hold the frontiers of Spain's territory in America against aggressors and to protect the missions. Presidios were forts or posts where soldiers lived with their familes, cultivating the surrounding land. The number of soldiers varied; along the northern frontier there were seldom more than fifty residing at a presidio. The presidios were not entirely self-supporting because they received subsidies from the viceroy of Mexico. They were located in California, Arizona, New Mexico, TEXAS, the West Indies, and Spanish Florida, which at the time included Georgia and the Carolinas.

BIBLIOGRAPHY

Benton, Lisa M. *The Presidio: From Army Post to National Park.* Boston: Northeastern University Press, 1998.

Lillian Estelle Fisher / A. R.

See also **San Antonio; San Diego; San Francisco; Tucson.**

PRESS ASSOCIATIONS, or news agencies, are news bureaus, such as wire services; which include syndication services that that supply text features such as columns and horoscopes, comics, games and puzzles, and print and interactive media. In the United States, the Associated Press (AP), a nonprofit newspaper cooperative of 1,500 member papers, and the privately owned United Press International (UPI) are the leading news agencies. The British-based Reuters (founded in London in 1851) is the world's largest international newsgathering and dissemination agency.

Among syndication services, the Hearst-owned King Features is the world's largest distributor of newspaper comics and text features. Its competitors are many, including Creator's Syndicate and McMeel Anderson Universal. The *New York Times, Washington Post,* Scripps-Howard News Service, Hearst Corporation, Tribune Media Services, and Gannett Company also offer news services and syndicated features.

Press associations were born out of nineteenth-century New York City's competitive newspaper industry, which found it could offset expenses through shared costs and cooperative newsgathering and reporting. The earliest agency, the Association of Morning Newspapers, was formed in New York City in the 1820s. In 1848, the seeds of the modern Associated Press (AP) were planted when David Hale, publisher of the *Journal of Commerce,* convinced five other competing papers—including the *New York Herald* and *New York Tribune*—to pool their resources. Making the most of the latest technologies, the AP opened the first "overseas" news bureau (in Halifax, Nova Scotia) in 1849 to telegraph news from foreign ships as they arrived. In 1858, the AP received the first transatlantic news cable message; in 1875, the AP leased its own telegraph wire (another first); and in 1899, it tested Marconi's wireless telegraph by reporting on the America's Cup yacht race.

The concept of a wartime correspondent pool was born during the Civil War, as AP reporters provided newspapers large and small with coverage from the war, no matter where it was being waged. After the war, regional Associated Press versions sprang up, including the Western Associated Press, created under the leadership of Joseph Medill of the *Chicago Tribune* in 1865. And in 1892, the Associated Press of Illinois was formed, initially to compete with the New York bureau.

The other major press association of the late nineteenth century, the United Press, was formed in 1882 and merged with the New York Associated Press a decade later. In 1900, after the Illinois Supreme Court ruled that the Associated Press of Illinois "must submit to be controlled by the public," the Illinois branch rechartered itself in New York, and the regional versions joined forces as a nonprofit newspaper cooperative, forming the modern Associated Press.

Flamboyant media mogul William Randolph Hearst founded the International News Service (INS) in 1906 to be an AP competitor. In 1913, recognizing a market for text features and comics—such as the popular "Yellow Kid" (which he'd stolen from competitor Joseph Pulitzer's *New York World* in 1896)—Hearst launched the Newspaper Feature Service.

The syndicate was incorporated two years later as King Features, renamed for Moses Koenigsberg (literally, "king mountain"), whom Hearst had dispatched on a cross-country mission in 1909 to lay the groundwork for what became the world's most successful syndication service. In 1907, the Scripps-McRae League of newspapers, owned by George Scripps and his brother-in-law, Milton A. McRae, combined three regional press associations into the United Press Association (UP). Scripps-McRae also formed the Newspaper Enterprise Association (NEA) as a syndication service to distribute comics and features. The UP shook things up by offering its services on an unrestricted basis (the AP initially restricted its members from buying news from competitors); it also gave its authors bylines and set up foreign bureaus to reduce reliance on foreign news agencies. The AP and INS eventually followed suit.

During World War I, UP president and manager Roy W. Howard wreaked havoc by prematurely reporting an armistice. But all was soon forgiven; in 1922, Howard partnered with George Scripps's son, Robert P. Scripps, and Scripps-McRae became Scripps-Howard. In 1958, Hearst's INS and Scripps's UP merged to form UPI (United Press International). With its combined resources, UPI offered the first wire service radio network, with correspondents around the world. UPI was purchased in 1992 by Middle East Broadcasting, Ltd.

During the twentieth century, press agencies brought news to the world not only in the form of print journalism reporting, but also with award-winning photojournalism (the AP has won 28 Pulitzer Prizes for photography) and global broadcasting. And as new technologies improve the speed and ease of global reporting, photography, broadcasting, and transmission—as well as new audience demands and competing media—are keeping news agencies and syndicates on their toes. Newsgathering, reporting, and distribution have become easier with secure servers, content management systems, and digital content provider services such as Screaming Media. And Internet users can now read digital versions of local newspapers from any computer, which is reducing the need for global reporting networks. Nevertheless, news organizations such as CNN have bred a generation of news junkies addicted to a constant stream of information, making news agencies and syndicates a necessity despite the wide availability of alternative news sources.

BIBLIOGRAPHY

Boyd-Barrett, Oliver, and Terhi Rantanan, eds. *The Globalization of News.* Thousand Oaks, Calif.: Sage Publications, 1998.

Fenby, Jonathan. *The International News Services.* New York: Schocken Books, 1986.

Gordon, Gregory, and Ronald E. Cohen. *Down to the Wire: UPI's Fight for Survival.* New York: McGraw Hill, 1990.

Gramling, Oliver. *AP: The Story of News.* Port Washington, N.Y.: Kennikat Press, 1969.

Schwarzlose, Richard Allen. *The Nation's Newsbrokers.* Evanston, Ill.: Northwestern University Press, 1990.

Laura Bergheim

See also **Mass Media; Newspapers.**

PRESS GANG. The British government never devised an orderly procedure for impressment, or conscription, for naval service. Instead, captains of shorthanded men-of-war sent armed details to scour British waterfronts or to board merchantmen to exercise direct and immediate conscription. Lieutenants commanding these "press gangs" were ruthlessly undiscriminating. Their use in colonial ports was only a minor cause of the American Revolution. However, Great Britain stepped up impressment efforts in the early nineteenth century to create a navy sufficiently large to fight France in the Napoleonic Wars. When British impressment was applied to American merchantmen after independence, impressment became a major cause of the War of 1812.

BIBLIOGRAPHY

Stagg, J. C. A. *Mr. Madison's War: Politics, Diplomacy, and Warfare in the Early American Republic, 1783–1830.* Princeton, N.J.: Princeton University Press, 1983.

Jim Dan Hill / A. E.

See also **Conscription and Recruitment; Impressment of Seamen; War of 1812.**

PRIBILOF ISLANDS. The Pribilof Islands, in the Bering Sea, were first visited in 1786 by the Russian explorer Gerasim Pribylov. The islands were ceded to the United States by Russia at the time of the purchase of Alaska in 1867. As the summer breeding grounds of the largest known herd of seals, they became the subject of a controversy between the United States, Great Britain, and other nations whose subjects were slaughtering the seals for their fur. In 1869 the U.S. Congress passed a law restricting the sealing. An American cutter seized Canadian vessels engaged in pelagic sealing in 1886. The British government vigorously protested, and an arbitration tribunal, agreed to in 1892, decided against the United States in 1893. The dispute was finally settled in 1911 by the North Pacific Sealing Convention between Great Britain, Russia, Japan, and the United States. The United States was given the right to regulate the killing of the seals, and the herd increased from a low of 127,000 in 1911 to more than 2.5 million in the 1960s. Japan withdrew from the convention in 1941, during World War II.

BIBLIOGRAPHY

Elliott, Henry Wood. *The Seal Islands of Alaska.* Kingston, Ontario, Canada: Limestone Press, 1976.

Jones, Dorothy Miriam. *A Century of Servitude: Pribilof Aleuts Under U.S. Rule.* Lanham, Md.: University Press of America, 1980.

Charles Marion Thomas / T. G.

See also **Galapagos Islands; Navy, Department of the; Sino-Japanese War; Taft-Katsura Memorandum.**

PRICE AND WAGE CONTROLS. The federal government uses price and wage controls to address the inflation of wages and prices. During wartime, wage and price controls function as a means of mobilizing resources. In a modern economy, inflation is usually stopped only by a recession or a depression, but the government can also decrease, or at least attempt to control, the rate of inflation by imposing price and wage controls.

Price and wage controls were used as early as the seventeenth century. In 1630, diminishing job opportunities and rising wages in Massachusetts Bay caused great consternation among workers and employers alike. To solve the problem, the Court of Assistants put a cap on wages for several categories of skilled workers and for common laborers in general. During the American Revolution, some colonies also imposed a maximum wage in the building trades to counteract labor shortages.

The federal government established price and wage controls during the Second World War by creating the Office of Price Administration (OPA) in 1942. The OPA set price ceilings on all commodities, with the exception of farm products; controlled rents in the areas where key defense plants were located; and held wartime price increases to a relatively low thirty-one percent. The agency also imposed rationing on certain scarce commodities such as automobile tires and gasoline. In the 1950s, President Harry S. Truman used the Office of Economic Stabilization to balance price and wage increases.

In response to the spiraling inflation of the early 1970s, Richard Nixon became the first president to use price and wage controls during peacetime. The strategy did help to stabilize the economy but proved to be only a temporary fix. Unfortunately, Nixon's attempt to subdue inflation and reduce unemployment resulted in limited goods for consumers and increased business bankruptcies, while doing little to curb joblessness. By the time Nixon resigned in 1974, inflation had reached double digits and the American economy was mired in a deep recession. When inflation reached eighteen percent in 1980, Americans clamored for mandatory price and wage controls. President Jimmy Carter steadfastly refused, stating that peacetime controls during the 1970s had proven a dismal failure.

Price controls were employed in 2001, when the Federal Energy Regulatory Commission—in response to the electricity shortage in California—voted to cap the wholesale price of electricity in the state for one year. Under this plan, price controls would be imposed whenever electricity reserves fell below 7.5 percent of demand.

BIBLIOGRAPHY

Rockoff, Hugh. *Drastic Measures: A History of Wage and Price Controls in the United States*, New York: Cambridge University Press, 1984.

Meg Greene Malvasi

See also **Agricultural Price Support; Prices; Wages and Salaries.**

PRICES. By "price" economists mean the rate of exchange of one good, typically money, for another. Prices convey information to producers, consumers, and government essential to efficient decision making. By attaching values to goods and factors of production, prices affect the allocation of resources and thereby shape the distributions of consumption and income across individuals and nations.

Setting and Measuring Prices

Some prices are set by custom, by bargains struck between individual buyers and sellers, by businesses with "market power" (such as monopolies), or by government fiat. However, in a large, capitalist economy like that of the contemporary United States, most prices are determined by the interchange of numberless and typically anonymous buyers (demand) and sellers (supply) in competitive markets.

To measure the overall level of prices, economists construct price "indexes," essentially weighted averages of prices of specific goods. The index is set equal to unity (or 100) in a base year, and prices in any other year are expressed relative to prices in the base year. An index of "producer prices" refers to prices received by supplies commodities. The "consumer price index" measures prices paid for goods and services purchased by consumers. In the case of the consumer price index, the weights refer to the relative importance of the goods in consumer budgets. Ideally, the introduction of new products, improvements in the quality of existing goods, and changes in the weights should be reflected in the construction of the indices. In practice, this may be difficult or impossible to do, particularly with historical data.

Over the course of American history, both the price level and the structure of relative prices have changed markedly. Most economists believe that sustained changes in the level of prices are caused primarily by sustained changes in the supply of money per unit of output, although other factors may be relevant in specific historical periods.

From the point of view of consumers, the single most important change in relative prices has been a substantial long-term rise in the "real wage": the money wage relative to the price level. Most economists believe that, in the long run, increases in real wages reflect increases in labor productivity. Other examples of changing relative prices include new products and regional differences. Typically, new products are introduced at high relative prices that moderate over time as the products are improved. A spectacular example is the computer: on average, computer processor prices declined by 20 percent per year from the early 1950s to the mid-1980s. Historically, there were significant regional variations in relative prices in the United States, but these differences have diminished as internal (and international) transport costs have fallen, and national (and global) markets have evolved.

Price Trends in American History

Economic historians and economists have charted the course of prices in the United States from the earliest settlements of the seventeenth century to the present day. Fragmentary information suggests that prices were falling throughout the seventeenth century as the demand for money (shillings) grew faster than the irregular supply. Variations in relative prices across colonies were common, as were localized, and often sudden, inflation and deflation. As trade expanded and as the money supply became more regular, prices began to rise and price fluctuations to moderate. The development of wholesale commodity markets in the major port cities—Boston, New York, Philadelphia, and Charleston—led to the regular publication of price information in broadsheets or in tabular form in local newspapers known as "Prices Current," and these have facilitated the construction of historical price indexes beginning in the early eighteenth century.

The revolutionary war witnessed one of the first (if not the first, the French and Indian War being a precursor) occurrences of wartime inflation in American history. Prices fell after the mid-1780s but soon rose again sharply beginning in the mid-1790s through the War of 1812. Prices fell sharply from their wartime peak in 1814, and continued to fall until reversing course in the early 1830s. The fall in prices that occurred after the panic of 1837 cemented in place a cyclical pattern in prices that, while hardly new to the economy, would be repeated several times up to and including the Great Depression of the 1930s—prices generally rose smartly during booms, but then fell, sometimes quite abruptly, during a recession.

Following the recession of the early 1840s, the last two decades of the pre–Civil War period were generally a period of rising prices. Beginning in 1843, prices rose more or less continuously until once again declining in the wake of the panic of 1857, but stabilized shortly thereafter. Despite the increases of the preceding twenty years, on the eve of the Civil War the overall level of prices was still well below that experienced in the late eighteenth and early nineteenth centuries.

The war years (1861–1865) witnessed substantial—uncontrollable, in the South—increases in prices due to the issuance of paper money by both the Union and Confederate governments. Prices rose sharply, and more importantly, relative to wages, created an "inflation tax" that helped both sides pay for the war effort.

Prices fell after the Civil War, and except for a minor upswing in the early 1880s, continued on a downward trend until the late 1890s, when an expansion in the worldwide supply of gold produced an increase in the money supply and a rising price level that stabilized just before the outbreak of World War I. As during the Civil War, prices rose rapidly during World War I, as the sale of war bonds fostered an expansion of the money supply in excess of the growth of production.

Prices fell sharply after the end of World War I and remained stable for the remainder of the 1920s. Stock prices were an important exception. Fueled by the postwar boom, these prices rose to unprecedented heights, before crashing down in October 1929. The depression that followed was by the far the worst in American history. Just as it had in previous downturns, the price level fell sharply between 1929 and 1933. Money wages also fell, but not as much as prices. Real output per capita decreased, and unemployment soared to nearly a quarter of the labor force in 1933. Prices began to recover after bottoming out in 1932, but fell again when the economy again went into decline late in the decade. In 1940, on the eve of U.S. entry into World War II, the price level was lower than it had been in 1930, and lower still than in the 1920s.

With the entry into the war, the nascent economic recovery accelerated, and unemployment, which had stood at nearly 15 percent in 1940, declined sharply. The war effort put severe upward pressure on prices that, officially at least, was checked through the imposition of wage and price controls in 1942. Unofficially, price rises exceed those recorded by the government: black market activity was rampant, and black market prices do not figure into the official price indexes of the period. After controls were lifted in 1946, the price level rose rapidly, reaching a level in 1950 slightly more than double the level in 1940.

Since 1950, the American economy has experienced a steady and substantial rise in price level, although the rate of increase—the inflation rate—varied across decades. Consumer prices rose by 23 percent in the 1950s and by another 31 percent in the 1960s. These increases were sufficient to prompt the Republican administration of President Richard Nixon to impose wage and price controls from 1971 to 1974. In the end, however, the controls did little to stem rising prices, particularly after an international oil embargo in 1973–1974 caused a sharp spike in energy prices. By the end of the decade, the price level had risen a stunning 112 percent over the level prevailing in 1970. The price level continued to rise in the 1980s and 1990s but at a much reduced pace. By the end of the 1990s, the cumulative effects of post-1950 increases in the price level were such that one 1999 dollar purchased the equivalent of $0.19 in 1950 prices.

Information on prices is routinely collected by government agencies and by the private sector. At the federal level, much of the responsibility is entrusted to the Bureau of Labor Statistics and the Bureau of Economic Analysis. Indexes produced by these agencies are published regularly in government documents such as *Statistical Abstract of the United States* and on-line at agency Web sites. For historical price indexes, readers are directed to the various editions of *Historical Statistics of the United States.*

BIBLIOGRAPHY

Cole, Arthur H. *Wholesale Commodity Prices in the United States, 1700–1861.* Cambridge, Mass.: Harvard University Press, 1938.

Gordon, Robert J. *The Measurement of Durable Goods Prices.* Chicago: University of Chicago Press, 1990.

Hanes, Chris. "Prices and Price Indices." In *Historical Statistics of the United States: Millennial Edition.* Edited by Susan B. Carter, Scott S. Gartner, Michael Haines, Alan L. Olmstead, Richard Sutch, and Gavin Wright. New York: Cambridge University Press, 2002.

McCusker, John J. *How Much Is That in Real Money? A Historical Price Index for Use as a Deflator of Money Values in the Economy of the United States.* 2d ed. Worcester, Mass.: American Antiquarian Society, 2001.

U.S. Bureau of the Census. *Statistical Abstract of the United States: The National Data Book.* 120th ed. Washington, D.C.: Government Printing Office, 2000.

———. *Historical Statistics of the United States: Colonial Times to 1970.* Washington, D.C.: Government Printing Office, 1976.

Robert A. Margo

See also **Business Cycles; Consumer Purchasing Power; Cost of Living; Inflation; Price and Wage Controls.**

PRIGG V. COMMONWEALTH OF PENNSYLVANIA, 41 U.S. 539 (1842). In 1837, a black woman named Margaret Morgan and her children, who were then living in Pennsylvania, were seized as fugitive slaves by Edward Prigg and three other men. The captors took the blacks back to Maryland without first obtaining a certificate of removal from a state judge, as required by an 1826 Pennsylvania personal liberty law. Prigg was subsequently convicted of kidnapping, but, in 1842, the U.S. Supreme Court overturned his conviction.

Writing for the Court, Justice Joseph Story concluded that 1) the federal Fugitive Slave Act of 1793 was constitutional; 2) all state personal liberty laws were unconstitutional because no state could pass any law adding additional requirements to that law which could impede the return of fugitive slaves; 3) the U.S. Constitution provided a common law right of recaption—a right of self-help—which allowed a slave owner (or an owner's agent) to seize any fugitive slave anywhere and return that slave to the master without complying with the provisions of the federal Fugitive Slave Act; 4) state officials ought to, but could not be required to, enforce the federal law of 1793; and 5) no fugitive slave was entitled to any due process hearing or trial beyond a summary proceeding to determine if the person seized was the person described in the affidavit or other papers provided by the claimant.

By striking down the Pennsylvania law, and, by extension, all other personal liberty laws, Justice Story left the northern states without the weapons or the legal authority to prevent the kidnapping of blacks. Story further endangered blacks in the North by asserting that the Constitution gave a master a right of self-help "to seize and recapture his slave" anywhere in the nation, regardless of state or federal statutory law.

Justice John McLean (of Ohio) dissented, arguing that states had a right and duty to protect their free black citizens from kidnapping. Chief Justice Roger B. Taney concurred in the majority opinion, but objected to Story's assertion that the northern states could withdraw their support for the law and leave its enforcement entirely to the federal government. When many northern states did this, southerners demanded a new law, which led to the adoption of the punitive and draconian Fugitive Slave Law of 1850.

BIBLIOGRAPHY

Finkelman, Paul. "Sorting Out *Prigg v. Pennsylvania.*" *Rutgers Law Journal* 24 (1993): 605–665.

———. "Story Telling on the Supreme Court: *Prigg v. Pennsylvania* and Justice Joseph Story's Judicial Nationalism." *Supreme Court Review* (1994): 247–294.

Paul Finkelman

See also **Fugitive Slave Acts.**

PRIMAL THERAPY, one of a cluster of "New Age" therapies that emerged during the 1970s, was pioneered by Dr. Arthur Janov. These therapies generally rejected the basic tenets of modern medicine and psychotherapy in favor of techniques and theories that purported to treat disorders holistically. Janov's primal scream therapy was based on the concept of repressed trauma. Janov suggested that early childhood trauma, perhaps even the trauma of birth itself, was the source of adult neurosis as well as a host of physical disorders, such as addiction, arthritis, and heart disease, he thought rooted in neurosis. His method for healing called for adults to re-experience the pain associated with early trauma, and in so doing, to release previously repressed memories about frightening or abusive experiences. Patients were encouraged to scream, cry, or otherwise express themselves to facilitate the therapeutic process. By unearthing these "primal" feelings and integrating them with memories, adults could move forward free of damaging psychic wounds thought to be the source of various physical and mental problems.

The concept of repressed memory of child abuse, which lies at the root of primal therapy, became highly controversial. A groundswell of popular interest in the theory led to a rash of claims by adults who believed they had, through primal therapies, uncovered memories of childhood trauma. Some of these claims even led to serious criminal charges; yet upon further investigation many examples of recalled abuse or trauma proved false. Further controversy surrounded practitioners of primal therapy who tried to re-create the birth trauma for their patients when a child died during the therapy. Thirty years after its introduction, primal therapy, and related techniques based on the concept of repressed traumatic memory, continued to attract patients interested in holistic healing. The near unanimous rejection of these techniques by mainstream therapeutic professionals, however, assured that they remained a cultural rather than a clinical force.

BIBLIOGRAPHY

Gardner, Martin. "Primal Scream: A Persistent New Age Therapy." *Skeptical Inquirer* 25:3 (May/June 2001): 17–19.

Janov, Arthur. *The Primal Scream: Primal Therapy—The Cure for Neurosis.* New York: Putnam, 1970.

Loren Butler Feffer

See also **New Age Movement.**

PRIMARY, DIRECT. Suspicious of public officials and of interest groups, Progressive thinkers of the early twentieth century sought to give individual voters a more direct role in government by curing "the ills of democracy (with) more democracy." Although not a new idea at the time, the direct primary became the most lasting Progressive reform and the most common form of primary election now used for all elected offices in the United States except the presidency. In the direct primary, party members who want to run for office file petitions to have their names placed on the ballot, allowing voters to vote directly for the candidates of their choice. Two types of direct primaries exist. A closed primary, used in almost all of the states, is limited to those people who have previously registered as members of a party in whose primary they are voting. An open primary allows individuals to vote across party lines as in the regular election process.

Before primary elections were used on a regular basis in the twentieth century, political parties nominated candidates for office at party conventions and caucuses. From the 1790s to the 1830s, the congressional and legislative caucuses made nominations for public office. From the 1830s until the early 1900s, the preferred method of nomination was by delegate conventions. Party primaries were introduced as early as 1842, when the Democratic Party of Crawford County, Pennsylvania, first used the system. Later, party primaries were used to nominate candidates for local offices in California and New York in 1866 and soon became the standard in other states throughout the rest of the nineteenth century. Primaries became the centerpiece of the Progressive movement when the first presidential primary law was passed in Florida in 1901. In 1905, Robert M. La Follette's Progressive Movement in Wisconsin gave impetus to the principle of nominating candidates by direct voting of party members. Oregon became the first state to adopt a preferential primary in 1910, a primary where voters voted for their favorite candidates and voted for convention delegates separately. Presidential primaries rose to popularity during the election of 1912, when at least thirteen primaries were held.

Primaries played a relatively minor role in presidential elections until the 1960s, when John F. Kennedy entered the West Virginia primary to test whether or not a Catholic could do well in a predominantly Protestant state. As of 2002, the presidential primary was used in about three-quarters of the states to choose delegates to the national party conventions. Several states, most notably Iowa, still use the caucus system to nominate presidential candidates.

BIBLIOGRAPHY

Diclerico, Robert E., and James W. Davis. *Choosing Our Choices: Debating the Presidential Nominating Process.* Lanham, Md.: Rowan and Littlefield Publishers, 2000.

Galderisi, Peter F., Marni Ezra, and Michael Lyons, eds. *Congressional Primaries and the Politics of Representation.* Lanham, Md.: Rowan and Littlefield Publishers, 2001.

Kendall, Kathleen E. *Communication in the Presidential Primaries: Candidates and the Media, 1912–2000.* Westport, Conn.: Praeger, 2000.

James F. Adomanis

See also **Elections; Caucus; Machine, Political; Political Parties.**

PRIMARY, WHITE. The white primary was one of several means used by white southern politicians in the first half of the twentieth century to control black political power. By preventing blacks from voting in Democratic primaries, southern whites effectively disfranchised them, since primaries are more important than general elections in one-party states. At first southern whites set up primary-election machinery so as to exclude most blacks, but without direct reference to race. In 1923 the Texas legislature enacted a law specifically declaring blacks ineligible to participate in the state's primary elections. In *Smith v. Allwright* (1944) the SUPREME COURT ruled that since the white primary was an integral part of the election process, the Texas Democratic party's decision to exclude blacks was unconstitutional. Supplemental decisions were handed down, and by midcentury the white primary was legally abolished not only in Texas but also in all other states.

BIBLIOGRAPHY

Branch, Taylor. *Parting the Waters: America in the King Years, 1954–1963.* New York: Simon and Schuster, 1988.

Payne, Charles M. *I've Got the Light of Freedom: The Organizing Tradition and the Mississippi Freedom Struggle.* Berkeley: University of California Press, 1995.

Weisbrot, Robert. *Freedom Bound: A History of America's Civil Rights Movement.* New York: Norton, 1990.

Monroe Billington / T. G.

See also **Ballot; Black Codes; Civil Rights Act of 1957; Emancipation Proclamation; Literacy Test; Suffrage, Exclusion from the.**

PRIMOGENITURE implies seniority by birth; legally, it denotes the right of the eldest son to inherit the estate of a parent to the exclusion of all other heirs. Its wide use in medieval England followed the introduction of continental feudalism by the Normans, who stressed the wishes of a lord to keep his holdings intact to ensure the rents, fees, and military services arising from these tenures. Otherwise, a vassal, the person holding land from a feudal lord, might distribute his tenure among his sons in a way that would defeat the economic basis of the feudal structure. By the fourteenth century practically all free tenures were subject to primogeniture. In 1540 the British Parliament passed a statute that allowed owners of land held in fee simple, as well as many feudal tenures, to pass their holdings to persons other than their eldest sons by will. Feudal tenures were abolished in 1662, after which all freehold land could be willed. By this time, feudalism, except for the manorial system, was in decline. Although feudalism influenced institutional development in America, it was chiefly in its manorial aspects that primogeniture affected the New World.

Primogeniture existed in almost all of the original thirteen colonies. In Massachusetts the earliest colonial laws provided for partible descent, or division of the property. In cases of intestacy, property was divided among all the children, with the eldest son getting a double portion. This rule was also in effect in Pennsylvania. In New England, except for Rhode Island, stout opposition gradually reduced inheritance through primogeniture, so that by the American Revolution it had practically disappeared and had been replaced by partible inheritance. In New York and the southern colonies, where economic and social forces favored large estates, primogeniture generally prevailed, much to the dissatisfaction of those who viewed the institution as an alien and undesirable practice. Its effect was limited, however, because families of the gentry tended to distribute property through wills.

The movement for free and equitable inheritance was fostered by those sponsoring the American Revolution. Stimulated by the democratic philosophy of Thomas Jefferson, the Virginia assembly attacked primogeniture and finally, in 1785, abolished it. Georgia and North Carolina had done the same in 1777 and 1784, respectively. The other states followed this lead, although it was not until 1798 that Rhode Island abolished primogeniture. Since that date, primogeniture has not been in effect anywhere in the United States.

BIBLIOGRAPHY

Brewer, Holly. "Entailing Aristocracy in Colonial Virginia: 'Ancient Feudal Restraints' and Revolutionary Reform." *William and Mary Quarterly.* 54, no. 2 (April 1997): 307–346.

Cantor, Norman F. *Imagining the Law: Common Law and the Foundations of the American Legal System.* New York: HarperCollins, 1997.

Haskins, George Lee. *Law and Authority in Early Massachusetts: A Study in Tradition and Design.* Hamden, Conn.: Archon Books, 1968. The original edition was published in 1960.

Morris, Richard B. *Studies in the History of American Law, with Special Reference to the Seventeenth and Eighteenth Centuries.* 2d ed. Studies in History, Economics, and Public Law, no. 316. Philadelphia: J. M. Mitchell, 1959. The original edition was published in 1930.

W. Freeman Galpin / C. P.

See also **Entail of Estate; Land Policy.**

PRINCETON, BATTLE OF (3 January 1777). Leaving three regiments at Princeton, New Jersey, the British general Charles Cornwallis arrived at the Delaware River near sunset on 2 January 1777 to avenge George Washington's defeat of the Hessians at Trenton. Cornwallis found Washington's army of five thousand men occupying a precarious position along Assunpink Creek. Ignoring Sir William Erskine's counsel to attack immediately, Cornwallis decided to "bag" Washington in the morning.

Advised by General Arthur St. Clair, Washington executed a brilliant military maneuver. At midnight, leaving his campfires burning, he quietly withdrew the main body of his army along an unpicketed road and gained the British rear. Approaching Princeton at daybreak, the Americans encountered a force, under Colonel Charles Mawhood, just leaving the village to join Cornwallis. General Hugh Mercer's brigade engaged Mawhood's troops but was driven back. Rallied by Washington and joined by new arrivals, the continental patriots drove the British from the field and village. British losses were between four hundred and six hundred killed, wounded, or captured. Cornwallis, outmaneuvered, withdrew his entire army in feverish haste to New Brunswick to save a £70,000 war chest. Washington, his army wearied, took up a strong position at Morristown, having freed most of New Jersey and infused new hope into a cause that appeared all but lost.

BIBLIOGRAPHY

Bill, Alfred Hoyt. *Campaign of Princeton, 1776–1777.* Princeton, N.J.: Princeton University Press, 1948.

Stryker, William S. *The Battles of Trenton and Princeton.* Boston: Houghton Mifflin, 1898. Reprint, New Jersey Heritage Series, no. 3. Spartanburg, S.C.: Reprint Company, 1967.

C. A. Titus / A. R.

See also **Delaware, Washington Crossing the; Revolution, American: Military History; Trenton, Battle of.**

***PRINCETON*, EXPLOSION ON THE.** The *Princeton*, the first warship driven by a screw propeller, carried a large gun known as the "Peacemaker," devised by R. F. Stockton, the ship's commander; at twelve inches in diameter, it was the largest gun yet forged for the American navy. On 28 February 1844, while a party of about two hundred government officials, including President John Tyler, were cruising down the Potomac aboard the *Princeton*, the crew fired the gun to entertain the company. It burst and killed several persons, including Secretary of State Abel P. Upshur and Secretary of the Navy Thomas W. Gilmer.

BIBLIOGRAPHY

Bennett, Frank M. *The Steam Navy of the United States: A History of the Growth of the Steam Vessel of War in the U. S. Navy, and of the Naval Engineer Corps.* Westport, Conn.: Greenwood Press, 1972.

Walter B. Norris / C. W.

See also **Gunboats; Navy, United States; Steamboats.**

PRINCETON UNIVERSITY. Founded in 1746 by religious reformers, Princeton University is one of the oldest and most prestigious universities in the United States. The fourth oldest school in the nation, Princeton's founders decided to establish the school after Harvard and Yale opposed the Great Awakening. Four Presbyterian ministers, all of whom were part of the New Light faction that was part of a split that took place in the Presbyterian Church in the 1740s, came together with three laymen to found the institution. It was originally called the College of New Jersey. The first classes were held in Elizabeth, New Jersey, in the parsonage of Jonathan Dickinson, its first president. The school was moved to Newark in 1747 and then in 1756 to Princeton, New Jersey. Like most eighteenth-century schools of similar stature, Princeton's curriculum emphasized the classics while the campus culture reflected the religious orientation of the school's founders. Throughout the eighteenth century, admission was based upon a knowledge of Latin and Greek. Attendance at prayer remained a requirement until the late 1800s.

In addition to establishing its place in colonial history as one of the academic institutions founded in response to the Great Awakening, Princeton was significant to the history of the early Republic because of its central role in both the American Revolution and in the development of Congress. Princeton was the site of an historic battle during the Revolution, the Battle of Princeton in 1777, and its president at the time, John Witherspoon, was a signer of the Declaration of Independence. Nassau Hall, which has been the center of Princeton's campus since 1756, briefly served as the meeting site for the Continental Congress in 1783. From its members, Princeton was able to claim nine graduates among the delegates to the Constitutional Convention of 1787. This was more than any other college could boast. In addition, ever since the first meeting of the House of Representatives in 1789, the school has had at least one alumnus sitting in Congress.

Since Princeton attracted a significant number of southern students during the nineteenth century, the school's work was largely disrupted during the Civil War. Nevertheless, following the conflict the students were able fully to resume their academic programming. In 1896, the College of New Jersey officially changed its name to Princeton University. In 1902, Woodrow Wilson became Princeton's thirteenth president. Under Wilson's administration, the university's curricular and administrative structures were revamped. Wilson created departments of instruction with administrative heads, unified the curriculum, and greatly increased the faculty by creating preceptorials. Preceptors allowed students the opportunity to interact more with professors by meeting with small groups. Preceptors would later be used at colleges and universities across the country. Wilson went on to become the second Princeton graduate, after James Madison, to become president of the United States.

Although Princeton established its Graduate School in 1900, it was during the presidency of Harold Dodds in the 1930s, 1940s, and 1950s that the school became highly focused on graduate education and research. In 1933 Albert Einstein took an office at Princeton when he became a life member of the nearby Institute for Advanced Study.

Like the rest of America, Princeton University was touched in many ways by the social movements of the 1960s. Although it graduated its first black students in 1947, not until the 1960s did Princeton begin actively to recruit students of color. The university also voted to admit women as undergraduates in 1969. In the year 2001, Princeton's student body consisted of 4,611 students, of whom 48 percent were female. American minorities, including African Americans, Asian Americans, Latinos, and Native Americans, represented 26 percent of the student body. One of America's most competitive schools, Princeton admits only 12 percent of its applicants.

As Princeton University entered the twenty-first century, it maintained the fourth largest endowment in the country (preceded by Harvard, the University of Texas, and Yale). It is also the first major research university to have women in its two highest positions: Shirley Tilghman as president and Amy Gutman as provost.

BIBLIOGRAPHY

"About Princeton." Available from http://www.princeton.edu.

Leitch, Alexander. *A Princeton Companion.* Princeton, N.J.: Princeton University Press, 1978.

"Women at the Top of Academe." *New York Times* (4 September 2001): A22.

Stephanie R. Sims

See also **Education, Higher: Colleges and Universities; Great Awakening; New Lights.**

PRINTER'S DEVIL. Printing was originally associated with black magic because of the marvelous uniformity of printed works as compared with handwritten manuscripts. Printers cherished their air of mystery and dubbed their young helpers evil spirits, or "devils." Also, some European apprentices were considered permanent menial laborers and so received a disreputable name.

In America the term lost its connotation of magic, but the chore boy or youngest apprentice was still called the printer's devil. Educated in setting type and working the handpress, these workers sometimes became master printers, publishers, or writers. With the mechanization of printing, apprenticeship declined, and the printer's devil became obsolete.

BIBLIOGRAPHY

Joyce, William L. *Printing and Society in Early America.* Worcester, Mass.: American Antiquarian Society, 1983.

Pasko, W. W., ed. *American Dictionary of Printing and Bookmaking.* Detroit, Mich.: Gale Research, 1967. The original edition was published in 1894.

Quimby, Ian M. G. *Apprenticeship in Colonial Philadelphia.* Outstanding Dissertations in the Fine Arts Series. New York: Garland, 1985.

Silver, Rollo G. *The American Printer, 1787–1825.* Charlottesville: University Press of Virginia, 1967.

Milton W. Hamilton / T. D.

See also **Apprenticeship; Publishing Industry.**

PRINTING INDUSTRY. The origin of printing would seem to be inextricably bound up with that of literacy. While that may indeed have been the case, at this remove it is difficult to be certain. The essence of printing is that multiple copies are made of a sample of written language. How large a sample is reproduced depends on the flexibility of the printing technique in question. The history of printing is to a great extent also the history of paper and of publishing.

Early History of Printing

In classical times, an edition of a written work was produced by having it copied by scribes, usually literate slaves devoted entirely to that purpose. The availability of slave labor made possible editions of up to several thousand copies of a poem or history, each written by hand on a papyrus or parchment scroll, the cost of each thus dependent on the value of the scribe's time.

The early steps toward printing, unlike those of many other arts and crafts, have left clear tracks, easily traced by archaeology. From the handprints dampened with mud and pressed directly on the walls of prehistoric caves, or outlined in blown pigments, to carved ring and cylinder seals used to impress designs in wax or clay, artifacts survive that clearly predate the invention of writing, probably in Mesopotamia, sometime in the fourth millennium B.C.

Perhaps the earliest extant example of printing involving language dates from the seventeenth century B.C. The Phaistos disk, discovered on Crete, bears over a hundred pictographs arranged in a spiral pattern, which have never been deciphered. Whether these characters were ideographic, syllabic, or protoalphabetic, the repeated characters are not merely similar, but in fact are identical impressions made by pressing stamps made of some unknown material into the soft clay—in effect, an example of early typewriting, but not of printing as it is understood today.

At about the beginning of the present era, printing on textiles and other materials was practiced in Europe and Asia. Wood, baked clay, stone, or other carved surfaces could be covered with parchment or fabric and rubbed with solid pigment, producing a positive impression of the incised design. But parchment, vellum, and other such materials were expensive, and papyrus was fragile. With the invention of paper in China, by Ts'ai Lun in A.D. 105, the printing of books from wooden blocks (xylography) became practical, for paper—made from rags, hemp, bark, rope, nets, and other fibrous, readily available materials—combined the qualities of cheapness and durability.

A page was written by hand, with or without illustration, and the thin paper was glued to the smoothed block of wood. The paper was dampened to make the reversed page visible, and the areas not covered by writing were cut away, leaving the printing surface. The block was inked, and a sheet of paper was laid over it and pressed down firmly to transfer the ink from the wood to the paper. Thus, a block had to be carved for each page to be reproduced.

The earliest movable type was produced in China, probably about the beginning of the present era, but Chinese, with approximately 40,000 so-called ideographs, presented an apparently insuperable challenge to this effort. Korean, which has the most purely syllabic form of writing of all languages on earth—has a comparatively concise 2,300 symbols. Cast in bronze, Korean movable type was being used in printing centuries before Europe moved beyond block printing.

Wooden blocks were being used in Europe for printing perhaps eight centuries before the apparently independent invention of movable type in northern Europe. Playing cards, illustrations, and even single pages of written matter were printed in presses derived from wine and fruit presses well before the mid-fifteenth century. But printing a page meant first carving—in reverse—the entire page, in a smoothed block of hardwood, and an error, once made, was virtually impossible to correct.

The growth of the monastery system contemporaneous with the collapse of the Roman Empire supplanted the slave-based system of copying manuscripts. Books to be transcribed were copied, one by one, and especially important works would be further embellished with decorative initials and marginal illustrations, with varying use of color and gilding. Throughout the Middle Ages, the scribes developed various "hands," or styles of lettering, ultimately adding to the classical Roman capitals the minuscule, or lowercase, letters. By the twelfth century, the production of books was becoming a business, as the centers of learning moved from the monasteries to the cities. As the universities arose, the demand for books increased.

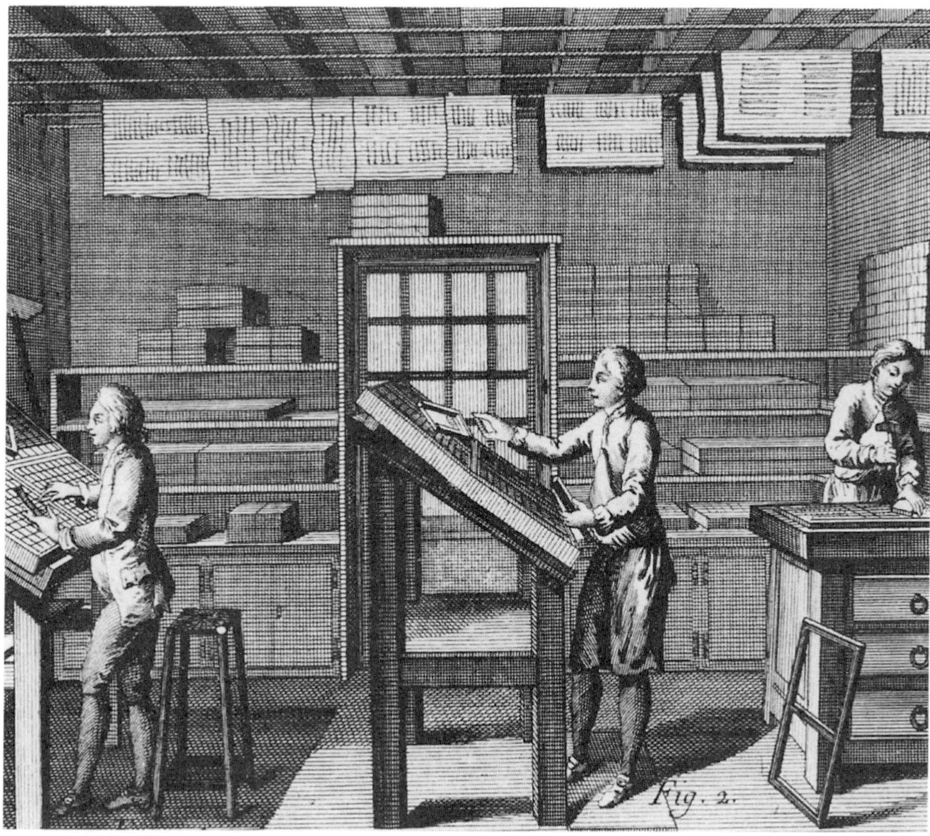

Printing Comes to America. In the mid-1600s, printing presses were large, intricate machines that required a great deal of work to produce books. Nonetheless, the demand for printed materials was growing, and so the first printing press was built in the American British colonies in 1638. The machine was set up at Harvard College by Stephen Daye and his son Matthew; within two years, they had published their first book, *The Whole Book of Psalmes Faithfully Translated into English Metre.* This engraving shows that first book being printed on the Dayes' press. LIBRARY OF CONGRESS

Gutenberg's Invention

Johannes Gutenberg, of Mainz, is generally credited with the invention of printing from movable type, beginning in the 1440s. His contribution was more than simply realizing that each letter could be cut as a separate piece rather than carved into the solid block that would make up a page. Trained as a goldsmith, and thus familiar with the techniques of fine metalworking, Gutenberg set out to create the first-ever mass product: an imitation of the individually produced books of his time. He imitated the black letter "gothic" writing style then current in northern Europe, complete with the ligatures, or combinations of letters, including the fi, fl, ff, ffi, and ffl still used today, as well as others. His font, or character set, including eight versions of the lowercase letter "a" and similar variations of other letters, along with all the scribal abbreviations in contemporary use, came to a total of 290 separate characters: capital and small letters, numbers, punctuation marks, and spaces.

To make these characters, Gutenberg invented the adjustable type mold. A letter was first cut and filed, in reverse form, in the end of a steel punch. Once the letter was completed and had been checked and approved, the steel was hardened, and then the cut letter was driven into a soft copper bar to make a positive. This copper impression was fitted into the adjustable mold, which for a given font had a constant height but a variable width, so that narrow letters, such as f, i, j, l, r, and t, could be cast as narrow pieces of type; wider letters—m and w, for example—could be cast correspondingly wider. The adjustable mold thus enabled Gutenberg to set letters in lines of readable words. Gutenberg further invented such "modern" features as hanging punctuation, in which end-of-line hyphens were placed in the margin, past the edge of the type area, and the pins used to position the paper sheet for proper registration of multiple pages.

Gutenberg is known to have printed single-sheet indulgences, which were sold to the Church in editions of several thousand for later individual distribution, many of which are still in existence, and he printed a Latin textbook by Donatus, which was so popular that only single sheets have survived to the present day. His most signifi-

Hoe Rotary Press. In 1871 Richard March Hoe revolutionized the printing industry when he invented the first continuous-roll press, which automatically placed a new roll of paper on the press and continued printing when the old roll ran out; previously, the machine had to be stopped and a new roll loaded by hand. His press, shown in this early engraving, could print 18,000 newspapers per hour, a tremendous improvement over existing web-fed presses. © Archive Photos, Inc.

cant printed book was in fact twofold: a thirty-six line and a forty-two line two-volume Bible, in an edition of perhaps a couple hundred, mostly in paper, but with perhaps as many as fifty printed on the more expensive vellum.

From Gutenberg's first efforts, book printing expanded at a prodigious rate. By 1501, the end of the "incunabulum" or "cradle" period of printing, over 6,000 books had been printed, in Latin, Greek, and Hebrew, as well as many of the various vernacular languages of Europe. The real measure of Gutenberg's achievement is how minor were the improvements made—or required—in his press, type, and other equipment, in the next three and a half centuries. These changes included the design of more easily readable roman and italic typefaces, which largely supplanted the black letter forms outside the Holy Roman Empire. Presses built of metal made possible the application of greater pressure, thus making it possible to print more pages in a single pass. The cumbersome screw of early presses, which limited the rate of printing to perhaps 250 impressions per hour, was replaced by a system using a complex sprung lever that brought the platen down onto the paper and chase of type somewhat more rapidly, but still only about 300 impressions per hour. In the 1770s, the English printer and inventor John Baskerville devised a system of hardening paper with heat and pressure before printing, which along with the typeface he designed, resulted in a remarkably clear, crisp, readable printed page—at a cost that slowed the adoption of his methods by most printers.

Printing in the New World

The first printing press in the New World was brought by the Spanish to Mexico City less than half a century after the first voyage of Columbus. The press was used in 1539 to print the first book in the Americas, *Breve y más compendiosa doctrina cristiana en lengua mexicana y castellana* roughly, *Brief and Most Compendious Christian Doctrine, in the Mexican and Spanish (Or Castilian) Languages.*

Printing came to North America in 1638, when the first press was set up at Harvard College by Stephen Daye and his son Matthew; within two years they had printed *The Whole Booke of Psalmes Faithfully Translated into English Metre*, familiarly known as the Bay Psalm Book. Within a decade, the press had been taken over by Samuel Green, who produced the first Bible printed in the thirteen British colonies, John Eliot's Algonquian translation, *Mamusse Wunneetupanatamwe Up-Biblum God.* Well through the eighteenth century, colonial printers relied on presses, type, and other equipment imported from England and Europe. The Declaration of Independence, for example, was printed in the type designed and cut by William Caslon in 1734. Language aside, Gutenberg would hardly have felt out of place in the print shop of an American newspaper or book publisher, as all printing continued to be done on a flat bed of type, which was inked by hand using a padded leather ball, then overlaid with a sheet of paper, before the pressure was applied by a flat metal platen. Illustrations in books, periodicals, and other printed matter were done primarily in the form of woodcuts, wood engravings (with the design cut into the end of the grain), and copper engravings.

Changes of the Nineteenth Century

The nineteenth century was a time of explosive change in printing, no less in America than in Europe. In Germany during the 1790s, Aloys Senefelder had invented lithography, the first planographic method of printing: a design was drawn on a flat slab of limestone in pencil, crayon, or other oil-based medium; the stone was dampened, an oil-based ink was applied, and a sheet of paper was laid across the stone. Within a few years, Senefelder had designed and built a press to handle the heavy limestone slabs, sufficiently mechanizing the process to allow him to print hundreds, even into thousands, depending upon the quality maintenance required for each job. In the first decades of the nineteenth century, Senefelder developed lithographic printing further, leading at quarter century to multicolor lithography. Heretofore, only relief printing, such as that from the raised surface of type and wood cuts, and intaglio printing, from engravings in which the ink was forced into lines cut or etched into a metal plate, had been available. When typographical headings and body text were added to pictorial matter, the seeds were firmly planted for a newly practical, efficient, feasible, cost-effective method: offset lithography, planographic printing from rotary blankets fully contiguous with the surface to be printed.

One problem in letterpress printing had always been the wear on the type from multiple impressions in the press, a problem exacerbated by the higher pressures of the metal-bodied presses of the eighteenth century. Furthermore, a printer had to have sufficient type on hand to make up new pages while others were in press. A considerable advance was the invention in the early 1800s of the stereotype, in which the typeset page was pressed into a plaster mold, which was then used to cast a solid plate for the press; the individual letters, punctuation marks, and other pieces of type could then be returned to the case for immediate reuse without having to withstand—or succumb to—the repeated force of the press. The electrotype, in which a wax mold of the type was electroplated with copper then filled with lead, was a further development away from printing letterpress directly from type.

Presses and paper changed as well during the Industrial Revolution. The first all-steel press was built in about 1800, and in 1803 in London the brothers Fourdrinier introduced the first paper-making machine to produce a continuous roll, or web, of paper. In 1814, Friedrich König invented the first steam-driven printing press. The cylinder press used a revolving cylinder to bring the paper against the flat bed of type. The rotary press put both paper and type—or rather the curved plate made from the type—on cylinders. The perfecting press made it possible for the first time to print both sides of the paper at one time. The combination of steam power and the paper web, along with stereotypes, revolutionized the industry, making larger editions of books, magazines, and newspapers feasible.

Even so, the presses were still sheet-fed; that is, the web of paper was cut into press-size sheets before it was printed—until 1863, with the introduction in the United States of William Bullock's web-fed newspaper press; a roll of paper was fed into the press, emerging as printed and folded newspapers. Bullock's press, like the later Walter press in England, had to be stopped to change paper rolls. In 1871, American Richard March Hoe's continuous-roll press could produce up to 18,000 newspapers per hour.

Type, however, was still set piece by piece as it had been since the mid-fifteenth century, with spaces added individually to justify (space out) the line to the proper measure, or line width. Various attempts at automating the process of typesetting met with frustration, until in 1886 American inventor Ottmar Mergenthaler introduced the Linotype, a keyboard-driven machine on which the operator set and cast each line as a single solid piece of type-high lead, complete with spacing for justification, automatically spreading the line out to full measure. The fact that each line produced by the machine had, only moments before, existed in the form of molten lead gave this method the apt nickname "hot type." Within a few years, Mergenthaler had improved his invention so that both roman and italic versions of a given typeface could be set on one machine. Once the lines of type had been used to make the stereotype of metal cast in plaster—later the electrotype, in which the type was cast in wax, which was then electrically plated with a thin but sturdy and precise replica of the original, from which these could be used to print, or yet later, to make camera-ready copy, or other form for printing—they could be melted down for reuse. The Linotype held its own as the typesetting method of choice well through the mid-twentieth century, and some were still in use in considerable numbers a century after the machine's introduction.

Innovations of the Twentieth Century

The first practical photocomposition (cold-type) devices appeared in the 1950s, and by the late 1980s had almost entirely displaced the Linotype. These produced a photographic image of the page rather than raised metal type. The pages were then photographed to produce negatives used to make lithographic plates. Modern offset lithography uses the oil-water principle of Senefelder's process, with the slab of limestone replaced by flexible plates of aluminum, steel, or plastic, treated with a light-sensitive chemical. When the plate is covered by a negative of the image to be printed and exposed to light, the image is photographically etched on the plate to accept the oil-based ink; areas not to print on the plate will take water but not oil. The plate is mounted on the press, and the image is offset onto a rubber roller, or blanket, which transfers the ink to the paper. Modern offset web presses have a throughput of over three thousand feet of paper per minute, with the webs changed "on the fly," the beginning of a new roll transferred to the tail of the old without stopping the press.

Offset lithography is the least expensive and most-used printing process. Gravure, in which the ink is trapped within tiny cells (as many as 50,000 per square inch) on the plate for transfer to the paper, is used for printing high-quality color, as for example in magazines and particular kinds of books. Flexographic printing, like letterpress, transfers ink from the raised surface of the plate to the material to be printed, but soft plates, originally rubber and more recently photopolymer, are used, and the ink is more fluid. Flexography allows printing on a wide variety of materials, including plastics, heavy cardboard, and other packaging. Screen printing, in which a fine porous sheet, originally of silk, is treated so that areas to remain unprinted are masked, permits printing on virtually any material, including clothing such as sweatshirts, T-shirts, and heavy plastic and foam-core boards used for signage.

In the 1960s, writer Marshall McLuhan predicted the demise of the "Gutenberg Age," that is, the coming disappearance of print. In fact, the advent of the computer revolution, more properly the microchip revolution, has brought an explosion of new forms of printing. So-called desktop publishing has brought the tools of typesetting that once required a massive investment in hardware and software within the reach of quite literally millions of people worldwide.

Office printers in the early twenty-first century possess multiple capacities, in scanning, duplicating, and assembling written materials, including graphic illustration, which formerly had to be outsourced to professional art studios. While many have bemoaned the falloff in quality that was to be expected when enthusiasm and a few weeks' practice took the place of years of apprenticeship, experience so far indicates that quality is still sought and, however haltingly, will tend to win out in the end. Indeed, the efforts of the amateur publishers in the late twentieth century have already borne fruit in the improved graphic productions of the early twenty-first century On-demand publishing, in which a single or a few copies of a book can be printed and bound as needed, obviating the need for warehouses full of seldom-required texts, has become a reality, with the cost reasonably comparable to that of a conventionally printed short-run book.

And contrary to predictions of a "paperless office," paper is being produced and used at an increased rate since the personal computer first became a familiar sight in homes and offices. Time will tell to what extent the Internet will affect the newspaper, magazine, and book businesses, but five and a half centuries after Gutenberg, over 135,000 new book titles were being published each year, in editions of from a few hundred to tens, even hundreds, of thousands. Just as films did not spell the end of legitimate theater, nor television that of films, it seems likely that the new forms of publishing—electronic in any of various ways—are more likely to supplement than to supplant the familiar.

BIBLIOGRAPHY

The Chicago Manual of Style. 14th ed. Chicago: University of Chicago Press, 1993.

Lawson, Alexander. *Anatomy of a Typeface.* Boston: David R. Godine, 1990.

Lee, Marshall. *Bookmaking: The Illustrated Guide to Design/Production/Editing.* 2d ed. New York: Bowker, 1979.

Nakanishi, Akira. *Writing Systems of the World: Alphabets, Syllabaries, Pictograms.* Rutland, Vt.: Charles E. Tuttle, 1982.

Olmert, Michael. *The Smithsonian Book of Books.* Washington, D.C.: Smithsonian Books, 1992.

Skillin, Marjorie E., Robert M. Gay, et al. *Words into Type.* 3d ed. Englewood Cliffs, N.J.: Prentice-Hall, 1974.

Dan Kirklin

See also **Publishing Industry.**

PRINTMAKING. The first print executed in the American colonies is a crude woodcut portrait of the Rev. Richard Mather, made by the Boston artist John Foster in 1670. Some fifty years later, Peter Pelham, the émigré British artist who settled in Boston, created several mezzotint portraits of New England personalities between 1728 and 1751. The most celebrated American print from the eighteenth century is the silversmith and patriot Paul Revere's *The Boston Massacre* (1770), based on a print by Henry Pelham. At the outset, prints were intended to convey information: portraits of notable people, maps, views of cities and towns. Even after the establishment of the United States of America, these practical requirements dominated graphic arts well into the first quarter of the nineteenth century, although the technical caliber of etching, engraving, and lithography was quite high.

In 1857, Nathaniel Currier and James Ives formed a partnership to print lithographs that could be distributed and sold in large numbers. Their scenes of farmhouses, frontier scouts and covered wagons, or life in America's growing cities, became synonymous with popular American taste. But it was not until Winslow Homer etched eight large copper plates in the 1880s, each reproducing a painting by him, that an American artist working in the United States undertook to create important original graphic works. Homer rethought his painted compositions in terms of black and white etchings that capture the drama and energy of his oils, and are in no sense reproductive.

During this same period, many American artists went to Europe to study and visit museum collections. Not surprisingly, these artists experimented with graphic media. Most notably, Mary Cassatt, who settled in Paris, made a series of color aquatints that are among the masterpieces of American graphic art. James A. McNeill Whistler also made etchings in France and England, and his set of Venetian views from 1879 to 1880 became immensely popular on both sides of the Atlantic, with the prices of his prints soon equaling those of Rembrandt. Although the expatriate status of Cassatt and Whistler was no obstacle to their work being known in the United States, their example did not stimulate other artists to create graphic works of comparable originality.

The most revolutionary art movement of the first decade of the twentieth century, Cubism, had virtually no impact on American graphic art, excepting some small woodcuts by Max Weber, and John Marin's few etchings and drypoints that capture the pace of urban life, such as his celebrated *Woolworth Building* (1913). In contrast, the artists associated with the ASHCAN SCHOOL did create prints that reflect their fascination with incidents from everyday life in overcrowded metropolises. John Sloan produced numerous etchings of urban life, whether shopping on Fifth Avenue or the grim realities of tenement living. George Bellows, whose preferred medium was lithography, covered a wider range of subject matter than Sloan, from his famous prizefight image *Stag at Sharkey's* (1917) to the atrocities of World War I. Although not part of the Ashcan School, Edward Hopper's etchings, such as *Evening Wind* (1921) and *Night Shadows* (1921), evoke the poetry of the urban experience. At this time, few modernist painters made prints, the notable exceptions being Stuart Davis's black and white lithographs, and Charles Sheeler's coolly observed views of urban and rural America, such as his *Delmonico Building* (1926).

By contrast, Regionalist painters sought their subjects in rural, Midwest America. Grant Wood and Thomas Hart Benton made prints that portrayed the isolation and independence of the people living on these vast stretches of farmland. The drama and energy of Benton's lithographs was studied by Jackson Pollock who, before he made his celebrated "drip" abstract canvases, executed several lithographs of Regionalist subjects in a style that closely parallels Benton's.

The Great Depression made life much more difficult for American artists, and many found some help in the Federal Art Project, administered under the Works Progress Administration (WPA). The program ran from 1935 to 1943 and included a section devoted to printmaking. The amount of activity was surprising: some 12,581 prints in editions of varying sizes, which were later placed on deposit in American museums. Artists employed by the WPA were expected to work in a representational style and to portray some aspect of American life. Overall, the graphic art produced under this program is unexceptional. It was only after World War II that American printmaking assumed a central position on the international scene.

World War II brought a number of European artists to America; for printmaking, the crucial figure was the British artist William Stanley Hayter, a gifted teacher whose "Atelier 17" in New York City introduced American artists to color intaglio techniques and the stylistic innovations of Surrealism. Another refugee artist was the Argentinean Mauricio Lasansky who arrived in the United States in 1943, and then founded his own graphic workshop at the University of Iowa in 1945. At Yale University the Hungarian Gabor Peterdi also ran a printmaking workshop. These printmakers shared the belief that the artist should be responsible for all aspects of a graphic work's creation, from the original conception to all stages of its execution and printing. In time, this quest for technical excellence was viewed as unexciting. By the late 1950s, print workshops were founded that aimed to create collaborative relationships between artists and printers. On the East coast, the Universal Limited Art Editions (founded in 1957) and the Pratt Graphic Arts Center in New York (founded in 1956) were complemented on the West coast by Los Angeles's Tamarind Workshop (founded in 1960). These workshops focused on the technically demanding medium of color lithography, which requires that an artist work in concert with a master printer.

American avant-garde painting stressed large size, bold gestures, and powerful colors, which placed formidable difficulties in the path of artists wanting to transpose these qualities into graphic works. Few early abstract expressionist painters were interested in printmaking, with the exception of Willem de Kooning. By the mid-1960s, however, most prominent abstract painters also made prints, emboldened by their fascination with the graphic media and guided by expert printers who often encouraged experimentation. A case in point is Robert Rauschenberg's color lithograph *Booster* (1967), an image that incorporates actual-size x-ray photographs of the artist's full-length skeleton. At the time it was one of the largest prints executed, and its scale, bold colors, and dramatic incorporation of photography as part of the graphic process, showed that prints could rival paintings in their impact.

American graphic art now claimed center stage wherever it was shown. Whether artists used Pop Art imagery of wire coat hangers (Jasper Johns), Campbell's Soup cans (Andy Warhol), or were inspired by comic strips and advertising (Roy Lichtenstein), their graphic works were seen on museum walls and in gallery exhibitions throughout the world. Even less approachable Minimalist painters such as Barnett Newman, Ellsworth Kelly, and Agnes Martin made their austere aesthetic more widely known through their graphic work, usually color lithographs. Contemporary artists have enlarged the scope of printmaking with computer-generated graphics, another innovation that has expanded the boundaries of graphic media.

BIBLIOGRAPHY

Beall, Karen F. *American Prints in the Library of Congress: A Catalog of the Collection.* Baltimore: Johns Hopkins Press, 1970.

Castleman, Riva. *American Impressions: Prints since Pollock.* New York: Knopf, 1985.

Shadwell, Wendy J. *American Printmaking: The First 150 Years.* New York: Museum of Graphic Art, 1969.

Victor Carlson

See also **Art: Painting; Pop Art.**

PRISONERS OF WAR

This entry includes 7 subentries:
Overview
Exchange of Prisoners
Prison Camps, Confederate
Prison Camps, Union
Prison Camps, World War II
Prison Ships
POW/MIA Controversy, Vietnam War

Overview

Throughout the colonial wars, French authorities imprisoned British and American colonial soldiers in Montreal. During the American Revolution, no accurate count was ever recorded, but it is estimated that more than 18,000 American soldiers and sailors were taken as POWs, with the majority kept aboard British prison hulks near New York City. Captured American privateers were kept in England, Ireland, and Scotland. Since the British never recognized the Continental Congress as a sovereign government, citizenship became a serious issue when the British captured American soldiers. The prisoners the British took faced severe conditions in captivity. Although the British continued to use prison hulks to some extent during the War of 1812, American POWs were treated humanely until their repatriation following the Treaty of Ghent (1814).

During the Mexican-American War (1846–1848), very few Americans fell into Mexican hands, but treatment was fair and humane. The U.S. Army paroled captured Mexicans in the field. During the Civil War (1861–1865), both Union and Confederate forces were unprepared for the enormous numbers of POWs: 211,400 Union prisoners in the South and 220,000 Confederates in the North. Exchanges took place regularly under the Dix-Hill Cartel until 1864, when General Ulysses S. Grant stopped them in order to further tax Confederate resources and bring the war to a swift conclusion. Thereafter, the South was glutted with huge numbers of starving Union prisoners it could not support.

By the time the United States entered World War I in April 1917, it had become a signatory to the Hague Convention (1899 and 1907), and of its 4,120 POWs, only 147 died in captivity, most from wounds received in combat. Treatment was fair and humane. World War II POW issues were covered by the 1929 Geneva Convention, which protected the 93,941 American POWs in the European theater. Only 1 percent died in captivity. Japan signed the Geneva Convention, but refused to ratify it at home. Japanese treatment of Allied POWs was criminal at best. Of the 25,600 American POWs captured in Asia, nearly 45 percent, or 10,650, died from wounds received in battle, starvation, disease, or murder. More than 3,840 died in unmarked transports, called "Hell Ships," sunk by American submarine attacks. Beginning in 1945 and lasting through 1948, the Allied international community conducted military tribunals to seek justice against those Japanese officers and enlisted men who deliberately mistreated POWs in the Pacific.

The captivity experience in Korea continued the kinds of savagery experienced by Allied POWs during World War II. More than 7,140 Americans became documented POWs; at least 2,701 died in enemy hands. After the Chinese entered the war in 1951, they took control of United Nations' POWs whenever possible, introduced a political reeducation policy, and attempted to indoctrinate prisoners with minimal success. In 1954, President Dwight D. Eisenhower issued Executive Order 10631, prescribing the Code of Conduct for Members of the Armed Forces of the United States, a set of principles that bound prisoners together into a POW community through a unified and purposeful standard of conduct.

In 1964, when the situation in Vietnam evolved into a major war, the International Red Cross Commission (ICRC) reminded the warring parties that they were signatories to the 1949 Geneva Convention. The Americans and the South Vietnamese affirmed the convention without reservations. The North Vietnamese and the National Liberation Front (NLF or Vietcong) refused to consider the convention, citing their reservation to Article 85 that permitted captors to prosecute prisoners for acts committed prior to capture. Between 1964 and 1972, 766 Americans became confirmed POWs, of whom 114 died in captivity. After the Paris Peace Accords (1973), 651 allied military prisoners returned to American control from Hanoi and South Vietnam.

In January 1991, hostilities erupted between a coalition of nations, including the United States and Iraq over the invasion and occupation of oil-rich Kuwait. In the one-month Gulf War, Iraq took twenty-three American POWs. In captivity, POWs suffered physical abuse that ranged from sexual abuse, electric shocks, and broken bones to routine slaps.

BIBLIOGRAPHY

Baker, C. Alice. *True Stories of New England Captives Carried to Canada during the Old French and Indian Wars.* Bowie, Md.: Heritage Books, 1990. Originally published in 1897.

Doyle, Robert C. *Voices from Captivity: Interpreting the American POW Narrative.* Lawrence: University of Kansas Press, 1994.

———. *A Prisoner's Duty: Great Escapes in U. S. Military History.* Annapolis: Naval Institute Press, 1997.

Robert C. Doyle

See also **Andersonville; Exchange of Prisoners; Geneva Conventions; Hague Convention; Prison Camps, Confed-**

erate; Prison Camps, Union; Prison Camps, World War II.

Exchange of Prisoners

Derived from the medieval custom of holding prisoners for ransom, the exchange of prisoners of war was an established practice by the American Revolution. Shortly after the battles at Lexington and Concord, Massachusetts authorities arranged for the exchange of captured British soldiers for Massachusetts militiamen, a precedent that other states soon followed. In July 1776 the Continental Congress authorized military commanders to negotiate exchanges, and in 1780 it appointed a commissary general of prisoners, thereby assuming from the states the responsibility for exchanging prisoners of war. British refusal to recognize American independence prevented agreement on a general cartel for exchanges, but American commanders used the authority vested in them by Congress to make several exchanges. In March 1780 a separate cartel arranged for the trade of American prisoners confined in Britain for British prisoners interned in France. In 1783 a general exchange of prisoners occurred after the cessation of hostilities and recognition of American independence.

During the War of 1812, battlefield exchanges happened under a general British-American cartel for exchanging prisoners. The United States and Mexico failed to negotiate a cartel during the Mexican-American War, but the United States released many Mexican prisoners on parole on the condition that they remain out of combat. The Mexicans released some American prisoners in "head-for-head" exchanges that occasionally took place during the war, but most American prisoners of war remained incarcerated until the ratification of the Treaty of Guadalupe Hidalgo.

During the Civil War the unwillingness of the federal government to enter into an agreement recognizing the Confederacy complicated the exchange of prisoners. The Dix-Hill Cartel provided for parole of captured personnel. The cartel became ineffective as the tide of battle changed, however, and commanders resorted to the traditional battlefield exchange of prisoners. At the end of the war, the North exchanged or released most Confederate prisoners. Except for the exchange of a few Spanish soldiers for American sailors, no exchange of prisoners occurred during the Spanish-American War.

Prisoner exchange during World War I followed the signing of the armistice. Throughout World War II the United States negotiated through neutral nations with the Axis powers for the exchange of prisoners. The United States and Germany never arranged a general exchange, but they traded sick and wounded prisoners on one occasion. Repatriation and exchange of prisoners took place after the defeat of the Axis nations.

During the Korean War the vexing issue of voluntary repatriation delayed the exchange of prisoners. Exchanges began after the Communist side accepted the principle of nonforcible repatriation. Operation Little Switch witnessed the exchange of sick and wounded prisoners, while a general exchange occurred during Operation Big Switch.

Each side occasionally released prisoners during the Vietnam War, but the North Vietnamese released the majority of American prisoners during the sixty days between the signing of the Paris Agreement and the withdrawal of all American military personnel from South Vietnam. A total of 587 Americans held in captivity in North Vietnam, South Vietnam, and Laos gained their freedom. American forces turned over North Vietnamese military prisoners to South Vietnamese authorities, and the responsibility for exchange of Vietnamese prisoners of war fell to the Vietnamese participants.

BIBLIOGRAPHY

Foot, Rosemary. *A Substitute for Victory: The Politics of Peacemaking at the Korean Armistice Talks.* Ithaca, N.Y.: Cornell University Press, 1990.

Gruner, E. G. *Prisoners of Culture: Representing the Vietnam POW.* New Brunswick, N.J.: Rutgers University Press, 1993.

Lech, Raymond B. *Broken Soldiers.* Urbana: University of Illinois Press, 2000.

Marvel, William. *Andersonville: The Last Depot.* Chapel Hill: University of North Carolina Press, 1994.

Whiteclay, John et al., eds. *The Oxford Companion to American Military History.* Oxford: Oxford University Press, 1999.

Vincent H. Demma / A. E.

See also **Prisoners of War.**

Prison Camps, Confederate

Approximately 200,000 prisoners were taken by the Confederates in the Civil War. Inadequate resources and no preparation for the task produced a severe drain on both the material and human resources of the South. An exchange of prisoners, arranged in 1862, was ended in 1863, and captives were held in scattered prison camps until near the end of the war. The larger prisons were, for officers, in Richmond, Va., Macon, Ga., and Columbia, S.C.; for enlisted men, in Andersonville, Millen, Florence (all in Georgia), and Charleston, S.C. Andersonville was by far the most infamous; over ten thousand prisoners perished there. Its commander, Capt. Henry Wirz, was later tried on charges of murder and conspiracy and was hanged. Deserters, spies, and political prisoners were incarcerated at Castle Thunder in Richmond or in Salisbury, N.C. Throughout most of the war the provost marshal of Richmond exercised a general but ineffective supervision over the prisons. The majority of the prisons consisted of either tobacco warehouses or open stockades. Poor quarters, insufficient rations and clothing, and lack of medicines produced excessive disease and a high death rate, which were interpreted in the North as a deliberate effort to starve and murder the captives. In retaliation, northern authorities reduced the allowances for rations and clothing to the prisoners they held. Some relief was obtained when southerners permitted the Union authorities to send food, clothing, and drugs through the lines, but conditions remained bad and the Confederate prisons became the major "atrocity" in northern propaganda.

BIBLIOGRAPHY

Hesseltine, William B. *Civil War Prisons.* Columbus: Ohio State University Press, 1930.

Marvel, William. *Andersonville: The Last Depot.* Chapel Hill: University of North Carolina Press, 1994.

W. B. Hesseltine/A. R.

See also **Andersonville Prison; Civil War; Prisoners of War; Prison Camps, Union; Prisons and Prison Reform;** *and vol. 9:* **Prisoner at Andersonville.**

Prison Camps, Union

Most captured Confederate soldiers were released on parole in the first year of the Civil War, but federal authorities confined captured officers and civilian prisoners in temporary prisons scattered across the North. Lt. Col. William Hoffman became the commissary general of prisoners on 7 October 1861. He hoped to consolidate the prisoners at a central depot for 1,200 inmates on Johnson's Island in Lake Erie, but the capture of 14,000 Confederates at Fort Donelson rendered the depot inadequate. Soon the already chaotic collection of prisons expanded to include four training camps across the Midwest. Compounding the confusion, guards and medical personnel changed frequently, so there was little continuity in administration.

Hoffman tried, but only partially succeeded, to regulate the disarray. An agreement to exchange prisoners in June 1862 cut the number of inmates from 19,423 to 1,286, enabling Hoffman to consolidate prisoners at three locations. When the prisoner exchange broke down in early 1863, the number of inmates increased and camp conditions deteriorated. Scarce clothing, unsatisfactory sanitation, overcrowded quarters, inadequate medical attention, and inclement weather contributed to widespread sickness. To consolidate and regulate facilities Hoffman established large permanent prisons at Fort Delaware, Del., Rock Island, Ill., Point Lookout, Md., and Elmira, N.Y., although the same problems that had plagued their more temporary counterparts continued to beset the newer prisons.

Starting in February 1865, when the Union prisons held over 65,000 inmates, the federal government began to return large numbers of soldiers to the Confederacy. After the surrender at Appomattox the Union prisons were closed quickly, so that by early July only a few hundred prisoners remained.

BIBLIOGRAPHY

Hesseltine, William B. *Civil War Prisons.* Kent, Ohio: Kent State University Press, 1972.

McAdams, Benton. *Rebels at Rock Island: The Story of a Civil War Prison.* DeKalb: Northern Illinois University Press, 2000.

United States. War Dept. *The War of the Rebellion: A Compilation of the Official Records of the Union and Confederate Armies.* Prepared under the direction of the Secretary of War by Robert N. Scott. Series 2. Pasadena, Calif.: Broadfoot, 1985.

Leslie Gene Hunter
Christopher Wells

See also **Exchange of Prisoners; Prison Camps, Confederate; Prisoners of War.**

Prison Camps, World War II

The experiences of the Allied troops held captive in prisoner-of-war (POW) camps during World War II varied according to time, place, and nationality of captor. For the first time in history, combatants captured by American troops were brought to U.S. soil and used as laborers in one of 155 POW camps. Japan held the majority of its war prisoners on the Asian mainland. Most of the German POW camps were located in the Third Reich and in western Poland. The Soviet Union probably administered some 3,000 camps. Most of the POWs captured by the British were held in England, with a small percentage held in Wales, Scotland, and Northern Ireland. While 15 million POWs were held at some point during World War II, by the war's end 220,000 Allied prisoners were in Japanese camps, and 260,000 Allied troops remained imprisoned by Germany.

The Third Reich administered concentration camps for political and minority prisoners and separate camps for military prisoners of war; POW camps were further subdivided into camps for officers and camps for nonofficers. Sometimes Allied troops were sent to concentration camps.

The treatment of POWs in Japanese camps was grueling. POWs were subjected to starvation diets, brutally hard labor, and sometimes execution. It is possible that as many as 27 percent of the 95,000 Allied troops taken prisoner by the Japanese died in captivity. By contrast, 4 percent of the 260,000 British and American POWs in German captivity died.

The imprisonment of POWs on U.S. soil was ordered by the U.S. Department of War and administered by the Army. At first POW labor in the U.S. was restricted to military installation service jobs, but by summer of 1943 it was contracted out to civilian projects, especially on farms.

BIBLIOGRAPHY

Dear, I. C. B., and M. R. D. Foot, eds. *The Oxford Companion to World War II.* New York: Oxford University Press, 1995.

Laqueur, Walter, and Judith Tydor Baumel, eds. *The Holocaust Encyclopedia.* New Haven, Conn.: Yale University Press, 2001.

Monahan, Evelyn M., and Rosemary Neidel-Greenlee. *All This Hell: U.S. Nurses Imprisoned by the Japanese.* Lexington, Ky.: University Press of Kentucky, 2000.

Martha Avaleen Egan

See also **World War II.**

Prison Ships

Americans and the British both used prison ships during the Revolution to confine naval prisoners. Conditions on the prison ships varied greatly, but the British vessels moored in Wallabout Bay, Brooklyn, particularly the *Jersey,* became notorious for the harsh treatment accorded the captives. Provisions were poor. Fever and dysentery prevailed and the guards were brutal. George Washington and the Continental Congress protested against this treatment, and Vice Adm. John Byron of the Royal Navy labored to better conditions. At least thirteen different prison ships were moored in Wallabout Bay or in the East or North rivers from 1776 to 1783. Up to 11,500 men may have died on these ships.

BIBLIOGRAPHY

Allen, Gardner W. *A Naval History of the American Revolution.* Boston: Houghton Mifflin, 1913.

Louis H. Bolander / F. B.

See also **Atrocities in War; Jersey Prison Ship; Revolution, American: Military History.**

POW/MIA Controversy, Vietnam War

POWs and MIAs are an important legacy of the Vietnam War, with ramifications for both American domestic politics and U.S. relations with Vietnam. By the terms of the Paris Peace Accords of 1973, which ended U.S. involvement in Vietnam, the Democratic Republic of Vietnam (North Vietnam) agreed to release all American POWs that it was holding. North Vietnam had acceded to the Geneva Convention of 1949, which classified prisoners of war as "victims of events" who deserved "decent and humane treatment." Nonetheless, North Vietnam insisted that the crews of U.S. bombers were guilty of "crimes against humanity," and returning POWs told stories of mistreatment by their captors. Evidence of mistreatment stirred emotions, which reports that North Vietnam had not returned all POWs and was still holding Americans captive only magnified. The plight of "boat people" fleeing Vietnam and Vietnam's invasion of Cambodia in 1978 reinforced these impressions of an inhumane Vietnamese government, officially called the Socialist Republic of Vietnam following the North's victory of 1975. These events helped to solidify public and congressional support for nonrecognition of Vietnam and a trade embargo.

The United States made "full accountability" of MIAs a condition of diplomatic recognition of Vietnam. At the end of the war, 1,750 Americans were listed as missing in Vietnam, with another 600 MIAs in neighboring Laos and Cambodia. The United States also insisted that Vietnam assist in the recovery of remains of MIAs who had died in Vietnam and in the return of any individuals who might have survived the war. Of particular concern were the "discrepancy cases," where individuals were believed to have survived an incident, such as bailing out of an aircraft and having been reportedly seen later, but were not among the returning POWs.

The POW and MIA controversy triggered a rigorous debate and became a popular culture phenomenon in the late 1970s and 1980s, despite Pentagon and congressional investigations that indicated there were no more than 200 unresolved MIA cases out of the 2,266 the Department of Defense still listed as missing and about a dozen POWs unaccounted for. By contrast, Vietnam still considers approximately 300,000 North and South Vietnamese as MIA. President Ronald Reagan, speaking before the National League of POW/MIA Families in 1987, stated that "until all our questions are fully answered, we will assume that some of our countrymen are alive." The Vietnam Veterans of America, which sent several investigating groups to Vietnam in the 1980s, helped renew contacts between the U.S. and Vietnamese governments. Accordingly, Vietnamese authorities and representatives of the Reagan administration reached agreements that resulted in cooperation in recovering the remains of American casualties. Beginning in the late 1980s, Vietnam returned several hundred sets of remains to the United States. In addition, progress occurred in clarifying "discrepancy cases." The question resurfaced in the 1990s about whether President Richard Nixon and Secretary of State Henry Kissinger had done all they could during peace negotiations to free servicemen "knowingly" left behind or whether they both were so desperate to get out of Vietnam that they sacrificed POWs. Both Nixon and Kissinger maintained that it was the "doves" in Congress at the time who prevented any effective military action to find out the truth about POWs when it was still possible to do so in the summer and spring of 1973. On 3 February 1994, with the approval of the Senate and business community, President Bill Clinton removed the nineteen-year trade embargo against Vietnam, and the Vietnamese government cooperated with veterans groups in locating the remains of U.S. soldiers and returning remains to the United States for burial, including those of nine soldiers in October 1995. As of June 2002, just over 1,900 Americans remained unaccounted for in Southeast Asia.

BIBLIOGRAPHY

Howes, Craig. *Voices of the Vietnam POWs: Witnesses to Their Fight.* New York: Oxford University Press, 1993.

Keating, Susan Katz. *Prisoners of Hope: Exploiting the POW/MIA Myth in America.* New York: Random House, 1994.

Philpott, Tom. *Glory Denied: The Saga of Jim Thompson, America's Longest-Held Prisoner of War.* New York: Norton, 2001.

Stern, Lewis M. *Imprisoned or Missing in Vietnam: Policies of the Vietnamese Government Concerning Captured and Unaccounted for United States Soldiers, 1969–1994.* Jefferson, N.C.: McFarland, 1995.

Gary R. Hess/A. E.

See also **Exchange of Prisoners; Geneva Conventions; Post-Traumatic Stress Disorder; Vietnam War; Vietnam War Memorial; Vietnam, Relations with; War, Laws of.**

PRISONS AND PRISON REFORM. Prisons are institutions in which persons convicted of criminal offenses are detained as punishment. Their penal raison d'être distinguishes them from other asylums, yet they share common characteristics with many familiar facilities. Like some hospitals for the mentally ill, for example, prisons are "total institutions" that dominate entirely the lives of their inhabitants. Prisoners' daily movements are tightly prescribed, and their compliance with routines is strictly enforced. The purpose of restrictions on inmates' freedom within the institution is said to be the maintenance of security. Yet regimentation accentuates the deprivations that imprisonment itself necessarily entails.

The earliest precursors of prisons were local gaols (jails), established in New England in the first half of the seventeenth century. Jails were not conceived as a means of housing wayward persons for any significant period of time. They were holding facilities in which persons charged with serious crimes were detained pending trial. Incarceration was not itself understood to be punishment but rather a prelude to the kinds of punishment employed in England. Upon conviction, offenders were either executed or else fined, tortured, or banished.

Some of the colonies also maintained almshouses, houses of refuge for juveniles, and workhouses in which people were confined for longer periods. Most of the inmates were impoverished or ill, but many were vagrants whose behavior was regarded as criminal. The conscious objectives were mixed. To some extent the idea was to provide a structured environment for people who had no families to support them. In addition, almshouses, houses of refuge, and workhouses fortified colonial "settlement" laws under which "rogues" and "vagabonds" were exiled. The living conditions were generally grim and the forced labor extremely hard. The threat of detention in a harsh environment discouraged people who were unproductive for whatever reason from entering or remaining in the colony.

In 1682 the province of Pennsylvania experimented with using confinement as a means of punishing both vagrants and serious criminal offenders. William Penn's "Great Law" restricted the death penalty to cases of murder and prescribed fines and hard labor in "houses of correction" as an alternative to torture for other crimes. The Pennsylvania program was formally in place for more than thirty years, but little evidence regarding its implementation survives. After Penn's death the Pennsylvania Assembly bowed to pressure from Parliament and reinstated the old corporal punishments.

"Separate" and "Silent" Systems

The first American prisons with staying power were established after the Revolutionary War. Influenced by European utilitarians, particularly Jeremy Bentham and Cesare Beccaria, Philadelphia Quakers proposed that offenders should be made to appreciate the immorality of their behavior. Specifically they should be removed from the temptations of free society, subjected to religious instruction, and forced to perform hard labor in solitude, meditating on their sins. The name the Quakers gave the institutions they had in mind, "penitentiaries," reflected that theory. The Pennsylvania Assembly initially created a prototype penitentiary in a section of the Walnut Street Jail. Prisoners lived in single-occupancy cells, where they labored at tasks that could be performed alone, typically sewing and weaving. Later the assembly established the Eastern Pennsylvania Penitentiary (known as Cherry Hill), which fully implemented the "separate system."

Contemporaneously, New York established similar prisons at Newgate in Greenwich Village and at Auburn in Cayuga County. There too inmates slept in single-occupancy cells. Yet the New York plan departed from the Pennsylvania "separate system" by organizing prisoners for employment together during the day. The two systems shared the common ground that if convicts congregated freely they would corrupt each other, but New York insulated prisoners from one another during working hours by compelling absolute silence. The warden at Auburn, Elam Lynds, implemented the "silent system" by forcing prisoners in striped uniforms to move from place to place in a laborious shuffle step with eyes downcast and by flogging any convict who dared to speak. Later Lynds extended the same program to New York's third prison, the infamous SING SING.

In their day the separate and silent systems were regarded as laudable attempts to devise a more humane means of dealing with crime. They were unique efforts actually to implement the most progressive thinking about punishment to date. Other nations sent emissaries to tour them. The most famous was Alexis de Tocqueville, who was dispatched from France not to critique the whole of American culture as he ultimately did but to appraise the new prisons in Pennsylvania and New York. Many foreign observers were especially impressed by Cherry Hill, which became the model for separate system prisons in Britain and on the Continent.

The rivalry between the separate and silent systems persisted in the United States until the Civil War. Pennsylvania and a few New England states maintained single-occupancy cells and at least the pretense of isolation. But most states in the northern and eastern regions of the country established prisons following the silent system model. Experience showed that prisoners laboring in groups could undertake more diverse projects, work more efficiently, produce more output, and pay for their own keep. Moreover, new prisons often became crowded, making single-occupancy cells impractical. As states built more prisons, they typically abandoned any effort to isolate prisoners from each other.

Southern states did not create prisons following the separate or silent system models. Instead, they either assigned convicts to chain gangs or leased them to private industry. Contract prisoners built railroads, picked cotton, and mined coal and iron ore. Everywhere they suffered under appalling living conditions, sickened, and died in large numbers. The tragedy was exacerbated by its demonstrable racism. Most contract prisoners in the South were African Americans who endured agonies little different from slavery.

By the middle of the nineteenth century, imprisonment had displaced capital punishment and torture as the general response to serious crime. Yet legislatures refused to finance institutions for criminal offenders on anything like the scale required. Accordingly prison managers concentrated on creating more acceptable prison industries to make ends meet. That was difficult, in part because organized labor resisted the resulting competition. In the succeeding fifty years the employment of prison inmates actually declined. In the 1920s, after most of the dreadful southern leases were abolished, only half the prisoners able to work were engaged in income-producing labor. Without self-generated funds, prisons deteriorated. Formally they still were charged to "rehabilitate" inmates rather than simply to hold them in detention. New prisons were sometimes called "reformatories" or "correctional" facilities to signal that function. Yet crowded and dilapidated physical plants frustrated efforts in that direction. Prisons became human warehouses for holding as many prisoners as possible at the least possible cost. To maintain order, guards resorted to torture. Refractory prisoners were whipped or confined in airless disciplinary cells on short rations.

Federal Involvement

The federal government began building prisons comparatively late and did not consolidate their administration under the Federal Bureau of Prisons until 1929. The most notorious federal facilities, Leavenworth and ALCATRAZ, became symbols of fortress prison architecture. Eventually the bureau operated dozens of federal facilities. Beginning in 1934 many inmates in federal facilities worked in prison factories operated by Federal Prison Industries, which sold prison-made goods exclusively to agencies of the federal government.

During and immediately following the Great Depression, the population of prison inmates in the United States expanded by 39 percent. There was a 29 percent decline during World War II (when many crime-prone youths served in the military), but between 1945 and 1961 the prisoner population rose by 72 percent. The Vietnam War accounted for another decline from 1962 to 1968. From 1973 to 1978, however, the prisoner population increased by 54 percent. In many states convicts were crowded together in loosely supervised dormitories with no outlet for their frustrations. Violence soon followed. In the 1970s prisoner uprisings occurred at institutions around the country.

Civil rights organizations responded to the crisis by filing lawsuits in federal courts contending that squalid prison conditions constituted cruel and unusual punishment in violation of the Eighth Amendment to the Constitution. The AMERICAN CIVIL LIBERTIES UNION and the NATIONAL ASSOCIATION FOR THE ADVANCEMENT OF COLORED PEOPLE (NAACP) Legal Defense and Education Fund were particularly active. Federal judges held that the prisons in Arkansas, Alabama, Texas, and other states were unconstitutional. To bring those institutions up to constitutional standards, the courts enjoined state officials to make extensive changes. The specifics of the court orders were modest. In the Alabama case, for example, Judge Frank M. Johnson ordered state authorities to assign prisoners to dormitories only if they posed no threat to each other and to provide every inmate with a bed, sixty square feet of living space, three wholesome meals per day, adequate medical care, meaningful employment, and access to educational and vocational programs. Nevertheless, it took years to obtain rough compliance with even those basic requirements.

Court orders requiring state officials to eliminate crowding presented a special challenge. In the near term, authorities in Alabama responded by leaving sentenced prisoners in county jails, thus exacerbating crowding at those facilities; pitching tents on prison grounds; and keeping scores of prisoners in buses traveling between penal facilities. When those stopgap measures failed to achieve results, Judge Johnson's successor, Judge Robert Varner, ordered state authorities to release nonviolent prisoners before their terms were complete. In the longer term, the Alabama legislature grudgingly constructed new prisons. Those facilities were Spartan structures of concrete and steel offering the minimum space the court required but little else.

Federal court supervision of state prisons was politically unpopular, short-lived, and only marginally successful. By dint of judicial intervention, prisons became cleaner, safer, and less crowded. Yet the courts stopped well short of requiring significant adjustments in penal policy. When, for example, Judge Johnson insisted that prisoners have jobs and access to self-improvement programs, his stated purpose was not to force prisons actually to fulfill their formal rehabilitative mission but rather to ensure that prisoners had some occasional escape from the grinding pressures of prison existence.

Confronting Crowded Conditions

In the final quarter of the twentieth century the number of prisoners in state and federal institutions increased by about 500 percent. There were many explanations. The federal government and most states prescribed new and extremely long terms of imprisonment for a wide range of criminal offenses. The "war on drugs" resulted in lengthy terms for numerous nonviolent offenders, particularly young African Americans. Innovations in sentencing policies also produced more prisoners with longer sentences. Congress and many states enacted statutes mandating minimum terms for some offenses and for offenders who committed multiple crimes, the so-called "three strikes and you're out" laws. Growing doubts about the death penalty also had an effect. When it became apparent that juries hesitated to spare violent defendants in the face of any chance those defendants might be released and commit violent crimes again, legislatures established the option of life imprisonment without possibility of parole. That innovation in turn invited juries to send offenders to prison for the rest of their lives, thus presenting the future prospect of a host of geriatric inmates.

To accommodate the rising tide of convicts, Congress and state legislatures authorized the construction of new prisons on a grand scale. In the 1990s alone more than three thousand new prisons were built at a cost of nearly $27 billion. At the beginning of the twenty-first century more than two million Americans were confined in some kind of penal institution, almost 500 in every 100,000 persons in the country. Most prisoners were adult males, and roughly half were African Americans. Among African American males, one in fourteen was either in prison or in jail awaiting trial and potential imprisonment. The incarceration rate for women was comparatively low but increased by a factor of twelve during the last quarter of the twentieth century.

The prisons of the twenty-first century take a variety of forms. Many, however, are large institutions accommodating thousands of inmates. The prisoner population is beset with difficulties. Two-thirds of the prisoners in custody have a history of drug abuse. Two-thirds are also illiterate. Over 16 percent of the prisoners in state institutions are mentally ill. Yet the primary mission of prisons is simply to house as many inmates as possible under minimally acceptable living conditions and to do it cheaply. Prison managers have employed four strategies to reduce costs.

One is to substitute sophisticated electronic devices for comparatively expensive human guards. At many facilities video cameras and microphones allow a few guards to monitor large numbers of inmates wherever they may be within the institution. Electronic security systems are not entirely successful. In some instances they are more expensive than more labor-intensive methods. Moreover, extensive electronic surveillance is controversial inasmuch as it denies prisoners even a modest measure of personal privacy.

Another is to consolidate especially aggressive inmates in designated facilities in hopes of reducing security concerns and the costs they entail at ordinary prisons. These "supermax" prisons exploit technology to isolate dangerous inmates from human contact. Prisoners are held in single-occupancy cells twenty-three hours per day with only an hour of solitary exercise in an adjacent yard. Guards and visitors communicate with them through two-way video equipment. Supermax prisons are controversial in that they subject inmates to extreme isolation with untold psychological effects.

A third strategy is to pool resources. Occasionally states develop unplanned excess space in their institutions and agree, for a price, to accept overflow prisoners from other jurisdictions. Some states deliberately make renting prison beds a routine feature of their operations. Texas, for example, contracts with private companies called "bed brokers" that arrange to house inmates from other states in much the way travel agents book hotel rooms for tourists. Prison-space brokerage reduces crowding in the states that export prisoners elsewhere. Yet it is controversial inasmuch as it disrupts any rehabilitative activities in which transported inmates may be engaged and separates prisoners from families and friends.

The fourth strategy is to transfer the responsibility for operating prisons to for-profit private companies that promise reduced costs. In some instances states maintain public facilities but hire private firms to manage them. That model recalls the contract labor schemes of the past. In other cases private firms construct their own facilities, then charge states for housing convicts. Private prisons are of a piece with a general "privatization" movement in American politics. Yet private penal institutions raise special ethical and economic questions. Critics charge, for example, that the public is best served by policies that reduce recidivism, while private firms have an interest in seeing prisoners return as repeat customers.

The rapid increase in the use of imprisonment and related innovations in prison management have made prison construction and maintenance a major industry in the United States. Prison administrators, guards, and other staff depend on the prisons they manage for their sustenance and careers. Economically depressed rural communities rely on prisons to employ their residents. Private prison firms necessarily depend on the demand for prison space. Investment bankers, architects, building contractors, and equipment vendors look increasingly to prisons as markets. Consequently, many sectors of the economy have a stake in the status quo, and efforts to change the prison industry in the United States face resistance.

BIBLIOGRAPHY

DiIulio, John J., Jr., ed. *Courts, Corrections, and the Constitution.* New York: Oxford University Press, 1990.

Feeley, Malcolm M., and Edward L. Rubin. *Judicial Policy Making and the Modern State: How the Courts Reformed America's Prisons.* New York: Cambridge University Press, 1998.

Foucault, Michel. *Discipline and Punish: The Birth of the Prison.* New York: Vintage, 1979.

Goffman, Erving. *Asylums: Essays on the Social Situation of Mental Patients and Other Inmates.* Garden City, N.Y.: Anchor Books, 1961.

Hawkins, Gordon. *The Prison: Policy and Practice.* Chicago: University of Chicago Press, 1976.

Jacobs, James B. *Stateville: The Penitentiary in Mass Society.* Chicago: University of Chicago Press, 1977.

———. *New Perspectives on Prisons and Imprisonment.* Ithaca, N.Y.: Cornell University Press, 1983.

McKelvey, Blake. *American Prisons: A History of Good Intentions.* Montclair, N.J.: Patterson Smith, 1977.

Morris, Norval. *The Future of Imprisonment.* Chicago: University of Chicago Press, 1974.

Morris, Norval, and David J. Rothman, eds. *The Oxford History of the Prison.* New York: Oxford University Press, 1995.

Playfair, Giles. *The Punitive Obsession: An Unvarnished History of the English Prison System.* London: Victor Gollancz, 1971.

Riveland, Chase. *Supermax Prisons: Overview and General Considerations.* Lompoc, Calif.: U.S. Government, 1999.

Rothman, David J. *The Discovery of the Asylum: Social Order and Disorder in the New Republic.* Boston: Little, Brown, 1971.

Schlosser, Eric. "The Prison-Industrial Complex." *Atlantic Monthly* (December 1998): 51–77.

Sherman, Michael, and Gordon Hawkins. *Imprisonment in America.* Chicago: University of Chicago Press, 1981.

Larry Yackle

See also **Capital Punishment; Punishment; Reformatories.**

PRIVACY. The notion of a right to have certain parts of one's life, one's home, and one's property protected against invasion by other citizens or by government is as old as America itself. Four of the first five amendments to the Constitution of the United States protect some aspect of the privacy of Americans, including the First Amendment's right to association, the Third Amendment's prohibition against the government quartering soldiers in private homes, the Fourth Amendment's protection against unreasonable searches and seizures, and the Fifth Amendment's protection from self-incrimination.

The specific idea of what was later recognized as the "right to privacy" began with British common law notions, such as "a man's home is his castle" and the right "to be let (or left) alone." A number of early U.S. Supreme Court decisions recognized these traditional rights to be free of unwanted personal or governmental invasions. Responding to some of the invasive journalistic practices of the day, a future justice of the Supreme Court of the United States, Louis D. Brandeis, and his coauthor and law partner, Samuel D. Warren, are credited with coining the phrase "the right to privacy" in their 1890 article of that name in the *Harvard Law Review.* When Brandeis was elevated to the Supreme Court, he took the opportunity in that Court's first wiretapping case to reiterate his strongly held views on the right to privacy. That 1928 case, *Olmstead v. United States,* involved the attempt by the federal government to tap the phone of a person without first obtaining a warrant. The majority of the Court ruled that this was not a violation of the Constitution. In his dissenting opinion, however, Brandeis said those who wrote and ratified the Constitution and the Bill of Rights did recognize the existence of a right to privacy:

> The makers of our Constitution . . . conferred, as against the Government, the right to be let alone—the most comprehensive of rights and the right most valued by civilized men. To protect that right, every unjustifiable intrusion by the government upon the privacy of the individual, whatever the means employed, must be deemed a violation of the Fourth [and Fifth] Amendment[s].

But Brandeis's view remained in the minority on the Supreme Court until the 1965 case of GRISWOLD V. CONNECTICUT. That case involved the constitutionality of an 1879 Connecticut law that banned the use of contraceptives, even by married couples. A seven to two majority opinion, vindicating Brandeis's view, held that the Constitution does contain a right to privacy and that the right is a fundamental one, even if that right does not appear in so many words anywhere in the text. While a majority of justices agreed that such a right was protected by the Constitution and its amendments, they disagreed over where in the text of the Constitution that right is found. Justice William O. Douglas's majority opinion claimed that various parts of the Bill of Rights have "penumbras" formed by "emanations" from specifically granted guarantees in the text. This kind of argument did not sit well with many other members of the Supreme Court then, and as the Court became more literal and conservative in subsequent years, more and more justices expressed their skepticism over the existence of such a right to privacy.

The announcement of the existence of a constitutional right to privacy resonated through American law, politics, and society in the years following the Supreme Court's 1965 decision in *Griswold.* This right to privacy was at the foundation of the Court's landmark ROE V. WADE decision in 1973, which brought a woman's right to have an abortion under the rubric of the right to privacy. William H. Rehnquist, then an associate justice of the Court, dissented from *Roe v. Wade,* arguing that abortion does not involve the issue of privacy. As chief justice Rehnquist has generally continued to argue against the existence of this constitutional right.

Other areas of American life have been impacted by this debate over the existence of the right to privacy. In 1967 in the case of *Katz v. United States* the Supreme Court overturned its 1928 ruling in *Olmstead.* In *Katz* the Court ruled that someone speaking on the phone, even on a public pay phone, has a reasonable expectation of privacy and that the government must secure a warrant prior to eavesdropping on that conversation. In 1969 the Supreme Court ruled in *Stanley v. Georgia* that the mere possession of obscene materials in the privacy of one's home could not be interfered with by government officials. However, in the 1986 case of *Bowers v. Hardwick* a sharply divided Supreme Court ruled that the right to privacy did not include the right to engage in homosexual sodomy in the privacy of one's home.

Certain professional and personal relationships are considered private and thus protected from various kinds of intrusion. The relationships between doctor and patient and between attorney and client are examples of professional relationships given special privacy protections under the law. Student grades and recommendations are also protected by various federal and state laws. In addition the spousal relationship is considered by many jurisdictions to be a generally private relationship, and husbands and wives are often protected from being compelled to testify against each other.

The advent of computers brought with it a new range of privacy concerns. Prior to computers, to intercept a piece of mail from one person to another, an actual letter had to be seized and then opened. In the information age intercepting an electronic mail message requires no physical interference but merely the accessing of data files in which E-mail is sent and stored. Consequently privacy invasions became not only easier but also less detectable. Cell phone calls are less secure than wire-based phone communications and more easily intercepted. Other privacy issues include the privacy of what an employee does on a workplace computer, the proliferation of video surveillance cameras in public and private spaces, access to personal information contained in electronic databases, and the "identity theft" that sometimes results from the stealing of such electronically stored personal information.

As communication occurs less in face-to-face exchanges and more in technological data exchange mediums, the opportunities for individuals and governments to eavesdrop on those virtual conversations increase. For example, in response to the terrorist attacks of 11 September 2001, the federal government passed legislation that made it easier for law enforcement officials to have access to previously private data and communication, even between lawyer and client. Privacy in the information age promises to be an important and contentious topic.

BIBLIOGRAPHY

Lessig, Lawrence. *Code and Other Laws of Cyberspace.* New York: Basic Books, 1999.

McLean, Deckle. *Privacy and Its Invasion.* Westport, Conn.: Praeger, 1995.

Rosen, Jeffrey. *The Unwanted Gaze: The Destruction of Privacy in America.* New York: Random House, 2000.

Akiba J. Covitz
Esa Lianne Sferra
Meredith L. Stewart

See also **Bill of Rights in U.S. Constitution.**

PRIVATEERS AND PRIVATEERING. Historians often consider the operations of Sir John Hawkins, Sir Francis Drake, and other sixteenth-century Elizabethan freebooters as the origin of privateering in America, but the participation of privately armed American colonists in the wars of England did not begin until more than a century later, with King William's War (1689–1697). During Queen Anne's War (1702–1713), the colonial governors commissioned a considerable number of privateers. Relatively few took to the sea during the short war with Spain in 1718, but under royal warrants the American governors again issued letters of marque and reprisal against Spain in 1739. In King George's War (1744–1748) privateering became a major maritime business, and some scholars contend that as many as 11,000 Americans engaged in such operations during the French and Indian War (1754–1763).

At the beginning of the American Revolution in 1775, most of the colonies issued letters of marque and reprisal. Three months before the Declaration of Independence, the Continental Congress sanctioned privateering "against the enemies of the United Colonies." The 1,151 American privateers operating during the Revolution captured about 600 British vessels, including sixteen men-of-war.

Although privateers had been invaluable during the revolution, the U.S. government soon joined the movement in Europe to abolish privateering. It reversed its position in 1798 when French vessels began harassing American shipping. In 1798 Congress passed acts allowing American merchantmen to arm themselves for defensive purposes and authorizing them to apply for special commissions to make war on armed French vessels. By the close of the year, the government had equipped at least 428 merchantmen; this number increased to upward of 1,000 vessels before the end of hostilities in 1801. Since the government did not allow armed merchantmen to prey on unarmed commerce, fighting was generally secondary to trading; nevertheless, there were some notable encounters and valuable captures. In the War of 1812, privateers working for the United States captured at least 1,345 British ships. All the seaboard states, from Maine to Louisiana, sent privateers to sea against Great Britain in either the Revolution, the War of 1812, or both.

With the return of world peace in 1815, many American and European privateers found service in Latin American revolutions, and others became pirates. For the next twenty-five years, the U.S. Navy struggled to check piracy on the high seas. The Republic of Texas resorted to privateering in the early stage (1835–1837) of its protracted war with Mexico. In 1856 the United States declined to accede to the Declaration of Paris's outlawing privateering among the principal world powers.

However, when the Confederate States of America began recruiting privateers during the Civil War, President Abraham Lincoln treated them as pirates. The privateers sailing from Louisiana, North Carolina, and South Carolina in 1861 enjoyed great profits, but Confederate privateering declined after the first year, and the

Confederacy instituted a volunteer naval system. Privateering ended throughout the world with the downfall of the Confederacy.

BIBLIOGRAPHY

Lane, Kris E. *Pillaging the Empire: Piracy in the Americas, 1500–1750.* Armonk, N.Y.: Sharpe, 1998.

Marley, David F. *Pirates and Privateers of the Americas.* Santa Barbara, Calif.: ABC-CLIO, 1994.

Swanson, Carl E. *Predators and Prizes: American Privateering and Imperial Warfare, 1739–1748.* Columbia: University of South Carolina Press, 1991.

William M. Robinson Jr. / E. M.

See also **France, Quasi-War with; Piracy.**

PRIVATIZATION. Privatization is the practice of delegating public duties to private firms. It is advocated as a means of shrinking the size of government, reducing deficits, and increasing efficiency in public services, although its success in these objectives is debated. Privatization takes several forms in the United States: the selling of firms that were once partly owned and regulated by government; the contracting out of public services to private companies for production; and the funding of vouchers for use in the private sector thus introducing competition between public and private agencies.

Historically the United States has maintained a distaste for federal government intervention in the economy, although the Constitution does grant Congress the power to regulate commerce. With the exception of the Progressive Era (1901–1921) and the New Deal (1933–1945), policy was guided by the principles of laissez-faire capitalism, articulated by economist Adam Smith in *Wealth of Nations* (1776).

After World War II, public agencies themselves began privatizing without legislative guidance. In 1955, the Bureau of the Budget officially discouraged federal agencies from producing any "product or service [which] can be procured from private enterprise through ordinary business channels." In the mid-1970s the Ford administration proposed legislation eliminating federal involvement in airline, trucking, banking, and gas industries, and one aspect of President Jimmy Carter's energy policy at the end of the decade was to end regulation of natural gas. But it was President Ronald Reagan who made the strongest postwar push for privatization on the federal level.

Reagan established the Private Sector Survey on Cost Control (often referred to as the Grace Commission) to "identify opportunities for increased efficiency and reduced costs in federal government operations." Congress supported the Commission's recommendations, and in the 1985 Deficit Reduction Act required "the President to report on progress in implementing [commission] recommendations." This led to the largest privatization in U.S. history, the sale of Conrail for $1.65 billion—and seventy-eight other recommendations for privatization.

Since the 1980s proposals to privatize Amtrak, the U.S. Postal Service, the prison system, health care, housing, welfare, Social Security, and education (among other programs), have been put forth, debated, and implemented in various forms. Allowing citizens to invest some of their social security funds in the stock market was hotly debated during the bull market of the 1990s, yet was generally unpopular with voters, while welfare-to-work programs tended to be supported by public opinion. By the turn of the twenty-first century, state and local governments were contracting services ranging from operation of public utilities to maintenance of public parks.

Perhaps the most intensely debated privatization proposals were in public education. School voucher programs, permitting parents to use public funds to send their children to private schools were implemented in Milwaukee, Wisconsin, and Cleveland, Ohio. In 1992, private firms began running public schools in cities across the county to mixed reviews, while efforts to privatize five of New York City's public schools were reject by parents in 2001.

Critics of privatization point out that the essential mandate of government is to work in the public interest, while that of private enterprise is to maximize profits; thus ideologically, public services are best handled by government. Others argue privatization disproportionately hurts minority populations because they tend to rely more heavily on employment in the public sector. When such jobs move to the private sector, workers often receive lower wages and fewer benefits.

BIBLIOGRAPHY

Pack, Janet Rothenberg. "The Opportunities and Constraints of Privatization." In *The Political Economy of Privatization and Deregulation.* Edited by Elizabeth E. Bailey and Janet Rothenberg Pack. Brookfield, Vt.: Edward Elgar, 1995.

Smith, Preston H. "'Self-Help,' Black Conservatives and the Reemergence of Black Privatism." In *Without Justice for All: the New Neo-Liberalism and Our Retreat from Racial Equality.* Edited by Adolph Reed Jr. Boulder, Colo.: Westview Press, 1999.

Swann, Dennis. *The Retreat of the State: Deregulation and Privitisation in the UK and US.* Ann Arbor: University of Michigan Press, 1988.

Margaret Keady

See also **Laissez-Faire.**

PRIVILEGES AND IMMUNITIES OF CITIZENS. The U.S. Constitution contains two clauses that address the privileges and immunities of citizens. The first, in Article IV, Section 2, guarantees that citizens of each state shall be entitled to all privileges and immunities of citizens in the several states. The Articles of Confederation included a similar provision, but neither the

Articles nor the drafters of the Constitution provided a clear meaning for this new section. They provided no definition of privileges and immunities, no test of state citizenship, and no indication whether the citizen was entitled to these privileges in his own state, when he was temporarily in other states, or both. Justice Bushrod Washington gave the first authoritative definition in *Corfield v. Coryell* (1823). The protected privileges and immunities, he said, were those "which are, in their nature, fundamental; which belong, of right, to the citizens of all free governments." As examples he suggested government protection and the right to acquire and possess property, to bring court actions, and to travel from one state to another.

Fifty years later, in the SLAUGHTERHOUSE CASES (1873), the Supreme Court ruled that whatever these rights were, the Constitution required that, as the states granted or established privileges and immunities to their own citizens, "the same, neither more nor less, shall be the measure of the rights of citizens of other States within [their] jurisdiction." However, states could treat out-of-state citizens differently from their own citizens when there were reasonable grounds for doing so. Thus, the right to vote was limited to citizens of the state. Out-of-state students could be charged higher tuition fees at state universities. Fees for hunting and fishing licenses could be higher for nonresidents, who did not contribute by local taxes to the upkeep of the public domain, but the fees could not be prohibitive. Practitioners of certain professions vital to the public interest, such as medicine and law, could not practice outside the state in which they were licensed without new certification, and corporations could not claim protection under the provision.

The second privileges and immunities clause appears in the Fourteenth Amendment (1868) and forbids states to make or enforce any law abridging the privileges and immunities of citizens of the United States. It was one of three standards written into the post–Civil War amendment for the purpose of, but not limited to, protecting the rights of the newly freed blacks. The other two provisions were the equal protection clause and the due process clause. Debates on the Fourteenth Amendment in Congress made it clear that the privileges and immunities clause was regarded as the most important of these three, and it was expected to be a major restraint on state denial of civil rights. However, in the Slaughterhouse Cases the Supreme Court interpreted the language narrowly to protect only those rights peculiar to national citizenship (such as access to the seat of government and the writ of habeas corpus) and made it inapplicable to property rights and to trials in state courts. Litigants later turned attention to the due process clause and the equal protection clause, with much greater success. The Court's wide interpretation of those two provisions made the privileges and immunities clause almost a dead letter.

BIBLIOGRAPHY

Finkelman, Paul. *An Imperfect Union: Slavery, Federalism, and Comity.* Chapel Hill: University of North Carolina Press, 1981.

Irons, Peter. *A People's History of the Supreme Court.* New York: Viking, 1999.

Lien, Arnold Johnson. *Concurring Opinion: The Privileges or Immunities Clause of the Fourteenth Amendment.* Reprint of 2d rev. ed. (1958). Westport, Conn: Greenwood Press, 1975. The original edition was published in 1957.

Pritchett, C. Herman. *The American Constitution.* 3d ed. New York: McGraw-Hill, 1977.

C. Herman Pritchett/C. P.

See also **Civil Rights and Liberties; *Minor v. Happersett.***

PRIVY COUNCIL was a body of advisers who provided policy advice to the British sovereign. The council contained the ministers of state who held leading administrative positions for the British Empire. The Crown performed all official business concerning Anglo-America at the Privy Council meetings. The council heard appeals from colonial courts, had veto power over colonial legislation, advised the monarch on the appointment of royal governors, and recommended the issuance of proclamations. Committees within the Privy Council for the oversight of the colonies were the Board of Trade and Plantations, the Council for Foreign Plantations, the Colonial Board, and the Committee for Trade and Plantations.

BIBLIOGRAPHY

Christie, I. R. *Crisis of Empire: Great Britain and the American Colonies, 1754–1783.* New York: Norton, 1966.

Turner, Edward Raymond. *The Privy Council of England in the Seventeenth and Eighteenth Centuries, 1603–1784.* 2 vols. Baltimore: Johns Hopkins University Press, 1927–1928.

Ubbelohde, Carl. *The American Colonies and the British Empire, 1607–1763.* New York: Crowell, 1968.

Michelle M. Mormul

See also **Appeals from Colonial Courts; Colonial Assemblies; Colonial Policy, British; Royal Colonies.**

PRIZE CASES, CIVIL WAR. In 1863 the SUPREME COURT upheld President Abraham Lincoln's exercise, at the outbreak of the CIVIL WAR, of emergency powers not previously authorized by Congress. After the firing on Fort Sumter in April 1861, Lincoln all but declared war, called for volunteers, suspended the writ of habeas corpus, and blockaded various southern ports. Not until July did Congress retroactively legalize these executive measures. Meanwhile, under the presidential BLOCKADE certain merchant vessels were captured as prizes by the Union navy for attempting to run the blockade. The Supreme Court upheld the seizures on the grounds that a de facto state of war had existed since April.

BIBLIOGRAPHY

Neely, Mark, Jr. *The Fate of Liberty: Abraham Lincoln and Civil Liberties.* New York: Oxford University Press, 1991.

Paludan, Phillip Shaw. *The Presidency of Abraham Lincoln.* Lawrence: University Press of Kansas, 1994.

Martin P. Claussen / T. G.

See also **Blockade Runners, Confederate; Habeas Corpus, Writ of; Sumter, Fort.**

PRIZE COURTS derive their name from their function, which is to pass on the validity and disposition of "prizes," a term referring to the seizure of a ship or its cargo by the maritime, not the land, forces of a belligerent. Jurisdictional pronouncements of prize courts have expanded the definition of lawful capture of property at sea to include the territorial waters and navigable rivers of occupied enemy territory and have accepted as legitimate the seizure of vessels in dry docks, ports, and rivers. According to the U.S. Prize Act of 1941, the seizure of aircraft may also fall under the jurisdiction of prize courts.

Although belligerents are operating under the rules of international law when conducting seizures, the prize courts themselves are national instrumentalities. Their structures, rules of procedure, and means of disposition of the prizes emanate from national law. They may apply the principles of international law to determine the validity of seizures and the liability to condemnation, but in many cases the rules of international law are applied by virtue of their adoption by the national legal system or incorporation into it. Domestic enactments and regulations may also modify prize courts. It is not surprising, therefore, that worldwide prize-court decisions have lacked uniformity and have not always reflected a high degree of recognition of, and respect for, international law regarding capture and condemnation. In the United States, jurisdiction in prize matters belongs to the federal district courts, with the right of appeal to the circuit court of appeals and ultimately the Supreme Court. The domestic courts have the authority to appoint special prize commissioners to act abroad. An international prize court has never been established.

BIBLIOGRAPHY

Bourguignon, Henry J. *The First Federal Court: The Federal Appellate Prize Court of the American Revolution, 1775–1787.* Memoirs of the American Philosophical Society, vol. 122. Philadelphia: American Philosophical Society, 1977.

Miles, Edward L. *Global Ocean Politics: The Decision Process at the Third United Nations Conference on the Law of the Sea, 1973–1982.* The Hague, Netherlands: Martinus Nijhoff Publishers, 1998.

Warren, Gordon H. *Fountain of Discontent: The Trent Affair and Freedom of the Seas.* Boston: Northeastern University Press, 1981.

Angela Ellis
Werner Feld

See also **Freedom of the Seas; Hague Peace Conferences; London, Declaration of; *Trent* Affair.**

PRIZEFIGHTING. Technically speaking, prizefighting is any physical contest that offers a prize or "purse" to one or more contestants. In the common vernacular, it refers primarily to boxing, the only form of prizefighting in the United States to gain some measure of prestige as well as commercial success. Boxing is a sport where two opponents, chosen by weight class, fight with their fists, usually wearing padded gloves. Contestants are judged based on the number and quality of blows delivered to their opponent's head and torso. Boxing history in the United States has been dominated by heavyweight boxers, but in recent decades boxers from lighter weight classes have occasionally grabbed the spotlight. Because of its nature as an individual sport, the peaks and valleys of the boxing world have been largely dependent on the personalities of the players.

Imported from England

John Graham Chambers, a British boxing official, drew up the Marquess of Queensberry Rules in the 1860s. The new rules became part of the British tradition, adding prestige to a sport favored by wealthy gentlemen who wagered considerable sums on contests or "bouts." The Queensberry Rules included gloves, in contrast to the more lowly form of bareknuckle fighting, and the introduction of three-minute rounds. The American tradition, however, was more associated with bareknuckle grudge matches in saloons and rural gathering spots. In slave states, boxing could be particularly gruesome, with some bouts involving several black slaves in the ring while white spectators wagered on which would be the last man standing. Its unsavory reputation resulted in the widespread prohibition of prizefighting in the mid-nineteenth century, led by northeastern states such as New Jersey, Massachusetts, and New York. Nearing the end of the nineteenth century, most states had banned prizefighting. Nonetheless, the sport remained popular and fights were still promoted and exhibited, especially in the western United States.

Patriotism and Race

Beginning in the early nineteenth century, some bouts between English and American fighters gained widespread attention, thanks in no small part to promoters encouraging nationalistic pride. Bill Richmond (1763–1829), the son of a Georgia-born slave, caught the attention of General Earl Percy, who took him back to England to fight in championship-level bouts. In 1910, Richmond beat English champion George Maddox in the fifty-second round, adding fuel to the rivalry between England and the United States. The same year, Tom Molineaux (1784–1818), a former slave from Virginia, fought England's Tom Cribb (and lost) in the first black-white title fight, gaining international attention.

John L. Sullivan. A photograph taken by J. M. Mora in 1882, the year the Great John L. became the bare-knuckle heavyweight champion; the hugely popular slugger lost ten years later to the younger, more tactical James J. "Gentleman Jim" Corbett in the first championship bout to follow the Marquess of Queensbury Rules—including gloves. LIBRARY OF CONGRESS

Later in the century, as American boxing became legalized and more institutionalized, promoters catered to the dominant white culture, who wanted blacks barred from the more prestigious heavyweight contests. As a result, blacks and whites generally fought in different circuits. Perhaps the most famous boxer of the era was Boston's John L. Sullivan (1858–1918), whose charisma and talent made him a star on the exhibition circuit. Sullivan's celebrity status increased the popularity of the sport and helped establish American dominance over British fighters.

In the later part of the nineteenth century, however, patriotic rivalries were replaced by racial rivalries. In 1908, black fighter Jack Johnson (1878–1946) defeated Canadian Tommy Burns for the heavyweight title. Johnson openly taunted white opponents and inflamed racial tensions, and promoters grew desperate to find a white fighter to beat him. In 1910, Johnson defeated white former champion Jim Jeffries in fifteen rounds, sparking race riots in the United States that left twelve people dead. Johnson's success as a fighter was eclipsed by his reputation for creating trouble for promoters and did not make it any easier for blacks to compete in prominent contests. Championship bouts were again dominated by whites until the 1930s, after which came the ascendancy of black fighters and, later, Hispanics.

The Highs and the Lows

In the 1920s, American heavyweight champ Jack Dempsey (1895–1983) became an international celebrity whose fights made front-page news. After Dempsey's retirement in 1927, however, boxing went into a lull. For the next decade, the title went to good but less exciting heavyweights such as Max Baer, Primo Carnera (Italy), James Braddock, and Max Schmeling (Germany).

The boxing hero of the 1930s and 1940s was Joe Louis (1914–1981), a black American originally from Alabama. Louis's talent in the ring, paired with his polite demeanor, made him one of the best-known boxers of all time, the reigning champion from 1937 to 1949. His most embarrassing defeat, to Germany's Max Schmeling in 1937, was avenged in a 1938 re-match that lasted just over two minutes, making "The Brown Bomber" a popular symbol of American superiority over Adolf Hitler's Germany.

The 1950s saw the emergence of popular boxers from lighter weight classes, including Sugar Ray Robinson (1921–1989), the virtually unstoppable welterweight champion of the 1940s. Robinson moved up to capture and retain the middleweight title in the 1950s and became a national celebrity. Heavyweight bouts continued to be the most publicized and most prestigious events, however. Heavyweight champs from the era included Rocky Marciano (1923–1969), who retired undefeated, and Floyd Patterson (b. 1935), who held the title from 1956 until 1959, and then again from 1960 until 1962, when he lost to Charles "Sonny" Liston (1932–1970).

Bold and brash challenger Cassius Clay (b. 1942) was the light heavyweight champion of the 1960 Olympics who moved up to beat Liston in the 1964 title bout. Clay, a black Muslim, changed his name to Muhammad Ali and went on to become one of the most famous athletes of the twentieth century. In 1967, Ali made headlines outside the ring when he was stripped of his title and lost his license to box for refusing on religious grounds to be inducted into the Army during the Vietnam War. Ali was later allowed to box again and was vindicated by the Supreme Court in 1971.

Joe Frazier (b. 1944) won a tough decision over Ali in 1970, but lost to George Foreman in 1973. Ali defeated Foreman in Zaire in 1974 and regained the title in a media spectacle dubbed "The Rumble in the Jungle." Ali's charisma made him a popular culture icon in both Africa and the United States, and the contest made the history books as one of the greatest comebacks in sports. Ali won in eight rounds by leaning against the ropes of the ring and taking punch after punch until, finally, Foreman exhausted himself. Ali called his strategy the "Rope-A-Dope," a term that immediately entered the popular lexicon. In another hyped bout in 1975, Ali fought Frazier in the Philippines—"The Thrilla in Manila"—one of the most brutal fights in modern history between two of the sport's most bitter rivals. Ali beat Frazier and held the championship title, but age was catching up to him. Ali lost in 1978 to Leon Spinks (b. 1953), regained the title briefly, then lost again to Larry Holmes (b. 1949) and retired in 1981.

Holmes won twenty straight title fights between 1978 and 1985, but never gained the superstar status of Louis or Ali, partly due to organizational chaos in the boxing industry. In the 1980s, the public turned its attention to lighter weight divisions and captivating personalities such as Sugar Ray Leonard (b. 1956), "Marvelous Marvin" Hagler (b. 1954), and Thomas Hearns (b. 1958), although big money matches were still the province of the heavyweights.

In 1987, Mike Tyson (b. 1966) became the undisputed world champion at the age of twenty, the youngest to ever hold the title. Short and stocky, "Iron Mike" overwhelmed opponents with strength and speed, but lost the crown in 1990 to James "Buster" Douglas (b. 1960) in one of boxing's biggest upsets. Douglas held the title for less than a year, then lost to Evander Holyfield (b. 1962) in a third-round knockout. Meanwhile, Tyson's most famous fights were outside the ring and inside the courtroom. After a brief marriage came a highly publicized divorce from actress Robin Givens, then a 1992 rape conviction that led to three years in prison. After jail, Tyson made a comeback, but in a bizarre incident, he bit the ear of Holyfield during a 1997 title fight. In spite of the controversy in his personal life and his strange antics in the ring, Tyson continued to generate millions of dollars for the boxing industry, thanks in large part to the advent of pay-per-view matches on cable television. In 2002, Tyson's last-ditch effort to gain respectability and the title fell short and he was soundly defeated by British champion Lennox Lewis (b. 1965), in what was popularly considered a contest between the gentleman (Lewis) and the brute (Tyson).

By the end of the twentieth century, professional boxing still hinged on the ability of fighters to excite the public, and heavyweight bouts continued to be the most publicized and the most lucrative. But the ascendancy of Hispanics, who generally fight in lighter weight divisions, helped hold the attention of fans in the absence of a captivating heavyweight fighter, and smaller fighters like Oscar De la Hoya (b. 1973) and Puerto Rico's Felix Trinidad (b. 1973) became stars in their own right.

BIBLIOGRAPHY

Andre, Sam E., and Nat Fleischer, updated by Dan Rafael. *Prizefighting: An Illustrated History of Boxing.* 6th rev. ed. New York: Citadel, 2001.

Mee, Bob. *Bare Fists: The History of Bare-Knuckle Prize-Fighting.* Woodstock, N.Y.: Overlook Press, 2001.

Pacheco, Ferdie, and Jim Moskovitz. *The Twelve Greatest Rounds of Boxing: The Untold Stories.* Kingston, N.Y.: Total/Sports Illustrated, 2000.

Seltzer, Robert. *Inside Boxing.* New York: MetroBooks, 2000.

Paul Hehn

See also **Sports.**

PRIZES AND AWARDS

This entry includes 5 subentries:
Academy Awards
Guggenheim Awards
MacArthur Foundation "Genius" Awards
Nobel Prizes
Pulitzer Prizes

Academy Awards

The Academy of Motion Picture Arts and Sciences was founded in May 1927 through the efforts of Louis B. Mayer of Metro-Goldwyn-Mayer Studios. Its purpose was to "establish the industry in the public mind as a respectable, legitimate institution, and its people as reputable individuals." Membership is by invitation of the academy board to those who have achieved distinction in the arts and sciences of motion pictures. Its original thirty-six members included studio executives, production specialists, and actors. At the beginning of the twenty-first century the academy had 5,467 voting members. The academy is supported by members' dues and the revenues from the annual Academy Awards presentation.

Pioneer. Hattie McDaniel (*left*) accepts the Academy Award for best supporting actress of 1939 from the previous year's winner, Fay Bainter, on 29 February 1940; McDaniel, honored for her work in *Gone with the Wind*, was the first African American to win an Oscar. AP/Wide World Photos

The Academy Awards, soon given the name "Oscars," were initially for "a dual purpose. One is that we want to recognize fine achievements, and the other is that we want to inspire those others to give finer achievements tomorrow" (Holden, *Behind the Oscar*, pp. 30–31). The Oscar is awarded by nomination from the several groups of members, including actors, directors, and so forth, and by election of all members of the academy. The categories of awards changed between the first Oscars in 1929, when thirteen awards were presented, and 2001, when twenty-three were presented. The first awards ceremonies were at private dinners for the members of the academy. This was amplified by partial radio coverage in 1931. Television was introduced in 1951, and the auditorium format of televised presentation evolved in the 1960s and 1970s.

The Academy Awards reflect the popular culture of the United States with an increasing international aspect as American movies earned acceptance around the world. Through 1939 the Best Picture Oscars were awarded to six historical films, ranging from World War I dramas to *Gone with the Wind* (1939). In the next decade eight contemporary social dramas, including *The Lost Weekend* (1945) and *Gentleman's Agreement* (1947), won Best Picture awards. In the following twenty years eight musicals and fantasies, including *An American in Paris* (1951) and *The Sound of Music* (1965); and seven historical dramas, including *From Here to Eternity* (1953) and *Patton* (1969), earned Best Picture. In the final three decades of the twentieth century ten historical dramas, including *Chariots of Fire* (1981) and *Shakespeare in Love* (1998); six mysteries, including *The French Connection* (1971) and *The Silence of the Lambs* (1991); and five social dramas, including *Kramer vs. Kramer* (1979) and *Forrest Gump* (1994), earned the award.

Through 2001 only 188 actors of the 608 nominated won Oscars. In 2001, of the 106 nominations made for the 23 Oscars, 37 nominees were not U.S. citizens. It is fair to say that by the early twenty-first century the Academy Awards were recognized globally as the symbol of achievement in the entertainment world.

BIBLIOGRAPHY

Holden, Anthony. *Behind the Oscar: The Secret History of the Academy Awards.* New York: Simon and Schuster, 1993.

Levy, Emanuel. *Oscar Fever: The History and Politics of the Academy Awards.* New York: Continuum, 2001.

Osborne, Robert. *Sixty Years of the Oscar.* New York: Abbeville Press, 1989.

Michael Carew

See also **Film; Hollywood.**

GUGGENHEIM AWARDS

The John Simon Guggenheim Memorial Foundation presents annual fellowships to assist research and artistic creation. United States Senator Simon Guggenheim and his wife, Olga, created the foundation in memorial to their son, who died on 26 April 1922.

The foundation offers fellowships to both artists and scholars in most disciplines, including the humanities, the creative arts, the natural sciences, and the social sciences. The conditions for applying for the award are broad and do not include applicants' race, sex, or creed. Awards are presented to those demonstrating exceptional scholarship or artistic creativity and must result in a specific project outcome, such as a work of art or a monograph. There are two annual competitions: one is open to citizens and permanent residents of the United States and Canada; the second is open to citizens and residents of Latin America and the Caribbean. Appointments are normally for one year and cannot be renewed.

Between 1925 and 2000 the foundation granted more than $200 million in fellowships to some 150,000 individuals. A variety of advisory panels reviews the applicants and make recommendations to the committee of selection. Final recommendations are then given to the board of trustees. Less than 10 percent of the applicants receive fellowships. The foundation maintains an active Web site and its headquarters is in New York City.

BIBLIOGRAPHY

The Foundation Directory. New York: Foundation Center, Columbia University Press, 2001.

Karen Rae Mehaffey

MACARTHUR FOUNDATION "GENIUS" AWARDS

In 1978, the will of John D. MacArthur, the Chicago billionaire owner of Banker's Life and Casualty Company, directed the establishment of the John D. and Catherine T. MACARTHUR FOUNDATION, a private, independent grantmaking organization devoted to improving the human condition, with a bequest of $700 million. The most publicized of its four programs has been the MacArthur Fellowships, popularly known as the "genius" awards. Each year between twenty and thirty individuals receive a five-year unrestricted grant of $500,000. Candidates are nominated by approximately one hundred anonymous "talent scouts," and then selected by a committee of leaders in a variety of fields. Fellows, who must be citizens or residents of the United States, are selected on the basis of their potential for extraordinary creative accomplishment as well as evidence of exceptional originality, dedication, and self-direction. By the end of 2001, more than six hundred writers, artists, scientists, activists, teachers, social scientists, and others have received the prestigious award. Perhaps because fellows are not evaluated or required to produce evidence of how they benefited from the awards, some critics question the fellowships' success in fostering significant creative advancement. The foundation believes, however, that by generously supporting talented individuals the fellowships enhance the creative and intellectual environment of society at large.

BIBLIOGRAPHY

Senior, Jennifer. "Winning the Genius Lottery." *Civilization* 4, no. 5 (October–November 1997): 42–49.

Megan L. Benton

Nobel Prizes

Since their inception in 1901, Nobel Prizes have stood as the cachet of international recognition and achievement in the areas of physics, CHEMISTRY, physiology or medicine, LITERATURE, and peace. Awards in economics were established in 1969. Nonetheless, the various Nobel Prize committees were slow to recognize Americans. During the first decade of the awards, Americans received only three prizes. In the second decade, Americans earned only four awards. In later decades, however, the number of prizes claimed by Americans grew remarkably.

In all, by 2001 seventy U.S. citizens had won or shared twenty-three awards in physics. Twenty-one prizes had gone to fifty Americans in chemistry. The United States won its greatest number of prizes in the area of physiology or medicine, receiving forty-six prizes among eighty-three recipients. Only eleven writers had won the Nobel Prize in the field of literature, the most elusive prize category for Americans. The Peace Prize had been awarded to eighteen Americans, who received or shared sixteen prizes. The prize in economics, awarded by the Central Bank of Sweden, had been won nineteen times by twenty-seven Americans. No American has ever declined an award.

American winners of the Nobel Prize are listed below.

Economics: Paul A. Samuelson (1970); Simon S. Kuznets (1971); Kenneth J. Arrow (1972); Wassily Leontief (1973); Milton Friedman (1976); Herbert A. Simon (1978); Lawrence R. Klein (1980); James Tobin (1981); George Stigler (1982); Gerard Debreu (1983); Franco Modigliani (1985); James M. Buchanan (1986); Robert M. Solow (1987); Harry M. Markowitz, William F. Sharpe, and Merton H. Miller (1990); Ronald Coase (1991); Gary S. Becker (1992); Robert W. Fogel and Douglass C. North (1993); John F. Nash and John C. Harsanyi (1994); Robert Lucas (1995); William Vickrey (1996); Robert C. Merton and Myron S. Scholes (1997); James J. Heckman and Daniel L. McFadden; A. Michael Spence, Joseph E. Stiglitz, and George A. Akerlof.

Literature: Sinclair Lewis (1930); Eugene O'Neill (1936); Pearl Buck (1938); William Faulkner (1949); Ernest Hemingway (1954); John Steinbeck (1962); Saul Bellow (1976); Isaac Bashevis Singer (1978); Czeslaw Milosz (1980); Joseph Brodsky (1987); Toni Morrison (1993).

Chemistry: Theodore Richards (1914); Irving Langmuir (1932); Harold Urey (1934); James Sumner, John Northrop, Wendell Stanley (1946); William Giauque (1949); Edwin McMillan, Glenn Seaborg (1951); Linus Carl Pauling (1954); Vincent Du Vigneaud (1955); Willard Libby (1960); Melvin Calvin (1961); Robert B. Woodward (1965); Robert S. Mulliken (1966); Lars Onsager (1968); Christian B. Anfinsen, Stanford Moore, William H. Stein (1972); Paul J. Flory (1974); William N. Lipscomb (1976); Herbert C. Brown (1979); Paul Berg and Walter Gilbert (1980); Roald Hoffmann (1981); Henry Taube (1983); R. Bruce Merrifield (1984); Herbert A. Hauptman and Jerome Karle (1985); Dudley R. Herschback and Yuan T. Lee (1986); Donald Cram and Charles J. Pedersen (1987); Thomas R. Cech and Sidney Altman (1989); Elias James Corey (1990); Rudolph A. Marcus (1992); Kary B. Mullis (1993); George A. Olah (1994); F. Sherwood Roland and Mario Molina (1995); Richard E. Smalley and Robert F. Curl, Jr. (1996); Paul D. Boyer (1997); Walter Kohn (1998); Ahmed H. Zewail (1999); Alan J. Heeger and Alan G. MacDiarmid (2000); William S. Knowles and K. Barry Sharpless (2001).

Peace: Theodore Roosevelt (1906); Elihu Root (1912); Woodrow Wilson (1919); Charles G. Dawes (1925); Frank B. Kellogg (1929); Jane Addams, Nicholas M. Butler (1931); Cordell Hull (1945); Emily G. Balch, John R. Mott (1946); American Friends Service Committee (1947); Ralph Bunche (1950); George C. Marshall (1953); Linus Carl Pauling (1962); Martin Luther King Jr. (1964); Norman E. Borlaug (1970); Henry Kissinger (1973); Elie Wiesel (1986); Jody Williams (1997).

Physics: A. A. Michelson (1907); Robert A. Millikan (1923); Arthur Holly Compton (1927); Carl Anderson (1936); Clinton Davisson (1937); Ernest Lawrence (1939); Otto Stern (1943); Isidor Rabi (1944); Percy Bridgman (1946); Felix Bloch, Edward Purcell (1952); Willis Lamb, Jr., Polykarp Kusch (1955); William Shockley, John Bardeen, Walter Brattain (1956); Emilio Segrè, Owen Chamberlain (1959); Donald Glaser (1960); Robert Hofstadter (1961); Maria Goeppert-Mayer, Eugene P. Wigner (1963); Charles H. Townes (1964); Julian S. Schwinger, Richard P. Feynman (1965); Hans A. Bethe (1967); Luis W. Alvarez (1968); Murray Gell-Mann (1969); John Bardeen, Leon N. Cooper, John Schrieffer (1972); Ivar Giaever (1973); James Rainwater (1975); Burton Richter and Samuel C. C. Ting (1976); Philip W. Anderson and John H. Van Vleck (1977); Arno Penzias and Robert W. Wilson (1978); Steven Weinberg and Sheldon L. Glashow (1979); James W. Cronin and Val L. Fitch (1980); Nicolaas Bloembergen and Arthur L. Schawlow (1981); Kenneth G. Wilson (1982); Subrahmanyan Chandrasekhar and William A. Fowler (1983); Leon M. Lederman, Melvin Schwartz, and Jack Steinberger (1988); Norman Ramsey and Hans G. Dehmelt (1989); Jerome I. Friedman and Henry W. Kendall (1990); Joseph H. Taylor and Russell A. Hulse (1993); Clifford G. Shull (1994); Martin Pearl and Frederick Reines (1995); David M. Lee, Douglas D. Osheroff, and Robert C. Richardson (1996); Steven Chu and William D. Phillips (1997); Robert B. Laughlin and Daniel C. Tsui (1998); Jack S. Kilby (2000); Carl E. Wieman and Eric A. Cornell (2001).

Physiology or Medicine: Karl Landsteiner (1930); Thomas Hunt Morgan (1933); George R. Minot, William P. Murphy, George H. Whipple (1934); Edward

Doisy (1943); Joseph Erlanger, Herbert S. Gasser (1944); Hermann J. Muller (1946); Carl and Gerty Cori (1947); Philip S. Hench, Edward C. Kendall (1950); Selman A. Waksman (1952); Fritz A. Lipmann (1953); John F. Enders, Thomas H. Weller, Frederick Robbins (1954); Dickinson W. Richards, André F. Cournand (1956); George W. Beadle, Edward L. Tatum, Joshua Lederberg (1958); Severo Ochoa, Arthur Kornberg (1959); Georg von Békésy (1961); James D. Watson (1962); Konrad Bloch (1964); Charles Huggins, Francis Peyton Rous (1966); Haldan K. Hartline, George Wald (1967); Robert W. Holley, H. Gobind Khorana, Marshall W. Nirenberg (1968); Max Delbruck, Alfred D. Hershey, Salvador E. Luria (1969); Julius Axelrod (1970); Earl W. Sutherland, Jr. (1971); Gerald M. Edelman (1972); Albert Claude, George E. Palade (1974); David Baltimore, Howard M. Temin, and Renato Dulbecco (1975); Baruch S. Blumberg and D. Carleton Gajdusek (1976); Rosalyn S. Yalow, Roger Guillemin, and Andrew V. Schally (1977); Daniel Nathans and Hamilton Smith (1978); Allan M. Cormack (1979); Baruj Benacerraf and George D. Snell (1980); Robert W. Sperry and David H. Hubel (1981); Barbara McClintock (1983); Michael S. Brown and Joseph Goldstein (1985); Rita Levi-Montalcini and Stanley Cohen (1986); Gertrude B. Elion and George Hitchings (1988); J. Michael Bishop and Harold E. Varmus (1989); Joseph E. Murray and E. Donnall Thomas (1990); Philip A. Sharp and Richard J. Roberts (1993); Alfred G. Gilman and Martin Rodbell (1994); Edward Lewis and Eric Wieschaus (1995); Stanley B. Prusiner (1997); Louis J. Ignarro, Ferid Murad, and Robert F. Furchgott (1998); Günter Blobel (1999); Paul Greengard, Eric R. Kandel, and Leland H. Hartwell (2001).

BIBLIOGRAPHY

Fant, Kenne. *Alfred Nobel: A Biography*, trans. Marianne Ruuth. New York: Arcade, 1993.

Friedman, Robert Marc. *The Politics of Excellence: Behind the Nobel Prize in Science.* New York: Times Books, 2001.

Levinovitz, Agneta Wallin and Nils Ringertz, ed. *The Nobel Prize: The First 100 Years.* London: Imperial College Press, 2001.

W. A. Robinson / A. E.

See also **Biochemistry; Medicine and Surgery; Physics; Physiology.**

Pulitzer Prizes

Joseph Pulitzer. The publisher of the tabloid *New York World;* his bequest established the prestigious Pulitzer Prizes. © CORBIS

In a bequest to Columbia University, Joseph Pulitzer (1847–1911), the Hungarian-born journalist and pioneering American newspaper publisher, provided for the establishment of the Pulitzer Prizes to encourage excellence in journalism, letters, and education. Recognizing the dynamic nature of American society and culture, Pulitzer also granted the prizes' advisory board significant powers to expand or alter the categories in which the prizes were to be awarded. Since their inception in 1917, the number of prize categories has grown from thirteen to twenty-one.

In 2002, prizes honored distinguished achievement in fourteen categories of journalism: meritorious public service for local, investigative, explanatory, and beat reporting; reporting on national affairs; reporting on international affairs; feature writing; commentary; criticism; editorial writing; editorial cartoons; and both breaking news photography and feature photography. Six categories recognized literary achievement in fiction, U.S. history, biography or autobiography, nonfiction in another category, poetry, and drama. In 1943 a prize honoring achievement in musical composition was added.

Each year the Pulitzer Prize competition receives more than two thousand entries for its twenty-one awards. To be eligible for the journalism awards, material submitted must have appeared in a U.S. newspaper published at least weekly. (Beginning in 1999, the board sanctioned the submission of electronically published material as well.) In the remaining categories, eligible writers or composers must be American citizens. Further preference is given to works dealing with American subjects. Appointed juries evaluate the entries for each category and nominate three finalists, in no ranked order, for final deliberation by the board. The nineteen-member board exercises considerable discretion; it may disregard a jury's recommendations or even decline to bestow an award.

Each winner receives a certificate and a cash prize of $7,500, except for the winner in public service, upon whom a gold medal is bestowed. Of greatest value, however, is the international recognition attached to the prizes—arguably the most prestigious and well-known in America.

BIBLIOGRAPHY

Brennan, Elizabeth A., and Elizabeth C. Clarage. *Who's Who of Pulitzer Prize Winners.* Phoenix, Ariz.: Oryx, 1999.

Megan L. Benton

See also **Newspapers.**

PRO-CHOICE MOVEMENT. The pro-choice movement has sought to keep abortion safe, legal, and accessible to women. Advocates of ABORTION rights began using the term "pro-choice" in the years after the 1973 SUPREME COURT decision in *Roe v. Wade*, which found that the CONSTITUTION OF THE UNITED STATES protects abortion rights. They adopted the term to emphasize that their cause is women's choice, not abortion per se, and to counter the antiabortion, or "pro-life," movement's description of them as "pro-abortion." People in the pro-choice movement believe that women should have control over their reproductive lives as a legal fact and fundamental right, and that abortion should be available to all women.

BIBLIOGRAPHY

Colker, Ruth. *Abortion and Dialogue: Pro-choice, Pro-life, and American Law.* Bloomington: Indiana University Press, 1992.

Craig, Barbara Hinkson, and David M. O'Brien. *Abortion and American Politics.* Chatham, N.J.: Chatham House, 1993.

Ginsburg, Faye D. *Contested Lives: The Abortion Debate in an American Community.* Berkeley: University of California Press, 1998.

Gorney, Cynthia. *Articles of Faith: A Frontline History of the Abortion Wars.* New York: Simon and Schuster, 1998.

Nancy B. Palmer / D. B.

See also **Birth Control Movement; Pro-Life Movement; Women's Health; Women's Rights Movement: The Twentieth Century.**

PRO-LIFE MOVEMENT. The pro-life movement is the movement to block women's access to legal ABORTION and to recriminalize the procedure. Abortion rights opponents coined the term "pro-life" after the SUPREME COURT ruled in 1973's *Roe v. Wade* that the CONSTITUTION OF THE UNITED STATES protects abortion rights. Its mem-

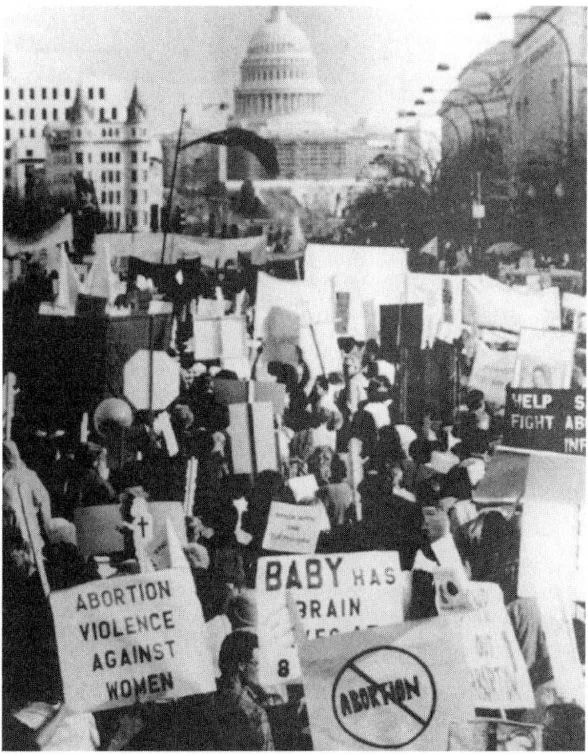

Pro-Life Demonstration. Abortion opponents rally in the nation's capital, as they do each January on the anniversary of the Supreme Court's 1973 *Roe v. Wade* decision legalizing abortion.

bers term themselves "pro-life" in contrast to supporters of women's right to the option of abortion, whom they call "pro-abortion." Some participants use direct action and the language of the civil rights movement to obstruct abortion clinics and harass personnel and clients. Since Randall Terry and Joseph Scheidler launched Operation Rescue in 1987, violence against clinics has escalated to the extent that the 1990s witnessed murders of doctors performing abortions and of clinic personnel.

BIBLIOGRAPHY

Colker, Ruth. *Abortion and Dialogue: Pro-choice, Pro-life, and American Law.* Bloomington: Indiana University Press, 1992.

Craig, Barbara Hinkson, and David M. O'Brien. *Abortion and American Politics.* Chatham, N.J.: Chatham House, 1993.

Ginsburg, Faye D. *Contested Lives: The Abortion Debate in an American Community.* Berkeley: University of California Press, 1998.

Gorney, Cynthia. *Articles of Faith: A Frontline History of the Abortion Wars.* New York: Simon and Schuster, 1998.

Nancy B. Palmer / D. B.

See also **Birth Control Movement; Pro-Choice Movement; Women's Health; Women's Rights Movement: The Twentieth Century.**

PROCLAMATION MONEY was coin valued according to a proclamation issued by Queen Anne on 18 June 1704 and in effect until 1775. Colonists and colonial governments reckoned their accounts in pounds, shillings, and pence but used a variety of coinages in their daily exchanges, including the Spanish pieces of eight and the French silver "dollars" (ecus). Under the proclamation, the various colonial valuations of Spanish pieces of eight, the most common coins in the American colonies, were superseded by a uniform valuation of six shillings. This attempt to unify the silver currency of the colonies failed in practice.

BIBLIOGRAPHY

Brock, Leslie V. *The Currency of the American Colonies, 1700–1764: A Study in Colonial Finance and Imperial Relations.* New York: Arno Press, 1975.

Stanley R. Pillsbury/A. R.

See also **Currency and Coinage; Pieces of Eight; Pine Tree Shilling.**

PROCLAMATION OF 1763, issued by the British government regulating the settlement of land in North America. It was prepared in part by William Petty Fitzmaurice, Lord Shelburne, and was proclaimed by the Crown on 2 October. By it, parts of the territory in America acquired through the Treaty of Paris earlier in the year were organized as the provinces of Quebec, East Florida, West Florida, and Grenada; the laws of England were extended to these provinces; and provision was made for the establishment of general assemblies in them. Settlement within the new provinces was encouraged by grants of land to British veterans of the French and Indian War.

The proclamation called for a new strategy to conciliate the Indians. The governors of the provinces and colonies were forbidden to grant lands "beyond the Heads or Sources of any of the Rivers which fall into the Atlantic Ocean from the West and North West." An Indian reservation was thus established south of the lands of the Hudson's Bay Company, west of Quebec and the Appalachian Mountains, and north of the boundary line of the Floridas. Settlement upon the Indian lands was prohibited, and settlers already on such lands were commanded "to remove themselves." Furthermore, private purchases of land from the Indians were forbidden; prior acquisitions in the Indian reservation were voided; and future purchases were to be made by licensed traders for the Crown alone.

For more than a decade successive ministries had been dissatisfied with the management of Indian relations by the different colonies. Rivalry among the colonies for Indian trade, and in some cases for western lands, had led to abuses by the governors of their power over trade and land grants, arousing a justified resentment among the Indians. The success of the French in conciliating the Indians strengthened the argument in favor of imperial control of Indian affairs.

The appointment in 1756 of two regional superintendents of Indian affairs had been the first step toward the British government's control of Indian relations. Sir William Johnson, superintendent of the northern Indians, urged the fixing of a line west of which settlement should be prohibited. The danger from the Indians during the French and Indian War automatically fixed such a line at the Appalachian Mountains. Settlers, however, disregarding the proclamations, swarmed over the mountains, and their encroachments were one of the causes of Pontiac's War. The Proclamation of 1763 was an attempt to check their advance until some agreement could be negotiated with the Indians. The proclamation was not intended to change the boundaries of the old colonies; nevertheless, many in the colonies resented it as an interference in their affairs. After Pontiac's War, negotiations with the Indians resulted in the treaties of Hard Labor, Fort Stanwix, and Lochaber, by which a new line was drawn. In 1774 the Quebec Act added the remainder of the Indian reservation north of the Ohio River to the province of Quebec. This aroused resentment in some of the thirteen colonies already close to rebellion, since it was seen as an attempt to deprive them of their claims to western lands.

BIBLIOGRAPHY

Jennings, Francis. *Empire of Fortune: Crowns, Colonies, and Tribes in the Seven Years War in America.* New York: Norton, 1988.

Sosin, Jack M. *The Revolutionary Frontier, 1763–1783.* New York: Holt, Rinehart, and Winston, 1967.

Solon J. Buck/A. R.

See also **Florida; Georgiana; Indian Policy, Colonial; Indian Reservations; Paris, Treaty of (1763); Western Lands; Westward Migration.**

PROCLAMATIONS. American government proclamations antedate independence. For example, on 16 March 1776, the Second Continental Congress, at the time of "impending calamity and distress when the Liberties of America are imminently endangered," issued a Proclamation "publicly to acknowledge the overruling providence of God." A "Day of Public Worship" was called for. Many proclamations like this followed in the centuries since then, including days of prayer and thanksgiving.

A far more recent example was President Bush's traditional Thanksgiving Day Proclamation of November 2001. Calling attention to the tradition, Bush mentioned that the Pilgrims gave thanks in 1621 and that President Washington's Proclamation in 1789 recounted "the blessings for which our new nation should give thanks." President Bush recalled that on "this day of Thanksgiving," we take note of those of "our fellow citizens who are grieving unimaginable loss" after the attack on 11 September 2001.

Not all proclamations, however, were appeals for God's grace or related to ceremonial occasions. The instrument was invoked often, sometimes with extraordinary and very visible results. Perhaps the first example of this occurred on 22 April 1793 when Washington issued his Neutrality Proclamation, reminding both Europe and the American citizens that the United States would follow "a conduct friendly and impartial toward the belligerent powers" locked in a struggle over the French Revolution.

While presidents, governors, and even mayors have always issued proclamations, most of these fall into the categories of trivial and even frivolous. They tout local products or pride or elevate some week—"Hog Calling Week," for example—to an official level. But the meaningless overuse of this executive authority, whatever the level of execution, should not diminish the supreme importance of the proclamation as an expression of executive might. Abraham Lincoln's Emancipation Proclamation of 1 January 1863 is a case in point. While it only freed the slaves in areas yet unconquered by the Union Army, its symbolism was huge as the first official act of the Civil War government to end slavery, and its stature has only grown over the years as a starting point in changing race relations. President Andrew Johnson's Proclamation of Amnesty in 1865, shortly after Lincoln's assassination, restoring the civil rights of most Confederate officials and belligerents, conversely touched off a firestorm of protest that resulted in the triumph of Radical Reconstruction (1867–1877), which also moved the nation to confront realistically its racial problems.

One of President Franklin Roosevelt's first acts of office during the Great Depression was to issue the Bank Holiday Proclamation of 1933. Not waiting for Congress to act, Roosevelt signaled a strong presidential response to the suffering that the American people confronted. He closed all the banks, stopping further failures in their tracks; they wouldn't open until Congress protected the deposits of the working classes through the Federal Deposit Insurance Act. The proclamation thus achieved a symbolic level of response that immediately began the process of restoring confidence in the American government. It was not unlike President Bush's reminder in November 2001 that the United States government was acting to redress an assault on the nation. The presidential proclamation can instantly do that, and it has over the course of American history.

BIBLIOGRAPHY

Leuchtenberg, William. *In the Shadow of FDR: From Harry Truman to George W. Bush.* Ithaca, N.Y.: Cornell University Press, 2001.

McPherson, James M. *Ordeal by Fire: The Civil War and Reconstruction.* Boston: McGraw-Hill, 2001.

Rakove, Jack N. *The Beginnings of National Politics: An Interpretive History of the Continental Congress.* Baltimore: Johns Hopkins University Press, 1982.

Carl E. Prince

PROCTER AND GAMBLE. Founded in 1837 in Cincinnati, Ohio, by British immigrants and brothers-in-law William Procter and James Gamble as a soap- and candle-making venture, the Procter and Gamble Company (P and G) incorporated in 1890 and is the largest manufacturer of household products in the United States, with over 250 brands of consumer goods. In 1879, P and G introduced Ivory and embarked on one of the earliest national advertising campaigns to sell the "99.44/100% pure" soap. The company became a leader in innovative and vigorous marketing that, in the 1930s and 1940s, included sponsorship of radio and television programs, nicknamed "soap operas." Research in P and G laboratories later produced Crisco, the first all-vegetable shortening in 1911; Tide, the first synthetic laundry detergent in 1946; Crest, the first fluoride toothpaste in 1955; and Pampers, the first disposable diapers in 1961. P and G also pioneered such business innovations as an employee profit-sharing program in 1887 and the brand management system in 1931. Acquisitions of smaller companies after World War II diversified the multinational conglomerate into coffee, paper products, pharmaceuticals, and cosmetics. In 2000 amidst a worldwide company reorganization, P and G, with 110,000 employees and operations in over seventy countries, achieved record revenue of nearly $40 billion, approximately half of which came from international sales.

BIBLIOGRAPHY

Jorgensen, Janice, ed. *Encyclopedia of Consumer Brands.* Detroit: St. James Press, 1994.

Schisgall, Oscar. *Eyes on Tomorrow: The Evolution of Procter and Gamble.* Chicago: J. G. Ferguson Publishing Company/Doubleday, 1981.

Jeffrey T. Coster

See also **Soap and Detergent Industry; Soap Operas.**

PRODUCT TAMPERING, the unauthorized altering of a consumer product without the knowledge of the product's owner or eventual user, is almost always treated as a threat to human health or safety, because it typically changes the contents of ingested products, such as foods or drugs, in a harmful manner. An exception to this pattern is fraudulently decreasing the odometer settings on used automobiles in an effort to increase the apparent value of a vehicle to a prospective buyer. Product tampering began in the 1890s. An especially bad case was the cyanide poisoning of Bromo Seltzer containers. The worst case of product tampering in America in the twentieth century happened in Chicago in 1982, when poison placed in packages of Tylenol killed seven people. Congress responded with the Federal Anti-Tampering Act of 1983, making it a crime to tamper with products or to make false claims of tampering. Tampering motives have included revenge, financial gain, and publicity for various causes. Tampering incidents have triggered false reports and copycat cases, both of which occurred in 1993 in response to a fabricated story that syringes were found in Pepsi-Cola cans. To combat tampering, manufacturers use science and technology to generate "tamper-evident" packaging and DNA testing to identify suspected tamperers.

BIBLIOGRAPHY

Kilmann, Ralph H., and Ian I. Mitroff. *Corporate Tragedies, Product Tampering, Sabotage, and Other Catastrophes.* New York: Praeger, 1984.

Logan, Barry. "Product Tampering Crime: A Review." *Journal of Forensic Sciences* 38 (1993): 918–927.

Monroe Friedman

PRODUCTIVITY, CONCEPT OF. The word *productivity* usually denotes the ratio of economic output to any or all associated inputs (in real terms), or output per unit of productive input. Increases in productivity mean that the amount of goods and services available per capita is growing, assuming a constant population. Factors that might lead to increases in productivity include technological innovation, capital accumulation, increased skill of workers, increased access to natural resources, changes in labor processes such as division and specialization, changes in business practices, and changes in patterns of trade. In fact, all of these factors propelled economic growth in the United States in the nineteenth and early twentieth centuries. Better machinery meant less farmers could produce more food. From 1870 to 1829, the actual output of crops increased while the proportion of the labor force on the farm decreased from 50 percent to 20 percent. Industrial productivity also surged at the same time. For example, the amount of steel produced per worker tripled between 1870 and 1900 and tripled again between 1900 and 1929.

Increasing productivity does not necessarily lead to comparable increases in wages or standard of living, however. During the 1920s, output per worker rose steadily in the manufacturing and mining sectors of the economy, but worker earnings did not keep up. In fact, yearly earnings in mining fell 13 percent between 1920 and 1929, despite a 43 percent increase in output per person during the same period. Higher productivity mainly translated into higher corporate profits rather than higher wages. Higher profits signaled an increasing income disparity that undermined the ability of the economy to recover when the stock market, fueled by higher profits during most of the 1920s, went bust in 1929.

The federal government began trying to understand U.S. productivity long before the economy sank in the 1930s. The earliest studies of output per man-hour in the United States were made in the late nineteenth century. The Bureau of Labor in the Department of the Interior, under the direction of Commissioner Carroll D. Wright, measured the labor-displacing effects of machinery. The next broad studies were made by the National Research Project of the Works Progress Administration in the 1930s, again because of concern with possible "technological unemployment." The Bureau of Labor Statistics in the U.S. Department of Labor made measurement of output per man-hour in major industries and sectors of the United States a regular part of federal government statistical programs in 1940. The focus after World War II was on (1) the contribution of productivity to economic growth and (2) the use of the trend-rate of productivity advance as a guide to noninflationary wage increases under the voluntary stabilization programs of the 1960s and the wage-price controls that were in effect from late 1971 to 1974. Estimates of productivity also were provided in a series of studies sponsored by the National Bureau of Economic Research beginning in the 1930s and expanded after World War II to include capital productivity and total productivity.

BIBLIOGRAPHY

Cochran, Thomas C. *Frontiers of Change: Early Industrialism in America.* New York: Oxford University Press, 1981.

Heibroner, Robert, and Aaron Singer. *The Economic Transformation of America: 1600 to the Present.* 4th ed. Fort Worth, Tex.: Harcourt Brace, 1999.

Kendrick, John W., and Elliot S. Grossman. *Productivity in the United States: Trends and Cycles.* Baltimore: Johns Hopkins University Press, 1980.

Lewis, Walter Edwin. *Yankee Ingenuity, Yankee Know-How.* New York: Vantage Press, 1998.

McElvaine, Robert S. *The Great Depression: America, 1929–1941.* New York: Times Books, 1993.

John W. Kendrick / C. R. P.

See also **Agricultural Machinery; Agriculture; Assembly Line; Capitalism; Computers and Computer Industry; Great Depression; Industrial Revolution; Labor, Department of; Standards of Living;** *and vol. 9:* **The Principles of Scientific Management.**

PROFESSIONS. *See* **Legal Profession; Medical Profession.**

PROFIT SHARING. The U.S. Department of Labor defines a profit-sharing plan as a "defined contribution plan under which the plan may provide, or the employer may determine, annually, how much will be contributed to the plan (out of profits or otherwise). The plan contains a formula for allocating to each participant a portion of each annual contribution."

Annual cash bonuses, particularly to white-collar or administrative workers, have a long history in Europe. Plans to distribute a percentage of profits to all workers appeared in the United States shortly after the Civil War. These plans were largely confined to medium-sized family or paternalistic companies and never became widespread before their general abandonment during the

Great Depression. The difficulties encountered in such plans were formidable: many employers feared the effect on prices and competitors from a public disclosure of large profits; it was hard for managers to see how a share in profits could raise the productivity of many types of labor; workers feared that a promise of a bonus based on profits was in fact an excuse for a low wage, antiunion policy; and most working-class families preferred a reliable to a fluctuating income. As a consequence, when unions became strong in the manufacturing field after 1940, their leaders proposed fixed fringe benefits such as group insurance, pensions, or guaranteed annual wages, rather than profit sharing.

An allied movement, particularly popular in the prosperous 1920s, was the purchase of stock in the company by employees. Management offered easy payments and often a per-share price lower than the current market figure. It was hoped, as in the case of profit sharing, that such plans would reduce labor turnover and give workers a stronger interest in company welfare. The decline in value of common stocks in the Great Depression to much less than the workers had paid for them, especially when installment payments were still due, ended the popularity of employee stock-purchase plans.

Annual bonuses in stock, cash, or both continued in many companies as an incentive to employees in management positions. Especially when managerial talent has been scarce, as in the booms of the mid-1950s or 1960s, options to buy large amounts of stock over a span of years at a set price were used to attract and keep executives.

In the 1960s, the Supreme Court ruled that professionals could incorporate, which meant that they could also take advantage of retirement benefits that paralleled plans available to people working in corporations. In 1963, Harry V. Lamon, Jr. drafted the first master Keogh plan, a tax-deferred retirement program for self-employed people and unincorporated businesses.

The Employment Retirement Income Security Act was passed in 1974 to protect retirement plan participants. This act established numerous reporting and disclosure rules and provided additional incentives for Keogh plan participants. Another important element of the act was the establishment of employee stock-ownership plans.

Retirement plans were simplified by the Revenue Act of 1978, which, among other changes, established the 401(k) retirement plans. A contributor to a 401(k) plan is not taxed on the income deposited in the year it was earned; the money is taxed at the time of withdrawal.

While each of the legislative changes over the last third of the twentieth century addressed different elements of profit sharing plans, the overall focus has shifted from a clearly defined benefit to defined contribution.

BIBLIOGRAPHY

Allen, Everett T. Jr., et. al. *Pension Planning: Pensions, Profit Sharing, and Other Deferred Compensation Plans.* 8th ed. New York: McGraw Hill/Irwin, 1997.

Kelly Boyer Sagert

See also **Employment Retirement Income Security Act, Retirement Plans.**

PROFITEERING, a term for making unconscionable or socially destructive profits, especially in times of economic stress and widespread shortages. For example, during the American Revolution speculators profited from fluctuations in paper currency. During the Mexican-American and Civil Wars, profiteers extracted excessive prices from the government for war matériel. During the panic of 1893, J. P. Morgan provided necessary assistance—and made $7.5 million on the deal. Both world wars saw profiteering in munitions, supplies, and commodities. During the 1973–1975 energy crisis, oil corporations reported annual profits ranging up to 800 percent. Governmental and private efforts to control profiteering have encompassed a wide range of techniques, with limited success.

BIBLIOGRAPHY

Brandes, Stuart D. *Warhogs: A History of War Profits in America.* Lexington: University Press of Kentucky, 1997.

The Industrial Reorganization Act, Hearings Before the Subcommittee on Antitrust and Monopoly of the Committee on the Judiciary, 93rd Congress, 1st session.

Profiteering, 65th Congress, 2nd session, Senate Document No. 248.

Norman John Powell
Christopher Wells

See also **Financial Panics; Munitions; Oil Crises; Revolution, American: Profiteering.**

PROGRESS AND POVERTY, the magnum opus of the American economist Henry George (1839–1897) and the bible of his Single Tax movement. The forty-eight-page essay on which the book was based, "Our Land and Land Policy," published in 1871, advocated the destruction of land monopoly by shifting all taxes from labor and its products to land. George began *Progress and Poverty* in September 1877 as "an inquiry into industrial depression and of increase of want with increase of wealth." Its publication in 1880 established a major American contribution to the literature of social reform and exerted an appreciable influence on modern theories of taxation.

BIBLIOGRAPHY

George, Henry. *An Anthology of Henry George's Thought.* Edited by Kenneth C. Wenzer. Henry George Centennial Trilogy, vol. 1. Rochester, N.Y.: University of Rochester Press, 1997.

Harvey Wish / c. w.

See also **Economics; Land Policy; Single Tax; Taxation.**

PROGRESSIVE MOVEMENT. The Progressive movement of the early twentieth century was an effort to form a majority coalition from interest groups alienated by the economic policy of the governing Republican Party. These groups—including farmers, a significantly immigrant working class, and middle-class consumers—hoped to sustain the successes of American industry while spreading its benefits more widely. Both of the major parties, and several of the minor ones, were home to politicians who hoped to capture this coalition. This diverse movement gave rise to a strain of political thought called Progressivism, whose creators sought to adapt the decentralized ideals of democracy to an age whose material pressures favored the concentration of money and power.

From the Civil War to 1900 the Republican Party, which dominated federal politics, adopted a strategy of national economic development favoring urban industry. A protective tariff nurtured manufacturers. The subsidized development of railroads and telegraph networks gave commerce access to the natural riches of the American continent. A commitment to a strong dollar through maintaining the gold standard kept financiers happy. The country had achieved the Republicans' goal by the turn of the century: the United States was the premier manufacturing nation in the world and was becoming the richest nation in total and per capita wealth.

But mere prosperity, unevenly spread, could not satisfy all segments of the population. Farmers objected to the tariff, which made them pay higher prices for manufactured equipment; to the gold standard, which made life harder for them as debtors; and to the policies that favored railroads, which charged far-flung rural shippers rates higher than urban producers paid. Laborers, against whom the federal government sided in every major union dispute, opposed the tariff, preferring an income tax that would raise public money from the pockets of the rich. In addition, unions sought decent working conditions and stability in employment. Also, university-educated professionals looked with alarm on the war of all against all that resulted from the encouragement of unfettered industry. Oilmen owned U.S. senators, railroad men plundered the public coffers, and public service appeared generally and increasingly beholden to private interests rather than being attentive to the national interest.

Despite this growing discontent, two major obstacles stood in the way of the Progressive movement. One was party loyalty. Even with formidable personalities seeking to woo voters away from traditional tickets, Americans tended to stick with familiar politicians. The other was the near impossibility of bringing together rural, Protestant farmers and urban immigrants who might be Catholic, Orthodox, or Jewish. Ultimately, these two factors spelled ruin for Progressivism; in 1917, anti-immigration sentiment found a home in the Democratic Party and fractured the coalition upon which reform depended. But between 1901 and 1917, the possibility of making this coalition permanent and giving it a partisan home energized politics and political thought, and generated legislation equipping the American state to manage a modern society.

The Republican Roosevelt

After William McKinley's two defeats of the Democratic and Populist candidate William Jennings Bryan in 1896 and 1900, conservative Republicans seemed set to perpetuate the political economy that had worked so well so far. In a speech at the Pan-American Exposition in Buffalo, New York, in September 1901, McKinley assured his constituents that the tariff would remain the principal economic tool of his administration. But while greeting visitors there, McKinley was fatally shot by the anarchist Leon Czolgosz. Vice President Theodore Roosevelt became president, and the character of politics dramatically changed.

Had McKinley not been assassinated, historians would not now have the concept of a Progressive movement to kick around, as without Roosevelt the dissenting constituencies could more easily have found homes in the Democratic or Socialist parties. But for personal and political reasons, Roosevelt used his presidency to give dissenters a place, however uneasy or temporary, in the Republican coalition. Identifying himself variously as a Progressive, liberal, radical, or insurgent Republican, Roosevelt claimed that as the only elected official with a national constituency, the president was the steward of the public welfare. He used his public addresses to call for a long list of reforms, including anti-corruption, anti-monopoly, democratizing, regulatory, and other novel measures that would use the government to rein in industry. Above all, he tried to define a national interest that would rise above the regional or commercial particularities that had hitherto characterized Republican efforts. Trying to find a middle ground between traditional Republicanism and reformist zeal, he nearly always equivocated; in *Americans* (1922), Stuart Sherman gave him the title of "greatest concocter of 'weasel' paragraphs on record." But he also, Sherman allowed, was responsible for the consequential rhetorical feat of "creating for the nation the atmosphere in which valor and high seriousness live." While president, Roosevelt used his executive authority to prosecute some trusts; to arbitrate between capital and labor, as in the anthracite coal strike of 1902; and to set aside national parks, preserving them from altogether free exploitation by industry. Aided by the 1904 election—which swept western, reformist Republicans into Congress, and also made Roosevelt president in his own right—he campaigned for and sometimes got reformist legislation. Chief among these laws were three measures passed in 1906: the Hepburn

Act, which gave the Interstate Commerce Commission the authority to set maximum railroad rates and to standardize railroad accounting; the Pure Food and Drug Act, which led to the creation of the Food and Drug Administration; and the Meat Inspection Act, which empowered the Department of Agriculture to grade meat products.

But as observers like Sherman noted, Roosevelt effected fewer changes in the law than he did in the atmosphere. He was the first president to identify himself with the changes that had long been brewing in city and state governments. When Robert La Follette was still in the Wisconsin statehouse and Woodrow Wilson was still a conservative Democrat who hated Bryan, Roosevelt was calling for reforms that he freely borrowed from Bryan's platform and using the government as an arbiter between capital and labor rather than a mere tool of capital. And as a Manhattanite who had lived in and identified with the West, Roosevelt straddled two streams of political thought that Progressives desperately wanted to see combined: the self-conscious consumerism of educated urban middle classes and the political rebellion of the West against eastern dominance.

The Basis for Dissent

To a considerable extent, the Progressive effort to trammel industry picked up where the strongly western Populist Party of the 1890s left off. Depression-wracked farmers identified the cozy relationship between industry and politics as the enemy of their security, and even as prosperity returned in the early twentieth century, they continued to support reforms intended to limit the influence of urban industry on government. Thus, railroad regulation and increased antitrust action enjoyed the support of congressmen representing farm districts. When Roosevelt promoted a federal income tax (which became constitutional with the Sixteenth Amendment, proposed in 1909 and ratified in 1913), he echoed farmers seeking to supplant the protective tariff as a method of funding government. Western farmers also supported the creation of a decentralized national banking system, which became law in the Federal Reserve Act of 1913. Western states led in adopting democratizing reforms like the enfranchisement of women and the primary election for senators and presidential candidates. And the Populists, like the Jacksonians before them, had supported the popular election of senators, which finally became law when the Seventeenth Amendment was ratified in 1913, ending the power of state legislatures to choose them. All of these measures would tend to limit the ability of extractive industry to exploit the political and financial capital of the West.

These reforms enjoyed as well the backing of urban reformers, who also sought to regulate industry. As consumers mindful of the health of their children and the children of their neighborhood, they favored health and safety codes to prevent overcrowding, the spread of disease, and the danger of fire. They pressed for public ownership of municipal utilities to prevent electric and gas companies from gouging ratepayers. And they sought to improve public education on the subject of modern political issues so as to encourage the poor to assert their rights. They favored antitrust and regulatory legislation to curb the exploitive power of industry. They supported the income tax, which recognizes actual inequalities of wealth among a people dedicated to an ideal of equality. To give greater democratic sanction to their reforms, they lobbied for the enfranchisement of women and direct democratic measures like the primary election, initiative, referendum, and recall. They also promoted a federal banking system that would limit the swings of boom and bust in business cycles, which would lead to steadier employment for nonprofessional workers. All of these measures would tend to reduce the ability of industry to exploit the cityscape without, reformers hoped, reducing American businesses' ability to make money and employ workers on a regular basis.

To the extent that the western agrarian agenda corresponded with the urban consumer agenda, Progressive reform provided a plausible basis on which to construct a political coalition, and because this constellation of interests crossed traditional party lines, it required a new definition of common interests to unify them. Journalists, politicians, and intellectuals inspired by Roosevelt's energy and by the political philosophy of the day stepped into the breach, giving rise to a variety of political thought called Progressivism. Whether categorized as journalist Herbert Croly's New Nationalism or as the contrapuntal New Freedom of lawyer Louis Brandeis, Progressive political thought deployed the same basic idea, namely that when more Americans lived in cities, when concentrations of capital and labor fought over the spoils of industry, the government had to stand above all as an agent of the public interest. Influenced by pragmatic philosophers like William James and John Dewey, Progressives believed the public interest could only emerge from the colloquy of individual citizens seeking to transcend their particular interests and open to the lessons of experience. Because social conditions were constantly changing, democratic opinion had to change, too, and a progressive democracy must be willing endlessly to experiment with social policy. As Croly argued, societies became democratic by acting as if they were democratic, and learning from the results. Even Christian theorists of the social gospel like Walter Rauschenbush argued that all earthly victories were conditional. In this era inflected by Darwinian thinking, adaptive ability was paramount. Fixed ideologies prevented creatures from adapting to new circumstances, so all arrangements were open to improvement.

The formulation that described most actual Progressive reforms was "Hamiltonian means for Jeffersonian ends," the paradoxical principle that those with authority and power must use more of it to produce more nearly democratic conditions: they must use their power so as ultimately to diminish it. Consequently, Progressives were especially optimistic about education and improved child-rearing as models for reform: the relationship between teachers and pupils or between parents and children matched their idea of the ideal relationship between the powerful and the powerless, between the government and its citizens. If government could modify the market principle that all buyers, although not equally equipped, must equally beware, and instead interpose its own judgment, then a truer equality might result. This idea underwrote the educational functions of government agencies like the Interstate Commerce Commission and the Bureau of Labor Statistics, which publicized and judged the fairness of business practices, and also of private efforts like the philanthropically funded settlement houses, in which educated middle-class women set themselves up as parents and teachers to the immigrant poor. All such enterprises, from bureaus of municipal information to experimental schools, operated on the principle that if people knew better, they could truly see their own interests and govern themselves.

Elections sorely tried this faith, as voters continued to exhibit party loyalty, irrespective of what reformers regarded as the public interest. But the Roosevelt presidency created a national nexus for Progressives of the urban and rural varieties, who formed countless organizations based on these principles. With an interlocking web of personnel and ideas developed in the United States and borrowed from similarly reformist European or Antipodean societies, these groups included the General Federation of Women's Clubs (1890), the Sierra Club (1892), the National Consumers League (1899), the National Conference on City Planning (1909), and the National Association for the Advancement of Colored People (1909), among others, dedicated to enlightening the public on its interest in a particular set of issues.

During the presidency of William Howard Taft, Progressives found themselves excluded from the White House, although they constituted a growing presence in Congress, especially after the elections of 1910 sent control of the Senate to an informal coalition of Progressive Republicans and Democrats. Congress passed the Mann-Elkins Act of 1910, which strengthened railroad regulation more than Taft wanted, and entirely without his help put before the country the Sixteenth Amendment for a federal income tax and the Seventeenth Amendment for the direct election of senators.

Both amendments, ratified by the states in 1913, yoked together key elements of the Progressive coalition and also showed how fragile and fleeting it was to be. Urban and rural consumers alike supported both measures because they diminished business influence on politics. But key support for the Seventeenth Amendment came from the heavily immigrant industrial cities and a coalition depending upon the common interests of immigrants and farmers could not hold. The campaign for Prohibition, which became law after the Eighteenth Amendment was ratified in 1919, served as a stalking horse for anti-immigrant sentiment and foretold the end of Progressivism.

The 1912 Election and the Wilson Presidency

In the two decades around the turn of the twentieth century, the United States took in some fifteen million immigrants. Progressive attitudes toward immigrants varied from the urbanely condescending approaches of intellectuals who valued diversity to the racist attitudes of labor unions and intellectuals who sought to exclude peoples who, they believed, were bred to live cheaply. Both attitudes tended to generalize unduly about immigrants. Some, like Russian Jews, hoped to make accommodations with American culture and rear their descendants in the United States; many others, like Italian peasants, hoped to make as much money as possible and go home as little tainted by American culture as possible. Return rates among some immigrant populations ran as high as 50 percent.

Between 1898, when Congress failed to pass a McKinley-backed immigration-restriction bill, and 1917, when Congress passed such a bill over President Woodrow Wilson's veto, it was possible for politicians to bid plausibly for the support of both farmers and immigrants. The 1898 bill was defeated by southern congressmen hopeful that immigration might contribute to the industrialization of their region. With time it became clear that immigrants avoided the South—partly because the racial terrorism that accompanied Jim Crow was often extended to foreigners—and instead swelled the cities and the congressional districts of the North. But during the two decades it took for southern leaders to change their minds, the immigrant-farmer coalition was workable and the need to woo southern voters meant national Progressives turned a blind eye toward Jim Crow.

As the 1912 election approached, Progressive Republicans who remembered Roosevelt gathered uneasily around La Follette, now a U.S. senator from Wisconsin who had carried the insurgent torch while Roosevelt was out of politics. Although an experienced Progressive governor, the self-righteous La Follette alienated the press and his supporters early in 1912, leaving room for Roosevelt to seize the leadership of the movement that the senator had husbanded in his absence. When the Republican convention at Chicago renominated Taft, Roosevelt led the insurgents out of the GOP to form a new Progressive Party, leaving fistfights and shouting delegates in his wake.

Roosevelt's split of the Republican Party created a golden opportunity for the Democrats to win a presidential election for the first time since 1892. They nominated Wilson, the governor of New Jersey and former president of Princeton University. On the Progressive ticket, Roosevelt came nearer the presidency than any other third-party candidate. But party loyalty combined with a Progressive-looking candidate prevailed, and enough of the dissenting coalition voted for Wilson to put him in the White House.

Robert La Follette Sr. The Progressive leader—as governor of Wisconsin from 1901 to 1906, then a U.S. senator until his death in 1925—addresses a crowd from a wagon in Cumberland, Wis., on 4 July 1897, starting a sixteen-month-long gubernatorial campaign (the last one he lost) and spreading his new Progressive message. State Historical Society of Wisconsin

Originally a Virginian, Wilson had always leaned toward the states rights interpretations of the Constitution, so much that he opposed basic Progressive measures like laws preventing child labor. But his years of dealing with privileged Princetonians and New Jersey corporate interests moved him nearer the Progressive position on economic regulation and the early years of his presidency saw a flurry of Progressive legislation. The Underwood-Simmons Act of 1913 lowered import tariffs and raised, for the first time, a constitutional federal income tax. The Federal Reserve Act of 1913 created a dollar regulated by a regional system of publicly supervised banks. The Clayton Antitrust Act of 1914 included detailed provisions for prosecuting anti-competitive business, and the Federal Trade Commission Act of 1914 created a strong regulatory agency to enforce Clayton Act provisions. In the midst of the 1916 election season, almost wholly on the president's initiative, Congress passed the Adamson Act mandating an eight-hour day for interstate railroad workers.

But the 1916 election spelled the end for the Progressive coalition. Democrats carried Congress and the White House, with rural congressmen promising their constituents anti-immigration legislation and the president promising urban immigrants he would oppose such legislation. The xenophobic influence of the European war drove anti-immigrant sentiment to new heights and in February 1917 Congress passed immigration restriction legislation over Wilson's veto. Two months later Wilson sought, and got, a declaration of war from Congress, and so the war displaced Progressivism altogether in the nation's politics.

The constellation of interests that comprised the Progressive movement would not align again until immigrants, farmers, and self-conscious urban consumers backed Franklin Roosevelt in 1932. In the meantime, Republican administrations, returned to office by traditional conservative constituencies, declined to enforce many Progressive laws. Aided by a Supreme Court that gutted regulatory decisions by subjecting them to judicial review, the conservative administrations and conservative judiciary of the 1920s laid Progressivism to rest. Theodore Roosevelt died in 1919 and Wilson suffered a debilitating stroke in the same year. The Progressive season had passed, leaving in place a partial legislative program and an experimental political philosophy that waited fulfillment.

BIBLIOGRAPHY

Hatton, Timothy J., and Jeffrey G. Williamson. *The Age of Mass Migration: Causes and Economic Impact.* New York: Oxford University Press, 1998.

Kennedy, David M. "Overview: The Progressive Era." *Historian* 37 (1975): 453–468.

Kloppenberg, James T. *Uncertain Victory: Social Democracy and Progressivism in European and American Thought, 1870–1920.* New York: Oxford University Press, 1986.

Kousser, J. Morgan. *The Shaping of Southern Politics: Suffrage Restriction and the Establishment of the One-Party South, 1880–1910.* New Haven, Conn.: Yale University Press, 1974.

McCormick, Richard L. "The Discovery that Business Corrupts Politics: A Reappraisal of the Origins of Progressivism." *American Historical Review* 86 (1981): 247–274.

Milkis, Sidney M., and Jerome M. Mileur, eds. *Progressivism and the New Democracy.* Amherst: University of Massachusetts Press, 1999.

Rauchway, Eric. *The Refuge of Affections: Family and American Reform Politics, 1900–1920.* New York: Columbia University Press, 2001.

Rodgers, Daniel T. *Atlantic Crossings: Social Politics in a Progressive Age.* Cambridge, Mass.: Belknap Press of Harvard University Press, 1998.

———. "In Search of Progressivism." *Reviews in American History* 10, no. 4 (December 1982): 113–132.

Sanders, Elizabeth. *Roots of Reform: Farmers, Workers, and the American State, 1877–1917.* Chicago: University of Chicago Press, 1999.

Sarasohn, David. *The Party of Reform: Democrats in the Progressive Era.* Jackson: University Press of Mississippi, 1989.

Sherman, Stuart P. *Americans.* New York: Scribners, 1922.

Skocpol, Theda. *Protecting Soldiers and Mothers: The Political Origins of Social Policy in the United States.* Cambridge, Mass.: Belknap Press of Harvard University Press, 1992.

Eric Rauchway

See also **Adamson Act; Bull Moose Party; Elections, Presidential; General Federation of Women's Clubs; Hepburn Act; National Association for the Advancement of Colored People; New Freedom; New Nationalism; Populism; Pragmatism; Sierra Club; Social Gospel.**

PROGRESSIVE PARTY OF 1924, LA FOLLETTE'S. The Progressive Party of 1924 originated in 1922 as the Conference for Progressive Political Action (CPPA), organized by leaders of the railroad brotherhoods. After liberal gains in the congressional elections of that year, state and local branches of the CPPA were organized, but the CPPA initially opposed the formation of a political party. The scandals of the Warren G. Harding administration altered its opinion and led it to view Senator Robert M. La Follette of Wisconsin as a suitable presidential challenger, though it did not officially nominate him, so that he could continue to run as an independent. The CPPA platform called for a reduction in the power of the judiciary, construction of the St. Lawrence Seaway, public control of money and credit, public ownership of waterpower and railroads, and the provision of federal public works at times of depression. It also attempted to empower the weak by seeking to give workers the right to organize and bargain collectively and by offering greater aid to farmers' cooperatives.

Interest groups formed a key component of the progressive movement, but not all were sympathetic to the idea of a third party. Railroad unions had come to advocate government intervention to improve their wages and working conditions, particularly after the railroads—which had been government-run during World War I—returned to private ownership in 1920. They were instrumental in creating the People's Legislative Service to support prolabor candidates and saw the La Follette candidacy as a means of exerting pressure in pursuit of their objectives. The American Federation of Labor (AFL) had also been interested in increasing workers' job control after World War I, but had been defeated by employers' resistance and various court decisions. The AFL worked for the election of Progressive candidates in 1922, and backed La Follette in 1924 because he was an independent rather than a third party candidate, viewing the movement as a chance to elect friendly members of Congress. Farming groups also saw in the La Follette candidacy a chance to advance their agenda of agricultural protection and farm subsidies. Such groups all saw their support for the Progressive campaign as a way to articulate their particular interests without sacrificing their independence.

By contrast, a number of state Farmer-Labor parties backed the movement in the hope of creating a national third party organization. The same was true of middle-class reformers in the Committee of Forty-Eight, who favored a broad-based liberal party. A clear division existed within the movement between those prewar Progressives (like La Follette) who inclined toward consumer-oriented political democracy and those who favored job-oriented economic democracy. La Follette's belief in the malignant power of economic monopoly meant that he was generally critical of all interest-group activity and often ignored the consumer benefits of economic concentration. Future New Deal theorists like Rexford Tugwell and Felix Frankfurter favored government planning and the involvement of interest groups in reform.

La Follette added to his appeal when he picked Democratic Senator Burton Wheeler of Montana as his running mate and carried out a major speaking campaign. Nevertheless, the campaign was poorly coordinated, had little funding, and lacked a strong precinct organization. La Follette received 4,814,050 votes, or 16.6 percent of the popular vote. Although he finished second in eleven states in the West and Midwest, he carried only his home state of Wisconsin. The ticket had sectional appeal and was also strong among Scandinavians and in certain Catholic communities in the urban Northeast. After the election, the progressive movement quickly dissolved as the unions abandoned it. It did, however, lay the groundwork for the New Deal coalition of the 1930s and served as a stepping-stone for the rise of interest-group liberalism.

BIBLIOGRAPHY

Briley, Ronald F. "Insurgency and Political Realignment: Regionalism and the Senatorial Elections of 1922 in Iowa, Nebraska, North Dakota, and Minnesota." *Mid America* 72, no. 1 (1990): 49–69.

MacKay, Kenneth C. *The Progressive Movement of 1924*. New York: Octagon Books, 1972. Reprint of original 1947 edition.

Waterhouse, David L. *The Progressive Movement of 1924 and the Development of Interest Group Liberalism*. New York: Garland, 1991.

Jeremy Bonner

See also **Farmer-Labor Party of 1920; Political Parties; Progressive Movement; Railroad Brotherhoods.**

PROGRESSIVE PARTY, 1948, founded to oppose the Harry Truman administration's Cold War policies and a rapidly escalating red scare. Its presidential and vice presidential candidates were the former vice president Henry A. Wallace and the Idaho senator Glen Taylor. The party hoped to draw millions of voters away from the Truman ticket and reorient U.S. politics back to New Deal policies of domestic economic and social reform and toward postwar cooperation with the Soviet Union.

The Progressive Party candidates and campaign called for a complete end to segregation in the South and to all forms of social discrimination. In the South, the Progressives faced terroristic violence when they held integrated meetings. The party also raised issues of women's rights in the workplace and, in its commitment to functional representation for women and minorities in its organization and national convention, prefigured affirmative action.

While early optimistic polls showed the Progressive Party receiving as many as 8 million votes, and party leaders privately considered 4 million as necessary for success, the Truman administration's sharp shift to the Left during the campaign brought millions of working-class and liberal voters back to the Democrats by the election, leaving the Progressive Party with slightly more than a million votes. The Democratic Party campaign song, "Don't Let Them Take It Away," summed up the Truman campaign against the Progressive Party: a vote for Henry Wallace was a vote for Tom Dewey, the Republican candidate, who, as president, would complete the policy of dismantling the New Deal begun by the Republican Eightieth Congress.

The immediate effects of the Progressive Party campaign were devastating to the issues it sought to raise. Domestically, the red scare intensified as purges of trade unions and blacklists of radicals and noncommunist liberals in the arts, sciences, and professions were institutionalized, both by private bodies such as the Motion Picture Association and by state and federal laws, especially the McCarran Internal Security Act of 1950. This domestic cold war peaked in the early 1950s, as Senator Joseph McCarthy both fomented and scavenged in an atmosphere of anticommunist political hysteria.

Internationally, the bipartisan foreign policy consensus that the Progressive Party challenged saw the formation of the North Atlantic Treaty Organization, the nuclear arms race, and the Korean War, institutionalizing a global Cold War that would last for nearly half a century, destroy the Soviet Union, and cost the United States trillions of dollars. Many Progressive Party activists became special targets of domestic cold warriors. Henry Wallace retired. Senator Glen Taylor was driven out of Idaho politics largely by the actions of the state and national Democratic Party. However, the Progressive Party's militant articulation of both civil rights and women's rights issues, and its call for ending the Cold War through Soviet-American negotiations and international cooperation, raised issues that would eventually revive in the last decades of the twentieth century, often with the help of activists whose first experience in politics had been in the Progressive Party campaign.

BIBLIOGRAPHY

Culver, John C. *American Dreamer: The Life and Times of Henry A. Wallace*. New York: Norton, 2000.

MacDougall, Curtis. *Gideon's Army*. 3 vols. New York: Marzani and Munsull, 1965.

Markowitz, Norman. *The Rise and Fall of the People's Century: Henry A. Wallace and American Liberalism*. New York: Free Press, 1973.

Norman Markowitz

See also **Cold War; New Deal; Political Parties; Third Parties.**

PROGRESSIVE PARTY, WISCONSIN. Officially established during a convention held at Fond du Lac on 19 May 1934, the Progressive Party of Wisconsin was primarily the creation of erstwhile Governor Philip F. La Follette and U.S. Senator Robert M. La Follette, Jr. The La Follettes were sons of the state's most legendary political figure, "Fighting Bob" La Follette, who founded and led the "progressive movement" within the Republican Party earlier in the century, and in 1924 ran for president under the Progressive banner. Upon Fighting Bob's death in 1925, "Young Bob" inherited his senate seat and rejoined the GOP, following in his father's footsteps as a severe critic of the Coolidge and Hoover administrations. With the advent of Franklin D. Roosevelt in 1933, Young Bob quickly emerged as a frequent supporter of New Deal measures, but a supporter who staunchly resisted blandishments to become a Democrat. Philip La Follette had been elected governor as a Republican in 1930, but was then defeated for reelection in the Democratic sweep of 1932. He conceived of the new party as a vehicle that would not only return him to the state house, but also secure his brother's reelection to the Senate. After much persuasion, he finally convinced his brother that running together as candidates of a new party was the surest way to tap into the state's progressive tradition without being swallowed up in Roosevelt's scheme to subsume all the country's liberals under the Democratic tent. Philip La Follette further overcame his brother's qualms that such action would cause many voters to reject "too much La Follette."

Bulking equally large in the decision of the La Follettes to form a third party was the desire to co-opt a movement being galvanized by former Congressman Tom Amlie and labor leader John J. Handley composed of Socialists, organized labor, and such militant agrarian organizations as the Farmers Union, the Wisconsin Cooperative Milk Pool, and the Farmers' Holiday Association. Backed by the national Farmer Labor Political Federation (FLPF), their organizing efforts paralleled those that led to the establishment of the powerful Farmer-Labor Party in neighboring Minnesota and of the Wisconsin Farmer-Labor Progressive Federation. Although considered "radicals" in many conservative circles, both generations of La Follettes and their progressive supporters had consistently eschewed class politics in favor of broad-based appeals to Wisconsinites as consumers, taxpayers, and citizens. As Philip La Follette told the Fond du Lac convention, the new party aimed to attract voters "as Americans and not by reason of their occupation." Much of the credit for holding together the tenuous coalition between the La Follette Progressives and FLPF belonged to Thomas Duncan, a Milwaukee Socialist who also served as Philip's right-hand man.

Although hastily cobbled together and internally conflicted, the new party swept the 1934 election, winning not only the Senate seat and the governor's chair, but seven of the state's ten Congressional positions, thirteen of the thirty-three seats in the state senate, and forty-five of the one hundred places in the assembly. However, their victory was more apparent than real, given the increasing dissatisfaction of the party's left wing, Roosevelt's overwhelming popularity, and disagreements between the La Follettes and among their respective advisers. Deciding to back Roosevelt during the 1936 presidential campaign and having persuaded the Socialists to withdraw from the ballot in Wisconsin, Philip La Follette was reelected with 48 percent of the gubernatorial vote, additionally the Progressives captured all statewide offices, seven of ten Congressional seats, and working majorities in both houses of the state legislature. But, as Philip La Follette's biographer, John E. Miller, has observed, the "election of 1936 marked the political apogee of both the New Deal and the Wisconsin Progressive party" (*Governor Philip F. La Follette*, p. 92).

Having resisted the temptation to form a national third party in 1936, Phil succumbed in 1938, despite growing factionalism, ideological splits, urban-rural conflict, the open skepticism of his brother, and escalating charges that he had become a virtual "dictator." Before a crowd of 5,000 at the University of Wisconsin stock pavilion, he proclaimed the National Progressives of America, unfurled its banner featuring a red circle surrounding a blue cross on a white background in the center of a blue field, and enunciated the party's six basic principles: public control of money and credit, the "absolute right" of every American "to earn a living by the sweat of his brow," reorganization of the federal government along lines of Wisconsin's newly adopted Government Reorganization Act, the guarantee of "a decent annual income" for all based upon "the contribution they were making," the use of government to restore opportunities for individual initiative," and the solidarity of the Western Hemisphere in the face of the coming European war.

Opposed by a de facto coalition of Republicans and Democrats in 1938, the Progressives lost every single state office, the U.S. Senate race, five of their seven House seats, five of their sixteen positions in the state senate, and sixteen of their forty-eight seats in the assembly. Philip La Follette himself was decisively repudiated, receiving only 36 percent of the gubernatorial vote and effectively retiring from politics. Although Young Bob was reelected to the Senate in 1940 and individual progressives continued to win elections over the next four years, more and more voters deserted to the two major parties. In a final irony, Orland S. Loomis was elected governor in 1944, only to die before he could take office. In 1946, Young Bob, running as a Republican, lost in the primary to a virtual unknown named Joseph R. McCarthy.

BIBLIOGRAPHY

Glad, Paul W. *The History of Wisconsin, Volume V: War, A New Era, and Depression, 1914–1940.* Edited by William F. Thompson. Madison: State Historical Society of Wisconsin, 1990.

Maney, Patrick J. *"Young Bob" La Follette: A Biography of Robert La Follette, Jr.* Columbia: University of Missouri Press, 1978.

Miller, John E. *Governor Philip F. La Follette, The Wisconsin Progressives, and the New Deal, 1895–1940.* Columbia: University of Missouri Press, 1982.

John D. Buenker

See also **Progressive Movement; Third Parties.**

PROHIBITION was a tool to which temperance reformers repeatedly turned during more than a century's efforts to change American drinking habits. The first attempts to ban alcohol consumption through government action appeared on the local and state levels during the 1830s. Local prohibition has flourished on and off ever since.

During the early 1850s, twelve states and territories followed the example of Maine by enacting statewide prohibition laws. Most of these, however, were struck down by the courts or repealed. After the Civil War, new organizations were formed to advance the prohibition cause: the Prohibition Party (1869), the Woman's Christian Temperance Union (1874), and the Anti-Saloon League (1893). During the early years of the twentieth century, many localities and states adopted prohibition. During the same period, per capita alcohol consumption rose, buoyed by the rising popularity of beer, which increasingly replaced distilled liquor in American drinking preferences. Rising consumption had two results. On one hand, it motivated prohibitionists to focus their efforts toward a national solution to a problem they perceived as intensifying. On the other hand, it persuaded brewers, who had previously cooperated politically with distillers, that their beverage enjoyed enough popular support to be spared by a federal prohibition law, and thus disrupted the liquor-industry coalition. The Anti-Saloon League's nonpartisan lobbying and balance-of-power approach was rewarded in 1916 by the election of a dry Congress, which approved a proposed prohibition constitutional amendment in December 1917. Three-quarters of state legislatures ratified within the next thirteen months, and national Prohibition came into force one year later, on 16 January 1920. World War I contributed to Prohibition's triumph by eliciting a spirit of sacrifice, restricting liquor production and sales, and discrediting German American antiprohibitionists, but most states ratified after the war's end.

The Eighteenth Amendment prohibited the manufacture, sale, transportation, importation, and exportation of intoxicating beverages and called for concurrent enforcement by the state and federal governments. The amendment's federal enforcement legislation, the Volstead Act, defined "intoxicating" as one-half of 1 percent alcohol by volume. Personal possession and consumption were therefore not proscribed, but Prohibition encompassed a wider range of alcoholic beverages than most Americans had expected. At the same time, the mechanics of concurrent state and federal enforcement were left vague. Prohibition's impact varied among beverage types and social classes. Beer, predominantly the drink of the urban working class, suffered most, and the more easily transported distilled liquors regained a larger place in American drinking patterns. Nevertheless, per capita alcohol consumption declined from its pre-Prohibition peak. Enforcement created political problems, both when it worked, by flooding courts and jails, and when it did not, as speakeasies replaced urban saloons. Federal support for enforcement was inadequate, and federal-state cooperation was consistently problematic. Nevertheless, Prohibition retained considerable popular support until the onset of the Great Depression in 1929.

Prohibition. Despite constant efforts to destroy the flow of liquor into the United States, Prohibition was widely considered a failure by 1933. LIBRARY OF CONGRESS

Leadership for the antiprohibitionist cause was provided during the 1920s by the Association Against the Prohibition Amendment, an upper-class lobby formed in 1918, but its ideological arguments, based upon opposition to centralized federal power, held little popular appeal. Mass support came late in the decade, primarily from the Women's Organization for National Prohibition Reform, led by upper-class women. The needs of the depression produced powerful new arguments for repeal, to generate liquor-industry jobs and government tax revenue. The Democratic Party became repeal's political instrument. After the Democrats' overwhelming victory in 1932, Congress submitted to the states a new constitutional amendment repealing the Eighteenth, and within ten months elected state conventions had ratified the Twenty-first Amendment. The states resumed primary responsibility for liquor control. A few states retained their prohibition laws after federal repeal; the last, Mississippi, abandoned its law in 1966. Per capita alcohol consumption did not regain the level of the pre-Prohibition years until the 1960s.

BIBLIOGRAPHY

Blocker, Jack S., Jr. *American Temperance Movements: Cycles of Reform.* Boston: Twayne, 1989.

Kerr, K. Austin. *Organized for Prohibition: A New History of the Anti-Saloon League.* New Haven, Conn.: Yale University Press, 1985.

Kyvig, David E.. *Repealing National Prohibition.* Chicago: University of Chicago Press, 1979.

Pegram, Thomas R. *Battling Demon Rum: The Struggle for a Dry America, 1800–1933.* Chicago: Ivan R. Dee, 1998.

Jack S. Blocker Jr.

See also **Alcohol, Regulation of; Speakeasy; Temperance Movement; Volstead Act.**

PROHIBITION PARTY, the oldest continuous third party in the United States, was founded in 1869 by temperance crusaders who broke with the Republican Party because they felt it was betraying its original spirit and aims. Men such as Neal Dow of Maine, Gerrit Smith of upstate New York, and James Black of Pennsylvania had backed the Republican Party during its early years because they saw it as an instrument of Christian reform. Although they were willing to let temperance take a back seat during the fight to end slavery, they expected prohibition to be the Republican Party's next great crusade. After the Civil War, however, Republicans increasingly focused on the economic issues favored by eastern business interests and even defended liquor sales because of the federal revenue derived from excise taxes on alcohol. When 500 delegates from nineteen states convened in Chicago to found the new party, the abolitionist Gerrit Smith declared, "Our involuntary slaves are set free, but our millions of voluntary slaves still clang their chains."

During its first several decades, the party was dominated by "broad-gauge" prohibitionists who believed that the party could help remake the social order and argued that it should embrace a wide range of issues in order to win broad public support. The party's platform in the late nineteenth century included the direct popular election of U.S. senators, civil service reform, and suffrage for all of voting age regardless of sex or race. In these years, the party helped mobilize thousands of women into the political process for the first time. In addition, since party leaders often came from affluent colleges and congregations in the Northeast, the Prohibition Party brought a reform agenda to areas that were comparatively insulated from the Greenback and Populist movements of the period. The party's first presidential nominee, Pennsylvania lawyer James Black, garnered only 5,600 popular votes in 1872. By 1892, however, John Bidwell of California attracted over 270,000 votes, becoming the party's most successful presidential nominee. (Although the party has fielded presidential and vice presidential candidates in every election since 1872, it has never won any electoral votes.)

In 1896 the controversy over maintaining the gold standard or issuing unlimited silver coins temporarily divided the Prohibition Party, and by the early twentieth century, its leaders no longer envisioned replacing one of the nation's major political parties. Instead, they joined forces with other temperance organizations, and focused on persuading the major parties to support or adopt their position on prohibition. They achieved this goal in 1919 with the ratification of the Eighteenth Amendment.

Popular support for the Prohibition Party fell off dramatically after 1919, although the party itself remained active in presidential politics. After the repeal of prohibition in 1933, the party increasingly came to be dominated by Protestant fundamentalists who felt alienated from modern American society and called for a return to the moral values of an earlier era. In the late 1970s, the party briefly changed its name to the National Statesman, but it reversed that move because it tended to confuse hard-core supporters. As the twenty-first century opened, the party's platform included the right to life, opposition to commercial gambling and the "homosexual agenda," the right to prayer and bible reading in public schools, opposition to the commercial sale of alcohol, and concern about the role of the United Nations and international trade agreements.

BIBLIOGRAPHY

Kobler, John. *Ardent Spirits: The Rise and Fall of Prohibition.* New York: Putnam, 1973.

Smallwood, Frank. *The Other Candidates: Third Parties in Presidential Elections.* Hanover, N.H.: University Press of New England, 1983.

Storms, Roger C. *Partisan Prophets: A History of the Prohibition Party.* Denver: National Prohibition Foundation, 1972.

Prohibition Party. Home page at http://www.prohibition.org/.

Wendy Wall

See also **Third Parties.**

PROMONTORY POINT, UTAH, was the site of the dramatic completion, on 10 May 1869, of the first transcontinental railroad, which linked the Union Pacific on the east and the Central Pacific on the west. A giant crowd gathered to witness the final ceremonies. Following prayers and brief but grandiloquent speeches, the president of the Central Pacific, Leland Stanford, using a silver sledgehammer, nervously drove the last spike, made of gold, into a polished California laurel tie. A Western Union telegraph apparatus was connected along with the spike, so that Stanford's final strokes were instantly heralded in all cities of the United States. Two locomotives, *Jupiter* and *119*, crept forward until their noses touched, and a cheering crowd confirmed a single-word telegram: "Done."

BIBLIOGRAPHY

Bain, David Haward. *Empire Express: Building the First Transcontinental Railroad.* New York: Viking, 1999.

Winther, Oscar Osburn. *The Transportation Frontier: Trans-Mississippi West, 1865–1890.* New York: Holt, Rinehart and Winston, 1964.

Oscar Osburn Winther / W. P.

See also **Central Pacific–Union Pacific Race; Railroads; Transcontinental Railroad, Building of.**

PROPAGANDA. The deliberate use of information, images, and ideas to affect public opinion, propaganda is a policy tool deployed by all governments, although its effectiveness is widely debated by scholars. The term acquired a pejorative connotation because of the exaggerated atrocity stories peddled by all sides fighting in World War I, and the horrifying accomplishments of the Ministry for Popular Enlightenment and Propaganda of Nazi Germany's Joseph Goebbels. Since then, most Western governments have eschewed the term in favor of "public information," "public diplomacy," and other similar euphemisms when discussing their own practices of attempted persuasion, and have applied the word exclusively to the statements of rival regimes.

Information analysts often classify propaganda into three categories: black, gray, and white. Black or covert propaganda consists of outright falsehoods or material falsely attributed to a source. Gray propaganda is unattributed material of questionable validity. White propaganda is the overt spreading of true information in the service of a cause. During the twentieth century, the U.S. government engaged in all three types of propaganda at various times.

The first official U.S. agency charged with developing and distributing propaganda was the COMMITTEE ON PUBLIC INFORMATION (CPI), created by order of President Woodrow Wilson on April 6, 1917, within a week of American entry into World War I. George Creel, a journalist who had written pamphlets for Wilson's 1916 re-election campaign, was made chairman. Creel hired reporters, novelists, and advertising copywriters for his sprawling organization that produced a daily newspaper, the *Official Bulletin*, with a circulation of 100,000, as well as press releases and editorials distributed to regular newspapers throughout the United States. The CPI printed millions of pamphlets for worldwide distribution of messages favorable to the United States, and sent 75,000 volunteers dubbed "Four Minute Men" to give patriotic speeches in movie houses. Other divisions of the CPI produced cartoons, drawings, and films, all designed to recruit soldiers, sell war bonds, and foster support for the war effort. In a military counterpart to the CPI, the U.S. Army Military Intelligence Division created a unit for psychological warfare, dropping leaflets behind German lines to demoralize enemy troops.

World War II

Postwar disillusionment soured the public on government-sponsored information programs, and it was not until World War II that a successor agency to the CPI was created. On June 13, 1942, President Franklin D. Roosevelt authorized the Office of War Information (OWI) to present government policies to the public both at home and abroad. The OWI engaged in activities similar to the CPI, producing printed materials, films, and newspapers; but it went beyond the CPI's legacy to introduce regular broadcasts over the government radio station, the VOICE OF AMERICA (VOA), and worked with Hollywood to ensure that privately produced movies were in harmony with government aims in the war. The OWI soon had twenty-six overseas posts known as the U.S. Information Service (USIS). On the military side, psychological warfare was the purview of the OFFICE OF STRATEGIC SERVICES (OSS), headed by William D. ("Wild Bill") Donovan. In addition to sabotage and intelligence work, the OSS engaged in propaganda in support of military operations, including spreading disinformation. In Latin America, Nelson Rockefeller directed an ambitious information campaign to shore up support for the Allies, placing articles in U.S. and Latin American periodicals and distributing approved films through the Office of the Coordinator of Inter-American Affairs (OCIAA).

The end of the war again brought about severe cutbacks in these agencies, and President Harry S. Truman eliminated OWI altogether, placing the VOA under the State Department. But the anti-Communist campaign of the Cold War required a continuing government information program. The CENTRAL INTELLIGENCE AGENCY (CIA), successor to the OSS, took over covert propaganda efforts, using black and gray propaganda to undermine the appeal of the French and Italian Communist Parties in elections. CIA funds supported the British magazines *Encounter* and *New Leader*, the French *Preuves*, the Spanish *Cuadernos*, the Italian *Tempo Presente*, and the Austrian *Forum*. A CIA front organization, the National Committee for a Free Europe, created Radio Free Europe (RFE) in 1949 for broadcasting to Eastern Europe; another CIA front set up Radio Liberty (RL) two years later. The Agency also funded Radio in the American Sector (RIAS) directed at East Germany, and created a covert radio station as part of its successful operation to overthrow President Jacobo Arbenz Guzmán in Guatemala in 1954.

Domestic Propaganda

Despite its mandate not to engage in domestic intelligence work, from the late 1940s at least until the mid-1970s, the CIA also placed propaganda in the American media, either directly or by sponsoring research and paying publication costs. CIA material was delivered, wittingly or unwittingly, by major television networks, wire service agencies, and major newspapers. Between 1947 and 1967, more than 1,000 books were written on behalf of the CIA, and published by reputable houses both in America and abroad.

In 1950, President Truman persuaded Congress to back a "Campaign of Truth" to wage psychological warfare against the Soviet bloc. He created the Psychological Strategy Board (PSB) within the NATIONAL SECURITY COUNCIL (NSC) to coordinate propaganda efforts from the Departments of State and Defense as well as CIA and the Joint Chiefs of Staff. Although the PSB's struggles for bureaucratic control were resisted by the individual departments, government information programs grew in scope. The VOA broadcast radio programs to one hundred countries in forty-six languages, and ten thousand foreign newspapers received daily materials from the U.S. press service.

President Dwight D. Eisenhower created the United States Information Agency (USIA) on June 1, 1953, as an independent agency controlling the VOA and other overt information programs formerly in the State Department. The USIA touted some of Eisenhower's favorite programs, such as Atoms for Peace, Food for Peace, and the People-to-People exchange programs, which brought private citizens into contact with foreigners. In the 1960s, President John F. Kennedy invited famed CBS broadcaster Edward R. Murrow to head the USIA.

Controversial Outcomes

Foreign propaganda work sometimes provoked controversy, as when Radio Liberty exhorted the people of Eastern Europe to overthrow their governments. When Hungarians revolted in 1956, many counted on help from the United States and complained bitterly that Radio Liberty had raised their expectations. The station's broadcasts grew more cautious after Soviet tanks crushed the revolt.

In the 1980s, with the sharpening of the Cold War, the USIA received a billion-dollar budget to support new programs such as Worldnet television broadcasts. From 1983 to 1986, the Office of Public Diplomacy for Latin America and the Caribbean was directed by Otto J. Reich, who reported to the National Security Council. Reich used white, gray, and black propaganda techniques to try to reverse the negative media coverage of the Reagan administration's policies in Central America, where Washington supported regimes with poor human rights records in El Salvador and Guatemala and underwrote the counterrevolutionary Contra forces seeking to overthrow the Sandinista government in Nicaragua. His staff of psychological warfare specialists from the CIA and the Pentagon claimed credit for placing ghost-written op-eds in the *Wall Street Journal*, *New York Times*, and *Washington Post* and intervening with editorial offices at CBS and NBC News and National Public Radio to alter their coverage of Central America. Reich's office spread the rumor that reporters who wrote articles critical of the Contras had been bribed by Sandinista agents with sexual favors, and his staff orchestrated a smear campaign linking the Sandinistas to anti-Semitism. The nonpartisan General Accounting Office later found that Reich's office "engaged in prohibited, covert propaganda activities."

Since 1985, radio and later television broadcasts have been beamed to Cuba by a government station named after nineteenth-century Cuban independence hero José Martí. Radio Martí and TV Martí largely adhered to VOA standards of objectivity until 1998, when pressure from Cuban exile political organizations led VOA to move the station from Washington to Miami, where it came under the influence of hard-line exile activists. The subsequent change in tone of the broadcasts led Senate critics to call the program an embarrassment to the United States, and listenership inside Cuba fell to an estimated level of eight percent.

The Gulf War

The end of the Cold War reduced the emphasis on propaganda broadcasts to Eastern Europe, but the military continued to apply psychological warfare during armed conflicts. During the Persian Gulf War in 1991, the U.S. military dropped some 29 million leaflets over Iraqi lines, and used radio and loudspeaker teams to urge enemy soldiers to surrender. Army officers tightly restricted access to the battlefield, guiding "pools" of journalists to approved sites for supervised reporting. The Pentagon provided compelling video footage to news organizations, famously demonstrating the capabilities of "smart bombs" that accurately hit their targets without causing collateral damage. Only after the war was it revealed that "smart" weapons made up a small fraction of the bombs dropped on Iraq. Covert CIA broadcasts to Iraq urged the Kurds in the north and the Shiites in the south to rise up against Iraqi dictator Saddam Hussein, but drew criticism when the revolts took place and were swiftly crushed without U.S. interference.

BIBLIOGRAPHY

Green, Fitzhugh. *American Propaganda Abroad.* New York: Hippocrene Books, 1988.

Hixson, Walter L. *Parting the Curtain: Propaganda, Culture, and the Cold War, 1945–1961.* New York: St. Martin's Press, 1997.

Jackall, Robert, ed. *Propaganda.* New York: New York University, 1995.

Schlesinger, Stephen, and Stephen Kinzer. *Bitter Fruit: The Untold Story of the American Coup in Guatemala.* Garden City, N.Y.: Doubleday, 1982.

Shulman, Holly Cowan. *The Voice of America: Propaganda and Democracy, 1941–1945.* Madison: University of Wisconsin Press, 1990.

Wagnleitner, Reinhold. *Coca-Colonization and the Cold War: The Cultural Mission of the United States in Austria after the Second World War.* Translated by Diana M. Wolf. Chapel Hill: University of North Carolina, 1994.

Max Paul Friedman

See also **Intelligence, Military and Strategic; Psychological Warfare; World War I; World War II.**

PROPERTY. Property lies at the center of Americans' minds and hearts. When they look around they see land, all of which is owned by someone. Ralph Waldo Emerson captured that reality when he wrote in 1841, "I cannot occupy the bleakest crag of the White Mountains or the Allegheny, but some man or corporation steps up to tell me it is his." While Emerson and other reformers questioned the system of property, the vast majority of Americans have embraced it. The American legal system is central to protecting individuals' rights to property, including the right to exclude trespassers; the right to have property free from excessive government regulation (which is also the right to use property in the manner the owner wishes); and the right to sell (alienate) property.

Restrictions on Property Rights

Property exists in conjunction (and often in conflict) with community rights. The federal and state governments, for example, have the right of EMINENT DOMAIN, which is the power to purchase property from owners for public use, even if they do not want to sell. The Fifth and Fourteenth Amendments to the United States Constitution require that the government pay "just compensation." The eminent domain power is used frequently to acquire property for highways, railroads, public parks, and urban renewal. Some of the most contentious property disputes in the late twentieth century have been over the appropriateness of eminent domain for urban renewal projects, such as the wholesale purchase of Poletown, a Polish community in Detroit, which was subsequently sold to General Motors in the early 1980s. Many questioned whether the property was being taken for public use. That case placed individual homeowners and their close-knit community against the larger community and General Motors. Other urban renewal projects have also been controversial because of their dislocation of communities. Yet the U.S. Supreme Court remains reluctant to intervene in a legislature's judgments about what constitutes public use.

Eminent domain is one example of the way that private property is subject to community rights. Zoning is another illustration. During the Progressive Era, local governments frequently imposed restrictions on the use that could be made of land, such as prohibiting the location of houses in industrial areas, limiting the size and height of buildings, and requiring minimum lot sizes for houses. Those restrictions on the use of property often had the effect of dramatically decreasing property value. The Supreme Court upheld zoning in 1926 in *Village of Euclid v. Ambler Realty Company*. The decision, issued by Justice George Sutherland—one of the most consistently conservative jurists of the twentieth century—rested on the principle of the police power, which is the state's power to regulate for the health, safety, and morality of the community. Since that case, courts have consistently given wide latitude to government decisions about zoning.

Euclid drew upon a long history of limitations on use of property for noxious purposes under the police power. It referred to a 1915, *Hadacheck v. Sebastian*, case that allowed Los Angeles to regulate a brick-making plant that was located near residences. As early as the colonial era, governments heavily regulated the use of property, such as by ordering the draining of swamps and by limiting the use of property for taverns, tanneries, and the storage of gunpowder. In the nineteenth century, many judges allowed significant regulation of property, as by imposing restrictions on building in a manner that might be dangerous, on using property for immoral purposes, and on locating businesses in residential areas. In some cases, the government ordered the destruction of property that was posing an immediate threat, such as blighted trees. Frequently, homes and businesses were burned during fires to create a firebreak and thereby stop the fire from spreading. In those cases, the government paid no compensation. Courts also restricted the rights of cemetery owners to exclude visitors. Despite sweeping statements, such as William Blackstone's that property consists of "that sole and despotic dominion which one man claims and exercises over the external things of the world, in total exclusion of the right of any other individual in the universe," property was frequently subject to regulation in the years leading up to the Civil War.

Compensation and Regulatory Takings

Some of the most important regulations of property related to property in human beings, known as slaves. Slaves who committed crimes were often punished without compensation to owners. Masters were also restricted in some of the "uses" they could make of slaves; they could not, for example, teach slaves to read, and harsh punishments were usually prohibited. In the aftermath of Nat Turner's 1831 rebellion in Virginia, the legislature discussed the abolition of slavery. One person likened slaves to dangerous property and urged that they be freed, without paying any compensation to their owners, on the theory that dangerous property could be destroyed without compensation. Later on, in environmental cases, federal and state statutes greatly restricted dumping hazardous waste on property and imposed even retroactive liability on the owners of contaminated property. When the Thirteenth Amendment confirmed the end of slavery, it also marked the wholesale termination of property rights.

On occasion, when there is significant limitation on the use of property, courts require the government to pay compensation. Those cases are called "regulatory takings," because the government's regulation has, in effect, taken the property owner's rights. Determining when a regulation becomes a taking is difficult and generated substantial debate in the twentieth century. The modern era of regulatory takings jurisprudence began with the *Pennsylvania Coal v. Mahon* decision of Justice Oliver Wendell Holmes in 1922. Justice Holmes struck down a state statute prohibiting coal companies from mining under houses in a way that caused the surface of the land to cave in. Holmes thought the regulation went "too far"; it deprived the coal mine owners of their right to property, he stated, for they had already purchased the surface rights. Justice Louis Brandeis's vigorous dissent argued that the state has the right to prohibit dangerous uses of property, such as prohibiting the sale of alcohol and margarine (which was then considered unhealthy).

Since the mid-1980s, the Supreme Court has revisited regulatory takings claims numerous times, in two contexts. First, landowners were asked to give up interests in their property in exchange for permission to build on it. The Supreme Court concluded that in those cases, known as exactions, the government must show a reasonable nexus between the burden imposed and the use being permitted and that the burden imposed by the state is reasonable in light of the proposed development. Thus, it is permissible to condition expansion of a parking lot, which will increase water run-off, on the grant of the right to expand a nearby floodplain onto property held by the owner of the parking lot. In a second series of cases, landowners argued that their property was taken when restrictions on building essentially prohibited all development of the land. The Supreme Court looks to a variety of factors to determine whether a regulation restricting development is permissible, including the economic effect of the regulation and whether it unreasonably interferes with owners' expected profits from their investments.

Balancing Interests

Property law balances competing interests between neighboring owners as well as between property owners and the community. The doctrine of "nuisance," for instance, limits owners from using their property in a way that unreasonably interferes with neighbors. So, a person living in a city may be prohibited from operating a feed lot on her property. At other times, when a use of property is particularly important, but it significantly harms a neighbor, nuisance law may award damages to the neighbor. Thus, a cement plant that provides significant employment, and would cost millions to relocate, may continue to operate, but it will have to pay for the interference it causes to the lives and property of neighbors. Frequently, owners also have rights in their neighbors' property, such as an easement to cross a neighbor's property. Covenants, or agreements, between neighbors also give them rights in the other's property, such as the right to prohibit the construction of a carport, or the right to veto architectural changes.

One covenant that was common among property owners in the years between 1900 and 1948 was the racially restrictive covenant. It took several forms: one prohibited an owner from selling property to members of certain races or religions; another allowed the sale, but prohibited members of certain races or religions from occupying the property. The U.S. Supreme Court's landmark 1948 decision in *Shelley v. Kraemer* declared the enforcement of those covenants unconstitutional because they violated the equal rights of members of the prohibited classes. After the case, the covenants were unenforceable, although some property owners and courts made feeble attempts to get around the decision until the Fair Housing Act of 1968 outlawed them completely.

Twentieth-Century Legislative Innovations

Federal legislation in the New Deal and civil rights eras imposed additional limitations on property rights. Thus, union organizers have the right to appear on private property for limited organizing efforts under the National Labor Relations Act of 1935. The federal Fair Housing Act of 1968 limits the right of owners to discriminate in the sale or renting of housing. Sellers, landlords, and real estate agents cannot discriminate in the terms, conditions, or availability of property based on race, gender, religion, marital status, or disability. Similarly, the CIVIL RIGHTS ACT OF 1964 limits the right of property owners who provide public accommodations to refuse service on the basis of race. Those federal acts realign the power held by property owners and the public.

From the late 1960s, property law became increasingly concerned with the welfare of tenants. In most jurisdictions, landlords must deliver and maintain habitable premises for residential tenants. If tenants fail to pay rent, the landlord can no longer forcibly remove them without a court order. When tenants move out before the lease expires, landlords must "mitigate" the harm by searching for substitute tenants.

There have been similar changes in marital property rights, which are designed to equitably divide property at divorce. A few states, for instance, consider an educational degree earned during marriage as marital property. Such a doctrine entitles the spouse who assisted in the acquisition of the degree some economic benefit from it. Another development, known as "palimony," allows those who contribute to a partner's acquisition of wealth to a share of that wealth, even if the couple was never married. Another important change since the 1960s is the movement to view many government entitlements, like welfare and pensions, as property. That view means that the government must provide recipients with due process in the award and termination of benefits.

Courts and the Protection of Property: Adverse Possession

Throughout American history, courts have been important in protecting property. They have consistently punished trespassers, although there were occasional squatter and tenant movements, such as the Anti-Rent movement in upstate New York in the 1840s, that supported the right of tenants to purchase the land they occupied on long-term leases. The courts have been perhaps most notorious in supporting the ouster of Native Americans from land. The most notorious case is *Johnson v. McIntosh*, decided in 1823. Chief Justice John Marshall seemed to recognize the inherent justness of the claim that the Plankasaw tribe once owned the land at issue in what is now Illinois, but he said the power of precedent constrained him. Marshall's frequently quoted opinion observed that "conquest gives a title which the Courts of the conqueror cannot deny, whatever the private and speculative opinions of individuals may be, respecting the original justice of the claim. . . ."

While property law protects owners, it also respects those who use property efficiently. The doctrine of adverse possession allows squatters who occupy property for an extended period of time to acquire title to the property if they make sufficient improvements on the property or otherwise use it, such as for farming. Adverse possession indicates a pro-development bias in the law that encourages the development of land. Similarly, many states have statutes that allow those who mistakenly build on land thinking it is their own to buy the land from the true owner. Such provisions demonstrate property law's preference for exploitation of the land.

Landscape art in the nineteenth century frequently confirmed Americans' desire to possess property—and put their footprints on the land. George Inness's painting, *The Lackawanna Valley*, places a railroad roundhouse in the center of New York farmland. Similarly, Thomas Cole's *Notch in the White Mountains* (1839) depicts a mountain pass in the fall, a beautiful scene of nature, along with a tree stump, a house with smoke rising from its chimney, and a rider on a horse, going along a well-worn road.

Changing Ideas About the Purposes of Property

Property served different purposes in the founding era, the antebellum period, and the years after the Civil War. Around the time of the Revolution, it was perceived as a way of ensuring independence. Thomas Jefferson spoke of the importance of widely distributed property, for property provided the independence that made virtuous citizenship possible. Following the Revolution, states changed their laws regarding distribution of property at death so as to provide for a more equitable distribution among children and grandchildren. The changes both reflected American values favoring wide distribution of property, and helped shape an ideology proclaiming that property should be widely distributed. That civic republican vision of property has some modern adherents, who sometimes reconceptualize the community's rights over property. One argument runs that workers have an interest in the factory where they work, which courts should protect.

In the antebellum period, beginning around 1820, American values began to change. Wide distribution of property grew less important; instead, Americans spoke about the virtues of property as a way of acquiring wealth and of disciplining government. Southern proslavery writers like Thomas Roderick Dew and Nathan Beverly Tucker told their readers that throughout history, property was important in securing freedom. When English kings needed money, for instance, they traded increased rights for tax revenue. Some still appealed to the need for wide distribution of property—and the evils of concentrated wealth. Abolitionists frequently criticized wealthy slaveowners as anti-republican. Because slaveowners had a disproportionate share of property in the community, they did not have the same values or interests as the community. Their great power over others—poorer whites as well as slaves—led them to act imperiously. The Homestead Act of 1862, passed during the Civil War, granted 160 acres of land to people who agreed to settle it for five years. It reflected the desire for wide distribution of land.

During the Reconstruction Era and the Gilded Age, judges placed a premium on the freedom of contract. Born of the Civil War–era ideology that labor should be freely alienable (rather than owned by others), property was viewed as a commodity that could—and should—be sold. Those ideas became transformed into a doctrine that businesses may make contracts free from governmental scrutiny. Often those contracts held employees to low wages. Under their terms, if employees left before the contract was up, they received no compensation at all.

In the twentieth century, property has received varying degrees of protection. During the Progressive Era there were sharp conflicts within the courts and society about the value of protecting property at the expense of workers. A 1905 Supreme Court case, LOCHNER V. NEW YORK, struck down a minimum wage, maximum hour law for bakers on the principal of freedom of contract. Over the next two decades, however, many cases upheld similar laws. During the New Deal, the Supreme Court went so far as to approve of a statute that extended the time that debtors had to pay their mortgages before they were foreclosed.

At the beginning of the twenty-first century, a period in which property rights will be given increased protection from regulations seems to be starting. Those sentiments appear in Congress as well as in the U.S. Supreme Court. For instance, in 1998 Congress extended the period of time that a work may have copyright protection to seventy years after the death of the creator. Another example of the increased respect for property is the dramatic reduction in the estate tax in 2001, which was advocated even by members of the Democratic Party, the major party typically less concerned with protecting wealth.

BIBLIOGRAPHY

Alexander, Gregory S. *Propriety and Commodity: Competing Visions of Property in American Legal Thought, 1776–1970.* Chicago: University of Chicago Press, 1997.

Brophy, Alfred L. "The Intersection of Property and Slavery in Southern Legal Thought: From Missouri Compromise Through Civil War." Ph.D. diss., Harvard University, 2001.

Donahue, Charles, Jr., Thomas E. Kauper, and Peter W. Martin. *Cases and Materials on Property: An Introduction to the Concept and the Institution.* Saint Paul, Minn.: West, 1993.

Fisher, William W. "Ideology, Religion, and the Constitutional Protection of Private Property: 1760–1860." *Emory Law Journal* 39 (1990): 65–134.

Hart, John F. "Colonial Land Use Law and Its Significance for Modern 'Takings' Doctrine." *Harvard Law Review* 109 (1996): 1252–1300.

Nedelsky, Jennifer. *Private Property and the Limits of American Constitutionalism: The Madisonian Framework and Its Legacy.* Chicago: University of Chicago Press, 1990.

Novak, William J. *The People's Welfare: Law and Regulation in Nineteenth-Century America.* Chapel Hill: University of North Carolina Press, 1996.

Plater, Zygmunt J. B., et al. *Environmental Law and Policy: Nature, Law, and Society.* Saint Paul, Minn.: West Group, 1998.

Rose, Carol M. *Property and Persuasion: Essays on the History, Theory, and Rhetoric of Ownership.* Boulder, Colo.: Westview Press, 1994.

Siegel, Stephen. "Understanding the Nineteenth Century Contract Clause: The Role of the Property-Privilege Distinction and Takings Clause Jurisprudence." *University of Southern California Law Review* 60 (1986): 1–119.

Singer, Joseph William. *The Edges of the Field: Lessons on the Obligations of Ownership.* Boston: Beacon Press, 2000.

———. *Entitlement: The Paradoxes of Property.* New Haven, Conn.: Yale University Press, 2000.

Treanor, William Michael. "The Original Understanding of the Takings Clause and the Political Process." *Columbia Law Review* 95 (1995): 782–887.

Williams, Joan. "The Rhetoric of Property." *Iowa Law Review* 83 (1999): 277–361.

Alfred L. Brophy

See also **Inheritance Tax Laws; Indian Land Cessions; Land Acts; Land Grants; Zoning Ordinances.**

PROPERTY QUALIFICATIONS. The Twenty-fourth Amendment to the CONSTITUTION OF THE UNITED STATES, which took effect on 23 January 1964, outlawed property qualifications for voting in federal elections by abolishing all poll or other taxes as requirements for voting. In 1966, the SUPREME COURT extended this prohibition to state elections when it held, in *Harper v. Virginia Board of Elections,* that state poll taxes violated the equal-protection clause of the Fourteenth Amendment. At the time of the American Revolution, almost all states had property requirements for voting. In the early nineteenth century newly admitted western states imposed few property requirements, and the eastern states moved to reduce their impediments to voting. By the time of the CIVIL WAR, the states had eliminated nearly all property requirements for voting. But, after the Civil War, many southern states reenacted poll taxes in order to disfranchise African Americans.

BIBLIOGRAPHY

Kousser, Morgan. *The Shaping of Southern Politics: Suffrage Restriction and the Establishment of the One-Party South, 1880–1910.* New Haven, Conn.: Yale University Press, 1974.

Rogers, Donald W., ed. *Voting and the Spirit of American Democracy: Essays on the History of Voting and Voting Rights in America.* Chicago: University of Illinois Press, 1992.

Williamson, Chilton. *American Suffrage from Property to Democracy, 1760–1860.* Princeton, N.J.: Princeton University Press, 1960.

John H. Fenton/C. P.

See also **Solid South; State Constitutions; Suffrage.**

PROPORTIONAL REPRESENTATION is an electoral device that seeks to make a representative body a faithful image of its electorate. Ideally, the system gives legislative voting strength proportionate to the electoral strength of every shade of societal opinion. Technically, proportional representation is achieved by devising a quota that determines the minimum number of votes required for election. The number of seats a party wins is the number of votes it receives divided by the quota. The simplest quota is the Hare quota, which is found by dividing the total number of votes cast by the number of seats to be filled. Such elections are usually at large or employ multimember districts. The greater the number of seats to be filled, the greater proportionality of representation possible.

Proportional representation dates at least to the French Revolution. Although it is the most common method of election in the Western democracies, the use of proportional representation in the United States has been rare. It has been tried by several cities, notably Cincinnati, Ohio; Boulder, Colorado; and New York City. Debate over the use of proportional representation has focused on the consequences of the system—especially instability of governments—rather than on its inherent logic or principle. Proponents argue that proportional representation prevents excessive centralization of government, strengthens parties by making candidates more dependent on them, and increases voter interest and participation in elections. Opponents contend that the system vitiates democracy on the interparty and intraparty levels.

BIBLIOGRAPHY

Barber, Kathleen L. *Proportional Representation and Election Reform in Ohio.* Columbus: Ohio State University Press, 1995.

David, Paul T., and James W. Ceasar. *Proportional Representation in Presidential Nominating Politics.* Charlottesville: University Press of Virginia, 1980.

Robert B. Kvavik/T. G.

See also **Apportionment; Caucus; Gerrymander; Majority Rule; Republic.**

PROPOSITION 13 was a California INITIATIVE constitutional amendment approved in June 1978 that started an American antigovernment tax revolt. The ballot measure set real estate property value for tax purposes at 1975–1976 market value, limited real estate taxes to 1 percent of that value, limited tax increases to 2 percent per year for continuing owners, provided for a full reassessed value base for new owners, required a two-thirds vote for legislative revenue increases, and made any local government tax increase dependent upon a two-thirds approval of the local voters.

Howard Jarvis and Paul Gann led this antigovernment crusade. Jarvis was chairperson of the United Organization of Taxpayers with an unsuccessful political record, including a failed, nonqualifying property tax reform initiative in 1972. Gann had a political career dating back to the 1950s. Active in the Republican Party, Gann organized People's Advocate, Incorporated, in 1974, focusing on crime issues. In 1977, Jarvis and Gann met and agreed to join forces to battle against rising property taxes. What they drafted with the early help of the Los Angeles assessor Philip Watson was Proposition 13, popularly known at the Jarvis-Gann Initiative. Working almost independently in the campaign with grassroots and county organizations, they gathered 1,263,000 signatures for the ballot measure. More than one million of those signatures, or about 81 percent, were deemed valid; it was the first time that more than a million signatures had ever been solicited for a ballot measure. Their main fund-raising group, Yes on 13, collected $1.5 million, with just under half of the contributions less than $50. The Jarvis-Gann campaign shook California's politics at its core.

The legislature responded with Proposition 8 to implement the Property Tax Relief Act of 1978, which was designed to give 30 percent property tax cuts, compared with Proposition 13's 50 percent cuts. This put a tax cut measure approved in Sacramento on the ballot as an alternative to Jarvis-Gann.

Jarvis-Gann forces launched an effective public campaign. They accused the state government of a political snow job. In particular, they contended that the 1 percent tax rate would provide more than enough to run the government and would encourage government to cut wasteful spending practices such as providing "phony sick leave grants," fat pension plans, and union-inflated prevailing wages for state workers. Further, the media loved Jarvis, who gave them quotable sound bites and memorable flourishes.

State Democrats, the Parents-Teachers Association, and labor unions opposed Proposition 13. They warned of closed libraries, crippled schools, abandoned paramedic services, and massive layoffs. They were on the defensive and saddled with a projected $3.6 billion budget surplus in Sacramento.

Voters turned out in near record numbers in 1978 and passed Proposition 13 with 65 percent of a 69 percent turnout. The turnout was the highest in an off-year election since 1916. The voters defeated Proposition 8 by 53 to 47 percent. What was most striking was the breadth of support for Proposition 13. Jarvis-Gann had touched a political nerve that set off a national phenomenon.

BIBLIOGRAPHY

Allswang, John M. *The Initiative and Referendum in California, 1898–1998.* Stanford, Calif.: Stanford University Press, 2000.

Schrag, Peter. *Paradise Lost: California's Experience, America's Future.* New York: New Press, 1998.

Gordon Morris Bakken

See also **California; Taxation.**

PROPOSITION 187, a California initiative statute, was a November 1994 ballot measure in the spirit of Proposition 13, designed to save the state $5 billion per year by reducing public services for illegal immigrants. The measure denied public social, health, and education services to illegal immigrants. It required state and local agencies to report suspected illegal aliens to state and federal authorities, and it declared that the manufacture, sale, or use of false citizenship or residency documents was a felony.

Popularly known as the "Save our State" initiative, Proposition 187 raised serious constitutional issues regarding illegal-alien access to public education as well as questions about the federal regulation of immigration. Regardless of these issues, Governor Pete Wilson and other Republican leaders, including Harold Ezell, President Ronald Reagan's western regional director of the Immigration and Naturalization Service, joined in support. Democratic and liberal leaders, Cardinal Roger Mahoney of Los Angeles, Los Angeles County Sheriff Sherman Block, and the League of Women Voters opposed the measure. Opponents outspent supporters three to one. Republican, moderate white, and African American voters passed the measure with 59 percent of the vote. Democratic, liberal, and Hispanic voters overwhelmingly voted against the measure.

Proposition 187 was quickly in the courts. In 1997, federal district judge Mariana R. Pfaelzer ruled that the denial of services to illegal immigrants was unconstitutional. In 1998 she made her injunction permanent, grounding her decision on the federal government's exclusive authority to legislate on immigration.

Proposition 187 created deep ill will in the Hispanic community, and many immigrants responded to the measure's threats by becoming citizens.

BIBLIOGRAPHY

Allswang, John M. *The Initiative and Referendum in California, 1898–1998.* Stanford, Calif.: Stanford University Press, 2000.

Gordon Morris Bakken

See also **Aliens, Rights of; California; Immigration Restriction; Proposition 13.**

PROPOSITION 209, a California initiative constitutional amendment, was a November 1996 ballot measure to end affirmative action in state programs. This measure was part of a national debate in the 1990s and of a Republican Party drive to end all affirmative action programs in California. Officially the "Prohibition Against Discrimination or Preferential Treatment by State and Other Public Entities" measure, it was the handiwork of Ward Connerly, a conservative African American businessman on the University of California Board of Regents, together with Governor Pete Wilson and Attorney

General Dan Lungren. Preferential admissions practices at the University of California were annual targets for critics of the system, particularly Connerly.

The public campaign was well funded. Supporters raised 5 million mostly Republican dollars, and opponents filled their chest with a similar amount from Democrats, unions, and feminists. The battle line between conservatives and liberals was clear. Although big business did not play a significant role in the campaign, national politics did. This was a presidential election year and the Republican candidate, Bob Dole, needed California. He came to California and spoke in favor of Proposition 209, a reversal of his prior support for affirmative action. The supporters of the Democratic candidate, Bill Clinton, and liberals called for the preservation of affirmative action as part of a civil rights ideology. The national rhetoric had a distinctly California twang with Protestants decisively in favor, Roman Catholics in the middle, and Jews slightly on the other side. African American and Hispanic voters decisively opposed Proposition 209, but 55 percent of the voters put it into law, at least for a day.

One day after the election, a federal civil rights suit on behalf of female and minority contractors, labor unions, and students found its way into court. Governor Wilson moved quickly to petition the federal judge to stay proceedings to allow the state courts to rule on the proposition. The court denied the governor and issued a temporary restraining order against the governor and attorney general because of the strong probability that the initiative was unconstitutional. The Clinton administration joined the suit against Wilson and Proposition 209, but in April 1997 the Ninth Circuit Court of Appeals overturned the trial judge, ruling Proposition 209 to be constitutional. In November 1997 the U.S. Supreme Court let stand the Circuit Court of Appeals ruling.

The correlation between the votes in favor of Proposition 187, the measure designed to drive illegal immigrants out of the state, and Proposition 209 was later manifested in the votes for Proposition 227 to end bilingual education in California's public schools. Research has demonstrated that increased wealth, increased education, and urban residency made one most likely to support such sociocultural measures. The old progressive politics designed to minimize the impact of political parties and make direct popular government possible came home to roost in urbanizing Eden.

BIBLIOGRAPHY

Allswang, John M. *The Initiative and Referendum in California, 1898–1998.* Stanford, Calif.: Stanford University Press, 2000.

Chávez, Lydia. *The Color Bind: California's Battle to End Affirmative Action.* Berkeley: University of California Press, 1998.

Gordon Morris Bakken

See also **Affirmative Action; California Higher Educational System.**

PROPRIETARY AGENT. A proprietary agent was a business representative of the proprietor of an American colony. The proprietors of New York, Carolina, MARYLAND, and PENNSYLVANIA all found it necessary to employ agents to attend to colonial business both in London and in America. Sir John Werden served as the Duke of York's agent in England, and John Lewin went to the colony as special agent to report on financial conditions. Before 1700 Henry Darnall served Lord Baltimore as a private agent in Maryland, and this office was continued through the colonial era. Proprietors frequently acted as their own agents in London.

BIBLIOGRAPHY

Burns, James Joseph. *The Colonial Agents of New England.* Washington, D.C.: Catholic University of America, 1935.

Lilly, Edward P. *The Colonial Agents of New York and New Jersey.* Washington, D.C.: Catholic University of America, 1936.

Lonn, Ella. *The Colonial Agents of the Southern Colonies.* Chapel Hill: University of North Carolina Press, 1945.

Wolff, Mabel P. *The Colonial Agency of Pennsylvania, 1712–1757.* Philadelphia, 1933.

Winfred T. Root / T. D.

See also **Colonial Agent; New York State; North Carolina; South Carolina.**

PROPRIETARY COLONIES were grants of land in the form of a charter, or a license to rule, for individuals or groups. They were used to settle areas rapidly with British subjects at the proprietors' expense during the costly settlement years. Also, they could be used by the Crown to repay a debt to, or bestow a favor upon, a highly placed person. Charters replaced the trading company as the dominant settlement device, beginning with Maryland's royal grant in 1632.

The land was titled in the proprietors' name, not the king's. The proprietors could appoint all officials; create

TABLE 1

Proprietary Colonies

Proprietary Colony	Date of Charter	Changed to a Royal Colony
South Carolina	3 April 1663	29 May 1721
North Carolina	3 April 1663	25 July 1729
Delaware	14 March 1681	
East Jersey*	4 July 1664	15 April 1702**
West Jersey**	4 July 1664	15 April 1702**
Maryland	30 June 1632	
Maine	1622	absorbed into Mass. 1691
New Hampshire	18 September 1680	absorbed into Mass. 1708
New York	12 March 1664	6 February 1685
Pennsylvania	14 March 1681	

*As New Caesarea
**Consolidated into New Jersey

Proprietary Colony. This engraving shows King Charles II *(left)* granting a charter to William Penn in 1681 for what would later become Pennsylvania (with Delaware added shortly afterward); the land grant settled a royal debt owed to Penn's father, for whom the king named the colony. Mary Evans Picture Library

courts, hear appeals, and pardon offenders; make laws and issue decrees; raise and command militia; and establish churches, ports, and towns. Proprietors had the opportunity to recoup their investment by collecting quitrents—annual land fees—from the settlers who had purchased land within these colonies. These vast powers were encapsulated in the Bishop of Durham clause, so-called because they were reflective of powers granted to the Lord Bishop of Durham when Scots invaders threatened his northern lands in fourteenth-century England. Proprietary colonies were the predominant form of colony in the seventeenth century, when the Carolinas, the Jerseys, Maine, Maryland, New Hampshire, New York, and Pennsylvania were handed down through hereditary proprietorship. By the 1720s, the proprietors were forced to accede to the insistent demands of the people and yield their political privileges and powers, making all but three—Maryland, Pennsylvania, and Delaware—royal colonies. After the Revolution, these three former proprietary colonies paid the heirs to the Calvert, Penn, and Grandville estates minimal amounts for the confiscated lands.

Carolina was bestowed to seven aristocrats and the governor of Virginia in 1663. South Carolinians, disgruntled with the proprietors, requested to be a Crown colony in 1719, the request granted in 1721. North Carolina was made a royal colony in 1729.

In March 1664, King Charles II granted his brother, the duke of York, a proprietorship between the Delaware and Connecticut Rivers, which included New Netherland, on the correct presumption that it would be taken over by the British. In July, the duke of York granted the Jerseys, between the Delaware and the Atlantic Ocean, to John, Lord Berkeley, and Sir George Carteret. Berkeley sold his half share of the West Jersey proprietorship to the Quaker partnership of John Fenwick and Edward Byllynge in 1674. Disagreement between the two resulted in a Quaker trusteeship in 1675, and later a joint stock company with over one hundred stockholders. Carteret's heirs sold the East Jersey lands in 1681 to twelve proprietors (including William Penn), who took in twelve associates in 1682. Disagreement between English settlers and Scottish proprietors in East and West Jersey from May 1698 to March 1701 forced the Scottish proprietors to beseech the Crown to take the responsibility for governing the two provinces. The proprietors still held the rights to unpatented lands when New Jersey became a royal colony in 1702.

The province of Maine was included in the 1622 proprietary grant to Sir Ferdinando Gorges and John Mason of all the land between the Merrimack and the Kennebec Rivers. The colony was then deeded to the government and company of Massachusetts Bay in 1679 and governed by Massachusetts colony as lord protector.

Maryland was established as a Catholic refuge under the proprietorship of Cecil Calvert, second Lord Baltimore, in 1632. Despite Maryland's Toleration Act of 1649 guaranteeing freedom of worship to all Christians, disgruntled Protestants overthrew the proprietary government in 1654. Parliament asserted Lord Baltimore's proprietary right in 1656. The Protestant Association led by

Prospecting on the Ute Reservation—An Ominous Meeting. An 1879 drawing by W. A. Rogers, a longtime artist for *Harper's Weekly*. North Wind Picture Archives

John Coode pushed Maryland's proprietary government out in August 1689; the lord proprietor, Lord Baltimore, was deprived of his political privileges in August 1691, and the new British monarchs, William III and Mary II, appointed a royal governor. In May 1715, Maryland was given back to the fourth Lord Baltimore, an Anglican Protestant, with the 1632 proprietary charter reinstated.

New Hampshire, originally part of Massachusetts, was given as a proprietorship to Robert Tufton Mason in 1680 through the proprietary rights of his grandfather, Captain John Mason. Because of political turmoil and the hardships of King William's War (1688–1697), New Hampshire sought reannexation to Massachusetts. A compromise was made when authorities in London allowed a joint governorship with Massachusetts. Finally, in 1708 British courts upheld the claims of local residents, ending any proprietary claims to New Hampshire.

New York became a proprietary colony in 1664, when Charles II gave the colony as a proprietorship to his brother James, Duke of York, upon the English claim to New York, formerly Dutch New Netherland. Only when its proprietor became King James II in 1685 did New York become a royal colony. In 1681, Charles II awarded William Penn the areas encompassing Pennsylvania and Delaware as a refuge for Britain's persecuted Quakers in repayment of a debt. William Penn's proprietary authority was revoked in March 1692 but returned in August 1694.

BIBLIOGRAPHY

Andrews, Charles McLean. *Colonial Self-Government, 1652–1689.* New York: Harper and Brothers, 1904.

Clark, J. C. D. *The Language of Liberty, 1660–1832: Political Discourse and Social Dynamics in the Anglo-American World.* Cambridge, U.K.: Cambridge University Press, 1994.

Henretta, James A., and Gregory H. Nobles. *Evolution and Revolution: American Society, 1600–1820.* Lexington, Mass.: D. C. Heath, 1987.

Middleton, Richard. *Colonial America: A History, 1585–1776.* Cambridge, Mass.: Blackwell, 1996.

Michelle M. Mormul
Winfred T. Root

See also **Assemblies, Colonial; Colonial Policy, British; Maine; Maryland; Middle Colonies; New England Colonies; New Hampshire; New Jersey; New York; North Carolina; Pennsylvania; South Carolina.**

PROSPECTORS are people who explore for minerals. For many nineteenth-century American prospectors, the hope of one day striking it rich was a lifelong preoccupation. Their explorations accelerated westward migration. The influx of miners and then settlers after gold discoveries forced the Cherokees from Georgia; the Sioux from the Black Hills of South Dakota; and the Arapahos, Cheyennes, and Utes from Colorado.

By the mid-twentieth century representatives of giant corporations, who relied heavily on geological research and sophisticated detection equipment, were doing most of the prospecting in the United States. Increasingly, the minerals that they sought were those related to energy production, notably petroleum and uranium.

BIBLIOGRAPHY

Johnson, Susan Lee. *Roaring Camp: The Social World of the California Gold Rush*. New York: W. W. Norton, 2000.

Trafzer, Clifford E., and Joel R. Hyer, eds. *Exterminate Them: Written Accounts of the Murder, Rape, and Slavery of Native Americans during the California Gold Rush, 1848–1868*. East Lansing: Michigan State University Press, 1999.

Percy S. Fritz / A. E.

See also **Gold Mines and Mining; Gold Rush, California; Lead Industry; Petroleum Prospecting and Technology; Silver Prospecting and Mining;** *and vol. 9:* **Roughing It.**

PROSTITUTION, the exchange of money for sex, was not regarded as a serious social problem in the United States until the last part of the nineteenth century. Previously, Americans had followed the practice of English common law in ignoring prostitution, which regarded it as a crime only when it became an offense to public decency. In most areas of America during the colonial and early national periods, prostitution was a more or less irregular occupation for a few women. Only where men greatly outnumbered women, as in the French colonies on the Gulf of Mexico, was it in any way institutionalized.

By the middle of the nineteenth century, the growth of industrial cities and the opening of the western frontier had led to an increase in prostitution, which tended to be concentrated in tacitly accepted "red-light" districts. The growth of these districts and the mounting concern over venereal disease resulted in two differing approaches to dealing with prostitution. One group, led by the New York physician W. W. Sanger, wanted to require compulsory medical inspection of prostitutes and to confine all prostitution to the red-light districts. During the Civil War some army commanders adopted such plans, but the only city to do so was Saint Louis between 1870 and 1874. Agitation against the Saint Louis plan came not only on moral grounds but also on public health grounds after an increasing number of physicians began to have doubts about their ability to detect venereal disease during the required inspection.

The second group wanted to abolish prostitution altogether. Josephine Elizabeth Butler, an English reformer, greatly influenced their efforts, but the group also had strong ties to the woman's suffrage movement. Many of the activists of the pre–Civil War antislavery movement joined the cause, and an increasing number of cities and states acted to curtail prostitution in the last two decades of the nineteenth century. The movement to outlaw prostitution gained immeasurably when a number of venereal specialists, especially Prince A. Morrow of New York, decided that the consequences of syphilis and gonorrhea were so horrible that traditional attitudes and institutions had to be changed. The result was the formation of the American Social Hygiene Association, which gave "scientific" backing to the movement to abolish prostitution. The Iowa Injunction and Abatement Law of 1909 took direct aim at law enforcement officials who were reluctant to move against established houses, and other states widely copied its provisions. Under this law any taxpayer might institute an action in equity against property used for prostitution. The U.S. federal government also entered the field in 1910 with the Mann Act, or White Slave Traffic Act, which outlawed procuring and transporting women across state borders for immoral purposes. The army's decision in World War I to inspect soldiers rather than prostitutes bolstered the campaign against tolerated houses. By the 1920s legally tolerated districts had mostly disappeared. For a brief period prostitution became a source of income for organized crime, but the difficulties of monopolizing what was essentially a free-lance occupation made prostitution only a minor aspect of the underworld's activities.

After the end of World War II, when effective cures for many venereal diseases had been developed, legal attitudes toward prostitution came under question again. The American Law Institute and the American Civil Liberties Union argued that sexual activities between consenting adults should not be subject to criminal penalties and advocated a return to the earlier common-law regulation of prostitution. In the mid-1970s several states considered action in this area, but only in Nevada did a state legally tolerate prostitution. Thirteen of the state's sixteen counties legalized the activity, but subjected it to careful regulation. In the context of changing sexual norms and more effective contraceptives, some authorities argued that even if legalized, prostitution would continue to decline because of the country's changing moral standards. As women began to gain equality—economically, politically, and sexually—the idea that prostitution was a necessary evil increasingly came under challenge.

Despite these changes, however, most states continued to enforce laws against prostitution and closely associated crimes, including pandering (procuring prostitutes) and pimping (living off the earnings of prostitutes). Between 1975 and 1991 there were an average of 89,000 annual arrests in the United States for male and female prostitution. Prostitution is now overwhelmingly an urban phenomenon, with most arrests in cities of more than 250,000 people. Unlike cities like San Francisco, where neither police nor prosecutors actively pursue prostitutes, most cities unofficially enforce a policy that confines sexual commerce to red-light districts. Most Americans do not worry greatly about prostitution unless activity is nearby. Prosecution can be politically advantageous for local politicians, but it is usually inconsistently pursued. Raids are often little more than symbolic gestures. Critics of current law enforcement policies also argue that prosecution and incarceration expenses should be applied to drug treatment and job training. In the politics of the United States, however, legalization of prostitution in the 1990s was as remote a possibility as it was in the 1890s. Officers arrest an average of 62,000 women, but few of their customers, each year.

Female prostitution tends to be hierarchical and male dominated. At the top are call girls, available by appointment through a madam or a high-class male pimp. Fees may run into thousands of dollars. A similar system involves escort services, through which customers may hire someone for companionship or sex. Escort services operate superficially within the law and may even advertise in newspapers or telephone directories. Far below escort services are strip joints and massage parlors, which often function in tawdry, unsanitary conditions. A related activity is telephone sex, which insulates both parties from disease, particularly AIDS, while providing customers with verbal stimulation. At the bottom of the hierarchy are streetwalkers. Protected only by a pimp, streetwalkers charge little, accept nearly all customers, and perform their work in cars, alleys, or cheap hotels. New York City authorities estimate that one-third of street prostitutes carry the HIV virus, which causes AIDS. Streetwalkers comprise only 10 to 20 percent of all prostitutes, but account for 90 percent of arrests; a disproportionate number of those who are detained are women of color.

Prostitution superficially involves a mutually agreed-upon transaction. Many young men still regard visits as rites of passage; older men ostensibly work out marital and sexual difficulties. Customers include disabled, single men unable to find legitimate sex partners. Women enter prostitution for myriad reasons, the fundamental nature of which is controversial. Some argue that prostitutes seek financial gain otherwise unavailable, or that they are pushed into this life because of high unemployment, particularly among minority women. Few still believe prostitutes are oversensual females, but a link with childhood sexual abuse at home is accepted. Prostitution is recurrently connected to other criminal activities, including credit card forgery and extortion. Little joy seems attached to the work, and interviews emphasize ancillary entertainment over sexual pleasure.

Despite disagreements within the feminist movement over whether prostitution should be legalized (women controlled by the state) or decriminalized (permitting women to control this oldest of professions themselves), the institution has entered politics. In 1973 Margo St. James, a San Francisco prostitute, organized COYOTE (Call Off Your Old Tired Ethics), urging decriminalization through the magazine *COYOTE Howls*. Priding itself as a union local, PONY (Prostitutes of New York) also favors decriminalization and works with United Nations groups to fight international trafficking in women and children. WHISPER (Women Hurt in Systems of Prostitution Engaged in Revolt) opposes prostitution, while other groups offer counseling to help young women quit the life. The political and legal impact of these organizations has been minimal. The most significant organization at the street level remains the exploitative control of the pimp.

The world of male prostitutes is more shadowy. They tend to be lone individuals, although many maintain connections with escort services. Arrests of male prostitutes and their male partners are on the rise, in part because law enforcement has become more gender-neutral as public acceptance of homosexuality has increased, giving homosexual prostitutes more visibility, and in part because male prostitution often has links to drug trafficking. Male prostitutes, like their female counterparts, work in a range of related areas, such as pornographic productions, strip houses, and phone sex.

The most notorious type of prostitution involves the child prostitute, who has left or been exiled from home, often fleeing sexual abuse or other mistreatment. The AIDS epidemic has made child prostitutes more desirable for customers who incorrectly believe that children are less likely to pass on the disease. Increasing numbers of streetwalkers are runaway children. In New York City in the early 1980s, the streets adjacent to the Port Authority Bus Terminal, the arrival point for many runaway children, became known as the "Minnesota Strip" because so many runaways worked there as prostitutes. In contrast to its ambiguous treatment of adult pornography, the Supreme Court grants no constitutional protection to child pornography, and because many of these children also work in child pornography media, police are especially vigilant toward child prostitution.

BIBLIOGRAPHY

Barry, Kathleen. *Female Sexual Slavery.* Revised ed. New York: New York University Press, 1994.

Burnham, John C. "Medical Inspection of Prostitutes in America in the Nineteenth Century." *Bulletin of the History of Medicine* 45 (1971).

Davis, Nanette J., ed. *Prostitution: An International Handbook on Trends, Problems, and Policies.* Westport, Conn.: Greenwood Press, 1993.

Ennew, Judith. *The Sexual Exploitation of Children.* New York: St. Martin's Press, 1986.

Miller, Eleanor M. *Street Woman.* Philadelphia: Temple University Press, 1986.

Riegel, Robert E. "Changing American Attitudes Toward Prostitution." *Journal of the History of Ideas* 29 (1968).

Steward, Samuel M. *Understanding the Male Hustler.* New York: Haworth Press, 1991.

Vern L. Bullough / c. w.

See also **Acquired Immune Deficiency Syndrome; American Civil Liberties Union; Antislavery; Common Law; Crime; Crime, Organized; Epidemics and Public Health; Mann Act; Narcotics Trade and Legislation; Pornography; Progressive Movement; Sexually Transmitted Diseases; Suffrage: Woman's Suffrage.**

PROTECTIONISM. *See* **Tariff.**

PROTESTANTISM. Martin Luther never set foot in North America, but the movement he unleashed in the sixteenth century profoundly shaped society and culture in America, informing everything from social policy and architecture to literature and health care. Protestantism has been, by far, the dominant religious tradition in America, although the denominational diversity of Protestantism has rendered its influence more diffuse.

Protestantism Defined

While Christianity remained fairly unified during its first millennium, cultural differences prompted a split between the Western church, based in Rome, and Eastern Christianity (Constantinople) in 1054. The Roman Catholic Church enjoyed both religious hegemony and considerable political influence in the West throughout the Middle Ages, but by the fifteenth century various reformers began to agitate for change. Some, like John Wycliffe and Jan Hus, wanted the Bible made available in the vernacular, while others called attention to ecclesiastical abuses, including simony (the buying and selling of church offices), nepotism, and general corruption among the clergy and the hierarchy.

Luther himself had been a loyal son of the church and an Augustinian friar. The combination of a visit to Rome, a spiritual crisis, and an itinerant emissary of the Vatican, however, dimmed his affection for the Roman Catholic Church. Luther returned from his sojourn to Rome in 1511 disillusioned with both the splendor of the church and the squalor of the city. A spiritual crisis over the salvation of his soul drove him to an intensive study of the New Testament, especially Paul's epistles to the Romans and to the Galatians, which convinced the restless monk that salvation was available by grace, through faith, not through the agency of priests or the church. Finally, the peregrinations of Johannes Tetzel, raising money for the completion of St. Peter's Church in Rome by selling indulgences (forgiveness of sins), convinced Luther that the Roman Catholic Church was sorely in need of reform.

On 31 October 1517 Luther posted his Ninety-five Theses to the castle church door at Wittenberg, inviting a debate with anyone who wished to engage him on the selling of indulgences. Word of Luther's defiance spread quickly throughout the Europe and led eventually to his excommunication from the Roman Church in 1521. In the meantime, while hiding from papal authorities, Luther translated the New Testament into German, drafted catechisms for teaching the rudiments of theology to the masses, and eventually set about solidifying a church free from papal control.

Luther believed, as do most Protestants today, in the priesthood of all believers; everyone is accountable for himself or herself before God, thereby obviating the necessity of priests as dispensers of grace. Whereas Rome taught the twin bases for authority—scripture and tradition (as interpreted by the church)—Luther insisted on *sola scriptura*, the Bible alone was the only authority on faith and practice. In worship, Luther emphasized the centrality of the sermon as a means of proclaiming the gospel and educating the laity. By implication, he rearticulated the importance of the Eucharist or Holy Communion; Catholics believe in transubstantiation, that the bread and wine actually become the body and blood of Jesus in the saying of the mass, while Luther believed that the real presence of Christ was in the bread and wine, assuring believers of God's grace.

Luther's spirited defense of sola scriptura, the vernacular Bible, and the priesthood of believers virtually ensured that the Protestant Reformation would become diverse and unwieldy. Within Luther's own lifetime various sects arose, each claiming the infallibility of its own interpretation of the Bible, some insisting, for instance, solely on adult baptism or on nonviolence.

Protestantism in America

All of these divergent Protestant groups found their way to North America. Anglicans, members of the Church of England, which had broken with Rome in 1534, settled in Virginia. The Pilgrims, who had separated from the Church of England, founded Plymouth Colony in 1620, the Dutch Reformed organized their first congregation in New Netherland (New York) in 1628, and Puritans began migration to Massachusetts Bay around 1630, followed by the QUAKERS. Swedish Lutherans settled along the Delaware River. A dissident Puritan, Roger Williams, adopted the belief in adult baptism in 1638, thereby initiating the Baptist tradition in America. The arrival of Scots-Irish in the 1680s brought PRESBYTERIANISM to North America, and the immigration of various Germanic groups planted PIETISM and the Anabaptist tradition in the middle colonies.

All of these groups functioned with relative autonomy until the mid-eighteenth century when a colonies-wide revival, known to historians as the GREAT AWAKENING, reconfigured Protestant life in America by eroding ethnic barriers and creating a new vocabulary of faith, known as the "new birth," or evangelicalism. Although evangelical refers to the first four books of the New Testament and also to Luther's "rediscovery of the gospel" in the sixteenth century, the term took on a special valence in America, combining the remnants of New England Puritanism with Scots-Irish Presbyterianism and Continental (especially Dutch) Pietism to form a dynamic, popular movement. Itinerant preachers during the Great Awakening summoned their listeners to obey the call of God and be "born again." Converts as well as those favorably disposed to the revival became known as NEW LIGHTS, whereas those who looked askance at the revival enthusiasm, included many of the settled clergy, earned the sobriquet Old Lights.

In the decades surrounding the turn of the nineteenth century another revival convulsed three theaters of the new nation: New England, the Cumberland Valley of Kentucky, and western New York, an area newly opened to settlement by the Erie Canal. The Second Great Awakening in the late 1820s and 1830s brought evangelical Protestantism to the frontiers, and in so doing it reshaped American society. In the South, camp meetings combined opportunities for socialization with fiery preaching, and many came away converted—even though some detractors noted that as many souls were conceived as converted. Methodist circuit riders organized congregations in the wake of the camp meetings, while Baptist congregations tended simply to ordain one of their own as their pastor.

The Second Awakening unleashed a flurry of reforming zeal in the new nation. Protestants believed that they could, by dint of their own efforts, bring about the kingdom of God here on Earth. Many believed that such efforts would usher in the millennium, the one thousand years of righteousness predicted in Revelation 20. This conviction animated sundry social reform initiatives during the antebellum period: the temperance movement, prison reform, women's rights, the female seminary movement, and (in the North) the crusade against slavery.

The carnage of the Civil War, however, began to dim hopes of a millennial kingdom, and the arrival of non-Protestant immigrants, most of whom did not share evangelical scruples about alcohol, convinced many Protestants to rethink their understanding of the millennium. Latching onto a mode of biblical interpretation called dispensationalism, imported from Great Britain, conservative Protestants decided that the teeming, squalid tenements no longer resembled the precincts of Zion. Jesus would not return after Protestants had constructed the millennial kingdom; he would return before the millennium, which meant that his return was imminent. This shift in theology effectively absolved conservatives from social engagement. If the world was on the verge of collapse, why bother with social and moral reform? The popularity of dispensational premillennialism signaled a turn on the part of conservative Protestants from the amelioration of society to the redemption of individuals. "I look upon this world as a wrecked vessel," the Chicago evangelist Dwight L. Moody famously declared. "God has given me a lifeboat and said, 'Moody, save all you can.'"

Liberal and Conservative

Adoption of this new formula of biblical interpretation also marked the deepening of a split in Protestantism between conservative and liberal. Whereas the liberal strain had been present since the eighteenth century and had manifested itself in such movements as Unitarianism and TRANSCENDENTALISM in the mid-nineteenth century, Protestant liberals at the end of the nineteenth century distinguished themselves by their insistence that Christianity redeemed not only sinful individuals but sinful social institutions as well. Marching side by side with other reformers during the Progressive Era, liberal Protestants engaged in what became known as the SOCIAL GOSPEL, working for the abolition of child labor, the eradication of poverty and political machines, and advocating the rights of workers to organize.

Liberal Protestants had also shown greater receptivity to new intellectual currents in the latter half of the nineteenth century, including Darwin's theory of evolution and an approach to the Bible called higher criticism, which cast doubts on the authorship of several books of the Bible. Conservatives, who tended to read the Bible literally, feared that these developments would undermine confidence in the Scriptures.

Fearing a slippery slope toward liberalism, conservatives countered with a series of pamphlets called *The Fundamentals*, published between 1910 and 1915. Financed by Lyman and Milton Stewart of Union Oil Company, *The Fundamentals* contained highly conservative affirmations of such traditional doctrines as the virgin birth of Jesus, the authenticity of miracles, the inerrancy of the Bible, and the premillennial return of Christ. Those who subscribed to the doctrines articulated in the pamphlets came to be known as fundamentalists. Liberals, also known as modernists, joined the battle in the 1920s in what became known as the fundamentalist-modernist controversy, a fight over control of many Protestant denominations.

Modernists, by and large, prevailed, and many conservatives, fearing contamination by association with what they regarded as heresy, separated and formed their own churches, denominations, Bible institutes, seminaries, publishing houses, and mission societies. Taken together, this vast network of institutions, largely invisible to the larger society, formed the evangelical subculture in America, and it served as the foundation for their reemergence later in the twentieth century.

Protestant liberalism became more or less synonymous with "mainline" Protestantism, the movement that dominated American religious life during the middle decades of the twentieth century. During a gathering in Cleveland in November 1949 mainline Protestants formed the National Council of Churches, an organization intended to underscore Protestant unity and avoid the duplication of efforts. Less than a decade later, on 12 October 1958, President Dwight D. Eisenhower laid the cornerstone for the monolithic Interchurch Center on the Upper West Side of Manhattan, thereby symbolizing the fusion of mainline Protestantism with white, middle-class values.

Challenges to Mainline Protestant Hegemony

While mainline Protestants celebrated their unity and their cultural ascendance, other forces conspired to diminish their influence. A young, charismatic preacher named Billy Graham, who hailed from North Carolina, caught the eye of newspaper magnate William Randolph Hearst, who instructed his papers to "puff Graham." The

Norman Vincent Peale. The Dutch Reformed minister was pastor of Marble Collegiate Church in New York City for more than fifty years and author of dozens of books—as well as countless sermons broadcast on radio and television—offering a blend of piety and self-confidence, most notably his best-seller *The Power of Positive Thinking* (1952). LIBRARY OF CONGRESS

evangelist's anticommunist rhetoric fit the temper of the McCarthy-era 1950s. Soon he was preaching to huge audiences throughout North America and the world, inviting them simply to "make a decision for Christ," to accept Jesus into their hearts and become "born again," a term taken from John 3, when Nicodemus visits Jesus by night and asks how to enter the kingdom of heaven. Graham consciously tempered some of the incendiary rhetoric of the fundamentalists; he preferred the moniker evangelical, and he sought to cooperate with all Protestants, conservative and liberal. Graham's knack for self-promotion and his adroit use of emerging media technologies earned him a large public following as well as recognition from major political figures. His popularity, moreover, prefigured the return of evangelicals to the political arena in the 1970s.

In Montgomery, Alabama, another expression of Protestantism rose to public consciousness in December 1955 after a diminutive seamstress, Rosa Parks, refused to surrender her seat to a white man and move to the "colored" section of the bus. African American preachers in the town quickly organized a boycott to protest the entrenched practice of segregation in the South, and they chose the young pastor of the Dexter Avenue Baptist Church, Martin Luther King Jr., as their leader and spokesman. Influenced by Mahatma Gandhi, King cloaked the teachings of nonviolence and social justice in the cadences of the King James Version of the Bible to shame a nation into living up to its own ideals. In so doing, King drew upon the long history of black Protestant activism; since the days of slavery the ministry was the only real avenue for the expression of leadership within the African American community, so the pastor served not only as the spiritual shepherd to his flock but also as guardian of their temporal interests.

The movement for civil rights stirred the nation's conscience, although the opposition of some Protestants occasionally turned violent, as when a bomb ripped through the basement of Birmingham's Sixteenth Street Baptist Church on 15 September 1963, killing four little girls, or when three civil-rights workers were murdered near Philadelphia, Mississippi, in June of 1964. Such events stiffened the resolve of King and a growing number of religious leaders. When King found himself incarcerated in Birmingham for civil disobedience in 1963, he responded to the criticism that a group of Protestant ministers had leveled against him for his leadership of the civil rights movement. King's "Letter from Birmingham Jail" remains a masterpiece of religious and political rhetoric, arguing that the biblical mandates for justice impelled him to work for desegregation and civil rights.

The Evangelical Resurgence

King's assassination at the Lorraine Motel in Memphis on 4 April 1968 deprived American Protestantism of one of its luminaries. By that time the United States was mired in the unpopular Vietnam War (which King had opposed shortly before his death), and the younger generation was rapidly becoming disillusioned with what Eisenhower had dubbed the "military-industrial complex" and with what the counterculture called "the establishment," including religious institutions. Attendance, membership, and giving in mainline Protestant denominations began a steady decline in the mid-1960s, a drop that would show no signs of leveling off until the end of the century.

At the same time, changes in the ways the Federal Communications Commission apportioned airtime for religious programming allowed evangelical preachers to purchase access to the airwaves. Enterprising evangelists, who became known as televangelists, used this opening to catapult them from obscurity to national prominence and, in the process, they pulled in millions of dollars in contributions. The televangelists' simple message and their uncompromising morality appealed to a nation still reeling from the counterculture, the ignominy of Vietnam, and Richard Nixon's endless prevarications.

In this context a Southern Baptist Sunday-school teacher, Jimmy Carter, emerged as a credible candidate for president. The former governor of Georgia declared that he was a "born again" Christian and that he would never knowingly lie to the American people. He captured the Democratic nomination and went on to win the 1976 election with the help of many newly enfranchised evangelicals. Within four years, however, many of these same evangelicals turned against him, led by the televangelists who became leaders of a loose coalition of politically conservative evangelicals known as the Religious Right. Jerry Falwell, pastor of the Thomas Road Baptist Church in Lynchburg, Virginia, formed MORAL MAJORITY in 1979, and he, together with other televangelists, anointed Ronald Reagan as their candidate in 1980. Throughout the 1980s the Religious Right enjoyed access to the corridors of power in Washington, and the success of the Religious Right emboldened another televangelist, Pat Robertson, to mount his own (unsuccessful) campaign for the presidency in 1988.

Protestantism in a New Millennium

At the close of the twentieth century American Protestants remained profoundly divided between liberal and conservative, mainline and evangelical. Liberal Protestants, although declining in numbers, continued their pursuit of ecumenism, elevating the standard of inclusivity to the status of orthodoxy. The leadership of mainline Protestant denominations supported racial desegregation, ordained women to the ministry, and endorsed the civil rights of gays and lesbians. The prospect of ordaining homosexuals or blessing same-sex unions, however, was more fraught and divisive, although denominational leaders pushed vigorously for such reforms.

Evangelical Protestants, on the other hand, generally hewed to more conservative stances on doctrine, social issues, and domestic arrangements. While mainline Protestants were debating gay ordination and same-sex unions, for example, evangelicals rallied behind an expression of muscular Christianity called Promise Keepers, which enjoined men to be good and faithful husbands, fathers, and churchgoers. Promise Keepers, founded in the early 1990s by Bill McCartney, a successful football coach at the University of Colorado, also demanded that men take control of their households. Feminists were aghast, but the movement proved enormously popular, drawing several million men to stadium gatherings across the country and to a massive "Standing in the Gap" rally on the Mall in Washington, D.C. As with all revivals in American history, the movement faltered soon thereafter, but its popularity underscored the continuing appeal of conservative values.

Protestantism and American Life

The terrorist attacks of 11 September 2001 illustrated the importance of Protestantism in American life. Almost immediately, convoys of relief workers arrived at the scene of both the World Trade Center and the Pentagon. Victims were rushed to hospitals, many of which had been founded by Protestant denominations decades earlier. Protestant congregations across the country collected money for the victims and their families, organized food and blood drives, and gathered for prayer. But the tragedy also demonstrated that Protestantism no longer enjoyed hegemonic status in American religious life. Members of other religious groups—Jews, Catholics, Hindus, Muslims, Mormons, Buddhists, and many others, including those who professed no religious convictions whatsoever—were amply represented among both the victims and the rescuers.

Protestantism, nevertheless, has cast a long shadow over American history and culture. A poll conducted in 2001 found that 52 percent of Americans identified themselves as Protestants. Although the internal diversity of the movement has attenuated somewhat its influence, it remains the dominant religious tradition in the United States.

BIBLIOGRAPHY

Balmer, Randall. *Mine Eyes Have Seen the Glory: A Journey into the Evangelical Subculture in America.* 3d ed. New York: Oxford University Press, 2000.

Balmer, Randall, and Lauren F. Winner. *Protestantism in America.* New York: Columbia University Press, 2002.

Butler, Jon. *Awash in a Sea of Faith: Christianizing the American People.* Cambridge, Mass.: Harvard University Press, 1990.

Hatch, Nathan O. *The Democratization of American Christianity.* New Haven, Conn.: Yale University Press, 1989.

Marty, Martin E. *Righteous Empire: The Protestant Experience in America.* New York: Dial Press, 1970.

Warner, R. Stephen. *New Wine in Old Wineskins: Evangelicals and Liberals in a Small-Town Church.* Berkeley: University of California Press, 1988.

Wuthnow, Robert. *The Restructuring of American Religion.* Princeton, N.J.: Princeton University Press, 1988.

Randall Balmer

See also **Baptist Churches; Calvinism; Lutheranism.**

PROVIDENCE ISLAND COMPANY. The Providence Island Company, which functioned from 1630 to 1641, was incorporated for the purpose of colonizing the Caribbean islands of Providence, Henrietta, and Association. Although profit was the main objective of the company's wealthy promoters, they were also interested in founding a colony for Puritans. From the outset the undertaking foundered. Soil and climate were unfavorable, and the location of the colony in the heart of Spanish territory was a constant source of danger. To attract settlers, the company's promoters tried to divert to Providence Island English Puritans planning to go to New England; they even encouraged disillusioned New England Puritans to migrate. A group headed by John Humphry left Massachusetts in 1641 to settle in Providence, but en route it was conquered by a Spanish expedition.

BIBLIOGRAPHY

Bridenbaugh, Carl, and Roberta Bridenbaugh. *No Peace Beyond the Line: The English in the Caribbean, 1624–1690.* New York: Oxford University Press, 1972.

Viola F. Barnes/A. R.

See also **Caribbean Policy; Chartered Companies; Colonial Charters; Colonial Settlements; Puritans and Puritanism; Trading Companies.**

PROVIDENCE PLANTATIONS, RHODE ISLAND AND. The Providence Plantations were the first white settlements in Rhode Island. The clergyman Roger Williams, banished by the General Court of Massachusetts Bay for propagating "new and dangerous opinions," founded the Providence Plantations in June 1636. Williams bought a large tract of land from the Narragansett Indians, and in 1638 joined with twelve other settlers in forming a land company. Their covenant provided for majority rule and allowed religious liberty. Other religious dissidents fleeing the Bay Colony's orthodox Congregationalism founded towns at Narragansett, Newport, Pawtuxet, Pocasset, and Warwick by 1643. To protect local land titles, Williams petitioned Parliament to recognize Providence, Newport, and Portsmouth as a charter colony, and the charter was issued on 24 March 1644 as the Incorporation of Providence Plantations in the Narragansett Bay in New England (adding Warwick in 1647). After the Restoration, Williams received a royal charter from Charles II in 1663 confirming the parliamentary charter.

The charter of 1663 declared religious liberty and became in the seventeenth century a haven for adherents of despised and persecuted religions, especially Antinomians, Baptists, Quakers, French Huguenots, and Jews, the latter gathering in a small community in Newport. The aim of Providence Plantations was to sever church-state connections to protect the church from the state's corrupting influence. Initially developed as individual farmsteads dispersed across the countryside, over time residents gathered into tight nuclear towns. Of all the colonies, Rhode Island experienced the greatest increase in land use during the first half of the eighteenth century, up from 9 percent in 1700 to 50 percent in 1750. The term "Providence Plantations" still remains part of the official title of the state of Rhode Island.

BIBLIOGRAPHY

Bridenbaugh, Carl. *Fat Mutton and Liberty of Conscience: Society in Rhode Island, 1636–1690.* Providence, R.I.: Brown University Press, 1974.

James, Sydney V. *The Colonial Metamorphoses in Rhode Island: A Study of Institutions in Change.* Edited by Sheila L. Skemp and Bruce C. Daniels. Hanover, N.H.: University Press of New England, 2000.

McLoughlin, William G. *Rhode Island: A Bicentennial History.* New York: Norton, 1978.

Michelle M. Mormul
Jarvis M. Morse

See also **Rhode Island.**

PROVINCETOWN PLAYERS was an avant-garde theater group of authors, artists, and actors that produced Eugene O'Neill's *Bound East for Cardiff* in 1916 in a renovated fishing shack, the Wharf Theater, in Provincetown, Massachusetts. First under the direction of George Cram Cook, the group went on to become well known for producing or otherwise supporting the experimental work of such authors as Djuna Barnes, Susan Glaspell, e. e. cummings, and Edna St. Vincent Millay, in addition to O'Neill. Dramatic productions and other endeavors were managed by the artists themselves or others more interested in advancing literary expression than in reaping commercial profits. Eugene O'Neill went on to win the Pulitzer Prize for four of his plays, and in 1936, he became the first playwright to receive the Nobel Prize for Literature. O'Neill's success brought attention and lasting credibility to, and nostalgia for, the Players, who had moved their work to Greenwich Village in New York City before they disbanded in 1929.

Works produced by the Provincetown Players, either in Provincetown or in Greenwich Village, include Millay's *The Princess Marries the Page* and *Aria da Capo;* Glaspell's *Inheritors;* Sherwood Anderson's *The Triumph of the Egg;* and e. e. cummings's *him.*

BIBLIOGRAPHY

Cook, George Cram, and Frank Shay, eds. *The Provincetown Plays.* Cincinnati, Ohio: Stewart Kidd, 1921.

Deutsch, Helen, and Stella Hanau. *The Provincetown: A Story of the Theatre.* New York: Russell and Russell, 1931.

Egan, Leona Rust. *Provincetown As a Stage: Provincetown, The Provincetown Players, and the Discovery of Eugene O'Neill.* Orleans, Mass.: Parnassus Imprints, 1994.

Sarlós, Robert Károly. *Jig Cook and the Provincetown Players: Theatre in Ferment.* Amherst: University of Massachusetts Press, 1982.

Connie Ann Kirk

See also **Theater.**

PROVINCIAL CONGRESSES. Between 1775 and 1776, the term "provincial congress" (in some colonies "provincial convention") was used to describe the primary revolutionary body managing the transition of power from traditional colonial legislative assemblies to independent state legislatures. Inasmuch as the traditional assemblies had been perceived as the "people's house," from the early seventeenth century on, it was natural that the popularly elected provincial congresses saw themselves as transitory representatives meeting in lieu of legally considered lower houses of the colonial legislatures. In sum, the Americans were inventing government as they went along. In most emerging states the provincial congresses were curious blends of revolutionary agencies and traditional conservators of representative self-government characteristic of colonial America. The provincial congresses took legitimacy from the recognition accorded them by the First and Second Continental Congresses, themselves the embodiment of revolutionary transitional government based on American understanding of traditional English liberties.

Within this overarching context, the colonial provincial congresses differed widely in form and in the perception of their roles as revolutionary bodies. In most colonies, beginning in 1774, the shift in terminology from the now-familiar committee of correspondence to "provincial congress" marked a linguistic acceptance of the dawning reality that the goal was independence, not merely the reform of colonial relations with the mother country. Benjamin Franklin articulated this when he wrote in 1773 "it is natural to suppose . . . that if the oppressions continue, a congress may grow out of that correspondence."

On the colonial level, Massachusetts was, as usual, the first to make the transition. When Governor Thomas Gage dissolved the increasingly rebellious lower house in October 1774, it met as the provincial congress; John Hancock was named as its president. It quickly took over the direction of the local communities of correspondence, and named a Committee of Safety to meet increasingly threatening efforts to impose crown authority by the local British masters in the now openly rebellious colony. In New York in the spring of 1775, the colony's provincial congress was organized by the Committee of One Hundred, in effect New York City's Committee of Correspondence. Under its extra-legal auspices, it stripped hastily evacuating British troops of arms and supplies; took control of the cannon at the Battery, a fort at the tip of Manhattan; and destroyed the presses of loyalist printer James Rivington. It committed these acts even as, in the course of the year 1775, it attempted to stave off a complete break with both New York loyalists and the English government.

The Second Continental Congress, meanwhile, lent its legitimacy to the provincial congresses in those colonies that still needed stiff encouragement to move closer to independence. To this end, it officially recognized shaky provincial congresses in New Hampshire, South Carolina, and Virginia in the fall of 1775, and urged them to take the next step and reconvene themselves as colonial governments. Even as late as May 1776, the Second Continental Congress was urging several provincial congresses to assume authority as the new governments of their respective colonies. This step had already been taken as much as a year earlier in the more revolutionary colonies of Massachusetts, New York, and New Jersey. In most colonies, members of the colony-wide committees of correspondence were popularly elected to the new provincial congresses. In New Jersey in the spring of 1775, for example, the membership was almost identical. The provincial congress in New Jersey, also a microcosm for the others, took over executive authority by making its own appointments to a wide range of positions, thus effectively usurping the authority of both Royal Governor William Franklin and the New Jersey colonial Legislative Council or upper house. These appointments included not only civil administrative posts but militia and judicial appointments as well.

Not all colonies moved so boldly. The provincial congresses still operated unevenly in 1776, even as the Second Continental Congress moved toward independence. Reflecting the quasi-legal terrain these congresses inhabited as late as June 1776, the provincial congresses of New York, Pennsylvania, Delaware, and North Carolina had still not instructed their delegates in Philadelphia how to vote on separation from the mother country. As the vote for independence approached, the New York Provincial Congress was hamstrung by the continuing violent activities of local New York City committees arrayed against each other along class lines. Although both the more conservative, merchant-dominated Committee of Fifty-one and the radical Mechanics Committee (made up of shopkeepers, artisans, and laborers) espoused revolutionary principles and independence, they differed on support for mob activity directed at the politically significant and sizable loyalist element in the city. The conflict between the two committees over utilizing crowd actions against suspected Tories rendered the New York Provincial Congress helpless. It dared not choose sides between revolutionary factions. Its activities ground to a halt as the vote on independence became imminent. This was the most extreme example of impotence among several colonies' provincial congresses. While most by June 1776 ruled totally and effectively (Massachusetts, Connecticut, and New Jersey were good examples), some in the South, while not helpless, remained only timidly in control of government as the question of separation from the mother country awaited a vote in Philadelphia. In the end all thirteen provincial congresses fell in line behind the DECLARATION OF INDEPENDENCE of 4 July 1776, largely because the national delegation to the Second Continental Congress was going to vote for it whether or not explicit instructions from home arrived in time.

It was no wonder then that, with independence, these provincial congresses dissolved in favor of regularly elected state legislatures, which in turn made provision for executive and judicial authority in the new state governmental agencies.

BIBLIOGRAPHY

Rakove, Jack. *The Beginnings of National Politics: An Interpretative History of the Continental Congress.* New York: Knopf, 1979.

Jensen, Merrill. *The Founding of a Nation: A History of the American Revolution, 1763–1776.* New York: Oxford University Press, 1968.

Gilje, Paul. *The Road to Mobocracy: Popular Disorder in New York City, 1763–1834.* Chapel Hill: University of North Carolina Press, 1987.

Prince, Carl E., et al., eds. *The Papers of William Livingston.* 5 vols. New Brunswick, N.J.: Rutgers University Press, 1979–1988.

Carl E. Prince

See also **Continental Congress; Revolution, American: Political History.**

PROZAC (or fluoxetine) was the first of a class of drugs known as selective serotonin reuptake inhibitors (SSRI) to be introduced for the treatment of depression and other psychological disorders. These drugs work by increasing the amount of serotonin, a neurotransmitter thought to be involved in the biochemical mechanism of depression, available in the brain. Researchers hoped that because these drugs specifically targeted serotonin without affecting other neurotransmitters, they would have fewer undesirable side effects than earlier generations of psychiatric drugs.

First introduced in Belgium by the Eli Lilly Company in 1986, Prozac was made available in the United States the following year. It enjoyed remarkable early success—within five years, 4.5 million Americans had taken Prozac. Although the Food and Drug Administration had only approved the drug to be prescribed for depression and obsessive-compulsive disorder, it soon became common for physicians and psychiatrists to prescribe Prozac for eating, anxiety, and panic disorders and posttraumatic stress as well.

With this rapid acceptance, Prozac became a cultural phenomenon. Patients using Prozac reported feeling beyond well, suggesting that the drug had not only eased their depression but had also led them to new levels of awareness of their personalities. Prozac users reported the loss of social inhibitions: the shy became bolder, the lazy more diligent, the cautious more confident. For the first time, a drug seemed as if it might be able to improve personalities and suggested a future where pharmaceuticals could allow patients to reshape themselves to meet social expectations.

Although usage of Prozac and related drugs remained high in the late 1990s (an estimated 40 million patients worldwide were treated with Prozac during its first fifteen years on the market), a cultural backlash did arise against its early success. Some patients claimed that the drug made them feel suicidal. Others made even darker claims, suggesting that Prozac led them to commit murder and other crimes. Popular belief that Prozac could perfect otherwise normal personalities waned, but the use of the drug did not.

BIBLIOGRAPHY

Kramer, Peter D. *Listening to Prozac.* New York: Penguin, 1997.

Wurtzel, Elizabeth. *Prozac Nation: Young & Depressed in America.* New York: Riverhead Books. 1995.

Loren Butler Feffer

See also **Mental Illness.**

PSYCHIATRY. Psychiatry, a branch of medicine, is a discipline that takes the full range of human behaviors, from severe mental illness to everyday worries and concerns, as its study. In the nineteenth century the discipline was largely concerned with the insane, with the mentally ill sequestered in large custodial asylums located largely in rural areas; as a result, psychiatrists were cut off from medicine's main currents. In the early twentieth century, under the leadership of such men as Adolf Meyer and E. E. Southard, psychiatry expanded to address both the pathological and the normal, with questions associated with schizophrenia at the one extreme and problems in living at the other. Psychiatrists aligned their specialty more closely with scientific medicine and argued for its relevance in solving a range of social problems, including poverty and industrial unrest, as well as mental illness. Psychiatry's expanded scope brought it greater social authority and prestige, while at the same time intermittently spawning popular denunciations of its "imperialist" ambitions. The discipline's standards were tightened, and, in 1921, its professional organization, formerly the American Medico-Psychological Association, was refounded as the American Psychiatric Association. In 1934, the American Board of Psychiatry and Neurology was established to provide certification for practitioners in both fields.

Over the course of the twentieth century, psychiatry was not only criticized from without but also split from within. Psychiatrists debated whether the origins of mental illness were to be found in the structure and chemistry of the brain or in the twists and turns of the mind. They divided themselves into competing, often warring, biological and psychodynamic camps. Psychodymanic psychiatry, an amalgam of Sigmund Freud's new science of psychoanalysis and homegrown American interest in a range of healing therapies, was largely dominant through the early 1950s. From the moment of its introduction following Freud's 1909 visit to Clark University, psychoanalysis enjoyed a warm reception in America. By 1920, scores of books and articles explaining its principles had appeared, and Freudian concepts such as the unconscious, repression, and displacement entered popular discourse. The dramatic growth of private-office based psychiatry in the 1930s and 1940s went hand in hand with psychoanalysis's growing importance; by the early 1950s, 40 percent of American psychiatrists practiced in private settings, and 25 percent of them practiced psychotherapy exclusively. The scope and authority of dynamic psychiatry were further expanded in World War II. Nearly two million American recruits were rejected from the services on neuropsychiatric grounds, and the experience of combat produced more than one million psychiatric casualties—young men suffering from combat neuroses. Only one hundred of the nations' three thousand psychiatrists were psychoanalysts, yet they were appointed to many of the top service posts. The prominent psychoanalyst William Menninger, for example, was made chief psychiatrist to the army in 1943, and he appointed four psychoanalysts to his staff. The immediate postwar period was psychodynamic psychiatry's heyday, with major departments of psychiatry headed by analysts and talk of the unconscious and repression the common coin of the educated middle class.

The cultural cachet of psychoanalysis notwithstanding, most psychiatric patients were institutional inmates, diagnosed as seriously disturbed psychotics. The numbers of persons admitted nationwide to state hospitals increased by 67 percent between 1922 and 1944, from fifty-two thousand to seventy-nine thousand. Critics charged psychiatrists with incompetence, neglect, callousness, and abuse. Both desperation and therapeutic optimism led psychiatrists to experiment with biological therapies, among them electroconvulsive shock therapy (ECT) and lobotomy. ECT was introduced to enthusiastic acclaim by the Italian psychiatrists Ugo Cerletti and Lucio Bini in 1938. Within several years it was in use in 40 percent of American psychiatric hospitals. Prefrontal lobotomy, first performed by the Portuguese neurologist Egas Moniz in 1935, involved drilling holes in patients' heads and severing the connections between the prefrontal lobes and other parts of the brain. More than eighteen thousand patients were lobotomized in the United States between 1936 and 1957. Psychosurgery promised to bring psychiatrists status and respect, offering the hope of a cure to the five hundred thousand chronically ill patients housed in overcrowded, dilapidated institutions. Instead, it was instrumental in sparking, in the 1960s and 1970s, a popular antipsychiatry movement that criticized psychiatry as an insidious form of social control based on a pseudomedical model.

Biological psychiatry entered the modern era with the discovery of the first of the antipsychotic drugs, chlorpromazine, in 1952. For the first time, psychiatrists had a means to treat the debilitating symptoms of schizophrenia—hallucinations, delusions, and thought disorders. Pharmacological treatments for mania and depression soon followed, and psychiatrists heralded the dawn of a new "psychopharmacological era" that continues to this day. The introduction, in the 1990s, of Prozac®, used to treat depression as well as personality disorders, brought renewed attention to biological psychiatry. The once-dominant psychodynamic model, based on the efficacy of talk, fell into disrepute, even though studies showed that the best outcomes were obtained through a combination of drug and talk therapies. The profession, divided for much of the century, united around the 1980 publication of the third edition of the American Psychiatric Association's *Diagnostic and Statistical Manual of Mental Disorders* (DSM-III), psychiatry's official manual of nomenclature that endorsed a descriptive, nondynamic orientation, thus signaling psychiatry's remedicalization.

Psychiatry has had to constantly establish its legitimacy within and beyond medicine. Despite enormous advances in the understanding and treatment of mental illness, in the mid-1990s psychiatry was one of the three lowest-paid medical specialties (along with primary care and pediatrics). Psychiatry's success has spurred increased demand for services. But with increasing pressure on health-care costs, and with the widespread adoption of managed care, psychiatry—that part of it organized around talk—has seemed expendable, a form of self-indulgence for the worried well that society cannot afford. Insurers have cut coverage for mental health, and psychologists and social workers have argued that they can offer psychotherapy as ably as, and more cheaply than, psychiatrists, putting pressure on psychiatrists to argue for the legitimacy of their domination of the mental health provider hierarchy. In this, psychopharmacological treatments have been critical, for only psychiatrists, who are medical doctors, among the therapeutic specialties have the authority to prescribe drugs. Advances in the understanding of the severe psychoses that afflict the chronically mentally ill continue to unfold, fueling optimism about psychiatry's future and insuring its continuing relevance.

BIBLIOGRAPHY

Grob, Gerald N. *Mental Illness and American Society, 1875–1940.* Princeton, N.J.: Princeton University Press, 1983.

Healy, David. *The Antidepressant Era.* Cambridge, Mass.: Harvard University Press, 1997.

Valenstein, Elliot S. *Great and Desperate Cures: The Rise and Decline of Psychosurgery and Other Radical Treatments for Mental Illness.* New York: Basic Books, 1986.

Elizabeth A. Lunbeck

See also **Mental Illness; Psychology.**

PSYCHOLOGICAL WARFARE. Joshua's trumpets at the battle of Jericho suggest that psychological warfare, also called *psywar,* is probably as old as warfare itself. Nonetheless, only during World War I did the major powers designate official agencies to oversee this effort, the first example of organized psychological warfare. The U.S. Committee on Public Information, otherwise known as the Creel Committee, marked the United States's foray into formal propaganda activities. In quite a different application, the propaganda section of the American Expeditionary Forces staff headquarters represented the first official U.S. experiment in the military use of psychological warfare.

Psychological warfare aims to complement, not supplant, military operations. It breaks down into two broad categories. First, strategic psychological warfare usually targets the enemy in its entirety: troops, civilians, and enemy-occupied areas. Second, tactical psychological warfare most commonly supports localized combat operations by fostering uncertainty and dissension, and sometimes causing the enemy to surrender.

American World War I psychological warfare techniques appear primitive by later standards. Following the lead of the British and French, the United States used the leaflet as the primary vehicle for the delivery of messages intended to demoralize the enemy and to encourage surrender. Hedgehoppers, balloons, and, to a lesser degree, modified mortar shells delivered these messages to the target audience. The goal was to alienate the German troops from their "militarist" and "antidemocratic" regimes. Later, the Nazis suggested that the World War I German army had not lost that conflict but instead that Allied propaganda had victimized it.

Psychological warfare activities fell into abeyance during the interwar period and did not resume until World War II. At that time the American government set up hastily improvised propaganda agencies, which jealously fought over spheres of interest and mission assignments. This infighting continued until the creation of the Office of War Information (OWI) and the Office of Strategic Services (OSS). On 9 March 1943, Executive Order 9312 redefined their respective functions.

On the theater level psychological warfare operations differed widely from one command to another because Executive Order 9312 required commander approval for all plans and projects. Under Gen. Dwight D. Eisenhower a joint British and American military staff, in cooperation with such propaganda agencies as the OWI and the OSS, managed all Allied psychological warfare activities. In the Pacific commands and subcommands, there were varying degrees of official acceptance for psychological warfare. Adm. William F. Halsey's command stood as the sole exception to this rule because he would have nothing to do with psychological warfare and would not allow OWI and OSS civilians to have clearances for this area. As the war progressed, this unconventional weapon of war slowly won grudging official approval and a place on the staffs of Pacific commands. Leaflets were by far the most prevalent means of delivery, but propaganda agencies also employed loudspeaker and radio broadcasts. The American military has continued to use increasingly sophisticated psychological warfare in more recent conflicts, such as the Korean War, the Vietnam War, and the Persian Gulf War.

BIBLIOGRAPHY

Katz, Barry M. *Foreign Intelligence: Research and Analysis in the Office of Strategic Services, 1942–1945*. Cambridge, Mass.: Harvard University Press, 1989.

Simpson, Christopher. *Science of Coercion: Communication Research and Psychological Warfare, 1945–1960*. New York: Oxford University Press, 1994.

Vaughn, Stephen. *Holding Fast the Inner Lines: Democracy, Nationalism, and the Committee on Public Information*. Chapel Hill: University of North Carolina Press, 1980.

Winkler, Allan M. *The Politics of Propaganda: The Office of War Information, 1942–1945*. New Haven, Conn.: Yale University Press, 1978.

Don E. McLeod/A. E.

See also **Committee on Public Information; Federal Agencies; Intelligence, Military and Strategic.**

PSYCHOLOGY. At the turn of the twentieth century, the German psychologist Hermann Ebbinghaus remarked that "psychology has a long past, but only a short history." He was referring to recent scientific interest in the experimental study of the mind and behavior that was characteristic of the "new" psychology. Beginning with a few laboratories in Germany and the America in the late nineteenth century, the field of psychology grew significantly throughout the twentieth century, especially in the United States. Psychological terms have infiltrated everyday language, a huge mental health industry has arisen, and psychological tests have become ubiquitous. Psychology is embedded in modern life. How are we to define this protean field and to explain its rise?

Interest in understanding and explaining human nature and actions is as old as the first stirrings of self-consciousness among humans. Western philosophy has a long tradition of thinking about causes and consequences of human action, both individual and social. Within that general field, psychology has drawn particularly from scholarship on ethics (i.e., moral rules of conduct) and epistemology (theory of the method or grounds of knowledge).

The advent of modern scientific inquiry and methodology in the seventeenth century transformed European culture as it spread to philosophical comprehension and technological practice during the Enlightenment in the eighteenth century. By the nineteenth century, science had become a legitimate and growing profession; the physical world, biology, and society became subject to scientific scrutiny.

Modern psychology as a discipline formed during this period. Psychology's conceptual roots can be found in the experimental laboratories of physiologists, in the medical practices of asylums and clinics, and in the statistical manipulations of mathematicians.

After 1870, college students in the United States gradually became aware of the "new" psychology: William James, a professor at Harvard University, introduced theories of mind and demonstrated empirical findings with a collection of so-called "brass instruments," borrowed from laboratories of physics and physiology. James wrote the classic *Principles of Psychology* in 1890.

James was associated with the functionalist school, which studied the mind's adaptation to its environment. Habits, consciousness, and the self were understood as adaptive functions, not as structural elements of the mind. The influence of Charles Darwin was evident in the functionalists' interest in evolutionary processes; they investigated the development of mind and behavior in other species as well as humans. Between 1870 and 1910, many students from the United States traveled to Germany to study. Attracted by low travel costs and inexpensive accommodations as well as the reputation of German universities, students were exposed to the ideas and practices of scholars such as Wilhelm Wundt, professor of philosophy at the University of Leipzig. A founder of modern psychology, Wundt wrote voluminously on psychology as an independent academic discipline and, in 1879, established the first psychological laboratory.

Conceptually, Wundt espoused a broad view of scientific psychology, ranging from individual psychophysiology and mental chronometry to human language and culture. Different topics needed different research methods. For instance, when measuring the speed of the nervous impulse, accurate mechanical timers gave readings of 1/1,000 of a second; when a colored light was used as a stimulus for a psychophysics experiment, precise introspection provided qualitative judgments about the light's color, intensity, and other characteristics; when religious practices were being investigated, historical and comparative methods of textual analysis were employed.

Wundt and James, both nonpracticing medical doctors, were recognized leaders of the new psychology; in Vienna, another physician, Sigmund Freud, was developing his own system of psychology and psychotherapy, which he called psychoanalysis. His system was spread through an apprentice method of "training analysis" before the psychotherapist began a private practice. Psychoanalysis in America became associated with the medical profession, developing separately from academic psychology.

An American Science

Fresh from their exposure to the new psychology, graduates adapted laboratory techniques and intellectual agendas to the rapidly changing landscape of higher education in the United States. During the last quarter of the nineteenth century, the research ideal was fused with values of social utility and liberal culture to give rise to the modern university. In 1876, only one university, Johns Hopkins, offered graduate instruction leading to the Ph.D.; by 1900, scores of institutions offered doctoral level studies and degrees.

More than forty psychological laboratories had been established in U.S. colleges and universities by 1900. Experimental work concentrated on sensation and perception, using the reaction-time method where a stimulus was presented to a subject and the speed of response was accurately measured. Professors published their research findings in the *American Journal of Psychology* beginning in 1887, the *Psychological Review* beginning in 1894, or other scientific periodicals. The field grew rapidly in American universities and colleges. The American Psychological Association (APA), a professional body dedicated to the advancement of psychology as a science, was formed in 1892, with 26 charter members. Psychologists were also active in the child-study movement and in trying to advance the art and science of pedagogy, newly significant with the rise of universal education. Differences in theory and methods gave rise to schools of thought (structuralism, functionalism, BEHAVIORISM, Gestalt, etc.) that were more apparent to insiders than to the public.

Applications of psychology and psychological theory to education expanded significantly with the spread of mental tests. Starting in 1905, French psychologist Alfred Binet published scales on testing for intelligence in children. Stanford University psychologist Lewis Terman subsequently revised the tests and included the ratio of mental and chronological ages, resulting in the "Intelligence Quotient" (IQ). In 1916 the "Stanford-Binet" debuted. Mental tests were widely used in World War I to classify soldiers for general intelligence and occupational specialties. After the war, personnel psychology, particularly in business and industry, became a recognized specialty.

By 1929, at the start of the Great Depression, psychology was firmly institutionalized in higher education. Although the APA reached 1,000 members that year, during the 1930s its dominance diminished as psychologists founded new organizations to pursue their scientific and professional interests. Occupational trends led to a split between academic and applied psychologists, and to marked gender differences, with the majority of females confined to low-status jobs in nonacademic settings.

The "Age of Learning"

By the start of the 1930s, psychology had matured to the point that the discipline generated internally a system of scientific priorities, preferred methods of investigation, and complex reward arrangements. Experimental research was dominated by the use of behavioristic methods in the service of a general theory of learning. In a seminal article in 1913 published in the *Psychological Review*, "Psychology as the Behaviorist Views It," John B. Watson strongly urged psychologists not to look within at unseen mental processes, but to concentrate on observable behavior. Watson had earned his doctorate from the University of Chicago in 1903 with a thesis on rat psychology. Later investigators made the white rat a standard laboratory subject, and Watson's ideas were reformulated into a variety of neo-behavioristic perspectives.

Among the prominent neo-behaviorists was B. F. Skinner (who earned a doctorate from Harvard in 1931), who developed a theory of behavior known as "operant conditioning." In contrast to the "classical conditioning" associated with the Russian physiologist Ivan Pavlov in which a stimulus is substituted for an already existing response, operant conditioning focuses on a class of emitted responses that are followed by reinforcement. For example, a rat in a "Skinner box" (an apparatus with a lever to obtain food and/or water) presses the lever (the operant) and eats (reinforcement). With each trial, the rat is more likely to repeat the action (response strength). Through a series of ingenious experiments, Skinner demonstrated the scientific utility of his approach in the laboratory before later extending it to the realm of teaching machines, social engineering (with the 1948 utopian novel *Walden Two*), and an air-conditioned baby crib, all of which engendered controversy.

The Aftermath of World War II

World War II was a watershed for psychology in many ways. The war gave rise to the practice of clinical psychology that was strongly supported by the federal government. New techniques and tools borrowed from other disciplines transformed the intellectual life of psychology. Increased funds were available for scientific research; the number of psychologists grew dramatically; and the APA reorganized to include all areas of psychological activity under a federated governing system.

The academic psychology department remained the basic unit for research, education, and training. The G.I. Bill, a robust economy, and a widespread consensus on the positive value of a college degree helped usher in a "golden age." Psychology grew on the broadening foundation of undergraduate education.

The introductory course exhibited the diversity of psychology while presenting the prevailing orthodoxy of scientific professionalism. A new wave of undergraduate textbooks was written. For instance, Ernest R. Hilgard published *Introduction to Psychology* in 1953. Firmly based in the research literature, the book attempted comprehensive coverage of topics ranging from the nervous system to personal adjustment. One innovation in format was the use of sidebars to break up the main mass of text and provide additional details on selected topics. Successful textbooks often went through multiple revisions over the course of 30 or more years.

By the early 1960s, employment trends had shifted decisively to nonacademic settings, thus the majority of psychologists found work in hospitals, schools, clinics, corporations, and private practice. That led to increased concern over the professional aspects of psychology, including interprofessional relations with psychiatrists and social workers who were a part of the expanding mental health industry. Some psychologists took their message directly to the general public, contributing to the literature of lay psychology or to the robust market in self-help books. For instance, B. F. Skinner explained his system of operant conditioning to the general public, beginning in 1953 with *Science and Human Behavior*, and Carl R. Rogers introduced his approach to psychotherapy with the mass-market textbook *On Becoming a Person* in 1961.

The Rise of Cognitive Psychology

Perhaps the most striking intellectual development of the post–World War II period was the rise of cognitive psychology. Cognitive psychology covers the whole range of human mental activity, from sense perception to memory and thought. With deep roots in nineteenth-century research on attention, memory, and language, cognitive psychology developed an institutional focus at Harvard University's Center for Cognitive Studies starting in 1962. In an influential survey of the field, psychologist Ulric Neisser explained in *Cognitive Psychology* (1967) that the physical stimuli that an object produces "bear little resemblance to either the real object that gave rise to them or to the object of experience that the perceiver will construct as a result." It is this constructive activity that provided the foundation for cognitive psychology.

Closely allied with the study of cognition is mathematical psychology. Curve-fitting, mathematical modeling, and inferential statistics are used to explain experimental results as well as a source for theory construction. By the early 1950s coursework in the analysis of variance became a common feature of graduate training in the United States. Its routine use, standardized and codified in textbooks, meant that psychologists did not have to understand the complexities of statistics to apply them to their work.

Statistics were useful in addressing quantitatively the inconsistencies of individual human behavior. People behaved differently at different times, and what they did in one experimental setting might have little relation to what they did in another. Statistical treatment of group data combined data from many individuals, enabling certain patterns to emerge that were characteristic of the statistical group, even though the actual behavior of any particular member of the group might not conform to the statistical "average."

Mainstream psychology was not without its critics. Some urged turning away from apparent "methodolatry," while others descried the "physics envy" that grew out of attempts to emulate the physical (and precisely measurable) sciences. A movement toward humanistic psychology was prompted by dissatisfaction with behaviorism's narrow methods and the psychoanalytic focus on childhood pathology. This so-called "third force" represented an attempt to place human values at the core of psychological theory and practice rather than mechanical virtues or developmental doctrine.

At the close of the twentieth century, psychology remains a protean discipline dedicated to the pursuit of scientific knowledge as well as a potent profession serving the mental health needs of Americans. Neither a single set of assumptions nor a common methodology unites the work of psychologists. How psychologists prospered by exploiting this diversity is an intriguing area for historical investigation.

History of Psychology

Psychologists and others have exhibited a sustained interest in the history of the field since the rise of the "new" psychology. In his three-volume *A History of Psychology* (1912–1921), George Sidney Brett traced the philosophical background of modern psychological thought, from the ancient Greeks to his day. Edwin G. Boring, considering Brett's work too philosophical, was motivated to write *A History of Experimental Psychology* in 1929; Boring argued for the primacy of scientific research, saying "The application of the experimental method to the problem of mind is the great outstanding event in the history of the study of mind" (p. 659). Boring's book became the veritable Bible for courses in the history and systems of psychology. History was also used as a resource for asserting the unity of psychology despite the proliferation of diverse viewpoints.

After World War II, the history of psychology was pursued for two decades mostly as a teaching subject within psychology departments. In the mid-1960s the field became increasingly professionalized with new university programs starting and the APA founding a history division. A specialized journal, *Journal of the History of the Behavioral Science* (1965), and a society, Chiron: The International Society for the History of the Behavioral and Social Sciences (1969), provided support for scholars. In addition, professional historians, notably historians of science and medicine, grew more interested in and paid more attention to the history of psychology.

In 1966, Robert M. Young published a scathing review of the literature in the history of psychology and related fields in the journal *History of Science.* Since that time, scholarship in the history of psychology has steadily deepened. Developments in the late twentieth century included the establishment of the Forum for History of Human Science, a special-interest group of the History of Science Society formed in 1988, and an APA-sponsored journal, *History of Psychology* established in 1998.

In the pages of an 1893 *McClure's* magazine, Herbert Nichols, one of the first students awarded a doctorate in psychology from an American university, boldly predicted that "the twentieth century will be to mental science what the sixteenth century was to physical science, and the central field of its development is likely to be America." In broad outline, Nichols's prediction came true. But the road leading from the era of brass instruments and introspection to the age of computers and cognitive science proved to be both long and with many byways. World wars, economic depression as well as prosperity, and the rise of American higher education provided the setting and context for the growth of psychological thought and practice. Psychology today is intellectually multiparadigmatic, professionally pluralistic, and ideologically diverse. Psychologists, more than a quarter million strong in the United States, have had and continue to have a tremendous impact on the culture of modern science.

BIBLIOGRAPHY

Boring, Edwin G. *A History of Experimental Psychology.* 2d ed. New York: Appleton-Century-Crofts, 1950. An influential account by a prominent psychologist-historian.

Burnham, John C. "On the Origins of Behaviorism." *Journal of the History of the Behavioral Sciences* 4 (1968): 143–151. The classic statement of the historical problem of behaviorism.

Capshew, James H. *Psychologists on the March: Science, Practice, and Professional Identity in American Psychology, 1929–1969.* New York: Cambridge University Press, 1999. A study of the impact of World War II on the profession of psychology.

Danziger, Kurt. *Constructing the Subject: Historical Origins of Psychological Research.* New York: Cambridge University Press, 1990. A penetrating account of the standardization of methodology and the resultant conceptual and professional power it generated.

Hale, Nathan G., Jr. *Freud in America.* 2 vols. New York: Oxford University Press, 1971–1995. A judicious and balanced historical narrative.

Heidbreder, Edna. *Seven Psychologies.* New York: Century, 1933. A sensitive contemporary account of the major schools of psychology.

Herman, Ellen. *The Romance of American Psychology: Political Culture in the Age of Experts.* Berkeley: University of California Press, 1995. A nuanced examination of the role of psychology in public affairs and policy from 1940 to 1975.

Hilgard, Ernest H. *Psychology in America: A Historical Survey.* San Diego: Harcourt Brace Jovanovich, 1987. An authoritative encyclopedic survey.

O'Donnell, John M. *The Origins of Behaviorism: American Psychology, 1870–1920.* New York: New York University Press, 1985. An analytic narrative focused on the transition from philosophy to psychology.

Smith, Roger. *The Norton History of the Human Sciences.* New York: Norton, 1997. Psychology is the backbone of this massive and informative synthesis that ranges from sixteenth-century thought to twentieth-century American institutions.

Sokal, Michael M., ed. *Psychological Testing and American Society, 1890–1930.* New Brunswick, N.J.: Rutgers University Press, 1987. Essays that explore the construction, use, and impact of mental testing.

James H. Capshew

See also **Intelligence Tests; Psychiatry.**

"PUBLIC BE DAMNED." On Sunday afternoon, 8 October 1882, as a New York Central Railroad train bearing W. H. Vanderbilt, president of the railroad, approached Chicago, two newspaper reporters boarded the train and interviewed Vanderbilt on various aspects of the railroad industry. In the course of the interview, Vanderbilt was asked whether he planned to match the "express passenger" service just inaugurated by the Pennsylvania Railroad. Vanderbilt remarked that such service was unprofitable; answering a follow-up question about "the public benefit," he is reported to have replied, "The public be damned." Vanderbilt later claimed that "both my words and ideas are misreported and misrepresented." Publication of the interview caused widespread critical comment.

Thomas Robson Hay / T. G.

See also **"Full Dinner Pail"; Locomotives; Pujo Committee; Railroads; Trust-Busting; Yellow Journalism.**

PUBLIC CREDIT ACT. The Public Credit Act was a federal statute enacted after Alexander Hamilton's "First Report on the Public Credit" of 14 January 1790. The act provided for the payment of the government's obligations at par with interest (except that Continental currency was to be redeemed at a hundred to one in specie); the assumption of state debts for services or supplies during the American Revolution; and the authorization of loans to meet these obligations. The act was approved 4 August 1790. The act helped get the support of security holders for the new government.

BIBLIOGRAPHY

Ferguson, E. James. *The Power of the Purse: A History of American Public Finance, 1776–1790.* Chapel Hill: University of North Carolina Press, 1961.

James D. Magee / A. R.

See also **Confederation; Money; Revolution, Financing of the.**

PUBLIC DOMAIN. The public domain differs from national domain and acquired land. National domain arises from political jurisdiction while the federal government either buys acquired land or receives it as gifts for national parks, monuments, forests, wildlife refuges, post-office sites, and other such purposes. Cessions of their western land claims by Massachusetts, Connecticut, New York, Virginia, North Carolina, South Carolina, and Georgia, seven of the original thirteen states, created the first portion of the public domain or public land. These seven states retained the ungranted land within their present boundaries as did the other original states and Maine, Vermont, West Virginia, Kentucky, Tennessee, and Texas. Between 1802 and 1867, huge additions to the national domain and the public domain occurred through the Louisiana Purchase in 1803, the Florida Purchase in 1819, the annexation of Texas in 1845 and the Texas cession of 1850, the division of the Oregon country in 1846, the huge purchase from Mexico in 1848, the Gadsden Purchase of 1853, the purchase of Alaska in 1867, and the annexation of Hawaii in 1898 (see Table 1).

TABLE 1

Summary of Accessions of the United States

	National Domain (acres)	Public Domain (acres)
Area conceded by Great Britain in 1783 and by the Convention of 1818 (Lake of the Woods boundary)	525,452,800	
Cessions of seven states to the United States		233,415,680
Louisiana Purchase (1803)	523,446,400	523,446,400*
Florida Purchase (1819)	43,342,720	43,342,720*
Red River Basin (Webster-Ashburton Treaty, 1842)	29,066,880	29,066,880
Annexation of Texas (1845)	247,050,480	
Oregon Compromise (1846)	180,644,480	180,644,480
Treaty With Mexico (1848)	334,479,360	334,479,360*
Purchase From Texas (1850)		78,842,880
Gadsden Purchase (1853)	18,961,920	18,961,920*
Alaska Purchase (1867)	365,481,600	365,481,600
Hawaiian Annexation (1898)	3,110,820	

* Between 40 million and 50 million acres included in the public domain were in private claims of land granted by Great Britain, France, Spain, and Mexico, which when proved valid were patented and were not subject to disposal by the United States.

From the outset, there were two views concerning the policy that should govern the disposal of the public lands. The first, sponsored by Alexander Hamilton, was that the government's need of money to retire its Revolutionary War debt and to meet its expenses required it to pledge the public domain for the payment of that debt and to extract from it the greatest possible income. The other view, held by Thomas Jefferson, was that farmer-owners with a stake in the land made the most responsible citizens and that they should have easy access to the public lands at little cost. Hamilton's view prevailed for a time, and Jefferson, who yielded to necessity, reluctantly accepted it. The basic established price varied from $1.00 to $2.00 per acre until 1820, when credit was abolished and the minimum price became $1.25 per acre. This may not have been a high price to the investors Hamilton hoped would purchase large tracts of land, but to frontier settlers lacking capital or credit, it was more than they could raise. Their solution was to squat on public land, improve it, and try to raise a crop or two to make their payments before the government discovered their trespass. Squatters wanted protection against speculators who might try to buy their somewhat improved tracts. Squatters protected themselves through claim associations, which provided mutual assistance to all members. Nonetheless, the squatters also wanted the legal recognition of their right of preemption; that is, a prior right to purchase their claim before auction at the minimum price, without having to bid against speculators. They won a number of special preemption acts and in 1841 sustained a major victory with the adoption of the Distribution-Preemption Act, which permitted persons to settle anywhere on surveyed land in advance of its official opening; to improve the land; and, when the auction was announced, to purchase up to 160 acres at the minimum price of $1.25 an acre. Squatterism had thus prevailed, and a major breach in the revenue policy occurred.

In 1854 the Graduation Act provided a further breach by reducing the price of land that had been on the market for ten or more years in proportion to the length of time it had been subject to sale. In 1862 the West gained its major triumph in the Homestead Act, which made public lands free to settlers who would live on and improve tracts of up to 160 acres for five years. Unfortunately, a substantial portion of the best arable lands had already been alienated through sale to speculators, grants to states, and direct grants to corporations to aid in the construction of canals and railroads. These new owners sold all this land for the market price, which was beyond the reach of many pioneer settlers.

Individual speculators and land companies invested heavily in land during boom periods, 1816–1819, 1833–1837, and 1853–1857. By anticipating settlers, investors, as well as land grant railroads and states, raised the cost of farmmaking; dispersed population widely on the frontier; delayed the introduction of roads, churches, and transportation facilities; contributed to the early appearance of tenancy; aggravated relations with the Indians; and in some regions, were responsible for the development of rural slums. On the other hand, they provided credit to hard-pressed pioneers, aided in bringing settlers to the West through their advertising and promotional works, and introduced improved farming techniques that by example contributed to better agricultural practices. At the time, public attention centered on the damaging effects of intrusions by speculators and led to demands for the limitation in the sale of public land and the halt to further grants to railroads. After the adoption of the Homestead Act, little newly surveyed land became available for unlimited purchase although unsold land that had been offered previously continued to be subject to unrestricted entry.

Farmers in the High Plains west of the ninety-ninth meridian, where the annual rainfall was less than 20 inches and where a portion of the land had to be left fallow each year, needed more than 160 or even 320 acres for the extensive cultivation that was necessary. Congress met this difficulty by increasing the quantity that farmmakers could acquire by enacting the Timber Culture Act of 1873, the Desert Land Act of 1877, and the Timber and Stone Act of 1878. Combined with the Preemption and Homestead acts, these measures permitted individuals to acquire up to 1,120 acres in the semiarid High Plains and in the intermountain and desert regions. Like all poorly drafted land legislation, the acts became subject to gross abuse by grasping persons anxious to engross as much land as possible through the use of dummy entry people and roving, uprooted people willing to serve their ends.

Growing criticism of the abuse of the settlement laws and the laxity of the land administration led in 1889–1891 to the adoption of a series of measures to restrict total acquisition of public lands under all laws to 320 acres, to halt all purchases of potential agricultural lands other than those specifically intended for farmmaking, and to eliminate or insert additional safeguards in acts most subject to abuse.

Notwithstanding the extensive abuse of the land system and its incongruous features that somewhat minimized the effectiveness of the measures designed to aid homesteaders in becoming farm owners, the public land states enjoyed a remarkable growth rate. In the 1850s, the first decade for which there are statistics, 401,000 new farms sprang up in the public land states. Thereafter, the number grew even more rapidly. By 1890 settlers had established an additional 2 million farms in the public land states. Never before had so many farmers subjected such a large area to cultivation.

The censuses of 1880 and 1890, giving alarming figures of mortgage debt outstanding on farms and the high proportion of farms that were tenant-operated, combined with the growing feeling that soils, minerals, and forests were being wastefully used, turned people's thoughts to further reform in land management and to conservation. Instead of a policy of transferring all public lands to individuals, railroads, and states as rapidly as possible, Congress determined to retain a portion of the land in public ownership. To this end, an amendment to the General Revision Act of 1891 authorized the president to withdraw from public entry forest lands on which organized management policies could be introduced. Under President Theodore Roosevelt's leadership, gross withdrawals reached nearly 160 million acres.

Next in the planned use of the natural resources by government was the Reclamation Act (Newlands Act) of 1902, which provided that the income from the sale of public lands be used for construction of high dams on western rivers to store water for the irrigation of dry lands and thus to provide for a new farmers' frontier. With supplementary appropriations for construction of dams, the government gave an enormous boon to the development of the eleven far western states, but the provisions of the act that aimed to make small farmers the major beneficiaries have proved ineffective. Instead, large individual and corporate owners have derived the greatest returns.

In 1916 the National Park Service came into existence to administer areas of superlative natural beauty that the federal government was setting aside from the public lands as permanent reserves: Yosemite, Yellowstone, Hot Springs, Glacier, Sequoia, Mount Rainier, Grand Canyon, and Crater Lake. Thus, curiousity seekers and commercials interests could not despoil these and other places of outstanding aesthetic, geologic, and historical interest.

Rapid and unscientific exploitation of mineral lands by destructive and wasteful practices induced Roosevelt to order the withdrawal of 66 million acres suspected of containing valuable coal deposits and a smaller acreage of suspected oil-bearing land. Lands having coal, potash, phosphate, and nitrate deposits also gained protection, although the surface rights might remain alienable. In 1920 the Mineral Leasing Act provided some control over the exploitation of these withdrawn lands for the first time. Moreover, as a sweetener to the West, it allocated 37.5 percent of the proceeds from leasing to the states in which the lands were located and 57.5 percent to reclamation projects, thereby ensuring a principal and growing source of funds for such projects. The remaining 5 percent went to the states in which lands were allocated for schools.

Roosevelt's conservation-minded advisers, notably Gifford Pinchot, also persuaded him to withdraw 3.45 million acres of public lands as possible sources for power sites. The Water Power Act of 1920 authorized a system of licensing the power sites, but it was not until the 1930s and 1940s that the federal government undertook great hydroelectric power development.

The last important withdrawal of public lands from entry took place in 1934. The harmful effects of overgrazing on the ranges of the West had become so evident that even the livestock industry recognized the need to accept federal control. This withdrawal provided that in the future, the remaining grazing lands in public ownership were to be leased under close supervision. To administer these lands, the federal government set up a Division of Grazing in the U.S. Department of the Interior. Congress preferred to create a new administrative agency rather than to permit the Forest Service, which had gained much valuable experience in administering the range lands within the national forests, because this latter agency had shown independence as well as excellent judgment in protecting its lands. The Division of Grazing started off well, but it also ran into bitter opposition for its failure to play politics. Congress virtually starved it by inadequate appropriations and later consolidated it with the General Land Office in the Bureau of Land Management (BLM). Before 1976 the BLM struggled to administer the land under its control following hundreds of separate and sometimes contradictory laws. In that year, however, Congress passed the Federal Land Policy and Management Act (FLPMA), which presented the BLM with its first coherent, unified mission. This piece of legislation overturned the Homestead Act and instructed the BLM to administer the public domain in accordance to the concept of multiple use management. This legislative mandate empowered the BLM to balance as it deemed best the commercial use of public lands, such as through mining and grazing, with environmental protection of the public domain and maintenance of the lands for recreational use.

Over a century and a half of unparalleled prodigality in managing the public domain had made possible the alienation of most of the best agricultural, forest, and mineral lands of the United States, but there still remains a noble fragment in federal ownership under organized management. By 2002, the Bureau of Land Management was administering just over 260 million acres of land, which equals about 13 percent of the total area of the United States. Most of these public lands are in the western states, including Alaska, which presents the BLM with one of its most pressing contemporary problems. This region of the United States has witnessed remarkable population growth in the last few decades. For instance, Nevada, where the federal government administers the highest percentage of land, 67 percent, of any state, also experienced the largest population explosion of any state, an increase of over 66 percent between 1990 and 2000. In response to such pressures, during both of his terms in office, President Bill Clinton took advantage of the powers granted to presidents by the Antiquities Act of 1906 to create numerous new national monuments out of land formerly part of the public domain. No consumptive activities, such as mining or logging, may take place in national monuments. Clinton's administration defended this tactic as a necessary, emergency step to protect threatened natural treasures while critics interpreted it as a way for the Democratic president to bypass potential opposition from a Republican-led Congress and unilaterally make decisions in which the public should have had a voice. Either way, the BLM clearly must develop less controversial yet still effective methods of protecting the public domain in western states while also making it available as a commercial and recreational resource for a burgeoning population.

BIBLIOGRAPHY

Durant, Robert F. *The Administrative Presidency Revisited: Public Lands, the BLM, and the Reagan Revolution.* Albany: State University of New York Press, 1992.

Feller, Daniel. *The Public Lands in Jacksonian Politics.* Madison: University of Wisconsin Press, 1984.

Goodman, Doug, and Daniel McCool, eds. *Contested Landscape: The Politics of Wilderness in Utah and the West.* Salt Lake City: University of Utah Press, 1999.

Lehmann, Scott. *Privatizing Public Lands.* New York: Oxford University Press, 1995.

Oberly, James Warren. *Sixty Million Acres: American Veterans and the Public Lands before the Civil War.* Kent, Ohio: Kent State University Press, 1990.

Robbins, William G., and James C. Foster, eds. *Land in the American West: Private Claims and the Common Good.* Seattle: University of Washington Press, 2000.

Paul W. Gates / A. E.

See also **Conservation; Interior, Department of the; Land Acts; Land Office, U.S. General and Bureau of Plans Management; Land Policy; Land Speculation; National Park System; Public Land Commissions; School Lands; Western Lands.**

PUBLIC HEALTH. *See* **Epidemics and Public Health.**

PUBLIC INTEREST LAW. The term "public interest law" describes a type of practice of law, carried out under the auspices of a nonprofit organization, in which the focus of the lawyer's work is the issues presented. It contrasts with civil and criminal legal aid or defense where the focus is on achieving justice for the individual client. Most of the work in public interest law is in civil rather than criminal cases, although the latter sometimes present issues that have broad application, such as a First Amendment defense to a charge of failing to obtain a permit for a demonstration.

The first group that can be said to have practiced public interest law is the American Civil Liberties Union, which was founded in 1920. Its principal mission has been to safeguard individual liberties, largely those found in the Bill of Rights. It has local offices in every state, and it employs both staff attorneys and volunteer lawyers to advance its goals. Its fidelity to the value of civil liberties, regardless of who is asserting them, is illustrated by its decision to defend the nazis who were denied a permit for a parade in Skokie, Illinois, where there was a very substantial Jewish population, including Holocaust victims.

Another early practitioner of public interest law is the National Association for the Advancement of Colored People, which undertook a systematic, long-term project to eliminate segregation in education and public accommodations through the court system. It took a very strategic approach, taking on the easiest cases first, and working slowly toward its major victory in *Brown v. Board of Education* (1954), which outlawed segregated schools.

Following these models, other organizations began to use similar approaches, focusing particularly on the failures of federal agencies to protect the public from the companies that Congress had told the agencies to regulate. Until that time, only a regulated company could go to court to challenge an agency's decision, which increased the likelihood that the agency would side with the industry. In the late 1960s, the courts accepted the notion that the intended beneficiaries of a law should also be able to sue the agency that enforces it, which made it possible for public interest groups to use the judicial system to redress the balance that had been created by agency capture by the regulated industries. Among the major interests that took advantage of this change in access to the courts were radio and television listeners, as well as consumers who were unhappy over the regulation of products ranging from unhealthy food and unsafe drugs to defective and risky consumer goods. In addition to direct challenges to an agency decision, the passage of the Freedom of Information Act, which makes available agency records to the public (with certain exceptions), and other related open-government laws has also been a source of significant public interest pressure on the agencies.

Perhaps the most significant area of new public interest law was the environment. Some of this growth was due to the recognition of a right to sue under existing laws, but much of it was based on new substantive laws governing pesticides, clean air, and clean water, plus the National Environmental Protection Act, which, for the first time, required all federal agencies to consider the environmental impacts of their decisions. Although much of the environmental work involved the courts, the efforts of environmental groups (and other public interest organizations as well) also focused on what the agencies were doing in reaching their decisions, as well as on how Congress writes and amends the law.

Federal agencies have not been the exclusive concern of public interest lawyers. They have worked in a wide variety of areas, such as reforming the legal and other professions; preventing abuses in class actions; protecting rights secured by the First Amendment in a variety of contexts; assisting dissidents in labor unions who are denied federally guaranteed rights by union leaders; promoting campaign finance reform; and protecting the rights of victims to sue companies that have injured them.

Because most clients of public interest organizations cannot afford to pay for legal services, and because most public interest cases do not involve claims that produce a sum of money from which a lawyer can take a portion as a fee, other methods must be used to fund public interest law firms. These include membership dues and other contributions, foundation grants, and, under certain statutes, awards of attorneys fees paid by the defendant. By contrast, legal aid for those accused of crimes is paid for by the government (although often at very low rates), and civil legal aid is partially government funded and partially supported by individuals and foundations. Raising money for public interest law firms is a major barrier to increasing their activities and in competing for legal talent in a marketplace where law firm salaries are greater by a factor of three or more.

BIBLIOGRAPHY

Aron, Nan. *Liberty and Justice for All: Public Interest Law in the 1980s and Beyond.* Boulder, Colo.: Westview Press, 1989.

Baum, Robert A. *Public Interest Law: Where Law Meets Social Action.* New York: Oceana Publications, 1987.

Epstein, Lee, et al., eds. *Public Interest Law: An Annotated Bibliography and Research Guide.* New York: Garland, 1992.

Alan B. Morrison

See also **American Civil Liberties Union; Consumer Protection; National Association for the Advancement of Colored People.**

PUBLIC LAND COMMISSIONS have been established on four occasions by the United States government to review federal land policies and to make recommendations for their improvement or redirection. In 1879 Congress authorized the first of them. At that time there was widespread abuse of the settlement laws, corruption prevailed in the local land offices and in the awarding of lucrative surveying contracts, the General Land Office was understaffed and far behind in its work, and a mass of conflicting land laws and administrative orders required revision. Five distinguished men long associated with public land administration made up the commission, the best known of whom was John W. Powell. The testimony they took during a three-month tour of the West revealed scandalous management of the surveys, illegal sale of relinquishments, and exploitative activities by land attorneys and agents; it further indicated that hydraulic mining was doing serious damage to rich valley lands in

California. Recommendations for change included abolition of the unnecessary receivers' office in each land district, better salaries for the staff of the General Land Office, classification of the public lands, sale of the grazing lands, and exchange of lands between the railroads and the government to block areas for more effective management. Congress failed to act, although some of the reforms came into effect in 1889–1891, by which time the best of the arable land had gone into private ownership. Thomas Donaldson, a member of the commission, left its most lasting contribution, *The Public Domain*, a 1,300-page history and analysis of land policies that has since become a basic source of information about land policies. It bore down heavily on the misuse of the settlement laws.

In 1903 President Theodore Roosevelt appointed the second commission with Gifford Pinchot, then head of the Bureau of Forestry in the Department of Agriculture, as its most important member. After hearings in Washington, D.C., and in the West, the commission recommended the repeal of the Timber and Stone Act of 1878, as had the first commission. It also urged the appraisal of timber and other lands before they were sold; the establishment of grazing districts under the administration of the Department of Agriculture, with fees for use of the public ranges for grazing; the repeal of the lieu land feature of the Forest Management Act of 1897; and additional safeguards in the Homestead Act of 1862 and Desert Land Act of 1877. Congress was not receptive, although it repealed the lieu land provision and transferred the forest reserves from the Department of the Interior to the Agriculture Department's Bureau of Forestry under Pinchot.

Western livestock, lumber, and mining interests did not like the dynamic leadership of Pinchot, one of the founders of the modern CONSERVATION MOVEMENT, and in 1910 they brought about his dismissal by President William Howard Taft. These interests were pressing for the ceding of the public lands to the states in which they were located, thereby reviving an issue that had agitated the public land states for a century. They also opposed executive withdrawals of public lands that protected them from entry by private individuals and companies. They wanted no more government controls on public lands. Until 1929 their influence was responsible for relaxation of controls in the Department of the Interior while livestock overgrazed the public lands, which seriously diminished their carrying capacity.

Conservationist forces were not moribund but rather were regrouping their forces to protect the national forests from passing into private hands and to provide management of the PUBLIC DOMAIN rangelands previously uncontrolled. President Herbert Hoover may have sensed this groundswell and shrewdly decided to anticipate it with a proposal to convey to the western states the remaining public lands not subject to controlled use by a government agency. In response to his request, Congress authorized the appointment of the third commission, known as the Committee on the Conservation and Administration of the Public Domain. A carefully picked committee, dominated by westerners, recommended that the public lands, minus mineral rights, revert to the states in the hope that they would establish grazing control but that if they did not, the United States should undertake to do so in the recalcitrant states. The committee also recommended a procedure to eliminate those portions of the national forests it was not deemed desirable to retain. Conservationists throughout the country, not agreeing with the president that the record of the states was better than that of the National Forest Service in administering both forest and rangelands under its jurisdiction, sprang to arms in opposition to the recommendations. Most western states were also distressed at the recommendations, for they felt that without the mineral rights, they would gain little from the ceding of the lands. No action occurred.

In 1964 the fourth and best-financed of the public land commissions came into existence, when many issues affecting the public lands needed serious attention and Congress was already considering measures relating to them. Rather than deal with these questions in a piecemeal fashion, Congress decided to create the Public Land Law Review Commission, which, through use of the best expert aid in the universities and government agencies, undertook an overall examination of the many overlapping and conflicting programs and make recommendations to the Congress for new legislation. Again, failing to recognize that the public lands belong to the nation and that people of all states are deeply concerned about their management, the commission was strongly slanted toward the western viewpoint. Its final report, *One-Third of the Nation's Land*, contained homilies about planning for future needs and multiple use but placed emphasis on giving commercial interests more leeway in utilizing and acquiring ownership of the public lands, although requiring that they pay more for those privileges. The report showed westerners' dislike of the use of executive authority to effect land withdrawals, opposition to higher fees for grazing privileges, and preferences for state, as opposed to federal, administrative authority. It also reflected the general public's concern for retaining public lands in government ownership and for multiple use of the lands, but it favored "dominant use," which generally meant timber cutting and mining above other uses. Conservationists long accustomed to regarding the National Forest Service as the best administrative agency dealing with land matters disliked the proposal to consolidate it with the Bureau of Land Management. Environmentalists feared that the commission's failure to recommend the repeal of the Mining Act of 1872, which had been responsible for some of the most serious errors of the past in land administration, showed a marked insensitivity to public attitudes.

BIBLIOGRAPHY

Boschken, Herman L. *Land Use Conflicts: Organizational Design and Resource Management.* Urbana: University of Illinois Press, 1982.

Bryner, Gary C. *U.S. Land and Natural Resources Policy: A Public Issues Handbook.* Westport, Conn.: Greenwood Press, 1998.

Burch, William R., et al. *Measuring the Social Impact of Natural Resource Policies.* Albuquerque: University of New Mexico Press, 1984.

Clarke, Jeanne Nienaber, and Daniel C. McCool. *Staking out the Terrain: Power and Performance Among Natural Resource Agencies.* Albany: State University of New York Press, 1996.

Nester, William R. *The War for America's Natural Resources.* New York: St. Martin's Press, 1997.

Taylor, Bob Pepperman. *Our Limits Transgressed: Environmental Political Thought in America.* Lawrence: University Press of Kansas, 1992.

Worster, Donald. *A River Running West: The Life of John Wesley Powell.* New York: Oxford University Press, 2001.

Paul W. Gates/A. E.

See also **Forest Service; Land Office, U.S. General and Bureau Plans Management; Land Policy; Public Lands, Fencing of; West, American.**

PUBLIC LANDS, FENCING OF. During the nineteenth century, Congress enacted several laws that allowed individuals to stake a claim to public land, yet none of the laws permitted a claim of enough acreage to sustain the raising of stock in the arid west. Therefore, the range cattle industry that emerged on the GREAT PLAINS after the CIVIL WAR was based on the use of the public domain for grazing purposes. Few objected to this practice as long as the range remained open and the country was not wanted by settlers.

During the 1870s, however, the number of settlers and the number of CATTLE increased substantially. Farmers and new cattlemen began to use public land that established cattlemen had considered theirs. After the invention of barbed wire, complaints began to pour into the General Land Office that large ranchers and cattle companies were making illegal enclosures of public land. A series of investigations revealed a startling situation. In 1884 the commissioner of the General Land Office reported thirty-two cases of illegal fencing. One enclosure contained 600,000 acres; another included forty townships. And one cattleman had 250 miles of fence. Investigations during the succeeding years showed a rapid increase in illegal fencing, until 531 enclosures were reported in 1888, involving more than 7 million acres of the public domain.

Cattlemen, sheepmen, and farmers who had been fenced out of public land sometimes responded by cutting the fences. In the mid-1880s, fence cutters in Colfax County, New Mexico, cut a line of wire almost ninety miles long. Unable to defend their claims to the public domain in court, large ranchers often responded with violence. Fence-cutters' wars erupted in several states.

Cattlemen's associations urged that Congress resolve the fencing conflicts by leasing public land to ranchers. Instead, on 25 February 1885, Congress passed a law prohibiting the enclosure of the public domain. And on 7 August 1885, President Grover Cleveland issued a proclamation that ordered the removal of the fences. These measures were not vigorously enforced, however. Bad weather, mismanagement, and overstocking of the range probably did more than the law to eliminate the illegal practice of fencing public land.

The FEDERAL GOVERNMENT allowed leasing and fencing of public lands for grazing in 1934.

BIBLIOGRAPHY

Dale, Edward Everett. *The Range Cattle Industry: Ranching on the Great Plains from 1865 to 1925.* Norman: University of Oklahoma Press, 1960.

Gates, Paul W. *History of Public Land Law Development.* New York: Arno Press, 1979.

McCallum, Henry D., and Frances T. McCallum. *The Wire That Fenced the West.* Norman: University of Oklahoma Press, 1965.

O'Neal, Bill. *Cattlemen vs. Sheepherders: Five Decades of Violence in the West, 1880–1920.* Austin, Tex.: Eakin, 1989.

Pelzer, Louis. *The Cattlemen's Frontier: A Record of the Trans-Mississippi Cattle Industry from Oxen Trains to Pooling Companies.* New York: Russell and Russell, 1969.

Dan E. Clark/C. P.

See also **Cattle Drives; Fencing and Fencing Laws; Land Acts; Land Office, U.S. General and Bureau Plans Management; Land Policy.**

PUBLIC OPINION has formed a part of American politics ever since the authors of the *Federalist Papers* declared that "all government rests on opinion." They drew on a long tradition stretching from before Machiavelli's counsel that princes should not ignore popular opinion through Hume's dictum that it is "on opinion only that government is founded." The idea that the right to govern is grounded in the consent of the governed led over time away from instrumental reasons for gauging public opinion (to avoid being overthrown) to normative ones (to govern rightly and justly). This democratic doctrine prevailed in the New England town meetings, although it was only in the latter half of the twentieth century that the "public" whose opinion was to be sought expanded to its present size, concomitant with the extension of the right to vote to almost all adult citizens. The struggles to obtain the franchise and to contest the view of someone like Alexander Hamilton that popular opinion is seldom right are well documented. Today, as Harold Lasswell wrote, the open interplay of opinion and policy is the distinguishing mark of popular rule.

Early Straw Polls and Social Surveys

A precondition of measuring public opinion is an awareness of who constitutes the public, the potential universe of those whose opinion is to be measured. One of the most authoritative descriptions of the public is the government census, which in the United States was first carried out in 1790. Popular attitudes were not surveyed until newspapers and magazines introduced "straw polls," a term that refers to determining the direction of the political winds, much as a farmer might gauge the direction of the wind by throwing a handful of straw into the air. The *Harrisburg Pennsylvanian* is held to have carried out the first straw poll in the United States in 1824, showing Andrew Jackson a clear winner over John Quincy Adams and Henry Clay in a survey of 532 respondents from Wilmington, Delaware. Other newspapers of the time carried out similar straw polls.

The development of more extensive public opinion surveys can be credited to the social surveys of the late nineteenth century. Inspired by the sanitary surveys of health and housing conditions conducted by the statistical societies established in England in the 1840s, American surveyors of social conditions sent letters to businesses and conducted door-to-door interviews. None of these efforts was comparable in scope to Charles Booth's *Life and Labour of the People in London*, the first volume of which was published in 1889. Booth developed the theory of a poverty line and produced a poverty map of London, color-coded for eight economic levels. American social reformers used Booth's methods to document poverty in American cities. In one study, Hull-House workers canvassed door to door in a Chicago neighborhood in order to produce maps of nationality and wages, collected in the *Hull-House Maps and Papers* of 1895. The following year, W. E. B. Du Bois undertook a study that was published in 1899 as *The Philadelphia Negro*, collecting data on nearly 10,000 residents of the Central Ward.

Encouraged by the example of these social surveys being undertaken by reformers, newspapers and magazines adapted straw polling to their business. In 1896, the *Chicago Record* mailed postcard ballots to every registered voter in Chicago and every eighth voter in twelve midwestern states. Based on the results, the *Record* predicted that William McKinley would win 57.95 percent of the Chicago presidential vote; he received 57.91 percent on election day. Outside Chicago, however, the results were far off the mark. Publishers focused on the marketing potential of straw polls; postcard ballots often included subscription offers intended to boost the sponsor's circulation.

At the same time, government began to take a more active interest in public opinion, combining detailed straw polls with methods from the social surveys. For example, the Country Life Commission organized by President Theodore Roosevelt sent out a questionnaire to over half a million rural residents in what is likely the first major quality-of-life survey. The results were starting to be tabulated by the Census Bureau when Congress cut its funding; later, the questionnaires were burned as useless. Undaunted, the Department of Agriculture several years later started its own surveys of farm conditions, collecting the attitudes and opinions of farmers as early as 1915.

George Gallup. The nation's leading pollster starting in 1936; he sought to apply scientific methods to public opinion surveys. GETTY IMAGES

Polling in Transition

Scientific research into public opinion proliferated in the 1930s with the development of new statistical techniques. The New Deal was characterized by a growing number of government contracts in applied research, some of which employed surveys. Market researchers also adopted the techniques of applied sampling, but newspapers and magazines tended to be concerned not with technique, but rather with how polls would boost their circulation. Despite methodological problems and errors of often over ten percent, straw polls continued to be published by newspapers and magazines until the 1936 election. The *Literary Digest*, the largest-circulation general magazine of the time, had claimed "uncanny accuracy" for its previous straw polls and, in 1936, predicted Alf Landon winning with 57 percent of the vote over Franklin Roosevelt. Roosevelt won the election with 62.5 percent of the vote. The *Digest* prediction, based on almost 2.5 million unrepresentative straw ballots, was off by nearly 20 percentage points, and the magazine soon went bankrupt. Meanwhile, pollsters George Gallup, Elmo Roper, and Archibald Crossley correctly predicted the outcome. In fact, Gallup had written in July—before the *Digest* had even sent out its ballots—that the magazine's straw poll would show Landon winning with 56 percent. A marketing whiz, Gallup encouraged newspapers that subscribed to his poll to run it alongside that of the *Digest*, and he sold his column with the money-back guarantee that his prediction would be more accurate. He also pointed out the reasons why the *Digest* would be wrong: sampling bias based on the above-average incomes of the *Digest*'s readership, and response bias inevitable in mail-in questionnaires. As a result of his success, Gallup quickly became the country's top pollster.

The Gallup, the Roper, and the Crossley polls relied on quota sampling, intended to ensure that the poll sample looks demographically like the general population. However, their polls had a persistent Republican bias. Although he had the outcome correct in 1936, Gallup had actually underestimated Roosevelt's win by 6.8 percent. The pattern continued until 1948, when the Gallup Poll, the Roper Poll, and the Crossley Poll all predicted that Republican Thomas Dewey would defeat Democrat Harry Truman. In a thorough investigation of these 1948 failures, the Social Science Research Council urged replacing quota sampling with probability sampling, the method still employed in contemporary public opinion polls.

The Application of Social Science to Polling

Before World War II, however, and encouraged by the clear superiority of his techniques of survey research over those of the *Digest*, Gallup famously declared that there was a "new science of public opinion measurement." Indeed, the government's manpower policy and wartime research needs attracted social scientists to work on social research problems. Some of these government units conducted polls and surveys, especially to study wartime morale. The units were interdisciplinary and problem-oriented, and social scientists worked alongside market researchers, advertising and media professionals, and specialists from the armed forces, the Bureau of the Census, the Federal Reserve Board, and the Treasury.

When the war ended, Congress stopped funding these government research groups, and the social scientists they had employed returned to their universities. Three key university research centers were founded: the Bureau of Applied Social Research at Columbia University, the National Opinion Research Center (NORC), originally at Denver and later at Chicago, and the Survey Research Center (SRC) at the University of Michigan. Before the war, government research funds had gone primarily to its own agencies. Between 1945 and 1959, however, government research funding to universities and colleges increased tenfold. Although almost all of this funding went into the physical and life sciences, the small share that went to the social sciences was substantial relative to existing standards. For example, the SRC's $230,000 of federal funding for its first year of operations in 1946 was over four times the University of Michigan's annual allocation to the Department of Sociology for salaries and operating expenses.

Modern Developments and Techniques

Polling spread around the world in the postwar decades, and by the 1960s there were several hundred survey organizations in the United States, many of them university-affiliated. The SRC started the National Election Studies (NES) in 1948, and the Studies are still carried out every two years. The NES asks respondents hundreds of questions in the autumn before elections and then interviews them again once the election is over. NORC started its General Social Survey in 1971, asking a general set of questions usually repeated from year to year alongside a changing topical module. Both the GSS and the NES interview respondents for several hours in their homes and are thus expensive to carry out, but the data are well-respected and widely used by social scientists.

New techniques for randomly sampling telephone numbers cut the cost of surveys, and the news media once again took an interest in polling: the *New York Times* and CBS News started polling together in 1976 and they were soon joined by the NBC/*Wall Street Journal* and ABC/*Washington Post* polls. Exit polls, developed in the late 1960s, were first used to predict the outcome of a presidential election in 1980, causing complaints that Democrats on the West Coast were dissuaded from voting by the news that President Jimmy Carter had already been defeated. Social scientists remain critical of many commercial and journalistic polls, for example, the popular "call-in" polls, which are the modern version of the straw poll: unrepresentative and self-selecting.

Other public opinion polls are connected with the marketing of political candidates and positions. The darker side of public opinion polling came to light with President Lyndon Johnson's use of polls to manipulate opinion rather than simply report it. In commissioning and interpreting polls, Johnson's staff employed shallow analysis and outright misrepresentation to exaggerate domestic support for the war in Vietnam. Instead of engaging them as a tool to judge public opinion, Johnson thus used poll results to convince the media and policymakers of his personal popularity and that of his policy proposals. A more recent innovation is so-called push polls, in which campaign staff posing as pollsters provide respondents with false information in an attempt to influence their opinion or their vote. The American Association for Public Opinion Research asserts that push polls constitute an unethical campaign practice. Another recent development is decreasing response rates as potential respondents refuse to take part in polls. This raises methodological concerns because people who decline to participate in a survey may differ in significant ways from those who do complete it. A related problem is incomplete surveys, as respondents refuse to answer particular questions on a survey. Pollsters tend to compensate for nonresponse by weighting their results, but the best way of doing so is the subject of much debate.

Conclusion

Although technical questions about the best way of measuring public opinion remain, there have been clear methodological advances since the days when utilitarians such as Jeremy Bentham emphasized the difficulty of even defining public opinion. Current public opinion research in sociology and psychology generally focuses on the ways in which individual beliefs interact with those of the wider community or of others within the individual's social network, since public opinion cannot form without communication and social interaction. Political scientists, by contrast, generally tend to study the influence of public opinion on public policy.

A question of an entirely different nature from technical concerns is that of the relationship between public opinion and public policy. Walter Lippmann argued that the "pictures in our heads" that form our opinions can be manipulated by organized interests. He concluded that the public should choose political leaders, but that policy ought to be set not by the public or their leaders, but by expert social scientists working within a "machinery of knowledge." Lippmann refused to consider that these policy specialists might also hold opinions divergent from pure reason, admitting only that the methods of social science were still far from perfect.

Recent research emphasizes the fact that most journalistic polls merely report horse-race information, such as between two or more candidates for office, and thus cannot actually influence policy. There is normative debate about the extent to which changes in public opinion should influence policy. Political leaders today rarely follow the model of Pericles, who thought the role of the leader was to convince the public to back policies they might originally have resisted. Advances in communications technology mean that modern democratic leaders can more often represent public opinion, which has led to calls for more direct democracy. However, a final argument is the suggestion that, simply by posing questions in a certain way, polls may actually create opinions about matters that had previously remained unexamined. The relationship between public opinion and democratic governance remains in question.

BIBLIOGRAPHY

Converse, Jean M. *Survey Research in the United States: Roots and Emergence, 1890–1960.* Berkeley: University of California Press, 1987.

Erikson, Robert S., and Kent L. Tedin. *American Public Opinion: Its Origins, Content, and Impact.* 6th ed. New York: Longman, 2000.

Key, V. O. *Public Opinion and American Democracy.* New York: Knopf, 1961.

Lasswell, Harold Dwight. *Democracy through Public Opinion.* Menasha, Wisc.: George Banta, 1941.

Lippmann, Walter. *Public Opinion.* New York: Harcourt, Brace, 1922.

Public Opinion Quarterly. A periodical publishing articles dealing with the development and role of communication research and current public opinion, as well as the theories and methods underlying opinion research.

Willem Maas

See also **Polling.**

PUBLIC OWNERSHIP. *See* **Government Ownership.**

PUBLIC SCHOOLS. *See* **Education.**

PUBLIC UTILITIES. In the United States, public utilities supply consumers with electricity, natural gas, water, telecommunications, and other essential services. Government regulation of these utilities considered vital to the "public interest" has waxed and waned. In the nineteenth century, canals, ferries, inns, gristmills, docks, and many other entities were regulated. However, in the early twentieth century, emerging electric companies initially avoided regulation These rapidly growing power companies often merged, creating monopolies that controlled the generation, transmission, and distribution of electric power. By 1907, entrepreneur Samuel Insull of Chicago Edison had acquired twenty other utility companies. He and others argued that building multiple transmission and distribution systems would be costly and inefficient. Nevertheless, reformers clamored for state regulation of the monopolies. By 1914, forty-three states had established regulatory polices governing electric utilities. Insull and other electric power "barons" found a way past regulation by restructuring their firms as holding companies. A HOLDING COMPANY is a corporate entity that partly or completely controls interest in another (operating) company. Throughout the 1920s, holding companies bought smaller utilities, sometimes to the point that a holding company was as many as ten times removed from the operating company. Operating companies were subject to state regulation, holding companies were not. Holding companies could issue new stock and bonds without state oversight. This pyramid structure allowed holding companies to inflate the value of utility securities. Consolidation of utilities continued until, by the end of the 1920s, ten utility systems controlled three-fourths of the electric power in the United States. Utility stocks, considered relatively secure, were held by millions of investors, many of whom lost their total investment in the stock market crash of 1929.

Public Utility Holding Company Act

With strong support from President Franklin D. Roosevelt, Congress passed the Public Utility Holding Company Act (PUHCA) in 1935. PUHCA outlawed interstate utility holding companies and made it illegal for a holding company to be more than twice removed from its operating subsidiary. Holding companies that owned 10 percent or more of a public utility had to register with the Securities and Exchange Commission and provide detailed accounts of all financial transactions and holdings. The legislation had a swift and dramatic effect. Between 1938 and 1958 the number of holding companies fell from 216 to eighteen. This forced divestiture continued until deregulation of the 1980s and 1990s.

Deregulation

Many politicians and economists argued that the marketplace, not government regulation, should determine utility prices. Many consumers also sought lower prices through DEREGULATION. Near the end of the twentieth century, while government oversight of safety remained, price and service regulation were removed from several industries, including telecommunications, transportation, natural gas, and electric power. As a result, new services and lower prices were often introduced. The increased competition among investor-owned utilities also led to mergers and acquisitions and a concentration of ownership. Deregulation is also credited with the rise of unregulated power brokers, such as Enron, whose historic collapse in 2002 laid bare the vulnerability of consumers and investors when corporations control essential public services. About a dozen states repealed or delayed their deregulation laws; many consumer groups maintained that PUHCA's protections should be reinstated.

BIBLIOGRAPHY

Euromonitor International. "Electric Power Distribution in the United States." http://www.MarketResearch.com.

Lai, Loi Lei. *Power System Restructuring and Deregulation.* New York: Wiley, 2001.

Warkentin, Denise. *Electric Power Industry in Nontechnical Language.* Tulsa, Okla.: PennWell Publishers, 1998.

Lynda DeWitt

See also **Monopoly; Robber Barons; Trusts;** *and vol. 9:* **Power.**

PUBLISHING INDUSTRY. Book publishing in the United States grew from a single printing press imported from England in 1638 to an industry boasting more than 2,600 publishing houses and generating nearly $25 billion a year in revenue in 2000. The country's most famous publishing houses, some of which date back to the 1800s, have been transformed from private, family-owned companies to multinational media conglomerates. With the advent of the World Wide Web in the 1990s and other advances in electronic publishing technology, the industry is at the cutting edge of the electronic revolution that is transforming the American economy.

Publishing in Early America

In 1638 a printing press was imported to Cambridge, Massachusetts, from England. Two years later Stephen Daye (also spelled Day) used that press to print the first English-language book in America, *The Whole Booke of Psalmes,* also known as the *Bay Psalm Book.* This printing press issued many other religious works, including John Eliot's *Indian Bible,* a 1663 translation of the Scriptures into the Algonquin language. The Boston-Cambridge area has remained a center of publishing since these colonial beginnings.

Philadelphia is another publishing center with origins dating to the colonial period. William Bradford, who had come to Pennsylvania with William Penn, established a press in Philadelphia in 1685. Five years later he built the first paper mill in the colonies on the city's outskirts. Bradford moved to New York in 1693, but his descendants remained in Philadelphia where they were leading publishers until the nineteenth century. Philadelphia's best-known publisher was Benjamin Franklin, who opened his print shop in 1728. In addition to the *Pennsylvania Gazette,* Franklin published numerous books, including the *Poor Richard's Almanack* (1732–1757), which had impressive sales of 10,000 copies per year.

In 1744 Franklin began publishing popular English novels in the colonies. He was a pioneer in this area, and his three editions of Samuel Richardson's *Pamela* rapidly sold out. Just prior to the American Revolution, Isaiah Thomas of Worcester, Massachusetts, became the most successful publisher of European books in the colonies. Thomas printed such popular English works as Daniel Defoe's *Robinson Crusoe,* John Bunyan's *Pilgrim's Progress,* and John Cleland's racy *Memoirs of a Woman of Pleasure,* better known as *Fanny Hill.*

Georgia was the last of the thirteen colonies to get a printing press, in 1762. The type of books published in the colonies varied by region: nearly half of the books printed on New England presses were religious titles, while more than half of the books published in the South dealt with law. During the colonial period, printers were often booksellers, selling books in their print shops. Some booksellers placed orders directly with printers.

The Rise of New York as the Publishing Capital

The nineteenth century set a pattern of trends in the publishing industry that would continue into following centuries. By 1850, New York City had surpassed Boston and Philadelphia to become the center of the publishing industry in the United States, a position that the city occupied into the twenty-first century. Such nineteenth-century New York publishers as Harper, Putnam, and Scribner were still important names in the industry in 2000. The 1840s saw the beginning of the royalty system, and international copyright protection enacted at the end of the century ensured authors payment of their royalties. The large publishing houses that made New York so prominent in the industry exercised so much influence throughout the county that they forced many of the local printers that flourished through the 1700s and early 1800s out of business. A similar scenario occurred in the late twentieth century, when large retailers placed many local bookshops out of business.

The first great New York City publishing house was Harper Bros., founded in 1817. By 1840 George Palmer Putnam, in partnership with John Wiley, had also established a publishing house in the city, and in 1846 Charles Scribner founded his publishing house in New York. Together, these three firms launched New York as the center of the U.S. book publishing industry. Like many of the city's manufacturers, these publishers took advantage of the Erie Canal, which opened markets in the West to New York in 1825. New York publishers offered better prices than local printers did, because they could reduce overhead costs by printing and shipping books in larger quantities. Many smaller printers could not compete with this competition from the large New York publishing houses.

Like many publishers of the 1800s, Harper Bros. took advantage of the lack of international copyright enforcement. The firm printed pirated copies of works by such British authors as Charles Dickens, William Makepeace Thackeray, and Anne, Charlotte, and Emily Brontë. Harper Bros.' best-selling pirated work by a British author was Thomas Babington Macaulay's *History of England from the Accession of James II.* The book sold approximately 400,000 copies, a figure that would classify it as a nonfiction bestseller at the turn of the twentieth century. Because international copyright laws were not enforced, U.S. publishers did not pay royalties to either the British authors or their publishers. The American market had grown to be so significant that, in 1842, Dickens traveled to the United States in an effort to secure royalties from the sale of his works. He was unsuccessful at recouping this money, but the trip did give Dickens the material for his book *American Notes for General Circulation,* which Harper Bros. promptly pirated.

The Constitution had granted the federal government authority to ensure that American writers and inventors were given exclusive rights to their work, and in 1790 Congress enacted legislation to advance domestic copyright protection afforded to U.S. authors. By the late nineteenth century, American authors had become sufficiently well known throughout the world that their works had significant sales abroad. To ensure that these American authors, as well as their publishers, received the royalties due them from sales outside the United States, Congress entered into the International Copyright Act of 1891. Although this secured American authors and publishers royalties from sales in other signatory countries, it also meant the end of U.S. publishers pirating works of foreign authors.

Until the mid-nineteenth century, most American authors published at their own expense. For example, Walt Whitman self-published and sold his 1855 edition of *Leaves of Grass.* However, a printer and bookseller might share costs with an author whose work appeared to have strong sales potential. When American publishers began to spend their own funds to print books, they generally paid authors no royalties until they had recovered the initial expense incurred in printing the book. George Palmer Putnam instituted the modern royalty system in 1846, offering authors 10 percent of a book's sale price for each copy sold.

The paperback was another innovation of the nineteenth-century book publishing industry. Although paperbound pamphlets and tracts had existed since the colonial era, the sales of paperbound novels exploded in the mid-1800s. In 1860, Erastus Beadle, a printer in Ostega County, New York, published *A Dime Song Book,* a paperbound collection of lyrics to popular songs. Sales of this book were so strong that in the same year Beadle published another 10-cent paperbound book, *Maleska: The Indian Wife of the White Hunter* by Anne S. W. Stephens. The book was an adventure novel, which became staples of the genre known as "dime novels." Whether a dime novel was a detective story, an adventure story, or an historical tale, it always featured an all-American hero who saved the day, triumphed over evil and vice, and was handsomely rewarded. Gilbert Patten created the hero figure Frank Merriwell, whose exploits helped sell 125 million copies of Patten's books. Although their literary merits were questioned, dime novels were a reading staple until the early 1910s, when pulp magazines and comic books surpassed them in popularity.

While readers of dime novels enjoyed wholesome tales, other readers of the mid-1800s indulged their tastes for the more salacious literature that had become a specialty of New York's publishers. Anthony Comstock, an anti-obscenity crusader and secretary of the New York Society for Suppression of Vice, led a successful campaign in 1870 that forced New York publishing houses to stop printing such racy fiction. Comstock, a special officer of the U.S. Postal Service, also succeeded in persuading Congress to pass the so-called Comstock laws that prohibited the postal service from carrying material deemed obscene. Comstock carried on his anti-obscenity campaign until his death in 1915, and he was so effective that New York publishers practiced self-censorship well into the twentieth century. Although the movement led by Comstock had as its goal the suppression of obscene publications, the entire literary and publishing community felt the effects of this censorship. George Bernard Shaw coined the term "Comstockery" for this form of censorship, and H. L. Mencken railed against Comstock and his movement for making it "positively dangerous to print certain ancient and essentially decent English words."

A New Generation in Publishing

The 1920s is generally acknowledged as the beginning of the Modern Age in American literature. In this decade, a new generation of American literary giants came to prominence. Their work was often too bold to be printed by the established New York publishers that still felt the censorial effects of Comstock and his campaigns. This new generation of writers required a new generation of publishers that would dare to champion new, modern American literature. The 1920s saw the founding of such important publishing houses as Simon and Schuster, Random House, Alfred A. Knopf, and Viking Press.

Although Random House would grow to be the largest and most successful publisher in the country, and would hold that position into the twenty-first century,

Simon and Schuster introduced some important industry innovations with long-term consequences. In 1939 the firm reintroduced mass-market paperback books with its Pocket Book imprint. Paperbacks received further attention in the early 1950s from Doubleday: The publishing house followed the lead set by British publisher Penguin Books and reprinted literary classics in paperback under its Anchor Books imprint. This helped to remove the low-brow stigma that had been associated with paperbacks since the days of the dime novel, and by the twenty-first century a wide range of books—from the Bible and other classics to professional references and textbooks—were available in paperback.

The Great Depression of the 1930s hit the book publishing industry as hard as it hit every other sector of the American economy. Booksellers at that time were mostly small local businesses, and to help them survive the economic hardships of the depression, Simon and Schuster invented a system allowing booksellers to return unsold copies of books for credit against future purchases. Other publishers quickly had to follow Simon and Schuster's lead, and the practice became the industry standard. At times booksellers have been able to use this system to their advantage to clear inventories or to "pay" for copies of new books by returning unsold copies. Publishers have adapted to the system of returns by adding costs of shipping, warehousing, and recycling returned copies into the price of books.

The 1920s also saw the establishment of book clubs as a new way to market books. The BOOK-OF-THE-MONTH-CLUB was the first, started in 1926, and was followed by the Literary Guild in 1927. By the 1970s, approximately 150 book clubs were in business, generating almost $250 million in sales, or 8 percent of the industry's revenue at that time. By the 1990s, though, book clubs were struggling to survive because of competition from national bookstore chains and Internet booksellers. At the turn of the twenty-first century, only a handful of book clubs were still in business.

Consolidation in the Industry

Beginning the 1960s, a major trend in publishing was the merging of houses, as well as the consolidation of retail sales outlets. One of the first mergers to occur was Random House's purchase of Alfred A. Knopf in 1960. In 1965 RCA acquired Random House for $40 million and added it to RCA's roster of media companies, which included NBC Radio and Television. In 1980, Random House was acquired by Advanced Communications and became part of the Newhouse family's media empire. During this time a number of publishers, including Crown, Fawcett, and Ballatine, were merged with Random House. In 1998 Random House was acquired by Bertelsmann AG, a German-based media conglomerate that, at the time of Random House's purchase, already owned the Bantam Doubleday Dell Group.

Simon and Schuster was acquired by Gulf + Western in 1975. From 1984 to 1994, the company acquired more than sixty companies, including Prentice-Hall, Silver Burdett, and Macmillan Publishing Company. With the addition of these educational, professional, and reference imprints, Simon and Schuster's revenue grew from $200 million in 1983 to more than $2 billion in 1997. In 1989, the Gulf + Western corporation restructured and emerged as Paramount Communications. In 1994, shortly after the purchase of Macmillan, Paramount was bought by Viacom Inc., which also owned MTV. In 1998 the company sold its education, professional, and reference units to Pearson PLC, which later merged with Longman.

This mass consolidation has made unlikely partners out of former competitors. For example, Prentice-Hall and Addison Wesley, which were rivals in the textbook and professional book markets, are owned by the same parent company, Longman-Pearson (which also owns Viking, Penguin, Putnam and Dutton). Consolidation has allowed a handful of major publishing conglomerates to dominate the industry. These include Bertelsmann, Viacom, Longman-Pearson, News Corporation, and Germany's Verlagsgruppe Georg von Holtzbrinck.

Consolidation was part of an overall economic trend of the late 1980s, 1990s, and early 2000s. Book publishers were also forced to consolidate because of the consolidation of retail outlets. Traditionally, booksellers were small, locally owned businesses. They were able to make a profit by maintaining low overhead costs such as rent. These booksellers usually stocked extensive inventories of books published in previous years (known in the industry as backlist titles). However, when shopping malls began to attract people in the 1960s and 1970s, many bookstores could not follow their customers, as rents in the malls were higher and retail space was at a premium.

In the 1970s, national chain bookstores such as Barnes and Noble and Waldenbooks began to open retail outlets in malls across the country. By buying in volume, chains could earn more profit on each copy of a book sold, allowing them to pay higher rents. Buying in volume also meant that they could negotiate deeper discounts from publishers. By passing this discount on to book buyers, the chains were able to attract customers away from the smaller independent bookstores.

Because the chains first opened stores in malls where retail space is at a premium, they could not carry an extensive inventory of backlist titles. This had a profound effect on publishers. Many publishers relied on backlist sales as a steady income stream that helped them weather years when newly printed titles (i.e., frontlist titles) did not sell as well as anticipated. As chains carried fewer and fewer backlist titles for sale, publishers were compelled to print ever-more successful frontlist titles. Thus, publishers had to cultivate a roster of authors whose books could almost always be counted on as instant bestsellers. In developing this roster, publishers had to pay premiums to attract and keep these authors. For example, in 1972, best-selling author Irving Wallace signed a contract with Bantam Books worth $2.5 million. At that time, Wallace's contract represented a little less than 0.1 percent of the entire industry's revenues. To be able to afford such a contract, a publisher like Bantam needed extensive financial resources; a lone publishing house may not have these resources, but a publishing conglomerate would.

During the 1980s and 1990s, chain booksellers changed their marketing tactics by creating what is known in the industry as the superstore. A prototype superstore was the original Borders Bookstore in Ann Arbor, Michigan. This store carried a large backlist inventory and had a library-like atmosphere that encouraged browsing. When the store was bought by Waldenbooks, then owned by K Mart, Inc., the original Borders formula was basically replicated nationwide, but with more emphasis on frontlist titles and bestsellers. In 1989 Barnes and Noble bought Bookstop, a chain of supermarket-style bookstores, and made its entrance into superstore book retailing. During the 1990s, Barnes and Noble and Borders rapidly expanded the number of their superstores, combining the deeply discounted bestsellers that were staples of mall stores with the extensive inventory of backlist titles that was the trademark of traditional independent bookstores. This combination provided stiff competition that many independent bookstores could not match, and the chains became the dominant bookselling outlets. This allowed the chains to negotiate even greater discounts from publishers, which further increased market share and drove an even greater number of independent bookstores out of business.

As the chains continued to discount prices, the industry as a whole came to rely more heavily on the bestsellers that guaranteed high-volume sales and profits. Because of their popularity and the reliability with which they produced bestsellers, a handful of authors came to dominate the book publishing industry. Between 1986 and 1996, Tom Clancy, John Grisham, Stephen King, Danielle Steel, and Dean Koontz wrote sixty-three of the one hundred bestselling books in the United States. J. K. Rowling, author of the *Harry Potter* series, later joined this elite group of super-selling authors.

Electronic Publishing

Just as consolidation was transforming the book industry in the 1990s, the World Wide Web and new electronic publishing technology were rewriting the rules for book publishers and sellers. Online booksellers, such as Amazon.com and BarnesandNoble.com, have had a profound effect on the way publishers market and sell books. These online bookstores offer the selection, availability, and price discounts that had been the marketing strengths of the book clubs and mail-order booksellers that now struggle to compete with the online retailers.

In the mid-1990s, many predicted the demise of the printed book, arguing that books would be supplanted by CD-ROMs, online books, and other electronic book (or e-book) technology. Although the printed book continues to flourish, CD-ROMs and Web-based technology has transformed many aspects of the book publishing industry.

For example, reference books traditionally have been multi-volume sets written by a team of authors and editors that could spend several years in preparing a new edition. Because these references took so long to be produced, they often contained outdated information by the time they were printed. Although time is still required to gather, write, and edit new reference information, electronic publishing technology has dramatically reduced the time needed to produce an updated reference. Often updates are published on a Web site and can be downloaded by subscribers. Web-based and CD-ROM technology has also greatly improved the way reference information can be searched. By enabling sound, color images, and video to be incorporated into a reference, electronic publishing technology has also transformed the very nature of this type of publication.

Another innovation of electronic publishing is print-on-demand. This type of technology allows a publisher to print a single copy of a book at the request of a customer. Textbook publishers offer this technology to teachers, allowing them to create custom textbooks for specific courses electronically. Print-on-demand has also extended the amount of time a book is available for purchase. Traditionally, a publisher stopped printing new copies of a book and declared it "out of print" when sales dwindled to the point that the firm could no longer afford to print more copies. Print-on-demand, however, allows customers to have printed copies of a book whenever they want, and a publisher may never have to declare a book out-of-print. This technology was still a premium service at the beginning of the twenty-first century, but many observers of the publishing industry believed all bookstores would have print-on-demand services eventually, giving readers an almost endless choice of titles to purchase.

E-book technology allows readers to download books onto a variety of personal computing systems. Still in its infancy, this technology had the potential to restructure the entire publishing industry. In September 2001, Random House, Penguin Putnam, HarperCollins, and Simon and Schuster, all rival publishing houses, entered into a agreement to bypass established online booksellers and sell e-books directly on the Yahoo! Web site. Many industry experts took this arrangement, which allows publishers to sell books directly to customers, to be a harbinger of the future online technology will create for book publishing.

BIBLIOGRAPHY

Epstein, Jason. *Book Business: Publishing, Past, Present, and Future.* New York: Norton, 2001.

Greco, Albert N. *The Book Publishing Industry.* Boston: Allyn and Bacon, 1997.

Korda, Michael. *Making the List: A Cultural History of the American Bestseller, 1900–1999.* New York: Barnes and Noble, 2001.

Schiffrin, Andre. *The Business of Books: How the International Conglomerates Took Over Publishing and Changed the Way We Read.* London: Verso, 2001.

John Wyzalek

See also **Literature; Printing Industry.**

PUEBLO is a Spanish word meaning "town" that refers to twenty aggregated Native American communities on the Colorado Plateau in northern New Mexico and Arizona. The basic characteristics of Pueblo culture—apartment-like traditional houses, maize agriculture, and pottery-making—have their origins in the Ancestral Puebloan (formally known as the Anasazi) occupation of the Colorado Plateau that extends back 2,000 years. Western Pueblos include Laguna, Acoma, and Zuni in northwestern New Mexico and Hopi in northeastern Arizona. Sixteen eastern Pueblos are clustered along the Rio Grande River valley in northern New Mexico. The eastern Pueblos are the focus of this discussion.

There are many similarities among the eastern Pueblos, but disparate origins are suggested by differences in language, patterns of kinship, and ritual details. Eastern Pueblo languages are divided into two groups. Keresan languages are spoken in Zia, Santa Ana, San Felipe, Santo Domingo, and Cochiti, as well as in Laguna and Acoma.

Pueblo Pottery. A stereograph, from a photograph by William H. Rau, of Indians selling crafts at the 1904 Louisiana Purchase Exposition in St. Louis. Library of Congress

Indian Service School. Arthur Rothstein's 1936 photograph shows two Pueblos at work in this school in Taos, N.M. Library of Congress

Kiowa-Tanoan languages include Northern Tiwa, spoken at Taos and Picuris; Southern Tiwa, spoken at Isleta and Sandia; Tewa, spoken at San Juan, Santa Clara, San Ildefonso, Nambe, Pojoaque, and Tesuque; and Towa, spoken at Jemez. Numerous ruins along the Rio Grande testify to the antiquity of native occupation. Pueblos such as Pecos, east of Santa Fe, were abandoned in historic times. Traditional architecture, such as that still seen at Taos, consists of multi-storied, apartment-like houses built of sandstone or adobe. Many traditional aspects of life have persisted through Spanish, Mexican, and U.S. domination over the past five centuries.

Puebloan peoples are traditionally farmers, growing maize, beans, squash, melons, and chiles. Trips are taken throughout the year to hunt, to gather plants and resources such as salt, and to visit shrines. Pueblos near the Great Plains, such as Taos and Pecos, traded with Plains tribes for buffalo hides and meat. The Spanish introduced wheat, oats, fruit trees, horses, cattle, pigs, chicken, sheep, and goats. By the latter part of the twentieth century, wage labor had replaced traditional agriculture as the primary source of income. A growing market for Native American arts has fueled the increasing production of arts and crafts for sale, including traditional crafts such as pottery-making, weaving, leatherwork, lapidary work, and carving and more recent introductions such as silver jewelry work.

Social institutions vary among groups. Among the Tewa communities, social structure takes the form of patrilineal, nonexogamous divisions, or moieties, associated with summer and winter. Among the Keresan groups, matrilineal exogamous clans, or clusters of related lineages, are more important, but moieties are also present. Today political control is strong and centralized in the form of a cacique and a tribal council. Strong notions of cyclicity and dualism underlie much eastern Pueblo social organization. Astronomical events such as solstices or equinoxes divide the year in two. There is a complex annual cycle of communal activities involving harvest, construction, and ritual events. Moieties take turns organizing these events. Summer dances tend to revolve around fertility and bringing rain for crops, whereas winter dances emphasize hunting.

Spiritual, ritual, and social order are manifested not only through ceremony and daily life but also in the organization and layout of the physical Pueblo world. Pueblos are oriented around central plazas where daily activities as well as community rituals take place. Subterranean kivas are used for society meetings and ritual events. Puebloans share the belief that people emerged through an opening from a previous world and arrived at their current villages after a series of migrations. The Pueblo is seen as a center place, located in the middle of a series of horizontal and vertical dimensions that have social and ritual meaning. Nested series of shrines and natural landmarks represent these dimensions in the physical world. Today many families dwell primarily in nuclear family residences outside the village center, but they often maintain residences in the old, central pueblo, where they return for ritual and festive occasions.

In 1540, Francisco Vásquez de Coronado led a band of conquistadores into the Rio Grande valley and quartered his men at a group of twelve Tiwa pueblos near modern Bernalillo. The Pueblos initially welcomed the Spanish, offering them food and supplies. Soon Spanish demands began to tax Pueblo resources and hospitality, and they took food and women by force. In 1598, Don Juan de Oñate arrived at the head of a group of settlers who established a colony with headquarters in Santa Fe. Spanish colonists lacked enough resources to work the land and feed their people, so they instituted the *encomienda*, which gave colonists tribute rights to food and blankets from the Pueblos, and the *repartimiento*, which forced Puebloans into labor on Spanish farms and haciendas.

Religion was another major point of friction. Spanish missionaries were on a holy quest to convert Native Americans to Christianity, even if the campaign required force. Catholic churches were raised with native labor, and Pueblo peoples were taught European trades. Missionaries had no tolerance for native religious practices. Dances were prohibited, sacred paraphernalia was confiscated, and religious leaders were tortured and executed. Pueblo rituals continued in secret beneath a veneer of Catholicism and did not openly re-emerge until the 1800s. Contemporary Pueblo religion contains Catholic elements. Secrecy continues to surround native beliefs and ceremonies.

Friendly, commercial relationships between the Pueblos and their Apache and Navajo neighbors were disrupted by escalating patterns of raiding involving the Spanish. By the mid-1600s, Pueblo populations had been decimated by disease, famine, raids, and ill-treatment. In 1680, the allied Pueblos under the leadership of Popé evicted the Spanish in the Pueblo Revolt. All Spanish objects and churches were destroyed. The Spanish fled south to El Paso, but respite was short-lived. In 1692, Diego de Vargas led the reconquest of New Mexico. The area remained in Spanish hands until Mexican independence from Spain in 1821. New Mexico became part of the United States in 1848.

Jemez Pueblo. A photograph by E. A. Bass of a characteristic pueblo structure, near Albuquerque, c. 1884. Library of Congress

BIBLIOGRAPHY

Sturtevant, William C. *Handbook of North American Indians.* Volume 9: *Southwest*, edited by Alfonso Ortiz. Washington, D.C.: Smithsonian Institution, 1979.

Trimble, Stephen. *The People.* Santa Fe, N.M.: School of American Research Press, 1993.

Ruth M. Van Dyke

See also **Ancestral Pueblo (Anasazi); Architecture, American Indian; Indian Religious Life; Indian Social Life.**

PUEBLO INCIDENT.

On 23 January 1968, twenty miles from Wonsan, North Korea, four North Korean patrol craft opened fire on the U.S.S. *Pueblo*, a spy ship, after it ignored an order to halt. The *Pueblo's* eighty-three crewmen surrendered, and the American and North Korean governments wrangled over their respective interpretations of the encounter. After the U.S. government secured the crew's release from North Korea, without their ship, the Navy seriously considered courts-martial against the ship's officers for having surrendered too quickly. The House Armed Services Committee then sharply criticized the Navy's command structures, and the Secretary of Defense ordered a review of the civilian military chain of command.

BIBLIOGRAPHY

Lerner, Mitchell B. *The Pueblo Incident: A Spy Ship and the Failure of American Foreign Policy.* Lawrence: University Press of Kansas, 2002.

Paul B. Ryan / s. c.

See also **Korea, Relations with; Navy, United States.**

PUEBLO REVOLT. After the Spanish established a colony in the RIO GRANDE valley in 1598, they seized Indian land and crops and forced Indians to labor in Spanish fields and in weaving shops. The Indians were denied religious freedom, and some Indians were executed for practicing their spiritual religion.

The pueblos were independent villages, and the Indians spoke many dialects of several distinct languages. Occasionally an uprising against the Spanish would begin in one pueblo, but it would be squashed before it could spread to neighboring pueblos. Leaders were hanged, others enslaved.

In 1675, the Spanish arrested forty-seven medicine men from the pueblos and tried them for witchcraft. Four were publicly hanged; the other forty-three were whipped and imprisoned. Among them was Popé, a medicine man from San Juan. The forty-three were eventually released, but the damage had been done and the anger ran deep. Through the use of multilingual Indian traders, Popé recruited leaders (including Saca, Tapatú, and Catiti) in other pueblos to plan the overthrow of the Spanish. He demanded extreme secrecy.

The date was set. On 10 August 1680, Indians attacked northern settlements, killed Spanish men, women, and children, took horses and guns, and burned churches. As word spread of the massacres, nearby Spanish settlers fled to Spanish Governor Antonio de Otermín's enclosure at SANTA FE.

In the southern area around Isleta, Indians spread rumors that the governor had been killed, leading settlers to flee. Meanwhile, Indians surrounded Santa Fe, and after a few days' siege, Otermín's settlers retreated south.

Although the Indians had killed 400 Spaniards and succeeded in driving the rest of the colonists out of the Rio Grande country, they did not continue their confederation. As a consequence, the Spanish were eventually able to re-establish their authority. By 1692 they had reoccupied Santa Fe, but they did not return to their authoritarian ways. The Spanish did not force the Indians to convert to Christianity and they tolerated the continuation of native traditions. Pueblo people have been able to maintain a great deal of their traditions because of the respect they won in the 1680 rebellion.

BIBLIOGRAPHY

Knaut, Andrew L. *The Pueblo Revolt of 1680: Conquest and Resistance in Seventeenth-Century New Mexico.* Norman: University of Oklahoma Press, 1995.

Riley, Carroll L. *Rio del Norte: People of the Upper Rio Grande from Earliest Times to the Pueblo Revolt.* Salt Lake City: University of Utah Press, 1995.

Veda Boyd Jones

See also **Conquistadores; New Mexico; Southwest.**

PUERTO RICANS IN THE UNITED STATES. Puerto Ricans have migrated to the continental United States as U.S. citizens since 1917. In the Jones Act of that year, the U.S. Congress made Puerto Ricans living on the island and the mainland American citizens. The United States took possession of Puerto Rico at the end of the Spanish-American War in 1898 and has retained sovereignty ever since. Before 1898, Puerto Ricans came to the United States as workers, as merchants, and as political exiles, struggling to end Spanish colonialism in Puerto Rico and Cuba. After 1898, Puerto Ricans came because U.S. investment in Puerto Rico had wrought economic changes. Displaced cigar makers settled in New York City, Philadelphia, and Tampa. Puerto Ricans were also recruited through labor programs. Between 1900 and 1901, 5,000 men, women, and children were recruited to Hawaii as low-wage workers for sugar plantations. Puerto Rican communities emerged in Hawaii and in various places along the long, brutal journey, especially California. At the turn of the twentieth century, Puerto Ricans' status was ambiguous. In 1904, the U.S. Supreme Court declared that Puerto Ricans were neither citizens nor aliens, but ruled that they were entitled to enter the United States without restrictions.

After World War I, Puerto Rican migration increased, creating a vibrant community in New York City. European immigration was restricted, and Puerto Ricans, now U.S. citizens, became a preferred source of labor. Women found garment industry jobs and earned income by taking in boarders and providing childcare. Men worked in light manufacturing, as well as in hotels and restaurants. Puerto Rican neighborhoods formed close to job opportunities, and were soon dotted by bodegas (small grocery stores), restaurants, rooming houses, and other businesses and professional services owned by and catering to the new arrivals. By the mid-1920s, there were at least forty-three Hispanic organizations, including mutual aid societies, hometown clubs, cultural societies, and civically oriented associations. Puerto Ricans also participated in trade unions and city politics. Musicians, who had served in the U.S. armed services' black regimental bands, settled in the city, enriching the cultural life of the Puerto Rican community and serving as symbols of national culture. By 1930, approximately 100,000 Puerto Ricans lived in New York City, accounting for 81 percent of all Puerto Ricans in the United States. During the 1930s, the hardships of the Great Depression caused some to return to Puerto Rico. Still, by 1940, almost 70,000 Puerto Ricans lived in the United States, with 88 percent in New York.

The peak period of Puerto Rican migration came after World War II. During the 1940s, the population grew from 70,000 to 226,000. By 1970, 810,000 Puerto Rican migrants and another 581,000 mainland-born Puerto Ricans lived in the United States. Puerto Rico's agricultural economies declined, while the industrialization program based on U.S. investment and labor-intensive industries failed to generate sufficient employment. Leaving rural areas in search of work, Puerto Ricans settled in urban areas in Puerto Rico and the United States. Labor recruitment and contract labor programs continued. During World War II, the U.S. War Manpower Commission recruited approximately 2,000 Puerto Ricans, mostly to work in the canneries in southern New Jersey and on the railroads. After the war, a short-lived contract labor program to bring women to work as domestics was replaced by a program to bring men to work in agriculture. During the 1950s and the 1960s, between 10,000 and 17,000 agricultural laborers were contracted each year. While some returned to Puerto Rico at the end of the season, others settled permanently. Puerto Ricans also came without labor contracts, relying on social networks of family and friends. Urban economies provided jobs for women in manufacturing, especially in the garment industry, and for men in light manufacturing and the services sector, especially in hotels and restaurants.

Puerto Ricans increasingly settled beyond the barrios of New York City. By 1970, over 60 percent of Puerto Ricans lived in New York, still the largest community. Chicago became the second largest, with more than 79,000 Puerto Rican residents, and Philadelphia was third with more than 14,000 Puerto Rican residents. Communities of more than 10,000 had also emerged in Newark, Jersey City, Paterson, and Hoboken, New Jersey; in Bridgeport, Connecticut; and in Los Angeles, California. Dispersed settlement continued, and by 1990, just one third of Puerto Ricans lived in New York. Communities continued to grow in the Northeast and the Midwest, while the Puerto Rican population in Florida and Texas witnessed new growth. By the 2000 census, 3,406,178 Puerto Ricans lived in the United States, with 23 percent in New York City.

Wherever they settled, Puerto Ricans sought to recreate their communities, to confront the challenges they encountered, and to affirm their culture and traditions. Incorporated in 1956 in New York, El Congreso del Pueblo included eighty hometown clubs. These clubs continued earlier efforts to provide shelter, jobs, and emergency financial help, while expanding their activities to lead demonstrations against discrimination and police brutality. During the 1950s, Puerto Ricans in several communities established social service organizations to meet their needs, including the Puerto Rican Forum in New York and the Concilio de Organizaciones Hispanas in Philadelphia. Founded in 1961, Aspira prepared youth for leadership roles by establishing high school clubs, providing counseling, and advocating for educational issues, such as bilingual education. Aspira had branches in many communities. In Chicago, Los Caballeros de San Juan were instrumental in organizing the Puerto Rican Day Parade. Parades became important cultural and political events in many communities. By the 1970s, radical youth groups, such as the Young Lords, formed grassroots community-based programs and called for the independence of Puerto Rico and for a socialist society.

Puerto Ricans had settled primarily in industrialized cities. The economic restructuring of the 1970s affected Puerto Ricans in the inner cities, as manufacturing jobs relocated in search of cheaper labor. Puerto Rican women, who had been overwhelmingly concentrated in manufacturing, were displaced. The impact was intensified by residential segregation, as whole neighborhoods confronted the loss of employment and an eroding tax base. Puerto Ricans responded to these new challenges through grassroots community organizing, national organizations, and electoral politics. Despite underrepresentation and redistricting issues, in the 1990s Puerto Ricans had three elected representatives in the U.S. House of Representatives, and there were electoral victories on the local and state levels. In popular culture, there was new visibility as Puerto Rican celebrities enjoyed a broad appeal. Puerto Rico's political status was still debated, and tensions erupted over U.S. military activities on the offshore island of Vieques. Puerto Rican "Americans" continued to be at home in Puerto Rico and in the many communities of the Puerto Rican diaspora.

BIBLIOGRAPHY

Center for Puerto Rican Studies. *Labor Migration under Capitalism: The Puerto Rican Experience.* New York: Monthly Review Press, 1979.

Glasser, Ruth. *My Music Is My Flag: Puerto Rican Musicians and Their New York Communities, 1917–1940.* Berkeley: University of California, 1995.

Sánchez, Virginia Korrol. *From Colonia to Community: The History of Puerto Ricans in New York City, 1917–1948.* 2d ed. Berkeley: University of California, 1994.

Torres, Andrés, and José E. Velázquez. *The Puerto Rican Movement: Voices from the Diaspora.* Philadelphia: Temple University Press, 1998.

Whalen, Carmen Teresa. *From Puerto Rico to Philadelphia: Puerto Rican Workers and Postwar Economies.* Philadelphia: Temple University Press, 2001.

Carmen Teresa Whalen

See also **Hispanic Americans; Immigration; New York City.**

PUERTO RICO is the easternmost and smallest of the Greater Antilles. Located between the Atlantic Ocean to the north and the Caribbean Basin to the south, the island is a crucial access point to hemispheric waters and coasts, representing a valuable acquisition for European powers and the United States. Columbus landed in Puerto Rico on his second voyage in 1493. The island and its indigenous people, the Taínos, were colonized by Spain, which in 1508 appointed Juan Ponce de León its first colonial governor. In 1897, after almost four centuries of colonial administration, Spain approved an Autonomic Charter for the island that entailed local self-government, elected legislators, and voting rights in the Spanish parliament. But its implementation was soon thwarted by war between Spain and the United States. The TREATY OF PARIS (1898) that ended the SPANISH-AMERICAN WAR placed Puerto Rico under U.S. colonial authority.

Previous Relations

The relationship between Puerto Rico and the United States did not begin with this war. By the eighteenth century, the Spanish and British colonies had long engaged in contraband trade. At the time a major producer of sugar and molasses, Puerto Rico exchanged these commodities for basic food staples produced by Anglo American colonists. Ongoing expansionism concerning the Spanish-speaking Caribbean paralleled these economic relations, becoming official policy by Jefferson's presidency in 1801. The initially clandestine economic exchanges were officially authorized in 1815 when Spain sanctioned commerce between its colonies and other nations. A declining colonial power, Spain no longer had the means to extract primary resources from its few remaining colonies—Cuba and Puerto Rico being the most productive among them—and benefited from their participation in international trade. The authorization of commercial ties facilitated U.S. intervention and claims of vested interests on the two islands. By the 1830s, Puerto Rico's (and Cuba's) relations with the United States were so extensive that Cuban and Puerto Rican merchants established a Sociedad Benéfica Cubana y Puertorriqueña (Cuban and Puerto Rican Benevolent Society) in New York City.

Ideological ties also emerged as nationalist struggles escalated in Puerto Rico. By the eighteenth century, Puerto Ricans were asserting a unique Creole identity that distanced them from their Spanish colonizers, who were increasingly designated *hombres de la otra banda* (men [sic] from the other side). Resistance against Spain during the nineteenth century, either through claims for autonomy and independence or for equality and incorporation as an overseas province of Spain, brought Puerto Rican political activists, exiled as subversives, to the United States. They settled mostly in New York City, where they established an organizational base from which to work against Spanish rule, often acting jointly with Cuban exiles who were struggling equally for sovereignty. Puerto Rican exiles developed local political and communal associations and pioneered in the northeastern United States the historic and sociocultural bases for *Latinismo*—the assertion of a Latino identity based on shared linguistic, historical, and cultural resources—that spread throughout the nation in the later twentieth century. They also founded the first of many Puerto Rican communities on the mainland.

The Spanish-American War was thus the culmination of long-standing political, ideological, and economic ties, as well as the instantiation of U.S. interests in the Caribbean. Although the war was ostensibly triggered by concerns over the struggle for Cuban independence, the Puerto Rican campaign figured from the outset as a major military target and political goal. Controlling the Caribbean was consonant with national interests and the ideological orientations embodied in such historic principles as the MONROE DOCTRINE and MANIFEST DESTINY.

Although an armistice had already been proposed, the United States invaded Puerto Rico on 25 July 1898, landing in the small southwestern town of Guánica. The American military forces made their way to Ponce, the island's second-largest city, through a series of skirmishes with Spanish militia. They marched on to Coamo, in the southeast, to engage in the most serious fighting of the Puerto Rican campaign, with casualties amounting to six dead and thirty to forty wounded Spanish soldiers, and six wounded Americans. The U.S. forces soon gained control of the island, aided by relatively small Spanish garrisons and an enthusiastic populace anticipating the speedy acknowledgment of Puerto Rican sovereignty by the United States. Puerto Ricans assumed that this invader would be different from Spain and expected that it would uphold anticolonial and democratic principles.

Establishing the Colony

The immediate outcome of the takeover, though, was military rule. Significantly, the drafters of the Treaty of Paris had not provided for Puerto Rico's incorporation into the nation through citizenship and implementation of the Constitution. Enactment of the Foraker Act of 1900 reaffirmed the island's territorial status and consequently its colonial relationship with the United States. Unlike Spain's Autonomic Charter, it did not give Puerto Rico voting rights in Congress. Neither did it confer U.S. citizenship on Puerto Ricans, whom Spain had recognized as Spanish citizens. It gave the president full powers of appointment over the offices of the governor, the local Supreme Court, and key executive branches—education, treasury, and justice. Unlike other "territorial" peoples—Mexicans after the 1848 Mexican-American War and Hawaiians upon their 1898 annexation and the 1900 grant of U.S. citizenship—Puerto Ricans would enjoy neither incorporation as citizens nor the automatic extension of the benefits of constitutional protections because Puerto Rico was not considered an "incorporated" territory. This fostered the continuation of the local separatist movements that emerged during the island's struggles against Spain. As under the previous colonial regime, Puerto Ricans were divided about whether to advocate outright independence or incorporation through statehood in parity with other states of the union. The period saw the continuation of political parties organized around these forms of political relationship to the United States, or "status formulas," as they have been called ever since.

Congress continued to respond to the situation with mixed signals and equivocal measures. In 1917, rather than terminate or redefine the colonial relationship, the Jones Act conferred U.S. citizenship on Puerto Ricans yet confirmed their continuing status as an "unincorporated" territory. The U.S. Supreme Court also determined as much in a series of cases decided between 1901 and 1922, collectively known as the Insular Cases, in which the debate centered on whether or not the U.S. Constitution automatically applied of its own force (*ex proprio vigore*) and "followed the flag" into any territorial expansion. Since Puerto Ricans began clamoring for a solution to their status from the moment that they were forcibly involved in the 1898 war, unilateral congressional actions and decisions were increasingly viewed as oppressive, cynical, and undemocratic. The unsolicited grant of citizenship authorized by the Jones Act was regarded as a convenient imposition that anticipated the nation's entry into World War I and its need for soldiers; citizenship subjected island youth to military draft by a federal U.S. government that Puerto Ricans had no right to elect or to participate in.

The tensions between Puerto Rico and the United States throughout the twentieth century were not only experienced at the level of government, legislation, and case law. They also reached everyday domains, issuing from how Puerto Ricans were being regarded. The United States saw itself as exercising a benign "modernizing" function upon a society that it considered backward, underdeveloped, and bereft of any civilizing trait as the product of Spanish oppression. Puerto Ricans were racialized as the product of centuries of intermarriage between Europeans, indigenous people, the African slaves that were imported for its plantation economy, and Asian laborers. Puerto Ricans saw U.S. efforts at "modernization" as eroding their culture, curtailing their autonomy, and negating their uniqueness; they were also conscious that they were being regarded and defined through the prejudicial terms of U.S. racial hierarchies.

Spain had initially neglected the island after the colonial power realized that Puerto Rico's wealth did not lie in gold and silver. For 300 years, Puerto Rico survived as a strategically located military outpost for Spain, supporting itself through contraband and piracy, trading cattle, hides, sugar, tobacco, and foodstuffs directly with other nations.

In the eighteenth century, though, the Spanish monarch initiated a series of reforms inspired by enlightened despotism. Puerto Rico's system of land tenure was reformed through the establishment of private ownership. The 1815 sanctioning of commerce with other nations fostered development, immigration, urbanization, and population growth. These changes also facilitated the emergence of a strong sense of cultural nationalism among Puerto Ricans that was compounded by increased political consciousness. Because Spain was subject to periods of liberal reform, Puerto Ricans were exposed to the experience of civil liberties, constitutional principles, and representative government. Unlike the backward and politically unsophisticated colony that the United States assumed it to be, Puerto Rico was a complex society with a persistent sense of uniqueness, definite culture, and an intricate historical experience.

The colonial situation was aggravated by capitalist practices. The U.S. government facilitated the island's economic exploitation by absentee mainland corporations, abetted by local landowning and merchant elites. The implantation of monopolistic agribusiness in the form of the single-crop cultivation of sugarcane eroded economic diversity and autonomy, impoverishing the local economy. The United States also instituted the exportation of Puerto Rican workers as cheap, unskilled migrant labor. Depicting the island as overpopulated and as lacking prime material resources, the U.S. government encouraged migration, with the consequent expansion of Puerto Rican communities throughout the United States.

Widespread Americanization efforts targeted other significant sociocultural domains. These included, among others, the imposition of English-only education in the implementation of an educational system modeled on that of the United States, the appointment of pro–United States local elites to government positions, the incorporation of Anglo-Saxon common-law principles and practices into the island's Continental legal system, massive importation of U.S. consumer goods, and the devaluation of the local peso with the introduction of U.S. currency, a measure that bankrupted many middle-class families.

The dependency that ensued fostered the resurgence of strong political resistance. In the late 1920s, the Nationalist Party was founded under the leadership of Pedro Albizu Campos, a Harvard-trained attorney. The 1930s brought much turbulence to Puerto Rico, exemplified by the 1935 murder of five Nationalists during a university strike; two party members countered by assassinating the chief of police and were beaten and killed while in police custody. In 1937, Albizu Campos was successfully tried for sedition by federal prosecutors and sentenced to ten years of imprisonment in a federal facility. A Nationalist demonstration in Ponce, organized to protest both the persecution of Nationalist leaders and colonial measures of Americanization, ended with the massacre of participants and bystanders when police fired into the assembled crowd. The Ponce Massacre remains a significant Puerto Rican historical and ideological landmark.

The Nationalist Party represented the most militant promoter of independence among Puerto Rico's political parties. Other political parties were organized by pro-statehood advocates and those moderate pro-independence advocates who did not join the Nationalists. The lack of resolution to the colonial situation, its very complexity, and the perceptions of exploitation at the hands of the U.S. government, representing a nation that ostensibly stood for fundamental democratic principles, generated complex and fluid party politics. Shifting alliances emerged during these decades, bringing together pro-independence and pro-statehood advocates in such bipartisan party formations as La Alianza (Alliance Party) that emerged in the late 1920s and subsisted through the 1930s.

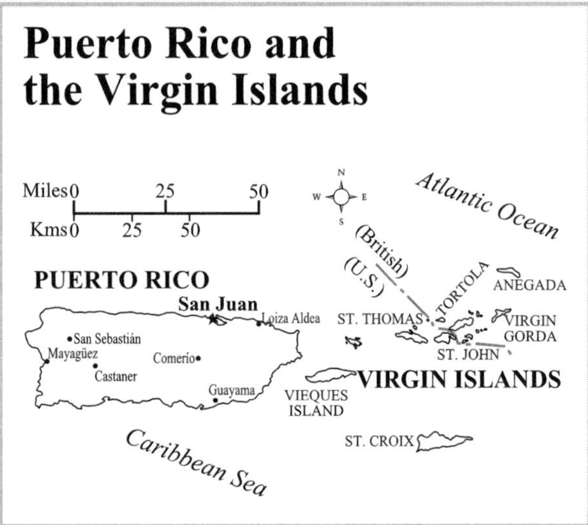

The Commonwealth

In 1938, Luis Muñoz Marín founded the Popular Democratic Party (PPD), which eventually proved to be the most significant political development for Puerto Rico in the twentieth century. The son of Luis Muñoz Rivera, a prestigious journalist, politician, and advocate for autonomy under both Spain and the United States, Muñoz Marín initially espoused independence and a socialist agenda of reform. He was incredibly successful in achieving control over the island's government by the mid-1940s and initiating local socioeconomic reforms. But he met congressional resistance when he attempted to gain any kind of resolution of Puerto Rico's colonial status.

Muñoz Marín devised the third "status formula"—the commonwealth—after World War II. Known in Spanish as Estado Libre Asociado (Free Associated State), it entailed the grant of greater control over local matters to Puerto Ricans. Its most evident change was to allow Puerto Ricans to elect their governor and to appoint local officials. It also provided for the enactment of a local constitution, but one subject to congressional approval. The colonial residues of commonwealth status were dramatically obvious when Congress rejected several dispositions of the Puerto Rican Bill of Rights that mandated universal education and health services because these rights were deemed too radical, even "communist," for the conservative postwar period. Finally, commonwealth status meant that island-based Puerto Ricans still could not vote in U.S. federal elections; they were and continue to be represented in Congress by a resident commissioner who can speak on their behalf but cannot vote. The situation has often been justified by appealing to the circumstance that island Puerto Ricans are not subject to federal taxes.

In 1952, Puerto Ricans went to the polls to approve their new constitution and commonwealth status. The change was consonant with both local claims for autonomy and the postwar situation, as the United States had become the leading world power and the Cold War had begun. The concession of commonwealth status persuaded the United Nations to drop Puerto Rico from its list of colonies, precluding both official UN support for its decolonization and the United States's status as a colonial power with regard to Puerto Rico. The short-lived Nationalist insurrection of 1950 was only the most dramatic resurgence of resistance at the time. Led by an aging Albizu Campos, Nationalists managed to take over some of the island's towns and attack both the governor's palace in San Juan and Blair House in Washington, D.C., in a failed attempt to assassinate President Harry S. Truman. The uprising had been anticipated by local legislation that curtailed freedom of speech in proscribing the use of media for advocating for independence; when it floundered, Nationalist and other pro-independence leaders were rounded up and incarcerated.

The commonwealth complemented limited local autonomy with industrialization programs to boost the island's economy, as embodied in Operation Bootstrap, the government's master developmental plan. Tax incentives and cheap but skilled labor brought many U.S. industries to the island, fostering a shift from an agriculture-based economy to one dependent on outside industrial investments. Consonant infrastructural changes included urbanization and suburbanization; improved public education, vocational training, and higher education to create a middle class and an educated and skilled labor force; the establishment of public medical services that reduced mortality and raised life expectancy; and the development of an island-wide network of modern highways and expressways.

By the late 1960s, Puerto Rico had achieved the highest standard of living in Latin America and had become a model for developing and newly decolonized nations. But it had also experienced steep social costs such as environmental pollution, social dislocation, wealth inequalities, consumerism, and more subtle forms of economic and political dependence. The end of tax incentives began to erode the economy, and U.S. economic cycles became even more intensely felt. As their ten-year tax exemption ended, U.S. industrialists fled to cheaper labor markets; ironically, labor legislation and educational campaigns had produced a protected, well-trained, educated, and thus expensive Puerto Rican labor force that was not competitive with unskilled labor in other nations. The rise of transnational business reduced the thrust of industrialization, since restrictive U.S. laws and policies concerning shipping, manufacturing, and tariffs, as well as U.S.-dominated banking and finance, limited Puerto Rico's ability to develop its own markets and attract more advantageous international business.

Puerto Rico remains economically dependent and reliant on manufacturing and services. The Puerto Rican government, a major employer, has fostered petrochemical and high-technology industries that capitalize on Puerto Rico's educated labor force. Pharmaceuticals, chemicals, electronics, medical equipment, and machinery are leading products. Tourism is the most important service industry.

Politically, the advent of the commonwealth has failed to end ongoing debates over Puerto Rico and its neocolonial condition. Muñoz Marín became Puerto Rico's first elected governor in 1948 and was reelected for four consecutive terms until he retired from the governorship in 1964. The PPD lost the 1968 elections, when a pro-statehood party, the New Progressive Party (PNP) won government control. The PNP had emerged in 1967, succeeding the old pro-statehood party, the Republican Party of Puerto Rico; along with the PPD, it remains one of the two strongest of the island's political parties. The leading independence party, the Puerto Rican Pro-Independence Party (PIP), was founded in 1948, when a PPD faction split off, disappointed at Muñoz Marín's failure to support independence and his "treason" in proposing, developing, and advocating for commonwealth status. Other short-lived political parties have waxed and waned under the commonwealth.

Since 1968, government control has alternated between the PPD and the PNP, indexing the ongoing struggle over the island's situation. Puerto Ricans are steadfast participants in the election process, practically the island's total adult population. The commonwealth's limitations and the lack of resolution in the island's relationship with the United States have increasingly led voters to overlook status preferences to support politicians on the strength of their immediate agendas rather than on the basis of status positions. The PIP's election returns peaked in 1952 when it was second only to the PPD, but it has since decreased to less than 5 percent of the vote. Nevertheless, the party and other independence advocates play important opposition roles in local politics. Concerns over the economy and quality-of-life issues have predominated over colonialism in elections, yet cultural nationalism, the fact of congressional control, and the ambiguities of the U.S.–Puerto Rico relationship have kept the colonialism issue from being fully disregarded.

On the occasions when Puerto Ricans have been consulted in plebiscite and referenda, they have to varying degrees supported commonwealth status. Yet incidents such as the widespread resistance, particularly in the 1990s, to the U.S. Navy's use of Vieques, one of Puerto Rico's outlying island extensions, for military maneuvers that include the use of live munitions, have brought to the fore the residual tensions between the two nations.

BIBLIOGRAPHY

Berman Santana, Déborah. *Kicking Off the Bootstraps: Environment, Development, and Community Power in Puerto Rico.* Tucson: University of Arizona Press, 1996.

Burnett, Christina Duffy, and Burke Marshall, eds. *Foreign in a Domestic Sense: Puerto Rico, American Expansion, and the Constitution.* Durham, N.C.: Duke University Press, 2001.

Cabán, Pedro A. *Constructing a Colonial People: Puerto Rico and the United States, 1898–1932.* Boulder, Colo.: Westview Press, 1999.

Carr, Raymond. *Puerto Rico: A Colonial Experiment.* New York: New York University Press, 1984.

González, José Luis. *Puerto Rico: The Four-Storeyed Country and Other Essays.* Translated by Gerald Guinness. Princeton, N.J.: Markus Wiener, 1993.

Lauria, Antonio. "'Respeto,' 'Relajo,' and Interpersonal Relations in Puerto Rico." *Anthropological Quarterly* 37, no. 1 (1964): 53–67.

López, Adalberto, and James Petras, eds. *Puerto Rico and Puerto Ricans: Studies in History and Society.* Cambridge, Mass.: Schenkman, 1974.

Maldonado-Denis, Manuel. *The Emigration Dialectic: Puerto Rico and the USA.* Translated by Roberto Simón Crespi. New York: International, 1980.

Rivera Ramos, Efrén. *The Legal Construction of Identity: The Judicial and Social Legacy of American Colonialism in Puerto Rico.* Washington, D.C.: American Psychological Association, 2001.

Steward, Julian H., et al. *The People of Puerto Rico: A Study in Social Anthropology.* Urbana: University of Illinois Press, 1956.

Trías Monge, José. *Puerto Rico: The Trials of the Oldest Colony in the World.* New Haven, Conn.: Yale University Press, 1997.

Vilma Santiago-Irizarry

PUGET SOUND is an inland waterway, connected to the Pacific Ocean through the Strait of Juan de Fuca, which borders Washington State and British Columbia, Canada. In 1787 the English captain Charles Barkley spotted the strait, and in 1792 another English captain, George Vancouver, sailed through the strait and explored the area. In 1898, Puget Sound was the jumping-off point for the Yukon and Alaska gold rushes. The Puget Sound Naval Shipyard was built at Bremerton, Washington, in 1891. The region was important during World War II, the Korean War, and the Vietnam War as a military center for the Pacific. More than half the population of Washington State ultimately settled on the shores of the sound.

BIBLIOGRAPHY

Schwantes, Carlos Arnaldo. *The Pacific Northwest: An Interpretive History.* Lincoln: University of Nebraska Press, 1996.

Laurie Winn Carlson

See also **Pacific Northwest; Vancouver Explorations; Washington, State of;** *and picture (overleaf).*

PUGWASH CONFERENCES. Summoned by an appeal from Albert Einstein and Bertrand Russell to work against the danger of nuclear war, twenty-two of the world's leading scientists attended a Conference on Science and World Affairs at Pugwash, Nova Scotia, in July 1957. Meeting at least annually thereafter and supported

Mount Rainier. The 14,410-foot peak looms over Lake Washington (the eastern boundary of Seattle), beyond Mercer Island (*left*) and what is now Seward Park, in this c. 1900 photograph of a now-urbanized area east of Puget Sound. Museum of History and Industry, Seattle

by philanthropist Cyrus S. Eaton, the loose association of scholars and public figures from both sides in the Cold War created an informal avenue for the exchange of ideas designed to combat the arms race and reduce the risk of international conflict. Whether high government officials or eminent academics, participants met as private individuals, not as representatives of their respective countries, and spoke off the record. Their conversations may have contributed to the realization of such arms control initiatives as the Partial Test Ban Treaty of 1963, the Non-Proliferation Treaty of 1968, the Anti-Ballistic Missile Treaty of 1972, the Biological Weapons Convention of 1972, and the Chemical Weapons Convention of 1993. In 1995, the Pugwash Conference and Joseph Rotblat, a Manhattan Project physicist who helped organize the first and subsequent meetings, jointly received the Nobel Peace Prize.

Since the Cold War, the Pugwash Conferences have broadened their concerns to include environmental and development issues. By the year 2000, some 10,000 people had attended Pugwash meetings.

BIBLIOGRAPHY

Blackaby, Frank. *A Nuclear-Weapon-Free World: Steps Along the Way*. New York: St. Martin's Press, 2000.

Ferry, Georgina. *Dorothy Hodgkin: A Life*. London: Granta Books, 1998.

Max Paul Friedman

PUJO COMMITTEE. In 1912 the House Committee on Banking and Currency launched an investigation into allegations that national financial and banking power had been concentrated in the hands of a few individuals, "a money trust." A subcommittee headed by Rep. Arsène Pujo of Louisiana conducted hearings at which J. P. Morgan, George F. Baker, and other financiers testified. After completing its investigation, the committee issued a majority report declaring that existing banking and credit practices resulted in a "vast and growing concentration of control of money and credit in the hands of a comparatively few men." This disclosure led eventually to the passage of the Federal Reserve Act (1913) and the Clayton Antitrust Act (1914).

BIBLIOGRAPHY

Heilbroner, Robert. *The Economic Transformation of America*. New York: Harcourt Brace Jovanovich, 1977.

Porter, Glenn. *The Rise of Big Business, 1860–1920*. Arlington Heights, Ill.: Harlan Davidson, 1992.

Strouse, Jean. *Morgan: American Financier*. New York: Random House, 1999.

Thomas S. Barclay / T. G.

See also **Codes of Fair Competition; Interests; Laissez-Faire; *Munn v. Illinois;* Open-Market Operations.**

PULITZER PRIZES. *See* **Prizes and Awards: Pulitzer Prizes.**

PULLMAN STRIKE. The Pullman Strike began on 11 May 1894, when workers at the Pullman Car Works in Chicago laid down their tools and walked off their jobs. Multiple factors precipitated their action. Pullman's preparations for the 1893 World's Columbia Exposition had raised wages and hours to new highs; the collapse of the national economy even as the exposition continued then drove them down to levels inadequate to meet basic needs. A harsh winter exhausted savings and left Pullman families vulnerable and angry. Exacerbating that anger was their complicated relationship with George M. Pullman and the town that bore his name. Almost half of the car works' employees lived in the Pullman Company's much-publicized planned community that provided residents with services and housing of a quality rarely found in working-class communities and bound their lives even more closely to company policies. Finally, recruiters for the American Railway Union (ARU), confident after the union's recent success against the Great Northern Railroad, promised the union's support for any action the Pullman manufacturing workers, if not its African American porters, took against the company.

George Pullman's refusal to intervene on their behalf and his apparent betrayal in laying off union leaders provoked the strike, but the hesitation of ARU's president Eugene V. Debs to launch a boycott of Pullman cars shaped its early weeks. Strikers realized that the company was too strong and Pullman too opposed to unionization of any kind for them to win alone. Helped by Chicago Mayor John P. Hopkins, himself a disgruntled former Pullman employee, strikers turned the company's publicity for the town on its head. Pointing to the poverty hidden within the town and recalling Richard T. Ely's critique of its undemocratic nature, they painted a portrait of an oppressive, closed environment that denied them and their families their rights as Americans. They especially targeted their message to the press and delegates to the upcoming ARU convention in Chicago.

Their strategy worked. At the end of June, the convention voted a boycott of all trains pulling Pullman cars. Rail traffic slowed and then stopped in the western United States; violence spread from Indiana to California. As the boycott grew, the struggle shifted from the Pullman Company to the ARU, the railroads' General Managers Association, and the U.S. government. Federal intervention ultimately decided the results. Federal judges issued an injunction prohibiting interference with trains and the mail they carried. President Grover Cleveland authorized federal troops to restore order from Chicago to California. ARU President Debs was jailed and later convicted of violating the provisions of the Sherman Antitrust Act.

Pullman Strike. This engraving of the 1894 railroad strike shows workers sabotaging switches in a rail yard as an engine approaches. Getty Images

Although the boycott collapsed by mid-July, the strike at Pullman continued well into August when the company gave most employees the opportunity to return to work if they abandoned the ARU. The legacy of both the company and the ARU, however, continued long after. Led by Governor John Peter Altgeld, the state of Illinois sued to force the company to sell the town. Debs embraced socialism and engaged the political system directly. The ARU and its industrial unionism receded until the federal government in the New Deal finally reversed its policies toward labor and unions forged during the Pullman Strike.

BIBLIOGRAPHY

Lindsey, Almont. *The Pullman Strike: The Story of a Unique Experiment and of a Great Labor Upheaval.* Chicago: University of Chicago Press, 1942.

Smith, Carl S. *Urban Disorder and the Shape of Belief: The Great Chicago Fire, The Haymarket Bomb, and the Model Town of Pullman.* Chicago: University of Chicago Press, 1995.

Janice L. Reiff

See also **Labor; Strikes;** *and vol. 9:* **The Pullman Strike and Boycott, June, 1894.**

PULLMANS were the railroad sleeping cars that, when introduced in the mid-nineteenth century, popularized long-distance rail travel. In 1836–1837, the Cumberland Valley Railroad of Pennsylvania installed sleeping-car service between Harrisburg and Chambersburg by adapting the ordinary day coach to sleeping requirements. Each car contained four compartments of three bunks each, built on one side of the car, and there was one rear section for washing facilities. Passengers could read only by candlelight, and box stoves warmed them. The seats and floors of most cars were filthy, and compartments were usually crowded. Passengers could only justify travel under such circumstances as a painful duty.

In 1855, a New York cabinetmaker, George M. Pullman, arrived in Chicago to apply his inventive ability to altering these conditions. Three years later, in Bloomington, Illinois, Pullman remodeled two Chicago and Alton coaches into sleeping cars, each of which contained ten sleeping sections, two washrooms, and a linen locker. Although this venture proved unprofitable, in 1864 Pullman decided to create a more elaborate car, which was equipped at a cost of $20,178.14, a huge amount for car construction in that day. The "Pioneer," as it was called, was bigger and wider than Pullman's first attempt and contained a folding upper berth, sliding seats, artistically decorated furnishings, special car springs, and better lighting, heating, and ventilation. In 1867 the Pullman Palace Car Company was incorporated with a capitalization of $1 million. In the same year the new luxurious sleeping-car model, the "President," included a kitchen, the predecessor of the dining car. In 1870 a Pullman car completed its first transcontinental journey. In 1883 the Pullman Company introduced to the United States the brilliant Pintsch gaslight as an illuminant and was a pioneer in the introduction of electric lighting.

Pullman Porter. While rail passengers slept, the porters cleaned their shoes and performed other tasks. GETTY IMAGES

Other improvements followed, and the Pullman Company outdistanced competitors. Indeed, the company proved so successful that an antitrust suit forced Pullman in 1947 to sell off its car-operating business and to concentrate solely on car manufacturing. By contrast, in the late nineteenth century, the Pullman Company ran into more difficulties when it experimented with industrial paternalism by building a company town outside Chicago for its workers. Workers resented their employer's attempts to impose bourgeouis culture on them and to control many facets of their private lives, and the famous Pullman Strike, beginning in 1893, eventually dissolved the community. Nevertheless, Pullman service, by introducing comfort to transportation, revolutionized travel both in the United States and abroad.

BIBLIOGRAPHY

Leyendecker, Liston E. *Palace Car Prince: A Biography of George Mortimer Pullman.* Niwot: University Press of Colorado, 1991.

Papke, David Ray. *The Pullman Case: The Clash of Labor and Capital in Industrial America.* Lawrence: University Press of Kansas, 1999.

Schivelbusch, Wolfgang. *The Railway Journey: The Industrialization of Time and Space in the Nineteenth Century.* Berkeley: University of California Press, 1986.

Harvey Wish/A. E.

See also **American Railway Union; Labor; Pullman Strike; Railroads; Transportation and Travel.**

PUMP-PRIMING is government spending during a recessionary period in an attempt to stimulate private spending and the expansion of business and industry. The phrase derives from the operation of an old-fashioned pump, in which a small leather suction valve must be moistened, or primed, with water so that it will function properly.

President Herbert Hoover began using the policy of economic pump-priming in 1932, when he passed a bill creating the Reconstruction Finance Corporation to make loans to banks, railroads, and other industries. During the Great Depression, President Franklin D. Roosevelt became convinced by the fall of 1933 that pump-priming was necessary to achieve economic recovery. Thereafter, through the Reconstruction Finance Corporation, the work-relief agencies, the Public Works Administration, and other organizations, the government spent billions of dollars to prime the pump. These expenditures averaged $250 million per month in 1934 and 1935 and about $330 million per month in 1936, but only about $50 million per month at the end of 1937. The recession of 1937 caused the Roosevelt administration to again resort to extensive pump-priming in 1938.

In the post–World War II period, the term "pump-priming" is rare in discussions of government economic policy, though the federal government intervenes in the economy in various ways. Some government programs, such as unemployment insurance, automatically act as pump-primers, since government expenditures must increase as people lose jobs during a recession. In the 1960s President Lyndon Johnson's War on Poverty increased such social programs. Since the 1960s administrations have leaned toward putting more disposable income into the economy by cutting taxes (as an alternative or supplement to raising government expenditures). In the 1980s President Ronald Reagan cut taxes to corporations and wealthy Americans, arguing that benefits would "trickle down" to the middle class and working class; nevertheless, the income gap between the richest and poorest Americans widened significantly.

BIBLIOGRAPHY

Nichols, Egbert Ray, ed. *Pump Priming Theory of Government Spending.* New York: H.W. Wilson, 1939.

Erik McKinley Eriksson/D. B.

See also **Council of Economic Advisors; Economics; Keynesianism; New Deal; Supply-Side Economics; Trickle-Down Economics.**

PUNISHMENT, in law, is the official infliction of discomfort on an individual as a response to the individual's commission of a criminal offense. That general definition invites attention to two related matters: the purposes for which punishment is visited upon an offender and the forms that punishment takes.

The purposes of punishment in American tradition cannot be determined from surviving records or inferred from experience but must be culled from the academic literature. That literature explains that government has punished offenders for reasons that fall roughly into utilitarian and nonutilitarian categories. Utilitarian objectives have in common the desire to prevent or to reduce crime. For example, government punishes criminals officially in order to preempt private retaliation by mob violence (vengeance), to restrain an offender while he or she undergoes discipline (incapacitation), to discourage an offender from misbehaving in the future (specific deterrence), to discourage others by making an example of the individual (general deterrence), and to dissuade an offender from committing more crimes by reforming him or her in some manner (rehabilitation). Nonutilitarian objectives are less eclectic. Governments punish an offender because the offender deserves to be punished for his or her crime and should be made to atone for it (retribution). The underlying Kantian idea is that a criminal has gained an advantage over others by virtue of his or her offense. That advantage must be eliminated via punishment to restore the proper balance of benefits and burdens in society.

The forms of punishment employed historically are fairly well documented. The colonists chiefly employed monetary fines and corporal punishments. They tortured slaves brutally and, outside the institution of slavery, they executed miscreants even for minor crimes. Offenders who were not hanged were whipped, branded, pilloried, ducked in water, placed in stocks, or banished from the colony (run out of town on a rail). It is difficult to say whether any of those punishments was consciously imposed to achieve utilitarian or nonutilitarian goals. Flogging slaves was part of the terror of slavery itself. Punishments of free colonists by public shaming may have had either utilitarian or nonutilitarian rationales. Punishments groomed to particular offenses may have been primarily retributive. Branding Hester Prynne with a scarlet letter *A* may have condemned her misbehavior more than it discouraged future illicit sexual liaisons.

Late in the eighteenth century the Quakers in Philadelphia conceived the notion that incarceration could substitute for the death penalty and physical torture. In the antebellum period custodial detention gradually became the preferred means of punishment in most states.

The Pennsylvania Quakers' rationale was utilitarian. They meant to confine convicts in penal institutions to "reform" them and thus to reduce the risk that they would commit additional criminal acts. The very name of the Quaker institutions, "penitentiaries," conveyed the message that their purpose was moral reform. Other proponents of incarceration expressed similar ambitions. As penal facilities of varying kinds were established over the next century, the theoretical justification was, by contemporary standards, humane: the ideal of rehabilitating citizens so they might become law-abiding and productive members of the developing industrial society.

The "rehabilitative ideal" dominated American penology throughout most of the twentieth century, implicating a variety of familiar policies, including the indeterminate sentence, probation and parole, vocational training, and educational programs for inmates. The working idea was that an offender should be incarcerated not for any fixed term but for as long as necessary to ensure rehabilitation. During and after confinement the offender should receive "treatment" to help foster a normal, law-abiding life. In 1949 the Supreme Court recognized that rehabilitation had become an important goal of criminal jurisprudence. In 1972 the National Council of Crime and Delinquency declared that convicts should be subject to reformative programs befitting their individual characteristics and circumstances.

Within a few years, however, many Americans discarded rehabilitation and embraced instead the competing idea that criminal offenders should be punished because they deserve it and for no other reason, pragmatic or humanitarian. Analysts have offered three explanations for the rapid shift to retribution. Critics on the right argued that rehabilitative programs rendered incarceration insufficiently punitive, critics on the left contended that rehabilitative programs constituted unacceptable ideological indoctrination, and professional penologists conceded that rehabilitation could not be shown to reduce recidivism.

Retribution's hegemony was not complete at the beginning of the twenty-first century. Imprisonment continued to serve forward-looking, preventive goals and conventionally was understood to be justified at least in part on utilitarian grounds. For example, prison terms for young offenders were commonly defended as a means of incapacitating young men during their most dangerous years. Retribution in 2002 is not necessarily regarded as meaningless or ineffective. When offenders are given sentences commensurate with their crimes rather than with their own individual circumstances and "need" for rehabilitation, individuals who committed roughly the same offenses received roughly the same penalties. That result in turn conforms to the American predilection for equality. After 1980 the federal government and many states adopted sentencing guidelines grounded in the idea that like crimes should be treated alike. In the punitive atmosphere of the times, however, the sentence for any given offense tended to be harsh. Moreover, repeat offenders often received enhanced sentences. Thus sentencing guidelines made prison terms not only more uniform but uniformly long, especially in nonviolent drug cases. Lengthy sentences to distant penal facilities in turn revived the colonial utilitarian policy of banishment.

The Eighth Amendment bars "cruel and unusual punishments." The Supreme Court has held that physical punishments once commonly accepted may become "cruel and unusual" as society's standards of decency evolve. Apart from the death penalty, corporal punishments are extremely rare and are probably unconstitutional when they occur. Political support for the death penalty has ebbed occasionally, but the Supreme Court has declined to hold that capital punishment necessarily violates the Eighth Amendment. Instead, the Court has held that the Constitution limits the death penalty to certain classes of homicides committed by especially culpable offenders.

BIBLIOGRAPHY

Allen, Francis A. *The Decline of the Rehabilitative Ideal: Penal Policy and Social Purpose.* New Haven, Conn.: Yale University Press, 1981.

Foucault, Michel. *Discipline and Punish: The Birth of the Prison.* Translated by Alan Sheridan. New York: Vintage, 1979.

Mitford, Jessica. *Kind and Usual Punishment: The Prison Business.* New York: Knopf, 1973.

Rotman, Edgardo. *Beyond Punishment: A New View of the Rehabilitation of Criminal Offenders.* New York: Greenwood, 1990.

Von Hirsch, Andrew. *Doing Justice: The Choice of Punishments: Report of the Committee for the Study of Incarceration.* New York: Hill and Wang, 1976.

Larry Yackle

See also **Capital Punishment; Prisons and Prison Reform; Reformatories.**

PURE AND SIMPLE UNIONISM. The expression "pure and simple unionism" was coined by Samuel Gompers, president of the American Federation of Labor (AFL), in a speech at the 1890 AFL convention in Detroit in which he opposed the inclusion of political parties in trade union organizations. Gompers argued that "the trade unions pure and simple are the natural organizations of the wage workers to secure their present and practical improvement and to achieve their final emancipation." The phrase came to represent the AFL's rejection of political action and social reform in favor of pragmatic economic strategies servicing the immediate needs of its members, such as wages, hours of work, and procedures for handling grievances.

BIBLIOGRAPHY

Gitelman, H. M. "Adolph Strasser and the Origins of Pure and Simple Unionism." *Labor History* 6, no. 1 (1965): 71–83.

Gompers, Samuel. *Seventy Years of Life and Labor.* Volume 1. New York: Dutton, 1925.

Greene, Julie. *Pure and Simple Politics: The American Federation of Labor and Political Activism, 1881–1917.* Cambridge, U.K., and New York: Cambridge University Press, 1998.

Thomas Chappelear

See also **American Federation of Labor–Congress of Industrial Organizations.**

PURE FOOD AND DRUG MOVEMENT. In the late nineteenth century, a reaction—the Pure Food and Drug Movement—set in against the growing scale of industry and its increasing freedom from government control. Before the mid-nineteenth century a large proportion of goods, especially consumables, were produced within the local communities where they were used, and peddlers who carried "foreign" goods were viewed with great suspicion. The advance of wage labor and the rise of large national producers battered down such localism, but the fears and suspicions of goods made by anonymous manufacturers, in far corners of the country, and in unknown conditions, remained.

Long before an organized movement for government regulation of the purity, safety, or labeling of food and drugs took root, Congress considered the problem of consumer protection. The consumers in this case were a select group, uniformed members of the U.S. military. After learning of the appalling death rates—due to disease and inadequate medicines—suffered by the Army during the Mexican War, Congress passed the Drug Importation Act of 1848, the first federal regulation of the quality of goods to be sold in the American marketplace. Though the law governed only imported articles, it was believed at the time that the rising quality of foreign drugs would pressure domestic drug makers to improve their standards to meet the competition.

Congress's first foray into the area of consumer protection was quickly undone by importers who exploited fine loopholes and party machines that staffed customs houses with cronies rather than chemists, but an important precedent was established. The federal government had asserted that it had a right to legislate to protect the public health and welfare. This ran counter to the trend in the 1850s at the state level, where the proliferation of medical disciplines, from homeopathy to magnetic therapies to faith healing, created public pressure to relax the previously strict medical licensing laws. Accompanying this trend was the increasing marketing of "patent" medicines; these concoctions of undisclosed ingredients promised to cure virtually every human ailment and were usually highly alcoholic or laced with addictive narcotics. For most of the nineteenth century these patent or "proprietary" medicines were widely used, and few objected to them. Even the *Journal of the American Medical Association* carried advertisements for them until 1905.

Although some colonial governments, following British practice, regulated the size, price, and purity of bread, it was when cities grew large that a significant number of people became dependent on middlemen or distant processors for their food supply, and the first public movement calling for government regulation of food appeared. In 1858 *Frank Leslie's Illustrated Newspaper* exposed the conditions in commercial dairies around New York City where diseased cows were fed distillery swill and their already thin milk was diluted with water and colored with chalk. The public outcry was loud enough to push the state legislature to pass the "Swill Milk Bill" but once the goal was achieved no lasting organization interested in food safety remained.

Until the end of the century most of the pressure for increased government oversight of the nation's food and drugs came not from public-spirited organizations but from private interests. Medical colleges and associations of pharmacists lobbied for restrictions on what were essentially their competitors. Butter makers and dairy interests tried to eliminate the cheap competition of oleomargarine. Kentucky bourbon distillers tried to throttle makers of blended whiskey. Cream of Tartar fought against Alum for control of baking powder. Sugar battled glucose. Meanwhile the public consumed an increasing array of foods laced with preservatives, dyes, perfumes, and cut with lard, cheap oils, by-products, and even sand and sawdust.

A few celebrated crusaders attempted to spark the interest of the public. George Thorndike Angell, better known for his founding of the movement for the humane treatment of animals, was an early advocate of government food-purity laws. Angell's loud warnings of the danger of adulterants to the public health made headlines but also were widely disputed by scientists and experts from both within and without the government. Angell cheered on Congressman Hendrick B. Wright, who introduced a broad food-purity bill in 1879, but such attempts died in every session of Congress for the next quarter century.

No comprehensive food regulation bill passed Congress before the twentieth century, however, farming interests triumphed over oleomargarine merchants in 1886, when Congress passed a special regulatory tax on margarine. Though of minor importance at the time, this proved a landmark in establishing a federal precedent for food regulation.

The struggle over this law marked the start of the career of Harvey Washington Wiley, widely considered the prime mover of food and drug regulation. As head of the Bureau of Chemistry within the Department of Agriculture, Wiley used margarine regulation as a lever with which to pry into the quality and safety of foods in general. With his newly expanded budget, Wiley purchased state-of-the-art photomicrography equipment and launched a sixteen-year investigation into food adulterants. Wiley also helped to found the Association of Official Agricultural Chemists and to place food safety at the top of its agenda.

The First Mass Movement

A mass movement calling for food and drug regulation first appeared at the state level in the 1880s. Massachusetts, New Jersey, and New York were all pressured to create more comprehensive systems of food inspection and regulation by a coalition of medical societies, women's clubs, temperance organizations, and civic organizations. By the end of the century most states had some food and drug regulations, though few seriously attempted to enforce them.

Women, especially those organized in the Women's Christian Temperance Union, were the base of a broadening movement calling for more effective protection of consumers. These reformers were alarmed at the drug addiction, alcoholism, and even death arising from routine use of patent medicines. State laws proved especially inadequate in dealing with medicine companies located in other states. Similarly, local food laws could not regulate conditions in canning plants and slaughterhouses in faraway Chicago or Baltimore.

Momentum toward a national food and drug bill built in the 1890s. A weak meat inspection law passed Congress in 1890 largely at the behest of meat packers themselves, whose products were mostly banned in Europe on the grounds of safety. In 1892 the Senate passed the Paddock Bill, which prohibited some additives and required accurate labeling, but it failed in the House. As outright food frauds multiplied during the long economic depression, the interest of civic organizations in the issue reached its height. Federal hearings exposed the rancid "embalmed beef" served to soldiers during the Spanish-American War of 1898.

Congress acted only after tragedy struck. In late 1901 thirteen children died after being given a tainted diphtheria vaccine in St. Louis. With almost no debate the Biologics Control Act became law the following year creating a tight licensing and labeling regime for makers of medical serums and antitoxins.

That same Congress also allocated money for Wiley's Bureau of Chemistry to begin investigations into the health effects of food preservatives. Wiley, by now experienced at manipulating the press, assembled a group of volunteers who were to dine on foods with established concentrations of preservatives and whose physical characteristics were carefully measured and charted over a period of months. Reporters dubbed the group Wiley's "poison squad" and followed the human guinea pigs over the course of their long experiment. The results published in 1904 were less impressive than the prolonged headline attention given to the issue of the danger of preservatives during the experiment itself.

The forces now lobbying for food and drug regulation had increased markedly from a decade before and included the American Medical Association, the trade journal *American Grocer*, the newly formed National Consumers' League, a number of influential food processors such as the H. J. Heinz Company, the very influential straight bourbon interests, and a number of western Senators finding political traction in condemning "eastern manufacturers." Yet, Congress still could not pass a bill through both chambers. The scales finally tipped when investigative journalists began to expose in detail food-industry practices. Samuel Hopkins Adams, a former medical student, uncovered the manipulative trade practices of patent medicine companies in a long series that ran in *Collier's*. Other widely read magazines of the day, such as *Ladies' Home Journal*, also ran exposés of food adulteration. President Theodore Roosevelt briefly mentioned the need for food and drug regulation in his State of the Union address that opened the legislative year of 1906.

Of all the so-called "muckrakers," none had a more profound impact than Upton Sinclair. When he published *The Jungle* in 1906, Sinclair hoped to awaken the nation's conscience to the plight of immigrant workers. Instead his stomach-turning passages depicting the conditions in Chicago's slaughterhouses caused the public to worry about its own health. As sales of Sinclair's book mounted, the split in the Republican Party between free-market stalwarts and regulation advocates widened, and worried party leaders applied pressure on the issue. After monumental wrangling, the different versions and amendments were finally reconciled, and the Pure Food and Drug Act and the Meat Inspection Act of 1906 became law.

These laws prohibited the interstate or foreign sale of adulterated (containing poisonous or spoiled ingredients) or mislabeled (including the removal of vital food constituents) foods, drugs that did not meet medical and pharmacological standards, or remedies that did not list on their labels the quantity of dangerous narcotics they contained. Meat was subject to federal inspection and condemnation.

The new system of federal food and drug regulation took a blow from the Supreme Court in 1911 in the case of *United States v. Johnson*, when the Court interpreted the 1906 statute to prohibit only false or misleading statements about a product's ingredients, not its therapeutic claims. But Congress partly closed that loophole with the Sherley Amendment in 1912. The Gould Amendment, requiring accurate labeling of the weight, measure, or numerical count of food packages, passed in 1913.

But there were countercurrents as well. Wiley was forced out of his post in 1912 after his vigorous enforcement against chemical preservatives and artificial sweeteners alienated him from the very agrarian interests that had helped propel the pure food movement before. After Wiley's ouster his successors trod carefully, focusing only on the most flagrant and threatening abuses that would be universally condemned. In the 1920s efforts shifted from prosecution to attempts to cooperate with manufacturers to improve their sanitation and standards, and the FOOD AND DRUG ADMINISTRATION (FDA) was created.

The New Deal and the Cold War

In 1933 a New Deal brain truster, Rexford G. Tugwell, helped promote a tough new revision of the 1906 law. It languished for several years, in spite of energetic lobbying from women's organizations, until a drug catastrophe involving Elixir of Sulfanilamide in 1937 killed 107 patients. The Food, Drug, and Cosmetic Act of 1938 gave the FDA the power to establish standards backed by the power to issue injunctions. The FDA's jurisdiction was expanded to cover cosmetics and medical devices, its regulatory authority over drugs was made proactive, and it was given tough new penalties and relieved of the need to prove criminal intent in all fields. The requirement that manufacturers get the FDA's approval before marketing a new good was expanded beyond drugs to include pesticides and other food additives in the late 1950s. The 1958 Delaney proviso placed a complete ban on any product shown to cause cancer in animals—a small amendment at the time, it became increasingly important with the advancing sensitivity of laboratory assayers.

During the Cold War the broad-based consumer movement that had pushed for powerful federal regulation lost voice to business interests, and Congress allowed the FDA's budget to stagnate in the face of greater regulatory responsibilities. This drift was quickly reversed when an approval review for a new tranquilizer for pregnant mothers, already in use in Europe, stretched out long enough to see the beginning of a wave of birth defects caused by the drug. Congress wasted no time in again expanding the FDA's oversight powers, requiring in 1962 that drug makers prove not only the safety but also the effectiveness of their products.

President John F. Kennedy proclaimed a "bill of consumer rights" in 1962, but it was the rise of a new consumer rights movement, now conscious of dangers from poorly designed products and led by Ralph Nader, that provided a new momentum for the expansion of regulation. Special protections were extended to children's products and fair labeling provisions were made to apply to all products in interstate commerce in 1966.

In spite of a generally conservative and antiregulation environment since the 1980s, the strength of consumer consciousness has remained strong and Congress has been wary of deregulating the food or drug industries. However, with new challenges to the existing regulatory regime from diseases such as AIDS, bioengineered foods, new factory technologies in the meat and poultry industries, food irradiation, and even potential terrorist attacks upon the safety of the food system, this issue returned to the forefront of public policy at the beginning of the twenty-first century.

BIBLIOGRAPHY

Anderson, Oscar E., Jr. *The Health of a Nation: Harvey W. Wiley and the Fight for Pure Food.* Chicago: University of Chicago Press, 1958.

Goodwin, Lorine Swainston. *The Pure Food, Drink, and Drug Crusaders, 1879–1914.* Jefferson, N.C.: McFarland, 1999.

Wiley, Harvey W. *An Autobiography.* Indianapolis, Ind.: Bobbs-Merrill, 1930.

Young, James Harvey. *Pure Food: Securing the Federal Food and Drugs Act of 1906.* Princeton, N.J.: Princeton University Press, 1989.

Timothy Messer-Kruse

See also **Food and Drug Administration; *Jungle, The;* Nader's Raiders.**

PURITANS AND PURITANISM. The terms "Puritans" and "Puritanism" originated in England in the 1560s, when they were used to describe the people who wished to reform the Church of England beyond the limits established by Queen Elizabeth I in order to "purify" it of what they considered the remnants of Roman Catholicism. Puritanism was first formulated as an ecclesiastical protest and was at the beginning devoted to attacking clerical vestments, the use of medieval ceremony, and the structure of the official hierarchy; Puritans wished to substitute a church government modeled upon the example of the apostles in the New Testament. However, this preoccupation with polity and ritual was an expression rather than the substance of Puritanism. Puritans were men of intense piety who took literally and seriously the doctrines of original sin and salvation by faith; they believed that true Christians should obey the will of God as expressed in divine revelation, and they condemned the Church of England because they found its order impious and anti-Christian. After 1603 their opposition to the church became allied with the parliamentary opposition to the royal prerogative; in the 1640s Puritans and Parliamentarians united in open warfare against Charles I.

Puritanism was thus a movement of religious protest, inspired by a driving zeal and an exalted religious devotion that its enemies called fanaticism but that to Puritans was an issue of life or death. At the same time, Puritanism was connected with the social revolution of the seventeenth century and the struggle of a rising capitalist middle class against the absolutist state. It was a religious and social radicalism that in England proved incapable of maintaining unity within its own ranks and, during the 1650s, split into myriad sects and opinions. The process of division began in the sixteenth century when "Separatists" broke off from the main body of Puritans. A small congregation of these extremists fled to America and established the Plymouth colony in 1620, although the major contribution of Puritanism to American life was made through the settlement established by the Massachusetts Bay Company at Boston in 1630. This band of Puritans was inspired to migrate by a conviction that the cause had become hopeless in England after the dissolution of the Parliament of 1629. Within the next decade some 20,000 persons came to MASSACHUSETTS and CONNECTICUT and there built a society and a church in strict accordance with

Puritans Going to Church. A traditional depiction of members of this intensely pious and theocratic sect of English Protestants, who settled primarily in New England. © BETTMANN/CORBIS

Puritan ideals. Ruled by vigorous leaders, these colonies were able to check centrifugal tendencies, to perpetuate and to institutionalize Puritanism in America long after the English movement had sunk into confusion and a multiplicity of sects. Yet insofar as Puritanism was but the English variant of CALVINISM and was theologically at one with all reformed churches, NEW ENGLAND Puritanism was merely one of the forms in which the Calvinist version of Protestantism was carried to America; its influence, therefore, must be considered along with that of Scotch-Irish, Dutch, or French Protestantism.

Historians have on occasion attributed the origins of the American democratic tradition to the New England communities that nourished Puritanism for more than a century. Puritan dislike for the Anglican church and Stuart monarchs contributed to the strong anti-British sentiment that typified Boston life in the mid-1700s. And the Puritan acceptance of theocratic hierarchies and notion of themselves as a covenanted people prepared New Englanders well for the CONSTITUTION OF THE UNITED STATES. However, beginning in the early twentieth century, historians increasingly tended to stress the undemocratic intolerance of Puritan theology—illustrated plainly in the banishment of Anne Hutchinson, the WITCHCRAFT prosecutions, and the brutal persecution of QUAKERS and Catholics.

Among some members of the literary avant garde in the early twentieth century, puritanism (uncapitalized) emerged as a pejorative term, a synonym for moral intolerance, prudery, and sexual priggishness. In the United States the word Puritanism (capitalized) has become practically synonymous with New England and its historical legacy, simply because New England (except for Rhode Island) achieved a social organization and an intellectual articulation that trenchantly crystallized the Puritan spirit. Puritanism can be said to have affected American life wherever Calvinism has affected it, but most markedly at those points where persons of New England origin have been influential.

BIBLIOGRAPHY

Bercovitch, Sacvan. *The American Jeremiad.* Madison: University of Wisconsin Press, 1978.

Breen, Timothy H. *Puritans and Adventurers: Change and Persistence in Early America.* New York: Oxford University Press, 1980.

Foster, Stephen. *The Long Argument: English Puritanism and the Shaping of New England Culture, 1570-1700.* Chapel Hill: University of North Carolina Press, 1991.

Gildrie, Richard P. *The Profane, the Civil, & the Godly: The Reformation of Manners in Orthodox New England, 1679–1749.* University Park: Pennsylvania State University Press, 1994.

Miller, Perry, and Thomas H. Johnson. *The Puritans.* New York: Harper and Row, 1963.

Morgan, Edmund S. *The Puritan Family: Religion & Domestic Relations in Seventeenth-Century New England.* New York: Harper & Row, 1966.

Reis, Elizabeth. *Damned Women: Sinners and Witches in Puritan New England.* Ithaca, N.Y.: Cornell University Press, 1997.

Perry Miller / A. R.

See also **Antinomian Controversy; Congregationalism; New England Way; Pilgrims; Religion and Religious Affiliation; Salem; Separatists, Puritan; Theocracy in New England;** *and vol. 9:* **Trial of Anne Hutchinson at Newton, 1637.**

PURPLE HEART. *See* **Decorations, Military.**

PYRAMID SCHEMES are frauds that pay a hierarchy at the top of a triangle out of investments made by those at the bottom. Often confused with legitimate multilevel MARKETING, pyramids are felonies in most states. In most scenarios a few people offer a seemingly attractive product or service and recruit people to sell it but require an investment for participation. Those investors are then encouraged to recruit still more participants. In legitimate multilevel marketing, profit comes from sales to actual customers; in pyramids profits come from cash investments of recruits and product sales to those recruits. Eventually, the pool of recruits dries up, leaving latecomers unable to recoup their investments. One popular small operation involves a plane scenario. A "pilot" sits atop the pyramid, the next level has two "copilots," the third level four "flight attendants," and the fourth and bottom level eight "passengers." Each passenger pays an entry fee, usually a few thousand dollars. The money is given to the pilot, who "jettisons" with huge profits. The plane then breaks into two new pyramids, with each copilot now sitting as the pilot. The new flight attendants then recruit fresh passengers, usually friends and relatives, and the scheme continues until it collapses under its own weight.

BIBLIOGRAPHY

Bulgatz, Joseph. *Ponzi Schemes, Invaders from Mars, and More Extraordinary Popular Delusions and the Madness of Crowds.* New York: Harmony Books, 1992.

Kathleen B. Culver / C. W.

See also **Crime.**

ISBN 0-684-80528-6

90000

9 780684 805283